First printing: December 2024

Copyright © 2024 by Ken Ham. All right reserved. No part of this book may be reproduced, copied, broadcast, stored, or shared in any form whatsoever without written permission from the publisher, except in the case of brief quotations in articles and reviews. For information write: Master Books, P.O. Box 726, Green Forest, AR 72638
Master Books® is a division of the New Leaf Publishing Group, LLC.

ISBN: 978-1-68344-397-1
ISBN: 978-1-61458-923-5 (digital)
Library of Congress Number: 2024947247

Interior and Cover Design by Diana Bogardus

Scripture quotations are from the ESV® Bible (The Holy Bible, English Standard Version®), © 2001 by Crossway, a publishing ministry of Good News Publishers. Used by permission.
All rights reserved. The ESV text may not be quoted in any publication made available to the public by a Creative Commons license. The ESV may not be translated in whole or in part into any other language.

WHERE NOTED:

Scripture quotations are from the King James Version of the Bible.

Scripture taken from the New King James Version®. Copyright © 1982 by Thomas Nelson. Used by permission. All rights reserved.

Please consider requesting that a copy of this volume be purchased by your local library system.

Printed in Canada

Please visit our website for other great titles: www.masterbooks.com

For information regarding promotional opportunities, please contact the publicity department at pr@nlpg.com.

TABLE OF CONTENTS

A WORD TO READERS FROM KEN HAM	5
JANUARY	6
FEBRUARY	68
MARCH	124
APRIL	186
MAY	246
JUNE	308
JULY	368
AUGUST	430
SEPTEMBER	492
OCTOBER	552
NOVEMBER	614
DECEMBER	674
INDEX	736

This collection of 365 daily readings is thoughtfully organized into key categories that highlight different aspects of Christian living, guiding you to apply biblical wisdom in every area of your life.

Science:	Discover the harmony between faith and science, with readings that delve into God's design of the universe, exploring the evidence of creation, natural order, and scientific apologetics.
Apologetics:	Gain insights into defending your faith and logic and reason, equipped with daily reflections that strengthen your ability to articulate the truth of the Gospel in a secular world.
Theology:	Deepen your understanding of Christian doctrines through Biblical theology, as you are guided through key concepts such as the nature of God, salvation, and the authority of Scripture.
Family:	Build a Christ-centered home with reflections on parenting, marriage, and family life, grounded in Biblical principles that nurture love, respect, and discipleship within your home.
Church:	Explore the vital role of the Church in the Christian life with an emphasis on community, worship, and mission, reminding believers of their purpose within the body of Christ.
Resources:	Dive into practical resources, including recommended books, tools for study, and strategies for engaging culture, to enhance your spiritual growth and Biblical worldview.

Ken Ham is the Founder and CEO of Answers in Genesis and the visionary behind the highly-acclaimed Creation Museum and the world-renowned Ark Encounter.

Each year, Ken speaks to hundreds of thousands of children and adults on the topics addressed in these dailies. He has authored over 40 best-selling books and resources and is a thought leader, upholding the authority of the Bible from the very first verse.

As husband, father of 5, and grandfather of 18, Ken has a heart for passing on a legacy of faith to the next generation as well as equipping this present generation to defend their faith and share the message of salvation.

A WORD TO READERS FROM KEN HAM

There are many daily devotionals available for Christians, but I want to offer something different for Christian families. This resource is truly unique. The 365 readings in this publication address the cultural and spiritual issues of our time, combining apologetics with teaching on a biblical worldview and sound doctrine. Each reading equips Christians to defend the faith and be effective witnesses in an increasingly anti-Christian culture. We could describe it as a daily reading that is:

- scientific yet devotional
- apologetics-based
- grounded in a biblical worldview
- culturally relevant
- designed for the whole family.

I envision this resource being used for personal devotions, in classrooms by teachers, for Sunday or Bible school classes, and more. My ultimate hope, however, is that it will be used for family devotions. Each reading offers a wonderful opportunity for fathers to take the lead in disciplining themselves to guide their families in daily teaching. It's like delivering a mini-sermon each day, with all the preparation already done for you.

These daily readings are based on articles I've written over my fifty years of active apologetics ministry, with editing help and contributions from others at times. I pray this resource will be a blessing to you and your family.

EXPRESSIONS OF GRATITUDE

I want to especially thank Answers in Genesis speaker and writer Avery Foley for her work in the initial editing of these daily readings, and the staff at Master Books for working so hard to get this publication produced in record time! I also want to extend my gratitude to everyone who contributed to these articles in various ways over the past fifty years.

JANUARY 1
John 3:19

Why Are We Seeing Intolerance and Hate Exhibited Increasingly Against Christians?

In recent times, we've experienced increased accusations against Christians that they are intolerant, use hate speech, and are unloving. This occurs particularly regarding issues surrounding the LGBTQ worldview involving gender issues, gay "marriage," abortion, etc. But what is really going on? Consider these verses before we analyze what is happening in our culture:

For behold, your enemies make an uproar; those who hate you have raised their heads (Psalm 83:2). Whoever is not with me is against me, and whoever does not gather with me scatters (Matthew 12:30).

We live in a time where we've seen a dramatic change in the dominant worldview in our culture. In the past, the Judeo-Christian ethic permeated the culture as a result of how the nation started. Certainly, not all the founding fathers of America were Christians, but nonetheless, they by and large adopted a worldview based on the Bible. Even most non-Christians in generations past adopted a Christianized worldview, believing marriage was between a man and a woman, abortion was murder and wrong, and there were only two genders of humans, for examples.

But as each generation became more indoctrinated in atheistic evolutionary humanism that permeated the public school system and as many church leaders gave up the history in Genesis 1–11 and adopted evolutionary ideas, the younger generations basically abandoned the Bible as a foundation for their worldview. Many became more consistent with the foundation that man determines truth and built a worldview of moral relativism that now permeates the culture.

In a culture where moral relativism is the dominant worldview, this clashes with the worldview based on the absolutes founded in the Word of God. This is similar to what we read in Judges 21:25, *In those days there was no king in Israel. Everyone did what was right in his own eyes.*

When there was no king to tell them what to do, everyone did what was right in their own eyes. In other words, when there's no absolute authority, anything goes. However, when anything goes, there is something that doesn't, and that is the absolutes of Christianity. This is the clash we now see in our culture. Two worldviews in conflict — moral relativism conflicts with the absolutes of Christianity. But, because moral relativism is now the dominant worldview, those holding to the absolutes of Christianity are considered the enemy!

Let me explain: I've spoken with people holding the LGBTQ worldview who accuse Christians of being intolerant and filled with hate speech. They claim all they want is freedom for their views and that Christians are intolerant of them, as they don't want them to have such freedom. Actually, I would claim from all we've seen in recent times that ultimately many of those with the LGBTQ worldview don't just want freedom for their views, they want total compliance and acceptance of their views by everyone. And those who don't comply and accept are then persecuted.

But regardless of that, I've had the following types of conversations with them. I'll use KH for my statements and LGBTQ for the statements of the person I was talking to. The conversation went something like this:

APOLOGETICS — JANUARY 1

LGBTQ: "We allow all views on marriage and gender. We only want freedom for all views, whereas you Christians are intolerant of this."

KH: "But you don't allow all views on these issues."

LGBTQ: "Yes, we do, but you won't tolerate people allowing all views, and you speak with hate against us."

KH: "But you are not allowing my view, which is built on God's Word that there's only one marriage – a man and a woman – and that there are only two genders – male and female – all based on God's Word."

LGBTQ: "But now you are intolerant of our views, as you are only holding to those views based on the Bible. And that's hate speech."

KH: "But you're not tolerant of my view, which states there is only one view, the view based on God's Word. And just because I hold a very different view to you isn't hate. You are interpreting my insistence on believing what God's Word states as hate. It is not hate."

We were at an impasse. Claiming to allow all views does not allow the view that there's only one right view, and that is God's! That clash is irreconcilable at the worldview level. The ultimate reason for this clash of worldviews is because there are two different foundations. One is founded on man's word and one on God's Word. Now, until the person with the foundation on man's word changes that foundation, they will not change their worldview. The only solution to this battle is for people to put their faith and trust in God's Word, receive the free gift of salvation, and build their worldview on what God has revealed to us.

In reality, those who claim they hold all views and thus are the supposed tolerant ones are the most intolerant of all, as they can't allow someone to have a worldview that states they are wrong. In fact, I've had such people say to me, "What gives you the right to claim you have the truth?" I answer, "But you claim you have the truth in claiming your position is the right one. So you're claiming you have the truth and I don't." There's that same clash again. When I explain to them that the God of the Bible is the absolute authority and determines what is absolute truth as He is our Creator, they have replied, "There is no such position as absolute truth." My response then is, "Are you absolutely sure about that?"

God's Word makes it clear one is either for or against Christ. There is no in-between. Those stating they allow all views are actually against what God's Word clearly states concerning how a person defines marriage, gender, etc. One can understand why this worldview clash is not going to be solved unless people change their foundation. The only answer is the truth of God's Word and the saving gospel. It's a spiritual solution that's needed.

Actually, I lay a lot of blame on much of the Church that has supported generations being educated in an anti-God education system; compromised God's Word in Genesis; and, in essence, allowed generations to have the wrong foundation of man's word instead of God's Word. A lukewarm Church, compromising Genesis with evolution and millions of years, has greatly contributed to the younger generations being captured by the world and permeated with a worldview of moral relativism.

> You are a part of the battle that began in a garden 6,000 years ago between good and evil, light and darkness, and those who build their house on the rock and those who build their house on the sand.

JANUARY 2
Daniel 3:5

Whom Should You Trust First? God or the Scientist? God or the Theologian? God or the Christian Academic?

Many times over the years, I've had a number of conversations with Christians who won't accept the days of creation as ordinary days and vehemently defend millions of years and other evolutionary beliefs. Often, the person talking to me has quoted various Christian academics, well-known theologians/Christian leaders, or certain church fathers, claiming that I should give up my literal Genesis position because these academics/famous Christians do not agree with me. My answer to them has been, "But what does God clearly state in His Word? I judge the people you quoted against God's Word, not the other way around."

I have certainly been scoffed at and mocked over the years because of my position. Now don't get me wrong. I respect scholarship. But regardless, we need to recognize that we could have 100 PhDs from Harvard University, but compared to what God knows, we would still know nearly nothing.

When I teach children about dinosaurs, creation, and evolution, I like to ask them these questions:

"Has any human being always been there?" They answer, "No."
"Has any scientist always been there?" They answer, "No."
"Does any human being know everything?" They answer, "No."
"Who is the only One who has always been there?" They shout out, "God."
"Who is the only One who knows everything?" They shout out, "God."

I then ask: "Who is the One we should always trust first? God or the scientist?" They call out, "God."

And I could add, "Whom should we always trust first: God, the scientist, the theologian, the teacher, the pastor, the professor?" And the answer will always be "God."

In a way, that sounds rather simplistic. In fact, I've had people who oppose my position claim that I have too simplistic a belief to just take Genesis 1–11 as it is written. Now when someone claims it's too simplistic, I believe this is showing a problem we all have to battle with because it's a part of our nature, the sinful nature we have, because we are descendants of Adam. The problem is pride. God's Word has a lot to say about pride:

When pride comes, then comes disgrace, but with the humble is wisdom (Proverbs 11:2).
Do you see a man who is wise in his own eyes? There is more hope for a fool than for him (Proverbs 26:12).

And God's Word tells how to gain wisdom and knowledge:
The fear of the Lord is the beginning of knowledge (Proverbs 1:7).
The fear of the Lord is the beginning of wisdom (Proverbs 9:10).

I would rather stand before the Lord and say that I'm guilty of simplistically believing what His Word states in Genesis than trust the word of fallible humans and reinterpret God's Word.

I'm reminded about this so-called "simplistic" approach when I read what Jesus said about children:
Truly, I say to you, unless you turn and become like children, you will never enter the kingdom of heaven. Whoever humbles himself like this child is the greatest in the kingdom of heaven (Matthew 18:3–4).

It is so much easier for children who have not had years of indoctrination from the world to believe God's Word as written. Reading Genesis for them is just like reading a history book. Well, it is history, and history

APOLOGETICS   JANUARY 2

as God had it recorded for us. Sadly, the more educated people become, many find it harder to believe God's Word as written in Genesis. And it's not because Genesis is literal history, but I believe it's because of pride. And a reason for that is we all have an underlying problem. It doesn't matter who we are, we all have sinful hearts.

[F]or all have sinned and fall short of the glory of God (Romans 3:23).

The origin of sin is found in Genesis 3 when Adam and Eve were tempted by the devil to disobey God. Now consider two elements of the temptation that help us understand our sin nature:

He said to the woman, "Did God actually say …?" (Genesis 3:1).

Note that the first attack by the devil was on the Word of God to get Adam and Eve to doubt God's Word so that doubt would lead to unbelief.

For God knows that when you eat of it your eyes will be opened, and you will be like God, knowing good and evil (Genesis 3:5).

The second part of the temptation was really to offer them to be their own god. We know Adam took the fruit and disobeyed God and brought sin and the judgment of death into the world. God's Word states:

Therefore, just as sin came into the world through one man, and death through sin, and so death spread to all men because all sinned—for sin indeed was in the world before the law was given, but sin is not counted where there is no law. Yet death reigned from Adam to Moses, even over those whose sinning was not like the transgression of Adam, who was a type of the one who was to come (Romans 5:12–14). So we have that sin nature. And Genesis 3:1 and 3:5 sum up that nature.

Our propensity will be to doubt the Word of God, as we would rather trust the word of man. I see that over and over again with Christian leaders/academics who would rather trust man's word (beliefs) about millions of years and evolution instead of God's Word as it's clearly stated in Genesis 1–11.

Also, we have this propensity to be our own god. We want to decide truth for ourselves. We see ourselves as being proud of what we know. We think we can reason correctly by ourselves, and so we have that problem of intellectual pride wanting intellectual respectability.

I believe this is why there is so much compromise in the Church when it comes to God's Word in Genesis. Our heart is such that we would rather trust man's word than God's Word, and so we have a problem with intellectual pride, and thus we cave to peer pressure. We must guard against this. However, none of us like being called anti-intellectual or anti-academic. And we will be called that if we believe in six literal days of creation and a young earth and universe.

But I often think about those in Hebrews 11 and the Christian martyrs of the past. They were sawn in half, thrown to lions, burned alive, lived in caves, were destitute, and suffered many atrocities. And yet, so many Christians today cave because they are belittled by secular academics for believing the "simplistic" account of creation, the Fall, the Flood, and the Tower of Babel as related in Scripture.

I wonder how many in the Church today would have stood with Shadrach, Meshach, and Abednego – would you?

JANUARY 3
Isaiah 40:28

Who Made God?

I have many secularists mock me as a Christian for believing in an eternal God. They've asked me the question, "So who made God?" They then claim it doesn't make sense to believe in an eternal God.

I do give them an answer, but then I ask them about what they believe.

So, what is the answer to the question of who made God? The Bible makes it clear that God exists in eternity. He has always existed. He didn't have a beginning. There are many verses of Scripture that attest to the fact that God is everlasting, eternal:

Have you not known? Have you not heard? The LORD is the everlasting God, the Creator of the ends of the earth. He does not faint or grow weary; his understanding is unsearchable (Isaiah 40:28).

Before the mountains were brought forth, or ever you had formed the earth and the world, from everlasting to everlasting you are God (Psalm 90:2).

To the King of the ages, immortal, invisible, the only God, be honor and glory forever and ever. Amen (1 Timothy 1:17).

The eternal God is your dwelling place, and underneath are the everlasting arms (Deuteronomy 33:27).

At a conference once, a young boy about 10 years of age came up and asked me, "Sir, if God created us, who created God?" How do you answer that question for a young child?

I then said to him, "If someone made God, then you would have to have a bigger God." The boy replied, "Yes, sir." I said, "But now, you have a problem: who made the bigger God? You would then need a bigger, bigger God who made the bigger God who made God." I then said, "Now, you have a problem." The boy said, "I know." I then went on, "Who made the bigger, bigger God? Now, you would need a bigger, bigger, bigger God who made the bigger, bigger God who made the bigger God who made God." The young boy understood. We could keep going back with bigger and bigger and bigger and bigger forever and then have to keep going. The only thing that makes sense is that you would have to have the biggest God of all, the infinite, eternal God of the Bible. The only one true God who has always existed. He had no beginning.

Now that is difficult, really impossible, for us to understand because we are created, finite beings. The space, mass, and time universe we live in was created. We think in terms of everything having a beginning because we are finite beings who have a beginning. This means there will always be a faith aspect to understanding who God is. We can't scientifically prove God exists because we don't have all information, only God does. That's why God's Word states, *And without faith it is impossible to please him, for whoever would draw near to God must believe that he exists and that he rewards those who seek him* (Hebrews 11:6).

However, it's important to understand this is not blind faith. It's a faith that makes sense of what we observe in this world, and observational science in many ways confirms this faith over and over again. The history recorded in the Bible makes sense of the evidence we observe in the present in biology, geology, astronomy, and so on.

THEOLOGY

JANUARY 3

Note that when you begin reading the first book of the Bible, it states, "In the beginning, God." In other words, God's Word starts with God. He exists. He is Creator. God's Word doesn't set out to prove God exists; it states God exists! As He states over and over again in Scripture, "I am."

I explain all that to secularists, including the faith aspect, when they ask me about who made God, but then I ask them questions.

After my debate with Bill Nye in 2014,[1] we took questions that were submitted by audience members. One of the questions came from a young boy who asked, "Where did matter come from?" Bill Nye responded, "I don't know, it's a great mystery." I answered, "There is a book [the Bible] that tells us where matter came from."

Atheists may mock Christians for believing in an eternal God, but what do they believe? Where did matter come from? Why does anything exist? Where did energy come from? Why does time exist? Why does space exist? Is matter eternal? Did matter suddenly come from nowhere for no reason? They have no answers! They can have all sorts of opinions and beliefs, but the bottom line is that they have no definitive answer at all.

I remember atheist Richard Dawkins claiming the possibility that life was seeded on earth by aliens from outer space. Obviously, atheists can't explain how life on earth could arise from matter by chance random processes, so one of their ways around this is to claim life came from outer space. All they did was shift the origin of life on earth to another planet. But then we could ask where the aliens from another planet that seeded life on earth originated. Well, maybe other aliens seeded life on that planet to become aliens to seed life on earth. But then where did the aliens that seeded life on that other planet come from? Were there other aliens that seeded life on that planet so aliens could arise to seed life on another planet so aliens could arise and seed life on earth? I think atheists would be happy to believe in eternal aliens but not an eternal God. How do atheists explain the laws of nature that are immaterial? And why do these laws stay the same and not evolve?

It's the atheists who have a blind faith. They believe that space, mass, and time somehow eternally existed or came into existence for some reason, and somehow, matter gave rise to life against everything we observe and know about the laws of nature.

As I've said many times, atheism is a religion, a belief system. There is no nonreligious position. Atheists have a faith, but it's a blind faith that lacks credulity. Christians have faith, but it's an objective faith that makes sense of life and the universe and a faith that observational science confirms.

The first man, the head of the human race, rebelled against God bringing sin and death into the world. But God loved man so much, He provided a way of salvation for man so his sin could be forgiven and be able to spend eternity with the eternal God.

For God so loved the world, that he gave his only Son, that whoever believes in him should not perish but have eternal life (John 3:16).

Where do you put your faith? In eternal matter? In eternal aliens?

> **Make sure your faith is in the eternal God who created all things and created the first man and woman.**

JANUARY 4
Genesis 9:11-15

Who Invented the Rainbow?

You can break up white light into its rainbow of colors using a prism to disperse the light rays. So, the rainbow is actually a result of the properties of light (refraction and dispersion) that God created on day one of creation week, when He said, *Let there be light* (Genesis 1:3).

He obviously created the entire electromagnetic spectrum, of which visible light is just a part. Now our eyes are designed to see seven colors with specific wavelengths divided out of visible light — red, orange, yellow, green, blue, indigo, and violet. Of course, there are many other visible colors made by mixing various combinations of these colors — such as pink, which can be made with the right mix of red and blue wavelengths. And if we consider all frequencies, there are as many colors (invisible to us) as the stars in the universe. But the true rainbow has seven colors.

God invented the rainbow. Who owns the rainbow? God! As God invented everything that enables a rainbow to exist, God obviously owns the rainbow. God owns everything. *Behold, to the LORD your God belong heaven and the heaven of heavens, the earth with all that is in it* (Deuteronomy 10:14).

Who gave the rainbow a special meaning? After the global Flood of Noah's day about 4,300 years ago, God made a promise. Pay close attention to what He says about ownership of the "[rain]bow":

"I establish my covenant with you, that never again shall all flesh be cut off by the waters of the flood, and never again shall there be a flood to destroy the earth." And God said, "This is the sign of the covenant that I make between me and you and every living creature that is with you, for all future generations: I have set my bow in the cloud, and it shall be a sign of the covenant between me and the earth. When I bring clouds over the earth and the bow is seen in the clouds, I will remember my covenant that is between me and you and every living creature of all flesh" (Genesis 9:11–15).

Note God said, "my bow." He owns it. The One who created light and its properties designated that from that time onward, the rainbow, "my bow" (resulting from light's created properties of refraction and dispersion), would serve as a reminder that God would never again judge the earth with a global Flood.

So the One who created light — and who created our eyes so we could see the colors that make up visible light — declared that the rainbow would have a special meaning after the Flood. God said, "I have set my bow in the cloud." Yes, God owns the rainbow and gave it special meaning about 4,300 years ago when He spoke to Noah after the Flood.

Anytime we see the rainbow and its seven colors, we should be reminded that:

1. God judged the wickedness of man at the time of Noah — and the evidence of that judgment is seen over the whole earth. Most of the fossil record is the graveyard of the global Flood of Noah's day.
2. God had Noah build an Ark of salvation, and it had one door. Noah and his family went through this door into the Ark to be saved. Jesus said, *I am the door. If anyone enters by me, he will be saved* (John 10:9). Noah's ark is a picture of Jesus, of salvation. In judgment, God provides salvation as a gift for those who will receive it.

THEOLOGY

JANUARY 4

3. There will never be another global Flood as a judgment, but there is another judgment coming when God will judge with fire and make a new heavens and earth. It's also a reminder that man can't destroy the earth — God will at the time He has appointed. But in the meantime, *While the earth remains, seedtime and harvest, cold and heat, summer and winter, day and night, shall not cease* (Genesis 8:22).

4. God has provided an ark of salvation for those who will receive it so we can spend eternity with our Creator and not suffer the consequences of our sin of rebellion by being cast into hell for eternity. Just as there was one door on the Ark, there is only one door by which we can go to heaven.

We need to worship the One who invented the rainbow, and every time we see it be reminded of its true message. However, be warned. The devil is the great liar and deceiver.

And the great dragon was thrown down, that ancient serpent, who is called the devil and Satan, the deceiver of the whole world—he was thrown down to the earth, and his angels were thrown down with him (Revelation 12:9).

You are of your father the devil, and your will is to do your father's desires. He was a murderer from the beginning, and does not stand in the truth, because there is no truth in him. When he lies, he speaks out of his own character, for he is a liar and the father of lies (John 8:44).

The devil takes whatever God has ordained and perverts it so that it is totally corrupted from what was first intended. For example, he perverts:

Marriage	corrupting this from the true created marriage of one man and woman to two men or two women or other perversions.
Sex	corrupting the created, rightful place for sex within marriage for one man and one woman to whatever is right in one's own eyes.
Gender	corrupting this from the created two genders – male and female – to however one wants to define gender.
Dominion	corrupting man's created dominion over the creation to the creation having dominion over man, as seen in the modern climate change religion.
Rainbow	corrupting this from the meaning of the seven-color rainbow given by God after the Flood to be associated with the anti-biblical LGBTQ worldview and other perversions.

Sadly, numerous churches and church leaders have adopted the devil's perversion of the rainbow and support the sinful lifestyles of those who reject true marriage as God created (one man and one woman) and reject God's created genders for humans (only two, male and female).

We must stand boldly against the devil's perversion of what God created and ordained:

I found it necessary to write appealing to you to contend for the faith that was once for all delivered to the saints (Jude 3).

God gives us in His Word the true meaning of the rainbow.

JANUARY 5
2 Timothy 3:16

Where Do You Draw the Line Between What Is Vital and What Is Not?

Often when I post on the vital importance of taking Genesis 1–11 as literal history, a number of Christians say the most important thing is the gospel, not what one believes about Genesis. They claim that whether or not Genesis is history is not a vital issue. They say it's not what is called a first-tier issue. Now, certainly, the gospel is the most important message in the universe, but there is a vital issue concerning how one takes Genesis that must be understood, nonetheless.

In Christian circles, a system exists, developed by theologians, that divides doctrines and other scriptural matters into first-tier, second-tier, and third-tier levels. This man-made categorization considers "first-tier" issues to be either "essential doctrines" or doctrines that are required for salvation or both.

I once heard a Christian leader's podcast where he declared that topics such as the days of creation and the age of the earth (and evolution) were not "first-order" issues. He essentially said that Christians could believe in millions of years and even theistic evolution (though he saw problems with that view) as long as they hold to the essentials of Scripture concerning doctrine and salvation. He does imply that there are people who hold to a literal Genesis (six literal days, young earth, etc.) and claim they use their views as a "litmus test" for whether one is a "real" Christian or not.

Now Romans 10:9 states: *[I]f you confess with your mouth that Jesus is Lord and believe in your heart that God raised him from the dead, you will be saved.*

Through the years, I have always emphasized in my teaching that salvation is not conditioned upon believing in six literal creation days or a young earth. Nowhere does God's Word state you have to believe such things to be saved. There are Christians who believe in millions of years and Christians who accept evolution. If they profess Christ as their Savior, I would not question their salvation in any way. So, I do not believe that what someone believes about the age of the earth or days of creation is a litmus test for whether they are a real Christian or not! Does it follow, then, that the days of creation, the age of the earth, and whether God used evolution are not important and thus are not first-tier issues?

Now, this is the problem with man-made systems imposed on Scripture. It's not as simple as the use of these systems would suggest. We have to understand the limitations of such man-made systems. So let me ask this instead: "Is biblical authority a first-tier issue?"

Let's consider the following. Does the Bible state you have to believe the following to be saved?

- Jesus walked on water.
- Jesus fed thousands as a miracle.
- Jesus healed the blind, deaf, and mute.
- The Israelites' shoes and clothes didn't wear out in the desert.
- Jonah was in a fish for three days.
- Jesus was born of a virgin.

APOLOGETICS

The list could go on and on. The answer to each question is "no" — the Bible doesn't say a person has to believe those accounts to be saved. So does that mean the list doesn't matter then? Of course not, as these accounts are plainly taught in Scripture when you take the text as written. Is it important to believe in the list? To reject them is to undermine biblical authority. It ultimately opens the door to reject anything in Scripture.

So where do you draw the line between what's vital (first tier) and what is not? Well, consider this verse: *All Scripture is breathed out by God and profitable for teaching, for reproof, for correction, and for training in righteousness* (2 Timothy 3:16).

Biblical authority is indeed a first-order (first-tier) issue.

What would be a litmus test to determine if someone is undermining biblical authority? Well, one way is to see if the person is working from the actual words of the text (exegesis) or if the person is taking ideas outside of Scripture and bringing them into the text and interpreting the words (eisegesis).

I've said so many times that it's true that in the Church, people have different views of eschatology, modes of baptism, speaking in tongues, the Sabbath day, etc. But all these issues involve people arguing primarily from Scripture to justify their positions, not basing their ideas on influences outside Scripture.

However, when it comes to Genesis, all the different views within the Church, such as day-age theory, framework hypothesis, theistic evolution, local flood, and so on, have one thing in common. Every one of these positions involves taking man's belief from outside the Bible, regarding millions of years (based on the religion of naturalism), and trying to fit old ages into Scripture. Many of these views involve adding biological evolution and astronomical evolution into Scripture. This approach uses eisegesis, not exegesis.

I assert that those who do not hold to a literal Genesis (i.e., six literal days, young earth, Adam made from dust and Eve from his side, global Flood, etc.) do so because they have been influenced by what the world is teaching regarding origins. This view permeates seminaries and Bible colleges, which produce most of our pastors. It is an attempt to add ideas into Scripture and force an interpretation on Genesis that undermines biblical authority. I believe this is a major contributing factor to the generational loss from the Church.

Now, how do I respond to Christian leaders who hold such a second-tier position on Genesis and biblical authority? Well, to quote the famous reformer Martin Luther:

"The 'Days' of Creation Were Ordinary Days in Length. We must understand that these days were actual days (*veros* dies), contrary to the opinion of the holy fathers. Whenever we observe that the opinions of the fathers disagree with Scripture, we reverently bear with them and acknowledge them to be our elders. Nevertheless, we do not depart from the authority of Scripture for their sake."[2]

I ask that you pray for Christian leaders who don't see Genesis and biblical authority as a vital issue. Pray that their hearts and minds would be opened so they can see how the authority of Scripture (especially its gospel message) is a "first-order" or "first-tier" issue. By not taking Genesis as it was written (as literal history), Christian leaders are undermining the authority of God's Word.

> **Taking the Bible naturally, as written, according to the literature and its context, is of great importance.**

JANUARY 6
1 Timothy 6:20

Man's Fictional Account of History vs. God's True Account of History

When I debated Bill Nye in 2014, Bill saw the debate as one of science versus the Bible. But it's not science versus the Bible! That's why one of the first things I did in the debate was to define terms.

In today's world, we often hear statements like "Science disproves creation" or "Science proves evolution." Whenever we hear such claims, the first thing we should ask is, "What do you mean by science?" When people talk to me about science and the Bible, I always start the conversation by asking them to define the word "science." Most look at me with blank faces. Others will give all sorts of different explanations. It's obvious that most people use the word "science," but they have a nebulous understanding of what it means.

The word "science" comes from the Latin *scientia*, which means "knowledge." When most people think of the word science, they tend to equate it with technology, yet secularists also equate the word science with molecules-to-man evolution and millions of years.

To help sort out the confusion, there needs to be an understanding that we can divide science into two categories:

Operational (or Observational) Science.	Historical Science.
This refers to knowledge gained by direct observation (using the five senses) and based on repeatable testing. Such "science" (knowledge) has enabled scientists to build modern technology like airplanes and rocket ships. Whether one is a creationist or an evolutionist, we all use the same operational science. Thus, both evolutionists and creationists can be honored for their observational science. Creationists love observational science. Often, I hear atheists claim that creationists can't be real scientists. Not only is that a ridiculous statement, but some of the most brilliant scientists in our history were creationists, such as Isaac Newton, Johannes Kepler, Michael Faraday, and many others.	This refers to knowledge about the past – in essence, history. This type of science cannot be observed directly or based on repeated testing, so we need other ways of finding knowledge. The Genesis account of origins gives us knowledge about the past, revealed by an infallible witness – God. Those who believe in Darwinian evolution claim to have knowledge concerning the past as well, but this knowledge is based upon the beliefs of fallible humans who did not witness the supposed evolutionary history. Genesis is the true account of historical science, whereas evolution is a fictional, historical science.

The Bible is really God's book of historical science, as it's primarily a book of history. And where it touches on biology, geology, astronomy, anthropology, etc., it is totally accurate.

Thus, the battle between creation and evolution (the Genesis account versus man's account of origins) is really a battle over historical science. The role of operational (or observational) science is that it can be used to confirm or refute one's historical science.

Observational science (in geology, biology, astronomy, anthropology, etc.) confirms the account of origins in Genesis and refutes the evolutionary account. (Many of these confirmations are available on our website, AnswersInGenesis.org.)

Thus, when an atheist claims the origins battle is one of science versus the Bible, they are incorrect. The origins battle is one of man's historical science versus God's historical science. It's a battle of man's fictional account of history versus God's true account of history.

When listening to arguments that supposedly support evolution, you have to learn how to separate observational science and historical science. Here is one example to get you thinking in this way: if you see a claim that sedimentary rock strata containing fossils are millions of years old, then you need to sort out what is observational versus historical science. The statement that rocks are sedimentary rocks is one of observational science. Both creationists and evolutionists agree on what is directly observed.

But the claim that the rocks are millions of years old falls under historical science. It is not observational but rather an interpretation of the past. Biblical creationists would not agree with this interpretation but instead interpret the fossils as a deposit from the Flood of Noah's day or some post-Flood catastrophe that occurred only thousands of years ago.

Thus, observational science cannot disprove the Bible. We agree on the observational science but totally disagree on the historical science. The problem is not with the operational science but with the mistaken interpretation of unobserved history.

We need to understand that all facts are interpreted, and they are interpreted based on one's worldview. And one's worldview has a foundation, either God's Word or man's word. I find most people don't really understand that all the facts are interpreted. That's why evolutionists will often say to me that it's a fact that rocks are billions of years old, or it's a fact that life arose by chance. They didn't see those rocks forming. They didn't see life arise on earth. What they are stating are not facts but interpretations based on man's word, and that has many fallible assumptions associated with it.

O Timothy, guard the deposit entrusted to you. Avoid the irreverent babble and contradictions of what is falsely called "knowledge" (1 Timothy 6:20).

The next time someone starts discussing issues of origins and science, ask them to define what they mean by "science." Before you can even discuss the topic, you all need to have the same understanding of that word, or you won't get anywhere. The same is true of the word "evolution." When someone is discussing evolution, ask them what they mean by that term. Some will say apelike creatures to man, others will say change. Unless one has the same definition of terms, discussions don't get anywhere.

Don't be led astray by man's false history/false knowledge.

JANUARY 7
Psalm 90:2

What Was God Doing All That Time Before Creation?

One reason some people have given me for rejecting a young universe is that they think it somehow limits God. After all, what was He doing all that time before creation? But this question reflects a basic misunderstanding of God and time.

Because of my stand on a young universe, a man approached me and said, "But it makes no sense to believe in a young universe. After all, what was God doing all that time before He created?"

I answered, "What time do you mean?"

The person answered, "Well, it doesn't make sense to say that God has always existed, and yet He didn't create the universe until just 6,000 years ago." Apparently, he was worried that God once had a lot of time on His hands with nothing to do.

I then went on to explain that because God has always existed, then it is meaningless to ask, "What was God doing all that time before He created?" No matter how far you were to go back in time, you would still have an infinite amount of time before He created! Even if the universe were billions or trillions or quadrillions of years old, you could still ask the same question.

I then answered, "But you are missing the fact that there was no time before God created." Time is actually a created entity. The first verse of the Bible reads: *In the beginning, God created the heavens and the earth* (Genesis 1:1).

A study of this verse reveals that God created time, space, and matter on the first day of creation week. No one of these can have a meaningful existence without the others. God created the space-mass-time universe. Space and matter must exist in time, and time requires space and matter. Time is only meaningful if physical entities exist and events transpire during time. "In the beginning" is when time began! There was no time before time was created!

When I'm teaching children, I like to explain it this way. There was no "before" God created. There was not even "nothing"! There was God existing in eternity. This is something humans, as finite created beings, can never really understand. That's why the Bible makes it clear there is always a "faith" aspect to our understanding of God. Now, biblical faith is not against reason, but such things go way beyond our finite understanding.

And without faith it is impossible to please him, for whoever would draw near to God must believe that he exists and that he rewards those who seek him (Hebrews 11:6).

In Psalm 90:2, we read, *Before the mountains were brought forth, or ever you had formed the earth and the world, from everlasting to everlasting you are God.*

So, what was "before" creation? God existing from everlasting to everlasting — God existing in eternity. Do you remember what God said to Moses when he asked God who he should say sent him to lead His people out of Egypt's oppression?

God said to Moses, "I AM WHO I AM." And he said, "Say this to the people of Israel: 'I AM has sent me to you'" (Exodus 3:14).

THEOLOGY

God is the great "I AM." He exists in eternity. He was not created.

In Revelation 1:8, we read, *"I am the Alpha and the Omega," says the Lord God, "who is and who was and who is to come, the Almighty."*

Isaiah 43:10 records these words from God: *"You are my witnesses," declares the Lord, "and my servant whom I have chosen, that you may know and believe me and understand that I am he. Before me no God was formed, nor shall there be after me."*

In other words, it's a mistake to talk about what God was doing "before creation" because the concept of time (before, during, and after) did not come to be until day one of creation week. God exists — He is — He is the eternal self-existent One. He is outside of time.

The Bible makes it clear that God's existence is completely separate from the history of this universe, which began in Genesis 1:1. In other words, there is no such thing as "prehistoric." History began when it was first recorded — the first verse of Genesis. Now when we understand this and then also understand that the whole of creation, including Genesis 1:1, was accomplished in six days, we can begin to calculate how long ago God created the world.

Exodus 20:11 makes it clear that the heavens and the earth (Genesis 1:1) and everything else (all that is listed in Genesis 1) were created in six days: *For in six days the Lord made heaven and earth, the sea, and all that is in them, and rested the seventh day. Therefore the Lord blessed the Sabbath day and made it holy.* Based on the way the word *day* is used in Genesis 1 (qualified by number, morning, evening, etc.), creation had to be six ordinary (approximately 24-hour) days. Many technical and popular articles show that the context requires this meaning.

Then the Bible lists very specific genealogies of the Messiah's line in Genesis 5 and Genesis 11. We are told that Adam was 130 years old when he begat Seth. When Seth was 105 years old, he begat Enosh — and so these lists continue. When one adds up all the dates and other time references throughout Scripture, it is clear that "In the beginning" was about 6,000 years ago.

Now some Christian leaders have claimed that the Bible doesn't give an absolute date for creation, so we can't know how old the creation really is. However, the Bible does give us something much better than a date — a very specific history that allows us not only to determine the age of the universe but also to know all the essential details about God's plan of redemption from the beginning of time, including the line of the promised Messiah.

One final point: Nowhere in the Bible do we find any suggestion of millions or billions of years. Belief in millions of years is really part of secular man's religion, which attempts to explain life without God, instead of believing the true account of origins in Genesis that begins "In the beginning." Our ability to trust God's promise of salvation relies upon our ability to trust everything He says about history, from beginning to end. Thankfully, we serve a God we can trust in every detail. Though He is beyond space and time, He humbled Himself to become a man and die on the Cross for our sins. He also has given us a record of this history in His Word so that we can know it's really true.

If we can't trust His claims about the past, how can we trust His promises about the future?

JANUARY 8
Revelation 7:9

What Should We Believe About "Interracial" Marriage?

One of the most-asked questions I've received when I talk about the origin of the so-called "races" is what I believe about what many call interracial marriage. When anyone asks me that question, I respond by saying, "Biologically, there is no such thing as interracial marriage."

When I speak on the race issue, I first of all go to God's Word to understand what God clearly teaches about the human race. We learn there was only one man to start with:

God made one man at the beginning: *[T]hen the Lord God formed the man of dust from the ground and breathed into his nostrils the breath of life, and the man became a living creature* (Genesis 2:7).

Thus it is written, "The first man Adam became a living being"; the last Adam became a life-giving spirit (1 Corinthians 15:45).

Then we learn there was only one woman to begin with:

So the Lord God caused a deep sleep to fall upon the man, and while he slept took one of his ribs and closed up its place with flesh. And the rib that the Lord God had taken from the man he made into a woman and brought her to the man (Genesis 2:21–22).

The man called his wife's name Eve, because she was the mother of all living (Genesis 3:20).

All human beings descended from Adam and Eve. This means there is only one race of humans biologically: *And he made from one man every nation of mankind to live on all the face of the earth, having determined allotted periods and the boundaries of their dwelling place* (Acts 17:26).

Yes, all humans belong to one biological race descended from the first man and woman.

In 2000, the Human Genome Project that mapped the sequence of the human genome released their findings to the world and stated: "Dr. Venter (head of the Celera Genomics Corporation, Rockville, MD) and scientists at the National Institutes of Health recently announced that they had put together a draft of the entire sequence of the human genome, and the researchers unanimously declared, there is only one race—the human race."[3]

Exactly what one would expect based on the Bible's revealed human history — there is only one human race.

This means all humans belong to one human family. We are all related to each other, and all have the same two ancestors from 6,000 years ago: Adam and Eve. There is only one race biologically according to Scripture and confirmed by observational science. This means there is no such thing as "interracial marriage" from a perspective of biology.

However, there is an issue in regard to interracial marriage spiritually. Consider this principle given in Scripture for us that also applies to marriage:

Do not be unequally yoked with unbelievers. For what partnership has righteousness with lawlessness? Or what fellowship has light with darkness? (2 Corinthians 6:14).

THEOLOGY

JANUARY 8

Applied to marriage, this principle means a Christian should never knowingly marry a non-Christian. Remember, one of the primary importances of marriage is to produce godly offspring. Sadly, many marriages end up in trouble because this principle of Christians only marrying Christians wasn't adhered to. Also, such spiritually mixed marriages can result in a godly legacy not being passed on to the next generation.

Some Christian leaders claim God teaches the claimed "races" of people be kept separate because he told the Israelites not to marry into other groups of people. For instance, God told the Israelites not to marry the Canaanites. But Rahab, a Canaanite who helped the Israelite spies at Jericho, is in the lineage leading to the God-man Jesus in Matthew 1 and is also listed in Hebrews 11 as a person of great faith.

It's obvious Rahab stopped being a Canaanite spiritually (rejecting the Canaanite pagan religion) and became an Israelite spiritually (believing and trusting in the one true God) and thus was free to marry an Israelite. This clearly shows there is no such thing as interracial marriage biologically. The interracial marriage the Bible speaks against is the marriage between the two spiritual races — the godly "race" and the ungodly "race." Whom a Christian should marry has nothing to do with biology but the spiritual state of one's heart.

When you then apply this, if two Christians get married and one has a light shade of skin and one a dark shade (all humans are the same basic color just different shades), this is not a biracial couple. This is a one-race couple! This also means there are no biracial children, as all of us belong to one race.

Christians should be using terminology consistent with God's Word and science to help people understand the truth concerning *homo sapiens*.

I urge people to not use the term "races" but to use the term "people groups" when referring to humans from different cultures. We also need to stop using terms like "biracial," as all humans belong to one race.

Because all humans belong to one race — all descendants of Adam — this means all humans are sinners, and all are in need of trusting Christ for salvation. That's why Christians need to proclaim the truth of the gospel to everyone, to all tribes and nations.

Then I saw another angel flying directly overhead, with an eternal gospel to proclaim to those who dwell on earth, to every nation and tribe and language and people (Revelation 14:6).

After this I looked, and behold, a great multitude that no one could number, from every nation, from all tribes and peoples and languages, standing before the throne and before the Lamb, clothed in white robes, with palm branches in their hands (Revelation 7:9).

> **What a difference it would make if every person started looking at everyone else as one of their relatives, a member of our extended family!**

JANUARY 9

James 2:1-4

What Should Christians Think About Critical Race Theory (CRT)?

As Christians, we need to ensure we look at everything through biblical glasses. We need to make sure we're using a truly Christian worldview starting with the foundation of God's Word to build our thinking in every area.

Instead of looking at CRT and then trying to fit it with the Bible, we need to ask, "Does CRT start with the foundation of God's Word or man's word?" It does not start with God's Word, which means there's only one other foundation: man's word.

This means CRT will not be in accord with a Christian worldview, which means it will not be a correct one. So we need to ask, "In what ways is it not Christian then?"

God's Word says we're identified as individuals made in God's image, equal in value, individually accountable to God.

CRT divides humans into two identity groups: oppressed and oppressors (essentially based on skin shade). In short, CRT says "whites" are guilty oppressors and "blacks" (non-whites) are the innocent "oppressed." Note, this is assigned guilt (or innocence) based solely on a person's shade of skin. CRT is racist and guilty of the sin of partiality.

Scripture says we are to show no partiality: *My brothers, show no partiality as you hold the faith in our Lord Jesus Christ, the Lord of glory. For if a man wearing a gold ring and fine clothing comes into your assembly, and a poor man in shabby clothing also comes in, and if you pay attention to the one who wears the fine clothing and say, "You sit here in a good place," while you say to the poor man, "You stand over there," or, "Sit down at my feet," have you not then made distinctions among yourselves and become judges with evil thoughts?* (James 2:1–4).

CRT has an emphasis on judging people by their outside appearances. But the Bible teaches us to *not judge by appearances, but judge with right judgment* (John 7:24).

And for right judgment, it has to be a judgment of their heart, their spiritual state. As God teaches us, *For out of the abundance of the heart the mouth speaks* (Matthew 12:34) and *The good person out of the good treasure of his heart produces good, and the evil person out of his evil treasure produces evil, for out of the abundance of the heart his mouth speaks* (Luke 6:45).

This is why God's Word records what happened when Samuel came to anoint the king and thought it was going to be David's brother: *But the LORD said to Samuel, "Do not look on his appearance or on the height of his stature, because I have rejected him. For the LORD sees not as man sees: man looks on the outward appearance, but the LORD looks on the heart"* (1 Samuel 16:7).

CRT divides people into those who are black and those who are white. And although there is much more behind this, it still relates to skin color. Yet all humans are the same basic color, brown, because of the main pigment for skin color, melanin. There are really no black or white people, but shades of brown from dark to light.

APOLOGETICS

CRT says only the oppressors are guilty. The Bible says we are all sinners and all guilty before a perfect and holy God.

CRT, in essence, seeks vengeance — reparations. But God's Word commands us to *Love your enemies and pray for those who persecute you* (Matthew 5:44) and *forgive us our debts, as we also have forgiven our debtors* (Matthew 6:12).

CRT says revolution and redistribution are the solution. God's Word tells us the only true solution is changed hearts through the gospel of Jesus Christ.

CRT and the Christian worldview are in total conflict. Sadly, there are even church leaders who have adopted aspects of CRT to mesh it with God's Word. That's no different than those who mesh evolution/millions of years with Genesis.

> **In an eternal sense, the Bible divides people into two groups too: the saved and the unsaved, which is the focus of God's justice and should be the focus of Christians as well.**

JANUARY 10
Romans 3:4

What Is the Bible?

What is the Bible?

Why do I ask that question? I have found a lot of people in the Church look on the Bible as just a guidebook to life and/or a book of spiritual and moral matters.

But the Bible is not just a book one adds to their thinking. The Bible has over 3,000 claims to be the Word of God. We are told that God knows everything, being infinite in knowledge and wisdom.

[F]or whenever our heart condemns us, God is greater than our heart, and he knows everything (1 John 3:20).

Great is our Lord, and abundant in power; his understanding is beyond measure (Psalm 147:5).

Have you not known? Have you not heard? The LORD is the everlasting God, the Creator of the ends of the earth. He does not faint or grow weary; his understanding is unsearchable (Isaiah 40:28).

The Bible is a revelation from God to man, from the One who knows all things. This means the Bible gives the key information God has revealed to us to enable us to have the right foundation to build the right way of thinking about everything. Without that key information, how would we as fallible human beings know how to understand anything?

Here's the problem for man. No matter how much we know, there's an infinite amount more to know. This means no matter how much we know, we don't know how much we do know or don't know in relation to whatever there is to know. That means we just don't know much at all.

That's the lesson God taught Job. When Job was going to argue with God concerning what had happened to him, God asked Job a series of questions to show him that he didn't know much at all compared to God. That's why after God had enabled Job to understand how finite his understanding was, Job said:

I know that you can do all things, and that no purpose of yours can be thwarted. "Who is this that hides counsel without knowledge?" Therefore I have uttered what I did not understand, things too wonderful for me, which I did not know. "Hear, and I will speak; I will question you, and you make it known to me." I had heard of you by the hearing of the ear, but now my eye sees you; therefore I despise myself, and repent in dust and ashes (Job 42:2–6).

Job recognized, as we all need to recognize, that we know next to nothing compared to God. How arrogant of humans to think they know better than God when they determine man's views of origins must be correct, and therefore, we have to reinterpret God's Word in Genesis to tell God what is supposedly true about the origin and history of life and the universe.

No, God's Word is a revelation from God, who doesn't lie, who knows everything. This means all our thinking in every area has to be founded on God's Word. We must use God's Word to judge what man is saying and not the other way around.

I remember my father telling me when looking at the notes in the Scofield Reference Bible about the supposed "gap theory" that we needed to always understand the notes were not inspired like the Word of God. He told me that God's Word should always be looked on as the commentary on the notes and not the other way

APOLOGETICS

around because only God knows everything, and it's God's Word we can totally trust. In other words, we should judge the notes by what God's Word states. And when we do — the gap theory fails! The notes were fallible; the text of Scripture is infallible.

Think about this in regard to forensic scientists trying to solve a murder. They may find someone's fingerprints and even blood type at the scene. The circumstantial evidence can overwhelmingly point to a particular person being the murderer. That person could be found guilty and put in jail. But these scientists didn't have all evidence. What happens if some evidence is found later that would throw a whole different light on the murder scene and that the murder was actually committed by someone else? This has really happened more than once in real life. There have been people found guilty of a crime based on circumstantial evidence, only to be found to be innocent later on when additional evidence comes along.

People may think that the evolutionists' view of history makes sense of the evidence of the present. But they don't know everything there is to know, so they don't know for sure they have the correct interpretation of the evidence. But God's Word is the Word of the One who knows everything and understands all the evidence. That's why we need to trust what God states in Genesis concerning origins and use what God reveals to judge the ideas of man — not the other way around, as has happened so much in the Church.

Sadly, many church leaders have exalted man's ideas above God's Word when they compromise man's evolutionary/millions of years beliefs with the Bible. In a way, those who do this are really looking at man, not God, as knowing everything. It's really a worship of fallible man.

That's why over and over again God's Word warns us to not trust in man's word, but trust in God's Word:

Thus says the Lord: "Cursed is the man who trusts in man and makes flesh his strength, whose heart turns away from the Lord" (Jeremiah 17:5).

It is better to take refuge in the Lord than to trust in princes (Psalm 118:9).

Trust in the Lord with all your heart, and do not lean on your own understanding. In all your ways acknowledge him, and he will make straight your paths (Proverbs 3:5–6).

It is better to take refuge in the Lord than to trust in man. It is better to take refuge in the Lord than to trust in princes (Psalm 118:8–9).

I must admit, when it comes to beliefs about origins, I'm immediately suspicious of views held by the majority of scientists because man knows nothing compared to God, and man has a sinful heart that does not want to believe God's Word.

I just can't understand (except it's a result of their sin nature) why so many Christians want to trust man's beliefs about evolution and millions of years instead of God's clear Word in Genesis. I would rather stand guilty before the Lord for believing His Word as written than for putting my trust in fallible man's word.

This trust in man's word has been catastrophic for the modern Church because of the devastating consequences in the coming generations doubting and ultimately rejecting God's Word.

As I often quote, "Let God be true though every one were a liar" (Romans 3:4).

JANUARY 11
Proverbs 31:30

What Is a Woman?

What is a woman? In 2022, a documentary hosted by conservative commentator Matt Walsh, host of *The Matt Walsh Show* podcast and columnist for *The Daily Wire*, was released.

This was an eye-opening documentary detailing the anti-God agenda regarding gender identity that is destroying many lives, including those of young children.

What the documentary didn't cover, though, was the answer to the question, "What is a woman?" from the One who created and designed women — our Creator God. The movie also didn't give the solution to the gender issue, which is the truth of God's Word and the saving gospel. (Now so much could be said about this documentary and this question, but I'm just going to highlight this one particular aspect.)

What do we learn from God's Word regarding the answer to the question, "What is a woman?"

Genesis gives an overview of the creation week, culminating in the creation of the first two human beings on day six: *So God created man in his own image, in the image of God he created him; male and female he created them* (Genesis 1:27).

We learn that God created only two genders of humans: male and female. And we know from the study of genetics that men have an XY pair of sex chromosomes and women have an XX pair. But God's Word tells us a lot about men and women and their differences.

God gives the details of why and how he created the first woman (female) in Genesis 2.

We learn that God created the first woman to be a helper for the first man, Adam: *Then the Lord God said, "It is not good that the man should be alone; I will make him a helper fit for him"* (Genesis 2:18).

So God made the first woman as Adam's wife. She was made from Adam's side. We then read in Genesis 3:20: *The man called his wife's name Eve, because she was the mother of all living.* So other than the first man, all people would be descendants of this first man and first woman.

God told the man and the woman to be fruitful and multiply, and both were to lead in having dominion over the creation: *And God blessed them. And God said to them, "Be fruitful and multiply and fill the earth and subdue it, and have dominion over the fish of the sea and over the birds of the heavens and over every living thing that moves on the earth"* (Genesis 1:28).

Are men and women equal? They are both equal in value, both sinners, both can receive the free gift of salvation, and both are commanded to live lives honoring to the Lord. So just like men, women need to be born again, to abide in Christ, and trust God's Word as the absolute authority in all areas.

However, God gave men and women different roles. Adam was created first, so he was given a headship role in marriage. Adam was given the instruction not to eat the fruit of the tree of the knowledge of good and evil. That's why Adam gets the blame for sin, not Eve, as in Romans 5:12: *Therefore, just as sin came into the world through one man, and death through sin, and so death spread to all men because all sinned.*

FAMILY — JANUARY 11

But I want you to understand that the head of every man is Christ, the head of a wife is her husband, and the head of Christ is God (1 Corinthians 11:3).

The man is given the role of pouring out sacrificial love on his wife: *Husbands, love your wives, as Christ loved the church and gave himself up for her, that he might sanctify her, having cleansed her by the washing of water with the word* (Ephesians 5:25–26).

Likewise, husbands, live with your wives in an understanding way, showing honor to the woman as the weaker vessel, since they are heirs with you of the grace of life, so that your prayers may not be hindered (1 Peter 3:7).

Marriage is a spiritual picture of Christ and the Church. The Church is to submit to Christ, as seen in teaching about the woman's role: *Wives, submit to your own husbands, as to the Lord. For the husband is the head of the wife even as Christ is the head of the church, his body, and is himself its Savior* (Ephesians 5:22–23). And the principle given in Ephesians 5:21 is a reminder for men and women in the Church to place themselves under each other's authority out of respect for Christ: *[S]ubmitting to one another out of reverence for Christ.*

Now because we no longer live in a perfect world, there will no longer be perfect relationships, and no longer perfect obedience to the roles God gave. We need to be warned about what can happen because of our sin nature. *To the woman he said, "I will surely multiply your pain in childbearing; in pain you shall bring forth children. Your desire shall be contrary to your husband, but he shall rule over you"* (Genesis 3:16).

Because of sin, now rules will be distorted. Our sin nature will try to master us. Because Adam sinned and Eve was deceived, now women will have pain in childbirth. Also, if a woman lets her sin nature master her, she will want to usurp the headship role of the man. The man will want to corrupt his headship role and lord it despotically over the woman, instead of sacrificially loving her. That's why the Apostle Paul reminds us this way in Colossians 3:18–19: *Wives, submit to your husbands, as is fitting in the Lord. Husbands, love your wives, and do not be harsh with them.*

God's Word instructs women this way: *Do not let your adorning be external—the braiding of hair and the putting on of gold jewelry, or the clothing you wear—but let your adorning be the hidden person of the heart with the imperishable beauty of a gentle and quiet spirit, which in God's sight is very precious* (1 Peter 3:3–4). And Proverbs 31:30 describes a godly woman: *Charm is deceitful, and beauty is vain, but a woman who fears the* Lord *is to be praised.*

Every woman should aspire to be described like this: *Strength and dignity are her clothing, and she laughs at the time to come. She opens her mouth with wisdom, and the teaching of kindness is on her tongue. She looks well to the ways of her household and does not eat the bread of idleness. Her children rise up and call her blessed; her husband also, and he praises her: "Many women have done excellently, but you surpass them all"* (Proverbs 31:25–29).

We can't fully answer the question "what is a woman" apart from the authority of God's Word.

JANUARY 12

Proverbs 3:5-6

What Happens to People Who Die but Have Never Heard the Gospel?

One of the questions Christians have debated through the ages is, "What happens to people who die but have never heard the gospel?" The same question is asked about young children. Skeptics have often used such questions to denigrate Christianity and stump Christians.

Now we are not going to have all the answers. But in building our thinking on God's Word, we should be able to have at least a big-picture answer, even if we don't have all the details. God hasn't revealed everything to us! We will always have an infinite amount more to know.

Now in regard to children, personally, I believe those children are a separate category for which the Bible doesn't really say much but does hint at the answer with David's comment when his son died, *I shall go to him, but he will not return to me* (2 Samuel 12:23).

In regard to both categories, we should always remember what Abraham said to God, *Shall not the Judge of all the earth do what is just?* (Genesis 18:25). And, yes, there are times we just have to admit we don't know for sure, and we do need to leave it to God.

However, the Bible does make it clear that *there is salvation in no one else, for there is no other name under heaven given among men by which we must be saved* (Acts 4:12). Salvation is only possible through trusting Jesus Christ as Lord and Savior.

But what if people haven't heard? God's Word teaches that God has made it evident to all that He is the Creator, *For what can be known about God is plain to them, because God has shown it to them. For his invisible attributes, namely, his eternal power and divine nature, have been clearly perceived, ever since the creation of the world, in the things that have been made. So they are without excuse* (Romans 1:19–20).

We are told that all humans have a conscience, as *They show that the work of the law is written on their hearts* (Romans 2:15).

All humans know God exists. And if they want truth, God will give it to them: *[I]f you seek it like silver and search for it as for hidden treasures, then you will understand the fear of the Lord and find the knowledge of God* (Proverbs 2:4–5).

In 1 Kings 10:1, we read that the Queen of Sheba came seeking. *Now when the queen of Sheba heard of the fame of Solomon concerning the name of the Lord, she came to test him with hard questions.* She is just one example of someone in the Bible who sought truth, and God gave it to her. It would seem from Matthew 12 when talking about the religious leaders who rejected him, Jesus refers to the Queen of Sheba as an example of someone who was pagan but recognized the truth of God.

The queen of the South will rise up at the judgment with this generation and condemn it, for she came from the ends of the earth to hear the wisdom of Solomon, and behold, something greater than Solomon is here (Matthew 12:42).

Every human is without excuse. If they want light, God will give them light. That's God's sovereignty. But then there's our responsibility: *How then will they call on him in whom they have not believed? And how are they to*

THEOLOGY   JANUARY 12

believe in him of whom they have never heard? And how are they to hear without someone preaching? And how are they to preach unless they are sent? As it is written, "How beautiful are the feet of those who preach the good news!" (Romans 10:14–15).

Responsibility and sovereignty work together. We must do everything humanly possible to reach as many people as possible with the truth of God's Word and the saving gospel. At the same time, we know our sovereign God will direct our paths, will open and shut doors, and will ensure those who want the light will receive the light.

An example of this is found in Acts:

And when they had come up to Mysia, they attempted to go into Bithynia, but the Spirit of Jesus did not allow them. So, passing by Mysia, they went down to Troas. And a vision appeared to Paul in the night: a man of Macedonia was standing there, urging him and saying, "Come over to Macedonia and help us." And when Paul had seen the vision, immediately we sought to go on into Macedonia, concluding that God had called us to preach the gospel to them (Acts 16:7–10).

Paul was going to a particular place to proclaim the gospel, but God shut the door and redirected him to others who needed and wanted the light.

We just can't comprehend God's ways. As we are told, *For my thoughts are not your thoughts, neither are your ways my ways, declares the Lord* (Isaiah 55:8).

Trust in the Lord with all your heart, and do not lean on your own understanding. In all your ways acknowledge him, and he will make straight your paths (Proverbs 3:5–6).

We should always do all we can to obey the Great Commission given in Matthew 28, with the understanding that God will direct our paths.

JANUARY 13
Joshua 4:21-24

What Do These Stones Mean?

Millions of people, including many Christian families, visit the Grand Canyon in America each year. As they stand on the edge of this stunning canyon, children and young people will ask their parents, "How did this happen? What formed all those rock layers and the canyon?" Now the signs and the park rangers will tell them the layers of sedimentary strata (some with lots of fossils) were laid down slowly over millions of years. They will then tell the story that the Colorado River eroded the canyon over millions of years.

In essence, the question asked was, "What do these stones mean?" Sadly, most hear a story based on the belief in (the religion of) evolutionary geology. But how many fathers answer the question by saying, "This canyon is a relic of a past catastrophic event, the event of Noah's Flood. The layers were laid down during the Flood, and then at the end of the Flood, God raised up the land surface, forming mountains (Psalm 104) and, in this area, formed a dam that held back leftover waters from the flood. Then the dam was broken, and the water gouged out the canyon to allow the river (called the Colorado River) to flow through it. The sediment was washed downstream into massive deposits called surge deposits. It's all a reminder of the judgment God brought on the earth because of the wickedness of man. It should remind us that God's Word is true, God judges wickedness because of our sin, and we all need to receive the free gift of salvation, as all humans are sinners."

Over and over again, children have not been given the correct answers by their fathers, even Christian fathers, when they have asked questions about the origin of the universe and life, as so many of all ages have been indoctrinated by the world's pagan evolutionary views.

One of my favorite passages in the Bible is in Joshua 4, where we read the account of the Israelites miraculously crossing the Jordan River. God told Joshua to get the people to have 12 men gather 12 stones from the river and build a memorial so that:

*When your children ask their fathers in times to come, "What do these stones mean?" then you shall let your children know, "Israel passed over this Jordan on dry ground." For the L*ORD *your God dried up the waters of the Jordan for you until you passed over, as the L*ORD *your God did to the Red Sea, which he dried up for us until we passed over, so that all the peoples of the earth may know that the hand of the L*ORD *is mighty, that you may fear the L*ORD *your God forever* (Joshua 4:21–24).

What a reminder! Make sure you tell this younger generation about the Lord and His Word so they will know who the true God is. And let this also be a witness to the world concerning the one true God.

When we opened the Ark Encounter attraction in 2016, the board members laid 12 stones next to the massive ship. I explained to the 8,000 in attendance that this life-sized Ark is our modern version of the 12 stones — to remind coming generations that God's Word is true and that the saving gospel in that Word is true. We built the Ark and the Creation Museum as our 12 stones, so to speak, to help parents pass on the truth of God's Word and the saving gospel to the coming generations.

We read one of the saddest passages in the Bible in Judges about when Joshua died, and then all that generation with Joshua died: *And there arose another generation after them who did not know the L*ORD *or the work*

FAMILY JANUARY 13

that he had done for Israel. And the people of Israel did what was evil in the sight of the LORD and served the Baals (Judges 2:10–11).

The children who were to ask about the meaning of these 12 stones rebelled and worshipped false gods! What happened? When we read Scripture, we find the fathers did not pass on the spiritual legacy to the next generation. This should be a warning to us today.

Psalm 78 instructs fathers to train their children to know the true God:

*… [H]e commanded our fathers to teach to their children,
that the next generation might know them, the children yet unborn,
and arise and tell them to their children, so that they should set their hope in God
and not forget the works of God, but keep his commandments* (Psalm 78:5–7).

And then we read:

*[A]nd that they should not be like their fathers, a stubborn and rebellious generation,
a generation whose heart was not steadfast, whose spirit was not faithful to God* (Psalm 78:8).

It's obvious these fathers of old did not obey the Lord and did not train up their children to fear the Lord as they should have. As a result, they lost the next generation after Joshua.

In essence, this is happening in the Church today. Statistics back in the early 2000s made it clear that two-thirds of young people in the United States were leaving the Church by college age (with very few returning).

Pew Research in 2010 clearly showed church attendance for millennials was down to 18%, and by 2021, Generation Z church attendance was down to less than 9%![4]

Research we have done at Answers in Genesis over the years shows clearly that parents and the Church have failed to raise generations who know what they believe, why they believe what they do, and how to defend the Christian faith.

Just like in the days after Joshua, we are now seeing the consequences of this lack of training as the secularization of generations has increased and an anti-Christian sentiment has grown in the culture.

I challenge fathers to commit to doing what God has commanded us to do in the spiritual training of our children. After all, each child is a human being who will live forever and ever in heaven or hell, which should convict each one of us concerning the time and resources we invest into each child.

Fathers need to be teaching their children to defend the Christian faith and give them answers to the evolutionary attacks of our day! They need to be teaching Genesis 1–11 as literal history, as it is the foundation of the rest of the Bible, of all doctrine, of the Christian worldview, and of everything. They need to be teaching against compromising God's Word in Genesis, as is happening in much of the Church.

[T]he father makes known to the children your faithfulness (Isaiah 38:19).

Fathers, do not provoke your children to anger, but bring them up in the discipline and instruction of the LORD (Ephesians 6:4).

Let's remember what God commands concerning our responsibilities to our children.

JANUARY 14

Philippians 3:7-8

What Can You Take to Heaven with You?

You can't take your car, your house, your bank account, or any other material item. So, it's not what you can take to heaven with you, it's whom!

Whom can you take to heaven with you? You can take your children, your friends, and your human family!

The point is, God's Son became the God-man to pay the penalty for our sin and provide the free gift of salvation to human beings.

Let me ask fathers a question. What is most important for your children? Is it their sports program? Is it their job in life? Is it the material goods they own? What is the most important thing for your children?

Consider this passage from Scripture:

But whatever gain I had, I counted as loss for the sake of Christ. Indeed, I count everything as loss because of the surpassing worth of knowing Christ Jesus my Lord. For his sake I have suffered the loss of all things and count them as rubbish, in order that I may gain Christ (Philippians 3:7–8).

The most important thing for any person is that they've trusted Christ for salvation. There is nothing more important than this in the whole universe. It is vital. It determines one's eternity.

There is nothing more important than your children knowing Christ. There is nothing more important for eternity. Eternity is forever, and ever, and ever, and ever, and ever, and … forever.

And Jeremiah reminds us that what is most important for all of us is that we know the Lord:

Thus says the Lord: "Let not the wise man boast in his wisdom, let not the mighty man boast in his might, let not the rich man boast in his riches, but let him who boasts boast in this, that he understands and knows me, that I am the Lord who practices steadfast love, justice, and righteousness in the earth. For in these things I delight, declares the Lord" (Jeremiah 9:23–24).

Now we all need to understand that no matter how we train our children, we can't guarantee their salvation. After all, *The soul who sins shall die. The son shall not suffer for the iniquity of the father, nor the father suffer for the iniquity of the son. The righteousness of the righteous shall be upon himself, and the wickedness of the wicked shall be upon himself* (Ezekiel 18:20).

However, at the same time, parents, and particularly the father as the spiritual head of the family, are to do all they can to train their children the way God instructs us to through His Word. There is always that balance between responsibility and sovereignty. We are to do all we can to train our children in the ways of the Lord. We must be diligent and teach them as the Scripture instructs us to. We are to pour in that biblical salt of truth and equip them with answers to defend the Christian faith. We must teach them to build a truly Christian worldview. We also must make sure they understand the gospel and the vital importance of receiving the free gift of salvation. And we pray God will open their hearts to the truth and save them. But we can't do the saving. It's God who does the saving. But our responsibility and God's sovereignty go hand in hand.

FAMILY — JANUARY 14

Our five children all have college degrees. We selected God-honoring colleges for them. And even though I'm thrilled they all have graduate degrees and one even a postgraduate degree, I would rather our children be ditchdiggers and go to heaven than some famous academic or wealthy person and go to hell. That's the bottom line.

Remember, our children are made in the image of God. They each have a soul that will live forever in heaven or hell. That should convict each one of us concerning how much diligence we put into training them as we should.

Wouldn't it be great if what Paul said to Timothy could be said of each of our children?

But as for you, continue in what you have learned and have firmly believed, knowing from whom you learned it and how from childhood you have been acquainted with the sacred writings, which are able to make you wise for salvation through faith in Christ Jesus (2 Timothy 3:14–15).

I praise the Lord my parents taught me God's Word from as far back as I can remember. They always took us to church and were highly involved in evangelistic outreaches to children. I remember my mother kneeling with us as she taught us to pray. I remember my father leading devotions at the breakfast table. And I'll never forget what they taught me.

My mother and father drummed into us, "God first, others second, and yourself last," and "It's only what is done for Jesus that lasts."

My parents were very involved with the church, always volunteering to help with various needs. And my father would also be teaching us the answers to liberal theology to make sure we would not be led astray by false teaching. He also filled in many times as the preacher when the pastor was away. We heard him teach God's Word authoritatively. And we heard people thank him for such great teaching that ministered to them.

And even though there was no guarantee of salvation, all six of their children received the free gift of salvation. And all our five children are Christians, and the four who have married have godly spouses. Now, all our children are raising their children by teaching the truth of God's Word and the saving gospel. What a blessing to see this generational impact.

So, fathers, hear God's Word:

Tell your children of it, and let your children tell their children, and their children to another generation (Joel 1:3).

And count the blessings:

The father of the righteous will greatly rejoice; he who fathers a wise son will be glad in him (Proverbs 23:24).

Remember: "It's only what is done for Jesus that lasts."

JANUARY 15
Job 38:4-7

Were You There?

In a presentation I give to children about dinosaurs, one of the fun things I do to teach them how to think in regard to origins is to teach them to ask, "Were you there?" when anyone talks about millions of years.

Now if you listen to my presentation, I do say to ask very politely. It's really one of those fun times during my talk that the kids, and adults too, love. I've had people come to me and introduce their children to me and say they remember going to one of my teaching sessions when they were a child, and they've never forgotten many things I taught them like, "Were you there?" I've even met many people and children over the years who will come up to me at the Ark or Creation Museum or in a church and look at me with a big smile on their face and say, "Were you there?"

Now over the years, evolutionists have mocked me for teaching children to ask this question. In fact, many blogs and even news items over the years have referenced me teaching children this and used it to malign me. Actually, I have been sort of surprised by the amount of attention this has received from atheists/evolutionists over the years. But I think the main reason they mock it is that it really is teaching children how to think correctly about science and origins. Sadly, much of education today doesn't teach children how to think. By doing this, they know children will start to recognize how they are being indoctrinated in evolutionary/millions of years beliefs.

Let me tell you where I obtained this idea from, why I teach children this, and why it's such a powerful question for them to learn to ask.

After Job's complaints and the dialogue with his friends, God spoke to Job:

*Then the L*ORD *answered Job out of the whirlwind and said: "Who is this that darkens counsel by words without knowledge? Dress for action like a man; I will question you, and you make it known to me"* (Job 38:1–3).

God was now going to help Job understand who God is. The first thing God said to teach Job was this:

Where were you when I laid the foundation of the earth? Tell me, if you have understanding. Who determined its measurements—surely you know! Or who stretched the line upon it? On what were its bases sunk, or who laid its cornerstone, when the morning stars sang together and all the sons of God shouted for joy? (Job 38:4–7).

God was making it clear to Job that he wasn't there when God made the earth. God asked, "Where were you when I laid the foundation of the earth?" It's significant that God began by speaking about the fact that He created the earth.

All the way through Scripture when God, through His Word, tells people who He is, we read statements like:

Worthy are you, our Lord and God, to receive glory and honor and power, for you created all things, and by your will they existed and were created (Revelation 4:11).

*Have you not known? Have you not heard? The L*ORD *is the everlasting God, the Creator of the ends of the earth. He does not faint or grow weary; his understanding is unsearchable* (Isaiah 40:28).

*Oh come, let us worship and bow down; let us kneel before the L*ORD*, our Maker!* (Psalm 95:6).

FAMILY — JANUARY 15

Job needed to be reminded that God is Creator. Also, God was teaching that Job wasn't there when God created, only God was. And then God goes on through the next chapters to ask Job lots of questions to help him understand that only God knows everything and man knows nothing compared to God. Job recognized this when he said later on:

I know that you can do all things, and that no purpose of yours can be thwarted. "Who is this that hides counsel without knowledge?" Therefore I have uttered what I did not understand, things too wonderful for me, which I did not know. "Hear, and I will speak; I will question you, and you make it known to me." I had heard of you by the hearing of the ear, but now my eye sees you; therefore I despise myself, and repent in dust and ashes (Job 42:2–6).

I base the question I teach people to ask, "Were you there?" on Job 38:4. The children and adults I teach understand that when it comes to origins, we weren't there, no scientist was there, no human was there, but God has always been there. Only God knows everything. So we need to believe God's Word about the past, not fallible man's word.

Really what I'm teaching them is that man's teaching about origins concerning evolution and millions of years are just beliefs. And those beliefs aren't true. Only God's Word is without error. We can trust God because He's always been there and is infinite in knowledge.

Sadly, secularists teach children that they, instead of God, know for sure what happened in the past concerning the origin of the universe and life. But now there are thousands upon thousands of children who know to ask the question God asked Job, "Were you there?"

I have had children come back to me and say, "We asked that question, 'Were you there?' and the person replied, 'No, but you weren't either.' What should we say then?" I said to them, "You would answer this way. 'No, I wasn't there, but I know someone who was, and I have His Word. Are you interested?' And then proceed to tell them about God's Word giving us the history of what happened when none of us were there."

That's what it's all about – understanding that the Bible is the Word of the One who has always been there and knows everything.

JANUARY 16
James 3:1

Judge All Actions and Beliefs and What Others Say Against the Absolute Authority of God's Word

God's Word has severe warnings for those of us who are teachers. God instructs us that teachers/leaders are going to be a problem. You see those who teach don't just teach facts per se. A teacher imparts a way of thinking, an interpretation of the facts, and a worldview to the people being taught. That's why God gives us this warning: *Not many of you should become teachers, my brothers, for you know that we who teach will be judged with greater strictness* (James 3:1).

My father was a schoolteacher, but he also loved to teach God's Word. But he would explain how he never wanted to lead anyone astray, which is why his favorite verses of Scripture began with, "Have you not read?" or "It is written." He taught me about study Bibles this way as an example of how we should evaluate what we are taught.

He would say, "Remember, the notes are not inspired like the text, so always use the text as the commentary on the notes." In other words, we need to judge what someone is teaching against the absolute authority of the Word of God. If we don't do this, we could easily be led astray.

God's Word has many warnings about shepherds who lead the sheep astray. In fact, there are numerous warnings, so we really need to take heed of this issue. For instance:

*"Woe to the shepherds who destroy and scatter the sheep of my pasture!" declares the L*ORD (Jeremiah 23:1).

Many shepherds have destroyed my vineyard; they have trampled down my portion; they have made my pleasant portion a desolate wilderness (Jeremiah 12:10).

Beware of false prophets, who come to you in sheep's clothing but inwardly are ravenous wolves (Matthew 7:15).

Think about how lukewarm much of the Church is today. Think about the fact that there's been a generational loss from the Church with Generation Z church attendance down to less than 9%. Think about the increasing number of churches going soft on the LGBTQ worldview, accommodating their views instead of lovingly explaining how our beliefs and behavior have to be judged against the absolute authority of the Word of God, and that such a worldview is sin.

In the era we live in, a major fact that has greatly undermined the impact of the Church and led to many of the younger generations leaving the Church for the world is the rampant compromise the majority of church leaders have made with evolution/millions of years, thus undermining Genesis as literal history. And this history in Genesis 1–11 is the foundation of all doctrine, our worldview, the rest of the Bible, and ultimately, of everything.

This compromise has had catastrophic consequences on the Church and the younger generations, who have become so secularized and anti-Christian that many leave the Church. Doubt in God's Word led to unbelief. Generation Z is now considered the first post-Christian generation.

Andy Stanley is a teacher who makes it very clear that Christians can accept evolution and say God used it to create. In fact, he's adamant Christians have to accept this. Thus, he is saying that God used death, suffering, disease, and violence over millions of years to bring man into existence. God calls all this death and disease

APOLOGETICS   JANUARY 16

"very good," as He describes everything He created in Genesis 1:31 this way. Stanley has also accepted the evolutionary history in regard to interpreting cultures of the past. He is saying that the ancient Hebrews were not as intelligent as us today and that God couldn't explain to them how He created everything because they didn't have all the "science" that we have today.

But this is not true. First of all, man has been intelligent right from the start. I'm sure Adam was highly intelligent with his perfect brain. Second, the Bible is not a book written to counter Near Eastern mythology as Stanley claims. No, the Bible is God-breathed (2 Timothy 3:16) and is for all people, for all ages, for all time! *The grass withers, the flower fades, but the word of our God will stand forever* (Isaiah 40:8). *Forever, O Lord, your word is firmly fixed in the heavens* (Psalm 119:89).

Third, God wrote His Word and knew that we in the twenty-first century would be the ones who would have trouble understanding it. Because of our intellectual pride in thinking we know a lot, we will think we are too sophisticated to believe God's Word as written. We would rather believe the fallible word of man than the infallible Word of God.

I judge Stanley's word against God's Word. Stanley is judging God's Word against his own word and the word of fallible scientists he has chosen to believe.

Such compromised teaching undermines the authority of the Word of God and results in lukewarm Christians at best. Sadly, over time, many doubt God's Word and end up walking away from the Christian faith.

I know a lot of people will be upset with me critiquing such a popular speaker. But all of us need to accept that Andy Stanley is not the absolute authority. He is a fallen human being like all of us. He has a sinful heart as we all do, and our sin nature is prone to exalt the word of man instead of the Word of God, which was the temptation the devil made to Eve in Genesis 3:1.

But we do have an absolute authority: God. He has given us His Word. So we need to judge our own actions and beliefs and what others are saying against the absolute authority of God's Word. When you do this with what Andy Stanley is teaching, you realize he is not teaching God's Word as written but imposing man's religion of evolution on God's Word.

Sadly, just like the Israelites, so many of our leaders have taken man's false religion and compromised it with God's Word. This is an attack on God's Word and an attack on the character of God by blaming God for millions of years of death, disease, violence, and suffering, as the evolutionary story details.

A verse I often think about in regard to such matters is this one: *Let God be true though every one were a liar* (Romans 3:4).

For the time is coming when people will not endure sound teaching, but having itching ears they will accumulate for themselves teachers to suit their own passions, and will turn away from listening to the truth and wander off into myths (2 Timothy 4:3–4).

> **Evolution is the religion of naturalism, which is atheism, and it is man's attempt to try to come up with a way of explaining life without God.**

JANUARY 17
Romans 10:17

Our Absolute Authority

How do we know Jesus rose bodily from the dead? Did any of us see it happen? No, it happened 2,000 years ago. But haven't people researched the Resurrection and found all sorts of evidence consistent with Him rising from the dead? Yes, but such evidence, though powerful, does not ultimately prove He rose from the dead.

In fact, no matter what evidence we point to in geology, biology, astronomy, etc., none of this proves in an ultimate sense that the Bible is true. Now, it is certainly true such evidence properly interpreted does confirm the Bible's history. For instance, the molecule of heredity, DNA, is a complex information system and language system. No one has seen matter produce information and a language from matter by natural processes. Our observations and experience show information and language have to come from an intelligence. Such evidence confirms an intelligence behind life. This certainly confirms the first verse of the Bible: "In the beginning, God created." But nonetheless, it's not absolute proof.

Think about it. We are finite beings living in the present. We don't know everything. We don't know how much we don't know. When we try to interpret evidence of the present in relation to the past, how do we know we have all the relevant information to make the correct interpretation? Some information we don't have could totally change our interpretation. That has certainly happened with scientists solving crimes using circumstantial evidence. When new evidence came along, some of the interpretations changed and certain people thought to be guilty were innocent. We need to have all the information needed. But we can't know everything and would never know how much we actually know.

However, we have a book that claims over 3,000 times to be the Word of God. This book claims that God moved people by His Spirit to write His Word about what He wants revealed to us regarding life, the universe, and history. This book, the Bible, tells us that God knows everything — He is infinite in knowledge and wisdom. He has all information.

[I]n whom are hidden all the treasures of wisdom and knowledge (Colossians 2:3).

If God's Word is what it claims, then the infinite Creator God has revealed to us the key information we need to know to have the ability to correctly interpret this world in relation to the past, present, and its purpose and meaning.

And we also thank God constantly for this, that when you received the word of God, which you heard from us, you accepted it not as the word of men but as what it really is, the word of God, which is at work in you believers (1 Thessalonians 2:13).

This means if we build our thinking on God's Word, we build a Christian worldview to enable us to look at the world through "biblical glasses" and have the ability to correctly interpret and understand it.

And Genesis 1–11 is the history that is foundational to the rest of the Bible and thus our worldview. So, when we start with God's Word, we learn that the God revealed to us in the Bible is the One who created all things. By just looking at the world — for instance, at DNA — we might deduce that there's an intelligence behind life. But we would not know who that intelligence is unless revealed to us. The Bible reveals who that

APOLOGETICS

intelligence is — God the Father, Son, and Holy Spirit. If we just looked at the world with all its death, suffering, and disease, we could assume that the intelligence behind life must be an ogre to make such a suffering world. But when we start from God's Word, we understand there was no death or disease to start with but entered the world because of sin. We also find that man has a problem called sin, which alienated him from God. We even find in Genesis that God promised someone would come to save us from our sin and restore our relationship with God (Genesis 3:15, 21). We learn later on that that "someone" is Jesus.

It's important to understand that we can't know anything absolutely unless an absolute authority has revealed to us what we need to know.

Now, Andy Stanley claims we don't know Jesus rose from the dead because the Bible tells us so, but claims it's the other way around — that because Jesus rose from the dead, we can believe what is said about this in the Bible. In reality, Andy Stanley is claiming he knows all the information about the Resurrection to know it's true so that he can proclaim what the Bible says about the Resurrection is true. This is nonsense. He accepts man's view of evolution and millions of years as true to declare that what Genesis records about creation is not all true.

Stanley, as a finite, fallen human being with very limited knowledge, starts outside the Bible to go to the Bible to make pronouncements over God's written Word. No wonder he rejects a literal Genesis.

Think about it. Really, Stanley is acting in accordance with the sin nature because of what happened in Genesis 3. Part of our sin nature concerns us wanting to be our own god. Consider Genesis 3:1 and Genesis 3:5, the temptation by the devil, where Satan tempted Adam and Eve to question God's Word and be like God to decide good and evil, truth, etc., for themselves. In actuality, the statements Andy Stanley is making about Christianity and God's Word reflect this sin problem we have. He is letting his sin nature master him in this instance instead of letting God's Word tell us clearly what we should believe.

The whole Bible is about Jesus — from the very first verse, Jesus is the Creator (Colossians 1:16, *For by him all things were created*), to the very last verse, *He who testifies to these things says, "Surely I am coming soon." Amen. Come, Lord Jesus! The grace of the Lord Jesus be with all. Amen* (Revelation 22:20–21).

We know Jesus rose from the dead because the Bible tells us so! We know we are sinners because the Bible tells us so. We know we can be saved through faith in Christ because the Bible tells us so. We know we need to repent of sin because the Bible tells us so. As Christians, we know we will spend eternity in heaven because the Bible tells us so.

So faith comes from hearing, and hearing through the word of Christ (Romans 10:17).

I still remember singing this chorus as a child:

"Jesus loves me; this I know, for the Bible tells me so."

Yes, the Bible tells me so — that's how we know who Jesus is.

God reveals all we need to know about Jesus in His Word.

JANUARY 18

Genesis 7:17-24

Was Noah's Flood a Global Event or Local?

Was Noah's Flood a global event or local? To be consistent, those Christians who believe in millions of years really have to make Noah's Flood just a local event. In fact, many have done so over the years. Let me explain why.

The idea of millions of years primarily came out of atheism of the 1800s. Secularists, in attempting to explain the fossil record by natural processes, promoted the (false) idea that the layers of fossils were laid down slowly over millions of years before man supposedly evolved.

Now, there are billions of dead things buried in rock layers laid down by water all over the earth. For those Christians who have accepted the belief in millions of years and attempt to add that into the Genesis account of origins, they have a major problem.

The flood continued forty days on the earth. The waters increased and bore up the ark, and it rose high above the earth. The waters prevailed and increased greatly on the earth, and the ark floated on the face of the waters. And the waters prevailed so mightily on the earth that all the high mountains under the whole heaven were covered. The waters prevailed above the mountains, covering them fifteen cubits deep. And all flesh died that moved on the earth, birds, livestock, beasts, all swarming creatures that swarm on the earth, and all mankind. Everything on the dry land in whose nostrils was the breath of life died. He blotted out every living thing that was on the face of the ground, man and animals and creeping things and birds of the heavens. They were blotted out from the earth. Only Noah was left, and those who were with him in the ark. And the waters prevailed on the earth 150 days (Genesis 7:17–24).

You can't read that passage and come to any other conclusion than this was a global Flood covering the highest mountains over all of the earth.

What do those who accept the millions of years then do with the account of the Flood of Noah's day? By accepting millions of years for the formation of the massive fossil record all over the earth, what did Noah's Flood do? If it really were a global catastrophic event as the Bible clearly describes, it would have eroded those layers of fossils and redeposited the sediment. In other words, it would have destroyed the fossil record. That's why some Christians claimed it must have been a tranquil flood. But I've never seen a tranquil flood. Floods of any size do catastrophic damage. Others claim it must have been a local flood. But the description given in Genesis 7 does not describe a local flood at all. It was a global catastrophic Flood.

Also, the description in Genesis makes it clear that all land-dwelling, air-breathing animals that weren't on the ark died, and only eight people survived the Flood. No other people survived as it was a global event. Even in the New Testament we read confirmation that only eight people survived the Flood:

[B]ecause they formerly did not obey, when God's patience waited in the days of Noah, while the ark was being prepared, in which a few, that is, eight persons, were brought safely through water (1 Peter 3:20).

Now the fossil record is not just one of death, with the remains of billions of creatures, but a record of disease, as there are many instances where evidence of diseases like cancer is found in fossil bones.

SCIENCE

For the Christian looking at the fossil record, how could one accept billions of dead things with evidence of diseases like cancer, tumors, arthritis, etc., millions of years before man when the Bible makes it clear that after man was created, God described everything He made as "very good"? Accepting millions of years is blaming God for death and disease and calling cancer "very good."

But the Bible states death is an enemy: *The last enemy to be destroyed is death* (1 Corinthians 15:26). Death will one day be thrown into the lake of fire: *Then Death and Hades were thrown into the lake of fire. This is the second death, the lake of fire* (Revelation 20:14). Death is an intrusion because of sin. Death did not exist before sin. Those who believe in millions of years are blaming God for death instead of blaming our sin.

And the Bible makes it clear that the world of death and disease we live in is one that's groaning because of our sin, *For we know that the whole creation has been groaning together in the pains of childbirth until now* (Romans 8:22).

It is actually a serious thing for Christians to accept millions of years, which is all part of the pagan religion of naturalism where people try to explain this world without God. Of course, evolutionists need millions of years, as, in a way, time is their god, because they have to have millions of years to try to propose an impossible process — evolution. Without time, they can't propose their evolutionary ideas.

Noah's Flood was not a tranquil flood. Noah's Flood was not a local event. Noah's Flood was a catastrophic event sent to judge a wicked world. *The Lord saw that the wickedness of man was great in the earth, and that every intention of the thoughts of his heart was only evil continually* (Genesis 6:5).

If there was such a Flood, we would find billions of dead things buried in rock layers laid down by water all over the earth. And that's exactly what we find.

Also, consider the covenant of the rainbow! After the Flood, God made a promise:

And God said, "This is the sign of the covenant that I make between me and you and every living creature that is with you, for all future generations: I have set my bow in the cloud, and it shall be a sign of the covenant between me and the earth. When I bring clouds over the earth and the bow is seen in the clouds, I will remember my covenant that is between me and you and every living creature of all flesh. And the waters shall never again become a flood to destroy all flesh" (Genesis 9:12–15).

We've had lots of local floods since then, so did God break His promise? NO! Noah's Flood wasn't a local event, it was a global cataclysmic event.

Is the fossil record the graveyard of millions of years of slow processes recording the supposed evolution of life? NO! Most of the fossil record is the graveyard of the Flood that occurred about 4,300 years ago.

And just as surely as God judged the wickedness of man with a global Flood, He is going to judge this earth again but by fire next time. And this will be a global event, not a local one.

> **The day is coming when God will judge the whole universe with fire and make a new heavens and earth.**

JANUARY 19
Genesis 1:29-30

Was Filet Mignon on Eden's Menu?

Today, many Christian leaders argue that the fossil record preceded Adam by millions of years. How does this view stack up against Scripture? In an effort to squeeze millions of years into the Bible, many Christians today are turning what the Bible clearly teaches about Adam, the Garden of Eden, the first animals' diet, and death's entry into the world on its head.

As more and more Christian leaders promote theistic (God-directed) evolution and/or millions of years, believers need to understand the plain teaching of Scripture about the origin of death. God's Word calls death "an enemy."

The last enemy to be destroyed is death (1 Corinthians 15:26). To the average Christian, the Bible's depiction of death seems pretty straightforward. Death as an "enemy" is an intrusion into this once-perfect world.

We take comfort knowing that in the future death will be *thrown into the lake of fire* (Revelation 20:14). Also, God promises that one day *death shall be no more, neither shall there be mourning, nor crying, nor pain anymore, for the former things have passed away* (Revelation 21:4).

That's what we would expect from a good God who created a perfect world. At the end of the sixth day of creation, *God saw everything that he had made, and behold, it was very good* (Genesis 1:31).

Yet we live in a world of life and death, joy and sorrow, love and hate — all at the same time. Only the history revealed in Genesis explains such a seemingly contradictory world.

As a test of obedience, God commanded the first man, Adam, *[O]f the tree of the knowledge of good and evil you shall not eat, for in the day that you eat of it you shall surely die* (Genesis 2:17).

In the saddest day in the history of the universe, Eve ate of the fruit and gave it to her husband, who also ate (Genesis 3:6). As a result, *sin came into the world through one man, and death through sin, and so death spread to all men* (Romans 5:12).

What is the nature of this "death"? The death that entered the human race wasn't only spiritual death (separation from God) but also physical death. Adam didn't physically die immediately, but he certainly began to, and he died 930 years later. In Genesis 2:7, we read where life came from: *[T]he LORD God formed the man of dust from the ground and breathed into his nostrils the breath of life, and the man became a living creature.* Then God's judgment on sin took away that life: *By the sweat of your face you shall eat bread, till you return to the ground, for out of it you were taken; for you are dust, and to dust you shall return* (Genesis 3:19).

This definition of death as a "return to dust" is confirmed in the New Testament: *The first man was from the earth, a man of dust … we have borne the image of the man of dust* (1 Corinthians 15:47, 49). Job also referred to death in this way: *[A]nd man would return to dust* (Job 34:15).

A minister once said to me, "I believe the dust referred to in Genesis 2:7 represents the animal [apelike creature] God used to form man." My response was, "Well, the Bible states we return to dust when we die, so what animal do we return to when we die?" No, when a human dies, that person's body returns to dust.

APOLOGETICS — JANUARY 19

Another church leader once said to me something like, "I believe dust-to-Adam represents molecules-to-man evolution." I then replied, "Well, what does the Bible mean when it says Adam's rib was 'made into' Eve [Genesis 2:21–22]?"

Now this fact of history — that the first woman was made from the man — is confirmed in the New Testament. For instance, *[M]an was not made from woman, but woman from man* (1 Corinthians 11:8), and *woman was made from man* (1 Corinthians 11:12). In Genesis 2:23, Adam describes another specific detail about his wife's physical existence: *This at last is bone of my bones and flesh of my flesh; she shall be called Woman, because she was taken out of Man.*

Adam's claim is confirmed in two New Testament passages. Quoting Genesis 2, Jesus concludes that all married couples *are no longer two but one flesh* (Matthew 19:5–6). Paul also quotes the Genesis account of Adam and Eve's union in Ephesians 5:31. Even Malachi 2:15 references Genesis 2 concerning Adam and Eve, who were "one" flesh: *Did he not make them one …?* What does all this have to do with filet mignon? Continue to bear with me, and it will become obvious soon.

The above is just a summary of Scripture verses to help substantiate that Genesis 1 and 2 are to be taken as literal history, established in other parts of God's Word, especially the New Testament. Adam and Eve were the first two people — real people in history — and the Fall was a literal event.

God told Adam to eat of *every plant yielding seed* and fruit trees (Genesis 1:29). He was originally vegetarian.

Some object that God doesn't say he couldn't eat animal flesh, but this objection is easily dealt with by God's words to Noah after the Flood: *Every moving thing that lives shall be food for you. And* as I gave you the green plants, *I give you everything* (Genesis 9:3; emphasis added). We could paraphrase: "Just as I gave you the plants to eat, now I make a change and I give you all things (everything)."

Adam didn't eat filet mignon — nor did any of the animals on the earth until after sin.

This substantiates that Adam's diet was vegetarian. Not until after the Flood did God allow humans to eat animals. So, Adam certainly did not eat filet mignon before the Fall. And if Adam obeyed God, he did not eat filet mignon after the Fall either. But Noah could have once God changed our diet after the Flood.

But how do you respond to Christians who believe animals could have eaten other animals before the Fall?

Genesis 1:30, written in the same way as Genesis 1:29, refers specifically to the animals: *And to every beast of the earth and to every bird of the heavens and to everything that creeps on the earth, everything that has the breath of life, I have given every green plant for food* (Genesis 1:30).

Just as humans were vegetarian originally, the animals were also vegetarian. Before the Fall, animals didn't eat animals, animals didn't eat humans, and humans didn't eat animals.

Romans 8:22, written in the context of the Fall's effects, tells us, *For we know that the whole creation has been groaning together in the pains of childbirth until now.*

> **There is no way a Christian can logically and consistently allow for millions of years of animal death, violence, and disease before Adam's sin.**

JANUARY 20
Job 42:1-6

Why Do Bad Things Happen?

When we hear of shocking tragedies like school shootings, usually I hear on the news lots of commentaries on why this happened. I hear church leaders interviewed and asked why this happened. Often, I hear answers like, "We don't know why this happened. We just have to trust God."

But we actually do know the ultimate cause of why this happened. If we believe and understand Genesis, we would know that our sin in Adam changed everything. We are living in a fallen world where *Your adversary the devil prowls around like a roaring lion, seeking someone to devour* (1 Peter 5:8). Also, *following the course of this world, following the prince of the power of the air, the spirit that is now at work in the sons of disobedience* (Ephesians 2:2).

So understanding this world correctly, our sin resulted in the terrible groaning we see happening around us (Romans 8:22). It's not God's fault, it's our fault — all our fault, as we sinned in Adam. We deserve nothing, but God, in His love and mercy, provided the gift of salvation through His Son to save us from this mess we caused.

We do understand the ultimate cause of this evil we see rampant around us, and we know God is in control. It's easy to say, but it's so hard for us as humans living through this. The pain is excruciating. And it's OK to groan and ask why. We're just humans. But in the end, we have to come to the position Job came to. Job had terrible tragedy in his life. His friends gave him bad counsel. Job wanted to argue with God, so God then spoke to Job and asked him if he knew this or that or this or that. God was showing Job he knew nothing compared to what God knows. We read:

Then Job answered the LORD and said: "I know that you can do all things, and that no purpose of yours can be thwarted. 'Who is this that hides counsel without knowledge?' Therefore I have uttered what I did not understand, things too wonderful for me, which I did not know. 'Hear, and I will speak; I will question you, and you make it known to me.' I had heard of you by the hearing of the ear, but now my eye sees you; therefore I despise myself, and repent in dust and ashes" (Job 42:1–6).

Job recognized that we have to let God be God. As hard as it is, we need to recognize that God knows an infinite amount more than we do. God can have morally good reasons for allowing something to happen that we don't know. And as humans, it is hard to let God be God. It's easy to say for someone not going through terrible tragedy, but in the end, that is what we have to do. We can grieve together, but there comes the time when we have to let God be God. Sometimes we can look back and see how God used these circumstances in astounding ways we did not understand at the time. Other times, we can't see it and won't find out until heaven.

Then there's the non-Christians who respond by claiming if there is a God, He is unjust to allow such a tragedy to occur. But a non-Christian has no basis for determining what is just or unjust. From their perspective of no God, they have no basis to determine what is right or wrong. They can't accuse someone of being unjust! From their perspective, everything is subjective, and morality is relative. Philosophically speaking, the problem of evil turns out to be a problem for the unbeliever. However, for the Christian, evil must be

THEOLOGY **JANUARY 20**

compatible with God's goodness. Therefore, evil events occur for reasons which are morally commendable (just) and good, even if we don't understand them. Think about it. The crucifixion was an evil event, but it had a morally good purpose — salvation!

In Luke 13, Jesus asked whether 18 who died from a tower collapse were worse sinners than others. His response, *No, I tell you; but unless you* repent, *you will all likewise perish* (Luke 13:3; emphasis added).

> Everyone has a time to die, so make sure you're ready, and make sure you have trusted Christ for salvation.

JANUARY 21
Why Is It Vital That We Take Genesis as Literal History?
John 5:45-47

The meaning of anything depends on its origin. And did you know that the book of Genesis gives us an account of the origin of all the basic entities of life and the universe? Let's start listing them:

- The origin of space, matter, and time
- The origin of the earth
- The origin of water
- The origin of the atmosphere and hydrosphere
- The origin of light
- The origin of plants
- The origin of the sun, moon, and stars
- The origin of the universe and solar system
- The origin of land animals, flying creatures, and aquatic creatures
- The origin of man
- The origin of man's dominion over the creation
- The origin of why man has to work hard
- The origin of woman
- The origin of marriage
- The origin of the family
- The origin of evil
- The origin of sin
- The origin of death
- The origin of clothing
- The origin of man's need for a Savior
- The origin of the sacrificial system
- The origin of thorns
- The origin of languages
- The origin of government
- The origin of culture
- The origin of people groups
- The origin of nations
- The origin of the chosen people

Let's consider marriage. God created marriage when he created the first man and woman:

Therefore a man shall leave his father and his mother and hold fast to his wife, and they shall become one flesh. And the man and his wife were both naked and were not ashamed (Genesis 2:24–25).

Marriage was not invented by judges or government leaders.

When Jesus as the God-man was asked about marriage, He responded this way:

Have you not read that he who created them from the beginning made them male and female, and said, "Therefore a man shall leave his father and his mother and hold fast to his wife, and the two shall become one flesh"? So they are no longer two but one flesh. What therefore God has joined together, let not man separate (Matthew 19:4–6).

APOLOGETICS   JANUARY 21

Jesus actually quoted the text of Genesis 1:27 (*So God created man in his own image, in the image of God he created him; male and female he created them*) and Genesis 2:24 in giving the foundation for marriage. Marriage is between one man (male) and one woman (female). Yes, there are only two genders.

To understand the meaning of marriage, we need to understand its origin. Sadly, many Christian leaders who compromised Genesis with evolution and millions of years haven't taught this foundational history to coming generations. If people don't have the foundation in Genesis concerning the origin of marriage, one can understand how they might be easily influenced by the LGBTQ worldview, which is sadly happening to many young people, even from the Church.

Satan knows that if he can cause people to reject the literal history of Genesis, then the foundation of the whole Bible, of all doctrine, of the Christian worldview, and, in fact, everything are undermined. That's why in our day, Genesis has been so attacked. Christians must stand against those who compromise Genesis. Even many conservative Christian leaders have been so intimidated by secular scientists and compromising Christian academics that many have not taught Genesis as literal history. As a result, biblical illiteracy permeates the Church. Many don't really understand Christianity as they should and can't explain what Christians really believe and how to defend the Christian faith.

How can a Christian explain the gospel without explaining where man came from, why we are accountable to God, what sin is, why we die, why we needed a Savior, and why Christ died and rose again, from the foundational history in Genesis?

Paul quotes or refers to Genesis many times when explaining the gospel message: *Therefore, just as sin came into the world through one man, and death through sin, and so death spread to all men because all sinned* (Romans 5:12).

Thus it is written, "The first man Adam became a living being"; the last Adam became a life-giving spirit. But it is not the spiritual that is first but the natural, and then the spiritual. The first man was from the earth, a man of dust; the second man is from heaven. As was the man of dust, so also are those who are of the dust, and as is the man of heaven, so also are those who are of heaven. Just as we have borne the image of the man of dust, we shall also bear the image of the man of heaven (1 Corinthians 15:45–49).

Paul goes back to Genesis in discussing the doctrine of marriage and the Church:

"Therefore a man shall leave his father and mother and hold fast to his wife, and the two shall become one flesh." This mystery is profound, and I am saying that it refers to Christ and the church. However, let each one of you love his wife as himself, and let the wife see that she respects her husband (Ephesians 5:31–33).

The above is just a tiny glimpse at why Genesis is so important and why it is vital that Christians take it as written — as literal history. No wonder Jesus said:

Do not think that I will accuse you to the Father. There is one who accuses you: Moses, on whom you have set your hope. For if you believed Moses, you would believe me; for he wrote of me. But if you do not believe his writings, how will you believe my words? (John 5:45–47).

> **Genesis is a very important book, as it provides the foundational knowledge for the rest of the Bible, for our Christian worldview, for all doctrine, and, in fact, for everything.**

JANUARY 22
Ephesians 6:12

Which Side Are You on in This Spiritual War?

One of the things I've observed (and experienced on social media and in other ways) is that those who claim tolerance are often the most intolerant. Those who claim others have hate speech often use the most hate speech. Those who claim they aren't religious are often the most fervent for their religion. Those who claim others are prejudiced are often the most prejudiced. Those who claim others discriminate are often the most discriminatory.

And such intolerance, hate, and discrimination are occurring against Christians.

Could it ever happen in America that we would see the government pass laws that would attempt to force the religion of sexual humanism on churches and Christian schools? The answer is not only could that happen, but in one state, it's about to happen.

The state of Michigan voted in legislation that is declaring war on Christianity in a major way. Lifesite news had an article titled, "Michigan Lawmakers Set to Pass LGBT 'Civil Rights' Bill with No Religious Exceptions."

The article states, "The Michigan State Senate passed SB 4 last week by a 23-15 vote, with three Republicans joining with their Democrat colleagues in support of the measure. The bill, which doesn't include exemptions for religious entities, adds 'sexual orientation' and 'gender identity' to the list of protected classes of persons who cannot be 'discriminated' against in the Wolverine State.... 'Every state that has amended its anti-discrimination law — 22 of them, and also the District of Columbia — has included protections for religious organizations. Unfortunately, Michigan appears to be going in an opposite and unprecedented direction,' the MCC pointed out in a statement published February 9."[5]

A pastor from Michigan wrote at the time, "God is moving among Bible-believing, Gospel preaching pastors all over Michigan who are uniting to stand together against increasing attacks on the Church. The most recent, and one of the most egregious attacks is Senate Bill 4 which will classify LGBTQ+ as a civil right. SB4 is in our state legislature right now, and if it passes, it will become illegal to preach and promote that God intended marriage to be between one man and one woman. It will also require that churches (as well as Christian schools, businesses, etc.) allow the use of gender identification to determine the choice of bathroom a person chooses to use. In the case of private Christian schools, this will allow the same for boys in girls' locker rooms."

As I've said many times, the LGBTQ movement does not just want freedom for their views, they want total compliance and acceptance by all. What's happening in Michigan shows the total intolerance these politicians who are passing this legislation have for Christianity.

There is increasing persecution of Christians in this nation as secularists in power increase their discrimination and prejudice against Christians. Are these same politicians going to allow the Bible to be taught in public schools? Of course not, as they claim such secular schools are not religious. But we all know that secular humanism and its resulting sexual humanism is the state religion of the public schools and the state religion of Michigan.

CHURCH   JANUARY 22

I still lay a lot of the blame for this on a by-and-large lukewarm Church that did not teach the truth of God's Word as they should have to generations, and many of the leaders compromised God's Word with the pagan religion of naturalism and evolution/millions of years.

What is happening is a spiritual war that has been heating up big time in this nation. Which side are you on?

For we do not wrestle against flesh and blood, but against the rulers, against the authorities, against the cosmic powers over this present darkness, against the spiritual forces of evil in the heavenly places (Ephesians 6:12).

Be prepared, for we are seeing the chasm between true Christianity and the world widening catastrophically.

JANUARY 23
2 Timothy 3:16-17

The Bible IS the Word of God

Can you recognize liberal theology? Do evolution and liberal theology go hand in hand?

In 1977, in Australia, the Uniting Church of Australia was formed. This involved the union of three churches: the Congregational Union of Australia, the Methodist Church of Australasia, and the Presbyterian Church of Australia.

I remember my father showing me wording in their basis of union that stated the Bible "contains" the Word of God. But does the Bible actually "contain" the Word of God?

My father was a teacher, and we were transferred to different towns in the State of Queensland every three years as my father was promoted. We encountered a number of pastors who were impacted by liberal theology. My father made sure he studied liberal theology to understand what was being taught and believed. He then made sure we had answers to what the liberal theologians were saying about the Bible so we wouldn't be led astray with doubt that could lead to unbelief in God's Word. These liberal pastors would reject Genesis as literal history (and accept evolution), try to explain away many of the miracles in the Bible, and some even rejected the virgin birth and bodily resurrection of Christ.

I learned to "smell" liberal theology from a million miles away!

As soon as my father and I saw the word "contain" in regard to the Word of God, we "smelled" liberal theology. And we were right. The Uniting Church by and large (of course, there are always exceptions depending on the leadership) became very liberal quite quickly. There was rampant compromise on Genesis, for instance, which led to compromise in regard to all sorts of doctrine. I find that if Christians accept Genesis as written, then they usually don't have problems with the rest of the Bible. But once they compromise Genesis, very often, all sorts of problems/compromises show up in regard to aspects of the rest of the Bible and Christian doctrine, etc. It all becomes a slippery slope.

The point I want to make is that the Bible actually IS the Word of God. It is God-breathed:

All Scripture is breathed out by God and profitable for teaching, for reproof, for correction, and for training in righteousness, that the man of God may be complete, equipped for every good work (2 Timothy 3:16–17).

And we also thank God constantly for this, that when you received the word of God, which you heard from us, you accepted it not as the word of men but as what it really is, the word of God, which is at work in you believers (1 Thessalonians 2:13).

The sum of your word is truth, and every one of your righteous rules endures forever (Psalm 119:160).

When one says the Bible "contains" the Word of God, then one could justify claiming that it contains truth but it's not all truth. That's what liberals do. They will explain away miracles and claim the accounts teach truth but didn't actually happen as recorded. And, of course, they do that in Genesis.

We hear so many church leaders today claiming that Genesis is not literal history but that it contains truth. Some even call it mythological language, that it's a type of myth that teaches truth. But who determines that "truth"? It's whatever that person determines that "truth" to be. In 1982, the *New Life Christian Newspaper* in

THEOLOGY JANUARY 23

Australia published an item about Josef Ton. He was a Romanian Baptist pastor imprisoned for his faith by the communists. He was quoted saying, "I came to the conclusion that there are two factors which destroyed Christianity in Western Europe. One was the theory of evolution, the other, liberal theology…. Liberal theology is just evolution applied to the Bible and our faith."[6]

That should be a warning to all Christians and church leaders who compromise God's Word in Genesis and accept evolutionary ideas.

Over the years I've had a lot of Christians claim it's not what Genesis says that's important but what it means. But how can it mean something if we don't take what it says as written? When we drive, do we come to a STOP sign and claim, "I know what it says, but what does it mean?" And then interpret it as saying we can go? That's really how many church leaders approach the Bible, particularly in Genesis.

For instance, I have had Christian leaders tell me that the important lesson to learn from Genesis is that God created everything. They then claim that the details don't matter and Genesis is not meant to be taken literally. I have responded to them like this, "So you believe 'In the beginning God created the heavens and the earth'?" They have always replied to me, "Yes." I then ask them how they know this, as that's the first verse of the Bible, so are they telling me to take this verse literally? And if we take that as written, where do we draw the line on how to determine which verses are to be taken literally and which are not? Is verse two to be taken literally, and if not, why not? What about verse three? How do we know anything about Genesis if the words don't mean what they clearly say in context of the rules of language/genre? And Genesis is written as historical narrative anyway.

I was at a conference once where a pastor was telling me that one couldn't take the first few chapters of Genesis literally. A man standing nearby said something like, "I'm a new Christian. So could you tell me when we do start believing the words in the Bible?"

Really those Christians compromising Genesis are acting in accord with liberal theology! I know there are a lot of fairly conservative pastors who compromise Genesis with evolution but maintain a non-liberal approach to the rest of Scripture. They suffer from what I call "intellectual schizophrenia." In essence, they are saying Genesis contains the Word of God, but the rest of the Scriptures are the Word of God.

And therein lies the major problem in much of the Church. Biblical authority has been undermined, and many no longer look on the Bible as the absolute authority of the Word of God. Thus, those who preach cannot speak boldly with authority!

And when Jesus finished these sayings, the crowds were astonished at his teaching, for he was teaching them as one who had authority, and not as their scribes (Matthew 7:28–29).

> How we need church leaders to have the courage to be bold in their preaching the Word of God as it really is – the authoritative Word of God, the absolute authority.

JANUARY 24
Psalm 14:1

Legacy

For all his fame (and fortune, I'm sure) for being a star in the popular *Star Trek* series, William Shatner basically says that at the end of his life, he and his legacy will amount to not much, if anything! How would you like to leave a meaningless legacy like that?

At least he is consistent with his evolutionary beliefs and rejection of God. Think about it: if this life is all there is, and when you die, you cease to exist and won't even know you were ever here, then life is ultimately purposeless and meaningless. But that is the logical outcome of the evolutionary atheistic religion that Shatner and millions of others hold to.

Shatner is releasing a new book about his life. But what's the point if it's all ultimately meaningless anyway? And why should people listen to the pontifications of an actor who rejects God and made his living pretending to be someone he is not? Why should people even take notice of him? What gives him the right to tell people how they should think about life? By whose authority? Actually, by his own authority.

When Shatner rode in the successful Blue Origin flight for 10 minutes in space, he saw the earth from space. If you listen to his interview with Neil Cavuto, you will recognize that he was amazed at how special Earth looked compared to everything else in space. Instead of seeing it as obviously a miracle of creation in the vastness of space, he saw it this way:

"'When I came out of the spaceship I was crying, just sobbing, and I thought, "Why am I crying?" ... I'm in grief ... I'm grieving about the world because I now know so much about what's happening. I saw the earth and its beauty and its destruction,' he continued. 'It's going extinct. Billions of years of evolution may vanish. It's sacred, it's holy, it's life, and it's gone. It's beyond tragic. We stupid ... animals are destroying this gorgeous thing called the earth. Doesn't that make you angry? Don't you want to do something about it?'"[7]

He said humans are "intricately connected" to the universe and we need to connect with the earth and universe. He even used the word "prayer." But he's not talking about praying to God, but to the universe. That's his religion! Of course, a lot of people would say, "Wow, that's profound." Neil Cavuto said his book was profound. But it's utter foolishness. *The fool says in his heart, "There is no God"* (Psalm 14:1).

Sounds like the modern climate change religion (and he refers to that movement) where people think they can save the planet and save themselves. But one day, God will destroy this planet by fire (2 Peter 3) and destroy the whole universe and create a new heavens and earth. Nothing Shatner can say or do will change that. And it's God who sustains the universe right now by the power of His hand (Colossians 1:17) and promised after the Flood, *While the earth remains, seedtime and harvest, cold and heat, summer and winter, day and night, shall not cease* (Genesis 8:22). Man cannot destroy the earth! Only God can.

At the recent World Economic Forum, John Kerry said there was an elite group of people who were out to save the planet and save mankind. It's a religion of worship to the creation and worship of man as his own god. There's only one who saves man, and that is the Lord Jesus Christ who came to Earth as the God-man to pay the penalty for our sin and offer a free gift of salvation. John Kerry and William Shatner will hopefully

APOLOGETICS — JANUARY 24

receive this free gift (and we should pray earnestly for them that they will), or they will not simply cease to exist when they die but will spend eternity separated from God under righteous judgment for their sin.

Shatner is reported as saying, "People ask about a legacy. There's no legacy. Statues are torn down. Graveyards are ransacked. Headstones are knocked over. No one remembers anyone. Who remembers Danny Kaye or Cary Grant? They were great stars. But they're gone and no one cares. But what does live on are good deeds. If you do a good deed, it reverberates to the end of time. It's the butterfly effect thing."[8]

Well, God does not forget us after death. As God's Word states, *And just as it is appointed for man to die once, and after that comes judgment* (Hebrews 9:27). William Shatner needs to change his legacy from what he calls "good deeds" to one of proclaiming salvation in Christ by faith!

> **Know that we are to look after the earth, as we were given dominion (Genesis 1:28), but we are to use it for man's good and God's glory.**

JANUARY 25

1 Corinthians 1:10-13

Unity on God's Word

Is the biblical creation ministry divisive?

Over the years, I've had several people, including Christian leaders, say negative things about the Answers in Genesis ministry, claiming what we do is divisive. They claim as Christians we shouldn't create division but unity. Now this may sound confusing and contradictory, but I say we need to create both division *and* unity. And I also claim that is what God's Word teaches.

Jesus said, *Do you think that I have come to give peace on earth? No, I tell you, but rather division* (Luke 12:51).

Let's consider division first of all. The light of God's Word will create two types of division.

Division from the world is one. We live in a world where there is a lot of darkness:

And this is the judgment: the light has come into the world, and people loved the darkness rather than the light because their works were evil (John 3:19).

God's Word has a lot to tell us about shining light in this darkness:

In an obvious reference to Christ, we read in Isaiah 9:2, *The people who walked in darkness have seen a great light; those who dwelt in a land of deep darkness, on them has light shone.*

You are the light of the world. A city set on a hill cannot be hidden. Nor do people light a lamp and put it under a basket, but on a stand, and it gives light to all in the house. In the same way, let your light shine before others, so that they may see your good works and give glory to your Father who is in heaven (Matthew 5:14–16).

The light shines in the darkness, and the darkness has not overcome it (John 1:5).

And light shines brighter the darker it gets. When you shine light in darkness, you see the stark division/contrast between the light and darkness.

Obviously, shining the light of God's Word in this dark world because of sin will create division. We will see the result of this division in those who will oppose those who shine the light:

Indeed, all who desire to live a godly life in Christ Jesus will be persecuted (2 Timothy 3:12).

Do not be surprised, brothers, that the world hates you (1 John 3:13).

Now there's another type of division, and that's division in the Church. There is division in the Church that is bad, and Scripture warns about it:

I appeal to you, brothers, to watch out for those who cause divisions and create obstacles contrary to the doctrine that you have been taught; avoid them. For such persons do not serve our Lord Christ, but their own appetites, and by smooth talk and flattery they deceive the hearts of the naive (Romans 16:17–18).

We must stop division created by those who teach error and do things contrary to Scripture. We must boldly stand against error and hold those people accountable who try to lead people astray by teaching error.

But there is division that must occur and has occurred over the years to help cleanse the Church of error and ensure the truth is being taught. That's why God through the Apostle Paul in 1 Corinthians 11:19 states,

[F]or there must be factions among you in order that those who are genuine among you may be recognized.

When truth is taught (light is shone), those who reject and oppose that truth will react against it, creating division. But this is the sort of division that will occur in a fallen world to show up those who reject the truth.

Christians need to be rightly dividing the Word of truth: *Do your best to present yourself to God as one approved, a worker who has no need to be ashamed, rightly handling the word of truth* (2 Timothy 2:15).

Unity. Yes, the Bible does talk about unity. For instance, *I appeal to you, brothers, by the name of our Lord Jesus Christ, that all of you agree, and that there be no divisions among you, but that you be united in the same mind and the same judgment. For it has been reported to me by Chloe's people that there is quarreling among you, my brothers. What I mean is that each one of you says, "I follow Paul," or "I follow Apollos," or "I follow Cephas," or "I follow Christ." Is Christ divided? Was Paul crucified for you? Or were you baptized in the name of Paul?* (1 Corinthians 1:10–13).

For this unity, we need to be in agreement by having the same mind in regard to God's Word. This can only happen when there is unity on God's Word. That's the unity we need and should always strive for.

Now when Answers in Genesis insists that we must take God's Word as written in Genesis and thus teach that God created in six literal days, death came after sin, Noah's Flood was global, the earth can't be millions of years old, and we must accept the account of creation as given in Genesis and reject evolution, some claim we are being divisive. We are told that we should allow people to have other views, such as believing in millions of years, theistic evolution, gap theory, and so on.

But when you analyze this, we are insisting on unity on God's Word in Genesis, but those who disagree want unity around man's word regarding millions of years and evolutionary processes. So, the division created by insisting on a literal Genesis is the right sort of division to stand up for the truth of God's Word. We need unity for all Christians to take God's Word as written and come against the belief that man's ideas, such as evolution and millions of years, can be used to reinterpret God's clear Word.

The bottom line is, the stand Answers in Genesis takes on Genesis is both one of creating division and unity! In this dark world and with so much compromise in the Church, if you are not creating the right sort of division for the right reasons, I suggest you need to analyze whether your stand on God's Word is the right one.

I find many pastors don't want to create any sort of division, as they don't want to lose people or finances from their congregation. But I suggest there needs to be a lot more division when we have so many church leaders and academics who compromise Genesis with man's ideas. We have such a lukewarm Church because of this rampant compromise and resulting very shallow teaching. There are exceptions, of course, but those who take the stand on God's Word as they should in Genesis are in the minority.

> **We need to challenge the Church concerning the truth of God's Word beginning in Genesis, creating the right sort of division to lead to much-needed unity on the infallible Word.**

JANUARY 26

Genesis 1:27

How Can Christian Creationist Ken Ham Have Any Common Ground with Atheistic Evolutionist Richard Dawkins?

Is it really so amazing that Ken Ham and atheist Richard Dawkins agree on something? Actually, it's not. But first, what do we agree on?

A recent news item headline stated, "Richard Dawkins Declares There Are Only Two Sexes as Matter of Science: 'That's All There Is to It.'" Well, I do agree with Richard Dawkins. He's right, there are only two sexes, male and female.

Dawkins is quoted in the article as saying, "During a recent interview with British journalist Piers Morgan, famed atheist and biologist Richard Dawkins declared that 'there are two sexes, and that's all there is to it.' He added that LGBTQ activists looking to discredit the reality of two biological sexes are pushing 'utter nonsense.'"[9]

The article reported on Piers Morgan's interview with Dawkins by stating, "Morgan was referring to a recent list of problematic words put out by the 'EBB Language Project,' a collection of academics looking to police words that could potentially be found to be politically incorrect. The proposed list contains gendered words such as 'male, female, man, woman, mother, father,' U.K. outlet *The Telegraph* reported. Dawkins had commented on the project last month, telling the paper, 'The only possible response is contemptuous ridicule. I shall continue to use every one of the prohibited words. I am a professional user of the English language. It is my native language.'"[10]

I actually admire Richard Dawkins' courage in responding this way.

Now, how could it be that Christian and biblical creationist Ken Ham could have any common ground with atheistic evolutionist Richard Dawkins?

Well, that's easy to comprehend when one has the correct understanding of science. There's no doubt that I and Richard Dawkins will also agree on a lot of other things as well. That shouldn't be surprising. Just because someone is an atheistic evolutionist doesn't mean they can't do some good science when it comes to observational science.

When I debated Bill Nye in 2014, the first thing I did at the beginning of the debate was define our terms. I explained that the word *science* means "knowledge." I then helped people understand that there's a big difference between observational science, where we use our five senses in the present to do repeatable experiments and develop technology. However, historical science concerns knowledge/beliefs about the past — about our origins, for instance. Such beliefs can't be investigated directly using our five senses, and we can't repeat the past.

So when Richard Dawkins does observational science, we can agree. Richard Dawkins and Ken Ham will actually agree on a lot of things involving observational science. That shouldn't be a shock to anyone. But when we discuss historical science, that's where we will vehemently disagree.

Concerning the sexes (gender), observational science in the present shows us that the information to build a human being is in 23 pairs of chromosomes made from that molecule of hereditary DNA. Each human

SCIENCE

JANUARY 26

has a pair of sex chromosomes. Males have an XY pair, and females have an XX pair. Now there can be some so-called exceptions, but they are a fraction of a percent. And such people have various problems because the created order is XX and XY. Christians understand such "exceptions" are because we live in a fallen world because of sin, so there can be mutations, copying mistakes, etc.

In Genesis 1:27, we are told God created humans *male and female*. So taking God at His Word, there are only two genders of humans: male and female. And the observational science Richard Dawkins and Ken Ham agree with confirms this fact: males with a pair of XY chromosomes and females with a pair of XX chromosomes.

The Bible and observational science agree. That's why Ken Ham and Richard Dawkins agree.

So God created man in his own image, in the image of God he created him; male and female he created them (Genesis 1:27).

And in the New Testament, Jesus as the God-man quoted the text of Genesis 1:27 as literal history: *Have you not read that he who created them from the beginning made them male and female …?* (Matthew 19:4).

There are people, including a number of Christians, that believe in a flat earth. I have a friend who is not only a dedicated Christian with an active ministry to proclaim God's Word and the gospel, but also is an astronaut. He has been on the space shuttle and the International Space Station. He has shown me photos and videos he has taken of the earth in space. He sent me a video that shows clearly the earth is round, not flat. He described the short video taken while on the Space Station this way:

"It was taken at the point in the earth's orbit around the sun where the International Space Station's (ISS) orbit around the earth is perpendicular to the sun, therefore the sun never sets. The 13-second video is sped up to show a complete 90-minute ISS orbit around the earth as it travels at 17,500 mph. The solar arrays are evident as they track the sun."

When I've explained this video to some who claim they are flat-earthers, they've said the video can't be real. In reality, they are accusing this Christian of lying.

> **As a Christian, not only do we believe in observational science, but we also know God's Word in Genesis is true.**

JANUARY 27
Romans 10:17

God's Word vs. Man's Word

When someone tells a Christian that if they could show them evidence that God exists, then they would believe, do they really mean this? In most instances, I have found, particularly with someone who says they're an atheist, they don't really mean this at all.

Over the years, I have had secularists claim that if I could show them evidence for God, they would believe. But what you will often find is when you give them evidence that confirms an intelligence behind life or the universe (confirming evidence for a Creator), they will claim it's not evidence at all and just reinterpret it within their secular worldview.

I've sometimes asked atheists what evidence they would be prepared to accept for God. I've had quite a number who have responded and said something like, "If there's a God, then why doesn't He show Himself to us? If God did that, then we'd believe."

My answer when they have made such a claim is to say, "Well, He did come to Earth and showed Himself to people, but the majority still rejected Him. In fact, they crucified Him on a Cross." I explain that the Bible states that God stepped into history in the person of His Son to become a man (the God-man) to show Himself to us and also deal with a problem we have — sin — and provide the solution in dying for our sin and being raised from the dead.

Remember what Jesus said to Philip in John 14:9, *Jesus said to him, "Have I been with you so long, and you still do not know me, Philip? Whoever has seen me has seen the Father. How can you say, 'Show us the Father'?"*

God's Word tells us in Romans 1:20 that *For his invisible attributes, namely, his eternal power and divine nature, have been clearly perceived, ever since the creation of the world, in the things that have been made. So they are without excuse.* Yes, they are without excuse if they don't believe.

I have often used the example of the molecule of heredity, DNA, which makes it obvious life had to be created by an intelligence and couldn't arise by natural processes. After all, DNA is an example of an information system and language system. Information and a language cannot arise from matter by natural processes. And yet, when challenged with this example, I find secularists scoff and claim DNA did arise by natural processes even if they can't prove that right now.

When I debated Bill Nye in 2014, one of the questions asked at the end concerned what evidence we would be prepared to accept to show our position was wrong. I answered "none" simply because I am committed to my stand on God's Word as truth. Certainly, models based on my foundation are subject to change, but not the foundation itself. Bill Nye answered by saying if someone found an out-of-place fossil, he would be prepared to question his evolutionary belief. I had already given such an example in my presentation, and he obviously rejected it. In other words, he was just as committed to his foundation that man determines truth as much as I was committed to my foundation that God's Word is truth.

At a conference where I talked on Noah's Ark and the Flood a few years ago, an atheist said to me, "I don't care if they find a big boat on Mt. Ararat and drag it down the main street, I will not believe in Noah's Ark."

APOLOGETICS — JANUARY 27

This reminds me of the scoffers in 2 Peter 3 who "willingly reject" (or deliberately disbelieve) creation and the Flood.

And think about the account of Jesus raising Lazarus from the dead. The religious leaders wanted to kill Lazarus and get rid of the evidence.

Now evidence is important to give people answers for what we believe as Christians (1 Peter 3:15), but in doing this, we should always be directing them to the Word of God that saves.

So faith comes from hearing, and hearing through the word of Christ (Romans 10:17).

Our evidence can't save people, only God's Word can.

JANUARY 28
Romans 1:28

Atheism Is a Religion

Atheists are religious people. Atheism is a religion. One of the definitions of *evangelism* from the *Merriam-Webster Dictionary* is "militant or crusading zeal."[11] Many atheists are evangelistic for spreading their religion of atheism.

One of the definitions of *religion* from the *Merriam-Webster Dictionary* is "a cause, principle, or system of beliefs held to with ardor and faith."[12] That certainly fits atheism. One could claim atheists have a blind faith, as there is no confirming evidence for atheism.

Atheism is based on naturalism and materialism. They believe all of reality came about by natural processes and the material universe is all there is. But the laws of nature are immaterial, so where did they come from? And there's zero evidence that matter by natural processes formed life. Besides, the DNA molecule is a complex information system and language system. Matter can't produce information or codes by natural processes. Such only come about as a result of an intelligence.

One could rightly say atheism is not just a blind faith, it's a faith that lacks credulity.

Now atheists can get very emotional and claim they don't have a religion, saying they don't worship a god and have no religious system. But everyone has a worldview, a way of thinking. The definition of *worldview* from the *Merriam-Webster Dictionary* is "a comprehensive conception or apprehension of the world, especially from a specific standpoint."[13] Atheists have a worldview based on naturalism. This determines how they understand reality. This is their religion. Atheists are very religious people, and many are zealous for their religion — zealous to impose it on others.

Now atheist bullies like those from the Freedom From Religion Foundation claim we can't have the Bible or creation taught in public schools or allow crosses or nativity scenes in public places. They claim such is allowing the Christian religion to be imposed on people. These atheists claim they want neutrality. Many people have succumbed to their bullying and taken the Bible, creation, crosses, and nativity scenes out so those places can supposedly be "neutral."

But they're not neutral. There is no such thing as neutrality! The Bible makes it clear one is for or against Christ (Matthew 12:30). Everyone has a worldview — a religion — based on certain presuppositions. Secular does not mean neutral: it means without God. In reality, when atheists remove Christian teachings or symbols from places, they are instead imposing their religion of atheism — no God, naturalism — on everyone!

Romans 1:28 describes these atheists, *And since they did not see fit to acknowledge God* ... They reject God. We are told what they worship: *[B]ecause they exchanged the truth about God for a lie and worshiped and served the creature rather than the Creator, who is blessed forever!* (Romans 1:25). They worship the "creature." They really worship the creation, including man. The current climate change cult is, by and large, a part of the religion of atheism, where man thinks he can save himself and save the planet. They believe man is his own god (Genesis 3:5).

APOLOGETICS   JANUARY 28

Atheists have worship centers, including many public schools and secular universities. They have priests, such as many university professors and teachers. They have high priests, including Charles Darwin. And they try to get converts by evangelistically proclaiming their anti-God religion to as many people as they can.

When I asked Bill Nye what happens when you die, he said, "When you die, you're done." Atheists believe that when you die, you won't know you ever existed. You remember nothing. So why fight Christians? Why care about anything? It's a spiritual issue. In their heart, they know God exists (Romans 1:19). They're in rebellion. Pray for them, as they have been blinded by the devil (2 Corinthians 4:4).

> **Atheism is a religion of ultimate total purposelessness and meaninglessness, but our God is the God of hope and purpose.**

JANUARY 29
Romans 10:17

Intelligent Design Arguments vs. Intelligent Design Movement

Over the years, I've had a number of church leaders and Christian college/seminary professors say how wonderful the ID (Intelligent Design) movement is and what a great help to the Church it is. But in some ways, I beg to differ.

First of all, we need to understand the difference between intelligent design arguments and the Intelligent Design movement.

At Answers in Genesis, we use various intelligent design arguments in a number of our presentations and articles. These arguments clearly illustrate Romans 1:19–20, *For what can be known about God is plain to them, because God has shown it to them. For his invisible attributes, namely, his eternal power and divine nature, have been clearly perceived, ever since the creation of the world, in the things that have been made. So they are without excuse.*

In other words, the evidence all around us makes it obvious that life and the universe were created by an intelligent designer. Whether it's DNA, the development of a baby in a mother's womb, the obvious design of feathers, and so on, the evidence itself only makes sense interpreted within the framework of an intelligent designer. This evidence does not in any way fit with the belief that life arose by natural processes.

Now the Intelligent Design movement does some great research concerning design arguments about life and the universe. And we certainly use these arguments. And we must applaud them for this great research. But here's the problem, the ID movement does not tell us who the intelligent designer is.

At AiG, we do not and will never separate design arguments from telling people who the designer is — the Creator God of the Bible. God's Word states, *So faith comes from hearing, and hearing through the word of Christ* (Romans 10:17); *For the word of God is living and active, sharper than any two-edged sword, piercing to the division of soul and of spirit, of joints and of marrow, and discerning the thoughts and intentions of the heart* (Hebrews 4:12); and *so shall my word be that goes out from my mouth; it shall not return to me empty, but it shall accomplish that which I purpose, and shall succeed in the thing for which I sent it* (Isaiah 55:11).

There's no point converting people to believe in an intelligent designer unless we are pointing them to our Creator and Savior to see them receive the free gift of salvation.

And then another real, important issue. If one just uses the evidence of the world to point to a designer without using the Bible as a foundation for the right worldview to understand the world, then one would conclude that intelligence must be an ogre. After all, look at all the death, suffering, and disease in the world. There are so many horrible things that happen in the world. There's so much evil.

It's only when we start with God's Word that we understand we are living in a fallen world because of sin. This world was once perfect ("very good," as stated in Genesis 1:31) but is now a broken world because of God's judgment of death because of our rebellion in Adam. It's only using God's Word that we can begin to understand that it's not the fault of the intelligent designer (God) that there's death, disease, and suffering in this world; it's our fault because we committed high treason against the God of creation.

SCIENCE

Also, because the ID movement does not use God's Word as the foundation for their worldview, many within that movement believe in billions of years and certainly would not stand with Answers in Genesis on a literal Genesis and a universe that is only about 6,000 years old.

Answers in Genesis is an evangelistic organization. Our emphasis has always been biblical authority and the saving gospel message. We do see that the teaching of evolution and millions of years are an attack on the authority of God's Word in Genesis, so we help equip people with answers to these attacks as part of defending the Christian faith in today's world. Our main messages have always been that the history in Genesis is true, and the saving gospel message based in that history is true.

Let's not divorce intelligent design arguments from the intelligent Designer, the God of the Bible who is our Creator and Savior.

JANUARY 30

1 Peter 3:15

The Role of Apologetics in Evangelism

I've had some Christians over the years claim that people who use apologetics are trying to prove the Bible is true. They insist all we need to do is preach the gospel.

Most churches actually don't teach apologetics and don't train people to use apologetics in evangelism. I believe the lack of teaching apologetics has been a contributing reason as to why so many of the younger generations have left the Church.

What is apologetics?

Consider this verse:

[B]ut in your hearts honor Christ the Lord as holy, always being prepared to make a defense to anyone who asks you for a reason for the hope that is in you; yet do it with gentleness and respect (1 Peter 3:15).

The word *defense*, or in some translations *answer*, is translated from the Greek word *apologia*, which means to give a logically reasoned defense of the faith. In other words, when people ask questions about our faith, we need to be prepared to be able to defend the Christian faith.

In 2 Corinthians 11:3, God, through the Apostle Paul, warns that the devil is going to use the same method on us as he did on Eve to get us to a place of not believing God's Word:

But I am afraid that as the serpent deceived Eve by his cunning, your thoughts will be led astray from a sincere and pure devotion to Christ.

We go back to Genesis 3:1 to find the method the devil used on Eve:

Now the serpent was more crafty than any other beast of the field that the Lord God had made. He said to the woman, "Did God actually say, 'You shall not eat of any tree in the garden'?"

The method the devil used was to create doubt so that doubt would lead to unbelief. In the era we live in, the devil uses evolutionary beliefs such as millions of years to cause people to doubt God's Word. We live in a time where, all around the world, people are told that science supposedly shows the Bible's account of history in Genesis is not true. It's important that we raise up generations with answers to defend the Christian faith against such attacks on God's Word.

That's a major reason why the ministry of Answers in Genesis exists. Our Mission Statement makes this clear:

"Answers in Genesis (AiG) exists to proclaim the authority of the Bible—from the very first verse—without compromise by using apologetics in its world-class attractions, dynamic resources, and creative media to communicate the message of God's Word and the gospel so that believers are equipped to defend the Christian faith, and nonbelievers are challenged with the truth of the Bible and its message of salvation."

Now note that we use apologetics, but the whole purpose of our mission is to proclaim the truth of God's Word and the saving gospel. We use apologetics to point people to the truth of God's Word, knowing that:

So faith comes from hearing, and hearing through the word of Christ (Romans 10:17).

APOLOGETICS   JANUARY 30

For by grace you have been saved through faith. And this is not your own doing; it is the gift of God (Ephesians 2:8).

So, we use apologetics to answer skeptical questions that can cause doubt in God's Word and to point people to the truth of God's Word so they will hear the message of salvation, understanding only God can save a person. We recognize that for non-Christians, they are *dead in the trespasses and sins* (Ephesians 2:1). Non-Christians are walking dead people. They cannot raise themselves from the dead, nor can any person raise them from the dead. Only Christ can raise people from the dead.

To explain how it works to use apologetics in evangelism, I like to use the account of Jesus raising Lazarus from the dead in John 11 as an analogy.

Jesus comes to the tomb of Lazarus. He asks people to move the stone away from the grave. Now Jesus could have done that with one word, but human beings can move the stone away. But then, no human could raise Lazarus from the dead, so Jesus (who is the resurrection and the life — John 11:25) raised Lazarus when he said, "Lazarus, come forth."

Using apologetics is like rolling the stone away. This is something we can do. We do our best to roll out of the way the stumbling blocks represented by various questions and accusations against God's Word. We do the best we can to answer their skeptical questions. We do our best to roll that stone out of the way. But we also point people to the truth of God's Word, as we know only God can raise the dead. This is also why one cannot give up God's Word when arguing with someone who rejects God's Word.

This represents responsibility and sovereignty. We see this all the way through Scripture. And we see it in regard to salvation as we preach the Word and do our best to convince people of the truth by answering their questions, but we understand it's only God who opens people's hearts to do the saving.

The sad thing is that many church leaders may teach God's Word but don't teach people how to defend the Christian faith by giving answers to those who question God's Word (apologetics).

> **I urge churches to teach people apologetics to defend the Christian faith so they can be more effective in witnessing and pointing people to the saving message of the gospel.**

JANUARY 31
Psalm 127:3

How to Train Up a Child

Children are not miniature adults.

We've seen shocking headlines lately about political leaders, including President Joe Biden, insisting children/youth should have the freedom to decide if they want to be a boy or want to be a girl.

For instance, Fox News, April 5, 2023:

"White House slammed for saying 'a child and their parents' should decide trans surgeries: 'This is madness.' Article states: "White House press secretary Karine Jean-Pierre alarmed Twitter users on Wednesday after insisting that the decision to receive gender treatments should be made by a child along with their parents."[14]

Other headlines:

"Biden signs order to protect transgender children as Texas continues efforts to restrict gender-affirming care. The executive order calls on the U.S. Department of Education and the Department of Health and Human Services to increase access to gender-affirming health care and develop ways to counter state efforts aimed at limiting such treatments for transgender minors."[15]

"Biden calls curbs on treatment for trans kids 'outrageous,' 'immoral.' President Biden has claimed states have no right to restrict treatments like hormone blockers or sex change operations for transgender children, claiming that recent measures passed by Republican-led legislatures were based in 'fear.'"[16]

It's amazing how young political leaders claim kids can decide if they want to try to change their gender, with some researchers claiming three years old is not too young!

As I stated at the beginning, children are not miniature adults. Let's consider what God's Word states about children:

When I was a child, I spoke like a child, I thought like a child, I reasoned like a child. When I became a man, I gave up childish ways (1 Corinthians 13:11).

Brothers, do not be children in your thinking. Be infants in evil, but in your thinking be mature (1 Corinthians 14:20).

There are many verses instructing parents to train up their children. When our children are born, they don't know about the Bible, they don't know answers to questions that attack God's Word, and they don't know anything about human life. We as parents have to train them. When it comes to practical issues, we have to potty train them; we don't let them decide how to do it. We train them not to cross busy roads; we have to warn them about danger. We also know that when they go through puberty, there are lots of changes that can occur, and so we need to help them through this time. As they grow into adulthood, they need training and advice to help them mature so they can understand more of the things of life and how to make decisions.

And, of course, for Christians, we need to train them to build their thinking on the Bible so they will understand that marriage is one man and one woman and God made only two genders: male and female. They need to know that they can't change their genetics nor trust their feelings because of our sin nature. They need

FAMILY

JANUARY 31

to know they have to judge their feelings against God's Word. They also need to understand that because we live in a fallen world, our bodies are not perfect and we can have all sorts of problems, but in no way does that mean we should think we can change our gender, which we can't do genetically anyway.

We've also seen headlines about teachers who influence children and young people, insisting they can hide a child's supposed wanting to transition from parents. But that's when we need to make sure parents and children understand that teachers don't own the children, the government doesn't own the children, God does. God owns us all, as He is the Creator. And that's why we need to obey what God tells us in His infallible Word.

Also, God has entrusted children to parents to train for Him, *Behold, children are a heritage from the LORD, the fruit of the womb a reward* (Psalm 127:3).

Any of those who claim they are *L* or *G* or *B* or *T* or *Q* or *I* or *A* (or any others) are all perverting the created order, which is a disaster for each one of them. Sadly, more people are realizing they were pressured and led astray when they were young and immature and are now detransitioning, but much irreversible damage has been done.

The only answer is for people to trust Christ for salvation and build their worldview on His Word.

FEBRUARY 1
Genesis 5:4

Where Did Cain Get His Wife?

I was in a restaurant in London a few years ago when the chef came to our table and said, "I heard you are doing a conference on the Bible?"

"Yes," I replied.

He said, "I don't believe the Bible."

I then asked, "Why don't you believe the Bible?"

He responded, "Well, the Bible says God made Adam and Eve, and they had Cain and Abel, so where did all the people come from?"

I then said, "Well, Genesis 5:4 tells us Adam had other sons and daughters."

He then blurted out, "Oh, I never read that far."

And that's a problem with many people. They don't read that far! They don't read the Bible as they should and then, like many atheists, make accusations against the Bible. And many times, when they are given answers, they won't accept them, as they don't want to accept them. The question about Cain's wife is very easy to answer and understand.

We don't know how many children Adam and Eve had, but it's interesting to note that Jewish tradition has Adam with 33 sons and 23 daughters. In 1 Corinthians 15:45 and Genesis 3:20, it is clear there was only one man and one woman to start with. So originally, close relatives obviously had to marry.

I was on a radio talk program once when a caller asked, "Where did Cain get his wife?" I answered, saying Cain's wife was his sister. The next caller identified himself as an atheist and said, "If you believe that, it's incest and it's immoral." I've heard many atheists make that accusation over the years.

First, an atheist can't make a moral judgment like that. If it was truly incest as we understand the word today, then why is incest immoral from an atheist's perspective anyway? If there's no God, no absolute authority, then "right" and "wrong" are subjective and can't be treated as moral absolutes. Also, from an atheistic evolutionist's perspective, humans are just evolved animals, so they could have sexual relationships with anyone (or any animal), as there's no such thing as marriage and morality is relative. And yet atheists try to claim Christians have a moral problem with Cain's wife being his sister! They can't see their own inconsistencies.

Now the word *incest* wasn't even invented until the thirteenth century. It's a modern word. But doesn't the Bible forbid marriage between close relations? It does, but the laws against marrying family members were initially given as part of the Mosaic covenant, approximately 2,500 years after God created Adam and Eve. Due in part to genetic mistakes, these laws were necessary to help protect offspring from mutations shared by both parents.

In today's world, close relations (e.g., brother and sister) marrying would be incest. The closer we go back to Adam and Eve, the fewer genetic mistakes people would have accumulated, so it would have been safer for close relatives to have children.

APOLOGETICS   FEBRUARY 1

Think about the fact that because we're all one race, descendants of Adam and Eve, then when a person gets married, they marry their relative. It's just today, we don't marry a close relative. Different countries have different laws in regard to how close relations can be for marriage.

Noah's grandchildren would have married brothers, sisters, or close cousins because there were no other people (1 Peter 3:20; Genesis 7:7). The Bible says that Abraham married his half-sister (Genesis 20:2, 12) and that Isaac married Rebekah, daughter of his cousin Bethuel (Genesis 24:15, 67). Jacob married first cousins Leah and Rachel. Clearly, the Bible did not forbid the marriage of close relatives until the time of Moses.

"Who was Cain's wife?" is not the supposed problem atheists and others try to make it out to be. When one understands the Bible's account of origins in Genesis correctly, the answer is obvious.

> **Originally, there was no problem with close relations marrying, providing it was one man for one woman, which is what the doctrine of marriage is all about.**

FEBRUARY 2

Genesis 3:15

What Does Genesis Have to Do with Easter?

What does Genesis have to do with Easter?

Well, at Easter, Christians especially remember Christ's death and Resurrection, as we should remember every day of the year. We call that the power of the gospel. After all, *if Christ has not been raised, then our preaching is in vain and your faith is in vain* (1 Corinthians 15:14).

Now I've had many Christians over the years claim that it's not important to take Genesis 1–11 as literal history, as it's the gospel that's the most important message.

The gospel is the vital message for every human being. But how does one fully understand the saving gospel message without a belief in and understanding of Genesis 1–11? Actually, the first time the gospel message is preached is Genesis 3:15.

When Adam disobeyed God, sin entered the world. God had warned Adam that if he disobeyed, death would be the consequence: *[B]ut of the tree of the knowledge of good and evil you shall not eat, for in the day that you eat of it you shall surely die* (Genesis 2:17).

We are told in Genesis 3:17–19 that because Adam did disobey, then our bodies would return to dust (die).

In Genesis 3:15, we read what God said to the serpent: *I will put enmity between you and the woman, and between your offspring and her offspring; he shall bruise your head, and you shall bruise his heel.* This verse tells us a number of things:

1. "Enmity between you and the woman." There is going to be a perpetual war between Satan and the Church because of the irreconcilable hatred Satan has against the Church.

2. "Enmity … between your offspring and her offspring." There will be a continual battle between, metaphorically speaking, the serpent's (devil's) offspring (demonic forces), the people who follow the devil, and those who trust in God. It's the perpetual war between good and evil. *For we do not wrestle against flesh and blood, but against the rulers, against the authorities, against the cosmic powers over this present darkness, against the spiritual forces of evil in the heavenly places* (Ephesians 6:12).

3. We have a prophecy concerning the virgin birth of the Savior, the babe in a manger, as Jesus would literally be the woman's offspring. This also refers to those who trust God.

4. "You shall bruise his heel" tells of the fact that the devil's actions would result in the wounding and death of Jesus.

5. "He shall bruise [crush] your head." The passage tells us of Jesus' victory over the devil. Jesus would triumph over sin and the devil on the Cross — the Resurrection!

And although Satan was defeated, he is still active in this world but one day will be thrown into the lake of fire when God brings in the consummation of all things.

In Genesis 3:21, God kills animals, sheds blood, and provides clothes for Adam and Eve. *And the L ord God made for Adam and for his wife garments of skins and clothed them.*

APOLOGETICS

Here God sets up the sacrificial system that looks forward to the ultimate sacrifice when Christ died on the Cross. This is the first blood sacrifice as a covering for their sin — a picture of what was to come in Jesus Christ, the Lamb of God who died and rose from the dead to take away our sin.

Because death was the penalty for sin, life had to be given to pay that penalty. *[W]ithout the shedding of blood there is no forgiveness of sins* (Hebrews 9:22). *For the life of the flesh is in the blood* (Leviticus 17:11). But *it is impossible for the blood of bulls and goats to take away sins* (Hebrews 10:4). Humans are not animals, so an animal's sacrifice can't take away sin. This was pointing to the time when a man, but a perfect man — God's Son — would come to take away our sin.

What does the special message Christians remember at Easter have to do with Genesis? Everything. Without the events of Genesis, we wouldn't understand where sin came from, what it is, why we are under the judgment of death, and why we need a Savior. Genesis 1–11 is the foundation for understanding the saving gospel message. Ultimately, Genesis 1–11 is the foundation for everything.

> **The answers are always ultimately in Genesis, which is why to properly understand the gospel, we must start with Genesis 1–11.**

FEBRUARY 3
Psalm 11:3

Genesis 1–11 Is Foundational to the Book of Revelation

What's more important, to teach on eschatology (end times) or Genesis (beginnings)?

I'm sure that will be a provocative question for some. Now, before I deal with this, let me remind us that all Scripture is inspired by God: *All Scripture is breathed out by God and profitable for teaching, for reproof, for correction, and for training in righteousness* (2 Timothy 3:16).

So from Genesis 1:1 to Revelation 22:21, we have the inspired, infallible Word of God. Of course, God's Word consists of different sorts of language. For instance, Genesis is written as historical narrative, the Psalms are poetry, and Revelation is apocalyptic literature (which means it will have a lot of symbolism).

When one thinks of the end times in the Bible, one would immediately think about the Book of Revelation. One of the observations I've made over the years is that there are a lot of churches that have quite a detailed statement of faith about Revelation and a specific view of eschatology. In fact, there are churches that will not let a person become a member if they don't hold to a specific view of eschatology.

However, many of those same churches are not as concerned about specific details of what they believe about Genesis as they do Revelation. In many instances, they will have general statements like, "God created all things." Some church statements of faith may state they believe in a literal Adam and Eve but no specific details as to what that actually means.

I also find a number of preachers who consider it more important to preach on end times because of what they see happening in the culture than to preach on Genesis. But here are some important facts:

- Revelation is not the foundation for the rest of the Bible, Genesis 1–11 is.
- Revelation is not the foundation of all doctrine, Genesis 1–11 is.
- Revelation is not the foundation for our Christian worldview, Genesis 1–11 is.
- Revelation is not the foundation for everything, Genesis 1–11 is.

That does not mean Revelation is not an important book. And this does not mean it's not important to preach on the end times and the book of Revelation.

But I claim that because so many church leaders and Christian academics gave up Genesis 1–11 and either ignored it, compromised it with evolutionary ideas, or decided it was too divisive to teach it, this is where the Church lost biblical authority in a major way in our era. This has been a major contributing factor to the generational loss from the Church. It's a major reason why much of the Church is so lukewarm and not impacting the culture like it did and should.

If the Church really understood the vital importance of the first 11 chapters of the Bible, they would have statements of faith that showed this. I encourage you to read the Answers in Genesis statement of faith to see how detailed it is in Genesis. We also know that if specific details are not given, then it makes it easy for people to justify compromising Genesis with man's evolutionary ideas.

For instance, if a church just states they believe in Adam and Eve, then people could agree to this and yet be ardent theistic evolutionists, believing God evolved humans from animals. One would need to state Adam

APOLOGETICS — FEBRUARY 3

was made directly from dust and Eve from his side, etc., to begin to ensure people (including pastors) would not bring compromising positions into the Church. Another example would be stating that God created everything in six days. If it is not stated clearly that they are six 24-hour days, then someone could justify believing they can interpret the days as millions of years long.

Here are some examples from the Answers in Genesis statement of faith: "The special and unique creation of Adam from dust and Eve from Adam's rib was supernatural and immediate. Adam and Eve did not originate from any other preexisting lifeforms (Genesis 2:7, 2:21–23, 3:19; 1 Corinthians 11:8–12, 15:47–49)."

"The days in Genesis do not correspond to geologic ages but are six consecutive, 24-hour days of creation; the first day began in Genesis 1:1, and the seventh day, which was also a normal 24-hour day, ended in Genesis 2:3 (Genesis 1:1–2:3; Exodus 20:8–11, 31:17; Hebrews 4:3–4)."

"The gap theory, progressive creation, day-age, framework hypothesis, theistic evolution (i.e., evolutionary creation), functionality–cosmic temple, analogical days, day-gap-day, and any other views that try to fit evolution or millions of years into Genesis are incompatible with Scripture."

Today we are seeing moral relativism permeate the culture. And the LGBTQ worldview seems to be driving the culture in many ways, from the leaders in the nation down. Even a number of churches/church leaders and Christian academics are softening their stand on God's Word to accommodate LGBTQ and other issues.

Now if one wants to deal with any issue as a Christian, then one has to start with Genesis 1–11. The first 11 chapters of the Bible give the origin of all the basic entities of life and the universe: The origin of the universe, life, animals, humans, gender, marriage, sin, death, clothing, work, dominion, seven-day week, nations, language — in an ultimate sense, everything.

Yet, Genesis has probably been the most mocked at, scoffed at, ridiculed, disbelieved, and attacked book of the Bible in our day and age. The devil knows if the foundation of everything is destroyed, the structure (of Christianity) will collapse (Psalm 11:3).

I challenge churches to take a stand on Genesis as they should and ensure their statements of faith are very detailed for the first 11 chapters of Genesis to ensure they won't compromise the foundation of all doctrine. The gospel message is founded in Genesis 1–11. Church leaders need to be teaching Genesis 1–11 as literal history, equipping people to have a truly Christian worldview, and providing answers (teaching apologetics) to defend against the attacks on the vital history God has given to us.

Only then will people be equipped to deal with the issues of our day, like abortion, transgenderism, racism, death, suffering, marriage, and the list goes on! Ultimately, to deal with any issue, one has to start with Genesis 1–11.

> **Genesis 1–11 is foundational to the Book of Revelation, for if man had not sinned, there would be no need for a book about the end times.**

FEBRUARY 4
Matthew 12:34

Upholding the Authority of the Word of God

What is your real motivation at AiG? Are you political activists? Are you trying to get creation taught in the public school classroom? Does your ministry aim to change the culture?

These are just a few of the many questions I've been asked by the secular media over the years, particularly during each media blitz surrounding the opening of the Creation Museum and the Ark Encounter.

In these interviews, I made it very clear that Answers in Genesis' thrust is to uphold the authority of God's Word, as we not only provide answers to the questions of skeptics but also preach the gospel of Jesus Christ and see people won to the Lord.

At Answers in Genesis, we understand that the Christianized culture we once had in America (and the once-Christianized culture of the West in general) has become increasingly secularized over the past few years.

AiG helps the Church understand that this societal change occurred from the foundation up — that is, instead of the culture generally being founded on the teachings in God's Word (when the Judeo-Christian ethic permeated the culture), generations were eventually taught instead to exalt autonomous human reason and build their worldview on that foundation.

And what has been the basic and most successful mechanism for this secularization of the culture? Over the decades, millions upon millions of people, one person at a time, have been indoctrinated to believe in the idea of evolutionary naturalism and millions (billions!) of years, and thus to doubt and ultimately disbelieve the Bible as true history — particularly in regard to the history in Genesis 1–11.

As generations began to reject God's Word as reliable and authoritative, they began to consistently build a secular worldview based on moral relativism.

As this change occurred, many such secular humanists moved into positions in education, the government, legal systems, etc. The worldview they adopted determined how they would vote in passing laws, establishing curricula, making moral choices, and so on.

For as he thinks in his heart, so is he (Proverbs 23:7; NKJV).

For out of the abundance of the heart the mouth speaks (Matthew 12:34).

The culture changed from predominantly Christianized in its worldview to increasingly secular. The West was changing.

As people repent, are converted to Christ, and are taught to build their thinking consistently on God's Word (and as Christians are challenged to de-secularize their own thinking and build a Christian worldview), they can make an impact on culture. In other words, the solution to what happened in the culture doesn't ultimately rely on government. The solution ultimately is God's Word and the saving gospel impacting hearts and lives.

APOLOGETICS

After all, God's people are told to be salt and light (Matthew 5:13–14) — and thus affect the world for good. Jesus said, *[L]et your light shine before others, so that they may see your good works and give glory to your Father who is in heaven* (Matthew 5:16). Lives impacted for Christ will impact others.

That's why I often explain to the secular media that the ministry of AiG, the Creation Museum, and the Ark Encounter is to preach the gospel and pray to see people converted to Christ and thus be salt and light in their daily living. As these people find themselves on school boards, are elected to local government, or obtain influential positions in the media, their worldview will govern the way they vote, which can lead to change.

The AiG ministry is providing answers to the skeptical questions of our day that cause people to doubt the Bible's historicity. And in this era of history, the most-attacked part of the Bible's history is Genesis 1–11. When people understand that they can trust the history in the early chapters of Genesis, they can better understand and be more responsive to the gospel — the gospel that is based in that history.

As Christians, our aim is not to change the culture. Changing the culture is a by-product of a much bigger and more eternally significant goal. As one life at a time is changed, each of those Christians can have an impact on the culture for the glory of Christ.

So, this is what Answers in Genesis, the Creation Museum, and the Ark Encounter are "on about" — and what we believe every Christian should be doing: presenting and defending the life-changing gospel message to see lives changed for the glory of God.

We all need to be doing our best to be "impacting the culture, one life at a time."

FEBRUARY 5
Psalm 11:3

The Real Battle Is at the Foundational Level

I've had many Christians express dismay at what they see as a plethora of problems in the culture, such as abortion, gender issues, LGBTQ, gay "marriage," racism, and so on. They have said to me, "There are so many problems to battle. How can we do it?" It's almost like they want to throw their hands in the air and give up because the many problems seem so overwhelming to them.

Sadly, many churches haven't taught people to think foundationally, and thus they do not understand that all these issues are, in reality, the same problems. They are different symptoms of that problem.

Had churches been teaching foundationally, then Christians would understand that our thinking starts with God's Word — in particular, Genesis 1–11, the foundation of everything. Sadly, because so many Christian leaders have compromised Genesis 1–11 with evolution/millions of years, most Church people have not been taught the foundation for their doctrine and for a true biblical worldview.

Many Christians just look at what they perceive as the "problems" and try to figure out how to take these to the Bible to try to understand what to do. But those Christians who understand what it means to have a biblical worldview do know that God's Word beginning in Genesis is the foundation for that worldview. They also would know that there are only two foundations ultimately for people's worldview (or religion). One either starts with God's Word or man's word.

For those who build their thinking on man's word (which is basically the foundation of the secular education system), the outcome of that thinking is a worldview of moral relativism. Thus, marriage is however they want to define it. Because man is seen as just an animal, abortion is not seen as killing a human being made in God's image but is more along the lines of thinking that you get rid of spare cats, so get rid of spare kids; there's no difference. People who are aged and infirmed are seen as a drain on the health system and, therefore, should use euthanasia to stop their suffering and costly care. Gender is however one wants to define it, and people can change their gender using drugs and surgery if they want.

But when people build their thinking on God's Word, then their worldview is determined by what God our Creator has determined. God created marriage, so there's only one marriage — one man and one woman. Humans are made in the image of God, so abortion after fertilization is murder. God made only two genders of humans: male and female.

Two foundations with two very different worldviews. Once one understands that the real battle is at the foundational level, then we can understand that to battle all the social issues (abortion, gender, gay "marriage," racism, etc.), one must understand they are the symptoms of a foundational problem. The problem is that people have built their worldview on the wrong foundation of man's word.

Now if all those social issues are the same ultimate problem, then they must have the same solution. And they do. The solution has always been the truth of God's Word and the saving gospel. Now for many, they have been indoctrinated to think the Bible is an outdated book of mythology, and science proves it can't be trusted — particularly in its history in Genesis 1–11. So that's where apologetics comes in to give answers to the attacks on God's Word to show we can defend the Christian faith. That's why at Answers in Genesis, we

APOLOGETICS

FEBRUARY 5

provide scientific and biblical answers to the questions of our day used to try to attack and undermine God's Word. So, the solution to the social issues is to battle at a foundation level. To do that, we need to raise up generations who know how to think foundationally and are equipped with apologetics.

Sadly, most churches do not do any of this, which is why most Christians don't know how to battle in the right way concerning all these social issues that are catastrophically changing the culture. One of the consequences of this lack of teaching is that we are going to see increased persecution against Christians who stand boldly on God's Word.

> The clash we see happening in our culture is a clash between two totally opposite worldviews, which at a foundational level is a battle between God's Word and man's word.

FEBRUARY 6
John 3:12

Is the Bible a Science Textbook?

During a radio talk show, a caller asked me the question, "Is the Bible a science textbook?" Of course, secularists would say the Bible is not a science textbook. They would claim it's a book of mythology. So, how did I answer the question?

I said, "Well, I'm glad the Bible is not a science textbook like the ones they use in school because those textbooks basically change each year, but the Bible doesn't change. The Bible itself states, *Forever, O Lord, your word is firmly fixed in the heavens* (Psalm 119:89)."

In fact, there are many verses of Scripture to tell us God's infallible Word, unlike man's fallible word, lasts forever: *"[B]ut the word of the Lord remains forever." And this word is the good news that was preached to you* (1 Peter 1:25).

The grass withers, the flower fades, but the word of our God will stand forever (Isaiah 40:8).

So, is the Bible a science textbook?

Well, first of all, we need to understand what the word *science* means. The word *science* comes from the classical Latin *scientia*, which means "to know." The Merriam-Webster online dictionary defines the word *science* as "the state of knowing: knowledge as distinguished from ignorance or misunderstanding."[17]

In other words, the actual meaning of the word *science* is "knowledge."

Now words get to be used in different ways. For instance, when people talk about doing chemistry experiments or studying cells under a microscope in biology, they will say they are studying science. But then, secular scientists studying the supposed evolution of life when they weren't there to see it happen also call that "science."

That's why when I debated Bill Nye in 2014 at the Creation Museum (you can see that debate on the Answers in Genesis YouTube channel or on Answers TV), I said the first thing we needed to do was define our terms. I made sure people understood the word *science* meant "knowledge."

Now to help people understand the different ways the word *science* is used, I wanted to correctly make sure I taught them *how* to think and not just *what* to think about this topic. I explained that being able to observe and repeat experiments in the present is very different from discussing the topic of origins, when humans weren't there to observe what was happening.

That's why I said doing experiments in the present so you can repeat those experiments to gain knowledge is called "observational science" or "operational science." But talking about the origins issue is a very different type of knowledge, and we call that "historical science," as we are talking about the past, trying to understand history. That's a very different type of knowledge indeed.

Sadly, the same word *science* is used by secularists and others for observational science and historical science. So, students are brainwashed to think that because studying science put man on the moon, a marvelous technological feat, then we have to believe scientists when they say science proves evolution. They don't realize there's been a type of "bait and switch" to use the same word (*science*) to mean very different things.

SCIENCE

FEBRUARY 6

When students use science textbooks in public school, these books usually cover biology, chemistry, physics, and so on. But they also cover topics about evolution and millions of years. The problem is evolution and millions of years involve "historical science," whereas studying biology, chemistry, and physics (providing it's not the origins issue) involves "observational science." Students aren't being taught how to think correctly about science. It's one of the reasons they get easily brainwashed to believe evolution and millions of years are true (as have many church leaders and Christian academics for the same reason) because they think science (and really scientists) have clearly shown this.

When I debated Bill Nye, I explained that if he and I were at the Grand Canyon, we would agree that we could observe layers of sandstone and limestone, and we could agree on how thick they were, as we could measure them, so that's "observational science." But we wouldn't agree on how old the layers are and how long they took to be laid down, as that's "historical science." He would believe in millions of years of slow processes to explain the layers, but I believe they were formed during Noah's Flood a few thousand years ago.

When it comes to the Bible, we need to understand that it is primarily a book of history, spiritual, and moral matters. It's God's history book to us. In a way, we could say it's God's textbook of historical science. However, the Bible also deals with geology, biology, astronomy, and so on. And when it deals with these topics, we can trust it, as it's God's Word. And unlike "science" textbooks in public schools, it never changes. What we can do is use observational science to see if experiments and observations in the present confirm the history God reveals in geology, biology, archaeology, etc. And the Bible's history is confirmed over and over again, as we've shown in many articles on our websites, in our magazines, in presentations, in books, etc.

The science of genetics confirms animals exist in kinds that never change into another totally different kind. The science of geology confirms catastrophic processes formed the fossil record over the earth, confirming the Flood of Noah's day. There are so many confirmations like this.

The exhibits at the Ark Encounter and Creation Museum attractions give lots more confirming evidence for the truth of God's Word in many different areas. And there are thousands of articles on the Answers in Genesis website that also give such answers.

Because the historical science (the "earthly things") in the Bible is true, the moral and spiritual teachings based in that history are true. Evolution and millions of years are false history.

If I have told you earthly things and you do not believe, how can you believe if I tell you heavenly things? (John 3:12).

Christianity is based on real history, the history God recorded for us in His Word – the Bible.

FEBRUARY 7
Isaiah 5:20

A Spiritual Health Problem

We're seeing the symptoms of a deadly disease sweeping the nation and sweeping through the entire Western world.

The disease is man's sin of rebellion against God and His Word. And it's resulting in a war on children like we've never seen before.

Who would have thought we would see headlines like these:

"Transgender Assistant Secretary of Health Rachel Levine Says Changing Kids' Genders Has the 'Highest Support' of the Biden Administration and Is Key to the Mental Health of Minors."

"Biden Calls Bans on Transgender Treatments for Children 'Close to Sinful'"

"Dr. Rachel Levine Says Changing Kids' Genders Will Soon Be Fully Embraced"

In March 2022, Dr. Rachel Levine, the assistant secretary of health in the USA, was named 1 of 12 "Women of the Year" by *USA Today*.[18] But he is not a woman! It's a biological man who claims he's a woman and is one of the people in charge of health in America.

What a mess. And Dr. Levine, along with Joe Biden, are ardent supporters of children, youth, and adults wanting to try to change their gender by using dangerous drugs and mutilating surgeries. This is not surprising given that Levine is a trans woman whose sex chromosome pair is XY. This means this person is a male. Science confirms that.

The Bible makes it clear God made only two types of humans: male and female. They are different physiologically, behaviorally, and genetically.

Let's judge what Joe Biden and Dr. Levine believe and support against God's Word:

So God created man in his own image, in the image of God he created him; male and female he created them (Genesis 1:27).

Male and female he created them (Genesis 5:2).

But from the beginning of creation, "God made them male and female" (Mark 10:6).

He [Jesus] answered, "Have you not read that he who created them from the beginning made them male and female ...?" (Matthew 19:4).

Scripture and science make it clear that there are only two genders of humans. And no matter what one tries to do, one can't change one's genetics!

Those who reject the worldview built on the Bible, regardless of what they do, can never change their genetics.

What is happening to this nation and its leaders? God's Word tells us clearly. We're observing Romans 1 happening before our eyes:

For although they knew God, they did not honor him as God or give thanks to him, but they became futile in their thinking, and their foolish hearts were darkened. Claiming to be wise, they became fools (Romans 1:21–22).

APOLOGETICS

Therefore God gave them up in the lusts of their hearts to impurity, to the dishonoring of their bodies among themselves, because they exchanged the truth about God for a lie and worshiped and served the creature rather than the Creator (Romans 1:24–25).

For this reason God gave them up to dishonorable passions. For their women exchanged natural relations for those that are contrary to nature; and the men likewise gave up natural relations with women and were consumed with passion for one another, men committing shameless acts with men (Romans 1:26–27).

Sadly, even certain church leaders have compromised God's Word to accommodate the sinful actions of people like those described in Romans 1.

We can sum up many of the leaders of this nation this way: *Woe to those who call evil good and good evil, who put darkness for light and light for darkness, who put bitter for sweet and sweet for bitter!* (Isaiah 5:20).

The solution to the world's ills is the truth of God's Word and the saving gospel. We need to pray that these rebellious leaders will repent of their sin, turn to Christ, and receive the free gift of salvation.

> **America and the rest of the West have a severe spiritual health problem, and to deal with it, we need to deal with the disease – the sin of rebellion that permeates hearts and minds.**

FEBRUARY 8
Galatians 5:9

The Catastrophic Consequence of Compromise: Part 1

A little leaven leavens the whole lump (Galatians 5:9).

How many of those Ivy League schools (Harvard, Yale, Princeton) were once Christian? All of them. How many are Christian today? None of them. All are now indoctrinating generations in an atheistic worldview.

How did this happen?

I suggest that a little compromise (leaven) on God's Word here and there, and particularly on Genesis, begins a slippery slide of unbelief.

It happens generation after generation. Sadly, most Christian institutions over time lose what their founders stood for in regard to God's Word. A little leaven begins the mission drift and usually within two to three generations, the original foundation they had is all but gone. There are exceptions, of course — but they are rare exceptions.

We also see this happening in church denominations, which is one of the reasons splits occur and new denominations arise. Think about the Methodist church of the John and Charles Wesley days. Most Methodist churches today are extremely liberal. But this has happened in Baptist, Lutheran, and Presbyterian churches. Even though some groups within such denominations maintain a stand on the truth of God's Word, most over time do not.

We see it happening in our day with Christian colleges. I suggest that institutions like Baylor, Biola, Calvin, and Wheaton, to name just a few, are well on their way to becoming the Yales and Princetons of the future. In certain areas, they are already there. And in our era (that began in the late 1700s–early 1800s), the "leaven" (the effects of naturalism) has been imposed on Genesis, which has had and is having catastrophic consequences.

Let me illustrate how this "leaven" undermines the authority of God's Word and results in doubt leading to unbelief. Wheaton College, with the financial help of BioLogos (an organization dedicated to getting the Church to accept evolution/millions of years and receives considerable financial support from the Templeton Foundation, known for supporting liberal causes), produced a college textbook.

This textbook is called *Understanding Scientific Theories of Origins: Cosmology, Geology and Biology in Christian Perspective* and was written by five Wheaton College professors.

Here is one quote from the book:

"Although some Christians have argued that the fall utterly disrupted some kind of original perfection of creation, there is no evidence from either the Bible or the creation, making that a foregone conclusion."

Now why would they say that? Well, consider this quote from the book:

"The age of the Earth, now understood to be 4.55 billion years (or 4.55 Ga) is really less a theory than it is a measurement."[19]

APOLOGETICS

They accept the billions of years for the age of the earth as fact. As part of those billions of years, they believe the fossil layers were laid down over millions of years, and the fossils represent a supposed record of the evolution of life.

Once a Christian accepts that there were millions of years of death (and diseases like cancer that are found in fossil bones) before man, and thus before man sinned, then to be consistent, the Fall (the entrance of sin and the judgment of death) could not have produced all the death and suffering we see today.

Now Romans 8:22 makes it clear that the whole creation groans because of sin, because of the Fall. One day, there will be a restoration of all things with a new heavens and earth. But right now, we live in a fallen world. But what did the Fall do? Those who take Genesis as literal history understand that the death and suffering we see today happened after Adam fell. The original world was perfect; it was "very good," as God describes in Genesis 1:31, but it's no longer very good. Now it is a groaning world.

However, you can see the dilemma for those who believe in millions of years. For them, the world with all its death, bloodshed, disease, and suffering has gone on for millions of years. So, what did the Fall do? That's why the authors of this textbook claim the Fall did not disrupt a world that originally had perfection!

The Bible actually describes death as an enemy (1 Corinthians 15:26). It's an intrusion because of sin. And the Bible tells us that one day *Death and Hades were* [will be] *thrown into the lake of fire* (Revelation 20:14).

The sad thing is that one of the most asked questions by the younger generations is, "How can there be a loving God with all the death and suffering in the world?" And it's only those who take Genesis as literal history (and that's certainly not these five Wheaton College professors) who can show that all this death and suffering is our fault because of our sin in Adam. It's not God's fault. But really, those Christians who believe in millions of years are actually saying it's God's fault because He has used death and suffering over millions of years as part of bringing lifeforms into existence.

Also, once one unlocks the door to take man's beliefs, like millions of years, and add them into Scripture (a little leaven), this begins to put people on a slippery slide of doubt leading to unbelief. As this continues to happen, an institution will lose the foundation of God's Word and eventually become more and more secularized and become like a Yale or Princeton, etc.

That's why I have a burden for Christians to understand that the Answers in Genesis ministry is a biblical authority ministry. We warn people about believing in millions of years because this undermines the authority of Scripture and can put people on that slippery slide of unbelief, and it also attacks God's character. I contend such compromise in our era has been a major contributing reason as to why we've seen such catastrophic generational loss from the Church.

Check the Christian colleges you support to see if they use this textbook or have any material or speakers from BioLogos. If they do, I suggest you challenge the leaders/professors of the college about the importance of standing on God's Word beginning in Genesis. If no success, then consider whom you should be supporting. And beware of compromising colleges and the destruction they can have on your own children.

A little leaven certainly does leaven the whole lump.

FEBRUARY 9
Proverbs 9:10

The Catastrophic Consequence of Compromise: Part 2

The majority of Christian colleges compromise God's Word in Genesis. This compromise undermines the authority of God's Word and has been a major contributing factor as to why we are seeing massive generational loss from the Church and the secularization of the culture. A major reason for this compromise is they put man's word before God's Word.

One such college is Wheaton College. A few years ago, five Wheaton College professors with funding (millions of dollars) from the liberal evolutionist organization BioLogos produced a textbook on origins in geology, biology, and cosmology. The textbook title is *Understanding Scientific Theories of Origins*.

One quote in the book really summarizes the reason these professors and so many other academics compromise God's Word in Genesis with evolution/millions of years. In the book, we read:

"A Bible-first approach devalues the meaningfulness of creation revelation."[20]

Now at Answers in Genesis, we have a Bible-first approach. We recognize that God is infinite in knowledge and wisdom. A word to sum up a Bible-first approach would be *exegesis*. We take God's Word as written (naturally) and let it speak to us through the literature, context, etc. As God's Word states:

[I]n whom are hidden all the treasures of wisdom and knowledge (Colossians 2:3).

As human beings, we really know almost nothing compared to our infinite Creator. Because the Bible is God's Word and Genesis 1–11 is the history in geology, biology, astronomy, and anthropology that God has revealed to us, we need to accept God's Word as truth and to judge man's word against the truth of God's Word.

We live in the present. When we are trying to understand what happened in the past to bring the present (whether it be in regard to biology, geology, astronomy, etc.) into being, we need to understand that God has revealed the events of history so we know what happened in the past. Knowing what happened in the past is a key to understanding the present and interpreting the evidence of the present correctly.

That's why, as Christians, we must have a Bible-first approach (exegesis). We must use God's Word as the foundation for our worldview so we can look at the present world through the lens of Scripture.

Now, in this textbook, the authors don't take a Bible-first approach, but in fact, it's really a man's-word-first approach. A word to sum this up is *eisegesis*. This means taking beliefs to Scripture to interpret the words in the light of what fallible man believes. In other words, reading ideas into the text. The authors of this textbook take the fallible word of man concerning his evolutionary beliefs based on naturalism (atheism) in the history concerning geology, biology, and astronomy and then reinterpret God's Word in Genesis to fit.

That's why (as quoted in Part 1 of this topic — see previous entry) these authors believe the earth is billions of years old and that it never had original perfection that is now marred by sin.

Now let me show another consequence of what happens with this man's-word-first approach when taking the belief in billions of years and adding that to Scripture. Once a Christian believes the fossil record was laid down over millions of years, then they would reject the global Flood of Noah's day. After all, if there really was such a Flood, one would expect to find billions of dead things buried in rock layers laid down by water all

APOLOGETICS — FEBRUARY 9

over the earth. But if all those billions of dead things were laid down over millions of years, then there could not have been a global Flood. That's why in this textbook, the authors state:

"Here it is enough to say that geological data to support a flood of massive proportion is lacking. Furthermore, no archaeological evidence lends support to such a flood."

Usually, such people claim Noah's Flood was just a local event, which is not what Scripture clearly teaches.

Another consequence of this man's-word-first approach would be in regard to how human beings came into being. Secularists claim man evolved from apelike creatures, and thus, man is just an animal, some sort of an ape. Therefore, man could not have been created directly from dust and Eve directly from the man's rib.

In this textbook," the authors state:

"Humans are hominoid primates [apes] in the hominin tribe with cognitive abilities that exceed those of all other primates, evidenced by our ever-advancing technology, cultural innovations, and adaptability to different environments."[21]

They are blatantly stating that humans are apes!

This sort of compromise has permeated the Church and Christian institutions, resulting in generations doubting and eventually not believing the Scriptures to be the infallible Word of God. As doubt in God's Word is created, this puts many on that slippery slide of unbelief.

Over the years, I've been asked many times why the majority of academics have a man's-word-first approach when it comes to origins. I have come to the conclusion that the issues have to do with academic respectability, academic pride, and peer pressure. For instance, to be published in the mainline theological and scientific journals, academics who believe in six literal days of creation and a young earth would in most cases be rejected for publication and certainly be scoffed at and mocked.

The fear of the LORD is the beginning of wisdom, and the knowledge of the Holy One is insight (Proverbs 9:10).

The fear of the LORD is the beginning of knowledge; fools despise wisdom and instruction (Proverbs 1:7).

We should always have a Bible, God's Word, approach first!

FEBRUARY 10

Genesis 1:27

What Is Abortion?

Is abortion really murder?

So the Supreme Court in the USA had to grapple over whether a drug used to kill (murder) children should be allowed to continue to be made available to murder children. They ruled that people should have access to this drug, thereby condoning the murder of children. I would claim they are condoning child sacrifice.

Well, for those who reject God and believe man is just an animal having evolved by chance, random processes, then who decides what's right or wrong anyway? Morality would be subjective. So why would the deliberate killing of another human being be wrong? How would murder be defined? Would it just be like the termination of the life of an animal? One of the things you will find is that secular evolutionists are always inconsistent when it comes to discussing morality, as they will (inconsistently) insist on some absolutes but be totally subjective in other areas. That's because when one builds their worldview on man's word, all is subjective.

For the Christian, how should we deal with the abortion issue? Well, to deal with any issue, we need to build our thinking on the Bible, beginning with Genesis 1–11. So let's do that.

1. God created humans in His image. *So God created man in his own image, in the image of God he created him; male and female he created them* (Genesis 1:27).

2. No animal was made in God's image. *And God said, "Let the earth bring forth living creatures according to their kinds—livestock and creeping things and beasts of the earth according to their kinds." And it was so* (Genesis 1:24).

3. Therefore, we need to conclude that humans are not just animals. Even though we have a body like a mammal's body, humans are made in the image of God. No animal was created that way. Remember, God's Son stepped into human history to be the God-man to die for the human family. Animals don't have salvation, only humans do. Humans are special, and God places a value upon them that animals do not have.

4. In sexual reproduction, DNA comes from the male and female to produce a fertilized egg. A fertilized egg has all the information to build a human being, and the combination of information is unique, being different from any other human being on earth or whoever has existed. A unique combination of information exists, and as that cell builds the person's body, no new information is ever added. This means a human being made in the image of God exists right from fertilization, so abortion at any stage is murder.

5. God's Word makes it clear that while a human body is developing in a mother's womb, it is a real person, a human being made in the image of God at every stage: *For you formed my inward parts; you knitted me together in my mother's womb. I praise you, for I am fearfully and wonderfully made* (Psalm 139:13–14); *Your eyes saw my unformed substance* (Psalm 139:16).

6. A fertilized egg is not part of a woman's body. In fact, the woman's body looks on the fertilized egg as foreign tissue to reject. Just like a human body looks on a kidney transplant as foreign tissue to reject (which is why the person will need anti-rejection drugs), God built an anti-rejection mechanism into

THEOLOGY

FEBRUARY 10

the uterus for the fertilized egg. Also, note that if the fertilized egg has XY as the pair of sex chromosomes, then this is a male. The Y chromosome is not part of the woman's body, so this is a reminder that a male-fertilized egg can't be part of a woman's body. When people claim a fertilized egg or any stage of human development is part of the woman's body, this is nonsense.

7. When people yell, "My body, my rights," then this is a false statement about a fertilized egg or any stage during the development of a child in a mother's womb.
8. When people call abortion "health care," they are hiding the fact that it's not health care for the child developing in a mother's womb, it is death for them.

So, what is abortion?

Abortion is the deliberate killing of a human being made in the image of God — right from fertilization. Abortion is murder. *You shall not murder* (Exodus 20:13). Abortion is, in reality, child sacrifice to the god of self. Abortion is no different than the Israelites sacrificing their children to pagan gods.

They sacrificed their sons and their daughters to the demons; they poured out innocent blood, the blood of their sons and daughters (Psalm 106:37–38).

[T]he LORD hates ... hands that shed innocent blood (Proverbs 6:16–17).

Many look back on cultures that sacrificed children to their pagan gods and are appalled at what happened. Yet our culture in the USA has sacrificed 60 million plus children by abortion since 1973 and millions more through abortion drugs. The number of abortions worldwide in our modern era is estimated at around 60 million per year. Do the math! It's a holocaust of astronomic proportions.

Now we also need to point out that God is a God of love, mercy, grace, and forgiveness.

If we confess our sins, he is faithful and just to forgive us our sins and to cleanse us from all unrighteousness (1 John 1:9).

[A]s far as the east is from the west, so far does he remove our transgressions from us (Psalm 103:12).

For I will be merciful toward their iniquities, and I will remember their sins no more (Hebrews 8:12).

So, why do men and women (including so many politicians) get so emotional about protecting what they call "abortion rights" (which should be called "murder of children rights")? It's because they don't want to be accountable to God. They don't want to obey God's rules in regard to sex. They want to do what they want to get rid of the consequences by murdering human beings in the womb. They are shaking their fist at God. They are being their own gods and want to decide "truth" for themselves and insist they own their bodies.

God owns us: *The earth is the LORD's and the fullness thereof, the world and those who dwell therein* (Psalm 24:1).

Those demanding abortion remind me of those spoken of in 1 Timothy 4:2, *[T]hrough the insincerity of liars whose consciences are seared.*

Yes, they have seared consciences.

> **Remember that in all of this, if people truly repent of sin (such as the sin of abortion), God will forgive their sin.**

FEBRUARY 11
John 10:9

How Do We Deal with Pride Month as Christians?

The secular world has designated June as the so-called "pride month." What does it really mean to celebrate "pride"?

From a truly biblical perspective, it is sadly a celebration of sin. Now, of course, because I stated that this is a celebration of sin, I will be called unloving and be accused of hate speech. Even a number of Christians, Christian leaders, churches, and Christian institutions celebrate "pride month." They say they are showing love and celebrating diversity. But is it unloving to call "pride month" a celebration of sin?

When the first man, Adam, disobeyed God, this brought sin into the world. How did God respond? God judged man's rebellion against a holy God by judging man's sin with death.

Therefore, just as sin came into the world through one man, and death through sin, and so death spread to all men because all sinned (Romans 5:12).

Man would now die a spiritual death, being separated from God, breaking the perfect relationship that existed before sin. Man would also die physically.

By the sweat of your face you shall eat bread, till you return to the ground, for out of it you were taken; for you are dust, and to dust you shall return (Genesis 3:19).

Our bodies die, but the real us, our souls, would live on, eternally separated from God.

However, in judgment, God provided salvation. He promised a Savior (Genesis 3:15) who would provide a way for man to come back to that relationship with God and spend eternity with Him.

For God so loved the world, that he gave his only Son, that whoever believes in him should not perish but have eternal life (John 3:16).

At the time of Noah, the wickedness of man was so great that God judged that wickedness with a global Flood.

The LORD saw that the wickedness of man was great in the earth, and that every intention of the thoughts of his heart was only evil continually. And the LORD regretted that he had made man on the earth, and it grieved him to his heart. So the LORD said, "I will blot out man whom I have created from the face of the land, man and animals and creeping things and birds of the heavens, for I am sorry that I have made them" (Genesis 6:5–7).

And the waters prevailed so mightily on the earth that all the high mountains under the whole heaven were covered. The waters prevailed above the mountains, covering them fifteen cubits deep (Genesis 7:19–20).

But in judgment, God also provided a way of salvation for those who would receive it. He told Noah to build an Ark for the saving of his family and the land-animal kinds. He instructed Noah to put one door in the Ark. Only those who went through that door into the Ark were saved. The Ark and the one door are a picture of salvation in Jesus Christ. As our promised Savior said:

I am the door. If anyone enters by me, he will be saved and will go in and out and find pasture (John 10:9).

The point is, God doesn't ignore sin/wickedness. He is a holy God. He judges sin, but He is also a God of love in providing salvation. He is a merciful God.

THEOLOGY
FEBRUARY 11

When the Israelites conquered Jericho, God provided salvation for Rahab, as she obviously put her faith in the true God. She's in the lineage leading to Jesus and in the Hebrews 11 chapter as an example of great faith.

Now God is our Creator, and therefore, He owns us. He has a right to set the rules and determine what is right and wrong. He created marriage as one man and one woman. He makes it clear that sex outside of marriage is sin. He also makes it clear that men lusting after men and women lusting after women is sin:

Now the works of the flesh are evident: sexual immorality, impurity, sensuality, idolatry, sorcery, enmity, strife, jealousy, fits of anger, rivalries, dissensions, divisions, envy, drunkenness, orgies, and things like these. I warn you, as I warned you before, that those who do such things will not inherit the kingdom of God (Galatians 5:19–21).

For this reason God gave them up to dishonorable passions. For their women exchanged natural relations for those that are contrary to nature; and the men likewise gave up natural relations with women and were consumed with passion for one another, men committing shameless acts with men and receiving in themselves the due penalty for their error (Romans 1:26–27).

The loving, merciful way to deal with "pride month" as a Christian is to warn people about sin — the need for repentance — and provide them with the wonderful message of a merciful God who does judge wickedness but provides salvation for those who will receive it. And for those who do trust Christ, He promises to provide a way to overcome temptation.

For God did not send his Son into the world to condemn the world, but in order that the world might be saved through him. Whoever believes in him is not condemned, but whoever does not believe is condemned already, because he has not believed in the name of the only Son of God. And this is the judgment: the light has come into the world, and people loved the darkness rather than the light because their works were evil. For everyone who does wicked things hates the light and does not come to the light, lest his works should be exposed. But whoever does what is true comes to the light, so that it may be clearly seen that his works have been carried out in God (John 3:17–21).

Whoever believes in the Son has eternal life; whoever does not obey the Son shall not see life, but the wrath of God remains on him (John 3:36).

[B]ecause, if you confess with your mouth that Jesus is Lord and believe in your heart that God raised him from the dead, you will be saved (Romans 10:9).

No temptation has overtaken you that is not common to man. God is faithful, and he will not let you be tempted beyond your ability, but with the temptation he will also provide the way of escape, that you may be able to endure it (1 Corinthians 10:13).

Now, none of this is hate. It is love. It is mercy. Christians can't celebrate sin, but celebrate those who repent of sin and trust Christ for salvation. And celebrate those who overcome temptation to sin through trust in Christ and the work of the Holy Spirit in their hearts.

> **It is unloving not to warn people about their sin and to teach them about God's love, mercy, forgiveness, and provision of salvation in Christ.**

FEBRUARY 12
Romans 8:18

God Is Not Mocked

Since the horrific shootings at a Christian school in Nashville and the resulting murder of children and adults, we've seen a number of extremely concerning headlines, such as "Trans Activists Are Calling for More Blood After the Nashville Shooting." Another stated, "Nashville Congressman Responds to Radical Trans Group Turning Shooter into 'Martyr' Is Beyond Disturbing."

There was a graphic posted that no one seems to know for sure if it's an April Fool's Day prank or real that advertised, "Trans Day of Vengeance."

Secular media outlets came across as having sympathy for the shooter because she said she was trans, and little or no sympathy was given to the victims and their families.

The media was also reported for mocking prayer in this headline: "Media Mockery of Prayer 'Subtle Smears' Against Christianity Coverage of Nashville Massacre." No doubt they did this because they know Christians, based on God's clear Word, teach there are only two genders of humans: male and female. To claim one can change their gender is a perversion of God's created order.

And, of course, many claimed guns were the problem instead of looking at the fact that it was a person using the gun that carried out this tragic crime. (I'm not getting into the gun debate but just making an important point.)

When the media mocks prayer, mocking Christianity, they are actually mocking God. Of course, they don't believe in God but seem to spend a lot of time mocking someone they don't believe in. They make moral judgments about issues but, in reality, have no basis to make moral judgments. Without the basis in an absolute authority, they have no basis to determine right or wrong or good or bad. As Jesus taught, *And Jesus said to him, "Why do you call me good? No one is good except God alone"* (Luke 18:19).

These mocking, anti-Christian people are so hypocritical. They gleefully condone the brutal killing of children every day in their mother's wombs. They wouldn't speak against the instruments (as they do guns) used by abortion doctors, as they demand child sacrifice to the god of self. Yes, they believe they are their own god and can do whatever they determine. In doing so, they are totally intolerant of Christians who trust the true God and obey His Word. After all, the God of the Bible is our Creator, and therefore, He owns us and has total right to tell us what is right and wrong.

These mocking people ignore the fact that they, and everyone else, are under the death penalty for our sin. Such mockers are trying to blame others, particularly Christians, for the reason this woman killed children and adults. They refuse to acknowledge that humans are sinners and are under the condemnation of death. In fact, none of us deserves life.

But God loves us so much, as undeserving as we are, that He provided a way of salvation for us. He stepped into history in the person of His Son to be the God-man, 100% God and 100% man, a sinless man, who suffered death on the Cross to pay the penalty for our sin. He rose from the dead, conquering death, conquering the devil, and offers a free gift of salvation to all who believe.

THEOLOGY   FEBRUARY 12

[B]ecause, if you confess with your mouth that Jesus is Lord and believe in your heart that God raised him from the dead, you will be saved (Romans 10:9).

Death is horrible. The Bible describes it as an "enemy." I can't imagine the grief those Christian parents are suffering. One day, death will be thrown in the lake of fire and be no more (Revelation 21:4), though for now, we grieve at death.

He will wipe away every tear from their eyes, and death shall be no more, neither shall there be mourning, nor crying, nor pain anymore, for the former things have passed away (Revelation 21:4).

For Christians, as hard as it is dealing with this world of death and suffering, we also understand what God tells us in Romans 8:18: "For I consider that the sufferings of this present time are not worth comparing with the glory that is to be revealed to us."

FEBRUARY 13
Romans 10:17

How Do You Argue Christianity with Someone Who Doesn't Believe the Bible?

Should you ever give up the Bible when speaking to people who don't believe the Bible?

My short answer is, "Absolutely not." Those who tell you to do this are simply wrong.

Before I answer this in detail to explain my position, let's ponder these verses of Scripture:

So faith comes from hearing, and hearing through the word of Christ (Romans 10:17).

For the word of God is living and active, sharper than any two-edged sword, piercing to the division of soul and of spirit, of joints and of marrow, and discerning the thoughts and intentions of the heart (Hebrews 4:12).

[S]o shall my word be that goes out from my mouth; it shall not return to me empty, but it shall accomplish that which I purpose, and shall succeed in the thing for which I sent it (Isaiah 55:11).

One of the questions I've been asked the most over the years is, "How do you argue Christianity with someone who doesn't believe the Bible? What are the best arguments to use when not using the Bible?"

I've also heard of Christian leaders who have said that one can't use the Bible when arguing with someone who doesn't believe the Bible.

Let me share why I believe if you give up the Bible when arguing with someone who doesn't believe the Bible, you have lost the argument before you even start the discussion.

Everyone has a worldview, a way of thinking. Our worldview is built upon the presuppositions we have. Ultimately, there are only two foundations for those presuppositions: God's Word or man's word. The battle beginning in Genesis 3 (the temptation and the Fall) began a battle between God's Word and man's word that's been raging for 6,000 years.

Our worldview is built upon the foundation we have. Those who build their thinking on God's Word beginning in Genesis build a Christian worldview on this foundation. This worldview determines not only how one views the earth, fossils, etc., but also determines one's morality. Thus, those with a Christian worldview believe marriage is one man and one woman, abortion is murder, and there are only two genders of humans — male and female — and so on. All biblical doctrine comes from this foundation.

Those who build their thinking on man's word believe everything is a result of natural processes and thus have a secular worldview. They then believe marriage is whatever you want it to be, abortion is health care, and gender is whatever you make it to be.

Now when those who build their thinking on God's Word are in conflict with those who build their thinking on man's word, there is a clash of worldviews because they each have a different foundation.

Now if these two are arguing concerning their worldviews, the real argument is actually at the level of man's word versus God's Word. So when someone who has the foundation of man's word says the Christian has to give up their foundation — God's Word — if they are to discuss the issues, then they retain their foundation, but the Christian does not then have the foundation for their worldview. So the Christian has already lost.

APOLOGETICS — FEBRUARY 13

When someone says they don't believe God's Word, instead of giving up God's Word, the Christian needs to challenge that person as to why they don't believe God's Word, how they determine truth, and give them answers to their arguments against God's Word. Using various questions, the Christian needs to get the argument down to the foundational level, as that's where the real argument is really at. If someone doesn't change their foundation (man's word) to God's Word, then they aren't going to agree at the worldview level.

Christians should never give up God's Word but explain that this is their foundation and challenge non-Christians that they have the wrong foundation. Christians should be using apologetics as a part of this discussion to show they can defend the truth of God's Word. As they do this, they should be pointing the non-Christian to God's Word and the truth of the gospel, understanding that it's only God's Word that saves! Also, Christians need to explain that the worldview they have comes from this foundation. Christians need to point out that the non-Christian has a wrong foundation.

Now one of the problems is that many people think that evidence alone can convince people about the God who created all things and is our Savior. And certainly, one can use observational science to show that evidence confirms God's Word. But it's only God's Word that saves people. We have to understand that non-Christians are, in essence, walking dead people:

And you were dead in the trespasses and sins (Ephesians 2:1).

Dead people cannot save themselves. *Faith comes from hearing, and hearing through the word of Christ* (Romans 10:17). We need to point people to the Word of the One who is the Resurrection and the life.

Non-Christians never give up their foundation of man's word when they are arguing against Christians, but Christians think they need to give up God's Word to successfully witness to them. This is just wrong. The trouble is that most Christian leaders have not taught people how to argue correctly. We need to learn to argue foundationally.

Do your best to present yourself to God as one approved, a worker who has no need to be ashamed, rightly handling the word of truth (2 Timothy 2:15).

The real argument comes down to this about God's Word: "Is this foundation the correct one?" – which it is.

FEBRUARY 14
Jeremiah 17:9

Man Is Not Neutral, and Man Is Not Inherently Good!

Should we totally accept the word of secular scientists? Do we really need law enforcement? Can we totally trust everything that Christian academics believe? Would people abuse drugs if they were allowed to be freely used? We have a problem that is having dire consequences in our culture. Man is not neutral, and man is not inherently good!

There seems to be this philosophy that to reduce criminal activity, all one needs to do is give people a great environment, freedom to do what they want, and use counseling. But there's a massive problem. This is how Jeremiah states the problem: *The heart is deceitful above all things, and desperately sick* [wicked]; *who can understand it?* (Jeremiah 17:9).

Jesus tells us, *For from within, out of the heart of man, come evil thoughts, sexual immorality, theft, murder, adultery, coveting, wickedness, deceit, sensuality, envy, slander, pride, foolishness. All these evil things come from within, and they defile a person* (Mark 7:21–23).

The Apostle Paul wrote, *[F]or all have sinned and fall short of the glory of God* (Romans 3:23).

The point is that Christians should understand that man's heart is not neutral. We are biased against God. In fact, because we sinned in Adam, our sin nature is really summed up by Genesis 3:1 (*"Did God actually say …?"*) and Genesis 3:5 (*"you will be like God"*). Thus, our nature is we don't want to obey God; we want to be our own god and be a law unto ourselves.

Man is not inherently good. Our nature is that we are in rebellion against all that is good. We inherently don't want the truth. Judges 21:25 describes what happens when there is no authority over people, and they look to themselves to decide truth: *In those days there was no king in Israel. Everyone did what was right in his own eyes.*

When people reject the absolute authority of God's Word and let their sin nature master them, they do what is right in their own eyes. Thus, morality is subjective.

Now originally, there was no need for civil government, as man was perfect. He was to delight in obeying his Creator. However, sin changed all that. After the Flood, God institutes civil government. He did this when he introduced capital punishment for murder: *And for your lifeblood I will require a reckoning: from every beast I will require it and from man. From his fellow man I will require a reckoning for the life of man* (Genesis 9:5). The first purpose of this civil government is the protection of human life. Remember, man is made in the image of God (Genesis 1:27).

So, a purpose of government is to maintain law and order. But here are two problems:

1. If those in power think man is basically good, they will not make right decisions in maintaining law and order.
2. If those in power do not understand the wickedness of man or their own wickedness, then their rule will be detrimental for people: *When the righteous increase, the people rejoice, but when the wicked rule, the people groan* (Proverbs 29:2).

APOLOGETICS

Now, it is true that humans have a conscience: *They show that the work of the law is written on their hearts, while their conscience also bears witness, and their conflicting thoughts accuse or even excuse them* (Romans 2:15). But it is also true that people can have consciences that are seared (1 Timothy 4:2).

If the wicked rule and they don't accept that man is not basically good, then we will see people groan under such rule as wrong decisions are made about what should happen to maintain law and order.

Now as Christians, we should understand the sin nature of man, but because we are redeemed by the blood of the Lamb, we should continually look to God, His Word, and the work of the Holy Spirit in our lives to not let our sin nature master us daily. Nonetheless, because we are sinful, fallible humans, we struggle with our sin nature as Paul did:

For I do not do what I want, but I do the very thing I hate. Now if I do what I do not want, I agree with the law, that it is good. So now it is no longer I who do it, but sin that dwells within me. For I know that nothing good dwells in me, that is, in my flesh. For I have the desire to do what is right, but not the ability to carry it out. For I do not do the good I want, but the evil I do not want is what I keep on doing. Now if I do what I do not want, it is no longer I who do it, but sin that dwells within me (Romans 7:15–20).

I say all this to make another very important point. Just because a person is a Christian does not mean we can totally trust everything they believe. That's why we always need to be like the Bereans: *[T]hey received the word with all eagerness, examining the Scriptures daily to see if these things were so* (Acts 17:11).

I've often found that one of the main reasons Christian professors and leaders compromise God's Word in Genesis is that they have a basic trust in the words of secular scientists. I've had a number of PhD scientists and Christian leaders who claim that secular colleagues or secular scientists really are searching for truth and wouldn't lead people astray. But that is simply not true. They are not searching for ultimate truth because their heart is in rebellion against God. Because of this, they can be blinded to the truth and pass on wrong interpretations of evidence. And, sadly, because of academic peer pressure, academic pride, and sinful hearts, even Christians can be blinded to the truth.

So, what does this all mean? Well, the answer to the world's troubles is the truth of God's Word and the saving gospel. Until people trust God's Word and trust Christ for salvation and build their thinking on God's Word, the problems of the world can't be solved. That's why it is vital we stand on and proclaim the truth of God's Word and the gospel without compromise.

Also, for Christians, until they all understand that God's Word, not man's word, is the ultimate authority, and they judge what anyone says against God's Word, we will not stop the compromise that so permeates the Church and undermines the authority of God's Word.

Trust in the LORD with all your heart, and do not lean on your own understanding. In all your ways acknowledge him, and he will make straight your paths (Proverbs 3:5–6).

I have stored up your word in my heart, that I might not sin against you (Psalm 119:11).

> **Once again, we understand the battle in this world is one over authority: Is God or man the ultimate authority?**

FEBRUARY 15
Matthew 7:24-27

Raising Up Generations with the Foundation of God's Word

Should church leaders who compromise Genesis be surprised if the younger generation of church attendees decide to reinterpret marriage and/or gender to mean whatever they want it to mean?

I would say no, they shouldn't be surprised if that happened because compromising Genesis with evolution/millions of years opens the door for marriage and gender to be reinterpreted. How could that be so?

Genesis 1–11 is the foundation of all doctrine — in fact, the foundation for everything.

Genesis 1–11 is the foundation for gender and marriage.

Genesis 1:27 records a summary of God making the first two people:

So God created man in his own image, in the image of God he created him; male and female he created them.

It's clear, God created only two genders of humans: male and female.

In Genesis 2, we are given the details of how God made the first male and female humans. After God made man from dust, and the first woman from his side, we read:

Therefore a man shall leave his father and his mother and hold fast to his wife, and they shall become one flesh (Genesis 2:24).

One man and one woman — a male and a female. This is the origin of marriage.

Jesus reiterated this in Matthew 19 and Mark 10 when he was asked about marriage:

"But from the beginning of creation, 'God made them male and female.' 'Therefore a man shall leave his father and mother and hold fast to his wife, and the two shall become one flesh.' So they are no longer two but one flesh. What therefore God has joined together, let not man separate" (Mark 10:6–9).

Now when Christians compromise God's Word in Genesis by taking man's ideas of evolutionary biology and geology (millions of years) and use that to reinterpret the creation account, they are unlocking a door — a door to undermine the authority of Scripture and reinterpret its clear meaning.

Now this is a major reason why we boldly challenge those Christians/Christian leaders who add millions of years to the Bible. What they are doing is taking man's belief about the past and using that to reinterpret the clear words in Genesis, such as reinterpreting the days of creation, reinterpreting the account of man made directly from dust and woman from his side, reinterpreting the Flood, etc.

Now, contemplate this carefully. Those Christians who believe in millions of years and other evolutionary ideas didn't get those ideas from reading Scripture. They didn't get those ideas from Genesis. They obtained those ideas outside of Scripture from fallible humans and then have taken those ideas to Scripture to force them upon the words of Scripture.

Many pastors have endorsed their young people going to public school, endorsing what these young people were taught at school about evolution and millions of years. So how do such people reconcile what is being taught at school about origins with the Scriptures? Well, sadly, these compromising church leaders tell the

APOLOGETICS

young people that Genesis is not meant to be literal history, or it's allegory, and what man calls "science" (evolutionary beliefs) can be used to reinterpret and give different meaning to the words in Genesis.

The point is that these young people are being taught that one can take what the world is teaching and use this to reinterpret and thus determine the meaning of Scripture. This is the dangerous door these leaders have unlocked that puts man's word in authority over God's Word, thus undermining the authority of Scripture.

Over time as the culture changes and emphatically now pushes the LGBTQ worldview along with gender identity and so on, many of these young people don't see any problem with taking man's views of gender and marriage, etc., and reinterpreting God's Word in Genesis in regard to these subjects. After all, if the Christian leader they respect said to reinterpret Genesis based on man's evolutionary ideas, why not reinterpret Genesis based on man's ideas about "marriage"?

Thus, two in marriage can be reinterpreted to mean two men or two women. Male and female genders can be reinterpreted to mean that one can define gender in various ways and change one's gender if one wishes.

I submit that when one considers the generational loss from the Church and how secularized the younger generations have become that a large part of the blame lies with the compromising Church that did not teach generations to stand boldly on the absolute authority of the Word of God and not to compromise God's Word with man's word.

And because those who have attended public school have been indoctrinated with the foundation of man's word for their worldview, they are easy prey for the world to capture their hearts and minds. The Christian worldview can't stand on the wrong foundation of man's word, but the secular worldview is a logical outworking of that foundation. We must build on God's Word, the strong foundation, for the house built on the sand of man's word collapses:

"Everyone then who hears these words of mine and does them will be like a wise man who built his house on the rock. And the rain fell, and the floods came, and the winds blew and beat on that house, but it did not fall, because it had been founded on the rock. And everyone who hears these words of mine and does not do them will be like a foolish man who built his house on the sand. And the rain fell, and the floods came, and the winds blew and beat against that house, and it fell, and great was the fall of it" (Matthew 7:24–27).

We need to be raising up generations with the foundation of God's Word, building our house on the rock.

FEBRUARY 16

Job 38:2

Should Christians Have an Answer for Everything?

A number of times over the years when being interviewed on radio or TV, I've been asked a question like this: "What is an example of a question you've been asked that you can't answer?" Another similar sort of question is, "What is one of the most difficult questions you've been asked that you can't really answer?"

Well, let's consider this: Should Christians have an answer for everything?

My answer to that question might surprise you because it is both yes and no. Yes, we should be able to give some sort of answer to every question, even if it's "I don't know." But actually, if we have a biblical worldview, we should be able to give answers to questions asked even if we can't give an answer. OK, so what on earth do I mean by that?

I remember taking a call on a radio talk show when the caller said that if snakes were created by an intelligent designer, then why do they have particular bones that don't have a function? Now, at the time, I had no idea what the person was referring to, as I had never studied snakes. So, in one sense, I had no idea of the specific answer to that question. However, because I build my thinking on God's Word and have a biblical worldview, I considered the question by applying my biblical glasses. A key is understanding that God is infinite in knowledge and wisdom, and man is finite. Man doesn't know everything. There are always things we don't know.

I said something like this: "Just because someone claims such bones don't have a function doesn't mean they don't have a function; it just means you don't know what the function is. We don't know everything there is to know about everything. The information we have is finite. There could be some more information that comes along in the future that shows it has a function we hadn't thought of. So don't use an argument around a lack of information to claim creation can't be true."

Remember what God said to Job, *"Who is this that darkens counsel by words without knowledge?"* (Job 38:2).

God asked Job many questions to show he didn't know everything and, in fact, knew nothing compared to what God knows:

"Where is the way to the dwelling of light, and where is the place of darkness, that you may take it to its territory and that you may discern the paths to its home? You know, for you were born then, and the number of your days is great!" (Job 38:19–21).

"Can you bind the chains of the Pleiades or loose the cords of Orion? Can you lead forth the Mazzaroth in their season, or can you guide the Bear with its children? Do you know the ordinances of the heavens? Can you establish their rule on the earth?" (Job 38:31–33).

When I was a student at university, I remember one of my professors giving us a list of what were called vestigial organs. These were organs in the human body that supposedly didn't have any function. One of those organs was the appendix. Vestigial organs were considered to be evolutionary leftover, functionless organs or structures.

APOLOGETICS

However, from a biblical worldview, understanding that God created everything, then I would assume such organs or structures either had a function that was unknown or had an important function for some stage of life that is not needed now, or it has degenerated because of the effects of sin in a fallen world and thus lost its created function. We have now found that the appendix has very important immunological functions before and after birth. It's not an evolutionary leftover. God designed it for important purposes.

When asked what was one of the most difficult questions I've been asked, I would often say it was the question about how light could travel from stars millions of light years away and yet the universe be only thousands of years old. Without getting into various ideas and models creationists have proposed concerning this matter, I like to answer from a big-picture perspective through my biblical worldview glasses.

I would ask the person posing this question, "Do we know everything about light? Do we know everything about space and how light travels through it? Is it possible there are things about light and space we just don't know and so it warps our understanding? Do we know the processes God used to create light and how it would be seen on earth from stars on the fourth day of creation? Because God finished His word of creation and is not currently using those processes, how does that affect our understanding of things in regard to this question?" And that's besides the fact that when skeptics ask this question, they don't realize that those who believe in the big bang billions of years ago, based on the same assumptions about light, only get light halfway across the universe. The point is that no one has definitive answers because we are dealing with so many unknowns. In other words, even when we don't know the specific answer, when we think the right way from the right foundation of God's Word, we can always give a big-picture answer admitting we can't give a detailed specific answer.

This really hit me when I read Job 38 through 41. I encourage you to read these chapters a number of times. This really reinforces the fact that we are so finite and know nothing compared to God. Think about God being infinite in wisdom and knowledge. Sadly, many church leaders/academics think they know more than God, as they reinterpret Genesis to fit with man's fallible evolution/millions of years ideas.

As my father taught me so well:

Just because something man states seems like what the Bible states can't be true doesn't mean Christians should reinterpret God's Word. First, you go to God's Word and read what it states in context, according to the rules of language (e.g., Hebrew or Greek, etc.). If you are sure that what it states is clear, and there is still conflict with what man is proposing, then we question man's word, not God's Word. If we don't have answers, we need to wait for those answers. More information may come along to show why what man said is wrong. And even if we don't get that information, we don't question God's Word when we are sure we are taking it as God intended.

Every word of God proves true; he is a shield to those who take refuge in him (Proverbs 30:5).

> **No matter how much we know, there is infinitely more to know, which is why it is so arrogant of fallible man to question God's Word and think we know better than God.**

FEBRUARY 17
Acts 1:9–11

Scoffers and the Last Days

Yes, we are in the last days. But how "last" are we? We don't know. We just know every day is more last than the day before. We've been in the last days for nearly 2,000 years, ever since the life and earthly ministry of Jesus as the God-man. When Jesus' earthly ministry was completed, we read:

And when he had said these things, as they were looking on, he was lifted up, and a cloud took him out of their sight. And while they were gazing into heaven as he went, behold, two men stood by them in white robes, and said, "Men of Galilee, why do you stand looking into heaven? This Jesus, who was taken up from you into heaven, will come in the same way as you saw him go into heaven" (Acts 1:9–11).

Jesus left earth for heaven and said He would return. We've been waiting for that return for about 2,000 years.

In 2 Peter 3, we read about scoffers in the last days who scoff at the idea that Jesus will return, as they say, *For ever since the fathers fell asleep, all things are continuing as they were from the beginning of creation* (2 Peter 3:4). They claim things have just gone on and on, so Jesus can't be returning, as it's been such a long time. But we're told in 2 Peter 3:8 that to God, a day is like a thousand years and a thousand years like a day. God is outside of time, and 2,000 years is not a long time for God, as He is not bound by time. And we're given the reason why Jesus is patient and has not returned:

The Lord is not slow to fulfill his promise as some count slowness, but is patient toward you, not wishing that any should perish, but that all should reach repentance (2 Peter 3:9).

Now consider what is told to us about these scoffers in the last days. They will reject creation:

For they deliberately overlook this fact, that the heavens existed long ago, and the earth was formed out of water and through water by the word of God (2 Peter 3:5).

They not only reject that God created the earth but that the earth was created covered with water, as it states in Genesis 1.

Then they will reject the Flood of Noah's day:

[A]nd that by means of these the world that then existed was deluged with water and perished (2 Peter 3:6).

And they will reject the coming judgment by fire:

But the day of the Lord will come like a thief, and then the heavens will pass away with a roar, and the heavenly bodies will be burned up and dissolved, and the earth and the works that are done on it will be exposed (2 Peter 3:10).

Let's apply this to the scoffers today:

They believe things on this earth have gone on for millions and millions of years.

They believe life and the universe evolved over millions of years by chance random processes.

They reject that God created the earth and believe it came about by a supposed big bang.

They reject that the earth was covered by water and claim it was a hot molten blob to start with.

THEOLOGY — FEBRUARY 17

They reject the global Flood of Noah's day.

They reject that Jesus is going to come back and judge this earth with fire.

So, scoffers down through the ages, just as scoffers in our day, reject God's Word! And why do they reject God's Word? Because they don't want to be accountable to God. If God created them (and He did), then God owns them and God has a right to set the rules and determine what's right and wrong. Then marriage is one man and one woman, there are only two genders of humans — male and female — the rightful place for sex is within marriage only, abortion is murdering a human being, and so on, as God's Word instructs clearly.

God's Word tells us that man is a sinner, and his sin nature is that he would rather believe man's word (e.g., millions of years of evolution) than God's Word in Genesis about creation, the Fall, and the Flood.

God's Word here in 2 Peter 3:5 tells us these scoffers will "deliberately overlook" the truth of creation, the Flood, and the coming judgment by fire. Some translations state they are "willingly ignorant."

These scoffers will reject the obvious evidence for creation and the Flood, which is exactly what we see happening today. It's so obvious that life had to be created when one looks at DNA, the most complex information and language system in the universe that could never happen by chance. It's so obvious there was a global Flood, as we find billions of dead things (fossils) buried in the rock layers laid down by water all over the earth.

Don't be led astray by scoffers, but simply believe God's Word.

FEBRUARY 18

Ephesians 2:8-10

How Should Christians Respond to Reparations?

There's a lot of talk about reparations in the media lately. How should Christians respond to this? Is it more important to talk about spiritual reparations?

In recent days, we have seen a lot of discussion in the media about sins of the past and the supposed need to pay reparations to modern-day people because of injustices committed by some members of past generations. How should we respond?

History is extremely complicated. There is much that we don't know, and it's always easy to look back and say they shouldn't have done this or that. When discussing the history of humanity, we will never be able to even begin to deal with issues of the past unless we have the correct history.

In reality, the only way to begin to deal with such complex issues regarding humanity requires us to know the detailed true history of humans. And there's only one infallible history book that we can turn to — God's infallible Word. Until people believe in the true history of the one human race as outlined in the Bible beginning in Genesis and build their worldview on the gospel, people will never be able to deal with issues of racism, prejudice, injustices, and reparations. Until we understand the sin nature of man and how that impacts how people see their fellow man, we just will not have the right starting point to deal with such issues.

Now that doesn't mean that governments shouldn't change some things to help people and stop prejudice. But without the foundation of God's Word, who determines what is right or wrong? And if you think about it, the reason there have been injustices over the years is that people did not obey God's Word but allowed their depraved (fallen) natures to determine how they acted. Again, unless people believe the true history of the human race and our sin problem from the Bible and build their worldview on this foundation, we will never be able to deal with these issues.

Before we consider how to deal with reparations in our culture, we must understand the spiritual reparations that we all owe but could never repay. Surely, the greatest injustice of all was when we, in Adam, committed high treason against the God of creation by disobeying His direct command (Genesis 3:6; Romans 5:12). Can sinful man pay "reparations" to God for his sin of rebellion? God's Word is very clear:

For by grace you have been saved through faith. And this is not your own doing; it is the gift of God, not a result of works, so that no one may boast. For we are his workmanship, created in Christ Jesus for good works, which God prepared beforehand, that we should walk in them (Ephesians 2:8–10).

Fallible, sinful humans can't pay "reparations" to God for our sin. But God paid those reparations for us. Salvation is a gift for those who receive it. Praise God for what He did for us. On the Cross, Jesus paid all those "reparations" we owe!

God shows his love for us in that while we were still sinners, Christ died for us (Romans 5:8).

APOLOGETICS — FEBRUARY 18

Understanding our sin problem and what God has done for us as Christians should totally transform the way we look at others who have wronged us:

[God] *saved us and called us to a holy calling, not because of our works but because of his own purpose and grace, which he gave us in Christ Jesus before the ages began* (2 Timothy 1:9).

After we understand that the answer to spiritual reparations is to receive God's free gift of salvation, we can build a worldview about the topic of reparations in our culture.

Jesus instructed His disciples how to treat people when they wrong us and are considered enemies.

I say to you, Love your enemies and pray for those who persecute you (Matthew 5:44).

You shall love the Lord your God with all your heart and with all your soul and with all your strength and with all your mind, and your neighbor as yourself (Luke 10:27).

Jesus taught us how to pray when dealing with those who mistreat us:

[F]orgive us our debts, as we also have forgiven our debtors (Matthew 6:12).

Now that is a hard one at times. We ask God to forgive our sins, as we have forgiven others who sin against us! We need to forgive and not hold grudges — not hold past sins against people.

We can also apply specific passages to build our biblical worldview of reparations, such as Ezekiel 18, to help us understand that the children don't pay for the sins of their fathers. Everyone answers for their own sins.

The soul who sins shall die. The son shall not suffer for the iniquity of the father, nor the father suffer for the iniquity of the son. The righteousness of the righteous shall be upon himself, and the wickedness of the wicked shall be upon himself (Ezekiel 18:20).

What should our answer be to those claiming injustices and calling for reparations? The ultimate answer is the Cross. Until they understand that answer and receive God's free gift of salvation and build their worldview on what God teaches, they will never be able to ultimately deal with such issues.

We all need to be reminded that each of us has committed the greatest injustice of all because we sinned in Adam. That's why each one of us needs to make sure we have responded to and received God's free gift of salvation and know that we will spend eternity with our Creator. That's the most essential message of all time. We can't trust our feelings but must be obedient to the One who created us and saves us.

I write these things to you who believe in the name of the Son of God, that you may know that you have eternal life (1 John 5:13).

> **As Christians, we need to ensure we don't let our sin nature master us and that we continually look to God's Word to be conformed to what God through His Son would have us do.**

FEBRUARY 19

Luke 19:12-13

Redeeming the Time

In recent times, I've had a number of Christians tell me that they get so depressed looking at what is happening in the culture concerning the moral decline, decreasing church attendance, and the seemingly lessening impact of the Church. Some have said they just want Jesus to come back now. Others have said they feel so helpless. How should Christians respond when we see such overwhelming evil permeate the government and culture?

Consider a parable Jesus told: *"A nobleman went into a far country to receive for himself a kingdom and then return. Calling ten of his servants, he gave them ten minas, and said to them, 'Engage in business until I come'"* (Luke 19:12–13).

Jesus is the nobleman, and we are the servants. Jesus entrusted resources to the servants. He entrusts resources to us, whether they be material resources or gifts of teaching, preaching, music, or the numerous other gifts and talents He has bestowed on people. Jesus ascended to heaven after His death and Resurrection. We are being commanded to the business of the King until He returns. This means we need to use whatever gifts, talents, and other resources we have been entrusted with to do the best we can to proclaim the truth of God's Word and the saving gospel, no matter how bleak things look.

We are to redeem the time we have to carry out the Great Commission. That's why at Answers in Genesis and through the two attractions, the Ark Encounter and Creation Museum, we try to do all we can to reach as many as possible with the most important message in the universe — the saving gospel.

Like many of the Apostle Paul's letters, the book of Ephesians is divided into beliefs (chapters 1–3) and practice (chapters 4–6). One of the "practice" verses I remember my father using is Ephesians 5:16 (NKJV): *[R]edeeming the time, because the days are evil.*

My parents took this verse to heart and did their best to take whatever opportunity arose to proclaim God's Word and the saving gospel message. As a young boy, when we visited my grandparents' farmhouse in North Queensland, I remember my mother telling us how as a young teen, she would ride her bicycle to pick up two young girls who didn't have any other way of getting to Sunday school. She would ride five miles with these children on her bike to ensure they could be taught God's Word.

Just that story had a great impact on my life. My mother's example challenged me to do whatever I could to ensure people heard the gospel message. So that I could help our children and our children's children understand their heritage, I interviewed my mother on video when she was 87 years old. I specifically asked her about those two girls. She had met them again just a couple of years before my interview. One of them was really going on for the Lord, and the other said she was going to come back to the Lord. Those Sunday school lessons had a real impact on them.

Since my father was a teacher and transferred every three years as he was promoted, I watched my parents start Sunday schools in several different country areas and bring in evangelists so that families could hear the truth of the Bible and the salvation message. As I look back on this, I realize that my parents were doing what God, through Paul, instructs us to do in Ephesians 5:16. Look at the verse and the meanings of the three main

THEOLOGY   FEBRUARY 19

Greek words: *Redeem* has a meaning akin to buying someone out of slavery, just as Christ redeemed us out of slavery because of our sin. We need to buy up every opportunity to help people out of their bad situations.

The Greek word translated *time* isn't about hours, minutes, and seconds. It's not about wristwatches or other timepieces. It really means "opportunity."

The Greek word translated *evil* means "hurtful, evil in effect, calamitous, diseased, derelict and vicious." These same adjectives could be applied in our own culture when we look at the news headlines.

So, we are being told in this verse to make the best of every opportunity, to do what we can to see people taken out of their bad situations. They are on the road to eternal separation from God as a consequence of sin and the effects of the evil world we live in.

And that's my challenge to each of us. What are we doing in "redeeming the time"?

The church at Ephesus is mentioned specifically among the seven churches that received letters from the Lord Jesus Christ in Revelation (2:1–7). The Christians in this church were diligent to hold to the doctrines of the faith. But our Lord warned, *But I have this against you, that you have abandoned the love you had at first* (Revelation 2:4).

I believe this means they no longer had the zeal to reach the culture as they once had. In Ephesians 4–6, Paul had earlier told these Christians to apply their beliefs practically in three areas: in the local church (which Revelation 2 indicates they were still doing), in their homes (and I believe they were doing this also), and in the world (and this is where I believe they had lost their first love).

Paul set the example when he first visited Ephesus. He boldly preached against the idolatry of the day. According to Acts 19, many turned away from their idols when Paul unashamedly confronted the pagan religion of his day. But this caused an uproar. Paul was persecuted because of his boldness in doing whatever he could to "redeem the time" so people would leave their evil ways and receive Christ's free gift of salvation.

Perhaps the Ephesians were no longer being bold in confronting the idolatry in their culture as Paul did. I suggest this is why they "left their first love."

Yes, "the days are evil," and our time here on earth is short. But reaching others with the saving gospel while we are here has eternal importance.

The battle between God's Word and man's word (that battle between good and evil), which started in Genesis 3, hasn't changed. The gospel message hasn't changed. The Book of Ephesians is as much for individuals as it is for the whole Church today. We need to stand on God's Word and adhere to the doctrines God has revealed to us. And we need to apply God's Word daily in our homes, in our local churches, and in the world.

What are each of us doing to "redeem the time"? Are we using every opportunity that comes before us to affect hearts and minds for the Lord, prayerful that many will receive His free gift of salvation and live in heaven with their Creator and Savior forever?

Let's focus on doing the business of the King until He returns.

FEBRUARY 20

2 Corinthians 11:3

Parents, Be Warned!

God, through the Apostle Paul, has given us a very important warning in 2 Corinthians 11:3: *But I am afraid that as the serpent deceived Eve by his cunning, your thoughts will be led astray from a sincere and pure devotion to Christ.*

Let me paraphrase it for you. God is saying, "I want to warn you that the devil is going to use the same method on you (which means on your kids and grandkids, and on everyone) as he did on Eve, to get you to not believe the things of God."

All Christian parents should be saying, "God is warning me about the method the devil will use on us, so I need to understand that method and make sure I'm preparing my kids and grandkids so that method won't lead them astray. I need to diligently understand this warning and how to counteract it."

First, note that the Apostle Paul references an event with Eve and the devil. He is referencing Genesis 3:1–7. This is another example of a passage in the New Testament that references Genesis as literal history.

So, what was the method the devil used on Eve? *"Did God actually say …?"* (Genesis 3:1). It was an attack on the authority of the Word of God to get Adam and Eve to doubt God's Word so that doubt would lead to unbelief. Adam (and Eve) succumbed. And so, sin entered the world, and the judgment of death by a righteous, holy God because of sin.

Now this should be a warning to all of us that the method the devil will use on us and our children is to attack the Word of God, to cause doubt and resulting unbelief. I call this the Genesis 3 attack.

The Genesis 3 attack, though always the same attack on the Word of God, manifests in different ways in different eras. Down through the ages, Christians have had to deal with many different sorts of attacks on God's Word as they defended the Christian faith.

The question we need to ask is, "How does the Genesis 3 attack manifest itself in today's world?" Our current Genesis 3 attack began in the 1800s when atheists (and deists) who rejected God's Word and rejected the global Flood of Noah's day began popularizing the idea that the fossil record was laid down slowly over millions of years. Their worldview is one of naturalism — totally rejecting anything supernatural, thus totally rejecting God.

Sadly, many Christian leaders took the millions of years and added them into Scripture, resulting in different compromising positions, such as the gap theory, day-age theory, and so on. Putting man's beliefs based on naturalism into Scripture is placing man in authority over God's Word and undermines (creates doubt in) the authority of the Word.

Darwin used the supposed millions of years in geology to help popularize his biological and anthropological evolutionary ideas. Sadly, many Christians then added these to Genesis, creating more doubt as God's Word is undermined.

The supposed millions of years (age-of-earth issue) is the Genesis 3 attack of our day, and most of our Christian leaders (and many in the Church) and most Christian academics have succumbed to this. It's a

THEOLOGY — FEBRUARY 20

major reason so many in the younger generations have been led through doubt in God's Word at the beginning to full-blown unbelief in the Scriptures and the Christian faith.

That's a reason why Answers in Genesis has been providing so many answers to the skeptical questions of our day, many of which relate to whether or not one can trust the history revealed in the first 11 chapters of Genesis. The devil knows if he can get generations to doubt Genesis, it will lead to unbelief in God's Word. And sadly, so many of our Christian leaders have, in essence, and maybe unwittingly for some, helped the devil in creating this doubt as they compromised Genesis with man's religion of evolutionary naturalism and millions of years.

As I've said many times, those who believe in millions of years are then stating that death, diseases (like cancer, as seen in the fossil record), violence, and suffering were part of the process God used to create. Thus, God is responsible for all the horrible things in the world instead of understanding it's our sin that did that!

Remember, Genesis 1–11 is foundational to the rest of the Bible, to all doctrine, our Christian worldview, and, in fact, everything.

FEBRUARY 21

Genesis 8:4

Do We Really Need to Find Noah's Ark?

Over the years, I've had many Christians say that if we could only find Noah's Ark on the mountains of Ararat, this would convince the world that the Bible's account of Noah and the Ark was true. But would finding the Ark really convince people of the truth of this scriptural account? Would this cause people to immediately repent and turn to Christ?

An atheist once said to me, "I don't care if you find a big boat on the top of Mount Ararat and drag it down the main street of our city, I still won't believe in Noah's Ark."

According to the Bible, the Ark landed on *the mountains of Ararat* (Genesis 8:4), which encompass the ancient region of Urartu (translated *Ararat*). This area included mountain ranges in eastern Turkey and likely extended farther east into Armenia. The Bible does not say the Ark landed on *the* Mt. Ararat.

There is already overwhelming evidence confirming the Flood of Noah's day — the massive fossil record over the majority of the earth's surface. This record exhibits evidence of a watery catastrophe consistent with the global Flood account as recorded in Genesis 6–9. But despite all this overwhelming evidence, the majority of people, including most scientists, reject the global Flood of Noah's day as a real event in history. The evidence for the Flood is staring them in the face, but they still reject it.

Why does the majority reject this evidence? The simple answer is that it's a spiritual issue. Because of their sinful hearts, those who reject God's Word don't want to accept the account of the Flood. In 2 Peter 3, we read that in the last days, people will willingly reject the account of creation, the Flood, and the coming judgment by fire.

For they deliberately overlook this fact ... the earth was formed out of water and through water by the word of God, and ... the world that then existed was deluged with water and perished. But by the same word the heavens and earth that now exist are stored up for fire ... (2 Peter 3:5–7).

I've had atheists tell me that if we can show them evidence for the Flood and creation, they will believe. But no matter what evidence these people are shown, they reinterpret it within their evolutionary secular worldview because of their sinful hearts. One must interpret the evidence of the present in relation to the past, and one's foundation of God's Word or man's word determines the worldview one has, by which such evidence is then interpreted.

The spiritual nature of this battle over evidence can be seen in the biblical account of Jesus raising Lazarus from the dead. The chief priests wanted to kill Lazarus to get rid of the evidence because they refused to acknowledge that Jesus was the Son of God. Yes, it's a spiritual issue.

In Luke 16, we have an account of a rich man and another man called Lazarus. Both had died. The rich man was in a place of torment, whereas Lazarus was with Abraham. The rich man wanted Abraham to send Lazarus back to warn his five brothers about the place of torment after death.

"But Abraham said, 'They have Moses and the Prophets; let them hear them.' And he said, 'No, father Abraham, but if someone goes to them from the dead, they will repent.' He said to him, 'If they do not hear Moses and

SCIENCE — FEBRUARY 21

the Prophets, neither will they be convinced if someone should rise from the dead'" (Luke 16:29–31). And we certainly saw this play out when Jesus rose from the dead. In Matthew 28, we read that the chief priests and elders gave money to the soldiers to tell people the disciples had stolen the body of Jesus while they were asleep (v.13)! Even though Jesus rose from the dead, the chief priests and elders refused to believe it.

Now it's true that evidence is important. Jesus said to the Jews, *"If I am not doing the works of my Father, then do not believe me; but if I do them, even though you do not believe me, believe the works, that you may know and understand that the Father is in me and I am in the Father"* (John 10:37–38).

Jesus gave people evidence of His divine nature by His works. But most still did not believe He was the Messiah because of the spiritual state of their hearts. We do need to give answers for what we believe, as we're instructed to in 1 Peter 3:15. We do need to do all that we can to show people the correct interpretation of the evidence and that it confirms the truth of God's Word. Thus, we use evidence to point people to the Word of God, understanding that it's not the evidence that will convince them but the word of the Holy Spirit on their hearts. There is always that balance between responsibility and sovereignty. Our responsibility is to do our best to convince people of the truth, but in doing so, we point them to the Word of God, as ultimately, it is God who does the convincing, not us.

Moses gave Pharaoh evidence that God was telling him to take the Israelites out of Egypt. But Pharaoh kept rejecting the evidence. The spiritual nature of the battle is seen in the biblical account when Pharaoh *hardened his heart* (Exodus 8:32) and refused to accept the evidence. But we are also told that God hardened Pharaoh's heart (Exodus 7:3, 10:20, 14:4). It's God who opens people's hearts to the truth, which is why it's important to understand that *faith comes from hearing, and hearing through the word of Christ* (Romans 10:17).

For by grace you have been saved through faith. And this is not your own doing; it is the gift of God (Ephesians 2:8).

Does it matter if we find Noah's Ark? No, it really doesn't. That doesn't mean it wouldn't be one of the greatest archaeological finds of our day if we did. But God has already allowed us to find the overwhelming evidence we need to confirm the Flood. God has given everyone enough evidence that He is the Creator. If they don't believe, they are without excuse (Romans 1:20). There's no "silver bullet" that will convince everyone, as it's really a spiritual issue. However, in ways I don't understand, God uses the answers we give (our responsibility) regarding evidence to impact people.

And actually, we have found the Ark! It's in Northern Kentucky, ready for you to visit. Well, it's the life-sized replica of the Ark with exhibits teaching lots of evidence that clearly confirms the Bible's account of the Flood and points people to the truth of God's Word and the gospel. We hope to see you at the Ark Encounter soon.

> **We know it's only God's Word (God's sovereignty) that saves, and so in answering questions about evidence, we must also point people to the Word of God.**

FEBRUARY 22

Isaiah 2:22

Battle Between Man's Word and God's Word

Some time ago, Tucker Carlson on Fox News made a very interesting statement.

Now, I do not believe (from all I've heard and read of Tucker Carlson) that he understands his statement in the context of the spiritual battle that I see as a Bible-believing Christian. But he does recognize a chasm in this nation that is widening.

He put it as a chasm between those who believe they are God and those who believe they are not God. Insightful.

I would put it this way: It's a battle between two religions — man's word and God's Word. It's a battle that began 6,000 years ago in the Garden and is detailed in Genesis 3. The beginning of this spiritual battle occurred when the devil, in the form of a serpent, tempted the first man and woman (Adam and Eve) to disobey God's Word. The devil said, *"Did God actually say ...?"* (Genesis 3:5). And then he said, *"[Y]ou will be like God."* In other words, reject God's Word and be your own god.

Actually, Genesis 3:1 and 3:5 sum up the sin nature of man. We know Adam succumbed, listened to the devil, and disobeyed God. That's the origin of sin, resulting in the judgment of death. Because Adam succumbed to the devil's temptation, the sin nature of man is that he would rather believe the word of man than the Word of God. Secondly, humans will want to be their own god, to decide "truth" for themselves.

Now those who trust Christ for salvation can look to Christ and the work of the Holy Spirit in their lives to not let their sin nature master them. We need to be sanctified as we daily conform our thinking and behavior to that of the Lord Jesus Christ.

But those who are not Christians, to one degree or another, allow the sin nature to master them as they act as their own god. We are seeing this play out before our very eyes as those who act as their own god determine "right" and "wrong" for themselves. God's Word describes man's sinful heart this way in Jeremiah 17:9: *The heart is deceitful above all things, and desperately sick; who can understand it?* The natural man has a depraved heart.

As humans allow their depraved hearts to master them, they will resort to all sorts of perversion and depravity as they attempt to exhibit their supposed god status. They will turn against everything that the Creator God who owns them has set down as His rules about life. The Bible describes them this way: *Woe to those who call evil good and good evil, who put darkness for light and light for darkness, who put bitter for sweet and sweet for bitter!* (Isaiah 5:20).

They will pervert marriage. We see that in their insistence of gay "marriage." (There is no such thing as gay "marriage," as there's only one marriage, the one that God created: one man [male] for one woman [female].) They will pervert gender. God created two genders only — male and female (and science confirms that). They will pervert that man is made in God's image. They pervert this as they do all they can to kill as many children as possible by abortion, which is nothing less than the child sacrifice to the god of self. And a major reason they are so emotional about demanding the ability to kill children is because they refuse to obey God's rules in regard to sex. They want to do whatever they want with whomever they want and get rid of any of the

APOLOGETICS

consequences, such as pregnancy, by any means possible. They have adopted sexual humanism and attempt to force this on everyone. They will pervert that God gave man dominion over the creation and will put the creation in dominion over man, as we see in the modern climate religion. They will worship the creation instead of the Creator.

Yes, we are seeing man being his own god and perverting God's Word in increasing ways with increasing exhibitions of depravity. It's a spiritual battle.

Stop regarding man in whose nostrils is breath, for of what account is he? (Isaiah 2:22).

Know that we are in a battle between those who believe they are God and those who trust in the real God.

FEBRUARY 23
Matthew 12:30

No Neutrality

I must admit, I get rather dismayed sometimes at the lack of discernment from certain people in the Church.

Secularists have attacked the ministry of Answers in Genesis since its founding. They attack all along the way as the ministry has grown. They have vehemently attacked the vision and building of the Creation Museum and Ark Encounter. And they continue to attack in various ways.

But should we really be surprised at this? Of course not. But what does surprise me, although in a way I should expect it, as it's happened ever since we started the creation apologetics ministry in our home in 1977, is that many in the Church seem to believe many of the secularists' false accusations.

Not long after the Ark Encounter was opened, a secularist posted a video showing the parking lot was empty and claiming no one was coming to the attraction. What the person didn't tell the audience was that he used a drone to take the video on a Sunday morning when the attraction wasn't open. Of course, that information is left out so people will be led to believe a lie. Now that is so typical of how many of these people operate.

But should we really be surprised at the world's tactics? Of course not! And this is something every Christian should understand.

Man is not neutral! Every person has an "agenda" in whatever they say. Consider the following verses:

Whoever is not with me is against me, and whoever does not gather with me scatters (Matthew 12:30).

"Enter by the narrow gate. For the gate is wide and the way is easy that leads to destruction, and those who enter by it are many. For the gate is narrow and the way is hard that leads to life, and those who find it are few" (Matthew 7:13–14).

"Everyone then who hears these words of mine and does them will be like a wise man who built his house on the rock.... And everyone who hears these words of mine and does not do them will be like a foolish man who built his house on the sand" (Matthew 7:24, 26).

[F]or at one time you were darkness, but now you are light in the Lord. Walk as children of light (Ephesians 5:8).

For the wrath of God is revealed from heaven against all ungodliness and unrighteousness of men, who by their unrighteousness suppress the truth. For what can be known about God is plain to them, because God has shown it to them (Romans 1:18–19).

For the mind that is set on the flesh is hostile to God, for it does not submit to God's law; indeed, it cannot (Romans 8:7).

For all have sinned and fall short of the glory of God (Romans 3:23).

The heart is deceitful above all things, and desperately sick [wicked] (Jeremiah 17:9).

There are many more verses than those above that tell us over and over again that no one is neutral. People are either for Christ or against Him. We live in a world where *the light has come into the world, and people loved the darkness rather than the light because their works were evil* (John 3:19).

Now whenever those who have dark hearts speak about things, we need to be reminded that *The good person out of the good treasure of his heart produces good, and the evil person out of his evil treasure produces evil, for out of the abundance of the heart his mouth speaks* (Luke 6:45).

So Christians should be suspicious of secularists who make accusations against Christians! They need to remember what Jesus said about those who oppose God and His Word:

You are of your father the devil, and your will is to do your father's desires. He was a murderer from the beginning, and does not stand in the truth, because there is no truth in him. When he lies, he speaks out of his own character, for he is a liar and the father of lies (John 8:44).

We shouldn't be surprised that secularists will lie because they don't believe there is an absolute authority, except for themselves. After all, for those who do this, the means (lying) justifies the end (attempting to undermine ministries like Answers in Genesis). And they can define a lie however they want to define it.

And don't believe everything you read in secular newspapers, magazines, etc. The same non-neutral understanding needs to be applied. It's very rare that we read a totally accurate news article about the ministry or some aspect of it that secularists consider supposedly newsworthy. The majority of such articles are written deliberately to attack us as a Christian organization. Even the terminology they use is chosen to try to put us in a bad light.

Now we do have a couple researchers who will research various posts by those who oppose AiG if needed when we're interviewed by the media (which happens on a regular basis) about a particular issue. So, we check out what has been claimed and prepare for the interview with relevant answers. That's normally how we even find out about such attacks. Otherwise, we just ignore them. Besides, for most of them, the number of followers they have is rather small. Most have no concept of how an organization like AiG is run.

Now sometimes, Christians will send us articles or links to videos by certain secularists and ask for our answer to what these God-haters are saying. That's a reminder that Christians have sinful hearts too! All Christians should be reminded that no one is neutral. If something appears to be a stumbling block to someone, we will check it out and get back to them with an answer. However, on many occasions when we've done that, we've found the person doesn't really want our answer, as they want us to be seen in a bad light! Usually, it's because the Christian has compromised God's Word with secular ideas, and they want us to be seen as the "bad guys," so to speak.

So, the big takeaway? No human heart is neutral! And remember, *In their case the god of this world has blinded the minds of the unbelievers, to keep them from seeing the light of the gospel of the glory of Christ, who is the image of God* (2 Corinthians 4:4).

Christians should know better than to totally trust secular news sources. They also have to be careful with liberal Christian news sources! In fact, always check things out carefully from any news source. The point is, we are in a battle every day. There's a war raging around us.

For we do not wrestle against flesh and blood, but against the rulers, against the authorities, against the cosmic powers over this present darkness, against the spiritual forces of evil in the heavenly places (Ephesians 6:12).

Be aware of the enemy's tactics in this war and don't succumb to them!

FEBRUARY 24

Nehemiah 13:8

Nehemiah Anger

The following verses of Scripture remind me of my father:

I was very angry when I heard their outcry and these words (Nehemiah 5:6).

And I was very angry, and I threw all the household furniture of Tobiah out of the chamber (Nehemiah 13:8).

Should verses like that remind us of our fathers? Actually, I believe they should.

Now don't misunderstand this anger of Nehemiah. It was not a sinful anger. It was a righteous anger, as he saw things that were very wrong and was burdened to make them right! But you also notice as you read through Nehemiah that most others did not seem to have that righteous anger that Nehemiah did. It seems so few are really prepared to stand boldly to make sure things are done correctly and in accordance with God's Word.

My father so reminded me of Nehemiah. In fact, as we were growing up, in one of the churches we attended, someone labeled my father with the title of "Merv the Stirrer" (his name was Mervyn). Now why was that? Let me give you examples. One week at church, the pastor handed out a daily devotion booklet for the month to every church family. As soon as my father opened the booklet, he noticed a devotion about Noah's Flood. As he read the text of this devotion, he found the writer was telling everyone that Noah's Flood was just a local event!

Well, my father had that Nehemiah anger. He went to the pastor and elders and said that they couldn't hand this out, as it was compromising God's Word, or, at the very least, he told them that the congregation needed to be informed that this particular devotion was incorrect and undermined the authority of Scripture. He said people needed to be told Noah's Flood was a global event. However, the pastor and the elders didn't want to rock the boat. They said it would be best to do nothing and let it go, as saying something would only stir up strife. My father then had that Nehemiah anger (righteous anger) at their response. He told them this devotion was opening a door to compromising God's Word. My father was right! Why was he the only one who said something about this? Others came and told him they agreed with him, but they weren't prepared to do anything about it. My father was prepared to stand for the truth. And for that, he was labeled "Merv the Stirrer."

Another time at a members meeting, those present spent a long time arguing about the color of paint to use on the restroom doors. It turned into a massive argument with different factions among the members arguing for different colors of paint. Most of the meeting was taken up with this issue. But then, it came time to approve the Sunday school curriculum for the coming year, so the head Sunday school teacher proposed they accept a particular curriculum, and they were ready to vote on it with virtually no discussion. My father stood up and said that they needed to be sure someone had checked out the content of this curriculum to make sure it did not compromise God's Word and to be confident the content was what we wanted to be taught to the children. Well, you would think my father had just committed some heinous crime. There was an outcry that they didn't need to do that. But my father knew that the devotion book handed out was from the same publisher, and a devotion in that book had compromised God's Word concerning Noah's Flood.

However, the elders just went ahead with a vote by the members and accepted the curriculum without knowing if it had been checked out thoroughly by the leadership and others. Again, my father was labeled as

CHURCH
FEBRUARY 24

"Merv the Stirrer." But in reality, my father had a burden to ensure the kids were going to be taught biblical truth and that this not be undermined by compromise.

Another time, a gay couple came to the church and said they would like to attend this church and also sing in the choir. The elders were going to let them sing in the choir, as they thought it was a great opportunity to impact them. Once again, my father stood up and said that by letting them sing in the choir, their sinful lifestyle was being condoned by the church. He said they should never be allowed to be in a position like this in the church. Well, once again, he was labeled as "Merv the Stirrer." Yes, we want to witness to such people, but we don't give them positions in the church where they minister to people! My father was right.

Basically, the Nehemiah anger means, "Why isn't someone doing something about this? We need to do something." My father's Nehemiah anger rubbed off on me in many ways. When I took my school students to museums and saw they were all from an evolutionary atheistic perspective, I would have that Nehemiah anger and say, "Why can't someone do something about this? Why can't we build a Creation Museum?"

I would say that the Nehemiah anger is part of what God used to establish the ministry of Answers in Genesis and all its outreaches, including the two leading Christian-themed attractions in the world. When I saw the lack of creation apologetics books in Australia, I said, "Why can't we do something about this?" So we started a bookstore in our home to import the books and make them available to people.

A few years ago, our eldest daughter founded the Answers in Genesis Christian school, Answers Academy. She trained to be a nurse, spent five years working as such, and then pleaded to work in the ministry of AiG. She became my executive assistant, and then after a few years, she told me she had a burden to establish a truly biblical worldview discipleship school, as there was a lack of such schools. She saw the lack in our area. She said, "Someone needs to do this." So she did! And it's really grown as a wonderful, unique, God-honoring school. Yes, that Nehemiah anger continues generationally.

Question: How many are prepared to stand boldly against compromise and do something about it regardless of how others think? Obviously, we need to act graciously, but nonetheless, courageously and biblically. Really, we could sum it up this way: *[C]ontend for the faith that was once for all delivered to the saints* (Jude 3).

How about we see more Nehemiah anger from our fathers! Let see more standing up to contend for the faith! And let's see that Nehemiah anger passed on generationally.

How many of us are prepared to have that Nehemiah anger when we need it?

FEBRUARY 25

Psalm 139:13-14

"My Body, My Rights"

In the last few years, we've increasingly heard this chant from those demanding abortion: "My body, my rights." In 2021, the vice president of the USA (Kamala Harris), in support of abortion, posted a tweet stating, "The right of women to make decisions about their own bodies is not negotiable. The right of women to make decisions about their own bodies is their decision, it is their body."

She was claiming in this tweet that a fertilized egg/developing human baby is part of a woman's body. Well, she was totally wrong scientifically and wrong biblically. It matters what we do with our bodies because they belong to the One who created them.

As part of the current battle over the abortion issue, we often hear women saying something like, "It's my body, so I can do whatever I want." For instance, the Amnesty International website featured a headline stating, "My Body, My Rights," followed by the words, "Being Able to Make Our Own Decisions About Our Health, Body, and Sexual Life Is a Basic Human Right."[22]

On the BBC website's Ethics Guide page, we read this statement: "Here are some of the women's rights arguments in favour of abortion: women have a moral right to decide what to do with their bodies."

But from a Christian perspective, human beings do not own their bodies. God owns everything because He is the Creator of all things. I believe the emotionalism over this issue from abortionists is because they want to do whatever they want with sex. They don't want a higher authority (i.e., God) telling them what is right and wrong. Their worldview is one of sexual humanism. They want to get rid of any consequences (e.g., pregnancy) of their sexual exploits. I believe that's really what it's all about in the majority of instances.

But from a Christian perspective, human beings do not own their bodies. We are not the product of natural processes. We came into existence because of the actions of our Creator God.

The earth is the LORD's and the fullness thereof, the world and those who dwell therein, for he has founded it upon the seas and established it upon the rivers (Psalm 24:1–2).

Yours, O LORD, is the greatness and the power and the glory and the victory and the majesty, for all that is in the heavens and in the earth is yours. Yours is the kingdom, O LORD, and you are exalted as head above all (1 Chronicles 29:11).

For every beast of the forest is mine, the cattle on a thousand hills. I know all the birds of the hills, and all that moves in the field is mine. "If I were hungry, I would not tell you, for the world and its fullness are mine" (Psalm 50:10–12).

Many Scriptures make it clear that God owns everything, including us. This means God has a right to tell us the rules. He is the absolute authority. He determines what is right and what is wrong.

Now, what about a fertilized egg, the developing human baby, in a woman's womb? From a perspective of observational science, is a fertilized egg and the resulting developing child a part of the woman's body?

No. In sexual reproduction, we know that DNA from the father and DNA from the mother come together when a sperm fertilizes an egg. The result is a unique combination of information — different from the mother, different from the father, and different from any other human being who has ever lived, is living, or will be

SCIENCE

FEBRUARY 25

living. As the cell then divides to build the human body, no new information is ever added. So, from a scientific perspective, a unique human being with information from both father and mother exists at fertilization.

And right from fertilization, genetic information for this human being determines whether this individual is male or female. Think about it — a fertilized egg with the sex chromosomes XY and all its future stages of development is a male being carried in a female's body. So how could this be a part of the woman's body anyway? The Y chromosome came from the male, not the female.

Another corroborating fact from science is that the mother's body would reject the developing baby as foreign tissue, but God has built an anti-rejection mechanism into the uterus and placenta so the developing body of this tiny individual can be accepted by the uterus and nourished until birth.

In a way, it's similar to the following situation: If a person has a kidney transplant, then that person must take anti-rejection drugs since the body does not recognize the tissue and would normally reject it. So, if a woman claims she can have an abortion because what is developing in her womb is her body and she therefore has the right to do what she wants, then she is wrong scientifically. She is a science denier.

Now, biblically, we know we don't own ourselves, because God owns us — He owns everything. And in Genesis 1:27, we read that God made humans in His image. *So God created man in his own image, in the image of God he created him; male and female he created them.* No animal was created in God's image. But with humans, right from fertilization, the new unique individual is made in God's image.

So, what is abortion? Abortion at any stage, from fertilization through birth, is the deliberate killing of a unique human made in God's image. And that is murder. Really, abortion is child sacrifice to the god of self.

At the Creation Museum, a stunning pro-life exhibit called *Fearfully and Wonderfully Made* opened in September 2020. This exhibit details the biblical and scientific aspects of human life beginning at fertilization and helps people understand the reality of abortion. The unique models show various stages of human development and powerfully teach the scientific and biblical truth about the unique individual developing in his or her mother's womb. It's the most powerful pro-life exhibit in the world.

Because women who have had an abortion will come through this exhibit and be convicted about what they see and read, the exhibit ends with teaching about God's forgiveness and love. And for those who have suffered from a miscarriage in this fallen world, we give encouragement and hope from God's Word.

Right from fertilization, we can exclaim with the psalmist, *For you formed my inward parts; you knitted me together in my mother's womb. I praise you, for I am fearfully and wonderfully made* (Psalm 139:13–14).

While your body was being formed, "knitted together," God referred to the person.

Before our body was formed, God's Word in Psalm 139:16 also states, *Your eyes saw my unformed substance; in your book were written, every one of them, the days that were formed for me, when as yet there was none of them.*

Wow, while our body was developing, God knew everything about the length of our life! Abortion is the deliberate termination of a human life. And here is a sobering warning: *So then each of us will give an account of himself to God* (Romans 14:12).

Always remember that we truly are fearfully and wonderfully made.

FEBRUARY 26

Matthew 7:1-5

As Christians, Should We Judge Others?

Many times over the years, and often on social media, I get accused of being judgmental because I speak against Christians who compromise Genesis with evolution. I also get accused of judging people when I show clearly from Scripture that sexual conduct outside of marriage is sin, or that abortion is murder, and so on.

Both Christians and non-Christians have told me that I shouldn't judge others and that I need to stop being judgmental. Interestingly, they are very judgmental against me when they accuse me of being judgmental.

I've often replied to Christians that when we tell someone they are a sinner, we are judging them. In making this statement about sin, we are using God's Word that tells us we are all sinners and in need of salvation (Romans 3:23). So, yes, we are judging people using the words of the only truly righteous Judge.

I've had many Christians (and even non-Christians) who will claim that the Bible states we are to "judge not." But when they do this, they are taking those words in the Bible way out of context.

Let's look at the passage where people quote "judge not" from:

"Judge not, that you be not judged. For with the judgment you pronounce you will be judged, and with the measure you use it will be measured to you. Why do you see the speck that is in your brother's eye, but do not notice the log that is in your own eye? Or how can you say to your brother, 'Let me take the speck out of your eye,' when there is the log in your own eye? You hypocrite, first take the log out of your own eye, and then you will see clearly to take the speck out of your brother's eye" (Matthew 7:1–5).

Here Christ is warning believers against making judgments in a hypocritical or condemning manner. He is not saying we are not to judge! A person can't just take the first two words "judge not" and claim this means Christians shouldn't judge! However, even when they say this, they are judging Christians themselves with verses taken completely out of context.

Hypocritical type of judging is a characteristic often associated with the Pharisees during the ministry of Jesus. Many people who quote "judge not" from Matthew 7:1 fail to notice the command *to* judge in verse 5 of this passage, where it says, *Then you will see clearly to take the speck out of your brother's eye.*

The point Jesus emphasizes here is to judge yourself first before you make judgments about others. So, this passage is definitely not saying a person can't judge. Think about this verse: *Do not judge by appearances, but judge with right judgment* (John 7:24).

Now should we make judgments about other believers, especially as it relates to their erroneous teachings on Genesis?

The Bible provides many examples of how God's people can be in error, dating back to (and before) the kings of Israel and Judah. Out of the 39 rulers in Israel and Judah after the time of Solomon, only eight of them (1 Kings 1–2, all from Judah) tried to reverse the evil their predecessors had introduced into the kingdom. Only eight of them saw the depravity around them and tried to do something about it. However, these godly kings had failures as well. These eight kings have their histories tarnished because they failed to take down

THEOLOGY

the high places (1 Kings 15:11, 14; 22:43; 2 Kings 12:2–3; 14:3–4; 15:3–4, 34–35). They didn't deal with the compromise like they should have.

Answers in Genesis points out that there are many Christians (including Christian leaders) who add evolution and/or millions of years to Scripture. We expose this compromise not to make harsh judgments about the person or his spiritual walk but to show the inconsistency (as we all can be) of a Christian leader toward Genesis — and the negative implications that it can have on the rest of Scripture and on the people they teach.

Now, the ministry of AiG is dedicated to upholding the authority of the Bible and giving answers to point out that such compromising positions are really undermining God's Word and its authority. When I do that, I'm often told that I'm unloving and that we should not be making judgments about others by pointing out errors in their teaching regarding Genesis.

Some people take offense and say that as believers, we should focus on loving others and not be divisive. We are, however, divisive if we do not correct error. Are we working toward *the unity of the faith* (Ephesians 4:13), or are we compromising God's Word by allowing for the world's "wisdom"? Remember, as believers, we are all part of *one faith* (Ephesians 4:5). We must establish our foundation in the truth of God's Word and not our own philosophies, making God the authority over our lives. Having the right foundation will help us to know the difference between truth and lies as well as right and wrong. Paul explained the need for truth and the divisive nature of lies in the following passage:

[S]o that we may no longer be children, tossed to and fro by the waves and carried about by every wind of doctrine, by human cunning, by craftiness in deceitful schemes. Rather, speaking the truth in love, we are to grow up in every way into him who is the head, into Christ, from whom the whole body, joined and held together by every joint with which it is equipped, when each part is working properly, makes the body grow so that it builds itself up in love (Ephesians 4:14–16).

We need unity on the truth of God's infallible Word, not unity on man's fallible word! As I've said many times, the truth is divisive in a world where "men loved darkness rather than light."

Think about it. Are we being loving if we allow our fellow brethren to remain in error and even deceive others? Of course not. Loving others requires that we graciously correct them when they fall into error (Matthew 18:15–17; 1 Corinthians 1:11; Galatians 6:1). Those who err do not necessarily know they are in error; they are possibly deceived or ignorant. So we gently and carefully correct the error in regard to teaching, no matter what the situation. After all, this is one of the responsibilities of the Church: to teach sound doctrine and correct erroneous teaching (2 Timothy 2:25, 3:16; Titus 2:1).

As Christians, we must point out that which is sin, or we are not being loving. We must tell people that all sexual conduct outside of marriage is sin, that abortion is sin.

So yes, Christians can and need to judge, but don't judge hypocritically, and judge using righteous judgment!

We must judge with gentleness and meekness, but also with boldness and courage.

FEBRUARY 27

Jeremiah 21:8

Life or Death?

"And to this people you shall say: 'Thus says the Lord: Behold, I set before you the way of life and the way of death'" (Jeremiah 21:8).

Let's think about this from the perspective of the Israelites. The Chaldeans (Babylonians) had besieged the city. They were described by God in Habukkuk 1:6 as a ruthless people.

So the people inside the city would be looking at these ruthless people who were outside the city and thinking that if the Chaldeans find them, they would kill them. Then God says they have a choice before them: life or death. If they surrender, they will live, but if they try to shelter in the city, they will die.

People looked at the evidence. The Chaldeans, a ruthless people, were outside the city. Then they looked at the city and saw themselves safe from these people. But had they remembered God's Word, it had already been prophesied to them that God would bring the Chaldeans to take the city. And now God was telling the people to obey His Word and if they would surrender and go outside the city to the Chaldeans, they would live. But if they sheltered in the city, they would die.

As you contemplate this, from a human perspective, it all seems illogical. Looking at the evidence, it doesn't make sense to surrender to the enemy, but instead, it makes sense to shelter in the city to be safe. However, God said something very different. Really, God was saying, "Don't look at the evidence and try to interpret it from your fallible, finite, human perspective. Listen to the infinite Creator God and trust His Word."

This reminds me of what happened in the Garden of Eden 6,000 years ago. God placed Adam in the Garden. But as a test of obedience, He placed two trees, the tree of life and the tree of the knowledge of good and evil. Then God said to the first man, Adam, *"You may surely eat of every tree of the garden, but of the tree of the knowledge of good and evil you shall not eat, for in the day that you eat of it you shall surely die"* (Genesis 2:16–17).

God put before Adam the way of life and the way of death. Then God showed Adam he was alone (no animal was made in God's image), so God made the first woman (Eve) from his side.

Now the devil in the form of a serpent came to Eve (Adam was with her) and tempted them to disobey God and eat the fruit they were told not to eat. Note we read in Genesis 3:6, *So when the woman saw that the tree was good for food, and that it was a delight to the eyes, and that the tree was to be desired to make one wise, she took of its fruit and ate, and she also gave some to her husband who was with her, and he ate.*

Eve (and obviously Adam, who was there) looked at the evidence — the fruit. It looked good. They decided to listen to the devil and interpret the evidence themselves and determined it was good for them to eat. But they should have remembered what God said and obeyed His Word and rejected the temptation to eat. Because Adam disobeyed, death came into the world.

Today, so many of our Christian leaders/academics listen to what fallible man says about the origin of life and the universe, and they trust man's interpretation of the evidence. It looks good to them. Then they accept *the lies* of the devil and reinterpret God's Word and partake in compromise that undermines Scripture and causes many to reject God's Word, thus leading to death, the second death — eternal separation from God.

APOLOGETICS

FEBRUARY 27

Sadly, today we also see an increasing number of Christians/Christian leaders looking at what the world says about transgenderism, gay "marriage," and other issues. They're told to comply and accept their lifestyles or they're not loving. They take this interpretation instead of judging such against God's Word and understanding true love is to point out that God calls these things sin. As a result, many choose the way of death — eternal separation from God — rather than eternal life because of salvation in Christ.

We should always listen to God first and judge what others are saying against God's Word and not the other way around.

FEBRUARY 28
Exodus 20:11

Why Is the Age of the Earth Important?

It always burdens me that many Christians are quick to speak out against evolution but often fall silent on the age of the earth. It just doesn't seem to matter. But when you talk to an evolutionist, which subject arouses the strongest reaction? Why is this so?

When the secular media visit the Creation Museum or Ark Encounter to interview me, they rarely ask about biological evolution. Typically, they will start by asking, "Why do you believe dinosaurs and people lived at the same time?" or "What do you believe about the age of the earth?" or even "Why do you reject science and believe God created the universe in six days, only thousands of years ago?"

Secularists sure scoff at those of us who only believe in thousands of years for the age of the earth and universe. I believe the media start the way I described above because they know biological evolution is impossible without billions of years of history. In fact, I find that secularists are very emotionally committed to the idea of millions and billions of years. They almost go ballistic when told the earth is only thousands of years old.

In my experience, I have found that secularists don't really care that much if Christians reject biological evolution. Yes, they still mock. But the minute people reject billions of years, they are labeled as anti-science, anti-academic, and anti-intellectual. The pressure to believe in an old earth is extremely great, and evolutionists become very emotional about it. Sadly, even many Christian leaders and academics become very emotional about insisting on billions of years for the age of the earth and universe.

Secularists understand something few Christians seem to grasp: biological evolution is not the heart of the issue, "millions of years" is. And besides, many don't seem to understand that millions of years is evolutionary geology. It primarily comes out of atheism. So, when someone says they don't believe in evolution but believe in millions of years, they are incorrect. What they mean is they reject evolutionary biology but not evolutionary geology! Now if they accept a history timeline as outlined in the Bible (around 6,000 years), secularists are forced to abandon biological evolution, and creation is the only viable alternative. But by accepting an old earth, it is easy for them to justify their rejection of God and the trustworthiness of His Word. After all, given enough time, anything can happen! Most conservative, evangelical pastors recognize that the Scriptures clearly teach that Adam was made from dust and Eve was made from his side. They realize how hard it would be to explain the gospel without referring to the origin of sin and death in Genesis. However, many such pastors do not consider the age of the earth an important issue.

Many Christian leaders tend to think it is very important to oppose biological evolution but it doesn't matter what you believe about the age of the earth. Let's face it, in the majority of evangelical churches in America, pastors won't preach that people evolved from apelike creatures. But many pastors will say they are not sure if the days of creation were long periods of time or literal days. Many will say the earth could be billions of years old. And that is a bigger problem. I believe many are pushed to this position to maintain academic respectability within academic circles. I also think there's an issue with intellectual pride. And it's important to note that all of the compromised positions on Genesis (the gap theory, framework hypothesis, theistic evolution, day-age theory, progressive creation, etc.) have one thing in common — they attempt to fit millions of years of history

SCIENCE

into Genesis. The major reason so many pastors, Christian academics, and Christians do not believe in six literal (24-hour) days of creation is ultimately because of their desire to account for the supposed billions of years.

Such compromise places mankind's fallible dating methods — beliefs about the past — in authority over God's Word. This opens a door to undermining biblical authority. Such compromise does not negate one's salvation, but it does affect how coming generations view Scripture. This compromise causes a generational loss of biblical authority. Loss of authority is a major reason why many young people doubt the Bible and ultimately walk away from the Church.

"Millions of years" flies directly in the face of the history God's Word clearly reveals. Ultimately, belief in millions of years attacks the character of God. If the fossil-bearing layers were laid down slowly over millions of years, then these layers contain the remains of dead creatures, fossil thorns, evidence of diseases (e.g., cancer), and animals eating each other — all supposedly before humans appeared on the planet.

How can a Christian fit this into God's Word, which tells us that everything was "very good" after God finished creating man? How can a good God call cancer "very good"? How could such history fit with Scripture, which tells us that thorns came after sin and that humans and animals were originally all vegetarian?

The old age of the earth is a much bigger problem than biological evolution. Not only is it a direct attack on the authority of Scripture that drives away the next generation, but it is also the child of the pagan religion of this age: naturalism, the atheistic philosophy that everything can be explained by natural causes without God. Secularists must cling to long ages in order to attempt to explain life without a Creator.

The belief in billions of years was originally postulated by materialists, atheists, and deists in an attempt to explain the geological record by natural processes rather than by a global Flood as revealed in the Bible.

Naturalism is the anti-God religion of this age, and "millions of years" is foundational to its false idea of biological evolution. George Wald, a biochemist and Nobel prize winner, explains why a long period of time is so important to evolution's story: "Time is in fact the hero of the plot. The time … is of the order of two billion years. What we regard as impossible on the basis of human experience is meaningless here. Given so much time, the 'impossible' becomes possible, the possible probable, and the probable virtually certain. One has only to wait: time itself performs the miracles."[23] Without the belief in millions of years, Charles Darwin could never have successfully postulated his ideas of biological evolution.

Standing against biological evolution only partly closes the door to biblical compromise. Refusing to compromise on the timeline of God's Word beginning in Genesis — while standing against mankind's fallible beliefs about millions of years — slams the door shut. As an analogy, the idea of millions of years is like a disease (although we know sin is everyone's ultimate disease). Biological evolution is merely the symptom. Many Christians are treating the symptom but fail to recognize the source disease. In Scripture, God has given us the infallible record of the true history of the universe, which shows how He has been working out His plan to redeem sinners since Adam brought death into the world around 6,000 years ago.

For in six days the Lord made heaven and earth, the sea, and all that is in them, and rested on the seventh day. Therefore the Lord blessed the Sabbath day and made it holy (Exodus 20:11).

Time may be the hero of the secular evolutionary plot, but the hero of real events is God.

MARCH 1
Matthew 19:4–5

What Does the Bible Say About Marriage?

Is there such a thing as gay marriage? No. It should be written as gay "marriage." It is not true marriage. Marriage is a union established by God that is legally or formally recognized.

Now the first such union was created by God when He made the first two people—Adam and Eve. God made the first man from dust and the first woman from his side:

Then the Lord God formed the man of dust from the ground and breathed into his nostrils the breath of life, and the man became a living creature (Genesis 2:7).

So the Lord God caused a deep sleep to fall upon the man, and while he slept took one of his ribs and closed up its place with flesh. And the rib that the Lord God had taken from the man he made into a woman and brought her to the man. Then the man said, "This at last is bone of my bones and flesh of my flesh; she shall be called Woman, because she was taken out of Man" (Genesis 2:21–23).

After this we read: *Therefore a man shall leave his father and his mother and hold fast to his wife, and they shall become one flesh* (Genesis 2:24). This verse is the creation of the first union of humans, in other words, the first marriage. It's important to note that neither the president of the USA, nor the prime ministers of Australia, Canada, or the United Kingdom, created marriage. God created marriage. This union was one between a male and a female—one man and one woman.

As God created marriage, He therefore gives marriage its meaning. After all, the meaning of anything is dependent on its origin. And the origin of marriage is in Genesis. After God created the first human union, He said: *And God blessed them. And God said to them, "Be fruitful and multiply and fill the earth and subdue it, and have dominion over the fish of the sea and over the birds of the heavens and over every living thing that moves on the earth"* (Genesis 1:28).

A primary importance of marriage is to produce offspring. And as Malachi 2:15 makes clear, to produce godly offspring. Only a man and a woman can do this. It requires a male and a female to produce offspring.

Thus, there is only one true marriage, that of one man and one woman—a male and a female.

Jesus as the God-man reiterated this when asked about marriage. He referred to the creation of marriage as we have recorded in Genesis:

Have you not read that he who created them from the beginning made them male and female, and said, "Therefore a man shall leave his father and his mother and hold fast to his wife, and the two shall become one flesh"? (Matthew 19:4–5).

Now the devil perverts everything God has created. We see that in marriage. Some people have defined "marriage" as one man and multiple women (polygamy). Some have defined "marriage" as two men or two women. These "marriages" are not marriage as God created this institution.

In today's world, some have determined that gay "marriage" is as valid as heterosexual marriage. But gay "marriage" is not how God defined marriage. So this can't be true marriage. It's interesting how in gay "marriage" people want there to be two human beings. Why two? Well, two actually comes from the Bible

FAMILY — MARCH 1

as the first marriage was between two people. But then the devil takes the two in marriage and perverts it to destroy it and totally undermine its meaning.

When courts rule that gay "marriage" can be legalized as a real marriage, they are redefining marriage, thus a door has been unlocked to redefine marriage in any way one wants to. It becomes totally subjective.

Once man defines marriage, instead of accepting the definition of marriage as the Creator of marriage defined, then ultimately anything goes in regard to defining marriage. Thus, not only two men or two women, but why stop at two? Why not any number of wives, husbands, or "partners" one wants?

Now it is true that the Bible records accounts of people who had multiple wives. The Bible doesn't hide man's behavior in this fallen world and clearly shows the negative consequences of not obeying God's created order. Marriage, as God ordained it, has always been one man and one woman.

But here's the bottom line. If a person builds their thinking on the Bible, then the worldview that comes from that foundation would define marriage as between one man and one woman. However, if one rejects the Bible and builds their thinking on man's word, that marriage can be defined any way a person determines. After all, on the foundation of man's word, everything is ultimately subjective.

Now when Christians disagree with gay "marriage," they are often accused of hate speech. But having a biblical worldview built on the foundation of God's Word does not mean when this worldview conflicts with the secular one built on man's word, we're spreading hate speech. It's a conflict of worldviews.

Secularists often claim that Christians disagreeing with gay "marriage" is hate speech because all the secularists want is freedom for all views in regard to what they call marriage. However, they don't want freedom for all views, as they don't want freedom for Christians who have their view built on the Bible and therefore believe that there is only one definition of marriage because God created and defines marriage. This means that the worldview conflict between biblical marriage and gay "marriage" can never be resolved at the worldview level.

So is a gay "marriage" valid? Well, from a Christian perspective, based on God's Word in Genesis, there is only one true marriage: a man and a woman. Therefore, a gay "marriage" is not a valid marriage. They can call it a gay union or whatever they want to call it, but not marriage! God created marriage as recorded in Genesis. Any union other than a man and a woman is sin:

Therefore God gave them up in the lusts of their hearts to impurity, to the dishonoring of their bodies among themselves, because they exchanged the truth about God for a lie and worshiped and served the creature rather than the Creator, who is blessed forever! Amen. For this reason God gave them up to dishonorable passions. For their women exchanged natural relations for those that are contrary to nature; and the men likewise gave up natural relations with women and were consumed with passion for one another, men committing shameless acts with men and receiving in themselves the due penalty for their error (Romans 1:24–27).

> **Unless people believe the truth of God's Word and build their thinking on God's Word beginning in Genesis, we can never resolve this conflict over who determines the definition of marriage.**

MARCH 2
2 Timothy 3:16

Is the Present the Key to the Past?

Is the present the key to the past? Or is knowing what happened in the past the key to the present?

Think of the dilemma for secularists who reject God and His Word. How do they figure out how the universe and life came into being? How do they explain how the fossil layers all over the earth were formed?

Back in the late 1700s and early 1800s, primarily out of atheism, came the belief that the layers of fossils were laid down over millions of years, trapping life-forms in the supposed evolutionary progression of life. The term "uniformitarianism" was used regarding this matter. Basically, this term was summed up by the phrase, "The present is the key to the past." In other words, it was observed that sediments today are laid down slowly under normal circumstances. Therefore, extrapolating backward, it was assumed that such present-day processes can be used to interpret how long these layers took to be laid down.

Now the problem is that, as well as "normal" processes, we also can observe "abnormal" processes such as catastrophic floods or pyroclastic flows (hurricane-force-steam-driven flows) from volcanic eruptions. Such floods and flows can carve canyons quickly and lay down thousands of individual sedimentary layers quickly. For example, such was observed as a result of the eruption of Mount Saint Helens in 1980.

So can we use the present as the key to the past? Well, which should we use, the slow processes or the catastrophic ones as we interpret the present sedimentary layers in relation to how they formed in the past? No matter how someone does this one has to make basic assumptions that may or may not be accurate. For the Christian who believes God's Word, the present is not the key to the past. Revelation is the key to the past, and knowing what happened in the past is the key to the present.

The Bible claims to be (and Christians know it to be) the revealed Word of the infinite Creator God. It is God-breathed (2 Timothy 3:16). The Bible is not just a guide to life or a book of stories. The Bible is a revelation from the One who is infinite in knowledge, to give us the key information in history that is foundational to building the right way of thinking about the present.

Because God reveals to us the events of the past that we need to know and because God's Word is totally truthful/trustworthy, these events are the key to understanding why things are as we observe them in the present. Now if these revealed events are true, then not only will they enable us to correctly understand the present, but we should be able to use observational science in the present to confirm this history.

This also means that evolutionary beliefs about the past can be tested this way. If those beliefs are true, then observational science should confirm them. Let's just consider a few items from Genesis 1–11, as this is the history to geology, biology, astronomy, and anthropology which is the key to understanding the present. This history is also the foundation for the rest of the Bible, for all doctrine, for a biblical worldview, and in fact, everything.

The Bible reveals that the earth has undergone a global Flood (Genesis 6–9). If such a Flood occurred in the past, we would expect to find evidence of it. Even local floods in the present lay down many feet of layers quickly. So looking at the present can give us some indication of what catastrophic processes can do. In other words, we are using observational science to understand processes.

SCIENCE — MARCH 2

If there really was a worldwide (global) Flood, you would expect to find billions of dead things (fossils) buried in rock layers, laid down by water, all over the earth. And that's exactly what we find in the present. And the more this has been investigated by creation scientists, the more we understand that these fossil-bearing sedimentary layers had to be laid down quickly, not slowly. What the Bible reveals concerning a global Flood is the key to understanding the present regarding most of the fossil layers.

Let's consider another example: Scientists know that life is built on the molecule of hereditary called DNA. The more DNA has been studied, the more we understand it is like a library of books filled with information. That information is read by a code system. We also know that information and code systems cannot arise from matter by natural processes. They can only come from an intelligence. Thus, DNA can only be explained by an intelligent designer. This does not prove it was the God of the Bible, but it does confirm what the Bible declares: *For by him all things were created, in heaven and on earth, visible and invisible, whether thrones or dominions or rulers or authorities—all things were created through him and for him* (Colossians 1:16).

Another example: God's Word in Genesis tells us that God created distinct kinds of animals "according to their kind." The implication is that each kind produces its own kind and cannot change into a different kind. We now know that the "kind" in most instances is at the family level of classification (from documented evidence showing which can breed with which). So the dog family always produces dogs. Although different species of dogs have formed because of the genetic diversity God created in the DNA of the dog kind, dogs will only ever produce dogs. The science of genetics confirms biblical kinds and does not confirm evolutionary beliefs that claim one kind can change into a totally different kind over millions of years.

We could then look at the topic of death. Revelation (God's Word) tells us that death is an intrusion because of sin. Thus, the present world, which is full of death, suffering, and disease, wasn't always like this. To understand this world, revelation (God's Word) is the key, and Genesis 1–11 is the key to understanding everything.

The sad thing is that most churches/church leaders have not taught God's revelation in Genesis 1–11 as literal history, which is why so many in the Church don't have a biblical worldview and thus have been indoctrinated by the secularists to interpret the evidence of the present within a secular worldview. That's why so many in the Church believe in millions of years, or add evolution to the Bible, and compromise God's Word in Genesis in numerous ways. And it's why so many in the Church (increasingly so of the younger generations) are impacted by LGBTQ, abortion, etc.

God's revelation is history. Man's beliefs about the past, such as evolution and millions of years, are fairy tales, not history. When Christians believe the fairy tales of man and compromise God's Word in Genesis, they undermine the history that is foundational to everything.

As Christians, we must always start with God's Word as the foundation for our thinking.

MARCH 3
Psalm 119:160-162

Is the Bible Just a Book of Stories?

If you perform an Internet search for the meaning of the word story, a top hit is this: "An account of imaginary or real people and events told for entertainment." The example they use is "an adventure story." The top synonym for story is tale. And the definition of tale is "a fictitious or true narrative or story, especially one that is imaginatively recounted."

When I attended Sunday school as a child, the Sunday school teacher would often tell us we were going to have a Bible story. We always understood the word story to mean a true event. Often in church, there was a segment of the service when someone would have a "Bible story time" for the kids.

Now the stories we heard from the Bible were passages about Jonah and the great fish, the feeding of the 5,000, Jesus on the Cross, the Resurrection, the crossing of the Red Sea, Noah and the ark, and so on. And, of course, it's important to know all that God's Word teaches concerning these events of the past.

God has those events in His Word to teach us spiritual and moral things and to teach us the gospel. Christianity is based in real history. If that history wasn't real, then neither is the Christian faith based in that history.

But, over time, the word story has become more associated with fiction. For instance, Aesop's fables are stories people enjoy. We have heard of the stories of Hansel and Gretel, The Three Little Pigs, Snow White and the Seven Dwarfs, Little Red Riding Hood, Cinderella, Beauty and the Beast, Jack and the Beanstalk, and many others. I think the advent of television and the fact that many of these stories or fairy tales were made into movies helped to shift the word story toward meaning fairy tale in our modern vernacular.

Regardless, for many today, the word story really equates more with something that's not necessarily true (which is actually one of the main meanings of the word).

There has definitely been a shift in our culture concerning the use of this word. But there's a problem: Many in the Church (particularly leaders) haven't taken a lot of notice of this.

Now at the same time, we've seen public schools (and around 85% or so of Church kids go to public school) teach generations naturalistic (atheistic) evolution and millions of years as fact. Sadly, many church leaders and Christian academics have also accepted such as fact and accommodated this into Genesis. Actually, I would say evolution is just a story, meaning it's a fairy tale.

I've found many kids have the idea that they learn real history at public school when they're taught evolution in science classes. To most of them, evolution is true history. They think millions of years is true history. Even many Christian schools sadly teach this. But at church or in Bible class, they have Bible stories. Now, with the word story not really being understood as something true or real and because many have been told the Genesis "story" is not really true and must be interpreted as supporting evolution (which is supposedly true history), we now have generations who look on what the Bible relates as a whole is not necessarily true. What we read about events in Scripture is more equated with interesting tales somewhat like fairy tales. So for many, the Bible is just a storybook, but they learn real history (evolution) at school.

THEOLOGY — MARCH 3

I do understand the word story is used in a number of the great old hymns. I love those hymns like: "Tell Me the Old, Old Story."

Or one of my favorites of all time is "I heard an old, old story / How a Savior came from glory / How He gave His life on Calvary / To save a wretch like me."

The context of those hymns is obviously teaching the "story" is true! So I'm not advocating at all that we stop using them. I love singing them, and many are full of great teaching, telling us truth in regard to God, His Word, and the saving gospel.

However, because we live at a time when the Bible as a book of history, particularly in Genesis, is vehemently attacked, I want to suggest that when we are teaching the Bible to children, teens, and adults, we emphasize it is a book of history.

I even suggest, instead of saying to those we're teaching that we are going to read a story in the Bible, we should consider saying something like, "We are going to read an account from the Bible." And explain that account means it is real history; this really happened. Christianity is based in real history. You could use terms like "record of" or "historical account" and so on.

When I am giving presentations to children, I tell them the Bible is the history book of the universe. I then get them to say it out loud, "The Bible is the history book of the universe." Yes, it's God's history book to us. It's important for them to understand that God's Word is the only infallible history book we have. And because the history is true, the gospel message based in that history is true.

That's why we help make this history come alive at our two attractions—the Ark Encounter and Creation Museum. These attractions present the Bible as history and give answers through the exhibits to the many questions people have about the accounts in the Bible, particularly in Genesis.

Atheists mock the Bible and call it a book of myths. Even many Christian leaders claim Genesis is mythology. No, Genesis is history, and we can use passages from the New Testament where Jesus quoted Genesis as history to reinforce this such as Matthew 19 and Mark 10. We can also use passages from the Apostle Paul in Romans 5 and 1 Corinthians 15.

The Bible is not just a book of stories; it's a book of history. Even if you use the word story, I urge you to explain you are using this to mean it's a real story, or history.

The sum of your word is truth, and every one of your righteous rules endures forever. Princes persecute me without cause, but my heart stands in awe of your words. I rejoice at your word like one who finds great spoil (Psalm 119:160–162).

> **Because of the attack on the Bible as a book of history, we really need to focus on the fact that the Bible is a book of history.**

MARCH 4
Zechariah 1:3

We Need an Uncompromising Stand on the Bible's Authority

Is compromise on Genesis akin to harlotry? The Bible uses strong language to describe any form of compromise with worldly thinking. And it doesn't just apply to the ancient Israelites.

Hosea 4:12 says, *My people inquire of a piece of wood, and their walking [wooden] staff gives them oracles. For a spirit of whoredom has led them astray, and they have left their God to play the whore.* Hosea used strong language against his fellow Israelites, calling them harlots because they had violated their vows to remain faithful to the One true God. Is it possible that Christians today, and particularly Christian leaders—in their zeal to make Christianity more enticing—are actually "playing the harlot" too?

Born-again Christians who love the Lord, preach the gospel, and insist on the inerrancy of Scriptures are saddened when they read how the Israelites compromised God's Word as they embraced more and more pagan beliefs (including idolatry) from the nations around them. God calls such compromise "harlotry." Over and over again, Scripture gives clear instructions concerning the worship of the one true God, and it condemns compromise with pagan beliefs as harlotry (Jeremiah 3:6).

Because of our sin nature, God knows how we humans are more likely to be influenced by that which is wrong than that which is right. God describes our hearts this way: *The heart is deceitful above all things, and desperately sick; who can understand it?* (Jeremiah 17:9).

Despite all the miracles many Israelites saw God do for them, many compromised their worship of God with idolatry and pagan rituals. As we read about this in the books of Jeremiah, Ezekiel, Hosea, and Amos, we shake our heads and say, "How could they do this? How could they play such harlotry, as God describes it?"

But I'm also reminded of the verse, *And there is nothing new under the sun* (Ecclesiastes 1:9). You see, ever since Adam sinned, man's sin-cursed nature hasn't changed. Certainly, those who are born again, as the Bible defines this, know that their sins are forgiven and that they will spend eternity with the Lord. Nonetheless, such Christians still have to deal with their sin nature daily while in these sin-cursed bodies. Even the Apostle Paul had this battle: *For I know that nothing good dwells in me, that is, in my flesh. For I have the desire to do what is right, but not the ability to carry it out. For I do not do the good I want, but the evil I do not want is what I keep on doing* (Romans 7:18–19).

All Christians have feet of clay. No matter how dedicated to the Lord and His Word, all are susceptible to being drawn into error because of our sin nature. Indeed, we are all guilty of "harlotry" (idolatry) to one degree or another every time we choose sin and love the world rather than loving God and following His rule (1 John 2:15).

Because of man's fallen nature, God frequently gave instructions to the Israelites such as this: *You shall not make gods of silver to be with me, nor shall you make for yourselves gods of gold* (Exodus 20:23).

In fact, because man is so likely to compromise God's Word, God gave further instructions in verse 25: *If you make me an altar of stone, you shall not build it of hewn stones; for if you wield your tool on it you profane it.*

APOLOGETICS

MARCH 4

Why is that? In Genesis 3, we read that the serpent said to Eve: *For God knows that when you eat of it your eyes will be opened, and you will be like God, knowing good and evil* (Genesis 3:5). Human nature is that we want to replace the true God with our own god, so God told the Israelites not to use any tool on the stone for an altar. In other words, He did not want them to be tempted to make a god or to compromise.

But sadly, the Israelites gave in to this temptation and did adopt the false gods of the pagan nations. They compromised God's Word. And we find how God responded:

He has withdrawn from them (Hosea 5:6).

I will send a famine on the land ... of hearing the words of the LORD (Amos 8:11).

I despise your feasts. ... Burnt offerings and grain offerings, I will not accept them. ... to the melody of your harps I will not listen (Amos 5:21–23).

My people are destroyed for lack of knowledge. ... I also will forget your children (Hosea 4:6).

Yes, their children rebelled against the Lord—the parents lost their children to the pagan world. As for all their offerings, praise, and worship, God did not hear or accept them.

I submit that there "is nothing new under the sun." The same situation, albeit portrayed in a different way and using different terminology, is happening today. Much of the Church today is really no different when we consider this sin of harlotry.

When I debated Bill Nye in February 2014, he was not just defending molecules-to-man evolution and millions of years; he was also defending naturalism. Naturalism is the belief that the whole universe, including the earth and all life, is explained by natural processes. This is Bill Nye's religion—the religion of the secularists.

Sadly, many Christians have adopted evolutionary geology, biology, astronomy, and anthropology, along with belief in millions of years, and they have mixed such beliefs with God's Word. Because such beliefs are founded on an anti-biblical, anti-God worldview, I humbly submit that such is harlotry no different than that of the Israelites.

I also state that salvation is conditional upon faith in Christ as the Scriptures teach, and not upon one's view on the age of the earth or evolutionary ideas. Certainly, many born-again Christians have adopted evolutionary beliefs, which doesn't mean they can't be saved. But they have played harlotry with man's religion that opposes God's Word, and they have undermined the authority of the Word of God.

What happened to the Israelites is happening today. There is a famine of hearing the Word of the Lord in our Western world, as many church leaders water down the teaching of the Word and adopt the world's views in regard to marriage, abortion, and so on.

We are losing most of the coming generations from the Church. Yes, churches all across our Western world have emotion-touching music and well-run programs—but in many instances God is not hearing them because they have not taken an uncompromising stand on the Bible's authority.

> **I end with this challenge that God gave to the Israelites: "Therefore say to them, Thus says the LORD of hosts: Return to me, says the LORD of hosts, and I will return to you" (Zechariah 1:3).**

MARCH 5
Revelation 21:4

Why Do Children Suffer?

It's heartbreaking to see children suffer, and our minds can wander to the inevitable question, "Why is someone so innocent suffering so badly?"

When we allow God's Word to inform our thoughts, we see a different picture. All children—in fact, all people—suffer to one degree or another because humanity is under the curse of sin (Romans 5:12). And no one is innocent, *for all have sinned and fall short of the glory of God* (Romans 3:23).

Because we, in Adam, committed high treason against the God of creation (when Adam took the fruit and disobeyed God's command), we deserve nothing. We don't even deserve to exist. But God, in His mercy, provided a way for us to be redeemed and brought back to a right relationship with God.

That's why God's Word emphasizes that all humans face the judgment of death. *It is appointed for man to die once, and after that comes judgment* (Hebrews 9:27). It's also important to understand that the whole creation suffers because of our sin in Adam. *For we know that the whole creation has been groaning together in the pains of childbirth until now* (Romans 8:22). By placing upon us the judgment of death, God provided the way for His Son to become a man (the God-man) and pay the penalty for our sin by dying on the Cross. He rose from the dead, conquering death, and provides a free gift of salvation for those who will receive it. Actually, without death, we couldn't be redeemed.

Now it's also true that some people hurt more than others physically, mentally, emotionally, and spiritually. Does that necessarily mean their suffering is a direct result of a specific sin? Of course not! In Luke 13, Jesus spoke about 18 people who were killed when a tower fell on them. *Or those eighteen on whom the tower in Siloam fell and killed them: do you think that they were worse offenders than all the others who lived in Jerusalem? No, I tell you; but unless you repent, you will all likewise perish* (Luke 13:4–5).

Those 18 weren't killed because they were worse sinners; it was their time to die. Jesus uses this to remind us that we are all under the judgment of death because of sin, and so all will face death. This is a stark reminder to make sure we have done what Jesus said: "Repent."

In other words, that was their time to die, so make sure you have received the free gift of salvation so you know with certainty that when you die, you will go to be present with the Lord for eternity. *But these are written so that you may believe that Jesus is the Christ, the Son of God, and that by believing you may have life in his name* (John 20:31).

We often hear news media discussing the top reasons for death. They list cancer, heart attacks, etc., as some of the top reasons people die. But they miss the most important fact that the top reason (the only reason) for death is sin! People don't want to admit they're sinners as that means they need to be reconciled to God.

Suffering is a result of living in this groaning creation affected by sin and the curse. We know suffering arose because of human sin. Suffering is not God's fault; it's mankind's fault! It's a sad reminder of how bad sin is and what it's done to the world. And we can grieve as we see the results of our sin. We can also be reminded that because we are responsible for the groaning creation, we have a responsibility to do whatever we can to help others who suffer.

APOLOGETICS

We can sometimes see specific ways God uses someone's suffering. How they cope with pain can be a witness to others who then listen to the gospel and receive the free gift of salvation. Think of people who have suffered, such as Joni Eareckson Tada. Yet even through her disability, Joni has had a spiritual impact on millions of people. Sometimes, God uses someone's suffering in their own life to bring them to Christ.

People sometimes look back over their lives and realize that, though they did not understand while they were suffering, they can now see the mighty hand of God working in marvelous ways through their suffering. Many times, we don't understand why someone suffers, but there's no doubt that God has purposes that are beyond our understanding on this earth.

For my thoughts are not your thoughts, neither are your ways my ways, declares the Lord (Isaiah 55:8).

God taught Job this lesson. When Job tried to show that he had been a righteous person and therefore really didn't deserve what happened to him, God stepped in to show Job that he knew nothing compared to God's infinite knowledge and wisdom. As God used various aspects of the creation to help Job see how little he knew and understood, Job began to recognize who God is. And we read:

Then Job answered the Lord and said: "I know that you can do all things, and that no purpose of yours can be thwarted. 'Who is this that hides counsel without knowledge?' Therefore I have uttered what I did not understand, things too wonderful for me, which I did not know. 'Hear, and I will speak; I will question you, and you make it known to me.' I had heard of you by the hearing of the ear, but now my eye sees you; therefore I despise myself, and repent in dust and ashes" (Job 42:1–6).

As hard as it is and it's awfully hard sometimes, we all need to step back and let God be God. But we have to understand the consequences of our sin. God as a righteous God had to judge sin. But in doing so, He Himself paid the penalty for our sin even though we deserved nothing. Wow.

Living through horrendous suffering—or seeing loved ones hurting—can be very hard. But Paul offers comfort: *For I consider that the sufferings of this present time are not worth comparing with the glory that is to be revealed to us* (Romans 8:18).

Our life on this earth is so short compared to eternity. Yet it's true that we struggle through this life, and our hearts go out to those who struggle more than others. We know that those who have trusted Christ have a beautiful future to look forward to when one day *[God] will wipe away every tear from their eyes, and death shall be no more, neither shall there be mourning, nor crying, nor pain anymore, for the former things have passed away* (Revelation 21:4). What a day that will be!

Only God's Word can give us answers about suffering – and offer comfort.

MARCH 6
Genesis 3:21

Origin of Clothing

In 2016, just after the Ark Encounter opened, I was showing Bill Nye, with his and our Answers in Genesis video teams, through the Ark exhibits. It turned into what we call "The Second Debate" (available on YouTube and Answers TV).

At one stage, I asked Bill Nye why humans wear clothes. He replied that there are hot places in the world where people don't wear clothes. I then told him it was hot that day and would he therefore take his clothes off? He looked rather shocked at what I said. I then went on to explain that humans wear clothes, but animals do not. So why is it that humans wear clothes? I then used this as a stepping stone to explain the saving gospel message. I told him humans wear clothes because of sin. He said he was skeptical that was so.

Evolutionists have written papers about when humans supposedly invented clothing. For instance, on April 25, 2023, a paper was published in the *Smithsonian* Magazine titled, "When Did Clothing Originate?" The author used the evolution story (yes, it's a fairy tale), discussing archaeological evidence based on man's fallible dating methods to suggest clothing was invented hundreds of thousands of years ago by humans dealing with the cold. In another paper published by "Science Alert" in 2021, the author suggested humans invented clothing 120,000 years ago.

Secular evolutionists, of course, must explain everything in the light of their atheistic worldview of millions of years and slow and gradual evolution, concluding that, at some point, humans evolved the intelligence to fashion clothes from animal skins and other available materials.

Now, humans making clothing is not a problem to explain from a biblical worldview. God's Word gives us the true account of the origin of clothing going back about 6,000 years. And it really does help us explain the gospel as I explained to Bill Nye on that day in 2016.

The first clothes humans (Adam and Eve) wore were made from fig leaves: *[The woman] took of its fruit and ate, and she also gave some to her husband who was with her, and he ate. Then the eyes of both were opened, and they knew that they were naked. And they sewed fig leaves together and made themselves loincloths* (Genesis 3:6–7).

But God gave Adam and Eve different clothes: *And the LORD God made for Adam and for his wife garments of skins and clothed them* (Genesis 3:21).

Clothing was invented not because we were cold, as evolutionists suggest, but because of sin and shame. Mankind was originally created naked and unashamed, but after their sin, they tried to cover that sin and shame with fig leaves. But God Himself made them clothes when He killed an animal—the first animal death in God's "very good" creation. These clothes and the sacrifice and spilled blood of that animal (or animals) covered over their sin and shame. God taught Adam and Eve that they couldn't cover their sin. Only God could do that.

When God made clothes from coats of skins, He was setting up the sacrificial system. He killed animals—the first blood sacrifice as a covering for their sin, a picture of what was to come in Jesus Christ, the lamb of God who came to take away the sin of the world.

APOLOGETICS

Now God's Word tells us that "without the shedding of blood there is no forgiveness of sins" (Hebrews 9:22). Because death was the penalty for sin, there had to be the giving of life (shedding of blood). Leviticus 17:11 states, "the life of the flesh is in the blood." Blood represents life. That's why God had the Israelites sacrifice animals over and over again, so they would understand this.

But "it is impossible for the blood of bulls and goats to take away sins" (Hebrews 10:4). An animal's sacrifice can't take away our sin because humans are not animals. Humans are made in the image of God. A man (Adam) brought sin and death into the world, so a man would need to pay the penalty for sin. All humans are descendants of Adam and Eve. But all humans are sinners.

A sinner can't pay the penalty for sin. So God stepped into human history in the person of His Son, to be born of a virgin, the sinless perfect Son of God. He became a man as the God-man. He lived a sinless life and died on a Cross. But He rose from the dead. That means He has ultimate power, the power over death. He suffered the penalty for our sin and paid our debt on that Cross. He offers a free gift of salvation to those who will repent of the sin and receive this free gift.

The origin of clothing is so much more amazing than humans stumbling upon leather one day: It's a picture of the gospel message, pointing us to the One who would one day take away the sins of the world through His death and Resurrection (John 1:29). To receive that free gift of salvation, we must repent and believe (Romans 10:9).

And as an aside: the origin of clothing is yet another way the evolutionary story and the biblical account of history clash. You can't harmonize the two! You can't add millions of years of death before man into Scripture. Christians believing in millions of years undermine the authority of God's Word and undermine the foundation of the gospel message. Our sin is the cause of death! God didn't use death for millions of years before man when He created life! The Bible—the history book of the universe written by the eyewitness to creation—is the true account of history, and evolutionary millions of years ideas are just fairy tales.

By the way, secular evolutionists wear clothes. From an atheistic worldview, morality is subjective and ultimately means anyone can do whatever they want if they can get away with it! I wonder how long it will be before politicians decide clothing is optional! You think they wouldn't do this? People thought they wouldn't try to legalize pedophilia either, but now we see moves to do that! Remember, man has a sinful, wicked heart and wants to do whatever is right in his own eyes! And the devil wants to implement the opposite of what God has ordained.

> **We need to always proclaim the truth of God's Word and the saving gospel with boldness in this increasingly evil culture.**

MARCH 7

Acts 17:26

The Human Race

If all Christians truly understood what it means to have a consistent biblical worldview, then in many instances, they would use different terminology than the world that can open up doors to enable a powerful witness to people.

Take the issue of so-called "races." Most people have really been impacted by the secular world concerning this issue. And, sadly, because most Christian leaders have not taught the history in Genesis 1–11 as the foundation for our Christian worldview, most Christians have no idea how to deal with the issues of "races" and racism and often just regurgitate what the world teaches.

I suggest if Christians started using terminology consistent with a biblical worldview found in Genesis, this could open up all sorts of conversations about the Christian faith. And this would be a part of Christians being light as they should. For instance, consider the following:

The term races. If the Bible's history is true (and it is), then there were only two people at the beginning of human history: Adam and Eve.

Thus it is written, "The first man Adam became a living being"; the last Adam became a life-giving spirit (1 Corinthians 15:45).

The man called his wife's name Eve, because she was the mother of all living (Genesis 3:20).

Because all humans are descendants of Adam and Eve, biologically there can only be one race of humans, not different races.

Imagine what would happen if any time people talked about races, the Christian explained there is only one race. This would give an opportunity to explain the gospel because we're all descendants of Adam, thus all sinners (all people) need to receive the free gift of salvation. And one can also explain that scientists studying genetics (e.g., Human Genome Project) found there's only one human race.

Maybe the next time you fill out those forms at the doctor's office, etc., where the question is asked, "What race are you?" write in "Adam's race." Who knows what conversations that could lead to.

Did you know humans are all the same basic color, just different shades of brown? The main pigment in a person's skin is melanin, a brown pigment. Because of the information in our genes (in our DNA), humans exhibit a whole range of skin shades from dark brown to light brown. Technically, there are no "black" or "white" people. Everyone (unless one is an albino who has a lack of pigment and thus medical issues) is a colored person. This could be a real conversation starter if someone was talking about black people and/or white people, and they were challenged that there aren't any truly black or white people. People don't have different skin colors but different shades of the one main color (brown). Again, this could lead to conversations about human history from the Bible.

When the human genome project in 2000 mapped the human genome after collecting samples of human DNA from different groups of people all over the world, the scientists involved publicly stated there was only one human race. It was the event of the tower of Babel that resulted in different groups of people moving

APOLOGETICS — MARCH 7

away from each other, forming different nations. Thus, there are not different "races" but different people groups. When someone is discussing what they think are different "races," they need to be told there is only one race but different people groups. Once again, this conversation could lead to talking about the history in the Bible about Adam, the origin of sin, the promise of the Savior, and so on.

I've had many people tell me they brought their relatives to the Ark Encounter and Creation Museum attractions. I then ask if they brought eight billion people with them. They look perplexed, but then I explain that all humans are related to each other, and they brought their close relatives to the attractions. All humans are one family, all descendants of Adam and Eve. This means all humans are sinners and all are in need of salvation. Challenging people concerning the right terminology from a worldview built on God's Word really can open up conversations about the Bible and the saving gospel.

Also, when Christians understand that everyone is related, it should make them realize that we need to pray for our lost relatives, that they would hear the gospel. It's convicting to realize that people we don't like (including many of our politicians) are our relatives. They are all members of the human family, and all need the gospel.

Think about what a difference it would make if children's Christian books represented the true history of the human race even in the illustrations. Most illustrated Christian children's books I've seen have Adam and Eve looking so-called "Caucasian white." But it would make much more sense that Adam and Eve were middle brown, with genetic diversity to enable their offspring to have the potential of a large range of skin shades from dark to light. That's why in children's books produced by Answers in Genesis we have Adam and Eve looking middle brown, and Noah's family that were on the ark having a range of skin shades.

In a way, Acts 17:26 sums all this up: *And he made from one man every nation of mankind to live on all the face of the earth, having determined allotted periods and the boundaries of their dwelling place.*

Because we are all one race—Adam's race—we are all sinners, and all in need of salvation. That's why the gospel message is for every human being on earth from every people group. And it's why God saves people out of every group.

Then I saw another angel flying directly overhead, with an eternal gospel to proclaim to those who dwell on earth, to every nation and tribe and language and people (Revelation 14:6).

After this I looked, and behold, a great multitude that no one could number, from every nation, from all tribes and peoples and languages, standing before the throne and before the Lamb, clothed in white robes, with palm branches in their hands (Revelation 7:9).

> **When we talk about the one human race, it can really pave the way for proclaiming the truth of the gospel.**

MARCH 8
Proverbs 30:5-6

Interpretation of Scripture

I realize the following statement could easily be taken out of context from what I'm about to communicate, and that some people no doubt will be very upset with me for saying it.

I believe that what those who compromise God's Word in Genesis with evolution/millions do is similar to what cults do to the Bible. Now before people get too upset, I recognize those who believe in the teachings of a cult cannot be Christians. However, I recognize there are true Christians who believe in millions of years and evolution. Now I do believe they are compromising and thus undermining the authority of Scripture, but I'm not saying they are not Christians.

My point is this: Anyone can force ideas into Scripture and claim they can interpret the Scripture in a particular way to fit their ideas, no matter how wrong they are. We are, after all, fallible, sinful human beings. Many times, we don't even recognize how our particular presuppositions cause us to ignore the obvious and believe something that is incorrect. Those in cults who deny the deity of Christ or many other orthodox Christian beliefs do this all the time.

Now why would I dare to say there is any similarity at all with those Christians who compromise Genesis and those people in cults? Let me explain it this way. I was being interviewed on radio by a minister who asked if I accepted that Christians can have different views of baptism, eschatology, speaking in tongues, Sabbath day, and a number of other issues. He said there are different Christian denominations that have differences in regard to theology in various areas. I acknowledged that this was so. He then said that, in the same way, Christians can have different views on Genesis.

Now, this is where I disagreed. I explained it this way. When Christians argue about different views of baptism, eschatology, speaking in tongues, and other such issues, they are primarily arguing FROM Scripture. They will say things like, "Scripture here states this." And the person they are arguing with might respond, "Yes, but over here, it states this." And so, the arguments continue. Mostly though, they are arguing FROM Scripture to try to justify their particular stand on an issue. And obviously, they can't all have the correct interpretation! But provided this doesn't affect major doctrines, Christians can live with each other and those differences. In a sense, they can agree to disagree because they are arguing using exegesis.

But, when Christians have different views of Genesis, they are primarily arguing from outside of Scripture taking beliefs TO Scripture. Mostly, they are trying to fit man's ideas of evolution and millions of years (based in naturalism) into the Bible. As they do this, they invent all sorts of creative ways of trying to fit such beliefs into Scripture, resulting in positions like the gap theory, theistic evolution, progressive creation, framework hypothesis, and so on. The main motive for these positions is not exegesis (out of), but eisegesis (into). They are trying to force beliefs from outside of Scripture onto Scripture.

There's no way you get millions of years FROM Scripture. There's no way you could ever get the idea of apelike creatures evolving into humans from Scripture. There's no way you could get the big bang idea of stars supposedly forming millions of years ago, then the sun and then the earth as a hot molten blob, from Scripture.

THEOLOGY

Now, this is the serious problem. Those who compromise Genesis are using beliefs from outside of Scripture to try to force them into Scripture and then reinterpret the words of Scripture to claim they fit with their beliefs. I assert that this is an undermining of the authority of Scripture. It's also an attack on the character of God when you understand that to believe in millions of years is to believe that death and diseases like cancer, as one sees in the fossil record, existed before man and before man sinned. God called everything He made as "very good" after He made man! Believing in millions of years would mean God called cancer, death, other diseases, and suffering "very good." No, the Bible makes it clear our sin is responsible for death, disease, and suffering, and why it's now a groaning world (Romans 8:22) because of sin.

I've had many Christian leaders who believe in millions of years tell me that it's just my interpretation of Scripture to say the universe is only thousands of years old. They tell me we all interpret Scripture, and their interpretation is valid.

It is true we all interpret what we read because we have presuppositions concerning the type of literature, the meaning of words in context, and so on. So, yes, we all interpret the words in Genesis, so whose interpretation then is correct?

My father taught me to always take Scripture the way it was meant to be taken. There are different sorts of literature in the Bible including historical narrative, poetic literature (the Psalms), apocalyptic literature, etc. I was taught to use the grammatical-historical interpretive method, which means to interpret the words according to the type of literature, language, words in context, and so on, searching for what the original author intended. We are to carefully observe the text, understand that context is key, look for clarity of Scripture, compare Scripture with Scripture, deal with classification of the text (type of literature), and search out the Church's historical view.

Now Genesis is written as historical narrative which seems to be structured on the recurrence of the Hebrew phrase *eleh toledoth* ("This is the book of the genealogy of . . ." or "This is the history of . . ."). This occurs 11 times throughout the book: six times in Genesis 1–11 and five times in chapters 12–50. Clearly, the author intended that both sections should be interpreted in the same way—as historical narrative. The New Testament treats Genesis 1–11 as historical narrative. At least 25 New Testament passages refer directly to the early chapters of Genesis, so we need to interpret Genesis literally. But what do I mean by "literally"? I mean naturally. If it's history, read it as history. If it's poetry, read it as poetry knowing it can use simile, metaphor, and figurative language.

But Genesis 1-11 must be read and interpreted as real history. And when we do, it is easy to understand and is in total conflict with man's evolutionary beliefs. *Every word of God proves true; he is a shield to those who take refuge in him. Do not add to his words, lest he rebuke you and you be found a liar* (Proverbs 30:5–6).

As you read Genesis, make sure you are letting God's Word speak to you and that you are not trying to impose outside ideas on the text.

MARCH 9
Amos 5:23

What Does God Reveal About "True Worship" That Pleases Him?

I love to worship God through music. At the Ark Encounter and Creation Museum, our resident artist, TrueSong (they are so great), performs concerts at these attractions on a regular basis. I join them on the piano at times, although I keep telling them that I'm a speaker, not a musician. The gospel is presented, and people worship God through music. I love it.

Many churches now place a heavy emphasis on praise and worship music in their services. But I want to express a concern. While God loves good music, it's important to make sure our priorities line up with Scripture. What does God reveal about "true worship" that pleases Him? One of my closest friends was Answers in Genesis' songwriter and singer, Buddy Davis. I encouraged Buddy over the years to produce CDs of the many songs he has composed and presented at concerts at the Creation Museum and churches around the world. Having said that, I want to address what I see as a problem—something that troubles me. I realize that when you begin to talk about music, it can evoke very emotional responses. But I don't want to address music styles or content in this article (not that such is not important). I believe something else needs to be addressed.

I am in a rather interesting position to view what is happening in much of the Church. I have traveled for over 30 years across the United States and to other parts of the world speaking at conferences and churches. I get to see patterns from a big-picture perspective. My observation holds true across denominations and national boundaries (with some exceptions, of course). I would like to suggest that in many instances—particularly from my personal observation in the larger churches—music has become the dominant part of church services, and the teaching of God's Word has become less of a priority. The same is true in certain Bible conferences, particularly those geared for young people. Let me share just some of my observations. I encourage you to consider them carefully.

There is what they call a "praise and worship" time, with a band usually on stage. The congregation, or audience, is asked to stand and sing for 30 to 40 minutes—sometimes for an hour or so. As I look around the room, I often find that many people are not singing. Many of the songs are sung over and over and over again. When people finally sit for a sermon or teaching, this time is often much less than the music. And many seem tired and distracted. Many times, the band's words cannot be understood. You can recognize them only if they are shown on the screen.

Let me share a couple of personal experiences that show how this mindset can hinder the teaching of God's Word. Sometimes a pastor says something like, "We tried to cut the praise and worship time so you could have the 50 minutes you wanted to speak, but I can't really control what the worship pastor will do." And so, I often end up with much less time than what I prepared for and what is needed and agreed to. Now, to be sure, not all churches are like this, and I'm not saying churches should not have a "praise and worship" time. But if young people and adults get the idea that music is more important than the study of God's Word, where will they and their churches be spiritually in the coming years?

Biblical teaching and worshipful music do not have to be in competition. When properly done, both are important aspects of true "praise and worship" that glorifies and pleases the Lord. I have had many pastors,

CHURCH

particularly youth pastors, tell me that music is where the kids "are at" today, and music helps keep them in church and attract others. But when I've been given opportunity to speak to these young people, I find they are filled with questions and doubts about God's Word, and they desperately want answers that can't be found in a praise chorus.

Let me give a specific example. I was asked to speak at a service for young people. I sat through almost an hour of loud music and couldn't understand most of the words. Then I was asked to speak for only about 20 minutes because, "Young people can't sit for long and listen to talks these days." Then I could have a question time afterward. So I did my best in 20 minutes and asked for questions. Those young people bombarded me: Where did Cain get his wife? How do you know the Bible is true? Why doesn't God show Himself to us? What about carbon dating? How do you explain dinosaurs? How could Noah fit the animals on the ark? We went on for over an hour. Afterward, the youth pastor said, "I've never seen them so interested. I never knew Billy could even ask a question, let alone the one he asked. What happened?"

What happened? Well, the beliefs of these young people are being challenged at public school. From my experience, I know many of their doubts, and from the research we conducted, we know that two-thirds of these young people will leave the Church by college age. So I began giving them answers to help them understand how we know God's Word is true.

Many church leaders have adopted music styles simply to attract people, instead of focusing on the things that most please God. What's the point of all this? I believe many church leaders have adopted music styles simply to attract people, instead of focusing on the things that most please God: music and vital teaching that most meet the flock's needs and glorify the Lord. People want to hear solid biblical truth and answers to the skeptical questions of this age. They want to know how to live Christ-honoring lives and proclaim and defend the gospel to people who are thoroughly "evolutionized."

Now, the Bible does not prescribe how much time should be allotted to teaching and music. But in a world that increasingly attacks the Bible's authority, I submit that the pastor, more than ever, needs to equip His people with biblical truths so that they can function as true Christ followers (2 Timothy 3:16–17). Furthermore, many churches tell their adults and young people that they can believe in evolution and history over millions of years, as long as they just trust Jesus. Or they totally ignore this topic. Yet I believe that today's attack on God's Word is the same strategy Satan employed in Genesis 3 when he asked Eve, "Did God really say…?" This attack on the Bible's trustworthiness is destroying the coming generations. Meanwhile, church members get together and have long "praise and worship" times that relegate Bible teaching to a much lesser role than music.

But is God hearing many of these churches? If we are compromising God's Word and not teaching and obeying His Word as we should, is it possible that God would say to these modern churches what He did to the Israelites of old? *Take away from me the noise of your songs; to the melody of your harps I will not listen* (Amos 5:23). *Has the Lord as great delight in burnt offerings and sacrifices, as in obeying the voice of the Lord? Behold, to obey is better than sacrifice, and to listen than the fat of rams* (1 Samuel 15:22).

> **By God's grace, may we get our priorities straight and help people to worship Him as He deserves – giving primacy to His Word in all aspects of our lives and church services.**

MARCH 10
Genesis 1:26

Are Humans Any Different to Animals?

It may seem like a radical idea, but from a biblical worldview I want to challenge Christians.

When students are taught in biology classes about the kingdoms of life, they're usually taught six different kingdoms, including the animal kingdom.

I am going to suggest we don't just use the system the secular world uses, particularly if there's a very important reason for making such a change. I believe there's a very important reason because of how students are being indoctrinated in evolutionary dogma that has great bearing on understanding humanity's place in this world.

When discussing abortion, I've had a number of secularists say something like, "Humans are just animals. We get rid of spare cats, so we can get rid of spare children in their mother's wombs."

Over the past 40 years, I've talked about the creation/evolution issue and warned that the more students believe they're just animals that evolved from apelike creatures, the more they'll view humans as having no more value than animals. The more human life is devalued, the more we'll see abortion and euthanasia as just getting rid of a living being having no more value than an animal.

A good example of how people are being brainwashed to believe humans are just animals comes from a local zoo. Think about all the children with their parents visiting an ape enclosure and being told on the signs that they're visiting their "family." As they read the sign, they're told, "There is no sharp line dividing us from the chimpanzees and the other apes.... We humans are a part of, and not separate from, the animal kingdom." Thus they're indoctrinated to believe they're of no more value than a chimp.

This is why we have Ararat Ridge Zoo at the Ark Encounter so we can teach guests to think about animals from a biblical worldview perspective. We also conduct live animal programs at the Ark and the Creation Museum (where we have a small zoo). We encourage Christian families to come to the Ark and Creation Museum to learn about animals so they won't be led astray by false evolutionary teaching that permeates zoos and museums, etc.

From a biblical worldview perspective, humans are different from animals. Only human beings are made in the image of God. *Let us make man in our image, after our likeness* (Genesis 1:26).

God made animals differently, *And God said, "Let the earth bring forth living creatures according to their kinds—livestock and creeping things and beasts of the earth according to their kinds"* (Genesis 1:24). When God created Adam, He brought animals to him to name to show that there was no one like him, as none of the animals were made in God's image, *But for Adam there was not found a helper fit for him* (Genesis 2:20).

Because the emphasis today that man is just an animal affects people's view of humanity and how they view various moral issues, I suggest Christians use the criterion "made in the image of God," for an additional kingdom. This would place man in his own kingdom, the human kingdom. We need our children to understand that humans are special and made in God's image, whereas animals are not made in God's image.

This will greatly help as we teach about the abortion issue. Right from fertilization, there exists a human being made in God's image. So abortion is not just killing an animal but killing a human being made in the image of

SCIENCE **MARCH 10**

God. And remember, God said, *You shall not murder* (Exodus 20:13). Also, when teaching about euthanasia, we must make sure all people understand that humans are made in God's image no matter how old they are or what problems they have.

God's Word never changes. But models that man has devised to understand the world, classify animals, etc., are subject to change.

> **Because of the way the secular world is indoctrinating students to believe man is just another evolved animal, we should change the way we teach about human beings.**

MARCH 11
2 Peter 3:8

A Day Is Like a Thousand Years?

I have to admit it. Every time I hear someone say it, it drives me nuts. What am I referring to?

Over the past 40 years, as I've spoken all over the world, and I've had many people in churches come up and say something like, "But how can the days of creation in Genesis 1 be ordinary days when the Bible says a day is like a thousand years?" Ugh!

This is when I groan internally and then set out to explain the many problems with what they stated.

1. They are quoting a small section from 2 Peter 3:8. Now this is a passage from the New Testament, and you cannot use such a passage to determine the meaning of a Hebrew word. The meaning of a Hebrew word in Genesis (e.g., yom used for the word day in Genesis 1) depends on the Hebrew language. One needs to use a Hebrew lexicon (dictionary) to determine the meaning of a Hebrew word.

2. When I've been asked this question, I can't remember a time when the person asking actually quoted that passage correctly. They usually say, "But a day is like a thousand years." That is not what the Scripture states. Let's look at 2 Peter 3:8: *But do not overlook this one fact, beloved, that with the Lord one day is as a thousand years, and a thousand years as one day* (2 Peter 3:8). Now note that the text actually states, "With the Lord one day is as a thousand years." In other words, the reference is to God, telling us that to God a day is like a thousand years. God is not limited by natural processes and time. God is outside of time. He created time. So, to God, a day is no different than a thousand years because God exists in eternity and is not bound by time.

3. I notice they always seem to quote the first part of the verse and not the rest. After "with the Lord one day is as a thousand years," the verse continues, "And a thousand years as one day." Now this in essence cancels out the first section. The whole point is to God a day is like a thousand years, or a thousand years like a day. Again, it's because God is outside of time. So to God, a day or a thousand years doesn't make any difference in regard to time. Now humans are created in time, and we measure time by days and years. To humans, a thousand years is so much longer than one day. But that is not so for God.

4. Now let's look at the context of 2 Peter 3. The passage leading up to verse 8 starting in verse 3 states, *Knowing this first of all, that scoffers will come in the last days with scoffing, following their own sinful desires* (2 Peter 3:3). The passage is discussing the second coming of Christ, the last days, and the scoffers who scoff at Jesus coming again: *They will say, "Where is the promise of his coming? For ever since the fathers fell asleep, all things are continuing as they were from the beginning of creation"* (2 Peter 3:4). So these scoffers are saying that things just go on and on, so Jesus is obviously not coming back. The passage is teaching us that for those scoffers who believe Jesus isn't coming back again as things just seem to continue on and on, to God a day is no different than a thousand years. So humans think it's been a long time since Jesus said He was coming back again, but to God, it's not a long time because He is not bound by time.

5. Then we are told why Jesus hasn't come back yet: *The Lord is not slow to fulfill his promise as some count slowness, but is patient toward you, not wishing that any should perish, but that all should reach repentance*

APOLOGETICS — MARCH 11

(2 Peter 3:9). God will decide when He will return, but in the meantime, people need to hear the gospel as it's not His will "that any should perish."

6. Now think about this. I have found the main reason many Christians try to reinterpret the word day in Genesis and use this passage from 2 Peter 3 to justify this is that they really are trying to fit the false millions of years belief into Scripture. But how will making each day 1,000 years help accommodate millions of years—it won't!

7. I also note something else. The Hebrew word for day, yom, is used hundreds of times in the Old Testament, but I don't hear anyone questioning what those days mean by claiming a day is like a thousand years. So why is it that they only single out the use of the word day in Genesis 1? Again, it's because they're impacted by millions of years, and they're trying to fit long ages into Genesis 1. Do we ever hear anyone claiming Jonah was in the great fish for 3,000 years because a day is like a thousand years? Of course not.

8. Now, if we take Genesis 1 as written, and look at the context for the word day, yom, for each of the days of creation, we can come to no other conclusion than those days are ordinary approximately 24-hour days. When yom is qualified by night, evening, morning, or number, it always means an ordinary day. All six days have yom qualified by evening, morning, and number. Day one also qualifies yom with night, and day seven is qualified with a number. All seven days in Genesis 1 are ordinary days.

Now, can you see why it drives me nuts when people rather glibly say, "Oh, the days of creation aren't ordinary days as a day is like a thousand years"? I find most say this because they heard it from a friend or their pastor or Bible school teacher or read it somewhere. Once I explain what I've listed above to them, most realize they have not been thinking about this correctly at all.

By the way, Psalm 90:4 states something similar to 2 Peter 3:8: *For a thousand years in your sight are but as yesterday when it is past, or as a watch in the night.* This is teaching us that with God a thousand years is like a day or a watch in the night which was four hours. So God is not limited by time, as He is outside of time.

We must study God's Word carefully before making off-hand statements, because we humans are so quick to question God's Word as that's our propensity because of our sin nature.

MARCH 12
Luke 10:27

Our Planet Is Doomed!

I have sad news for you. The planet is doomed! Now, we can't ultimately fix the planet, despite all the rhetoric from politicians. And there's no hope for this planet as it is. God's Word tells us this planet will have all sorts of problems physically and politically until Christ returns. Then the planet will be judged by fire; a new heavens and earth will be created; and Christ will rule His eternal kingdom. So humans can't fix this planet—it's doomed in its current state.

And God did ordain government to maintain law and order—although governments have intruded on many issues (e.g., the definition of marriage) that are not part of their ordained role. I applaud Christians in politics who can be salt and light in the political arena, influence the culture for the Lord, and help maintain religious liberty so that we can freely share the gospel.

Well, it may surprise you, but I thought about this theme after I read what a reporter (who states he is a Christian) had written for a secular newspaper about a conference I once spoke at on race. The themes of my talks included race relations, racism, and prejudice. Along with my good friend Dr. Charles Ware (an African American Bible college president emeritus and leader of the organization Grace Relations), we based our presentations on our coauthored book, *One Race One Blood*. My presentations were also based on the same information seen in the exhibits at both the Creation Museum and Ark Encounter.

Now, the newspaper reporter was an African American man who stated that he was a "devout evangelical Christian." But he was lukewarm about the content presented at the conference he attended. Here's what the reporter wrote in his newspaper about what I taught that day: "While I respect many of Ham's religious views, his sessions generally veered from the advertised topic. He would discuss an unrelated (or tangentially related) topic for 10 minutes or so before appearing to remember that he was supposed to have been discussing race and racism."

Now to me, this reporter either didn't get the point I was making or didn't want to! I started my presentation by discussing what it means to build a truly Christian worldview using God's Word, and Genesis 1–11 in particular, as the foundation of that worldview. I was making the point that issues like gay "marriage," gender, abortion, and racism are not the real problems—they are actually the symptoms of a foundational problem.

In the conference, I pointed out that until Christians understand that the geological, biological, anthropological, and astronomical history in Genesis is foundational to our entire worldview, they will never be able to deal with any of the issues before us—such as racism, gay "marriage," abortion, etc. The reporter ended his column with, "In short, Ham's spiritual gaze was fixed beyond the sky to an ethereal future. Ware understood that people of color must endure an existential crisis on earth—in the here and now.... After sitting through the presentations, I was frustrated that there was no clear charge or challenge to dismantle the structural edifice of racism." Well, the point I try to make in my talks on racism is that there is no way to humanly fix the systems of this world in regard to racism! But there is a way to help "fix" each individual.

Regardless of what issue I'm addressing in public talks, one of the main points I make in all my presentations (in a variety of ways) is that we can't fix things (politically, socially, etc.) on this earth! And sadly, the majority

SCIENCE MARCH 12

of people are also doomed, but there's real hope! What we can do is proclaim the "fix" for each individual—and that "fix" is to respond to the gospel and build all of one's thinking on God's Word! And the more we see individuals building their thinking on God's Word, the more impact we will have on the culture. Each of us needs to recognize what it means that we sinned in Adam (Romans 5:12), committing high treason against the holy Creator God. We deserve God's wrath yet get grace: *He does not deal with us according to our sins, nor repay us according to our iniquities* (Psalm 103:10).

Just think of what God has done for each of us and what that means: *For while we were still weak, at the right time Christ died for the ungodly. For one will scarcely die for a righteous person—though perhaps for a good person one would dare even to die—but God shows his love for us in that while we were still sinners, Christ died for us. Since, therefore, we have now been justified by his blood, much more shall we be saved by him from the wrath of God. For if while we were enemies we were reconciled to God by the death of his Son, much more, now that we are reconciled, shall we be saved by his life. More than that, we also rejoice in God through our Lord Jesus Christ, through whom we have now received reconciliation* (Romans 5:6–11).

All I can say is, "Wow! God did this for me!" And He offers this free gift of salvation to all who will freely receive it! And responding to the gospel is something each individual must do on their own. We can't force people to receive God's free gift. And God doesn't force Himself on anyone. *For by grace you have been saved through faith. And this is not your own doing; it is the gift of God* (Ephesians 2:8).

Now, in what I think was a rather condescending statement, the reporter wrote, "There were two headliners: Ken Ham, who is white, and Dr. Charles Ware, who is black. (I should note that Ham explicitly rejects describing people by color, which is not all that uncommon among well-meaning people who endeavor to combat racism.)" But it's scientifically true that all humans are the same basic skin color from a brown pigment called melanin. There are no truly black or truly white people. That's why Dr. Ware puts it this way, "Ken Ham is of the lighter hue, I'm of the darker hue." In my talks, I explain how the various shades of melanin correspond to the genetic diversity God built into each human being. This is all part of understanding the event of the Tower of Babel that helped produce different ethnic/people groups—and understanding that all humans belong to one biological race. This is why the gospel is for each individual and is to be proclaimed to every tribe and nation.

Then I saw another angel flying directly overhead, with an eternal gospel to proclaim to those who dwell on earth, to every nation and tribe and language and people (Revelation 14:6).

We also deal with social issues and past injustices in our books, lectures, and exhibits inside the Ark Encounter and the Creation Museum. We deal with these issues by presenting the truth of God's Word and the gospel so that each individual—from every tribe and nation—will be challenged to respond and affirm the words of Jesus. The planet may be doomed, but let's do all we can to share the truth of God's Word and the gospel with every tribe and nation.

You shall love the Lord your God with all your heart and with all your soul and with all your strength and with all your mind, and your neighbor as yourself (Luke 10:27).

> **Please pray with me that many will respond and not be doomed to eternity in hell but will be saved for eternity with their Creator God.**

MARCH 13
Galatians 3:24

True Love from a Biblical Perspective

I have heard a number of people, including some pastors, claim that Christians should never be negative. To them, showing love is not saying anything negative to people. But showing love for a Christian is to warn people about sin and its consequences, including the eternal consequences of separation from God in a place of judgment called hell.

I've heard LGBTQ people claim Christians give hate speech because such Christians, based on God's Word, teach people that God made only two genders of humans—male and female—and there's only one true marriage—the one created by God, a man (male) and a woman (female). Some Christians claim that to tell LGBTQ people such things is not loving and means they are promoting negativity. But what is the truth concerning such matters?

I remember as a child hearing the schoolmaster warning us about things we should not do unless we wanted to be disciplined. There sure were a lot of rules—a lot of negativity from the schoolmaster. Don't do this or that, and if you do this, you will be disciplined this way, and so on. I wondered, "Why so many rules?"

Then as I read the Bible, I understood that God gave the Israelites numerous laws (rules). In fact, there are a lot of warnings and "do nots" throughout Scripture.

Galatians 3:24 in the King James Version reads, *Wherefore the law was our schoolmaster to bring us unto Christ, that we might be justified by faith.* We needed our "schoolmaster" to understand what is right and wrong. But we have a problem called sin. (No wonder the schoolmaster had a lot of rules for us, as he knew we weren't perfect and were liable to do things we shouldn't.)

The purpose of the law was to expose our sin (Romans 3:23 says "all have sinned") and to show us that we can't save ourselves since we can't keep the law perfectly. The law was given to point us toward the righteousness that comes through faith in Christ alone. As the Apostle Paul states in Romans 5:1, *Therefore, since we have been justified by faith, we have peace with God through our Lord Jesus Christ.* I remember my father drumming into us that justification means "just as if I hadn't sinned."

In Genesis 4:7, God warns Cain, *If you do well, will you not be accepted? And if you do not do well, sin is crouching at the door. Its desire is contrary to you, but you must rule over it.* Cain wanted to do things his way, and God was warning him that sin was about to have mastery over him. Cain didn't listen to the warning God gave, and out of jealousy, he killed his brother Abel.

My point is that, in a sense, there are a lot of negativities throughout Scripture because we live in a fallen world. As a result of our sin nature, we are more prone to do what is wrong than what is right. We are more prone to be influenced by the fallen world than to impact the world with what is right. Jeremiah gave such a message to God's people. Actually, I've heard people accuse Jeremiah of being too negative. But Jeremiah was a prophet of the Lord, and what he spoke is part of the inspired, inerrant, written Word of God.

Jeremiah warned the people, *Thus says the Lord: "Learn not the way of the nations"* (Jeremiah 10:2) and *The gods who did not make the heavens and the earth shall perish from the earth and from under the heavens* (Jeremiah 10:11).

THEOLOGY — MARCH 13

Speaking of the true God, Jeremiah proclaimed, *It is he who made the earth by his power, who established the world by his wisdom, and by his understanding stretched out the heavens* (Jeremiah 10:12). Speaking of those who were worshipping false gods, Jeremiah stated, *Every man is stupid and without knowledge* (Jeremiah 10:14).

Many in the Church today would claim that Jeremiah was being too negative. But Jeremiah, as a prophet, was pointing out the wrong things people were doing and then pointing them to the true God they needed to worship. And he was giving the people the words God instructed him to give them.

There is a great need today for us to warn people about the evil happening around us in the culture *"so that we may no longer be children, tossed to and fro by the waves and carried about by every wind of doctrine, by human cunning, by craftiness in deceitful schemes"* (Ephesians 4:14). Because of our sin nature, we must be diligent to ensure we don't become captive to the evil ways of the world. We can so easily be influenced by that which is wrong.

We do need to warn people and give them the "negative" message. For instance, we need to warn people that they are sinners and, as such, would spend eternity separated from God. But to go with that, we teach the good (positive) news that our God, through His Son, provided a means of salvation for those who will receive it so that we can spend eternity with the Lord.

We also need to warn people about the evils of certain movements that are impacting generations of kids (for example, LGBTQ, critical race theory, social justice, and gender issues) but also point them to the Word of God to help them build a truly Christian worldview and impact people around them—including their children and grandchildren—with the truth of God's Word and the gospel.

So should Christians be negative? In a fallen world, we need to be negative for the right reason—to help people understand the evil consequences of sin and point them to the positive message of the saving gospel through the Lord Jesus Christ.

As God's Word warns: *But as for the cowardly, the faithless, the detestable, as for murderers, the sexually immoral, sorcerers, idolaters, and all liars, their portion will be in the lake that burns with fire and sulfur, which is the second death* (Revelation 21:8).

True love in this world means we will be giving some negative messages.

MARCH 14
Genesis 6:20

Building Our Thinking on the Bible

A multiple-choice question for you:

Did kangaroos once live in the Middle East?

A. They've always lived in Australia

B. We don't know where they've always lived

C. Yes

D. None of the above

When I give this question to a church audience, I find most answer A.

The correct answer is C.

This question is one of many I ask to help people learn how to develop a truly Christian worldview.

After finding most people give A as the answer, I ask a series of questions. How many of you believe in Noah's ark? Most hands go up. How many believe two of each kind of land animal, including the kangaroo kind, went on board the ark? Most hands go up. How many believe there was a global Flood? Most hands go up. How many believe the ark landed on the mountains of Ararat in the Middle East? Most hands go up. How many now believe kangaroos once lived in the Middle East? People laugh as their hands go up.

Most have not been taught to think with a biblical worldview by building their thinking on the Bible. Most have been very secularized. Most churches haven't taught how to develop a true biblical worldview.

When trying to understand the past, secularists have the basic philosophy that the present is the key to interpreting the past. For example, they look at present processes such as how quickly sediments are laid down, etc., to interpret the past to try to explain how the layers were laid down at the Grand Canyon.

For the Christian, the present is not the key to understanding the past. Revelation is the key to the past, and understanding the past is the key to the present.

Let me explain this in regard to the kangaroo question. We look at Australia today and see the kangaroo kind (with different species) lives there. But what is the history that led to them living there?

Starting with Genesis 6, we read the account of God calling Noah to build an ark because He was going to judge the wickedness of man with a global Flood. God brought two of each kind of land-dwelling, air-breathing animal (seven pairs of some) to the ark to survive the Flood.

Two of every sort shall come in to you (Genesis 6:20).

That would have included two of the kangaroo kind. We know the ark landed in the area we today call the Middle East. The land-animal kinds on the ark, including the kangaroos, came off the ark. Animals then began to move away from the ark.

THEOLOGY

We also believe Noah's Flood generated an ice age. That's another topic and information can be found at the Answers in Genesis website. As a result of the ice age, ocean levels would have been lowered, forming land bridges connecting Australia with New Guinea and Indonesia to Southeast Asia.

As animals competed with each other, they moved to various areas. Kangaroos are marsupials and can travel with their young when they're very immature. They eventually arrived in Australia and were isolated there as the ice age receded and ocean levels rose. Over time, the kangaroo kind formed various species.

Why don't we find kangaroo fossils in the Middle East? Why don't we find fossils of millions of buffalo that once lived in the USA? Fossilization is a unique event requiring a catastrophic event to quickly preserve a creature. That's why most fossils were formed from the global Flood. When animals die today, they decay quickly and aren't fossilized.

So when I'm asked how kangaroos got to the Middle East, with tongue in cheek, I say, "They hopped."

Biblical history gives us the key information to build the big picture of our thinking (our worldview) to then look at the present world in the correct way. The Bible doesn't give us all the information, but based on the key information, we can build models to answer such questions about kangaroos. Now, models are always subject to change, but God's Word is not. So kangaroos lived before the Flood, during the Flood on the ark, after the Flood in the Middle East, and today in Australia.

> **To deal with any topic, Christians need to make sure the foundation for their worldview is God's Word, beginning in Genesis.**

MARCH 15
Psalm 115:16

Is There Intelligent Life in Outer Space?

In recent times, there has been a lot of talk about UFOs and supposed evidence of alien spacecraft. If the people who are so focused on UFOs and aliens were as focused on God's Word, they would be focusing on matters of eternal value.

Actually, I do believe in UFOs. But, no, I don't believe in aliens! Why do I believe in UFOs? Well, any flying object that can't be identified is a UFO. But do I believe in UFOs piloted by Vulcans, Klingons, or Cardassians? The answer to that question is a definite no, even though I am a fan of (some) science fiction.

But if I don't believe in aliens flying around in UFOs, does that mean I reject the idea that intelligent life could exist in outer space? As one of my friends once said, "Looking at the mess people get themselves into in this world, sometimes I wonder if there's intelligent life on Earth, let alone outer space."

A good friend of mine back in the 1980s was Dr. Clifford Wilson, author of the million-copy bestseller *Crash Go the Chariots*. He did a lot of research on UFOs. He once told me that he concluded that, by far, the majority were either misunderstood natural phenomena or misinterpreted man-made objects. However, concluded there was a very small percentage that couldn't be explained, and he allowed the possibility of some supernatural origin—albeit evil. But regardless, he, like me, did not believe in intelligent physical beings on planets other than our earth. There can always be some evidence we don't have which could give a logical explanation for claimed sightings and objects.

A number of leading evolutionists, like the late Dr. Carl Sagan, have popularized the idea that there must be intelligent life in outer space. From an evolutionary perspective, it would make sense to suggest such a possibility. People who believe this possibility contend that if life evolved on earth by natural processes, intelligent life must exist somewhere else in the far reaches of space, given the size of the universe and the millions of possible planets. One can postulate endlessly about possibilities of intelligent life in outer space, but I believe a Christian worldview, built on the Bible, rejects such a possibility. Here is why.

During the six days of creation in Genesis 1, we learn that God created the earth first. On day four, He made the sun and the moon for the earth, and then "he made the stars also" (Genesis 1:16; KJV).

From these passages of Scripture, it would seem that the earth is special—it is center stage. Everything else was made for purposes relating to the earth. For instance, the sun, moon, and stars were made "for signs and for seasons, and for days and years" (Genesis 1:14).

Throughout the Old Testament, many passages distinguish between the heavens and the earth. Psalm 115:16 states, *The heavens are the Lord's heavens, but the earth he has given to the children of man.*

Many other passages single out the earth as being special, made for humans to dwell on, and a focus of God's attention, such as Isaiah 66:1, *Thus says the Lord: "Heaven is my throne, and the earth is my footstool."*

Isaiah 40:22 likens the heavens to a curtain that God basically stretches around him: *It is he who sits above the circle of the earth, and its inhabitants are like grasshoppers; who stretches out the heavens like a curtain, and spreads them like a tent to dwell in.*

SCIENCE

Such verses certainly imply that the earth is to be considered separate and special when compared to the rest of the universe, so they suggest that the earth alone was created for life. So far, based on man's limited exploration of space and the solar system, this certainly holds true.

But there is a theological reason that I believe rules out the possibility of intelligent life in outer space.

Once when I wrote an article on this, secularists posted headlines saying that I believe aliens were going to hell! Well, the point of what I want to say from a theological perspective is that this is one of the reasons I don't believe in aliens. I don't believe aliens are going to hell as I don't believe aliens exist!

The Bible makes it clear in Romans 8:22 that "creation has been groaning" because of Adam's sin. When Adam fell, the entire universe was affected. Not only this, but one day in the future, there will be "a new heaven and a new earth, for the first heaven and the first earth had passed away" (Revelation 21:1).

Isaiah 34:4 states, *All the host of heaven shall rot away, and the skies roll up like a scroll. All their host shall fall, as leaves fall from the vine, like leaves falling from the fig tree.*

Now here is the problem. If there were intelligent beings on other planets, then they would have been affected by the Fall of Adam because the whole creation was affected. So these beings would have to die because death was the penalty for sin. In the future, their planet would be destroyed by fire during God's final judgment, but they cannot have salvation because that blessing is given only to humans.

If intelligent beings lived on other planets, they would suffer because of Adam's sin but have no opportunity to be saved through Christ's sacrifice.

When Jesus Christ stepped into history, He became the God-man. The Bible calls Him "the last Adam" and the "second man" (1 Corinthians 15:45, 47). He became the second perfect man (Adam was perfect before he sinned), and He took the place of the first Adam by dying for the human race. As the first Adam was the representative head of the human race, so Jesus became the new head, the last Adam. So there can be no other Savior, only Christ. Jesus now sits in the heavens, still in human form, sitting on His throne next to the Father. If Jesus stepped out of His human form, we would no longer have a Savior. He remains the God-man forever.

But note, Jesus didn't become a "God-Klingon," a "God-Vulcan," or a "God-Cardassian"—he became the God-man. And, regarding animal life and plants, we cannot be so dogmatic because the Bible does not state whether life exists elsewhere in the universe. Based on the passages about the heavens and earth, however, I strongly suspect that life does not exist elsewhere.

So the next time you hear someone talking about UFOs, think on the Scripture passages quoted above, and use them to segue into a presentation of the gospel: *For as by a man came death, by a man has come also the resurrection of the dead. For as in Adam all die, so also in Christ shall all be made alive* (1 Corinthians 15:21–22).

> **It wouldn't make sense theologically for there to be other intelligent, physical beings who suffer because of Adam's sin but cannot be saved.**

MARCH 16

Genesis 1:27

Gender from a Biblical Worldview Perspective

How many genders of humans are there? Generations ago in the West, whether Christian or non-Christian, most people would immediately respond with the answer, "Only two: male and female." But now we live at a time when there is much confusion around gender. It used to be considered that gender and biological sex were the same thing. However now, even in elementary public schools, students are being taught that the following are divisions for humans:

Biological sex

1. Gender
2. Sexual Orientation

A biblical worldview (based on God's revealed Word in the Bible) makes it clear that God made two sexes of humans, male and female: *So God created man in his own image, in the image of God he created him; male and female he created them* (Genesis 1:27). There are only two options given here: male or female. When asked about marriage, Jesus, who is God, replied: *Have you not read that he who created them from the beginning made them male and female* (Matthew 19:4). Jesus quotes the text of Genesis 1:27, attesting to the fact that God made only two sexes (two genders) of humans: male and female.

Now science confirms there are only two sexes. We now know that humans have 23 pairs of chromosomes. Males have a pair of sex chromosomes, XY, and females have a pair of sex chromosomes, XX. So the Bible and observational science make it clear that there are only two biological sexes of humans: male and female. By the way, for the tiny fraction of a percent of humans that have XXX or XXY, etc., as part of their sex chromosomes, this is because we live in a fallen world resulting from our sin. As a result, there are mutations (e.g., copying mistakes, etc.). These so-called "exceptions" are a small fraction and certainly don't negate the created order.

Can a human being change their biological sex? No! Impossible. They can't change their genetics. This is why trans women will always be males, and males are different from females in various ways. This is also why trans women (males) will almost always beat females in sports. Now anyone who goes against God's created order is sinning against our Creator.

But what about gender? The definition of this now has become complex in the world. However, one aspect of it is how one feels. But can a person trust their feelings? What if a male feels his gender should be a woman? This is where those with a secular worldview based on man's word will conflict with a biblical worldview founded in Genesis 1–11. Only a Christian will understand a person can't trust their feelings.

The natural person does not accept the things of the Spirit of God, for they are folly to him, and he is not able to understand them because they are spiritually discerned (1 Corinthians 2:14).

God's Word makes it clear that all humans suffer from a problem called sin. *For all have sinned and fall short of the glory of God* (Romans 3:23).

That's why God describes the human heart this way: *The heart is deceitful above all things, and desperately sick; who can understand it?* (Jeremiah 17:9).

APOLOGETICS

Because of our sin nature, we can't trust our feelings. *Whoever trusts in his own mind is a fool, but he who walks in wisdom will be delivered* (Proverbs 28:26).

We must always judge our feelings against the absolute authority of God's infallible Word. *I have stored up your word in my heart, that I might not sin against you* (Psalm 119:11).

Just as God warned Cain in Genesis 4:7 to not let sin master him, we must not let our sin nature master us. And even though desires and temptations can be very strong because of our sin nature, God promises us that:

No temptation has overtaken you that is not common to man. God is faithful, and he will not let you be tempted beyond your ability, but with the temptation he will also provide the way of escape, that you may be able to endure it (1 Corinthians 10:13).

When it comes to sexual orientation, then once again, the secular worldview conflicts with the biblical worldview. God's Word makes it clear that the rightful place for sex is within marriage only, between one man and one woman. Anything else is sin.

But because of the temptation to sexual immorality, each man should have his own wife and each woman her own husband (1 Corinthians 7:2).

Let marriage be held in honor among all, and let the marriage bed be undefiled, for God will judge the sexually immoral and adulterous (Hebrews 13:4).

Flee from sexual immorality. Every other sin a person commits is outside the body, but the sexually immoral person sins against his own body. Or do you not know that your body is a temple of the Holy Spirit within you, whom you have from God? You are not your own, for you were bought with a price. So glorify God in your body (1 Corinthians 6:18–20).

Or do you not know that the unrighteous will not inherit the kingdom of God? Do not be deceived: neither the sexually immoral, nor idolaters, nor adulterers, nor men who practice homosexuality, nor thieves, nor the greedy, nor drunkards, nor revilers, nor swindlers will inherit the kingdom of God (1 Corinthians 6:9–10).

So, for the Christian, from a biblical worldview perspective, biological sex, gender, and sexual orientation are all the same, and there are only two types: males or females. A male can't change to a female and a female can't change to a male. Those who use surgery and/or chemicals to try to change one's gender are attempting to force something that is impossible and will greatly harm their lives in various ways. We all need God's saving grace.

Because, if you confess with your mouth that Jesus is Lord and believe in your heart that God raised him from the dead, you will be saved. For with the heart one believes and is justified, and with the mouth one confesses and is saved (Romans 10:9–10).

Therefore, if anyone is in Christ, he is a new creation. The old has passed away; behold, the new has come (2 Corinthians 5:17).

No one born of God makes a practice of sinning, for God's seed abides in him; and he cannot keep on sinning, because he has been born of God (1 John 3:9).

> **The only solution to this for those with unregenerate hearts is to receive the free gift of salvation, turn their lives around, and build their thinking on God's Word.**

MARCH 17
Deuteronomy 6:6-7

How Long Does It Take to Produce a "Primitive" Culture?

How long does it take to produce a "primitive" culture?

Well, it depends on what one means by "primitive." For evolutionists, it takes millions of years, but for creationists, it takes one generation!

For many people when they think of the word "primitive," they are thinking in terms of an evolutionary worldview. They would think of so-called "primitive cavemen" who are evolving upward from apelike creatures to eventually become modern man.

For instance, evolutionary scientists used to consider neanderthals to be unintelligent, subhuman brutes in human evolution. But creation scientists recognized that neanderthals had all the hallmarks of being human. They used fire, buried their dead with rituals, and used tools to hunt. And more research has revealed that neanderthals likely wore jewelry and makeup and could even bind up broken bones.

Also, neanderthal homes, which were often in caves, were divided into specific rooms . . . and even had hot water! And they did cave paintings. Few scientists today think they were nonhuman brutes. For a time, it seemed God's Word couldn't be trusted. But, like always, science eventually caught up with what God's Word had said all along—that humans were highly intelligent from the start!

So they obviously weren't "primitive" in an evolutionary sense at all.

But think about this, neanderthals had an ancestor called Noah. Noah trusted in God. Noah had ship-building technology. Neanderthals still showed all the hallmarks of human intelligence but didn't have ship-building technology as far as we know. And there was no evidence that they worshipped the God of creation. They didn't leave any paintings, etc., indicating such.

Now think of the Australian Aboriginal people. When they were first discovered, they were an animistic culture. They didn't know the true God. Yet their ancestor also was Noah back to Adam. They were considered very "primitive" in an evolutionary sense. In fact, because of Darwinian evolutionary beliefs, evolutionists believed the Australian Aboriginals were the missing links in human evolution because they were supposedly closer to the apelike creatures. They used stone tools and also did cave paintings, etc.

But here's the point: From a biblical worldview perspective, they weren't "primitive" in an evolutionary sense but "primitive" in the sense that they had lost what their ancestors once had. They obviously had lost technological skills and also an understanding of the true God.

Now the Australian Aboriginal people (like other cultures around the world) had legends passed down from their ancestors. And many of these legends sound like one is reading Genesis 1–11. They have legends about a global flood, three sons on a raft, a rainbow at the end of the flood, and many other elements similar to *the Genesis Flood* account. They also have legends about a forbidden tree and that the first woman tasted some honey from the tree, and death came into the world. Sounds familiar, doesn't it?

There are flood legends in cultures all over the world. We have an exhibit on such flood legends on the third deck of the Ark at the Ark Encounter attraction.

SCIENCE

MARCH 17

When I went to university, I had a professor who said that the Jews had stories about a flood like the Babylonians. He claimed that it's obvious the Jews borrowed their stories from the Babylonians. Many seminary professors sadly also teach this secular view of history.

But this doesn't make logical sense, and it certainly doesn't make biblical sense!

If one reads the Babylonian stories, they sound fanciful and not real. But when one reads the Genesis account, it reads as real history with a ship with dimensions that make sense! I would say the Babylonian account is a perversion of the original account which is preserved in Scripture.

As people increased on the earth after the Flood, they went through an event called the Tower of Babel. God judged by giving different languages because of their rebellion, so people then dispersed over the earth. They took the account of the Flood and other events about creation and the Fall and, over the years, changed them to become the fanciful legends that abound in people groups over the earth. Somewhere in their history, they did not retain the truth and also lost technology they once had, etc. They became "primitive" in the sense of losing what they had, not "primitive" in the sense of evolving upward.

So how long does it take to produce such a so-called "primitive" culture? It only takes one generation! That should be a reminder to fathers who have the responsibility to be the spiritual head of their homes. If they don't train their children as they should, then in one generation the spiritual legacy of the truth of our Creator God can be lost!

We learned in Judges when those who crossed the Jordan River as a miracle were told to tell the next generation who God is and pass on that spiritual legacy. They even built a monument of 12 stones so that the next generation would ask what they meant. The fathers were then to tell them about God and who He is and what He had done for them. But we read that the next generation served false gods. They lost it in one generation! And Psalm 78 tells us about the fathers who did not teach their children as they should.

And the people served the Lord all the days of Joshua, and all the days of the elders who outlived Joshua, who had seen all the great work that the Lord had done for Israel (Judges 2:7).

And there arose another generation after them who did not know the Lord or the work that he had done for Israel. And the people of Israel did what was evil in the sight of the Lord and served the Baals. And they abandoned the Lord, the God of their fathers, who had brought them out of the land of Egypt. They went after other gods, from among the gods of the peoples who were around them, and bowed down to them. And they provoked the Lord to anger. They abandoned the Lord and served the Baals and the Ashtaroth (Judges 2:10–13).

What a warning to fathers! I pray this passage of Scripture will be taken to heart by every father:

And these words that I command you today shall be on your heart. You shall teach them diligently to your children, and shall talk of them when you sit in your house, and when you walk by the way, and when you lie down, and when you rise (Deuteronomy 6:6–7).

It only takes one generation to lose a spiritual legacy.

MARCH 18
Proverbs 31:26-31

Godly Mothers

*Honor your father and your mother, that your days may be long in the land that the L*ORD *your God is giving you* (Exodus 20:12).

I want to honor two special mothers—both godly mothers and godly wives. And I can say that the ministries of Answers in Genesis, Creation Museum, and Ark Encounter would not be here today without their dedication to the Lord, His Word, and sacrificial love.

I'll never forget my godly mother teaching us over and over again, "God first, others second, and yourself last." And she didn't just teach this; she lived it. I saw her sacrificial love not just for her family but for others. She would always put others before herself—and always God first.

My wife, Mally, is just like my mother in many ways. She always puts God first, others second, and herself last. She overflows with generosity and sacrificial love. She has always supported me a million percent in this ministry. She has never complained about me being away or spending too much time in the ministry. As she says, "God brought us together to support each other in this ministry. I want to support you with whatever God has called you to do." She has also devoted herself to our five kids and their spouses (and now 18 grandkids and spouses for two of them). Our kids and grandkids adore her. She has been such a godly example to them all.

My mother had such a heart for reaching others of all ages with the gospel. I remember as we moved to different towns when my father was transferred in the state of Queensland in Australia, my parents would start Sunday schools. They would invite evangelists to come and conduct evangelistic rallies to reach children, teens, and adults with the gospel. I will never forget when I was about 10 years old, we were visiting my mother's parents who live on a sugar cane farm in north Queensland. My mother told me how she started a Sunday school to reach kids in this country area with the gospel. She even rode her bicycle a mile up the road to collect two girls and put them on her handlebars and bar and rode two miles to Sunday school and then two miles to take them back home and a mile back to her house. She did this for a long time so those two girls would be taught God's Word and the gospel. I remember thinking, If my mother did that to reach people with the gospel, what can I do?

I can still hear my mother saying, "It's only what is done for Jesus that lasts." I have never forgotten that. She, along with my father, would teach us Bible verses to memorize. One of the first verses I remember my mother teaching me was, *Trust in the* LORD *with all your heart and do not lean on your own understanding* (Proverbs 3:5). It was one of her favorite Bible verses.

And I will never forget the prayer she taught me as a little child as she knelt beside me, and we prayed the words of a hymn written as a night prayer for children in 1839 and published in 1841:

Jesus, tender Shepherd, hear me;
Bless Thy little lamb tonight;
Through the darkness be Thou near me;
Watch my sleep till morning light.

FAMILY — MARCH 18

> All this day Thy hand has led me,
> And I thank Thee for Thy care;
> Thou hast clothed me, warmed and fed me,
> Listen to my evening prayer.
> Let my sins be all forgiven;
> Bless the friends I love so well;
> Take me when I die to Heaven
> There with Thee to dwell.

My mother was bold in her faith and witnessed to everyone she could, even in the last years of her life as she suffered physical ailments. Her faith never wavered! Her desire to tell people about Jesus never waned.

My mother had a phenomenal spiritual impact on her kids and countless others. And her legacy lives on in the ministry of Answers in Genesis, Creation Museum, and Ark Encounter, impacting tens of millions of people a year. She passed away in November 2019, just two months before her 92nd birthday. On her gravestone is this verse: *Trust in the Lord with all your heart* (Proverbs 3:5).

Our five children all love the Lord. The four that are married, married godly spouses. They are now bringing up their children (our 18 grandchildren) to love the Lord. And the two grandchildren who are married have godly spouses. Mally has had such a phenomenal spiritual impact on our children, and that spiritual legacy is now being passed on to our grandchildren. She is a counselor to our children and to our grandchildren.

Mally is not one for "stuff." She says, "We don't need stuff. You can't take it with you to heaven." She is not one to gather up material goods. She would rather be generous and help our families and others with their needs. She truly understands that, *You do not know what tomorrow will bring. What is your life? For you are a mist that appears for a little time and then vanishes* (James 4:14).

Mally, in so many ways, is like my mother as she desires to put God first, others second, and herself last. And she lives out that it's only what's done for Jesus that lasts.

Why did my mother and Mally have such things in common? Because of their love for the Lord Jesus and His infallible Word.

As I think about these two godly mothers and praise the Lord for them, I think of this passage of Scripture that describes them:

She opens her mouth with wisdom, and the teaching of kindness is on her tongue. She looks well to the ways of her household and does not eat the bread of idleness. Her children rise up and call her blessed; her husband also, and he praises her: "Many women have done excellently, but you surpass them all." Charm is deceitful, and beauty is vain, but a woman who fears the Lord is to be praised. Give her of the fruit of her hands (Proverbs 31:26–31).

> **Praise the Lord for godly mothers, and praise the Lord for the legacies of these two who I want to honor today.**

MARCH 19
Genesis 6:1-4

Who Were the Nephilim?

I'm sure this will get me into "trouble." I find this is a very emotional issue for some, and often, some Christians' views of eschatology and Genesis 6 are intricately intertwined. I find there are certain topics where people passionately (sometimes aggressively) respond, and no doubt this will be one of them. But all of us need our thinking to be challenged.

So I swallow hard, and here goes. Let's talk about Nephilim! I've been asked about my views many times, so I decided to give them. Of course, sometimes people ask for my views on something, so I give them, and then they get upset with me.

Genesis 6:1–4 has been a much-debated passage. Christian scholars have taken a number of different positions on what these verses mean. As this section doesn't impinge on any major doctrines, the ministry of Answers in Genesis doesn't take an official position on the identity of the Nephilim, but speakers and researchers have their own personally preferred positions. The position I personally lean toward is given below, as I have done my best to negotiate through these verses, including reading many different scholars' commentaries on these verses. Remember, God has put these verses in Scripture for our learning, so there must be an important reason for them to be included.

The context of these verses is to relay the extent to which wickedness had come to prevail on the earth. One of the ways this happened has something to do with people marrying. I like to take as straightforward an interpretation as possible without trying to complicate things (e.g., Proverbs 8:8–9; 2 Corinthians 4:2).

It seems to me the simplest explanation is that the line of Seth (which could have been referred to as "sons of God" because they were godly and called upon the name of the Lord) started marrying the line of Cain (the "daughters of men"—women who were beautiful but ungodly). Such mixing of spiritual light and darkness destroys families. We see a warning of this with the godly Israelites entering into ungodly Canaan (e.g., Deuteronomy 7:1–4; 1 Kings 11:2). In the New Testament, we are also warned in 2 Corinthians 6:14: *Do not be unequally yoked with unbelievers. For what partnership has righteousness with lawlessness? Or what fellowship has light with darkness?* Malachi was warning about such marriages (godly and ungodly) in Malachi 2.

Because of the sin nature of every human being, such mixing could easily lead to increasing ungodliness. As an example, that was the case of the wise and godly King Solomon who was led into idolatry and sin by his pagan wives (1 Kings 11:1–11; Nehemiah 13:26). Therefore, God judged him. That should be a stern warning for us to ensure we obey God's rules in regard to marriage and the training of children.

Associated with all this is the mention of Nephilim. We read, *The Nephilim were on the earth in those days, and also afterward, when the sons of God came in to the daughters of man and they bore children to them. These were the mighty men who were of old, the men of renown* (Genesis 6:4).

Who were the Nephilim? Certainly, the description may imply that they were of great stature (perhaps giants in the build of their bodies), greatly feared, and well-known, presumably for extreme wickedness. Perhaps they were certain individuals of the offspring resulting from this mixing of "the sons of God" and the "daughters

THEOLOGY — MARCH 19

of men" who became extremely evil. An interesting point concerning the Nephilim is the phrase, "and also afterward." It seems this is referring to after the Flood, as Nephilim are mentioned once again in Numbers 13:33 (though it is spelled differently in Hebrew): *And there we saw the Nephilim (the sons of Anak, who come from the Nephilim), and we seemed to ourselves like grasshoppers, and so we seemed to them.* The Nephilim in Numbers 13 were indeed giant in stature as the text indicates.

By the time of the Flood, there was so much ungodliness that God describes it this way:

The LORD saw that the wickedness of man was great in the earth, and that every intention of the thoughts of his heart was only evil continually. And the LORD regretted that he had made man on the earth, and it grieved him to his heart. So the LORD said, "I will blot out man whom I have created from the face of the land, man and animals and creeping things and birds of the heavens, for I am sorry that I have made them." But Noah found favor in the eyes of the LORD (Genesis 6:5–8).

So certainly, the first four verses of Genesis 6 are a lead-up to this situation of rampant wickedness. Personally, I can't accept, as some do, that wicked angels mated with humans. Angels don't reproduce and don't have human DNA. To me, it makes a much more logical and simpler explanation that when godly and ungodly mix in marriage, it doesn't take long for the godly legacy to be lost! Thus, by the time of Noah, there was extreme wickedness.

But, regardless of the position one takes on understanding these verses, it is certainly a warning from God as to what happens when sin is allowed to rule over us. It's a reminder to make sure we raise up godly generations who call upon the name of the Lord and have boldness and courage to stand for God and His Word without compromise.

All the way through Scripture, we read of examples where the people of God compromised God's Word with the pagan beliefs of the nations around them and it destroyed them, and God judged them for it. We also see examples where the people of God married ungodly people, and it destroyed families. This has been a problem since the beginning.

> This is a reminder to know God's Word, obey what He instructs us to do, and be aware of how sin is crouching at the door for each one of us to destroy us.

MARCH 20
Zechariah 1:3

Revival or Reformation?

Does the Church need a revival? Or does it need reformation first? The spirit of compromise sadly permeates much of the Church. I submit we need a new reformation honoring the authority of God's Word starting with Genesis 1:1 before there can be real revival. So much of the Church in our Western world has become rather lukewarm. Church attendance is waning with a catastrophic generational loss resulting in church attendance for Generation Z now down to less than 9%.

Consider how the Church's influence has greatly waned in Europe. In the United Kingdom, church attendance has dwindled, and many church buildings have been abandoned and turned into secular facilities. Church attendance in England is down to about 4%, and the same will happen in the USA if the current trends continue.

In 2009, Answers in Genesis released the results of a survey commissioned through America's Research Group that documented that the Church in America was in big trouble. The results were published in three major books: *Already Gone, Already Compromised,* and *Ready to Return.* Research on millennials at that time confirmed previous research from the Barna group that around two-thirds of young people were leaving the Church by college age, with few returning. Most millennials who still regularly attended church were very secularized. Forty percent declared they were not born again, 65% believed being good would get them to heaven, and 40% openly supported gay "marriage." Now that was some years ago, and things have deteriorated since then.

From my years of experience interacting with churches and church leaders and reading research conducted on Christian institutions, a spirit of compromising God's Word in Genesis with evolutionary ideas permeated much of the Church. I predicted we would continue to lose generations from the Church if God's people didn't return to God's Word beginning in Genesis.

Secular thinking has permeated Western cultures, and there's been a generational change in worldview within the Church and the culture as a whole. In America, Christian symbols have been, by and large, removed from much of the culture, and prayer, Bible, and creation have been all but eliminated from the government education system. Public schools have thrown out God, creation, prayer, and the Bible and now impose the religion of atheism and sexual humanism on generations of kids. An increasing number of Christian leaders are becoming soft on LGBTQ, support gay "marriage," are impacted by critical race theory, and compromise in many other ways.

I've met many of those who remember how Christianized the West used to be and have called for a revival in our churches. Along with the psalmist, they cry: *Will you not revive us again, that your people may rejoice in you?* (Psalm 85:6). However, I contend there needs to be reformation before there can be real revival. What is the difference between reformation and revival? In the 1866 Sword and Trowel, C. H. Spurgeon defined revival: "The word revive . . . may be interpreted thus—to live again, to receive again a life which has almost expired; to rekindle into a flame the vital spark which was nearly extinguished." Notice the condition for revival. You can only revive something that was once healthy. While I agree that we need a new revival to sweep the land, I suggest something needs to come first.

CHURCH

Much decay has occurred as generations (and many church leaders) have been abandoning the authority of God's Word beginning in Genesis. I suggest the Church body has a cancer that is attacking its life, and this needs to be dealt with, so the body can be revived. In this era, compromise on the historical truths of Genesis, which leads to further compromise throughout Scripture, is a cancer. Much decay has occurred as generations (and many church leaders) have been abandoning the authority of God's Word. This has opened the door for secular thinking to permeate the Church, including antibiblical views of marriage, gender, and other areas.

It is my contention that for God to bring a revival, there needs to be a new reformation. Reformation is a call of the Church back to honoring the absolute authority of the Word of God, from the very first verse in Genesis. We need a new reformation today—a reformation where God's people, particularly Christian leaders, repent of compromising God's Word and stand boldly on God's infallible Word.

I'm reminded of the words of the prophet Jeremiah addressing the people of his day: *You have played the whore with many lovers; and would you return to me? declares the* LORD (Jeremiah 3:1). Also, the words of the prophet Zechariah: *Return to me, says the* LORD *of hosts, and I will return to you* (Zechariah 1:3). These messages are just as pertinent for the Church today.

I would love to see God bring a revival in our churches. But how can this happen if God's people, and particularly many of its leaders, are not honoring God's Word as they should? Because of the rampant compromise, many in the Church (and particularly the younger generations) don't understand that the Bible, God's Word, is the absolute authority. *Come, let us return to the* LORD (Hosea 6:1).

I love how the great expositional teacher of the twentieth century, Martin Lloyd Jones, put it: "The Church, after all, is the Church of God.... We are a people for God's own peculiar possession. And why has he called us out of darkness into his own marvelous light? Surely it is that we may show forth his praises, his excellencies, his virtues. And, therefore, we should be concerned about this matter [of revival] primarily because of the name, and the glory, the honor of God himself. Whether we like it or not, it is a fact that the world judges God himself, and the Lord Jesus Christ, and the whole of the Christian faith, by what it sees in us. We are his representatives, we are the people who take his name upon us,... and the man outside the Church regards the Church as the representative of God."[24]

At this point in time, the world sees much of the Church accepting secular thinking and compromising God's Word with the pagan religion of evolution, which the world uses to justify rejecting God. How can the Church impact the world when church members dishonor God by treating His Word so glibly? Compromising Christians are helping the secularists attack God's Word.

To impact the world, I strongly believe we need a new reformation in our churches. Pray that when such reformation occurs, God will then bring revival in the land, and we will see people fall on their knees before a holy God, recognizing their sinfulness and need for repentance and salvation.

Revival needs a foundation of rock, not sand! (Matthew 7).

If the foundations are destroyed, what can the righteous do? (Psalm 11:3).

Surely, true revival can only be built on the foundation of the absolute authority of God's Word.

MARCH 21
Mark 16:15

Are Cavemen Real?

Do I believe in cavemen? Of course, I do.

Cavemen are people that lived in caves. Actually, there are people today that live in caves in certain parts of the world. For instance, in central Australia where they mine opals, it is so hot that people live in caves. Some of the Native Americans used to live in caves in areas around the Grand Canyon. So there were ancient cavemen, and there are modern-day cavemen! But despite popular opinion to the contrary, ancient "cavemen" were completely human and in need of a Savior, Jesus Christ, just like every other human being.

We've all heard about "missing links"—supposed races of humanlike people who were similar to us but not as intelligent or skilled. While differences among people do exist, the only important difference has nothing to do with body shape, intelligence, or skill.

When many people hear the term cavemen, they usually think of primitive-looking, hairy (even apelike), cave-dwelling brutes. That is how they have often been depicted in secular museum dioramas, illustrating man's supposed ancestors or ancient relatives. For instance, neanderthal man was often depicted this way.

Because of this evolutionary type of propaganda, many people are confused about cavemen. However, as I stated above, there is a very simple definition for this term: "Cavemen" are people who live (or lived) in caves!

After Noah's Flood, eight people came off the ark, and from Noah's three sons and their wives came all the people who live or have lived on this earth. The genealogies in Genesis make it very clear that these eight people descended from the first couple, Adam and Eve. This means that every person who has ever lived is a relative of everyone else. We are all members of the one human race—Adam's race—which means we are all sinners in need of salvation.

Now consider what happened at the time of the Flood. A massive amount of technology was lost. Except for what Noah took on the ark, the pre-Flood world's technology, architecture, and other expertise were completely destroyed. It took time for humans to restore knowledge and rebuild technology after the Flood. For instance, the Bible tells us that Noah initially lived in a tent (Genesis 9:21).

As time progressed and the population increased on the earth, perhaps some people built homes out of stone. Some may even have taken pieces of the ark to build wooden structures to live in. Others may have found or dug caves to live in. If I had been one of those people, I would have found a cave to live in as I don't have a talent to build things!

Throughout history, people have lived in different types of structures, depending on the available natural resources, the talents of individuals, and the amount of accumulated knowledge for technological advances.

Now because of the indoctrination in evolutionary beliefs, many people believe that man evolved from slime, and as he did, he first learned to grunt and then eventually speak. Then he developed stone tools that gradually became more sophisticated as he supposedly evolved.

However, from a biblical perspective, man was highly intelligent right from the start. Adam's immediate descendants were soon inventing musical instruments and working with brass. No doubt, Noah and his

THEOLOGY MARCH 21

family began reinventing some of the technology lost at the Flood. As time went on, their descendants developed new technologies as knowledge about the elements and laws of nature increased.

Some people (such as the group we call neanderthals) probably became isolated from other humans. They lived in caves, invented musical instruments, made jewelry, and buried their dead. Yes, they were "cavemen," but they were our relatives—descendants of Noah. They certainly had some external features that made them look a little different from people today, but they were still members of the human race. They may have looked slightly different on the outside, just as Australian Aboriginal people look different from northern Canada's Inuit, but their genetics clearly show they are all members of the human race.

This brings us to the most important point. In 2000, the Human Genome Project announced to the world that all humans biologically belong to one race. Although the people heading this project did not acknowledge it, they confirmed the Bible's account of the creation of man—that all people are descendants of Adam and Eve and all belong to one biological race. Now, because of the immense variability God placed into the genome of each kind of creature, including humans, there is enormous potential for differences on the "outside" (e.g., physical traits). Sadly, many people see these outside differences as major and important whereas, in reality, these differences only reflect the genetic differences that God placed in the genes of each type of creature. However, humans have a difference inside that is vitally important. There are actually two "races" of people! There is only one race biologically, but there are two races spiritually. You are either for Christ or against Him (Matthew 12:30); you either walk in light or in darkness (1 John 1:5).

The Bible makes it clear that the two spiritual "races" can be distinguished ultimately only by what is on the inside—the state of one's heart. In 1 Samuel, we read the account of Samuel going to anoint a king. He did not know God had chosen David. From the text, we are given the impression that Samuel saw one of David's brothers and was convinced that he would be the king because of his physical characteristics. However, that was not to be. In 1 Samuel 16:7, we read, *But the LORD said to Samuel, "Do not look on his appearance or on the height of his stature, because I have rejected him. For the LORD sees not as man sees: man looks on the outward appearance, but the LORD looks on the heart."*

It is easy for us as humans to focus on the outside as we look at people—their physical characteristics, their clothing, their lifestyle—but God reminds us that the inside makes all the difference. As we think about all this regarding the great commission, *Go into all the world and proclaim the gospel to the whole creation* (Mark 16:15), we need to remember that the saving power of the gospel is for all our relatives—every human being. So whether they live in apartments in New York City, in caves in Coober Pedy (real cave people who have TV sets) in Australia, in caves in France, or in ice houses in the Arctic, all humans are descendants of Adam and are thus sinners in need of salvation.

The next time we hear the term cavemen, it will make a difference if we consider the fact that all humans, regardless of where they live or what they look like, are our relatives. We need to do our best to obey the great commission so that the good news of the gospel will reach the hearts of every human being.

> **We need to lovingly challenge others to deal with their heart problem and become members of the spiritual race of the Lord Jesus.**

MARCH 22
Psalm 104:6-9

Understanding the Difference Between Historical Science and Observational Science

Did you know that creationists and evolutionists have the same facts? That Christians and non-Christians have the same facts? The facts are not what people argue/debate over. It's the interpretation of the facts that people argue about. And one's interpretation depends on one's worldview. And one's worldview depends on the presuppositions they have. Ultimately, there are only two foundations our worldviews: God's Word or man's word.

When a scientist digs up fossils, are they digging up the past or digging up the present? They are digging up the present. Fossils exist in the present. They certainly existed in the past, but we only have the present, so events that happened in the past resulted in the fossils being where they are found in the present. This is a point I made to Bill Nye "the Science Guy" when I debated him at the Creation Museum in 2014.

I explained this point in the context of discussing the meaning of the word science. The word itself means "knowledge," and I wanted people to understand the difference between knowledge about past events when we were not there to see them versus knowledge gained in the present through observation (using our five senses) and repeatable testing that leads to our wonderful technology.

Knowledge about the past is called historical science. Knowledge gained in the present through observation and repeatable testing is called observational science.

Now secularists often get very emotional over this issue as they don't want to acknowledge such a distinction. They want to use the one word, science, for discussing their beliefs (like evolution) about the past and for observation and repeatable testing when discussing technology.

The reason they get so emotional is that they don't want to admit that naturalistic evolution is a belief. It is in the realm of historical science, not observational science. Evolution in fact is an anti-God religion attempting to explain the past regarding how the universe and all life came into being by natural processes.

I've encountered many pastors and theologians who will state that they trust science because they use computers, fly in airplanes, and drive motor cars. So, when a secular scientist states that science has proved evolution/millions of years, they think they have to believe and trust these scientists because this is also "science." But they don't understand, and it's certainly not taught in the secular education system, that the word "science" when used for technology and evolution is being used to mean two totally different things.

The example I gave Bill Nye went something like this: If I went with Bill Nye to the Grand Canyon, we could agree on the fact that there are different sedimentary layers laid down on top of each other. We could agree one such layer is called the Coconino Sandstone. We could measure the thickness of the sandstone layer, and we could agree on that. We could also agree on the size of the grains that make up this sandstone. Now that's observational science. We have the same facts.

What we disagree on is how long ago the sandstone layer was laid down and how long it took to be laid down. Neither of us were there in the past to see the layers form. Now we are talking about historical science. Bill Nye believes the layers of the Grand Canyon were laid down slowly over millions of years, millions of years ago. I believe the layers were laid down quickly around 4,300 years ago from the Flood of Noah's day.

SCIENCE

We have different interpretations about the same facts in the present regarding how those facts connect to the past.

Neither of us can scientifically prove our beliefs. However, I contend that for many reasons the observations of the various layers and their grains and other factors confirm the layers were laid down catastrophically just thousands of years ago, not slowly over millions of years.

A creation scientist and a secular scientist can agree on how deep the Grand Canyon is. They agree the Colorado River flows through the canyon and any such river does cause some erosion of the rocks. This is observational science. However, when secularists claim the Colorado River eroded the canyon over millions of years, that is now in the realm of historical science. No one was there to see what actually happened. It's possible the canyon was formed by processes that allowed the Colorado River to flow through it. In fact, creationists point to a number of factors that confirm the area was uplifted toward the end of Noah's Flood, forming a dam. Because the layers were weakened by this uplift and lots of leftover water from the Flood was behind the dam (one observes evidence such as water was once in existence in that area), the dam broke, and the canyon was eroded catastrophically. This canyon then allowed the Colorado River to flow through. So the river didn't form the canyon. That's a different interpretation of the same facts of the present in relation to the past.

Secularists are not teaching students in education to think correctly about science and the past. Sadly, generations of students are being brainwashed by secularists who are committed to their religion of evolution and don't want students to think critically about the origins issue.

Some Christians believe Psalm 104 describes what happened at the end of the Flood:

You covered it with the deep as with a garment; the waters stood above the mountains. At your rebuke they fled; at the sound of your thunder they took to flight. The mountains rose, the valleys sank down to the place that you appointed for them. You set a boundary that they may not pass, so that they might not again cover the earth (Psalm 104:6–9).

Creation scientists believe God ended the Flood by raising the mountains and lowering the ocean's basins, so the water poured off into the oceans we have today. It is believed the mountains were not as high or the ocean basins as deep before the Flood. This also explains why marine fossils are found on mountain tops like in the Himalayas. The fossil layers were laid down and uplifted toward the end of the Flood (or as part of post-Flood events).

Young people must be prepared with knowledge so they won't be brainwashed by secularists attempting to convert them to their anti-God evolutionist religion—a religion of meaninglessness and hopelessness.

Make sure you teach your children and/or students to understand the difference between historical science (or origins science) and observational science (or operational science).

MARCH 23
Revelation 21:4

How Can a Christian Explain This World of Death, Disease, and Suffering and Yet Believe in a Loving God?

It's an age-old question. How can a Christian explain this world of death, disease, and suffering and yet believe in a loving God?

Well, only those who take Genesis as literal history can explain the condition of the world today.

Earthquakes, tsunamis, hurricanes, tornadoes, diseases, violence, and death—we see these catastrophes and tragedies each day on this earth. Surely, no one would call a world like this "good." In reality, Christians who compromise Genesis with millions of years have to justify describing all this as "very good."

In 2019, the website of BioLogos, the organization that actively tries to get churches and Christian institutions to believe in evolution and millions of years, stated: "We're thrilled to announce the release of an important new book, *Understanding Scientific Theories of Origins: Cosmology, Geology, and Biology* in Christian Perspective. This book—a textbook—was written by five Wheaton College professors. [It is] the fruit of a 3-year grant they received from BioLogos in 2013."[25]

Now the professors who wrote this book promote evolution and millions of years, demonstrated by saying, "Although some Christians have argued that the fall utterly disrupted some kind of original perfection of creation, there is no evidence from either the Bible or the creation, making that a foregone conclusion."[26]

At Answers in Genesis and in the Ark Encounter and Creation Museum exhibits, we teach the opposite of this statement. AiG teaches that the Fall utterly disrupted the original perfection, and we show directly from Scripture that we now live in a groaning world because of sin.

For the creation was subjected to futility, not willingly, but because of him who subjected it, in hope that the creation itself will be set free from its bondage to corruption and obtain the freedom of the glory of the children of God. For we know that the whole creation has been groaning together in the pains of childbirth until now. And not only the creation, but we ourselves, who have the firstfruits of the Spirit, groan inwardly as we wait eagerly for adoption as sons, the redemption of our bodies (Romans 8:20–23).

So why do these Wheaton College professors claim the Fall did not disrupt "some kind of original perfection of creation"? Well, to put it simply, because they believe in millions of years!

In the 1700s and 1800s, atheists and deists wanted to explain the fossil record by natural processes to get rid of any explanation from the Bible, such as the global Flood of Noah's day, so they claimed the fossil layers over the earth were laid down millions of years before the existence of man. Now since that time, many people in the Church have accepted these supposed millions of years to explain the fossil-bearing layers and tried to fit them into Scripture before humans (before the creation of Adam and the entrance of sin).

It's important to understand that the fossil record with its billions of dead things is not just a record of death but a record of disease and violence. The fossil record holds numerous documented examples of diseases like cancer in bones, evidence of animals eating other animals, and fossil thorns—all supposedly millions of years old. However, the Bible teaches that before man sinned, the animals were vegetarian (Genesis 1:30), thorns came after the curse (Genesis 3:18), and everything was "very good" (Genesis 1:31).

APOLOGETICS — MARCH 23

After creating everything, including the first two people (Adam and Eve), *God saw everything that he had made, and behold, it was very good* (Genesis 1:31).

Originally, before sin, there was no death, disease, bloodshed, carnivory, or thorns. God described everything as "very good." But those who accept millions of years (like these Wheaton College professors) believe the death, disease, and bloodshed we observe today is all part of how God created everything. Thus, those things must be "very good."

One of the most-asked questions by the younger generations today is, "How can Christians believe in a loving God with all the death, disease, and suffering in the world?" Sadly, most of our church leaders have told these young people that's how God created everything. Only those Christians who take Genesis as literal history, as it is meant to be taken, can explain that the world we live in today has been affected by sin. It's a fallen, groaning world full of death. In fact, God describes death as an "enemy" (1 Corinthians 15:26). This fallen world is not God's fault, it's our fault because we sinned in Adam.

In Acts 3:21, we read that one day in the future, all things will be restored. In other words, when God makes the new heavens and earth, it will be restored to be like it was before the Fall. And how is this restoration described?

He will wipe away every tear from their eyes, and death shall be no more, neither shall there be mourning, nor crying, nor pain anymore, for the former things have passed away (Revelation 21:4).

Of course, those who accept millions of years and believe that the original "very good" creation was full of death, disease, pain, and suffering must also believe that the restoration will be one of death, disease, pain, and suffering. That would not be "good" and certainly not "very good"!

Only those who take Genesis literally can rightly understand the origin of sin, what it has done to the world, and even more importantly, what it has done to each of Adam's descendants. Only then can we truly understand the message of the saving gospel and why Jesus' death and Resurrection were needed so that humans can be saved for eternity.

> What a difference it would make if all pastors and Christians leaders were teaching Genesis as literal history and equipping generations with answers to defend the Christian faith against the attacks by secularists who fervently preach (yes, preach) the religion of evolutionary biology, geology, astronomy, and anthropology.

MARCH 24
Mark 10:17-18

Could God Use Evolution to Create?

Could God use evolution to create? Could God use millions of years as part of creating life?

I've had many Christians and Christian leaders tell me they believe God used evolution and millions of years to create life. I've also had many Christians say to me that God could have used evolution and millions of years if He wanted to.

But my answer is that God could not use evolution and millions of years. Now some are shocked when I say this as they say, "But God can do anything. He's the infinite Creator." Others have said, "But Luke 1:37 states, 'For nothing will be impossible with God.'"

That's true. But isn't it impossible for God to lie? God's character is a truthful one, as many verses of Scripture attest to. In fact, Proverbs 12:22 states that *lying lips are an abomination to the LORD*. Numbers 23:19 states, *God is not man, that he should lie*. It is irrational to think God would lie. He can't because of who He is, because of His very character.

Now I would say that for the same basic reason, God could not use (or have used) evolution and millions of years. To do so would go against His character. In fact, I would claim that for those Christians who believe in evolution and millions of years, they are condoning a process that is a direct attack on God's character. It would be impossible for God to use evolution and millions of years.

Let me explain. In Mark 10, we read this account: *And as he was setting out on his journey, a man ran up and knelt before him and asked him, "Good Teacher, what must I do to inherit eternal life?" And Jesus said to him, "Why do you call me good? No one is good except God alone"* (Mark 10:17–18).

God Himself is the definition of good. The attributes of God (all loving, all merciful, etc.) are part of what "good" means. When God stepped into history in the person of His Son, He healed people of diseases. He raised people from the dead. After all, God's Word describes death as an "enemy" (1 Corinthians 15:26).

Now today we live in a world of death and disease. This is described in Romans 8:22 as a groaning world because of our sin. God didn't create the world this way because after He finished creating He said everything was "very good" (Genesis 1:31). Our sin messed up this "very good" world resulting in death (which is an enemy, an intrusion), disease, and suffering.

Now evolution involves a process of death, violence, and suffering over millions of years to supposedly produce all life including humans. The fossil record, which is supposedly a record of the evolution of life over millions of years, is replete with remains of all sorts of animals, with many bones showing evidence of diseases like cancer, abscesses, arthritis, and more.

For those Christians who take man's ideas of evolution and millions of years (which is really a pagan religion to try to explain life without God) and add it into the Bible, they are saying all these supposed millions of years of death and disease existed before man. Now after God created everything, including man, He said everything He made was "very good." In other words, one would have to then accept that God is calling diseases like cancer and violence "very good." That is an attack on the character of God.

APOLOGETICS

Let me though state something very clearly. I am not saying people who believe in evolution and millions of years can't be Christians. Salvation is not conditional upon what one believes about the age of the earth or evolutionary processes but is conditional upon faith in Christ. I have never said the age of the earth and evolutionary processes, etc., are salvation issues.

> Evolution and millions of years are issues that undermine biblical authority and attack the character of God, which I consider very serious issues indeed.

MARCH 25
Romans 1:19-25

Clash of Worldviews

I've had a lot of interesting conversations with people at various conferences, our attractions, and other places over the years. I thought I would summarize some of them for you. There was a news story with this headline: "Drag Queens, Including Anti-Catholic 'Nuns,' March Chanting, 'We're Coming for Your Children.'"

I've met LGBTQ people over the years, and I've had them tell me that all they want is freedom for their views. I claim most of them really want total compliance and acceptance of their views by everyone. And the headline quoted above confirms that!

As I've spoken to some LGBTQ people, they have said that Christians like me are intolerant of other views and that's hate speech. I told them that they were intolerant of my views. They then insisted that they allowed all views but Christians didn't. Then I explained to them that they didn't allow the Christian worldview built on the Bible that there are only two genders of humans—male and female—and only one marriage—the one God created, one man and one woman. They then claimed that holding such views was being intolerant of their view. But as I showed them, they are intolerant of my view built on the Bible.

What we were experiencing was a clash of worldviews. And we were at an impasse. Why? One worldview was based on man's view and one based on God's Word. And while we had different foundations for our worldviews, we would not be able to resolve the conflict unless we had the same foundation and built the same worldview.

It's a reminder to Christians that ultimately the only resolution to the LGBTQ worldview and all other issues built on man's word (abortion, racism, etc.) is for people to trust Christ for salvation and build their worldview on God's Word. God's Word and the gospel have always been the only solution ultimately to the worldview conflict we are experiencing.

A second conversation: At one conference, I explained that the laws of nature (law of biogenesis, laws of chemistry, laws of planetary motion, laws of physics, laws of mathematics, laws of logic, uniformity of nature, universal constants, etc.) were immaterial and could not be explained by natural processes within a purely materialistic approach to the universe. Such laws can only be explained within a biblical worldview, that God created them. They are the logical, orderly way God upholds all things in the universe:

And he is before all things, and in him all things hold together (Colossians 1:17).

Thus says the LORD: *If I have not established my covenant with day and night and the fixed order of heaven and earth* (Jeremiah 33:25).

After I had spoken, a young man came to me and said something like, "Sir, I heard your talk, but I still think we all evolved by chance, random processes. I can believe that, right?"

I responded, "Well, if we all evolved by chance, then our brains also evolved by chance, random processes. That means our logic evolved by chance, random processes. If our logic evolved by chance, then we don't know it evolved the right way. Son, you don't even know if you are asking me the right questions."

His reply? "What was the name of that book you mentioned?"

APOLOGETICS

It's interesting that I've had some secularists claim that the laws of nature must be eternal. So I asked them if could there be an eternal God then. They immediately responded with, "No, not at all."

Why wouldn't they be prepared to consider an eternal God? Because that would mean God owned them as He created them, and God has a right to set the rules and determine right and wrong. People are in rebellion against God. It is a spiritual issue.

A third conversation:

At a church once, I had a high school student say something like, "Sir, I believe in evolution, and I believe we have a right to set our own rules."

I responded with, "Well, do I have a right to set my own rules then?" He said, "Yes, everyone has a right to set their own rules."

I then said, "Well, what if one of my rules is that types like you are dangerous, and I believe you should be eliminated?"

He said, "That's not right."

"Why is it not right?" I asked.

He said, "Well, it's wrong."

I said, "Why is it wrong?"

He said, "Well, it's not right."

Secularists cannot be consistent with their worldview of moral relativism. Sadly, more and more we see generations who mostly believe there is no God and that man is his own authority. And when man is his own authority, anything goes except the absolutes of Christianity. Secularists become intolerant of Christianity as the Christian worldview is built on the absolute authority of God's Word and thus God determines right and wrong! I think of these passages when I see where our culture is heading:

In those days there was no king in Israel. Everyone did what was right in his own eyes (Judges 21:25).

For what can be known about God is plain to them, because God has shown it to them. For his invisible attributes, namely, his eternal power and divine nature, have been clearly perceived, ever since the creation of the world, in the things that have been made. So they are without excuse. For although they knew God, they did not honor him as God or give thanks to him, but they became futile in their thinking, and their foolish hearts were darkened. Claiming to be wise, they became fools, and exchanged the glory of the immortal God for images resembling mortal man and birds and animals and creeping things. Therefore God gave them up in the lusts of their hearts to impurity, to the dishonoring of their bodies among themselves, because they exchanged the truth about God for a lie and worshiped and served the creature rather than the Creator, who is blessed forever! Amen (Romans 1:19–25).

Without an absolute authority, anything goes, and it would lead to the collapse of society.

MARCH 26
Romans 1:21-25

Climate Change

Climate change has become a big topic in Western countries. But I say it's not just a topic, it's a religion—a religion that worships the creation with man acting as God. The climate change cultists have rejected the God of creation and His Word (the Bible).

What is happening today regarding the climate change religion can be summed up by this passage of Scripture: *For although they knew God, they did not honor him as God or give thanks to him, but they became futile in their thinking, and their foolish hearts were darkened. Claiming to be wise, they became fools, and exchanged the glory of the immortal God for images resembling mortal man and birds and animals and creeping things. Therefore God gave them up in the lusts of their hearts to impurity, to the dishonoring of their bodies among themselves, because they exchanged the truth about God for a lie and worshiped and served the creature rather than the Creator, who is blessed forever! Amen* (Romans 1:21–25).

When people reject the true God and His Word, the Bible, they will misinterpret why the world is changing—including the climate. Do I believe in climate change? Yes, I do, though very differently to what is being discussed by politicians and the media. I believe in biblical climate change. What do I mean by that?

There are two types of climate changes the world needs to understand. One concerns spiritual climate change. Now, the media reporters don't discuss it this way, but as they write and talk about issues that are increasingly permeating the culture, such as gay "marriage," transgender, abortion, and euthanasia, they are actually reporting on spiritual climate change.

The second climate change concerns the changing physical climates on the earth, and discussions of whether man has caused these changes and whether this will lead to a doomsday scenario in the very near future.

Now, there is a connection between these two types of climate changes that we need to understand. And it's God's Word that explains what I call biblical climate change.

The secular education systems of the entire world are, by and large, teaching generations of students that science has supposedly proved the universe and all life (including humans) arose by natural processes. Students are indoctrinated to believe that astronomical, biological, geological, and anthropological evolution are fact. As a result, increasing numbers in each generation believe the Bible is not a true book of history but is a book of mythology.

The more people believe that there is no God and that they arose by natural processes, the more they will build a worldview consistent with this belief. The best way to summarize their worldview is to apply this verse of Scripture to their situation: *In those days there was no king in Israel. Everyone did what was right in his own eyes* (Judges 21:25).

In other words, when people reject the absolute authority of God's Word, ultimately, anything goes regarding their worldview. Right and wrong are a matter of their subjective decision. As a result of such a worldview, we would expect to see moral relativism permeating the culture—which is exactly what we see. This is resulting in a massive spiritual climate change, particularly in the West, that has had a predominantly Christianized worldview built on the Judeo-Christian ethic found in the Bible.

SCIENCE

MARCH 26

Now, when people reject the Bible (including the Book of Genesis) as a book of history, they are rejecting the account of a perfect creation that has been affected by the entrance of sin and God's judgment of death and the curse. They also reject the account of the geological, globally catastrophic event of the Flood of Noah's day.

God's Word tells us that, because of man's Fall, the whole of creation now groans: *For we know that the whole creation has been groaning together in the pains of childbirth until now"* (Romans 8:22).

God no longer "holds together" the creation by the power of His hand (Colossians 1:17) in the perfect way it was originally made. Everything is running down because of the effects of sin. This affects every aspect of the physical creation, including climate.

Approximately 1,600 years after creation, we read in the Bible that God judged the earth with a cataclysmic event—the global Flood. This Flood devastated the surface of the earth and led to dramatic climate changes. After the Flood, there were warmer oceans (due to plate movements, heat from the earth's mantle, and so on) and lots of ash and other particles in the atmosphere (such as from volcanic activity). This led to a catastrophic ice age with the formation of massive glaciers. Along with such drastic changes would come severe storms, hurricanes, and other weather disturbances.

But we need to understand that if people reject the Flood and the resulting one major ice age, they will not understand what has been happening to climates over the past 4,300 years since the Flood. And many people don't understand that ocean currents and phases of the sun's activity have a major bearing on Earth's climates too.

Now, this is not to say that humans are free to pollute the earth as much as they want. Man was given dominion over the earth, but this means we need to look after the creation, using it for man's good and God's glory. We need to do the best we can to take care of this fallen, cursed world.

To build a way of thinking that correctly interprets spiritual and physical climate change, one must start with the true history of the earth and all life as recorded in Genesis 1–11. One cannot disconnect the history in the Bible from understanding spiritual and physical climate changes. And one cannot disconnect the Bible from the changes God says are coming—such as the final judgment of this earth by fire. But it's God, not man, who is in charge of this massive change to come.

So, *Let God be true though every one were a liar* (Romans 3:4).

Now, when people reject God's Word concerning the past, they also reject God's Word concerning the future. We hear a number of politicians today claiming man is going to destroy the earth in a few years. But for those who believe God's Word, we know man will never and can never destroy the earth.

While the earth remains, seedtime and harvest, cold and heat, summer and winter, day and night, shall not cease (Genesis 8:22).

God is the One who will destroy the earth in the future. Yes, another judgment, not by water but by fire.

Only by believing God's Word and building a worldview on what God has revealed will we understand true climate change.

MARCH 27
John 4:14

Digging "Wells"

Christians needs to be digging "wells"! In fact, there used to be a lot of "wells" giving water in America, but many are now filled up or gone. If we don't start re-digging "wells" and digging new "wells," there will be a massive famine in the land.

In the Bible, water is symbolic of the gospel, the Holy Spirit, and the Word of God. For instance:

With joy you will draw water from the wells of salvation (Isaiah 12:3).

But whoever drinks of the water that I will give him will never be thirsty again. The water that I will give him will become in him a spring of water welling up to eternal life (John 4:14).

That he might sanctify her, having cleansed her by the washing of water with the word (Ephesians 5:26).

People down through the ages have dug wells to obtain a supply of water. The water of the Word of God once permeated much of the West. America had much such water from different sources. In a way, we could say that lots of different "wells" were dug across the nation so the water of the Word could flow freely. And it did flow freely.

In Genesis 26, we read about a famine in the land. We also read the account of Isaac and how he dug again the wells that Abraham had dug because the Philistines had filled them in.

And Isaac dug again the wells of water that had been dug in the days of Abraham his father, which the Philistines had stopped after the death of Abraham (Genesis 26:18).

Applying this to our present culture, we see that many of the "wells" the fathers (previous generations) dug have been filled by the "Philistines," the secularists who have captured generations away from God's Word and infiltrated many churches and Christian organizations with their anti-biblical worldview.

Now there really is a famine in the land, a famine of the teaching of the Word of God. Reminds me of Amos 8:11: *"Behold, the days are coming,"* declares the Lord GOD, *"when I will send a famine on the land—not a famine of bread, nor a thirst for water, but of hearing the words of the LORD."*

So many church leaders have compromised Genesis with evolution/millions of years or ignored teaching Genesis, and this really has contributed greatly to the famine in the land. So many pastors have encouraged parents to send their kids to the pagan, secular education system to be trained, and most of these kids have walked away from the Church.

One of the most-asked questions I receive these days is by people who ask, "Do you know a church in our area where we live that takes the same stand on God's Word as Answers in Genesis, as we can't find one?" Now such churches exist, but they are the minority. Yes, there's a famine in the land. Many churches now have such shallow teaching and an emphasis on performance on stage. We also see a catastrophic generational loss from the Church with church attendance for Generation Z down to less than 9%.

Yes, the "Philistines" have filled in the wells. We need to be digging those "wells" and digging new "wells" so we can see the water of the Word flowing freely across the nation again. That's what we are doing

THEOLOGY — MARCH 27

through Answers in Genesis, the Creation Museum, and the Ark Encounter. We are doing our best to equip Christians so they can impact their church, family, and friends. We also are providing various resources as part of digging the "wells."

Answers in Genesis does this in many ways by providing books, videos, a streaming platform (Answers TV), curricula for church and home, presentations, conferences, workshops, the Ark Encounter and Creation Museum attractions, and so much more.

Now, when Isaac began to dig the wells again, he did get opposition.

But when Isaac's servants dug in the valley and found there a well of spring water, the herdsmen of Gerar quarreled with Isaac's herdsmen, saying, "The water is ours" (Genesis 26:19–20).

As we challenge church leaders/academics concerning believing God's Word in Genesis, we get opposition from those who vehemently intend on continuing their compromise on Genesis. As we challenge the culture concerning God's Word, the gospel, and the moral issues permeating the culture, we get opposition from the world.

But regardless, we will never stop doing our best to dig "wells" and help others dig "wells." If we are being bold about the truth, we can expect opposition from the enemy. Actually, if as Christians we are not getting opposition to our Christian faith, we should be examining what we are doing and why we are not getting such opposition. As God tells us in His Word:

Indeed, all who desire to live a godly life in Christ Jesus will be persecuted (2 Timothy 3:12).

Blessed are you when people hate you and when they exclude you and revile you and spurn your name as evil, on account of the Son of Man! (Luke 6:22).

> Let's get as many people active in digging "wells" as we can and pray the water of God's Word will flow more than it's ever flowed and impact lives for the Lord Jesus Christ.

MARCH 28
Matthew 7:28-29

Speaking with Authority on Genesis

Should Christians speak with authority?

And when Jesus finished these sayings, the crowds were astonished at his teaching, for he was teaching them as one who had authority, and not as their scribes (Matthew 7:28–29).

Over the 40 years I've been involved in the Answers in Genesis ministry, I've had many Christians/Christian leaders accuse me of saying a person had to believe in six literal days of creation and a young earth to be saved.

Such an accusation is simply not true and can be documented as false from my many talks and articles I've written over the years clearly showing I have never equated salvation with believing in a young earth and literal creation days. What my accusers don't like is the fact I speak with authority on what Genesis clearly says. They want me to allow other views. But there's only one view: God's Word as written.

Now salvation is conditioned upon faith in Christ, not what a person believes about the age of the earth or days of creation. People respond saying it's not an important issue then.

But, even though it's not a salvation issue, it's a very important matter indeed, as it's one of authority.

The following examples represent the types of conversations I've had over the years with various Christians and Christian leaders as I've discussed this topic as I ask questions.

Question: "Do you believe Jesus bodily rose from the dead?"

Answer: "Of course, yes."

Question: "Did you see it happen? Do you have a movie of the event? How do you know?"

Answer: "Because the Bible says so."

Question: "Do you really believe Jesus fed thousands as a miracle?"

Answer: "Yes."

Question: "Did you see this event? How do you know?"

Answer: "Because the Bible says so."

Question: "Do you believe Jesus healed the blind, lame, and deaf, and even raised people from the dead?"

Answer: "Yes."

Question: "How do you know?"

Answer: "I know because the Bible says so."

Question: "Do you believe the Israelites crossed the Red Sea as a miracle, and when wandering in the desert, their clothes and shoes didn't wear out?"

Answer: "Yes."

Question: "How do you know?"

APOLOGETICS

Answer: "Because the Bible teaches this."

Question: "Do you believe a man was swallowed by a fish for three days and survived?"

Answer: "Yes, God's Word says so."

I then move to Genesis and ask, "Do you believe God created in six literal days, death came after sin, and that Noah's Flood was a global event, and we must take Genesis 1–11 as literal history?"

I often get answers like, "Well, no, because of what the scientists tell us about millions of years, big bang, and evolution. The days must be long periods of time. Noah's Flood might have been a local event. God used evolution."

And here is my point! For other events in the Bible, Christians usually accept the accounts as written. But when it comes to Genesis, so many Christians and Christian leaders will go outside of Scripture and use what secular scientists are saying to then claim we can't take Genesis as written on these matters.

And therein lies a major problem. They are putting man's word over God's Word and making man the authority, not God. Sadly, many pastors and Christian academics have taught generations of young people this. In doing so, they've unlocked a door that one can take man's word over God's Word. So if you can take millions of years and reinterpret God's Word, why not take man's word on marriage and gender and reinterpret God's Word to allow gay "marriage," etc. And this is happening.

Over the years because so many Christian leaders have compromised God's Word in Genesis, many have been led to doubt God's Word, and that doubt leads to compromise and unbelief.

We can and should speak with authority on Genesis, just as we can with the rest of Scripture because it is the infallible Word of God!

I am saying their compromise on Genesis is wrong, as there's only one view: God's! And I'll continue speaking with authority (God's) on this.

Are you taking God at His Word or putting man's word over God's Word?

MARCH 29
Isaiah 44:6

Is Your Religion Based on Man's Word or God's Word?

Atheism is a religion. Evolution/millions of years is a religion. Climate change is a religion. Abortion is a religion. LGBTQ is a religion.

The *Merriam-Webster Dictionary* includes part of the definition of *religion* as: "A cause, principle, or system of beliefs held to with ardor and faith."[27] The *Merriam-Webster Dictionary* defines *worldview* as: "A comprehensive conception or apprehension of the world especially from a specific standpoint."[28]

Everyone has a worldview. Everyone has beliefs about life and the universe. One's beliefs determine one's worldview. Your worldview is the way in which you look at the present world and how you interpret the evidence of the present in relation to the past, its purpose, and meaning. Your worldview also determines your morality. Really, your worldview is your religion, and its foundation is either man's word or God's Word.

Thus, ultimately, there are only two religions in the world: one based in man's word and one based in God's Word. Because God is infinite in knowledge and wisdom, those Christians who compromise man's word concerning evolution and millions of years have introduced man's fallible ideas into God's infallible Word. Thus, in reality, the foundation for their worldview is now man's word, because it is now fallible! Such Christians can inconsistently hold to Christian morality and doctrine founded in God's Word, but they can't ignore that their foundation is really man's word, as they've compromised God's Word.

I say all this to make a very important point. As we consider issues before us such as atheism, evolution, millions of years, climate change, abortion, and LGBTQ, we have to recognize these are all part of the religion based on man's word and thus a religion that, in essence, worships man.

Atheists believe (yes, it's a belief) there is no God and that everything can be explained by natural processes. They are really claiming they are God as they don't have infinite information, yet they make absolute statements about rejecting God. It's exactly as Romans 1 states, *Because they exchanged the truth about God for a lie and worshiped and served the creature rather than the Creator, who is blessed forever! Amen* (Romans 1:25).

Evolution/millions of years is a religion. Darwin's motivation was that he wanted to come up with a supposed mechanism for explaining life by natural processes—naturalism is atheism. Naturalistic evolution over millions of years (based on man's fallible beliefs) is a religion. These constitute the pagan religion of the age to try to explain life without God. As we read in Romans: *Claiming to be wise, they became fools, and exchanged the glory of the immortal God for images resembling mortal man and birds and animals and creeping things* (Romans 1:22–23).

This is also a religion that worships man, and yet, so many Christian leaders have compromised this religion with God's Word. Sad!

The modern climate change agenda is a religion. After John Kerry came back from the World Economic Forum in 2023, I heard him on a news conference say that an elite group of people are going to save mankind and save the planet. This is man thinking he can save himself. It's man being his own god (Genesis 3:5). It's a religion that worships man. Of course, if they don't believe the history concerning the Fall and the Flood from God's Word, they will not interpret the evidence they present correctly and will make wrong decisions of man—which is what is happening. Man can't save himself. Only God can save us. The climate change religion is permeating politics and the world. As Romans 1 states: *For although they knew God, they did not honor him as God or give thanks to him, but they became futile in their thinking, and their foolish hearts were darkened. Claiming to be wise, they became fools, and exchanged the glory of the immortal God for images resembling mortal man and birds and animals and creeping things* (Romans 1:21–23).

Abortion is people's attempt to justify doing whatever they want with sex and get rid of any consequences they don't like. It's people being their own god and determining whether a human being (and we are human beings from fertilization) lives or dies. They are prepared to sacrifice (murder) children to the god of self as part of their worship of man. Of course, it's only murder from a Christian worldview perspective. Those who reject God have no absolute basis for morality, so everything is subjective, and morality is relative. Thus, they can justify in their own mind doing whatever is right in their own eyes (Judges 21:25).

As Romans states: *And since they did not see fit to acknowledge God, God gave them up to a debased mind to do what ought not to be done. They were filled with all manner of unrighteousness, evil, covetousness, malice. They are full of envy, murder, strife, deceit, maliciousness* (Romans 1:28–29).

The LGBTQ movement is based on the foundation that man can do whatever he or she wants to do with his or her body. In other words, anything goes, except the absolutes of Christianity to which they are adamantly opposed to and intolerant of. They act as their own god, claiming they own themselves, not God, thus they can do whatever they want. This is also a worship of man. As Romans teaches:

For this reason God gave them up to dishonorable passions. For their women exchanged natural relations for those that are contrary to nature; and the men likewise gave up natural relations with women and were consumed with passion for one another, men committing shameless acts with men and receiving in themselves the due penalty for their error (Romans 1:26–27).

What we are experiencing at the present is that the religion of man, the worship of man, is the dominant religion in the culture. This worship of man is in total conflict with those who worship the one true God. It's the battle that started in Genesis 3 between God's Word and man's word.

Sadly, we also live at a time where the majority of church leaders and Christian academics have compromised God's Word with man's religion, such as evolution and millions of years. And an increasing number are compromising with man's religion of LGBTQ, abortion, and climate change.

Thus says the LORD, the King of Israel and his Redeemer, the LORD of hosts: "I am the first and I am the last; besides me there is no god" (Isaiah 44:6).

And he said with a loud voice, "Fear God and give him glory, because the hour of his judgment has come, and worship him who made heaven and earth, the sea and the springs of water" (Revelation 14:7).

Start challenging people about their religion of worshipping man and point them to the true God.

MARCH 30
Romans 8:22

Does the Universe Really Look Old?

As I have spoken at conferences over the years, people have often come up to me and said:

"When I am talking to someone who believes in an old earth, one of the things I say to them, as a young-earth creationist, is that God didn't make Adam a baby—he made him an adult. And when he created the universe, he created it fully functional, with the appearance of age—even though it wasn't old."

But does the creation look old? Do we know what a young one looks like?

My response often shocks these speakers: "By saying the universe looks old, you are trusting that dating methods can give us an apparent old age for the universe—but they can't."

Let me explain. When people say the universe has "apparent age," usually they are assuming, for whatever reason, that the universe "looks old." I have often found that, unconsciously, such people have already accepted that the fallible dating methods of scientists can give great ages for the earth/universe. So, if they believe what the Scripture says about a young universe, they have to explain away this apparent great age.

But does the universe really look old, or have we simply been indoctrinated to believe it looks old? Would the Creator God of the Bible, who does not lie, really deceive us into thinking that the universe looks old—when according to the Bible's account of history (taking Genesis as literal historical narrative), He created it only about 6,000 years ago? What would a "young universe" look like anyway?

Creation scientists have written many articles to clearly show that all dating methods (other than the record of history given in the Bible) are based on fallible assumptions and can't be trusted to give absolute dates about the past. Also, dozens and dozens of dating methods contradict an old universe and actually support a young age. (For example, the oceans would be much saltier if salts had been accumulating in them for hundreds of millions of years, and many short-lived comets circling the sun should have broken up if they were more than a few thousand years old.)

When God finished creating the heavens and earth, everything was fully formed. The stars burned brightly, the trees were laden with fruit, and animals were ready to bear young. The earth and its inhabitants were designed to last forever, without aging or dying. The first animals and humans were ageless—you couldn't even tell whether they were alive only one day or alive for one thousand years. In short, God created a mature universe.

When God created the stars, He obviously created them mature and fully functional and for a specific purpose: to be for signs and for seasons. When God created Adam and Eve and told them to be fruitful and multiply, He gave them mature bodies that were ready to produce children.

Some people conclude that God would have created them with the appearance of age, say 20 or 30 years old. But would "age" have any effect on Adam's body before he sinned? If the first people—and the universe—were originally designed to last forever, would you expect to see any difference between a man at age 30 or at age 3,000?

SCIENCE

When doctors look at the human body today, they can estimate age from various evidences in the body. But before sin, nothing aged—everything was created "very good." The human body did not experience the effects of sin or aging.

What would a doctor from today's fallen world say if he looked at Adam's and Eve's bodies just after they were created? This doctor would be very confused. Such perfect bodies would show no degenerative aging, and he would be shocked to learn that these adults were less than a day old.

Now it is true that when God created the earth on the first day of creation week, it wasn't fully functional. God deliberately prepared the earth and created various kinds of living things over six days. However, at every stage of creation, everything God did was "good," and all was functional for His created purposes, even when not totally finished.

The creation was then finished and called "very good"—mature but not with so-called "apparent age." When Adam and his first descendants looked at the earth, they did not assume apparent age because they knew, based on God's Word, that creation had taken place recently.

The sun, moon, and stars would be in place fully formed and functioning perfectly.

The dry land would have soil ready for plants. The various original plants, including trees, would have mature fruit to nourish Adam and Eve and the animals. Perhaps trees even had tree rings as a regular part of the tree's structure (for strength, etc.). Adam and Eve and the animals were created mature and fully functional so they could reproduce. But none of these things were "old" or "looked old."

God is not man, that he should lie (Numbers 23:19). God did not deceive us by making a universe that looks old. No, He gave mankind the truth about creation. Only later did the devil deceive Eve about the accuracy of God's Word. Her husband, Adam, then rebelled against God, bringing a curse upon the whole universe. This curse radically changed the appearance and function of the universe. *The whole creation has been groaning together in the pains of childbirth until now* (Romans 8:22).

The world is now an aging, fallen creation—not a creation with great age. We can't look at an aging, fallen creation and understand what the original perfect creation was like. We are living in this fallen world.

We've never experienced a perfect world; only Adam and Eve did.

MARCH 31

1 Corinthians 6:18

What Does God's Word Say About Fornication?

As a Christian, if you were asked to be a best man or bridesmaid at a wedding but found out the groom would be wearing a T-shirt stating, "I'm a proud fornicator," would you agree to do this? First, we need to understand what God's Word says about fornication (premarital or extramarital sex):

Flee from sexual immorality. Every other sin a person commits is outside the body, but the sexually immoral person sins against his own body (1 Corinthians 6:18).

Let marriage be held in honor among all, and let the marriage bed be undefiled, for God will judge the sexually immoral and adulterous (Hebrews 13:4).

I would say the right answer would be to not only politely decline the invitation but to also explain that from a Christian worldview, sexual immorality is a blatant sin. I would also say that even attending the wedding would be condoning such sin, so a Christian should not attend. Christians can't endorse blatant sin.

OK, then what if you were invited to be a best man or bridesmaid at a wedding but found out the bride would be wearing a sign saying, "I love abortion"?

Well, from a Christian perspective we know that abortion, right from fertilization, is killing a human being made in the image of God. It's murder (child sacrifice). God hates "hands that shed innocent blood" (Proverbs 6:17).

There is no way a Christian should accept such an invitation to participate because of the flaunting of such sin. In fact, I suggest a Christian shouldn't even attend such a wedding. A Christian can't condone blatant sin.

Now, what if a Christian was invited to be a best man or bridesmaid at a gay "marriage"? Well, first of all, we need to see what God's Word states about marriage. The reason I put "marriage" in quotes is that there is only one true marriage, the one God created in Genesis when He made the first man from dust, the first woman from the man's side, and then we're told:

Therefore a man shall leave his father and his mother and hold fast to his wife, and they shall become one flesh (Genesis 2:24). This is the creation of marriage. God created marriage, and there's only one true marriage: one man and one woman. Anything else is sin. There is no such thing as gay "marriage." They can call it gay union or whatever else they want to call it, but it's not marriage.

Now what does the Bible say about homosexual behavior?

In the Old Testament we read, *You shall not lie with a male as with a woman; it is an abomination* (Leviticus 18:22). The New Testament confirms this as we read, *Or do you not know that the unrighteous will not inherit the kingdom of God? Do not be deceived: neither the sexually immoral, nor idolaters, nor adulterers, nor men who practice homosexuality, nor thieves, nor the greedy, nor drunkards, nor revilers, nor swindlers will inherit the kingdom of God* (1 Corinthians 6:9–10).

Other passages such as Romans 1 make it very clear that homosexual behavior is sin. So on the basis of this and how God defines true marriage, a Christian can't endorse such sin as gay "marriage." A gay "wedding" is certainly flaunting blatant sin. So again, just as we discussed above for fornication and abortion, a Christian

THEOLOGY   MARCH 31

can't endorse blatant sin. So I would say that a Christian should not participate in such a ceremony or even attend it. Now as soon as I say this I will be accused of hate. No. I do not hate such people. God's Word tells us to love people. And for a Christian, true love is warning people, with gentleness and meekness, about their sin and pointing them to the truth of God's Word and His warning about such blatant sin.

However, it seems even a number of church leaders have determined that homosexuality is not a sin or shouldn't be treated as such. I suggest they do this because there's enormous pressure from the culture to legitimize gay relationships. But Christians should never soften their stand on Scripture to accommodate what the world is demanding.

Christians need to judge what the world is claiming against the absolute authority of the Word of God.

APRIL 1
Romans 3:4

Genesis 3 Attack

Are those who compromise Genesis 1–11 with millions of years and other evolutionary ideas actually helping atheists? Why would I even make such a claim?

Atheists believe *the lie* that there is no God. They reject the supernatural. They believe *the lie* that materialism is all there is, and everything related to the origins of life and the universe came about by natural processes. Now who is the father of lies?

You are of your father the devil, and your will is to do your father's desires. He was a murderer from the beginning, and does not stand in the truth, because there is no truth in him. When he lies, he speaks out of his own character, for he is a liar and the father of lies (John 8:44).

Satan (the devil) is the father of lies. The first attack he made on humanity was when he tempted Adam and Eve by saying, "Did God actually say?" His first attack was on the authority of the Word of God, to get Adam and Eve to doubt God's Word so that doubt would lead to unbelief. It was an attack on the authority of the Word of God.

Now we are warned in the New Testament that the devil will use the same attack on us that he used on Eve to get us to not believe the things of God. In other words, the attack will be on the authority of God's Word.

But I am afraid that as the serpent deceived Eve by his cunning, your thoughts will be led astray from a sincere and pure devotion to Christ (2 Corinthians 11:3).

I call this the Genesis 3 attack. We are warned the devil will use this type of attack to get people to doubt God's Word, knowing doubt leads to not believing God's Word.

Now when you consider history, you will find that the devil has used different attacks down through the ages. In other words, the Genesis 3 attack will manifest itself in different ways at different times. There have been times when the deity of Christ, the Resurrection, or salvation by grace through faith have come under attack. We need to ask ourselves, How is the Genesis 3 attack being manifested in the era we live in?

I have found no matter where I travel throughout the world, in this era (that I believe began in the late 1700s–early 1800s), when people hear those like me teaching God's Word, the gospel, and biblical Christianity, many scoff by saying that science in our day has proven the Bible is not true. They will bring up topics like fossils, evolution, geological dating methods, the age of the universe and earth, millions of years, ape-men, and much more to claim the Bible has been discredited. They will also ask questions like:

How did Noah fit all the animals on the ark? Where did the "races" come from if we all go back to Adam and Eve? Don't dinosaurs disprove the Bible? And many more.

The idea of millions of years primarily came out of atheism of the 1800s when secularists attempted to explain the fossil record without the supernatural (rejecting God's Word and the account of the Flood) and claimed the fossil layers were laid down slowly over millions of years.

Sadly, certain church leaders then adopted the millions of years and attempted to force them into the Scriptures by inventing the gap theory, day-age theory, and other compromise positions. While there are

CHURCH APRIL 1

many problems as a result of such compromise positions, a major one is that by adopting such positions, they are placing man's word in authority over God's Word, unlocking a door that one can take man's ideas and reinterpret God's Word. It's called eisegesis (taking ideas from outside of Scripture to reinterpret Scripture). And it's been a pandemic in the Church that has led to so many of the younger generation doubting God's Word and being put on a slippery slope toward unbelief and eventually leaving the Church. This has been a major attack on the authority of God's Word in our era.

When we look at statistics today, we see a catastrophic generational loss from the Church with current statistics showing less than 9% of Generation Z now attend church.

Atheists want people to doubt and not believe God's Word. Their father is the devil who uses this method to accomplish this. Sadly, many church leaders, unwittingly in many instances I'm sure, have helped atheists by succumbing to the Genesis 3 attack of our time by accepting man's beliefs (based on naturalism) of millions of years. I'm sure many will object to me saying this, but I urge them to consider what such compromises are really doing. They need to examine their approach to the Scriptures to see if they really are getting what they believe from Scripture itself or from outside Scripture—from fallible, sinful man, who does not want the truth!

Christians compromising with millions of years are undermining biblical authority. Yes, it's an authority issue. And that's why Christians believing in millions of years is compromise—it's contamination. *You are the salt of the earth, but if salt has lost its taste, how shall its saltiness be restored? It is no longer good for anything except to be thrown out and trampled under people's feet* (Matthew 5:13).

Taking God's Word as written makes it clear the universe can only be thousands of years old and that death and disease came after sin.

Now let me emphasize something I've said many times. Salvation is conditioned upon faith in Christ, not what one believes about the age of the earth. That does not mean it doesn't matter. It does matter as it's an authority issue.

There's been massive generational loss from the Church and a culture that is deteriorating daily as moral relativism permeates. Much of the Church is lukewarm and weak. Much of the Church has resorted to shallow teaching and experiential entertainment. Something is dreadfully wrong.

By no means! Let God be true though every one were a liar (Romans 3:4).

Wake up, Church, stand back, and look at the big picture.

APRIL 2
1 John 5:13

Are Muslims Going to Hell?

Are Muslims going to hell? OK, so some of you may gulp at me asking that question so bluntly. Actually, this question was asked of me.

I was being interviewed by a secular news reporter about the Ark and Creation Museum attractions, but the first question the reporter asked was, "Are Muslims going to hell?"

That caught me off guard a little, but I'm sure that was the agenda of the reporter. I've had quite a lot of experience dealing with the secular media and realize that the majority of times I'm interviewed, the reporter has an agenda to attack and denigrate Christianity. I'm sure this reporter wanted me to say outright, "Yes," so they could put the headline, "Ken Ham Says Muslims Are Going to Hell" to try to portray us in an unloving, negative light.

When I am being interviewed by such reporters, I want to give answers for the sake of those who will be listening to or watching the program, but I also want to be a witness to the reporter. So, when asked this question, how did I respond?

I said something like, "Well, it doesn't matter if one is a Baptist, Presbyterian, Lutheran, Catholic, Mennonite, Muslim, Orthodox Jew, or any other denomination or religious group. If a person has not repented of sin and received the free gift of salvation offered through the Lord Jesus Christ (being 'born again'), they will be separated from God for eternity in a place the Bible calls hell."

And, sadly, the majority of people will go there as Jesus warned, *Enter by the narrow gate. For the gate is wide and the way is easy that leads to destruction, and those who enter by it are many* (Matthew 7:13).

I made sure the reporter understood that everyone needs to be born again, including the reporter, as I referenced the passage in John 3 about Nicodemus:

Now there was a man of the Pharisees named Nicodemus, a ruler of the Jews. This man came to Jesus by night and said to him, "Rabbi, we know that you are a teacher come from God, for no one can do these signs that you do unless God is with him." Jesus answered him, "Truly, truly, I say to you, unless one is born again he cannot see the kingdom of God." Nicodemus said to him, "How can a man be born when he is old? Can he enter a second time into his mother's womb and be born?" Jesus answered, "Truly, truly, I say to you, unless one is born of water and the Spirit, he cannot enter the kingdom of God" (John 3:1–5).

Water is often used in Scripture as a symbol of the Word of God. Jesus is telling Nicodemus he must be "born again" or redeemed by the Word of God and the work of God's Spirit on his heart to save him for eternity. This is consistent with, *for by grace you have been saved through faith. And this is not your own doing; it is the gift of God* (Ephesians 2:8). In other words, Jesus was explaining to Nicodemus that we are born as human beings, born of a woman, but we need to be born again, to be born from above!

In summary, the message about being born again is:

For God so loved the world, that he gave his only Son, that whoever believes in him should not perish but have eternal life (John 3:16).

THEOLOGY — APRIL 2

Because, if you confess with your mouth that Jesus is Lord and believe in your heart that God raised him from the dead, you will be saved (Romans 10:9).

Repent therefore, and turn back, that your sins may be blotted out (Acts 3:19).

If we confess our sins, he is faithful and just to forgive us our sins and to cleanse us from all unrighteousness (1 John 1:9).

Instead of the hell we deserve for our sin against a holy God, by repenting and believing, we receive new and eternal life with Christ. What a glorious message of mercy, grace, hope, and love! So, anyone who is not born again, regardless of what label you have, will be separated from God in hell for eternity.

There's another aspect to this. We also need to judge what people believe against the absolute authority of God's Word and challenge them if their beliefs are incorrect. For instance, with Muslims, we need to be aware of the following so we can lovingly point out the problems with their beliefs when judged against God's Word:

The Quran's teachings regarding salvation are inconsistent. On the one hand, the Quran teaches that salvation is based on purification by good deeds (Quran 7:6–9). A Muslim can become righteous through prayer, almsgiving, fasting, and living according to the Quran. Yet the Quran also teaches that Allah has predetermined every person's destiny, and one's righteous acts may or may not affect Allah's decision (Quran 57:22). It teaches that everyone, both the righteous and the unrighteous, will be led into hell by Allah before the righteous will enter heaven (Quran 19:67–72). Therefore, no Muslim can know his or her eternal destiny in this life. Even Muhammad himself was unsure of his salvation (Quran 31:34, 46:9).

Allah loves only those who first love him (Quran 3:31–32) or who do good deeds (2:195). God first loved us while we were yet sinning (1 John 4:10; Romans 5:8). The Quran's Allah and the Bible's Yahweh are simply not the same deity with the same attributes.

Muslims believe Jesus was a real person, but they think He only came to teach and do miracles like any other prophet. They don't believe that He's the true Son of God. But Jesus is God; He's the Creator (Colossians 1:16).

As Christians, we need to show love to everyone and share the vital news with them that *Jesus said to him, "I am the way, and the truth, and the life. No one comes to the Father except through me"* (John 14:6).

We need to diligently study God's Word, know how to defend the Christian faith, and study to know what others believe so we can point out what God's Word clearly teaches compared to what they believe. And we need to lovingly point out that we are all sinners in need of salvation through Christ.

I write these things to you who believe in the name of the Son of God, that you may know that you have eternal life (1 John 5:13).

Hell is a real place. We don't want to see anyone go there! Receive the free gift of salvation through Jesus Christ.

We can know where we will spend eternity.

APRIL 3
1 Corinthians 14:8

The Church Needs to Stop Giving an Uncertain Sound

And if the bugle gives an indistinct sound, who will get ready for battle? (1 Corinthians 14:8).

I believe much of the Church today is giving an indistinct or uncertain sound. Because of this, much of the Church is lukewarm and, sadly, not impacting generations with the truth of God's Word as should be happening. This is a major contributing factor as to why there's a generational loss from the Church. The younger generations are much more secular and impacting the culture against Christianity.

If you ask the secularists in the world where the universe and humans come from, by and large, they will give you a distinct message. Even though there may be differences in the details, the basic message is the same:

- A big bang brought the universe and subsequently the earth into existence billions of years ago.
- Somehow matter over millions of years formed the molecule of heredity.
- Through natural processes, eventually, life evolved.
- Life began in the oceans and evolved into terrestrial creatures.
- Amphibians over millions of years evolved into reptiles.
- Fish evolved into amphibians.
- Reptiles evolved into birds and mammals.
- Mammals evolved into apelike creatures.
- Fossils were laid down over millions of years as life evolved.
- Apelike creatures evolved into man.
- In summary, the universe and life were formed over billions of years as a result of naturalistic evolutionary processes.

The above is basically taught as fact in education systems of the world, through the media, museums, and so on. This message permeates the world.

Now, if you ask Christians and Christian leaders and academics how the universe and life, including humans, came into existence, there will be a variety of answers that go something like this:

- God created but over millions of years.
- God created like Genesis states.
- God used evolution to evolve animals but created man directly.
- God used evolution to evolve man from apelike creatures.
- Noah's Flood was just a local event.
- God created billions of years ago and then recreated the earth and life in six days.
- God created in six days, but the days were long periods of time.
- Fossils were formed during the Flood of Noah's day.
- Fossils were laid down over millions of years.
- And many other variations.

As you look at the above, we see the Church giving all sorts of positions in regard to Genesis and the origin of life and the universe. And though a small minority proclaim Genesis as they should, the majority are preaching a message that Genesis is not to be taken literally, but man's evolutionary beliefs are to be taken literally!

Think about that! So many people take man's words literally but God's Word allegorically! No wonder so many in the Church are confused about what to believe concerning Genesis. Sadly, many of the young people have rejected God's Word and walked away from the Church.

CHURCH — APRIL 3

In one way, much of the Church is giving a "certain" and "distinct" sound, but it's the wrong certain sound. In reality, much of the Church has compromised a pagan religion with God's Word. Yes, they are taking man's word literally but rejecting God's Word. I challenge those compromising Christians/Christian leaders to stop being yoked with unbelievers in what they believe concerning origins. We should not allow the secular worldview based on man's word to contaminate God's Word. Christians need to separate from the pagan religion of the age.

Do not be unequally yoked with unbelievers. For what partnership has righteousness with lawlessness? Or what fellowship has light with darkness? What accord has Christ with Belial? Or what portion does a believer share with an unbeliever? What agreement has the temple of God with idols? For we are the temple of the living God; as God said, 'I will make my dwelling among them and walk among them, and I will be their God, and they shall be my people. Therefore go out from their midst, and be separate from them, says the Lord, and touch no unclean thing; then I will welcome you, and I will be a father to you, and you shall be sons and daughters to me, says the Lord Almighty (2 Corinthians 6:14–18).

In the Old Testament, God used many different ways to teach the Israelites not to be impacted (contaminated) by the world but to be there to impact the world with the truth. As God said to Jeremiah, we are here to influence the world, not have the world influence us. *Learn not the way of the nations* (Jeremiah 10:2).

I believe much of the Church has been contaminated by the world by accepting evolutionary ideas and compromising Genesis. The Church needs to stop giving an uncertain sound. The certain sound the Church needs is the sound of unity on God's Word beginning in Genesis:

- The Bible is God's Word.
- God is the infinite eternal Creator God.
- God created as is stated in Genesis just a few thousand years ago (around 6,000 years).
- God created everything in six literal days.
- God created distinct kinds of animals and plants to reproduce their kind.
- One kind of animal cannot change into a totally different kind.
- God created the first man and woman, two genders, the first marriage—a man and a woman.
- There was no death or disease in the world, as everything was "very good."
- Man did not evolve from apelike creatures, as the first man was made from dust and the first woman was made from the man's rib.
- Man rebelled against God, bringing sin and the judgment of death into the world.
- God promised a Savior to save us from our sin.
- God judged the world with a global Flood because of man's wickedness.
- Most of the fossils were formed as a result of Noah's Flood around 4,300 years ago.
- Man rebelled again at the time of the Tower of Babel.
- God gave different languages as a judgment that dispersed people to form nations/people groups.

Observational science confirms the history in Genesis over and over again in geology, biology, astronomy, and anthropology.

> Imagine the impact on generations of people if the Church gave that certain and distinct sound! That's how the Church can equip generations for the spiritual battle raging around us.

APRIL 4
2 Timothy 2:15

Calvinist or Arminian?

Am I a Calvinist or Arminian? I knew that would get your attention!

People define those terms in various ways. But some define Calvinist as "the Protestant theological system of John Calvin and his successors" and Arminian as "doctrines of Jacobus Arminius... a Dutch Protestant theologian who rejected the Calvinist doctrine of predestination."

I heard someone tell the difference between a Calvinist and an Arminian this way: A Calvinist and Arminian were riding through the woods when a tree branch knocked them both off their horses. The Arminian said, "What a fool I was not to duck in time and get knocked off by that branch." The Calvinist said, "I'm glad that's over and done with."

Over the years, I have had people ask me my position in regard to being Calvinist or Arminian. Because I emphasize the sovereignty of God and presuppositions that build my thinking, I've had some say I must be a Calvinist. Then I've had others say that I must not be a Calvinist because I challenge people to commit their lives to the Lord. Some have told me I confuse them, and they can't figure out if I'm a Calvinist or an Arminian. So what am I? Well, I'm both Calvinist and Arminian, and I'm neither Calvinist nor Arminian. If you are confused, then that's good.

You see, I personally don't like man-made labels such as Calvinist or Arminian in regard to a position on Scripture. When I say I'm both, it's because in many ways I agree with both. When I say I'm neither, I'm saying I'm not one or the other.

I want to be a biblical Christian, and that's the emphasis I want to bring. To the best of our ability, we need build our way of thinking on God's Word without bringing our own ideas to Scripture. I realize that's hard and many times we don't recognize our own biases from the way we have been impacted by others.

I also want to say that as fallible, finite humans who know next to nothing compared to what God knows (He is infinite in wisdom and knowledge, Colossians 2:3), we have to understand our own limitations, and the fact that there are things we just won't be able to explain.

We do have to be careful about defining things in human terms when we are dealing with a sovereign, infinite God. For instance, can we really understand Jesus was fully man and fully God? He became the God-man—100% human and 100% God. I can't and never will understand this. I have to accept it as a finite human being. I know it's true because God's Word tells me so. Remember, God spoke to Job and used many illustrations to help Job learn the lesson that he knew nothing compared to God: *I know that you can do all things, and that no purpose of yours can be thwarted. "Who is this that hides counsel without knowledge?" Therefore I have uttered what I did not understand, things too wonderful for me, which I did not know. "Hear, and I will speak; I will question you, and you make it known to me." I had heard of you by the hearing of the ear, but now my eye sees you; therefore I despise myself, and repent in dust and ashes* (Job 42:2–6).

What I see all the way through Scripture is that man's responsibility and God's sovereignty work hand in hand. I can't explain how it works, but it does because God is the infinite Creator, and He brings them together.

THEOLOGY — APRIL 4

For instance, when it comes to salvation, there's man's responsibility:

And he said to them, "Go into all the world and proclaim the gospel to the whole creation" (Mark 16:15).

How then will they call on him in whom they have not believed? And how are they to believe in him of whom they have never heard? And how are they to hear without someone preaching? And how are they to preach unless they are sent? As it is written, "How beautiful are the feet of those who preach the good news!" (Romans 10:14–15).

Because, if you confess with your mouth that Jesus is Lord and believe in your heart that God raised him from the dead, you will be saved (Romans 10:9).

There are, of course, many other verses we could point to. But then we consider God's sovereignty:

We know that non-Christians are "dead in the trespasses and sin" (Ephesians 2:1), and no human being can raise a dead person to life.

So faith comes from hearing, and hearing through the word of Christ (Romans 10:17).

For by grace you have been saved through faith. And this is not your own doing; it is the gift of God (Ephesians 2:8).

There are, of course, many other verses we could use for this too.

But here we have man's responsibility and God's sovereignty in salvation. God brings them together. I can't explain it. But I know I need to be faithful to do all I can to preach God's Word, to convince people of the truth, to give them answers to their skeptical questions knowing I don't do the convincing, God does.

God opens people's hearts to the truth. God also hardens the hearts of people who harden their hearts, as we see from the example of the Pharaoh of the Exodus. *But Pharaoh hardened his heart this time also, and did not let the people go* (Exodus 8:32); *But the LORD hardened the heart of Pharaoh* (Exodus 9:12).

Yes, we need to pray for these lost people and do all we can to convince them of the truth of God's Word and the gospel, but we don't do the convincing, God does. We can't raise a dead person to life, only God can.

When you understand this, I find it relaxing really, knowing that as long as I'm diligent to study God's Word, learn the answers to skeptical questions, honor His Word and His Son, defend the Christian faith to the best of my ability and knowledge, and point people to the gospel, then I leave the saving of the souls to God!

Do your best to present yourself to God as one approved, a worker who has no need to be ashamed, rightly handling the word of truth (2 Timothy 2:15).

And he said to them, "Go into all the world and proclaim the gospel to the whole creation" (Mark 16:15).

But in your hearts honor Christ the Lord as holy, always being prepared to make a defense to anyone who asks you for a reason for the hope that is in you; yet do it with gentleness and respect (1 Peter 3:15).

> Let's make sure we are all biblical Christians and understand we won't be able to define and explain how responsibility and sovereignty work together, but rest in knowing that God does.

APRIL 5
Genesis 2:24

A Father's Role

What is one of the primary importances of marriage? God created marriage when He made the first man from dust and the first woman from the man's side (rib).

Therefore a man shall leave his father and his mother and hold fast to his wife, and they shall become one flesh (Genesis 2:24).

Now in Malachi 2, there was a situation where Israelite men were divorcing their wives and marrying pagans or taking on multiple wives. They were perverting marriage as God ordained it to be. The prophet Malachi (under the inspiration of God) spoke to these people and stated:

Did he not make them one, with a portion of the Spirit in their union? And what was the one God seeking? Godly offspring (Malachi 2:15).

Let's analyze this verse: *Did he not make them* [a reference to the first two humans, Adam and Eve] *one* [one flesh, a reference to Genesis 2:24 that God made the woman from the man, and so in marriage, they become one as they were one flesh], *with a portion of the Spirit in their union* [what was the purpose of this union of two who become one]*? And what was the one God seeking? Godly offspring.*

Note, a primary purpose of this union was not just to produce offspring but to produce "godly offspring."

How does one go about producing "godly offspring"?

As a Christian, as I emphasize over and over, we need to ensure we build all our thinking on God's Word to ensure we have a truly biblical worldview in every area. So in regard to marriage and producing godly offspring, we need to make sure we understand what God has instructed for the roles of the man and woman in marriage and the methods and priorities for raising children.

The family is the first and most fundamental of all human institutions God ordained in Scripture. The family is actually the educational unit God uses to transfer a spiritual legacy to the next generation and to impact the world for the Lord Jesus Christ. So, let's summarize one of the basic principles God gives us for raising a family.

But I want you to understand that the head of every man is Christ, the head of a wife is her husband, and the head of Christ is God. Every man who prays or prophesies with his head covered dishonors his head (1 Corinthians 11:3–4)

The father (husband) is to be the spiritual head of the home. Remember, God made Adam first and gave him the instruction not to eat the fruit of the tree of knowledge of good and evil. That's why Adam gets the blame for sin, not Eve.

There are many Scriptures that make it plain that the father is to be the spiritual head:

Fathers, do not provoke your children to anger, but bring them up in the discipline and instruction of the Lord (Ephesians 6:4).

The father makes known to the children your faithfulness (Isaiah 38:19).

FAMILY — APRIL 5

Which he commanded our fathers to teach to their children, that the next generation might know them, the children yet unborn, and arise and tell them to their children, so that they should set their hope in God and not forget the works of God, but keep his commandments; and that they should not be like their fathers, a stubborn and rebellious generation, a generation whose heart was not steadfast, whose spirit was not faithful to God (Psalm 78:5–8).

Not only does Psalm 78 remind fathers to teach their children, it tells us that Israelite fathers were rebellious and didn't do what God had commanded them. We see the result of this in the generation produced by the generation that saw God's miraculous hand in taking them across the Jordan River—they served pagan gods. In one generation, the spiritual legacy was lost because fathers didn't train their children as they should have.

We have a similar situation in the Church today. Sadly, most fathers do not carry out their God-given role to be the spiritual head of their family and ensure they are leading the family spiritually. Most have abdicated their spiritual headship role and leave it up to the church or others. And most kids from church homes attend public schools where mostly (there are exceptions, of course) pagan teachers have the greatest impact on shaping the kids' thinking.

There has also been a great lack of teaching from the pulpits to train fathers concerning their God-given role in the family. And there is a devastating situation today in that there are a massive percentage of single-parent homes, homes with major marriage issues, or homes where a Christian married a non-Christian, resulting in all sorts of problems.

The devil knows the family is the backbone of the culture and has used many different means to attack and destroy the family. I challenge Christian fathers to kneel humbly before the Lord and commit to be the godly husband and godly fathers they should be and be obedient to the Lord and His clear instruction in Scripture to take charge of the spiritual upbringing of his family.

I challenge fathers to teach their children that a Christian should never knowingly look to a non-Christian regarding marriage. I also challenge church leaders to teach men how to be godly husbands and fathers and to help those families where there are issues undermining the family.

And I challenge godly wives to encourage their husbands toward the godly leadership of their family that God requires of them.

I challenge fathers to carefully consider who really is shaping their children's thinking and make the right decisions for the children's education, understanding the most important part of their education is the spiritual input, as that impacts them for eternity.

Take to heart what God through the Apostle Paul states:

But whatever gain I had, I counted as loss for the sake of Christ. Indeed, I count everything as loss because of the surpassing worth of knowing Christ Jesus my Lord. For his sake I have suffered the loss of all things and count them as rubbish, in order that I may gain Christ (Philippians 3:7–8).

There's nothing more important than your children knowing Christ.

APRIL 6
Proverbs 13:22

A Father's Legacy

At the Creation Museum, in the lobby of the Legacy Hall auditorium, there is an exhibit called the *Ham Family Legacy Exhibit.* This exhibit features my father and mother and tells of the phenomenal spiritual impact they had on their family.

Inside a glass case is my father's Bible, opened at Genesis, showing his many notes he had written beside the text. He would use such notes as he taught Bible studies, not just on Genesis but through the whole Bible.

There is also a wooden model of Noah's ark that he built me many years ago, not knowing that one day we would build a life-size Noah's Ark attraction.

I've had the opportunity to speak to people who were at the exhibit contemplating what was being conveyed. I've asked them, "What does this exhibit mean to you?" The answers go something like this, "It's challenging us about what legacy we are leaving in our children and what legacy we are leaving in this world."

I've told people that really the ministry of Answers in Genesis, the Ark Encounter, and Creation Museum that impacts (conservatively estimated from our research) 30 million people directly and tens of millions more indirectly each year is a legacy of parents who taught their children to stand boldly and uncompromisingly on the authority of the Word of God.

My father was a teacher, a school principal. Because he excelled at what he did, he was promoted every three years to a bigger school with more responsibility. We were transferred to different towns around the state of Queensland in Australia. My father was a great spiritual leader for our family.

My parents had such a love for the Lord and His Word, they were always seeking ways to reach people with the saving gospel message. If they found a town where they were to live didn't have a Sunday school, they would start one!

They were a great example to us in supporting various missions and missionaries, as they wanted to do all they could to proclaim the truth of God's Word and the saving gospel. They would also invite missionaries to come to an area and run evangelistic campaigns. We often had missionaries staying in our home.

When I was 10 years old, my parents were involved with a missionary from the Open Air Campaigners organization (which was founded in Australia) who was going to run a program for children at the church we were attending. My parents would invite children from the local area to come to the program, and they would offer to pick them up and drive them to and from the program. Those were the days when there were no seatbelts in cars, and you could pack as many people in a car as you could!

During this particular outreach program, the missionary gave a challenge to the kids. I remember him saying something like, "For those of you who have put your trust in Jesus and are willing to do whatever He wants you to do and go anywhere He wants you to go, I want you to sign this piece of paper with this commitment on it."

FAMILY — APRIL 6

I remember saying to myself, "Yes, I trust the Lord Jesus to save me. I want to be like my parents and tell people about Jesus and His Word in the Bible. I want to do whatever He wants me to do and go wherever He wants me to go." I really meant this.

I did not know that I would become a schoolteacher, and God would call me to start a creation apologetics ministry in our home. I did not know that the Lord would call me and my family to go to America and eventually start the Answers in Genesis ministry that also would build the two leading Christian-themed attractions in the world.

Yes, truly, the Answers in Genesis ministry is a legacy of parents who loved God's Word and had a burden to reach souls for the Lord.

My father heard about the plans for the Creation Museum, but he never got to see this God-honoring attraction, and he never knew about the Ark Encounter attraction, yet his legacy lives on in these attractions and in the ministry of Answers in Genesis that is reaching millions around the world.

My parents never had much materially, but they used whatever material means they had and time they specially put aside to teach their own children the truth of God's Word and the gospel and reach so many others with this vital message of God's Word and the saving gospel.

And their legacy not only lives on in the AiG ministry, but the Lord brought a godly woman into my life (Mally) and gave us five wonderful children who all have trusted Christ for salvation. And they all are passionate about defending the Christian faith and never compromising God's Word. Four of them have married godly spouses (we are still praying for a godly man for one daughter), and they are raising their children (18 grandchildren) to stand on the authority of God's Word. Two of our grandchildren have married godly spouses, and now, we have our first great grandchild who will be taught by godly parents.

What a legacy.

A good man leaves an inheritance [legacy] to his children's children (Proverbs 13:22).

We often think about material inheritance when we read this verse, but I want to challenge all of us that the most important "inheritance" is that spiritual legacy that we can pass on to the next generation, and to the next, and next, and so on.

What legacy are you leaving in this world and in your children?

APRIL 7
Matthew 7:29

A Father's Impact

Fathers have a vital impact on their families. It's well-known that because so many fathers have abdicated their spiritual headship role in their family, there is a great lack of godly young men available to marry godly young ladies.

I praise the Lord for the impact my father had on our family and on me as one of his sons.

When my father was dying in a hospital in 1995 at age 66, one of my younger brothers was with him and asked him, "Why did you love God's Word so much?" All of us knew that our father would never knowingly compromise God's Word. He hated compromise. He taught us to spot compromise regarding God's Word at a million miles away!

My father answered with something like this: "My father died when I was 16, so then I didn't have an earthly father, so I turned to the words of my heavenly Father and read them and studied them over and over again." He became a student of the Word! He knew what God's Word stated. And he wanted to make sure he let God speak to him through His Word.

He understood that once someone used ideas outside of Scripture to begin reinterpreting parts of God's Word, that was unlocking a door to undermine the authority of Scripture. He knew that once the door was unlocked, it could easily be pushed open further and further as doubt led to unbelief.

Our father always stood boldly on the authority of God's Word. When he was asked to preach in church or was teaching a Bible study group, I can still see and hear him as he would get so excited about quoting Scriptures such as, "Have you not read, 'it is written'" and "Thus says the Lord." When he quoted such verses, he would remind everyone of the authority of God's Word.

When the pastor of a church we were attending (I was about 12 years old at the time) stated from the pulpit that a Christian can believe in evolution and just reinterpret Genesis, my father met with the pastor to challenge him and explain that such a position was compromising God's Word. Because the pastor wouldn't change his position, my father led his family away from that church to a different one. He didn't want us as children being led astray by this church leader. He took very seriously his responsibility as the spiritual leader of our home.

At my father's memorial service in 1995, each of the six children gave a brief testimony about their father. We all independently prepared what we were going to say. As each of us gave our testimony honoring our father, we all said many different things in different ways, but we also said the same thing! What came through each of the testimonies was the impact our father had on each of us regarding standing uncompromisingly and boldly on the authority of the Word of God. Yes, our father's stand on biblical authority came through loud and clear.

After the service, one of my good friends came up to me and said something like, "Wow! What phenomenal testimonies about a father's impact on children concerning the authority of the Word of God. I'm going home to ask my children, 'What are you going to say about me when I'm dead?'"

FAMILY — APRIL 7

I thought to myself, that would be a great title for a book. Imagine this title, "What Are Your Children Going to Say About You When You're Dead?"

That certainly is something to ponder. What spiritual impact are you having on your children and others? I'll never forget the things my father taught me about handling God's Word.

For instance, regarding study Bibles, my father taught me this: "Always remember the notes in study Bibles are not inspired like the text. And always use the text as a commentary on the notes." He was teaching us that man's word is fallible and only God's Word is infallible. While the notes may have some great explanations to help us understand the text, they can also have incorrect information.

One example that we discussed were the notes in the Scofield Reference Bible about the gap theory. The gap theory is a compromise position to try to accommodate the supposed millions of years into the Bible and come up with an explanation for the fall of Satan. When one uses the text of Scripture to judge these notes, it's easy to see that what is proposed about the so-called gap theory is unscriptural.

Another example was when my father taught us about something that supposedly contradicted what the Bible states. My father taught something like this:

"If a person claims that something contradicts Scripture, then go to the Scripture first and study the passage carefully, in context, and according to the type of literature and language. (He taught us the grammatical-historical interpretive method). If you are then sure you know what it is clearly teaching and this supposed contradiction still exists, then there must be something wrong with what this person is claiming. And just because we can't resolve the supposed contradiction at that time doesn't mean the Bible is wrong, it means we just don't have all the answers. We need to keep searching for the answers as there may be something we will find that will show us why what that person is stating is wrong. But you don't compromise God's Word just because something outside of Scripture seemingly contradicts Scripture."

I think all this (and much more) had a great impact on me! Whenever I say that while giving my testimony, I find people laugh. They realize that my father had a phenomenal impact on me and why I and the Answers in Genesis ministry stand so boldly on God's Word today. Yes, our father certainly had a great impact on his family.

There are many verses of Scripture that remind me of my father, but one of them is:

For he was teaching them as one who had authority, and not as their scribes (Matthew 7:29).

I remember my father telling people that because Jesus is God, and we have His Word, the absolute authority of the Word of God, then when we teach God's Word without compromise, we can speak with authority!

And people loved my father's preaching and his teaching at Bible study! He always spoke with authority because He believed with a passion the authority of the Word of God.

What are your children going to say about you when you're dead?

APRIL 8
Ezekiel 33:7-9

Stand Boldly Against Compromise

You may be surprised to learn this, but there is something I really, really dislike about being in the ministry of Answers in Genesis! Now what would that be? Actually, it's something that should burden our hearts as Christians.

First, let me tell you about what I love about the Answers in Genesis apologetics ministry. I love the opportunities the Lord has opened for us, including building the Creation Museum and Ark Encounter attractions, reaching millions of people with the truth of God's Word and the gospel as thousands pour in daily.

I'm so thankful we can reach tens of millions of people a year through our websites, see thousands of churches use AiG's Answers Bible Curriculum, and have thousands of churches adopt AiG's Answers Vacation Bible School (VBS) program to reach hundreds of thousands of children each year.

I'm thrilled that millions of books, DVDs, gospel tracts, and other resources have been purchased from Answers in Genesis or given away by AiG. My heart is so warmed when the Lord gives me opportunities to speak to adults, teens, and kids at churches and conferences.

Even though it was a stressful and nerve-racking debate, I praise the Lord I was able to debate Bill Nye "the Science Guy" publicly and be a witness for God's Word and the gospel to many millions. Another stressful time is when I'm able to speak at secular institutions or interact with liberal theologians—but it's all a part of what the Lord has called AiG to do.

I'm saddened when we experience attacks from secularists and read *the lies* they spread about us—but that's all to be expected in a fallen world. I groan when I'm about to be interviewed by the secular media, knowing the majority of the published stories will misquote, mock, and attack us. But again, this is all a necessary part of contending for the faith in a world where people "loved the darkness rather than the light" (John 3:19).

But even with all these challenges, there is one thing I really dislike about being in this ministry! And as I said, it's something every Bible-believing Christian should hate. I hate it when we have to publicly oppose, debate, and challenge sincere Christians who, while they believe the gospel (and would even say they believe in biblical inerrancy), compromise God's Word in Genesis. That is what I'm most saddened and stressed about. And all Christians should be saddened by this, as Genesis 1–11 is the foundation for everything: for all doctrine, for our Christian worldview, and for the gospel.

I hate it when the world sees this contention among believers. But at the same time, it's very important for Christians and non-Christians to see us boldly, uncompromisingly, and unashamedly standing on the authority of God's Word from the very first verse.

As I've stated many times, and as we have documented with research published in various books, compromise on Genesis (particularly with Christians who add millions of years into the Bible) has had a devastating impact on how this generation views the Bible. And sadly, this compromise has been a major factor as to why so many people are leaving the Church and are now secularized in their thinking.

CHURCH — APRIL 8

It must be perplexing to many people that Christians with a heart for the gospel, who say they believe in inerrancy, battle each other over their views on Genesis. But it's our contention that compromising Christians (as I call them) have an inconsistent approach to Scripture that unlocks a door to undermine biblical authority in Genesis—and puts people on a slippery slope toward unbelief through the rest of Scripture. Such compromising Christians are trusting man's word over God's Word in Genesis. They are doing what I call eisegesis, not exegesis.

In fact, because we are so burdened by the rampant compromise in the Church regarding Genesis, we work hard in contending for the faith by exposing and challenging this compromise. This is particularly true when it comes to Christian leaders and Bible college/seminary professors.

This compromise is really no different from what the prophets dealt with as recorded in the books of Isaiah, Jeremiah, Hosea, and others, as we read about leaders who compromised God's Word with man's fallible beliefs. That's why, as much as I hate it, it's so important for us at AiG to do all we can to passionately reach out to these leaders and challenge them.

We plead with Christian leaders to apply a consistent hermeneutic to Scripture and reject compromise that undermines the authority of the Word, which has such a negative impact on the people they influence.

Now when we do stand against Christian leaders who compromise, I sometimes get accused of being unloving and have people tell me that I should be going to these leaders personally as per Matthew 18. But it's not a personal matter. It is not a Matthew 18 situation. When Christian leaders make public statements and teach compromising positions on God's Word beginning in Genesis publicly, then we need to judge what they teach against God's Word publicly. We need to warn people. It's not a personal conflict situation.

Now I'm not saying all those who compromise God's Word are not Christians. But those who are compromising God's Word are not only undermining its authority but unlocking a door for a stumbling block to be placed in people's way in regard to trusting God's Word. I believe many in the younger generations have been led astray by Christian leaders who have compromised God's Word.

I have often been reminded of the watchman in Ezekiel:

Whenever you hear a word from my mouth, you shall give them warning from me. If I say to the wicked, O wicked one, you shall surely die, and you do not speak to warn the wicked to turn from his way, that wicked person shall die in his iniquity, but his blood I will require at your hand. But if you warn the wicked to turn from his way, and he does not turn from his way, that person shall die in his iniquity, but you will have delivered your soul (Ezekiel 33:7–9).

> **When we have the opportunity to do so, we must stand lovingly, graciously, with gentleness, but boldly against compromise to warn people, knowing such compromise can put people on a slippery slide of unbelief.**

APRIL 9
Matthew 5:14-16

Even the Court System Is Not Above the Constitution

A number of years ago, an item made international news that a U.S. federal judge ruled in favor of Answers in Genesis in its religious freedom lawsuit against the state of Kentucky! Although this is an American situation, there is teaching and warning here for every nation.

Kentucky state officials, including the governor, had denied AiG's and the Ark Encounter's right to participate in a state tourism tax-incentive program available to all qualifying groups. The federal judge also confirmed that as a religious organization, AiG had a right to use a religious preference in hiring at the Ark. In other words, we can require employees to sign our Statement of Faith.

It was a huge win for the freedom of religion in America and for the free exercise thereof. It was a major win for the U.S. Constitution, the First Amendment, and the 1964 Civil Rights Act and its Title VII on hiring for religious groups. It was a huge win for Answers in Genesis and the Ark project, and it helped set a precedent that has been and will be cited for years to come. It's really a huge win for Christendom in America!

So why were so many of the Ark's opponents shocked and dismayed with the judge's sensible ruling? Not only were the usual aggressive secularists/atheists stunned, but even some in the church decried the judge's decision. They claimed the judge did not abide by the so-called "separation of church and state" and/or that it was illegal for AiG to use a religious preference in hiring.

I have come to realize that many in the Church and the secular world are suffering the consequences of a particular problem. Hosea 4 really sums it up with the verse that states that people suffer from a "lack of knowledge" (Hosea 4:6). I have found that many do not have the knowledge they should about the U.S. Constitution or the 1964 Civil Rights Act.

When discussing the state of the Western culture, I've often used the example from Joshua 4 of the miracle of the Israelites crossing the Jordan River and then building a monument of 12 stones. The 12 stones were meant to remind the Israelites to pass on the knowledge of God to the next generation. Because they failed to do so, the Israelites lost the culture in just one generation.

Not only has much of the Church today failed to instruct the current generation on the things of the Lord as they should have, but many people in both the Church and the secular world do not have an understanding of history. As a result, they may be doomed to make the same mistakes of the past. Ignorance abounds!

We've all heard the phrase "separation of church and state," but it's just not in the U.S. Constitution! The phrase is used by secularists and others to explain away the establishment clause of the First Amendment, which reads: "Congress shall make no law respecting an establishment of religion."

Of course, the First Amendment was written to prevent a state-sponsored church from being imposed on people, as it was in England. Now, the rest of the U.S. First Amendment reads: "Congress shall make no law respecting an establishment of religion, or prohibiting the free exercise thereof; or abridging the freedom of speech, or of the press; or the right of the people peaceably to assemble, and to petition the government for a redress of grievances."

CHURCH APRIL 9

Secularists often dismiss the phrase "the free exercise" of religion. They want to treat Christians as second-class citizens! Just because an organization like AiG is a Christian one doesn't mean it can't receive a tax-rebate incentive offered to any organization that will bring economic impact and jobs to a state. That's what the Tourism Development Program in Kentucky offers.

We said all along that to deny AiG this right to participate is viewpoint discrimination and violates our First Amendment rights to the free exercise of religion. On the basis of the Constitution, the federal judge ruled that the state must allow AiG the opportunity for its incentive application to move forward. That's what we expected would happen if a judge ruled according to the U.S. Constitution and the law.

The judge stated in his ruling, "The Court finds the Commonwealth's exclusion of AiG from participating in the program for the reasons stated (i.e., on the basis of AiG's religious beliefs, purpose, mission, message, or conduct) is a violation of AiG's rights under the First Amendment to the federal Constitution."

He also stated the following: "Title VII of the Civil Rights Act prohibits employers from discriminating because of 'race, color, religion, sex or national origin.'"

He then added, "In order to protect the constitutional rights of religious organizations, however, Title VII has expressly exempted religious organizations from the prohibition against discrimination on the basis of religion."

The judge then cited the exception found in Title VII of the Civil Rights Act (which, it seems, most secularists and even many American Christians don't even know exists):

"This subchapter shall not apply to . . . a religious corporation, association, educational institution, or society with respect to the employment of individuals of a particular religion to perform work connected with the carrying on by such corporation, association, educational institution, or society of its activities."

The judge went on to acknowledge something we have never hidden, that "AiG is clearly a religious organization with a particular religious mission" and "it can choose to hire people who adhere to certain religious beliefs while still being in compliance with state and federal law."

Actually, the main reason that AiG filed the lawsuit was because we believed we had to make a stand for what this great nation of the USA has prided itself in: freedom of speech, freedom of religion, and the free exercise of religion. One of the reasons these constitutional guarantees are being undermined is that so many people (including many in the court systems) are so ignorant of what the Constitution and laws really say.

I believe the life-size Ark is one of the greatest reminders on this planet of the truth of God's Word and the saving gospel. That's why we stepped out in faith to build it. And the Lord has mightily blessed. Because the Ark project received so much attention, we believe it is more vital than ever that we ensure everyone has the opportunity to clearly hear the gospel message.

You are the light of the world. A city set on a hill cannot be hidden. Nor do people light a lamp and put it under a basket, but on a stand, and it gives light to all in the house. In the same way, let your light shine before others, so that they may see your good works and give glory to your Father who is in heaven (Matthew 5:14–16).

You are the light of the world.

APRIL 10
Acts 4:12

One Way, One Door, One Savior

And there is salvation in no one else, for there is no other name under heaven given among men by which we must be saved (Acts 4:12).

How would you answer if someone asked you if a particular group of people were going to hell?

During an interview with a secular reporter, I was not all that surprised when I was asked, "Do you believe Muslims are going to hell?"

The answer I gave went something like this: "My authority is the Bible—God's Word. God tells me in His Word that 'unless one is born again he cannot see the kingdom of God' (John 3:3). We're also told in Romans 10:9 that 'if you confess with your mouth that Jesus is Lord and believe in your heart that God raised him from the dead, you will be saved.'"

I concluded: "So, whether you're a Baptist, Catholic, Presbyterian, Muslim, or Hindu—if you're not born again as the Bible states and have not received the free gift of salvation in Christ, the Bible clearly teaches you will not spend eternity in heaven with our Creator and Savior. You will be in hell, separated from God—forever."

I also shared a number of other verses, such as:

- *Jesus said to him, "I am the way, and the truth, and the life. No one comes to the Father except through me"* (John 14:6).
- *Jesus said to her, "I am the resurrection and the life. Whoever believes in me, though he die, yet shall he live"* (John 11:25).
- *I [Christ] am the door. If anyone enters by me, he will be saved* (John 10:9).

Thus, the Bible clearly teaches there is only one way, only one door, to heaven—Jesus Christ.

In 2008, a survey from the Pew Forum[29] (a nonpartisan, non-advocacy organization) showed that 57% of people in America who attend what they call an "evangelical church" believed there is more than one way—or door—to heaven! This should have caused preachers across this land to do an "emergency series" on basic Christianity. The situation sadly has probably worsened over time. In part 2 of the Pew research results, we read:

"The survey finds that most Americans [including Christians!] have a non-dogmatic approach to their faith; for example, most do not believe their religion is the only way to salvation. The survey also finds that religion is closely linked to political ideology."

A staggering 57% of evangelicals believe there is more than one doorway to heaven.

Those who said they attend an "evangelical church" were asked:

"Tell me whether the FIRST statement or the SECOND statement comes closer to your own views even if neither is exactly right. First/next: My religion is the one, true faith leading to eternal life, OR: many religions can lead to eternal life."

THEOLOGY — APRIL 10

Again, 57% of "evangelicals" (supposed Bible-believing Christians) answered, "Many religions lead to eternal life." But John 14:6 and the other verses above clearly show that Christianity is an admittedly exclusive religion. There is only one way—only one door—to heaven.

Many people in today's secular society (and even in the Church) accuse Christians who hold to this exclusive teaching of being intolerant and dogmatic. I wish to point out, however, that those who insist there are many ways to heaven are intolerant themselves: of God's Word, which states there is only one way. People who assert their view of many ways leading to heaven—and who reject the Bible's teaching that there is only one way—reveal their own intolerant dogmatism.

Ultimately, there are only two ways to look at this: A person is either for Christ or against Him. That person walks in light or darkness. This is the real nature of the "culture war" in America. Yet it is really the same war that started in the Garden of Eden over 6,000 years ago when Satan tempted Eve—God's Word was not accepted, and humans decided to determine truth for themselves.

The basic sin nature of man is that we don't want to trust God's Word, and we want to be our own god and decide "truth" for ourselves. This is the nature we need to fight against daily. God's Word through Paul informs us of this battle:

For I do not do the good I want, but the evil I do not want is what I keep on doing. Now if I do what I do not want, it is no longer I who do it, but sin that dwells within me. So I find it to be a law that when I want to do right, evil lies close at hand. For I delight in the law of God, in my inner being, but I see in my members another law waging war against the law of my mind and making me captive to the law of sin that dwells in my members. Wretched man that I am! Who will deliver me from this body of death? Thanks be to God through Jesus Christ our Lord! So then, I myself serve the law of God with my mind, but with my flesh I serve the law of sin (Romans 7:19–25).

This is the battle that began in the Garden of Eden when the devil tempted Eve:

Now the serpent was more crafty than any other beast of the field that the Lord God had made. He said to the woman, "Did God actually say, 'You shall not eat of any tree in the garden'?" And the woman said to the serpent, "We may eat of the fruit of the trees in the garden, but God said, 'You shall not eat of the fruit of the tree that is in the midst of the garden, neither shall you touch it, lest you die.'" But the serpent said to the woman, "You will not surely die. For God knows that when you eat of it your eyes will be opened, and you will be like God, knowing good and evil" (Genesis 3:1–5).

Because Adam and Eve succumbed to the devil's lies, and we are descendants of them, our sin nature is really summed up by Genesis 3:1 and 3:5—we want to trust man's word above God's Word, and we want to be our own god. Thus, instead of listening to God's clear Word that there is only one way to heaven, sinful man wants to allow for other ways!

But how many salvation doors are there? Only one! As the Bible states, *And there is salvation in no one else, for there is no other name under heaven given among men by which we must be saved* (Acts 4:12).

There are only two religions in conflict: one which is based on the authoritative Word of God, and one built on man's fallible ideas/opinions.

APRIL 11
Romans 10:13-17

True Aliens

I believe in aliens! I knew that would get your attention.

When our family moved to the United States and eventually obtained our permanent resident cards, the government labeled each one of us as a "Resident Alien." So we were resident aliens for many years until we finally were granted citizenship. We are no longer "aliens." Now non-Christians are considered to be "aliens," and when they become Christians, they are no longer "aliens." Let me explain.

At the Creation Museum, we have a number of programs we show in our state-of-the-art planetarium. One of these programs deals with aliens—but not resident aliens! This program deals with the topic of whether there are intelligent aliens on other planets.

You don't have to spend hundreds of millions of dollars, as NASA and others are doing, to try to meet a (nonexistent) alien. You can meet one at the Creation Museum!

Yes, the alien at the Creation Museum is a fictional one—and we make that very clear—yet we use this made-up alien to explain the gospel to the real "aliens"! Let me explain.

Answers in Genesis' talented animators and other staff produced a planetarium program for our museum called Aliens: Fact or Fiction? As museum guests sit in our state-of-the art planetarium, they travel the universe and discover scientific and biblical answers to questions about the possibility of extraterrestrial, intelligent life. They meet some new friends (including our friendly fictional alien) who have lots of questions, such as:

Are we alone in the universe?

Does life exist on other planets?

Did your neighbor really see a UFO?

Are there answers in the Bible to the question of aliens in our universe?

Visitors to the Creation Museum learn why there may be water on other planets, but there can't be intelligent beings because of the meaning of the gospel. You see, the Bible makes it clear that Adam's sin affected the whole universe. This means that any supposed aliens would also be affected by Adam's sin. But because the supposed beings are not Adam's descendants, they can't have salvation.

One day, the whole universe will be judged by fire, and there will be new heavens and a new earth. But God's Son, Jesus Christ, has stepped into history as the God-man to be our relative and to be the perfect sacrifice for sin—as the Savior of mankind.

Jesus did not become the "God-Klingon" or the "God-Martian," as only descendants of Adam can be saved. God's Son remains the God-man as our Savior. In fact, the Bible makes it clear that we see the Father through the Son (and we see the Son through His Word, the Bible). To suggest that aliens could respond to the gospel is wrong.

The gospel makes it clear that salvation through Christ is only for the Adamic race—human beings who are all descendants of Adam.

THEOLOGY   APRIL 11

Now, I'm not contradicting myself when I write the following, but I actually do believe in aliens! In fact, Christians were once "aliens." God's Word states:

So then you are no longer strangers and aliens, but you are fellow citizens with the saints and members of the household of God (Ephesians 2:19).

Once people become Christians, they are no longer "aliens" or foreigners in this world—they are citizens of heaven!

The whole purpose of the Creation Museum is to present the truth of God's Word—and the gospel most of all—so that people will receive Jesus as their Savior and no longer be "aliens" but become a part of the family of God.

So I encourage as many "aliens" as possible to come to the Creation Museum and learn how to stop being "aliens" themselves!

In 2014, when I wrote an article explaining why I didn't believe in extraterrestrial aliens (using the message of the gospel as I did above), secularists wrote many articles mocking me. They included bizarre headlines like, "Creationist Ken Ham Says Aliens Will Go to Hell, So Let's Stop Looking for Them."

In fact, "aliens," those people who are not of the family of God, will go to hell if they don't repent of their sin and receive the free gift of salvation. That's why we at Answers in Genesis seek out as many "aliens" as we can so we can present them with God's Word and the gospel. There are billions of "aliens" on planet earth who need to hear the message of the gospel and be saved from hell.

We show our museum visitors that even nonexistent aliens can be used to bring the truth of salvation to real "aliens"! Even some Christians are more concerned about discussing and looking for nonexistent aliens instead of being burdened for real aliens—those alienated from God who desperately need the gospel.

For "everyone who calls on the name of the Lord will be saved." How then will they call on him in whom they have not believed? And how are they to believe in him of whom they have never heard? And how are they to hear without someone preaching? And how are they to preach unless they are sent? As it is written, "How beautiful are the feet of those who preach the good news!" But they have not all obeyed the gospel. For Isaiah says, "Lord, who has believed what he has heard from us?" So faith comes from hearing, and hearing through the word of Christ (Romans 10:13–17).

> **I urge you to consider how you can reach more "aliens" with the truth of God's Word and the saving gospel.**

APRIL 12
Luke 18:8

We Need to Stand Boldly and Unashamedly on the Gospel!

Whenever I read this verse in the Bible, I think about some of the greats of the past who were prepared to die for their faith. I wonder how many people in the Western Church would be prepared to stand so boldly and confidently: *Nevertheless, when the Son of Man comes, will he find faith on earth?* (Luke 18:8).

I have visited England many times over the years. On a couple of occasions now, I have visited Oxford and, while there, stood at the exact place where Latimer, Ridley, and Cranmer were burned at the stake for their faith. It's believed that as Latimer and Ridley were burning to death, Latimer said to Ridley, "We shall this day light such a candle, by God's grace, in England, as I trust shall never be put out."

This event was all part of the Reformation that swept Europe. Those great men didn't get to see the fruit of their labor and martyrdom, but the light of God's Word and the freedom to spread the gospel swept England!

Sadly, that light has greatly dimmed in the United Kingdom today (as it has through the entire West). Although there is still freedom (though significantly undermined) to preach God's Word and the gospel (for which Latimer and Ridley fought and were then martyred), the free exercise of Christianity has come under immense attack in the United Kingdom.

And here's a great irony. The Latin phrase written on the side of one of the buildings in Oxford, Dominus Ilumina Tio Mea, is the motto of the University of Oxford and cites the opening words of Psalm 27, "The Lord is my light." The motto appears on the university's arms and has been used since the second half of the sixteenth century. But sadly, there is very little light at Oxford University anymore. It's a pagan institution. The same could be said of the Ivy League schools in the USA. They once had a Christian foundation; now, they are leaders in spreading the atheistic worldview.

There's no doubt the United Kingdom and the rest of Europe have become spiritually dark. Yet we find there is an enthusiastic remnant in countries throughout the Western world who are hungry for the truth of God's Word. It's a reminder that as God told Elijah (and even the Apostle Paul may have alluded to this), we are to remind people that God always has His remnant who trust Him: *Yet I will leave seven thousand in Israel, all the knees that have not bowed to Baal, and every mouth that has not kissed him* (1 Kings 19:18). *So too at the present time there is a remnant, chosen by grace* (Romans 11:5).

Almost every time I speak at the Ark Encounter or the Creation Museum, I have people tell me how encouraging it is to see so many guests visiting these Christian attractions. Sometimes they tell me how lonely they feel as hardly anyone in their church takes the stand Answers in Genesis does on God's Word. Guests often tell me that visiting the Ark and Creation Museum reminds them of that passage in 1 Kings, where God told Elijah He had a remnant who trusted Him. We seek to give our visitors increased confidence and zeal to be more fervent in proclaiming His Word and to challenge non-Christians and compromising Christians concerning the truth of Scripture.

It's easy to get discouraged when you look at the exodus from the Church in America and notice the increasingly secularized worldview with its moral relativism permeating the culture. And yet, I often ponder the fact that God has let us build the ministry of AiG, the Ark Encounter, and the Creation Museum to impact tens of

CHURCH   APRIL 12

millions of lives across the USA and around the world each year. God has opened these doors, so we need to do our part and do all we can to reach as many people as possible with the truth of His Word and the gospel.

We have also found a hunger for God's Word in Latin America that we don't see in the rest of the world. At some of the conferences we've been invited to in Latin America, tens of thousands of people will flock to the meetings. God is doing something amazing in those countries south of the USA, and as He has opened this door for us, we will go and do whatever we can to minister to these spiritually hungry people. The people don't complain about the length of our presentations. They want to stay the whole time and not miss out on anything! In many ways, much of the Church in most of the Western world is lukewarm, compromised, and more interested in entertainment than Scripture and apologetics. Many church leaders are oblivious as to why they're losing up to 80% of their younger generations! Praise the Lord for allowing us at AiG to be a cutting-edge ministry to challenge the Church in these difficult days.

While in the United Kingdom, we stayed for one night in an Oxford hotel. Inside was a wall full of photographs of famous people who stayed there. One was of Professor Richard Dawkins. He was educated at Oxford and is one of the most aggressive atheists in the world today. His goal in speaking and writing is to lead as many people away from God as he can.

When I and one of our AiG scientists gave a public presentation in the famed Sheldonian Theatre in Oxford, we were told Richard Dawkins had recently given a lecture in that very hall. He was there to summarize his new book, *Outgrowing God*. We pray our presentations helped those in attendance outgrow the bankrupt atheist religion of Richard Dawkins.

Many who attended our presentation in the Sheldonian Theatre told us how grateful they were to hear our messages. Many had never heard this kind of information before. A number of non-Christians attended the event and also many theology students. One of the theology students told me how he's trying to grapple with all he's being taught in his theology classes that undermines Genesis. Another told me he was at Oxford to study the New Testament, and that he had heard me speak in the United Kingdom many years ago. He said that our teaching helps him to stand boldly on God's Word as he attends Oxford classes.

Sadly, many people in England said they wanted to impact their church with apologetic teaching, but the pastor didn't stand on a literal Genesis. They wanted to know how best to challenge and equip the people in their church with the answers they were so excited about from the conference. I often wonder if those pastors would have stood with Latimer and Ridley or run in the other direction! Usually, I find those who compromise God's Word just don't have the same commitment to stand boldly amidst persecution.

I've often wondered why God has let AiG build such a ministry, which includes two large attractions in the USA. I believe it's because of the faithfulness of so many Christians in the past and the faithfulness of a large remnant of millions today. And God has blessed people materially to support the spread of the gospel around the world. Sadly though, we see so much compromise in the Church and a lukewarm Church in the USA as it is in the rest of the West. Remember to: *Contend for the faith that was once for all delivered to the saints* (Jude 1:3).

In the midst of everything, we need to be found faithful.

APRIL 13
Acts 17:26

The Human Race

Whenever I give my presentation called "One Race, One Blood," people tell me they have never heard this message before. Many tell me their church has never taught such a message. And yet, the message is not complicated. When you believe the history of the human race as given in Genesis 1–11, it really is quite easy to build your worldview on this foundation and correctly interpret humanity. Then one can understand where humans came from, what their problem is, and what the solution is.

Now Genesis is clear that there is only one race biologically: the human race. So why isn't the Church leading the fight against racism? Shouldn't the Church be leading the way?

And the secular scientific world confirmed there's only one race in the year 2000 when they released their findings to the world concerning the sequencing of the human genome:

"Dr. Venter [head of the Celera Genomics Corporation, Rockville, MD] and scientists at the National Institutes of Health recently announced that they had put together a draft of the entire sequence of the human genome, and the researchers unanimously declared, there is only one race—the human race."[30]

Sadly, it seems most politicians ignore this fact of one human race as they want division for the sake of control/power. Words like race, racism, prejudice, blacks, and whites in the media seem to be almost an everyday occurrence. But where is the Church regarding the "race" issue?

I suggest that if the Church believed God's Word in Genesis, had taught creation apologetics, and raised up generations with the right foundation, it would be leading the way in dealing with such issues.

In my 40 years' experience of traveling and speaking in churches and other Christian institutions (and from research we've conducted), I've found that the majority of Christian leaders compromise Genesis with evolution and/or millions of years. And sadly, Darwinian evolution is inherently a racist philosophy. There's no doubt Darwin fueled racism, even in the Church, with his ideas of lower and higher races. In his book, *The Descent of Man*, certain dark-skinned people were closer to the supposed apelike ancestors of man than those with light skin.

Darwin taught that those closer to the apes (he considered the Australian Aboriginal people in this group) were lower on the mental scale than so-called "Caucasians" which he considered to be higher on the mental scale. Where's the cancel culture? Shouldn't they be canceling Darwin from libraries and educational institutions? Of course, they won't do that as Darwin is protected because he is their high priest of the evolution/atheist religion.

Many conservative Christian leaders avoid teaching Genesis because it's considered too controversial or too divisive or they don't know how to deal with what they perceive as scientific issues. As result of these factors (and others), most people in churches really don't understand the foundational importance of the book of Genesis, and they don't understand the true history of the world. Because of this, they really have no basis to effectively deal with topics like racism. The fact is, Genesis 1–11 is the foundation for everything. The only way to deal with any issue is to start with Genesis 1–11 to build a truly biblical worldview in every area.

APOLOGETICS — APRIL 13

Now, I've seen research showing that people reading the Bible spend much more time toward the end and not much time reading the beginning (for instance, Genesis). This to me reinforces the fact that most people really don't see the history behind the gospel as important—yet it's foundational to all doctrine and foundational to dealing with any issue including racism.

It is my contention that if the Church had stood uncompromisingly on the Book of Genesis and taught creation apologetics to equip people to defend the Christian faith and thus the history in Genesis, the Church would be leading the way in combatting racism. And the Church should be!

Because much of the Church is not doing this, we at Answers in Genesis are doing all we can to get the message of one race, etc., to the Church. We need to make sure we are reaching the younger generations with this message.

For instance, I wrote a book for kids ages eight through teens titled, *One Blood for Kids: What the Bible Says About Race*. In this book, I teach that all humans are descendants of Adam and Eve, so there are no biological races because all people belong to the same race—we're all one family. I also explain that because of the Tower of Babel event after the Flood, the human population was dispersed into different language groups that resulted in different people or ethnic groups over time.

Also, the book explains that all humans have the same basic skin color because of a pigment called melanin. This pigment is manufactured in special structures at the bottom of the outer layer of our skin, and the instructions come from the genes we have in our DNA. Thus, there are no truly "black" or "white" people. All people are shades of brown.

These basic truths from God's Word also help people to understand that all humans are equal before God. All are sinners and need salvation. Adults and kids need to understand this message.

The answer to racism (and to any issue) is to see people converted through the saving power of the gospel and build their thinking on the true history of the world that God reveals to us in His Word beginning in Genesis.

Yes, the Church could be leading the way in fighting prejudice and racism if God's people were motivated to do so, but so many lack the information they need. AiG is doing its best to help equip the Church in this area so many more voices will speak out with the truth from God's Word, which deals powerfully with the problems of racism and prejudice so ingrained in our culture. Most people in the Church lack teaching on this topic, so they don't know how to deal with racism.

And he made from one man every nation of mankind to live on all the face of the earth, having determined allotted periods and the boundaries of their dwelling place (Acts 17:26).

The answer to racism is simple. People need to be saved and build their worldview on God's Word beginning in Genesis, but it will require people to become biblically and scientifically literate and to earnestly "contend for the faith" (Jude 3).

I urge God's people – let's lead the way and deal with the sin of racism.

APRIL 14

Ephesians 6:11-13

A New Reformation

When you look back in history, there are certain people who really stand out in regard to the Christian world. Now whenever I mention the names of some of these people, I always get objections from various Christians because they don't agree with certain aspects of the theology of these historical figures, or they want to point out inconsistencies or errors, etc. But you know what? None of us are perfect. And sometimes you have to look at what these people came out of or where they were living to understand their times. And, of course, we must not stray from orthodox Christian beliefs.

But regardless, one cannot ignore that God has used these greats of the past to do amazing things for Him. And remember that God used Samson with all his problems and even Moses who killed someone and so the list goes on.

I'm amazed at how God chooses to use imperfect, fallible, finite people like us for His purposes. I stand in awe of Him. He doesn't need any of us, but He chooses to use us with all our frailties and other issues.

One of the great Christian men of the past was Martin Luther. The Reformation was initiated by this German priest and professor. And it was continued by others such as Calvin and Zwingli. Luther's nailing of his famed 95 Theses to a church door in Wittenberg began the Reformation in October 1517.

It was a movement that called the Church back to the authority of God's Word and away from the fallible opinions of man, which had severely compromised the clear teaching of the Word of God. The Bible-upholding movement was so powerful that today we are still experiencing the effects of this historical earthquake that spread from Germany to the world.

One of the special moments of my life was when my wife and I stood near a plaque in Germany in the area where Martin Luther would have stood when he uttered those famous words, "Here I stand (on Scripture). I can do no other, God help me."

Throughout history, whenever we witness a great work of God, our adversary, the devil, "the prince of the power of the air, the spirit that is now at work in the sons of disobedience" (Ephesians 2:2), aggressively tries to undo this work.

I believe one of the major tactics that Satan uses to counter the good effects of the Reformation relates to the Book of Genesis. It began with a claim that the earth was very old, based on supposed geologic evidence (that grew out of a belief in naturalism and spread widely in the early 1800s) of slow, natural processes, with nothing supernatural involved. An old age for the earth was necessary to justify the ideas behind naturalism, and the publication of Darwin's book on evolution titled *On the Origin of Species* soon followed in 1859.

Darwin's book was an attempt to explain how animals and plants arose by natural processes, not the supernatural means revealed and documented for us by the Creator Himself in Genesis. Ultimately, this led to the idea that man evolved from apelike creatures. Armed with this cache of scientific "evidence" that the earth was supposedly millions/billions of years old and that molecules eventually gave rise to man, compromising theologians permeated the Church, teaching that Genesis should be treated as myth.

THEOLOGY
APRIL 14

I warn people today that Darwin's evolutionary ideas and millions of years are really part of the religion of naturalism (atheism) to try to explain all of reality without God! It's so sad that so many Christian leaders have tried to compromise this pagan religion with God's Word.

From both inside and outside the Church, the Darwinian revolution changed the hearts and minds of generations concerning biblical authority. To this day, most church leaders and Christian academic institutions are infected by the religion of naturalism.

The result has been devastating in our churches. The majority of the younger generations have left the Church in America, and in fact the whole Western world, and very few are returning. Our nationwide study through America's Research Group showed that the lack of trust in biblical authority, starting in Genesis, has been a major reason.

In England, church attendance has declined from around 50% of the population three generations ago to about 5%. In the USA, church attendance for Generation Z is less than 9%. (Overall church attendance was around 70–80% in the 1700s.)

America's once very Christianized culture is now divided between an aggressive secularist philosophy and a Christianized worldview (the Judeo-Christian ethic that is really based on the Bible).

Sadly, compromise in Genesis has undone much of what the Reformation had accomplished. It's why at Answers in Genesis we want to ignite a new reformation. We need to see a new reformation in the hearts and minds of God's people in our churches before a much-needed spiritual revival can occur in this nation—a country that's becoming increasingly hostile toward God's Word.

I urge God's people to help us start a new revolution—a new reformation, a creationist revolution—to undo the destructive consequences of the Darwinian revolution.

Hosea the prophet observed, *My people are destroyed for lack of knowledge* (Hosea 4:6). Indeed, a lack of knowledge exists among God's people today. We need to raise up soldiers for the King who have on the whole armor of God.

Put on the whole armor of God, that you may be able to stand against the schemes of the devil. For we do not wrestle against flesh and blood, but against the rulers, against the authorities, against the cosmic powers over this present darkness, against the spiritual forces of evil in the heavenly places. Therefore take up the whole armor of God, that you may be able to withstand in the evil day, and having done all, to stand firm (Ephesians 6:11–13).

We need to equip people to know God's Word, understand *the times,* **and be equipped with apologetics to defend the Christian faith.**

APRIL 15
Jeremiah 23:1

We Need to Be Rescuing Our Children!

When we look at those undermining the Christian faith, we can't just look at atheists! We can't just look at those outside the Church, but we need to look inside the Church as well.

Christians need to rescue children and teens from the destructive teaching of shepherds who compromise God's Word and lead our children astray. And as Ecclesiastes states:

What has been is what will be, and what has been done is what will be done, and there is nothing new under the sun (Ecclesiastes 1:9).

Down through the ages, so many shepherds have been a problem, undermining the authority of God's Word. In many ways, I think compromising shepherds are worse than secularists!

I remember the time a few years ago when I wrote blogs and Facebook posts about an atheist website that was targeting children. Interestingly, the launch of this anti-God website that was seeking to capture kids for atheism coincided with AiG's ministry theme for that year which was "Standing Our Ground, Rescuing Our Kids" (Galatians 1:4).

More than ever in our increasingly secularized culture, Christians need to be rescuing our children. Galatians 1:4, regarding Christ, says that He *gave himself for our sins to deliver us from the present evil age, according to the will of our God and Father.*

Now, when we consider this "rescue," believers usually think of rescuing children from non-Christians, like the atheists operating the website I mentioned above—humanists who actively try to pull children away from the truth of God's Word.

The Bible warns us about shepherds that our children need to be rescued from: *"Woe to the shepherds who destroy and scatter the sheep of my pasture!" declares the* L<small>ORD</small> (Jeremiah 23:1).

I thought of this verse recently when someone brought a segment of a Christian TV program to my attention. A lady had written the following which the host read on air:

"I have three teenage boys and now two of them are questioning the Bible. This scares me! They tell me if the Bible is truth, then I should be able to reasonably explain the existence of dinosaurs. This is just one of the many things they question. Even my husband is agreeing with them. How do I explain things to them that the Bible doesn't cover? I am so afraid that they are walking away from God. My biggest fear is not to have my children and husband next to me in God's Kingdom."

The TV host gave an answer on the air that so burdened me that I just have to warn you again about compromising shepherds in the Church and the kids who need to be rescued from them.

His answer:

"Look, I know people will probably try to lynch me when I say this, but Bishop Ussher, God bless him, wasn't inspired by the Lord when he said that it all took 6,000 years. It just didn't. And you go back in time, you've got radiocarbon dating. You got all these things and you've got the carcasses of dinosaurs frozen in time out in the

Dakotas ... They're out there and so there was a time when these giant reptiles were on the earth, and it was before the time of the Bible. So, don't try to cover it up and make like everything was 6,000 years. That's not the Bible. ... If you fight real science, you're going to lose your children, and I believe in telling it the way it was."

Well, I pray this lady didn't accept this host's destructive advice. This televangelist did not understand that the Bible includes references to huge land-dwelling creatures—what could possibly be dinosaurs (e.g., Job 40 about Behemoth)—that lived at the same time as man; furthermore, he does not understand the difference between historical and observational science. Plus, he obviously does not understand carbon dating at all, which has nothing to do with millions of years. His answer was a complete mess! But it sadly reflects the state of so many of the shepherds in the Church.

Notice how he mocked those of us who take a stand on a young earth. He was essentially telling this concerned woman to make sure her kids believed what the secularists said about Earth history. Sadly, this kind of approach is a major reason children are walking away from Christ and from the Church in unbelief, not because of the teachings of biblical creationists who take God's Word as written. Generation Z is considered the first truly post-Christian generation in the USA.

To be frank, this shepherd and others like him are the compromising shepherds we discussed in my 2009 book *Already Gone*. This coauthored book, with the renowned researcher the late Britt Beemer, summarized the detailed research into why two-thirds of young people had been walking away from the Church.

One of the major reasons for the exodus we discovered in our research was that young people saw such biblical compromise (the kind seen with this TV host) as hypocrisy. On the one hand, this shepherd tells people to believe the Bible, but on the other hand, he tells them they shouldn't believe Genesis as written. Instead, he argues that our children should believe what the atheists and other anti-God secularists say about earth history.

As we continue in the Answers in Genesis apologetics ministry which reaches millions around the world, AiG will be doing its best to bring groups together to help rescue kids (and adults) from this present evil age. The majority of shepherds in our churches have compromised Genesis in various ways with evolutionary/millions of years beliefs. This has undermined the authority of God's Word and put a stumbling block in the way of many in the younger generations being receptive to the truth of God's Word and the saving gospel.

> **We need to rescue children and teens from the destructive teaching of shepherds who compromise God's Word and lead our children astray.**

APRIL 16
Genesis 2:21-22

One Big Human Family

When my hair and beard were darker, I would often have people stop me and say, "You look like Abraham Lincoln." After this happened a number of times, I decided to reply by saying, "Yes, he's one of my relatives." People would often exclaim, "You're related to Abraham Lincoln?" I would reply, "Yes, we all are." And then I would use this as a witnessing tool to talk about the fact that all humans are related, all are one race, and therefore, all are sinners in need of salvation.

What a huge difference it made when as a teacher, I saw the excitement from students from the Australian Aboriginal community in my class when they learned from Genesis that we're all one big family.

Back in the late 1970s when I was visiting Mossman, North Queensland, Australia, not that far from where my mother was born and grew up (Babinda), I met a missionary who was in charge of a settlement for Australian Aborigines.

The missionary told me that one day he read to the people the Bible's account of the creation of the first woman, Eve: *So the LORD God caused a deep sleep to fall upon the man, and while he slept took one of his ribs and closed up its place with flesh. And the rib that the LORD God had taken from the man he made into a woman and brought her to the man* (Genesis 2:21–22).

After he read this, one of the older Aboriginal elders said, "How come you have a story about the creation of woman like we do, only your story's better?"

It was amazing to me to read through these legends and find quite a number that sounded very similar to certain events in the Genesis account.

Because of my special interest in the Genesis account of origins, I had already collected some books—obtained from the secular natural history museum in Brisbane—on Aboriginal myths and legends. It was amazing to me to read through these legends and find quite a number that sounded very similar to certain events in the Genesis account.

For instance, there were flood legends. One told about three sons on a boat who survived the flood. In another one, the boat landed on a mountain at the end of the flood and a rainbow appeared in the sky.

They also have a legend about the origin of death as a result of the first woman. The creator told her not to touch his special tree, but she took sweet honey from it anyway, and death entered the world as a result. Another legend said that woman was made while man was asleep, only she was made from some sort of plant.

No doubt the elderly Australian Aboriginal had heard many such legends from his parents, and he recognized the similarity between the Genesis account of the creation of the first woman and the legend he knew.

The missionary then used this opportunity to help the Aborigines understand that the Genesis account was the original one and that their legends were changed versions of the original. This enabled the missionary to help them understand the truth of God's Word and point them to the saving gospel.

APOLOGETICS

I experienced a similar event a few years earlier in 1975, during my first year as a science teacher in Dalby, Australia. During the class dealing with human origins, I happened to mention that all humans are descended from two people (Adam and Eve) and because of what happened after the Flood—at the Tower of Babel with the giving of different languages—families moved away from each other, forming different nations and cultures. I explained that all humans are one biological race and are related, and therefore, we're all just one big family.

After the class, three students from the Aboriginal community came up to me and asked if I could explain this in more detail. They were extremely interested in all I had to say. As I talked to them, I realized that Darwin taught in his book *The Descent of Man* that the Australian Aborigines were closer to apes than light-skinned people in the supposed evolutionary story of man. It is also true that scientists in England sent people to Australia to collect specimens of Aborigines to display in museums, and sometimes the Aborigines were illicitly killed—all in the name of evolution!

What a difference it made to those students to learn that they were all part of the one big human family, related to me and their classmates and everyone else in the world but certainly not to apes!

Ever since that time, I have had a real burden to teach everyone I can the truth about the one human race—that all humans belong to one race, all are related, all are one color just different shades of brown. We all have the same problem—sin. God's Son became a member of the one human race (as the God-man, the Lord Jesus Christ). Jesus died and rose again for the entire race, and He offers the free gift of salvation to all members of the human race who will receive it.

That's why so many people are fascinated by the Creation Museum's and Ark Encounter's detailed exhibits on the Tower of Babel, the one human race, the origin of nations, and the evil of racism and prejudice.

By the way, in the year 2000, the Human Genome Project (headed by an atheist) announced to the world, after mapping the entire sequence of the human genome, "There is only one race, the human race."[31] Observational science confirms the Bible's account of one race!

The battle over racism and prejudice is actually a battle of two worldviews—one based on man's word (man's false evolutionary story about the origin of life and the universe) and one based on God's Word (the true account of origins as given in Genesis). The correct way to begin the battle against racism is to start with Genesis 1–11, which gives the true account of the history of the human race.

> "And he made from one man every nation of mankind to live on all the face of the earth, having determined allotted periods and the boundaries of their dwelling place" (Acts 17:26).

APRIL 17
Psalm 19:7-11

Godly Parents

When I was 12 years old (which seems like millions of years ago now), I went to a fancy dress party (American translation: costume party) at the school in Australia where my father was the principal. I've never forgotten what I was dressed as—it is indelibly imprinted on my mind!

I think you will laugh when you hear what it was, but it represented one of those many defining moments in my life, especially considering the ministry God clearly led me into at Answers in Genesis.

We had moved to a country town in North Queensland and had started attending a local church. My parents were so upset when they heard the pastor of that church telling the congregation they could believe in evolution. My father told us we could not stay in that church as adding evolution to the Bible was an attack on the authority of God's Word. My father understood and taught us that Genesis 1–11 was the foundation of all doctrine and for the rest of the Bible. I grew up understanding the foundational importance of Genesis from my father, sadly, not from the Church!

My father understood that the idea of evolution and millions of years is not just a side issue or just about how people understand Genesis 1–11 but has an impact on the Bible's authority. What we believe about Genesis has consequences for how we read and understand the entire Bible—including the New Testament and especially the gospel! I am so grateful my father never wavered and always stood for the truth of God's Word. He loved verses stating phrases like, "Have you not read?" and "It is written." He was adamant about the absolute authority of Scripture. He saw compromise with God's Word as putting people on a slippery slide toward doubt and unbelief in Scripture. He was so adamant about never undermining God's Word. That's why he was so passionate about biblical authority.

In June 1995, my late brother, Robert, was sitting with my father in the hospital (my dad died on June 9, 1995). Robert asked Dad, "Why did you love God's Word so much?" My dad explained that his father had died when he was 16, so he didn't have an earthly father to talk to any longer. This caused him to turn to the words of his heavenly Father and read them over and over again. He saturated himself in the Word of God.

Growing up in our family, we could all see that our father hated compromise. In 2 Timothy 1:14, the Apostle Paul gave Timothy the following command: *By the Holy Spirit who dwells within us, guard the good deposit entrusted to you.* My father guarded every word of God's truth and entrusted that Word to his children.

He was often studying what the liberal scholars were saying and then explaining to his children why they were wrong. He didn't want us to be led astray and doubt or not believe God's Word because of false teaching. As I've often told people, I learned to smell liberal theology a million miles away because of how our father trained us.

This gives you a little background as to why my father was so distressed with this pastor's teaching that evolution was God's supposed way of bringing life into existence. Well, needless to say, we quickly changed churches!

FAMILY — APRIL 17

I remember all this, but most of all I remember my parents' uncompromising stand on God's Word! They taught me to stand up for all the teachings of Scripture, no matter what anyone else might say. What an impact this had on me!

Well, with evolution on our minds, the school's annual fancy dress (costume) party date was approaching. My creative mother used to make the costumes we would wear to such events.

For this particular event, my parents came up with what we could call a "pun costume," to poke fun at evolution. I certainly knew this costume meant that evolution was not true!

I was dressed as an ape (with an ape mask on my face and brown clothing), holding a pot with a small tree in it with a sign stating, "Our Family Tree." People thought it was hilarious as it was a poke at evolution.

Sort of ironic, isn't it, that I wore such a costume and now see the ministry the Lord called me to that proclaims the truth of creation and exposes *the lie* of evolution? How grateful I am that God led me into a ministry to help counteract the false teaching of evolution in the Church and the culture!

When people see the ministry of Answers in Genesis, the Creation Museum, and the Ark Encounter, they are amazed at what God has done. So many have asked me to share with them how all this came about. I did produce a video of my testimony that is available on our streaming platform, Answers TV. It's called Fire in My Bones.

It's amazing for me to look back and see the Lord's hand in my upbringing to prepare me for the ministry I've been involved in since the '70s.

One event from my past that I remember well is the time my mother's mother (we called her Nanna) was standing on the steps of her farmhouse—Bible in her hand—preaching to Jehovah's Witness representatives who came visiting.

I can still see her walking down the stairs following them as they turned to leave, and she kept following them, holding up her Bible, as she continued to teach them from the Bible! I could tell of many other events, but so many like this had such an impact on my life in regard to standing boldly, unashamedly, and uncompromisingly on the authority of God's Word from the very first verse.

I thank God for godly parents who raised children to believe God's Word as the absolute authority. This powerful evangelistic ministry started with them and continues with the millions who have been and continue to be impacted by this Bible-upholding ministry.

The law of the LORD is perfect, reviving the soul; the testimony of the LORD is sure, making wise the simple; the precepts of the LORD are right, rejoicing the heart; the commandment of the LORD is pure, enlightening the eyes; the fear of the LORD is clean, enduring forever; the rules of the LORD are true, and righteous altogether. More to be desired are they than gold, even much fine gold; sweeter also than honey and drippings of the honeycomb. Moreover, by them is your servant warned; in keeping them there is great reward (Psalm 19:7–11).

> **Think about what impact your life is having spiritually on others, on your children, grandchildren, and so on.**

APRIL 18
Colossians 3:23

Set the Standard High!

When I visited Disneyland (before it became so woke) and various Smithsonian museums back in the 1980s when I first visited the USA, I would often think to myself, "Why can't Christians build museums and parks the quality of these secular places? After all, we have the most important message in the universe to tell the world." Yes, the message of the truth of God's Word and the message of salvation.

A Bible verse that has always stood out to me in regard to these thoughts is this one:

Whatever you do, work heartily, as for the Lord and not for men (Colossians 3:23).

My father went to be with the Lord in 1995. These many years later, I still remember the principles he taught me from God's Word and also the principles he set by example.

My father was the principal of primary schools in Australia (i.e., for Americans, elementary/middle schools). Even though he worked in a secular environment (there were no Christian schools in Australia in those days), my father was well-known to students and parents as a Christian. And in whatever he did, he excelled. School inspectors always gave him top marks. He was promoted every three years.

As my father ran his schools with excellence, he was determined to never knowingly, in any way, compromise his stand on God's Word. I remember the time I talked to my father about how he ran his schools and about many of the special events he organized (sports activities, fairs, etc.). He told me that "whatever you do, do it heartily, as to the Lord." I'll also never forget both my father and mother teaching me (based on God's Word) how we should look at ourselves and others: God first, others second, yourself last. In my mind, I can still hear both of them saying that.

I praise the Lord that God has brought hundreds of like-minded, Bible-believing staff members to the ministry of Answers in Genesis. That's one major reason AiG, the Creation Museum, and Ark Encounter have been able to impact so many lives.

You see, many of those visiting our attractions have told me about our wonderful staff members. Our visitors are made to feel special and truly welcome here. And guests (and media) always comment on how first-class the exhibits are. In fact, many are amazed at the quality of everything we do at the attractions.

Over the years, many have told me that Christians have been known for doing things in a cheesy way. No one would consider Christians doing anything like the quality of Disney. And yet, the Creation Museum and Ark Encounter are every bit the quality of a Disney attraction, and I believe in many ways even better! Some have told us that when the Creation Museum first opened, they realized this set a new standard for a Christian attraction! There are other Christian attractions now that exhibit excellence in what has been built (e.g., Museum of the Bible, Washington, DC; Billy Graham Library, NC; and others).

For Christians who visit, our staff wants to help them be better equipped to defend our Christian faith in these increasingly secular times. For the non-Christians, we want them to be introduced to the truth of God's Word and its gospel message. We recognize that it's all the Lord's ministry. In whatever they do, the AiG staff members seek to give the very best of their abilities and talents. Why should God have our second best?

RESOURCES — APRIL 18

Many journalists from the secular media have commented on the high quality of the Creation Museum and Ark exhibits and the special programs we hold. They often note the hospitality of our professional staff. It actually causes non-Christians to take the ministry and our message more seriously. One secular reporter, while I was touring him through the Ark, said, "This is not the quality of Hollywood; this is way above Hollywood. For a start the wood is real." I had to smile when I heard that.

But the accolades are not just for the Creation Museum and Ark Encounter. The overall ministry of AiG has won many awards over the years from both the secular and Christian worlds for excellence in advertising, web design, videos, magazine publication, etc.

Our *Answers* magazine has picked up numerous awards from the Evangelical Press Association. In the most-esteemed category, Answers once received EPA's top award for general excellence—two years in a row! Hundreds of publications make up the EPA.

As the quality of AiG's outreaches continues to be recognized, the Lord is being honored. Most of our very talented AiG staff no doubt could receive much higher salaries in the secular world. Yet they choose to work at this apologetics ministry to share the gospel.

The following verse applies to our excellent staff and how they view AiG's reputation:

A good name is to be chosen rather than great riches, and favor is better than silver or gold (Proverbs 22:1).

I praise the Lord for our hundreds of staff for whom we can say that whatever they do, they "do it heartily, as to the Lord and not to men."

I say all this to remind us that as Christians we are soldiers of the King of kings. We are ambassadors on Earth for the God of creation. And whatever we do, we should do to the best of our ability as a witness to others and to glorify our Creator God.

I must admit I do dismay sometimes at some in the younger generations and the work ethic of many of them. So let me challenge us all once again:

Whatever you do, work heartily, as for the Lord and not for men (Colossians 3:23).

Do nothing from selfish ambition or conceit, but in humility count others more significant than yourselves (Philippians 2:3).

Let's set the standard as high as we can for what the Lord has called us to do.

APRIL 19
Mark 16:15

What Is the Best Motivation to Learn a Foreign Language?

The event at the Tower of Babel, where God gave different languages, was a judgment because man rebelled against God. Today, we have to work hard to deal with the fact that we need to communicate the gospel to people of different languages.

When I began grade nine in Australia, it was mandatory to take a foreign language class for two years. The only language offered at our school was French. I didn't know anyone who spoke French, so I couldn't see the point in studying this language. So, yes, I had a great lack of motivation. At the end of year ten, my parents, at a parent/teacher night, were told that their son (yes, me!) should not pursue the study of foreign languages! C'est la vie!

I wish I could go back and show my teachers how proficient I am now at foreign languages! I speak a number of them—Australian-English, Canadian-English, American-English, English-English, and so on! But it is true today that I'm motivated to pursue foreign languages! You see, as a 13-year-old, I hadn't grasped that in order to carry out the Great Commission to *"go into all the world and proclaim the gospel to the whole creation"* (Mark 16:15), Christians need to learn many different languages. We need to proclaim the truth of God's Word and the gospel to all these groups.

I eventually learned that the Tower of Babel dispersed people and resulted in many different language groups, with subgroups forming within each group. Now, we need to proclaim the truth of God's Word and the gospel to all these groups.

My parents understood this need. During my first year of university, Dad became a member of the board of an organization called "Japan Evangelistic Band," and my parents started supporting a missionary who had a burden to reach the people of Japan with the salvation message.

Over the years, as I have traveled across the world giving presentations on the creation/gospel message, I've had so many people speak to me through interpreters, pleading for our books to be made available in their own languages. When I was in France many years ago, I remember thinking, "I wish I had been motivated to learn French when I was in high school!"

We now have quite an intensive translation outreach at AiG. In fact, various AiG publications have been translated into Spanish, French, German, Hebrew, Arabic, Russian, Japanese, Chinese, Italian, Romanian, and many more languages. Because of the large number of people who speak Spanish in the USA, and our extensive outreach to Latin America, Spanish has become our biggest translation ministry. I didn't realize as we embarked on translating many of our resources into Spanish, what an incredible impact this ministry would have on Latin America. AiG is also assisting creation-apologetics ministries in many countries. As well as having offices in the United States, United Kingdom/Europe, Canada, and Australia, AiG also supports full-time missionaries in Peru. And we now have a full-time office in Mexico.

When our speakers began traveling to Latin American countries, we were astonished at the response. Thousands (and sometimes tens of thousands) of people come eagerly to hear the messages—and they "vacuum up" the books and DVDs off the tables! Because so many of these people don't have the resources, we greatly subsidize this part of the ministry. Actually, people in Latin America have a hunger for hearing God's Word way above what I've experienced in the United States.

One of the most exciting and startling things is that in Latin America, our speakers are invited into public universities and public schools to speak to professors, teachers, and students. There is so much more freedom to speak on campuses in these countries than in America—and the rest of the once-Christianized West! We now have many such open doors into these countries, so we need to take these opportunities while they are available to us. Over time, the Lord brought together a team to head up our Spanish-language ministry at AiG. This ministry is led by staff member Joe Owen.

At eight years old, Joe heard South American missionaries speak, and God placed a burden on his heart to learn Spanish. In high school, he fell in love with the Spanish language while he and his older brother competed to see who could pick it up the fastest! During college, Joe fell in love with Maria Elizabeth Montes Rodarte from Zacatecas, Mexico. They married, had six children, and now live in Mexico. When Joe speaks English, he still sounds American, but people tell me that when he speaks Spanish, he doesn't have an American accent at all!

Joe has translated for me many times when I've spoken in Spanish-speaking countries like Mexico, the Dominican Republic, and Bolivia. I praise the Lord that Joe has such a burden to reach Latin America while the doors are still wide open to the gospel. He has been traveling and speaking all over Latin America (sometimes in front of massive crowds) and providing AiG resources that are now readily available in Spanish.

AiG's Vacation Bible School (VBS) is now available in Spanish, and we are translating our four-year Answers Bible Curriculum into Spanish as well. At the same time, AiG is working with our publisher to make many more of our resources available in various languages.

AiG also has an in-house team of Spanish translators. We often have fun (at my expense) as the staff has come to learn that the only Spanish words I know are *burrito*, *enchilada*, *taco*, and so on! But at least my Spanish is better than my French!

I pray that you will grasp the excitement and magnitude of what God is doing through AiG in Latin America. Yes, we all should have a burden to reach people around the world with the gospel.

AiG is finding that people from many different language groups are visiting the Ark Encounter and the Creation Museum. Some groups bring their own translators with them. But with smartphones and Google Translate, people can now read signs and hear words in their own language. Yes, technology can be used to reach people with the truth of God's Word and the gospel.

We also hold special Deaf Days at the Ark and Creation Museum, with translators who can sign for the Deaf. And we are introducing more ways to assist the visually impaired in experiencing our attractions and understanding the teaching in each exhibit.

So I wasn't motivated to learn French 50+ years ago, but the Lord eventually motivated me to proclaim the truth of His Word and the gospel in many languages—to millions of people! I wish I could go back and let my teacher know that this is the best motivation one could ever have in learning a foreign language!

"Go into all the world and proclaim the gospel to the whole creation" (Mark 16:15).

APRIL 20
John 10:9

What Was the Real Reason Answers in Genesis Built a Life-Size Noah's Ark Attraction Called Ark Encounter?

The life-size Noah's Ark that Answers in Genesis constructed in Northern Kentucky is a spectacular sight—it is the largest free-standing timber-frame structure in the world. This 510-foot-long Ark is an architectural and engineering marvel.

But there is one aspect of the Ark's construction that is ultimately more important than its impressive size. In fact, it's the real reason we built this life-size Ark. This crucial aspect had (and still has) the atheists up in arms. It became the reason the state of Kentucky, at the time we began the project, tried to prevent us from the opportunity to participate in a tourism sales-tax incentive. However, through a federal lawsuit, it was ruled conclusively the Ark could participate in this tourism incentive.

Actually, the state government officials who opposed us would have been very happy if we had just built the life-size Ark as a tourist attraction that had no real message. I believe the atheists wouldn't really have cared that much if we just built a huge wooden ship.

So what is it that the secularist organizations—like the Freedom from Religion Foundation and the Americans United for the Separation of Church and State—were (and still are) really upset about? And what were some officials in Kentucky really objecting to with the Ark?

In a letter to Answers in Genesis, state officials at the time tried to pressure us to guarantee that "no visitor to the attraction would be subject to religious proselytizing." Now the word "proselytizing" can have many definitions, but we believe the state means that the Ark project can't share the gospel. (Certainly, AiG would never force the gospel on guests.)

In a letter, Kentucky officials detailed why they decided to deny AiG access to the tourism incentive, one that is offered to any organization that wants to build in Kentucky and meets the tourism requirements (which the Ark certainly did). Here are some of the reasons for that initial denial found in the state's letter to us:

"On February 27, 2014, in a press conference streamed live from the Creation Museum, Mr. Ham described how the Ark was designed to further AiG's evangelical mission. He has stated that he wanted people to come and have an encounter with Noah's Ark, but at the same time to have an encounter with the Lord Jesus Christ."

"Patrick Marsh, AIG's Director of Museum Design, in describing the Ark's design has said that the Ark Encounter will present an evangelical, yet entertaining, Gospel message, and that the project is really about evangelism to the unchurched."

"At the Hammer & Peg ceremony on May 1, 2014, supporters were reminded that Deck 3 of the Ark would contain the Christ Theater and referred to Ark Encounter as 'this Gospel-proclaiming project that will stand as a monument to biblical authority, reminding people of God's judgment on sin as well as His great mercy.'"

"One speaker proclaimed 'that the new Ark Encounter would save people to Jesus just as the original Ark saved Noah, his family and the animals.' In addition to these statements, the current design schematic for the Ark featured on its webpage shows the Christ Theater and a room called, 'Why the Bible is True' as prominent features on the third floor."

RESOURCES
APRIL 20

"In the November 19 fundraising letter, Mr. Ham characterized the purpose of the Ark and its exhibits as a mechanism to 'point people to God's Word and the gospel,' and stated his belief that 'it is going to be one of the most effective evangelical outreaches of our era.'"

You can clearly see what the bottom line was for the state regarding its tourism incentive program and the Ark Encounter. It wasn't the physical Ark as a tourist attraction that certain officials (and secularists around the country) objected to—it's the message inside the Ark that they didn't want guests to see and consider. It came down to discrimination against Christianity.

This brings me to what I consider to be the most important aspect of the life-size Ark project: the three floors of walk-through exhibits inside this huge wooden structure. These excellent exhibits cover a wide variety of topics, like how Noah fit the animal kinds on board, how he and his family could care for them, and so on. These displays answer the many questions people have about the feasibility of such an Ark (and the Flood event) as outlined in the Bible in Genesis 6–9. But there's no point in merely answering people's questions about the feasibility of the Ark and what the Bible says about this structure if we don't unashamedly engage people with the spiritual message of the Ark.

Like we do at the Creation Museum, we share the salvation message with guests. Just as Noah and his family had to go through a door to be saved, so we too need to go through a door to be saved for eternity.

Jesus said, *I am the door. If anyone enters by me, he will be saved and will go in and out and find pasture* (John 10:9).

And like we do at the Creation Museum, we share the message freely, with no attempt to compel anyone into believing the messages we share. People are free to come to the museum and consider what we present—guests are free to accept, reject, or be challenged by what we share.

In fact, people from all sorts of religions, from atheists to Bible-believing Christians, have visited the Creation Museum and the Ark. And the overwhelming feedback we have received is that while we do not hide what we believe concerning God's Word and the gospel, guests say that we share it all in a professional way with no attempt to force the messages on visitors.

When guests walk through the life-size Ark, they are challenged to consider the answers we give that point to the Flood/Ark being a real event in history. We then share the gospel with visitors in a powerful but loving way.

And he said to them, "Go into all the world and proclaim the gospel to the whole creation. Whoever believes and is baptized will be saved, but whoever does not believe will be condemned" (Mark 16:15–16).

There would be no point building a life-size Ark unless we are answering skeptical questions, sharing the truth of God's Word, and proclaiming the gospel.

APRIL 21
2 Timothy 4:2

What Should the Main Message of a Biblical Creation Apologetics Ministry Be?

On many occasions, I have shared that while Answers in Genesis, the Creation Museum, and the Ark Encounter specifically deal with topics relating to the history in Genesis and the creation/evolution/millions of years issues, our main thrust is really one of biblical authority and the gospel. Yes, we are overtly Christian and overtly evangelistic. There would be no point if we weren't. The most important message in the entire universe is the message of salvation through Jesus Christ, and the message of the gospel begins in Genesis.

Ultimately, AiG and its various outreaches boldly and uncompromisingly stand on the truth of God's Word, beginning in Genesis. And we preach the saving gospel of Jesus Christ—that's the message I have been proclaiming for 40 years now. There's no point just seeing people converted to be creationists! Creationists will end up separated from God for eternity if they have not trusted the Creator for salvation. We praise the Lord for the thousands of churches that are now using AiG's apologetics curricula, Sunday school curriculum, Vacation Bible School (VBS) program, DVDs, books, magazines, and so on.

At the same time, we are seeing many megachurches and prominent church leaders not taking a stand on God's Word in Genesis. Many of them have also become soft on issues like gay "marriage" that are blatantly against God's Word. And, of course, there's a connection between not taking a stand on a literal Genesis and increasing watered-down teaching and acceptance of anti-God positions like LGBTQ, etc.

Overall, the Church is not impacting the culture as it did in our once-very-Christianized Western nations. There's no doubt we are seeing Western cultures becoming more secular and more anti-Christian. Teens and young adults are less churched and more secularized. It's a sad state of affairs. A number of researchers have produced studies that have exposed what's happening in America's churches. Christian researcher George Barna conducted a nationwide survey of Americans (Christians and non-Christians) and presented an analysis of the spiritual condition of the United States in 2016. Here are some of his shocking conclusions (and it's only deteriorated since then):

- "Americans are losing faith in all aspects of their Christian heritage and commitment. During the past decade alone there have been huge declines in the proportion of people … who claim to have made a personal commitment to Jesus Christ."
- "Belief in God, trust in the Bible, and reliance on Jesus alone for salvation have all declined precipitously. Fewer than one in five adults believe that absolute moral truth exists and is defined in the Bible."[32]
- "The unchurched population is growing like cancer."
- "The Bible is taking a big hit. … Only one out of three adults believe it is totally accurate in all of the principles it teaches."
- "The nation's morals and values are a mess. … A majority argues that co-habitation, sexual fantasies, sex outside of marriage, giving birth outside of marriage, divorce, doctor-assisted suicide, homosexual relations, and same-sex marriage are morally acceptable endeavors."
- Barna concluded by noting that these massive cultural changes provide "the cultural context for the battle for who is in control in politics."[33] What a spiritual mess this country and the whole West is in.

CHURCH — APRIL 21

Now, what's the real problem? And then what's the solution?

Contrary to what many people think, politics is not the solution. The remedy is that people need to believe God's Word and respond to the saving gospel. Only the gospel changes hearts and minds, and then the culture follows. Now that doesn't mean Christians shouldn't try to be involved in government. If they can, I certainly encourage that the more people with a Christian worldview involved in government, the more such can have a positive impact on legislation, etc. So, yes, I applaud Christians getting involved in politics.

Herein though lies a major problem in Western churches. You see, I believe that the Church is to blame for much of what has happened in our former Christianized cultures. Certainly, there are many churches and pastors that stand on biblical authority as we do at Answers in Genesis and use the resources we produce. Sadly, they are the minority.

The majority of churches have departed from an uncompromising stand on God's Word, starting in Genesis. This has led to undermining biblical authority and losing generations from our churches. This goes hand in hand with the increasing secularization of the culture.

I have written about an influential pastor in Georgia and his response to what's happening in America. He wants to take the focus off the Word of God and concentrate instead on telling people about Jesus and the Resurrection. This strategy doesn't make sense to me, as we get the message of Jesus and His glorious Resurrection from the Word. And *So faith comes from hearing, and hearing through the word of Christ* (Romans 10:17). So many Christian leaders today are impacted by the world's teaching on evolution, millions of years, etc., and treat the Word of God as a fallible document that should be interpreted to fit with the world's teaching. That's a major problem in the Church.

Over the years, I've seen the Church try to respond to the increasing exodus of people from the Church and the growing secularization of the culture. We've seen the "seeker-sensitive" approach, the growth of the "emergent church," the emphasis on entertainment, and making music the dominant feature of church services as they become more performance based. At the same time, the teaching of God's Word often has become very shallow. And none of that has worked. The generational loss from the Church continues.

I contend that the Church needs to raise up generations who know what they believe, know why they believe it, are equipped with answers to defend the Christian faith against secular attacks (like evolution/millions of years), and know they can trust God's Word from the very first verse. AiG continues to move ahead to reach millions of souls each year (and, prayerfully, billions) with the gospel. That's what the creation apologetics ministry is all about.

Preach the word; be ready in season and out of season; reprove, rebuke, and exhort, with complete patience and teaching (2 Timothy 4:2).

And God's people need to be reminded: *All Scripture is breathed out by God and profitable for teaching, for reproof, for correction, and for training in righteousness, that the man of God may be complete, equipped for every good work* (2 Timothy 3:16–17).

> We need reformation, transformation, and revival in our churches so they will once again impact the culture and raise generations of godly people.

APRIL 22
1 Corinthians 15:1-4

What Is the Gospel?

Over the years, I've heard of pastors who have told their congregation they need to go out and witness to people in their communities, but I believe they give instructions that are detrimental to doing this.

People have told me of pastors who have said things like, "When you present the gospel to people, if they bring up questions like evolution, treat that as a red herring. Don't deal with that but just tell them about Jesus and what He did on the Cross."

I've had others tell me of a pastor who said, "When you are witnessing to people, don't bring up Genesis as it only causes problems. Keep away from Genesis but just concentrate on the New Testament and the message of Christ and the Resurrection."

Imagine a scenario something like this as a Christian is witnessing to a non-Christian:

Christian (C): "I'm here to tell you the good news that Jesus died on the Cross for you."

Non-Christian (N): "Who is Jesus and why did He die?"

C: "Jesus is God's Son, and He died on the Cross to save you."

N: "Save me from what? And which god are you talking about?"

C: "Well, Jesus died for your sin."

N: "What do you mean by sin?"

C: "We are all sinners."

N: "How do you know that and what does it mean?"

C: "Don't worry about that, just know you're a sinner and need to be saved."

N: "What do I need to be saved from? And you still haven't told me which god you are talking about."

I could go on, but how does one explain the gospel without the foundational history in Genesis?

We need to ask ourselves, "What is the gospel?"

When I ask that question of many Christians, the answer I get is often something like this: "Well, the gospel is the message that Jesus died on the Cross for us and was raised from the dead. If we put our faith and trust in the Lord Jesus, we will be saved."

But the gospel is much more than that. The gospel consists of three major parts. When I am explaining any aspect of Christianity to someone, I look on it like building a house. You don't start with the roof; you have to build the foundation first.

The gospel consists of: The foundational history. God created everything (Genesis 1). He created the first man and woman (Genesis 1 and 2). The first man Adam was given an instruction to obey God's Word and not eat the fruit of one particular tree. Adam disobeyed God, and that is called sin. Thus, that's the origin of

THEOLOGY APRIL 22

sin (Genesis 3). And the judgment of sin was death (the origin of death): *Therefore, just as sin came into the world through one man, and death through sin, and so death spread to all men because all sinned* (Romans 5:12).

Because we are all descendants of Adam and he was the head of the one human race, we all have that sin nature. We are all sinners and all under the judgment of death. And that death is physical death as our bodies die and return to dust. It's also spiritual death, separation from God. Our soul, which will live forever, would be eternally separated from God because of sin.

However, in Genesis 3:15 and 3:21, God promised a solution to the sin problem. These verses really prophesize that one would come to pay the penalty for our sin. The prophecy tells us about One (Jesus) who would be victorious over death, the consequence of our sin, thus paying the penalty for our sin.

As we go on through Scripture, we find more prophecies concerning this One who would come, and then we learn in the New Testament who this One is. God steps into history in the person of His Son to become Jesus Christ the God-man. He became a member of the human race, born of a virgin, a perfect man—sinless. He then died on a Cross to suffer the penalty for sin and rose from the dead. He offers a free gift of salvation to those who will receive it:

If you confess with your mouth that Jesus is Lord and believe in your heart that God raised him from the dead, you will be saved (Romans 10:9).

This is the power of the gospel.

The Bible tells us that one day Jesus will return to make a new heavens and new earth. This is called the consummation—the restoration of all things. This is called the hope of the gospel—that sure hope that Christ will one day restore all things to what they were like before sin. In the meantime, we live in this sin-cursed creation. To truly understand the gospel, we need to preset the foundational history—the power of the gospel and the hope of the gospel. When Paul expounded the gospel, he referred back to the history recorded in Genesis to ensure people understood it:

Now I would remind you, brothers, of the gospel I preached to you, which you received, in which you stand, and by which you are being saved, if you hold fast to the word I preached to you—unless you believed in vain. For I delivered to you as of first importance what I also received: that Christ died for our sins in accordance with the Scriptures, that he was buried, that he was raised on the third day in accordance with the Scriptures (1 Corinthians 15:1–4).

For as by a man came death, by a man has come also the resurrection of the dead. For as in Adam all die, so also in Christ shall all be made alive. But each in his own order: Christ the firstfruits, then at his coming those who belong to Christ. Then comes the end, when he delivers the kingdom to God the Father after destroying every rule and every authority and power. For he must reign until he has put all his enemies under his feet. The last enemy to be destroyed is death (1 Corinthians 15:21–26).

> You can't be an effective witness for the gospel unless you proclaim the whole gospel, not just part of it.

APRIL 23
1 Corinthians 14:8

How to Proclaim God's Word with a Spiritual Battle Raging Around Us

The more I look at the state of much of the Church, the more I believe we need to be more intentional than ever in challenging the Church to take back the Bible's clarity . . . from the very first verse. So much of the Church in the West today is lukewarm. And so many church leaders have compromised God's Word beginning in Genesis.

A verse that reminds of this situation states, *And if the bugle gives an indistinct sound, who will get ready for battle?* (1 Corinthians 14:8). The Church needs to be giving a certain sound, proclaiming the truth of God's Word in Genesis. However, much of the Church gives an uncertain sound because of the many compromise positions on Genesis as church leaders try to fit evolution/millions of years into the text. Sadly, it's the world, not much of the Church, that gives the certain sound, as the secular world is united in proclaiming evolution and millions of years as fact.

Now, the Word of God is clear and needs to be proclaimed to all. It's for all people for all time, regardless of their level of education! And when we take God's Word as written in Genesis, we can and should be giving a clear, certain sound.

I was once asked to engage in a "dialogue" with a seminary professor at a large apologetics conference in North Carolina. It really turned into an informal debate! Looking back on it, I believe the Lord orchestrated the event (as is always the case) as there was a lot of positive impact that came out of the interaction. It helped people wake up to the compromise by the majority of academics in Christendom.

This "debate" highlighted a major problem that permeates most Christian seminaries and Bible colleges and the thinking of many Christian academics. It's a plague in the Church.

This national apologetics conference had many old-earth creationists, who compromise on Genesis, give presentations.

I debated one professor who was a young-earth creationist, but to me, he seemed rather weak in his convictions and not very knowledgeable of the biblical and scientific arguments in favor of young-earth creation. And he was very opposed to the way that I, and AiG in general, defend Genesis. I don't think he really understood our approach to apologetics—as is true of many seminary professors.

Unfortunately, this professor, like the old-earth creationists, insisted that the issue over the teachings of Genesis was not the authority of Scripture but the interpretation of Scripture. I kept hammering away that it was an authority issue—that the battle over the age of the earth came down to God's infallible Word versus man's fallible word. And this determines how one interprets Genesis. It's biblical authority first! I challenged him and the audience many times that if they accepted millions of years, God should be blamed for cancer, brain tumors, arthritis, and other diseases found in the fossil record—a record, they would say, of millions of years before man.

Now, this professor was very eloquent and spoke much about philosophical and hermeneutical issues. I just tried to be my usual self, using down-to-earth, practical examples to help make the issues clearer. I also said that research we conducted (and published in various books) made it obvious that the Church was

APOLOGETICS

losing generations because so many young people doubt or disbelieve God's Word because of issues like the supposed millions of years for the fossil record and the earth's age.

At the end, I made sure that the audience understood once again that this was an authority issue. Afterward, many people (primarily young adults and teens) swarmed around to thank me for standing for the truth and the clarity with which the Scriptures present God's Word to all. Overall, I believe the "debate" was a profitable time of planting seeds and encouraging those who do believe in Genesis to stand for the truth. A number of people told me they were glad that AiG was represented at this apologetics conference.

After the "debate," I discussed with colleagues the issue that really dismayed me. As I listened to many of these seminary professors at the conference who held millions of years, it was sad to see them sending an unclear message to the Church concerning God's Word.

They made it confusing regarding how to read and understand God's Word. My "opponent" kept emphasizing man's interpretation of God's Word. But under the premise that academics can interpret Genesis as teaching millions of years and that it is not an important issue, he stated that we can all agree to have different interpretations—and just dialogue together!

We are seeing a trend in which it seems many of these academics are saying that the average person can't fully understand the Word of God for themselves but has to listen to what these "learned" people are saying. In fact, during the "debate," my opponent made reference to the fact that "everyone should have a Hebrew scholar in their life" to help them fully understand Scripture!

That's why during this "debate" I said that God's Word is for all people for all time. And its message (even though there are difficult passages) is easy for anyone to understand—and it's not difficult to understand Genesis if we just read it and take it as written, as did Jesus, Peter, and Paul in the New Testament. That's how most orthodox Christian scholars accepted Genesis up until the nineteenth century when the idea of millions of years (which came out of deistic and atheistic naturalism) began to infiltrate the Church.

Compromise positions on Genesis are permeating our seminaries and other Christian institutions. Many academics have come up with all sorts of fanciful ways to twist the Scriptures to try to fit in millions of years. It's almost like the gnostics who claimed some sort of special knowledge. Many of these academics are telling the average person, "Trust us. We've done in-depth theological study, and you need to reinterpret God's Word as we tell you to."

There's so much compromise about Genesis today. And now we see compromise on marriage and gender, as people increasingly compromise other parts of the Bible. The message the Church presents is not clear—it's not certain. And as 1 Corinthians 14:8 tells us, when there's an uncertain sound, people will not be prepared for the battle.

There's a spiritual battle raging around us, and many in the Church are not prepared for that battle with a clear understanding of the Word of God. Read this verse again and ponder it:

And if the bugle gives an indistinct sound, who will get ready for battle? (1 Corinthians 14:8).

> **Are you and your church giving a clear, certain sound or an uncertain sound in regard to proclaiming God's Word, particularly in Genesis?**

APRIL 24

2 Timothy 4:2-5

We Need to "Wake Up" the "Sleeping Giant"

Secularists now control most of the secular education institutions, much of the court system, branches of government, and so on. Yet activist atheists (who vocally oppose Answers in Genesis and Bible-believing Christians) constitute a minority in society. This small segment of atheists/secular humanists has become very aggressive in promoting atheism (through the courts, media, schools) and getting Christian reminders (crosses, Ten Commandment displays, Nativity scenes, creation teaching and Bible in schools) removed from public places. And now trying to normalize LGBTQ worldview, abortion, etc. If the millions of Christians in America were to "wake up" and become more assertive in standing up for the Christian faith, they could have a great positive effect on the culture.

Christians have been intimidated by the constant attacks from scholars and intellectuals on the accuracy of the Bible. Most believers don't know how to answer their skeptical questions about God's Word. Furthermore, many Christians have been brainwashed into thinking that the so-called "separation of church and state" means that the public (secular) schools are now neutral because they have, by and large, eliminated God and the Bible from the classroom. But secular really means anti-God. One is either for or against Christ; there is no neutral position. And, sadly, many Christian leaders have accommodated to secularist views of evolution/millions of years, and some have even adopted heretical views in regard to the Bible.

Christians are a "sleeping giant" in our culture. I believe the Lord has been "awakening" them in many ways, and He often uses biblical apologetics ministries to do it. It is amazing to look back and realize what the Lord has been doing in recent times: Consider the publication of *The Genesis Flood* by Drs. Morris and Whitcomb in 1961. Really, Answers in Genesis and the Creation Museum are part of continuing their legacy. This creation movement in our modern era helped "wake up a sleeping giant," as so many in the Church had been "asleep" in regard to the compromise with God's Word in Genesis that has so undermined biblical authority. Actually, many organizations/people, such as the American Family Association, the late Dr. D. James Kennedy/Coral Ridge Ministries, and numerous others were raised up to help in "waking up" the "sleeping giant" in regard to moral issues like abortion and gay "marriage." They helped alert the Church that the Christian worldview was under a massive attack.

In 2009, our publisher released the book *Already Gone* (I am a coauthor). This book detailed the results of an AiG-commissioned study by Britt Beemer's America's Research Group to find out why two-thirds of young people were exiting the Church when they leave home. This book was (and continues to be) a "wake-up" call to pastors and the Church as a whole. Many churches/homes introduced creation and general Bible apologetics into their programs as a response to the book. As a result of this research, AiG recognized the dire need to produce a Bible curriculum from kindergarten through adult that emphasizes biblical authority, teaches apologetics, and proclaims the gospel. We produced the curriculum called Answers Bible Curriculum that is now used in thousands of churches to teach apologetics, biblical worldview, doctrine, and the gospel as all ages are taught chronologically through the Bible.

A number of years ago, AiG (boldly, unashamedly, and respectfully) stood against compromise teaching that was occurring at particular homeschooling conferences (run as a for-profit business, not a ministry). At this

APOLOGETICS — APRIL 24

homeschool convention, anti-biblical teaching was being presented in workshops and resources in the expo hall. I spoke at two of these conferences, and then I was disinvited from speaking at the rest of this company's conferences. My expulsion from these homeschool conferences caused a big "shock wave" through the Christian homeschool community in America (and even in Canada). Many homeschoolers began to "wake up" to the fact that false teaching had been creeping into the homeschool movement through speakers and their Bible-compromising resources. Many leaders told us that this was a watershed moment for the homeschool movement nationwide. In addition to these homeschool leaders, many parents commented to us that they will now need to look very carefully at homeschool resources and protect their children from teaching that undermines biblical authority. Being expelled from the convention caused thousands to join my Facebook page. One representative of the many thousands of comments was this one: "Thank you for standing for the truth, and for bringing to light the teachings of some of the other homeschool curriculums. We will be much more vigilant in choosing curriculum for our children based on this new knowledge."

I groan when I look at many of the vendors at most homeschool conferences. So many of them sell compromised resources! There is such a lack of discernment here. Or perhaps, because of the need for funds, the standards are greatly lowered to allow vendors who shouldn't be there to display their materials. One person observed that the expulsion caused a "light to shine on the entire homeschool network in America and has awakened many people of the need to re-evaluate who is being allowed into the vendor halls, speaking at the podium, etc."

Our publisher released a sequel to *Already Gone* titled *Already Compromised* (also coauthored by me). America's Research Group (ARG) was again commissioned by AiG and our publisher, this time to research what is being taught in Christian colleges. The research resulted in an eye-opening indictment of Christian colleges across America. In this unprecedented 2010 study, these colleges were polled on core faith questions . . . and the results were both revealing and shocking! Compromise was rampant. The views, responses, and answers to basic questions about biblical authority from these leaders at Christian colleges should alarm every Christian. ARG interviewed Christian college presidents, academic deans/vice presidents, science department heads, and theology/religion department heads. We discovered how these institutions address the cultural battlefields of science, Christianity, and the accuracy of the Bible, including views on the inspiration, inerrancy, and infallibility of the Word of God.

With this college survey, AiG quickly saw the need to help parents and students with tips for choosing Christian colleges. We wanted to equip them with the questions to ask colleges to ensure that their children will be instructed to stand boldly on God's Word. Yes, let's all get actively involved in the spiritual battle raging around us and:

Preach the word; be ready in season and out of season; reprove, rebuke, and exhort, with complete patience and teaching. For the time is coming when people will not endure sound teaching, but having itching ears they will accumulate for themselves teachers to suit their own passions, and will turn away from listening to the truth and wander off into myths. As for you, always be sober-minded, endure suffering, do the work of an evangelist, fulfill your ministry (2 Timothy 4:2–5).

Every Christian needs to stand firm and without compromise on God's Word.

APRIL 25
Matthew 7:21

False Prophets

In Matthew 25, we read the parable of the ten virgins. Five wisely kept their lamps lit as they awaited the return of the bridegroom and five were foolish. From the context of this chapter and the preceding one, this passage helps expose the difference between nominal Christians (i.e., in name only) and true Christians.

John Gill, in his well-known Bible commentary, discusses the nominal and real Christians referred to in Matthew 25. He writes that there will be those who make "a profession of religion, and yet, at last, [will] be shut out of heaven."[34]

The word *virgins* in the parable describes those who are betrothed to Christ. Five neglected their steadfast preparation and let their lamps go out and missed the joyful return of the bridegroom. They represent those who outwardly look like believers but inwardly are not true Christians.

I have sometimes wondered whether the "foolish virgins" could apply to a number of church leaders/academics today—those who say they are Christians but have rejected the authority of God's Word and basic biblical doctrines. They have relied instead on man's fallible ideas to determine truth. These leaders may have never truly been born again as the Bible teaches and, among other things, have put their trust in "the scholars" or other religious leaders rather than the Word, Jesus Christ.

Now don't misunderstand me here. I know there are many Christians who compromise God's Word in Genesis with evolution/millions of years. I'm not saying one has to believe in a young earth to be saved. Salvation is conditioned upon faith in Christ, not what one believes about the age of the earth. But we are finding other church and academic leaders in Christendom rejecting the very basics of the Christian faith.

We must keep our lamps lit (Matthew 25) and also continue in our prayers for those who are not prepared for the return and judgment of Christ.

In essence, such "Christians" have placed their faith in the writings of man over the clear teachings of the Word—and also over many biblical doctrines, including the Fall of Adam and Eve into sin (Genesis 3). Yes, there is an increasing number of liberal people in Christendom that are rejecting such basic doctrines.

Sadly, we are seeing more and more "false prophets" arising in the Church today. These teachers deny the literal Fall and dismiss a sin nature inherited from a real Adam. Thus, they ultimately deny the true saving gospel that everyone needs to heed.

These church leaders and academics outwardly profess to believe in Christ, but like the false prophets of Jeremiah's day (e.g., Jeremiah 23:9–40) and the Pharisees of Jesus' day (Matthew 23:13–36), they are leading God's people astray. One day they will find that "the door is shut." It's all so very sad.

Not everyone who says to me, "Lord, Lord," will enter the kingdom of heaven, but the one who does the will of my Father who is in heaven. On that day many will say to me, "Lord, Lord, did we not prophesy in your name, and cast out demons in your name, and do many mighty works in your name?" And then will I declare to them, "I never knew you; depart from me, you workers of lawlessness" (Matthew 7:21–23).

THEOLOGY

I pray that none of the readers of this article would be counted among the "foolish virgins" and that the door to heaven is not shut to them. Make sure your heart is truly right with God, that you are truly born again and believe God's Word. I believe there are more than we think in our churches who are Christian in name only and have never been truly born again.

In Genesis 7, we read the account of Noah and his family (eight people total) who went through the door of the ark to be saved from a watery judgment. These were the only people living in the pre-Flood world whose hearts were right with God and who believed God's promises.

And the Lord shut him in (Genesis 7:16).

Noah is also mentioned in the New Testament. In 2 Peter 2, the Apostle Peter warns us about false prophets in the Church—leaders who profess that their hearts are committed to the true God but are really false teachers. Outwardly they were prophets/teachers, but inwardly, their hearts were not right.

In verse 5, Peter describes Noah as a "preacher of righteousness" and someone who was saved. But Peter points out that false teachers cannot expect to escape divine vengeance. Just as God shut the door when Noah and his family were on the ark and just as those whose hearts were not right with God suffered the judgment of the Flood, false teachers will not be on board today's ark of salvation, Jesus Christ, when He comes again (this time in judgment). The door will be shut to them.

Jesus, the Son of God said, *I am the door. If anyone enters by me, he will be saved* (John 10:9).

I believe there is a great danger today in the Church: an increasing number of "Christian" academics and pastors who may intellectually believe in God, but inwardly (and only God knows), their hearts may not be right with God—like the "foolish virgins." And certainly, only Jesus, who is the Word, can ultimately judge their hearts (Hebrews 4:12).

Now I am not saying that if a person denies the creation account of origins and believes in evolution/millions of years, he or she can't be truly saved. After all, God's Word simply states that *if you confess with your mouth that Jesus is Lord and believe in your heart that God raised him from the dead, you will be saved* (Romans 10:9). I'm talking about people who reject basic doctrines like the Fall. Some church leaders seem to be more concerned with shallow messages and being popular and providing entertainment. Only God knows their heart, but we all need to examine our hearts in regard to where we stand in the Christian faith.

Please pray for those academics and pastors in Christendom who are leading so many people astray. Pray that the Lord will convict them to make their hearts right with God while the "door" (the Lord Jesus) is still open. Remember, *Not everyone who says to me, "Lord, Lord," will enter the kingdom of heaven, but the one who does the will of my Father who is in heaven* (Matthew 7:21).

> **We are burdened to proclaim the gospel of Christ and the fact that only those who go through the open door can be saved.**

APRIL 26
Psalm 119:30

Communicating Christianity to Our Anti-Christian, Woke Culture

In 2018, a national media event occurred and involved a lot of personal stress. But looking back, I see some great lessons for us as Christians in regard to communicating Christianity to our secularized and increasingly anti-Christian, woke culture.

I was invited to give a lecture for a Christian group at a university in Oklahoma, but because of opposition from the LGBTQ group on campus, the invitation was rescinded. Then, due to enormous public pressure, I was re-invited to speak!

Media across the nation covered the event. As you know, there are ongoing battles in the USA in public universities over First Amendment rights involving freedom of speech—and such battles have been heating up. As a result of intense media coverage and politicians getting involved over freedom of speech issues, I was invited by the president of the university to give a public lecture. What's interesting is that the LGBTQ group thought they had shut me down from speaking to a Christian group on campus, but as a result, I was invited back to give a public lecture at the university.

Reminds me of the situation with Joseph: *But Joseph said to them, "Do not fear, for am I in the place of God? As for you, you meant evil against me, but God meant it for good, to bring it about that many people should be kept alive, as they are today"* (Genesis 50:19–20).

I've often used that verse in regard to situations in our ministry where those opposing us thought they had hurt us in some way, only to find out God is using those situations for purposes we could never have imagined. But back to the invitation to give this public lecture at a secular university. When the evening came, the auditorium was packed. The LGBTQ group that opposed me were there, as well as many students and professors, people from the general public, and a number of media outlets.

Before we spoke (I had also brought one of our PhD scientists with me to give part of the presentation), the vice president gave a disclaimer concerning what they were about to hear from us. I'm sure they were concerned we were going to come in as "Bible thumpers" and call out the sin of homosexual behavior, etc. But I know you can't impose a Christian worldview on people who don't have the foundation of God's Word. For my presentation, I told the audience I wanted them to understand why we as Christians believe the way we do. I explained that I do believe the Bible is God's Word and that Genesis 1–11 is history. I then showed that I use that history as the foundation for my worldview. I gave a summary of the Bible's message from creation, through the Fall, the Flood, the Tower of Babel, and the message of the gospel, including the consummation.

I said that if someone doesn't have the same foundation that I do, they will not have the same worldview. I explained that did not mean I hated them but that I had a different worldview. I showed that what I believe about marriage, gender, abortion, etc., all comes from the foundation of Genesis 1–11, so I covered these moral issues from a foundational perspective. After the presentation, I had a number of people say things such as:

- You really disarmed the LGBTQ group!

APOLOGETICS — APRIL 26

- We think they were hoping you would say something against them so they could accuse you of hate speech. But the way you handled those issues was so disarming.
- Every church needs to learn how to address these volatile issues regarding gender, as was done here.

After the event, a person who watched online said to me, "I've grown up in the church but have never been taught to think foundationally, as you presented. This makes so much sense and has really challenged me to change the way I speak to people about issues like abortion, gender, and gay 'marriage.' I wish everyone in the church could hear the presentation and especially see how the question time was handled."

There were many media articles about this university talk. One such report came from the Religion News Service and was published by several media outlets across the nation. In this article, specific reference was made to a question I answered, one that many people have since commented on. This was the answer that many told me was disarming for the LGBTQ group—in fact, the head of the group on campus was in the audience for my talk. Here are excerpts from the RNS syndicated article:

One questioner—a self-described "spirit-filled Christian" and member of the LGBTQ community—said: "I sought the Lord and churches for why I feel attracted to the same sex. I found the Church nor churches' traditional view on (LGBTQ) fit my experience of hearing the Lord speak directly to me. Science, not the Church, gave me peace. How can you say my experience of still being a child of God isn't valid?"

Ham said he would start by asking how the person heard from God: "My way of dealing with that would be to say, 'Let's judge what the actual written word of God says. Let's judge what you're saying against what it says.'

"Because I have a different worldview in relation to marriage and gender doesn't mean I hate that person," Ham added. "Sometimes, people accuse us of hate speech because we disagree with them. It's a clash of worldviews. That doesn't mean we hate someone. In fact, the Bible commands us to love everyone, and that's what we do."

I said much more than this, of course. I explained that if people don't build their thinking on the Bible as I do (and if they don't have the same interpretation of Genesis as I do), then we're not going to agree on how we view marriage, gender, abortion, and so on.

I wanted people to understand that the essence of the battle comes down to the foundation that their worldview is built upon—and until we can sort that out, we are not going to agree regarding how we view such culture issues. As I explained in my talk, whether it's racism, gay "marriage," gender battles, abortion, or other issues, they all involve one overall issue: Where does your worldview come from? Many people have told me the way we presented our worldview beliefs took a lot of the emotionalism out of the arguments.

> "The unfolding of your words gives light; it imparts understanding to the simple" (Psalm 119:130).

APRIL 27

Luke 11:4

Let's Rescue Coming Generations from the Evil One!

From my experience of over 40 years in ministry and from the research we've done, it's obvious most of the youth in our churches have not been taught general Bible apologetics, much less creation apologetics. They haven't been taught how to defend the Christian faith and how to answer the skeptical questions of our day that attack the Bible. In fact, many of them have been taught not to take Genesis 1–11 as literal history.

My heart became burdened when so many young people came up to talk to me after I spoke to their group in one of my teaching tours in California. They said positive things about the talks, but some teens also stated:

- "I grew up in the church and thought we had to believe in evolution. You rocked my world."
- "I've grown up in church but never heard this information before. Thank you, thank you."
- "I was taught Bible 'stories' for years in church. I've never heard answers like this. You've changed my life—thank you, thank you."

These young people seemed to be dedicated Christians who loved the Lord. At the same time, they had a very shallow understanding of Christianity. They had no idea how to answer the skeptical questions of this age—questions that are intended to create doubt in people's minds about the Christian faith. For children and teens in our churches, lacking answers can put them on a slippery slide toward unbelief. These young people hadn't been taught Genesis 1–11 as literal history and really had no understanding this history was foundational to all doctrine, to our worldview, to everything. Without that they would never be able to deal properly with issues like gender, abortion, homosexuality, racism, and so on.

During the question time after my presentation, these teens asked about the usual topics, like carbon dating, Cain's wife, dinosaurs, etc. But there were also lots of questions like, "Why doesn't God show Himself to us?" "What about all the other books that aren't in the Bible (like the Apocrypha)?" "How can we know God exists?" Over time, I've noticed young people adding in questions about gender and other LGBTQ issues. Of course, lack of teaching on Genesis 1–11 leads people to not understanding what they should believe and why about all these questions. But back to this particular group of young people.

This Q&A session confirmed what I had seen time and time again throughout America: The youth in our churches have not been taught general Bible apologetics, much less creation apologetics (which are core in truly understanding, believing, and defending the gospel). While most of these teens at the California conference seemed to be blessed by the "praise and worship" time, it struck me, based also on what I heard from their leaders, that these teens just didn't have an in-depth understanding of the Christian faith.

After I spoke, much to the surprise of the conference organizers, several hundred young people purchased thousands of our books, including those in the New Answers book series.

Yes, I was overwhelmed at the positive response but also burdened. I was reminded of the importance of AiG's creation apologetics ministry and our emphasis on "Standing Our Ground, Rescuing Our Kids" that's based on Galatians 1:4 and that passage's reference to rescuing people from this "present evil age."

APOLOGETICS APRIL 27

As I pondered these young people I spoke to in California, I thought of categories of "people rescue" that we can be involved in: Rescuing the non-Christians of the world. We need to do our best to proclaim the truth of God's Word and the gospel, praying the Lord will save our kids for eternity. The huge Creation Museum and Ark Encounter attractions are two such major evangelistic outreaches.

Rescuing the Christians! So many young people, like those I mentioned above, need to be "rescued" from their church's teachings or lack of them (i.e., churches that either compromise on Genesis or don't equip young people and adults with solid answers). As we revealed in our 2009 book *Already Gone*, a lack of training in biblical apologetics is a major reason why two-thirds of today's youth leave the Church.

Rescuing those who were brought up in the Church and have now walked away (the two-thirds I just mentioned). To give you an example of the effectiveness of such rescue efforts, here is what a person once posted to my public Facebook page: "Ken: I am so glad you are in this great work of the Lord. My son came home from college a while back and told me that two of his friends that he grew up with no longer believe in God because of evolution. [But] your work is helping to bring their hearts back to the truth...I wish your light was taught in all colleges."

Rescuing those young people who are still in the Church but are attending a Christian college or seminary where Bible-undermining professors are training many of them to be compromising pastors. (Most of the "top" Christian colleges are now in this sad category! There are exceptions, but they are a small minority.) These future pastors will only perpetuate the horrible compromise already in our churches, and we'll continue to see generations of young people leave the Church and turn their backs on God. This youth exodus is a major problem in our churches.

The ministry of AiG, with all its various outreaches (including the phenomenal Creation Museum and Ark Encounter), are set up to "rescue" as many people as we can from this present evil age. We provide resources to help others in rescuing kids. I encourage you to check out our rescuing resources.

> Let's all remember to pray, as Jesus taught us in Luke 11:4 (NKJV), what is called the Lord's Prayer, to "deliver us from the evil one," for Christians need to be diligently working to help rescue coming generations from the evil one.

APRIL 28
2 Corinthians 11:3

The Battle Doesn't Change!

Times have changed over the last 500+ years, but some basic challenges never change. Also, God's Word never changes. The gospel never changes. But the culture has changed.

When Martin Luther nailed those 95 theses on the Castle Church in Wittenberg (Germany) 500 years ago, on October 31, 1517, what questions might people have asked him?

Do you think anyone came up to him and asked, "Dr. Luther, it's all very well and good to nail these theses on the church door. But explain how you can trust the Bible when carbon dating gives dates that contradict its genealogies?" Or, "Did dinosaurs go on Noah's ark?"

Well, of course, no one asked him such questions. Carbon dating was invented over 400 years later, in the 1900s. Similarly, he wouldn't have been asked about dinosaurs (a term invented in 1841), Lucy (discovered in 1974), the big bang (coined in 1949), Charles Darwin (born in 1809), and so on.

Martin Luther was dealing with a different set of questions, which he understood as attacks on the authority of God's Word in his era. He was confronting people who were using man's fallible ideas and imposing them on the unchanging, infallible Word of God. It was an authority issue. Who is the ultimate authority? God or man? This is the battle that began in Genesis 3 and has been raging ever since. The battle doesn't change, but it does manifest in different ways in different eras.

What Martin Luther boldly accomplished was to start a movement to challenge the Church to return to the authority of God's Word. He specifically was defending justification by faith. And so out of the Reformation came the cry for Sola Scriptura—Scripture alone.

Actually, five solas (Latin phrases) came out of the Reformation. Sola Scriptura (Scripture alone) means the Bible alone is our highest authority. The other solas were Sola Fide (faith alone), Sola Gratia (grace alone), Solus Christus (Christ alone), and Soli Deo Gloria (to the glory of God alone).

I've often said that the ministry of Answers in Genesis is helping to ignite a New Reformation. This stresses the first sola—Sola Scriptura. In fact, God warns us that Sola Scriptura is the focus of the devil's ongoing attacks on God's Word in every generation. Second Corinthians 11:3 warns: *But I am afraid that as the serpent deceived Eve by his cunning, your thoughts will be led astray from a sincere and pure devotion to Christ.*

In other words, the devil will use the same method on us that he used on Eve to get people to not believe the Word of God.

So, what method did he use on Eve? We read about it in Genesis 3:1: *He said to the woman, "Did God actually say?"* Another translation puts it this way: *"Did God really say?"* Notice the first attack was on the authority of the Word of God to get Adam and Eve to doubt and disbelieve God's Word.

The warning then is that the devil will attack the authority of God's Word by creating doubt in His Word, which in the end can lead to unbelief. I call this the Genesis 3 attack. That attack has never let up; it never changes. But what does change is how the attack manifests itself.

APOLOGETICS — APRIL 28

Down through the ages, believers have dealt with various attacks on God's Word. For example, the early Church faced attacks on the deity of Christ, Martin Luther's era faced attacks on justification by faith, and the Enlightenment period of the 1800s faced attacks on Christ's bodily Resurrection.

But what is the main "Genesis 3 attack" today? I suggest the teaching of evolution/millions of years, based on naturalism (atheism), that permeates the culture and Church. Evolution is really the pagan religion of this age, which secularists push as their justification for rejecting God and His Word.

Compromise with this pagan religion is a major reason the Church is losing so many in the current and coming generations. It's also a major reason our once-Christianized West is becoming less Christian every day, at least from a worldview perspective.

Today's Genesis 3 attack has resulted in a loss of respect for the Bible's authority. So many in the Church no longer believe God's Word in Genesis because they believe evolutionary ideas. As a result, the culture doesn't see why they should trust the Bible on anything it speaks about. And so many Christians don't really understand what they believe and why and don't know how to defend the Christian faith.

Thus, this attack on Genesis' creation account opened the door for coming generations to reject biblical authority. As a result, many people are careening down a slippery slide toward doubt and unbelief, resulting in a generational loss from the Church, and a very secularized worldview permeating the Church and culture.

That's why I believe we need a new Reformation. We need (symbolically, of course) people across this nation and the world nailing Genesis 1–11 on doors of churches and Christian institutions to call God's people back to the authority of God's Word, beginning in Genesis. We need to question what's being taught and hold the teachers accountable. We need to shut the door of compromise in Genesis, or we will continue to see the Church's impact on the culture lessening and the culture's impact on the Church increasing!

Sadly, most churches (not all of course), and most Christian colleges, seminaries, and Bible colleges have been impacted by the religion of naturalism by compromising Genesis with evolution and/or millions of years.

Stop regarding man in whose nostrils is breath, for of what account is he? (Isaiah 2:22).

Trust in the Lord with all your heart, and do not lean on your own understanding. In all your ways acknowledge him, and he will make straight your paths (Proverbs 3:5–6).

> Yes, once again, we need to be proclaiming *Sola Scriptura* in our generation and confront the rampant compromise in the Church, which makes man's fallible ideas (evolution/millions of years) the authority over God's infallible Word.

APRIL 29

Deuteronomy 4:9

What Will Your Legacy Be?

I want to highlight the legacies of four very different people. The first is Martin Luther, the great reformer who is credited with sparking the Protestant Reformation. While certainly not a perfect man (no one is), he loved God's Word and encouraged those of his day to start their thinking with God's Word, pointing them toward the saving gospel. His legacy lives on even today, many hundreds of years later. I love those words attributed to him, "Here I stand [on God's Word], I can do no other, God help me."

Here is one of my favorite quotes from Martin Luther:

"When Moses writes that God created heaven and earth and whatever is in them in six days, then let this period continue to have been six days, and do not venture to devise any comment according to which six days were one day. But, if you cannot understand how this could have been done in six days, then grant the Holy Spirit the honor of being more learned than you are."[35]

I wonder how many Christians leaders today would be willing to stand as Luther did, knowing it would result in placing his life in jeopardy. While some may criticize various aspects of what he taught and stated, one cannot deny the astounding impact he had on the Church.

The second person is Charles Darwin, the man credited with popularizing the idea of evolution. His legacy lives on today as his naturalistic (atheistic) ideas have permeated not only Western culture but much of the rest of the world and much of the Church. But his legacy is not a good one. He popularized a philosophy that attacked (and was intended to destroy—but that can never happen, of course) the authority of the Word of God. Sadly, many churches adopted his ideas and reinterpreted the Book of Genesis. This led to an undermining of the authority of God's Word and generations doubting its truth and walking away from the Christian faith. Darwin's legacy is a destructive, evil legacy, and it lives on, not only in the secular culture and teaching but, sadly, also in many churches.

Darwin's legacy in the Church can be seen in the fact that he was buried in the church (Westminster Abbey in London) and honored by the Church. Actually, his grave is in the floor of the church. This, to me, is a reminder that a man who popularized a philosophy to undermine the foundation of the Church is honored by the Church and buried in the foundation of the church!

The last two legacies are my own parents, Mervyn and Norma Ham. My father and mother are both now at home with the Lord. Answers in Genesis, the Ark Encounter, and the Creation Museum are really a result of their legacy, which is impacting tens of millions of people a year with the truth of God's Word and the saving gospel. Now, that's a legacy!

You see, my parents taught their children to stand boldly, unashamedly, and uncompromisingly on the authority of the Word of God. They loved God's Word, and in many places we lived, they started Sunday schools and brought in evangelists to make sure children and their families were able to hear the message of the gospel.

When I was a child, I watched my dad read the Scriptures and passionately declare, "Thus saith the Lord!" He was always researching what the liberal critics of the day were saying so that he could find answers and

FAMILY   APRIL 29

equip us to defend our faith. If he came across an argument he couldn't answer, he would emphasize that our knowledge is nothing compared to God's. He taught us to always go back to God's Word to make sure that we were correctly understanding the passage in its context and literary genre and that our interpretation was indeed correct because God's Word is true—not the argument. Eventually, God's Word would be vindicated, he said, and he was right! It always is!

Since we moved frequently for my father's work, we attended many different churches. If my parents ever heard a pastor teach something that went against what God's Word clearly teaches, they would take all of us kids, along with a Bible, up to the front after the service and graciously challenge the pastor with God's Word. They emphasized the authority of God's Word and never knowingly compromised on its truth. This greatly impacted all their family.

The work of AiG, the Ark Encounter, and the Creation Museum are the legacy of this teaching. My parents never had much in the way of material things, but they left a rich spiritual legacy for their children and our children—and our children's children!

And their legacy isn't just impacting our immediate family. It has affected the family of Christ through our VBS, Answers Bible Curriculum, thousands of books, DVDs, and other apologetics materials that have been distributed through the AiG conferences and website, the gospel-centered teaching and answers at the Ark Encounter and the Creation Museum, and more. These resources have impacted literally millions of people (including many non-Christians), encouraging them to stand on the authority of God's Word—something many have taught their children, who are now teaching their children!

So I challenge you: What legacy are you leaving behind? Are you leaving a legacy that will long outlive you and be felt in subsequent generations? Will your legacy impact your immediate family, local believers, unbelievers, or even the body of Christ around the world?

A strong spiritual legacy doesn't happen by accident. Be intentional about what kind of legacy you want to leave behind. Let how you spend your time and money speak clearly to what that legacy will be. If you have children and grandchildren, pour into them. Spend time with them. Engage in meaningful, spiritual conversations. Encourage them; share your story; offer wisdom; always point them to Christ and God's Word.

Too many grandparents waste the precious years they have with their grandchildren. Instead of recognizing that their race is not yet finished, they leave the spiritual instruction of their grandchildren completely up to the child's parents or church and instead focus solely on building memories or retirement. But God doesn't say age 65 is when our race is run! We have a calling to declare God's works to our children and their children (Deuteronomy 4:9). You have a unique perspective and wisdom you can pass along to encourage the next generation. Don't waste your latter years!

Only take care, and keep your soul diligently, lest you forget the things that your eyes have seen, and lest they depart from your heart all the days of your life. Make them known to your children and your children's children (Deuteronomy 4:9).

What will your legacy be?

APRIL 30
2 Peter 3:9

Hope for Atheists

When I read some of the atheist blogs, Facebook posts, and news articles that display a sheer hatred against Christians (really, it's a hatred against God), it can seem, humanly speaking, hopeless to try to reach these secularists with the truth of God's Word and the salvation message it presents.

And yet, we can be encouraged to read of the incredible conversion of Saul (who severely persecuted Christians) in Acts 9 and realize that God's Word can penetrate even the most hardened heart. *For the word of God is living and active, sharper than any two-edged sword, piercing to the division of soul and of spirit, of joints and of marrow, and discerning the thoughts and intentions of the heart* (Hebrews 4:12).

As I read many of the comments posted on my social media by atheists (blasphemous, perverse, and vitriolic as some of them are), I understand that they have been indoctrinated in evolutionary naturalism. Most of them have probably never heard a clear, logical defense of the Christian faith that would answer many of their skeptical questions. It's important to remember that God's Word commands us to *honor Christ the Lord as holy, always being prepared to make a defense to anyone who asks you for a reason for the hope that is in you; yet do it with gentleness and respect* (1 Peter 3:15).

At the same time, it's vital that we never divorce any arguments/defense we could present to atheists from the powerful Word of God: *So faith comes from hearing, and hearing through the word of Christ* (Romans 10:17).

At Answers in Genesis, through our resources, conferences, and other outreaches, we do our best to defend the Christian faith using apologetics against the secular attacks of our day. But in doing so, we need to also point people to the truth of God's Word and challenge them concerning the saving gospel. We use apologetics to answer questions and direct people to God's Word and its message of salvation.

There's no greater thrill than to hear how God has used what has been taught by AiG to touch someone's life—for eternity. Years ago, I was introduced to one of our new volunteers, who was helping sew some of the costumes for the figures that were placed inside our full-size Ark. She had responded to my Facebook post asking for a seamstress.

I discovered that she became a Christian in 1993 after attending one of my seminars in Ohio. The Bible-upholding seminar was such an eye-opener to her about the reliability of the Bible that she became a Christian.

I asked if she would share her testimony. She wrote:

"The Lord opened up this atheistic evolutionist's eyes decades ago, through exposure to Ken's ministry.

"I was a die-hard evolutionist, completely convinced that the fossil finds in Olduvai Gorge supported the 'evidence' that we evolved from less-complicated, early hominid creatures, like the so-called 'Lucy.'

"To keep a long story short: I attended a Creation Seminar at Cedarville College [now Cedarville University], sat in rapt attention as Ken Ham told me 'the rest of the story,' and I realized that all of the fossil finds I believed supported evolution were, in all cases, misinterpreted. I was blown away! So, learning the truth about evolution preceded my realizing that God was real (after all!) and that the Bible was His Word. I became a creationist before I became a believer in Christ.

APOLOGETICS — APRIL 30

"I was raised and educated Roman Catholic. My parents took all seven of us to church every Sunday. And for all that religiosity, we never spoke of Jesus at home.

"After twelve years of Catholic schools, and being taught that Noah's Ark, for example, was just an allegorical way to relay the story that 'if you come on board with belief in God, He'll keep you through the storm,' that there probably was no actual Noah's Ark, and probably no actual Adam and Eve, it was easy to throw out the Bible as any believable 'Word of God.'

"I became a non-Christian. I used to say, 'How can I believe a book that's been copied over and over and over, translated in so many different versions, when it probably doesn't even look like the original, like a Xerox copy of a Xerox copy of a Xerox copy?' It was easy to walk away from what little faith I'd been taught.

"But then being exposed to creation [apologetics ministry], I had to look honestly at what I'd come to believe about God. I can't name a specific date that I came to saving knowledge of what Christ had done for me—it was more of a season. I was that thick headed. It took a while for it all to unfold.

"Today, I am feasting on apologetics, Christian music, and the inerrant Word of God. I never thought the Bible could make so much sense. Christ has loved and protected me through my years of doubt, even though I never deserved it. I know where I came from, and I know exactly where I'm going. I am free of the fears and superstitions of religion, because I have a deep, personal relationship with the most awesome Creator of the Universe!

"By the way, my twin daughters are both graduates of Cedarville, and one is a pastor's wife!

"I am so honored to be doing any little thing to make the presentation at the Ark Encounter come alive, and look forward to many more days helping with the sewing effort."

The above is a great example of using apologetics in evangelism.

In explaining how we conduct apologetics evangelism at AiG, I like to use the account of Jesus raising Lazarus from the dead (John 11). When Jesus came to the tomb of Lazarus, He told people to roll the stone away. Now, Jesus could have moved the stone with one command—but what people could do for themselves, He asked them to do. Then what people couldn't do, He did with a command—His Word. He raised Lazarus from the dead.

At AiG, we know that non-Christians are really walking dead people—"dead in the trespasses and sins" (Ephesians 2:1). Only God's Word can raise the dead. So when we are witnessing to "dead" people, we do the best we can to give answers (1 Peter 3:15) to defend the faith and, in so doing, to point them to the Word of God that saves! God is the One who opens people's hearts (including atheists) and who "has shone in our hearts to give the light of the knowledge of the glory of God in the face of Jesus Christ" (2 Corinthians 4:6).

Yes, God's Word reaches even the most hardened heart. There is hope for every atheist, for the Lord *is patient toward you, not wishing that any should perish, but that all should reach repentance* (2 Peter 3:9). And *blessed be the God and Father of our Lord Jesus Christ! According to his great mercy, he has caused us to be born again to a living hope through the resurrection of Jesus Christ from the dead* (1 Peter 1:3).

Never give up on praying for and sharing the gospel with hardened hearts.

MAY 1
John 17:17

My Stand on Genesis 1–11

When people ask me what position I take on Genesis 1–11, I answer by saying I take the biblical one! I start with Scripture and let the words in context speak to me according to the rules of the language. I don't impose outside ideas from man onto the Scripture which is sadly a problem across Christendom.

There are several compromise positions about Genesis that permeate the Church. All these views have one thing in common: They try to accommodate what the secularists believe about origins/millions of years. Consider this verse: *And they were astonished at his teaching, for he taught them as one who had authority, and not as the scribes* (Mark 1:22).

A Christian member of parliament once appeared on one of Australia's most-watched national TV programs. He was on a panel that included famed atheist Richard Dawkins of England. The moderator asked the Christian, "Where did human beings come from?" The Christian gently put his hand on Richard Dawkins' arm and replied, "You may want to ask this guy. He's got firm views on it."

Sadly, the way in which this Christian answered a legitimate question represents the origins view of most Christians today. Essentially, this well-known Australian Christian declared that secularists know what they believe, but Christians don't. Secularists have firm views, but Christians don't when it comes to origins. Sadly, this represents a major problem in the Church and Christian institutions.

Think about it! When most Christians—including Christian academics, pastors, and other Christian leaders are asked what they believe about Genesis, the answers can be one or more of the following:

- "There is a gap of millions of years between the first verses of Genesis."
- "We don't know what the days of Genesis mean."
- "The Flood was a local event. Fossils are probably millions of years old."
- "God used evolution to evolve Adam and Eve."
- "The framework idea fits millions of years into Genesis."
- "Genesis 1 is a poem."
- "Adam and Eve don't have to be literal people."
- "God made races of people to start with."
- "Genesis 1 represents the cosmic temple, not material origins."

And that's just a few of them! I could go on and on. The point is, there are many compromise positions about Genesis that permeate the Church. All these views have one thing in common: They all try to accommodate what the secularists believe about millions of years into the Bible.

Think about this: Most children from church homes attend public schools, where their textbooks and lectures give our young people a very specific history. (They also get this from watching TV documentaries and going to secular museums, etc.). Here is what they are almost always taught as fact: "The universe began with a 'big bang' 15 billion years ago. The stars formed 10 billion years ago. The sun formed 5 billion years ago, and the molten earth 4.5 billion years ago. Water formed on the earth 3.8 billion years ago. And over millions of years,

APOLOGETICS — MAY 1

life formed from non-life, and then evolved to fish, then amphibians, reptiles, to birds and mammals, then apelike creatures, and then man—a process involving death over millions of years."

Secularists insist they know all of this happened in the unobservable past. They claim to know the true history of the universe. They believe and preach their worldview with zeal. They are adamant about their main views on origins even if there are some differences.

On the other hand, Christians have the benefit of a very specific history that has been revealed to them by someone who was there at the beginning and throughout history—and who doesn't lie. And this history is recorded in a book (the Bible) for everyone to read. Yet believers say they aren't sure what God said in Genesis? There is an uncertain sound being blared by many in the Church.

How come Christians, who have God's clear infallible words in Genesis, can't give a certain sound? After all, God knows everything and has always been there. Yet the secularists who weren't there in the past and don't know everything give a certain sound!

No wonder we are seeing a mass exodus of young people from our churches! They begin to doubt the Bible in Genesis, reject it as God's Word, and then leave the Church. Not surprising since many church leaders and Christian academics told them to believe the secular world's views on origins and not what the Bible clearly states. The devil has been very successful in getting generations to doubt God's Word, and the doubt leads to unbelief.

The Bible declares, *If the bugle gives an indistinct sound, who will get ready for battle?* (1 Corinthians 14:8).

There is an uncertain sound about the Bible being blared by much of the Church, including in Christian academia. Young people and adults in our churches are hearing (and often heeding) this uncertain sound about the accuracy of the Bible from its very start. As a result, many Christians are not really sure what they believe. Meanwhile, they hear the secular world—speaking with authority—telling them they know exactly what to believe! And many Christians believe the secular world and question the Word of God. It should be the other way around. In reality, these church leaders are giving an uncertain sound about the Bible but a certain sound about the secularist worldview!

In Mark 1:22, we read that many people were astonished with Christ's teaching, for He spoke as one having authority. Today, we can speak with this same authority because we have the Word of God! Jesus Christ, the Creator and the Word, has given us the Bible, and He told us how He created all things. We need to be speaking with the authority of God's Word beginning with Genesis. We need to be giving that certain sound to tell the world God's Word is true. Don't trust man's fallible word.

Furthermore, He has given us a very specific history from the Old Testament to the New Testament—a history that is foundational to all doctrine, including the gospel (in Genesis 3). It's the true history of the world that tells us where we all came from, what our problem is (sin), and the solution—salvation through Christ.

What a difference it would make if Christians started speaking with authority (the authority of the Word) and then witnessed to the world that we do know what we believe – and it is the truth because it is the Word of God!

MAY 2

Hebrews 4:12

Yes, the Bible Says

For the word of God is living and active, sharper than any two-edged sword, piercing to the division of soul and of spirit, of joints and of marrow, and discerning the thoughts and intentions of the heart (Hebrews 4:12).

A number of years ago, an article in *Christianity Today* titled, "Should Pastors Stop Saying, 'the Bible Says'?"[36] caught my eye. The article began as follows: "It's time to stop saying, 'the Bible says.' At least according to Andy Stanley." At Exponential, a church-planting conference attended by 5,000 in late spring (with another 20,000 watching via video), the senior pastor of North Point Community Church in Alpharetta, Georgia, said pastors should instead use phrases like "Paul says" and "Jesus says" when citing Scripture.

Further, the article reports that "the main reason for his injunction is 'to keep people who are skeptical of the Bible's authority engaged in the sermon.'" Stanley also reportedly states that "it's a question of evangelism, not theology," and one of Pastor Stanley's assertions is that his "goal is to lead [people] to the place where they acknowledge Jesus to be who he claimed to be."

Now although I have reasons why I vehemently disagree with the approach taken by Andy Stanley, I do understand that to reach the world with evangelism, Christians need to ensure they are using methods that communicate to them in a way they understand.

You see, we live in a time that is often called "a scientific age" when God's Word has come under a massive attack from secularists who claim "science" has disproven the Bible's historical accounts of beginnings found in Genesis. Of course, what they mean by "science" is actually the "historical science" (beliefs) in regard to fallible man's beliefs concerning evolution and millions of years.

As a result of this attack on God's Word (and sadly much of the Church has helped this attack by compromising God's Word in Genesis with evolution and/or millions of years), generations have been led to doubt God's Word at the beginning. This leads to doubt and ultimately unbelief in the rest of Scripture.

When we are presenting the truth of God's Word and the gospel today, increasing numbers in this generation are already doubting God's Word and rejecting it entirely. Understanding this phenomenon as a major cause of today's youth exodus, I believe we need to give them apologetics arguments confirming the truth of God's Word as a part of our defense of the Christian faith. To us, this approach would deal with the problem of how to reach today's people with the gospel. However, we must always remember that *"faith comes from hearing, and hearing through the word of Christ"* (Romans 10:17).

An analogy AiG has often given to illustrate the use of apologetics in proclaiming the truth of God's Word and the gospel relates to the account of Jesus coming to the tomb of Lazarus in John 11. When Jesus came to Lazarus' tomb, He told the people to "take away the stone" (John 11:39). Jesus could have moved the stone with one word! But what people can do, He had them do. What people couldn't do—raise Lazarus from the dead—Jesus with His Word did! The analogy is this: Moving the stone is akin to us doing all we can to reach people—giving apologetics arguments to help them understand God's Word is true. But we must never divorce this approach from sharing the Word of God, as it is God's Word that convicts and saves through the power of the Holy Spirit. The two go hand in hand. Because increasing numbers of people do not believe

THEOLOGY

God's Word can be trusted, we need to give apologetics answers to defend the faith and point them to the truth of the Word, but always share the Word (Christ) that saves.

Now understanding this, I want to explain why I don't agree with what is purported to have come from Andy Stanley—that pastors should stop saying "the Bible says" and instead use introductory phrases like "Paul says" or "Jesus says."

In many ways, God's Word is treated merely as words of the humans who wrote it, so we can reinterpret it any way we like. This is one of the reasons I believe we now see young people in the Church defending the LGBTQ worldview and abortion. You see, if they have been told they can take man's ideas about origins and reinterpret God's Word, why shouldn't young people take man's ideas about marriage and gender and reinterpret God's Word on these matters?

I see an increasing trend in the Church to treat God's Word like a book written by fallible people, just like other books. Instead, we need to be reminded of what we read in Thessalonians: *And we also thank God constantly for this, that when you received the word of God, which you heard from us, you accepted it not as the word of men but as what it really is, the word of God, which is at work in you believers* (1 Thessalonians 2:13).

And we also need to remember that all of Scripture is God-breathed: *All Scripture is breathed out by God and profitable for teaching, for reproof, for correction, and for training in righteousness, that the man of God may be complete, equipped for every good work* (2 Timothy 3:16–17).

Because of the compromise in the Church with man's fallible ideas and the intense attacks on Christianity by secularists, I recognize that many people don't respect the Bible as the Word of God as they did in the past. But I do not agree with Pastor Stanley in emphasizing that "Paul says" or "Peter declares," etc. I believe it's important to emphasize that this is what God has said through Paul or Peter. I am convinced of the need to help people understand that the Bible is not just the word of men—but that it is, in truth, the Word of the living God. So these days at AiG, we often say things like, "Now, God has a warning for us here in 1 Corinthians" or "God, through Paul, tells us."

When you think about it, the first attack (which we read about in Genesis 3:1) was on the Word of God when the devil asked Eve, "Did God really say?" God warns us through Paul that the devil will use the same method on us as he did on Eve to get us to a position of not believing His Word: *But I am afraid that as the serpent deceived Eve by his cunning, your thoughts will be led astray from a sincere and pure devotion to Christ* (2 Corinthians 11:3).

I believe our response to skeptics today should be to show we can defend the Christian faith, answer skeptical questions (1 Peter 3:15), confirm the truth of God's Word, and help people understand that the Bible is the Word of God (God-breathed), not just a book written by humans.

> **Even though God used humans to write the Scriptures, these men were specially "carried along by the Holy Spirit" to ensure every Word was God-breathed (2 Peter 1:20-21).**

MAY 3

Leviticus 18:21

Child Sacrifice

You shall not give any of your children to offer them to Molech, and so profane the name of your God: I am the LORD (Leviticus 18:21).

If people today were found sacrificing children, as the Canaanites and others did in the Old Testament, I'm sure the public and its elected officials would be aghast. Such people would be prosecuted for brutality and murder.

It is my contention that, in essence, abortion is another form of child sacrifice! But because killing children in the womb has been legalized in the United States, so many elected officials and many other pro-abortionists condone this brutality and murder! They are condoning child sacrifice.

And, sadly, it would seem abortion is the key factor in the United States in regard to who wins elections. Exit polls indicate a significant number of those who call themselves evangelical Christians vote for those in favor of abortion. Seems unbelievable, but that's the state of the culture.

Many times in Scripture, God's people are warned not to be like the pagan peoples of other nations who sacrificed their own children. As we read of this abomination in Scripture, the so-called "civilized West" would claim that such vile behavior as child sacrifice should not be tolerated. But they do! In numbers, abortion makes the child sacrifice of the past pagan cultures pale in significance.

In Psalm 106:35–38, we read the following: *But they mixed with the nations and learned to do as they did. They served their idols, which became a snare to them. They sacrificed their sons and their daughters to the demons; they poured out innocent blood, the blood of their sons and daughters, whom they sacrificed to the idols of Canaan, and the land was polluted with blood.*

Such an abomination as child sacrifice does occur in our Western nations and, in fact, the whole world. In America alone, there is so much child sacrifice that it makes what Hitler did during the Holocaust (as horrific and evil as that was) pale by comparison.

Now abortion is not called child sacrifice. And the victims are not called children. Different terms are used in an attempt to hide the reality of what is actually happening in this modern-day holocaust. Terms like fetal tissue, abortion, pro-choice, women's rights, women's health care, reproductive rights, and other words are used to hide a reality: the killing of a human being made in the image of God! It's murder! It's child sacrifice.

Daily in America, thousands of children are being sacrificed.

Since the impact of *Roe v. Wade* in 1973, it is estimated that over 60 million children have been sacrificed. This holocaust of abortion has victims who are called mere tissue or fetuses, but these children are made in God's image, and that is being ignored as children are being killed in a holocaust of unimaginable proportions.

We all think that the Canaanites and other pagan cultures were barbaric because of their ritual child sacrifice. But the brutality and bloodshed happening in the Western nations today makes the Canaanites look mild by comparison.

THEOLOGY   MAY 3

We live in a country where most of the political leaders applaud the work of probably the world's largest child-sacrificing machine, Planned Parenthood. In 2013, President Obama thanked Planned Parenthood, stating (and when he says "health care" and "woman's right" in this context, he means abortion—the murdering of children): "As long as we've got to fight to make sure women have access to quality, affordable health care, and as long as we've got to fight to protect a woman's right to make her own choices about her own health, I want you to know that you've also got a president who's going to be right there with you, fighting every step of the way. Thank you, Planned Parenthood. God bless you."[37]

As he says, "God bless you," he cannot be talking about the God of the Bible. The only god he can be referring to is the god of self and the god of this world, the devil! Is he not in reality saying, "May the god of self bless you for sacrificing so many children"? He was exalting the work of Satan. Remember too that President Obama was a supporter of partial-birth abortion (really, it's partial-birth murder).

Romans 1 makes it clear that God will pour out His wrath in judgment upon a culture that rebels against Him. And one sign that God is judging a society and withdrawing His restraining influence of the Holy Spirit is the acceptance of increasing homosexual behavior, as Romans 1 teaches. LGBTQ issues are prominent in the culture today and have greatly contributed to an increasingly secularized worldview among the population and increasing anti-biblical, anti-Christian, and anti-God emphasis. Although many people might not want to consider it, I suggest that perhaps God is now judging the nations that have shed the blood of millions of children sacrificed to the god of self.

The LORD hates . . . hands that shed innocent blood (Proverbs 6:16–17).

We are observing the dismantling of the Christian influence in this nation (and the whole Western world) that had led to its greatness in the world.

In the United States in 1962, school prayer was ruled unconstitutional. In 1963, Bible reading in public schools was deemed unconstitutional. In 1973, abortion was legalized. In 1985, nativity scenes on public land were ruled to violate the supposed separation of church and state. In 2015, gay "marriage" was legalized. Next, euthanasia is coming and, yes, pedophilia too (now called minor-attracted persons to attempt to hide the truth). We read about this regularly in the news.

Blessed is the nation whose God is the LORD (Psalm 33:12).

This nation needs to repent of the wickedness of worshipping the god of self.

MAY 4

Judges 2:10

One Generation at a Time

And all that generation also were gathered to their fathers. And there arose another generation after them who did not know the L<small>ORD</small> or the work that he had done for Israel (Judges 2:10).

It only takes one generation to lose a culture! It only takes one generation to lose a godly legacy!

Over and over again in Scripture, God instructs His people to make sure they train up the next generation. For instance, when God miraculously enabled Joshua to lead the people through the Jordan River, the first thing He told Joshua to do was to take 12 stones from the riverbed to build a memorial. But what was the memorial for?

Joshua explained, *And he said to the people of Israel, "When your children ask their fathers in times to come, 'What do these stones mean?' then you shall let your children know, 'Israel passed over this Jordan on dry ground.' For the L<small>ORD</small> your God dried up the waters of the Jordan for you until you passed over, as the L<small>ORD</small> your God did to the Red Sea, which he dried up for us until we passed over, so that all the peoples of the earth may know that the hand of the L<small>ORD</small> is mighty, that you may fear the L<small>ORD</small> your God forever"* (Joshua 4:21–24).

The stones were to remind parents to make sure they taught the next generation about the true God. They were instructed to pass on the knowledge and fear of God to their children.

I think one of the saddest passages in the Bible is Judges 2:10–12: *And all that generation also were gathered to their fathers. And there arose another generation after them who did not know the L<small>ORD</small> or the work that he had done for Israel. And the people of Israel . . . abandoned the L<small>ORD</small>, the God of their fathers, who had brought them out of the land of Egypt. They went after other gods, from among the gods of the peoples who were around them, and bowed down to them. And they provoked the L<small>ORD</small> to anger.*

After Joshua and all the first generation of parents who entered the promised land died, the next generation served false gods! It took only one generation to lose the spiritual legacy that should have been passed on.

What happened? In Deuteronomy 6:6–7, God had given clear instructions to the fathers: *And these words that I command you today shall be on your heart. You shall teach them diligently to your children, and shall talk of them when you sit in your house, and when you walk by the way, and when you lie down, and when you rise.*

Obviously, the parents in Joshua's day did not teach their children as they should have—and in one generation, the devil had those kids! While it's ultimately a matter of God's grace that anyone is saved, God has given parents an immense responsibility to do their part. Over and over, the Jewish fathers were told about their crucial role, but they shirked it (see Psalm 78).

Sadly, this same situation is happening now in Western nations once influenced by Christianity. Many fathers today are not carrying out their God-given, God-commanded role to be the spiritual head of their house and take responsibility for training their children in spiritual matters.

In England, at least two-thirds of young people say they don't believe in God—in a culture where most people once went to church.

APOLOGETICS — MAY 4

In America, a major poll indicated that two-thirds of young people were leaving the Church once they lived on their own. Answers in Genesis commissioned America's Research Group to find out why this is happening and published the results in the book *Already Gone*. It showed clearly these kids were doubting the Bible at a very young age.

We also established that around 90% of those who leave Church attended public schools, where, by and large, God, creation, the Bible, and prayer have been thrown out. Atheistic evolution (naturalism) is taught as fact. The vast majority of these students were not taught apologetics on how to give a reasoned defense of the Christian faith in their homes or churches, so they didn't believe it themselves and certainly couldn't defend it to others. Eventually, most kids will leave the Church.

Joseph Stalin knew the power of education as a propaganda tool. In just one generation, he converted hordes of the deeply religious Russian people into followers of atheistic Marxism.

Sadly, most of the people who control the West's education, and publishing and video/video streaming industries, today reject the God of the Bible, and they are winning over the next generation, indoctrinating them in evolutionary humanism. Day after day, our children are bombarded with their message. And it continues to get worse each year though there is a large godly remnant who are becoming more on fire for Jesus too.

For years, I have been warning churchgoers about this danger in my presentations. Despite the fact that America has many megachurches and more Christian resources than any other country in history, America as a culture is becoming more secular every day. America is heading down the same path as Europe and England.

In an article by a staffer from the National Center for Science Education (an organization begun in 1983 for the explicit purpose of attacking the influence of creationism and now headed by ardent atheist Amanda L. Townley), it is very clear that the atheists today are out to get our kids.

The last paragraph of the article reads, "What we can do is work toward the day when American schoolchildren are taught evolution in the same way as any other well-established scientific idea, without caveats or apologies. With evolution at the center of biology, and thus important to the success of medicine, biotechnology, and agriculture, we can't afford to keep it bottled up or to kick the can."[38]

Atheists don't want Christians teaching kids about God—they want to teach your kids there is no God! They are out to get your kids, and they are using the public schools, secular media, museums, and other outlets to do this. The public schools (despite a minority of Christian teachers who are trying to be missionaries in the system) have become churches of secular humanism/atheism. Yes, the atheists, like Hitler and Stalin, know that if they can capture the next generation (through the education system, media, etc.), they will have the culture.

Christians need to take heed of God's Word and ensure they are capturing the next generation for the Lord—passing that spiritual legacy along to the children so they will not be captured by the world!

God's people need to wake up and understand a battle for their kids is raging around them—a battle that is being won, at the present time, by those who seek to destroy the next generation spiritually!

> Yes, it takes only one generation to lose a culture.

MAY 5
Genesis 8:22

Is the Climate Changing?

While the earth remains, seedtime and harvest, cold and heat, summer and winter, day and night, shall not cease (Genesis 8:22).

After the Bill Nye debate in 2014, I was interviewed live on CNN by Piers Morgan. The first question he asked me was, "Why don't you believe in climate change?" I answered, "I do believe in climate change." At that stage, Bill Nye interjected to claim that I reject climate change. I went on to say that I didn't reject climate change, and that "there's been climate change ever since the Flood." I don't believe the interviewer knew how to proceed, and we ended up going in a different direction.

Not only do I believe in climate change, but I'm a climate change alarmist! We hear a lot from climate change alarmists these days. In fact, it seems every day someone is on the news talking about this topic, even warning that humans could become extinct within 12 years (or less) if we don't deal with climate change.

Well, I admit it. I am also a climate change alarmist, and I do believe humans have caused climate change. But "climate alarmism" should be properly understood. Yes, it's true we need to warn people about the coming catastrophic climate changes that will affect all of humanity. We need to proclaim this from the rooftops. It's an urgent message. In fact, the Bible prophetically refers to its coming:

But by the same word the heavens and earth . . . are stored up for fire, being kept until the day of judgment and destruction of the ungodly. . . the heavens will pass away with a roar, and the heavenly bodies will be burned up and dissolved, and the earth and the works that are done on it will be exposed (2 Peter 3:7, 10).

Now that's the ultimate catastrophic climate change everyone should be aware of—when one day in the future, Jesus will return, and the earth (and whole universe) will be judged with fire, and God will make a new heavens and earth: *But according to his promise we are waiting for new heavens and a new earth in which righteousness dwells* (2 Peter 3:13).

It's important to understand that humans are the cause of this coming catastrophic climate change. Because of our sin in Adam, we recognize that the whole creation is now groaning, awaiting this massive change.

For the creation was subjected to futility, not willingly, but because of him who subjected it, in hope that the creation itself will be set free from its bondage to corruption and obtain the freedom of the glory of the children of God. For we know that the whole creation has been groaning together in the pains of childbirth until now (Romans 8:20–22).

But even though the creation is groaning because of our sin (think of earthquakes, tidal waves, hurricanes, floods, tornadoes, cyclones, death, and disease), God gave us a promise about 4,300 years ago after the Flood: *While the earth remains, seedtime and harvest, cold and heat, summer and winter, day and night, shall not cease* (Genesis 8:22).

So man is not going to destroy the earth! A similar promise was given by the prophet Jeremiah over 2,500 years ago:

SCIENCE — MAY 5

Thus says the LORD: If you can break my covenant with the day and my covenant with the night, so that day and night will not come at their appointed time, then also my covenant with David my servant may be broken. ... If I have not established my covenant with day and night and the fixed order of heaven and earth (Jeremiah 33:20–21, 25).

Even though we live in such a groaning world, God gave humans dominion over the environment, not the environment over humans, so we can boldly proclaim that humans aren't going to destroy themselves or destroy the earth because God is in complete control, and He will determine when the ultimate catastrophic climate change will occur. The climate change countdown clock is absurd! We need to understand and believe in climate alarmism in a biblical context.

In the meantime, it's important to understand that we do live in a world where sin, the curse, the Flood, and the ice age (which was generated by the Flood) have all contributed to climate changes that have been going on during the past 6,000 years of Earth's history. And in this world, He gave us dominion.

Then God said, "Let us make man in our image, after our likeness. And let them have dominion over the fish of the sea and over the birds of the heavens and over the livestock and over all the earth and over every creeping thing that creeps on the earth" (Genesis 1:26).

As Christians, we need to have a biblically based worldview regarding environmental issues. To have this worldview, we must understand our role as having dominion over creation as both mankind and the rest of creation suffer the effects of sin, the curse, and past catastrophic events (such as the Flood of Noah's day). The bottom line is that we are to live in this world and use what God has entrusted to us for humanity's good (doing our best not to abuse it) and God's glory.

And remember, humans are finite. Based on our limited understanding, we might not know many factors, which can lead us to interpret past and future things incorrectly. That's why we must ensure that we have the right foundation for our worldview, the foundation of the revelation of One who knows all things—the foundation of the authority of the Word of God. And God's Word never changes.

We need to help people understand that the climate alarmism from many of our politicians is based on a religion—a religion that trusts man as his own god, and a religion that worships the creation instead of the true Creator. We are seeing Romans 1 played out before our eyes:

For although they knew God, they did not honor him as God or give thanks to him, but they became futile in their thinking, and their foolish hearts were darkened. Claiming to be wise, they became fools, and exchanged the glory of the immortal God for images resembling mortal man and birds and animals and creeping things (Romans 1:21–23)

> **We will never sort out all the claims about climate change until we all agree to begin with the right foundation – the Word of the infinite Creator God.**

MAY 6
Genesis 1:24

What About Dinosaurs?

And God said, "Let the earth bring forth living creatures according to their kinds—livestock and creeping things and beasts of the earth according to their kinds." And it was so (Genesis 1:24).

An aura of mystery surrounds dinosaurs. Where did they come from? Did they evolve? Did they really live millions of years ago? What happened to them? Are there any living today? Has any human being ever seen a live dinosaur? The truth of the matter is that there are no real mysteries at all, once you have key information that is not generally known and is withheld from the public. Dinosaurs certainly did roam the earth in the ancient past! Fossils of dinosaurs have been found all over the world, and their bones are displayed in museums for all to see. Scientists have been able to reconstruct many of their skeletons, so we know much about how they may have looked.

The story of their discovery began back in the 1820s, when Gideon Mantell, an English doctor, found some unusual teeth and bones in a quarry. Dr. Mantell realized there was something different about these animal remains and believed that he had found an entirely new group of reptiles. By 1841, about nine types of these different reptiles had been uncovered, including two called Megalosaurus and Iguanodon. At this time, Dr. Richard Owen, a famous British scientist, coined the name Dinosauria, meaning "terrible lizard," for this is what the huge bones made him think of. Some were as small as chickens; others were even smaller. Of course, some dinosaurs were very large, weighing in at an estimated 80 tons and standing 40 feet high! The average size of a dinosaur, however, was probably about a large sheep or bison.

According to evolutionists, the dinosaurs "ruled the earth" for 140 million years, dying out about 65 million years ago. However, scientists do not dig up anything labeled with those ages. They only uncover dead dinosaurs (i.e., their bones), and their bones do not have labels attached telling how old they are. Creation scientists have a different idea about when dinosaurs lived.

The first book in the Bible—Genesis—teaches us many things about how the universe and life came into existence. Genesis tells us that God created everything—the earth, stars, sun, moon, plants, animals, and the first two people. Although the Bible does not tell us exactly how long ago it was that God made the world and its creatures, we can make a good estimate of the date of creation by reading through the Bible and noting some interesting passages:

God made everything in six days. He did this, by the way, to set a pattern for mankind, which has become our seven-day week (as described in Exodus 20:11). God worked for six days and rested for one as a model for us. Furthermore, Bible scholars will tell you that the Hebrew word for day used in Genesis 1 can only mean an ordinary day in this context. We are told God created the first man and woman on day six. Many facts about when their children and their children's children were born are given in Genesis. These genealogies are recorded throughout the Old Testament until the time of Christ. They certainly were not chronologies lasting millions of years.

As you add up all the dates and accept that Jesus Christ, the Son of God, came to Earth almost 2,000 years ago, we come to the conclusion that the creation of the earth and animals (including the dinosaurs) occurred

APOLOGETICS   MAY 6

only thousands of years ago (perhaps only 6,000!), not millions of years. Thus, based on the Bible's history, dinosaurs must have lived within the past thousands of years.

The Bible tells us that God created all the land animals on the sixth day of creation. Because dinosaurs were land animals, they must have been made on this day, alongside Adam and Eve who were also created on day six (Genesis 1:24–31). Because God designed and created dinosaurs, they would have been fully functional, designed to do what they were created for, and would have been 100% dinosaur. This fits exactly with the evidence from the fossil record.

Evolutionists declare that no man ever lived alongside dinosaurs. The Bible, however, makes it plain that dinosaurs and people must have lived together. The Bible teaches (in Genesis 1:29–30) that the original animals (and the first humans) were vegetarian. It was an unblemished world, with Adam and Eve and animals (including dinosaurs) living in perfect harmony, eating only plants.

But Adam rebelled against his Creator, bringing sin into the world (Genesis 3:1–7; Romans 5:12). Because of this rebellion, Adam, and thus all of his descendants (you and me), gave up the right to live with a holy (sinless) and just God. God, therefore, judged sin with death. The Bible plainly teaches from Genesis to Revelation that there was no death before Adam sinned. This means there could not have been any animal fossils (and no dinosaur bones) before sin.

In Genesis 6, we read that all flesh (man and animals) "had corrupted their way on the earth" (Genesis 6:12). Perhaps people and animals were killing each other; maybe dinosaurs had started killing other animals and humans. In any case, the Bible describes the world as "wicked." Because of this wickedness, God warned a godly man named Noah that He was going to destroy the world with a Flood (Genesis 6:13). God therefore commanded him to build a great ship (the ark) so that all the kinds of land animals (which must have included dinosaurs) and Noah's family could survive on board while the Flood destroyed the entire earth (Genesis 6:14–20).

God sent two of most (seven of some) land animals into the ark (Genesis 7:2–3, 8–9)—there were no exceptions. Therefore, dinosaurs must have been on the ark. Even though there was ample room in the huge ship for large animals, perhaps God sent young adults into the ark that still had plenty of room to grow. What happened to all the land animals that did not go on the ark? Very simply, they drowned. Many would have been covered with tons of mud as the rampaging water covered the land (Genesis 7:11–12, 19). Because of this quick burial, many of the animals would have been preserved as fossils. The Flood of Noah's day occurred just around 4,300 years ago; thus, the dinosaur fossils were formed as a result of this Flood, not millions of years ago.

Dinosaurs can remind us that God judged the rebellion in Noah's day by destroying the wicked world with water, resulting in the death of millions of creatures. The Bible teaches us that He will again judge the world, but next time by fire: *But the day of the Lord will come like a thief, and then the heavens will pass away with a roar, and the heavenly bodies will be burned up and dissolved, and the earth and the works that are done on it will be exposed* (2 Peter 3:10).

> **Dinosaurs are "Missionary Lizards" because they help us tell people about creation, sin, death, our need for a Savior, and the salvation provided for us in Jesus Christ.**

MAY 7

Genesis 3:1

Genesis Relevance

Now the serpent was more crafty than any other beast of the field that the LORD God had made. He said to the woman, "Did God actually say, 'You shall not eat of any tree in the garden'?" (Genesis 3:1).

Over the years, people have asked me what was the core message that built the ministry of Answers in Genesis. In the late 1970s and early 1980s, I developed what I called "The Relevance of Genesis" message. This has been the core message of the ministry. It was after I developed this message that we saw people in the Church say they hadn't realized how important Genesis 1–11 is.

In 1986, I wrote out this message for a book titled, *The Lie: Evolution*. And when I upgraded and expanded it for the 25th anniversary of the book's publication, I didn't have to change a lot of what I'd written, as God's Word doesn't change, and the fact that Genesis 1–11 is the foundation for everything doesn't change. I basically added to the message and made it current. The core message of the book is still the classic "Relevance of Genesis" message that in many ways built this ministry.

At AiG, we want to make Christians aware of the destructive effects that evolutionary ideas and a belief in millions of years have on the gospel, the Church, and scriptural authority in the culture as a whole. Now, the "lie" is more than evolution or millions of years. It speaks to a deeper issue—one that has plagued humanity since Adam and Eve took that first bite of the forbidden fruit. It begins with the question, "Did God actually say?" (Genesis 3:1). I like to call this the "Genesis 3 attack" of our age—one that causes people to question what God has revealed to us in His Word. We are warned in 2 Corinthians 11:3 that Satan will use this same Genesis 3 attack on us as he did to Eve—to make us disbelieve the Word of God.

When sinful human beings believe *the lie* that God's Word is not authoritative, we put ourselves in a position of authority over God, disregarding and even rewriting His Word. Our culture is answering the question, "Did God really say?" with a resounding "No!" Those who question His Word are denying the full authority and accuracy of the Bible from its very first verse. This has had devastating effects on our Church and culture.

Every major doctrine of Scripture is ultimately (directly or indirectly) found in Genesis, so when believers dismiss Genesis 1–11 as myth or as unreliable, we are left with human opinions, which at the root are just man's ideas lifted up as an authoritative standard over God's Word. Thus, humans can make doctrines mean whatever they want them to mean.

When a Christian accepts the secular belief of millions of years, he is blaming God for death, suffering, bloodshed, and disease. Why? The idea of millions of years came out of naturalism—a belief system to explain the fossil record. Secularists claim the fossil layers over the earth were laid down slowly over millions of years before man appeared on Earth. The fossil record is one of death, disease (e.g., brain tumors, cancer, and arthritis are found in fossil bones), and suffering—all supposedly before humans existed. However, the Bible tells us that after man was created, God called everything "very good." God would certainly not call brain cancer very good!

Also, the Bible is clear in Genesis 3:18 that thorns came into existence as a result of the curse. Yet in the fossil record, there are many examples of fossilized thorns. So how could such fossils have existed before the curse?

CHURCH MAY 7

One of the most devastating effects of believing *the lie* of evolution and millions of years is that both of them teach our children that the Bible cannot be trusted as it is written. As we discovered in the research for my coauthored book *Already Gone*, two-thirds of young people were walking away from the Church by the time they reached college age. The majority of these young people do not believe that Genesis 1–11 is accurate or reliable, or they have at least been led to doubt the history in Genesis in some way. In fact, many church leaders compromise on Genesis by mixing evolution and/or millions of years with Scripture. When they do this, they are essentially teaching our children that the Word of God is fallible and that man's word is infallible. Our children suffer the most from the results of such thinking.

We have seen a generational loss of regard for biblical authority in our culture. The result is that the dominant worldview is changing from a primarily Christianized worldview to a secular worldview with moral relativism. This is the fault of church leaders for not standing on biblical authority, thereby losing the coming generations to the world.

Many children in this culture grow up learning about *the lie*s of evolution and millions of years, so they never gain a proper foundational understanding of Christianity. This is one reason it is important to present the gospel from the very beginning of Scripture. People need to comprehend why they are sinners. They need to understand the origin of sin in Genesis. To understand why they need to be saved, they first must know they are lost—as the history in Genesis reveals. To know why Jesus died on the Cross for them, they need to understand that death is the penalty for sin—as recorded in Genesis. We need to use what we call "creation evangelism." This type of evangelism involves presenting the gospel as God does in the Bible: by starting at the beginning and providing answers to the secular attacks of our day on the history in Genesis. As a result of using this type of evangelism, many people have had their eyes opened to the truth of God's Word and responded to the gospel.

Jesus Christ and the Apostle Paul treated Genesis 1–11 as literal (Matthew 19:3–6; Romans 5:12–17; 1 Corinthians 15:45–49). They even affirmed that death entered the world through Adam's sin. So were they lying or misinformed? Of course not! But if Christians believe *the lie* that Genesis cannot be trusted, they are paving the way for a questioning of the trustworthiness of the gospel message, and the barriers people have to the gospel will remain firmly in place.

As I was revising *The Lie* for the 25th anniversary, I said to myself (a number of times): "Wow. I'm using the same arguments from the Bible today as I was back in 1987 to counter the arguments of people in the Church who compromise evolution/millions of years with the Bible." I put the book down and wondered why. But the answer quickly became clear. The Bible's teachings haven't changed. God's Word remains the same today as it was yesterday. So, yes, if you stick with Scripture, the arguments against compromise don't change!

As Christians, if we want to leave a legacy of faith to our children and grandchildren, we must rescue them from the faith-destroying compromise happening all around us. To do this, we must restore the right foundation to the gospel—the authority of God's Word from the very first verse—and stand our ground in defending the truth of the entire Bible. That's the heart of the message at Answers in Genesis.

Genesis is foundational to the gospel.

MAY 8
Romans 8:28

Overcoming the Opposition

And we know that for those who love God all things work together for good, for those who are called according to his purpose (Romans 8:28).

Not all things are "good," but God's Word promises that "all things work together for good." So even those who troll me on social media help things "work together for good." And a lot of people who oppose Christianity attack me on social media almost daily. They stalk us! They're obsessed. They hate, lie, mock, blaspheme. And they troll. On Twitter (X) and other social media, those who oppose us post angry comments, blaspheme, use derogatory statements, post sexually perverse statements, and so on.

These people have put Answers in Genesis, the Ark Encounter, and the Creation Museum (and a guy named Ken Ham!) in the national news on a number of occasions. Why should secularists/atheists even care what Christians believe? After all, if one ceases to exist at death and therefore all their memories will be gone and they won't even know they ever existed, what does it matter what anyone believes? Life ultimately is meaningless and purposeless. And yet, many of these people aggressively oppose Christians. God said in Romans 1 that He has made the fact that He is Creator obvious to all. Also, Romans 2 tells us everyone has a conscience and inherently knows what is right and wrong. That's why atheists get so emotional about active Christians. They can't stand Christians having the freedom to spread their message, as it convicts them of the truth. By opposing Christians, they are in essence putting their hands on their ears and "yelling" to try to stop hearing God's Word. They don't want to recognize they are sinners and need salvation. They refuse to believe God created them, owns them, and sets the rules. They want to be their own gods, which is what the devil's temptation was all about in Genesis 3. Their reasons go deep—really deep—but God uses their actions in various ways, including to publicize our ministry!

These attacks remind me of how important the ministry of AiG is. I've said it before, and I think often of the person who said to me, "When you stand on the devil's toes, he reacts. You guys must be kicking him in the shins!" The stalking of AiG (and me personally) by secularists began in earnest in 1996 when we announced AiG was rezoning land to build a Creation Museum. A local atheist group went berserk. How dare we build such a place! Suddenly, without any effort on our part, we were thrust into the media spotlight. One of the arguments an atheist attorney used against us at a public rezoning meeting was that building such a museum was against the so-called "separation of church and state." OK, let me get this straight: We were building a Creation Museum on private property with private funds (from our supporters), but that was somehow against the law and the Constitution?

Now because of the opposition stirred up by this small group of atheists, local officials ruled against our rezoning, and we had to find a different piece of property. But God was in control. We ended up with a far superior piece of property that was right off Interstate 275, where the Creation Museum is located today. And we built a far bigger Creation Museum. Yes, "all things work together for good." Just as important, because of all the opposition, our support base grew exponentially. Many people donated specifically to the museum because of this opposition and the news coverage it received. In fact, one family contacted me while I was speaking in Australia and said we must be doing something right to stir up such opposition. The family had

RESOURCES

been reading the newspapers about those who opposed God and our museum, and they gave a million-dollar donation to the Creation Museum project! The stalking has continued, and it's not just from local atheists. National atheist groups and individuals across the nation and around the world are now stalking us. They protested outside the Creation Museum when it opened in 2007. They vehemently opposed the Ark Encounter receiving the same tourism incentive other attractions receive. These groups protested the opening of the Ark in 2016, and they have continued protests at the Ark.

These anti-Christian organizations spread false claims that the two attractions were failing. (By the way, if we're supposedly failing, why would they even bother with all their activism?) All this opposition results in more publicity for AiG and more people finding out about our attractions and coming to visit. We couldn't afford to pay for such widespread marketing! Yes, "all things work together for good."

With the thousands of secular attractions and secular museums (usually tax-funded) in the USA and around the world, these atheists are deeply troubled by two Christian attractions that use stunning exhibits to proclaim biblical history and the gospel message. It would take pages (actually a whole book!) to detail all the secularist opposition. But here, I'll just share some events.

- The Freedom from Religion Foundation (a group of anti-Christian atheists) and the American Atheists (AA) have been aggressive in their attacks against AiG. Such groups are well-known for using fearmongering, bullying, and strong-arm tactics to intimidate public schools, local authorities, government officials, and so on against Christians. These organizations attempt to eliminate any access to and mention of anything remotely Christian to students and the general public. They are the definition of intolerance.
- In 2016, after the Ark Encounter opened, the FFRF sent threatening letters to 1,000 public schools within driving distance of our attraction, warning them not to organize a school field trip. FFRF implied a legal threat if they did.
- In 2018, a local atheist group connected to AA sent threatening letters to public schools in three counties, making similar threats.
- In 2017 and 2018, FFRF sent more threatening letters to various state parks and recreation departments that had scheduled trips to our two attractions. Bus tours from Illinois and Virginia were canceled because of these implied legal threats.

This sort of battle with secularists has been going on since we began AiG and continue to this day—in fact, such opposition has been happening since I started speaking on creation-apologetics in 1975! It would be easy to tire of this, but we're in a major spiritual battle, and AiG won't retreat. I often think of what Jesus taught us in the parable of the 10 minas: *Engage in business until I come* (Luke 19:13).

Yes, it's a spiritual battle. God's Word also makes it clear that in a world where there are more souls on the broad way than the narrow way, there will be opposition. And, yes, I'm glad we are facing these battles day after day. If we weren't engaged, I would be questioning whether the AiG ministry was actually being effective!

In all this, "all things work together for good."

MAY 9
Hosea 4:6

Answering Difficult Questions

My people are destroyed for lack of knowledge (Hosea 4:6).

I have been traveling around the world and speaking for over 40 years. I've also been on many media interviews and radio talk shows. I've met thousands of people. You can imagine that I have been asked a lot of questions relating to what I teach concerning Genesis 1–11, the authority of Scripture, and the gospel. Surely, by now, you would think I've heard every question possible. But, no, I think almost every week I hear a question I haven't been asked before.

During one of my trips to Australia a reporter with a Christian media outlet had some different questions for me. I think you'll be very interested in these questions and how I did my best to answer them. Often, after answering certain questions, I say to myself, "I need to remember how I answered that for next time!" I always pray for wisdom and ask the Lord to help me answer new questions, and I believe He also helps me recall things I've heard or read. Every time I hear a question that I don't know the answer to, I follow up with research, sometimes meeting with our resident scientists/theologians at AiG. We discuss the topic to ensure I can answer the question even better next time.

The media outlet heard I was speaking at a conference in Sydney and contacted the church to ask if a reporter could talk to me. The reporter called me a couple of days later, and I spent nearly an hour on the phone with her. I wasn't able to record the conversation, but I took careful notes and compiled them to the best of my ability. It didn't take long for her to ask a question about whether I believe someone has to believe in six literal days and a young earth to be a Christian. I emphatically stated that salvation is not conditional on the age of the earth or the six literal days but on faith in Christ. I explained why it's really a biblical authority issue, and I gave her many examples of how incompatible millions of years are with Genesis.

But then she asked a question that I had never been asked before: "Can you love theistic evolutionists?"

I told her I had recently spoken at a secular university (the University of Central Oklahoma), with many from the LGBTQ group present. I told the crowd that I didn't hate them, because I'm a Christian. And as Jesus tells us, we are to love our neighbor as ourselves. However, I told the audience that I disagreed with the LGBTQ worldview—but that should never be interpreted as hate. I then said to the reporter, "I can love LGBTQ people, and I can love theistic evolutionists."

Sensing why the reporter might be asking the question, I added that because I speak boldly about what I believe, sometimes people will falsely interpret my beliefs as hate. I often find that those who don't take AiG's stand on Genesis will demand we agree that people can have different views. I told the reporter that Christians can have different views, but I'll tell them why I believe those views are wrong—and how they undermine biblical authority! Sometimes people get angry when I respond like this, and they may even, ironically, show hate toward me! They want me to say their position is a valid one. But I can't do that if I do not believe it!

The reporter asked me many other questions, and she got to the topic of climate change. Now, I would say that this was the only time during the interview when I believe things became somewhat contentious with this Christian reporter. (Climate change can be an emotional topic.)

APOLOGETICS

First, I told her there's been climate change ever since the Flood. I said I didn't deny climate change, but the details as to why it's happening and how serious it is (or isn't) were matters that needed to be discussed. I referred to one of the articles in our *Answers* magazine where a scientist shows that there have been warming and cooling periods in the past and that our current (quite small) warming trend could be a normal fluctuation.

I further explained that we don't have enough data to know for sure what has really been occurring. I added that scientists know the sun's activity has a significant effect on climate change and that the main greenhouse gas is not actually carbon dioxide but water vapor. Then it became a bit tense. I said that if you ask most people who are climate change alarmists to explain the data and give the facts behind what they're claiming, most of them have no clue. They just regurgitate what they've heard.

She then said something to the effect that she didn't need to do that. The reporter said that she could rely on the experts who have done the research. I replied that this is not the correct approach and that, as Christians, we all need to search things out and be prepared to give reasons (1 Peter 3:15) for what we believe.

I told her my father wanted his kids to know why we believed what we did and wanted us to be able to defend our beliefs. She then essentially accused me of refusing to accept what the majority of scientists are saying: that man-made climate change is a big problem.

I replied by saying that the majority of scientists say there's no God and that life arose by naturalistic evolution. Should we then say we have to reject God because the majority of scientists say so? I emphasized that we are obligated as Christians to check things out.

I also explained that after the Flood, God told Noah, *While the earth remains, seedtime and harvest, cold and heat, summer and winter, day and night, shall not cease* (Genesis 8:22).

She responded with, "Are you saying we should do nothing then?" Well, of course, I wasn't saying that. I responded that God gave man dominion over the environment, not the environment over man, and that Christians should have a biblically based worldview in regard to environmental issues. We should responsibly use the creation for man's good and God's glory.

I gave an example that in the United States, trees are harvested for various reasons, but more trees are planted than are harvested. I also said that we need to understand how sin and the curse of Genesis 3:14–19 have affected the world. I recalled the verse, *My people are destroyed for lack of knowledge* (Hosea 4:6).

Actually, that's a major problem in the world and in the Church! Sadly, many churches have not taught their congregations how to think about these issues from a biblical worldview perspective and how to defend the Christian faith against the secular attacks of our day (by equipping with apologetics).

> One of the reasons so many young people are being led astray by evolutionary ideas, climate change alarmists, abortionists, the LGBTQ movement, and so forth is that they have been told what to believe and not taught how to think about such issues or look at all the evidence available.

MAY 10
1 Peter 3:15

Give People Answers

But in your hearts honor Christ the Lord as holy, always being prepared to make a defense to anyone who asks you for a reason for the hope that is in you; yet do it with gentleness and respect (1 Peter 3:15).

Answers are important. As Christians, we are instructed to be ready to give answers to people to show we can defend the Christian faith. Doing so is a witness to these people.

At a speaking engagement, a man once asked me something like this:

"I don't have all the knowledge you have to be able to answer skeptical questions. So what should I do if I witness to people and they bring up objections and questions? How can I respond to them when I don't know all these answers?"

I admitted to him that I have been in creation ministry for many years, and so I have had the time to accumulate a lot of information to be able to answer people. I acknowledged that his question was a legitimate one. What about Christians who haven't been immersed in the Answers in Genesis ministry, like our speakers, writers, and researchers? What should they do when challenged?

I remember when I was going to college in Australia and was taught evolution and millions of years as fact. I knew this wasn't what the Bible taught, and I really wanted answers so I could defend the Christian faith. I also wanted to be a witness to my fellow students—and even the professors.

It was at that time (the 1970s) when I came across a fascinating booklet, originally published in England. It provided answers to questions about the fossils and Noah's Flood—and the supposed millions of years of earth history. I then came across the now-famous book by Drs. Henry Morris and John Whitcomb, *The Genesis Flood*. It was packed full of answers! I then began to search around the world for other books that had scientific and biblical answers to the origins issues. I found a few.

When I became a science teacher, I began using the information from these books and started teaching creation apologetics (answers) to my students—and also to people in churches. People kept asking me how they could buy these same books.

The Lord gave me an intense burden to get this Bible-defending information into people's hands. So my wife and I (and another teacher) began a creation-apologetics bookshop in our Australian home. We soon discovered that more and more Christians had a hunger for this vital information.

Today, as I stroll through the large bookstores inside our Creation Museum and Ark Encounter and see all the books and curricula sitting on shelf after shelf, my heart rejoices. I think back to the time when I had just one little booklet. But today, there are so many apologetics resources available.

The massive number of resources AiG provides today reflects the burden the Lord gave to me a few decades ago to get this critical faith-affirming and gospel-proclaiming information out to people. At the same time, I soon realized that the world wants to censor and restrict these Bible-upholding resources.

That's why AiG today is a content-rich, information-disseminating ministry focused on proclaiming the truth and authority of God's Word—and the life-changing gospel message.

APOLOGETICS — MAY 10

One of those "fires" the Lord has put in my bones was to research and produce resources with as much content as possible and then disseminate them far and wide. I have such a burden to provide these life-changing and equipping resources at our speaking engagements, through our newsletter, website, at the Creation Museum, and so on.

And that brings me back to the question I was asked at the conference: "How can I possibly get the knowledge needed to answer the skeptical questions of the age?" I shared these things with the man:

Most skeptics really don't know how to defend what they believe. These secularists just regurgitate what they were taught at school, read in a book, or saw on some TV program. Now, these people can come across as bold when they speak. But as soon as you ask them specific questions, insist on the "evidence," or ask them to explain why they believe what they do, not many can actually do it!

If Christians take the time to read our basic apologetics books, they will be thoroughly equipped with the answers to many of the questions people ask today. Even if you can't remember the detailed answers, if you have read the books, you will at least know there are answers—and you can probably give a big-picture type of answer and point skeptics to the books and to AiG's information-packed website. AnswersInGenesis.org has several thousand articles (and a great search engine) to help people get the answers to the skeptical questions of our day.

I remember when I was on BBC television a number of years ago while in the United Kingdom. I was on a panel with a leading evolutionary geneticist. I asked him in front of a TV audience of probably millions of viewers to give the best evidence he could to convince people of evolution—something that would be very obvious. He gave the example of a certain type of salmon producing different species of salmon. I remember saying something like, "But they are still salmon."

From my many years of experience in this ministry, I believe one of the problems in the Church is that many Christians are easily intimidated by non-Christians, especially by confident-sounding professors. Many of these skeptics come across as if they have all this scientific evidence that has proven evolution and an earth that is millions of years old.

But when you are equipped with solid information, you can challenge Bible-doubters to present their evidence and then ask them to logically defend their position. They almost always flounder. It's often easy to point out inconsistencies in their position. They will borrow from a Christian worldview using words like good, etc. They will resort to "rescuing devices" based on beliefs one can't prove or disprove, or often begin ad hominem attacks. That inability opens the door for you to answer questions and point them to the Word of God—and the gospel.

> I urge you to get equipped with good solid answers so you can be an effective witness in today's world.

MAY 11
John 15:18

No God Allowed

If the world hates you, know that it has hated me before it hated you (John 15:18).

What an anti-Christian time we live in. Really, though, I guess we shouldn't be all that surprised when the secular world does all it can to attack the Bible. After all, God's Word tells us that men *loved the darkness rather than the light* (John 3:19) and that *the heart is deceitful above all things, and desperately sick; who can understand it?* (Jeremiah 17:9). We sure see evidence of that all around us, including in some surprising places. I have observed a growing campaign over the years by the secular world to mislead the public about those of us who stand boldly and uncompromisingly on the authority of the Word of God. It's an anti-Christian propaganda campaign. Let me give you just a few examples.

I read an article once about the science standards for public schools in Kansas. The writer expressed concern that citizens may try to get evolution banned from the curriculum, as was supposedly done in 1999. But this was total disinformation. I had heard the bogus claim over and over again (even in *Time* magazine) that the Kansas Board of Education in 1999 "expunged" evolution from the curriculum. But what actually occurred? First, evolution was never removed from the standards! You can read the 1999 document yourself and see references to the teaching of evolution on pages 53, 79, 87, etc. The board decided that it would not test students at the state level on what they know about evolution. You see, Kansas was a strong local-control state when it came to education, and the decision on testing students on evolution was left to the local districts.

The state board also decided that it would not mandate the teaching of the origins of the universe, but that instructors had the academic freedom to teach macroevolution if they chose to do so. The Kansas effort was thus only a mild attempt to de-emphasize the intensive, one-sided program indoctrinating students with evolution. But the secularists got the media to believe evolution was outlawed in Kansas!

I have often heard leaders in public education and the media claim that in 1987 the Supreme Court voted not to allow the teaching of creation in the public school science classroom. However, this is yet more misinformation. This is what really happened:

- The 1987 court noted (in *Edwards v. Aguillard*) that teachers are "free to teach any and all facets of this subject" of all scientific theories about the origins of humankind (p. 9).
- The ruling actually provided a "green light" for alternatives to be taught, even though its teaching cannot be mandated, and even though it prohibits the teaching of biblical creation.
- In their powerful dissent, Chief Justice Rehnquist and Justice Scalia also acknowledged that "evolution is not unquestionable fact" (p. 25). They also chastised the majority for its "Scopes-in-reverse" "repressive" position (p. 25).

The secular media claimed over and over again that a supposed "creationism bill" was passed in Tennessee. But again, this was misinformation. What really occurred? The Teacher Protection Academic Freedom Act allowed teachers to help students understand and critique the "scientific strengths and scientific weaknesses" of various scientific theories. Teachers were not allowed to promote religious belief, although everyone has a religious belief and evolution is a religion!

APOLOGETICS MAY 11

I once went on an intensive 10-event speaking tour of England and Northern Ireland. A firestorm erupted just before I left over a well-known tourist attraction in Northern Ireland—the Giant's Causeway—and a new exhibit about it. Secularists and the media were claiming that the National Trust had allowed creationists to have their explanation of the Giant's Causeway included in the exhibition—and they wanted it removed! But this was highly misleading. What was the truth?

First, the Giant's Causeway exhibition didn't really give "creationist explanations." In fact, the display presented the typical evolutionist explanation for this unique geological formation; namely, Giant's Causeway took millions of years to form. It was taught as fact. In an interactive audio part of the exhibit, there is a passing mention of the history of how this feature may have been formed. It's stated in one part of the audio history that "Young Earth Creationists believe that the earth was created some 6,000 years ago. This is based on a specific interpretation of the Bible and in particular the account of creation in the Book of Genesis." Even though the exhibition was set up to indoctrinate people in millions-of-years thinking and calls its presentation "mainstream science," just a mention of the history of what people have believed about its formation—including the creationist view of a young earth—evoked remarkable fury from secularists! It became headline news across the United Kingdom. If evolutionists are sure their views are right, why is there such emotion when someone even hints at others having different views?

After having visited the United Kingdom at least 20 times, I have come to the conclusion that secularists want no mention of Christianity or the Bible in the culture—not even in the context of reporting historical facts that might involve Christianity. They want Christianity outlawed. I find that the secularists have become more and more aggressive in their disinformation propaganda campaign to malign Christians. They know the old adage, "If you throw enough mud, after a while some will stick." Sadly, I have also seen many examples of people who claim to be Christians tell us we are unloving because we insist on a literal Genesis and believe true marriage can only be between a man and a woman.

Just as I was leaving for the United Kingdom after the tour mentioned above, I read a distressing commentary by a former Church of Scotland minister that defended gay "marriage." He tried to use the Bible to make that defense, but in doing so, this church leader promoted teachings that are anti-biblical!

The public education system, by and large (yes, there are a few "missionaries" in the system), has indoctrinated young people with the teaching of evolution and millions of years as indisputable fact. In most cases, churches and homes did not teach apologetics to their young people! As a result, our children have been told that the Bible can't be trusted. Over time, they began doubting the truth of the Bible, and millions of people eventually walked away from the Church.

We need to be challenging the Church to return to the Bible. The secularists' misleading propaganda effort continues to increase in the West.

> We need to work harder than ever before to reach people with the truth.

MAY 12
Colossians 1:19-22

Martians Aren't Going to Hell
(Because They Don't Exist)

For in him all the fullness of God was pleased to dwell, and through him to reconcile to himself all things, whether on earth or in heaven, making peace by the blood of his cross. And you, who once were alienated and hostile in mind, doing evil deeds, he has now reconciled in his body of flesh by his death, in order to present you holy and blameless and above reproach before him (Colossians 1:19–22).

In 2014, if you believed many of the news headlines, you would believe that I said aliens are going to hell. But I don't believe aliens are going to hell because I don't even believe in aliens. But many headlines stated something similar to this one from a major Kentucky newspaper: "Ken Ham: Forget Aliens, They're Going to Hell Anyway."

Now consider this statement: "That's messed up." That's how Neil deGrasse Tyson (host of the modern Cosmos TV series) responded to statements TV commentator and comic Bill Maher (falsely) claimed I had said about the possibility of life in outer space and aliens supposedly going to hell. So what did Tyson mean when he said on Maher's HBO program that I was "messed up"? Well, as is usual, there can be a number of definitions, including wrong, crazy, weird, or being intoxicated.

In context, I suspect Tyson meant "messed up" in the sense that he believed I was just plain wrong and considered what I supposedly said also to be weird. Assuming Tyson was saying I was just wrong, I would say that Bill Maher was "messed up" and Tyson was also "messed up"! Maher, in typical style, told outright untruths on his HBO TV program Real Time to demean me and try to get some laughs for his vulgar TV show. A website called MEDIAite reported about the segment on this atheist's TV show, with this headline: "'That's Messed Up': Neil DeGrasse Tyson Responds to Creationist Ken Ham's NASA Claims."

Here is what Maher said: "Creationist Ken Ham who runs the Creation Museum . . . said this week that we should call off the search for extraterrestrial life because aliens haven't heard the word of Jesus and thus are going to hell anyway."[39] He then had astronomer and Cosmos TV host Tyson respond, and Tyson said, "That's messed up." By the way, as a scientist, you would think Tyson would carefully research something before making pronouncements. But when it comes to creationists, he just believes whatever his secularist friends say regardless.

Yes, it is messed up. Maher outright lied (but then, to an atheist who has no basis for morality, what is a "lie" anyway?). As anyone who has read my post about supposed alien life knows, I didn't say, "Aliens haven't heard the word of Jesus and thus are going to hell anyway." I used a theological reason (as well as other reasons) to argue that I did not believe there were aliens in outer space. In a short blog post, I stated: "I do believe there can't be other intelligent beings in outer space because of the meaning of the gospel . . . . An understanding of the gospel makes it clear that salvation through Christ is only for the Adamic race—human beings who are all descendants of Adam." I also stated, "I'm shocked at the countless hundreds of millions of dollars that have been spent over the years in the desperate and fruitless search for extraterrestrial life." I didn't say doing space research was a waste of time and money. I said searching for extraterrestrial life was a waste of money. Many secular websites (including *Huffington Post* and Salon.com) also spread Maher's false information as part of their ongoing attempts to malign me and the ministry of AiG. We shouldn't be surprised.

THEOLOGY — MAY 12

Science (observational science) can't be used to disprove the Bible—in fact, it confirms it! So what do these secularists do instead? They propagate untruths and attack us personally. The popular website Salon.com spread the same lie. In an article about Tyson's statement, a Salon author stated the following: "Last week Ken Ham, president and founder of creationist organization Answers in Genesis and the Creation Museum, called for the end of the U.S. space program. The pseudo-science promoter does not believe we should be searching for extraterrestrial life. Why? Well, for starters, if we found alien life it would be damned to hell."[40] That's just absurd!

I challenged Salon.com to document where I actually said that I "called for the end of the U.S. space program," and where I supposedly said that "if we found alien life it would be damned to hell." I have made no such statements. In regard to what I did say about aliens, these secularists have not only taken my comments completely out of context, but they actually made up false quotes attributed to me. It is an obviously deliberate attempt to denigrate biblical creationists! I guess we shouldn't be surprised that Tyson actually seemed to believe what Maher claimed. After all, Tyson also believes the fairy tale of evolution, so he is easily deceived.

What's interesting is that if you do an Internet search, you will find many examples over the years of both Christians and non-Christians who have made comments similar to what I said, in essence saying that Bible-believing Christians would have a problem with a belief in aliens because Jesus died for the human race, and thus only humans in this universe can be saved—thus Bible-believing Christians don't (or can't) accept the belief there are aliens on other planets.

So, do I believe aliens are going to hell? I don't believe in aliens, so there will be no aliens in hell! But unless people like Bill Maher, who are alienated from God because of their blatant rebellion against Him, repent before a Holy God and receive the free gift of salvation, they will end up in a real place called hell. Actually, everyone in this world is "messed up" because we are sons and daughters of Adam and Eve: *For all have sinned and fall short of the glory of God* (Romans 3:23). And so every one of us needs to repent and live in Christ:

Now this I say and testify in the Lord, that you must no longer walk as the Gentiles do, in the futility of their minds. They are darkened in their understanding, alienated from the life of God because of the ignorance that is in them, due to their hardness of heart. They have become callous and have given themselves up to sensuality, greedy to practice every kind of impurity. But that is not the way you learned Christ!—assuming that you have heard about him and were taught in him, as the truth is in Jesus, to put off your old self, which belongs to your former manner of life and is corrupt through deceitful desires, and to be renewed in the spirit of your minds, and to put on the new self, created after the likeness of God in true righteousness and holiness (Ephesians 4:17–24).

Let's pray that one day the following can be said of both Maher and Tyson: *For in him all the fullness of God was pleased to dwell, and through him to reconcile to himself all things, whether on earth or in heaven, making peace by the blood of his cross. And you, who once were alienated and hostile in mind, doing evil deeds, he has now reconciled in his body of flesh by his death, in order to present you holy and blameless and above reproach before him* (Colossians 1:19–22).

> **Pray with me that God will open such skeptics' hearts to the truth of His Word and the saving gospel.**

MAY 13
Luke 18:8
Pandemic of Unbelief

When the Son of Man comes, will he find faith on earth? (Luke 18:8).

Have you heard of the "epidemic" that is hitting the Church worldwide? Did you know that many Christian leaders are doing exactly what the atheists are encouraging them to do? It's incredible. You see, there's an "epidemic" that is infecting and destroying many churches around the world. It is the epidemic of Christians (including many church leaders) who are adopting man's religion of evolutionary ideas and adding them to Scripture—thus undermining the authority of the Word of God and helping atheists.

As we see the loss of the foundation of the authority of God's Word in our Western nations, we are also seeing a massive decline in Christian morality in society. Even the great nation of America is on a downward spiral, as we see the absolutes of Christianity being eliminated from the culture (on an almost daily basis).

We spoke to a prominent Christian leader once who was the pastor of a large church in a generally conservative denomination (though many of its churches allow for millions of years). He shared with us that within his denomination, he saw the next big theological debate being whether or not Adam and Eve were literal human beings! And we've certainly seen this play out. Such rewriting of Scripture is sadly coming to this denomination. But is it at all surprising? Once the door was opened, as many of its churches (and affiliated seminaries) began to compromise on the foundations, adding millions of years to Genesis, then the slippery slide toward unbelief in other areas of Scripture began to escalate—even whether there was a real Adam. This has happened in many churches of different denominations.

At AiG, we have been saying for years that as churches compromise with millions of years and evolution, eventually they will begin to compromise other parts of Scripture. They will give up on Adam and Eve and original sin—then maybe a literal hell, bodily resurrection, and virgin birth. Sadly, we are now seeing that happening more and more in the Church. Several years ago, *Christianity Today* published a cover story about the battle over a literal Adam and Eve. Yes, now even that question is beginning to infiltrate theologically conservative churches. We also hear of Christian leaders giving up a belief in a literal hell. And there are those who are beginning to question aspects of the Resurrection and so on.

Yes, what is happening in the Church today is exactly what the atheists want to see happen. The atheists know that if they can get Christians to compromise God's Word in Genesis, eventually there will be a generational decline in the acceptance of the authority of all of God's Word.

For instance, a professed atheist, Dr. Eugenie Scott, once mailed a fundraising letter on behalf of the organization called NCSE (National Center for Science Education). This group was set up primarily to oppose biblical creation organizations like Answers in Genesis. In this letter, Dr. Scott (who at that time headed up NCSE) told blatant untruths about what AiG was doing. But then again, one shouldn't be surprised when atheists don't tell the truth. After all, if they don't believe in an absolute authority, they have no basis for truth—except for how they decide to define it as such! She was obviously greatly concerned about the effect of AiG in society. Well—we can praise the Lord for that! But in her letter, designed to cause alarm and raise funds for her anti-Christian organization and "motivate the secular troops" to oppose creationist organizations like

AiG, Dr. Scott made a statement similar to the one she had previously made before on the NCSE website about how she seeks to recruit religious people to help her atheist group. She stated: "Find common ground with religious communities and ally with them to promote the understanding of evolution."

And back in 2008, Dr. Scott's NCSE website made these statements in an article entitled, "How You Can Support Evolution Education?" One section listed these ideas:

- "Suggest adult religious education projects focusing on evolution with your religious leaders."
- "Encourage your religious leaders to endorse the Clergy Letter Project and to participate in Evolution Weekend."
- "Encourage your religious leaders to produce educational resources about evolution and religion, and to take a formal stand in support of evolution education."

The "Evolution Weekend" referred to above was founded by an atheist professor. He recruited thousands of clergy to sign a statement that agreed with the concept of millions of years/evolution and agreed to conduct an "Evolution Sunday," when they would preach the "truth" of evolution to their congregations.

Now, Dr. Scott, back in September 2000, in her opening statement at the American Association for the Advancement of Science Conference titled, "The Teaching of Evolution in U.S. Schools: Where Politics, Religion, and Science Converge," said: "You can't win this by scientific arguments . . . our best allies were members of the mainstream clergy.... The clergy went to school board meetings and said, evolution is OK with us ... they didn't want the kids getting biblical literalism five days a week either, which meant they'd have to straighten them out on the weekends."[41]

In 2005, in an article on our AiG website, I wrote about a supporter of AiG who attended a seminar conducted by Dr. Scott on how to teach evolution in public schools. When dealing with the issue of what to do with Christian students, she offered this sad advice. Our supporter reported: "I attended the 'Teaching Evolution' seminar yesterday led by Eugenie Scott. The teachers were advised to suggest to the Bible believers to consult their clergy who would usually assure them that belief in evolution is OK!!" In her fundraising letter, this atheist continued her tactic of trying to influence churchgoers to believe in evolution/millions of years.

Atheists understand that if they can get the Church to compromise with millions of years/evolution, this will undermine the authority of the entire Bible . . . and lead to unbelief about Christianity. The atheists know that by getting the Church to compromise today, then coming generations may be won over to atheism. And more of our church leaders are doing exactly what the atheists (gleefully) want them to do. One verse of Scripture I have often used to remind me of the constant battle we are in (and the stand we should be taking) is 2 Corinthians 6:14: *Do not be unequally yoked with unbelievers. For what partnership has righteousness with lawlessness? Or what fellowship has light with darkness?*

When I look at the state of the Church, I think of Luke 18:8, *When the Son of Man comes, will he find faith on earth?*

> **When Christians compromise with the belief system of millions of years and evolution (in reality, a pagan religion), they are being unequally yoked with unbelievers.**

MAY 14
Jude 3

Earnestly Contend for the Faith

Contend for the faith (Jude 3).

I hear so many testimonies when I'm out speaking or at a meet and greet after I speak at the Ark and Creation Museum. I wish you could be there when people share their exciting testimonies with me or when I open the mail or receive emails detailing testimonies about how God has used Answers in Genesis to change people's lives. I wish you could be with me as I read every thrilling email and letter and listen in on every phone call we receive. So let me share just one testimony from a scientist to understand the importance of the AiG message and how it impacts lives.

A scientist wrote to me:

- "I was first introduced to AiG about 5 or 6 years ago when a friend invited me to attend a local AiG conference hosted by a nearby church. We sat through a day's worth of lectures and bought a whole stack of books and magazines to devour later. I spent the last few years intrigued by the information but never really experienced the 'aha' moment.
- "That moment came when I had the opportunity to visit your Creation Museum for the first time with my husband. Even though I was familiar with AiG, I was not prepared for the personal experience that the museum would offer me. I was absolutely blown away by the exhibits!
- "We spent two full days there, reading all the [signs] we could ... and even staying after hours to listen to guest speakers. The biggest thing I remember, though, is not any one particular exhibit or lecture, but rather the life-changing paradigm shift of worldviews that I experienced."

This scientist continued:

- "My academic background is biology. I graduated from Penn State with a biology/genetics & development degree ... so I'm quite well-versed in molecular and cellular processes, as well as natural selection and evolution. I have always had a difficult time knowing what to believe about the origins of the earth and natural earth processes, given that the majority of my science teachers and professors were atheists, and, of course, were promoting their own agenda as well as the 'universally accepted' science curricula.
- "However, when I attended the Creation Museum, somehow everything changed in my mind. I'll be honest and say that there are many topics that I still don't grasp and some that I'd like to explore further. What changed in my mind was the realization [of what I] needed to know—knowing that God's Word is absolute truth. Period.
- "It's hard for me to admit that I am just now really starting to believe that, because I would like to say that I always have believed God. But the truth is that I didn't fully believe God before. Now, I know that I can and I do, thanks to your ministry!
- "I plan to visit the museum again with some [friends] who are members of my small group from church. ...If it strengthened my faith in God and changed my worldview, it can certainly do the same for them!"

I get so excited when I read such thrilling testimonies. And this is just one of hundreds of such accounts I have received over the years.

APOLOGETICS

Around the time I was reading this letter from the scientist, I was burdened at the publication of a book by a Christian academic. The author, Dr. Peter Enns, was a professor at what was described as a Christian university (Eastern University in Philadelphia). He had just released a book intended to influence the Church not to believe there was a literal Adam and Eve and that there wasn't a literal Fall into sin. You shouldn't be surprised then to learn the book's title: *The Evolution of Adam*. Beyond this heresy of not believing in a literal Fall, Dr. Enns in essence also accused Jesus Christ of lying and being a sinner! Here's how: AiG researchers have posted an article on our AiG website about a statement Dr. Enns wrote in *The Evolution of Adam*. We reported that Dr. Enns rejected Moses as the author of the Pentateuch. And in dealing with Bible passages where Jesus directly attributes the authorship of these books to Moses, Dr. Enns stated: "Rather, Jesus here reflects the tradition that he himself inherited as a first-century Jew and that his hearers assumed to be the case."

Our researchers wrote in their review: "The idea advanced by Dr. Enns here is known as the accommodation theory and was first advanced in the eighteenth century by Johann Semler, the father of German rationalism. The accommodation theory is very popular among liberal theologians and basically asserts that Jesus accommodated (accepted and taught) the various ideas of His day, even if they were wrong." Our writers added that according to the accommodationists, "since Jesus was allegedly primarily concerned with spiritual matters, He didn't bother to correct some of their false historical or scientific beliefs because they might have sidetracked Him from His real message."

Our AiG authors then state: "So what's the big deal if Jesus accommodated the errors of His day? Well, if Jesus taught error, then He would have lied to His listeners, in which case He would have been a sinner. If He unwittingly taught error, then He would have misled His followers, and would have been a false teacher."

Our researchers further observed: "Either option leaves us with a Jesus who is sinful and less than God. If Jesus had sinned, then He could not have been the spotless Lamb who appeased God's wrath by His sacrificial death on the Cross, because He would have needed to die for His own sins. If Jesus did not die for our sins, then we are still in our sins and are headed for an eternity in the lake of fire."

A book like *The Evolution of Adam* serves to remind Bible-believing Christians that there are two battlefronts that are being played out every day: the world and the Church. AiG is doing our best to counter the pagan religion of evolution and millions of years that so permeates the education system and culture as a whole—and which has had devastating effects on the hearts and minds of millions of young people in our churches. But praise the Lord, just as with the testimony I shared above, the Lord is using AiG to get Christians "on fire" for Him.

Sadly, we have to also engage in a battle within the Church as an increasing number of Christian academics are now publishing a plethora of materials to convince people that they should deny a literal Adam, a literal Fall, a literal Genesis, etc. As I once said to someone, "Who needs enemies from outside the Church when we have enough compromisers within the Church to cope with?" We need to be engaging an increasingly secularized culture and Church and be active in the fight for the Bible's authority as we:

Contend for the faith (Jude 3).

How much are you involved in the battle to contend for the faith?

MAY 15
Matthew 7:15

Ravenous Wolves

Beware of false prophets, who come to you in sheep's clothing but inwardly are ravenous wolves (Matthew 7:15).

Both the building of the Creation Museum and Ark Encounter certainly created a buzz—in Christian as well as non-Christian circles. Both resulted in different but similar sorts of responses, but I want to focus on the Ark Encounter (life-size Noah's ark) and the lessons that showed us the spiritual nature of the battle in this world we live in today.

When we announced we would be building a full-scale, all-wood Noah's ark in Northern Kentucky, together with exhibits that answer the most-asked questions about the Flood, post-Flood events, and this huge vessel (the centerpiece of an amazing 160-acre history-based theme park called Ark Encounter), it received remarkable media attention.

For instance, a feature story on ABC-TV's World News with Diane Sawyer and a lengthy article in *the New York Times* (plus an item in *Newsweek*) started a media frenzy that quickly went international. Two reporters from German newspapers came to Kentucky to interview us, and stories also appeared in newspapers in India, Israel, Italy, Hong Kong, Norway, Czech Republic, United Kingdom, my native Australia, etc. It showed amazing interest.

But as might be expected when a project of this size and growing popularity affirms the truth of the Bible, many in the secular media (plus bloggers, etc.) reacted quite negatively. Misinformation and outright false accusations were made about how the Ark was to be built and operated. The same sort of thing happened back when we were building and then opening the Creation Museum.

Sadly, even some church leaders blasted the project or made ill-informed, negative comments. So typical. Opposition to Christian work comes within and without the Church!

Of course, atheist bloggers poured forth hatred as they wrote (and have continued to write quite regularly) emotional, error-laden blogs and articles against the Ark and Creation Museum. There were also hundreds (by now many thousands) for-and-against letters and web comments in newspapers and on the Internet.

The Ark Encounter project certainly created a buzz! And it's a buzz that should remind us of lessons we should have already learned in regard to the spiritual nature of the battle raging around us.

Before I get to those lessons, here are just a couple of negative reactions we received back at that time to the Ark Encounter and the Creation Museum, typical of the sorts of responses from opponents:

"The most tragic part of the Creation Museum on both of my visits was the intellectual child abuse. There's some heartbreaking stuff in this video [on the Ark Encounter website]…plus a preview of the idiotic Noah's Ark nonsense that Kentucky will soon be known for around the globe if Ark Encounter is built."

"Not only will the state of Kentucky give $40 million in tax breaks to Ken Ham [that is an outright lie that has been told many times in the secularists' propaganda war against us] so we can be an accomplice to such intellectual child abuse, we're also going to spend many millions on road construction to help them out as well. Based on the numbers in Ken Ham's insanely inflated fake study, of course."

RESOURCES — MAY 15

And here is one coauthored by a Baptist minister back then who was in the state of Kentucky where we built the Ark:

"We represent lay and clergy leaders from the Christian, Jewish, Islamic, Baha'i, Quaker, Buddhist, Hindu and other faith groups practicing in Central Kentucky. As an organization that has been promoting and practicing interfaith engagement and understanding here in the Bluegrass [State] for over 10 years, we have serious concerns about the recent announcement of the proposed Ark Encounter theme park sponsored by Answers in Genesis.... We know many people still hold anti-scientific views. However, when Kentucky presents even the appearance of advancing or promoting one particular version of faith over other faiths, or over none, it does enormous damage to the future of interfaith understanding, respect and hope for peace that so many have worked so hard to ensure."

Now here are the lessons for believers to learn—or to be reminded of—as we see how biblical Christianity is being attacked in an increasingly secular world.

First, don't be surprised at how the world reacts. Romans 1 tells us that the ungodly "by their unrighteousness suppress the truth." The reason so many atheist bloggers and secular reporters/editorial writers reacted so negatively and wrote so furiously against the project (and AiG) is that they know in their hearts that there is a God—and they actively suppress that.

What we are seeing today is just the outworking of this active suppression. Right before our eyes, the warnings from God's Word are being illustrated.

Also, remember that *the heart is deceitful above all things, and desperately sick* (Jeremiah 17:9). Proverbs 1:29 also reminds us that these scoffers "hated knowledge."

Second, we should not be surprised when religious leaders oppose those of us who stand for the truth of God's Word. When Jesus the "God-man" walked on Earth, He had to deal with—and rebut—the religious leaders of the day.

I think of these verses: *Beware of false prophets, who come to you in sheep's clothing but inwardly are ravenous wolves* (Matthew 7:15) and how *shepherds have led them astray* (Jeremiah 50:6).

One of the thrilling lessons from all the opposition is that God's people saw this attack on biblical authority and became excited to be part of a project that would boldly and publicly take a stand for the truth of God's Word in this culture. Thankfully, there are thousands upon thousands in this nation (and others around the world) who haven't "bowed the knee to Baal." God always has a remnant. The remnant in America I would say actually numbers in the millions. And an enormous number of people did get behind this project to fund it and enable it to become a reality.

And let's remember the lesson from Jude 3, where we are told to *contend for the faith that was once for all delivered to the saints.*

> Make sure you have on the full armor of God so you are ready to be an active soldier for the King.

MAY 16
Genesis 50:20

God Meant It for Good

I have often thought about this verse over the years in the Answers in Genesis ministry:

As for you, you meant evil against me, but God meant it for good, to bring it about that many people should be kept alive, as they are today (Genesis 50:20).

This was Joseph talking to his brothers. But I've often pondered this verse as we have encountered opposition over the years. Examples from our ministry I trust will help you as a Christian who encounters opposition. We can apply that verse to our own situations today as it's a reminder that God is in total control of every situation. He is the sovereign Creator.

It's good at times to be reminded of some remarkable events that have shown us how God has truly blessed this creation/gospel ministry of Answers in Genesis and even used the opposition to it for His glory.

When the Creation Museum (the first of our two attractions) was opened in 2007, it was interesting to read statements made by secular news sources. Here's a sample:

- "The museum, a 60,000-square-foot menace to 21st century scientific advancement, is the handiwork of Answers in Genesis."[42]
- "The museum may be the biggest collection of kitsch in God's entire world."[43]
- "The Creation Museum is more frightening than Disney's Haunted Mansion."[44]

The irony is that this sort of opposition actually helped advertise the Creation Museum to so many people! Since 2007, we continue to see people from all across America and around the world visit the museum and now the Ark too. Many millions have visited Northern Kentucky to come to these Christian attractions. Many told us that hostile statements like those from the secular media made them want to find out about these facilities. Some said something like, "To get the sort of opposition we saw you receiving in the secular media, we thought there must be something good here."

We decided to make a TV commercial with a voice saying (including visuals on the screen): "The *LA Times* calls the Creation Museum a '60,000-square-foot menace to 21st century scientific advancement.' *Vanity Fair* calls it 'the biggest collection of kitsch in God's entire world.' *Architectural Record* says it's more 'frightening than Disney's Haunted Mansion.'"

And then with me saying: "There are nearly 200 natural history museums that teach evolution, so why is the media so hateful to our museum that teaches creation from a biblical perspective? Think for yourself and prepare to believe." Yes, what the media intended for evil God used for good—it gave us marketing material to get people to come and hear the truth of God's Word and the saving gospel.

When I read media articles attacking AiG and the museum and the Ark attractions, I do think of that verse I quoted at the beginning of this chapter. The more the media and others make statements they intend for evil, the more I hear from our "troops" (our supporters) rallying around us. And the more I hear of people finding out about our ministry who never knew it existed. So, when you get opposition, remember how God can use it for good.

APOLOGETICS — MAY 16

Consider more examples of opposition. As I've mentioned many times, more and more we are seeing secularists accusing AiG of "child abuse" with our Bible-affirming teachings. One time I put up a short video on my Facebook page where I was teaching children about dinosaurs at a conference in Wisconsin. Some secularists responded with charges of "child abuse." Here are just a few representative comments from these secularists that appeared on the web):

- "Intellectual child abuser Ken Ham doesn't like being called that."
- "For his child abuse on a massive scale (Answers in Stupidity, Magical Creationism Museum, preaching [expletive deleted] in churches), I vote for world-class [expletive deleted] and subhuman Ken Ham."
- "Ken Ham is proud that he is retarding the education of innocent vulnerable minds whom will later require years of remedial education should they choose to take a career in the sciences.... This is child abuse. It needs to end."
- "It's child abuse. And every adult in that [conference] room is unwittingly guilty of it."
- "I hate Ken Ham. I'm not going to be nice or PC about this. The man is a disaster for the world and for the state of Kentucky. He and his creation museum and ark theme park make me fear for my state."

As we continue to reach millions of adults and children with the creation/gospel message, the secularists absolutely hate it! But we must continue, as the enemies of the gospel want to destroy the lives of these children. They want to point them away from the Bible's teachings. And in this world where men loved darkness rather than light (John 3:19), we will be opposed and persecuted for proclaiming the truth of God's Word. Expect it to happen. Don't be intimidated by such opponents.

Despite all this opposition and nasty, profane words, we also receive many encouraging comments. God is so gracious in allowing us to see these. Consider these wonderful words in an email sent to us from a senior pastor, received after an Answers conference was held at his church:

- "Tell your board a huge thanks from all of us little guys. You and your team were a shot in the arm of spiritual energy, hope, and confidence in the authority of the Word and the sheer power and awesome glory of the gospel.
- "You and your board have launched out with God-sized vision that demands God-sized faith. We all need it but often the rest of us are content to be in the kiddie pool of life. Actually we are fearful and have grown comfortable with our little safe visions that don't demand much courage or faith.
- "Your unbelievable boldness (and that of the board) in going to build an ark may do as much to rescue the church from ourselves as it will to reach the Lost.
- "Tell them again that all of us 'no-name guys' out there are counting on them and have been strengthened to greater faith and courage. [The AiG Conference] breathed new life and gospel energy into us."

Well, we are definitely all about boldly proclaiming the authority of God's Word and the vital creation/gospel message! I hope you are too.

For I am not ashamed of the gospel, for it is the power of God for salvation to everyone who believes, to the Jew first and also to the Greek (Romans 1:16).

Be bold for God's Word and the gospel!

MAY 17
Proverbs 18:13

Listen First

One verse of Scripture that I have reminded many people of over the years is this one: *If one gives an answer before he hears, it is his folly and shame* (Proverbs 18:13).

So many times people have made accusations (or heard accusations) about people or ministries but have never heard those being accused give their account of things. Many times I've found the differences between the two sides can be massive. And one has to be discerning and conduct research before being able to come to a conclusion as to what to do or not do in response.

What dismayed me the most about the attacks on the Ark and Creation Museum was the response from certain Christians.

Some of the comments have been rather shocking. Let me explain further. First, I want to discuss the situation regarding secularists.

Many Christians were astounded at how the secular media and atheist bloggers responded so harshly to the announcement about our full-size Noah's ark to be built in Northern Kentucky. But really, we shouldn't have been all that surprised. As Christians, we know that non-Christians "suppress the truth" and "hate knowledge," as the Scripture tells us. Secularists have reacted the way we would expect based on what the Bible teaches us about the heart of man.

As examples, let me share a few responses to a guest column written by three of AiG's PhD scientists that was published in a secular newspaper. Our article was intended to correct false information contained in an opinion piece that the paper had published about the Ark and creation vs. evolution. Here's a sampling of comments to our rebuttal column:

- "Why do you idiots make a living abusing innocent children? Are you too stupid to get a real job, or is being a dishonest [expletive deleted] more lucrative for you?"
- "The problem is, Mr. Moron-For-Jeebus, your new facility is going to mentally abuse innocent children and it's going to make idiot America even more stupid."
- "You three idiots should be put in prison for child abuse and excessive stupidity. You're a disgrace to your profession and a disgrace to the human race."

As nasty as these responses are, they are just the tip of the iceberg. So much more has been written negatively about AiG and the Ark Encounter and Creation Museum over the years. Such attacks continue. It reminds us of how anti-Christian the enemies of Christ are. Sadly, this anti-Christian sentiment has been growing in our culture.

But what dismays me the most about attacks on our ministry is the response from Christians for two totally different reasons.

First, there have been Christian leaders—even theologically conservative ones—who have written against the Ark Encounter (as some did for the Creation Museum). Some Christian leaders used the Ark project to voice their opposition to the literal Book of Genesis and to speak out against AiG and our Creation Museum.

APOLOGETICS

Second and most saddening, there were Christians—even a few who had supported AiG—who contacted us to express opposition to the Ark Encounter because they believed some of the false information in a secular newspaper or website.

Because of these unfortunate responses, I thought I should use this opposition to the Ark Encounter as a teaching point and to offer a reminder for all of us when we hear people at church talking about others.

One of the most practical verses in the Bible is Proverbs 18:13. To paraphrase, it cautions believers not to hear just one side of a controversy and perhaps come to a (wrong) conclusion no matter how convincing it would seem. Sometimes we can hear people give what sounds like a convincing case for their side of a controversy, but when we don't hear the other side, we don't really get the full story—and perhaps don't hear how unbiblical the "convincing" side might be. Circumstantial evidence can make a person look guilty of something, but one tiny piece of evidence unknown to them could change the entire interpretation. How many times has someone been convicted and jailed for a crime only to be released later when new research on DNA found they were totally innocent?

As you hear about new developments in the fight for biblical authority within the Church and in the secular world, you might hear something negative about AiG—and perhaps even about our attractions. As I alluded to above, some Christians, reading articles in the secular press, have believed what they read and then wrote us to criticize the Ark project. But they didn't consider asking us first to see if the report was true. Frankly, these people violated Proverbs 18:13.

Sadly, jumping to conclusions occurs too often among Christians. You can probably recall a few disputes within your church—and between high-profile Christian leaders. As Christians, we need to follow Proverbs 18:13 (and other Scriptures) to make judgments about personal conduct, biblical soundness, etc. We really need to ensure we are like the Bereans of Acts 17 who searched the Scriptures to see if things were so.

Daily, as Christians, we are in an immense spiritual battle. We battle with the world and, sadly, we struggle with much of the Church too. We live at a time when we see so much of the Church going "woke" (soft on LGBTQ, etc.) and being rather lukewarm in regard to proclaiming God's Word. We see so many church leaders who have compromised God's Word in Genesis.

As a ministry, we continue to do battle in this spiritual war and create the "armaments" for God's people like you to defend His Christian faith. When one does this, people will raise all sorts of accusations to try to denigrate or undermine. But don't forget to remember that passage I quoted above from Proverbs 18:13:

If one gives an answer before he hears, it is his folly and shame (Proverbs 18:13).

> Understand the nature of the raging battle around us, be diligent, and ensure you check things out carefully so you don't even unwittingly help the enemy.

MAY 18

Ephesians 5:16

Are You Burdened for Your Relatives?

Making the best use of the time, because the days are evil (Ephesians 5:16).

Whenever my wife, Mally, and I return to our homeland of Australia, one of our favorite things to do is to go into Brisbane City. We enjoy walking around the Queen Street Mall in the heart of the city.

While Mally is shopping, I will sit in the mall and observe all the people walking by. Often I sit there counting the people. Why? When I reach 100 people, I remind myself that statistics in Australia have revealed that probably only one out of that 100 is likely to be a born-again Christian. My heart sinks when I look around the mall. I realize that almost all of the thousands of people I see in that mall are heading to a Christless eternity. Probably only about 1% of 20 million people in Australia are truly born again.

In the United States, because of the history of Christian influence here, there is a greater percentage of Christians. But I wonder what the real percentage is. Various statisticians/organizations have researched this question, but they admit that many people who call themselves "Christian" define the word in various ways. Some suggest around 20% of Americans are truly born-again Christians, but others suggest the percentage is much less.

A number of years ago, we commissioned America's Research Group (ARG) to conduct a nationwide study of millennials who regularly attend church (i.e., at least three times a month). We discovered that 40% stated outright that they were not born again, and 65% said they believed being a "good" person would get someone into heaven. So it's not just those outside the Church we should be concerned about in regard to being saved!

Such sad statistics burden me. Remember, we are all related. Doesn't this weigh heavily on your heart too, as you realize that so many of our family members are on a path to destruction?

I've shared a message various times based on Ephesians 5:16 and its phrase *"making the best use of the time, because the days are evil."* I explained to the audiences that this verse, in the context of Ephesians 5, instructs us to use every opportunity we have to shine the light of the truth of God's Word and the gospel as much as we are able.

I then shared an example from my own upbringing that had a great impact on me. When I was growing up, my parents used to take us to my mother's parents' home in North Queensland. On one of those trips, my mother shared with me about the time when, as a teenager, she used to ride a bike five miles each Sunday (over many months) to carry two girls to Sunday school! She wanted to make sure they heard God's Word and the life-changing gospel.

Some 60 years later, my mother met those same ladies again! One was a strong Christian, and the other said she had wandered away a bit but was turning around.

I've never forgotten this anecdote about my mother and the bicycle, and I think to myself, "If my mother, as a teenager, was prepared to help people get to Sunday school for the sake of the gospel, why shouldn't I do whatever is needed to help people hear the saving message of the gospel? Their eternity is at stake."

THEOLOGY

I've often used 2 Peter 3:9 over the years concerning Answers in Genesis (our speakers, resources, website, and so on), the Creation Museum, and the Ark Encounter to share the following truth: There's no point in trying to just convince people to believe in God/creation because, even if they are creationists, they will end up in hell just like an atheist if they don't believe and trust in the Lord Jesus Christ for salvation.

I'm reminded of James 2:19: *You believe that God is one; you do well. Even the demons believe—and shudder!*

When we first opened the Creation Museum and its "walk through the 7 C's of history" (Creation, Corruption, Catastrophe, Confusion, Christ, Cross, and Consummation), we produced a powerful movie called The Last Adam. This well-done film clearly presented the saving gospel. And after a few years, we opened a large "Christ, Cross, Consummation" exhibit in the museum to present the message of salvation, starting from the foundational Book of Genesis and sharing the truth of the power of the Cross and Resurrection.

Eventually, we opened the "Why the Bible Is True" exhibit, a 2,500-square-foot exhibit on the third deck of our life-size Noah's ark. The stunning exhibit presents a unique, captivating graphic-novel approach to share the gospel, using commonplace situations that apply to today's culture. For our guests, it's like walking through the pages of a book—you just can't wait to read the next page and find out what happens. This kind of approach is used to clearly explain the gospel message.

With visually striking artwork, we explain the various "doors" in Scripture (e.g., the ark door, the door the Israelites put blood on before their exodus from Egypt, the door to the sheepfold, the door to the tomb, and so on). We challenge each Ark visitor concerning whether they have gone through the "door" (the Lord Jesus) to be saved. And, of course, we deal with the ark door which is a picture of Jesus. Noah and his family had to go through that door into the ark of salvation as we have to go through a door, the Lord Jesus, into our "ark" of salvation.

You certainly can't leave the Ark or Creation Museum without understanding the gospel message. Christians and non-Christians from all over the world visit our two attractions. As we greet them, we are unashamed of what we stand for as Christians and, therefore, boldly (in a sensitive yet challenging way) present God's message of salvation at our attractions.

So let's use every opportunity we can as we "redeem the time" to ensure as many of our "family members" (around 8 billion of them) as possible are challenged to receive the free gift of salvation.

You may not get the opportunity to carry two kids on a bicycle to Sunday school like my mother did, but we have so many ways available to us today to carry out the Great Commission, such as sharing AiG's website, books, videos, events—or bringing friends and family to the God-honoring Ark Encounter and Creation Museum! And so much more!

Let's all be "making the best use of the time."

MAY 19
Genesis 11:9

Babel Is History!

Therefore its name was called Babel, because there the Lord confused the language of all the earth. And from there the Lord dispersed them over the face of all the earth (Genesis 11:9).

Over the years, people have asked me why we built a Creation Museum and a life-size Ark. Why build other attractions to expand these projects?

Not only is the building of the Creation Museum and life-size Noah's Ark a way to challenge people to accept the truth of God's Word, but just as important are the other exhibits we hope to build at the attractions, such as possibly the Tower of Babel to finish off the history in Genesis 1–11.

These attractions can have such a tremendous impact in challenging people to think about the Bible and its message of salvation, based in true history. It helps bring the historical events recorded in Scripture alive.

I happened to be skipping through the TV channels (surfing with a remote control is a male thing I am told!) and heard commentator Glenn Beck discussing the Genesis 11 account of the Tower of Babel with a rabbi.

My ears pricked up because of this topic from Genesis. But I was dismayed to hear comments like these from this well-known commentator and the rabbi:

"And then the mortar that holds it [the tower] together is the stuff, the material. Not the—not their common experiences of spiritualist or even history …. And I urge people to read the story and to listen to us, not as if we're describing some long forgotten historic event …. " [Me: In other words, the Tower of Babel wasn't a historical event?]

"But the bricks represent people." [So the bricks weren't real bricks but supposedly symbolized people?]

"The mortar is very related—same word really as the word materialism …. The mortar that will hold those bricks together is materialism." [So the mortar represented materialism?]

"After the Great Flood, everybody on Earth was getting together and then, all of a sudden, somebody had a different idea: Hey, how about we all speak one language and we'll build a tower to reach the sky?" [In other words, people spoke different languages before the Tower of Babel, and then they were led to speak one?]

"Rabbi, the very first time socialism or communism or new world order was tried was the Tower of Babel, right?" [So Babel is really about socialism?]

Beck: "They think they are doing good and that's why God didn't punish them. He blessed them by making them stones again, right?"

Rabbi Lapin: "Correct."[45] [Therefore, God didn't judge the people at the Tower of Babel? He actually blessed them by making them individuals again (represented by the different languages)?]

My heart sank as I heard this from such a well-known conservative broadcaster. Even though he said he respected the Bible, his comments were an outright attack on the history of this Babel event recorded in the Book of Genesis. The Bible makes it clear: People rebelled against God as they built this tower. They had disobeyed God's directive. God judged them by causing them to speak different languages. Genesis 10 gives

APOLOGETICS — MAY 19

details of how the 70 family groups moved away from each other because of their different languages to form different cultures/nations, etc., as a result of this event.

The Tower of Babel enables us to understand why there are different people groups (not races) in the world. It is a major event in history. It helps us show that all humans are descendants of Adam (all are related). Therefore, all are sinners and in need of the gospel. The Son of God stepped into history to become our relative—the "God-man," the perfect man—to die on a Cross and pay the penalty for our sin. Thus, He offers a free gift of salvation.

The Tower of Babel wasn't a fable written as a metaphor for socialism! The bricks were bricks, and the mortar was mortar.

What I watched made me realize how we need to be doing all we can to help people understand that the history in the Bible is true. As I teach children in my talks, "The Bible is the history book of the universe."

Now there's something I need to say to bring home a very important point about the Bible. At times, I have shown video clips of Christian leaders who compromise God's Word. I do this to warn others to be on the lookout for such compromise and to ensure their children (and friends, etc.) are not led astray by such leaders who compromise. I've had people tell me I shouldn't be doing this and only teach about the positive things.

But God in His Word does not hide us from error. God gives us truth but also warns about error and gives us examples of error so we can learn. God also warns us about shepherds that lead the sheep astray and metered out judgment because of this. So surely we can and should also warn people about shepherds who compromise and can lead people in the wrong direction.

I've also had people tell me we shouldn't build Noah's ark and talk about the Flood as it was a judgment on the world. But God details these events in the Bible to warn us about wickedness and to see God's hand of judgment and mercy. These are events in the Bible, so surely we can do all we can to show people these events were true and to learn the lessons God wants us to learn. The same is true for the event of the Tower of Babel.

My point is, the Bible is a book that doesn't hide wickedness from us. It doesn't hide people's weaknesses no matter how great a person they are. David was a man after God's own heart, and the greatest human king the Israelites had, yet his sin of adultery and other sins are not hidden from us. And we read how God judged David because of these sins.

Is it right therefore to say because certain events in the Bible are about judgment we shouldn't build exhibits to explain them to people? We all need to understand and believe the history God has revealed to us in His Word. And this can be done in various ways through books, teaching programs, exhibits, and so on.

Millions have come to our two attractions to be challenged about the truth of God's Word concerning creation and the Fall, as well as the account of Noah's ark, the Flood, the truth concerning the actual event of the Tower of Babel and what it means to our world today. And they are challenged to believe the history in God's Word and also the gospel based in that history.

For I did not shrink from declaring to you the whole counsel of God (Acts 20:27).

We need to teach all of God's Word.

MAY 20
Romans 8:22

Where Is God in Tragedy?

For we know that the whole creation has been groaning together in the pains of childbirth until now (Romans 8:22).

Tragedies beyond description occur all over the world. The question often comes up when this happens: Where is God in the midst of the loss of life and property?

For instance, on TV news in 2011, we were watching the terrible devastation, loss of life, homes, crops, businesses, etc., in Queensland, Australia, because of historic flooding. Tragedies beyond description had hit Queensland, where I lived most of my life. I still have many family members there who kept me apprised of flood-related developments. While I had first-hand accounts, you could grasp something of the extent of the catastrophe on the internet from Australian news sources. We learned just how much greater the catastrophe was than by merely watching a brief report on TV.

As an aside, for those Christians (including pastors and theologians) who believe that the fossil record was supposedly laid down over millions of years before Adam, they have a major problem dealing with the question, "Where is God in the midst of all this death and suffering?"

If death, disease, suffering, and catastrophes have been going on for millions of years before Adam's Fall, and God described all those bad things as "very good'" (the description God gave the creation when He finished it on the sixth day of creation), then God said death, struggle, suffering, disease, catastrophes, etc., are also "very good." It is only the Christian who takes Genesis as literal history who can provide the biblical answer. The creation was perfect but is now marred by sin. It was once "very good" but is now changed because of man's sin—our rebellion against the Creator. We live in a world where we have a little (though often horrible) taste of what life is like without God! The "groaning" (Romans 8:22) we experience daily and the extra groaning in times of terrible disaster are a reminder that we are not living in a world as God made in Genesis—but a world suffering because of the Fall. One can't imagine how horrible it would be to live for eternity without God! What a reminder to turn to the living God.

I was pleased to see the Australian prime minister at the time who, even though she was an avowed atheist, showed sincere care and concern for the people of Queensland. But as an atheist, why would she do that? She may claim that her worldview prompts her to care for people, but in an ultimate sense, what purpose would this have in a purposeless universe? And in reality, whether she liked it or not, she was borrowing from Christian presuppositions to incorporate such care into her worldview. In fact, even though she said she was an atheist, in reality, she was not! God's Word in Romans 1 makes it clear that the knowledge of God is written on our hearts. People who call themselves atheists actually "suppress the truth" (Romans 1:18–21). There really are no atheists.

Romans 8:22 reminds us we live in a groaning world because of sin. We do not live in a perfect world, as Adam and Eve did before the Fall. Whether we are Christians or non-Christians, all of us are under the curse pronounced in Genesis 3:17–19 because of sin. We suffer the effects of the curse in many ways: we age, get sick, and so on.

THEOLOGY — MAY 20

We are reminded in Matthew 6:19 to *not lay up for yourselves treasures on earth, where moth and rust destroy.* The things of this world, including material goods, are temporary. They will not last. Eternal matters are most important and should always be our priority. Of course, we do need to share one another's burdens, as the Scripture teaches us in Galatians 6:2.

Because we know we are made in the image of God, Christians should be showing care and love to others—helping them with their material needs. However, we need to understand that spiritual needs are of utmost importance, and they have to deal with the truth of God's Word and the gospel. There has been a terrible loss of material goods—homes, belongings, and so on—and as God's people, we should do all we can to help such people get back on their feet. But we should be reminded that material goods do not last, and we should consider what will be our eternal state.

We mourn when we hear of the death of anyone, but we must remember that the question is not, "Why did those people die?" but, rather, "Why does death exist?" (After all, everyone will eventually die.) Hebrews 9:27 points out that *it is appointed for man to die once, and after that comes judgment.* Furthermore, Romans 5:12 indicates that by one man—Adam—came sin, and with sin, came death. It is not God's fault that there is death in the world; it is our fault because we sinned in Adam and thus have separated ourselves from our Creator. God stepped into history in the person of Jesus Christ, the "God-man," to pay the penalty for our sin and offer us a free gift of salvation (Ephesians 2:8). He did a special work to save us from what we did in rebelling against our God. Yes, we mourned with people over those sad deaths in Australia. But we need to be reminded that death is the ultimate end for all, and the question we need to ask ourselves is, *Where will we stand in regard to what happens to us after death?* (Matthew 25:46).

God's ways and God's timing are not our ways and timing. Many accounts in the Bible remind us that though something at the time seemed to be unfair and without reason (from our human perspective), we are only fallible and finite human beings. We know nothing compared to an infinite God (Colossians 2:2–3). Such a God would have morally commendable and just reasons for something way beyond what we could imagine. Certainly, there are those who will get angry at God over what has happened. But instead, we should be angry at sin—our sin. And then, like the Apostle Paul, fall on our knees and cry out, *Wretched man that I am! Who will deliver me from this body of death?* (Romans 7:24).

Through all this, and as hard as it may be for those in the midst of tragedy, God is a God of love. It is only because there is a God that there is such a thing as love anyway. And even though we ask why and we do have to suffer in this world, ultimately, we have to come to the point that Job did where he fell before the Lord in dust and ashes and recognized that God is God (Job 42:6). Who are we to question His ways?

> We need to acknowledge who we are (i.e., sinful, finite, fallible creatures) and throw ourselves at His feet, knowing He is an all-merciful, all-loving God – a heavenly Father who wants us to live with Him in eternity.

MAY 21
Acts 17:11

Fallacies of the Modern Church: Part 1

Now these Jews were more noble than those in Thessalonica; they received the word with all eagerness, examining the Scriptures daily to see if these things were so (Acts 17:11).

As I have traveled around the world and spoken in numerous churches, I have encountered some interesting situations. On quite a number of occasions, more so in the United Kingdom than any other country, I had church leaders tell me I couldn't sell books in their church on Sunday. Many times they would tell me it's because Jesus drove out those selling things on the Sabbath in the temple.

It always dismayed me that the world is marketing their anti-God message to people 24 hours a day, and yet in certain churches, I was not given the opportunity to provide resources to equip people with the truth of God's Word so they can learn how to defend the Christian faith in a hostile world. And in those churches, young people were leaving because of the indoctrination by the secular world. Yet I couldn't give them an opportunity to obtain resources to overcome this indoctrination. So how should we respond to those who are concerned about the sale of resources within the church building—particularly at what are called "worship" services? Young people and adults in our churches are hungry for answers. Therefore, the question must be asked: Is the sale of Christian resources to proclaim the truth of God's Word at services or at any meeting in a church prohibited by John 2 or any other Scripture?

Three relevant questions must be addressed as we study John 2:13–22: What is the context of the teaching regarding money changers in the temple? Are church buildings the same as the temple of the old covenant? What is the correlation between worship in the temple and the church gathering? These questions will be answered in a three-part series beginning with this one.

What Is the Context of the Account Regarding the Money Changers in the Temple?

Jesus came to the Jerusalem temple during the time of the Passover. For the Jews, Passover was a big deal. It was the celebration of God's deliverance of His people from Egypt. Through the blood of a lamb on the doorpost, the Jews escaped judgment and experienced freedom. Exodus 12:1–11 reveals that Jews were to provide an unblemished lamb—the best of the best—for sacrifice. (If a family was too small to provide their own lamb, they were to join with their neighbor in this provision.)

Exodus 30:13–14 also discusses a tax to be paid to the sanctuary. This is echoed in Matthew 17:24–27 where Jesus talked to Peter about the temple tax. The money-changers exchanged foreign coinage for the accepted currency. John wrote, *In the temple he found those who were selling oxen and sheep and pigeons, and the money-changers sitting there* (John 2:14). Why did they sell oxen, sheep, and pigeons when the Jews were required to bring their own? What had become of the significance of choosing the unblemished lamb when one could simply buy something at the temple? To make matters worse, the sellers seemed to be cheating and taking advantage of guests. Essentially, they were stealing from others who sought to worship. Worship had become commerce.

In other references to money-changers in the temple (Matthew 21:13; Mark 11:17; Luke 19:45–47), Jesus rebuked them for defiling His house of prayer. The sad fact is that the temple should have been a place of prayer and worship but had become more of a convenient way for people to simply buy access to God and for others to cheat them in the process. The significance of the blood sacrifice had been reduced to consumerism for convenience.

The disciples watched Jesus overturn tables and draw out a whip of cords, and they remembered the Scripture, *For zeal for your house has consumed me* (Psalm 69:9). The Jewish sacrifices pointed to the one eternal and all-encompassing sacrifice of atonement for salvation: a Savior. By making access to God a matter of commercial convenience, these people were bringing dishonor to Christ and a rebellious spirit toward the Father.

In John 2:19, Jesus brought great significance to this encounter. He said, *Destroy this temple, and in three days I will raise it up.* As the ultimate Passover Lamb, Jesus would negate the need for the physical temple and animal sacrifices. Verse 21 reveals that Jesus has become for us the temple access to God, and we come to the Father through Him.

The temple and the sacrifices performed in it pointed to Jesus Christ and His future work on the Cross. Therefore, when the Jews desecrated the purpose of the temple, they were desecrating the person of Christ. Christ was in their very midst watching them do it. True worship in spirit and truth has never been something to be bought or commercialized. Salvation is free, and Christ, our true access to God, cannot become a consumer's appeasement of convenience.

In short, the passage about the money-changers in the temple has nothing to do with the provision and sale of resources that equip people to become more intimate worshippers in spirit and truth. In reality, the money-changers rejected the main point of the temple—pointing to the coming Messiah. This passage is about the commercialization of the sacrifice that was pointing to the Lamb of God. Lastly, it shows that God's people failed to acknowledge His presence among them. Today, however, the presence of God is not in a temple structure located in Israel but in Jesus Christ in our hearts and lives. The accusation that ministries like AiG shouldn't sell resources at church meetings because of the so-called "money-changers" argument is a false one built on an incorrect understanding of what is outlined in God's Word.

Also, the physical church building today is not a temple. A church building is a gathering place for Christians who themselves have become "the temple." Sadly, AiG is often restricted or denied the opportunity to equip Christians at Sunday church gatherings, which are optimal times to reach the largest number of people (including young people). Meanwhile, each day of the week, the secular world is marketing an anti-God philosophy to church attendees through television, the internet, secular textbooks, advertising avenues, etc. Oh, how we need to be diligent in getting life-changing resources into the hands of God's people so they can defend the Christian faith and help overcome the doubt that leads to unbelief (which is resulting in a catastrophic generational loss from the Church)!

Let's be like the Bereans in Acts 17 and judge what we think we believe against what Scripture clearly teaches.

Now these Jews were more noble than those in Thessalonica; they received the word with all eagerness, examining the Scriptures daily to see if these things were so (Acts 17:11).

> **Let's get rid of incorrect views of the Church that are hindering getting the much-needed answers to an increasingly skeptical generation.**

MAY 22
Acts 17:11

Fallacies of the Modern Church: Part 2

Now these Jews were more noble than those in Thessalonica; they received the word with all eagerness, examining the Scriptures daily to see if these things were so (Acts 17:11).

Many times, when I've gone to speak, I've heard people and even pastors refer to the church as the temple. I've heard them use words like temple, altar, and Sabbath as they talk to the congregation in the context of their church. We do have to be careful how we use such terms so people do not misunderstand. I've also found that many non-Christians who don't understand Christianity often think that Christians should be obeying all the Old Testament laws. Sometimes, I think the Church has used terminology that has given them that impression. So let's consider some of this terminology.

Are our church buildings the same as the temple of the old covenant?

The first article of this three-part series focused on the truth about the money-changers in the temple as recorded in John 2. We will now look more closely at the distinctions between the temple and the church buildings we use today. The final entry in this three-part series will examine the functions of these places as they relate to worship. Each of these subjects affect the way we think about providing edifying Christian resources in our church buildings and gatherings there.

Since the Cross, the definition of the word temple for the church has drastically changed. When Jesus cried, "It is finished" (John 19:30), the entire work of the substitutionary atonement for sin had been completed. Jesus had taken the full brunt of the wrath of God for our sin upon Himself. He had always planned to do this, and every aspect and activity of the tabernacle and temple pointed to this event.

God's presence in the midst of His people had changed. No longer did the temple signify the dwelling place of God with His people. Our access to God had radically changed, and the temple was no longer necessary for sacrifice.

As a result of Christ's work on the Cross, "The curtain of the temple was torn in two, from top to bottom" (Mark 15:38), which signified that our access to the Father had been directly given through the Son. The place of ongoing sacrifice of bulls and lambs had been replaced by the once-and-for-all sacrifice of the Lamb of God, Jesus.

The Book of Hebrews provides great confirmation that the temple was a shadow or copy of the heavenly things. In other words, the temple foreshadowed the true substance that we have in Jesus Christ. Through His work on the Cross, Jesus fulfilled and thus replaced the sacrificial system—the temple system of worship and the very dwelling place of God.

But when Christ appeared as a high priest of the good things that have come, then through the greater and more perfect tent (not made with hands, that is, not of this creation) he entered once for all into the holy places, not by means of the blood of goats and calves but by means of his own blood, thus securing an eternal redemption. For if the blood of goats and bulls, and the sprinkling of defiled persons with the ashes of a heifer, sanctify for the purification of the flesh, how much more will the blood of Christ, who through the eternal Spirit offered himself without blemish to God, purify our conscience from dead works to serve the living God (Hebrews 9:11–14).

CHURCH — MAY 22

Jesus was now once and for all our sacrifice and our access to the Father. The temple is now fulfilled and out of commission for every believer in Christ. Not only this, the Apostle Paul has given wonderful news for every Christian. *Do you not know that you are God's temple and that God's Spirit dwells in you?* (1 Corinthians 3:16).

Every Christian is the dwelling place of the Spirit of God. Our life is His, and He dwells within us. This has intimidating consequences when we understand its significance. Look at what Paul tells us further about this:

What agreement has the temple of God with idols? For we are the temple of the living God; as God said, "I will make my dwelling among them and walk among them, and I will be their God, and they shall be my people" (2 Corinthians 6:16).

If Jesus has fulfilled the temple function and if the living God now dwells within us and if the curtain has been torn and there is no more sacrifice required, then to treat our church buildings today as sacred places like the Jewish temple is to effectively reject the work of the Cross and flirt with idolatry.

It is amazing to us that many people we meet in churches (and of different denominations), by the very terminology they use and by their actions, exhibit that they really view the church building as a temple! Sadly, this has consequences concerning decisions that can greatly impinge on equipping the saints—for example (and as mentioned in part one), by restricting access to powerful apologetics resources. I've often had people, particularly from the older generation, tell me I shouldn't be selling books on Sunday. And these are books that help equip people and give answers to the attacks on God's Word. I just can't understand why they would rather have the young people in their church not have access to these powerful materials and yet say nothing about the fact that most of them go to secular schools where they are indoctrinated in naturalistic evolutionary humanism (atheism)!

> **It is so important that God's people have the right view of the church building to ensure they understand who Christ is and what He has done – and to ensure right decisions are being made to enable God's people to be equipped to defend the faith as is so sorely needed.**

MAY 23
Acts 17:11

Fallacies of the Modern Church: Part 3

Now these Jews were more noble than those in Thessalonica; they received the word with all eagerness, examining the Scriptures daily to see if these things were so (Acts 17:11).

We were created in the image of God as perfect worshippers of our Creator. Unfortunately, in the ultimate act of self-worship (man wanting to be his own god reflecting Genesis 3:5), we sinned, and ever since, mankind has had a major worship problem. In setting apart a people of His own, God gave the Jews the ability to worship Him through keeping His law and sacrificing in the temple. All of this pointed to the One who would fulfill the law and be the once-and-for-all sacrifice. While the Jews had a shadow of things to come, we see clearly that all worship is now in and through Jesus Christ. In Him, we now have the substance of what the temple once only foreshadowed. God, in the midst of His people in the temple, is now in the midst of His people in our hearts and lives.

When the woman at the well was talking to Jesus about the proper place to worship, Jesus said the following to her: *But the hour is coming, and is now here, when the true worshipers will worship the Father in spirit and truth, for the Father is seeking such people to worship him. God is spirit, and those who worship him must worship in spirit and truth* (John 4:23–24).

Jesus has also made it clear that the only way to the Father is through the Son. For a Christian to worship in spirit and truth is to worship in and through Jesus alone. In reality, worship is engaging with our God on His terms alone, and the Father's terms require that the Son is our only way. The temple is out of commission.

The Church is made up of believers in Jesus Christ—not bricks and mortar. Christ is the better, greater tabernacle. We come together to be edified and encouraged to serve Him more effectively. Indeed, the primary purpose of the church gathering is to be equipped and edified. This is brought out in 1 Corinthians 12–14, where the Apostle Paul instructs believers to have orderly gatherings whose purpose is the edification and the building up of the saints.

If we truly understood the purpose for the gathering of the saints, as borne out in 1 Corinthians 12:7, 25; 14:4–5, 12, 17, 26, 31, then we might change the name of our gatherings from worship services to "edification services." Here worshippers come together corporately and are built up through songs of praise, ordinances, and fellowship around the teaching of the Word of God. There is certainly no denying that there is something truly special about the gathering of the saints.

The New Testament does not tell Christians that we must come to a certain place on a certain day to worship God as the Jews did under the old covenant. We do not need to go to a building to worship. Instead, we gather as the Church because we are already worshippers through Christ. Neither do we come together to sacrifice as the Jews did in the Old Testament, but we come because of the once-and-for-all sacrifice of Christ. We do not come to the house of God; we are the house of God. We do not seek God through a priest; we are a royal priesthood (1 Peter 2:9).

So why do so many churches use unhelpful terms? Many churches call their auditorium a sanctuary and treat it as if it were a holy place. We fail to realize that when the people leave the building, it is just another

CHURCH MAY 23

empty room. The true sanctuary is the dwelling place of our Lord in the hearts and lives of His children—the true Church. We need to understand that our church gatherings are to be times when we are equipped for spiritual battle and trained to fulfill the Great Commission given to us by our Lord and Savior (Matthew 28:18–20).

So, let us ask the final question in this series: When Answers in Genesis comes to a church with resources to help people answer the critics of the gospel, does this have anything to do with an attempt to commercialize worship? No, not in the slightest. We are here to support the church gathering in its purpose to edify and strengthen worshippers and to reach out to those who may become worshippers. We come to give them even greater confidence in God's Word and pray that non-Christians will receive God's free gift of salvation.

Church buildings are not the same as the temple. The curtain has been torn in two, and Christ is now the free and only access to worshipping our Creator God.

In a time when our churches are losing our children at an alarming rate and in a culture that is becoming less Christian every day, we are grateful that the Lord has provided us with such incredible answers from His Word on how to live in an anti-God culture. The world is penetrating the minds of Christians, especially younger believers, with humanist dogma through various media. We face a barrage of humanist propaganda that markets secular ideology through television, schools, movies, and many more avenues.

We are so thankful to be in a ministry that defends the gospel of Jesus Christ and supports the church with God-glorifying resources that proclaim the foundational truths of the Bible. The Church needs to be thoroughly equipped for the battle in our increasingly secular culture and to lead people to Christ.

Sadly, AiG is often denied the opportunity to equip congregations because of a false view of the Church and temple. Sunday morning services are sometimes the only opportunity the Church has to reach the majority of its people. The culture's influence on the flock compared to the church's influence is terribly disproportionate in most Christian families.

So come on, Church! Let's not just welcome the provision of Bible-defending, equipping resources, but let's actually see pastors encouraging their people to get the resources that will help them defend the faith against the daily indoctrination of the secular onslaught. (And we praise the Lord for the church leaders who have already been doing this.)

The message we really should get from John 2 about the money-changers is to ask ourselves whether we view our faith with a heart to worship our Savior and Creator through His great sacrifice or whether we see our faith through a consumer's mindset and as a form of transaction to get us to heaven.

> If Christ were to walk into our hearts, would He be at home, or would He pull out a whip and turn our tables?

MAY 24
Hebrews 5:12-14

No More "Fluff and Stuff"

For though by this time you ought to be teachers, you need someone to teach you again the basic principles of the oracles of God. You need milk, not solid food, for everyone who lives on milk is unskilled in the word of righteousness, since he is a child. But solid food is for the mature, for those who have their powers of discernment trained by constant practice to distinguish good from evil (Hebrews 5:12–14).

Biblical illiteracy seems to be the norm these days in most of our churches. We live in a time when it seems the basic ABCs of Christianity are not being taught in America as they once were. When we think about learning our ABCs, the alphabet and the basics of language come to mind—all vital for communication. I suggest most people in our churches don't know how to defend their faith and don't have a true biblical worldview. This is certainly what a lot of the latest research confirms in regard to people who call themselves Christians.

Over the years, I've met many people who teach Sunday school (or lead a youth or adult Bible study) who have told me that so much of their material now seems watered down. In fact, as someone said to me, "I'm tired of the fluff and stuff." A lot of it is very shallow and doesn't teach apologetics or what it means to have a true biblical worldview.

Indeed, much of the currently available curricula being used for Sunday schools, youth outreaches, adult Bible studies, and so on, waters down the basic truths of the Bible. And much of it concentrates on spiritual aspects, relationship building, and devotional thoughts. (Of course, some of that is needed, but it's in much heavier doses today.) What is missing is teaching the Bible as a book of history, and equipping people with answers to the attacks on God's Word today. Also missing is teaching Genesis 1–11 as literal history that is the foundation for all doctrine, the gospel, our biblical worldview, and in fact, for everything.

The 2009 "Beemer Study" (from America's Research Group) that we commissioned helped explain why two-thirds of young people were leaving the Church by college age. (The study became the basis of our best-selling book *Already Gone*.) The late Britt Beemer discovered that young people were beginning to doubt the truth of the Bible at a much younger age than we all believed.

The research concluded that even Bible-believing churches were not teaching their children and adults how to use apologetics to defend the faith so that they wouldn't be intimidated by the attacks of the world against Christianity.

Actually, when you think about it, students are taught a form of apologetics in the public (secular—anti-God) school system. Even though there is a minority of Christians serving as "missionaries" in this system, by and large, students are being taught an apologetic to defend naturalism/atheism. For instance, they are being told:

- There never was a global Flood.
- The evidence is against creation.
- The universe formed through a big bang and is billions of years old.
- Fossils show how people evolved from apelike creatures.
- And much more!

At the same time, most churches and Christian homes have tended to treat the Bible as a book of stories; in today's vernacular, the word story is often taken to mean a fairy tale.

As a result, recent generations have been doubting the Bible's history. This doubt leads to unbelief. No wonder we have been experiencing such a massive exodus of youth from our churches. Generation Z is considered to be the first truly post-Christian generation.

In response to the alarming exodus, many church leaders have tried to make curricula more entertaining. But all it does is water down the content.

It's my contention (based on the response to AiG's well-received summer VBS programs) that children don't want "fluff and stuff." In addition, our other "meaty" materials for teens and adults have shown the same thing. People want answers—real answers—so they will know they can trust the Word of God in its recorded history and thus trust the Bible in what it says about the gospel.

We've discovered that whatever the age, people need to be taught the basics of Christianity in a way that enables them to not only understand what they believe and why, but how they can logically defend the Christian faith in this increasingly hostile secularized world.

In response, AiG committed to stepping out in faith to produce a basic but powerful "ABC" approach to deal with this problem. As a result, we produced our Answers Bible Curriculum—a chronological approach to teaching Genesis to Revelation with apologetics and teaching doctrine and biblical worldview. As far as we can determine, there is nothing truly like this curriculum anywhere in the world. It is totally integrated from kindergarten through adult. It emphasizes:

A: Apologetics. In a practical way, all ages are equipped to answer the skeptical questions of this age, which are used in an attempt to get people to doubt the authority of God's Word (leading to unbelief).

B: Biblical authority. All ages are taught chronologically through the Bible (with continual references to the New Testament) as they are taught how to build a Christian worldview based on Scripture. Yes, real meat! Our field tests of this curriculum have already shown that even young children love the "meaty" content!

C: Christ-centered. At every age level, people are taught to focus on Christ and His gospel message. Even when we study Bible characters, we exalt God and His attributes instead of teaching mere moralism. Pastors tell us it is revolutionizing their churches.

But in your hearts honor Christ the Lord as holy, always being prepared to make a defense to anyone who asks you for a reason for the hope that is in you; yet do it with gentleness and respect (1 Peter 3:15).

> I urge you to teach the ABCs of our Christian faith in your home, Sunday school, youth group, Bible study, homeschool, and Christian school.

MAY 25

Hebrews 11:6

Responsible Faith

As humans, we are finite, fallible beings. God is infinite and sovereign over all things. Yet, all the way through Scripture I see man's responsibility and God's sovereignty working hand in hand. I have to recognize that I cannot explain how these two work together; I just know I'm to be obedient and do what God has told me to do (for example, preach the gospel), but it's God who saves people. God instructs us to give reasons for what we believe, and He somehow uses what we say as we defend the Christian faith in opening the hearts of people to the truth of His Word. At the same time, it is only God's Word that convicts and saves.

So faith comes from hearing, and hearing through the word of Christ (Romans 10:17).

For the word of God is living and active, sharper than any two-edged sword, piercing to the division of soul and of spirit, of joints and of marrow, and discerning the thoughts and intentions of the heart (Hebrews 4:12).

In pioneering the AiG ministry from its humble beginnings in our house in Australia to where it is today, I've always been mindful of the fact that all through Scripture there's a balance between man's responsibility and God's sovereignty.

Before I resigned from teaching to go full-time into the beginning of this apologetics ministry, I wrote to friends and asked if they would commit to supporting us financially and prayerfully. Back then, we had no guarantees. But enough people said they would support us that we believed the Lord was leading me to resign and go full-time into building and running the ministry. After we launched, I began sending regular letters to inform our supporters what we were accomplishing as God was blessing and what our needs were.

We had our struggles and lean times, from which we learned many lessons, but we've never looked back! And just see where the ministry is today! I stand in awe of how He has provided—and how He matured us through many battles and other struggles (at times very difficult ones). We did our best to do all we could to build the ministry and let people know our needs but trusting by faith God would supply those needs.

While building the Creation Museum in the early 2000s and subsequently the Ark Encounter, we recognized that not only did we have to raise the money to build these facilities, but we had to be realistic (responsible) about the daily costs of running them. Most people probably don't understand how much it costs to run these attractions each day, including maintenance and repair, and the expenses to refurbish technology and exhibits over time. It's enormous!

We are living in a time when many children are being killed through abortion. Yet there are many families God has blessed with children to be raised for the Lord, and we want to encourage them. So, yes, we do all we can to help with genuine needs. But at the same time, those who can afford to pay need to pay the admission prices which are very reasonable anyway so the facilities can exist. And we do give children 10 and under free admission to our two attractions as part of our helping to impact the coming generations. We have a deep responsibility as we carry out the mission God has called us to.

The Creation Museum vision was birthed out of my burden as a high school science teacher to reach youth with the truth of God's Word, instead of *the lie* of evolution they were being taught. It also came out of a spiritual legacy my father and mother passed on to me. As I grew up and watched my parents, I saw the

RESOURCES

burden the Lord laid on them to reach children with the gospel. I had a burden to build a Creation Museum, but I knew only God could make it happen.

I saw my parents do all they could to reach people with the gospel (responsibility), at the same time trusting God to save them through their mission outreaches. My parents did all they could to teach their children God's Word, trusting they would receive the free gift of salvation. That's why in the Creation Museum near Cincinnati, we feature an exhibit of my late father's Bible, a wooden Noah's ark he built for me many years ago, and a photo of my father and mother. This small but powerful display has challenged many guests as to what kind of legacy they're leaving their children—and the culture. Are they doing all they can to teach their children the truth (responsibility) and trusting God to save them (sovereignty).

One can't just sit back and say, "God will save people." It's true, God doesn't need any of us, but He uses us and expects us to be responsible and obey His instructions on how to reach people with the truth of God's Word.

On opening day at the Ark Encounter in 2016, the AiG board and founders put 12 stones in place (based on the 12 stones of Joshua's day recorded in Joshua 4). The stones were a reminder that the truth of God's Word and the gospel needs to be proclaimed to our children and to all the world (that's our responsibility). At the Ark's grand opening, I stated that the Ark was our "12 stones"—to remind the world of vital biblical truths. We trust God's sovereignty to change hearts through all the exhibits.

After we published the book *Already Gone* in 2009, which detailed why there is such a huge exodus of the younger generations from the Church, I was so burdened that we produced an evangelistic apologetics Sunday school program. This curriculum was designed to help churches reach the coming generations and give them a solid foundation in God's Word. Already, around 10,000 churches are using this kindergarten through adult Answers Bible Curriculum! This is all part of our responsibility to reach people with the truth. At the same time, we trust God in His sovereignty to use the curriculum to equip, convict, and save people.

Because I never had apologetics resources when I was growing up (though, praise the Lord, I had a father and mother who taught me never to knowingly compromise God's Word and to be able to answer skeptics), I've always had a burden to produce as many resources as possible for all ages. That's another big part of what Answers in Genesis does.

All this to say, my burden to reach the younger generations is stronger than ever. It saddens me to see how the truth of God's Word is being censored from so many kids today. And it distresses me to watch so much rampant compromise with evolutionary beliefs in many of our churches and Christian institutions.

Of course, building two attractions with the quality of Disney was, for me, a way to reach kids, teens, and adults with the truths they needed to hear. And it has involved big steps of faith, doing all we can to make them a reality, but trusting God to supply our needs through His people as we let them know the needs for these projects. There it is again, a burden to do something (responsibility) and trusting God to lead and provide the needs (sovereignty).

And without faith it is impossible to please him, for whoever would draw near to God must believe that he exists and that he rewards those who seek him (Hebrews 11:6).

We can never understand how God makes them work together, but that is the way He works.

MAY 26

Genesis 3:1

Has God Said?

Now the serpent was more crafty than any other beast of the field that the L<small>ORD</small> God had made. He said to the woman, "Did God actually say, 'You shall not eat of any tree in the garden'?" (Genesis 3:1).

As we look around at the shambles of Western civilization, a question seems to be on everyone's mind: What happened? Many people—Christian and non-Christian—are asking the question, "What happened?" Why do they ask this question? In the USA, in the 1700s, 70–80% of the population attended church. But by 2010, 56% of what's called the greatest generation (those born before 1928) attended church. Now, only about 18% of millennials do.[46] In 2021, Generation Z church attendance was down to less than 9%.

In Britain, total church attendance in 2015 was down to 5% of the population.[47] The percentage of millennials and post-millennials that attend church is probably much less, considering that the younger generations are much more atheistic.

In Australia, total church attendance in 2011 was only 6%.[48] We have seen the same trends across Europe, New Zealand, Canada—across the whole Western world.

Also, we can observe the changing worldview in these cultures from a more Christianized one (permeated with the Judeo-Christian ethic based on the Bible) in the past to a very secularized/atheistic worldview of moral relativism in our present day. For instance, in America, 78% of the greatest generation believed same-sex relations were always wrong. However, in the millennial generation, this belief was down to 43%, and it seems Generation Z is much less than that.

We see similar statistics regarding same-sex relationships in Britain. And notably, in 1983, about 60% of those in Britain who claimed they had "no religion" (but they do have a religion—the religion of atheism/agnosticism) believed same-sex relationships were always or nearly always wrong. But by 2013, that figure was down to about 10%.[49] Similar changes have been observed in people's attitude toward abortion, euthanasia, and many other issues. So many people ask the question, "What happened?"

The answer is simple but is missed even by many in the Church. I assert these major reasons for this change:

- So much of the Church (and its leadership) has compromised God's Word in Genesis, thus undermining the authority of the Word of God and undermining a Christian worldview.
- Most church leaders and Christian academics have not taught generations how to develop a truly Christian worldview beginning with the foundation of Genesis and the rest of God's Word.
- The teaching of apologetics to combat the secular attacks of our day has been largely neglected in churches. After all, Genesis 1–11 is the foundation for everything!

In churches, 80–85% of the kids have been indoctrinated by the secular education system to doubt and not believe the Word of God beginning in Genesis—but to believe the pagan religion of evolution as fact. Public schools have become churches of atheism, imposing the atheistic worldview of moral relativism on generations of kids. What happened in our Western world is really nothing new. It's the raging spiritual battle that began 6,000 years ago in a garden—a battle between two religions.

APOLOGETICS MAY 26

God instructed Adam to obey His Word: *And the L*ORD *God commanded the man, saying, "You may surely eat of every tree of the garden, but of the tree of the knowledge of good and evil you shall not eat, for in the day that you eat of it you shall surely die"* (Genesis 2:16–17).

The devil successfully tempted Eve—and Adam followed her—to disobey God's Word and be their own gods (to build their thinking on man's word): *Now the serpent was more crafty than any other beast of the field that the L*ORD *God had made. He said to the woman, "Did God actually say, 'You shall not eat of any tree in the garden'?" . . . But the serpent said to the woman, "You will not surely die. For God knows that when you eat of it your eyes will be opened, and you will be like God, knowing good and evil"* (Genesis 3:1–5).

Thus, the battle between God's Word and man's word ensued! This battle is seen all the way through Scripture (light/darkness, good/evil, for/against Christ, build house on rock/sand).

Much of the Western world's worldview came out of the Bible. Therefore, most people believed that marriage was between one man and one woman, homosexual behavior was wrong, and there were only two genders of humans: male and female.

So what happened? The foundation for the dominant worldview of the West was changed.

Generations of kids, now particularly reflected in the younger generations (e.g., millennials and Generation Z), have been indoctrinated against the Bible to believe that man's fallible word is the foundation for their thinking. So if there's no absolute authority, then ultimately anything goes! The resulting moral relativism and the growing intolerance of Christianity is a sad reflection of this foundational change. We are seeing the symptoms of this foundational change in the cultural change from a predominant Judeo-Christian worldview to one permeated by moral relativism.

So to answer the question, "What happened?" the foundation for the dominant worldview of the West was changed, and as a result, the worldview has changed from a primarily Christianized worldview to a secular worldview!

Can the culture ever reverse direction and change back? Of course, that's always a possibility, but only through the power of God's Word and the gospel to change lives so people will be committed to building their thinking on the Word of God. God's Word and the saving gospel are the ultimate solutions to this foundational change.

And regardless of whether the culture could reverse direction, we need to be about the business of the King until He returns! God has entrusted resources to each of us, whether material resources and/or talents (writing, speaking, music, etc.). *Engage in business until I come* (Luke 19:13).

> **We need to do our best to use what God has entrusted us with to reach as many people as we can with the truth of God's Word and the gospel.**

MAY 27
Romans 8:28

God Uses Persecution

As you ponder this verse, take note it doesn't say "all things are good," but "all things work together for good."

We certainly have seen our share of "hate mail" and other forms of opposition over the construction of the Creation Museum and Ark Encounter. But at the same time, we also see how God used these battles to work together for good in so many ways. Take this example: The Creation Museum ended up on a far better piece of property than the first one that the atheist groups successfully lobbied against, as they helped to stop the land's rezoning approval. The opposition drew free publicity worldwide for the Creation Museum. The support we received from our ministry friends, who rallied to our side, led to increased donations and allowed the Creation Museum to be much bigger and more high-tech than we originally planned. Although it was stressful to go through it all, things worked out in ways we would never have imagined but praise the Lord for.

Now when we made the announcement about the construction of a second attraction, the life-size Ark, we knew we would receive opposition as we did for the Creation Museum. And that's exactly what happened! AiG has now seen hundreds of worldwide major media reports on the Ark Encounter project, and I wanted to give you one example of the lengths some people will go to attack Answers in Genesis and our attractions because of their hatred of God and His Word. In fact, we can almost sense that these people are gnashing their teeth and shaking their fists at God—doing whatever they can to try to stop such evangelistic outreaches.

Of course, regardless of what the opponents do, God is in control. He will only allow them to do what He permits! We must remember this in regard to our personal lives. One particular man at the time seemed to have made his life's mission to do whatever he could to denigrate the name of Answers in Genesis and the Creation Museum in an attempt to undermine the announcement about the Ark Encounter attraction. He misquoted, misrepresented, told untruths, and did whatever he could to try to stop the building of the Ark Encounter outreach. He also tried to influence state authorities against it.

I can't reproduce much of what he had written. You see, his blogs often contained vile language. At the same time, I want to give you the specifics of one particular action he concocted. It was an attempt to set us up, hoping that his actions would result in a landslide of opposition to the Ark project. This man heard about our Creation Museum's "Date Night" as we called it back then, a romantic evening for couples around Valentine's Day. It was a celebration of Christian marriage. The man wrote on his website that he wanted to raise money to send the most "flamboyantly gay" couple to the dinner as part of his "patriotic" duty. It was an obvious attempt to disrupt this event.

His underlying motive? He wanted to send a message to the Kentucky authorities that Answers in Genesis (and he assumed the Ark Encounter) would not allow gays inside the Creation Museum. By the way, AiG certainly stands on the biblical view of marriage—one man for one woman. We are not "anti-gay" in the sense of being against gay people personally. We welcome everyone to come to the Creation Museum (and now to the Ark Encounter too) and be influenced/impacted by the messages proclaimed through the exhibits. We certainly do not agree with gay "marriage" and consider such to be a sin against God's clear teaching on marriage in Genesis.

RESOURCES MAY 27

On the evening of "Date Night," two men and a woman arrived at the Creation Museum for the event. One of the men turned out to be a reporter for a pro-gay alternative weekly newspaper from Louisville (90 minutes from the museum). The other man said he was waiting for his male friend to arrive—the name he gave was of the man who devised the scheme to set up the Creation Museum with a manufactured stunt to disrupt the evening. This man and his male "date," who came later, were turned away from the event since they had declared their premeditated intent to act "flamboyantly gay" and provoke an incident.

The two men (both of whom later acknowledged they were not even gay) then claimed to the media that the Creation Museum had turned a gay couple away and gave other false reports of what happened at the museum dinner. Thankfully, some reporters recognized it all as a hoax (including one gay writer), but some reporters uncritically accepted what the plotters reported and printed their false accusations. The reporter from the alternative newspaper who attended the event also wrote error-filled articles against us. There was much more to the attempted "party-crashing," of course—but as you can see, this was a deliberate attempt to try to discredit Answers in Genesis, the Creation Museum, and particularly the Ark Encounter. In fact, the main perpetrator of this hoax told outright lies in his account of what happened, and then later on his website wrote: "The intellectual child abusers at AiG admit to AP that they discriminate against gays, yet call me 'intolerant.' Ken Ham and the good folks at Answers in Genesis are in full out damage control mode. Getting caught red-handed discriminating against what they perceived to be a gay couple, they now realize that their chance to get a $40 million welfare handout from the government to build a giant Dineysore Boat is now seriously in jeopardy." And then his real motive becomes obvious: "I think you can pretty much put the nail in the coffin on their $40 million government welfare handout to build a giant boat and tell kids that a 600-year old man herded T-Rexes and Sauropods onto it a few thousand years ago."

By the way, the "handout" he referred to is the sales tax rebate the Ark Encounter project applied for (and was subsequently granted) as a tourism incentive under the Tourism Development Act of Kentucky. And none of the sales tax rebates funded the construction of the Ark Encounter because any rebate would occur only after the Ark Encounter opened and generated sales tax for the state. The sales tax rebate comes from new money to be generated at the Ark Encounter attraction itself.

This man was spreading misinformation all over the Internet in hopes that he could stop the Ark Encounter project! Sadly, many people believed him and still do. These atheists are outraged that something so Christian could have such a public impact. They want to stop it at all costs. They angrily work to "suppress the truth" (Romans 1:18). They shake their fists at God! We need to pray for such people—and pray that what they were doing to try to stop the Ark Encounter will be used for good. We know the Lord can soften the hardest of hearts. Just consider this testimony we received: "Because of [God using] AiG, I am now a Christian. I was formerly a hardened evolutionist who HATED the Creation Museum when I first saw it on the news on its opening day [May 2007]. However, after reading many of the articles on the AiG website two and a half years ago, I started questioning my faith in evolution and soon gave my heart to Jesus Christ, and am now a fervent young-earth creationist." —G.H. (Facebook comment) Praise God for the many testimonies that we receive like this one on a regular basis!

> "And we know that for those who love God all things work together for good, for those who are called according to his purpose" (Romans 8:28).

MAY 28
Psalm 119:16

What the Church Needs

At a church conference, a pastor was asked publicly, "What would you do if you were the 'Pope' of the entire evangelical church?" This pastor replied: "I would ask preachers, pastors, and student pastors in their communication to get the spotlight off the Bible and back on the Resurrection. Let's get people's attention back on Jesus as soon as possible, that the issue for us is always who is Jesus, [and] did He rise from the dead? And that we would leverage the authority we have in the Resurrection as opposed to Scripture, not because I don't believe Scripture's inspired in terms of reaching this culture."

Now what this pastor wanted to see happen in our churches is very different from what I have been seeking in all my years of creation-apologetics ministry. My response to this question would be as follows: God's Word warns us in 2 Corinthians 11:3 that the devil is going to use the same attack as he did on Eve to get people not to believe the things of God. When we go to Genesis 3:1, we find this first attack was on the authority of the Word of God.

I call it "the Genesis 3 attack" of our day. The devil said to Eve, "Did God really say?" This first attack (which was successful) was to get Adam and Eve to doubt him and then not believe the Word of God. We are warned by God's Word through the Apostle Paul that the devil will use this same attack on us and our children and friends. The devil is very clever. In a sense, he has been saying the following to the Church: "You can go on and teach your kids about Jesus and the Resurrection and about miracles like walking on water, feeding thousands, healing the blind and the lame, and raising the dead. You can teach them about the miracles of the Israelites crossing the Red Sea and Jordan River and of Jonah living in a fish for three days. Yes, teach these Bible stories. But I'm going to attack the integrity of the Word. While you may teach them the wonderful Bible stories, I'm going to work hard to get them not to believe the Book from which these accounts come. And once they don't believe the Book, they won't believe any of those accounts and their messages anyway. They are just stories, fairy tales, not real accounts. That's what I would tell them," the devil might say.

That's exactly what I believe has happened in the culture. Whether it's through the public education system, the media, or even through compromised teaching in churches, the devil has been able to convince generations of people that the written Word cannot be trusted—particularly beginning with the Book of Genesis. When I have asked audiences how many of them have heard questions and statements like the following, usually all the hands in the room go up:

- Who made God?
- Noah couldn't fit the animals on the ark, so it couldn't have really happened.
- Where did Cain get his wife?
- What about all the ape-men? And the "races"?

The questions and statements above relate to the fact that the historicity of Genesis has been undermined for many generations. This generation is facing even more Genesis 3 attacks.

By and large, government schools present evolution and millions of years as fact. Such teaching has resulted in many young people doubting (and ultimately not believing) God's Word. Sadly, most Christian families

THEOLOGY

and churches have not been teaching creation and general biblical apologetics (although I rejoice that increasing numbers of families are beginning to realize the importance of doing this). Because generations have not been taught to defend the Christian faith and thus don't understand they can trust the Word, they have also rejected the primary message of the Word: salvation through Jesus Christ. At Answers in Genesis, we recognize that the focus of Scripture from Genesis to Revelation is on our Savior, Jesus Christ. It's the most vital message in the universe for us to proclaim. Because of our sin, God's Son became the God-man to pay the penalty for our sin by dying on the Cross and being raised from the dead.

But think about it: Where do we get the message of salvation and the message of who Jesus is and His Resurrection? We find them in the written Word. How do we find out about our need for salvation? From the written Word. How do we find out what sin is and why we are sinners? From the written Word. I'm reminded of the account (note, I don't use the word story which today means fairy tale) of the rich man and Lazarus in Luke 16. They both died, and Lazarus went to be with Abraham while the rich man went to a place of torment. The rich man wanted to send a warning to his surviving brothers. He asked for Lazarus to return from the dead to tell them. He believed this would convince the brothers. We then read: *And he said, "Then I beg you, father, to send him to my father's house—for I have five brothers—so that he may warn them, lest they also come into this place of torment." But Abraham said, "They have Moses and the Prophets; let them hear them." And he said, "No, father Abraham, but if someone goes to them from the dead, they will repent." He said to him, "If they do not hear Moses and the Prophets, neither will they be convinced if someone should rise from the dead"* (Luke 16:27–31).

Many of our Christian leaders seem to be oblivious to what's been taught in the education system and media. They apparently aren't aware that, as a result, increasing numbers in this generation do not believe the writings of Moses (particularly Genesis). They don't understand why we are losing teens and young adults from the Church. As I've stated many times, this exodus of young people from our churches has already happened in England and much of the rest of the Western world. If you want to know where the United States is headed, look at England. One of the major contributing factors to this exodus is that much of the Church did not teach apologetics and ignored (or compromised with) what kids were being taught at school concerning evolution/millions of years. They just kept on teaching about the Resurrection alone; all the while the devil was indoctrinating young people not to believe the Book—from which the message of the Resurrection comes. I will never apologize for standing on the authority of the Word of God. My father not only instilled the Christian worldview in his children from the foundation of God's Word, but he would also research what the critics of the Bible were saying. And then he would give us the answers so we would not doubt and disbelieve God's Word.

Those of us who lead Answers in Genesis all have the same burden. We will teach the message of Jesus, the Resurrection, and the living Word, and, along with the Psalmist, we will proclaim:

I will delight in your statutes; I will not forget your word (Psalm 119:16).

I have stored up your word in my heart, that I might not sin against you (Psalm 119:11).

> **Ultimately, we all need to remember that "faith comes from hearing, and hearing through the word of Christ" (Romans 10:17).**

MAY 29
Psalm 139:13-16

Fearfully and Wonderfully Made

At the Creation Museum, our design team constructed what I believe is the most powerful pro-life exhibit in the world. We also have produced books and videos dealing with the topic of life in a mother's womb and the issue of abortion.

Increasingly, we live in a culture that loves death! Now, I don't mean that people are doing it formally and intentionally—of course, most would not see death as desirable. Rather, this love of death is the result of that which people love and brings much death to the culture—and, ultimately, the second death (eternal separation from God) for them (Revelation 21:8).

As I was thinking about this observation, I was reminded of Proverbs 8:35–36: *"For whoever finds me finds life and obtains favor from the LORD, but he who fails to find me injures himself; all who hate me love death."*

The majority of politicians in the United States and the Western world sadly gleefully shout their "love of death." How? By promising to bring death to mothers' wombs! It's a shocking state of affairs—downright evil! I believe abortion is the greatest holocaust ever! In our modern era, at least 1 billion children have been slaughtered by abortion worldwide, and over 60 million of those murders have occurred in the United States since the sacrifice of children to the "god of self" was legalized in 1973.

In fact, I call abortion "child sacrifice"—because that's what it really is! The sacrifice of a child to the god of self. To me, there's no such thing as a so-called "pro-choice movement"—it is a pro-murder movement.

And consider just a couple of the many passages where God addressed child sacrifice in His dealings with the Israelites, such as:

"When you present your gifts and offer up your children in fire, you defile yourselves" (Ezekiel 20:31).

"Declare to them their abominations . . . blood is on their hands. With their idols they have committed adultery, and they have even offered up to them for food the children whom they had borne to me. . . . For when they had slaughtered their children in sacrifice to their idols" (Ezekiel 23:36–39).

Really, what the Israelites did in sacrificing their children to idols is no different from what's happening with abortion today—only it's called "health care" or some other name to try to hide the fact that it's actually the ruthless killing of human beings made in the image of God in their mother's wombs.

Let me walk you through an outline of the message proclaimed at the Fearfully and Wonderfully Made exhibit at the Creation Museum. This is done through the use of 3D models, signage, videos, and other creative and innovative displays.

We start with The Wonder of Life. Here, the powerful words of the Psalmist are brought to life. *"For you formed my inward parts; you knitted me together in my mother's womb. I praise you, for I am fearfully and wonderfully made. Wonderful are your works; my soul knows it very well"* (Psalm 139:13–14).

Once this Scriptural foundation is established, our guests then learn what it means that every person is created in the image of God. It's what makes us distinct from animals. In fact, we are created to rule over them (and to live forever):

THEOLOGY — MAY 29

"Then God said, 'Let us make man in our image, after our likeness. And let them have dominion over the fish of the sea and over the birds of the heavens and over the livestock and over all the earth and over every creeping thing that creeps on the earth.' So God created man in his own image, in the image of God he created him; male and female he created them" (Genesis 1:26–27).

Because all people are made in the image of God, everyone is inherently valuable. And the unborn child (right from fertilization) is just as valuable as anyone else (Exodus 21:22). As a child in the womb, John the Baptist leaped in the presence of the unborn Jesus (Luke 1:41). Also, God has made each person unique! From the moment of fertilization, every person has a one-of-a-kind combination of DNA, half of which comes from the mom and the other half from the dad.

The exhibit features medical and scientific information about the sanctity of life. Some 3D-printed models, vivid images, and informative videos show the various stages of the baby growing in the womb. Signage explains certain key points of development, focusing on God's intricate design. We then further highlight the sanctity of human life. All human life (regardless of age, ethnicity, physical condition, etc.) is created in the image of God and therefore has inherent value. Thus, we must oppose abortion and euthanasia. The exhibit addresses the common objections raised by our culture against those who stand for a biblical pro-life view. Answers are given to the following questions to help visitors gain the proper perspective and learn how to address these issues when they face them. (As Christians take a stand for the unborn, equipping them is essential.)

- Is it inconsistent to be pro-life while being in favor of the death penalty?
- "It's my body," so shouldn't it be my choice?
- What do you do in cases of rape and incest?
- God wiped out the entire world with a global Flood, except Noah's family, and He ordered Joshua to destroy entire cities. How does that fit in a pro-life position?

Yes, we all need to know how to answer such questions. And we give those answers.

The exhibit concludes with a clear message of God's forgiveness. The gospel is clearly shared, with a special section directed toward those who have had an abortion. No doubt there will be people who will walk through this exhibit who need to hear the message of 1 John 1:9: *"If we confess our sins, he is faithful and just to forgive us our sins and to cleanse us from all unrighteousness."*

Let's declare with the psalmist:

For you formed my inward parts; you knitted me together in my mother's womb. I praise you, for I am fearfully and wonderfully made. Wonderful are your works; my soul knows it very well. My frame was not hidden from you, when I was being made in secret, intricately woven in the depths of the earth. Your eyes saw my unformed substance; in your book were written, every one of them, the days that were formed for me, when as yet there was none of them (Psalm 139:13–16).

All Christians need to stand against the abortion holocaust.

MAY 30
1 Timothy 6:20

False "Knowledge": Part 1

O Timothy, guard the deposit entrusted to you. Avoid the irreverent babble and contradictions of what is falsely called "knowledge" (1 Timothy 6:20).

It's so important to teach people how to think, not just what to think. I find atheistic evolutionists do not want any talk of "critiquing" or "thinking critically" about evolutionary ideas because evolution is their way of explaining life without God. They are committed to this religion based on naturalism which requires some sort of evolutionary belief to try to attempt to explain life without the supernatural.

Students are being brainwashed with evolutionary ideas in almost all public (government) schools and museums, and they are expected to accept it uncritically. I've made this point many times over the years. Think about this example of blatant brainwashing. In 2008, Louisiana passed a bill that would allow teachers in the public school system to "use supplemental materials . . . to help students critique and review scientific theories." Such critical thinking skills should be a part of an education process and are part of many state education standards.

Well, a then 19-year-old student at Rice University, Zack Kopplin, was on a mission to repeal that law. He was praised by the secular world for his ambition, as evidenced in an article about him.

Atheistic evolutionists do not want any talk of "critiquing" or "thinking critically" about evolutionary ideas, because it is their way of explaining life without God, which is why we call the evolutionary worldview a religion. Despite their claims to the contrary, atheists use evolutionary ideas as their religion to replace God. The evolutionary worldview is a foundation for their set of beliefs about life and how it arose, just as the biblical creation worldview, as described in Genesis, is our (Christian) set of beliefs about how life arose. Atheists blindly hold to evolution because of their rejection of Christ. Zack Kopplin seemingly declined to talk about his personal beliefs about God, but many atheists basically claimed him as one of their own.

Now, the news reports on Kopplin at the time could be critiqued in many aspects, but one of the key sections concerned Kopplin's statements on science: "Creationism is not science, and shouldn't be in a public school science class—it's that simple," he claimed. "Often though, creationists do not, or are unwilling, to recognize this." Science, he argues, "is observable, naturalistic, testable, falsifiable, and expandable—everything that creationism is not."[50]

First, Kopplin makes the assumption that science has to be "naturalistic." Now, there's no reason that science must be naturalistic—this is simply an assertion made by Kopplin and atheistic evolutionists! And really, that's the legacy of brainwashing. Atheists use the philosophy of naturalism to explain life without God. In the naturalistic view, the world and human beings are the result of chance processes. In reality, equating science with naturalism is an arbitrary definition applied to the word science by those who reject the supernatural. As a result of adopting these ideas, Kopplin has gone a step further, insisting that science must be naturalistic. And he wants this arbitrary definition of science imposed on the culture. Really, he wants his religion of naturalism imposed on education.

What's more, Kopplin—like almost all evolutionists—confused historical science with operational (observational) science. Operational science is indeed observable, testable, falsifiable, and so on—but none of those words describe evolutionary ideas! While biblical creation may not be provable through tests and observation, neither is molecules-to-man evolution (or astronomical evolution). In fact, the evidence that is available to us concerning our origins makes sense in the biblical creation-based worldview, not the evolutionary one. Of course, secularists mock creationists for separating out historical science and operational science. But they do that because the secularists want the word science to apply to both historical and operational science so that they can brainwash people (like Kopplin) into the false thinking that to believe in creation is to reject science.

Kopplin also claimed that biblical creation inhibits students' abilities to perform operational science: "Creationism confuses students about the nature of science," he says. "If students don't understand the scientific method, and are taught that creationism is science, they will not be prepared to do work in genuine fields, especially not the biological sciences. We are hurting the chances of our students having jobs in science, and making discoveries that will change the world."[51]

We're now seeing this sort of claim more and more from evolutionists. They, like Kopplin, believe that if a student is taught or believes in biblical creation, he will never be able to understand or achieve anything in the realm of science. And yet, here at Answers in Genesis and the Creation Museum, we have a number of researchers on staff with earned PhDs in their respective fields of science. The scientist who invented the MRI machine was an ardent biblical creationist! The person said to be the greatest scientist of all time, Isaac Newton, was an ardent creationist.

In reality, evolutionary ideas are not necessary for understanding and performing operational science. A biblical creationist can design and build a bus just as well as an evolutionist. Actually, a creationist may do it better if the evolutionist, acting consistently with his worldview, applies the principles of chance processes to the engineering of the bus!

Kopplin continued his thoughts, drawing more faulty connections between evolution and operational science: He worried that, if Louisiana (and any other state that had a similar law) insisted on teaching students creationism, students will not be the ones to discover the cure to AIDS or cancer. "We won't be the ones to repair our own damaged wetlands and protect ourselves from more hurricanes like Katrina," he says.

> **The idea that without a belief in evolution, research for the cure for cancer will cease is the kind of faulty logic that accepts naturalistic explanations for our origins.**

MAY 31
1 Timothy 6:20

False "Knowledge": Part 2

O Timothy, guard the deposit entrusted to you. Avoid the irreverent babble and contradictions of what is falsely called "knowledge" (1 Timothy 6:20).

More than that, Kopplin was really saying that he was against critical thinking in the science classroom. His desire was to prevent students from being exposed to any alternative to evolution. But if evolutionary ideas have so much scientific support, then why work so hard to exclude any other ideas about our origins? Allowing an examination of creationist and evolutionary ideas about the history of the universe would only make evolutionary ideas more popular if it was so obvious that they were confirmed by operational science. Actually, evolutionists want legislation to protect their teaching of evolution, because they know that if students were allowed to critically analyze the evidence, they would begin to question the molecules-to-man evolutionary belief.

An evolutionist blogger (who had also written for the *Chronicle of Higher Education*) named Adam Laats addressed this fallacy, as it has been made by Kopplin, TV host Bill Nye, and a number of other prominent evolutionists. Laats explained that even though he does not agree with the views of biblical creation, it cannot be denied that creationists are good scientists. He stated:

"For those of us who want to understand creationism, we need to get beyond this naive assumption that creationists don't know what science is, or that they are somehow hypocritical in their use of technology. … Many creationists have studied mainstream science. In many cases, such as that of leading creation science author Henry Morris, they have earned advanced technical degrees. And, beyond such stand-out leaders such as Morris, many rank-and-file creationists have extensive science educations. … Also, as creationists often remind themselves and their evolutionist foes, belief in evolution is not necessary for sophisticated engineering. Dobzhansky's claim that nothing in biology makes sense except in the light of evolution may be true, but that would not stop creationists from traveling to the moon, perfecting airplanes, or inventing the internet. In the end, I think it makes a big difference whether Americans with creationist beliefs have 'forgotten what science is' or if they have a distinctly different definition of science. Building an anti-creationist argument on the foundation that creationism disables technical education, as does Tanenbaum and other prominent pro-science voices such as Bill Nye [and I would add 'and Kopplin'], is both a false claim and poor strategy."[52]

In other words, even Laats can see that it is patently false to claim that a disbelief in evolutionary ideas somehow hinders the advancement of operational science.

Besides, the teaching of evolution is not being hindered in public school classrooms in America or in secular universities, because in those institutions, all aspects of evolution are basically presented as fact. That has been the case for decades.

In an attempt to explain why creation should not be taught, Kopplin stated, "These creationists," he argues, "would be horrified to see the Vedas being taught in science class." However, we at AiG do not advocate that government-mandated classes in creation be taught in schools. We do support students being taught to examine the claims of any idea, such as evolution, critically with all available views and evidence at their disposal. Students need to be taught the difference between operational and historical science. When they are taught how to think correctly about science, then they will be equipped to properly understand the origins issue and the evidence used.

Moreover, we would be no more horrified of the Vedas being taught in schools than we are of the anti-God religion of evolution. It is hypocritical to demand the religion of evolution be exclusively taught in the classroom while denying the presentation of other views. Secularists just do not want evolution to be critiqued! Are they afraid people will start realizing the truth of God's Word if we start thinking critically? Whether he realizes it or not, what Kopplin wanted was more brainwashing, plain and simple. And that's because he himself has been totally brainwashed by the system.

To that end, Kopplin also attacked the state government school voucher programs across the United States, claiming that because of vouchers, belief in biblical creation is being promulgated. In an article from MSNBC, Kopplin attacked private Christian schools that could possibly benefit from state vouchers who take field trips to the Creation Museum and use the Answers in Genesis website (which contains thousands of articles written by expert scientists and Bible scholars) in their science classes. By the way, I would urge Christian schools to be careful about the voucher program as they usually have strings attached that can result in the government forcing certain ideas on the school.

Kopplin concluded, "We must speak out to prevent funding these creationist schools with our public money." In multiple posts on Twitter and Facebook, Kopplin claimed that "our kids are funding the creation museum [sic] with public money." But his accusations are both unfair and unfounded. He provides no evidence that state money was ever used to fund field trips to the Creation Museum, outside of the fact that some schools accept vouchers. Furthermore, if the schools he listed are using voucher money for these field trips (and there was no evidence provided to substantiate that claim), that is entirely outside our control.

Kopplin may have been offended at the very thought of government money from school vouchers going to schools that teach biblical creation, but we find it equally offensive that our (as Christians and creationists) tax dollars go to fund the teaching of the religion of evolution.

Claiming to be wise, they became fools (Romans 1:22).

> **Why should Christians, who want their children educated in biblical creation, be forced to fund public schools and secular museums that teach evolution?**

JUNE 1
1 Timothy 6:20

False "Knowledge": Part 3

I left off yesterday asking this question: Why should Christians, who want their children educated in biblical creation, be forced to fund public schools and secular museums that teach evolution?

In essence, what Kopplin and many other evolutionists have done over the years is build all these "creationist straw men" and then proceeded to tear them down by making outlandish, false statements about creation. One news headline stated, "Meet Creationists' Nightmare—The Teen Who Is Combating Christians & Defending Evolution in Public Schools." One of our nightmares is that this teen, like many others, was spreading *the lie* of evolution and millions of years, which causes many to doubt the authority of Scripture. Kopplin had publicly misrepresented biblical creation, and we wanted to set the record straight. Would Kopplin, obviously an intelligent young man, ever consider a debate with one of our scientists to look at the question of whether God's Word, starting in Genesis, is true? However, we suspected he would use the same rhetoric used by most evolutionists when responding to such an invitation and claim creationists should not be debated because they are not "real scientists." We could probably even have drafted his refusal letter for him based on what other secularists had written when they refused to debate a creation scientist.

Biblical creation is actually consistent with operational science, not contradictory, and we want people to know that they can trust the Bible. The Bible is God's Word, the true history book of the universe, and God is the Creator of the universe. As the Creator, He made the rules and laws of the universe. Christianity is not a blind faith but a defensible one. Observational science confirms the Bible's history in geology, biology, astronomy, etc.

God's Word exhorts us to *honor Christ the Lord as holy, always being prepared to make a defense to anyone who asks you for a reason for the hope that is in you; yet do it with gentleness and respect* (1 Peter 3:15).

Sad news reports like those above are one of the reasons Answers in Genesis wants to help parents to be "Standing Our Ground, Rescuing Our Kids." It is high time we stand our ground and stop letting the secular world influence our children. Instead, we need to teach them about *the lies* of the anti-God religion of evolution and show them why we can trust the Bible on creation and, more importantly, on salvation.

Our Lord Jesus Christ *gave himself for our sins to deliver us from the present evil age, according to the will of our God and Father* (Galatians 1:4), so let us do our part to raise our children *in the discipline and instruction of the Lord* (Ephesians 6:4).

Kopplin had sadly been brought up to believe in evolution as fact, and we sincerely hope that he would come to believe the authority of Scripture and submit to God as the Author of creation just as God said in His Word — and also that Kopplin would come to know the Lord as Savior (if he has not done so already). The battle is being fought in the hearts and minds of each individual. Imagine if all Christians had the passion that Zack Kopplin had for evolution, but instead for the cause of Christ and the authority of Scripture. Each of us needs to be doing our part, just as the Apostle Paul described in Ephesians 4:15–16: *Rather, speaking the truth in love, we are to grow up in every way into him who is the head, into Christ, from whom the whole body, joined*

SCIENCE — JUNE 1

and held together by every joint with which it is equipped, when each part is working properly, makes the body grow so that it builds itself up in love.

Evolution and millions of years are in direct contradiction to God's Word. As Christians, we need to remain strong on the authority of Scripture, showing our children that God's Word is trustworthy and giving them answers to the many questions the world throws at them on a daily basis.

What a sad state of affairs to see a young man who desired so strongly that generations of children and teens would believe they are just animals who developed by natural processes. If we really are just animals, why is violence, murder, cheating, or lying wrong? Who determines what's "moral" and what's not? In an evolution-based culture, moral relativism would permeate — as we see happening more and more in America and other Western nations.

This example should be a warning to parents. Kopplin was a product of the secular education system — a system that is also indoctrinating generations of children from church homes.

Therefore, if anyone is in Christ, he is a new creation. The old has passed away; behold, the new has come (2 Corinthians 5:17).

We urge parents to recognize that their kids need to be rescued from this evil age.

JUNE 2
Psalm 139:13-16

Atheists Hate God

Why do many atheists rant and rage over what we as biblical creationists believe? In their worldview, when you die, you then won't even know you ever existed. And eventually, from their worldview, everything dies anyway, and that's the end! So why do they get so emotional about opposing Christians? Because, as God's Word makes clear in Romans 1 and 2, God has made it evident to all that He's the Creator and we all have a conscience. The bottom line is that it's a spiritual issue, and that's why they battle so hard because, deep down, they're actually convicted. They suppress the truth (Romans 1).

Let me give you an example of the lengths such people sometimes go to in the belief they are harassing us. Imagine my surprise when I saw an envelope addressed to me personally from Planned Parenthood!

Now, I've written a number of tweets and other social media posts accusing this organization of murdering millions of children. I've described it as being one of the biggest human-murdering machines in the world. And I've stated that abortion is no different from child sacrifice — in fact, it's sacrificing children to what I call the "god of self"!

I opened the letter and was quite perplexed. It was thanking me for inspiring support of Planned Parenthood. It was a letter thanking me for a donation. The letter from Planned Parenthood thanked me for inspiring support of their "care" of women.

As I read the letter, it soon became clear. Because of my very public statements about this evil organization (which is subsidized by U.S. tax dollars), someone who opposes me and the ministry of Answers in Genesis sent a donation to Planned Parenthood in "honor" of me! I guess this person thought it was a way to rile us up because of our anti-abortion stand based on God's Word. I was so disgusted to read the following hypocritical statements in this "thank you" letter:

"Thank you for inspiring them [the donor] to make a gift to help us in our commitment to reproductive justice." In reality, "reproductive justice" means murder and making sure there is no justice for the unborn! The letter continued:

"PPINK [Planned Parenthood of Indiana and Kentucky] … Our tag line, 'Care. No matter what,' is more than a slogan. It is a way of life for everyone involved with us, you included."

Now they do care passionately, and they are tireless — about eugenics and free sex.

> How many babies never saw their first birthday because of their so-called "reproductive justice"?

JUNE 3
Psalm 14:1

Atheist Propaganda: Part 1

Atheists are certainly experts at building a propaganda machine to malign Christianity! And because humans have a sin nature, that is not such a hard thing to do.

Christians need to understand that many secularists have put together a very effective propaganda machine as a part of their effort to impose their atheistic religion on the Western culture, intimidate Christians, and influence the government to limit freedom of religion (particularly in regard to Christianity).

To help counteract this aggressive effort, Christians — wherever they are in the West — need to be aware of the terms being used in the secularist campaign and what Christians need to be doing to help counter their campaign. Secularists know the adage that if you "throw enough mud at the wall, some of it will stick." If enough false information and misleading accusations are spread, people will begin to believe them. This has happened in a number of places:

1. The use of the word *science*

Here is how I discussed the word *science* during my debate with Bill Nye "the Science Guy" in February 2014: "Public school textbooks are using the same word *science* for observational and historical science. They arbitrarily define science as naturalism and outlaw the supernatural. They present molecules-to-man evolution as fact. They are imposing the religion of naturalism/atheism on generations of students."

I also stated the following during the debate: "The word *science* has been hijacked by secularists in teaching evolution to force the religion of naturalism on generations of kids…. The creation/evolution debate is really a conflict between two philosophical worldviews based on two different accounts of origins or historical science beliefs."

The word *science* is defined as "the state of knowing: knowledge as distinguished from ignorance or misunderstanding." Scientific pursuit needs to be broken into two parts: experimental (observable or operational) science and origins (historical) science. Both creation and evolution involve historical science (beliefs) and observational science (such as the study of genetics).

Experimental science that builds our modern technology is accomplished through the scientific method. And origins, or historical, science is the non-repeatable, non-observable science dealing with the past — which enters the realm of beliefs (really, religion).

In almost all of today's government-run educational systems, the religion of secular humanism — with its foundation of naturalistic evolution based on man's word/beliefs about the past (molecules-to-man evolution) — is guised in textbooks, lectures, and secular museums as so-called "science."

But the same word *science* is used for the experimental science that helps build technology. Because students aren't taught the difference between historical and observational science, they are brainwashed into thinking that molecules-to-man evolution is the same science as what has built technology — which it is not. It is what we call a "bait-and-switch fallacy" (a fallacy in logic). It's really a conflict between two philosophical worldviews that are based on two different accounts of origins, or historical scientific beliefs.

Because of this misuse of wording by the secularists, Christians need to be using the terms *observational science* and *historical science* over and over again! The secularists hate these terms, for they don't want people to know they actually have a religion (a worldview) that they are trying to impose on the masses. Their propaganda campaign, which confuses the meaning of the word *science* and attempts to indoctrinate people in evolutionary ideas, has been very successful. To help counter their efforts, we need to keep delineating between "observational" and "historical" science as much as we can — much to the consternation of the secularists!

2. The use of the word *religion*

The word *religion* has a variety of definitions. But one of the main definitions (as given by the Merriam-Webster Dictionary) is "an interest, a belief, or an activity that is very important to a person or group," and "a cause, principle or system of beliefs, held to with ardor and faith."[53] That's atheism.

Atheists have effectively propagandized the culture to indoctrinate people to think that if you believe in God as Christians do, then that is religion — however, if you don't believe in God and believe the universe and all life arose by natural processes, then supposedly that is not a religion! But as we constantly point out, atheism and humanism are religions — they are beliefs meant to explain life by natural processes, without supernatural involvement.

Atheists go ballistic when I say in many articles that they are trying to impose their religion of naturalism on the culture. But the point is, they are! Just because atheists refuse to acknowledge it does not mean they are not doing it. In fact, due to the atheist propaganda effort, it's one of the reasons we are losing Christian symbols (crosses, Nativity scenes, and so on) across the nation. Furthermore, in the U.S. and other Western countries, the government is imposing a religion on millions of children when they insist that schools only teach evolution in science classes and not biblical creation. Officials insist that evolution is deemed to be "science" and creation is "religion." Evolutionists have been indoctrinating people with a false view of the words *science* and *religion*.

"There is no fear of God before their eyes" (Romans 3:18).

When a secular group like the Freedom from Religion Foundation or Americans United for the Separation of Church and State lodge a lawsuit to get a cross removed from a public place or a statue with someone praying, and so on, then we need to make sure to be vocal about the fact that secularists have imposed their religion of atheism.

> I am encouraging Christians, as much as they can, to use the word religion to describe secularism/atheism.

JUNE 4
Psalm 14:1

Atheist Propaganda: Part 2

People deny that humanism and atheism should be considered religions, but even various U.S. courts have ruled and described in their decisions that humanism should be viewed as a religion. In Oregon, an inmate sued, with the assistance of the American Humanist Association, to have a humanist study group recognized as a religious study group along with Bible studies in the prison. Arguing based on the Establishment Clause of the First Amendment, the inmate won the right, as the district judge ordered secular humanism to be viewed as a religion. While humanism was previously viewed as a nontheistic religion in the rationale for the Supreme Court case of *Torcaso v. Watkins*, this is the first ruling that clearly establishes atheistic secular humanism as a religion whose practice should be protected under the First Amendment. Additionally, the U.S. Army has commissioned humanist chaplains to serve those soldiers who deny God's existence.

3. The word *intolerance*

Intolerance[54] is defined in the *Merriam-Webster Dictionary* this way: "Unwilling to grant equal freedom of expression, especially in religious matters; unwilling to grant or share social, political, or professional rights."

Secularists often accuse Christians, who, for example, take a stand on marriage being one man for one woman based on the Bible, as being intolerant. But, in fact, Christians are the ones who are tolerant of others. You see, Christians who stand on God's Word will authoritatively speak against gay "marriage," but they should not be intolerant of the people who disagree with them. I find that those who call Christians "intolerant" are really the ones who are intolerant! So when a fire chief in Atlanta, Georgia, is fired by a city council because his personal beliefs concerning marriage are based on the Bible, Christians need to be vocal about the city council's being intolerant!

4. The word *proselytize*

The Merriam-Webster Dictionary has this definition of *proselytize*[55]: "To try to persuade people to join a religion, cause, or group."

Actually, America's courts have not been able to give an accepted definition of this word. Some people claim that just telling someone about the gospel of Jesus Christ is supposedly trying to force one's belief on someone (their definition of *proselytizing*). Christians will certainly share their beliefs and the hope of forgiveness of sins with others, but they recognize that they cannot force someone to become a Christian. Only God can change people's hearts.

In reality, it's the secularists who are trying to force their religion on others as they intimidate people to accept the basic tenets of their religion, such as evolutionary naturalism. Many atheists don't necessarily use the word *proselytize*, but they claim that a Christian working in a government institution or a government-funded place cannot bring their Christianity into the workplace. Yet many professors at government-subsidized universities will openly proclaim their atheism (and even attack the Bible and the Christian faith) in their classes. But if a professor were to admit he was a Christian and make statements about his religious beliefs to the students, he would likely be disciplined or fired.

SCIENCE JUNE 4

More and more, we see intolerant secularists trying to limit the Christian influence by attempting to intimidate Christians not to bring their Christianity into their workplace. They ultimately want Christianity eliminated altogether from the public arena. Meanwhile, secularists are free to exercise their religion wherever they want to.

As secularists are successful in getting the governments to teach evolution as fact to millions of students in Western nations and will not allow biblical creation to be taught in science classes, we should be pointing out their deceptive use of terms. Indeed, the secularists continually misuse the word *science* as they indoctrinate people into a false worldview of naturalism so they can impose that religion on young people. At the same time, they exhibit their intolerance of Christianity and Christians in the culture. The secularists want to express their beliefs throughout society and want Christians to keep their beliefs inside their churches. In reality, governments are sanctioning the religion of naturalism and that it be imposed on millions of children and teens. Western nations have supported a growing intolerance of anything Christian and are limiting free speech and the freedom of religion in trying to squelch the free exercise of Christianity.

As we stand firmly and boldly on the truths of Jesus Christ as the Creator and Savior in our apologetic arguments, we must also use correct terms like *historical science, observational science, religion,* and *intolerance* when engaging the secularists in the ongoing war against Christianity in Western nations. It's why you will find Answers in Genesis using these terms in our articles, billboards, and other outreaches as we do our best to help undo the work of the atheists' propaganda campaigns and point people to the hope that we have in Jesus Christ as we give a defense of the Christian faith.

The fool says in his heart, "There is no God." They are corrupt, they do abominable deeds; there is none who does good (Psalm 14:1).

> I challenge Christians, especially Christian leaders, to be more vocal in this battle, boldly proclaiming the gospel to unbelievers and calling Christians back to the authority of the Bible.

JUNE 5
Isaiah 8:20

No Light Inside

Back in 2011, just as we were announcing the Ark Encounter project, I had an informal TV debate on the *Anderson Cooper 360* program with Rev. Barry Lynn, who was then head of Americans United for Separation of Church and State. This is a real-life example that illustrates Isaiah 8:20. The reason people don't shine the light of truth is because they reject God's Word. *To the law and to the testimony: if they speak not according to this word, it is because there is no light in them* (Isaiah 8:20; KJV).

My debate with this clergyman centered on the Ark Encounter, which we had announced would feature a full-scale, all-wood Noah's Ark in Northern Kentucky. The Ark was opened in 2016 and has become the biggest attraction in Kentucky. Over 20 hotels have now been built because of the Ark and the Creation Museum attractions — the two leading Christian-themed attractions in the world. Millions of guests have visited Northern Kentucky to see these attractions. In fact, over 92% of visitors to these two attractions come from outside of Kentucky and have brought billions of dollars into the state of Kentucky.

I want to give you a real-life example of what I would call a "wolf in sheep's clothing." We all need to be reminded to be on the lookout for such people who will lead others astray. Rev. Lynn's main argument was that Kentucky was subsidizing religion if the state granted incentives to the Ark Encounter, LLC. In the full debate, he went on to state (falsely) that if Kentucky grants the incentives, the state would not get the full money needed for education, fire stations, etc.

First, everyone has a religion, a worldview, that comes from one's foundation (presuppositions). One is either for or against Christ. There's no in between. Now in order to counter this wrong information that the Ark project would be a drain on Kentucky's state revenues, I made it clear that the tourism incentives would not be a grant of state funds to help build the Ark Encounter. No funds would be taken from the state budget and away from its programs (e.g., social services, schools, etc.) to help construct or operate the Ark Encounter.

Who then pays? The key thing that is almost always omitted by the press and by Ark opponents like Rev. Lynn is that the sales tax tourism incentive is from sales tax generated within the attraction (e.g., on tickets, food, books, etc. — new money generated), that the state would rebate a portion of this sales money to the Ark Encounter (based on meeting attendance-performance standards) for a period of 10 years. This is because the tourist facility generates a lot of new money in the state. So, no money comes from the state budget.

The reason the state has an economic tax incentive to attract tourist-related projects is to bring money into the state — which is exactly what the Ark Encounter and Creation Museum do. If we hadn't built the Ark in the state and had gone elsewhere, Kentucky would have lost billions of dollars of revenue from sales tax and other sources. That's why Kentucky has a Tourism Development Act — to bring in tourist dollars. And the Ark and Creation Museum have brought in billions of dollars to Kentucky. The state tourism tax incentive is really the state saying, "Thank you for building this in our state instead of another one, so we can reap the financial benefit." I want to give this information to show how these people who are against taking God at His Word will say anything to try to stop a biblical attraction that presents the truth of God's Word and the gospel from being built.

During this "debate," I tried my best to make the point that if there were no Ark Encounter in the state, there would be no sales tax generated to be handed over to the state. I added that if the Ark Encounter attracted at least one million people in year one (as our independent study projected), it would have an economic impact in just the first year of around $250 million for Kentucky's economy. And the state government collects all the sales tax outside the attraction (plus the payroll taxes) from businesses that would be created as a result of a major tourist destination being in the area.

I also pointed out during the TV debate that a 2009 ruling by the U.S. Court of Appeals for the Sixth Circuit (which includes Kentucky) declared that as long as such projects endorse "all qualified applicants," they endorse "none of them, and accordingly [do not] run afoul of the federal or state religion clauses." Also, I indicated that Kentucky in no way was establishing a specific religious view that would be in violation of the U.S. Constitution's Establishment Clause. The state would not be compelling anyone to visit the Ark Encounter. Furthermore, the Tourism Development Act does not discriminate according to the subject matter of a theme park. Thus, there would be no constitutional problem. In fact, the nondiscriminatory aspect of the Act was even acknowledged by Bill Sharp of the American Civil Liberties Union (ACLU) when he told *USA Today* (December 5, 2010) that "courts have found that giving such tax exemptions on a nondiscriminatory basis does not violate the establishment clause, even when the tax exemption goes to a religious purpose."[56]

The whole debate really had nothing to do with the rebate incentive. As he mocked biblical history that evening, Rev. Lynn revealed that he didn't want the account of Noah's Ark (believed by tens of millions of people in this country) to have a high profile. The irony is that as he opposed the Ark Encounter with his blatant discrimination, he gave the Ark even more national publicity for an attraction that has a theme that appeals to so many people. Just as we saw with our Creation Museum and the opposition it received years ago, we rejoice in the exposure we received — even before construction started! So, God uses such circumstances to work together for good (Romans 8:28). Lynn reminded me of this passage of Scripture:

[K]nowing this first of all, that scoffers will come in the last days with scoffing, following their own sinful desires. They will say, "Where is the promise of his coming? For ever since the fathers fell asleep, all things are continuing as they were from the beginning of creation." For they deliberately overlook this fact, that the heavens existed long ago, and the earth was formed out of water and through water by the word of God, and that by means of these the world that then existed was deluged with water and perished (2 Peter 3:3–6).

Another irony was that the government was already supporting the religion of secular humanism to the tune of billions of dollars per year through tax-supported public (secular) schools/universities, science museums, zoos, PBS TV, etc. Secular humanism is an actual religion that denies the one true God and worships self or science (or other idols). The third irony is that here we have a man who called himself a reverend (associated with the United Church of Christ) who opposed biblical Christianity and supported secular humanism.

> Oh, how the Church needs to repent of such compromise. "Beware of false prophets, who come to you in sheep's clothing but inwardly are ravenous wolves" (Matthew 7:15).

JUNE 6
Daniel 2:21

God Controls the Nations

Back in 2015, the then-president of the United States, President Obama, made an interesting statement from which we can glean some important teaching points for Christians. In his address to the American people, the president made statements about the threat of terrorism. At the end of his speech, President Obama said:

"Let's not forget that freedom is more powerful than fear; that we have always met challenges — whether war or depression, natural disasters or terrorist attacks — by coming together around our common ideals as one nation, as one people. So long as we stay true to that tradition, I have no doubt America will prevail. Thank you. God bless you, and may God bless the United States of America."[57]

First of all, if what he calls "common ideals" are not built on the authority of the Word of God, then the common ideals are just man's fallible opinions — which, frankly, will mean that America will not prevail. A fallible human being like the president can claim all he wants that America will prevail, but there's a God in heaven who is in absolute control of the affairs of the nations! I think of the verse from Daniel 2:21: *He changes times and seasons; he removes kings and sets up kings; he gives wisdom to the wise and knowledge to those who have understanding.*

Sadly, the president, even though he stated that he wanted God to bless America, did not acknowledge the Creator God of the Bible — in fact, he had done the opposite: actively supported the removal of the one true God from the public arena. His belief in this regard was seen, for instance, in the lighting of the national Christmas tree in Washington, D.C., when this president began his speech by saying "happy holidays" — twice.

While he used the word *Christmas* on occasion, we all know that when a president says, "Happy holidays," like in his speech, it's largely a deliberate way to keep Christ out of Christmas. He turned Christmas-related events into secular ones, instead of acknowledging the Babe in a manger — the One who came to be our Savior over 2,000 years ago.

Now, Christians should respect the office of the presidency and pray for our elected officials. But when their actions go contrary to the absolute authority of God's Word, then we should say something. We need to judge their actions/beliefs against the absolute authority of God's Word.

Also, at the Christmas tree lighting, the first lady, along with the Muppet character Miss Piggy, read a story from the children's book *A Visit from St. Nicholas* — a story about Santa Claus. The president and the first lady told Americans that the real reason for the season is to have a happy holiday and enjoy stories about Santa.

Now, at our Christmas programs at the Creation Museum and Ark Encounter from the end of Thanksgiving to the end of December each year, we celebrate Christmas in the right way: We reflect on the greatest gift God gave to mankind — the gift of His Son, Jesus — and worship Him. He was the Babe in a manger — the God-man — who came to earth to provide the only way for humans to live forever with their God.

Christmas is a time to celebrate Jesus Christ (as we should do every day of the year) and remember the true account (the historical record) of the birth of a Baby. He was the incarnation of the Son of God — the Son of God who took on a fleshly, bodily form.

APOLOGETICS — JUNE 6

Second, did God hear President Obama at the end of his speech when he said, "God bless you, and may God bless the United States of America"? I suggest God did not. Hear God's Word from Isaiah 59:2–3: *[B]ut your iniquities have made a separation between you and your God, and your sins have hidden his face from you so that he does not hear. For your hands are defiled with blood and your fingers with iniquity; your lips have spoken lies; your tongue mutters wickedness.*

God's principles do not change. What He said to the rebellious Israelites, He also says to us today.

Yes, the iniquities of this nation are great and seem to get greater daily. The teaching of the true God and the reminders of the Christian faith are being removed from this nation. Crosses, Nativity scenes, and displays of the Ten Commandments are being taken down from public places. Also, prayer, the Bible, and the teaching of creation have been largely removed from public schools.

Furthermore, this president mocked God's design for marriage and endorsed the gross sin of gay "marriage" and homosexual behavior. He endorsed *the lie* of a false doctrine in regard to marriage. And so many of our political leaders continue to do this to a much greater extent. It seems even some of the Church is now becoming soft toward LGBTQ issues. There is a lack of teaching about sin and the need for repentance.

This president also helped this nation be "defiled with blood." He (like so many politicians and judges continue to) condoned the murder of millions of children in their mothers' wombs. The same president who said, "God bless the United States of America," in a previous speech, said, "God bless Planned Parenthood." In other words, he asked God to bless the biggest child-murdering machine in America! Will God ever bless a nation that is so guilty of defiling this land with the shed blood of millions of children (Proverbs 6:16–17)?

I humbly suggest that God "will not hear" these leaders when they ask for God's blessing on this nation! How could God hear such a plea when the iniquities of this nation and many of its leaders are so great? May God have mercy, and may God raise up people to repair the breach in this nation — a breach that has allowed rampant sin and the mocking of God's Word to permeate the culture.

The prophet Isaiah declared, *And your ancient ruins shall be rebuilt; you shall raise up the foundations of many generations; you shall be called the repairer of the breach, the restorer of streets to dwell in* (Isaiah 58:12).

This nation as a whole, along with many of its leaders, needs to repent before the one true God and return to His Word as the absolute authority in all matters of life and conduct. God's Word in Jeremiah chapter 18 is a reminder to us that He is in total control of the nations, just as a potter controls the clay in his hands. In Jeremiah it says:

Then the word of the Lord came to me: "O house of Israel, can I not do with you as this potter has done? declares the Lord. Behold, like the clay in the potter's hand, so are you in my hand, O house of Israel. If at any time I declare concerning a nation or a kingdom, that I will pluck up and break down and destroy it, and if that nation, concerning which I have spoken, turns from its evil, I will relent of the disaster that I intended to do to it. And if at any time I declare concerning a nation or a kingdom that I will build and plant it, and if it does evil in my sight, not listening to my voice, then I will relent of the good that I had intended to do to it" (Jeremiah 18:5–10).

May God's people be emboldened to stand for Him in this nation.

JUNE 7
Genesis 2:21-22

Genesis Is History

Over the years, flood legends have been collected from cultures around the world. Many of those legends have elements that show a similarity to the Flood account in Genesis. Books of such legends have been published, and at the Ark Encounter attraction, there is an exhibit on the third deck featuring a number of such legends.

Now as a Christian, I would say the reason for the similarities is that the real record of the Flood account has been preserved in God's Word. The other versions around the world are changed versions of the original, as they were handed down from the time of Noah through the Tower of Babel event and then to various people groups that formed the various cultures around the world. Now such legends, not just about the Flood but also legends about creation, reflect elements similar to the Genesis account.

Back in the late 1970s when I was visiting a town in North Queensland, Australia, not that far from where my mother was born and grew up, I met a missionary who was in charge of a settlement for Australian Aboriginal people. The missionary told me that one day he read to the people the Bible's account of the creation of the first woman, Eve: *So the Lord God caused a deep sleep to fall upon the man, and while he slept took one of his ribs and closed up its place with flesh. And the rib that the Lord God had taken from the man he made into a woman and brought her to the man* (Genesis 2:21–22).

After he read this, one of the older Aboriginal elders said, "How come you have a story about the creation of woman, like we do, only your story's better?"

Because of my special interest in the Genesis account of origins, I had already collected some books — obtained from the secular natural history museum in Brisbane — on Aboriginal myths and legends — legends the Aboriginal people say were handed down from their ancestors. It was amazing to me to read through these legends and find quite a number that sounded very similar to certain events in the Genesis account. For instance, there were a number of flood legends. One told about three sons on a boat who survived the flood. In another one, the boat landed on a mountain at the end of the flood and a rainbow appeared in the sky.

They also have a legend about the origin of death as a result of the first woman. The creator told her not to touch his special tree, but she took sweet honey from it anyway, and death entered the world as a result. Another legend said that woman was made while man was asleep, only she was made from some sort of plant.

No doubt the elderly Australian Aboriginal had heard many such legends from his parents, and he recognized the similarity between the Genesis account of the creation of the first woman and the legend he knew.

The missionary then used this opportunity to help the Aboriginal people understand that the Genesis account was the original one and that their legends were changed versions of the original. This enabled the missionary to help them understand the truth of God's Word and point them to the saving gospel.

I experienced a similar event a few years earlier in 1975, during my first year as a science teacher in a country town in Australia. During the class dealing with human origins, I happened to mention that as a Christian, I believed all humans are descended from two people (Adam and Eve), and because of what happened after the Flood (at the Tower of Babel with the giving of different languages), families moved away from each

APOLOGETICS

other, forming different nations and cultures. I explained that all humans are one biological race and are related, and therefore, we're all just one big family.

After the class, three Aboriginal students came up to me and asked if I could explain this in more detail. They were extremely interested in all I had to say. As I talked to them, I realized that Darwin taught in his book *The Descent of Man* that the Australian Aborigines were closer to apes than light-skinned people in the supposed evolutionary story of man. It is also true that scientists in England sent people to Australia to collect specimens of Aborigines to display in museums — and sometimes they were illicitly killed, all in the name of evolution! It's a sad part of Australia's history. But what a difference it made to those students to learn that they were all part of the one big human family — and related to me, their classmates, and everyone else in the world, and certainly not to apes! Actually, the account of creation in the Bible fits much more with the Aboriginal culture than the evolutionary story did!

Ever since that time, I have had a real burden to teach everyone I can the truth about the one human race — that all humans belong to one race, all are related, and all are one color but different shades of brown. So we all have the same problem: sin. God's Son became a member of the one human race (as the God-man, the Lord Jesus Christ). Jesus died and rose again for the entire race, and He offers the free gift of salvation to all members of the one human race who will receive it.

That's why so many people are fascinated by the detailed exhibits on the Tower of Babel, the one human race, the origin of nations, and the evil of racism and prejudice at both the Creation Museum and Ark Encounter attractions.

By the way, in the year 2000, the Human Genome Project announced to the world, after mapping the entire sequence of the human genome, "There is only one race, the human race." Observational science confirms the Bible's account of one race! The science of genetics confirmed the history in the Bible concerning the fact that all humans belong to one biological race, as all humans are descendants of the first two people.

The battle over racism and prejudice is actually a battle of two worldviews: one based on man's word (man's evolutionary story about the origin of life and the universe) and one based on God's Word (the true account of origins as given in Genesis). The only place to begin the battle against racism is Genesis, which gives the true history of life!

And he made from one man every nation of mankind to live on all the face of the earth, having determined allotted periods and the boundaries of their dwelling place (Acts 17:26).

People need to believe the truth of God's Word and build their worldview upon that.

JUNE 8
Acts 17:26

One Blood, One Race

The core message of the Answers in Genesis biblical apologetics ministry is what I've always called "The Relevance Message." It's a message about the relevance of Genesis 1–11, that this is foundational to everything. This is the core message that I've preached in hundreds of churches across the world. And this is the message that I find really resonates with on-fire, born-again Christians. And it's the message all Christians need to be giving to the coming generations.

I'm sure you sometimes get weighed down (as I do) by the continual string of sad news regarding the spiritual state of the Church and our nations. For example, we all know about the terrible exodus of young people from the Church. We published the book *Already Gone* in 2009 to present the eye-opening results of a study conducted by America's Research Group as to why about two-thirds of young people are leaving the Church.

The researchers found (among other things) that most churches and Christian homes were not teaching young people how to defend the faith — how to be prepared for the secular attacks of our age. Pastors and Sunday school teachers weren't giving them the vital apologetics training to equip their young people to stand boldly and unashamedly on the Word of God ... and answer the skeptical questions of this age that cause them to doubt and ultimately disbelieve God's Word. And these young people weren't being taught how foundational Genesis 1–11 is to all doctrine, our worldview, the gospel, and, in fact, everything.

These results compelled AiG to step out in faith and produce additional much-needed curricula that are biblical-authority based, with an apologetics thrust, and, of course, evangelistic. As part of this teaching vision of ours, we also determined to produce an entire multi-year, fully integrated Bible curriculum for preschool through adult called Answers Bible Curriculum (ABC). All of these resources really emphasize the vital relevance message.

Be encouraged as you read some wonderful feedback as to how such apologetics worldview curricula and other materials have helped God's people raise up generations of dedicated young adults who can make a difference for the Lord in our cultures. I trust this is a challenge to all of us concerning the importance of the relevance message. Below is an email we received from a church that used the AiG Foundations video curriculum that emphasized the relevance message:

"Listed below are some of the comments made by our group of young people in regard to the Foundations series.... It is information that you do not derive by attending church or even in Sunday school. It goes so much deeper, which is why we called our group Digging Deeper.... As you will see from the comments, the young people definitely feel they are now more prepared as they continue in their daily walk and their educational process."

Here is just some of the exciting, representative feedback from this group — clearly demonstrating that this approach, using AiG resources, is sorely needed:

- "Before this series I had trouble standing up for the hope that I have. That was very unfortunate because I'm a talker. I'm very quick to want to jump in a conversation, but would find myself falling short in words on this subject. Not anymore! I now have no trouble answering someone's questions about my faith or the Bible and standing up for the hope I have. I can now more effectively witness to non-believers and my brothers and sisters in Christ. Thank you so much." —B.C., high school junior

- "The Foundations series has taught me how to intelligently defend my faith. I am so grateful for this as I make my transition into the college world and come into contact with many people who can 'intelligently' argue against my faith." —S.E., high school senior
- "I have thoroughly enjoyed [the Foundations] series. It has boosted my confidence in being ready to give an answer." —C.J., high school junior
- "Foundations really made me ponder different things about why I do believe the Bible and how to defend my faith. It really made an impact." —T.J., 8th grade
- "WOW! Never knew 'genes' could help me explain the reason why there is just ONE race. Thanks … for giving me a better understanding." —K.G., college freshman
- "The Foundations lessons have really helped me be able to better explain why I believe Christianity is the way. With what we have learned, I have been able to defend my points when conversations arise about why I'm a Christian." —T.L., high school senior

We continually receive encouraging testimonies like those as an increasing number of churches are adopting AiG's VBS curricula and other biblically based apologetics worldview curricula that AiG produces. This shows the hunger there is for this vital relevance message.

AiG once gave a church the opportunity to do a trial run and provide crucial feedback for one of the three-month sections of the Answers Bible Curriculum, as we were first developing it. At the end, the excited teachers told us that the children were upset! Why? The youngsters didn't want to go back to their old curriculum because they had learned so much from ABC!

After one of AiG's Children's Ministry Leaders' Conferences, where the Answers Bible Curriculum was explained in detail, we were told that the ABC approach (i.e., teaching with creation and general biblical apologetics, worldview, and the relevance message) "rocked the world" of an experienced Christian curriculum writer — and that he was committed to taking the information learned through ABC and apply it to his own curricula in the future.

This ABC curriculum approach (apologetics, foundations, relevance, worldview) is so needed. But sadly, there are not many Christian organizations/churches prepared to take the stand AiG does.

As I often say to people, our daily battles remind me of the Israelites conquering the Promised Land — and God had them do it "little by little." Well, that's how we have been approaching the production of God-honoring resources — "little by little." And we believe AiG is making a huge impact on the Church through ABC and the other resources God has burdened us to produce.

"Do not think that I will accuse you to the Father. There is one who accuses you: Moses, on whom you have set your hope. For if you believed Moses, you would believe me; for he wrote of me. But if you do not believe his writings, how will you believe my words?" (John 5:45–47).

> And I would encourage you to begin, little by little, reaching your own children, Sunday school classes, Bible study, youth groups etc., with the relevance message.

JUNE 9
Matthew 5:13

Christian College Compromise

For my wife and me, our favorite place to be in the United States (other than where the Ark and Creation Museum are located, of course) is Jackson Hole, Wyoming. We have some very special friends there involved in running a small Bible college with a one-year apologetics worldview program, Jackson Hole Bible College. We love the magnificent Grand Teton Mountains and the spectacular Yellowstone National Park in this area. This region is actually one of our favorite spots on the entire planet.

Back in 2011, when we were in Jackson Hole and I taught some apologetics classes at the Bible college, I tasked the students with reviewing the book that was just about to be published that year called *Already Compromised*. I had 30 young people in my course on biblical apologetics. The main assignment I gave them was to read the book *Already Compromised* and write two papers about it. I presented each student with a preprint, spiral-bound copy. The final book was being printed during the days I was teaching this class. The book compiled research we had commissioned on Christian colleges and showed rampant compromise on Genesis and the Scriptures in general through most Christian colleges/seminaries. I decided to use excerpts from some of the student papers to see their appraisal of this Christian college situation (some minor editing was done to help ensure ease of reading).

- "The book begins by discussing the legacy of the Ivy League. The colleges in the League, such as Harvard, Yale, Princeton, and Dartmouth, were at first established by Christian men with solid views of Scripture. However, through naturalistic textbooks and liberal professors being brought into the system, these universities wandered further and further from the truth. Within roughly 200 years from the time they were founded, each school was already compromising the Christian faith. This is relevant and important today because even when a college or university starts out with strong Christian leaders, over time they are likely to be compromised by teachers who add their own interpretation to Scripture and influence others to do so as well."

- "*Already Compromised* discusses the reality that many Christian colleges have become no better than secular schools when it comes to a true view of Scripture. Though evolutionary and humanistic teachings are to be expected from secular schools, the amount of this compromise we see in Christian colleges is astounding. This book shows the increasing departure from Scripture in higher education today, and what to look for when seeking a college to attend." —Micaela R.

- "The focus of *Already Compromised* is to expose the infiltration of the same thought in Christian campuses across the country, and why the students who are not '*already gone*' when they get to college are leaving the faith when they reach these '*already compromised*' Christian colleges." —Cort T.

- "The foundation of this book is based on a study run by [the late] Britt Beemer of America's Research Group. Beemer conducted a survey of Christian institutions of higher learning, asking questions of people in four different positions: president, vice-president, head of science, and head of theology/religion. This survey resulted in getting a big picture of what is happening on the general Christian college campus, and it brought to light some specific issues of concern."

RESOURCES

- "It is encouraging to discover that nearly all of the participants in the survey answered positively when asked questions about foundational New Testament theology. However, the answers given for the questions concerning truths of the Old Testament are rather disheartening. They seem to have different definitions of important words such as *literal, infallible,* and *inerrant* when referring to Scripture."
- "Eighty-three percent of those [leaders/professors] surveyed stated that they 'believe the Genesis 1–2 account of creation is literally true.' However, only 59.6% responded yes when asked, 'Do you believe in God creating the earth in six literal 24-hour days?' A shocking 10.9% claimed that their institutions teach evolution as truth!" —Heather Y.
- "Unfortunately, many schools do not want the public, especially parents, to know what they are teaching." —Jessica M.
- "In my opinion, the reason a book like *Already Compromised* is necessary is because the church has become lazy. Parents spend thousands of dollars to send their child to a Christian university because they want them to have a Christian education — and that's not wrong. But what is wrong (and lazy) is assuming because the school is religiously affiliated or has the word 'Christian' in the name, makes it a doctrinally sound institution."
- "Parents do not investigate universities thoroughly enough. On the surface, it looks like the school's statement of faith is generally what the family agrees with. However, what parents should be doing is taking the time to ask questions of the individual professors that their child will be studying under. They should use the questionnaire given in *Already Compromised* and discover truly what the instructor believes and therefore teaches in the classroom." —Kaitlyn B.
- "*Already Compromised* caused me to respond by searching myself, judging my own thinking against Scripture, affirming what I believe, and by researching how to better give answers about the truth to those who question it."
- "I cannot wait to share the information I learned in this book with others, as many as I can, to help reverse some of the damage this way of thinking, teaching, and learning has led to." —Elisha P.

I thank God that there are some Christian colleges/seminaries that teach their students the full authority and accuracy of the Bible from the very first verse. Sadly, they are a small minority! Parents need to do much more research before entrusting their students to a particular Christian institution. Compromise destroys. As God's Word states:

"I know your works: you are neither cold nor hot. Would that you were either cold or hot! So, because you are lukewarm, and neither hot nor cold, I will spit you out of my mouth" (Revelation 3:15–16).

> "You are the salt of the earth, but if salt has lost its taste, how shall its saltiness be restored? It is no longer good for anything except to be thrown out and trampled under people's feet" (Matthew 5:13).

JUNE 10
Genesis 1:26

Creationists and Climate Change

Biblical creationists are often accused by secularists of denying climate change. The truth is we don't deny climate change, but we do deny the climate change being claimed by today's climate change religion! It's a religion where man worships the creation (and worships man) and believes man can save himself and save the planet. It's a religion where the creation has dominion over man instead of the other way around. Biblical creationists certainly believe there has been massive climate change since the Flood, and in a fallen world, there will continue to be climate change.

Bill Nye, TV's popular "Science Guy" and vocal evolution defender, visited Australia in 2015. News stories indicated that he would be spreading evolutionary propaganda in an attempt to influence educators and politicians to indoctrinate school children in evolutionary naturalism (really, an atheistic view of origins — his religion). On the *Sydney Morning Herald*'s (Australia's largest newspaper) website, an article presented an interview with Nye about his Australian speaking tour. In this article, Nye was reported as stating the following:

- "Climate change is the biggest problem facing humankind. But keep in mind that Mr. Ham and his Answers in Genesis group deny climate change routinely. It's part of their big picture. The denial of climate change seems to be very important to him."
- "Generally, climate change is generational. That is to say, there are very, very few young people who are in denial of climate change.
- "My concern with Ken Ham and his people is that they work so very hard to indoctrinate schoolchildren. They have a very expansive education program; they want to raise a generation of kids in denial of climate change."

Bill Nye also appeared on the American TV news program *CBS Mornings* to talk about his anti-creationist book, saying, "It's not a coincidence that the creationists also deny climate change. It's this really important thing to them."

Well, we do have a number of articles on our AiG website that deal with climate change. Anyone can easily search out our views and read them. More important as it relates to Bill Nye is that immediately after our evolution/creation debate in February 2014, he and I were interviewed by CNN's Piers Morgan (who no longer hosts the program due to poor ratings) on live TV. Here is what I wrote about that CNN interview in an April 16, 2014, article:

"First, the CNN interview with Piers Morgan was a setup. Our understanding was that the interview was to be about the just-concluded debate. But Morgan launched into climate change, which had nothing to do with the debate topic. From statements Bill Nye made in the interview, I am quite sure he and Morgan set this up ahead of time. Also, I did not deny climate change. I observed that there had been climate changes ever since the flood of Noah's time. What I did say was that the debate over what has caused climate change is somewhat like the creation/evolution debate. You see, how you interpret the evidence in regard to the past about what causes climate change depends on the person's assumptions."

Furthermore, here is what I wrote on my blog in 2013 and well before my debate with Nye in response to statements about climate change made by President Obama: "Now, we at Answers in Genesis certainly don't deny the reality of climate change—we just have a different idea about why the climate changes and what causes it. After the catastrophic global flood, the earth was dramatically changed, and much of the change in climate over the centuries has been due to the changes from the flood."

So Bill Nye — who sat beside me during the CNN interview — knew full well that we did not deny climate change. We just didn't agree with his particular views of climate change. As Piers Morgan interviewed Nye and me after the debate, I said plainly that I did not deny climate change!

Unfortunately, though, many websites and news outlets repeat *the lie* that creationist researchers deny climate change — and many news outlets made that claim because of Nye's insistence that we deny climate change.

As an author of an article published in our *Answers* magazine stated: "The key controversy seems to be 'do human activities significantly affect climate?' If so, changing those activities (for example, reducing our output of greenhouse gases) would have a measurable effect on climate. On the other hand, if human impacts are insignificant, controlling human emissions will have a negligible effect."

If the *Sydney Morning Herald*, read by millions of people, quoted Bill Nye correctly, then his statements that Answers in Genesis and I supposedly deny climate change are simply untrue — and if he was quoted accurately, Bill Nye knows it is not true, since he sat just a foot away from me on TV when I stated that I acknowledge that the climate can change. Moreover, if he did any research at all on the AiG website, Nye would know that, while we do not deny certain types of climate change, we would disagree about its major causes.

I had to smile and shake my head at this statement in the *Sydney Morning Herald*: "My concern with Ken Ham and his people is that they work so very hard to indoctrinate schoolchildren. They have a very expansive education program; they want to raise a generation of kids in denial of climate change."

Nye was upset that we at Answers in Genesis teach children and teens about God's Word on creation, just as he aggressively indoctrinates children in his naturalistic (atheistic) worldview. And to claim we want to "raise a generation of kids in denial of climate change" is ridiculous because we say the opposite. Really, he is against our Christian message and that's what it's all about.

Of course, our emphasis at AiG is not climate change. We are promoting biblical authority and the gospel, and we are equipping children, teens, and adults to defend the Christian faith against the secular attacks of people like Bill Nye. And we teach people to have a truly biblical worldview and, therefore, a correct understanding of climate change. Understanding how humans should interact with the environment must begin with this understanding:

Then God said, "Let us make man in our image, after our likeness. And let them have dominion over the fish of the sea and over the birds of the heavens and over the livestock and over all the earth and over every creeping thing that creeps on the earth" (Genesis 1:26).

> **Remember, the climate change movement of today that has brainwashed so many people, including most in the younger generations, is a religion.**

JUNE 11
2 Timothy 4:1–5

Biblical Authority Is Ultimate

You may be surprised to learn this, but there is something I really, really dislike about being in the ministry of Answers in Genesis!

Now, I love the opportunities the Lord has opened for us, including building a Creation Museum and the Ark Encounter, reaching millions of people with the truth of God's Word and the gospel. I'm so thankful we can reach 30 million people a year directly and tens of millions more indirectly. I love to see thousands of churches using AiG's Answers Bible Curriculum and adopting AiG's Answers Vacation Bible School (VBS) program to reach hundreds of thousands of children. I'm thrilled that millions of books, DVDs, gospel tracts, and other resources have been purchased from Answers in Genesis or given away by AiG. My heart is so warmed when the Lord gives me opportunities to speak to adults, teens, and kids at churches and conferences. Even though it was a stressful and nerve-racking debate, I praise the Lord I was able to debate Bill Nye "the Science Guy" publicly and be a witness for God's Word and the gospel to many millions. Another stressful time is when I'm able to speak at secular institutions or interact with liberal theologians — but it's all a part of what the Lord has called AiG to do.

I'm saddened when we experience attacks from secularists and read *the lies* they spread about us — but that's all to be expected in a fallen world. I groan when I'm about to be interviewed by the secular media, knowing the majority of the published stories will misquote, mock, and attack us. But again, this is all a necessary part of contending for the faith in a world where people *loved the darkness rather than the light* (John 3:19).

But even with all these challenges, there is one thing I really dislike about being in this ministry! I hate it when we have to publicly oppose, debate, and challenge Christians who, while they might believe the gospel (and would even say they believe in biblical inerrancy), compromise God's Word in Genesis. That is what I'm most saddened and stressed about. But we do have to contend for the faith (Jude 1:3).

I hate it when the world sees this contention among believers. But at the same time, it's very important for Christians and non-Christians to see us boldly and unashamedly standing on the authority of God's Word from the very first verse. As I've stated many times, and as we have documented with research published in books like *Already Gone* and *Ready to Return*, compromise on Genesis (particularly with Christians who add millions of years into the Bible) has had a devastating impact on how this generation views the Bible. And, sadly, this compromise has been a major factor as to why so many people are leaving the Church and are now secularized in their thinking.

It must be perplexing to many people that Christians with a heart for the gospel, and who say they believe in inerrancy, battle each other over their view on Genesis. But it's our contention that compromising Christians (as I call them) have an inconsistent approach to Scripture that unlocks a door to undermine biblical authority in Genesis — and puts people on a slippery slope toward unbelief through the rest of Scripture. And I'm passionate about not compromising biblical authority. In fact, because we are so burdened by the rampant compromise in the Church regarding Genesis, we work hard in contending for the faith by exposing and challenging this compromise. This is particularly true when it comes to Christian leaders and Bible college/seminary professors. This compromise is really no different from what the prophets dealt with as recorded

APOLOGETICS

in the books of Isaiah, Jeremiah, Hosea, and others, as we read about leaders who compromised God's Word with man's fallible beliefs. That's why, as much as I hate it, it's so important for us at AiG to do all we can to passionately reach out to these leaders. We plead with Christian leaders to apply a consistent hermeneutic to Scripture and reject compromise that undermines the authority of the Word, which has such a negative impact on the people they influence.

I recall the time I debated a professor from a Christian college over the age of the earth. I kept emphasizing it was a biblical authority issue. He refused to accept that. But for those listening, it was obvious it was an authority issue. One lady who brought her husband to the program wrote this:

"You see, my husband is a skeptic, and I'd been praying for the Lord to reveal himself in a mighty way during this conference experience. And while we attended many ... sessions [by an old earth creationist] and my husband was almost convinced of the Old-Earth Creationist stance [and bought some old earth books] ... we both felt the conviction of the Lord in the stance Ken Ham took during the 'God's Word vs Man's Word' debate. He spoke with such compassion, clarity, and truth."

She then told us that her whole family would be coming to visit our Ark Encounter and Creation Museum, and they did just that.

The rampant compromise among Christian scholars is also why I agreed to participate in a different kind of "debate." I was approached to contribute a chapter — and provide responses to other chapters — in a book titled *Four Views on Creation, Evolution, and Intelligent Design* published by Zondervan. I felt it was very important that, because this book would promote compromising views on Genesis and because we were given the opportunity to present our stand on God's Word regarding the origins issue, we should take the opportunity to participate.

In our interaction with two editors, it was very obvious they didn't share our views on a literal Genesis! In fact, the main editor made a negative comment about me in the book's conclusion over the length of my section. But in the end, my main chapter was only one page longer than one of the other authors (who had some diagrams).

The point we stressed with the editors was that, of the three other authors, two of them in this "debate" totally accepted the idea of millions of years, and the third person allowed for the possibility of it. So, in a sense, it was three against one (and with not-so-neutral editors!) when it came to Genesis as literal history. This book does help expose what is (sadly) happening in the Christian world.

I charge you in the presence of God and of Christ Jesus, who is to judge the living and the dead, and by his appearing and his kingdom: preach the word; be ready in season and out of season; reprove, rebuke, and exhort, with complete patience and teaching. For the time is coming when people will not endure sound teaching, but having itching ears they will accumulate for themselves teachers to suit their own passions, and will turn away from listening to the truth and wander off into myths. As for you, always be sober-minded, endure suffering, do the work of an evangelist, fulfill your ministry (2 Timothy 4:1–5).

> **Let's be bold about defending the Christian faith and standing against compromise that undermines biblical authority.**

JUNE 12
Luke 1:37

God Makes All Things Possible

Many said it couldn't be done. Others said it would fail if done. Others said it was a waste of money and time. Others claimed it would have no impact. But *nothing will be impossible with God* (Luke 1:37). And I believe with all my heart God called us to do it. If that is so, then nothing could stop it. And it happened!

I believe two historic moments in Christendom occurred when the Creation Museum and Ark Encounter Christian-themed attractions were opened in Northern Kentucky. I am convinced these attractions are two of the greatest Christian outreaches of our era. When I read many of the secularist attacks on the building of the Creation Museum and Ark (including occasional criticisms from self-described Christians), I saw one theme coming up over and over again: our motive!

Most secularists, who are in rebellion against God, just can't get their heads around why we would build a Creation Museum and replica of the massive wooden ship as described in the Bible. Many claimed we must have done it for the money! Well, those of you who know Answers in Genesis understand that, while money is certainly needed to build and then maintain such massive projects and to construct future phases, money is not our motive in the slightest degree.

Some critics who say they are Christians declare that we're building idols (a bizarre claim), supposedly because we are worshipping the Bible and not God! False claim. Of course, anyone who has visited the Creation Museum and the Ark understands that these Bible-upholding facilities are not idols in any way. The museum and Ark unashamedly direct people to the Word of God and the gospel of Jesus Christ.

Others accused us of building these attractions out of pride, claiming we just want to build something for the sake of getting our name in the news! Amazing! What was our real motive for building the Creation Museum and the Ark Encounter? Let me answer with this background.

A number of years ago in Australia, my wife Mally and I attended the commencement ceremony held at a secular university, as one of our family members was graduating. A local judge gave the commencement address. Her speech went something like this: "Students, you are graduating from university. You're thinking of your future. Eventually, you will die. So, what do you do until you're dead?"

At this point, I turned to Mally and said, "Wow, this is going to be a message of hope and encouragement!"

Well, the judge went on to say, "In my life, there were books that greatly influenced my life." She named *Zen and the Art of Motorcycle Maintenance* and *The Hitchhiker's Guide to the Galaxy* (where a computer came up with the meaning of life as the number 42). The judge explained how these books influenced her life. She then encouraged students to find what would influence their lives to be impactful until they are dead! She sat down to a standing ovation by the faculty!

I turned again to Mally and said, "If I were a student, I would feel compelled to jump off a cliff right now and get life over and done with." What a message of meaninglessness, hopelessness, and purposelessness she offered. As a Christian, doesn't a speech like that make you just want to stand up and declare to the audience that there is a message of real hope — not only for this life but for eternity?

RESOURCES   JUNE 12

What the judge presented was the ultimate message of the world. And sadly, it is being given daily to millions of students in public/secular schools, universities, and through most of the media and the entertainment industry! Doesn't your heart ache when you think about this hopelessness? No wonder the suicide rate is rising in America. No wonder younger generations turn to sex and drugs.

I remember saying to Mally after the commencement speech, "I wish we had a way to get the Bible's teaching of the hope of the gospel to these students. How can we get out the message of truth concerning God's Word and our hope in Christ to this lost world?"

And really, what I shared that day with Mally sums up our motive! You see, every human being is one of our family — we're all related going back to Noah (and then back to Adam). We're all sinners in need of salvation. We're all under the judgment of death. But God reminds us:

The Lord is ... not wishing that any should perish, but that all should reach repentance (2 Peter 3:9).

[B]ecause, if you confess with your mouth that Jesus is Lord and believe in your heart that God raised him from the dead, you will be saved (Romans 10:9).

Our real motive for building the Creation Museum and the Ark can be summed up in these verses:

And he said to them, "Go into all the world and proclaim the gospel to the whole creation" (Mark 16:15).

Go therefore and make disciples of all nations (Matthew 28:19).

[B]ut in your hearts honor Christ the Lord as holy, always being prepared to make a defense to anyone who asks you for a reason for the hope that is in you; yet do it with gentleness and respect (1 Peter 3:15).

[T]o contend for the faith (Jude 3).

"Engage in business until I come" (Luke 19:13).

Yes, our motive is to do the King's business until He comes. And that means preaching the gospel and defending the faith so that we can reach as many souls as we can with the greatest message of purpose, hope, and meaning — that even though we rebelled against our Creator, He provided a way for us, a free gift, so we can spend eternity with Him. Oh, how we want to see as many as possible receive this free gift of salvation!

When I think about the Creation Museum and the Ark, I often ponder the fact that millions of souls will hear the most important message of all — not one of hopelessness from a human judge, but a message of hope from the holy, righteous Judge who, despite our sin, wants us to spend eternity with Him! Wow! Now that's a motive to build these attractions.

> Pray that millions will learn the truth of God's Word and its life-changing gospel message through these unique facilities, and ask yourself what you are doing to spread the most important message in the universe – the message of salvation.

JUNE 13
Joel 2:13

The United States Needs Repentance

Back in 2012, in the USA, we were all shocked by the horrific shooting of several children and adults in the state of Connecticut. My heart was so heavy — so burdened — as I watched reports of the carnage. After these tragic events and then President Obama's State of the Union speech, I must admit that the hypocrisy of this nation's leadership stirred my heart. What is the real state of this nation? In fact, what is the real state of Western nations?

I can't imagine what the parents and other loved ones of those killed by an evil man must be going through. I'm a father, grandfather, and great-grandfather, and I shudder at the thought of such an unimaginably painful time in dealing with a tragedy like this. Now even though the wicked gunman (who took his own life) will answer to the God of creation for his sins, we know that such tragedies occur because of our sin in Adam. That's why there is so much evil in the world. When horrible things happen, we must remember, it's not God's fault — it's our fault. God's Word is clear about this: *For we know that the whole creation has been groaning together in the pains of childbirth until now* (Romans 8:22).

Therefore, just as sin came into the world through one man, and death through sin, and so death spread to all men because all sinned (Romans 5:12).

With such a tragedy, I think, "Oh Lord — look what our sin has done to this world!" This horrific shooting happened just before Christmas — a time when we especially remember the event of God's Son becoming the God-man and God Himself providing the sacrifice for our sin and offering a free gift of salvation: *For God so loved the world, that he gave his only Son, that whoever believes in him should not perish but have eternal life* (John 3:16). But as I pondered these truths from Scripture and watched the evening news, I must admit I became a little angry with the U.S. president. What he said after the shooting was good, and many of us shed a tear with him, so why be angry? Because he was being hypocritical. You see, the president had supported and signed legislation (since revoked by the Supreme Court in regard to Christian convictions) to force companies — and even ministries like Answers in Genesis — to provide a pill to employees that would terminate the life of a baby. Such abortion pills stop a fertilized egg from implanting in the mother's womb. Once it's fertilized, that's a human being. Answers in Genesis, of course, worked with our legal team to deal with this shocking, immoral government mandate. On the same day that this horrific killing of 20 beautiful children (and some adults) took place, probably 3,000 children (who didn't have names) were brutally killed in their mothers' wombs. Now, did President Obama shed tears for them each day?

On January 22, 2010 (the anniversary of the *Roe v. Wade* Supreme Court decision), the White House website quoted President Obama: "Today we recognize the 37th anniversary of the Supreme Court decision in *Roe v. Wade*, which affirms every woman's fundamental constitutional right to choose whether to have an abortion, as well as each American's right to privacy from government intrusion. I have, and continue to, support these constitutional rights."[58]

The same president, at a press conference to discuss the shocking school shooting, quoted the Bible. He read: *So we do not lose heart. Though our outer self is wasting away, our inner self is being renewed day by day. For this light momentary affliction is preparing for us an eternal weight of glory beyond all comparison, as we look not to the things that are seen but to the things that are unseen. For the things that are seen are transient, but the things that are unseen are eternal. For we know that if the tent that is our earthly home is destroyed, we have a building from God, a house not made with hands, eternal in the heavens* (2 Corinthians 4:16–5:1).

I don't recall atheists objecting to the president for quoting Scripture in public. Now, how could he get away with that, as God is not allowed in our public schools — including the school where this massacre took place? With President Obama quoting Scripture, I considered this extremely hypocritical and inconsistent. Let me quote another Scripture: *He answered, "Have you not read that he who created them from the beginning made them male and female, and said, 'Therefore a man shall leave his father and his mother and hold fast to his wife, and the two shall become one flesh'? So they are no longer two but one flesh. What therefore God has joined together, let not man separate"* (Matthew 19:4–6). Now, would President Obama ever quote that passage from Matthew? Of course not. He has made comments like the following that he stated (taken from the White House website): "I think same-sex couples should be able to get married." So, for his own purposes, the president picked and chose his Bible verses!

As I pondered the massacre and the president's attempt to console people by quoting the Bible, another news item caught my eye. Atheists had sponsored a billboard in New York City's Times Square. It had a picture of Santa Claus with the words, "Keep the Merry," but there was also a picture representing Christ with the words, "Dump the Myth." The atheist group's mission was to essentially stop the real message of hope from getting out to this dying world. They spent hundreds of thousands of dollars to promote a belief in, well, nothingness! And a belief that people are nothing but animals! America is increasingly shaking its collective fist at God and His Word (as the Obama administration was doing), as it:

- Removes God from the education system
- Deletes reminders of God's Word from public places
- Abandons Christian morality
- Makes it legal to kill thousands of unborn children every day.

As a result, we will see God removing the restraining influence of the Holy Spirit in this nation. Romans 1:18–32 is a description of what will happen. This nation continues to shake its fist at God by rejecting the truth that the only true marriage is between one man and one woman. That president, along with Joe Biden, have been ardent supporters of gay "marriage," which is an abomination to the Lord (see Romans 1).

This is what really needs to be shouted to our Western nations: *"[A]nd rend your hearts and not your garments." Return to the Lord your God, for he is gracious and merciful, slow to anger, and abounding in steadfast love; and he relents over disaster* (Joel 2:13).

Our nation's problems are spiritual ones! God's people need to repent of the rampant compromise regarding His Word and return to the Bible. Our nations need to repent of the shocking disregard of God's Word, including the sanctity of life and marriage. At Answers in Genesis, we will do our best to call the Church and our nations back to the authority of the Word of God!

> **We need to pray for our leaders, that they will repent of their sin of disregarding God's Word and then commit their lives totally to Him.**

JUNE 14
1 Corinthians 15:21-22
Could God Have Used Evolution?

Could God have used evolution? Well, first of all, it's not a matter of what God could have done but what He said He's done. Secondly, if a Christian truly understands evolution and its process of death, disease, and violence over millions of years and understands the attributes of a Holy God, then no, God couldn't have used evolution to create life. To do so would be against His own character.

Many Christians today claim that millions of years of earth history fit with the Bible and that God could have used evolutionary processes to create. This idea is not a recent invention. For over 200 years, many theologians have attempted such harmonizations in response to the work of people like Charles Darwin and Scottish geologist Charles Lyell, who helped popularize the idea of millions of years of earth history and slow geological processes. When we consider the possibility that God used evolutionary processes to create over millions of years, we are faced with serious consequences: the Word of God is no longer authoritative, and the character of our loving God is questioned.

Already in Darwin's day, one of the leading evolutionists saw the compromise involved in claiming that God used evolution, and his insightful comments are worth reading again. Once you accept evolution and its implications about history, then man becomes free to pick and choose which parts of the Bible he wants to accept. The leading humanist of Darwin's day, Thomas Huxley (1825–1895), eloquently pointed out the inconsistencies of reinterpreting Scripture to fit with popular scientific thinking. Huxley, an ardent evolutionary humanist, was known as "Darwin's bulldog," as he did more to popularize Darwin's ideas than Darwin himself. Huxley understood Christianity much more clearly than did compromising theologians who tried to add evolution and millions of years to the Bible. He used their compromise against them to help his cause in undermining Christianity.

In his essay "Lights of the Church and Science," Huxley stated: "I am fairly at a loss to comprehend how anyone, for a moment, can doubt that Christian theology must stand or fall with the historical trustworthiness of the Jewish Scriptures. The very conception of the Messiah, or Christ, is inextricably interwoven with Jewish history … what about the authority of the writers of the books of the New Testament, who, on this theory, have not merely accepted flimsy fictions for solid truths, but have built the very foundations of Christian dogma upon legendary quicksands?"

Huxley argued that if we are to believe the New Testament doctrines, we must believe the historical account of Genesis as historical truth. Huxley was definitely out to destroy the truth of the biblical record. When people rejected the Bible, he was happy. But when they tried to harmonize evolutionary ideas with the Bible and reinterpret it, he vigorously attacked this position. Huxley quoted 1 Corinthians 15:21-22: *For as by a man came death, by a man has come also the resurrection of the dead. For as in Adam all die, so also in Christ shall all be made alive.* Huxley continued, "If Adam may be held to be no more real a personage than Prometheus, and if the story of the Fall is merely an instructive 'type,' comparable to the profound Promethean mythos, what value has Paul's dialectic?" Thus, concerning those who accepted the New Testament doctrines that Paul and Christ teach but rejected Genesis as literal history, Huxley claimed, "The melancholy fact remains, that the position they have taken up is hopelessly untenable."

APOLOGETICS

He was adamant that science (by which he meant evolutionary, long-age ideas about the past) had proven that one cannot intelligently accept the Genesis account of creation and the Flood as historical truth. He further pointed out that various doctrines in the New Testament are dependent on the truth of these events, such as Paul's teaching on the doctrine of sin, Christ's teaching on the doctrine of marriage, and the warning of future judgment. Huxley mocked those who tried to harmonize evolution and millions of years with the Bible because it requires them to give up a historical Genesis while still trying to hold to the doctrines of the New Testament. If we compromise on the history of Genesis by adding millions of years, we must believe that death and disease were part of the world before Adam sinned.

The Book of Genesis teaches that death is the result of Adam's sin (Genesis 3:19; Romans 5:12, 8:18–22) and that all of God's creation was "very good" upon its completion (Genesis 1:31). All animals and humans were originally vegetarian (Genesis 1:29–30). But if we compromise on the history of Genesis by adding millions of years, we must believe that death and disease were part of the world before Adam sinned. You see, the (alleged) millions of years of earth history in the fossil record show evidence of animals eating each other, diseases like cancer in their bones, violence, plants with thorns, and so on. All of this supposedly takes place before man appears on the scene and thus before sin (and its curse of death, disease, thorns, carnivory ...) entered the world.

Christians who believe in an old earth (billions of years) need to come to grips with the real nature of the god of an old earth — it is not the loving God of the Bible. Even many conservative, evangelical Christian leaders accept and actively promote a belief in millions and billions of years for the age of rocks. How could a God of love allow such horrible processes as disease, suffering, and death for millions of years as part of His "very good" creation? The God of the Bible, the God of mercy, grace, and love, sent His One and only Son to become a man (but God nonetheless), to become our sin bearer so that we could be saved from sin and eternal separation from God. As 2 Corinthians 5:21 says, *For our sake he made him to be sin who knew no sin, so that in him we might become the righteousness of God.*

Now, it is true that rejecting six literal days doesn't ultimately affect one's salvation, if one is truly born again. However, we need to stand back and look at the big picture. In many nations, the Word of God was once widely respected and taken seriously. But once the door of compromise is unlocked, once Christian leaders concede that we shouldn't interpret the Bible as written in Genesis, why should the world take heed of God's Word in any area? After all, if the history in Genesis is not correct, how can one be sure the rest is correct? Jesus said, *If I have told you earthly things and you do not believe, how can you believe if I tell you heavenly things?* (John 3:12).

The battle is not one of young earth vs. old earth or billions of years vs. six days or creation vs. evolution — the real battle is the authority of the Word of God vs. man's fallible opinions. Is God's Word the authority, or is man's word the authority? So couldn't God have used evolution to create? The answer is no. A belief in millions of years of evolution not only contradicts the clear teaching of Genesis and the rest of Scripture but also impugns the character of God. He told us in the book of Genesis that He created the whole universe and everything in it in six days by His word: "Then God said." His Word is the evidence of how and when God created, and His Word is incredibly clear.

There's no doubt – the god of an old earth destroys the gospel.

JUNE 15
Ecclesiastes 1:9

Human Nature Has Not Changed

By using Bible references and secular sources, I want to help you understand cultures, past and present, and where they stood spiritually and morally. It's a reminder that the sin nature of man has not changed! Let's consider the past:

Idolatry — The Israelites were warned about idolatry over and over again. For instance, we read: *[W]ho say to a tree, "You are my father," and to a stone, "You gave me birth." For they have turned their back to me* (Jeremiah 2:27).

Child Sacrifice — Many examples are cited in the Old Testament about this evil (2 Kings 16:3, 17:17, 21:6; Ezekiel 20:31; Jeremiah 32:35). Of course, it is well known that thousands of years ago, the Canaanites conducted human sacrifice, using children. There's much evidence the Aztec, Mayan, and Inca societies were conducting child sacrifice just a few hundred years ago.

Euthanasia — It appears that ritual euthanasia was practiced by numerous ancient cultures. The Phoenicians were known to poison their older individuals. Both the Spartans and the Romans would leave children that they deemed disabled to die in the elements. Also, ancient Indian cultures were known to throw elderly adults in the Ganges River to drown.

Sexual Sin/Homosexual Behavior — Scripture teaches against such behavior (Leviticus 20:13) and records examples as warnings for us (Genesis 19:1–14; Judges 19:15–30; Romans 1:26–27). Homosexual behavior was a running theme in the literature of the ancient Greeks and Romans. And you've heard of the judgment God meted out on Sodom and Gomorrah!

Bestiality — This behavior was known in ancient cultures, and the Bible warned the Israelites against this evil (Leviticus 18:23, 20:15). Bestiality seems to have been a form of punishment in ancient Rome, used in the arena to humiliate a prisoner before death. Ancient Egyptians also appear to have engaged in it based on their hieroglyphics. In addition, bestiality appears in the mythology of numerous cultures.

Pedophilia — This sin was also a common practice in the ancient world. Greek and Roman men were notorious for taking boys as their "lovers" (in the Roman world, it was limited to slaves, not freeborn citizens).

Transgenderism — There appear to be references to transgenderism in the ancient world. Apparently, ancient Assyria had transgender prostitutes. Ancient Greece and later Rome had a cult religion that was transgendered (at least in the priesthood). Transgenderism is found in Roman poetry as well. The Roman Emperor Elagabalus is known to have identified as a woman and requested primitive gender reassignment surgery.

The Bible makes it clear that the nature of sin has not changed. Jeremiah reminds us that *The heart is deceitful above all things, and desperately sick* (Jeremiah 17:9). God also warns us in Romans 1 that as people rebel against God, He turns them over to their depraved natures — and a sexual revolution, homosexual revolution, and gender revolution will follow. My point is this: Because of sin, if we don't work and pray hard to raise up generations on the foundation of God's Word and its life-changing gospel message, their naturally depraved sin natures will again exhibit the same behaviors as those listed above. That's why God warned the Israelites over and over again, and why He instructed them to raise up godly offspring.

APOLOGETICS

Now consider the present: We now see that all the perverse behaviors above are permeating our "civilized" Western culture. Just like the Israelites of the Old Testament, parents have failed to raise up godly generations, so now we increasingly see young and old behave as described in Judges 21:25: *In those days there was no king in Israel. Everyone did what was right in his own eyes.* Actually, Romans 1 is happening before our very eyes.

Idolatry — The teaching of evolution/millions of years (which many church leaders have condoned for the next generation to believe) is no different from Jeremiah 2:27. People are really saying, "Matter — you are my father; you gave birth to me." Coming generations are no different from past generations who *worshiped and served the creature rather than the Creator* (Romans 1:25), thus *God gave them up* (Romans 1:26). So we are observing all the following behaviors again:

Child Sacrifice — It's called by different names in our culture, such as abortion, "health care," and women's reproductive rights. But they are just hiding the fact that abortion is nothing less than sacrificing children to the "god of self." Over 65 million babies have been murdered in the USA since 1973. Now I ask you this: Which is the more barbaric culture? Those of the past or the present?

Euthanasia — This practice is becoming another prominent issue in our Western world, with more and more countries making this freely offered to adults — and even children!

Sexual Sin/Homosexual Behavior — In the last few years, this has become a dominant issue in our culture. The pressure to welcome and accept such behavior has become pervasive in the media, schools, and government.

Bestiality — We've even seen some recent news articles about this happening in our culture. One article gave an example of an atheist's refusal to label bestiality as an immoral act, illustrating what happens when there are no objective moral standards.

Pedophilia — Recent calls have gone out to legalize pedophilia. Some people even try to justify such behavior in academic articles. Again, what would we expect when a culture lets go of any objective moral standards?

Transgenderism — This has also become a dominant issue in our society. Drag queens are now giving children talks in public libraries. Some parents are stating that they are bringing up their children to be "gender fluid." A few government agencies (and other groups) are adding alternatives to "male" and "female" on various forms and documents. In some places (as has happened in one instance with a committee in California recently), people are being told not to use *he, she, her,* or *him* in referring to people.

But I must make this point so clear: Our culture is no different from those of the past that we call barbaric! And that's because the sin nature of unregenerate man hasn't changed. And that's the problem.

Now, the solution has never changed, and that solution is the truth of God's Word and the saving gospel. I often remind people that what we see happening around us today is the consequence of a battle that began 6,000 years ago in a garden. It's a battle between God's Word and man's word. It began when the devil came to Eve and asked, *"Did God actually say ...?"* (Genesis 3:1).

> **The basic attack in this battle is on the authority of the Word of God, and we need to understand how this battle manifests itself today so we can be effective soldiers for the King.**

JUNE 16

Genesis 6:11-12

Days like Noah

I've had many Christians tell me they believe we are living in days like Noah in the Western world. They say this because the moral revolution and hostility toward Christianity make it seem that the world today is as bad as Noah's day.

As I've traveled across the United States and other countries around the world, speaking at conferences and in churches, a number of people have made comments to me that can be summarized like this:

"The Western world is so permeated by moral relativism. Who would have thought generations ago that the worldview of the culture would be driven by such issues as gender, gay marriage, abortion, and so on? And whereas the Church was once held in high esteem in the West, we now see an anti-Christian sentiment growing and Christian symbols being removed from public places. Once, the Bible was held in high regard in our government schools, but now it's almost banned from such educational institutions. And so much of the Church (including Christian educational institutions) has compromised God's Word in Genesis and also supports antibiblical positions like gay marriage and transgenderism."

After such comments, many people then say something like this to me: "Surely the Lord must be coming back soon. We must be living in days just like those of Noah when there was so much rebellion."

But are we really living in days like Noah? I may shock some by saying that I don't believe things are anywhere near as bad as the days of Noah. For all the ungodly behavior and rampant rebellion against God's Word, I believe we are far from what it must have been like in Noah's day. Even with the rampant evil we see in our Western world, I contend that our culture is far from that of Noah's day. I would say that what's happening in our Western world gives us somewhat of a small glimpse of what it may have been like in Noah's day. Let's read a description of what it was like in Noah's day from God's Word:

The Lord saw that the wickedness of man was great in the earth, and that every intention of the thoughts of his heart was only evil continually (Genesis 6:5).

Now the earth was corrupt in God's sight, and the earth was filled with violence. And God saw the earth, and behold, it was corrupt, for all flesh had corrupted their way on the earth (Genesis 6:11–12).

And then we find out:

These are the generations of Noah. Noah was a righteous man, blameless in his generation. Noah walked with God (Genesis 6:9).

[B]ecause they formerly did not obey, when God's patience waited in the days of Noah, while the ark was being prepared, in which a few, that is, eight persons, were brought safely through water (1 Peter 3:20).

[I]f he did not spare the ancient world, but preserved Noah, a herald of righteousness, with seven others, when he brought a flood upon the world of the ungodly (2 Peter 2:5).

It's very obvious from all these Scriptures that the whole world, except for Noah (and his family) had rebelled against God. Think about this for a moment. Can we even imagine a world where the entire population

APOLOGETICS   JUNE 16

(perhaps tens of millions or even billions of people), except for eight people, totally rebelled against God? And as God's Word describes, "Every intention of the thoughts of his heart was only evil continually."

I can't even begin to imagine how bad it must have been! That's why I stated that I think we get maybe a small glimpse of what it must have been like when we look at our culture today. There are millions of Christians in the West and millions more in the rest of the world. Can we even begin to understand what it must have been like to have only eight people who believed in God? I don't think so.

I think about this as I see thousands daily flocking to the Ark Encounter and Creation Museum attractions. Even though up to 30% are non-Christian, there are thousands upon thousands of people who love these Christian-themed attractions and want their families and friends to be impacted spiritually by them.

And that brings me to a point I've contemplated many times. God places Noah in the godly Hall of Fame in Hebrews 11: *By faith Noah, being warned by God concerning events as yet unseen, in reverent fear constructed an ark for the saving of his household. By this he condemned the world and became an heir of the righteousness that comes by faith* (Hebrews 11:7). We also read of Noah, *And Noah did all that the Lord had commanded him* (Genesis 7:5).

Just meditate on this for a moment. The entire population (except for Noah and his family) exhibited evil, as they rebelled against God! Yet Noah obeyed God. I can't even think about what sort of mocking, scoffing, and attacks he received for building the Ark. In the face of such wanton disobedience, Noah trusted God, obeyed His word, built the Ark, and then went through the door of the Ark with his family, believing God would do what He said He would — judge the unbelieving world of his day! What faith!

Oh, Lord! If, in the face of such adversity from the entire world, Noah stood for You as he did, surely we can put up with the mocking, scoffing, and ridicule God's people receive today and be prepared to do great things for You. Surely we can stand for Your Word without compromise and be prepared to be counted worthy of such persecution, whether it's from the secular world or the Church.

> **God, please grant us faith like Noah had so we can be a witness for You that would result in saving many from the judgment to come.**

JUNE 17
Romans 10:9

Gospel Gift

Did you know Bill Nye once sent me a gift? I was surprised but pleased that Bill Nye took the time to send me a gift before Christmas 2014. You will be very interested in what he sent me. My wife and I were on an extended stay in Australia at the time, due to the passing of my wife's dad. And, yes, I sent a gift back to Bill Nye, as I will explain below.

Both Bill Nye and AiG came out with books that covered the topics dealt with in the well-publicized Nye/Ham debate on February 4, 2014, and other aspects of the debate. The inscribed book he sent me was titled *Undeniable*, and the inscribed book I sent him was titled *Inside the Nye Ham Debate*.

Now on Lawrence O'Donnell's MSNBC show *Last Word* on the evening of the debate, Nye stated at one point that he had "respect for Mr. Ham and his beliefs." Also, on ABC TV's *Nightline* program about the debate, Nye stated that the two of us were "more alike" than different. When the correspondent Dan Harris asked the two of us if we were seeing the birth of a friendship, Nye stated that he has a "mutual respect for colleagues" who hold passionate beliefs.

But on the HBO interview with Bill Maher on Friday, February 14, 2014, Mr. Nye's tone had changed quite a bit. At the 44-second point, when Nye was asked about having some "respect" for me, he caved in to Bill Maher and stated, "If I said that, I may have misspoken." He then clarified that he really meant he respects my "passion." Nye went on to say that I'm not a charlatan, as he thought I was — but admitted that I really do believe what I presented.

Actually, from a lot of articles and posts I read, Bill Nye received a lot of flak from his peers for even debating me. Evolutionists don't want a debate with creationists, as they don't want people to hear creationist arguments! They want censorship. And they certainly didn't want Bill Nye saying complimentary things about me. Today, basically the only people who want to debate creationists are atheists who want to use *ad hominem* arguments and malign and slander the Christian.

I remember telling Dan Harris (ABC Television) in front of Bill Nye that I believed we could be friends. I was brought up in Australia, which has a very small percentage of Christians, so most of my best friends at school and university were not Christians — but we had a great respect for each other. I believed the same could be true of Bill Nye and me. Yes, we would oppose what each other teaches — and speak very forthrightly about those beliefs publicly — but we could still have a mutual respect for one another. Personally, I do believe Bill has a respect for me, as he knows that I do sincerely believe what I am saying and am prepared to publicly defend my beliefs.

So what did he send me before that Christmas? Well, he sent me an autographed copy of his book with a special message in it for me: "For Ken, Here's hoping you find your way someday. You would be welcomed in the world of reason — We could celebrate the science together! Bill Nye, 6 Dec. 2014."

Now, as I said above, the debate with Bill Nye really illustrated the clash of two worldviews — the clash that began in Genesis 3 when Adam chose to decide truth for himself, instead of trusting God's Word. The clash has been going on for 6,000 years — a battle between two worldviews: man's word vs. God's Word.

To me, the two books (Bill Nye's new book and the book AiG produced about the debate, coauthored by my son-in-law Bodie Hodge and myself) illustrate this same clash. As I read Bill's note to me, I thought the best way to respond was to send Bill a copy of our book, *Inside the Nye Ham Debate*, with a special message to Bill from me.

So what message did I send Bill? Well, I wanted to illustrate once again the worldview clash between the two of us. Also, I know that *Faith comes from hearing, and hearing through the word of Christ* (Romans 10:17) and that we read of God's Word, *[S]o shall my word be that goes out from my mouth; it shall not return to me empty* (Isaiah 55:11).

Now, read Bill's message to me again: "For Ken, Here's hoping you find your way someday. You would be welcomed in the world of reason — We could celebrate the science together! Bill Nye, 6 Dec. 2014."

Here is what I wrote in the book for Bill: "For Bill, Here's earnestly hoping you find THE WAY someday. You would be welcomed in the world of the redeemed. We could celebrate the salvation together. John 14:6 — Jesus said, I am the way, the truth and the life. Ken Ham, Jan 6, 2015."

If you have never watched the debate, I encourage you to do so on YouTube or on our Answers TV streaming platform. Millions have watched it, and the positive feedback has been and continues to be astounding.

The Lord is not slow to fulfill his promise as some count slowness, but is patient toward you, not wishing that any should perish, but that all should reach repentance (2 Peter 3:9).

[B]ecause, if you confess with your mouth that Jesus is Lord and believe in your heart that God raised him from the dead, you will be saved (Romans 10:9).

I am thankful Bill sent that gift. It gave me the opportunity to respond and once again lovingly challenge him concerning the gospel. I really want Bill and everyone in the world to know that the greatest gift in the universe is the one God offers us in the person of His Son: *And the Word became flesh and dwelt among us, and we have seen his glory, glory as of the only Son from the Father, full of grace and truth* (John 1:14).

> We need to be praying earnestly for Bill. God has brought him into my life, so even though I will publicly respond to his wrong beliefs when deemed necessary, I will pray for him and ask others to do the same.

JUNE 18
1 Corinthians 1:23

Generational Language Gap

Did you know many in the younger generations speak a different language than the older generations? OK, so in the United States, Australia, New Zealand, and the United Kingdom, English is the main language, right? Yes, that's true, but it's also true the younger generations are increasingly speaking what I would call a different language. Recently, I've been increasingly using words like:

- communication chasm
- millennial speak
- Greekized
- de-Greekized

Why am I using such unusual terms? I believe such words can help show how vital it is for Christians to understand the massive problem we have in effectively communicating the gospel and the Christian worldview in our secularized culture. Now, if I told you that someone was out by the "black stump" and "stone the crows" and boil the "billy" and cook a few "spuds," would you understand this Aussie slang? And if I said I was taking the "trouble and strife" and the "billy lids" out, can you guess what that means? Those words are from Australian slang — yes, that's a different language.

As I found out when our family moved to the United States 31 years ago, American English and Australian English are two different languages! I had to learn the words Americans used so I could communicate better. For instance, I had to learn to say "dead battery," not "flat battery." And "nursing a baby" in Australia means holding a baby, but it doesn't mean that in America, as I embarrassingly found out one day! These are communication problems due to differences within the English language. And communication is basically impossible if two people speak totally different languages, such as Chinese and English (unless, of course, you've learned to speak both languages).

Today, we have an increasing language problem in regard to communicating Christian messages, even as we use the same words. It often occurs between the older and younger generations. Many words have changed meaning! Words like *race, identity, story, gender, gay, health care, rainbow,* and many others have changed meaning or have been redefined by the secular culture. If you follow news reporters on TV and read newspaper columns of those who generally hold to conservative views (and they seem to be rare these days), you see this generational problem. I've noticed how they report on the problem in different ways, such as stating: "There's a great divide in this nation. We are seeing a Civil War happening before our eyes."

There's an intolerance to anything conservative in the younger generations that we haven't seen before: they recognize a change has occurred. There's definitely a growing communication chasm widening in the West. From a big-picture perspective, it seems to me there's a division between the older generation (age 35 and above) and the younger generation (millennials and Generation Z). My own observations (after extensive travel across the United States and much of the Western world) have led me to conclude that there's a growing chasm in the West between our past Christianized cultures and today's very secularized cultures (or what I call Acts 17 "Greekized"-type cultures). It's analogous to the way the Apostle Paul presented the gospel to the secular Greeks (Acts 17). This difference of worldviews is also seen today in the various ways millennials and Generation Z interpret certain words and give them different meanings, as opposed to how past generations understood the terms! For instance, millennials can express themselves in what I call "millennial

APOLOGETICS

speak." (Think "newspeak" from Orwell's book *1984*, where people would say one thing but mean another.) Those using "millennial speak" will claim they are tolerant of all beliefs, yet their "tolerance" often exhibits itself as being extremely intolerant of anyone who disagrees with them. Generation Z are the most atheistic generation, and that affects how they interpret words.

There are major language differences on either side of this chasm. Here are two examples: Generations ago, if someone said the word *God* in a public (government) school, most teachers and students would have immediately interpreted this word to mean the God of the Bible. However, when you say the word *God* today, many in the younger generation will interpret it by asking, "Which god?" The Muslim god? A Hindu god? A Buddhist concept of god? Which god? Today, the younger generation thinks in terms of many gods — and at the same time has been brainwashed to believe the Christian God is not allowed in the public arena!

And then there's another major problem in the culture! Increasingly, the younger generations are biblically illiterate. Many millennials who attended church as children or teens no longer go to church, and there's a growing number of them and Generation Z who say they are one of the "nones." Nones describe themselves as (supposedly) having no religion!

Many in the younger generations have no knowledge of the origin of sin and death and, therefore, have no understanding of who Jesus is and what He did on the Cross. In one of the most important messages I present in churches, I explain that the older generations grew up in more of what I call an "Acts 2"-type culture. When Peter preached to the Jews as recorded in Acts 2, he concentrated on the message of the death and Resurrection of Christ. The Jews of Acts 2 believed in one Creator God and understood the origin of sin and death and the need for a Savior. Their stumbling block was recognizing Jesus as the Messiah.

I then explain that the younger generations today are more like the Greeks in Acts 17. When Paul preached the message of the Resurrection to the Greeks, they didn't understand it. In their culture, there were atheists, pantheists, polytheists, and so on, with temples and idols. The Greeks were essentially evolutionary in their thinking and didn't have the foundational knowledge to understand the gospel. Paul had to define who the real God is and then give them the right foundation so they would truly understand the message of the gospel.

I suggest that the younger generations today are more like the Greeks in Acts 17 than the Jews in Acts 2. As such, we need (adding a new word to our vocabulary) to de-Greekize them. Meaning: we need to undo why they think the Bible can't be trusted. We need to explain to them the foundation of the gospel and answer their skeptical questions so they will truly understand the message of the Cross.

I call this approach "creation evangelism." Many believers have told me that this method has changed their whole approach to leading Sunday schools and Bible studies and preparing sermons. Pastors have told me that using "creation evangelism" to "de-Greekize" (i.e., teaching creation apologetics) is stopping an exodus of young people from their churches. I believe most churches are still stuck in an Acts 2 approach to evangelism.

Christians need to know how to effectively share the gospel in a hostile world, just like Paul did in Acts 17, through the process of "de-Greekizing." We must give non-Christians the proper starting point for their thinking. *[B]ut we preach Christ crucified, a stumbling block to Jews and folly to Gentiles* (1 Corinthians 1:23).

Without that correct foundation, people will never understand their need for a Savior.

JUNE 19
1 Peter 5:8

Weather Forecasting

Weather forecasters don't always get it right. But there's a type of weather forecasting that is accurate when you understand a true biblical worldview. Did you know that Answers in Genesis is engaged in a form of weather forecasting?

Just as when people hear the forecast of a huge storm approaching and they batten down, we at AiG want to give you a forecast of a different sort of storm and get you prepared. Actually, it's a storm that's been raging for 6,000 years, but it's now intensifying. Thankfully, God has given us instructions in His Word, the Bible, on how to weather this kind of storm.

As you have probably guessed, the storm I'm talking about has a spiritual dimension. The spiritual storm raging around us is described in many verses, including the following: *Be sober-minded; be watchful. Your adversary the devil prowls around like a roaring lion, seeking someone to devour* (1 Peter 5:8).

And I'm sure you are familiar with this related verse: *For we do not wrestle against flesh and blood, but against the rulers, against the authorities, against the cosmic powers over this present darkness, against the spiritual forces of evil in the heavenly places* (Ephesians 6:12).

There are times when this storm intensifies, particularly when God's people do their best to put on the whole armor of God (Ephesians 6:10–18) and actively fight against spiritual wickedness.

At Answers in Genesis, we experienced a huge spiritual storm after we announced the Lord had called us to build a Creation Museum. Secularists bent on attacking the Lord and His Word used lies and even a lawsuit to try to stop the museum project. But, just as God did with the wicked, He will (as explained by the psalmist) have the victory: *The wicked draw the sword and bend their bows to bring down the poor and needy, to slay those whose way is upright; their sword shall enter their own heart, and their bows shall be broken* (Psalm 37:14–15).

Yes, the work of the opponents of God will be fruitless. In fact, AiG can look back on the massive opposition to the museum and say (now seeing the success of the museum), *As for you, you meant evil against me, but God meant it for good, to bring it about that many people should be kept alive, as they are today* (Genesis 50:20).

As a result of this museum opposition, we were blessed to obtain a much better piece of property in a prime location right off an interstate and also build a far bigger facility. And the media attention was enormous, giving the museum a high profile before it opened. Praise God, we've seen many people saved and the faith of tens of thousands of Christians revived and emboldened as they've been equipped. There are now many more soldiers ready and active to battle in a raging storm.

When we announced our next major outreach — a life-sized Noah's Ark (something the Lord through various circumstances clearly called us to build) — we once again predicted the weather. AiG expected that in a nation where the spiritual storm was intensifying (perhaps even more than what we had seen in the past), the Ark would be in the middle of it. And this is exactly what happened.

The storm that continues to build in this nation is the secularists' overall attempt to rid the culture of the reminders of the Christian heritage of the USA. The storm clouds are not just gathered above Northern

APOLOGETICS — JUNE 19

Kentucky and the Ark Encounter. The storm has been slowly spreading over the entire nation and, in fact, over the entire Western world, as secularists have intensified their propaganda campaign to undermine biblical Christianity. Along the way, they have even blinded many Christians to the true nature of the storm.

The secularists' storm seeks to impose the religion of atheism on the culture. In one of their most blatant displays of intolerance, as they undercut the "free exercise of religion" guaranteed under the U.S. Constitution, they targeted our Ark Encounter project.

We had to go to court over a major First Amendment matter because: 1) The state of Kentucky had violated both federal and state laws by engaging in viewpoint discrimination against the Ark project, and 2) more importantly, if we had allowed the state's decision to go unchallenged, the door would have remained open wider for secularists to be allowed to undermine the free exercise of religion for other groups, including churches.

Kentucky at the time denied AiG a possible tourism incentive involving some rebate of sales generated by a tourist facility, one that was made available to any organization in Kentucky that fulfilled certain objective criteria that would bring tourist dollars into Kentucky. And why did the state deny this to our Ark Encounter attraction? Because the state said the project was deemed as religious and thus ineligible to participate in the Kentucky Tourism Development Act rebate program.

AiG launched a legal challenge because ultimately this issue affected not just those who stood with AiG, but all Christians — and indeed, people of all faiths. Our most fundamental freedoms as Americans were at issue: freedom of speech and the free exercise of religion. We are grateful that God blessed us with two attorneys with a great deal of experience in religious liberty cases who provided their services to AiG at no charge. We won this federal court case. Because we know that this spiritual storm will continue to rage against the AiG ministry, we need to learn to weather the storm continuously. *For you have been a stronghold to the poor, a stronghold to the needy in his distress, a shelter from the storm and a shade from the heat; for the breath of the ruthless is like a storm against a wall* (Isaiah 25:4).

God never promises there won't be such storms for His followers. In fact, those who are actively doing battle for the King of creation will encounter such storms. Thankfully, He does promise to be a refuge from the storm, and by His power and providence, He will fight for us against the flood of persecution.

If you have never had storms, maybe you should be looking at what impact you are making.

JUNE 20
2 Timothy 3:14–17

No Neutral

Did you know that everyone has a worldview and no one is neutral? Our worldview is not neutral. The Bible teaches we are either for Christ or against, we walk in light or darkness, we gather or scatter, we build our house on the rock or the sand. There are many verses of Scripture reminding us over and over again that there is no neutral position. Not only that, but we have a biased heart to begin with, as we are all sinners. I was reminded of this when a pastor produced a two-part video series against the position I hold on Genesis concerning six literal days and young earth. This pastor claimed that those Christians who reject the six literal days and young earth do so because of the text of Scripture. He then cited Augustine as an example, saying that Augustine said that explaining the light on day one was a problem; therefore, this couldn't be an ordinary day. But what Augustine did was start outside Scripture by using his own fallible logic to say he had a problem with the light on day one. He wasn't starting from Scripture. This pastor then said he rejected the thousands of years age for the earth and accepted millions of years. He said that "science" had shown clearly the earth is billions of years old. He then concluded that those who believe in six literal days and a young earth, as we do at Answers in Genesis, must be misinterpreting the text. He said this to attempt to justify his assertion that he was starting with the text, not coming to the text with outside ideas. But he was starting with the presupposition that the earth was millions of years old. Despite his claim to the contrary, he was starting outside Scripture and taking ideas to Scripture. He was then interpreting the text on the basis of the beliefs he already had.

However, such Christians have a different principle for interpreting Genesis 1–11 than they do for the rest of God's Word. If they applied the same logic above to the Resurrection, we would have to reject the bodily Resurrection of Christ because no scientist has shown a person can be raised from the dead. And the same would be true of the virgin birth and so many other miraculous accounts in Scripture. All of us need to examine our presuppositions to determine if we are letting the words of Scripture in context speak to us, or whether we are imposing ideas from the outside. Now it is true that even letting Scripture speak to us involves an interpretation. So we are taking an interpretive method to Scripture. I admit that my interpretive method is that of the grammatical-historical interpretive method. I let the words of Scripture and their context, according to the genre in which they are written and the rules of grammar, etc., for that language tell me what they are saying. Actually, Genesis is written as typical historical narrative. Some Christians claim it is written as "mythohistory" or poetry, etc. But they are imposing these ideas on Genesis to justify their rejection of a young earth, six literal days, etc. If we take Genesis as written, it is written as history, and Genesis is quoted as history throughout the Scriptures. We must also use Scripture to interpret Scripture to ensure we are interpreting it correctly.

So what does Genesis mean? Imagine if we approached everything we read like this. For instance, if you were driving and came upon a sign that says STOP, you might think, "It says, 'Stop,' but what does that really mean? My personal interpretation is that it means slow down and stop only if you see other cars coming." We know better. We're supposed to think, "Oh, a stop sign. I have to obey what it clearly says. It means to come to a full stop." Sadly, today we see Christians applying the first approach to the Bible, particularly to the Book of Genesis — and specifically to the age of the earth and universe.

APOLOGETICS — JUNE 20

I was on a radio program, and the pastor interviewing me asked something like this: "You agree Christians can have different views of baptism, eschatology, speaking in tongues, Sabbath day, and Calvinism?" I answered in the affirmative. The pastor continued, "And Christians can have different views of Genesis; it's the same thing."

"No, it's not the same thing," I replied. I then explained that when Christians disagree on issues like eschatology and baptism, they are arguing from Scripture and within Scripture. However, I contend that the different views of Genesis come from people taking outside ideas — beliefs from fallible man — and interpreting the clear words of Scripture to fit those beliefs.

Many different views persist within the Church, particularly among church leadership and academics, on how to take Genesis. The list of positions includes theistic evolution, evolutionary creation, progressive creation, framework hypothesis, day-age theory, local flood, and the gap theory. There are also new ideas, like those who state that Genesis 1 describes the creation of some "cosmic temple."

Now, I've actually had people come to me when I speak at conferences and say, "Our pastor is a gap theorist," or "My daughter's college professor is a theistic evolutionist," and so on, and then someone asks me, "What is your position on Genesis?" My answer? "The biblical one, of course: six literal days, young earth, literal Adam, and global Flood. I take it as written." I have looked into every one of the positions on Genesis that contradict the "biblical one" listed above, and I've found one common factor. Every single one in some way attempts to incorporate the "millions of years" belief into Genesis.

Here's what's so disheartening to me. Many Christian leaders and academics who hold one of these positions on Genesis would, by and large, take God's Word the same way I do from Genesis 12 onward! Yes, we may have some theological disagreements, arguing from within Scripture, and we may differ on the Book of Revelation. But from Genesis 12 onward, we don't use outside beliefs from the secular world to force a particular view on God's Word — but this is what they are doing in Genesis with the millions of years belief.

And therein lies the issue — they have one hermeneutical principle for interpreting Genesis 1–11 (forcing man's beliefs in millions of years into Scripture) and a different one for the rest of God's Word (taking God's Word as written and interpreting Scripture with Scripture). And yet most of them can't see this or don't want to. Why not? I believe it's primarily because of academic peer pressure, academic pride, and a desire for academic respectability.

If you read Genesis 1–11 to a child, he or she will understand the basic message and would never get the idea of millions of years from this account. No! The idea of millions of years comes from fallible man's beliefs and is imposed upon Genesis by many who would never impose man's rejection of Christ's physical Resurrection or virgin birth on the New Testament!

But as for you, continue in what you have learned and have firmly believed, knowing from whom you learned it and how from childhood you have been acquainted with the sacred writings, which are able to make you wise for salvation through faith in Christ Jesus. All Scripture is breathed out by God and profitable for teaching, for reproof, for correction, and for training in righteousness, that the man of God may be complete, equipped for every good work (2 Timothy 3:14–17).

Genesis means what it so clearly says it means.

JUNE 21
Matthew 5:13

Disease in the Church

There's a disease that has permeated the Church, and sadly, the majority of church leaders/Christian academics have been spreading it! Let me say this bluntly! The idea of millions of years is like a disease, and biological evolution is like the symptom. Many Christians are willing to deal with the "symptom" but not the "disease."

Although we know sin is the ultimate disease/reason for the secularist naturalistic (anti-God) position, I say again, millions of years is like a disease and biological evolution is like the symptom. Christians need to not only deal with the "symptom" but also the "disease." Here are some conclusions I have come to after 35 years of ministry: Many Christian leaders think that as long as they reject biological/anthropological evolution, then it doesn't really matter about the age of the earth. These pastors and theologians believe that by rejecting Darwinian evolution, they have shut the door to compromise regarding the authority of the Scriptures.

The reality, however, is that by allowing for millions of years, these Christian leaders have kept a "compromise door" open. If that door is not completely shut, then the next generation of leaders will push the door open further.

This compromise has led to a catastrophic loss of biblical authority in the Church (and culture as a whole) — which includes the devastating consequence of moral relativism permeating the Church. It has also greatly contributed to the generational loss from the Church.

Did you know that more often than not, when the secular media report on our Creation Museum or Ark Encounter, the reporters don't even mention our stand against evolution but are more focused on the issue of the age of the earth/universe?

For instance, in 2010, one secular news source, in covering our Creation Museum and Ark Encounter, stated: "The ministry, Answers in Genesis, believes the Earth is only 6000 years old — a controversial assertion even among many Bible-believing Christians." This news item was written to focus on the age of the earth issue rather than all that is taught by the various exhibits in these attractions.

A 2010 *Vanity Fair* magazine article about the Creation Museum declared: "Science has given itself millions of years — eons — to play with, but the righteous have got to get the whole lot in, home and dry, in less than 6,000 years, using just a pitchfork and a loud voice. It's like playing speed chess against a computer and a thousand people with Nobel Prizes."

When ABC TV's *Good Morning America* broadcasted live during the opening of the Creation Museum (May 2007), ABC reported: "Exhibits at almost every natural history museum teach that dinosaurs are millions of years old, and that they died out long before human beings existed. But at the Creation Museum, they say God created dinosaurs and humans at the same time." Over and over again, I've seen the media focus on the age issue. Why is the issue of time so important in the secular world? Well, without the supposed millions/billions of years, secularists cannot even propose biological evolution. An old age is absolutely crucial for the secularists in their attempt to explain life without God — by natural processes. Time is the hero of the plot for the secularist evolution religion.

CHURCH JUNE 21

It is vital for Christians to understand that: The Bible does not even hint at millions or billions of years. If you take the Bible as written, it's obvious God created in six literal days. With the specific history given in the genealogical lists, it's very clear that there have been only about 6,000 years of history since time began.

All dating methods devised by humans are fallible; they are based on fallible assumptions. The only true reliable dating method is the historical record that God prepared for us: the Bible.

When Christian leaders try to add millions of years into God's Word, then they are making God responsible for death, disease, thorns, carnivory, and suffering millions of years before sin. The Bible makes it clear such things are a result of man's sin! Ultimately, the issue over the age of the earth/universe is one of authority: Will it be fallible, sinful man's authority, or will it be God's? Should we take man's fallible understandings about the past and reinterpret God's Word, or do we judge man's beliefs against the absolute authority of Scripture?

The secular world has intimidated so many pastors and Christian/Bible college and seminary academics to believe in millions of years, for if they don't accept an old earth, they will be accused of being anti-intellectual and anti-science. It's largely a problem of academic and intellectual pride, as so many of these church leaders and academics don't want to be called anti-intellectual or anti-science by the world.

So why such intimidation from the world? Because the idea of an earth/universe that is billions of years old is the foundational religion of this age for secularists who need to explain the universe and all of life without God. The foundation of their religion is naturalism. These atheists and agnostics must have billions of years to support evolutionary naturalism. Without the supposed millions of years, they could not even begin to propose their evolution of life ideas. They need an incomprehensible amount of time (millions of years) to try to justify their impossible idea (naturalistic evolution for the formation of all life).

Compromising Christian leaders need to give up not only biological evolution but geological and cosmological evolution (i.e., billions of years). I call on Christians everywhere to shut the door to this compromise that is undermining the Church and culture and undermining biblical authority. Indeed, we are seeing the collapse of biblical Christianity in the West as scriptural authority is questioned.

Do not be unequally yoked with unbelievers. For what partnership has righteousness with lawlessness? Or what fellowship has light with darkness? (2 Corinthians 6:14).

"I know your works: you are neither cold nor hot. Would that you were either cold or hot! So, because you are lukewarm, and neither hot nor cold, I will spit you out of my mouth" (Revelation 3:15–16).

"You are the salt of the earth, but if salt has lost its taste, how shall its saltiness be restored? It is no longer good for anything except to be thrown out and trampled under people's feet" (Matthew 5:13).

> **The idea of millions of years is like a disease in the Church; biological evolution is just a symptom, and we need to do all we can to help prevent the disease from spreading further.**

JUNE 22

Hebrews 11:1

Who Has Faith?

Do evolutionists have faith? Do creationists have faith? What is the meaning of faith? Many, including Christians with the best of intentions, claim, "It takes more faith to believe in evolution than it does to believe in creation." But is this a proper use of the word *faith*? On the surface, this sounds like a plausible argument. But how does it correspond to the teaching of Scripture? How does the Bible define the word *faith*?

The Book of Hebrews offers a definition of faith that most believers should be familiar with: *Now faith is the assurance of things hoped for, the conviction of things not seen* (Hebrews 11:1). Here, *assurance* relates to the essence of truth ("what really is"). The Greek word pictures something that "stands fast under," such as a foundation or substructure, which provides a firm support for what we think and do. "Conviction of things not seen" refers to an assurance or evidence not based primarily on personal experience or empirical evidence but upon the character and purposes of God. This definition characterizes the lives of the believers mentioned in Hebrews 11, who relied on nothing but the promises of God without any visible evidence that the promises would be fulfilled (e.g., Hebrews 11:10, 11, 13, 39–40). Faith, then, generally involves trust or belief in someone or something — in this case, God — that is faithful:

Know therefore that the Lord your God is God, the faithful God who keeps covenant and steadfast love with those who love him and keep his commandments, to a thousand generations (Deuteronomy 7:9).

Let us hold fast the confession of our hope without wavering, for he who promised is faithful (Hebrews 10:23).

Scripture teaches that God is true (John 3:33) and cannot lie (Titus 1:2). He has communicated His truth through the apostles and prophets: *And we also thank God constantly for this, that when you received the word of God, which you heard from us, you accepted it not as the word of men but as what it really is, the word of God, which is at work in you believers* (1 Thessalonians 2:13).

Let's apply this biblical definition of faith to the claims of John 3:16, where it is written: *For God so loved the world, that he gave his only Son, that whoever believes in him should not perish but have eternal life.* Here we see that the eternal, transcendent God took on the form of human flesh, Jesus Christ. He came to earth to live a perfect life, to die a criminal's death, and to rise again three days later — all because "God so loved the world." Furthermore, anyone who believes that Christ is Lord and that He was raised from the dead will have "everlasting life" (cf. Romans 10:9). These are some extravagant claims! But we believe them. Why? We believe because we have faith in a God who is faithful (Deuteronomy 7:9; 1 Corinthians 1:9; 2 Timothy 2:13; Hebrews 10:23, 11:11; Revelation 3:14).

We as believers can have faith in God's Word because God is who He claims to be (Hebrews 11:6), and He has given us His revelation through His Word so we can know about Him. He promised that His words would never pass away (Matthew 24:35), and we know that God never fails (Joshua 21:45). Therefore, we regard Scripture as the reliable and sufficient revelation of the one true God. Moreover, God has proven Himself true over and over again. We expect this since He is the standard of proof and truth! We read eyewitness accounts and fulfilled prophecies recorded in the Word of God. We also find that operational science (observable, testable, and repeatable experimentation) is consistent with Scripture. The basis for our faith comes from God and His Word, as Romans 10:17 says, *So faith comes from hearing, and hearing through the word of Christ.* Things like fulfilled prophecies and eyewitness accounts help show that our faith is not blind. However, evolution does not qualify for faith, only blind faith.

Based on the Bible's description of faith, it does not seem accurate to say that it takes more faith to believe in evolution and millions of years. In fact, it's not likely that it takes any faith at all. Biblical faith is based on someone or something that is faithful, but evolutionary ideas are anything but faithful. Additionally, Romans 10:17 clearly indicates that evolution — which does not come from Scripture — is not based on biblical faith. Merriam-Webster's Dictionary has multiple definitions for *faith*. And there is a definition of *faith* that describes the evolutionists: "firm belief in something for which there is no proof."[59] Clearly, this definition of "blind faith" has a much different meaning than biblical faith.

Unlike biblical faith, blind faith has no substance, and there is no evidence or assurance of things "not seen." Biblical faith is defensible because our Creator is faithful. Using God's infallible and inerrant Word as our starting point, we can teach the truth about the world around us and show how the evidence we see is consistent with His Word. As Scripture states, *[A]lways being prepared to make a defense to anyone who asks you for a reason for the hope that is in you; yet do it with gentleness and respect* (1 Peter 3:15). In other words, we must be prepared to defend the substance of things in which we have hope. Of course, we all have a limit to what we will believe. In other words, every person is willing to accept some things based solely on the word of another. For example, a stranger might tell you that he flipped a coin three times and that it came up heads all three times. Would you believe him? Most likely — it does not take much convincing to believe such a claim. But what if the same person then told you that he flipped a coin 100 times and it came up heads every time — would you believe him then? Because of the improbability that what he is saying is true, it's unlikely that anyone would believe the coin came up heads 100 times in a row by chance. You might suspect that he somehow rigged the coin toss or that he was lying to you. At that point, you have reached your limit of blind faith. The above example, however, only demonstrates a very small amount of chance. If a person is not convinced that a coin could come up heads 100 times in a row (for which the chance is 1 in 2^{100}, or 1 followed by 30 zeros), then how could he possibly believe in the evolutionary idea that the entire universe came about by chance?

Scripture gives us the best evidence for creation — an eyewitness account from the Creator Himself. Furthermore, the Bible tells us that the experiential evidence for God's handiwork has been made plain to man so that he is without excuse: *For the wrath of God is revealed from heaven against all ungodliness and unrighteousness of men, who by their unrighteousness suppress the truth. For what can be known about God is plain to them, because God has shown it to them. For his invisible attributes, namely, his eternal power and divine nature, have been clearly perceived, ever since the creation of the world, in the things that have been made. So they are without excuse* (Romans 1:18–20).

So the next time you hear someone say, "It takes more faith to believe in evolution than creation," remember that biblical faith is based on the faithfulness of someone or something — specifically, the Creator God and His Word — and without that, all you have is blind faith.

> Not only do we have the Word of God, but we also can see and experience the evidence of creation all around us, from the birds of the air to the fish of the sea.

JUNE 23
Jeremiah 17:9

Atheists and Morality

When I was answering the question of who Cain's wife was on a radio talk show, an atheist told me I was immoral for saying close relations married in early history. But can an atheist make that claim? Secularists frequently accuse Christians of behaving "immorally" and religion of being "evil." But such objections bring up an interesting question: How do secular humanists or atheists define evil and morality and by what authority do they make such statements?

For the atheist or secular humanist, there is no foundation for morality besides his or her own subjective opinion. These individuals often throw around words such as *evil, immoral, moral,* or *ethical,* often in the context of Christianity or Christian individuals. They will say things such as "religion is evil" or that teaching creation to children is "child abuse," but what do they mean by these phrases?

In their worldview, what makes anything immoral or wrong? Really, it boils down to nothing more than their opinion. They claim that something is wrong. But who is to say that their opinion is the right one? After all, there are many different opinions on what is right and wrong. Who decides which one is right and which one is wrong?

Some atheists will argue that morality is simply decided by the society. For example, here in America, our society has decided that murdering an innocent human being is wrong, and therefore, that action is morally wrong. But this kind of thinking simply does not hold up to scrutiny.

Society often changes its opinion. One clear example of this is in regard to gay "marriage." What was considered morally wrong by most of society is now legal, applauded, and celebrated by some groups. In this view, homosexual behavior went from being morally wrong to being morally acceptable.

What if our society decides that murder is acceptable, as it did in the case of *Roe v. Wade* when America legalized the killing of unborn children? Does murder suddenly become morally acceptable too? What about adultery, stealing, lying, or any other manner of morally reprehensible actions? Would the atheist or humanist accept a society that decides that society can kill all atheists and humanists? If society is the moral compass, then the compass never points north but rather jumps all over the place and changes with every generation.

Also, if society determines morality, how can one society tell another society what is right or wrong? Most people would agree that the abhorrent actions of the Nazi death camps were morally wrong. But why? Nazi Germany decided as a society that these actions were morally acceptable. What right does our society have to judge their society if morality is simply a societal preference?

Or what about certain radical Muslim groups? Few would agree that blowing up innocent civilians, slaughtering hundreds of people from other religious groups, kidnapping and enslaving young women, or using children as suicide bombers is morally acceptable. Yet if morality is simply a societal preference, what right does our society have to tell their society that their actions are wrong and must be stopped?

The consistent atheist or humanist can say nothing if that is the ethic a society has decided is right. In this view, the atheist, based on his arbitrary opinion, might not agree with their ethic, but he has no rationale to

APOLOGETICS

say anything or try to put a stop to it. If morality is simply decided by societal preference, it fails to make any sense and becomes arbitrary, subject to change by time and culture.

The problem only gets worse when you break it down to a personal level. Some secularists will argue that morality is an individual decision and no one has the right to tell another person what to do (this is called "autonomous human reason"). Of course, the irony of such a statement should be evident. By saying that no one should tell someone else what to do, they have just told someone else what to do! If secularists really believed this, then they couldn't say "religion is evil" in the first place since it is not their place to say.

If this view of morality is true, then our justice system cannot exist. After all, why should one judge, legislative assembly, or government body impose their view of morality on another individual? If stealing, killing, raping, or abusing is right for one individual, what gives another individual the right to say that view of morality is wrong?

Now this personal morality or human reasoning view stems from the idea that people are basically good and that, left on our own, humans tend to do right and not wrong. (Again, who defines right and wrong?) But humans aren't basically good! Human experience shows that throughout history, humans have committed atrocities, even in our supposedly enlightened Western world. The Bible describes the fallen human heart this way:

The heart is deceitful above all things, and desperately sick; who can understand it? (Jeremiah 17:9).

And when the Lord smelled the pleasing aroma, the Lord said in his heart, "I will never again curse the ground because of man, for the intention of man's heart is evil from his youth. Neither will I ever again strike down every living creature as I have done" (Genesis 8:21).

Autonomous human reason simply does not provide a sufficient foundation for morality.

JUNE 24
Psalm 127:3

Education Controls the Future

Do you know who said this? "He alone, who owns the youth, gains the future!" It sounds like something a modern-day atheist might say. You see, the line reminds me of the time 285 atheists visited our Creation Museum in 2009! One of them later wrote, "For me, the most frightening part was the children's section. It was at this moment that I learned the deepest lesson of my visit to the Museum." He went on to say, "It is in the minds and hearts of our children that the battle will be fought!"

Now, who wrote, "He alone, who owns the youth, gains the future"? It was Adolf Hitler! And remember, he was able to capture the culture!

Secular humanists in America totally grasp the concept that if they are able to "own the youth," they will "gain the future." Because of secular influences that press on our societies, God, through His Word, has instructed parents over and over again to train their children (e.g., Deuteronomy 6:7). Sadly, many parents don't understand that the atheists and other secularists are out to capture the hearts and minds of generations of our children — and unfortunately, they aren't aware that the secularists have been very successful in our schools, media, museums, etc.

Yes, our children are under a fierce attack by secularists. We've already seen the horrible results of this attack. There's been a catastrophic generational loss from the Church. Generation Z is said to be the first post-Christian culture.

In 2012, Bill Nye "the Science Guy" of PBS TV and Disney released a video on YouTube titled, "Creationism Is Not Appropriate for Children." It received about five million views because it was publicized by the world's major media. Toward the end of this anti-creationist video, Bill Nye said the following: "And I say to the grownups, if you want to deny evolution and live in your world, in your world that's completely inconsistent with everything we observe in the universe, that's fine, but don't make your kids do it because we need them. We need scientifically literate voters and taxpayers for the future. We need people that can — we need engineers that can build stuff, solve problems."

Of course, what Bill Nye claimed about the importance of teaching evolution to kids — that if we don't, we won't have engineers, scientists, etc. — is ludicrous. More than that, Nye wants your children to be taught the religion of atheistic evolution as fact. Now Bill Nye was given the "Humanist of the Year" award in 2010.

Just a few weeks later, atheist Richard Dawkins was on CNN and made the following claims:

"You can't even begin to understand biology, you can't understand life, unless you understand what it's all there for, how it arose — and that means evolution. So I would teach evolution very early in childhood ... I think it needs serious attention, that children should be taught where they come from, what life is all about, how it started, why it's there, why there's such diversity of it, why it looks designed. These are all things that can easily be explained to a pretty young child. I'd start at the age of about 7 or 8. There's only one game in town as far as serious science is concerned ... No serious scientist doubts that we are cousins of gorillas, we are cousins of monkeys, we are cousins of snails, we are cousins of earthworms. We have shared ancestors with all animals and all plants. There is no serious scientist who doubts that evolution is a fact."

APOLOGETICS

In recent times, we have also seen an increase in the number of atheists who accuse Answers in Genesis, and Christians in general, of forms of "child abuse" because we teach kids to believe God's Word in Genesis. The atheists continue to be more aggressive than ever. They have a zeal to capture the hearts and minds of your children. They want to own the culture. I wish people in the Church had as much zeal to evangelize people.

These atheists and secularists have already been very successful in using the public (government) school system to win children over to their side. Think about it: they have been successful in throwing out creation, the Bible, prayer, and the Christian God from the public school system. Today, millions of kids are taught atheistic evolution as fact, just as Richard Dawkins wants.

Remember, God's Word says, *Behold, children are a heritage from the Lord* (Psalm 127:3). They are a gift from the Lord and are entrusted to us to train them up for Him — for their eternal ministries. We need to do all we can to reach these children and teens with the truth of God's Word and the gospel most of all. They need to be equipped with the armor of God so they can fight off the "fiery darts" of the wicked one, who is out to entrap them.

Therefore take up the whole armor of God, that you may be able to withstand in the evil day, and having done all, to stand firm. Stand therefore, having fastened on the belt of truth, and having put on the breastplate of righteousness, and, as shoes for your feet, having put on the readiness given by the gospel of peace. In all circumstances take up the shield of faith, with which you can extinguish all the flaming darts of the evil one; and take the helmet of salvation, and the sword of the Spirit, which is the word of God (Ephesians 6:13–17).

For the sake of the gospel, the Church faces an urgent task. We must rescue people from this "evil age." Aware of this urgency, Satan is also after the minds of this current generation. His tactic is to deceive our youth into believing lies that discredit the Bible's authority and accuracy, from which we get this gospel message. The true rescue from this evil world can only come through the gospel of Christ. The attack on the Bible from the ideas of evolution and millions of years causes doubt about the Bible, and the message of the gospel is thus undermined.

I pray your heart is filled with the same urgency as mine to see future generations rescued from the coming judgment of this world. We must rescue them from secular humanism — a worldview that is leading millions of people to reject the gospel, with eternal consequences. There is no greater urgency today than to stand our ground and rescue our children. Together, we must reach children and teens with the truths of Genesis, equipping them to defend the Bible against the onslaughts of evolutionary indoctrination in schools and the media. We are in a battle, in an intense spiritual war. This struggle began in Genesis, when the question was asked, *"Did God actually say …?"* (Genesis 3:1).

> **We need to diligently reach children with the message that "God really did say," and teach them the life-changing truths found in God's Word.**

JUNE 25
Romans 1:16

Taking Back the Rainbow

Do you notice that Satan always takes what God has created/ordained and then perverts it? This has happened with marriage, man's dominion, gender, work, and so on. And it's also happened with the rainbow.

I caused a stir (among secularists) some time ago concerning the rainbow. Yet it wasn't that many years ago I would not have had such scathing responses in talking about God's rainbow. As you know, in Genesis 9, God made a covenant with Noah's family, their descendants, and the animals. God promised He would never judge the world again with a global Flood. He said that whenever a rainbow appeared, it would be a reminder of that covenant. So this special meaning of the rainbow goes back about 4,300 years — just after the Flood of Noah's day. Since the 1970s, the rainbow (though not all of its colors) has been increasingly associated with what is called the "gay" movement — known today worldwide as the LGBTQ movement.

After the Ark was opened, as part of our Christmas lights, we lit up the huge ship with a rainbow of colors. I wrote an article that declared that we are "taking back the rainbow." I publicly reminded people that the meaning of the rainbow was given by God, for He is the One who created it in the first place. That caused something of an uproar from many secularists who were upset that Christians were using the rainbow. Now I tweeted and posted to Facebook that we installed permanent lights at the Ark Encounter to light up the ship each night with a spectacular rainbow of colors. In my posts, I also stated that we were taking back the rainbow, since it belonged to God!

LGBTQ people and their supporters "blew up" my Twitter and blanketed my Facebook with nasty comments. Now, that wasn't totally unexpected in today's environment of growing secular intolerance to anything Christian. But even though I've seen the rising anti-Christian sentiment in our Western cultures, I was somewhat surprised at how vitriolic these people were in response to my rainbow tweets. In fact, the degree of hate was off the charts compared to what I'd seen in the past. The tweets and comments were filled with hatred, expletives, threats, blasphemy, and sexual perversion. This response made me realize what's been simmering in our cultures and is now bubbling to the surface. It is erupting in ways we would never have predicted just a few years ago. It seems the LGBTQ movement, which represents a small percentage of the population, is manipulating the culture in many ways — even much of the Church! This furor over my news item declaring we were taking back the rainbow ended up on numerous news sites across the nation and around the world. Even many newspapers picked it up. Atheist bloggers went berserk, and, of course, gay newspapers made it a major story! A few Christian leaders called and told me of their support. They said that more Christians need to be taking such stands publicly. And we do need this boldness!

Sadly, because so many Christians have not been prepared to stand boldly for the authority of the Word of God and have allowed all sorts of compromises, we are losing the once great Christian influence in the United States and many other Western countries. If Christians aren't more active in proclaiming biblical authority, we will continue to lose influence (and our freedoms), as we see happening currently. Think of all the Christian symbols that have been removed from public places in the United States and elsewhere. And consider the way Christianity has been largely edited out of the government education systems. Look at how secularized our Western cultures have become, where an increasing number of people are calling good evil

THEOLOGYJUNE 25

and evil good (Isaiah 5:20). I never thought I would see that verse playing out in the culture we live in. *Woe to those who call evil good and good evil, who put darkness for light and light for darkness, who put bitter for sweet and sweet for bitter!* (Isaiah 5:20).

Another aspect of this rainbow story really burdened me. I met a lady at a church who said she was so pleased to see us taking the rainbow back. Then she declared how dismayed she was to find out that when she spoke to teenagers in church, they didn't know about the covenant of the rainbow in Genesis 9. They thought the rainbow was just associated with the LGBTQ movement. Yes, this generation of young people in many of our churches is biblically illiterate! There has been such an emphasis in many churches on entertainment and shallow Bible teaching, and a lack of teaching Genesis, or on compromising Genesis with evolution/millions of years, that so many young people today really have a limited understanding of Christianity.

That's why when we opened the Ark Encounter, the AiG board laid 12 stones to represent the 12 stones of Joshua (Joshua 4) — to challenge Christians to remind the coming generations of the truth of God's Word and the gospel. And those 12 stones are now a permanent exhibit near the entrance to the Noah's Ark attraction. Also, the rainbow lights are now a permanent feature at the Ark — to remind us of the true meaning of the rainbow: that God keeps His Word. Actually, the Ark and the Creation Museum were built to very boldly, publicly, and unashamedly remind everyone of the truth of God's Word and the saving gospel message. Those messages need to be heard not only by the secular world but also the Church. So many Christian leaders have compromised God's Word in Genesis and are compromising biblical doctrines concerning marriage.

I personally believe there's a supernatural aspect (judgment) to the massive influence of the LGBTQ movement, which represents only a small part of the population. However, it does represent the state of the culture — and sadly, the state of much of the Church. Activists in the LGBTQ community are growing increasingly hostile, particularly toward Christians who stand on God's Word and advocate for biblical marriage. In the past, the gay community largely claimed they just wanted tolerance. Today, however, they want everyone to celebrate and approve of their lifestyle. They are growing increasingly intolerant of those who refuse. They want total compliance and acceptance from everyone for their worldview. I certainly saw this when AiG proclaimed we were taking back the rainbow.

I don't hate those who call themselves gay. No Christian should. Yet in this day, when you disagree with this movement based on what Scripture teaches, you will be falsely accused of hate — often, ironically, in a hateful way! The ministry of Answers in Genesis and our Creation Museum and Ark Encounter attractions are reaching millions each year across North America and around the world. My burden is to do whatever we can to reach even more people and to be more active, more public, and more bold for the Lord and His Word.

For I am not ashamed of the gospel, for it is the power of God for salvation to everyone who believes, to the Jew first and also to the Greek (Romans 1:16).

And now, Lord, look upon their threats and grant to your servants to continue to speak your word with all boldness (Acts 4:29).

> **We still have the opportunity right now to proclaim truth and be active in taking back what the enemy has captured.**

JUNE 26
Mark 16:15

Focus on the Gospel

Should we just be trying to convert people to be creationists? Do you realize that creationists will end up in hell just like an atheist unless they've received the free gift of salvation?

Over the years, many people, particularly Christian leaders/pastors, have told me that creation is just a side issue, and instead of dealing with the creation and evolution issues, we should be just presenting the gospel. This tells me they have no understanding of what the ministry of Answers in Genesis is all about. Such people told me we shouldn't be spending (they said "wasting") money on building the Ark and Creation Museum, as they wouldn't attract non-Christians and there's no point trying to convert people to be creationists. That's what many falsely think Answers in Genesis is all about.

Now I agree that there's no point in trying to convert people just to be creationists. And that's not what we do at the Ark, Creation Museum, and the Answers in Genesis ministry. But when I explained to such people that the Ark and Creation Museum would present the truth of God's Word and proclaim the gospel very boldly, then they told me our attractions wouldn't draw non-Christians if we were overt about the gospel and it would be a waste of time and money. In other words, no matter what we do, we are criticized.

I told them that the whole purpose of building these attractions was evangelistic. I added that if we just presented evidence for creation and the Flood, there was no point in constructing these venues. So regardless, we were going to present the gospel clearly. I had no doubt that if we built these attractions in a first-class manner, with quality like that seen at Universal or Disney, and presented biblical messages tastefully but boldly, people, both Christian and non-Christian, would indeed come. And they have by the millions! Those who have already visited AiG's attractions know that the gospel is plainly and powerfully presented at both locations and in numerous places. We don't just try to convert people to be creationists! We unashamedly present the gospel, as we are burdened to see people converted to Christ. We estimate that around 30% of those who visit the Ark Encounter are non-Christians. Also, 80% of the bus tours that bring tourists to the Ark are not church tours but secular ones. (Of course, there are probably many Christians on those buses.)

I've spoken to non-Christians who have visited both the Ark and Creation Museum and asked what they thought of these Christian-themed attractions. The general feedback they've given me can be summarized like this: "We are impressed by the quality and attention to detail seen in the exhibits. We also found the teaching content fascinating and challenging. My friends and I were discussing the fact we've never heard some of these arguments before. It's certainly made clear what you believe and that these are very Christian facilities, but you present it all in a very tasteful way. We're going to recommend it to our friends."

We also get another (and even better) type of feedback. One of the Ark Encounter guests was recorded on video, telling us about his unsaved son-in-law. He watched the *As in the Days of Noah* movie that is shown on the third deck of the Ark:

- "My son-in-law was not saved, and we had been praying for him for so long.... We got to the Ark and [watched the movie] ... and he surrendered to the Lord Jesus.... It was just a wonderful moment for us...."

RESOURCES   JUNE 26

> "We're all indebted to y'all for putting together that wonderful place for him to find the Lord Jesus…. I have just an average old testimony…. I'm envious of him now because he has that wonderful testimony about finding salvation on the Ark."

I've often heard non-Christians discuss the teaching content of various signs at the exhibits. And many guests have told us they are amazed at the diversity of people who visit the Ark and the Creation Museum. As you walk around, you will notice people from different countries and hear several languages spoken. On just one day during a busy summer, I observed the following groups of people at the Ark Encounter: Roman Catholic nuns, Muslims from Baghdad, Orthodox Jews, Amish and Mennonites, people from India — and the list goes on. You wouldn't see such a mix of people attending the average church in America. But they are at the Ark and Creation Museum! The AiG attractions are bringing in people to hear God's Word and the gospel and be given a defense of the Christian faith. And Christians are being equipped to be better able to witness to non-Christians.

Now, not only are AiG's attractions reaching millions of people with God's Word and the gospel, but our websites also have about 30 million visits a year from people all over the world. And our books, DVDs, and curricula are being distributed to thousands upon thousands around the world, and all with one purpose: to see people directed to the truths of the Word of God and its message of salvation most of all. If you have heard me or one of our talented speakers give talks at conferences, churches, and other places, you know we all present the message of biblical authority and the saving gospel.

After Bill Nye "the Science Guy" debated with me in 2014, many people commented to me how thrilling it was to see the gospel presented (more than once) to Bill Nye and the millions who watched my debate presentation. I also clearly presented the gospel to Nye during the "second debate" when we filmed our two-hour walk through the Ark the day after it opened. I would see no point in having an apologetics ministry like Answers in Genesis if we weren't proclaiming the gospel of Jesus Christ.

I was brought up in a home with parents who worked very hard (in different sacrificial ways) to reach as many people as they could with God's Word and the gospel. I can't emphasize enough the phenomenal impact this example had on my life. We are not just trying to convert people to creationists. The Ark and Creation Museum have impacted millions of lives, and we've received many salvation testimonies as a result. Now that's an investment with eternal value!

When I spoke at a home educators conference in Washington State, two ladies came up to me after one of my presentations. They said something like this: "We've never heard you speak before. We came thinking we were going to hear talks on the evidence for creation. But we heard talks that also emphasized the Bible and a biblical worldview. We now want to use AiG's Bible curricula and other resources." The Ark proclaims the wonderful message of Christ's salvation. There was one door into the Ark that allowed Noah and his family to be saved from the Flood. Similarly, there is only one "door" that can save us today from eternal judgment. Jesus Christ is that door.

I am the door. If anyone enters by me, he will be saved and will go in and out and find pasture (John 10:9).

> **Yes, we don't want to see people just believe in creation. We want to see them experience the life-changing gospel of Christ and become Christians.**

JUNE 27
2 Corinthians 4:4

Is Christianity a Virus?

Is Christianity a "virus"? Are Christians "infected" by a disease that they are passing on to their children? Well, read what well-known atheist Daniel Dennet once said in an interview with the BBC.

BBC HOST STEPHEN SACKUR: It seems to me you posit the idea that religions are evolving that, in essence, they're evolving in a way which is going to leave them extinct. They are no longer necessary or useful for human beings. Am I right?

DANIEL DENNETT: Well, first of all, even if they're no longer necessary or useful, they might not go extinct. The common cold is not necessary or useful; it's not going extinct, is it?

SACKUR: Richard Dawkins talks of religion in a way — to think of it almost like a virus.

DENNETT: That's why I used that example. There are lots of symbiotes, lots of parasites and viruses and bacteria that thrive on us and other species, and some of them are very useful to us. We couldn't live without them. The flora in our guts, for instance. We couldn't digest our food without it. Some are just along for the ride; they don't hurt. And a few of them — a small minority — are really harmful. They're bad for us.

SACKUR: And in that sense, in the intellectual sense, in the idea sense, religion is bad for us, and therefore we need a cure. Is that what you're saying?

DENNETT: A cure ... yes, yes indeed, I think a lot of people are really afflicted by their religion, and I would love to see them cured.

In recent times, we have observed many atheists who increasingly use the term "child abuse" to describe the efforts of Christians who train their children in the truth of God's Word. We also see more secularists using terms like *drug, disease, virus*, and other similar words to describe Christianity. Atheist Lawrence Krauss (of Arizona State University) hinted that children who are taught from the Bible shouldn't be allowed to be home educated by their parents. Atheist and well-known anti-creationist Richard Dawkins stated the following in 2006: "Let me explain why, when it comes to children, I think of religion as a dangerous virus. It's a virus which is transmitted partly through teachers and clergy, but also down the generations from parent to child to grandchild. Children are especially vulnerable to infection by the virus of religion."[60]

Atheist Jillian Becker, an author and contributor to newspapers and periodicals such as the *Wall Street Journal* and the *Telegraph* (UK), wrote in 2012: "Has anything caused as much human suffering as religion? You might say disease, but religion itself is a disease, of the human race and of individual minds. Persecution, war, torture, terror, bodily pain, mental anguish, profound misery, wasted lives are the chief products of religion."[61]

Atheist Darrel Ray wrote something similar in 2009: "The best [defense against] god viruses, especially the fundamentalist variants, is science education. The more science is taught or discussed, the fewer tools a god virus has to infect populations."[62]

And in a *Time* magazine article titled "Can Your Child Be Too Religious?" we read the following: "Religion can be a source of comfort that improves well-being. But some kinds of religiosity could be a sign of deeper mental health issues ... So if your child is immersed in scripture after school and prays regularly throughout

APOLOGETICS   JUNE 27

the day, you may breathe a sigh of relief. She's such a good girl. My boy is OK. Or maybe not. Your child's devotion may be a great thing, but there are some kids whose religious observances require a deeper look. For these children, an overzealous practice of their family faith — or even another faith — may be a sign of an underlying mental health issue or a coping mechanism for dealing with unaddressed trauma or stress."[63]

These quotations are examples of what is being stated over and over again in various ways in this secularized culture. I believe it's all part of a propaganda war to marginalize Christians and make them appear to be the enemy. This is a sobering reminder that we need to be more diligent than ever in preparing our children and grandchildren for the world they'll be living in. I thought of this aggressive atheist campaign as our family gathered for dinner on Easter Sunday one year with many of our grandchildren.

My wife and our married children have all commented on how concerned they are by the state of the world in which they are raising their children. They have expressed their concern to me about what is going to happen as they see the Western world not only abandoning Christian morality but also experiencing an increasing anti-Christian sentiment.

At the same time, they know that the Lord has never revoked His command to be "fruitful and multiply" and that one of the primary purposes of marriage is to produce godly offspring. In Malachi 2:15, referring to the oneness in marriage (based on the "one flesh" teaching in Genesis 2), we read, *Did he not make them one, with a portion of the Spirit in their union? And what was the one God seeking? Godly offspring* (Malachi 2:15).

We see a battle all around us — and the Bible describes the struggle to capture coming generations away from the true God in this way: *In their case the god of this world has blinded the minds of the unbelievers, to keep them from seeing the light of the gospel of the glory of Christ, who is the image of God* (2 Corinthians 4:4).

I do believe God has raised up the unique apologetics ministry of Answers in Genesis, Answers Academy, the Creation Museum, and the Ark Encounter to be shining lights in the increasing spiritual darkness all around us. What a thrill it is to see so many families bringing their children and grandchildren to our two attractions. It's a part of training them to stand boldly and uncompromisingly on God's Word. What a blessing it is to know that thousands of families and churches are using AiG's Answers Bible Curriculum and other apologetics resources to train children solidly in the truth of God's Word — and prepare them to defend the Christian faith throughout their lives.

There are only a few Christian organizations like AiG that can discern *the times* and will not swerve from their bold stand on God's Word beginning at Genesis. I trust you also can discern *the times* and stand with us!

Of Issachar, men who had understanding of the times (1 Chronicles 12:32).

> We are in a tremendous spiritual battle today – a battle that has never let up since Genesis 3 when Adam succumbed to the temptation of the devil and rebelled against God.

JUNE 28
2 Timothy 4:14–18

Sifting the Church

I think God is sifting the Church in the West. The increasing anti-Christian attacks should be a warning to the Church that the chasm is widening between what is Christian and what is not in these nations. People can no longer straddle both sides of the chasm. It's getting very wide. They will have to finally decide which side they are on! And if those who are on God's side stand their ground on His Word without compromise, then they no doubt will face persecution in various forms.

But who will be strong enough to stand with the Lord? Who will be prepared to do what Martin Luther did when he is reported to have said, "Here I stand [on Scripture]. I can do no other. God help me." Luther knew that such a stand could result in imprisonment and even death. If we were in such a position today, would we be willing to risk our freedom or even our lives for the sake of God's Word? I sadly already see a number of church leaders succumbing to the secular world by becoming soft on LGBTQ, etc. Yes, the Lord is certainly sifting the Church. Could it come to that in the once "free" West? I suggest this country is moving closer to that terrible time. Increasingly, orthodox Christians are being looked on as the enemy in our Western world. We are being called "child abusers," "intolerant," and "judgmental."

Arizona State University professor and well-known atheist Lawrence Krauss once went on a crusade of sorts in the United States and Australia. As other secularists have often done, he accused Christian parents who teach their children about creation or hell of committing "child abuse." Furthermore, Krauss strongly implied that homeschooled children of such Christian parents should be taken away from home. This belief is becoming prevalent. Could the U.S. government ever take children away from their parents if authorities deem parents to be unfit because they are homeschooling their children and teaching about creation or hell? Look at what is happening in Canada.

Yes, the chasm between secular and Christian is widening. And as it widens, we are seeing that the minority who are prepared to stand their ground for God's infallible Word are increasingly being attacked or marginalized in the culture. For instance, the football star Tim Tebow canceled a speaking engagement at First Baptist Church in Dallas. Apparently, he bowed to political and other pressures and dropped out because the church's pastor takes a bold stand on the gospel and biblical marriage: a male and female, one man and one woman. In the days before the cancellation, many in the secular press attacked the pastor (as can often happen with AiG) and twisted the pastor's statements. They persecuted the pastor and his church, and Tebow pulled out of an agreed engagement with them.

Dr. Al Mohler, president of the Southern Baptist Theological Seminary (Louisville, Kentucky), responded to the cancellation. In a column in *Christianity Today*, he wrote the following:

"Now, take out Tebow's name and insert your own. The massive moral shift taking shape around us is fast eliminating any neutral ground on this issue. Those celebrating the moral normalization of homosexuality will demand an answer from us all. [Louis] Giglio [who was originally scheduled to pray at the president's inauguration] and Tebow withdrew from controversial appearances, but they will not evade the demand to answer the fundamental question, and any Christian who will not join the moral revolution will be marginalized as a moral outlier in the larger society."

CHURCH JUNE 28

All Christians need to be standing our ground, rescuing our kids (Galatians 1:4). Our emphasis should be to boldly stand on God's Word and help rescue children from this evil generation. My challenge to all of us is this: are we all prepared to stand our ground on God's Word, regardless of how the culture may mock and attack us?

AiG has stood out in society as we have boldly and unashamedly stood our biblical ground ... beginning in Genesis. Because of this stand, we often get attacked by secularists — and even by many who call themselves Christians.

An atheist once wrote a scathing article about AiG and me personally. It was full of misinformation, untruths, and mocking. This article was predicting (actually hoping for) the demise of AiG, the Creation Museum, and the Ark Encounter. The misinformation and prediction of our supposed downfall were reposted by several secular blogs — and even got into news sources in my homeland of Australia! One secularist reprinted most of the article with the headline, "The Rise and Fall of the Ken Ham Empire."

Sadly, I'm sure many people (including Bible-compromising Christians who would love to see AiG fail) believed the false information. I did write some blogs to point out the blatant errors and misrepresentations in this particularly savage item. Of course, we can't counter every error, or we would do little else! The tide of false information is enormous. Yes, the enemy tries to marginalize Bible-upholding, evangelistic ministries like AiG.

It would be easy to become despondent at the state of this nation and the untruths that are promulgated about AiG and other Christians — as well as the attacks we receive from compromising Christian leaders and academics. But then I quickly realized that we are so much better off than the Apostle Paul. I can't imagine what Paul felt as he wrote:

Alexander the coppersmith did me great harm; the Lord will repay him according to his deeds. Beware of him yourself, for he strongly opposed our message. At my first defense no one came to stand by me, but all deserted me. May it not be charged against them! But the Lord stood by me and strengthened me, so that through me the message might be fully proclaimed and all the Gentiles might hear it. So I was rescued from the lion's mouth. The Lord will rescue me from every evil deed and bring me safely into his heavenly kingdom. To him be the glory forever and ever. Amen (2 Timothy 4:14–18).

God has a remnant in our nations of people who are prepared to stand their ground. We need to remain bold! We need the world to see we are not going to shrink from their mocking and be afraid of forms of persecution. And we need compromising church leaders and academics to see that we will not bow to the pressure to compromise.

> As we stand and proclaim the truth of God's Word and defend the Christian faith against secular and Christian attacks, we pray the Lord will use our witness to save many for the kingdom – and to rescue many children from this evil age (Galatians 1:4).

JUNE 29
Acts 17:31

Judge Not?

When I point out church leaders and their Genesis compromise, I've had people tell me I should not judge. I notice they are very judgmental when they say that. But there is no neutral position when it comes to judging. We do it every day. Scripture makes it very clear that there is one supreme Judge of all — the Lord God — and that He alone has the authority to determine right and wrong motives and behaviors. Many Old Testament passages attest to the truth of God as Judge:

God is a righteous judge, and a God who feels indignation every day (Psalm 7:11).

[A]nd he judges the world with righteousness; he judges the peoples with uprightness (Psalm 9:8).

The heavens declare his righteousness, for God himself is judge! (Psalm 50:6).

For the Lord is our judge; the Lord is our lawgiver; the Lord is our king; he will save us (Isaiah 33:22).

The Old Testament is rife with passages that establish God as the ultimate Judge. When we come to the New Testament, we find that the Father has committed authority and judgment to the Son. Jesus spoke of this authority before He ascended to heaven after the Resurrection (Matthew 28:18).

For the Father judges no one, but has given all judgment to the Son (John 5:22).

I have come into the world as light, so that whoever believes in me may not remain in darkness. If anyone hears my words and does not keep them, I do not judge him; for I did not come to judge the world but to save the world. The one who rejects me and does not receive my words has a judge; the word that I have spoken will judge him on the last day (John 12:46–48).

"[B]ecause he has fixed a day on which he will judge the world in righteousness by a man whom he has appointed; and of this he has given assurance to all by raising him from the dead" (Acts 17:31).

As these passages and many others demonstrate, the Bible makes it very clear that one day Jesus will rightly judge all humanity based on each individual's faith in — or rejection of — the Son of God. For a world filled with people who believe in moral relativism — and for many professing Christians who practice morality in an attempt to earn righteousness — this day will be filled with fear and trepidation. The Judge of the universe has made a judgment about salvation, echoed by the Apostle Peter in Acts 4:12: *"And there is salvation in no one else, for there is no other name under heaven given among men by which we must be saved."*

Let us consider the idea of judging as it relates to believers and unbelievers. The methods are different when dealing with these two groups, but the goal is reconciliation. Unbelievers need to know Christ and be reconciled to Him, and believers need to grow in Christ and be reconciled to each other. When a Christian lovingly and graciously presents the gospel to unbelievers, a judgment is made regarding their standing with God. The Bible clearly declares that all men are sinners, have fallen short of the glory of God, and are in need of redemption from their sins (Romans 3:23). This judgment is not made from the opinion of the Christian who is presenting the gospel but rather by what the Bible clearly declares.

The claim that Christians are not to judge is often made when dealing with issues such as abortion, adultery, homosexual behavior, and same-sex marriage. When a Christian says, for example, that homosexual behavior

THEOLOGY   JUNE 29

is a sin and that same-sex marriage is wrong, he or she is often met with objections like the following:

- "Who are you to judge two people who love each other?"
- "Someone's private life is none of your business. Don't judge them."

Some people will even quote Matthew 7:1, where Christ said during the Sermon on the Mount, *"Judge not, that you be not judged."* Of course, when they quote this verse in regard to such situations, they take it out of context to support their fallacious claims. When we consider the concept of judging, especially as it relates to the Sermon on the Mount, Christ tells us to be discerning, not condemning. There are significant logical problems with the claim that believers should not make judgments. The first becomes evident when we read the context of Matthew 7:1.

"Judge not, that you be not judged. For with the judgment you pronounce you will be judged, and with the measure you use it will be measured to you. Why do you see the speck that is in your brother's eye, but do not notice the log that is in your own eye? Or how can you say to your brother, 'Let me take the speck out of your eye,' when there is the log in your own eye? You hypocrite, first take the log out of your own eye, and then you will see clearly to take the speck out of your brother's eye" (Matthew 7:1–5).

Here, Christ is warning believers against making judgments in a hypocritical or condemning manner. That type of judging is a characteristic often associated with the Pharisees during the ministry of Jesus. Many people who quote *"Judge not"* from Matthew 7:1 fail to notice the command to judge in Matthew 7:5, when it says, *"[A]nd then you will see clearly to take the speck out of your brother's eye."*

Remember, as believers we are all part of *one faith* (Ephesians 4:5). We must establish our foundation in the truth of God's Word and not our own philosophies, making God the authority over our life. Having the right foundation will help us to know the difference between truth and lies as well as right and wrong.

Realistically, people make judgments all the time. Now, if one person commits murder, should a Christian look at that action and say, "That was wrong because God's Word says not to murder," or should he say, "I'm not supposed to make a judgment"? And what if someone steals from you? Would you say, "That was wrong because God's Word says not to steal," or would you say, "I'm not supposed to make a judgment"? Furthermore, when someone tells us that we need to stop judging others, they have actually just judged us. So they are guilty of doing the very thing they tell us not to do.

We make judgments on various teachings and ideas every day, including our own. The biblical mentality of making judgments applies to any situation where a person is openly committing an error against God and His Word — whether that person is living in sin, such as adultery or homosexual behavior, or compromising God's Word and causing others to stumble and doubt His Word. We even make judgments of our children's actions as we work to help them see their sinful condition before God and point them to the gospel, in order that they might be saved and grow in obedience to God and His Word.

The key is making righteous judgments so that we can point people to the gospel. God's Word gives us a clear standard to abide by, and the Holy Spirit guides us in what is right, wrong, true, and false.

> **In order to make judgments righteously, we should be striving to live righteously and allowing the Word of God to be our foundation in every area of our thinking.**

JUNE 30
Mark 10:17-18

Is Cancer "Very Good"?

Does God call cancer "very good"? Would God call the world we live in "very good"? Obviously not. Yet many Christians are unwittingly (or even wittingly sometimes) accusing God of saying cancer, brain tumors, and other diseases are "very good."

"Surely not!" you may exclaim. However, I would assert that the majority of churchgoers (most unwittingly) are doing just that.

First of all, some background. What do Christians mean when they say God is love? When they answer this question regarding our Creator God, they use verses like these:

So we have come to know and to believe the love that God has for us. God is love, and whoever abides in love abides in God, and God abides in him (1 John 4:16).

For God so loved the world, that he gave his only Son, that whoever believes in him should not perish but have eternal life (John 3:16).

But what other attributes of God enable us to understand what it means that God is love? For one thing, everything God does is good. Many verses describe God's absolute goodness. For example:

You are good and do good (Psalm 119:68).

Praise the Lord, for the Lord is good; sing to his name, for it is pleasant (Psalm 135:3).

In fact, God Himself, in the person of the God-man Jesus, speaks about God being good: *And as he was setting out on his journey, a man ran up and knelt before him and asked him, "Good Teacher, what must I do to inherit eternal life?" And Jesus said to him, "Why do you call me good? No one is good except God alone"* (Mark 10:17–18).

So, the definition of good is related to the attributes of God Himself. And as Jesus is God, let's consider how He displayed God's goodness during His life on earth. When He came to the tomb of Lazarus, who had been dead for four days, we read: *Jesus wept. So the Jews said, "See how he loved him!" But some of them said, "Could not he who opened the eyes of the blind man also have kept this man from dying?" Then Jesus, deeply moved again, came to the tomb. It was a cave, and a stone lay against it* (John 11:35–38).

But why did Jesus weep? Yes, He was grieved at the unbelief of many of the Jews. He was also grieved to see dedicated people like Mary and Martha distraught over the death of a loved one. Yet Jesus knew He was going to raise Lazarus from the dead. He knew that Lazarus, like all people, did not cease to exist when his body died. So why, before He raised Lazarus to life, did He still "weep" and feel "deeply moved"?

I suggest that Jesus, because He is good, was deeply angry at death itself. We know death is called the *last enemy* (1 Corinthians 15:26). The Scriptures tell us that one day death will be cast into *the lake of fire* (Revelation 20:14). We learn that death was the penalty for sin (Genesis 2:17, 3:19; Romans 5:12). Death is an intrusion into this once "very good" world!

THEOLOGY

JUNE 30

In His desire to do good, Jesus chose to suffer the penalty for sin and death and conquered death by rising from the dead (Romans 6:9–10). Ponder this: Opposing death is at the heart of God's goodness.

God's Word also teaches that something bad has happened to our bodies. Right now, they are "perishable" (disease-ridden and under the penalty of death), so in the future, there will be a restoration when God's people will receive bodies that are "imperishable," and our mortal bodies will become "immortal" (1 Corinthians 15:53–56). Romans 8 teaches us that the whole of the present creation groans because of sin and its effects. So it's obvious God would not call death, diseases (like cancer, brain tumors, or arthritis), suffering, or bloodshed "very good." That's a reason why I believe those who add millions of years into God's Word are actually making a mockery of God's character.

And remember, the idea of millions of years came primarily out of atheism of the early nineteenth century. Atheists were involved in coming up with the idea that the fossil record was laid down slowly over millions of years before man supposedly evolved. These people rejected God's Word and the Flood of Noah's day. They wanted to explain everything by natural processes. Sadly, many Christian leaders have adopted the idea of millions of years and attempted in many different ways to force this into the Genesis account.

As a result, so many Christians have been led to believe that it doesn't matter if a Christian believes that the earth was around for millions of years before God created man. But this idea came out of deistic and atheistic naturalism, as people attempted to explain the fossil record without God. Many Christians took this belief in millions of years and added it into the Scriptures. But the fossil record is replete with death and many documented instances of evidence of diseases like cancer, brain tumors, and arthritis in the bones of creatures, and animals having eaten other animals.

Here's the problem. After God created man, He said "everything" He had made was "very good." Animals and man were vegetarian (Genesis 1:29, 30). So if Christians believe in millions of years, then they are in reality accusing God of calling cancer, brain tumors, death, and so on "very good." They are undermining God's character and God's Word.

My point is, you cannot add millions of years into God's Word, or else you make a mockery of God's basic character, including His goodness!

Most of the fossil record is the graveyard of the Flood, not a graveyard of millions of years.

JULY 1

Romans 10:9

Tragedies

Dealing with tragedy is one of those issues both Christian and non-Christians struggle with. For instance, each year on September 11, Americans recall the horror of the 2001 terrorist attacks against the USA that occurred at the two towers of the World Trade Center in New York City and the Pentagon in Washington, DC, and also the crashing of a hijacked plane in rural Pennsylvania. In addition, people all over the world are also reminded of these four terrible events and the loss of thousands of American lives.

For me personally, it was quite moving when I visited New York City and made sure I paid a visit to Ground Zero. Now two skyscrapers and a memorial park stand there as reminders of that tragic day.

People rightfully continue to grieve with the nation years after the events of 9/11. Christians in particular should reach out with compassion to the families affected. After all, thousands of our relatives were killed during these terrorist attacks. (You see, we are all related to each other because we are all descendants of one man, Adam.)

Since 9/11, people have often asked why God would allow such a terrible tragedy that killed "so many innocent people." Now, while I do not in any way want to take away from the grievous nature of these horrible events and the devastating impact on so many families and friends, I wanted to take this opportunity to remind us of one of the realities of this life—that all of us will die one day!

In Luke 13, Jesus gave two examples where people were killed in "tragic" events, and both times He asked the question as to whether the victims were "worse sinners" than others. We read the following:

There were some present at that very time who told him about the Galileans whose blood Pilate had mingled with their sacrifices. And he answered them, "Do you think that these Galileans were worse sinners than all the other Galileans, because they suffered in this way? No, I tell you; but unless you repent, you will all likewise perish. Or those eighteen on whom the tower in Siloam fell and killed them: do you think that they were worse offenders than all the others who lived in Jerusalem? No, I tell you; but unless you repent, you will all likewise perish" (Luke 13:1–5).

Now, notice something from the passage. The answer Jesus gave was the same for both examples here in Luke 13. He said, *No, I tell you; but unless you repent, you will all likewise perish.*

Let's put it this way. Noting that people were killed by Roman soldiers and by a falling tower, Jesus asked if they were worse sinners and that's why they died. He answered "No" and then said to "Repent."

In a modern context, we could take this passage and apply it this way: Those people at the World Trade Center, the Pentagon, and Pennsylvania who were killed by the terrorists—were they worse sinners than others? The answer would be, "No, not at all. But you need to repent!" We could apply this to any tragic situation in any country.

Digging deeper, we need to understand that every person is a sinner.

For all have sinned and fall short of the glory of God (Romans 3:23).

THEOLOGY   JULY 1

This teaching from the Apostle Paul reminds us that there are no "innocent" people, in the sense that everyone is a sinner and therefore accountable to the One we have sinned against—our Creator God. No one is without sin. The Bible makes it clear that all sinners (which means all human beings) are under God's judgment for sin, and the penalty for sin is death.

Therefore, just as sin came into the world through one man, and death through sin, and so death spread to all men because all sinned (Romans 5:12).

When Jesus spoke during His earthly ministry about those people killed by the soldiers and the falling tower, He was reminding His listeners that they were all sinners. He didn't say, "Were they sinners?" but "Were they worse sinners?" He was reminding people that there is a time for everyone to die: *A time to be born, and a time to die* (Ecclesiastes 3:2). The Bible also makes it clear that *it is appointed for man to die once, and after that comes judgment* (Hebrews 9:27).

Because everyone is a sinner, we will all stand before the holy God one day. But those who have been born again as the Scripture states in Romans 10:9, having confessed with their mouth the Lord Jesus and believed in their heart that God has raised Him from the dead, will be saved for eternity and live forever with their Creator in heaven.

And we must understand that as sinners, we deserve nothing! We don't deserve life. But God in His love and mercy provided a way for our sin to be dealt with so those who repent and put their faith and trust in Him will spend eternity with the Lord.

It's important for us to acknowledge that people perish every day. They die of old age, horrible diseases, catastrophes, and so on. There have been many terrible tragedies such as the tsunamis that hit Japan and Indonesia, devastating fires in Australia, or hurricanes that devastated various places like the Gulf Coast in the United States. Of course, such tragedies are the consequences of our sin and God's subsequent curse on the creation (Genesis 3:14–19). As Paul tells us in Romans, *For we know that the whole creation has been groaning together in the pains of childbirth until now* (Romans 8:22).

Such horrible tragic events should remind us that everyone is a sinner, and everyone will die (unless the Lord returns first), that we need to "weep with those who weep" (Romans 12:15), that all people need to repent, and that death is a reminder of our sin and the fact that sin has separated us from our God. We will be eternally separated from God if we are not born again. What a reminder that everyone has to face death, and how important it is that all people respond to the gospel to know that they are saved for eternity.

> "Because, if you confess with your mouth that Jesus is Lord and believe in your heart that God raised him from the dead, you will be saved" (Romans 10:9).

JULY 2
1 Peter 1:18-19

Evolution and Morality

Let me make something very clear. Evolution is not the cause of racism, abortion, gay "marriage," or any other such issue. Sin is the cause of such issues. But there is a connection between evolution and morality.

I believe the message of the AiG ministry has been in a sense very "prophetic." Even when I began teaching creation vs. evolution back in 1975, I was already asserting that atheistic evolution and morality were connected and that, over time, immorality would grow as people rejected God's Word and accepted naturalistic evolution. Not because evolution was the cause of the immorality, but the more generations believed evolution and rejected God's Word, the more their morality would be subjective. This would result in moral relativism permeating the culture. I taught that the more people believed that life arose by natural processes, the more they would also believe that life was ultimately meaningless and purposeless—and morality could be whatever a person determined. Or, as Judges 21:25 states, when there was no king (or absolute authority) in the land, "Everyone did what was right in his own eyes." The late Dr. Henry Morris (considered the father of the modern biblical creation movement) had also been writing about this connection between evolution and morality in most of his early books.

Over the decades, evolutionists have often mocked me for tying evolution to morality. They claim that evolution has to do with "science," not morality. But notice that as generations have been indoctrinated into believing naturalistic evolution, Christian morality has declined. Armed with so-called "science," secularists have become bolder in opposing Christian morality. In our Western world, we are seeing more and more people who boldly claim that evolution is "science" and are using it to promote an anti-Christian worldview. More than ever, secular activists are vehemently opposing Christian morality, such as marriage being between only one man and one woman and abortion being murder. And we are seeing very amoral and immoral behavior growing across the culture, especially, it seems, among the younger generations. While we do not argue that evolution directly causes immorality, people can use Darwinian thinking to justify their immoral behavior.

Now, it's a challenge to read Charles Darwin's books. His writings can be convoluted and difficult to follow. But what is clear is that Darwin believed humans are not special as the Bible states (i.e., made in God's image) but just animals. As a result, he declared that morality was a result of evolution, shaping man into a highly social species through the process of natural selection.

In *The Descent of Man*,[64] Darwin wrote, "Nevertheless, the difference in mind between man and the higher animals, great as it is, certainly is one of degree and not of kind." My point is that there has always been a connection between evolution and morality. Over the years, I've heard many evolutionists and even some Christians claim that evolution is all about "science." They vigorously rejected my insistence that evolution involves a worldview that helps build a relative/subjective morality. That's why many people were shocked (though I wasn't at all) when Bill Nye released a series on Netflix some years ago that pushed shocking immorality and is sometimes overtly anti-Christian.

Kids and adults enjoyed Nye's TV series years ago where he did lots of fun things to teach science. Even back then, you would have noticed how he promoted evolutionary ideas in biology and geology, but he did it in such a way that most children would not have really noticed—and many parents probably didn't see those

APOLOGETICS — JULY 2

pro-evolution sections. But kids were subtly indoctrinated. Even before his famous "Science Guy" program, Bill Nye had his television debut when he performed a comedy routine which included a number of sexual innuendos.

For those who saw my 2014 debate with Bill Nye (available uncut on my Youtube channel or our Answers TV streaming platform), you will remember how I emphasized that the creation vs. evolution issue was actually a clash of two worldviews. Nye rejected this, of course, claiming I was the one who was talking about religion, but he was supposedly all about "science." In that debate, I revealed the connection between naturalistic evolutionary beliefs and morality. Nye totally rejected this view. But many people now see that what I stated in the debate is being played out before their very eyes.

An article in The *Christian Post* reported (please excuse the crudeness): On his Netflix show "Bill Nye Saves the World" on Sunday, the man famous for his 1990s series "Bill Nye the Science Guy" cheerily featured "Crazy Ex-Girlfriend" star Rachel Bloom performing a lewd number called "My Sex Junk" and a video called "Ice Cream Sexuality," a clear derision of Christian sexual ethics. Nye's new show occasionally references science and scientific language with the purpose of promoting left-wing causes.

But really, this is what the belief in naturalistic evolution has always been about! I'm sure many of you have heard of the book *Brave New World* by Aldous Huxley. He was an English novelist and grandson of the famous contemporary of Darwin, Thomas Huxley. Thomas Huxley was known as "Darwin's bulldog," who, as an aggressive secular humanist, heavily promoted Darwin's evolutionary ideas. He clearly saw Darwin's naturalistic evolution as a justification for his secular humanist worldview.

Encyclopedia Britannica states the following about *Brave New World*: "The novel presents a nightmarish vision of a future society in which psychological conditioning forms the basis for a scientifically determined and immutable caste system that, in turn, obliterates the individual and grants all control to the World State."[65]

In 1937, Aldous Huxley made this statement in his book *Ends and Means*[66]: "For myself, as, no doubt, for most of my contemporaries, the philosophy of meaninglessness was essentially an instrument of liberation. The liberation we desired was simultaneously liberation from a certain political and economic system and liberation from a certain system of morality. We objected to the morality because it interfered with our sexual freedom; we objected to the political and economic system because it was unjust. The supporters of these systems claimed that in some way they embodied the meaning (a Christian meaning, they insisted) of the world. There was one admirably simple method of confuting these people and at the same time justifying ourselves in our political and erotic revolt: we could deny that the world had any meaning whatsoever."

We've often said that this worldview struggle is ultimately one that started in the Garden of Eden over 6,000 years ago. And the only way to ultimately win this struggle is for people to be redeemed by the blood of the Lamb: *Knowing that you were ransomed from the futile ways inherited from your forefathers, not with perishable things such as silver or gold, but with the precious blood of Christ, like that of a lamb without blemish or spot* (1 Peter 1:18–19).

We are in a battle between God's Word and man's word – a battle between two worldview religions.

JULY 3

Ephesians 5:31

One Flesh

Can we trust God's Word in Genesis concerning the details of how He made the first man Adam (from dust) and the first woman Eve (from Adam's rib)? Were Adam and Eve humanlike animals before God transformed them into His image?

Ever since the time of Darwin, many church leaders and academics have attempted various ways to harmonize Genesis with "millions of years" and Darwin's ideas of common descent. Consider a proposal by a Christian academic (Bill Dembski) who claimed that Adam and Eve came from "humanlike beings" who lived outside the Garden of Eden. He stated, "For the theodicy [defense of God's goodness in an evil world] I am proposing to be compatible with evolution, God must not merely introduce existing human-like beings from outside the Garden. In addition, when they enter the Garden, God must transform their consciousness so that they become rational moral agents made in God's image.

"Any evils humans experience outside the Garden before God breathes into them the breath of life would be experienced as natural evils in the same way that other animals experience them. The pain would be real, but it would not be experienced as divine justice in response to willful rebellion. Moreover, once God breathes the breath of life into them, we may assume that the first humans experienced an amnesia of their former animal life: Operating on a higher plane of consciousness once infused with the breath of life, they would transcend the lower plane of animal consciousness on which they had previously operated—though, after the Fall, they might be tempted to resort to that lower consciousness."[67]

Now you can test these claims against several scriptural teachings. But just one—the biblical teaching of "one flesh"—is more than sufficient to show how Dembski's position undermines key biblical doctrines, including marriage, the Church, and ultimately the authority of God's Word in the Old and New Testaments.

The first step in evaluating any claim is to look closely at what Scripture actually states. In Genesis 2, we read, *So the Lord God caused a deep sleep to fall upon the man, and while he slept took one of his ribs and closed up its place with flesh. And the rib that the Lord God had taken from the man he made into a woman and brought her to the man. Then the man said, "This at last is bone of my bones and flesh of my flesh; she shall be called Woman, because she was taken out of Man"* (Genesis 2:21–23).

If one takes this as literal history, then God made Adam first (from dust—Genesis 2:7), then put the man to sleep, and from his side (a rib), made the first woman. Note Adam's words that this woman was "flesh of my flesh." They were one flesh. In Genesis 2:24, God explains that marriage is to be a bond between a man and a woman and that they shall "become one flesh." In marriage, a couple is to be spiritually one and physically one—based on the one flesh aspect of how woman was created.

Jesus refers directly to the historical account of Genesis 2 when He was asked about God's view of marriage. He replied, *Have you not read that he who created them from the beginning made them male and female, and said, "Therefore a man shall leave his father and his mother and hold fast to his wife, and the two shall become one flesh"?* (Matthew 19:4–5). Jesus was quoting the literal account of Eve coming from Adam and being "one flesh" with the first man as we read in Genesis 2:24.

APOLOGETICS

Paul also quotes from Genesis 2 in his discussion about God's view of marriage: *Therefore a man shall leave his father and mother and hold fast to his wife, and the two shall become one flesh* (Ephesians 5:31). So when a Christian academic proposes that God allowed an evolutionary process to generate soulless animals then used two of those animals or supposedly humanlike creatures from an existing pool to make them into Adam and Eve—this totally undermines the teaching of "one flesh" in the Old and New Testaments. It also means Jesus and Paul did not tell the truth, which undermines biblical authority!

Another plain teaching of Scripture concerning the relationship between Adam and Eve needs to be considered when evaluating this recent claim. Because Eve was made from Adam, then Adam was made first—and obviously, the woman came from the man—just as Adam stated in Genesis 2:23. The New Testament refers to Adam being first:

- *For Adam was formed first, then Eve* (1 Timothy 2:13).
- *For man was not made from woman, but woman from man* (1 Corinthians 11:8).
- *For as woman was made from man, so man is now born of woman. And all things are from God* (1 Corinthians 11:12).

If you deny that the first man was created before the first woman and if you deny that the first woman came from the man (not from an existing animal or humanlike creature), you undermine the biblical doctrine of marriage and ultimately the authority of the Old and New Testaments.

No matter how respected a leader might be, God's people must carefully compare his or her ideas to Scripture. Paul says of the Church, *Because we are members of his body. "Therefore a man shall leave his father and mother and hold fast to his wife, and the two shall become one flesh." This mystery is profound, and I am saying that it refers to Christ and the church* (Ephesians 5:30–32).

And earlier in the chapter Paul says, *For the husband is the head of the wife even as Christ is the head of the church, his body, and is himself its Savior* (Ephesians 5:23).

Consider how significant this is to our faith. The Church's doctrine is that the redeemed of the human race are one body with Christ, and He is the head! We are "one flesh" with Him. In fact, the Bible makes it obvious that the Church is the "bride" of Christ, and Christ is likened to a "bridegroom" (Matthew 25:1).

The Church's relationship with Christ is explained in terms of the doctrine of marriage, which is founded in Genesis' literal "one flesh" history of woman's creation from the man. To teach that Adam and Eve came from a preexisting group of animals or humanlike creatures is to totally undermine the doctrine of the Church.

Adam and Eve—From One Flesh or Two? The Bible makes it obvious from Genesis to Revelation—they were from one flesh! Any teaching to the contrary is unbiblical and an attack on the authority of God's Word—and ultimately an attack on the "Lamb's wife."

Then came one of the seven angels who had the seven bowls full of the seven last plagues and spoke to me, saying, "Come, I will show you the Bride, the wife of the Lamb" (Revelation 21:9).

The "one flesh" teaching in Scripture, based on the historical "one flesh" of the first man and woman, is also the foundation of the doctrine of the Church.

JULY 4
Luke 24:27

Radical Gospel

Therefore, just as sin came into the world through one man, and death through sin, and so death spread to all men because all sinned (Romans 5:12). Sharing the gospel can be tough these days. No matter what new witnessing method comes along, none of them seem to work like they once did. I would like to offer what may seem a radical proposal that appears to have been overlooked.

The first time I traveled to Japan to speak, I sat down with my translator. He explained that Japan never had a Christian foundation (as has most of our Western world). So I could not assume that people understood Christian terminology. He explained that the Shinto religion dominated Japan, so when I used the word *God*, most people would assume I was talking about another "god" just like their thousands of gods. The translator explained that he would need to define the Bible's God so that they could understand this was different from the many gods of their pagan religion. I began to understand that most people in Japan wouldn't understand about Jesus dying on the Cross or the essence of the gospel, because they had no understanding of the account of Adam and Eve and the Fall. They needed this historical background to understand the entrance of sin and our need for a Savior. As my translator said, "To explain the gospel, you will actually need to start at the beginning."

I thought to myself, "Wow, what a radical idea! I need to present the gospel to these people the way God does it in His Word, the Bible! Who would have ever thought of that?" When I explain this to audiences today, people usually laugh. They especially chuckle when I say it this way: "Here is a radical approach to presenting the gospel: let's do it the way God does it for us in His Word." Think about it. Why is Genesis (which means "beginning" or "origin") the first book in the Bible, God's written revelation to man? It is because the first 11 chapters of this book outline a history that is foundational to the rest of the Bible. In fact, Genesis 1–11 is foundational to all doctrine, to the gospel, and ultimately, to everything.

Genesis gives an account of the origin of all the basic entities of life and the universe: the origin of space, matter, time, earth, light, water, atmosphere, dry land, plants, sun, moon, stars, sea creatures, flying creatures, land creatures, the first humans (Adam and Eve), clothing, sin, death, marriage, nations, languages, and much more. Without this historical revelation, how would we understand the reason for Jesus' life, death, and Resurrection? Or how would we understand what our problem is (sin) and the consequences (death) and therefore why the solution is in what Jesus did on the Cross? Imagine teaching a group of Christians that they need to go out and witness to non-Christians, with one stipulation: They are not allowed to refer to the first 11 chapters of Genesis or to Genesis in any way. Imagine a possible conversation:

- "You need to trust in Jesus for salvation," the Christian says.
- "Why do I need salvation?" the non-Christian responds.
- "Well, you do because you are a sinner."
- "Why am I a sinner?"
- "Well, just accept that you are."
- "Where did sin come from?"

APOLOGETICS

- "Don't worry about that—just accept it. Jesus died for your sin."
- "Why did He die?"
- "Because death is the penalty for sin."
- "Where did that originate?"
- "Don't worry about that—just accept it."

I could go on and on—but I trust you understand the point. How can a Christian explain the gospel to someone who has no background understanding of God's truth revealed in Genesis? It is impossible. Genesis' account of history explains that all humans are descendants of one man, Adam, who rebelled against God, thus bringing sin and death into this once-perfect creation. As a result, Adam and his descendants were separated from their Creator. However, the Creator God had a plan from eternity for man's salvation.

As Paul deals with the gospel in Romans 5 and 1 Corinthians 15, he goes back to Genesis to lay the foundational information so that all who read these crucial passages will understand the gospel. The missionary organization Ethnos360 (previously called New Tribes Mission) has led the way in what it describes as a "chronological approach" to teaching the Bible to pagan cultures that have no understanding of God's Word. This approach starts at the beginning in Genesis and works through the true history of the world. When the missionaries eventually present the message of Christ on the Cross, they find that the people to whom they are ministering understand the essence of the gospel! Sadly, many Bible colleges, seminaries, and other Christian institutions now train missionaries to present the gospel beginning in the Book of John or somewhere else in the New Testament. However, even in our Western world, we are now seeing generations of unchurched young people come through a secular education system that is devoid of the teaching of God's Word.

Increasingly, people even in our once-Christianized West don't understand the foundational history that is necessary to understand the gospel. Regardless of what background someone has in regard to Christianity, I suggest that we should always present the gospel the way God does it for us in His Word—starting at the beginning. That way our hearers will grasp the foundational history that enables us to understand what the message of salvation is all about.

Sound radical? It shouldn't. But it does sound radical in today's church environment, where so many churches have avoided Genesis (or consider it unimportant or even reject it as symbolic poetry or myth). The secularists have made incredible inroads in infiltrating Christian minds with false ideas about evolution and Earth history over millions of years. Because so many Christians (including many Christian leaders) have disregarded Genesis, even many church people do not truly understand the gospel. Also, the coming generations increasingly have little understanding of God's Word from the beginning. Many just "shrug their shoulders" at the message of salvation and end up walking away from the Church.

The gospel of Jesus Christ is truly amazing. But in our increasingly secular society, people don't recognize the good news until you first explain the bad news. That requires going back to the very beginning and telling the whole true account, as God Himself tells it. Jesus Christ, the God-man, set the example. We read in Luke 24:27 how He approached the subject when He was walking with two men on the road to Emmaus: *And beginning with Moses and all the Prophets, he interpreted to them in all the Scriptures the things concerning himself.*

It's not radical to present the gospel beginning in Genesis – it is vital!

JULY 5
Revelation 2:4

Finish Well

But I have this against you, that you have abandoned the love you had at first (Revelation 2:4).

How will you "finish"?

A well-known pastor once told me that in his conservative denomination, there was a major battle looming. It grieved me when he said that his denomination was about to tackle the question as to whether or not there really were a literal Adam and Eve!

I guess I shouldn't have been too surprised, though. After all, I have been seeing a number of Christian colleges and seminaries, which once took a stand on a literal Genesis, waver . . . and many have even given up the biblical view on Adam and Eve. There are a few that stand solidly on Genesis, but they are the exception sadly.

Think about *colleges* like Harvard, Princeton, and Yale which were founded to train preachers in the Word. But now they produce different kinds of preachers: aggressive secularists—promoters of naturalism (atheism).

Today, some denominations that once defined marriage as between a man and a woman have changed their view to support "gay marriage." Even in evangelical churches, we now see a number who are departing from offering their flock in-depth teaching on the Word of God. Instead, they have become more entertainment oriented. And some church leaders are now denying a literal hell. The list could go on and on. When I think of such state of affairs, a certain verse resounds in my head: *When the Son of Man comes, will he find faith on earth?* (Luke 18:8).

As I consider the growing compromise in churches and notice their general lack of authoritative biblical teaching, I am thankful for how God has blessed AiG and the Creation Museum and Ark Encounter attractions. But then I begin to wonder: Where will AiG be in the future? Can anything be done to safeguard this ministry from compromising God's Word in any way or from starting to lose its boldness in standing on the authority of the Word of God?

Over the years, I have observed many Christian organizations that were once so zealous for the Lord become ineffective (and even irrelevant). I've also seen pastors who, as their churches have grown, eventually lose their zeal and become more businesslike in running their church (like the CEO of a company).

I've also seen examples of Christian leaders who have become less bold in preaching the Word and have adopted ideas/beliefs they would not have done in the early exciting years of their ministry. And in their congregations, the people become less reliant on God—they end up looking more to themselves and others for their main sources of guidance and wisdom. Many of them also seem to have forgotten their history (i.e., *the times* when they sought the Lord with tears, and He provided miracles of provision).

"Oh Lord," we cry out, "how can we do our best to guide AiG and our staff so we don't end up like so many others?"

Of course, ultimately, the ministry is all in God's hand. But we still have a human responsibility to do what we can to watch over a ministry the Lord has entrusted to our daily care. And we have put a number of things in place to hopefully not let the ministry ever drift.

CHURCH

At the time I was considering all of this, I was reading through the Book of 2 Chronicles about the various kings of Judah and Israel. Wow! What lessons we can learn from this history! They can directly relate to how we are to consider AiG's future and to each one of us personally (and to our families).

While reading 2 Chronicles, I wrote down a number of notes and constructed a talk I did for the AiG staff. I read to them the accounts from 2 Chronicles 14–16 about King Asa. Then, I went through 2 Chronicles 24 concerning King Joash and 2 Chronicles 25 about King Amaziah. Lastly, it was 2 Chronicles 26 and Uzziah.

What lessons we can learn from these accounts! These kings started well, doing that which was right before the Lord. But they didn't end well. These kings did evil and turned against the Lord in a variety of ways.

And why did they not end well? Well, power, riches, and success led to an increase in human pride. Instead of trusting in God as they did in their early years, these kings looked to themselves for guidance and wisdom. God had blessed them with power, success, and riches, but because of their sinful, human heart, they became prideful. They did not end well at all.

I challenged the AiG staff about how each one of us will "end" and also collectively as a ministry. Will we end well? Will we keep the zeal for the Lord? Or will we look to ourselves and let pride destroy us?

It was a sobering time for our staff but so needed.

I have also noticed that when ministries become flush with funds or they become large and "successful," they can also become proud—and forget to rely on the Lord. Once these leaders begin looking to themselves and not the Lord and don't agonize before the Lord in prayer, it seems the effectiveness of the ministry begins to wane. They often become more accommodating with the world—often more businesslike. The zeal with which they started is dying. Now I do wholeheartedly support responsibly putting aside some finances for difficult times, etc. and planning for the future, but I also believe the funds the Lord provides us for impacting people with God's Word and the gospel need to be used for that.

I told our staff that it's good to be reminded of our ministry's history—of God's many miracles over the years. In tears, many times we have sought the Lord for certain needs and have asked for His direction and wisdom to make various decisions. I also explained that one of the reasons I believe the Lord has kept us on the edge financially is so that we don't become proud. In this way, we'll know that AiG is HIS ministry, not ours. I am certainly watchful that this ministry will not stray from its "first love": an uncompromising stand on God's Word.

Pray that none of us would ever be like those kings I mentioned and lose "our first love."

JULY 6
Matthew 5:13–14

Culture Changers?

Here is an interesting and probably provocative question for some: Are Christians commanded to change the culture?

The United States Supreme Court and gay "marriage" were in the news a lot back in 2014. The Supreme Court had turned away appeals from five states looking to prohibit gay marriage, effectively legalizing same-sex marriage in those states and likely others—but also leaving the issue unresolved nationally. The justices rejected appeals from Indiana, Oklahoma, Utah, Virginia and Wisconsin. The court's order immediately ended delays on gay marriage in those states. By doing this, the Supreme Court justices effectively endorsed gay "marriage" by allowing the rulings in favor of gay "marriage" in the lower courts to stand in those jurisdictions.

Then, on June 26, 2015, unsurprisingly the U.S. Supreme Court held in a 5–4 decision that the Fourteenth Amendment requires all states to grant same-sex "marriages" and recognize same-sex "marriages" granted in other states. It was a sad day for America from a Christian perspective. Over the years, Christians have spent millions of dollars trying to change the culture in regard to the abortion issue and the very high-profile gay "marriage" debate—but the culture continues to become more secularized every day. And it's a reminder that government legislation and courts are not the ultimate answers to moral issues.

Now Christians do need to publicly stand on the authority of God's Word and judge such moral issues accordingly—and be prepared to publicly and unashamedly, but with boldness and gentleness, proclaim the truth that God reveals in His Word. God's Word clearly teaches that marriage has its origin in the creation account in Genesis and, thus, is one man for one woman (Matthew 19:4–7). God's Word also teaches that humans are made in the image of God; therefore, abortion is deliberately taking a human life. Tens of millions of children have been murdered in their mother's wombs in the United States since 1973. And, just because Christians believe and obey God's Word, teaching against gay "marriage" and abortion doesn't mean they are intolerant of people who disobey God's Word. Christians have every right to stand by their convictions in regard to all moral issues—stealing, murder, marriage, adultery, fornication, and so on.

Now the Lord Jesus Christ gives God's people two commands:

And he said to them, "Go into all the world and proclaim the gospel to the whole creation" (Mark 16:15).

Go therefore and make disciples of all nations, baptizing them in the name of the Father and of the Son and of the Holy Spirit, teaching them to observe all that I have commanded you (Matthew 28:19–20).

We need to understand that the gospel changes people—their hearts and minds. And it's hearts and minds that change a culture. In Proverbs 23:7 (NKJV), we learn, *For as he thinks in his heart, so is he*. We are also told that, *"You are the salt of the earth, but if salt has lost its taste, how shall its saltiness be restored? It is no longer good for anything except to be thrown out and trampled under people's feet. You are the light of the world. A city set on a hill cannot be hidden"* (Matthew 5:13–14). Christians are to be salt and light, influencing the culture for good as they reflect the Lord Jesus Christ in everything they do. The emphasis for Christians is to be shining the light of God's truth and proclaiming the gospel, as that is what will impact culture.

CHURCH JULY 6

Now please don't misunderstand. I applaud when Bible-believing Christians are in Congress, the Senate, etc. and use their influence/votes to impact the culture from a biblical worldview. We need so many more like this involved in the political system. That's part of being salt and light as we are commanded to be. If we don't do this, secularists will. Secularists understand that if they can capture people's hearts and minds by instilling in them the foundation that man's opinion determines what is true and what is right, then such people will build a secular worldview. Secularists do not just believe that people have a right to believe what they choose, but rather that there are no absolute standards of right and truth. They believe that right and truth are matters of opinion. And they argue that when Bible-believers insist that there is an absolute standard that comes to us from an authority higher than man, from God the Creator of all, those who stand in opposition to God's standards are somehow being persecuted or having their rights violated.

Many of the founding fathers of America were Christians (or people who had a high respect for the Bible) and built their thinking to one degree or another on God's Word. Thus, they had a Christianized worldview (by and large reflecting the Judeo-Christian ethic). The worldview of people was reflected in the culture. People were salt, which affected the nation. Even many non-Christians inconsistently held to a Christianized worldview and thus helped influence the culture. But God's Word warns that if salt becomes contaminated, it is no longer good for anything.

People now have much more of a secular worldview that is permeating the culture. Over the years, the secularists have cleverly indoctrinated generations, even from the Church, to abandon God's Word as the absolute authority and make man the authority (the very temptation the devil gave to Adam and Eve in Genesis 3—"You will become like God"). The "salt" of God's Word that was once prevalent in the nation has been contaminated. Yet the Bible's Book of Judges illustrates the horrible mess that develops when, instead of following God, "everyone did what was right in his own eyes" (Judges 21:25). Isaiah 5:20–21 warns of the harm that comes to people and nations as a result of this attitude, substituting man's "anything goes" opinion for God's stand on what is and is not acceptable, saying, *Woe to those who call evil good and good evil, who put darkness for light and light for darkness, who put bitter for sweet and sweet for bitter! Woe to those who are wise in their own eyes, and shrewd in their own sight!* The Supreme Court has certainly not helped the people of this country or its stand, or rather their lack of a stand, on this important issue.

The Christian response to what is happening in regard to the gay "marriage" debate (and abortion and other moral issues) should be to stand uncompromisingly on God's Word, preach the gospel, make disciples, and teach them to obey the commands of Jesus Christ. It is not our mission to hate or mistreat anyone, but we must take a stand on the absolute truth that sin is still sin even if the law endorses it. I do have a very clear message for the leaders of our countries and the court judges: "You did not invent marriage—God did! You did not create life—God did! God is the absolute authority, not man. God created us, owns us, and therefore has the right to set the rules of what is right and wrong." *He answered, "Have you not read that he who created them from the beginning made them male and female, and said, 'Therefore a man shall leave his father and his mother and hold fast to his wife, and the two shall become one flesh'? So they are no longer two but one flesh. What therefore God has joined together, let not man separate"* (Matthew 19:4–6).

Jesus Christ came into the world to save people from their sins, not to condone their sins.

JULY 7

2 Chronicles 30:26

Hezekiah

One of the great reformers of all time was King Hezekiah. God ensured that details about his life and reforms were written down in His holy Word, so we could learn from what he did and be challenged in our own walk of faith.

God's Word says about the magnitude of Hezekiah's amazing reforms: *So there was great joy in Jerusalem, for since the time of Solomon the son of David king of Israel there had been nothing like this in Jerusalem* (2 Chronicles 30:26). Hezekiah carried out reforms to destroy idol worship and restore temple worship. He reinstituted the Passover and did whatever he could do to get people back to obeying God's Word.

How we need reformation in our churches, because so many believers in this era have compromised God's Word, beginning in Genesis! We are also seeing the sad consequences (abortion on demand, gay "marriage," LGBTQ, increasing violence, and so on) of a Western world that is becoming more anti-Christian and attempting to remove any vestiges of Christian influence and heritage.

What was different about Hezekiah compared to so many of the other kings of Israel and Judah who came before him? At the beginning of the Chronicles account of Hezekiah, we read: *And he did what was right in the eyes of the Lord, according to all that David his father had done* (2 Chronicles 29:2).

And after Hezekiah instituted many of his reforms, we read more about his godly character: *Thus Hezekiah did throughout all Judah, and he did what was good and right and faithful before the Lord his God. And every work that he undertook in the service of the house of God and in accordance with the law and the commandments, seeking his God, he did with all his heart, and prospered* (2 Chronicles 31:20–21).

If we want to impact the world around us, God's people first need to seek God and be obedient to His Word. Sadly, many Christians and Christian leaders today exalt man's word by taking man's religion of evolution and millions of years and adding it to God's infallible Word. This is no different from the efforts by the people of Judah and Israel to adopt the pagan religion of their age and mix it with what God had instructed. Reformation begins with a return to the authority of the Word of God and obeying God's revelation to man. Now we read about some of Hezekiah's specific initiatives in 2 Chronicles 30:1 and 30:5:

Hezekiah sent to all Israel and Judah, and wrote letters also to Ephraim and Manasseh, that they should come to the house of the Lord at Jerusalem to keep the Passover to the Lord, the God of Israel. . . . So they decreed to make a proclamation throughout all Israel, from Beersheba to Dan, that the people should come and keep the Passover to the Lord, the God of Israel, at Jerusalem, for they had not kept it as often as prescribed.

Now here is a serious warning for all of us: the problem of pride. Even as great a man of God as Hezekiah was, his pride let him down. At first, he was humble, and God greatly blessed his faith. After the many reforms Hezekiah instituted, God allowed the king of Assyria to come against Judah, intent on war against Jerusalem. Hezekiah fortified the city, made weapons, and prepared for the battle. But most important, he encouraged the people to trust in God, who was on their side:

Be strong and courageous; do not be afraid nor dismayed before the king of Assyria, nor before all the multitude that is with him; for there are more with us than with him. With him is an arm of flesh; but with us is the Lord our God, to help us and to fight our battles. And the people were strengthened by the words of Hezekiah king of Judah (2 Chronicles 32:7–8; NKJV).

When the king of Assyria sent people to taunt the Jews and mock their God, Hezekiah did what we should all do for every challenge, every day: *Then Hezekiah the king and Isaiah the prophet, the son of Amoz, prayed because of this and cried to heaven* (2 Chronicles 32:20).

And because of this God gave Hezekiah great victory:

And the Lord sent an angel, who cut off all the mighty warriors and commanders and officers in the camp of the king of Assyria. So he returned with shame of face to his own land. And when he came into the house of his god, some of his own sons struck him down there with the sword. So the Lord saved Hezekiah and the inhabitants of Jerusalem from the hand of Sennacherib king of Assyria and from the hand of all his enemies, and he provided for them on every side (2 Chronicles 32:21–22).

But now comes the lesson every one of us must learn. After the great victory God gave Hezekiah, we read this sad situation: *In those days Hezekiah became sick and was at the point of death, and he prayed to the Lord, and he answered him and gave him a sign. But Hezekiah did not make return according to the benefit done to him, for his heart was proud. Therefore wrath came upon him and Judah and Jerusalem* (2 Chronicles 32:24–25).

Because of the wonderful defeat of the Assyrian army, Hezekiah became proud! This should have been his downfall, *But Hezekiah humbled himself for the pride of his heart, both he and the inhabitants of Jerusalem, so that the wrath of the Lord did not come upon them in the days of Hezekiah* (2 Chronicles 32:26).

When we are involved in serving the Lord, no matter how great or small our role, we always need to remember to give God the glory and honor and to recognize it is easy for any of us to be lifted up in pride and set the wrong example for those looking at us.

One's pride will bring him low, but he who is lowly in spirit will obtain honor (Proverbs 29:23).

Hezekiah died, and we read that his son Manasseh became king in his place. But we are told: *And he did what was evil in the sight of the Lord, according to the abominations of the nations whom the Lord drove out before the people of Israel* (2 Chronicles 33:2).

It is hard to fathom how such a godly king as Hezekiah could end up with such an evil son as Manasseh to take his place. It's sad to observe the fact that most Christian institutions in our Western world have lost the biblical stand of their founders as compromise creeps in. Many such institutions have now become leaders in indoctrinating generations against the authority of the Word of God. Yes, we need Hezekiah-type reformers today. But we need to understand the sober lessons from Hezekiah's life, which God put in His Word for our learning.

> **Our focus needs to be on God's infallible Word, and we must always remember that hope for true reform rests in God alone.**

JULY 8
Joshua 24:15

Building a (Worldview) House

Homophobic. Misogynist. These are just two of the many terms used to (falsely) describe Christians who stand for the authority of God's Word in regard to gender, marriage, and, in fact, everything. How do Christians address the criticism that they're hate-filled bigots?

Many Christians have answered questions about such matters as gender, gay "marriage", and abortion in the wrong way, sometimes coming across as intolerant of people who hold different views. Most don't understand that to be Christian means to have a Christian worldview that is built upon the Bible as the foundation for that worldview. Yes, they may use the Bible and quote passages, but that doesn't mean they understand how to explain their worldview foundationally.

Most secularists (wrongly) don't think they have a worldview, and they think what they believe comes from just looking at evidence. Many misinterpret a Christian's disagreement with their worldview as being intolerant of them personally, instead of understanding there's a clash of worldviews because of the difference foundationally and where those worldviews come from.

For a Christian, the Bible makes it clear that one is either for or against Christ (Matthew 12:30) and that one walks either in light or in darkness (Matthew 6:22–23). As we read in Matthew 7:24–27, one builds a house either on the rock or on sand.

I've found that the best way to explain all this is to use the analogy of building a house. A carpenter doesn't start with the roof, then the walls, and then the foundation. No, he builds the foundation first, then the walls and roof. And he has to have the right type of foundation fit for that building.

A worldview is like the walls and the roof of a house, but every worldview has a foundation. And ultimately, there are only two foundations. One starts with the Word of the One who knows everything and who has revealed to us all we need to know to build the correct worldview. The other one starts with the foundation that fallible man determines truth. Remember what Jesus taught about building a house on rock or sand.

The Bible claims to be (and I know it to be) the revealed Word of God who knows everything. For Christians, this is the only foundation upon which they can build a truly Christian worldview. Thus, founded in God's Word beginning in Genesis, marriage is one man and one woman (Genesis 2:24); there are two genders—male and female (Genesis 1:27); abortion is murder because man is made in God's image (Genesis 1:27); and murder is wrong (Genesis 9:6).

It's important to explain to a secularist why we as Christians believe the way we do about these issues. We need to explain that our thinking comes from the Bible. Now they will often object and say the Bible is not true. When they do this, we need to pause to ask them why they believe this and what arguments they have against the Bible. Then we do our best to answer their claims (using apologetics) to show we can defend the claim that the Bible is true—it is God's Word. Then we can get back to explaining that our worldview comes from the Bible.

It's vital we show them that they have a starting point too, a foundation for their worldview. Often secularists claim they start with evidence, but the Bible is evidence and they reject that (Romans 1:21–22)! Explain to

APOLOGETICS — JULY 8

them that if they reject the Bible and believe all life arose by natural processes, then that foundation totally determines what worldview they have built upon it and how they look at evidence. Thus, we can understand why we have such different worldviews in regard to all these issues.

Once we've explained all this, we can point out that the reason there is a clash of worldviews is that we have two different starting points. Until we both have the same starting point, we won't have the same worldview. This will also help them understand that when a Christian disagrees with them on gay "marriage," abortion, or multiple genders (other than male or female), they are not being hateful; they have a different worldview, and that's where and why the clash is occurring.

Now there will be those who say they are Christians and agree with gay "marriage" and/or abortion. If they claim they are Christians, then we need to make sure they understand their worldview has a starting point—and it has to be the Bible. If they agree to that, then we have to talk about why they interpret the Bible differently (particularly in Genesis) than other Christians do. Until we can solve that issue, the worldview clash will not be alleviated. But explaining this all foundationally does help disarm skeptics of all types and enable many to understand the disagreement is not personal and, therefore, not hateful. It usually greatly helps take the emotionalism out of the argument.

Ultimately, it's all about foundations—God's Word or man's fallible, finite word. The battle started in Genesis 3:1, when the devil tempted Adam and Eve to doubt God's Word and decide truth for themselves, thus becoming their own gods. This battle has raged for 6,000 years and continues to rage.

It's described as a battle between

- Good and evil
- Light and darkness
- A house built on the rock and one built on sand
- For Christ and against Christ
- Gather and scatter
- Life and death

And if it is evil in your eyes to serve the Lord, choose this day whom you will serve, whether the gods your fathers served in the region beyond the River, or the gods of the Amorites in whose land you dwell. But as for me and my house, we will serve the Lord (Joshua 24:15).

Make sure you know how to contend foundationally.

JULY 9
2 Peter 3:3-7

How Long Do We Have?

How long will the opportunity to preach biblical truths be available to us? Well, consider excerpts from an article "Christians, Prepare for Persecution."[68] It was written by a well-known socially conservative political commentator in Australia, Andrew Bolt. Here are just a few excerpts, which I see as a warning to the United States also: "CHRISTIANS, prepare for persecution. Open your eyes and choose stronger leaders for the dark days. I am not a Christian, but I am amazed that your bishops and ministers are not warning you of what is already breaking over your heads."

The columnist gave a number of examples in Australia where those in authority are moving against Christians, including the education department in Queensland. In that state where I grew up and taught science, schools are being directed not to allow students (ages 4–12) to share with other kids about Jesus or give them Christmas cards with a Christian message.

There are also examples of the persecution of those who speak against gay "marriage," including two pastors in Tasmania arrested for preaching against gay "marriage." And things have continued to deteriorate since Andrew Bolt wrote that article.

We hear similar reports from Canada and the United Kingdom. America has already seen instances of Christians persecuted for their free exercise of the Christian religion—and it is only increasing.

Christian researcher in the United States George Barna noted that Generation Z is the first truly post-Christian generation and twice as likely to be atheists as any previous generation. We are seeing increasing numbers of people in the West skeptical of and antagonistic to Christianity.

The Apostle Peter warned that a skeptical philosophy would prevail in our day, claiming that *all things are continuing as they were from the beginning of creation* (2 Peter 3:4). Don't be troubled—he encouraged us. *Knowing this first of all, that scoffers will come in the last days* (2 Peter 3:3).

We are in the last days! Ever since God's Son stepped into history to become Jesus Christ the God-man, we have been in the last days. We don't know how "last" we are. We just know we are more "last" than we were. We do know that one day Jesus will return and there will be a final judgment—and the last days will then end.

It's fascinating that nearly 2,000 years ago, Peter (under the inspiration of the Holy Spirit) wrote about scoffers in the last days. As we read about these scoffers, we realize that there is "nothing new under the sun" (Ecclesiastes 1:9). The basic sin nature of man is the same today as it was 2,000 years ago—and as it was approximately 6,000 years ago when our ancestor Adam rebelled against God.

Peter explains that these scoffers will scorn those who believe Jesus is returning and will exclaim, *Where is the promise of his coming? For ever since the fathers fell asleep, all things are continuing as they were from the beginning of creation* (2 Peter 3:4). The philosophy of the scoffers is that physical processes just go on and on without any miraculous intervention.

We are then told the scoffers will reject creation, the Flood of Noah's day, and the coming judgment by fire: *Knowing this first of all, that scoffers will come in the last days with scoffing, following their own sinful desires.*

THEOLOGY

They will say, "Where is the promise of his coming? For ever since the fathers fell asleep, all things are continuing as they were from the beginning of creation." For they deliberately overlook this fact, that the heavens existed long ago, and the earth was formed out of water and through water by the word of God, and that by means of these the world that then existed was deluged with water and perished. But by the same word the heavens and earth that now exist are stored up for fire, being kept until the day of judgment and destruction of the ungodly (2 Peter 3:3–7).

The passage in 2 Peter 3 is an apt description of those in today's world who have adopted the religion of evolution and attempted to brainwash generations of students to deny the existence of the Creator God. In place of God, they teach that natural processes over eons brought the universe and all life into existence.

Today's secularist scoffers indoctrinate generations of students through the education systems, television programs, and natural history museums to reject creation and the Flood and, of course, the coming judgment by fire. These scoffers teach that the world has continued on and on for millions of years without any intervention by an all-powerful God. They are rejecting God's Word and the gospel.

Now Peter goes on to warn, *You therefore, beloved, knowing this beforehand, take care that you are not carried away with the error of lawless people and lose your own stability* (2 Peter 3:17). The scoffers will try to get each one of us to reject the truth of creation and the doctrines, the Flood, and the coming judgment.

We need to heed this warning. In today's world, the scoffers have caused many young people to "fall" and reject the truth of God's Word. Sadly, generations of young people from church homes have been indoctrinated in the secular education systems to believe in an evolutionist view of origins. Much of the Church has been lulled into complacency while the scoffers have captured the hearts and minds of many in the coming generations. And now they are very anti-Christian.

Later in his epistle, however, Peter explains that 2,000 years of "the last days" is not long to God. These scoffers may claim it's a long time, so God's Word can't be true concerning creation, the Flood, and the coming judgment by fire. But Peter responds, *With the Lord one day is as a thousand years, and a thousand years as one day* (2 Peter 3:8). Since God is outside of time, to God a thousand years is like a day—or a day is like a thousand years. God is not limited by natural processes and time.

However, the real reason God has delayed for what seems a long time to humans (2,000 years) is that God is patient and longsuffering. He is "not wishing that any should perish, but that all should reach repentance" (2 Peter 3:9; NKJV). Our stand on God's infallible Word needs to remain steadfast.

And just as surely as God created the earth and all life and as surely as He sent the global Flood in Noah's day as judgment, He will surely bring the final judgment by fire at the right time. Those of us who have believed God's Word concerning His message of salvation through Jesus Christ can say, *But according to his promise we are waiting for new heavens and a new earth in which righteousness dwells* (2 Peter 3:13).

> **We need to reject the philosophy of the scoffers and be diligent in spreading the wonderful gospel message of salvation for all to hear and respond to regardless of the persecution we receive.**

JULY 10
John 7:24

Voting and Christians

How should Christians vote in elections for government or for any position or anything for that matter? How can our vote count every day of the year?

Should Christians in Australia vote for the Liberal/National parties, Labor party, the Australian Greens, or some other party? What about American Christians? Should they vote Republican, Democrat, or Independent? What about Christians in the United Kingdom? Which of the many parties should they vote for?

Usually, when someone brings up the topic of voting, people think of politics and political parties. But the reality is that all of us vote every day in many different ways. When we buy food at the grocery store, we "vote" regarding the brands we think are the best based on whatever criteria we use to make decisions. We also vote when we determine who should be our close friends, whose children we allow to mix with our own, what programs we watch on television, what movies we allow our children to see, which church we decide to attend—and so much more.

Members of churches "vote" when they make decisions about what curriculum they should use for their Sunday school, Christian school, or homeschool; who will be elders or deacons; who should be appointed as a Sunday school teacher/Bible teacher; who should be the head teaching pastor; and so on. But whether it's politics, curricula, movies, or TV programs, I suggest that in any situation with worldview consequences, we should use the same basic principle to direct the decisions we make. It's vital for Christians to understand that the Bible is not just a guidebook to life. The Bible is a written revelation that is God-breathed:

All Scripture is breathed out by God and profitable for teaching, for reproof, for correction, and for training in righteousness, that the man of God may be complete, equipped for every good work (2 Timothy 3:16–17).

As we're told in 1 Thessalonians 2:13, it is not just the word of men but, in truth, the Word of God: *And we also thank God constantly for this, that when you received the word of God, which you heard from us, you accepted it not as the word of men but as what it really is, the word of God, which is at work in you believers.*

Think about it. The Bible is the Word of One who is infinite in knowledge and wisdom and doesn't ever tell a lie. It's the Word of the One who is "the truth." Jesus said, *I am the way, and the truth, and the life. No one comes to the Father except through me* (John 14:6). The Bible describes Jesus as being the Word: *In the beginning was the Word, and the Word was with God, and the Word was God* (John 1:1).

The only way we as fallible humans can be sure we have the right foundation to develop the correct way of thinking (our worldview) is to start with the revelation from Christ. He knows everything there is to know and has revealed the key information we need for the right foundation of our worldview. A truly Christian worldview is not one where we add passages from the Bible to our thinking, but we start with the Bible (and ultimately Genesis 1–11) as the foundation for all our thinking in every area.

When we start with God's Word, we learn that there is no such thing as a neutral position. The Bible tells us that we are either for or against Christ (Matthew 12:30), we walk in light or darkness (1 John 1:5–7), we build our "house" on the rock or the sand (Matthew 7:24–27), and we either gather or scatter (Luke 11:23).

APOLOGETICS   JULY 10

We are told that those who are not Christians are not neutral; they are, in fact, at enmity (at war) with God. *You adulterous people! Do you not know that friendship with the world is enmity with God? Therefore whoever wishes to be a friend of the world makes himself an enemy of God* (James 4:4). This principle enables us to understand that whenever we have opportunity to be of influence (to vote) if we do nothing, we are not being neutral!

Also, we are instructed in God's Word that we are to be "salt" and "light" in this world of darkness. *"You are the salt of the earth, but if salt has lost its taste, how shall its saltiness be restored? It is no longer good for anything except to be thrown out and trampled under people's feet. You are the light of the world. A city set on a hill cannot be hidden. Nor do people light a lamp and put it under a basket, but on a stand, and it gives light to all in the house. In the same way, let your light shine before others, so that they may see your good works and give glory to your Father who is in heaven"* (Matthew 5:13–16).

When we have opportunity to "vote," we need to have a standard by which to judge the situation and vote accordingly. We do have a standard—the absolute authority of the Word of God. And as I have said many times, when it comes to politics, Christians shouldn't vote for someone based simply on their identity or background. They shouldn't vote for someone just because they are Republican, Liberal/National, Democrat, Independent, or whatever! Christians should judge a candidate's worldview (even non-Christian candidates) against the absolute authority of the Word of God and vote accordingly, knowing we will not agree with everything—but we can do our best to be salt and light.

And, yes, we have to judge—in fact, we do every day when we make decisions. But *do not judge by appearances, but judge with right judgment* (John 7:24).

We judge by the absolute authority of the Word of God.

JULY 11
2 Corinthians 11:3

Reformation 2.0

Just over 500 years ago, the Reformation was initiated by a German priest and professor named Martin Luther and continued by others such as Calvin and Zwingli. Luther's nailing of his famed 95 Theses to a church door in Wittenberg in October 1517 began the Reformation.

It was a movement that called the Church back to the authority of God and away from the fallible opinions of man, which had severely compromised the clear teaching of the Word of God. The Bible-upholding movement was so powerful that today we are still experiencing the effects of this historical earthquake that spread from Germany to the world.

Throughout history, whenever we witness a great work of God, our adversary, the devil, *the prince of the power of the air, the spirit that is now at work in the sons of disobedience* (Ephesians 2:2), aggressively tries to undo this work. The devil's first temptation in Genesis 3:1 was to attack the Word of God and to get Adam and Eve to doubt God's Word so this would lead to unbelief. The Apostle Paul warns us in 2 Corinthians 11:3 that the devil will use the same method on us to get us to not believe God's Word. The devil would hate a movement like the Reformation and do all he could to get people away from believing in the authority of the Word of God.

I believe one of the major tactics that Satan uses to counter the good effects of the Reformation relates to the Book of Genesis. It began with a claim that the earth was very old, based on supposed geologic evidence of slow, natural processes, with nothing supernatural involved. An old age for the earth was necessary to justify the ideas behind naturalism, and the publication of Darwin's book on evolution soon followed in 1859. Another word for naturalism is atheism. Sadly, much of the Church (the majority of church leaders) has succumbed to this attack.

Darwin's book was an attempt to explain how animals and plants arose by natural processes, not the supernatural means revealed and documented for us by the Creator Himself in Genesis. Ultimately, this led to the idea that man evolved from apelike creatures. Armed with this cache of scientific "evidence" that the earth was supposedly millions/billions of years old and that molecules eventually gave rise to man, compromising theologians permeated the Church, teaching that Genesis should be treated as myth.

From both inside and outside the Church, the Darwinian revolution changed the hearts and minds of generations concerning biblical authority. The result has been devastating in our churches. Today, the majority of our young adults are leaving the Church in the West, and very few are returning. Our nationwide study through America's Research Group showed that the lack of trust in biblical authority, starting in Genesis, has been a major reason. In England, church attendance has declined from around 50% of the population three generations ago to about 5%. In the United States, 53% of millennials who used to go to church no longer do, and less than 9% of Generation Z attends church. America's once-Christianized culture is now divided between an aggressive secularist philosophy and a Christianized worldview.

Sadly, compromise in Genesis has undone much of what the Reformation had accomplished. It's why at Answers in Genesis I've often said our ministry is helping to ignite a new reformation. We need to see a new

APOLOGETICS　　　　　　　　　　　　　　　　　　　　　　　　　　　　JULY 11

reformation in the hearts and minds of God's people in our churches before a much-needed spiritual revival can occur in this nation—a country that's becoming increasingly hostile toward Scripture. So many of our church leaders (including many academics) need to repent of compromising God's Word.

A few years ago, one of our AiG scientists Dr. Nathaniel Jeanson (PhD in cell and developmental biology from Harvard) launched what I consider a groundbreaking book, *Replacing Darwin: The New Origin of Species*. I believe that this is the first major book to carefully research and offer a direct frontal attack on the very essence of the arguments Darwin used to promote evolution—arguments that have become popularized in our culture (including in much of the Church).

Dr. Jeanson states: "The goals of *Replacing Darwin* are audacious: to affect a scientific revolution and to set the research agenda for the next 50 years. In other words, *Replacing Darwin* seeks to accomplish a goal as big as its title—provoke a scientific shift of the same magnitude as Darwin's seminal work did."

He added: "*Replacing Darwin* is a unique and unprecedented book in modern literature. It draws on the latest scientific research and tells three scientific accounts that have never been put together in one volume anywhere. Furthermore, the book is structured in such a manner that anticipates and answers evolutionary objections to its claims. Since the origins debate inevitably converges on spiritual themes, the afterword presents the gospel in a manner that flows directly from the preceding chapters."

Dr. Jeanson further explains: "Since the vast majority of the scientific community rejects creationist science, *Replacing Darwin* not only challenges and equips Christians with powerful and startling scientific information, but it is written in a way to especially reach non-creationists. Free of Christian and creationist jargon, this book assumes a readership that is resistant to its message. Via 10 chapters of detailed scientific content, the book begins at ground zero in 1859, and then builds the case for creation while building credibility with the reluctant reader."

Yes, this groundbreaking book includes in-depth scientific content. But even if you don't understand some of the technical material, you will grasp the basic arguments against evolution that people need to learn today. So I urge you to help us start a new revolution to undo the destructive consequences of the Darwinian revolution.

Beware of the devil's attack: *Now the serpent was more crafty than any other beast of the field that the Lord God had made. He said to the woman, "Did God actually say"* (Genesis 3:1).

But I am afraid that as the serpent deceived Eve by his cunning, your thoughts will be led astray from a sincere and pure devotion to Christ (2 Corinthians 11:3).

Hosea the prophet observed, *My people are destroyed for lack of knowledge* (Hosea 4:6). You can help solve this major problem by becoming equipped with the information AiG provides and disseminating it to as many people as possible.

Don't let a lack of knowledge continue among God's people today.

JULY 12

Deuteronomy 6:5-7

War on Family

There's been a war on the family ever since sin entered the world. The devil knows how important the family is. The family is the first and most fundamental institution God ordained in Scripture. The family is the unit God uses to transfer a spiritual legacy from one generation to the next and to impact the world. The family is the educational unit of the nation. The devil knows that if you destroy the family, you destroy the backbone of the culture. The family is coming under increasingly aggressive attacks in America. Here are just some of the ways—and reasons:

Gay "Marriage":	Actually, there's no such thing as same-sex "marriage." That's why I have the word marriage in quotes. Marriage is a Christian institution God created when He made the first man and woman, Adam and Eve (Genesis 2:24). So-called gay (or same-sex) "marriage" is an attack on the family God instituted in Genesis. They can call it gay union or whatever they want to call it, but it's not marriage. There's only one marriage: the one God created–a man (male) and woman (female).
Gender Issues:	Almost daily we read news stories about transgender controversies, sex-change operations, restroom-gender issues, and the like. This is all an attack on the basis of the family structure God designed and ordained in Genesis when He created the first man and woman (Genesis 1:27). The secular culture has redefined "gender" to be what one feels they are as distinguished from one's biological sex! But that's absurd. Besides, Christians know we can't trust our feelings because of our sin (depraved) natures.
Feminism :	Much of the feminist movement pushes an idea of female superiority. When God created Adam and Eve, He created them in His image with equal value. God gave different roles to husband and wife–they are to submit to each other as they submit to God and the roles He ordained (Ephesians 5; Genesis 3:16, 17). Actually, in Genesis 3:16, God warns that because of our sin nature, women will have the propensity to want to be the head, and men will want to lord it despotically over the woman.
Abortion:	One of the primary reasons for marriage is to produce godly offspring (Malachi 2:15; Genesis 1:28). Not only is abortion the murder of a human being made in God's image, but the act is destructive to the purpose of marriage and the family as ordained by God. Abortion is actually child sacrifice to the god of self. The devil wants man to worship him and offer sacrifices to him, and that's really what abortion is.
Evolution:	The teaching of molecules-to-man evolution and millions of years has sadly resulted in countless young people doubting the Word of God (including its teachings about the family) and eventually leaving the Church. AiG published an eye-opening study of this youth exodus in my coauthored book *Already Gone*. Evolution and millions of years, in essence, are the pagan religion of the age as man attempts to explain life and the universe by natural processes. Naturalism is atheism. Generations of kids are being indoctrinated in the public school system in the religion of evolutionary atheism.

FAMILY   JULY 12

The devil knows that if he can get one generation to doubt and disbelieve God's Word starting in Genesis, he can destroy one of the main purposes of the family: to pass on a spiritual legacy to the next generation and to the world.

There are many other attacks on the family. Frankly, it shouldn't be all that surprising. As stated above, the family is the first and most fundamental of all human institutions God ordained. God created the family with the first man and woman (the first marriage), and He told them to be fruitful and multiply.

The family—especially a Christian family—is also the educational unit God uses to transmit a spiritual legacy to the next generation and to be a witness to the world. Throughout Scripture, we can find much practical teaching on training our children and passing on a godly legacy to the next generation (e.g., Deuteronomy 6; Joshua 4; Malachi 2; Ephesians 6).

Sadly, many families in the Church have succumbed to attacks on the family and have compromised in various ways. This is one of the reasons that AiG built the Creation Museum and the Ark Encounter and that we hold special lectures and hands-on science programs for families and formed our Answers Academy Christian school. We want to help parents raise godly offspring who are equipped to withstand the attacks of this evil world.

God's Word gives clear instructions on the structure of a family and the roles of mothers and fathers in raising godly offspring. Sadly, many in the Church have ignored these instructions. Many fathers have abdicated their responsibility to be the spiritual head of their home. We also live at a time where many homes don't have fathers for many reasons, and this has had a devastating impact on kids and on the culture. This is where the Church needs to be stepping up to help.

Sadly, many parents have handed their kids over to the pagan educational system to educate them, not understanding the kids are being indoctrinated in a secular worldview with the foundation of man's word. And even more sadly, many pastors have endorsed this system and have told generations they can believe what they're taught at school about evolution/millions of years, etc. But these kids realize if the Bible is not true at the beginning, how can you trust any of it? No wonder there's been a generational loss from the Church.

You shall love the Lord your God with all your heart and with all your soul and with all your might. And these words that I command you today shall be on your heart. You shall teach them diligently to your children, and shall talk of them when you sit in your house, and when you walk by the way, and when you lie down, and when you rise (Deuteronomy 6:5–7).

We need to train up godly generations.

JULY 13
Ephesians 6:11-17

Spiritual Warfare

I have a true story to share with you that involves a former Army Ranger. But first some background.

When I began giving apologetics presentations on biblical creation in Australia (1970s), some people in the Church were rather discouraging toward me. For instance, they would tell me that the teaching of evolution and millions of years was so pervasive in the culture (and the Church) that it would be hopeless to have any impact. I remember one person telling me I should just concentrate on "getting as many people saved as possible without trying to deal with such issues as creation/evolution, because everything would get worse anyway"! I recall telling one person something like this: "If you start digging a coal mine with a teaspoon, it will take a long time to dig a hole. But the more people who start digging with you, the faster and greater the hole will become."

And then I started to tell people something like this: "God's Word is like a major weapon. For me, it's as powerful as a 'nuclear bomb'—the more that we can see people motivated to stand on God's Word and proclaim the creation/gospel message and the authority of Scripture, the more the impact can resound around the world."

I am often reminded that God's Word uses a lot of military-type imagery to help us understand the real spiritual battle we are in—and how Christians need to be actively involved.

Here are some Scriptures in this regard: *Put on the whole armor of God, that you may be able to stand against the schemes of the devil. For we do not wrestle against flesh and blood, but against the rulers, against the authorities, against the cosmic powers over this present darkness, against the spiritual forces of evil in the heavenly places. Therefore take up the whole armor of God, that you may be able to withstand in the evil day, and having done all, to stand firm. Stand therefore, having fastened on the belt of truth, and having put on the breastplate of righteousness, and, as shoes for your feet, having put on the readiness given by the gospel of peace. In all circumstances take up the shield of faith, with which you can extinguish all the flaming darts of the evil one; and take the helmet of salvation, and the sword of the Spirit, which is the word of God* (Ephesians 6:11–17).

When I have read passages about the Israelites conquering the promised land, I have noticed that they can also be a picture of what the Christian life is like. We are, in essence, soldiers for the King—the King of creation (our Creator God). And just like the Israelites, we have our own Jericho and Ai battles. There are many "giants" to do battle with.

I am also reminded that God told the Israelites that *the LORD your God will clear away these nations before you little by little* (Deuteronomy 7:22).

Ever since the Lord directed me into the creation-apologetics ministry, I have had a burden to produce as many resources as we can and get them into as many people's hands as possible.

I firmly believed that, little by little, as people are equipped with the tools and weapons needed in the battle, they would impact the current and coming generations. And that's what I have seen happening. After working hard to proclaim the creation-gospel message around the world for many years, I have found it so thrilling for all of us at AiG to hear testimonies from people who have been impacted by the ministry. Furthermore, they are now teaching their children and impacting their church and friends. Indeed, we at AiG have done our best to obey the calling God has given us. And I praise the Lord for the incredible impact of so many outreaches that God has blessed.

In 1993, an incredible rescue operation and battle in Somalia became famously known as "Black Hawk Down." It is recognized as one of the most intense battles ever fought by U.S. forces. Although several of his comrades died and dozens were injured in the city of Mogadishu as hundreds of Somali militia swooped down on the American soldiers, Buck Wilford, an Army Ranger, came away unscratched from this intense firefight. Buck, who retired as a Green Beret, became a church planter and pastor of a church in Ohio.

Pastor Buck once visited AiG and the Creation Museum to speak at a conference. Our staff, as well as the Christian leaders attending our pastors' conference, had the privilege of hearing Buck give an account of his experience in Somalia. I must admit, after learning what he and his comrades went through, I felt physically exhausted. But Pastor Buck shared something else. He told us how God graciously spared his life and used his experiences to bring him to a point of committing his life to Him totally—and to give him a burden for reaching the lost.

Buck also shared how the ministry of AiG had impacted him and that he used AiG resources to reach souls for Christ. He told us how the Lord enabled him to attend the debate I had with Bill Nye "the Science Guy" in 2014—and how that event was life-changing for him.

Just as we have seen with Pastor Buck, the Lord is using AiG to help equip thousands of "soldiers"—all doing battle for our King. At AiG, we do all we can to enable this ministry—yes, little by little—to influence lives for Him. Praise God, the impact is growing exponentially.

How are each of us impacting lives for the Lord Jesus?

JULY 14
Psalm 90:2

Whose Beliefs Are Right? Part 1

Christians and atheists have beliefs. But which beliefs are the right ones? I have found that atheists, by and large, are either blinded to their own presuppositions or they refuse to acknowledge them! I find most just can't bring themselves to the point of acknowledging they have beliefs—in fact, a religion. And they are good at propaganda. They spread the narrative that Christians have a belief—a religion—but atheism is a scientific fact! The reality is that atheists have a blind faith that lacks credulity, but Christians have a faith that makes sense of the facts around us.

A well-known atheist in the United States was interviewing me in my office concerning the creation/evolution issue and the Book of Genesis. The conversation went something like this:

"So you admit that you start with the Bible?" she asked me.

"Yes, of course," I replied.

"And you are not prepared to change anything the Bible states, are you?" she asked.

"No," I said. "The Bible's statements concerning creation, the Flood, and so on are not subject to change—God's Word cannot be altered. Models based on the Bible are subject to change, but what the Bible clearly states is not subject to change."

"Ah," she then responded, "that's why creationists like you can never be real scientists. You see, real scientists like myself start with evidence and develop our theories. Then, as new evidence comes along, we modify our theories accordingly. You start with the Bible, not evidence, and you are not prepared to change your views. I start with evidence and am prepared to change or modify theories as new evidence comes along. That is real science."

I then responded by asking, "You are an atheist, correct?"

"Yes," she responded.

"And you don't believe in God and don't believe the Bible's account of Genesis has any part in science and in discussing the origins issue—is that right?"

"Yes," she again responded.

"Are you prepared to change that?" I asked.

Now I can't prove it because I didn't have a video camera running at the time, but I believe I saw a slight smile on her lips as she ignored the challenge and went on asking more questions. You see, I believe this atheist realized that I had caught her—that she started with beliefs that she was not prepared to change. And those beliefs determined how she approached evidence in regard to the origins issue.

I was making the point that no one ever starts with just evidence. We all have presuppositions that determine how we approach evidence. Now when we discuss the topic of origins particularly, we are dealing with history—what happened to bring the universe and life on this earth into being. The big problem is that no

APOLOGETICS — JULY 14

human being was a witness to record what happened. All the evidence that humans have access to exists in the present.

When we are dealing with the issue of origins, we are trying to answer questions such as:

- How did the universe come into existence?
- What happened to form the stars?
- How did life come about on Earth?
- How did humans come into existence?
- What processes formed the fossil record?

Forensic scientists know only too well the limitations of working with evidence in the present to reconstruct the history of the past. For instance, quite a number of people have been convicted of a crime based on circumstantial evidence, only to be declared not guilty when new evidence (such as DNA) came along to disprove the initial interpretation.

You may have experienced a similar situation in a murder mystery, such as a book or television program about Sherlock Holmes or some other famous detective. It can go like this: Halfway through, you are convinced the butler is guilty. Three-quarters of the way through, you are still convinced by the circumstantial evidence the butler did it. Close to the end of the book or television program, the circumstantial evidence still points to the butler's guilt. Then, just before the end, a piece of information is revealed that totally changes your conclusions. You suddenly realize the butler is innocent and a person you didn't expect is guilty! As I often say after reading such a book or watching such a program, "That was a waste of time!"

The problem is that fallible humans, who don't know everything, who weren't present everywhere in the past, can come to totally wrong conclusions in trying to reconstruct the past. You can never know you have all relevant evidence. One piece of evidence can totally change one's conclusions.

When visitors enter the Creation Museum in the Cincinnati area, one of the first exhibits they enter is called the Starting Points room. In this teaching exhibit, people are taught to understand that everyone has basic starting beliefs, or "presuppositions," which form their worldview (the way of thinking that they use to understand reality). Ultimately, there are only two starting points:

There is someone who knows everything about everything, who has always been there, who never tells a lie, and who reveals to us the information we need to know to come to right conclusions about this universe.

Somehow, fallible man, who doesn't know everything, who hasn't always been there, who doesn't always tell the truth, has to figure out the universe. The only place we find a claim about someone who fits the first description is the Bible:

From everlasting to everlasting you are God (Psalm 90:2).

His understanding is beyond measure (Psalm 147:5).

> We need to understand what the Bible actually is, as well as getting to the position Job arrived at in Job 42.

JULY 15
Romans 10:9

Whose Beliefs Are Right? Part 2

Atheists have the wrong foundation, the wrong religion. We need to get to that position Job arrived at when he stated: *I know that you can do all things, and that no purpose of yours can be thwarted. "Who is this that hides counsel without knowledge?" Therefore I have uttered what I did not understand, things too wonderful for me, which I did not know. "Hear, and I will speak; I will question you, and you make it known to me." I had heard of you by the hearing of the ear, but now my eye sees you; therefore I despise myself, and repent in dust and ashes* (Job 42:2–6).

Now the Bible not only claims to be a revelation from the infinite Creator, but it gives a very detailed history concerning origins, to enable us to come to right conclusions. No other book does this. If this book is what it claims to be, then we have a revelation from an omnipotent God, who gives us the history we need to know so we can interpret the evidence of the present correctly.

For instance, the Bible gives us an account of the origin of space, time, matter, earth, dry land, water, plants, stars, sun, moon, sea creatures, flying creatures, land animals, humans, marriage, the seven-day week, clothing, sin, death, languages, nations, and much more! We learn about the Tower of Babel and the global Flood of Noah's day. No evolutionist book covers all these topics. No other book does this—not the Koran or any Hindu book. Only the Bible gives such a detailed account of history.

If the Bible is really what it claims to be, a revelation from an omnipotent Creator, then the history that is revealed to us will make sense of the evidence of the present, and observational (empirical) science should confirm this history—and it does!

- The design in living things confirms an incredible intelligence behind the universe.
- The six-day creation week (and one day of rest) makes sense of the seven-day week we all adhere to.
- The giving of clothes after Adam and Eve sinned makes sense of why we wear clothes.
- Adam's original sin and its consequence explain why we all die.
- The Flood of Noah's day makes sense of most of the fossil record over the earth.
- The Tower of Babel makes sense of the different languages and nations, and yet genetics confirms we are all one race—consistent with humans being descendants of Adam and Eve.

The difference between me and the atheist who was interviewing me (see Part 1) was that I have built my worldview on the biblical revelation, whereas she has built her worldview on her atheistic beliefs. We approach the same evidence differently because we have different starting points.

Sadly, most Christians have been educated in a secular education system that indoctrinates them to believe that humans start with evidence to determine beliefs about the past. That is simply not true! Everyone starts with certain beliefs that determine how the evidence is interpreted, even though most people have not consciously thought about what their starting beliefs are.

APOLOGETICS

Because Christians have been indoctrinated in a secular system, they don't know how to approach answering questions about dinosaurs, the age of the earth, and so on. By and large, they don't realize that the secularists who taught them start with presuppositions that disallow the Bible's revelation.

These Christians, who may be real born-again Christians, are secularized in their thinking. When we understand the right way to think as a Christian, we know that we should start with the Bible (the revelation from our infinite Creator) and build our thinking (worldview) upon that. Then we have the right way to look at the evidence of the present.

The Bible's account of the creation of land animals, their diet before the Fall, the Flood of Noah's day, and so on gives us the right foundation to approach the topic of dinosaurs.

Now don't misunderstand me here. The Bible is not a scientific textbook, per se. The word *science* basically means "knowledge." Observational science, based on repeatable tests, is what builds technology. However, historical science (knowledge concerning the past to explain the present) is based on beliefs concerning history. The Bible is primarily a history book—an account of historical science, if you like—to enable us to think correctly concerning the origin of the universe, the meaning of life, the dilemma of sin, and the solution in Jesus Christ.

A number of qualified scientists are not ashamed to stand before this world and boldly proclaim that their starting point is the Bible. Among them are scientists at the Answers in Genesis ministry and Creation Museum. As you read various articles by these godly people, you will see over and over again how observational science confirms that the Bible really is the right starting point and reveals the inconsistency of starting with secular ideas.

Why is this ultimately important? If the history in the Bible concerning our origins were not true, then we would have no reason to trust the gospel message, which is based in that history. And the gospel is the heart of what Christians, such as those at Answers in Genesis, do.

Because, if you confess with your mouth that Jesus is Lord and believe in your heart that God raised him from the dead, you will be saved (Romans 10:9).

> Help bring the saving message of the gospel to a fallen world so that people may be convicted of their sin and repent and be saved for eternity.

JULY 16
Ezekiel 33:7

Watchmen on the Wall

Sometimes I despair at what some Christians complain about and what some support. But we need to be proclaiming the gospel and being watchmen to warn people of false teaching. I must admit there are times when I believe I have gotten a tiny inkling of what the prophet Jeremiah felt after he warned people about their departure from God's Word. He was probably hitting his head against a wall!

A number of Christians were upset with me about my debate with Bill Nye "the Science Guy" in 2014. I made a very public stand on the Bible's authority in the debate and proclaimed the gospel a few times. These Christians argued that I should have just used what they called "scientific evidences" during the debate. Now I did use some evidence but I wasn't going to concentrate on just giving evidence! Instead, I had prayerfully decided (and with the counsel from others) to concentrate on helping people understand that the creation/evolution conflict is a battle between two worldviews with different starting points (i.e., God's Word vs. man's word).

You see, there's no point in just seeing people converted to become creationists. We want them to be converted to be born-again Christians. Non-Christians will be saved by the power of the Word and its gospel message, not by evidence. (Evidence can be used in evangelism, but it's God's Word that ultimately convicts.) And, after the debate, we published a book dealing with all the supposed "evidences" Bill Nye brought up. But I used the debate platform to present the gospel clearly to the millions watching, and I make no apology for doing that.

I was shocked at the number of Christian leaders who supported the terrible 2014 secular movie *Noah* and even encouraged Christians and non-Christians to go see it! And they were upset with me for my negative statements about it.

You know, every time I read through the books of the prophets in the Bible, I am convicted about something: the importance of boldly standing on God's Word as the prophets did, even as they received varying degrees of opposition. For example, when I read Ezekiel, I am challenged about whether we as God's people are being the watchmen we need to be, as we contend for the faith in this secularized culture: *And if he sees the sword coming upon the land and blows the trumpet and warns the people, then if anyone who hears the sound of the trumpet does not take warning, and the sword comes and takes him away, his blood shall be upon his own head. He heard the sound of the trumpet and did not take warning; his blood shall be upon himself. But if he had taken warning, he would have saved his life. But if the watchman sees the sword coming and does not blow the trumpet, so that the people are not warned, and the sword comes and takes any one of them, that person is taken away in his iniquity, but his blood I will require at the watchman's hand. "So you, son of man, I have made a watchman for the house of Israel. Whenever you hear a word from my mouth, you shall give them warning from me"* (Ezekiel 33:3–7).

The amount of national media attention *Noah* received before it was even released was remarkable. More remarkable was the promotion it received from Christian leaders, who claimed that the movie would spur a dialogue with non-Christians regarding their need for a Savior. Because I knew that the movie would be unbiblical, blasphemous, and an attack on the character of Noah (and on God's character), I could not keep

APOLOGETICS JULY 16

silent before *Noah* was released. As the movie was being heavily promoted to churches, I believed we had an obligation to be "watchmen"—to warn Christians about what we had discovered about the film's content.

After watching this movie, I wondered if some of those Christian leaders who had been heavily promoting the movie had really watched it. Or were they just shown snippets that made it look like a "Bible" movie? If you read the Genesis narrative and watched the *Noah* movie, there is no way to conclude that this Hollywood production stayed true to the Scriptures—except for using some of the same Bible names!

Can Christians use a movie like *Noah* to point people to the true narrative of the Scriptures? Well, of course, it is possible—but that doesn't mean we should be promoting it!

While it is true that Christians can use things in the culture to point people to the Scriptures, they should show how the gospel is true because it's based on the history presented in the Bible (going back to Genesis 3) that is true.

The Church has been given the tremendous responsibility of carrying out the Great Commission to the uttermost parts of the earth. This commission predates the *Noah* movie or any other supposedly "Bible" movie. We already have numerous tools to enable us to be actively witnessing to people.

The *Noah* movie was not just inaccurate but a major distortion of the true biblical narrative. In Genesis 6:9, Noah is described as "a righteous man, blameless in his generation. Noah walked with God." Also, the writer of Hebrews describes Noah as a man of faith. Hebrews 11:7 states, *By faith Noah, being warned by God concerning events as yet unseen, in reverent fear constructed an ark for the saving of his household. By this he condemned the world and became an heir of the righteousness that comes by faith.*

In the movie, Noah is pictured as a homicidal psychopath whose main mission is to save the animals, while having no regard for human life. At one point, Hollywood's Noah almost kills his own granddaughters because their survival would go against his plans of reducing (or really eliminating) the human population. I truly fear that churches that took their young people to watch this movie, and failed to do a thorough follow-up using resources like the ones Answers in Genesis produces, would have caused a great deal of harm to the next generation. The culture is already indoctrinating our children with evolutionary and post-modern beliefs, and the last thing we need are churches and Christian leaders promoting such anti-biblical movies. Also, most non-Christians who watched this movie would most likely have not checked out the Bible. If anything, the gross distortions to the biblical text will do more damage than good concerning how they view Christianity.

The Church in America needs to wake up and understand that the increasing secular attacks against Scripture are only the start of the persecution that is headed to America. It is inevitable for the Church. Our brothers and sisters in Christ around the world are already being attacked for their faith and commitment to the Word of God. We are losing this and future generations from the Church. The Church is not influencing the culture as it once did—in fact, the culture has actually infected the Church.

> **Christians need to be defending the Christian faith and proclaiming the gospel boldly, doing their best to be "watchmen," and must warn the Church of the dangers that can undermine God's Word and our ability to reach people with the saving truth of the gospel.**

JULY 17
Matthew 16:18

Modern Reformers

I often ponder how God used special people to call people back to the authority of God's Word. It's a recurrent theme in history. As God's people drift from His Word, God raises up a person or persons to call people back to the authority of the Word of God. I think of men like Martin Luther, Dwight L. Moody, John Wesley, George Whitefield, and others who impacted so many people. Luther started the Reformation. Now, none of them were perfect, as we all have feet of clay as God reveals in His Word with David, Samuel, Samson, and so on. But God used them in mighty ways. But then, however, the enemy (the devil) raises up people to try to thwart God's call.

This ongoing spiritual battle started just over 6,000 years ago in the Garden of Eden. We've seen this battle rage over and over again in history, as recorded in the Bible and as seen in the last 2,000 years of church history. We saw it during the Reformation 500 years ago, and we're seeing it happen before our very eyes today. To help illustrate the spiritual battle in recent times, I want to share a real-life example with you. Here is the background.

In 2007, a historic event occurred: the opening of the world's first major Creation Museum. Then nine years later, another historic event in Christendom happened. And I truly believe it is one of the greatest outreaches of our era—the opening of the Ark Encounter!

In an interview with me about our life-size Ark attraction, a reporter for a major national media network inquired about Christian attractions that are appearing in different places. This reporter mentioned the Museum of the Bible in Washington, DC; the Sight and Sound Christian theater in Lancaster, Pennsylvania; the Creation Museum; and the Ark Encounter. He commented that it seemed to be the era for building significant Christian-themed attractions, and the reporter wanted to understand why it was happening.

Let me explain to you why I believe it's occurring in this era. We live in a time when we see the increasing secularization of our culture. We've also seen much of the Church (particularly leaders in Christian colleges, seminaries, and Bible colleges) drift from God's Word, beginning in Genesis. Much of the Church has become lukewarm resulting in a generational loss from the Church.

In this era, there has been an undermining of the authority of God's Word, particularly in Genesis 1–11, because of the teaching of millions of years/evolution. As a consequence, we are watching much of the Church compromise God's Word in other areas, such as the biblical teaching on the doctrine of marriage being one man and one woman. We see certain church leaders/Christian academics becoming soft on the LGBTQ movement.

As we have observed this drift happening in the Church across the world, we praise God that He has raised up the biblical creation apologetics movement, which is calling God's people back to the authority of the Word of God.

The Lord called men like the late Drs. Henry Morris and John Whitcomb to write a book called *The Genesis Flood* that started much of the modern biblical creationist movement. This Bible-upholding movement has spread around the world as many creation-apologetics organizations have been founded (and denominations and other groups have been greatly influenced). The Church has been impacted in many positive ways.

As the biblical creationist movement has grown enormously and has seen such a positive influence on millions of people (and thousands of churches), we have seen certain people within the Church who have tried to counteract this great work.

The Templeton Foundation has given millions of dollars to help an organization called BioLogos. The purpose? "BioLogos invites the church and the world to see the harmony between science and biblical faith as we present an evolutionary understanding of God's creation."[69]

Yes, this well-funded movement involving scientists (some well-known) is actively trying to influence the Church to believe in evolutionary geology, biology, anthropology, astronomy, and so on. They use millions of dollars to try to get God's people to compromise God's Word! And their emphasis is certainly not evangelism, to see people saved and won to the Lord Jesus Christ.

I don't believe it's coincidence that this pro-evolution undermining of biblical authority effort is happening when organizations like Answers in Genesis (with its various outreaches including the Creation Museum and the new Ark Encounter) have seen a great impact on the Church worldwide.

Much of the Church is not impacting the culture as it once did in our Western world. Sadly, many church leaders have compromised with evolutionary ideas and now are also compromising on moral issues like gender and marriage. But I believe God is raising up special people within the Church to impact the culture in unique and powerful ways, including through Christian attractions like the four I mentioned above (and I trust many more attractions in the future).

Although I explained it in a somewhat different way to the secular reporter, I believe God is moving in mighty ways to proclaim the truth of His Word and the gospel—as His Word promises:

I will build my church, and the gates of hell shall not prevail against it (Matthew 16:18).

I see God raising up Christian attractions as part of equipping Christians to defend their faith, challenging non-Christians with the gospel, and calling the Church back to the authority of the Word of God. Because much of the Church is not doing what it should, I believe God is using Christian attractions to bring people in to equip them so they can impact lives and their own churches.

> **I pray millions will be impacted and lives changed for eternity as a result of the era of Christian attractions.**

JULY 18
Genesis 1:26

Humans Have Dominion Over the Earth

I read a news article once about PETA (People for the Ethical Treatment of Animals) that wanted to erect a memorial where a tractor trailer filled with lobsters had an accident. The animal rights people wanted to erect a memorial to the lobsters that died in the accident. It's not uncommon to see animals exalted and valued far above humans. Animal rights groups, such as PETA, vehemently fight against the use of animals for anything, saying things such as, "Animals are not ours to eat, wear, experiment on, use for entertainment, or abuse in any other way" and "When it comes to pain, love, joy, loneliness, and fear, a rat is a pig is a dog is a boy. Each one values his or her life and fights the knife." What should a Christian's response be to these arguments?

Well, it's important to first note the inconsistency of most animal rights groups. These groups claim to be against animal abuse, but are these same people against the abuse of millions of children who are brutally murdered in their mothers' wombs through abortion? It's rather ironic that in PETA's evolutionary worldview humans are just animals, yet PETA does not petition against the "animal cruelty" of killing unborn children. And what about a Save the Tapeworms Society or People for the Preservation of Fruit Flies?

Now some animal rights people claim they are Christians. If so, then they need to understand that God gave man dominion over creation (Genesis 1:26), including over the animals. This dominion does not mean we can deliberately abuse, neglect, or harm creation, but rather, we're to use what God has made for our good and His glory. In Genesis 1:29 and 30, God told man to eat plants/fruits. But in Genesis 9:3, after the Flood, God said we could eat all things (plants and animals).

Animal rights groups really want animals to have dominion over man. Yet, ironically, most would claim that man is just an animal. So if they want equal rights for animals, what rights should humans have if they believe man is just an evolved animal? For example, if animals kill other animals, do animal rights groups think humans (if we're just animals) should have equal rights to kill too? Why should we be held to some higher standard or different moral code from other animals?

In an evolutionary worldview, what makes animal rights activists think that rights exist in the first place? Rights are an abstract concept that comes from a biblical worldview, which is denied by the evolutionary position. The evolutionary position, which comes out of naturalism and materialism, cannot account for the concept of rights, because they are not material. In other words, the evolutionary materialist must borrow the concept of rights from Christians to argue against the Christian position of man being superior and in dominion over animals. Those who start with an evolutionary view of mankind have no absolute basis for morality. Because they have no foundation, they are forced to construct a moral code that is "right in his own eyes" (Judges 21:25). This leads to all kinds of inconsistencies. Evolutionists arbitrarily create or hold to a moral code for humans—which, in their view, includes not using anything that comes from or was even tested on animals—yet they believe we are just animals. Consider if evolutionary animal rights groups are right in saying there is no distinction between man and animals. Then what is to say there is a distinction between animals and plants? Perhaps the argument should be to also refrain from any plant use. It wouldn't take long for the animal/plant rights activists to die of starvation. An evolutionary view of mankind and morality leads to inconsistency and confusion. It's only when we start with God's Word that we get a firm

APOLOGETICS

foundation for morality. We are not animals; we were specially and uniquely created in the image of God, separate and distinct from the animals. (In a similar fashion, animals are not created like plants either).

We are morally accountable to our Creator, and His Word has provided us with clear guidelines of how we are—and are not—to behave. Murder and theft are wrong because our Creator has decreed that we are not to kill (Genesis 4:8–11; Exodus 20:13) and we are not to steal (Exodus 20:15). Eating meat is not morally wrong because, after the global Flood, God gave mankind permission to eat meat (Genesis 9:3). Jesus Himself ate fish (Luke 24:41–43) and partook of the Passover lamb (Luke 22:7–22). We are not left drifting in an inconsistent moral sea of man's opinions. Starting with God's Word, we have a firm foundation for morality.

Most animal rights groups start with an evolutionary view of mankind. They view us as the last to evolve (so far), as a blight on the earth, and the destroyers of pristine nature. Nature, they believe, is much better off without us, and we have no right to interfere with it. This is nature worship, which is a further fulfillment of the prophecy in Romans 1 in which the hearts of sinful man have traded worship of God for the worship of God's creation.

Now all of creation groans, waiting for the coming day when Jesus will liberate it from the curse (Romans 8:20–22; Revelation 22:3). Creation was never designed to live in disharmony. We, and the animals, were originally created to be vegetarian (Genesis 1:29–30) and to live forever without any suffering or disease. But because sin changed all of that, we battle its effects every day. This doesn't mean that humans are a blight or disease. Despite our sin, we are the only ones created in the image of God, utterly unique from the rest of creation. We were granted dominion over the earth and its inhabitants (Genesis 1:26). This was part of our "very good" (Genesis 1:31), pre-Fall purpose and mission, and it stems out of our position as image bearers of the Creator.

But does having dominion mean that we can treat animals any way that we want to? No! Such a view stems from a misguided view of our dominion over creation. It exalts humans while devaluing the rest of God's creation. You see, God takes great joy in His creation. Six different times before He created mankind, God looked at what He had made and called it "good" (Genesis 1:4, 10, 12, 18, 21, 25). Scripture is full of celebrations of creation's beauty and God's care for what He has made (Matthew 6:30, 10:29). In Proverbs 12:10, we read, *Whoever is righteous has regard for the life of his beast*. The testimony of Scripture as a whole paints the picture of a Creator who loves and cares for all that He has made. As those made in His image, we should love and care for what He has made too. So the response here is not to point out that all of what animal activists are saying is wrong. We need to be discerning based on God's Word. The problem is that the activists have gone too far, to a point where they are essentially worshipping animals. In our world of harsh, contrasting sides, it's often difficult to find a balance. There's a temptation to fall into either ditch: exalting animals above humans or devaluing God's other creations.

As Christians, we need to find a proper balance based on Scripture. Humans alone are made in the image of God. We're unique and therefore have a unique place in God's creation. Jesus Himself became a man and died on the Cross to save mankind, not the animals.

> **We need to reflect the heart of the One whose image we are made in and treat His creation with kindness, directing glory to our Creator and Savior.**

JULY 19
Ephesians 4:14

We Need More Jeremiahs

I sometimes feel sorry for the prophet Jeremiah. He had to give the people such negative messages. And most of the people who heard his messages didn't like what they heard. Personally, I believe we need more people like Jeremiah today giving negative messages about where the culture and Church are at! Now that will horrify people who say we should never give negative messages.

For instance, I've heard certain Christians claim that I shouldn't be negative as I point out the LGBTQ movement, abortion activists, gender perversion, critical race theory, social justice, and the many other issues swirling around the culture in a tornado of moral relativism. I'm told I should stop being so negative, as that's just "hate speech," and talk about love. Well, if this were correct, I would have to stop quoting God's Word! Jeremiah would have had to stop his prophetic messages that God instructed him to give!

I remember as a child hearing the schoolmaster warning us about things we should not do unless we wanted to be disciplined. There sure were a lot of rules—a lot of negativity from the schoolmaster we could say. Don't do this or that, and if you do this, you will be disciplined this way, and so on. As a child, I wondered, "Why so many rules?"

Then as I read the Bible, I understood that God gave the Israelites numerous laws (rules). In fact, there are a lot of warnings and "do nots" throughout Scripture.

Galatians 3:24 in the King James Version reads, *Wherefore the law was our schoolmaster to bring us unto Christ, that we might be justified by faith.* We needed our "schoolmaster" to understand what is right and wrong. But we have a problem called sin. (No wonder the schoolmaster had a lot of rules for us. He knew we weren't perfect and were liable to do things we shouldn't.)

The purpose of the law was to expose our sin and to show us that we can't save ourselves because we can't keep the law perfectly. The law was given to point us toward the righteousness that comes through faith in Christ alone. As the Apostle Paul states in Romans 5:1, *Therefore, since we have been justified by faith, we have peace with God through our Lord Jesus Christ.*

In Genesis 4:7, God warns Cain, *If you do well, will you not be accepted? And if you do not do well, sin is crouching at the door. Its desire is contrary to you, but you must rule over it.* Cain wanted to do things his way, and God was warning him that sin was about to have mastery over him. Cain didn't listen to the warning God gave, and out of jealousy, he killed his brother Abel. He let his sin nature master him. We need to remember that about our sin nature daily.

There's a lot of negativity throughout Scripture because we live in a fallen world. As a result of our sin nature, we are more prone to do what is wrong than what is right. We are more prone to be influenced by the fallen world than for us to impact the world with what is right. Jeremiah gave such a message to God's people. And I've heard people accuse Jeremiah of being too negative. But Jeremiah was a prophet of the Lord, and what he spoke is part of the inspired, inerrant, written Word of God. He warned the people, just as we need to be warned today, about not letting our sin nature get the better of us.

THEOLOGY JULY 19

Jeremiah warned the people, *Thus says the Lord: "Learn not the way of the nations"* (Jeremiah 10:2) and *The gods who did not make the heavens and the earth shall perish from the earth and from under the heavens* (Jeremiah 10:11). Speaking of the true God, Jeremiah proclaimed, *It is he who made the earth by his power, who established the world by his wisdom, and by his understanding stretched out the heavens* (Jeremiah 10:12). Speaking of those who were worshipping false gods, Jeremiah stated, *Every man is stupid and without knowledge* (Jeremiah 10:14). How is that for a negative message!

Many in the Church today would claim that Jeremiah was being too negative. But Jeremiah was pointing out the wrong things people were doing and then pointing them to the true God they needed to worship.

There is a great need today for us to warn people about the evil happening around us in the culture: *So that we may no longer be children, tossed to and fro by the waves and carried about by every wind of doctrine, by human cunning, by craftiness in deceitful schemes* (Ephesians 4:14). As we bring up children, we have to give them negative messages about not crossing busy streets the wrong way, not playing in dangerous areas, not eating or drinking poisonous substances, and so on.

Because of our sin nature, we have to be diligent to ensure we don't become captive to the evil ways of the world. We can so easily be influenced by that which is wrong. We do need to warn people and give them the "negative" message. For instance, we need to warn people that they are sinners and, as such, would spend eternity separated from God. But to go with that, we teach the good (positive) news that our God, through His Son, provided a means of salvation for those who will receive it so that we can spend eternity with the Lord.

We also need to warn people about the evils of certain movements that are impacting generations of kids (for example, LGBTQ, critical race theory, social justice, gender issues, and many more) and also point them to the Word of God to help them build a truly Christian worldview and impact people around them—including their children and grandchildren and great-grandchildren—with the truth of God's Word and the gospel.

> **In a fallen world, we need to be negative but for the right reason – to help people understand the evil consequences of sin and point them to the positive message of the saving gospel through the Lord Jesus Christ.**

JULY 20
Isaiah 55:11

Foundations vs. Models

There's a big difference between changing one's models built on beliefs and changing those beliefs. So let's consider this: If creationists are unwilling to change their basic beliefs, does that mean they're not true scientists? When I quote secular articles claiming some new evidence that "rewrites" certain parts of the evolutionary story, evolutionists claim this is a good thing because change is part of the self-correcting mechanism of science. In contrast, such evolutionists usually claim that creationists aren't prepared to change, and because they don't allow for any such "self-correction," they aren't scientific. However, secular evolutionists will not change their basic belief of naturalism! They are committed to those beliefs just as Christians are committed to God's Word.

When the Creation Museum opened in 2007, I was interviewed by a well-known U.S. evolutionist whom the BBC had contracted for a radio program. (See this brief conversation on the July 14 entry.)

All evolutionists believe the universe and all life came about by natural processes. That's a foundational belief they are not prepared to change, no matter what the evidence. And naturalism is atheism, which is a religion.

I find that many people (whether creationists or evolutionists) don't seem to understand the difference between presuppositions (foundational beliefs on which we build our worldview) and the models built on those presuppositions. Now for Christians who build their thinking on the Bible, the presupposition that the Bible is the infallible Word of God and the foundation for our worldview is not subject to change. (This should be the stance of all Christians.) However, models built on God's Word are man-made, so they're subject to change. For instance, when the famous book that started the modern creation movement—*The Genesis Flood*—was published in 1961, it promoted a model that became very popular among creationists. Based on the authors' interpretation of Scripture, regarding the second day of creation, they proposed that the original earth was surrounded by a protective vapor canopy.

Now many in the next generation of biblical creationists rejected the canopy based on theological and scientific objections. What Scripture states concerning the second day of creation (our presupposition) has not changed, but the model built on Scripture has changed or even been rejected by many modern creationists. We need to be prepared to change models but stand firm on God's Word.

I explained to this evolutionist that she, like me, had certain basic views she was not prepared to change. When I debated Bill Nye in February 2014, I publicly admitted my presupposition of building my worldview on the Bible. I challenged Bill Nye to admit publicly his presupposition of building his thinking on evolutionary naturalism. However, as is usual for evolutionists, he would not admit his starting point of naturalism. He kept insisting his view was "science" based on evidence. That's why I kept emphasizing that there's a big difference between historical science (our interpretations based on beliefs about the past, such as God's revelation in the Bible concerning origins) and observational science (knowledge we can gain through direct observation, using one's senses, and based on repeatable testing in the present). In an ultimate sense, as a fallible human, I cannot absolutely prove my presupposition concerning the truth of Scripture. Only God can ultimately reveal that truth to someone: *And without faith it is impossible to please him, for whoever would draw near to God must believe that he exists and that he rewards those who seek him* (Hebrews 11:6). And only God can change

APOLOGETICS   JULY 20

someone's presuppositions: *For by grace you have been saved through faith. And this is not your own doing; it is the gift of God* (Ephesians 2:8). Now when I was debating Bill Nye and when I was being interviewed by the evolutionist, I recognized that I couldn't change their presupposition concerning naturalism and their rejection of God's Word. But I also understood that I needed to do my best to answer their objections to what I believe: *But in your hearts honor Christ the Lord as holy, always being prepared to make a defense to anyone who asks you for a reason for the hope that is in you; yet do it with gentleness and respect* (1 Peter 3:15).

Above all, I needed to point them to the Word of God that *is living and active, sharper than any two-edged sword, piercing to the division of soul and of spirit, of joints and of marrow, and discerning the thoughts and intentions of the heart* (Hebrews 4:12).

We are to do our best to convince those who don't believe the truth of God's Word, understanding that only the One who is the Resurrection and the life can change both their presuppositions and their eternal destiny: *Jesus said to her, "I am the resurrection and the life. Whoever believes in me, though he die, yet shall he live"* (John 11:25). Creationists have to be prepared to change mistaken interpretations and models, but not change the Word of God: *Forever, O Lord, your word is firmly fixed in the heavens* (Psalm 119:89).

And creationists always need to remember that the point of giving answers in regard to the creation-evolution issue is ultimately to point people to the Word of God that saves: *So shall my word be that goes out from my mouth; it shall not return to me empty, but it shall accomplish that which I purpose, and shall succeed in the thing for which I sent it* (Isaiah 55:11).

Therefore take up the whole armor of God, that you may be able to withstand in the evil day, and having done all, to stand firm (Ephesians 6:13).

We need to be prepared to change models but stand firm on God's Word.

JULY 21
Jude 3

Banning Christianity?

If secularists had their way, do you think they would outlaw Christianity? Well, it has happened many times in history. And, yes, I believe this is the outcome most secularists want. The Christian worldview and the secular worldview are in total conflict.

Back in 1986, I was filmed for a movie called *The Genesis Solution*. In my presentation, recorded in front of a live audience, I stated: "Our declining society is an outward expression of an inward rejection of our Creator. And our freedoms are being eroded as Christianity is being slowly eliminated. Christians may wake up one day to find Christianity outlawed."

Now, there were people back then, 30 years ago, who said to me, "Christianity outlawed in America? No way." But, little by little, Christianity is being eroded in the nation, in fact in the whole Western world. The free exercise of religion is under attack, particularly concerning the Christian faith.

The teaching of creation, the Bible, and prayer have been outlawed from most public (government) schools. Christian reminders, like crosses, Ten Commandments displays, and Nativity scenes are being outlawed from public places. The word *Christ* is being outlawed from Christmas in some places. We've already seen instances where people have not been able to carry out the free exercise of their Christian convictions in their businesses. The secularists, little by little, have been imposing their anti-God religion on the culture. Christians need to wake up to what is happening regarding their legal rights. And, yes, the secular worldview is a religious worldview. Everyone has a religion, a set of beliefs that determine how they think and behave about life.

Another example of hostility toward Christianity pertains to atheist groups attacking the Ark Encounter. For instance, they have bullied public schools in an attempt to outlaw students from having the opportunity to visit the attraction.

Now what these atheists claim is not correct and, in fact, is illegal. But because their lawyers constantly bully educators and threaten lawsuits, most school administrators cave in because of the hassle (and cost) to legally contest the issue.

One bullying letter stated: "The Ark Encounter, which is opening this week in Kentucky, is a Christian ministry run by the creationist Ken Ham, who also built the notorious Creation Museum."

And why are we so notorious? Well, this is why: "Ham has been clear … 'Our motive is to do the King's business until He comes. And that means preaching the gospel and defending the faith, so that we can reach as many souls as we can.'"

And, yes, we've always said that! Indeed, the Ark and Creation Museum present the Christian message! But then the atheist group's letter states: "Ham is free to erect monuments to the bible, but public schools are not permitted to expose the children in their charge to religious myths and proselytizing. So, public schools cannot organize trips for students to either the Creation Museum or the Ark Park. Doing so would violate the students' rights of conscience and the U.S. Constitution."

APOLOGETICS — JULY 21

Note the emotional language: "religious myths" and "proselytizing" (as if we are forcing our messages on people). But is it really correct that government-run schools would be in violation of the law if students were brought to a Christian facility as part of their school curricula? Not at all. Christian attorneys who battle such cases all the time sent me this statement: "Once again, [the atheist group] is wrong. Public schools are free to take students on field trips to any place they find educationally beneficial, which can include parks, museums, and even churches that have religious connotations. The Constitution demands the state be neutral—not hostile—toward religion. To deny students the unique opportunity to see and experience a full-scale model of Noah's Ark—just because its existence is described in the Bible—would be decidedly hostile."

Little by little, the secularists have been outlawing Christianity from the culture. Through misinformation, bullying, and intimidation, they have been succeeding. And because so many Christians have been secularized by the public education system, they have largely not put up a fight. If this trend keeps happening, we will see declining church attendance and increasing secularization of the culture. This is happening all across the Western world.

God's people have not been standing on God's Word from its beginning. In this era, the compromise between evolution/millions of years and Genesis began in England and spread around the world. Really, what's happened to the Church throughout the West is actually the outworking of a Church that has compromised God's Word with man's fallible ideas. Furthermore, the Church has largely handed over the education of generations to the state and its schools that have increasingly outlawed anything Christian.

I believe this is why the Lord has raised up ministries like Answers in Genesis, the Creation Museum, and the Ark Encounter. God is using these outreaches to equip Christians to stand against the secular attacks of our day and to challenge (in a very public and bold way) non-Christians with the truth of God's Word and the gospel.

God has allowed AiG to build the Creation Museum and the Ark because I believe there are many godly people who will take a stand on the authority of the Word of God. While we still have the freedom to boldly proclaim the message of God's Word to the world we need to help embolden God's people and reach millions with the saving gospel. I urge you to stand boldly against those who would try to completely outlaw Christianity from the culture.

You probably recall the famous quote by Edmund Burke, an eighteenth-century British statesman, parliamentary orator, and political thinker: "The only thing necessary for the triumph of evil is for good men to do nothing." God said it this way in His Word: *Beloved, although I was very eager to write to you about our common salvation, I found it necessary to write appealing to you to contend for the faith that was once for all delivered to the saints* (Jude 3).

If God's people don't contend for the faith, we will see Christianity outlawed even further in our culture! I implore you to stand up for your faith. In a very public way (with an increasing number of scoffers trying to stop us), AiG is contending for the faith through many ministries like the Creation Museum and the Ark Encounter.

Remember, we can all contend for the faith.

JULY 22
Ephesians 6:12

Everyone Is Religious

If you don't go to church and don't believe in God, does this mean you are not a religious person? Well, the answer is no! Everyone has a worldview, which means everyone has a religion.

Almost all atheists claim that, because (supposedly) there is no God, their own worldview is not a religion. Many of them would argue that they have a "nonbelief."

One of the definitions of religion in the *Merriam-Webster Dictionary*, however, is this: "a cause, principle, or system of beliefs held to with ardor and faith."

Atheism certainly fits that definition, and many of its adherents are quite zealous about their faith system.

Atheists have an active belief system with views concerning origins (that the universe and life arose by natural processes); no life after death; the existence of God; how to behave while alive; and so much more. Honest atheists will admit their worldview is a faith. Atheism is a religion!

One candid atheist wrote, "My attitude is not based on science, but rather on faith. … The absence of a Creator, the non-existence of God is my childhood faith, my adult belief, unshakable and holy."

This secular (anti-God) religion of atheism is growing. Atheism is all around us in various forms. It is practiced (and funded) by almost all government schools. In essence, atheism has become the religion of the state, and it pervades the media, courts, museums, textbooks, the internet, and science journals, and influences many people you encounter.

About 85% of children from our Church homes attend government (atheistic) schools. Your kids and grandkids have likely been adversely influenced by this religion—and they may not have even realized it.

Actually, however, there are no true atheists—just those who claim to be. The all-knowing God of the Bible informs us that He has made it evident to all people that He exists, but unbelievers try to suppress that knowledge (Romans 1:18). In Romans 2, we read that God has given everyone a conscience about right and wrong.

While atheism is a blind faith (really a faith that lacks credulity), its followers will still cry out, "We are not part of a religion!" Why do they plead this? First, if atheism were identified as a religion, atheists fear that their views might get kicked out of public places, like government-run schools. Second, these secularists will be less likely able to deceive children into thinking that their teachings (supposedly "neutral") are not in conflict with the religious beliefs of students. Secular is not neutral; it is anti-God. The Bible nowhere teaches neutrality but informs us that one is either for or against Christ. There is no in-between.

Secular humanistic religions—like evolution, atheism, and agnosticism—are part and parcel of the same belief system. These worldviews have free reign with tax-supported dollars, not only in America but also in the United Kingdom, Australia, Germany, and many other countries. It's ironic that under the rallying cry of "let's keep religion out" of the public arena, secularists have kicked Christianity out of the classroom and have replaced it with another religion (their religion): the religion of naturalism, which is atheism.

APOLOGETICS

There is a simple way to test this claim that a worldview is not "nonreligious." If atheism really isn't religious, then why do atheists strongly oppose religious claims? Their approach is illogical! That's because it is a spiritual issue—a religious issue.

Does the atheistic view of origins (big bang, millions of years, and evolution—each involving supposed natural processes) oppose the religious view of special creation by God in six days? Yes. Therefore, secular views of origins are religious.

Anyone who claims that they are not religious and then makes judgments about religious topics (e.g., the deity of Christ, the existence of God, the morality regarding adultery, the truthfulness of the Bible, and so on) has made a religious statement. Though they may "claim" to be irreligious, they reveal that they are indeed religious when they attempt to refute another religious view.

Does atheism oppose the religious claim that God exists? Again, yes. Thus, atheism is religious. Popular atheist John Dunphy, writing for a secular magazine, admitted:

"I am convinced that the battle for humankind's future must be waged and won in the public school classroom by teachers who correctly perceive their role as the proselytizers of a new faith: a religion of humanity that recognizes and respects the spark of what theologians call divinity in every human being.

"These teachers must embody the same selfless dedication as the most rabid fundamentalist preachers, for they will be ministers of another sort, utilizing a classroom instead of a pulpit to convey humanist values in whatever subject they teach, regardless of the educational level—preschool day care or large state university.

"The classroom must and will become an arena of conflict between the old and the new—the rotting corpse of Christianity, together with all its adjacent evils and misery, and the new faith of humanism."[70]

When it is financially beneficial or otherwise helpful to their cause, atheists want to receive the benefits allowed for groups that are widely seen as religious. For example, atheistic and other secular groups are eligible to receive tax benefits that other religious groups get. In addition, secular and atheist chaplains function within the military. These atheists want to have their cake and eat it too. The atheist worldview is religious because its adherents behave in religious ways.

Ultimately, the battle is between two religions: God's true religion and man's false religion. This battle has been raging for 6,000 years and won't end until Jesus returns and makes new heavens and a new earth.

Atheists believe they cease to exist when they die. Why then do they even bother to oppose Christians and aggressively work to impose their religion on the culture if all is futile anyway? The Apostle Paul pointed out the very real battle around us:

For we do not wrestle against flesh and blood, but against the rulers, against the authorities, against the cosmic powers over this present darkness, against the spiritual forces of evil in the heavenly places (Ephesians 6:12).

The atheists' battle against Christianity clearly illustrates the spiritual struggle raging around us.

JULY 23
Romans 1:28-32

Arkophobia

If you've never heard of the term Arkophobia, you will learn all about it in this article. I made up the word, but we can learn a lot from it.

We've all heard of the word arachnophobia, a fear of spiders and other arachnids such as scorpions. Well, there is a new phobia that's been showing up for years on countless blogs, on X (formerly Twitter), and in news sources. And it has a similar-sounding name: Arkophobia. It's a fear of the life-size Ark Answers in Genesis built in Williamstown, Kentucky, that opened in 2007.

The *Merriam-Webster Dictionary* defines a phobia as "an exaggerated usually inexplicable and illogical fear of a particular object, class of objects, or situation."[71]

Well, the Arkophobia we see all around us is certainly "illogical." But it's actually not "inexplicable." Let me explain. Arkophobia hit an all-time high the week of January 2016, just before the Ark attraction opened. That's when a federal judge issued a major ruling that gave a huge win to Answers in Genesis in our religious freedom lawsuit against the state of Kentucky and the actions of the liberal governor involved.

The judge ruled that Kentucky could not deny the Ark project participation in the state's tourism tax-incentive program. Such a denial would be discriminatory based on the U.S. Constitution and its First Amendment. The judge also ruled in accordance with the Civil Rights Act of 1964 and Title VII of that act, confirming that, as a religious organization, AiG can use religious preferences in Ark hiring.

Well, that federal decision was too much for the secularist/atheist bloggers. That's when Arkophobia was at its height. Many secularists were already livid that a Christian organization was building such a massive tourist facility that would have (and has had) a huge impact on the culture as it proclaims a Christian message! They just can't stand it! Their hatred against Christianity was so clear after the ruling.

In bemoaning the judge's decision, one atheist blogger mocked: "In case you don't know, Ken Ham is building a big boat in Kentucky and planning to tell people it's a replica of Noah's Ark. This, he believes, will make people want to become Christians and stop being gay. Ham's God really likes spending millions of dollars on vanity woodwork projects but really hates people who love other people of the same gender. Ham's God is apparently ambivalent about giving some of those millions of dollars to those who most need it."

These hateful statements helped to reveal Arkophobia. What is the real reason for such vehement opposition to a project that has become so beneficial to the state by bringing in hundreds of millions of tourist dollars into Kentucky for hotels, restaurants, and much more, and creating thousands of jobs? It's because of the message of the Ark. It's what the Ark represents! It is the message that is taught at the Ark.

The opposition to the tax incentives, which are offered to any tourism project that will have a positive economic impact in Kentucky and create jobs (called a "neutral purpose"), is illogical. Furthermore, such censorship violates the U.S. Constitution's guarantee of the freedom of religion and its free exercise. The opposition we have been encountering is due to a heart issue.

RESOURCES — JULY 23

Romans 3:23 teaches us that *all have sinned and fall short of the glory of God*. And Romans 3:10–18 states: *"None is righteous, no, not one; no one understands; no one seeks for God. All have turned aside; together they have become worthless; no one does good, not even one." "Their throat is an open grave; they use their tongues to deceive." "The venom of asps is under their lips." "Their mouth is full of curses and bitterness." "Their feet are swift to shed blood; in their paths are ruin and misery, and the way of peace they have not known." "There is no fear of God before their eyes."*

The bottom line with the secularist opposition? It's Arkophobia. And it means a hatred of anything Christian. And this Arkophobia is so widespread because *the heart is deceitful above all things, and desperately sick; who can understand it?* (Jeremiah 17:9).

Secularists are in rebellion against their Creator. The fact that He has the right to tell them, through His Word, what is right (e.g., marriage is one man for one woman, and there are only two genders of humans—male and female) and what is wrong (e.g., abortion is murder) angers them.

Secularists oppose the Ark because they are afraid of the Ark's goal: to proclaim the everlasting gospel. Revelation 14:6–7 declares: *Then I saw another angel flying directly overhead, with an eternal gospel to proclaim to those who dwell on earth, to every nation and tribe and language and people. And he said with a loud voice, "Fear God and give him glory, because the hour of his judgment has come, and worship him who made heaven and earth, the sea and the springs of water."*

Those opposing Christian organizations like Answers in Genesis and our two attractions may use arguments about money and so on, but the bottom line is they are opposed because it's a spiritual issue. They have a heart problem. They are opposed to the message. And they just can't tolerate an organization or attraction proclaiming a message that goes against their anti-God worldview. So we shouldn't be surprised at all when such people oppose anything Christian, particularly if it is going to have a major impact on hearts and lives.

And since they did not see fit to acknowledge God, God gave them up to a debased mind to do what ought not to be done. They were filled with all manner of unrighteousness, evil, covetousness, malice. They are full of envy, murder, strife, deceit, maliciousness. They are gossips, slanderers, haters of God, insolent, haughty, boastful, inventors of evil, disobedient to parents, foolish, faithless, heartless, ruthless. Though they know God's righteous decree that those who practice such things deserve to die, they not only do them but give approval to those who practice them (Romans 1:28–32).

One has to understand the spiritual dimension to those coming against Christianity.

JULY 24
Romans 3:4

Why Is the Age of the Earth/Universe Such an Emotional Issue?

In all the years I've been in the biblical creation apologetics ministry, I've discovered that the issue of the age of the earth and the universe is an extremely emotional topic for secularists. That's even true for some church leaders who believe in millions of years and vehemently attack our Bible-affirming ministry as well.

And there's a phenomenal intimidation factor from the world directed toward Christians regarding this topic. I've heard over and over again that people who reject the supposed millions/billions of years for the age of the earth and universe are accused of being anti-intellectual, anti-scientific, and anti-academic. This intimidation is so great that the majority of Christian academics compromise with the millions of years. Personally, I believe it comes down to an intellectual pride problem. If an academic rejects the millions of years, they won't be published in what are deemed the mainstream journals in theology or science.

Now for biblical creationists, the age of the earth is an issue that should lead Christians to a different kind of strong emotion—a real zeal for the authority and accuracy of the Word of God. Ultimately, the issue of the age of the earth/universe is an authority issue. Who is the ultimate authority? Fallible, finite man or God?

This all hit home to me as I watched a video clip of famed atheist Richard Dawkins who once appeared on the well-watched TV program *Q & A* in my homeland of Australia. Prof. Dawkins, perhaps surprisingly at first, came across as quite tolerant of Church people who believe in evolution. But when it came to the topic of the age of the earth, Dawkins changed his tone dramatically. On the program, he openly mocked those who believe in a young universe and earth (i.e., just over 6,000 years old). Now, he could somehow manage to sort of tolerate Church people who didn't accept evolution. But with the age of the earth, that's different. He scoffs and mocks. It was obviously a very emotional issue with him.

I've also observed that when the secular media have visited our Creation Museum or Ark Encounter and interviewed me or other staff, they usually concentrate on asking us questions about the age of the earth—including why we believe dinosaurs lived alongside people. The reporters often act as if it's ridiculous not to accept the supposed billions of years. And to them, that's the main issue.

Increasingly, I've noticed that when the media write reports about us, they often don't mention the scientific points we present in our rebuttal of evolution but instead state something like this (these words appeared in our local newspaper):

"The Creation Museum employs scientists of its own but has been criticized by the larger scientific community for positions it takes that conflict with mainstream scientific belief. For example, the museum contends the Earth is 6,000 years old, rather than about 4.5 billion. It also shows humans living at the same time as dinosaurs, which most scientists say never happened."

In fact, sometimes I wonder if all the secular media have this paragraph and then just paste it into any article that may refer to us. They certainly try to make this a big issue and ensure they are ridiculing us for believing in a young earth/universe no matter what other topics we deal with.

So why is the age of the earth such a big issue with secular scientists and the media? And why is it that after biblical creationists have written so many books and scientific peer-reviewed papers that contradict the

APOLOGETICS — JULY 24

supposed billions of years for the age of the earth/universe and expose the fallible dating methods devised by man, secularists still scoff?

Well, here's the bottom line: For secularists to even postulate the idea of evolution, they have to also postulate an incomprehensible amount of time (billions and billions of years) so that the universe and life might have enough time to supposedly evolve by an impossible process (e.g., matter giving rise to information and a language system as seen in the molecule of life DNA, which is impossible). Even with billions of years, though, evolution is impossible—mathematically and scientifically. But secularists aggressively promote billions of years to make evolution a plausible idea. After all, as humans, we can't really comprehend billions of years. So therefore, people are brainwashed to think that given enough time anything can happen.

The late famed evolutionary biologist Ernst Mayr said the following: "[The Darwinian] revolution began when it became obvious that the earth was very ancient rather than having been created only 6000 years ago. This finding was the snowball that started the whole avalanche."

For such scientists, it doesn't matter how good the creationist research is about the age issue. They have already rejected the possibility of a young earth and universe before considering it, as billions of years is integral to the religion of naturalistic evolution.

Frankly, they have to reject what biblical creationists state concerning the age of the earth because even allowing the possibility that the earth is only a few thousand years old is tantamount to admitting that biological evolution is totally wrong. And the alternative? Creation? No, they can't allow it at all! If creation is true and the God of the Bible is the Creator, then it means He sets the rules. He decides what is right and wrong. He owns us, and we need to obey Him. It means we are sinners in need of salvation. It also means marriage is one man for one woman, and there are only two genders of humans.

Why are biblical creationists so adamant that the earth is young? It's because we're zealous for the Bible, and God's Word clearly indicates (through the specific genealogical history) that the earth is thousands, not billions, of years old. The only reliable dating method for the age of the earth/universe would come from someone who knew everything, who had always been there, who knows when it started—and then revealed it to us!

Of course, there is such a ONE—the God of the Bible! The Bible is the only trustworthy dating source. It presents a detailed history from the beginning, about 6,000 years ago.

Also when a Christian believes in millions of years, they then accept that death and diseases like cancer (as seen in the fossil record which supposedly formed millions of years before man) existed before sin, and God calls that "very good." No, this undermines God's character and is an attack on biblical authority.

"Let God be true though every one were a liar" (Romans 3:4).

JULY 25
Psalm 119:105-113

The Battle Has Not Changed

Many things have changed since we started the biblical apologetics ministry that became Answers in Genesis in our home in Australia in 1977. The culture has changed. But God's Word has not changed and never will. Man's word about origins has continued to change in various ways over this time.

While we were still living in Australia, I read a report that the Assemblies of God denomination had adopted a "Doctrine of Creation" which stated the following: "This Bible record of creation thus rules out the evolutionary philosophy which states that all forms of life have come into being by gradual, progressive evolution carried on by resident forces. It also rules out any evolutionary origin for the human race, since no theory of evolution, including theistic evolution, can explain the origin of the male before the female, nor can it explain how a man could evolve into a woman.

"The account of creation is intended to be taken as factual and historical. Our understanding of God as Creator is rooted in a revelation that is historical in nature, just as our understanding of God as Redeemer is rooted in the revelation of God's dealings with Israel in history and in the historical events of the life, death, and resurrection of His Son."

But by 2010 (we had moved to the United States in 1987), this all changed. A new "Doctrine of Creation" was adopted by that same denomination's governing body, the "general presbytery."

Here is what they stated: "The advance of scientific research, particularly in the last few centuries, has raised many questions about the interpretation of the Genesis accounts of creation. In attempting to reconcile the Bible and the theories and conclusions of contemporary scientists, it should be remembered that the creation accounts do not give precise details as to how God went about His creative activity. Nor do these accounts provide us with complete chronologies that enable us to date with precision the time of the various stages of creation. Similarly, the findings of science are constantly expanding; the accepted theories of one generation are often revised in the next.

"As a result, equally devout Christian believers have formed very different opinions about the age of the earth, the age of humankind, and the ways in which God went about the creative processes. Given the limited information available in Scripture, it does not seem wise to be overly dogmatic about any particular creation theory. We urge all sincere and conscientious believers to adhere to what the Bible plainly teaches and to avoid divisiveness over debatable theories of creation."[72]

My heart was heavy as I read that statement: "The findings of science are constantly expanding; the accepted theories of one generation are often revised in the next." Well, the Bible hasn't changed, but man's ideas certainly have!

The message from this denomination was essentially this: Because of the beliefs and conclusions of contemporary scientists regarding origins, Christians must change their interpretation of the Bible in Genesis! This low view of Scripture and esteeming man's ideas is a major problem within many denominations in churches and Christian academic institutions. In fact, the tragedy of reinterpreting God's clear words to fit in man's beliefs has always existed with God's people. The same problem is recorded in Genesis when the serpent tempted Eve asking, "Did God really say?" It's the same problem the Israelites had as they adopted aspects of pagan religions into their worship system.

By the way, this situation is similar in most denominations, whether Assembly of God, Baptist, Presbyterian, Methodist, and so on! Now within any of these denominations, including the AG one quoted above, there are often churches led by pastors who stand on God's Word as we do at Answers in Genesis. But sadly, they are in the minority.

Creating doubt on God's Word has greatly undermined biblical authority in society as a whole, and even in many churches. We live in an era of great scientific advancement. But remember: Science means "knowledge." There is a big difference between knowledge gained by observation that builds our technology in the present ("operational science") and knowledge concerning the past ("historical science"), which cannot be observed directly. "Historical science" (man's beliefs) is being used as the authority over God's Word.

The AG denomination as quoted above was insisting that fallible man's historical science (beliefs about the past concerning origins) must be used to reinterpret God's clear and infallible Word. By the way, I thank God for the many pastors in Assembly of God churches who cringed at their denomination's position and support Answers in Genesis. I often find many of the average pastors are prepared to stand on God's Word in Genesis, but so many of the leaders in their denominations are not.

Our mission statement declares that we are to be "a catalyst to bring reformation by reclaiming the foundations of our faith which are found in the Bible, from the very first verse."

What can the righteous do as the foundations of Christianity are being destroyed? We need a new reformation in our churches. Christians need to be figuratively nailing Genesis 1–11 on the doors of churches and Christian colleges/seminaries, challenging God's people to return to the authority of the Bible.

Your word is a lamp to my feet and a light to my path. I have sworn an oath and confirmed it, to keep your righteous rules. I am severely afflicted; give me life, O Lord, according to your word! Accept my freewill offerings of praise, O Lord, and teach me your rules. I hold my life in my hand continually, but I do not forget your law. The wicked have laid a snare for me, but I do not stray from your precepts. Your testimonies are my heritage forever, for they are the joy of my heart. I incline my heart to perform your statutes forever, to the end. I hate the double-minded, but I love your law (Psalm 119:105–113).

> We will continue to see a decline in our nation, churches, and families – unless God's people repent of compromise and return to His Word.

JULY 26
Luke 15:10

Who Is Imposing Religion?

Various secular/atheist groups make the claim that if people mention the Bible, God, or creation in public (secular) schools, they are imposing religion (Christianity) on the students. Thus, they claim that eliminating the Bible, God, and creation from these schools eliminates religion and makes them neutral. However, I've discussed many times that no one has a neutral position as everyone has a worldview based on certain presuppositions. And from a biblical perspective, one is either for or against Christ. Everyone has a religion, a way of thinking about life and the universe. Now secularists aren't removing religion from public schools by eliminating the Bible; they're simply forcing their religion (of naturalism) onto students. Consider a past attack against Christianity (and also against parents' rights). Incredibly, this attack was conducted by a group that was headed at that time by an ordained minister! He and others were trying to stop students not only from hearing God's Word but preventing them from being influenced by Christians in any way. Their anti-Christian religion was showing!

In fact, in the group's newsletter, its leaders at that time pleaded for funds so they could continue to be aggressive in stopping any influence in public schools by various Christian groups including the Gideons who distribute free copies of the Bible. Just knowing that a Christian organization may be conducting a program in a public school was enough for this minister to use fear tactics against school principals to stop Christians from coming into the school. They will intimidate the school with threats of lawsuits. And usually, such threats (bullying) are enough to cause the school to comply with their anti-God worldview. In the same newsletter, the group told parents that their children shouldn't be allowed to be influenced by what they call "fundamentalist" or "evangelistic" groups or by those involved in "evangelism" (which they call "proselytizing"). Such terms were used about a dozen times in the letter in a derogatory manner. Ironically, this ordained minister stated that parents should be the ones deciding what religions their children should learn about, so that outside religious groups should not be given access to the public schools. In other words, this group is telling parents that they have the right to decide what their children are taught while at the same time, the group's actions are directly impacting what their children are allowed to be taught in school! How hypocritical.

This movement was led at the time by the "Reverend" Barry Lynn, an ordained minister with the United Church of Christ. He was the leader of this group called Americans United for Separation of Church and State. I heard Lynn at a conference once gleefully tell the audience how his group had successfully stopped Chuck Colson's Prison Fellowship outreach from ministering in certain prisons. Can you imagine being in "Reverend" Lynn's shoes standing before the Lord (as will happen one day) and bragging about how he stopped people from hearing the gospel? He shows no fruit of being a true born-again Christian. What the American people (and Barry Lynn) need to understand is that public school education is not neutral at all. While God, creation, and prayer have been thrown out of the public schools, that does not mean that religion has been tossed out. It means Christianity has been all but eliminated and replaced with the anti-God religion of naturalism/atheism. Barry Lynn didn't want any Christian influence in the public schools; he wanted the students to be indoctrinated by the secularist religion. And because various Christian groups had programs to present students with teachings about Christian morality or in some way give young people the opportunity to hear a Christian perspective on life (or study the Bible for themselves), Barry Lynn was telling parents that they needed to let him decide what their children are allowed to hear. It is people like Lynn who don't want parents to have rights in regard to their children. But Bible-believing Christians know that it is the parents who have the responsibility before God as to how they train their children. Now, of course, a minority of secularist parents will object when children are taught about Christianity. But what about the Christians whose children are being indoctrinated in secularism/naturalism/atheism in government-run schools?

In our AiG library, we have many of the major biology and earth science textbooks used in public schools across this nation. To give you an idea of how children in public schools are being indoctrinated in the atheistic religion of naturalism, let me share with you just a few examples from these texts. One biology textbook suggested that science be restricted to examining natural causes, since supernatural explanations for those things that are natural are outside what science can explain. In other words, "science" (which really means "knowledge") cannot allow the supernatural. Thus, by this definition, God and His Word are eliminated. The biology textbook then attempted to undermine those people who don't believe in millions of years of history. In making an obvious reference to the biblical view of creation (which they totally misrepresent, stating that species are "fixed" and that the earth is "relatively unchanging"), there is a blatant attempt to discredit the Christian view. The biology textbook further teaches students that they are nothing but animals and that evolution is fact. Then, in one of the earth science textbooks, the students were exposed to the idea that the earth's age of 6,000 years is a completely outdated idea (again, another hit at biblical creationists). The book then spends pages and pages presenting millions of years/evolution as fact, yet without any hint that such assertions could even be slightly wrong.

For the most part, what are our public schools doing? Well, they are trying to convert children to an atheistic, evolutionary, secularist worldview! Studies in the United States reveal that around 85–90% of students from Church homes attend public schools. Many of those reading this article probably have students who attend (or have attended) public schools. Praise the Lord, we've had numerous testimonies over the years from young people whose lives have been transformed by Answers in Genesis' apologetics resources, or the Creation Museum and Ark attractions. One such person sent this:

- "When I was in junior high school, our teacher taught us evolution as fact.
- "So when our teacher told us life originated by a single cell coming to life on its own, and that it had then evolved into all the life on this earth, time seemed to stop for me. I immediately realized that this meant science had disproved the Bible. Life and death had no meaning; everything was merely the result of natural physical processes. I lost my faith in Jesus Christ.
- "I was an atheist for ten years, but by the grace of God, I was given Answers in Genesis videos after that decade of darkness. As I watched Ken Ham give biblical answers to evolution, I realized how the atheist/public education system in America had brainwashed me. I am now a passionate Christian in love with my Lord and Savior Jesus Christ." —J.B.

I give all praise and glory to the Lord for this and the other many testimonies we regularly receive at Answers in Genesis!

"Just so, I tell you, there is joy before the angels of God over one sinner who repents" (Luke 15:10).

JULY 27
Colossians 1:15

Attacks on the Son

When Christians compromise God's Word (like adding millions of years and other evolutionary beliefs into the Bible), isn't it really an attack on *the* Son? You see, I am making the claim when you compromise the Word of God, it is also an attack on the Son of God, whose Word it is.

A Christian philosopher stated the following: "Dating methods, in my view, provide strong evidence for rejecting this face value chronological reading of Genesis [chapters] 4–11."

Another contemporary Christian philosopher/theologian stated the following in answer to a question: "Why not receive God's transforming grace yourself and then be better than the Young Earthers? You know that I don't hold their views about the age of the universe. Neither do most evangelical Christians, despite the high profile of their movement in churches."

And why did philosopher #2 say what he did about Christians who take Genesis literally? On a video you can watch on YouTube, this theologian (Dr. William Lane Craig) explains that "I'm going with the flow of what contemporary cosmology and astrophysics supports."

In other words, it's ideas from outside the Bible, not the plain reading of Scripture, which determine his view on the age of the earth. Such compromise is sadly the norm in the majority of our Christian colleges and seminaries.

Many times over the years, I have stated that such compromise is really an attack on the authority of the Word, in spite of some scholars' sincere intentions to the contrary. It is what I call "The Genesis 3" attack (i.e., creating doubt in regard to God's Word and asking "Did God actually say?"), and it ultimately undermines the authority of the Scripture. Although such beliefs as those above don't affect the scholars' salvation as such, they do have a great influence on the students and other Christians these professors influence. It impacts others in regard to how they view the Word of God, and that can (and does) have catastrophic consequences on people.

Many young people in our churches are already doubting and disbelieving God's Word. The result? At least two-thirds of children raised in theologically conservative churches have been walking away from the Church (or even the Christian faith altogether). Church attendance for Generation Z by 2021 was down to less than 9%.

Do you realize how serious such compromise really is?

Consider the following truths:

- We can only know the Father through the Son.
- We know the Son (Jesus Christ) through the Word.
- Jesus is the Word.

THEOLOGY   JULY 27

Then consider these verses:

- *Jesus said to him, "Have I been with you so long, and you still do not know me, Philip? Whoever has seen me has seen the Father. How can you say, 'Show us the Father'?"* (John 14:9).
- *He is the image of the invisible God, the firstborn of all creation* (Colossians 1:15).

Here are two more verses that help show the connection between the Word and the Son of God.

- *Long ago, at many times and in many ways, God spoke to our fathers by the prophets, but in these last days he has spoken to us by his Son, whom he appointed the heir of all things, through whom also he created the world* (Hebrews 1:1–2).
- *In the beginning was the Word, and the Word was with God, and the Word was God. He was in the beginning with God. All things were made through him, and without him was not any thing made that was made* (John 1:1–3).

Since Jesus is God, then God's Word (the Old and New Testaments of the Bible) is Jesus Christ's Word. Christ said, *Heaven and earth will pass away, but my words will not pass away* (Matthew 24:35).

He also declared, *If you abide in my word, you are truly my disciples* (John 8:31; see also John 5:24, 8:37, and Revelation 3:8). And Jesus clearly demonstrated that He accepted Genesis 1–11 as true literal history:

- *Do not think that I will accuse you to the Father. There is one who accuses you: Moses, on whom you have set your hope. For if you believed Moses, you would believe me; for he wrote of me. But if you do not believe his writings, how will you believe my words?* (John 5:45–47).
- *He answered, "Have you not read that he who created them from the beginning made them male and female, and said, 'Therefore a man shall leave his father and his mother and hold fast to his wife, and the two shall become one flesh'? So they are no longer two but one flesh. What therefore God has joined together, let not man separate"* (Matthew 19:4–6).

What's the bottom line?

When Christian leaders deliberately reinterpret God's Word on the basis of man's fallible ideas (taken from outside the Bible), not only are they undermining the Word of God, they are actually (though unwittingly) conducting an attack on the Son of God! This is very serious. Yes, when you compromise the Word of God, it is also an attack on the Son of God, whose Word it is.

May God help each of us to cling to—and tremble before—His Word (Joshua 1:6–9; Isaiah 66:1–2). And may He help us not to follow the teachings that compromise His Word and thereby (even unknowingly) attack His Son.

> "All these things my hand has made, and so all these things came to be, declares the Lord. But this is the one to whom I will look: he who is humble and contrite in spirit and trembles at my word" (Isaiah 66:2).

JULY 28
Proverbs 30:6

The Paganization of the West

Back in the sixteenth century, William Tyndale was persecuted, imprisoned, strangled, and his body burned at the stake. Why? Because he worked to translate the Scriptures into English and get copies of the Bible to the average person. Influenced by Luther and others, Tyndale was an integral part of the Reformation that spread God's written Word throughout the world—particularly to the Western world.

At that time, many church leaders believed the Bible should not be in the hands of the common person and that only appointed and scholarly church leaders should tell the public what they should believe. But the spread of God's written Word in the 1500s changed all that as it permeated many nations. It resulted in what we called the "Christian West." However, today we see the Christian influence in our Western world waning. Europe (especially the United Kingdom) is nearly dead spiritually. In America, the once-Christianized worldview is collapsing before our very eyes.

So why has this change occurred? First, let me point out that we need to be like the men of Issachar, who had "understanding of *the times*" (1 Chronicles 12:32). The Reformation was a movement to call people to the authority of the Word of God. Almost 500 years later, we believe the teaching of millions of years and evolution (particularly since the beginning of the nineteenth century) has been the major tool in this era to undo the work of the Reformation. To understand *the times* in which we live, we need to know how this sad transformation has come about. The majority of church leaders have adopted the secular religion of the age (i.e., millions of years/evolution) and have compromised God's Word beginning in Genesis—thus undermining its authority to coming generations.

Statistics are clear that most people in churches do not study their Bibles as they should. Frankly, we have a very biblically illiterate Church today. We also observe Church academics of our age beginning to impose a similar philosophy to that seen in Tyndale's time—that it is these learned leaders (most of whom have compromised God's Word) who determine what the public should believe. Increasingly, churchgoers are not like the Bereans who were "examining the Scriptures daily to see if these things were so" (Acts 17:11). I want to give you just two specific examples of this dramatic change—though there are so many such examples we could look at. The first comes from a professor who held the Clarence L. Goodwin Chair in New Testament Language and Literature at Butler University in Indianapolis. He wrote a blog item concerning AiG's stand on a literal Genesis: First, he quoted another writer: "Some may excuse Mr. Ham on the ground that he has no theological or biblical training (he has a bachelor's degree in applied science). I am not so inclined for one reason: by assuming the pulpit of churches and declaring he intends to interpret the Bible, he de facto sets himself up as a Bible teacher, and should be held accountable to know not only the relevant facts, but the proper way to exegete and teach a passage of scripture.

"If he does not want to give up seven years of his life and tens of thousands of dollars to get training in the Bible, theology, and the ancient languages (the standard degree program for clergy) then that is perfectly understandable. What is not so understandable is his desire to set himself up as a Bible teacher without getting Bible training." Then, he followed with his own comments about the above statements: "Amen! . . . I think that the best course of action is for those who are well-informed about the Bible to debunk, refute and if necessary 'repudiate' the statements of those who have no expertise in any field of scholarship related to the Bible, and yet believe that without any real knowledge of the original languages, historical context, and other relevant factors, their pontifications will do anything but harm the souls of believers and the Christian faith itself."

Well, it is true that I personally don't have formal theological training—but there are those at Answers in Genesis who do. And we do have quite a number of other highly qualified theologians whose counsel we seek to ensure we are accurate in handling God's Word. By the way, I'm glad I have not been theologically trained in the way this professor has (and like many who are now being trained in Bible colleges and seminaries). Otherwise, I might have ended up believing what he wrote below: "So why am I a Christian? ... given that I do not espouse Biblical literalism and inerrancy, some might ask whether I am still a Christian ... I am a Christian in much the same way that I am an American ... the tradition that gave birth to my faith and nurtured it is one that has great riches (as well as much else beside) ... Why am I a Christian? Because I prefer to keep the tradition I have, rather than discarding it with the bathwater and then trying to make something new from scratch."

The second sad example is from someone who was a professor at what was known as a conservative seminary in the south in the United States. What he proposed in his book, *The End of Christianity*, is an undermining of biblical authority, and it's an unfortunate example of the sort of compromise often taught to our future pastors. Here are a few excerpts from his book: "For the theodicy I am proposing to be compatible with evolution, God must not merely introduce existing human-like beings from outside the Garden. In addition, when they enter the Garden, God must transform their consciousness so that they become rational moral agents made in God's image" (page 159). He also states: "The young-earth solution to reconciling the order of creation with natural history makes good exegetical and theological sense. Indeed, the overwhelming consensus of theologians up through the Reformation held to this view. I myself would adopt it in a heartbeat except that nature seems to present such a strong evidence against it" (page 55).

By "nature," he is, in essence, accepting fallible scientists' interpretations of evidence (such as evolutionary interpretation of fossils, geologic layers, and so on). His statement concerning "good exegetical and theological sense" is the point exactly! In other words, we know what the clear teaching of Scripture is—and what the great Reformers knew. But this professor rejected it. We would say this person (who may be a fine Christian man) is taking the belief in billions of years (obtained by man's fallible interpretations of the present in an attempt to connect to the past) as infallible and, in reality, making God's Word fallible.

This is an example of what I call the "Genesis 3 attack" ("Did God Really Say?") in our era—undoing what the Reformation accomplished. We need a new Reformation to call our Church (and culture) back to the authority of the Word of God. The battle before us is one about authority: Is God's Word the authority or is man's word? *Do not add to his words, lest he rebuke you and you be found a liar* (Proverbs 30:6).

> **We need to hold compromising church leaders accountable and stand unashamedly and uncompromisingly on the authority of the Word of God.**

JULY 29
1 Kings 19:18

7,000 Who Have Not Bowed the Knee

Do you often feel rather alone for standing on the authority of God's Word without compromise?

You probably recall the passage in 1 Kings 19:14, where Elijah was described as very discouraged. He was thinking that he was very alone in his stand for the Lord: *He said, "I have been very jealous for the Lord, the God of hosts. For the people of Israel have forsaken your covenant, thrown down your altars, and killed your prophets with the sword, and I, even I only, am left, and they seek my life, to take it away."*

But then the Lord encouraged him in 1 Kings 19:18: *Yet I will leave seven thousand in Israel, all the knees that have not bowed to Baal, and every mouth that has not kissed him.*

I have quoted this passage a number of times over the years when I've been traveling and speaking in various cities. Why? You see, people have often come to me to say they feel so alone in their stand on the authority of God's Word beginning in Genesis as their church is so lukewarm and the culture very anti-Christian. They tell me that the leadership in their church won't support them, and others in their congregation just don't understand why Answers in Genesis supporters are so strong about their biblical stand.

They often go on to tell me they feel so alone. These Christians then usually ask: "Do you think there are many people in America any more who believe as we do?"

It's then that I remind them about Elijah, and that there are many more than 7,000 people in our Western nations who are prepared to stand uncompromisingly and unashamedly on God's Word—beginning with the very first book of the Bible. And it is so encouraging for them to be there at an AiG conference and realize there are many like-minded people in their area.

A typical response I receive (and I have heard this many times now) from guests I meet at our two attractions (the Creation Museum and Ark Encounter) on crowded days, goes something like this:

"Oh, we don't mind the crowds at all—we're just so thrilled to know there are so many others who understand the importance of this ministry. It's so encouraging for us to see this many people visiting the Ark and Creation Museum."

So I've come to realize that crowded days at the Creation Museum and Ark are really an encouragement to others, particularly amidst the serious moral and economic problems our nations are facing.

Be encouraged! There are millions of Christians in our nations who stand boldly on the truth of God's Word and the saving gospel. God always has a remnant. Now in the West, the remnant is still a large one, though certainly a minority compared to the population. And there are other large remnants in countries like China. And there is something else I am finding—something that is ever so encouraging.

I've been active in the apologetics ministry since 1975. I've heard so many testimonies from people who have been set "on fire for the Lord," or who have received the gift of salvation as a result of the messages given or reading resources, etc.

I loved it when a 16-year-old girl told me she read the book *Already Gone* and realized she wasn't a Christian. So she asked her parents to pray with her, and she committed her life to the Lord. Also, a young man told me

CHURCH — JULY 29

that he was heavily into pornography, but after watching AiG videos, he got back on track and became an on-fire Christian. I have heard so many testimonies like this over the years.

After having been in the creation apologetics ministry for many years and having spoken thousands of times, I have been hearing one particular kind of testimony that really tugs at my heartstrings.

A young mom or dad will often come up and tell me that they had attended an Answers in Genesis conference as a child—and/or that their parents purchased Answers in Genesis books for them as children. They grew up on our apologetics resources, and they meant so much to them and their stand on God's Word. They then introduce me to their children (who were brought to the conference) and tell me how they are now bringing their children up on AiG resources!

And what a thrill it is to speak to these children! I'm blown away by their enthusiasm for the Lord. Many of them tell me they want to be creation scientists, evangelists, and so on—they have such a love for God and His Word.

Yes, the effects of proclaiming God's Word spread—not just across the nation and around the world, but from generation to generation. I believe the generation of "creationist kids" is going to be a formidable force in our culture. And who knows? Maybe they will be the ones to launch a new Reformation to bring the Church and culture back to the authority of God's Word?

I've often thought how discouraging it must have been for Noah when he saw only eight people (his own family!) going on the ark—he must have felt so alone. And how discouraged Abraham must have been when he found there were not even 10 righteous people in Sodom.

But praise the Lord, we live in an era where millions are standing up for biblical authority beginning in Genesis—and the "troops" are rallying!

Yet I will leave seven thousand in Israel, all the knees that have not bowed to Baal, and every mouth that has not kissed him (1 Kings 19:18).

But what is God's reply to him? "I have kept for myself seven thousand men who have not bowed the knee to Baal." So too at the present time there is a remnant, chosen by grace (Romans 11:4–5).

> **The culture around us may seem like we are in days like Noah, but from a perspective of the number (though a minority) of Bible-believing Christians we are far from the days of Noah.**

JULY 30
2 Timothy 1:5

My Parents' Legacy

Back in 2015, while visiting my homeland of Australia, I asked my elderly mother (she had just turned 87) if I could record her thoughts on video. I wanted to "interview" my mum about her life. It turned out to be a fascinating time.

In particular, I wanted to learn about the influences on her life that allowed her and my father to pass on a wonderful spiritual legacy to me (and my siblings). I also wanted to understand a little more about how, as parents, they were such an influence on countless others.

I only regret not having recorded my father. I think of the time when my father was dying, in a hospital at age 66 in 1995, that my late younger brother Robert asked him why he was so bold in his stand on God's Word and hated compromise with the Bible. How I wish we had recorded his reflections.

My father told my brother that his own father had died when my father was 16. And because he didn't have an earthly father to turn to, he turned to the words of his heavenly father and read and studied those Scriptures over and over again. That's why our family has had such a strong emphasis on biblical authority.

Those conversations he had with my brother helped me understand why he took the strong stand on God's Word that he did. It had a great influence on my own life and ministry.

My interview with my mother went for about two hours. I thought the "interview" would encourage others to consider doing a recording of any of their parents/grandparents. I often wonder about the history of my grandparents in regard to the Christian legacy they left to our family.

My mother shared some very challenging things with me. For instance, we had a frank talk about death. She passed away not long before her 92nd birthday. Even one of our video editors at AiG said, as he was going through this interview, that "she really challenged me about the death issue—I had never thought about it like that before."

My parents never had much in the way of material possessions, and yet the Lord used them mightily to influence others in regard to salvation in Christ and to stand uncompromisingly on the Word of God. It's a reminder that it's a spiritual legacy that is the most important one to leave behind—not a material one.

I want to give you some insights into how the Lord was working in people's lives long before I was born in preparation for what the Lord would do in enabling the ministry of AiG, the Creation Museum, and the future Ark Encounter to come into existence.

When I was a little boy (and as far back as I can remember), my mother taught me a prayer based on the hymn "Jesus, Tender Shepherd, Hear Me," written by Mary L. Duncan in 1839. Duncan's hymns, primarily composed for her children, were written during a six-month period just before the end of her life.

To this day, I can still recite the words (shown on the next page). As we videotaped my mother, I asked her about the hymn of prayer, and she recited it for me. That was one of the most touching moments of our time together, as I heard my mother recite the words she taught me so many years ago:

FAMILY — JULY 30

Jesus, tender Shepherd, hear me;
Bless Thy little lamb tonight;
Through the darkness be Thou near me;
Watch my sleep till morning light.
All this day Thy hand has led me,
And I thank Thee for Thy care;
Thou hast clothed me, warmed and fed me,
Listen to my evening prayer.
Let my sins be all forgiven
Bless the friends I love so well;
Take me, when I die, to Heaven,
Happy there with Thee to dwell.

Now, when you visit our Creation Museum, there is a small exhibit located in what we call Legacy Lobby, just outside our Legacy Hall auditorium. It consists of a photograph of my mother and father, my father's heavily marked-up Bible, and a little model of Noah's ark that my father built for me many years ago, not knowing that one day we would build the life-size Ark for the Ark Encounter attraction.

This small exhibit helps illustrate the stand that Answers in Genesis (and its various outreaches including the Creation Museum and Ark Encounter) unashamedly takes on God's Word. Our outreaches would not have been possible without the spiritual legacy that my parents passed on to the next generation.

Because of my mother's age and her health problems, she was never able to travel to see the Creation Museum. However, she watched from afar, as I video called her regularly and kept her up to date with the news on the ministry in general, the Creation Museum, and the Ark Encounter.

She also kept current by going on the AiG website and to our Facebook sites. Even in an advanced age, she learned how to use a MacBook computer to do this! She would read every AiG book, newsletter, *Answers* magazine, and watched all the videos I sent to her.

My mother also followed my speaking calendar. She knew every flight I was on, and when I was traveling, she prayed for every trip. Mum often told me, "I knew you were flying last night, so I was awake praying for you." She asked me about every conference I spoke at—she wanted to know what happened and how God blessed. I sure miss her and my dad. But I know I will meet up with both my Mum and Dad one day in heaven.

AiG, the Creation Museum, and the Ark Encounter have already touched tens of millions of lives around the world as God has blessed. Millions have been reached as a result of this spiritual legacy from my parents.

In the video, my mother talked about the Christian faith of her mother (as well as her father). I learned for the first time that my mother was mocked at school by other students because they knew that her mother was unashamedly Christian!

As I listened to my mother, I gained a deeper understanding of what the Apostle Paul said to Timothy:

> "I am reminded of your sincere faith, a faith that dwelt first in your grandmother Lois and your mother Eunice and now, I am sure, dwells in you as well" (2 Timothy 1:5).

JULY 31
Isaiah 40:8

Scopes Trial

In 2017, a statue of Clarence Darrow was installed opposite the 2005-erected statue of William Jennings Bryan at the Dayton, Tennessee, courthouse, where the famous "Scopes Monkey Trial" took place nearly 100 years ago. In 1925, Darrow was the agnostic/atheist lawyer who defended Scopes, who allegedly broke the law by teaching that man evolved from lower animals. Scopes never taught evolution but volunteered to claim he did so that Darrow's anti-Christian beliefs could be heard in the courtroom and be covered nationally by newspapers. It was really a setup by the ACLU to come against Christianity and its impact on the culture.

Bryan, a great Christian orator, was greatly maligned because of his public stand on believing God's Word. However, Bryan, like all of us who have feet of clay, didn't understand all the issues involved regarding the Book of Genesis, just as many in the Church don't today.

Now, Darrow lost the case because, in the end of the trial, he pled guilty on behalf of Scopes. This was a deliberate ploy to ensure that Bryan didn't get to question Darrow on the stand, as Darrow had done to Bryan (a promise Darrow reneged on)! Bryan certainly would have exposed Darrow's utter contempt for Christianity and his blind faith in human reason, had he been given the opportunity. Darrow was victorious, in the sense that, while his client was found guilty, Darrow got Bryan (the prosecutor and a "spokesman" for the Bible and the creation of man) to say he believed that the Genesis account of creation could have taken millions of years. Bryan also had difficulty answering the question of where Cain got his wife. Now there were actually reports of threats of possible protests and violence at the courthouse over the new statue of Darrow, but nothing happened, except for a protest banner posted on the courthouse that said, "Read your Bible."

This whole statue unveiling had me asking a few questions: Why all the excitement over this statue, and why all the upset over it? Well, I can tell you that some saw this new statue as a "win" for evolution because they consider it another publicly accepted (and quite prominent [Darrow's statue is 10 feet tall!]) symbol of the acceptance of evolution in the culture. Some people (falsely) considered it symbolic of the downfall of biblical Christianity.

Zenos Frudakis, the Darrow sculptor, had this to say: "This is a time when we need a voice of reason more than ever. We need the voice embodied in bronze, because bronze lasts forever unlike most things." Well, we know that bronze doesn't last forever (2 Peter 3:10), but contrast this statement with what does last forever, according to the Bible:

The grass withers, the flower fades, but the word of our God will stand forever (Isaiah 40:8).

Such comments as those by Frudakis certainly show that this new statue is not just about portraying a historical event of 1925: It's about secularists wanting to celebrate reason (i.e., worship of man) and attack anything to do with Christianity. It's about proclaiming the religion of man, where man is his own god (Genesis 3:5).

Now, some believers were understandably upset by what is clearly an "in your face" declaration of "you're irrelevant"—or worse. In fact, an opinion piece in the *USA Today* newspaper at the time was titled, "Creationism support is at a new low. The reason should give us hope," discussing the addition of the Darrow statue outside the Dayton courthouse. The columnist was clearly happy to report a recent Gallup poll showing that there

APOLOGETICS — JULY 31

had been a drop to 38% of Americans who believe in a Creator who made humans in the past 10,000 years. The article goes on to say: "It's endlessly frustrating to secular and religious liberals, but the creationist view has held strong sway in this country in the decades since the famous Darrow-Bryan courtroom duel. Over recent decades, percentages in the upper-40s have taken the creationist position; the figure stood at 46% in Gallup's 2012 survey."[73]

And at Answers in Genesis, we continue to pump out information to proclaim the truth of God's Word beginning in Genesis. Millions of books, articles, and other pieces of information have been distributed, impacting tens of millions of people a year.

Certainly, violent protests aren't the answer to offensive statue unveilings. The answer isn't to merely protest such removals [or in this case, additions]—or to simply protest other anti-Christian actions (e.g., abortion, euthanasia, gay "marriage")—but to teach people why they can believe the Bible is true in every area it touches on. We need to provide Bible-based answers to the questions the world asks about the Christian faith. (Who was Cain's wife? Isn't the earth millions of years old? Weren't the days in Genesis 1 long periods of time?) As we do this, people will begin to see that they can trust the Bible when it speaks of "earthly" things, and thus, when it speaks of "heavenly" things (salvation, absolute moral standards, etc.), as Jesus teaches in John 3:12.

If I have told you earthly things and you do not believe, how can you believe if I tell you heavenly things? (John 3:12).

So who did win the Scopes trial? Well, the take-home lesson is that it's not about "wins." And if it were, we have nothing to worry about (Psalm 2; Romans 8:31.) After all, Bryan "won" the case: Scopes pleaded guilty (to something he did not do) and had to pay a fine (though that was later overturned on a technicality). It's not about plaques, statues, or court cases. It's about truth. It's about authority. It's about the Creator of the universe and His love for mankind, and it's about sharing that. That's a message of hope that the world doesn't have, as evidenced by this loveless and bankrupt supposed victory.

Ultimately, this statue unveiling is not about secularists having their say and promoting their heroes. It's more than that. Secularists actually want to impose their anti-God religious views on the culture. This strategy can be seen clearly in many ways regarding their actions toward AiG. This includes their opposition to our Ark Encounter and Creation Museum. Atheists and others tried to prevent the Creation Museum from being built and protested the opening of this privately funded facility, built on private land, because it's a Christian attraction. They have held a number of protests at the Ark also. To justify their intolerance about the Ark, they made up lies about taxpayer funds supposedly being used to build the ship! The intolerance of secularists and their fake news seem to have no bounds.

For we do not wrestle against flesh and blood, but against the rulers, against the authorities, against the cosmic powers over this present darkness, against the spiritual forces of evil in the heavenly places (Ephesians 6:12).

This is a reminder: it's all a spiritual battle.

AUGUST 1
Joshua 24:15

Two Worldviews

In an ultimate sense:

- How many foundations are there to build worldviews?
- How many worldviews are there?
- How many religions are there?
- The answer to all three questions is "two."

The Bible makes it clear there are only two worldview positions a person can hold: We're either for Christ or against Him. *Whoever is not with me is against me, and whoever does not gather with me scatters* (Matthew 12:30). There's no neutral position.

Also, God's Word makes it clear there are only two ways to build a worldview: on the rock or on the sand. There are only two foundations. *Everyone then who hears these words of mine and does them will be like a wise man who built his house on the rock. . . . And everyone who hears these words of mine and does not do them will be like a foolish man who built his house on the sand* (Matthew 7:24–26).

We're also told there are only two ways to walk in this world: in light or in darkness. *Again Jesus spoke to them, saying, "I am the light of the world. Whoever follows me will not walk in darkness, but will have the light of life"* (John 8:12).

These teachings reflect the fact that, in an ultimate sense, there are only two religious views in the world—beliefs built on man's fallible word (darkness/sand) and the one that's built on the infallible Word of God beginning in Genesis (light/rock). Christians who compromise God's Word with man's word really make their foundation man's word!

These two views—God's Word and man's word—have been in conflict for about 6,000 years, and the battle that began in the Garden of Eden continues to rage before us today. After God made Adam, He gave him an instruction to obey and then presented the consequences if he didn't. *The Lord God took the man and put him in the garden of Eden to work it and keep it. And the Lord God commanded the man, saying, "You may surely eat of every tree of the garden, but of the tree of the knowledge of good and evil you shall not eat, for in the day that you eat of it you shall surely die"* (Genesis 2:15–17).

In other words, Adam, who was to be the head of the entire human race (as from him all human beings would descend), was told to obey God's Word. It was a test of obedience.

The devil, however, came to Eve. Genesis 3 records: *Now the serpent was more crafty than any other beast of the field that the Lord God had made. He said to the woman, "Did God actually say, 'You shall not eat of any tree in the garden'?" And the woman said to the serpent, "We may eat of the fruit of the trees in the garden, but God said, 'You shall not eat of the fruit of the tree that is in the midst of the garden, neither shall you touch it, lest you die.'" But the serpent said to the woman, "You will not surely die"* (Genesis 3:1–4).

In other words, the devil claimed that you don't need to obey God's Word. You can be your own god and decide truth for yourself. Adam and Eve did just that, and they disobeyed God. *So when the woman saw that*

APOLOGETICS — AUGUST 1

the tree was good for food, and that it was a delight to the eyes, and that the tree was to be desired to make one wise, she took of its fruit and ate, and she also gave some to her husband who was with her, and he ate (Genesis 3:6).

And so began the battle of the only two religions. A battle between God's Word and fallible, sinful man's word—a religion of man being his own god and trusting his own word. The same battle is raging today. Sadly, in our Western world, God's Word has been denigrated and, by and large, has been thrown out of public schools. Now we have generations who largely believe they are their own god, and their worldview is predominantly one of moral relativism.

Once you cease building your thinking on the absolute authority of God's Word, then ultimately anything goes (except the absolutes of Christianity), if you can get away with it.

Now, religions based on man's word take on many different forms: Hinduism, Buddhism, New Age, Baha'i faith, Zoroastrianism, Satanism, Jehovah's Witness, Deism, Taoism, Shinto, Unitarianism, Atheism, Agnosticism, Materialism, Christian syncretism with evolution, and other belief systems.

It's so important for believers to know how to engage people who hold to a false, man-based religion. And that's one of the reasons Answers in Genesis produces all sorts of powerful resources to help you engage those who hold a false religion.

Battles about worldviews and religions are all ultimately battles over two foundations: God's Word or man's word. Sadly, because many churches have not taught this, so many Christians don't know the best way to powerfully dispute with those who reject the truth of God's Word. And because so many church leaders have compromised God's Word with man's word, particularly in Genesis, they have undermined the very foundation (God's Word) they purport to believe in.

Choose this day whom you will serve, whether the gods your fathers served in the region beyond the River, or the gods of the Amorites in whose land you dwell. But as for me and my house, we will serve the Lord (Joshua 24:15).

> **Once you understand that a person's thinking has a foundation, then you will be able to help those who have the wrong foundation of man's word to understand they need the foundation of God's Word.**

AUGUST 2
Romans 10:9

The Message

In August each year, our grounds crew (along with others) begins placing hundreds of thousands of lights on various trees and buildings at our attractions. It takes months to prepare the grounds with the stunning Christmas lights and events. And then in January, they spend weeks taking many of the lights down again as Christmas is over.

During the Christmas season, there is a particular emphasis on an event that occurred over 2,000 years ago in the town of Bethlehem. Christmas commemorates the birth of Jesus, prophesied in the Old Testament. But we shouldn't just celebrate this event once a year. In reality, we need to remember and celebrate this event all year long. Yes, we can have a special celebration at the end of each year, but let's never forget this event all year long.

To fully understand the significance of Christmas, we need to understand the history of the Old Testament that led up to this greatest of events. Following the creation of the world, we read of the creation of the first man, called "Adam," from whom all of mankind is descended. When God created Adam, He didn't make him to be a puppet; Adam had the ability to choose and make decisions. God gave Adam an instruction to obey in Genesis 2.

And the Lord God commanded the man, saying, "You may surely eat of every tree of the garden, but of the tree of the knowledge of good and evil you shall not eat, for in the day that you eat of it you shall surely die" (Genesis 2:16–17).

Adam, however, chose to disobey God by eating the fruit of the one tree God had told him not to eat from. Because Adam was the first member of the human race, what Adam did affected all of humanity. The punishment for Adam's sin was death (bodily death and spiritual death with our immortal souls separated from God)—not only for Adam but for all his descendants. And note that Adam gets the blame for sin because Adam was given the instruction by God not to eat the tree. Eve took the fruit first as she was deceived, but it was Adam who received the blame because he was given the role of headship—the head of the human race and the spiritual head of his marriage to Eve:

For as by the one man's disobedience the many were made sinners, so by the one man's obedience the many will be made righteous (Romans 5:19).

In Genesis 3:15, God made a statement that provided hope to Adam and Eve and their descendants (us) and actually sums up the message of the entire Bible: There is a way to be saved from the effects of sin. This declaration summarizes the whole meaning of Christmas: *I will put enmity between you and the woman, and between your offspring and her offspring; he shall bruise your head, and you shall bruise his heel.*

The words "her offspring" are actually a prophecy concerning the One who, conceived by God Himself, would be born of a woman (actually a virgin): the baby who was born in Bethlehem—the last Adam. The first Adam was the father of humanity and endowed all his descendants with sin and death (Romans 5:12). The last Adam, Jesus Christ, the baby of Bethlehem, communicates life and light to all people, and gives eternal life to those who receive Him and believe on His name—to become the sons of God (John 1:1–14). The

THEOLOGY

phrase "he shall bruise your head" points to the victory Christ will have over Satan on the Cross. The phrase "you shall bruise his heel" concerns the fact Satan will wound our Savior by having Him nailed on the Cross.

Genesis 3:15 is the message of Jesus' birth in Bethlehem. It starts with the creation of a perfect world and then, because of our sin in Adam, leads to our need of a Savior—which is why Jesus stepped into history 2,000 years ago. Our Creator became our Savior.

Today, we talk about "keeping Christ in Christmas," but do we communicate clearly enough why this is so important? If we discount the account of creation, we remove the significance of Christmas. And, sadly, generations of young people are being educated in schools and by the media with evolutionary ideas about our origins. The erosion of Christianity in society is directly linked to the attack on the history of Genesis and the increasing indoctrination in a false history—that man is a result of millions of years of evolutionary processes. And sadly, many church leaders have rejected Genesis as literal history, thus totally undermining the true message of the babe in a manger! If we discount the account of creation, we remove the significance of Christmas.

The message of the two Adams is what life is all about, but if we want people to understand this message, we need to clearly show them that the history in Genesis is true, for otherwise, they will not understand or listen to what is said about the babe of Bethlehem. Yes, the history in Genesis is true which is why the message of the gospel based on that history is true.

Many of the younger generations today haven't been taught the foundational knowledge given in Genesis to truly understand the message of why we need a Savior, and why our Savior stepped into history to become a member of the human race and die on a Cross and be raised from the dead.

The point is, the message we celebrate at Christmas does not start with the New Testament account of the babe in a manger. The message starts in Genesis.

And the message doesn't end with Jesus' death on the Cross. The message goes on to tell us Jesus rose from the dead and offers a free gift of salvation. And we are warned in Scripture that if we don't receive this free gift of salvation, we will live for eternity, separated from God. But for those who repent of their sin and put their trust in Jesus and what He did on the Cross for them, they will spend eternity with their Creator.

If we confess our sins, he is faithful and just to forgive us our sins and to cleanse us from all unrighteousness (1 John 1:9).

Because, if you confess with your mouth that Jesus is Lord and believe in your heart that God raised him from the dead, you will be saved (Romans 10:9).

And these [the unsaved] will go away into eternal punishment, but the righteous into eternal life (Matthew 25:46).

Where are you going to spend eternity?

AUGUST 3
Jeremiah 23:16

False Prophets

In reading the Book of Jeremiah recently, it hit me that in many ways the outreach of Answers in Genesis and the ministry of Jeremiah are similar. AiG could also easily despair as we look around our decaying Western cultures. But no matter what, we must still *contend for the faith that was once for all delivered to the saints* (Jude 3)! AiG fights for the truth of God's Word on many battlefronts. But two really stand out for me. Many people see us fighting on one obvious battlefront, yet there is another one that others don't see.

As background, I want to remind you that AiG built the two leading Christian-themed attractions in the world. In addition, the outreaches of Answers in Genesis include our worldwide teaching ministry (reaching hundreds of thousands of people in churches and other venues each year), popular websites (millions of unique visitors a year), VBS program (now one of the leading programs in the world), Sunday school/Bible curriculum (thousands of churches using it), homeschool and Christian school curricula, books, DVDs, radio broadcasts, and other programs to reach both Christians and non-Christians.

Boldly, yet with love, these outreaches to the general public and local churches proclaim the truth of God's Word and the gospel. We bring the biblical messages God has laid on our heart to as many people as we can around the world. But because of the intense secular propaganda machines that operate in the media, education systems, and other places, we need to overcome a challenge first described by Hosea in the Old Testament: *My people are destroyed for lack of knowledge* (Hosea 4:6).

There is a deceptive and very dangerous battle on another front: in Bible colleges and seminaries. You may remember June 26, 2015, as the date of the U.S. Supreme Court decision to legalize same-sex "marriage." But something else happened on that date that went unnoticed in much of the Church. One of the leading evangelical seminaries in America, Trinity Evangelical Divinity School in Illinois, announced a new project entitled "Evangelical Theology and the Doctrine of Creation Project." This initiative was actually funded by a $3.4 million grant from the John Templeton Foundation (a group not known to support those ministries who stand for the truth of God's Word beginning in Genesis). It's largely a secular, pseudo-religious foundation that generously supports the spread of evolutionary beliefs. The John Templeton Foundation has been a significant supporter of the BioLogos Foundation, the leading proponent of theistic evolution (or "evolutionary creation" as BioLogos labels it). On the website of the BioLogos website, we read: "BioLogos invites the church and the world to see the harmony between science and biblical faith as we present an evolutionary understanding of God's creation."

Two AiG speakers and researchers, Dr. Terry Mortenson and Dr. Nathaniel Jeanson, attended a yearly Evangelical Theological Society (ETS) conference. For many years, AiG has sent key personnel to this conference to host a booth, present papers, and be involved in strategic meetings to do our best to encourage and challenge ETS members to trust God's Word in Genesis and reject evolutionary compromises.

At the ETS conference in 2014, three groups had booths (including BioLogos) that pushed millions of years and evolutionary ideas to the attendees. Only one group, Answers in Genesis, was there to oppose compromising destructive views of Genesis. BioLogos has been aggressive in an attempt to influence theologians and students in Bible colleges and seminaries to reject the clear truth of Genesis that AiG defends. On the BioLogos blog about the ETS conference, one blogger wrote: "The great majority of the people who came to the [BioLogos] booth—mostly pastors, Christian academics, and graduate students—had heard of BioLogos. This was a massive change even from last year's ETS conference. Sometimes, sitting here in front of a computer, I can lose a sense of how much BioLogos is impacting the evangelical conversation on faith and science, but it's fantastic to see our influence firsthand."

"Among those who had heard of us, a majority didn't agree with our position. However, even among these people, we heard many varieties of the following statement: 'I can't support evolutionary creationism, but I understand your position and I appreciate your contribution to the conversation.' Whenever we heard this, Jim and I traded huge smiles, because this is exactly what we want to accomplish at BioLogos. Of course, we'd love for everyone to embrace an evolutionary understanding of God's creation because we think it is true, but we fully understand that for conservative Evangelicals, this is a long-term proposition. In the meantime, we count it a huge victory for the BioLogos perspective to be understood and respected as a legitimate position for evangelical Christians to hold." This sad account grieves me. But I bring it to your attention to help you understand that what happened at ETS is just the tip of the iceberg as to what is occurring elsewhere and behind the scenes year after year. BioLogos and other groups want to see theologians (who train future pastors, missionaries, and theologians) adopt evolutionary ideas and reject a literal Genesis. The result is that many theological leaders now doubt or even deny a literal Adam and a literal Fall, which undermines the gospel message.

Answers in Genesis has been doing much behind the scenes to reach theologians. Using solid apologetics resources, we challenge Christian leaders not to compromise God's Word. Now, we can't publicly give details about all these efforts, as some people might want to disrupt these very important outreaches. One such program costs us a considerable amount of money each year. But it has been worth it, as it has been so integral in reaching a large number of influential Christian academics. AiG is fighting a vital battle behind the scenes, and it must continue. I started this article with a reference to Jeremiah. Chapter 23 begins with, *Woe to the shepherds who destroy and scatter the sheep of my pasture!* Yes, so many shepherds today are leading the sheep astray. And really, I believe Jeremiah 23:16 should be applied to many of today's shepherds, church leaders, and academics, Christians though they may be: *Thus says the Lord of hosts: "Do not listen to the words of the prophets who prophesy to you, filling you with vain hopes. They speak visions of their own minds, not from the mouth of the Lord."*

The compromisers who are trying to influence Christian leaders and who dominate the theological world are speaking "visions of their own minds, not from the mouth of the Lord," for they are exalting man's evolutionary ideas over God's clear Word! So even though the life-size Ark, the Creation Museum, and many other AiG programs are reaching (and will continue to reach) millions of people with God's Word and the gospel, AiG is also involved in an intense battle behind the scenes: countering the shepherds who are negatively influencing the Church worldwide. I plead with you to understand how important this battle is over biblical authority. It's really a type of guerilla warfare.

All Christians need to be involved in this spiritual war raging around us.

AUGUST 4
2 Timothy 3:15

Train Up Your Child to Give an Answer

It's never too early to train your children in the way they should go.

After our first child was born, my wife and I would pray with our baby son—even singing some of our favorite hymns to him. After a few weeks, as our son became more aware of his surroundings and began responding to light, colors, and other things, we began showing him pictures in books.

Each of our five children grew up with creationist resources, such as *Dinosaurs: Those Terrible Lizards*—the first major children's book on dinosaurs written by a creationist (Dr. Duane Gish). Now, just because children can't read a book at a young age doesn't mean you can't use it to begin teaching them—particularly if the books have large, colorful illustrations.

We would summarize to them what was written in the book, also pointing to the pictures that accompanied the text. As they gained more understanding, we would read the actual words of the books to them. Eventually, of course, they would be able to read the books themselves. In addition, the Bible was always a major resource we used with them (daily).

Our children grew up enjoying apologetics books that we used to intentionally prepare them to handle the attacks on Christianity and the Bible that they would experience as they grew older. And, of course, we taught them the whole counsel of Scripture. We equipped them with creation apologetics, general Bible apologetics, doctrine, worldview, and so on. We helped them understand the gospel message very clearly from the foundations in Genesis to the message of the Resurrection and the sure hope to come. We taught them to pray as my parents taught us as children to pray. We spent time with them daily, teaching them the truth of God's Word and the saving gospel.

Although reading such books is not a guarantee of salvation, we do praise the Lord for our children who today still love the Lord and are saved in the ark of salvation—the Lord Jesus Christ. And remember: *So faith comes from hearing, and hearing through the word of Christ* (Romans 10:17).

Accordingly, it shocked and then greatly burdened me when I read an alarming statistic from pollster George Barna that approximately two-thirds of young people in our churches will walk away from the Church. We commissioned Britt Beemer's America's Research Group to conduct a national survey to find out why this horrible exodus was happening.

The findings as I've stated many times were both very revealing and at times quite shocking. The reasons behind the departure of our young people from the Church are a real wake-up call for all of us.

One of the most revealing discoveries was that, contrary to what most of us may have believed, we are not losing most of these young people during college. Actually, it's around 40% by the end of middle school and over 40% more by the end of high school; in other words, before college, over 80% were "*already gone*" from the Church in their hearts and minds.

What was the "big picture" reason for their departure (or impending departure)? It came down to their belief concerning the Scriptures. The research showed that, for the most part, these young adults now in their 20s

FAMILY AUGUST 4

were not taught the Bible as a true book of history, and they were not taught how to defend the Scriptures against the faith-shattering attacks of this age (e.g., evolution/millions of years, etc.).

It's important to note that about 85–90% of children and teens from church homes go to public (secular) schools, where biblical Christianity has been eliminated or undermined. Much of the public school curricula (especially in science classes) are contrary to the Bible's clear teachings.

What an awesome and serious responsibility God requires of us as parents to train our children. The family is the educational unit that God created to transmit the knowledge of godly, biblical teachings to the next generation. That's why Answers in Genesis has provided so many resources that parents can use in teaching God's Word to their children, building a Christian worldview, and instructing them to defend their faith in an anti-Christian world. I pray you will consider an investment in such resources as an investment in eternity—your children's and grandchildren's eternity.

I trust each one of us might be able to say of our children, as the apostle Paul did of Timothy: *And how from childhood you have been acquainted with the sacred writings, which are able to make you wise for salvation through faith in Christ Jesus* (2 Timothy 3:15).

Here is a great passage to remind us to be diligent in training our children: *And these words that I command you today shall be on your heart. You shall teach them diligently to your children, and shall talk of them when you sit in your house, and when you walk by the way, and when you lie down, and when you rise* (Deuteronomy 6:6–7).

> It's never too early to begin training your children, knowing that if you don't do it, someone else will.

AUGUST 5

Deuteronomy 20:3-4

Teaching Them to Defend the Faith!

Many Christians in the West are increasingly aware of the spiritual epidemic that has all but wiped out the Christianized West of previous generations. A terrible "virus" has permeated the cultures.

One year, I attended Sunday services at an impressive nineteenth-century church in London. In a building with seating for 3,000 in ornate pews, a handful of elderly people sat inside—in chairs set up in the foyer.

The service, held in a vibrant city full of millions of people, reminded me of a funeral—not the funeral of a person, the funeral of a once-great institution. Now, regardless of how bad things look, I do know and understand that: *And Jesus answered him, "Blessed are you, Simon Bar-Jonah! For flesh and blood has not revealed this to you, but my Father who is in heaven. And I tell you, you are Peter, and on this rock I will build my church, and the gates of hell shall not prevail against it"* (Matthew 16:17–18).

Hundreds and hundreds of churches in England, with hundreds of years of ministry behind them, have shut their doors, according to an architectural preservation group called the Victorian Society.

Today, it seems not many Americans are aware of the spiritual epidemic that wiped out the land of our Christian forefathers. Even fewer seem to be aware that the same epidemic has reached our own shores, spreading like a virus, although I think many are awakening to realize something catastrophic is happening spiritually. American Christianity could become extinct in less than two generations if Christians don't act quickly and decisively. Respected pollster George Barna was one of the first to put numbers to this epidemic, finding that six out of ten 20-somethings who were involved in a church during their teen years are *already gone*. Since that research was published in 2000, survey after survey has confirmed the same basic trend. In 2021, church attendance for Generation Z was down to less than 9%.

Young people see through the hypocrisy of those who claim to believe the Bible—just not as it's written. And when they do, they leave the Church—and their trust in God's Word—behind. Hear what they have to say from the revealing book *Already Gone*.

"The problem, in both the United Kingdom and America, began when the Church basically disconnected the Bible from the real world. Churches in America are not places where people typically talk about dinosaurs, fossils, or the age of the earth—that is left up to the secular schools and colleges. Effectively, the Church concentrates on the spiritual and moral aspects of Christianity.

"But the Bible is not some 'pie in the sky' theoretical book. It's a real book connected to the real world. It has everything to do with history, geology, biology, anthropology, and sociology. It provides the true history of the world, as opposed to evolution over millions of years.

"The 'disconnect' between faith and fact is an illusion created by an overwhelming misinterpretation of the facts. Observational science confirms the Bible's history and, thus, also the Christian doctrines (like the gospel) that are based in that history.

"As I travel around the world teaching how to defend biblical principles and history, I find that whether my audience is secular or Christian, they ask the same questions, such as:

CHURCH

- "How do you know the Bible is true?
- Hasn't science disproved the Bible?
- Isn't the world millions of years old?
- How did Noah get all the animals on the Ark?

But don't we observe evolution because we see animals change—bacteria become resistant to antibiotics?

"God's Word is confirmed by observational science: for example, a study of geology confirms that most rock layers and canyon systems are best explained by catastrophic process (such as those associated with Noah's Flood a few thousand years ago), rather than gradual processes over millions of years.

"The Word of God has never changed, but the Church's perception of the Word of God changed when it failed to engage the evolutionist scientific community on matters of evidence as well as faith. Typical churches use resources that are more geared for what could be called the 'Jew in Jerusalem' who has developed a religious background and lives in a religiously friendly society.

"We are now in the era of the 'Greeks'—like the secular philosophers the Apostle Paul encountered on Mars Hill—yet our churches and Sunday schools are still teaching us like Jews.

"See the problem?

"Our society is immersed in secularism. It's essential that we learn how to defend the Bible and the Christian faith for our sake and our children's. If we don't, the empty and obsolete churches in England will foreshadow the future in America.

"The Victorian Society's magazine recently carried a headline that read, 'Redundant Churches: Who Cares?' Churches in the United Kingdom have been turned into theaters, restaurants, museums—even mosques and temples. I have a whole series of photographs that I have taken of such buildings that were formerly churches."[74]

Where England is today, America and the rest of the West will be tomorrow, if most are not already there—unless we act now and pray for God's blessing. It's time for a new Reformation in the Church—to call the Church back to the authority of the Word of God, beginning in Genesis.

And shall say to them, "Hear, O Israel, today you are drawing near for battle against your enemies: let not your heart faint. Do not fear or panic or be in dread of them, for the Lord your God is he who goes with you to fight for you against your enemies, to give you the victory" (Deuteronomy 20:3–4).

> We can apply these words to our own lives today that God gave to the Israelites as they prepared for battle.

AUGUST 6

1 Timothy 6:20-21

What Kind of Science Do You Mean?

O Timothy, guard the deposit entrusted to you. Avoid the irreverent babble and contradictions of what is falsely called "knowledge," for by professing it some have swerved from the faith (1 Timothy 6:20–21). The Bible's account of beginnings cannot be tested in a laboratory, so secular scientists—and even some Christians—believe it is not science and must be classified as religion.

It is helpful to distinguish between operational (or observational) science and origins (or historical) science and compare how each one seeks to discover truth. When I debated Bill Nye in 2014, the first thing I did was to define terms like science and religion. I find most people have never done this. And most don't understand that the word science means knowledge, and there are different kinds of knowledge. People are generally unaware that dictionaries give a root meaning, or etymology, of science similar to this one from Webster's: "from Latin scientia, from scient-, sciens 'having knowledge,' from present participle of scire 'to know.'"

Although there are other uses of the word, the root meaning of science is basically "knowledge." In fact, in the past, philosophy and theology were considered sciences, and theology was even called the "queen of the sciences." But over the past 200 years, during the so-called Scientific Revolution, the word science has come to mean a method of knowing, a way of discovering truth. Moreover, many people assume that modern science is the only way to discover truth.

Operational science uses observable, repeatable experiments to try to discover truth. Origins science relies on relics from the past and historical records to try to discover truth. To assist people in clearing up the confusion, we have found it helpful to distinguish between two types of modern science and compare how each one seeks to discover truth:

Operational science (or observational science)	Origins science (or historical science)
uses the so-called "scientific method" to attempt to discover truth, performing observable, repeatable experiments in a controlled environment to find patterns of recurring behavior in the present physical universe. Both creationists and evolutionists use this kind of science, which has given rise to computers, space shuttles, and cures for diseases.	attempts to discover truth by examining reliable eyewitness testimony (if available) and circumstantial evidence, such as pottery, fossils, and canyons. Because the past cannot be observed directly, assumptions greatly affect how these scientists interpret what they see.

So, for example, how was the Grand Canyon formed? Was it formed gradually over long periods of time by a little bit of water, or was it formed rapidly by a lot of water? The first interpretation is based on secular assumptions of slow change over millions of years, while the second interpretation is based on biblical assumptions about rapid change during Noah's Flood. Such interpretations involve origins or historical science. Both creation scientists and evolution scientists have religious (or faith) components to their scientific models about origins. Yet both types of scientists are equally capable of doing both operational science and origins science.

Operational (observational) science, whether done by an evolutionist or a creationist, has benefited mankind in many ways, particularly through technology. Creationists have contributed greatly to this area of science,

SCIENCE   AUGUST 6

including nineteenth-century physicists Michael Faraday and James Clerk Maxwell, and more recently the late Dr. Raymond Damadian, who invented the MRI imaging used by medical doctors. In origins science, creationists are discovering many things that honor the Creator's wisdom and confirm biblical history. Dr. Raymond Damadian was an ardent young-earth creationist who was also credited by many as "the man who invented the MRI scanner."

At this point, most people realize that the debate between creationists and evolutionists is not about operational science, which is based in the present. The debate is about origins (historical) science and conflicting assumptions, or beliefs, about the past and thus conflicting interpretations of that evidence. Molecules-to-man evolution is a belief about the past. It assumes, without observing it, that natural processes and lots of time are sufficient to explain the origin and diversification of life. Until quite recently, many geologists have used studies of current river erosion and sedimentation to explain how sedimentary rock layers were formed or eroded slowly over millions of years. In the past few decades, however, even secular geologists have begun to recognize that catastrophic processes are a better explanation for many of the earth's rock layers.

After we explain these two types of science, people usually begin to recognize the potential problems with the statement, "Evolution is science, but the Bible is religion." Molecules-to-man evolution is not proven by operational science; instead, it is a belief about the past based on antibiblical assumptions. The Bible, in contrast, is the eyewitness testimony of the Creator, who tells us what happened to produce the earth—the different kinds of life, the fossils, the rock layers, and indeed the whole universe. And observational science confirms this. The Bible gives us the true, "big picture" starting assumptions for origins science.

Thus, creationists and evolutionists develop totally different reconstructions of history. But they accept and use the same methods of research in both origins and operational science. The different conclusions about origins arise from different starting assumptions, not the research methods themselves. So the battle between the Bible and molecules-to-man evolution is not one of religion versus science. Rather, it is a conflict between worldviews—a creationist's starting assumptions (a biblical worldview) and an evolutionist's starting assumptions (an antibiblical worldview).

Let us be clear. Accurate knowledge (truth) about physical reality can be discovered by the methods of both operational science and origins science. But truth claims in both areas may be false. Many so-called "proven facts" (statements of supposed truth) about how things operate (in physics, chemistry, medicine, etc.), as well as about how things originated (in biology, geology, astronomy, etc.) have been or will be shown to be false. So, as best we can, we must be like the Bereans in Acts 17:11 and examine every truth claim against Scripture and look for faulty logic or false assumptions.

There are many ways to test the accuracy of the biblical worldview against naturalistic atheism (the worldview that controls most origins research). However, evolutionary interpretations don't fit what we see and are not confirmed by observational science.

> When our research is based upon biblical truths about the past, we find that our interpretations of the biological and geological facts make sense of what we see in the real world, and observational science confirms such.

AUGUST 7
Acts 17:11

Here We Stand

Now these Jews were more noble than those in Thessalonica; they received the word with all eagerness, examining the Scriptures daily to see if these things were so (Acts 17:11).

I've found that young people see through the hypocrisy of those who claim to believe the Bible—just not as it's written. And when they do, they leave the Church and their trust in God's Word behind.

In 2009, Answers in Genesis released an eye-opening book where we asked Christians to symbolically nail Genesis 1–11 on the doors of churches, Christian colleges, and seminaries.

From your history classes, you may recall that in 1517 a young monk, Martin Luther, boldly nailed 95 theses on the church door in Wittenberg, Germany. He was calling the Church back to the authority of the Bible and away from the opinions and traditions of fallible man.

Four years later, Luther stood before the emperor, princes, and others in the Bishop's Palace in Worms, Germany, where he was told to recant his theses and books. The next day, after a long night of prayer and counsel, Luther famously replied that he would not recant unless it could be shown from the Scriptures that he was in error. He is then reported to have said: "Here I stand; I can do no other. God help me. Amen."

In the book *Already Gone* which was published in 2009, Christians learned about a major research study that we believed could help lead to a revolution—another reformation, if you will—for a desperately needed transformation of the Church in the West. This research detailed why young people were leaving the Church. Major reasons included the lack of apologetics teaching and rampant compromise by church leaders on the first 11 chapters of Genesis, which is nothing less than an attack on the authority of God's Word. Genesis 1–11 is the foundation for all doctrine, the gospel, for everything.

For years, we have been challenging the Church to stand without compromise on the authority of God's Word, beginning in Genesis. We have insisted that Christians should be like the Bereans in Acts 17:11.

Similarly, we have been encouraging Christians to be like Martin Luther, who stood before the authorities of his day and insisted that we judge our beliefs against the absolute authority of the Word of God—regardless of what the majority might say (e.g., like scientists of today who hold to evolution and millions of years).

In articles and in my lectures over the years, I have insisted that Christians who compromise by accepting the idea of an earth supposedly millions of years old (or who are indifferent to whether or not that is even a problem) have greatly contributed to the decline of the Church and its influence. Most churches lack apologetics teaching for their young people (and their adults, for that matter). As a result, a very significant number of young people are leaving the Church—and thus the decline of the influence of Christianity in the West continues.

The research for *Already Gone* consisted of survey questions to find out why so many young adults were being lost from the Church ... plus why Christians were not having the influence on the culture that they once had (and thus why we are ultimately losing the "culture war" in the West). The results shocked many Christians—and should have shocked the church as a whole.

CHURCH

For example, our national survey discovered that children who grew up in evangelical homes were being "lost" from the Church as early as elementary school, not primarily in college (as most might expect). Furthermore, in one of the biggest and most distressing surprises of the research, something you might call the "Sunday school syndrome" was contributing to the epidemic! Kids who went to Sunday school regularly were overall spiritually worse than those who did not go to Sunday school.

Already Gone was an alarming wake-up call for the Church, because it reported on this research that showed how church programs and approaches to Christian education were failing—and thus millions of our young people were leaving the Church. While the research statistics revealed the root issues of a huge problem, *Already Gone* showed how to fight back and reclaim our families, our churches, and our society for biblical truths.

I believe that once Christians understand what the researchers uncovered, they will be motivated to symbolically nail Genesis 1–11 on the doors of churches and Christian organizations. We need many "Luthers" nailing this on church doors throughout America. And I praise the Lord that many in the Church did take up this battle and, in a sense, started nailing Genesis 1–11 on the doors of their churches.

As we finished writing that book, I knew that it could bring a tidal wave of disbelief and frustration from those who didn't want to accept its findings. But I couldn't help but exclaim from the bottom of my heart: "Here we stand; we can do no other."

May God help us reach the Church with a crucial message of reformation—and may God raise up generations who will stand on His Word and be the salt and light that this culture so desperately needs.

   Please pray that we'll see a new reformation in the Church.

AUGUST 8

Philippians 2:8

Our Culture Needs the Violence of the Cross

And being found in human form, he humbled himself by becoming obedient to the point of death, even death on a cross (Philippians 2:8).

Many people will recall one of the most horrific acts of school violence in America in 1999. Beginning at 11:19 a.m. at suburban Columbine High School in Littleton, Colorado, high school seniors Eric Harris and Dylan Klebold killed 12 students and a teacher and wounded 23 others. It was a massacre that shocked the United States—and the world. Serial killer Eric Harris wore a T-shirt that day that simply declared "NATURAL SELECTION." Such acts as this—and numerous others since—sent a warning that something was happening in our culture—something many were perplexed about. Why would such situations occur?

From a biblical perspective and an understanding of a sovereign God, the ultimate answer, of course, is sin. Because of the effects of sin and the curse, we now experience violence, suffering, disease, catastrophes, and so on. But on the individual level, what could lead people like Harris and Klebold to kill their fellow students?

In 2007, Pekka-Eric Auvinen, a teen in Finland, shot and killed students at a high school in another shocking act of school violence. In a video posted on YouTube prior to the shooting, Auvinen stated: "I am prepared to fight and die for my cause.... I, as a natural selector, will eliminate all who I see unfit, disgraces of human race and failures of natural selection. No, the truth is that I am just an animal, a human, an individual, a dissident . ... It's time to put NATURAL SELECTION & SURVIVAL OF THE FITTEST back on track!"[75]

We live in an era of history in which the idea of atheistic evolution is taught as fact in most of the education systems of the world. If one studies the major biology textbooks used in the United States and other governments' schools, one will find that students are taught how the universe and life (including the origin of humans) are explained in terms of natural processes. Students are taught that man is just an animal. One needs to consider what would happen if a student's entire worldview were built on the foundation of atheistic evolution. If man is just an animal, and there is no God—if we are "all animals, descendants of a vast lineage of replicators sprung from primordial pond scum,"[76] as stated in a *Scientific American* article on social Darwinism in 1995—then what one bag of biological chemicals does to another bag of biological chemicals is ethically irrelevant. After all, if we are just chemicals arranged in no particular way, then there is no ultimate purpose and meaning in life—except one's subjective view of things while alive. And it's not likely that others will have the same subjective opinion.

So the more that generations are taught they are just animals and that life is a result of natural processes—with no ultimate purpose or meaning in life and with no absolute authority—then the more consistent they become in building their thinking on this foundation. We should expect to see people doing what is described in the book of Judges: *In those days there was no king in Israel; everyone did what was right in his own eyes* (Judges 21:25).

We live in a culture where increasing numbers of each successive generation have been taught there is no absolute authority. They believe that there is no Creator to whom we are accountable—and everyone has a right to do what is right in his own eyes.

THEOLOGY AUGUST 8

If we truly just evolved from apelike ancestors, then why should we fight for the sanctity of life and protect and cherish it at all costs? Why is it important for us to exercise self-control when we are angry or frustrated? If the Ten Commandments are ripped off the walls of our schools and courtrooms and disregarded as a basic, ethical God-given code of conduct, then who should care if kids are killing kids or if anyone is attacked for any reason? We watch animals hunt and tear each other apart on TV documentaries. If you don't matter to God, then tell me—do you truly matter to anyone? If God doesn't care about what happens to you, is anyone else obligated to care?

But the truth is, you do matter to God, and, therefore, your life and your existence on this planet that we all share ought to matter to everyone. If someone does you harm or violates your human rights, we, as your neighbors and community and church and government, need to be quick to come to your defense and aid and fight for justice and dignity at all costs. You are created in the image of an amazing, loving God, and you matter. There is such hope in that promise. Yes, there's light and hope when there is an understanding that God loves each and every individual and that every single solitary life matters to Him. Now, don't misunderstand me. I am not saying that evolution is the cause of violence. Sin is the cause. However, the more generations are taught they are just animals and that there is no Creator God, the more people will act consistently in accordance with who (or what) they believe they are.

I am not saying that every atheist/evolutionist will commit violent acts. The Bible makes it clear in Romans 1–2 that man has a God-consciousness and a conscience knowing right and wrong. People inherently know it is wrong to murder and commit violent acts against others. Actually, atheists have to borrow Christian presuppositions when they say that murder and violent acts are wrong! Atheists have to live inconsistently. The problem comes about when people act more consistently with their atheistic presuppositions!

While the bankrupt religion of evolution does not directly lead to horrible violence by young people, I suggest that if they were told that there is a Creator who gives a purpose and a meaning for His Creation, then this cannot help but provide young people with some meaning to their lives. In the Book of Genesis, we read that God created a perfect world—that is, a world that did not know death, suffering, or any kind of evil. In this perfect world lived two people who took it upon themselves to try to become like God. In doing so, their sin led to the Fall from grace that this world and everyone on it has experienced ever since.

Our world is not perfect—in fact, it's very broken. If God withdrew His sustaining power completely from the world, it would cease to exist. God is paying attention and is actively involved in His creation, but He doesn't always protect mankind from its own actions. Even the earth itself was cursed after the first sin. God is paying attention—so much so that he sent His Son, Jesus Christ, to pay the penalty for mankind's sin and offer forgiveness to all. God has promised everything will be made right again. He will wipe away every tear, and death, pain, and suffering will be no more.

Have you ever thought about the fact that the supreme act of violence was carried out (against Jesus) because of sin and the resulting wickedness of men, but God used that to pour His love out on us?

For God so loved the world, that he gave his only Son, that whoever believes in him should not perish but have eternal life (John 3:16).

Jesus paid the penalty for our sin and offers us the free gift of salvation.

AUGUST 9
2 Timothy 2:15

In Apologetics, Stick with the Bible!

"Problematic apologetics?" What does that term mean? The word *apologetics* comes from the Greek word *apologia*. It is usually translated as "answer" or "defense" in 1 Peter 3:15: *But in your hearts honor Christ the Lord as holy, always being prepared to make a defense to anyone who asks you for a reason for the hope that is in you; yet do it with gentleness and respect.*

If Christianity is true, and the Bible is the infallible, inspired Word of God, Christians should be able to defend their faith when asked skeptical questions. This doesn't mean that Christians must have all the answers—but from a big-picture perspective, they should be able to give a reasoned argument to counter attacks on the Christian faith. Unfortunately, I often see two major problems in Christian apologetics:

- Most Christians have not been taught practical, basic apologetics, so they don't know how to defend the Christian faith when it is challenged.
- Some Christians use incorrect or problematic arguments in their response. Bad arguments then become a stumbling block once the hearer sees the flaws.

Problematic apologetics comes in different forms, such as promoting urban legends or taking quotations out of context. Here is an illustration: A person made claims about how to interpret some scientific evidence and then quoted a Bible verse to justify his argument. But when the verse was checked in context, it did not support the claim. This is called eisegesis (a big word for "reading into the text"). Instead of letting God's Word speak to us through the style and context of the passage, many people try to force their own ideas into the Bible to justify their beliefs.

Cults are masters at eisegesis, but it's also a danger for Christians. In fact, every time a Christian defends compromise ideas about earth history and evolution, such as the gap theory, theistic evolution, progressive creation, and many other similar positions on Genesis, they are imposing their own ideas on Scripture. Then they claim that Scripture teaches their position. Such "eisegesis problematic apologetics" ultimately undermines the authority of Scripture and causes unbelievers to stumble. And such is rife in Christendom, churches, Christian colleges, etc. Let's consider just two examples to see whether they slip into eisegesis problematic apologetics.

1. Days of Peleg: Continental Breakup?

When looking at the earth, we find evidence that continental plates have moved great distances and are still moving (albeit slowly) today. If such major geologic change occurred in the past, wouldn't it be recorded in the Bible? Concerned about these scientific findings, Christians sometimes claim that the continents split apart during the days of Peleg, soon after the Flood. They usually cite Genesis 10:25, which says "the earth was divided" in the days of Peleg. If you look carefully at the context, however, you see that this verse appears in the middle of a detailed account of the division of languages, when people were divided and spread over the earth. In fact, the Hebrew word translated *Earth* in Genesis 10:25 is the same word used in Genesis 10:32 to describe the nations being divided. The same word appears again in Genesis 11:1, which says the whole *earth* spoke the same language. In each context, the word refers to the people living on the land, not the land itself.

APOLOGETICS — AUGUST 9

Genesis 8:3–4 raises another problem. The ark ran aground on the "mountains of Ararat" on day 150 of the Flood. These mountains in the region called Ararat appear to have been caused by the collision of the Eurasian plate, Arabian plate, and African plate. If the mountains were formed by continental plates moving in the days of Peleg, then the region of Ararat couldn't have existed when the ark ran aground! It makes more sense to believe that these continental shifts occurred catastrophically during the Flood, prior to day 150.

Another problem is that a continental breakup at the time of Peleg would have resulted in a global catastrophe similar to Noah's Flood, with devastating earthquakes, earth movements, and tsunamis wiping out all life on the land. The context of Genesis 10:25 is the division of nations. The context rules out the idea that the continents broke up at the time of Peleg.

2. Mt. Ararat: Have Remains of the Ark Been Found?

If Noah's ark really landed on Ararat, shouldn't it have been found? Many expeditions have attempted to locate the ark on modern Mt. Ararat, and some people claim they have found remains. But is it really necessary—or likely—to find anything? So far, no hard evidence has come to light, and if you look closely at the biblical text, it doesn't even say that the ark landed on Mt. Ararat. The ark landed on "the mountains of Ararat" (Genesis 8:3–4), which is a much larger range than just the one mountain known today as Mt. Ararat.

The argument for Mt. Ararat as the ark's landing place is based on assumptions about geology. Genesis 8:5 says, *The waters continued to abate until the tenth month; in the tenth month, on the first day of the month, the tops of the mountains were seen.* Since modern Ararat is much larger than other mountains in the area, some Christians believe the ark must have landed there. However, they are assuming that modern mountains had reached their current height during the Flood, which is extremely unlikely. Mountains were still rising and falling long after the Flood, even as they are doing more slowly today. In fact, Mt. Ararat is a very large volcano, which sits on top of other rock layers laid down during the Flood, so it was apparently formed at the end of the Flood. Since the volcano continued to be active until 1840, we know the mountain has continued to change since the Flood. Rushing to accept evidence of ark remains, when there is no hard evidence, is not good apologetics. In fact, it is probable that the ark has been destroyed over the course of about 4,300 years (by natural or human agents), perhaps even destroyed by the same violent post-Flood volcanic eruptions that built modern Mt. Ararat! Arguments that lack significant support from the Bible and other evidence can actually undermine biblical authority.

Such claims have been used to "defend" the faith and supposedly uphold Scripture—but in doing so, they can undermine biblical authority. When discussing such topics, we should always proceed with caution and hesitation, understanding not only the limitations of evidence but also what the Bible states clearly in context. The Bible is the most defensible historical document of antiquity. So we don't need to confuse our friends and loved ones with problematic apologetics.

Do your best to present yourself to God as one approved, a worker who has no need to be ashamed, rightly handling the word of truth (2 Timothy 2:15).

> Let's each work hard to use the best arguments that honor our Lord and "rightly divide" His Word of truth.

AUGUST 10
Proverbs 22:6

Sunday School Syndrome

Train up a child in the way he should go; even when he is old he will not depart from it (Proverbs 22:6).

Our research has revealed what we call the Sunday school syndrome. In a survey (results were published in 2009) conducted by a behavioral research group, we discovered that we are losing kids from Church in grade school—not just college. And we found out that Sunday school is one of the reasons why.

I have spoken across America and other parts of the world summarizing to audiences the shocking results of the national survey we conducted. Answers in Genesis commissioned this poll to ask 1,000 people who were in their 20s and grew up regularly attending a Bible-believing church, why they no longer go to church at all. The results of this nationwide poll have appeared in the coauthored book (with highly respected researcher Britt Beemer) *Already Gone*.

Two stunning and disconcerting results came out of this survey:

We discovered that we were losing our kids in church in elementary school, middle school, and high school ... not just in college (which is the conventional thinking); the large majority are "*already gone*" in their hearts and minds before college. Sunday school was one of the reasons why.

Indeed, as our survey revealed, there is a "Sunday school syndrome" contributing to the epidemic of young people leaving the Church. Our survey numbers were statistically significant (and are absolutely contrary to what most would have expected). This was a brutal wake-up call for the Church, showing how our programs of Christian education were failing dismally.

I do, however, thank those of you who are committed to Christian education inside and outside the Church. I sincerely commend you for giving your time, skills, and best efforts to invest in the future generation.

Nevertheless, when compared to those who never went to Sunday school, more Sunday school attendees who no longer went to church believed the church was less relevant—and more had become increasingly anti-church over the years. They were more inclined to accept abortion, gay "marriage," and other unbiblical activities of our day.

Young people saw through the hypocrisy of those who claim to believe the Bible—just not as it's written, particularly in Genesis. And when they did, they left the Church—and their trust in God's Word—behind. Hear what they had to say in this very revealing book, *Already Gone*.

"The startling conclusion is that, on the whole, the Sunday school programs of today are statistical failures—and are even detrimental.

"I know that's going to hurt many of you who are dedicated to Sunday school programs—as well as those of you who are depending on these programs to properly influence your children. But listen: if you are depending on these programs to properly teach and influence your children, it is just not happening.

"Out of the 1,000 interviews, 606 were former Sunday school students. The church failed these people miserably. As children and teenagers, these 606 were there almost every Sunday; they were present; they heard the lessons ... and it had a nominal and even negative effect on their beliefs about Christianity.

CHURCH   AUGUST 10

"If I were a church leader, I would sit down and pour my heart out to the Lord. I would then find a new Sunday school curriculum that better prepares young people to maintain their faith. ...

"There is no single inoculation that will make us immune to the Sunday school syndrome. The truth of the matter is that the epidemic affects each of us as individuals—because each of us is part of the great Body of Christ. Together, working as a body, a multifaceted response to the disease can materialize. Lord willing, the mass exodus can be slowed, if not reversed, and be transformed into something more powerful than the typical, traditional forms we are now using.

"Imagine if we started raising generations of children who stood uncompromisingly on the Word of God, knew how to defend the Christian faith, could answer the skeptical questions of this age, and had a fervor to share the gospel from the authority of God's Word with whomever they met! This could change the world."

Of course, Christian education begins in the home, and that is where the responsibility for it ultimately lies (and with the father in particular—see, for example, Isaiah 38:19; Ephesians 6:4). The education of our young people must be built upon the following biblical principle: the family is the first and most fundamental of all human institutions that God ordained in Scripture (in Genesis), and it is the educational unit that God uses to transmit His knowledge from one generation to the next.

> **With such families working with the assistance of their churches' educational programs, we could see the world changed.**

AUGUST 11
1 Peter 3:15

Christians Should Always Have an Answer

Why did someone exclaim, "Man ... that was radical!"

From the beginning of my creation apologetics speaking ministry that had its origin in Australia, I began to see a pattern. Wherever I spoke, regardless of the country, people were asking the same basic questions.

I remember once I had just given a presentation on the campus of Cardiff University in the country of Wales. I'll never forget it. A young man who had been in the audience came down to the front to speak to me. He leaned forward on the high bench at the front of the auditorium, looked at me, and exclaimed: "Man ... that was radical!"

I asked, "What was so radical?"

He replied, "Christians having answers!"

Looking back over the many years of my speaking on creation vs. evolution, I have noticed that after most talks, a long line forms with people wanting to ask questions.

- Where Did Cain get his wife?
- Who made God?
- How did Noah fit the animals on the ark?
- Why Christianity? Why not Buddhism?
- Does it really matter if Christians believe in millions of years and evolution?
- How do you know the Bible is true?

And there were many more!

Now as time went on, similar questions are asked, but new questions such as, "What's your position on gay 'marriage' and the LGBTQ movement?" "Should Christians attend a gay 'wedding' or a transgender 'wedding'?" and "How should we approach the abortion issue?" There's also been an increase in people asking how to deal with the identity issue—how people can determine who they are, what gender they are, and so on. But the point is, they ask many questions pertaining to how a Christian should respond to such matters.

Back in the 1980s, I thought it would be a good idea to compile the most-asked questions (and their answers) and publish them in a booklet. The first *Answers Book* was born. It quickly became extremely popular.

We then expanded the answers and turned this publication into an actual book. Well, this book proved to be so popular that we expanded it even more—and a few editions later, it is now known as *The New Answers Book*.

Over time, we continued to compile the questions people were often asking about the Book of Genesis. With ongoing creationist research to bolster our case, *The Answers Book* itself was expanded—and we published what we today call *The Answers Book 1*, answering over 25 tough questions. Since then, we continued to publish additional books in this series, answering the most-asked questions in our day concerning God's

APOLOGETICS — AUGUST 11

Word, science, and so on. God has blessed this series to become the biggest-selling creation apologetics book in the world since it was released.

And then, after we did some serious research into why so many young people were leaving the Church when they became adults (as reported in the book *Already Gone*), we created a series of children's books to give kids (and parents) answers for their faith: *The Answers Book for Kids*.

One of our "theme verses" as a ministry is 1 Peter 3:15:

But in your hearts honor Christ the Lord as holy, always being prepared to make a defense to anyone who asks you for a reason for the hope that is in you; yet do it with gentleness and respect (1 Peter 3:15).

The word *defense* or **answer** comes from the Greek word *apologia*. It can mean:

- a verbal defense; speech in defense
- a reasoned statement or argument

We live, of course, in a very skeptical age. Many accusations are leveled by non-Christians against the Bible—its authenticity and authority. But Answers in Genesis is at the forefront of equipping believers with answers so that they will be more effective as they share the gospel of Jesus Christ. We all need to be equipped to give answers to skeptical or enquiring questions.

Christians who are able to give answers shouldn't be seen as "radical"—actually, they should be the norm. I urge you to become equipped with the latest answers in order to be more effective in being a witness for the Christian gospel. And let's all start sharing these answers as part of our teaching in churches at all levels!

> We need generations equipped to be able to defend the Christian faith so they can "contend for the faith" (Jude 3).

AUGUST 12
Matthew 18:6

Teach Children Truth, Not Child Abuse

Many of those opposing the Christian faith accuse Christians of supposed "child abuse" for teaching them about the Creator God. Secularists often claim Christians should not be allowed to teach children as they are indoctrinating them in Christianity.

What do you think would happen if atheists took a group of children to a summer camp and gave them lessons that mocked the Koran and the Islamic faith? Would there be an outcry? Would Muslims remain silent? Well, we all know that such a camp would not be tolerated. And we also know that atheists in America would not attempt to insult Muslims like this.

Yet atheists can take children to a camp and make a shocking mockery of the Christian faith, and that's apparently OK! According to an edition of the *American Atheist* magazine, a "mass de-baptism" was held at a camp for children that was run by atheists. Over "100 humans [mostly children] were cleansed of religious folly."

This makes people realize that atheists don't want Christians teaching children because they want to be able to indoctrinate against God's Word/Christianity.

Camp Quest was described in the magazine as a place:

- "To provide children of freethinking parents a residential summer camp dedicated to improving the human condition through rational inquiry, critical and creative thinking, scientific method, self-respect, ethics, competency, democracy, free speech, and the separation of religion and government guaranteed [sic] by the Constitution of the United States ..."
- "Camp Quest is the first residential summer camp in the history of the United States for the children of Atheists, Freethinkers, Humanists, Brights, or whatever other terms might be applied to those who hold to a naturalistic, not supernatural world view [sic]."
- In addition, according to the group's website, "Campers at Camp Quest are encouraged to think for themselves and are not required to hold any particular view. We do emphasize critical and scientific thinking over faith though."

So these children, whose worldview was being formed by those who teach them at the camp, were supposedly "encouraged to think for themselves"? Is that why the young people were given a free T-shirt that stated, "It's OK To Be An Atheist"? And why a "nine-year old Camp Quest camper, who after being De-Baptized [using a hairdryer], raised her arms skyward and loudly proclaimed, 'I can see!'"?

Of course, they were not being taught to think for themselves, as any "bright," true "free-thinker" could easily see. These children were being indoctrinated against Christianity, especially with their adult-led mockery of Christian baptism. They were explicitly taught to reject God!

Ironically, you can find numerous examples on the web, in books, and in magazines where those who oppose the Christian faith accuse Christians of supposed "child abuse" for teaching them about God, creation, etc.

For instance, atheist Richard Dawkins in his book *The God Delusion* states the following concerning the biblical teaching of hell: "I am persuaded that the phrase 'child abuse' is no exaggeration when used to

FAMILY
AUGUST 12

describe what teachers and priests are doing to children whom they encourage to believe in something like the punishment of unshriven [unforgiven] mortal sins in an eternal hell."

On a well-known anti-creationist website, we read this statement by a person commenting on our Creation Museum: "I have no doubt that brain washing children with deliberate lies about the processes of science should indeed be viewed as child abuse."

You can find many similar quotes with child abuse accusations against Christians, especially those who teach children about God and creation.

And sadly, I've had a number of people tell me that when atheists make that accusation of "child abuse" against Christians, they are undermining the fact that there is real child abuse in the culture that destroys children.

I believe, however, that the ultimate "child abuse" (to use the term many God-haters use) is to take young children—who in their hearts know there is a God, for the knowledge of God is written on their hearts (Romans 1)—and teach them that there is no God; humans are just animals; there is no purpose in life; when you die, that is the end of you.

We must not forget the sobering verse where Jesus declares, *But whoever causes one of these little ones who believe in me to stumble, it would be better for him to have a heavy millstone fastened around his neck and to be drowned in the depth of the sea* (Matthew 18:6).

Let's praise God for tools like the maligned, yet amazingly effective Creation Museum, and the arsenal of Bible-affirming books, DVDs, and other resources that so powerfully present biblical truth to young people! And let's teach as many children as we can the truth of God's Word—that they are special and made in God's image. They are so special that God sent His Son, the Lord Jesus, to die on the Cross to pay the penalty for their sin so they can receive the free gift of salvation. What a different message to the one the atheists teach children as they tell them they're just animals, life is ultimately meaningless and purposeless, and when they die, they cease to exist.

We need to work hard to stop atheists from destroying the minds of children.

AUGUST 13
Matthew 7:28-29

Authority Is the Issue

In recent times, we've sadly seen many pastors and other church leaders (and whole denominations) change their stance on marriage, abortion, and other social issues. We've seen a number of church leaders and academics in Christian institutions become soft in regard to the LGBTQ movement by supporting them in various ways. Of course, the ultimate reason for their changes is sin! However, there is also a foundational reason why these changes have been happening.

In July 2019, headlines appeared in Christian and secular media concerning a person named Joshua Harris. Here is just a tiny sampling of what was being said:

"Joshua Harris falling away from faith: 'I am not a Christian'".[77]

"'I Am Not a Christian': Former 'Pastor,' Author Joshua Harris Kisses Christianity Goodbye".[78]

Atheist bloggers were almost giddy with excitement over this sad situation. Now, Harris was well known in many Christian circles for his bestselling book, *I Kissed Dating Goodbye*. He was also known for holding a key position with the Gospel Coalition and for pastoring a megachurch in Maryland for ten years. Harris was homeschooled and was brought up by parents who were considered pillars of the homeschool movement in the 1990s.

I was not familiar with Harris or his book (maybe because of my age!), but I discovered that three years before, a headline in *The Christian Post* read, "Abstinence Author, Pastor Joshua Harris, Apologizes for Telling Christians Not to Date in 'I Kissed Dating Goodbye'".[79]

The July 2019 *Christian Post* article quoted Harris from his Instagram post, saying: "I have undergone a massive shift in regard to my faith in Jesus. The popular phrase for this is 'deconstruction,' the biblical phrase is 'falling away.' By all the measurements that I have for defining a Christian, I am not a Christian." All this news coincided with an announcement that he and his wife were divorcing. So what contributed to Harris's falling away personally and theologically?

Now, before we get to what I believe is the heart of the matter, I must make one more observation. Unless you are immersed in a particular situation, you can never be sure of all the facts so that you can understand things completely. I know from my own experience over the years in regard to accusations against AiG, staff issues, etc., that unless you were intimately involved in the issue, you can't fully understand the reality of a situation. I don't know all that happened in Joshua Harris's life—and I can never find all that out. Regardless, I'm reminded of this Scripture that teaches that each of us will answer for our own sins: *The soul who sins shall die. The son shall not suffer for the iniquity of the father, nor the father suffer for the iniquity of the son. The righteousness of the righteous shall be upon himself, and the wickedness of the wicked shall be upon himself* (Ezekiel 18:20).

I found a 2017 TED talk (as this type of public lecture is called) in which Joshua Harris said he was wrong in his famous book about dating. I watched the entire talk and have two observations: Not once in this entire talk did Harris cite Scripture. He mentioned evolution (so he was impacted by this belief) and that evolution involves death as his analogy for his evolving views. He addressed how people should be thinking about

APOLOGETICS

things. But not once did he indicate that he even considered God's Word as an anchor for his worldview. It seemed to me from watching the video that he was acting as his own authority. He made this statement: "But at the end of the day, I know that I can't be controlled by someone else's viewpoint." Well, it's true that we can't just accept a fallible human's view on something unless we have an absolute standard against which we can judge it. For Christians, all of our thinking is to be controlled by a worldview anchored in the absolute authority of the Word of God. Without the foundation of God's Word, we have no basis except our subjective opinion (which permeates Harris' talk) to determine what we believe.

My father taught me many things that I have never forgotten, and I have applied them many times over the years. He taught me that what I believe has to be judged against the absolute authority of God's Word. My father also told me that whenever someone made statements that contradicted what we read in the Bible, I needed to do three things:

1. Go to Scripture and make sure I'm reading the words correctly according to the literature, the context, the grammar, etc. If I'm sure that I'm taking Scripture as God meant it to be taken, then I'm to question any of man's fallible views that say there are contradictions in Scripture.

2. Search for answers as to why claims about contradictions in Scripture are wrong. Not finding a solution doesn't mean that Scripture is wrong. It just means that at this stage, I don't have all the answers and need to wait and see if God allows me to find them.

3. When you use a study Bible, you need to remember that the notes at the bottom are not inspired like the text—the text should actually be looked at as the commentary on the notes!

How I praise the Lord for godly parents who taught me to acknowledge that the Bible is the absolute authority and the Word of God. They also reminded me over and over again that man's word changes, but God's Word never changes! And how I praise the Lord for my wife of almost 47 years, who is one with me on this stand on God's Word. It's always important to distinguish between what Scripture clearly teaches and what it doesn't. Yes, the culture is changing, and attitudes toward issues like gay "marriage" are changing (and, sadly, many church leaders have changed their views to accommodate unbiblical positions). But AiG won't change its stand on biblical marriage because God's Word hasn't changed. And it's always important to distinguish between what Scripture clearly teaches and what it doesn't. Another principle my father taught me was to understand that only God knows everything! Compared to what God knows, I know next to nothing! That's why I get so frustrated with Christians who compromise God's Word with man's fallible ideas about the age of the earth, biological evolution, and so on. How arrogant of us to tell God where He got it wrong in His Word! That's why we're so zealous at AiG for standing on the authority of the Word of God.

The Answers in Genesis ministry is not just dealing with creation, evolution, fossils, the Flood, the age of the earth, and so on. Ultimately this ministry is all about proclaiming the truth of the absolute authority of the Word of God and the gospel of Jesus Christ. *"And when Jesus finished these sayings, the crowds were astonished at his teaching, for he was teaching them as one who had authority, and not as their scribes"* (Matthew 7:28–29).

We can speak with the same authority, as we have the Word of God.

AUGUST 14
Acts 5:39

Progressive Christians Are Atheists' Allies

It really happened. Intolerant pastors united with secularists against a biblical Christian outreach! When it comes to the ministry the Lord has called us to, I have a "fire in my bones" that I can't explain. I can't help but get excited. I know the Lord has called my wife and me to this creation/gospel ministry—and He has confirmed that calling over and over again. Yes, I am passionate about this ministry. That's because I believe Answers in Genesis and its various outreaches are at the cutting edge of the spiritual battle for the hearts and minds of people today. I want to see as many people as possible become as fired up as we are! Let me tell you about a situation that occurred in our history that reminds me of the importance of this ministry and a reminder to not waver in our stand on God's Word.

The anti-Christian group Americans United for Separation of Church and State (AU) had put a great deal of pressure on Kentucky state government officials to deny the Ark Encounter the opportunity to participate in a state tourism sales tax rebate incentive program—one that is available to any group that meets certain criteria (all of which the Ark Encounter met and, in fact, way exceeded). The liberal Kentucky governor at the time and the secretary of the Tourism, Arts and Heritage Cabinet bowed to these pressures and decided to deny the Ark Encounter the opportunity to participate in the tourism incentive program. Their action was clearly religious discrimination—blatant viewpoint discrimination. Such attacks on religious freedom are on the rise in America. In response to the state's unconstitutional actions, AiG/Ark Encounter filed a religious discrimination lawsuit against Kentucky—which we subsequently won.

Now, the Americans United for Separation of Church and State, as part of its ongoing attack on AiG's ministry and life-size Noah's Ark project, lodged a motion with a federal court to intervene in our lawsuit with the state of Kentucky. The group wanted to be part of this legal action—on the side of the state—to try to stop AiG from being allowed to participate in the sales tax rebate. AU had found people to be the intervenors: "four Kentucky taxpayers who oppose the use of their tax dollars to promote religion," declares AU, and who "pay taxes, including sales and income taxes, to the Commonwealth."

Sadly, according to AU's court motion, two of the four intervenors are stated to be "ordained Christian ministers." One of them stated, "I am a minister ordained in the Baptist Faith and I serve as pastor at Broadway Baptist Church." He went on to declare, "The tax rebates sought for Ark Encounter would effectively compel me, as a Kentucky taxpayer, to subsidize a religious ministry against my will." This same statement was made by three other Kentucky residents, including a person on the faculty at the University of Louisville and a "minister ordained in the Baptist faith." He stated he has "served as pastor and interim pastor at a number of churches in Kentucky."

Now Americans United for Separation of Church and State knew very well that no one would be compelled "to subsidize a religious ministry against … [their] will." Contrary to popular—but wrong—opinion, the sales tax rebate incentive is not some kind of government grant to help Answers in Genesis in constructing the Ark Encounter. AU has been guilty of helping to perpetuate this myth a number of times on its website and in its dealings with the media. In a press release, AU stated, "in a motion to intervene and a proposed motion to dismiss the lawsuit, filed last night in a federal district court, Americans United says it wants to prevent taxpayer dollars from being used to unconstitutionally finance a religious ministry."

The very wording of the intervenor's motion repeats the tired old myth that taxpayers' money would be used to build the Ark. This was simply not true and was a blatant (and very likely intentional) misrepresentation on the part of AU. Absolutely no unwilling taxpayers would see a single penny of their tax dollars go toward the Ark Encounter. The tax incentive program refunds a portion of the sales tax collected from those who voluntarily chose to buy a ticket to tour the Ark Encounter. In other words, this is new money generated in Kentucky by the attraction itself. The reason for this incentive is that such a tourism project brings a large amount of new money into the state through sales tax, etc. The amount generated at the tourist facility is small compared to the state's overall net gain.

It is completely inconsequential that these four intervenors are taxpaying residents of Kentucky unless they ever choose to visit the Ark and pay sales tax on their tickets. If they don't choose to visit, none of their money (or taxes) will ever be used in any way to subsidize the Ark Encounter. They would not be compelled to "subsidize a religious ministry against [their] will." So, if these Baptist ministers didn't want any of their money finding its way back to Answers in Genesis, then they just should never visit the Ark Encounter. (They probably wouldn't pay to visit anyway.)

Now, AU knew the truth about the sales tax rebate and that no unwilling taxpayers would see their dollars used to build the Ark. So why would AU have these four people claim something that is totally untrue? From what I've witnessed over the years, I suggest AU engages in such dishonest misinformation campaigns for its own fundraising purposes. Over and over again, AU misrepresents or implies things that aren't true—or tells outright untruths. I believe the AU leadership does this because they want to rally their supporters to give them more donations. (By the way, their donors receive a tax deduction; AU is a 501(c)(3) organization and, therefore, it receives a number of tax benefits from the government!)

I suppose that AiG and the Ark are AU's "villains" for fundraising purposes. They wanted their supporters to send them money to help them stop Christians from their free exercise of religion. The repeated attacks against the Ark Encounter from secular groups, the media, and the state of Kentucky highlight that this struggle is ultimately not an earthly, physical battle. Just like when the Creation Museum was being proposed and construction began, AiG is facing an ongoing battle. *For we do not wrestle against flesh and blood, but against the rulers, against the authorities, against the cosmic powers over this present darkness, against the spiritual forces of evil in the heavenly places* (Ephesians 6:12). But I have a message for AU and groups like them. I'm reminded of what Gamaliel said to the people about the work of the Apostles: *but if it is of God, you will not be able to overthrow them. You might even be found opposing God!* (Acts 5:39).

At Answers in Genesis, we do believe that the Creation Museum and Ark Encounter are of God! He called us to establish these creation/gospel outreaches. And thousands visit them every day. Such opposition fires me up even more! It makes me even more passionate about the AiG ministry so we can proclaim the truth of God's Word and the gospel to as many as possible. In His own special way, the Lord has used AU to once again intensify that fire in my bones!

May you also become more emboldened to spread the truth of God's Word and the gospel.

AUGUST 15
1 Corinthians 2:14

Facts and Evidence vs. Worldview

In the ongoing war between creation and evolution, Christians are always looking for the strongest evidence for creation. They are looking for the "magic bullet" that will prove to their evolutionist friends that creation is true and evolution is false. Sadly, this craving for evidence, for that "magic bullet," has led some Christians to be drawn to what we might call "flaky evidence." Over the past several years, some so-called evidence for creation has been shown not to be reliable or, at the very least, questionable for various reasons.

Most well-meaning, informed creationists would agree in principle that things that are not carefully documented and researched should not be used. But in practice, many of them are very quick to accept the sorts of facts mentioned here without asking too many questions. They are less cautious than they might otherwise be because they are so keen to have "our" facts/evidence to counter "theirs." What they don't understand is that it's not a matter of "their facts vs. ours." All facts are interpreted, and all scientists have the same observations—the same data—available to them.

The point is, creationists and evolutionists, Christians and non-Christians, all have the same facts. Think about it: We all have the same earth, the same fossil layers, the same animals and plants, the same stars; the difference is in the way we interpret the facts. And why do we interpret facts differently? Because we start with different presuppositions. These are things that are assumed to be true without being able to prove them. These then become the basis for other conclusions. All reasoning is based on presuppositions (also called axioms). This becomes especially relevant when dealing with past events. Some Christians do claim they have, in a sense, a time machine. They have a book called the Bible, which claims to be the Word of God—the words of the Creator who has always been there and has revealed to us the major past events that we need to know. On the basis of these events (creation, the Fall, the Flood, Babel, etc.), we have a set of presuppositions to build a way of thinking which enables us to interpret the facts of the present.

Evolutionists have certain beliefs about the past/present that they presuppose, so they build a different way of thinking to interpret the facts of the present. Thus, when Christians and non-Christians argue about the facts, in reality, they are arguing about their interpretations based on their presuppositions. That's why the argument often turns into something like:

"Can't you see what I'm talking about?"
"No, I can't. Don't you see how wrong you are?"
"No, I'm not wrong. It's obvious that I'm right."
"No, it's not obvious."

These two people are arguing about the same facts, but they are looking at the facts through different glasses. It's not until these people recognize the argument is really about the presuppositions (the foundation for their worldviews) they have to start with that they will begin to deal with the foundational reasons for their different beliefs. A person will not interpret the facts differently until he or she puts on a different set of glasses—which means to change one's presuppositions. A Christian who understands these things can put on the evolutionist's glasses (without accepting the presuppositions as true) and understand how he or she looks at facts. However, for a number of reasons, including spiritual ones, a non-Christian usually can't put

APOLOGETICS — AUGUST 15

on the Christian's glasses—unless he or she recognizes the presuppositional nature of the battle and is thus beginning to question his or her own presuppositions. And really, God is the One who opens their eyes to see the truth if they sincerely seek after truth.

It is sometimes possible that just by presenting "evidence," one can convince a person that a particular scientific argument for creation makes sense of "the facts." But usually, if that person then hears a different interpretation of the same facts that seems better than the first, that person will swing away from the first argument, thinking he or she has found "stronger facts." However, if that person had been helped to understand this issue of presuppositions, then he or she would have been better able to recognize this for what it is—a different interpretation based on differing presuppositions (i.e., starting beliefs).

Often, people who don't believe the Bible will say that they aren't interested in hearing about the Bible. They claim to want real proof that there's a God who created. They'll listen to our claims about Christianity, but they want proof without mentioning the Bible. If one agrees to a discussion without using the Bible as these people insist, then we have allowed them to set the terms of the debate. In essence, these terms are: "Facts" are neutral. However, there are no such things as "brute facts"; all facts are interpreted. Once the Bible is eliminated from the argument, the Christians' presuppositions are gone, leaving them unable to effectively give an alternate interpretation of the facts. Their opponents then have the upper hand as they still have their presuppositions. In essence, they have rejected the evidence of the Bible itself. However, the Bible states: *The fear of the Lord is the beginning of wisdom* (Psalm 111:10); *The fear of the Lord is the beginning of knowledge* (Proverbs 1:7); *The natural person does not accept the things of the Spirit of God, for they are folly to him, and he is not able to understand them because they are spiritually discerned* (1 Corinthians 2:14).

A Christian cannot divorce the spiritual nature of the battle from the battle itself. A non-Christian is not neutral. The Bible makes this very clear: *Whoever is not with me is against me, and whoever does not gather with me scatters* (Matthew 12:30); *And this is the judgment: the light has come into the world, and people loved the darkness rather than the light because their works were evil* (John 3:19). Agreeing to such terms of debate implicitly accepts the proposition that the Bible's account of the universe's history is irrelevant to understanding that history! 1 Peter 3:15 and other passages make it clear we are to use every argument we can to convince people of the truth, and 2 Corinthians 10:4–5 says we are to refute error (as Paul did in his ministry to the Gentiles). Nonetheless, we must never forget Hebrews 4:12: *For the word of God is living and active, sharper than any two-edged sword, piercing to the division of soul and of spirit, of joints and of marrow, and discerning the thoughts and intentions of the heart.*

Also, Isaiah 55:11 says, *so shall my word be that goes out from my mouth; it shall not return to me empty, but it shall accomplish that which I purpose, and shall succeed in the thing for which I sent it.* Even though our human arguments may be powerful, ultimately, it is God's Word that convicts and opens people to the truth. All of this should be a lesson for us to take note of the situation when we read the newspaper. We are reading someone's interpretation of the facts of world history. There very well could be a different way of looking at the same "facts." One can see this in practice on television when comparing a news network that's currently considered fairly liberal with one that is more conservative.

In all of our arguments, we must not divorce what we are saying from the Word that convicts.

AUGUST 16
Genesis 2:24

What Is Marriage?

On June 26, 2015, the U.S. Supreme Court ruled (5-4) that the Fourteenth Amendment required all states to grant same-sex "marriages." This opened a door that continues to be opened wider and wider. There was no doubt that the then president of the United States, Barack Obama, had been a driving force behind this movement, not only in the USA but also in other parts of the world. As one news report stated, "Ireland was not ready for the massive influx of gay activist funding from America. Sadly, from President Obama down, America has been an aggressive force for normalizing homosexuality, and without American funding and vision, it is doubtful that Ireland would have voted so strongly for such radical change."[80] But here is a question that needs to be asked: Why only two? Why legislate to define marriage as two men or two women? Where did the idea of two come from? In fact, where did the idea of marriage come from in the first place?

There are many articles that have been published using animals to justify homosexual behavior in humans. After all, if humans are just evolved animals, then why shouldn't one look to animal behavior to justify what the human species does? For instance, an associate professor of anthropology at Duke University is the co-author of an article from 2014 that states:

"But in the debate over whether gay marriage, or any other non-reproductive sexual relationship, is 'natural,' no other animal holds more importance.

"Homosexuality in bonobos is not cultural...and wild-born bonobos in captivity—over the past two decades has demonstrated that bonobo sexuality is just part of who they are."[81]

Another article appeared on LiveScience.com in 2011 with the heading "Female Lemurs Benefit from Multiple Mates, Study Suggests." The article stated the following:

"While it may not be as socially acceptable among humans, a female choosing to take multiple mates is a common phenomenon in the animal kingdom. But why the practice of polyandry (a female having more than one male mate at a time) is so prominent is still a mystery in most species."[82] So why not use this behavior to defend a woman having multiple men in a relationship?

So now a question arises: Why has the Western world, until recently, been predominantly unanimous in supporting monogamous marriage between a male and female?

An article in *Scientific American* stated, "Are we humans (Homo sapiens) set up to be set up for life? Well, it's complicated. One study found evidence that women pass along more genetic information to their offspring, suggesting that for much of our evolutionary history, men were fathering children with more than one woman."[83] So, in this interpretation of supposed evolutionary history, monogamy is not the best option. On PBS.org, a 2010 article stated the following: "In the animal kingdom, when it comes to mating, promiscuity is the rule rather than the exception. About 90 percent of mammals have multiple mates, and cheating on social mates is observed in almost all species. In fact, only 3 to 10 percent of mammals are even socially monogamous."[84] According to evolutionists, monogamy is not the rule in the animal kingdom. And if humans are just animals in this evolutionary system, then why was monogamy in our Western world accepted as the norm until recently?

APOLOGETICS — AUGUST 16

Actually, the very idea of marriage between a male and female comes from the Bible. It's God who invented marriage in Genesis when He made the first man and woman, male and female (Genesis 1:27), and told them to *Be fruitful and multiply and fill the earth and subdue it, and have dominion over the fish of the sea and over the birds of the heavens and over every living thing that moves on the earth* (Genesis 1:28). In Genesis 2, we read the details of the creation of man and woman. God made the first man (Adam) from dust and put him to sleep to make the first woman (Eve) from his side. We then read about the first marriage that God, not man, invented: *Therefore a man shall leave his father and his mother and hold fast to his wife, and they shall become one flesh* (Genesis 2:24).

In Matthew 19, Jesus, as the God-man, in responding to a question about marriage, stated this: *He answered, "Have you not read that he who created them from the beginning made them male and female, and said, 'Therefore a man shall leave his father and his mother and hold fast to his wife, and the two shall become one flesh'?" So they are no longer two but one flesh. What therefore God has joined together, let not man separate* (Matthew 19:4–6).

The idea of monogamous marriage being between a man and a woman comes from the Bible. Until recently, the Western world had primarily adopted this worldview of marriage based upon the Judeo-Christian basis. However, the more generations that have been led to believe the Bible is just a storybook and that its account of origins is not true, the more we should expect to see people redefining marriage or abandoning it altogether. And since the younger generations have been told by many church leaders that they can take man's ideas of evolution and reinterpret Genesis, why should they not now be consistent and take man's ideas of marriage and reinterpret the doctrine of marriage in Scripture?

Why is it that we currently see this push for gay "marriage"—involving two men or two women? If there is no absolute authority, and if man determines what is right and wrong, why should there be any limits? Why not three people? Why not four? Why not adults and children? Why not anything anyone desires? Once the door has been pushed open to say that man can define marriage, then ultimately, that door will be pushed open wider. And if humans are just products of evolution, then why not polyamory, polyandry, polygamy, or whatever? It's a reminder of what we read in the Book of Judges: *In those days there was no king in Israel. Everyone did what was right in his own eyes* (Judges 21:25).

The devil deceives us by counterfeiting what God has done—as is being done with marriage. He takes that which is true and then imitates it in such a way that many people are deceived (2 Corinthians 11:14). The only way you won't be led astray by this is to judge what is happening against Scripture. *But test everything; hold fast what is good* (1 Thessalonians 5:21). And Timothy warns us what will happen in this world: *While evil people and impostors will go on from bad to worse, deceiving and being deceived* (2 Timothy 3:13).

Gay "marriage" is not the problem! It's just one of many issues that consequentially come out of a different worldview that has a man-devised foundation. We need to return to the foundation of the never-changing Word of God instead of the ever-changing word of man. *Forever, O Lord, your word is firmly fixed in the heavens* (Psalm 119:89).

> God's people need to return to God's Word and raise up generations who stand uncompromisingly on the authority of the Scriptures.

AUGUST 17
Romans 1:18-23

Intolerant Tolerance

Have you noticed that those who claim tolerance can be the most intolerant of all? Intolerance against Christians' freedom to express their Christian worldview is increasing from secularists who are in positions of authority in education, research, and so on. What happens when you briefly reference a creator (without even specifically explaining who this creator is) in a scientific paper for a secular publication? Well, watch out, for intolerant secularists will become incensed and get the paper censored.

Four scientists (three from China and one from Massachusetts) once published an article entitled, "Biomechanical Characteristics of Hand Coordination in Grasping Activities of Daily Living" in the journal *PLOS ONE*. In their article, they mentioned that "our study can improve the understanding of the human hand and confirm that the mechanical architecture is the proper design by the Creator for dexterous performance of numerous functions following the evolutionary remodeling of the ancestral hand for millions of years." Near the end of the paper, the researchers added, "Hand coordination should indicate the mystery of the Creator's invention."[85]

Now, it's even possible that the authors meant that nature (or evolution) was the creator! Some people use such wording about nature/evolution. When it became known that the word "creator" was used, the outrage on the Internet and social media was swift and fierce. People bemoaned the "unacceptable," "harmful disgrace," "absolute joke," and "sloppy job" of the editors and their journal for allowing this word to go through. Some secularists threatened to boycott the open-access journal, and some editors declared that they would resign if the article wasn't retracted. The intolerance shown by the secularists over the use of the word "creator" in the article was astonishing. The very idea that there could be an intelligence behind life was unacceptable and expressed with such anger that it only exposed how passionate secularists are in defending their religion of humanism and naturalism (atheism). The lead author of the paper, after he was contacted about the firestorm it was creating, reportedly said, "We are not native speakers of English, and entirely lost the connotations of some words such as 'Creator.' I am so sorry for that." After discussion and thought, the journal decided to retract the article.

It's ironic that creationists are frequently accused of not being "real" scientists because they supposedly "don't publish in peer-reviewed journals" (of course, by this common accusation, they mean secular peer-reviewed journals), this recent episode is a perfect example of why this doesn't happen! In their paper, these scientists made very brief mentions of a "creator's" design—in the same sentence mentioning evolution and millions of years—yet there was a vocal demand that if this paper was not retracted, a boycott might be called. It doesn't matter how sound and well-researched your observational science is or how technical the paper might be, if it even dares to mention a word like "creator," it will be censored. This is one reason Answers in Genesis has its own peer-reviewed journal where creationists can submit their articles to possibly be published. Many creationists are not allowed to publish in secular journals, regardless of the quality or soundness of their research and the author's credentials, simply because what they write isn't based on the religion of naturalism! It would immediately be declared "wrong"— simply because it may be influenced by the Christian worldview instead of evolutionary naturalism. Yes, that's the intolerance that abounds and is increasing.

APOLOGETICS

Now, this isn't to say that creationists never publish in secular, peer-reviewed journals. Many of the scientists at Answers in Genesis have been published in secular journals because they do solid observational science. However, they aren't permitted to mention the Creator or that their starting point is God's Word because their work would automatically be thrown out—regardless of the high-quality observational science they present. The intense prejudice and intolerance continually on display by secularists is almost unbelievable. We see this attitude in our personal lives and the culture as a whole. Anyone who dares to think biblically about origins, the nature of marriage, gender, or the sanctity of life is often treated with intolerance, anger, and prejudice and faces ad hominem attacks—just for starting with God's Word!

We saw a similar intolerance regarding the debate I had with Bill Nye "the Science Guy" in 2014. Many secularists openly admitted that they were against the debate because they didn't want creationists to be able to present their teachings to the public. It's the same reason atheist groups constantly attack the Creation Museum and Ark Encounter: They can't tolerate Christians having such a public presence to present their message in a world where so many people have been brainwashed by the religion of naturalism. Secularists don't want their monopoly on education and research to be broken, and thus, they resort to censorship.

Really, this outrage directed against the secular journal mentioned above shows how intolerant most secularists are to anything even remotely Christian. They don't want people to even hear any possibility of something that might support creation. They immediately resort to becoming censors. Now, something is wrong with your worldview if you have to censor other views and not let people hear the alternatives! Whatever happened to freedom of speech and freedom of religion? Secularists ultimately don't want freedom of religion; they want freedom from Christianity. And they want total compliance with and acceptance of their views without question. If secularists were to be honest, they would fully acknowledge that from their perspective, when they die, that's it—they're dead. Then why do they fight so vehemently against God? Why do they care if someone mentions a creator in a research paper? What is it that irks them so much about this? The bottom line is that they know that if there is a God who created them, and if He is the God of the Bible, then He owns them, He sets the rules, and they are accountable to Him. It means, for example, that marriage is one man for one woman, that abortion is murder, that there are only two genders of humans, and so on.

Because the human heart does not want to submit to Christ, secularists actively suppress the truth in unrighteousness (Romans 1:18). Romans 1 makes it clear that God is clearly seen through what He has made (Romans 1:20). But instead of submitting to Him, people reject that truth and do everything they can to ignore His witness in nature and through His Word. *For the wrath of God is revealed from heaven against all ungodliness and unrighteousness of men, who by their unrighteousness suppress the truth. For what can be known about God is plain to them, because God has shown it to them. For his invisible attributes, namely, his eternal power and divine nature, have been clearly perceived, ever since the creation of the world, in the things that have been made. So they are without excuse. For although they knew God, they did not honor him as God or give thanks to him, but they became futile in their thinking, and their foolish hearts were darkened. Claiming to be wise, they became fools, and exchanged the glory of the immortal God for images resembling mortal man and birds and animals and creeping things* (Romans 1:18–23).

Ultimately, life comes down to a heart issue.

AUGUST 18
Romans 10:9

Salvation or Gospel Issue?

Because Answers in Genesis and other biblical creationists take an authoritative stand on six literal (approximately 24-hour) days of creation and a young (approximately 6,000-year-old) age for the earth and universe, some have mistakenly taken our unwavering stand to mean these beliefs are salvation issues.

However, nowhere does the Bible even imply salvation in Christ is conditioned upon one's belief concerning the days of creation or the age of the earth or universe. Romans 10:9 states, *because, if you confess with your mouth that Jesus is Lord and believe in your heart that God raised him from the dead, you will be saved*. It does not state, "If you confess with your mouth the Lord Jesus and believe in your heart that God has raised Him from the dead and believe in six literal days of creation and a young earth and universe, you will be saved." Salvation is conditional upon faith in Christ—not a belief about the six days of creation or the earth's age. So, these are not salvation issues per se. But it is a salvation issue in an indirect sense. Let me explain.

Many Christians, including Christian leaders, believe fossils, the earth, and the universe are millions or billions of years old. I contend that when they accept this timeframe and try to fit millions of years into the Bible, they are violating three vital issues.

An Authority Issue: One cannot get the idea of millions of years from the Bible. This idea comes from outside of Scripture. When a Christian adds millions of years to the Bible and reinterprets the days of creation or tries to fit this extra time into the first verse in Genesis or a supposed gap between the first and second verses, he is allowing fallible man to be in authority over God's Word. Such compromise is setting an example for others that fallible man can take ideas outside of Scripture and reinterpret God's Word to fit these in. Ultimately, accepting this view means God's Word is not the final authority and is not without error. It also opens the door to others doing this with other historical claims of Scripture—such as the Resurrection and virgin birth.

A Gospel Issue: *For we know that the whole creation has been groaning together in the pains of childbirth until now* (Romans 8:22).

Let me set this up with three major points.

1. Genesis 1:29–30 teaches that man and animals were originally vegetarian (before Adam's sin). How do we know this for sure? Humans weren't told they could eat meat until after the Flood in Genesis 9:3. Verse 30 of Genesis 1 (about animals' diet) is worded in the same way as verse 29 (man's diet), so it makes sense that originally the animals were vegetarian too.

2. At the end of the creation week, God described everything He had made as "very good" (Genesis 1:31). Later, death is described as an "enemy" (1 Corinthians 15:26).

3. Genesis 3 makes it clear that the animals (v. 14) and the ground (v. 17) were cursed. And verse 18 makes it clear that thorns came into existence after sin and the Curse: *Thorns and thistles it [the ground] shall bring forth for you.*

Now, the idea that things have been around for millions of years came from the belief that the fossil record was laid down slowly over millions of years, long before man's existence. So, when Christians accept millions of years, they must also accept that the fossil layers were laid down before Adam—before sin. Yet the fossil record contains fossil thorns—claimed by evolutionists to be hundreds of millions of years old. How could that be if thorns came after Adam's sin? The fossil record also contains examples of animals eating other animals—bones in their stomachs, teeth marks on bones, and so on. Also, the fossil record contains examples of diseases, such as brain tumors, cancer, and arthritis. But if these existed before man, then God called such diseases "very good." Taking all this into consideration, it seems obvious that bloodshed, death of animals and man, disease, suffering, and thorns came after sin. This means the fossil record had to be laid down after sin too. Noah's Flood, approximately 4,300 years ago, would easily account for most fossils.

But what does this have to do with a gospel issue? The Bible calls death an "enemy" (1 Corinthians 15:26). When God clothed Adam and Eve with coats of skins (Genesis 3:21), a good case can be made that this was the first death—the death and bloodshed of an animal. Elsewhere in Scripture, we learn that without the shedding of blood, there is no remission of sins (Hebrews 9:22), and the life of the flesh is in the blood (Leviticus 17:11). Because Adam sinned, a payment for sin was needed. Because sin's penalty was death, death and bloodshed were needed to atone for sin. Genesis 3:21 would, therefore, describe the first blood sacrifice as a penalty for sin—looking ahead to the One who would die "once for all" (Hebrews 10:10–14).

The Israelites sacrificed animals over and over again as a ceremonial covering for sin. But Hebrews 10:4 tells us that the blood of bulls and goats can't take away our sin—we are not physically related to animals. We needed a perfect human sacrifice. All this animal sacrifice was looking ahead to the One called the Messiah (Jesus Christ). Now, if there was death and bloodshed of animals before sin, then this undermines the atonement. Also, if there were death, disease, bloodshed, and suffering before sin, then such would be God's fault—not our fault! Why would God require death as a sacrifice for sin if He were the one responsible for death and bloodshed, having created the world with these bad things in place?

One of today's most-asked questions is how Christians can believe in a loving God with so much death and suffering in the world. The correct answer is that God's just curse because of Adam's sin resulted in this death and suffering. We are to blame. God is not an unloving or incompetent Creator of a "very bad" world. He had a loving plan from eternity to rescue people from sin and its consequence of eternal separation from God in hell. So to believe in millions of years ultimately impugns the character of the Creator and Savior and undermines the foundation of the soul-saving gospel.

An Indirect Salvation Issue: Many Christians believe in millions of years and are truly born again. Their belief in millions of years doesn't affect their salvation. But what does it do? It affects how other people, such as their children or others they teach, view Scripture. Christians who compromise on the idea of millions of years can encourage others toward unbelief. For instance, telling young people they can reinterpret Genesis to fit in millions of years sets a deadly example: They can start outside Scripture and add ideas into Scripture. I suggest that such people can, over time, get the idea that the Bible is not God's infallible Word. This creates doubt in God's Word—and doubt often leads to unbelief. Since the gospel comes from a book they don't trust or believe to be true, they can easily reject the gospel itself. Christians who compromise over millions of years can, sadly, encourage others toward unbelief concerning God's Word and the gospel.

The age of the earth and universe is not a salvation issue per se, but it is a salvation issue indirectly.

AUGUST 19
Genesis 1:28

Earth Day

It happens every year. It's really a call to worship, to worship the creation. It reminds me of this passage of Scripture.

For although they knew God, they did not honor him as God or give thanks to him, but they became futile in their thinking, and their foolish hearts were darkened. Claiming to be wise, they became fools, and exchanged the glory of the immortal God for images resembling mortal man and birds and animals and creeping things. Therefore God gave them up in the lusts of their hearts to impurity, to the dishonoring of their bodies among themselves, because they exchanged the truth about God for a lie and worshiped and served the creature rather than the Creator, who is blessed forever! Amen (Romans 1:21–25).

April 22 each year has been designated as "Earth Day." But there is more behind what has been designated as Earth Day than planting trees, reducing pollution, and conserving natural resources. Of course, a lot of what is promoted on this day certainly sounds admirable. Furthermore, Christians are to be good stewards in caring for the earth (Genesis 1:28). God gave man dominion over the creation. Now this doesn't mean to abuse the creation, but to use it as part of the dominion mandate.

And God blessed them. And God said to them, "Be fruitful and multiply and fill the earth and subdue it, and have dominion over the fish of the sea and over the birds of the heavens and over every living thing that moves on the earth" (Genesis 1:28).

There is a lot more to Earth Day than meets the eye. For instance, at some Earth Day celebrations, you will find New Age crystals for people to "channel" through, and material can be found on how to worship "Mother Earth." For many people, this day is really a religious service for the New Age movement (and it's often based on evolutionary thinking). While we may be responsible for caring for the earth, we are not to worship it but to use it for man's good—and to God's glory.

When people reject God's Word, they redefine what God defined. Instead of many taking dominion over the creation, they make the creation have dominion over man!

The founder of Earth Day, Gaylord Nelson, believed: "The fate of the living planet is the most important issue facing mankind." In reality, the most important issue facing mankind is that everybody needs to recognize their sin and need for salvation in Jesus Christ.

Also, the fate of the planet is, ultimately, not in the hands of mankind. While we are responsible for earth care, we are not in control of the earth. It belongs to the Creator (Psalm 24:1), and we are His stewards. We care for the creation, which was once "very good" (Genesis 1:31) but now suffers from the curse of sin (Genesis 3). And we need to be reminded that God won't allow man to destroy the earth, but God will do that at the time He has appointed. *While the earth remains, seedtime and harvest, cold and heat, summer and winter, day and night, shall not cease* (Genesis 8:22).

One of the prominent debates regarding the earth today concerns climate change. Christians need to know how to look at the earth and deal with various questions, such as climate change, through the lens of the Bible. For instance, whether one is a Christian or non-Christian, or even a creationist or evolutionist, all people can legitimately believe that over various times of the earth's history, the climate has changed and will continue to do so.

And certainly, Noah's Flood, which generated the ice age after the Flood, caused considerable climate change that affects us to this day. If people reject the Bible's history concerning the Fall and the Flood, they will not interpret what is happening on this earth correctly. Thus they will make wrong decisions that affect the quality of life for humans.

As stated above, we live in an abnormal world because the once-perfect creation is now affected by sin and the curse: *For we know that the whole creation has been groaning together in the pains of childbirth until now* (Romans 8:22). So, climate can change, and does.

Now, there are disagreements over when various changes (like climate change) occurred on this earth, what type of changes have occurred, and to what extent—and whether humans were responsible and can do anything to reverse the effects of such changes.

As a biblical creationist, let me illustrate how I would deal with a specific issue like climate change, which can serve as a useful example of how we should use biblical principles when we approach any issues associated with Earth Day.

I argue that the earth's climate has gone through a few major periods of change, but in every case, humans did not produce the change. Ever since the Flood of Noah's time, about 4,300 years ago, people have seen an unsettled earth in its sin-cursed state. Many smaller climate changes have occurred and continue to occur (perhaps in cycles). Whether humans have contributed significantly in a detrimental way is just not suggested by the evidence we have at hand.

Of course, if humankind's impact on the climate is small, this does not mean that we should not look after the environment. To the contrary, we need to do the best we can to use the environment for man's good and God's glory as good stewards of what God has entrusted to us. But good stewardship requires us to avoid rash decisions based on inconclusive evidence.

The bottom line is that if people build their thinking on man's beliefs about the past instead of the history God has revealed in His Word, then they will have the wrong worldview and interpret climate changes incorrectly. They will then make wrong decisions that can have disastrous effects on various people. The climate change movement today is an anti-biblical/anti-God religious movement where man is acting as his own god and believes he can save mankind and save the planet.

> This is a worship of the creature, a worship of man, and a worship of the creation based on the religion of evolutionary naturalism.

AUGUST 20
Isaiah 27:1

Dragon Legends

In that day the Lord with his hard and great and strong sword will punish Leviathan the fleeing serpent, Leviathan the twisting serpent, and he will slay the dragon that is in the sea (Isaiah 27:1).

Just as there are many flood legends around the world, there are also many dragon legends. There are sculptures of dragons in various places. The national emblem of Wales is a dragon.

Just as global flood legends have a basis in a real flood, could dragons have a basis in real animals? Is it possible that some of the dragons in those legends might be references to real animals, such as dinosaurs? Now, of course, we can't say for sure, but it is interesting to think about this.

There are many ancient descriptions and images of dragons. Many of these descriptions and images are similar to drawings and depictions of how scientists believe dinosaurs would have looked.

God made all the land-dwelling, air-breathing animals on day six. The word dinosaur refers to a group (we would say about 80 different kinds) of animals that lived on the land. Flying reptiles like Pterodactyls and sea creatures like the Plesiosaur are not dinosaurs.

When did God make all the land-dwelling, air-breathing animals? On the sixth day of the creation week. And He made the first man and woman on the same day.

And God said, "Let the earth bring forth living creatures according to their kinds—livestock and creeping things and beasts of the earth according to their kinds." And it was so. And God made the beasts of the earth according to their kinds and the livestock according to their kinds, and everything that creeps on the ground according to its kind. And God saw that it was good. Then God said, "Let us make man in our image, after our likeness." . . . So God created man in his own image, in the image of God he created him; male and female he created them. . . . And there was evening and there was morning, the sixth day (Genesis 1:24–31).

When visitors come to the Creation Museum they will see a series of exhibits in the Portico about dragons. A sign visitors see asks: "Were Dinosaurs Dragons?" We also call the Creation Museum gift store, Dragon Hall Book and Gift Store. Inside the bookstore people see a carving of St. George and the dragon based on the famous legend most are familiar with. We also have a sculpture of a large dragon.

Now, I've experienced atheists who make all sorts of emotional accusations over what we say about dragons and dinosaurs. Why? Let me give you some background.

A number of years ago, headlines blared about the idea that there must have been a global flood on Mars in order to explain its canyons. Now there's no liquid water on Mars, yet scientists were happy to propose a global flood on the Red Planet. The atheists didn't go ballistic over this idea.

Here is the irony: Secular scientists were happy to propose a global flood on a planet that has no liquid water, but they refuse to allow the possibility of a global Flood on a planet that is mostly covered by water: Earth! In fact, secularists mock those of us who believe in a global Flood on Earth, and they call such an idea "anti-science." Why is this so?

THEOLOGY

Well, the simple answer is that to believe in a global Flood on Earth is to agree, heaven forbid, with what the Bible teaches! And man's unregenerate heart doesn't want to believe.

Reinforcing Genesis 8:21, the prophet Jeremiah says: *The heart is deceitful above all things, and desperately sick; who can understand it?* (Jeremiah 17:9).

To admit that the Bible might be true means to acknowledge that man is a sinner in need of salvation. Not only that, but there are also other Bible teachings they would have to acknowledge, such as marriage is only between a man and a woman; abortion is killing a human being; God owns us and has a right to tell us what is right and wrong, etc.

There is much evidence that confirms the Bible's account of a global Flood. Not only is most of the massive fossil record evidence of the Flood, but there are hundreds of flood legends in cultures around the world that have elements similar to the Bible's account. Past cultures (e.g., Babylonian) also have such legends. This is all consistent with the real Flood account being handed down from Noah through the people at the Tower of Babel. As people spread around the earth, they took this account with them; over time, the account was changed and embellished. Yet there are still elements in most of these accounts that are quite similar to the true account in Genesis.

Globally, there are many ancient descriptions and images of dragons. Interestingly, many of these descriptions and images are similar to drawings and depictions of how scientists believe dinosaurs would have looked. It makes sense: Just as flood legends have a basis in a real event, dragon legends also have a basis in reality—that people saw animals they called "dragons." Furthermore, God's Word clearly teaches that all the land animals (which included what we call dinosaurs), along with Adam and Eve, were made on the sixth day of creation. Dinosaurs and humans lived together. Atheists go ballistic when we say this because they reject the Bible.

Now, secularists mock the idea that dragons (such as those mentioned in Psalm 91:13 and Isaiah 27:1) were real and that some of them could have been dinosaurs. This is because it would mean dinosaurs once lived with people, and evolutionists are adamant in their religion that dinosaurs died out millions of years before humans supposedly evolved.

Now it's fascinating to note that in November 2023, a scientist published an article suggesting dinosaurs might be alive in the present, because they may have evolved on another planet. In other words, these secularists are happy to have dinosaurs living with people as long as they are on a different planet! But as soon as a Christian proposes something that makes sense about dinosaurs, evolutionists attack it as outlandish and anti-science.

Praise the Lord, we have a Creation Museum and other resources that present the truth of God's Word to the public. All this helps overcome the censorship and blatant atheistic, evolutionary domination seen in education, museums, and media.

> **To believe dinosaurs lived with people would mean that evolution and its millions of years are not true. And secularists just cannot allow that.**

AUGUST 21
Ephesians 6:12

Active Duty?

A friend of ours, knowing that my wife and I enjoy watching detective programs on TV, once sent us an intriguing DVD series set in World War II. As we watched the programs, I thought about what is happening today in the Church. You see, while soldiers were at the battlefront overseas in WWII, people back home in England were, by and large, going about their daily business.

The British people knew a war was going on, but they were quite oblivious to much of what was happening. When soldiers came home, some with horrific wounds and startling stories, it was clear that the general population did not know what terrible things were happening on the front lines.

I must admit that sometimes I wonder if the average churchgoer really understands that there is a spiritual war raging around him—in his home, church, school—well, everywhere! How many people are asleep and don't understand this war? The New Testament contains a lot of war terminology. I was particularly reminded of this passage in Ephesians: *For we do not wrestle against flesh and blood, but against the rulers, against the authorities, against the cosmic powers over this present darkness, against the spiritual forces of evil in the heavenly places* (Ephesians 6:12).

And then this instruction follows to make sure Christians are equipped for the battle: *Therefore take up the whole armor of God, that you may be able to withstand in the evil day, and having done all, to stand firm. Stand therefore, having fastened on the belt of truth, and having put on the breastplate of righteousness, and, as shoes for your feet, having put on the readiness given by the gospel of peace. In all circumstances take up the shield of faith, with which you can extinguish all the flaming darts of the evil one; and take the helmet of salvation, and the sword of the Spirit, which is the word of God* (Ephesians 6:13–17).

It seems to me that many Christians are virtually asleep while a battle rages all around them. They go to church, send their kids to school, and come home and watch TV or whatever they like to do—all seemingly oblivious to a shocking and destructive war that is capturing many of their kids and grandkids for the enemy.

Many Christians support the "war" effort abroad through their church's mission fund or by personally supporting missionaries. Many Christians seem to think the battle is only overseas—but the battle is everywhere. I am burdened by the thought that every Christian must understand they are all soldiers in a battle—and they all need to be at the front line and equipped to engage the enemy, who is set to drag them down and capture the coming generations of children.

Statistics show the enemy is winning a battle in our churches. The majority of our young people are walking away from the Church by the time they reach college age. By 2021, church attendance was down to less than 9% for Generation Z. Secularism is on the rise in America, while thousands of churches have been closing their doors each year in the West. And atheists are becoming more aggressive as soldiers for the enemy—out to capture the hearts and minds of children. The casualties are huge.

Through the ministry of Answers in Genesis, we do our best to "fire up" Christians in this battle. AiG also equips believers with the "weapons" they need so they can put on the "whole armor of God" and be involved in this spiritual war that is raging around us more than ever. I suggest that the battle lines are in our homes,

CHURCH   AUGUST 21

churches, Sunday schools, VBS programs, Easter pageants, Christmas pageants, schools (whether public or private), workplaces, courts—in fact, everywhere in the culture.

I believe AiG is a leading supplier of the most advanced "weaponry" designed to counter the enemy's attacks in this era. We work hard to stay on top of the news and trends to provide key information on what is needed for the latest "counterattacks" of the enemy. It's hard work, and it's costly and time-consuming—but what price can one put on a soul regarding eternity?

I praise God for the advances that many believers are making on various battlefronts. We are thrilled that despite the lethargy of many Christians, God has an army of people that is becoming more and more engaged in the battle—and we are raising up "soldiers" to teach and equip their children. We will never know how many people this ministry has been blessed to impact until we get to heaven. But here are excerpts from typical testimonies we receive regularly:

"I wanted to thank AiG from the bottom of my heart for opening my eyes to my terrible sin of compromising the Word of God. Without even realizing it, I had let atheistic, secular views alter my perception of Scripture. After watching a video of Ken Ham's talk on biblical authority, I cried and got down on my knees to pray for forgiveness from the Lord. I have a six-month-old son.... I've realized that the most important thing I can do with my life is to raise godly offspring to influence the world for Jesus Christ. Your website and resources give me inspiration daily, and I thank God for leading me to your blessed ministry."

"Because of what I have learned through AiG, it has changed my relationship with God and with people. I am able to help others that are in my life to understand the truth of God's Word and to stand on the foundations found in Genesis. Because of your work I have learned the truth about God and myself."

"I have a family member going through a really hard time right now and because I understand God's authority and His Word much better now, I am able to help her to stand on God's Word.... She is beginning to see that God loves her and that He wants more for her."

"I was encouraged by my wife to come to church. I was not a Christian at the time, but she was. You were the guest speaker. It was in... about 1992, I think. Your presentation and the material I purchased convinced me that I could trust the Bible from the first word. Shortly afterwards I confessed my sin, accepted Jesus as my Savior and His forgiveness. Your presentation started my way to becoming a Christian. Thank you.... I now teach Scripture in schools and use creation materials to help. It is amazing how most of the kids' questions can be answered from Genesis."

I trust you are as burdened as I am concerning the state of the Church and the great need to reach people with the truth of God's Word—especially its life-changing gospel message.

> Are you an active soldier for the King?

AUGUST 22
Romans 1:16

Scopes 2.0?

In 2014, I debated Bill Nye at the Creation Museum. As I meet people at the Ark or Creation Museum attractions, and as I travel to speak, I often have people tell me they saw the debate and how it impacted them. I have many young people tell me they recently watched the debate. There's no doubt that debate has had, and continues to have, a phenomenal impact. I've also heard from people who have become Christians as a result of the debate. I thought it would be good to share some thoughts about the heavy responsibility of representing Christianity to both the Christian and secular world.

As we approached what some people had dubbed the "debate of the century," "an historic debate," and even "Scopes 2," I wanted to share some personal thoughts that were going through my mind. The Scopes trial in 1925 was a turning point in the history of America, and not just for the creation/evolution debate. The man representing Christianity (William Jennings Bryan), a fine man, sadly did a poor job defending the Christian faith as he went against ACLU attorney Clarence Darrow. Bryan didn't know how to answer questions like, "Where did Cain get his wife?" and he also compromised the Bible with millions of years.

Even though Bryan technically won the trial, in the scheme of things, it was a win for the secularists. The well-publicized trial showed the world that Christians couldn't defend the history in the Bible—and that they were willing to give in to the secular teaching of millions of years. As some bloggers and media reports were comparing this evolution/creation debate to that of the Scopes trial, I must admit I shuddered. You see, I thought of the heavy responsibility of representing Christianity to both the Christian and secular world who would be watching. I truly felt inadequate. Yet I knew the Lord had put me in that position. Many people have told me that "God had obviously orchestrated this debate." Frankly, I did feel the pressure—immense pressure. The debate was on my mind day and night leading up to the big event. Yes, I trusted the Lord, but from a human perspective, it was a very stressful time as I felt the enormity of the responsibility.

I wanted to do the best I could. I wanted to be bold. I never want to knowingly compromise God's Word, and yet I'm not an expert in every area of science and theology. What about questions I may not be able to answer? I also did not see the point of doing such a public debate if the gospel was not clearly presented. I made sure this happened more than once. The pressure only increased when we found out that several Christian colleges and seminaries (and we found out later that a number of public schools and secular universities also) would be live streaming the debate. Also, many churches and organizations had told us they were going to use the debate as an outreach to their communities and would be live streaming the debate at special meetings in their facilities. Many families have told me they made sure their children watched this debate online at home.

The debate turned into something we could never have orchestrated ourselves. Lots of people were praying for me and for the debate. Special prayer groups were formed, but it still was a challenge to deal with the incredible pressure I felt, as I wanted to ensure I made the best possible presentation I could.

As for the debate presentation itself, how could anyone present what needs to be said on such a broad topic of creation and evolution in one evening? Here's what else was fascinating. I received countless emails, Facebook posts, letters (some even by certified mail), phone calls, and voicemail messages giving me advice on what I needed to include in my presentation. If I included all their ideas (over 100 of them!), my presentation would have been 12 hours long!

I knew that after the debate, I'd receive lots of emails, letters, and phone calls telling me what I should have included and what I did wrong! And that's exactly what happened. I did seek counsel from others as I prepared, but I had to do what the Lord had trained me to do and ensure I gave the most powerful presentation I could.

Because Bill Nye was so well known and had largely become a spokesperson for evolution in the secular media, this debate created huge media interest. And Answers in Genesis and the Creation Museum had become publicly known for our stand on Genesis. Also, just before the debate, the Pew Research Center released a headline-grabbing report. Pew presented the results of a survey that purportedly showed that about one-third of Americans believe as AiG does regarding Genesis. In addition, Pew stated that the majority of people believed that God had something to do with the creation of the universe and life.

For Bible-believing Christians, another factor that drove interest in the debate was because biblical Christianity had been losing its influence on the culture over the decades—particularly since the election of President Obama and his pro-gay "marriage" agenda and pro-abortion stance. And don't forget how atheists have been successful in imposing their worldview on the culture. They have successfully removed Christian symbols like crosses, Ten Commandments displays, and nativity scenes from many public places. And prayer, Bible reading, and creation have all but been eliminated from schools.

Another sad aspect was the number of Christian leaders and bloggers who, because they had gravely compromised God's Word with evolution and/or millions of years, were siding with Bill Nye. These Christians would rather have children be influenced by a secularist who publicly speaks against biblical truths and promotes naturalism than to have them listen to someone who believes God's Word in Genesis. What a terrible problem this is in the Church—one of epidemic proportions.

As I prepared for it, I was not setting out to "win" or "lose" but to present the truth of God's Word beginning in Genesis and the gospel, to the best of my ability as the Lord led, having bathed all this in prayer.

In the short time I had to present biblical truths that are confirmed by science, I wanted to honor God's Word. I sought to challenge people concerning the truth of the history in Genesis and the saving gospel message based in that history.

At the very least, the debate saw people across the world talking about God's Word and the creation account more than ever. I pray God will continue to use this debate to let His Word be clearly heard by millions of people. I believe this debate was a significant event in the history of Answers in Genesis—and perhaps in Christendom. Because of our current technologies that have given us social media and the Internet, this debate came at a time when people around the world could hear about it—and the live streaming gave me the opportunity to reach millions of people with the creation/gospel message. I am zealous for God's Word and want to see people saved and won to the Lord. That's what the ministry of Answers in Genesis is all about.

> "For I am not ashamed of the gospel, for it is the power of God for salvation to everyone who believes, to the Jew first and also to the Greek" (Romans 1:16).

AUGUST 23

Hebrews 10:29-31

Creation and Technological Advances

Back in 2013, in an interview with Big Think, a group that describes itself as "a knowledge forum featuring the ideas, lessons, stories and advice of leading experts from around the world," atheist Dr. Krauss explained his remarkably negative view of teaching biblical creation.

He got to the point of calling the teaching of biblical creation a form of "child abuse" and made the fallacious claim that if children are not taught evolution, technological advancement will cease. Such a charge is ridiculous. This is yet another example of a university professor who just does not fully understand science, or if he does, he does not want the public to know how he is portraying science incorrectly. By attempting to connect evolution (meaning "big-bang"-molecules-to-man evolution) with "technological advancement," he is mixing historical science (beliefs about the past) with operational (observational) science, which is what is used to develop our modern technology.

Dr. Krauss is a prolific author and a cosmologist in the secular world. Sadly, he operates from an atheistic worldview and thus accepts evolutionary ideas as fact. He has become known for his book *A Universe from Nothing*, in which he makes his beliefs clear: "In the interests of full disclosure right at the outset I must admit that I am not sympathetic to the conviction that creation requires a creator, which is at the basis of all the world's religions."

In other words, for complete clarity—he is an atheist. Knowing that Krauss is "not sympathetic" to the idea that there is a Creator God, it comes as no surprise that he also opposes outright the goal of parents who wish to educate their children that God created the universe and everything in it. This atheist argues against Christianity and biblical creation in *A Universe from Nothing* and also in his lectures, claiming that the universe already had the potential for creation on its own.

For Krauss, evolutionary ideas play the role of "god" in the universe. We at Answers in Genesis have noted many times before how the evolutionary worldview is really a religion, for it is a set of beliefs intended to explain the world we live in and how it operates without God. Some secularists vehemently voice their opposition to our assertion, but Dr. Krauss' statements praising evolutionary ideas make it all the more clear that evolutionary beliefs comprise a form of religion for those who hold them. By the way, if this is a world "without God or purpose,"[86] why does Krauss even bother to spend so much time and energy attacking Christians?

At the beginning of the Big Think interview, Krauss claimed, "It amazes me that people have preexisting notions that defy the evidence of reality ... and one of them is the notion of creationism." In other words, he believes that biblical creation is absurd. So, he puts forth what he considers to be his superior idea. During a lecture a couple of years ago, Krauss presented his belief about human origins in a quote that was widely circulated. Of course, his view is best described as wild and blasphemous, rather than as a viable alternative to the clear historical account provided in Genesis: "Every atom in your body came from a star. We are all "stardust," he argues—the result of stars "kind enough to explode." That explanation, for Krauss, supposedly makes more sense than an infinite Creator God who not only created the universe but also left an eyewitness account for us in His Word. But Dr. Krauss goes a step further—he ended his statements with outright blasphemy (which was met with collegial laughter from the audience): "So, forget Jesus. The stars died so that you could be here today."

Not only has Dr. Krauss attacked the God of the Bible, denying His existence and His creative work, but he has also directly attacked the atoning work of Jesus Christ on the Cross. His view treats stars as though they are objects of worship because he believes they have given life to humanity. There is a verse that sums up Krauss and his beliefs:

Claiming to be wise, they became fools (Romans 1:22).

While Dr. Krauss' mocking statements about Christianity are infuriating to believers, his ardent atheism makes them an expected (albeit unfortunate) outcome. And, really, what he claims only reinforces the truth of Romans 1:18, that there is a real spiritual battle going on: *… who by their unrighteousness suppress the truth.* The Bible makes it clear that the enemies of God will actively suppress the truth. They will fight with all their might against what they know in their hearts to be true! If this truly were a universe without purpose, why would these atheists bother to fight like this? Why would it matter at all to them?

There has been a rash of statements from evolutionists claiming (falsely) that technological advancement is tied to a belief in evolution and millions of years. In his Big Think interview, Dr. Krauss claimed that teaching biblical creation to students would cost them their competitiveness in the workforce: "Technology and biotechnology will be the basis of our economic future, and if we allow nonsense to be promulgated in the schools, we do a disservice to our students, a disservice to our children. And we're guaranteeing that they will fall behind in a competitive world that depends upon a skilled workforce able to understand and manipulate technology and science."

Operational science is observable, testable, and falsifiable. It is the kind of science one practices when engineering buildings or bridges or when designing computers or space shuttles. Operational science is what advances society technologically. And whether a person is a Christian or an atheist, that person can be a great scientist when using operational science. The evolutionary worldview falls under the umbrella of historical science (or origins science)—ideas about the origin of the universe. Biblical creation is also historical science, but the evidence that we have available to us in the present day and is gathered through operational science actually confirms the biblical creation-based worldview and does not confirm evolutionary beliefs.

Secularists like Krauss, however, want the word *science* applied generally to both operational and historical science without making the distinction. This results in confusion and much misunderstanding, which we believe is a deliberate attempt by secularists to deceive the public into falsely thinking that the belief in evolution and technology go hand in hand. Dr. Krauss will be held to account by the Creator of the universe for his blasphemous words and his intentional misleading of generations of children.

How much worse punishment, do you think, will be deserved by the one who has trampled underfoot the Son of God, and has profaned the blood of the covenant by which he was sanctified, and has outraged the Spirit of grace? For we know him who said, "Vengeance is mine; I will repay." And again, "The Lord will judge his people." It is a fearful thing to fall into the hands of the living God (Hebrews 10:29–31).

Please pray that he repents before he faces that judgment.

AUGUST 24
Proverbs 13:22

Leaving a Legacy

A good man leaves an inheritance to his children's children (Proverbs 13:22).

Legacy! Now, that's a word to ponder. We often think of "inheritance" in terms of money, valuable possessions, or property. But we leave our children and grandchildren so much more than that. When God takes us home, we leave behind a "spiritual inheritance," a legacy that will long outlive us. This legacy can be either positive or negative. What legacy are you leaving behind?

I want to highlight the legacies of four very different people. The first is Martin Luther, the great reformer who is credited with sparking the Protestant Reformation. While certainly not a perfect man (no one is), he loved God's Word and encouraged those of his day to start their thinking with God's Word, pointing them toward the saving gospel. His legacy lives on even today, many hundreds of years later. My wife and I once visited Germany, and we stood by a plaque in the ground purported to be the place where Luther would have stood when he uttered those words, "Here I stand [on Scripture], I can do no other, God help me." Now that's a legacy we all need to leave!

The second person is Charles Darwin, the man credited with popularizing the idea of evolution. His legacy lives on today as his naturalistic ideas have permeated not only Western culture but much of the rest of the world. But his legacy is not a good one. He popularized a philosophy that attacked (and was intended to destroy—but that can never happen, of course) the authority of the Word of God. Sadly, many churches adopted his ideas and reinterpreted the Book of Genesis. This led to an undermining of the authority of God's Word and generations doubting its truth and walking away from the Christian faith. Darwin's legacy is a destructive, evil legacy, and it lives on not only in the secular culture and teaching but, sadly, also in many churches. In fact, Darwin was honored by the church in England and was buried in the church! What a sad indictment on the church.

The last two people are my own parents, Mervyn and Norma Ham. My father and mother are now both home with the Lord. I can say that Answers in Genesis, the Ark Encounter, and the Creation Museum are really a result of their legacy — a legacy that impacts tens of millions of people directly and indirectly each year with the truth of God's Word and the saving gospel.

You see, my parents taught their children to stand unashamedly and uncompromisingly on the authority of the Word of God. They loved God's Word, and in the many places we lived in Queensland, they started Sunday schools and brought in evangelists to make sure children and their families were able to hear the message of the gospel.

When I was a child, I watched my dad read the Scriptures and passionately declare, "Thus saith the Lord!" He was always researching what the liberal critics of the day were saying so that he could find answers and equip us to defend our faith. If he came across an argument he couldn't answer, he would emphasize that our knowledge is nothing compared to God's. He taught us to always go back to God's Word to make sure that we were correctly understanding the passage in its context and literary genre and that our interpretation was

FAMILY — AUGUST 24

indeed correct, because God's Word is true, not the argument against it. Eventually, God's Word would be vindicated, he said, and he was right! It always is!

Since we moved frequently for my father's work, we attended many different churches. If my parents ever heard a pastor teaching something that went against what God's Word clearly teaches, they would take all of us kids, along with a Bible, up to the front after the service and graciously challenge the pastor with God's Word. They emphasized the authority of God's Word and never knowingly compromised on its truth.

The work of AiG, the Ark Encounter, and the Creation Museum is the legacy of this teaching. My parents never had much in the way of material things, but they left a rich spiritual legacy for their children and our children—and our children's children!

And their legacy isn't just impacting our immediate family. It has affected the family of Christ through our VBS, Answers Bible Curriculum, Answers TV streaming platform, thousands of books, DVDs, and other apologetics material that have been distributed through the AiG conferences and website, the gospel-centered teaching and answers at the Ark Encounter and the Creation Museum, and more. These resources have impacted literally millions of people (including many non-Christians), encouraging them to stand on the authority of God's Word—something many have taught their children, who are now teaching their children!

So, I challenge you: What legacy are you leaving behind? Are you leaving a legacy that will long outlive you and be felt in subsequent generations? Will your legacy impact your immediate family, local believers, unbelievers, or even the body of Christ around the world? And what sort of legacy is it?

A strong spiritual legacy doesn't just happen by accident. Be intentional about what kind of legacy you want to leave behind. Let how you spend your time and money speak clearly to what that legacy will be. If you have children and grandchildren, pour into them. Spend time with them. Engage in meaningful, spiritual conversations. Encourage them; share your story; offer wisdom; always point them to Christ and God's Word. After all, there's nothing more important than where each person will spend eternity.

Too many grandparents waste the precious years they have with their grandchildren. Instead of recognizing that their race is not yet finished, they leave the spiritual instruction of their grandchildren completely up to the child's parents or church and instead focus solely on building memories or retirement. But God doesn't say age 65 is when our race is run! We have a calling to declare God's works to our children and their children (Deuteronomy 4:9). You have a unique perspective and wisdom you can pass along to encourage the next generation. Don't waste your latter years!

What will your legacy be?

AUGUST 25
Genesis 18:14

Tapestry of Life

Over the years, I've heard many people relate the Christian life to something like a tapestry. When you examine the back of a tapestry, it looks like a messy jumble of thread. It seems to be random and all tangled, with no apparent image or meaning. But when you turn the tapestry over, you see the beautiful pattern. Likewise, life can be messy, and we find it hard to see the full picture and understand why certain situations occur. Oftentimes things seem to be a messy, tangled web. Yet, when looking back over the years, we can often see the other side: God's miraculous hand has weaved a beautiful tapestry.

My wife Mally and I stepped out in faith in 1979 to go full-time into a creation-apologetics ministry that began in our house in 1977 in Australia. Over the years, we've experienced many difficulties, faced perplexing situations, encountered seemingly impossible roadblocks, and had some heartache. We have had numerous "Red Sea Events"—seemingly impossible situations, yet God opened a way through them. We can now look back and see God's hand as He has weaved a superbly designed tapestry.

The Bible gives us a number of examples that help enable us to understand this tapestry concept, including in the lives of Joseph, Moses, Ruth, Esther, Job, and others. The lives of these biblical figures are a reminder to us that in all circumstances God is weaving a beautiful pattern beyond what we could ever imagine. I was brought up in a home with a godly dad and mum who taught me never to compromise God's Word and to have a heart for the gospel. My father taught me to defend the Christian faith and be prepared to stand for the truth of God's Word regardless of what others say. He inspired me to have a "Nehemiah spirit"—to be prepared to step out and do the seemingly impossible from a human perspective and trust God.

God raised up scholars like Dr. Henry Morris, Dr. Duane Gish, Dr. John Whitcomb, and others to start the modern creationist movement. I was privileged to get to know each of these godly leaders who are now all in Heavenly homes.

The Lord gave me a beautiful wife who has always supported me 100% in this ministry God called me to. Mally was prepared to move our family to America in 1987 as we believe God called us to be missionaries to the USA. I ministered with Drs. Morris and Gish for many years.

Back in Australia, the Lord had given me a burden to build a Creation Museum. I and a board member of our ministry stood on a piece of property and prayed for a Creation Museum in 1980. That passion came about because of my teaching days in the public schools of Australia and seeing my students going to evolutionist museums and being adversely affected. The Lord brought Mark Looy, Mike Zovath, and me together in San Diego, California, and God burdened all three of us to start the Answers in Genesis ministry in December 1993. I met Buddy and Kay Davis in 1994 and saw the dinosaurs Buddy had sculpted. I heard their burden to see Buddy's exceptional dinosaur models displayed for God's purposes. As a result, God used our encounter to intensify my burden to build a Creation Museum.

In the mid-1990s, we faced many battles in getting property for our Creation Museum, even involving a court case. The result was finding a piece of property far better than we ever hoped for, on land that allowed for bigger plans than we first envisioned for a Creation Museum. AiG began preparing the land and building the Creation Museum in 2001. But we didn't have anyone to design the museum's exhibits. Well, Patrick Marsh wrote to us from Japan, indicating that he had heard about the Creation Museum. Patrick asked if he could design the museum's exhibits. He had worked for Universal Studios, the Summer Olympic Games in Los Angeles, and theme parks around the world. So, Patrick moved back to America to use his talents for the Lord. Other artists noticed and followed him here. They, too, wanted to use their talents and experience to spread the truth of God's Word. At about the same time, God brought the marketing firm of Joseph David Advertising into our lives. The creativity of this talented group has taken the marketing of the ministry, museum, and Ark to levels we never thought possible. Perhaps you saw their excellent national TV spots on various cable channels in the USA.

In 2004, we began discussing building a life-size Ark once the Creation Museum was opened. In 2008, we had America's Research Group conduct a general population study to determine if people (both Christians and non-Christians) would visit an Ark. The nationwide results were so astounding that we began master planning the Ark in 2010. Soon, highly qualified artists, sculptors, and fabricators came on board the Ark project to use their gifts and talents for the Lord.

Through one of our board members, we met a theme park consultant, who, in turn, introduced us to Leroy Troyer, an architect in Indiana. Leroy had spent much of his life determining how one could build Noah's ark as a timber-frame structure. Leroy had designed what was, at the time, the largest timber-frame structure in America. Leroy then connected us to Orie and Ernie Lehman, two of the leaders of the Amish crew that built the timber-frame structure in Indiana. After I gave these Amish brothers the vision for the Ark, one of them said, "I believe God has been preparing us all these years just for this." Leroy then introduced us to Colorado Timber Frame, a mill near Denver that had the largest CNC cutting machine, as well as the business contacts to enable us to obtain and prepare timber for the Ark's construction. Leroy said designing Noah's ark and seeing it built was the fulfillment of God's purpose for him on this earth. Leroy is now in his Heavenly home.

Tens of thousands of people were to become a part of the Creation Museum and Ark projects. In addition to the hundreds of people who have become staff members, there have been contractors involving hundreds of their workers. Many other people with special contacts and expertise have come alongside. We have also been blessed with several hundred Ark volunteers and tens of thousands of donors.

I look back at the past years of AiG's history since its inception in 1993 and really the early beginnings in 1977, and marvel at what God has done. And the history above is just a small part of the wonderful threads God has woven into our lives and ministry to make a beautiful tapestry—the ministry of AiG, the Creation Museum, and Ark Encounter.

After walking through the Creation Museum and the Ark, many visitors have asked me, "How did these incredible places come into existence? How did all of this happen?" Our guests find it remarkable that such world-class attractions, which proclaim the truth of God's Word and the gospel, could actually be built.

How do I respond to them? Well, I offer the verse from Genesis 18:14 where the Lord spoke to Abraham when the seemingly impossible was going to happen (i.e., Sarah having a baby at an old age): "Is anything too hard for the Lord?"

> Nothing is too hard for the Lord!

AUGUST 26
Galatians 5:9

The Leaven in the Bread

A little leaven leavens the whole lump (Galatians 5:9).

Many Christians can have evolutionary assumptions that determine how they interpret evidence, and they may not even realize it. Because of our sinful nature, fallibility, and being finite, it is easy to be led astray. Several research staff, writers, reviewers, and editors for Answers in Genesis produced a series of articles on what we call "Young Earth Evolution" (or YEE). You can find them on the Answers in Genesis website. This is because of a sincere burden we have to uphold the absolute authority of the Word of God. These articles were written to warn others that once a door to undermine that authority is cracked open, it can lead to an eventual domino effect. In other words, a small error can result in a major issue over time. It's a warning for all of us.

While the series was running, we received quite a few emotional negative responses with accusations of ad hominem attacks by our authors, claims of false information, and so on. And the reason this happened is because we were warning people about certain creationist scientists who we believe are wrong in some of the ideas they are spreading. We all have feet of clay and need to be reminded that any of us can easily be contaminated by the world's teachings. Christians need to recognize that models, even those based on Scripture, are subject to change. Scripture itself, however, is not subject to change. We all need to acknowledge there is no neutral position in the way people view things. Everyone has a worldview through which they interpret the world around them, and that worldview is based on presuppositions. As Christians, our worldview should always be founded on God's Word.

Now, I earnestly believe, after checking things with others (taking counsel in the wisdom of many, as Proverbs 15:22 instructs) and spending considerable time in discussion with our researchers at AiG, they had found what they call "young-earth evolution" ideas—where creationists have accepted some false evolutionary assumptions that have led to what we believe is error in a number of areas. So this series of articles on "young-earth evolution" had an overarching theme of responding to instances in which we believe some creationist researchers have, for unknown reasons, accepted various secular evolutionary assumptions unnecessarily (e.g., supposed feathers on dinosaurs). We believe this is opening a door to undermine biblical authority and could lead to others accepting more evolutionary assumptions and eventually giving up biblical authority.

Some of the main items we are concerned about are summarized as follows:

1. Many have used terms and definitions influenced by the evolutionary worldview to support the hypothesis that dinosaurs had feathers.
2. Certain creationists are using the term evolution in a way that can cause people to think secular evolutionists are correct in saying the evidence supports molecules-to-man evolution.
3. There are creationists who accept the order of the fossils in the geological record as being the order in which certain creatures came into existence.

Some creationist researchers use the term *evidence* to imply that the supposed evidence found in nature (rather than certain interpretations of that evidence) supports evolution. And despite some of what is stated in these "young earth evolution" ideas, the evidence confirming the creation account in Genesis isn't ambiguous—it's

APOLOGETICS — AUGUST 26

overwhelming. That's why God's Word states He has made it evident to all that He's the Creator, and people are without excuse if they don't believe. But this is not just evidence for creation itself; evidence confirming the Flood and a young earth and universe is also overwhelming.

There are a number of other areas that are concerning, but the above gives a summary. Our scientists/researchers/writers at AiG (as well as others outside our own ministry) understand that we should always be suspicious when the secular world proclaims anything at odds with a plain reading of Scripture. Not all of what they say is untrue, of course, but there is a spiritual component that cannot be overlooked. No secular scientist, no matter how qualified or gentle or sincere they seem to be, is neutral, though they may truly believe they are and try to be. The fact is, God's Word says that man's heart is deceitful (Jeremiah 17:9). And we are warned that the devil blinds the eyes of those who are not Christians (2 Corinthians 4:4). Even scientists who are Christians still have a sin nature that can master them and result in wrong actions or beliefs (Romans 7:19).

Another factor related to our sinful nature is that someone having a PhD from a famous university doesn't exempt them from having their beliefs examined very carefully. And the fact that someone is a friend or a great professor still doesn't mean their views shouldn't be challenged. Not one of us is infallible in what we believe and say. All of us need to be prepared to have our ideas challenged. All Christians need to be "Bereans" and judge everything anyone says against the absolute authority of Scripture (Acts 17:11).

So why make these articles our staff wrote so public? Well, the proponents of YEE ideas have certainly made what they believe and teach very public, and we are aware of people being influenced or confused by their ideas, so this is not a personal issue. One person said this was a Matthew 18 issue for me because I'm the CEO of Answers in Genesis. But Matthew 18 has to do with personal issues between two people in a church situation. This situation is not a personal issue; it's about judging other Christians' publicly stated beliefs against Scripture for the sake of bringing problems to their and others' attention. AiG has also been accused of personal attacks because we have quoted various creationists to detail the views that they are publicly stating (views that impact people). Critiquing their beliefs is not a personal attack. I would challenge everyone to stand back, let go of all the emotions we might have, and consider carefully what our staff have researched and have claimed. And we do take the admonition given in regard to the principle of being a watchman seriously.

The word of the Lord came to me: "Son of man, speak to your people and say to them, If I bring the sword upon a land, and the people of the land take a man from among them, and make him their watchman, and if he sees the sword coming upon the land and blows the trumpet and warns the people, then if anyone who hears the sound of the trumpet does not take warning, and the sword comes and takes him away, his blood shall be upon his own head. He heard the sound of the trumpet and did not take warning; his blood shall be upon himself. But if he had taken warning, he would have saved his life. But if the watchman sees the sword coming and does not blow the trumpet, so that the people are not warned, and the sword comes and takes any one of them, that person is taken away in his iniquity, but his blood I will require at the watchman's hand" (Ezekiel 33:1–6). And let's also take the warning from 1 Corinthians 14:8: *And if the bugle gives an indistinct sound, who will get ready for battle?*

> **So here is my challenge to everyone: Consider carefully what our staff have researched and written and check it out diligently.**

AUGUST 27
Psalm 135:3

What Is Good?

What does the word "good" mean? Many Christians believe in millions of years because they have heard Christian leaders (pastors, professors at colleges, etc.) say that believing in millions of years doesn't matter. But it does matter. There are grave consequences for those Christians who believe in millions of years for the age of fossils, etc.

Does God call cancer "very good"? Would God call the world we live in "very good"? Obviously not. Yet many Christians are unwittingly (or even wittingly sometimes) accusing God of saying cancer, brain tumors, and other diseases are "very good." "Surely not!" you may exclaim. However, I would assert that the majority of churchgoers are doing just that. And it's because of the issue of the supposed millions of years. First of all, some background. What do Christians mean when they say God is love? When they answer this question regarding our Creator God, they use verses like these:

God is love, and whoever abides in love abides in God, and God abides in him (1 John 4:16).

For God so loved the world, that he gave his only Son, that whoever believes in him should not perish but have eternal life (John 3:16).

But what other attributes of God enable us to understand what it means that God is love? For one thing, everything God does is good. Many verses describe God's absolute goodness. For example:

You are good, and do good (Psalm 119:68).

Praise the LORD, for the LORD is good (Psalm 135:3).

In fact, God Himself, in the person of the God-man Jesus, speaks about God being good: *A man ran up and knelt before him and asked him, "Good Teacher, what must I do to inherit eternal life?" And Jesus said to him, "Why do you call me good? No one is good except God alone"* (Mark 10:17–18).

So, the definition of good is related to the attributes of God Himself. And as Jesus is God, let's consider how He displayed God's goodness during His life on Earth. When He came to the tomb of Lazarus, who had been dead for four days, we read: *Jesus wept. So the Jews said, "See how he loved him!" But some of them said, "Could not he who opened the eyes of the blind man also have kept this man from dying?" Then Jesus, deeply moved again, came to the tomb. It was a cave, and a stone lay against it* (John 11:35–38). But why did Jesus weep? Yes, he was grieved at the unbelief of many of the Jews. He was also grieved to see dedicated people like Mary and Martha distraught over the death of a loved one. Yet Jesus knew He was going to raise Lazarus from the dead. He knew that Lazarus, like all people, did not cease to exist when his body died. So why, before He raised Lazarus to life, did He still "weep" and feel "deeply moved"?

I suggest that Jesus, because He is good, was deeply angry at death itself. We know death is called the "last enemy" (1 Corinthians 15:26). The Scriptures tell us that one day death will be cast into the "lake of fire" (Revelation 20:14). We learn that death was the penalty for sin (Genesis 2:17; Genesis 3:19; Romans 5:12).

In His desire to do good, Jesus chose to suffer the penalty for sin and death and conquered death by rising from the dead (Romans 6:9–10). Opposing death is at the heart of God's goodness. After all, He is the Resurrection

THEOLOGY

and the life: *Jesus said to her, "I am the resurrection and the life. Whoever believes in me, though he die, yet shall he live, and everyone who lives and believes in me shall never die. Do you believe this?"* (John 11:25–26).

God's Word also teaches that a bad thing has happened to our bodies. Right now, they are "perishable" (disease-ridden and under the penalty of death), so in the future, there will be a restoration when God's people will receive bodies that are "imperishable," and our mortal bodies will become "immortality" (1 Corinthians 15:53–56). Romans 8 teaches us that the whole of creation groans because of sin and its effects.

For we know that the whole creation has been groaning together in the pains of childbirth until now (Romans 8:22). So it's obvious God would not call death, diseases (like cancer or brain tumors or arthritis), suffering, or bloodshed "very good." Most Christians have been led to believe that it doesn't matter if a Christian believes that the earth was around for millions of years before God created man. But this idea came out of deistic and atheistic naturalism, as people attempted to explain the fossil record without God. Many Christians took this belief in millions of years and added it to the Scriptures, but the fossil record is replete with death and evidence of diseases like cancer, brain tumors, and arthritis in the bones of creatures and animals having eaten other animals. Such diseases, as shown in the fossil record, have been well documented.

Here's the problem. After God created man, He said "everything" He had made was "very good." So, if Christians believe in the millions of years, then they are accusing God of calling cancer, brain tumors, death, and so on "very good."

My point is, you cannot add millions of years into God's Word, or else you make a mockery of God's basic character, including His goodness! Most of the fossil records are from the graveyard of the Flood, not a graveyard of millions of years. Now, I am not saying a person who believes in millions of years cannot be a Christian. Salvation is conditioned upon faith in Christ, not what one believes about the age of the earth.

For by grace you have been saved through faith. And this is not your own doing; it is the gift of God (Ephesians 2:8).

However, for those Christians who believe in millions of years, they are undermining the authority of the Word of God, attacking God's character, and, as a consequence, leading people away from God's Word. And remember, one day, there will be a restoration of all things:

Whom heaven must receive until the time for restoring all the things about which God spoke by the mouth of his holy prophets long ago (Acts 3:21).

What will that restoration entail? If there have been millions of years of death, suffering, and disease on Earth, and God called that "very good," then will heaven be full of death, suffering, and disease? Of course not.

He will wipe away every tear from their eyes, and death shall be no more, neither shall there be mourning, nor crying, nor pain anymore, for the former things have passed away (Revelation 21:4).

> Christians who believe in millions of years need to abandon this compromise position, for only God is truly good.

AUGUST 28
Romans 10:17

Is Genesis Important?

Many Christians, particularly pastors, have insisted that Genesis is not important, as the most important thing to do is preach the gospel. But how do you preach the gospel without the foundational knowledge in Genesis to understand the gospel?

One person told me their pastor told them to go and witness to people but don't use Genesis as it will only cause people to bring up questions. He told them to just tell people about Jesus. But what if they don't know who Jesus is? And if someone tells a person they are a sinner, do they know what sin is? And when they hear that Jesus died on the Cross, do they know who Jesus is, why He died, and why we all die? Where did death come from, and what's its importance?

Besides the fact that everyone needs to understand the foundational knowledge in Genesis to truly understand the gospel, we live in a culture where, increasingly, the younger generations don't understand the Christian terminology used. These younger generations are very secularized, and many have little or no concept of the Christian faith.

Now, Christians celebrate Christ's death and Resurrection every day of the year and especially set aside the time called Easter for special services to emphasize the vital importance of this historic event and boldly proclaim the "good news," the saving gospel. But do people today really understand this "good news"? Can they understand the "good news" if they don't understand the "bad news"?

Now no one can truly understand the meaning of the crucifixion and Resurrection of Christ without understanding the historical events outlined in Genesis 1–3. This is the foundational history that teaches us that God created the first two humans: Adam and Eve. We learn that Adam disobeyed God's instruction, and we call that disobedience sin.

Because we are all descendants of Adam, all humans are sinners. The penalty for sin is death. That's why all humans will die. But because humans are made in God's image, our bodies die, but our souls—the real us—will live for eternity. However, sinners can't live with a holy God, so God promised One (God's Son) who would step into history to become a man—a perfect man—and pay the penalty for our sin by suffering death and then being raised from the dead, thus conquering death. Christ then offers the free gift of salvation to those who will receive it by faith. This is the essence of the gospel.

Two verses in Genesis, in particular, not only promise the Savior but also point to the message of the Cross. Genesis 3:15 is a promise that God will send a Savior who will suffer but conquer the devil: *I will put enmity between you and the woman, and between your offspring and her offspring; he shall bruise your head, and you shall bruise his heel.* Actually, this is the message of the Bible in one verse!

Genesis 3:21 sets up the sacrificial system (the Israelites sacrificing animals), pointing to the One who would die for our sins. The first blood sacrifice as a covering for sin is a picture of what was coming in Jesus Christ. He is the Lamb of God who takes away our sins. He is the ultimate and perfect sacrifice.

Hebrews 10:4 says, *For it is impossible for the blood of bulls and goats to take away sins.* The shedding of animal blood can't take away our sins since animals aren't made in the image of God. Genesis 3:21 is pointing

APOLOGETICS   AUGUST 28

to God's Son who would become a man, the God-man, a perfect man, to fulfill the promise of Genesis 3:15 and die for sin, "since he did this once for all when he offered up himself" (Hebrews 7:27).

How can any Christian reject Genesis as historical narrative or claim that a person doesn't need to believe and understand Genesis to understand the gospel? After all, the gospel is not only founded in Genesis but the essence of the meaning of the gospel is given in the two crucial verses: Genesis 3:15 and 3:21.

When I am teaching, I always think of communication in terms of building a house. One has to start with the foundation, then build the walls, and then the roof. When teaching the gospel, I start with the foundational knowledge from Genesis and then build the walls and roof, the power and hope of the gospel, on top of that.

I believe we should always start with the foundation in Genesis, as even Christians need to be reminded of the foundational knowledge of the gospel. And as I remind people, why did God have Genesis as the first book of the Bible? Well, Genesis means origins, and the first eleven chapters give an account of all the basic entities of life and the universe. Genesis 1-11 is the foundation for the rest of the Bible, for all doctrine, for our Christian worldview, and ultimately for everything. We learn from Genesis the origin of sin, the origin of death, our need for a Savior, and the promise of the Savior.

In a way, we could say that previous generations in the West had, to a degree, an understanding of the foundational knowledge of the gospel. So evangelists could assume most people understood words like sin, etc. But now we have generations who don't have that knowledge as they need the gospel explained from the beginning. However, I would claim we should have always taught the gospel starting with the foundational terms to make sure people did understand it, and to make the point, we should always start with the foundation. Now, having said, that we also need to understand that:

So faith comes from hearing, and hearing through the word of Christ (Romans 10:17).

I once heard that a man became a Christian after hearing God's Word in Genesis 5 concerning the genealogies read. He kept hearing the phrase, "and he died." He realized he was going to die and called out to God to save him.

> Just as that man needed to be taught the gospel from the foundation so he understood it and could clearly communicate it to others, so must all of us learn the gospel from the beginning.

AUGUST 29
Colossians 3:23

Marketing in the Church

I've found that many Christians think "marketing" is something the Church shouldn't be doing. But let's discuss this. Did you know that the average person sees or hears 4,000 to 5,000 marketing messages per day? The secular world is expert at marketing their messages (often anti-Christian ones) to us. Shouldn't we, as Christians, be just as aggressive, if not more so, in marketing the message of truth to the world? Not with a Spirit of timidity, but power, love, and discipline:

For God gave us a spirit not of fear but of power and love and self-control (2 Timothy 1:7).

One day I'd like to write a book titled *Anti-Marketing in the Church*! You see, I do get frustrated at times about something: We have the most important message in the universe to get out to the world, and yet it seems (from my experience interacting with people over the years) that many Christians think it's wrong to "market" things. By that term, I mean actively disseminating/advertising information to the public.

Some Christians have even told me that marketing the Church and its messages is sinful. They appear to associate marketing with a shady salesman who is trying to make a sale, regardless of the product's quality and usefulness.

In spite of how it's sometimes characterized, a lot of advertising is entertaining and technically truthful. Unfortunately, many secularists market a worldview that is contrary to God's intention for our lives. And increasingly we are seeing the anti-Christian worldview marketed as part of advertising items like cars, drinks, etc. As believers we have what everyone needs the most—the saving message of the gospel.

The American Marketing Association defines marketing as: "The activity, set of institutions, and processes for creating, communicating, delivering, and exchanging offerings that have value for customers, clients, partners, and society at large."[87] There is nothing more valuable than the saving gospel message!

At Answers in Genesis, we recognize the Lord has entrusted us with resources like books, DVDs, curricula, a world-class website, radio program, streaming platforms, and so on. Also, the Lord has enabled us to open the Creation Museum and the Ark Encounter, the two leading Christian-themed attractions in the world. But what would be the use of all these wonderful outreaches if people didn't know about them?

The Scriptures in Jude 3 instruct us "to contend for the faith that was once for all delivered to the saints."

I have never been one to be content with merely advertising our resources and attractions. To me, if we are going to "contend for the faith," then we must also publicly challenge those who oppose God's Word in the culture, in boldness but gentleness and respect at the same time:

But in your hearts honor Christ the Lord as holy, always being prepared to make a defense to anyone who asks you for a reason for the hope that is in you; yet do it with gentleness and respect (1 Peter 3:15).

We must also unashamedly challenge those Christians (particularly Christian leaders) who compromise God's Word and lead the "sheep" astray.

Answers in Genesis has publicly challenged church leaders and secularists as we have proclaimed God's Word with boldness. Over the years, AiG has used billboard campaigns to advertise the Creation Museum and the Ark and contend for the faith. We have also used television advertising (both secular and Christian) and other media to advertise various aspects of the ministry.

Now, this may sound radical to some, but I think local churches should be more involved in such bold marketing (and some are). Christians need to have more of a public voice in the culture, particularly as we see so many secularists trying to restrict the free exercise of religion, as guaranteed in the U.S. Constitution! And as we see the secular world aggressively attempting to impose the LGBTQ worldview on everyone.

At Answers in Genesis, we have used an outside advertising agency that has enabled us to professionally and succinctly "market" our resources and message to the world. Our marketing agency describes itself this way: "a full-service advertising, strategy, media and branding agency that specializes in doing mighty things with excellence that effect change in our world."

That's what we want to do: effect change in our world and do it with the excellence we should before our Holy God: *Whatever you do, work heartily, as for the Lord and not for men* (Colossians 3:23).

We have done this in various ways to challenge the increasingly intolerant secularists who have been hammering away at Christians—and specifically aggressively fighting Answers in Genesis and our attractions. You see, we are burdened to reach souls with the truth of God's Word. We want to see everyone come to the Creation Museum and the Ark Encounter and use our resources. We unashamedly proclaim God's Word and the gospel through all we do. We want to reach as many children, teens, and adults as we possibly can with biblical truths.

I want to challenge each of us how we could be more publicly proclaiming the truth of God's Word. How could our churches be doing more to help people hear the most important message in the universe? What marketing methods could we employ personally? What more could our churches be doing?

Now, in doing this, we need to make sure we are not watering down the message of God's Word! I am burdened that some churches have tried to make the Church look more like the world in many ways to attract people. At the Ark and Creation Museum, we have never hidden that we are bold about presenting God's Word and the gospel. And because we have done this with excellence, Christians and non-Christians pour in.

Marketing, used in the right way with the right motives, can be very effective in doing what we've been commanded to do:

And he said to them, "Go into all the world and proclaim the gospel to the whole creation" (Mark 16:15).

And when they saw him they worshipped him, but some doubted. And Jesus came and said to them, "All authority in heaven and on earth has been given to me. Go therefore and make disciples of all nations, baptizing them in the name of the Father and of the Son and of the Holy Spirit, teaching them to observe all that I have commanded you. And behold, I am with you always, to the end of the age" (Matthew 28:17–20).

> **We need to be doing all we can to let the world hear and/or want to hear the message of truth God has for each of us.**

AUGUST 30
Psalm 119:160

The Age of the Earth Is the Issue

I've often found many Christians are quick to speak out against evolution but often fall silent on the age of the earth. It just doesn't seem to matter. But when you talk to an evolutionist, which subject arouses the strongest reaction?

When the secular media visit the Creation Museum to interview me, they rarely ask about biological evolution. Typically, they will start by asking, "Why do you believe dinosaurs and people lived at the same time?" or "What do you believe about the age of the earth?" or even, "Why do you reject science and believe God created the universe in six days only thousands of years ago?"

I believe they start this way because they know biological evolution is impossible without billions of years of history. In fact, I find that secularists are emotionally committed to the millions and billions of years. They almost go ballistic when told the earth is only thousands of years old. I have found that secularists don't really care as much if Christians reject biological evolution. Yes, they still mock. But the minute people reject billions of years, they are labeled as anti-science, anti-academic, and anti-intellectual. The pressure to believe in an old earth is extremely great. And sadly, most Christian leaders have succumbed. Secularists understand something few Christians seem to grasp—biological evolution is not the heart of the issue. "Millions of years" is. If they accept a history timeline as outlined in the Bible (around six thousand years), secularists are forced to abandon evolution, and creation is the only viable alternative. But by accepting an old earth, it is easy for them to justify their rejection of God and the trustworthiness of His Word.

Most conservative evangelical pastors recognize that the Scriptures clearly teach Adam was made from dust and Eve was made from his side. They realize how hard it would be to explain the gospel without referring to the origin of sin and death in Genesis. However, many such pastors do not consider the age of the earth an important issue. A U.S. poll found that more pastors and other Christian leaders believe in millions of years than believe in biological evolution or theistic evolution. LifeWay reported about its December 2011 survey of 1,000 Protestant pastors: "Pastors overwhelmingly believe that God did not use evolution to create humans and think Adam and Eve were literal people... [but] ministers [were] almost evenly split on whether the earth is thousands of years old."[88]

My 2011 book *Already Compromised* details the view of Christian college presidents, vice presidents, heads of religion or Bible departments, and heads of science departments. Overall, the majority believe the earth is billions of years old. Almost 78% of the heads of the religion departments are old earthers. So it is not surprising that most pastors accept an old earth.

All of the compromised positions on Genesis (the gap theory, framework hypothesis, theistic evolution, day-age theory, progressive creation, etc.) have one thing in common: They attempt to fit millions of years of history into Genesis 1. The major reason so many pastors, Christian academics, and Christians do not believe in six literal (24-hour) days of creation is ultimately their desire to account for the supposed billions of years. Such compromise places mankind's fallible dating methods—his beliefs about the past—in authority over God's Word. This opens the door to undermining biblical authority. Such compromise does not negate one's salvation, but it does affect how coming generations view Scripture.

APOLOGETICS   AUGUST 30

This compromise also causes a generational loss of biblical authority which is a major reason many young people doubt the Bible and ultimately walk away from the Church. This was documented in research published in my book *Already Gone* in 2009, which showed clearly why and when the Church is losing about two-thirds of the next generation.

"Millions of years" flies directly in the face of the history God's Word clearly reveals. Ultimately, belief in millions of years attacks the character of God. If the fossil-bearing layers were laid down slowly over millions of years, then these layers contain the remains of dead creatures, fossil thorns, evidence of diseases (e.g., brain tumors), and animals eating each other—all before humans appeared on the planet.

How can a Christian fit this into God's Word, which tells us that everything was "very good" after God finished creating man? How can a good God call brain tumors "very good"? How could such history fit with Scripture, which tells us that thorns came after sin and that humans and animals were originally all vegetarians?

The belief in billions of years was originally postulated by materialists, atheists, and deists in an attempt to explain the geological record by natural processes rather than by a global Flood, as revealed in the Bible. Naturalism is the anti-God religion of this age, and millions of years is foundational to its false idea of biological evolution. George Wald, a biochemist and Nobel prize winner, in 1954 explained why a long period of time is so important to evolution's story: "Time is in fact the hero of the plot. The time…is of the order of two billion years. What we regard as impossible on the basis of human experience is meaningless here. Given so much time, the 'impossible' becomes possible, the possible probable, and the probable virtually certain. One has only to wait: time itself performs the miracles."[89]

One figure who probably did more than anyone else to popularize belief in millions of years is Charles Lyell, who published his ideas in *The Principles of Geology* (1830). Charles Darwin took Lyell's work with him in his five-year voyage aboard the ship *HMS Beagle*. Lyell's book convinced Darwin and gave him the foundation to propose millions of years of small changes in biology.

If you visit museums, zoos, and amusement parks like Disneyland, EPCOT, and Universal Studios, you will hear and see the phrase "millions of years" much more than the word evolution. You only have to watch one or two documentaries on Discovery Channel, the Learning Channel, or the History Channel to hear the words "millions [or billions] of years" multiple times. Even the leading children's museum in the USA, the Indianapolis Children's Museum, has numerous signs in its dinosaur exhibit with the words "millions of years." But one will be hard-pressed to find the word evolution.

The idea of millions of years is like a disease. Biological evolution is merely the symptom. Many Christians are treating the symptoms but fail to recognize the source of the disease.

In Scripture, God has given us the infallible record of the true history of the universe, which shows how He has been working out His plan to redeem sinners since Adam brought death into the world around six thousand years ago.

The sum of your word is truth, and every one of your righteous rules endures forever (Psalm 119:160).

    Time may be the hero of the secular evolutionary plot, but the hero of real events is God.

AUGUST 31
Matthew 5:13

Missionaries to a Pagan Culture

Before Mally and I moved to the USA in 1987 with our children, our church in Australia set us apart as missionaries in "creation evangelism." Our church actually saw us as missionaries to the USA. Over the years, I would often begin my presentations in U.S. churches with something like, "My wife and I, and our children, moved to America as missionaries to a pagan culture." Usually, people laughed at the comment. After all, there are so many churches, Bible colleges, Christian radio stations, etc., that one wouldn't normally think of someone being called to be "a missionary to the USA." Americans tend to think of missionaries as those people who go to other countries where there isn't much of a Christian influence.

Today, when I tell an audience that Mally and I came to America as missionaries to a pagan country, I don't hear as many people laughing. Instead, I sometimes hear words like "thank you" or "amen," and so on. You see, more and more people in the Church today are recognizing that America, like the rest of the West, is becoming increasingly pagan every day! Our nations have all but abandoned God and His Word. In fact, in many ways, these nations have shaken their fists at God in defiance of His Word. They are redefining everything God ordained and created, redefining marriage, gender, life, family, and the list goes on. Since the call that God placed in our hearts back in the 1980s, I have always said that our calling was not primarily to the culture as a whole but to the Church. I earnestly believe the call on our lives was to be missionaries to the Church, and our first priority was to call the Church back to the authority of the Word of God. There has been so much compromise in the Church, and much of the Western Church is lukewarm to basically dead.

God has ordained the Church for the edification of believers and for God's people to be the salt and light in the culture so that people would hear the truth of God's Word and the gospel. But the Scripture states the following: *You are the salt of the earth, but if salt has lost its taste, how shall its saltiness be restored? It is no longer good for anything except to be thrown out and trampled under people's feet* (Matthew 5:13). Salt loses its flavor when it is contaminated. Sadly, much of the "salt" in the Western Church today is contaminated with secular beliefs such as evolution and millions of years, and now consequentially, impacted by the LGBTQ movement. Much of the Church either rejects or doesn't teach Genesis 1–11 as literal history. As a result, these churches aren't wokeproof and often get soft on the LGBTQ worldview. When a church stands on a literal Genesis 1–11, they are basically wokeproof.

On my first speaking tour of America in 1980, I came to what I considered to be a great Christianized nation (especially compared to my homeland of Australia, which was quite pagan). But while there was significant Christian influence in the country in 1980, I discovered that America had many Christian leaders who had either compromised God's Word in Genesis with millions of years and/or evolution, or else they did not think it even mattered what people believed concerning Genesis. I have been speaking in the USA for over 30 years now with this major message: God's people need to stand on the truth of God's Word beginning in Genesis 1:1 and not compromise with the secular religion of the day—evolution and millions of years. The more this compromise runs rampant in the Church, the more we will see people doubt God's Word in Genesis and be put on a slippery slope to unbelief about the Christian faith, the more they will be impacted by the "woke" movement and go soft on biblical doctrines like marriage.

In fact, I've often said that we need to call for a new reformation in the Church, that Christian leaders and God's people need to repent of compromise and return to the full authority of the Word of God. Really, the ministry of Answers in Genesis was set up as a missionary outreach to impact the Church first and then the world by presenting the message of the authority of the Word of God beginning in Genesis and the salvation message. I've often asked my seminar audiences, "How can we tell the world that they need to believe God's Word when much of the Church is saying something like, 'Well, we don't have to believe in Genesis'?" That point really hit home to me when I first heard the news about BioLogos, an organization dedicated to promoting theistic evolution (or "evolutionary creation") to the Church founded by ardent Theistic Evolutionist Francis Collins. This group was set up to infiltrate the Church with compromise teaching. This goal of BioLogos was demonstrated in an announcement years ago that accompanied the appointment of its president and a senior scholar. The two new appointees to this pro-evolution group were from two well-known Christian colleges!

Dr. Deborah Haarsma, a professor of physics and astronomy at Calvin College in Grand Rapids, Michigan (a Christian college) for many years, took on the role of president of BioLogos. Dr. Jeffrey Schloss, professor of biology at Westmont College in Santa Barbara, California (also a Christian college), came on as the senior researcher. Dr. Haarsma is well known for her shocking treatment of God's Word in Genesis. She had been actively pursuing her mission of rewriting the word of God as a co-director of The Ministry Theorem, a program of Calvin Seminary and Calvin College that helped pastors "engage" their congregations with evolutionary ideas. Actually, I think it's helpful to show you what Dr. Haarsma believes in her own words. In a video of one of her presentations, she states the following about Genesis 1: "[It] is a message of how God interacts with His creation and of our role in creation. It's several key theological messages. But it is not a message about the how and the when of creation. God didn't bother to teach the ancient Hebrews that the world was actually round. He didn't bother to teach them that it was actually atmosphere in the sky instead of a solid sky dome. He let them keep believing that. He accommodated the message to where they were at. And I find that so comforting to us today that God is willing to accommodate His message to our limited understanding. We don't have to have a perfect scientific understanding of the world to get God's message for us. And for that reason, I don't think we need to draw from Genesis 1 a chronology of how God created, a timeline of specific physical events, but rather these very important theological views."

She is actually claiming that God is not telling the truth—that He "accommodates" His message to where people are at. She based her interpretation of Genesis on a secular worldview! Dr. Schloss also wholeheartedly accepts evolutionary ideas. Drs. Haarsma and Schloss are not promoting evolutionary ideas alone. What they're doing is helping to promote the blending of Christianity with an atheistic religion. As a consequence, they are undermining the authority of the Word of God with a form of syncretism.

The evolutionary worldview is the secularists' primary way of explaining the world without God. Two professing Christians, employed by two Christian colleges, were appointed leaders in the charge against biblical authority. The mission of Drs. Haarsma and Schloss, and BioLogos as a whole, is absolutely destructive to the Church. In fact, I would say their mission is a part of the enemy within the Church.

> Our Western nations need their own internal missionaries to call the Church and culture back to the authority of the Bible.

SEPTEMBER 1

Titus 1:15

Secular Moral Foundations? Part 1

The war between Hamas and Israel is in daily headlines. We hear many non-Christians making statements about how evil Hamas is. And they are right. But ultimately, how does one decide what is evil?

Secularists and atheists frequently accuse Christians of behaving "immorally" and religion of being "evil." But such objections to religion bring up an interesting question: How do secular humanists or atheists define evil and morality, and by what authority do they make such statements?

For the atheist or secular humanist, there is no foundation for morality besides his or her own subjective opinion. These individuals often throw around words such as *evil, immoral, moral,* or *ethical,* often in the context of Christian religion or Christian individuals. They will say things such as "religion is evil," or that teaching creation to children is "child abuse," but what do they mean by these phrases?

In their worldview, what makes anything immoral or wrong? Really, it boils down to nothing more than their opinion. They believe that something is wrong, and therefore, it must be. But who is to say that their opinion is the right one? After all, there are many different opinions on what is right and wrong. Who decides which one is right and which one is wrong?

That atheism and secular humanism cannot provide a foundation for morality is a strong argument. Here are a few responses that you may hear if you bring up this objection.

Some atheists argue that morality is simply decided by society. For example, here in America, our society has decided that murdering an innocent human being is wrong and therefore, that action is morally wrong. But this kind of thinking simply does not hold up to scrutiny.

Society often changes its opinion. One clear example of this is in regard to gay "marriage." What was considered morally wrong by most of society is now legal, applauded, and celebrated by some groups. In this view, homosexual behavior went from being morally wrong to being morally acceptable. What if our society decides that murder is acceptable, as it did in the case of *Roe v. Wade* when America legalized the killing of unborn children? Does murder suddenly become morally acceptable too? What about adultery, stealing, lying, or any other manner of morally reprehensible actions? Would the atheist or humanist accept a society that decides that society can kill all atheists and humanists? If society is the moral compass, then the compass never points north but rather jumps all over the place and changes with every generation.

Also, if society determines morality, how can one society tell another society what is right or wrong? Most people would agree that the abhorrent actions of the Nazi death camps were morally wrong. But why? Nazi Germany decided as a society that these actions were morally acceptable. What right does our society have to judge their society if morality is simply a societal preference?

Or what about certain radical Muslim groups? Few would agree that blowing up innocent civilians, slaughtering hundreds of people from other religious groups, kidnapping and enslaving young women, or using children as suicide bombers is morally acceptable. Yet if morality is simply a societal preference, what right does our society have to tell their society that their actions are wrong and must be stopped?

APOLOGETICS

The consistent atheist or humanist can say nothing if that is the ethic a society has decided is right. In this view, the atheist, based on his arbitrary opinion, might not agree with their ethic, but he has no rationale to say anything or try to put a stop to it. If morality is simply decided by societal preference, it fails to make any sense and becomes arbitrary, subject to change by time and culture.

The problem only gets worse when you break it down to a personal level. Some secularists will argue that morality is an individual decision and no one has the right to tell another person what to do (this is called "autonomous human reason"). Of course, the irony of such a statement should be evident. By saying that no one should tell someone else what to do, they have just told someone else what to do! If secularists really believed this, then they couldn't say "religion is evil" in the first place since it is not their place to say.

If this view of morality is true, then our justice system cannot exist. After all, why should one judge, legislative assembly, or government body impose their view of morality on another individual? If stealing, killing, raping, or abusing is right for one individual, what gives another individual the right to say that view of morality is wrong?

Now, this personal morality or human reasoning view stems from the idea that people are basically good and that, left on our own, humans tend to do right and not wrong (again, who defines right and wrong?). But humans aren't basically good! Human experience shows that, throughout history, humans have committed atrocities, even in our supposedly enlightened Western world. The Bible describes the fallen human heart this way:

The heart is deceitful above all things, and desperately sick; who can understand it? (Jeremiah 17:9).

And when the Lord smelled the pleasing aroma, the Lord said in his heart, "I will never again curse the ground because of man, for the intention of man's heart is evil from his youth. Neither will I ever again strike down every living creature as I have done" (Genesis 8:21).

To the pure, all things are pure, but to the defiled and unbelieving, nothing is pure; but both their minds and their consciences are defiled (Titus 1:15).

From human experience, we seem to naturally and intuitively know that actions such as murder, stealing, and child abandonment are wrong for all people everywhere. But where does this intuitive sense come from?

Autonomous human reason simply does not provide a sufficient foundation for morality.

SEPTEMBER 2

Romans 3:23

Secular Moral Foundations? Part 2

Evolutionists, by necessity, believe that morality (along with everything else) is simply the result of evolution. Somehow, after billions of years of death, struggle, atrocities, disease, and suffering, man realized that we should strive to do the opposite! Mankind should oppose the survival of the fittest and try to be moral. In their worldview, we are nothing more than highly evolved animals and our brains are nothing more than chemical reactions. We are simply the product of our DNA.

This view raises the question of how the strictly naturalistic process of evolution leads to the development of an immaterial, absolute moral conscience that somehow applies to all people everywhere. What happens if this conscience evolves? Does morality change again? And furthermore, if we are simply animals, why are we held morally accountable? After all, we certainly don't hold animals accountable for their actions. No lion court exists to punish lions that maul gazelles to death and then eat them. No one jails a female cuckoo for abandoning her babies or forces male rabbits to pay child support. These are simply the things animals in this cursed world do, and no one faults them for doing it. If we are just animals, what makes humans so different?

The problem gets even worse if you argue that our brains are nothing more than random chemical reactions and that we are at the mercy of our DNA. If we are just programmed DNA, then how can we be held accountable for any of our decisions? Because there is no free will in a view such as this, there is no accountability for decisions or actions.

Morality simply cannot be the result of naturalistic processes over millions of years. This view does not hold up to close examination, and really, it is the opposite of what we know to be true from human experience and the Bible's teachings.

When faced with their worldview's inability to provide a foundation for morality, many atheists respond by claiming that you don't have to be religious to be moral. It's true that plenty of atheists are moral citizens. But those who argue this way have missed the point. Atheists certainly can be moral. Actually, starting with a biblical worldview, this is to be expected. God has put His law in all our hearts (Romans 2:15), so even atheists, who claim that they don't believe in the Creator God, can adhere to this law and be moral. The point is that they have no foundation for this morality in their own worldview. They have no basis for saying something is right or wrong, moral or immoral.

Secular humanism and atheism cannot account for the existence of morality in their worldview. But what about the biblical view? According to God's Word, humans were specially created in the image of God (Genesis 1:27). We are not animals, nor are our brains simply chemical reactions. As He has from the very beginning, our Creator holds us accountable for our actions (Genesis 2:17) and expects us to choose and distinguish between right and wrong.

As Creator, only God has the authority to tell us what is right and what is wrong. And this standard is not arbitrary. It is based on the unchanging character of the righteous, holy, and perfect Judge of the universe. For example, all murder is wrong because God has created us in His own image and forbids the taking of a human life (e.g., Genesis 9:6; Exodus 20:13; Romans 13:9).

APOLOGETICS — SEPTEMBER 2

God, the Creator, has given us the Bible, His revealed Word, which clearly lays out what is morally acceptable and what is not. The Creator provides a firm foundation on which we can base our morality. What is more, God has placed His law in all our hearts (Romans 2:15). We know right from wrong because of the conscience that God has given all of humanity. We are held accountable to Him for our actions and decisions (Romans 2:1–16) based on this knowledge of Him that we have.

It should be obvious to anyone who has lived in this world that no one fully obeys God's law. We all fall short of God's perfect standard, as Scripture makes abundantly clear (Romans 3:23). We even fall far short of imperfect human standards! Why is this? Genesis gives us the answer.

The first two people, Adam and Eve, were created morally perfect, but they chose to rebel against their Creator (Genesis 3). No longer were they morally perfect; now they had a sin nature, which they passed on to each of their children (Romans 5:12–21). All of their descendants — every person on earth — are now slaves to sin (John 8:34) and in rebellion against God.

The Bible provides a firm foundation for morality and provides the answer to why all people have a moral conscience and why we cannot live up to this knowledge of morality. But there's more. The ultimate solution is the gospel.

Not only does the Bible explain why there is a universal moral code, why everyone knows it, and why no one can consistently live up to it, but the Bible also provides the solution to our shortcomings.

When Adam and Eve sinned, they received the penalty that their rebellion deserved: death (Genesis 2:17). We all sinned and continue to sin in Adam, so we all deserve the penalty of death (Romans 5:12). No matter how hard we try, we can never live up to God's perfect moral standard (Romans 3:23). We certainly are in a dire position, deserving nothing but condemnation and death.

But because of His great love for us and according to His mercy (Ephesians 2:4), the Creator came to Earth as the God-man, a descendant of Adam just like us (1 Corinthians 15:45). But unlike us, He perfectly kept God's law (Romans 10:4). He then chose to become sin for us (2 Corinthians 5:21), taking the sins of the whole world upon Himself when He died on the Cross (1 John 2:2).

He took death — the penalty that we all deserve — for us (Romans 4:25, 5:8). But He didn't stay dead. He rose victoriously from the grave, defeating death (2 Timothy 1:10; Hebrews 2:14). He now offers forgiveness and eternal life to all who will repent (Acts 3:19), believe (John 3:18), and trust in Him (Romans 10:9).

> **Only the Bible provides a consistent foundation for morality that applies to all people everywhere, and only the Bible provides the hope that we need through the person of Jesus Christ, our Creator, Savior, and Lord.**

SEPTEMBER 3
Genesis 2:10-14

Where Is the Garden of Eden?

Most Bible commentaries state that the site of the Garden of Eden was in the Middle East, but what does Scripture actually tell us? Exactly where was the Garden of Eden? Many times, we just believe something because someone told us or we read it somewhere. But as Christians, we should always be reminded to be like the Bereans described in the book of Acts:

Now these [Berean] Jews were more noble than those in Thessalonica; they received the word with all eagerness, examining the Scriptures daily to see if these things were so (Acts 17:11).

Now, most Bible commentaries state that the site of the Garden of Eden was in the Middle East, situated somewhere near where the Tigris and Euphrates Rivers are today. This is based on the description given in Genesis 2:10–14:

A river flowed out of Eden to water the garden, and there it divided and became four rivers. The name of the first is the Pishon. It is the one that flowed around the whole land of Havilah, where there is gold. And the gold of that land is good; bdellium and onyx stone are there. The name of the second river is the Gihon. It is the one that flowed around the whole land of Cush. And the name of the third river is the Tigris, which flows east of Assyria. And the fourth river is the Euphrates.

Even the great theologian John Calvin struggled over the exact location of the Garden of Eden. In his commentary on Genesis, he states:

"Moses says that one river flowed to water the garden, which afterwards would divide itself into four heads. It is sufficiently agreed among all, that two of these heads are the Euphrates and the Tigris; for no one disputes that ... (Hiddekel) is the Tigris. But there is a great controversy respecting the other two. Many think that Pishon and Gihon are the Ganges and the Nile; the error, however, of these men is abundantly refuted by the distance of the positions of these rivers. Persons are not wanting who fly across even to the Danube; as if indeed the habitation of one man stretched itself from the most remote part of Asia to the extremity of Europe. But since many other celebrated rivers flow by the region of which we are speaking, there is greater probability in the opinion of those who believe that two of these rivers are pointed out, although their names are now obsolete. Be this as it may, the difficulty is not yet solved. For Moses divides the one river which flowed by the garden into four heads. Yet it appears, that the fountains of the Euphrates and the Tigris were far distant from each other."[90]

Calvin recognized that the description given in Genesis 2 concerning the location of the Garden of Eden does not fit with what is observed regarding the present Tigris and Euphrates Rivers. God's Word makes it clear that the Garden of Eden was located where there were four rivers coming from one head. No matter how one tries to fit this location in the Middle East today, it just can't be done. Interestingly, Calvin goes on to say: "From this difficulty, some would free themselves by saying that the surface of the globe may have been changed by the deluge...."

This is a major consideration that needs to be taken into account. The worldwide, catastrophic Flood of Noah's day would have destroyed the surface of the earth. If most of the sedimentary strata over the earth's

APOLOGETICS — SEPTEMBER 3

surface (many thousands of feet thick in places) is the result of this global catastrophe as creationists believe, then we would have no idea where the Garden of Eden was originally located — the earth's surface totally changed as a result of the Flood. Not only this, but underneath the region where the present Tigris and Euphrates Rivers are located, there exists hundreds of feet of sedimentary strata — a significant amount of which is fossiliferous. Such fossil-bearing strata had to be laid down at the time of the Flood. Also, creationists believe there was one major continent before the Flood, which was totally changed by various processes during and after the Flood. The continents today bear little or no resemblance to what existed before the Flood. Therefore, no one can logically suggest that the area where the present Tigris and Euphrates Rivers are today is the location of the Garden of Eden, for this area is sitting on Flood strata containing billions of dead things (fossils). The perfect Garden of Eden can't be sitting on billions of dead things before sin entered the world! This being the case, the question then is, Why are there rivers named Tigris and Euphrates in the Middle East today?

In my native country of Australia, one will recognize many names that are also used in England (e.g., Newcastle). The reason is that when the settlers came out from England to Australia, they used names they were familiar with in England to name new places/towns in Australia. Another example is the names given to many rivers in the United States. There is the Thames River in Connecticut, the Severn River in Maryland, and the Trent River in North Carolina — all named for prominent rivers in the United Kingdom.

In a similar way, when Noah and his family came out of the ark after it landed in the area we today call the Middle East (the region of the Mountains of Ararat), it would not have been surprising for them to use names they were familiar with from the pre-Flood world (e.g., Tigris and Euphrates) to name places and rivers, etc., in the world after the Flood.

Ultimately, we don't know where the Garden of Eden was located. To insist that the Garden was located in the area around the present Tigris and Euphrates Rivers is to deny the catastrophic effects of the global Flood of Noah's day and to allow for death before sin. That's why I believe this question is important. We live at a time where secularists deny a global Flood, and sadly, many Christians have relegated Noah's Flood to some local event because they've been impacted by the belief in millions of years.

> **Let's be Bereans and make sure we test our beliefs against the absolute authority of the Word of God.**

SEPTEMBER 4
1 Chronicles 12:32

Reformation Needed

God's people need to have an understanding of *the times*!

Back in 2014, I read a very disturbing (though sadly not surprising) report. It was from the group Association for Christian Retail, summarizing research by the Hartford Institute for Religion Research. The report stated: "As many as 200,000 churches of approximately 350,000 in the U.S. are in stagnation or decline and more than 4,000 close every year…. [W]hile 40% of Americans say they attend church weekly, only 20% do, based on actual attendance. Only some small churches (with less than 200 attendance) and some mega-churches report growth." The article continued: "Churches in the middle are either stagnant or declining, research shows. Most mega church growth is from absorbing attendance of closed churches. It's not caused by growth of the Christian faith."[91]

At AiG, we have been sounding the "alarm bells" for years now in regard to sad trends in the Church. Back in 2009, we published the book *Already Gone*, detailing a survey we commissioned from America's Research Group (ARG) into why two-thirds of young people are leaving the Church by college age.

In essence, what ARG and AiG found is that undermining the authority of God's Word beginning in Genesis (including through rampant compromise with evolution/millions of years) has greatly contributed to generations of young people in the Church doubting God's Word — and then walking away in unbelief. We have now seen a catastrophic generational loss from the Church. In 2021, church attendance by Generation Z was down to less than 9%. Churches and Christian organizations continue to shut their doors.

Mission statement of Answers in Genesis

Goal:	To support the Church in fulfilling its commission.
Vision:	Answers in Genesis is a catalyst to bring reformation by reclaiming the foundations of our faith which are found in the Bible, from the very first verse.
Mission:	We proclaim the absolute truth and authority of the Bible with boldness. We relate the relevance of a literal Genesis to the Church and the world today with creativity. We obey God's call to deliver the message of the gospel, individually and collectively.
Core Values	We resourcefully equip believers to defend their faith with excellence. We willingly engage society's challenges with uncompromising integrity. We sacrificially serve the AiG family and others. We generously give Christian love.

I was reminded of our mission statement when we officially launched the Ark Encounter project on May 1, 2014. The Ark Encounter's full-size Noah's Ark with all of its exhibits was another big step (opened in 2016) in boldly presenting God's Word and the gospel message to the culture and helping bring reformation to the Church that is so needed.

In our June 2014 newsletter, I stated the following in an article about the "Hammer and Peg" ceremony as we officially launched the Ark Encounter project: "Fifty-five years after the book *The Genesis Flood* (that really started the modern biblical creation movement) was published, a life-size Noah's Ark is scheduled to open

CHURCH   SEPTEMBER 4

(projected summer 2016).... In a very real way, the publication of *The Genesis Flood* laid the foundation for a new reformation — to call Church (and culture) back to the authority of the Word of God."

To me, when the AiG staff, board, and local officials used wooden mallets to hammer wooden pegs into big wooden beams (that were cut from the very property the life-sized Noah's Ark was to be built upon) — it reminded me of when Martin Luther nailed his theses onto the wooden door of that church in Germany, starting the Reformation. I personally believe, when the wooden pegs were hammered into the beams on May 1, this was us being part of continuing the Reformation that Luther launched in 1517. A reformation that is so needed today, as so much of the Church has compromised God's Word in Genesis — undermining the authority of His Word. God's people need to return to the authority of God's Word.

As a result of this loss of biblical authority, generations have been leaving the Church, and the Church in our Western world is no longer impacting the culture as it once did because the culture has infected the Church. If you were to ask me to sum up the ministry of Answers in Genesis (and all of its outreaches, including the Creation Museum and Ark Encounter) in just five words, I would say it this way: biblical authority and the gospel. That is the message for the world. We are an evangelistic, biblical-authority ministry, teaching people to understand *the times* we live in so we can equip Christians to defend the Christian faith against secular attacks of our day — and to challenge non-Christians concerning the truth of God's Word and its saving gospel message. God's people need to be like the men of Issachar: *Of Issachar, men who had understanding of the times, to know what Israel ought to do* (1 Chronicles 12:32).

We are now observing a culture and Church that are facing some enormous challenges. There is an increasing:

- acceptance of homosexual behavior and gay "marriage" in the culture and Church
- flood of gender issues that have permeated the culture
- talk of pedophilia and bestiality now being published in articles
- intolerance of Christian morality in the culture
- removal of biblical authority from the Church (e.g., denial of a literal hell, acceptance of evolution and millions of years, denial of a literal Adam and Eve, shallow presentations of the gospel, etc.)

The list could be much longer. We can all see these shifts happening. We know they are happening. And when you think about it, when generations of young people are brought up in a church that tells them they can reinterpret Genesis in order to fit in evolution and/or millions of years — then should we be surprised when they use man's ideas outside of Scripture to reinterpret marriage and gender, and defend abortion? The massive challenges in the culture and the Church are why I believe God has raised up ministries like Answers in Genesis — to stand uncompromisingly and boldly on the authority of the Word and challenge Christians to take a stand. We are equipping Christians to defend the Christian faith against the onslaughts of secular attacks in our day that are aimed at undermining the authority of the Word, from which we get the gospel. It's sad that a ministry like AiG is even needed to help bring reformation to the Church! But the reality is that much of the Church needs reformation so that it will return to the authority of the Word of God.

> **When we see what is happening, we should be more emboldened than ever to help bring reformation to the Church and to challenge the culture concerning the truth of God's Word and the gospel.**

SEPTEMBER 5
1 Kings 8:23

Origin of the Attractions

At times, many have asked me how the Ark Encounter and Creation Museum really came about. In a way, they're shocked that such world-class attractions that are overtly Christian and evangelistic could be built, let alone attract millions of visitors, including a large percentage of non-Christians.

The Creation Museum opened on May 28, 2007. As I ponder this event, I can't help but be reminded of a Bible passage. At the completion of the temple, King Solomon's first words were a prayer: *"O Lord, God of Israel, there is no God like you, in heaven above or on earth beneath, keeping covenant and showing steadfast love to your servants who walk before you with all their heart"* (1 Kings 8:23).

In meeting thousands of visitors at the Creation Museum over the past years and also at the Ark Encounter (which opened in July 2016), many guests have expressed utter amazement that such God-honoring, high-quality facilities exist. I've been asked many times a question that goes something like, "How could these world-class attractions have even come about, with the quality of other themed attractions as well as Hollywood studios (or better), yet instead proclaim the truth of God's Word and the gospel?" Millions have already visited and continue to pour in from across the nation and around the world.

I often hear people say that they are so used to the secular world having leading attractions — like the Smithsonian museums, Disney World, Universal Studios, and so on — and they thought it was remarkable that solid, true-to-the-Bible Christian attractions could ever be built to compete with what the world has constructed. But, yes, they have been built, and it's all because we acknowledge (as Solomon did with the temple) that "there is no God like you, in heaven above or on earth beneath."

The burden of building a Creation Museum goes back to my public school teaching days in the 1970s in Australia. I saw the intense evolutionary indoctrination that took place inside the secular museums my students visited. In the early '80s in Australia, John Thallon (a board member of the ministry that started in our home in Brisbane) and I prayed over a block of land for a possible Creation Museum. We didn't know then that God would answer this prayer in a whole different way than we could ever imagine. The Creation Museum opened in 2007 in Kentucky, USA. Yes, truly, there is no God like you:

For my thoughts are not your thoughts, neither are your ways my ways, declares the Lord. For as the heavens are higher than the earth, so are my ways higher than your ways and my thoughts than your thoughts (Isaiah 55:8–9).

So God answered that prayer many years after we prayed in Australia, but in ways that had never entered our minds. Looking back, I can see why God brought us to the United States, eventually to meet the other two founders of the AiG ministry, Mark Looy and Mike Zovath, and talented designer Patrick Marsh. Soon, God brought many gifted staff members to AiG, sometimes in miraculous ways.

Over the years, incredulous news reporters have often asked me how we ever managed to find so much talent to build the Creation Museum and the massive Ark Encounter. The first time I was asked this question by a member of the media was on the opening day of the Creation Museum in 2007. I answered the reporter, "Well, just as God brought the land animal kinds to Noah for the Ark, God brought gifted people to us in

RESOURCES — SEPTEMBER 5

ways we never thought possible." Looking back, we can truly say, as the angel said to Mary, *"For nothing will be impossible with God"* (Luke 1:37).

I've read 2 Chronicles 2 over the years and marveled at how God provided AiG with all the skilled artists and craftsmen. I look back at the design and construction of the museum exhibits (and now the Ark exhibits) and feel a little sense of what it must have been like for Solomon to have seen God collect gifted people to construct the temple, a very special building that was meant for God Himself. Many millions of people have now visited the Creation Museum and the Ark Encounter.

How do I answer people when they ask me why the Creation Museum and Ark Encounter are so successful? I tell them that it's because God is blessing these attractions, for we proclaim the truth of His Word and the gospel — and we honor His Son, the Lord Jesus Christ: *... for those who honor me I will honor ...* (1 Samuel 2:30).

To honor God's Son, our Creator and Savior (Colossians 1), our designers produced many stunning exhibits, including one installed at the Creation Museum — a large "Christ, Cross, Consummation" exhibit. With many startling pieces of artwork, this exhibit offers in-depth teaching on Christ, from Genesis to Revelation. Yes, it honors His Son! The stunning exhibit illustrates the miracles of Christ, including creating the world, healing the sick, raising the dead, and resurrecting from the dead. The message of salvation is clearly explained and illustrated for our guests.

We pray that as AiG continues to honor Christ, He will bless the Creation Museum and Ark, equip believers, and encourage Christians to bring the lost to our attractions and see them saved. *For I am not ashamed of the gospel, for it is the power of God for salvation to everyone who believes, to the Jew first and also to the Greek* (Romans 1:16).

> Then he knelt on his knees in the presence of all the assembly of Israel, and spread out his hands toward heaven, and said, "O Lord, God of Israel, there is no God like you, in heaven or on earth, keeping covenant and showing steadfast love to your servants who walk before you with all their heart" (2 Chronicles 6:13-14).

SEPTEMBER 6

Hebrews 11:7

Hollywood's Noah vs. the Real One

Did you know that over 270 cultures around the globe still have distant memories of Noah's Flood? People all over the world have heard of Noah's Ark and the Flood. Now, many details of these legends have been lost. But most of them share common themes: man became corrupt, the flood was worldwide, eight people survived, representatives of all land animals were saved, a bird was released to seek dry land, the survivors came down from a mountain to repopulate the whole world, and so on.

When I attended university, I remember my professor telling our class that the Bible's account had borrowed from earlier myths. But the truth is, it was actually the other way around. The Bible offers the only true account of the Flood. Thus, the reason the flood myths use names and elements similar to the Bible's is because they borrowed them from God's Word or were handed down generationally from the time of Noah. The true record is recorded in the Bible. That's why Noah-like names such as Nu-u, Nu-Wah, Noh, Nos, and Nuh are preserved in so many of the flood legends.

Back in 2009, CBS-TV News made this comment on its website: "Noah's Ark continues to capture the imagination of the general public, and this interest spans all social, religious, and economic segments. The Ark and the flood is one of the few historical events which are well known in the worldwide global circle."[92]

People all over the world have heard of Noah's Ark and the Flood and remain fascinated by this event. In 2009, Answers in Genesis commissioned a study by the highly respected America's Research Group (ARG), headed by the late, renowned researcher Britt Beemer, to conduct a general population survey to find out how many people (Christians and non-Christians) would visit a full-scale Noah's Ark if such a massive ship were built. Beemer's research found that a minimum of 1.2 million people per year would visit such an Ark. And that would increase over time as exhibits were added.

AiG then stepped out in faith to build a full-sized Noah's Ark, based on the account in Genesis. We called it "Ark Encounter." We wanted Ark visitors to have an encounter with Noah's Ark and, in so doing, have an encounter with God's Word and ultimately an encounter with the Lord Jesus Christ — to have guests respond to the message of the soul-saving gospel.

By faith Noah, being warned by God concerning events as yet unseen, in reverent fear constructed an ark for the saving of his household. By this he condemned the world and became an heir of the righteousness that comes by faith (Hebrews 11:7). *Also, if* [God] *did not spare the ancient world, but preserved Noah, a herald of righteousness, with seven others, when he brought a flood upon the world of the ungodly* (2 Peter 2:5).

The Lord saw that the wickedness of man was great in the earth, and that every intention of the thoughts of his heart was only evil continually (Genesis 6:5).

"I am the door," Jesus said. *"If anyone enters by me, he will be saved"* (John 10:9).

A few weeks after we made this announcement to build the Ark, Hollywood released its awful film version of Noah's Ark and Flood, called *Noah*, starring actor Russell Crowe. Now, what are the differences between how Hollywood portrayed the account of the Ark and Flood in Genesis chapters 6–9 and how AiG and the Ark Encounter portray it? It's like comparing some of the flood legends with the account in the Bible!

THEOLOGY

	Hollywood	Ark Encounter
Event	Some elements are similar to the account in Genesis, but Hollywood's version is like the other flood legends: a twisting (a major twisting) of the original account.	We present the account of Noah, the Ark, and the Flood as accurately as can be done, accepting the account in Genesis 6–9 as historical.
Life	Life began on Earth as a result of evolution.	Life came through the Creator God of the Bible.
Noah	Noah is an angry man who is not really interested in saving humans. Russell Crowe in Noah is depicted as a madman.	Noah is a preacher of righteousness who carried out what God called him to do with reverence. He warned people of the coming judgment because of their wickedness. The Noah of the Bible was a great godly man of faith (2 Peter 2:5).
Animals	Noah's Ark was built to save animals for environmental reasons; Noah really wasn't interested in saving people.	Noah's Ark was constructed to show the Ark as a vessel that saved representatives of the land – animal kinds and humans; God judged the earth because of man's wickedness. Only eight people were saved on the Ark (Genesis 6:5).
Space	The Ark is unrealistically crammed with all sorts of different species, including multiples within the same kind.	We teach that God sent two of each KIND (in most instances, "kind" means "family" in classification) of land-dwelling, air-breathing animals. There was plenty of room on the Ark for the estimated 1,000 land animal kinds, as our careful scientific research has revealed.
Cost	Producers spent $150 million to make and then promote a fictional movie for the purposes of entertainment.	We spent around $100 million (from donations and a bond offering) to build a huge Ark with high-tech exhibits with the purpose of affirming the Bible and reaching millions of souls with the gospel of Christ.

Now, which kind of Ark would you rather support: the fictional movie that is nothing but a grossly distorted perversion of the original or the accurate account that is based on the history presented in Genesis? *Every word of God proves true* (Proverbs 30:5). The account of the Ark is a reminder that God judges wickedness, but in judgment, God provides salvation. When He judged our sin with death, He promised a Savior (Genesis 3:15). When He judged the wickedness of man at the time of Noah, He provided an Ark of salvation for those who would go through the door to be saved.

God is holy and a God who judges, but at the same time, He is a God who saves!

SEPTEMBER 7

2 Peter 3:3-7

The Real Noah's Ark

Noah built the Ark about 4,300 years ago. This event was both a judgment and a message of salvation. The Flood was a major geological, anthropological, and biological event in the history of the earth and humanity. If the Flood really happened, which it did, then most of the fossil record is the graveyard of that event. Yet evolutionists use the fossil record as supposed evidence of millions of years as part of the evolutionary story regarding the earth and life. Secularists claim the Ark Noah built couldn't have fit all the land animal kinds as the Bible teaches. They, therefore, say this event never happened. But the Bible makes it clear that the building of the Ark and the Flood of Noah really did happen in history. If the events of the Ark and Flood are true, then all humans are descendants of Noah (who built the Ark) back to the first man, Adam.

To deal with these issues and more, Answers in Genesis decided to build a life-sized Ark based on the dimensions in the Bible and fill it with exhibits answering the attacks people level at the Bible's account of Noah's Flood. The building of this Ark was done to remind people of the truth of God's Word and call them to salvation. *For as were the days of Noah, so will be the coming of the Son of Man* (Matthew 24:37).

Regardless of how Christians may interpret Matthew 24 regarding eschatology, there's no doubt that this verse refers to the rebellion and judgment of Noah's day. Christ used the catastrophic Flood that occurred over 4,300 years ago to warn of impending judgment. Many Christians believe this verse also alludes to the coming final judgment when Christ returns and makes new heavens and a new earth.

What was it like in Noah's day? Genesis 6:5 states, *The Lord saw that the wickedness of man was great in the earth, and that every intention of the thoughts of his heart was only evil continually.* I believe it has been the right time to build a full-scale model of Noah's Ark!

But why an Ark? Hebrews 11:7 declares, *By faith Noah, being warned by God concerning events as yet unseen, in reverent fear constructed an ark for the saving of his household. By this he condemned the world and became an heir to the righteousness that comes by faith.* Noah built the Ark to provide a way of salvation. He and his family went through a door to be saved. But the Ark was also a visual warning of the condemnation that was coming — a judgment of those who had rebelled and would not turn their hearts to God. The Ark is a picture of Jesus, who said He is the "door." Just as Noah and his family had to go through a door to be saved, we must enter a door — the Lord Jesus Christ — to be saved.

Why was the time right to build another Ark? Well, today, there is a great rebellion against God and His Word in the land. With increasing homosexual behavior and a growing acceptance of abortion and other moral evils (gender transition, etc.), God's hand of judgment is being seen as He withdraws the restraining influence of His Holy Spirit.

Consider the state of the Western nations. In many ways, Genesis 6:5 could be used to describe what's happening in our once-Christianized Western world: *"The Lord saw that the wickedness of man was great in the earth, and that every intent of the thoughts of his heart was only evil continually."*

Today, rebellion against God and His Word is rampant. By and large, God and His Word have been thrown out of government schools, public places, courthouses, etc. In addition, many Christian leaders are rejecting

God's Word, especially in Genesis, as they compromise with the pagan religion of our day: evolution and millions of years. Many of these Christian leaders and academics are even rejecting the literal Adam and Eve and the literal Fall. And a number are becoming soft on the LGBTQ worldview! This atheistic religion of the day leads to a mindset that justifies the killing of millions of children through abortion. Many people are more concerned about animal life than human life.

There is no doubt God is judging America and the rest of the Western world. One major recent sign of God's judgment is that homosexual behavior is permeating the culture as God gives "people up" (or turns them over), according to Romans 1:24 and 26. Many political leaders and judges (and even some church leaders) are increasingly legalizing (and celebrating) same-sex "marriage," which is an abomination to the Lord.

Even though there is a remnant of true believers, most of the culture and many in the Church are in rebellion against God, His authority, and His Word. For instance, consider a news item that was published about the Supreme Court ruling on gay "marriage," which must have been anathema to our holy God:

"The National Cathedral is pealing its church bells, along with some other Washington churches, to celebrate the Supreme Court's decisions on gay marriage.... Bells also rang at other Episcopal, Methodist, Presbyterian, Unitarian and other Christian churches."

So why rebuild the Ark, then? Just as in Noah's day, the building of a full-sized Ark can stand as a reminder to the world of salvation — that people need to go through a doorway to be saved: *I am the door. If anyone enters by me, he will be saved and will go in and out and find pasture* (John 10:9). An Ark would also stand as a warning of coming judgment — to condemn those who reject God's clear Word:

[K]nowing this first of all, that scoffers will come in the last days with scoffing, following their own sinful desires. They will say, "Where is the promise of his coming? For ever since the fathers fell asleep, all things are continuing as they were from the beginning of creation." For they deliberately overlook this fact, that the heavens existed long ago, and the earth was formed out of water and through water by the word of God, and that by means of these the world that then existed was deluged with water and perished. But by the same word the heavens and earth that now exist are stored up for fire, being kept until the day of judgment and destruction of the ungodly (2 Peter 3:3–7).

Yes, it certainly has been the right time to rebuild Noah's Ark. We believe that God called AiG to construct an Ark according to the dimensions in the Bible to remind people of the truth of God's Word and call them to salvation. Make sure you visit our Christian-themed attractions, the Ark Encounter and Creation Museum, in Northern Kentucky, USA.

> "For as were the days of Noah, so will be the coming of the Son of Man" (Matthew 24:37).

SEPTEMBER 8
Revelation 14:6-7

A Picture of Salvation

Noah's Ark is a picture of salvation. There was one door in the Ark, and there is only one door by which we can be saved. Noah and his family went through the one door into the Ark of salvation. This is a reminder we need to go through the "door" (Jesus) to be saved. There will never be another global Flood. That was God's promise to us in Genesis 9:15 when He gave us the rainbow as a sign of His covenant with man and all living creatures. And that is the real meaning of the rainbow.

"I have set my bow in the cloud, and it shall be a sign of the covenant between me and the earth. When I bring clouds over the earth and the bow is seen in the clouds, I will remember my covenant that is between me and you and every living creature of all flesh. And the waters shall never again become a flood to destroy all flesh. When the bow is in the clouds, I will see it and remember the everlasting covenant between God and every living creature of all flesh that is on the earth." God said to Noah, *"This is the sign of the covenant that I have established between me and all flesh that is on the earth"* (Genesis 9:13–17).

The Bible makes it clear, however, that there will be another global judgment: next time by fire. As God's Word states, it will be the Final Judgment: *waiting for and hastening the coming of the day of God, because of which the heavens will be set on fire and dissolved, and the heavenly bodies will melt as they burn!* (2 Peter 3:12).

Today, we don't need another Ark to save animals and people from a global Flood. But we can experience another kind of Noah's Ark and take people on what we call "a voyage of discovery." More than ever, people need to discover the truth of God's Word beginning in Genesis and the saving gospel of the New Testament. That is especially true today for the younger generations (including those inside the Church). Our culture needs to take a voyage of discovery and discover that:

- God's Word concerning the history of the universe and all life is true.
- God's Word concerning man's sinful state and his need for salvation in Christ is true.

Just like the angel in the Book of Revelation, we need to be preaching the gospel and warning people about the judgment to come:

Then I saw another angel flying directly overhead, with an eternal gospel to proclaim to those who dwell on earth, to every nation and tribe and language and people. And he said with a loud voice, "Fear God and give him glory, because the hour of his judgment has come, and worship him who made heaven and earth, the sea and the springs of water" (Revelation 14:6–7).

In this very secularized time, I believe one of the best and most effective ways to reach tens of millions of people with the gospel message is to build another Ark — a gospel-focused, life-sized Ark — and show the world that science confirms the Bible and that God's Word is true, and we all need to come to repentance.

Other than the Cross, I believe Noah's Ark is the greatest reminder of the soul-saving gospel. Just as Noah and his family had to go through the one Ark door to be saved, so we need to go through the one door, Jesus Christ, to be saved. Jesus said: *I am the door. If anyone enters by me, he will be saved, and will go in and out and find pasture* (John 10:9).

RESOURCES — SEPTEMBER 8

In 2016, Answers in Genesis opened the life-sized Ark attraction, Ark Encounter, one of the greatest Christian outreaches in the world of this era. This huge ship takes visitors on a very special voyage:

- To experience the most authentic reconstruction of Noah's Ark, built according to the dimensions in the Bible.
- To get an idea of what it was like in Noah's day.
- To get answers to questions about the Ark and Flood.
- To be taught the truth of God's Word, beginning with its history in Genesis.
- To be challenged concerning the need for every person to go through the "door" (Jesus Christ), be saved from the coming judgment, and live for eternity with their Creator and Savior.

Because of our conviction that we need to reach the masses with an evangelistic message — the most important message in the universe — we use as many marketing techniques as we can to let people know about this attraction. The world massively markets its atheistic message to the world. Christians need to be actively marketing, in the sense of doing all we can to get the message out, the message of truth to the world.

Answers in Genesis has a decade-long history of utilizing the mass media in a high-profile way, in both Christian and secular outlets, to promote the various initiatives of this Bible-affirming ministry. Because the Ark Encounter is every bit the quality of a major attraction like Universal Studios or Disney World, yet with an unmistakable and bold Christian message, I believe it's vital we do our best to convince people across America and around the world to visit. But I believe the Church should also be doing all it can to get the message of truth to the masses. Just because the devil uses mass media doesn't mean Christians shouldn't!

I once had a lady tell me we shouldn't be using color in our books, as the devil uses color. I told her God invented color. My point is that any media can be used for good or evil. I believe we should be doing all we can to use media to challenge people with the truth of God's Word and the saving gospel. Personally, I think much of the Church is very introverted and self-focused. I believe we should be more aggressive (in a nice way) in contending for the faith in our culture. That's one of the reasons we built the two attractions, the Ark Encounter and the Creation Museum. We want to be very public about our stand on Scripture and bold about proclaiming God's Word and the gospel.

When the secular media ask me (constantly) about the purpose of Answers in Genesis, the Creation Museum, and the Ark Encounter, I tell them that our message is simply this: The history in the Bible is true, and the gospel based on that history is true!

We also share with the media this gospel verse: *because, if you confess with your mouth that Jesus is Lord and believe in your heart that God raised him from the dead, you will be saved* (Romans 10:9).

There is no more vital message than the message of salvation in Jesus Christ. That's the most important message in the universe.

> We need to be doing all we can to courageously proclaim God's Word and the gospel to as many people as we can around the world.

SEPTEMBER 9

Deuteronomy 6:5–7

Preparing Children for War

Normally, we wouldn't think of training children to be soldiers in a massive battle. But actually, that's exactly what we should be doing as Christians as we raise up generations in a world where a massive spiritual war is raging around us. In fact, as Christians, all of us are soldiers and have to be involved in doing battle in this war. It's a war over the hearts and minds of people. And the war over the hearts and minds of children, in particular, has been vicious.

How diligent we must be to teach children the truth of God's Word and equip them with the armor they need so they won't believe *the lie* of evolutionary naturalism (atheism) and *the lie* the devil wants them to believe — that you can't trust God's Word and you can be your own god. I get so excited when the Answers in Genesis VBS program is being used in churches each year to impact tens of thousands of children. These programs are designed to help children put on the armor of God and be equipped with weapons to be able to fight the spiritual war where the devil is out to capture their hearts and minds. They need to be equipped to know how to put on *the whole armor of God* so that they would be equipped to fend off the flaming darts of the wicked one (Ephesians 6:11, 13, 16). Not just the VBS program but also our Sunday school/Bible program and other curricula geared toward children are making a phenomenal impact.

The Bible warns us that the devil (the wicked one) is *like a roaring lion, seeking someone to devour* (1 Peter 5:8). We are also warned that the devil *is a liar and the father of lies* (John 8:44).

God's Word instructs us to teach our children the Scriptures and to equip them so they won't be led astray by the wicked one. Thankfully, we are told that Christ has paid for our sins so that we can be rescued from this *evil age* (Galatians 1:4). Yes, the wicked one is out to get our children, and one way he does this is through spreading lies. One of the devil's greatest lies is that there is no God and that His Word is not true. Sadly, tens of millions of children are being taught *"the lie"* in schools, museums, and the media on a daily basis — that they are just evolved animals and that everything in the universe is explained by natural processes, not supernatural acts. They are being indoctrinated in *the lie* of evolutionary atheism, which permeates the culture. *The lie* of evolution is one of the greatest delusions of our age. That's why the title of my best-known book is *The Lie*.

The Bible warns us: *Therefore God sends them a strong delusion, so that they may believe what is false* (2 Thessalonians 2:11). Today, we see so many people rebelling against God's Word. They are rejecting true marriage, rejecting their created gender, supporting the wanton killing of unborn babies, and rejecting creation. God has turned them over to the wickedness of their hearts. They are spreading the great "lie" that God's Word is not the authority. We must be diligent in teaching children the truth of God's Word and equip them with the armor they need so they won't believe *"the lie."*

Sadly, the vast majority of this generation of kids is being captured by the enemy. That's why, as Christians, we need to know how to rescue our children from the following:

- The evil one
- This evil generation

FAMILY — SEPTEMBER 9

- Secularists out to capture our youth
- Churches teaching bad apologetics
- Churches and their compromise over biblical authority
- Many Sunday school programs that teach "fluff and stuff" and compromise Genesis
- Many Christian institutions, like compromising Christian schools and Christian colleges

It's not only the world we have to be concerned about influencing our children. You see, much of the Church has compromised God's Word with the pagan religion of our age. That religion is a vain attempt to explain life without God (through evolution/ millions of years), thus undermining the authority of Scripture.

I often ponder the fact that thousands of churches across the USA and other parts of the world are now using AiG's uniquely powerful VBS programs and the incredible Answers Bible Curriculum (Sunday school program), as well as the other curricula AiG has been able to produce over the years.

The uniqueness of AiG curricula is that they don't just entertain and they don't teach Bible accounts the way the world teaches fables. AiG's curricula teach children and adults about the importance of believing and accepting the full history and authority of God's Word. And we teach how to defend the Christian faith in today's secularized world. Our resources are full of "meat," and yes, children love the in-depth teaching (so do the adults)! It's all part of helping them put on the armor of God to know how to ward off the attacks of the devil.

Children and adults are getting saved through these curricula, and many are now on fire for the Lord! How I praise the Lord for that. And they understand what it means to have a true Christian worldview built on God's Word beginning in Genesis 1–11. More than ever, Christians need to be equipped to be in the full armor of Ephesians 6 so that they can be properly engaged in the spiritual battle raging all around us. Part of that battle is a war on children. Let's make sure we are training our children just as God's Word instructs:

You shall love the Lord your God with all your heart and with all your soul and with all your might. And these words that I command you today shall be on your heart. You shall teach them diligently to your children, and shall talk of them when you sit in your house, and when you walk by the way, and when you lie down, and when you rise (Deuteronomy 6:5–7).

To help train your children, bring them to the two leading Christian-themed attractions in the world: the Ark Encounter and Creation Museum.

> **Generations of children are being brainwashed against the truth of who they are, where they came from, and what their purpose and meaning in life are all about, based on God's infallible Word.**

SEPTEMBER 10
John 5:45-47

Old Testament and New Testament

In recent times, we've heard a well-known pastor of a large church claim the New Testament needs to be unhitched from the Old Testament. I claim one reason young adults are leaving the Church is that they don't understand the Old Testament.

It comes as no shock to hear that young people — especially Millennials — are leaving the Church in the United States in great numbers. George Barna reports that "more than two-thirds of skeptics have attended Christian churches in the past." Less than 9% of Generation Z attend church, so most of that generation have nothing to do with church. So, what happened?

Well, according to research conducted by America's Research Group for one of my past books, *Already Gone*, one major issue is a lack of apologetics teaching. Millennials were not taught to defend their faith, and the world's scoffing at the Bible and arguments against the truth of God's Word have drawn them away. But it goes deeper. Our young people don't even know what the Bible teaches or that its grand narrative, beginning in Genesis, points to salvation through Jesus Christ (Genesis 3:15). These biblically uninformed young people do not understand the purpose of the Old Testament, so they think the Church is just picking and choosing what parts of the Bible to obey. When pastors use Old Testament terminology such as "come to the altar," they reinforce that idea.

Now, there's nothing wrong with using Old Testament terminology. Indeed, New Testament authors frequently did. But if a writer was addressing a largely Gentile audience (people not acquainted with Jewish history and beliefs), he would avoid using Old Testament terms or would explain them carefully. If he was writing to a Jewish audience, he could easily refer to the temple, sacrifices, priests, and so on because they had the foundational knowledge to understand him.

In the Book of Acts, we read two very different sermons — one by Peter and one by Paul. At Pentecost, Peter delivered a powerful sermon in Jerusalem (Acts 2:14–40). This sermon was full of Old Testament quotations and themes because the audience was Jewish and had an Old Testament background. In Acts 17, Paul addresses the Greeks in faraway Athens. Although he started with the Creator revealed in Genesis, his sermon was not full of Old Testament quotations because his Gentile audience knew little or nothing of the Old Testament. Though highly educated, they were biblically illiterate. Paul understood his audience and tailored his message accordingly.

In a sense, we could say the West used to be a "Jewish"-type audience. Many unbelievers knew biblical history and largely believed the Bible had at least some authority. But today, most young people who have grown up in the Church do not know the Old Testament well. They are no longer "Jewish" but "Gentile" in their thinking. Most have been thoroughly indoctrinated in evolutionary teaching. To minister to modern-day Gentiles, we need to help them understand the vital nature of the Old Testament. It provides the history on which the New Testament and the life of Christ on Earth are based. It reveals the origin of our sin and our desperate need for Jesus the Savior.

CHURCH

In Genesis, we learn that God created a perfect world, but Adam and Eve brought death and suffering by their sin. Their descendants likewise chose disobedience. The world became so wicked that God judged it with a global Flood. Only righteous Noah and his family survived. Just a few generations later, at the Tower of Babel, mankind rebelled again. Eventually, God chose a covenant people and gave them His law. They failed to live by it time and time again. This history clearly shows we cannot keep God's laws on our own.

With this backdrop, the New Testament teaching of salvation and restoration through the death and Resurrection of Jesus Christ makes sense. Salvation is by faith alone (Ephesians 2:8), in Christ alone (Acts 4:12). What we could never do on our own, Christ did for us (Ephesians 2:9). Throughout the Bible we see the unfolding of God's plan of salvation. It's about Jesus from beginning to end!

The Mosaic Law does the same thing. It highlights our inability to keep God's commands. The sacrifice of animals and the priesthood were pictures of Christ, who was to come. Jesus, through His death, burial, and Resurrection, has made the first covenant obsolete (Hebrews 8:13) and has brought us into the new covenant (Luke 22:20) foretold by the prophet Jeremiah (Jeremiah 31:31).

God does not change (Hebrews 13:8), but this doesn't mean that rules or punishments can't change. For instance, man was created vegetarian (Genesis 1:29). But following the Flood, God made a new covenant with Noah, allowing man to eat meat (Genesis 9:3). The Mosaic Law included dietary restrictions (Leviticus 11:47), but the new covenant lifted them (Acts 10:9–16). Since there won't be any death in the new heavens and new earth, we know we will be vegetarian once again (Revelation 21:4). Did God change? Not at all. But God's rules for us can change under various covenants.

The Old Testament, especially the Mosaic Law, seems to be a big stumbling block to many young people because they aren't receiving the instruction fundamental to understanding the redemptive history of the Old Testament and how it undergirds the person and work of Jesus. Christian leaders, pastors, teachers, and parents need to teach others how to view the Old Testament and the Law as Christians under the new covenant.

Jesus said, *"Do not think that I will accuse you to the Father. There is one who accuses you: Moses, on whom you have set your hope. For if you believed Moses, you would believe me; for he wrote of me. But if you do not believe his writings, how will you believe my words?"* (John 5:45–47).

> Be sure to use the Old Testament – it forms the basis for our theology – but make sure your audience understands how to view it so they can grow in the knowledge of Christ and in godliness.

SEPTEMBER 11

Hebrews 4:14

Purpose of the Old Testament

As I've spoken across America and other parts of the Western world, answered questions, and read research and atheist writings, I've noticed a common stumbling block that comes up continually. Most of the younger generations of biblically illiterate young people do not understand the purpose and place of the Old Testament. They've never been taught how to properly understand and apply the first thirty-nine books of the Bible, especially the ones dealing with the Mosaic Covenant and Law.

Because they lack a proper understanding, many in the younger generations will accuse the Church of being hypocritical for what they perceive as following some laws and not others. We hear accusations such as, "So you think homosexuality is wrong, but does that mean we should kill gay people?" (Leviticus 20:13) and "Why do you wear clothes made from two different kinds of fabric since Leviticus 19:19 says not to?" These young people don't understand the role of the Old Testament because, to them, Christians seem to pick and choose which laws they want to obey. Now, there's nothing wrong with using Old Testament terminology to communicate truth. After all, the Old Testament is a foreshadowing of what was to come in Jesus Christ and is a vital part of, and foundation for, our theology. Indeed, New Testament authors not only quoted from the Old Testament and referenced its history but also frequently pointed their Jewish readers back to Old Testament themes by using words and motifs from the former writings:

I appeal to you therefore, brothers, by the mercies of God, to present your bodies as a living sacrifice (Romans 12:1; see Psalm 50:13–14).

Since then we have a great high priest who has passed through the heavens, Jesus, the Son of God (Hebrews 4:14; see Leviticus 21:10–15).

Draw near to God, and he will draw near to you. Cleanse your hands, you sinners, and purify your hearts, you double-minded (James 4:8; see Psalm 24:4).

What the New Testament writers understood was the importance of knowing your audience. If a writer was penning a letter or a gospel to a largely Gentile audience that didn't have much knowledge of Jewish customs or the Old Testament, he would avoid using Old Testament terms and motifs or would explain them carefully. If he was writing to a largely Jewish audience, he could easily use references to the temple, sacrifices, priests, or Jewish customs and feasts because his audience would have the foundational knowledge to understand what the writer was communicating. In a sense, the West used to be a "Jewish" audience. In days gone by, even many unbelievers knew biblical history, believed in a Creator God, and largely believed the Bible had at least some authority. If a pastor referenced something from the Old Testament or used a cliché with Old Testament connotations, the audience understood what was meant. This is not so anymore. Even many of the younger generations who have grown up in the Church do not know the Old Testament, except perhaps a few scattered accounts such as "Daniel in the Lions' Den" or "David and Goliath." So, how do we effectively minister to a Gentile audience? First, we need to help our audience understand the purpose and place of the Old Testament, particularly the Old Testament Law. The Old Testament provides the history that the New Testament is based on. It points out our sinfulness, hopelessness, and desperate need for a Savior.

APOLOGETICS   SEPTEMBER 11

In Genesis, we learn that God created a perfect world, but Adam and Eve chose not to obey God's command and marred the world by their sin. Their children likewise chose disobedience, as did their children after them. Eventually, the world became so wicked that God judged it with a global Flood. Only righteous Noah and his family survived. But, just a few generations later, mankind rebelled against God again. Eventually, God chose a covenant people — Israel — for Himself and gave them His law. They failed to live by it time and time again. This pattern of failing to keep God's law repeats itself throughout the whole Old Testament. The history of mankind and the nation of Israel clearly shows that we cannot keep God's commands and laws on our own.

With this backdrop, the New Testament teaching of salvation through the death and Resurrection of Jesus Christ makes sense. Salvation is by faith alone (Ephesians 2:8), in Christ alone (Acts 4:12), because sinful human beings have fallen short of God's law (Romans 3:23) and can never keep it. So Christ kept it for us (Matthew 5:17). What we could never do on our own, Christ did for us because it's impossible for us to earn our own salvation (Ephesians 2:9). Throughout the Bible, we see the unfolding of God's plan of salvation that culminates in the person and work of Christ. It's about Jesus from beginning to end!

The Mosaic Law — the law that was given to the Israelites under the old covenant — does the same thing as the history of the Old Testament. It highlights our inability to keep God's commands. The law served as a tutor to lead us to Christ (Galatians 3:24) by showcasing our sinfulness (Romans 3:19) and showing us what sin was (7:7). The Law was also designed to keep Israel completely separate and distinct from her pagan neighbors (Leviticus 20:26). Some laws which seem strange to us — such as not mixing fabrics or types of crops — were designed to emphasize the holiness of God (Leviticus 19:2) and the need for Israel to keep herself separate from her neighbors (something she consistently did not do). The sacrifice of animals and the priesthood, which were so integral to the old covenant, were types and shadows of Christ, who was to come (the author of Hebrews lays this out beautifully in his letter). Now that Jesus has come, these types have been completely and utterly fulfilled. We are no longer under this old covenant (Romans 6:14). Jesus, through His death, burial, and Resurrection, has made the first covenant obsolete (Hebrews 8:13) and has brought us into the new covenant (Luke 22:20) foretold by the prophet Jeremiah (Jeremiah 31:31). We are no longer bound by the old covenant — it has been utterly fulfilled and nailed to the Cross.

So why don't Christians advocate stoning homosexuals and ban clothing with more than one fiber? Simply because we aren't under the Mosaic Law — the old covenant — anymore. This doesn't mean the Mosaic Law holds no value for us. The principles of the law still offer guidance for believers, and many have been carried over (Romans 13:9) and are now part of *For the law of the Spirit of life has set you free in Christ Jesus* (Romans 8:2). The Mosaic Law certainly has great value for new covenant believers (1 Corinthians 10:11), but it is no longer binding to us because we are under a different covenant (Hebrews 8:6–7). Now, some people have argued that if God's laws can change throughout history, then the Bible cannot be relied upon as an absolute foundation for morality. After all, if putting homosexuals to death was the right thing to do in Old Testament times but isn't now, doesn't that show morality changes with time?

> We don't get to decide what is moral – God does, and we must submit to Him and His law.

SEPTEMBER 12
Psalm 11:3

Foundational Collapse

What has happened to America? What has happened to the entire Western world? Spiritually and morally, there's been a catastrophic change. At one time in the past, the people of the United States generally knew who ruled over the affairs of men — the Creator God of the Bible. They even put His name on their coins and currency. In just one generation, that attitude has changed. What happened? But it's not just America; the entire Western world is changing. Whereas the West was once permeated by Christian thinking (the Judeo-Christian ethic) with a predominantly Christianized worldview regarding morality, there has been a dramatic shift.

Abortion was once, by and large, considered to be killing a human being (murder) and was basically outlawed. Marriage was once considered to be between one man and one woman only. But now, gay "marriage" is increasingly accepted and legalized. The LGBTQ worldview has exploded in acceptance through Western culture. Why has this change occurred? What are the foundational reasons for such a dramatic shift in worldviews? These same changes (and many more, such as the removal of Christian symbols from public places) are occurring and continuing to gather momentum in what was once considered the greatest Christianized (from a worldview perspective) nation on earth — the United States of America.

The changes in America are fundamentally the same as in the rest of the Western world. So, in understanding what is happening in America, one can understand why this dramatic shift is occurring in so many countries. The reasons for this change have been bubbling under the surface for quite some time in regard to the increasing acceptance of evolutionary naturalism and increasing compromise of God's Word in the Church. The bubble has been growing. But I believe a particular person was, in many ways, a catalyst that caused this bubble to burst and catastrophically affect America and the rest of the Western world.

In 2006, at Call to Renewal's "Building a Covenant for a New America" conference, then-Senator Barack Obama stated: "Whatever we once were, we are no longer a Christian nation; we are also a Jewish nation, a Muslim nation, a Buddhist nation, a Hindu nation, and a nation of nonbelievers." He repeated this same message in his book *The Audacity of Hope* and later in his inauguration address. During a trip to Turkey in early 2009, President Obama reiterated a similar message to Turkey's Muslim president: "I've said before that one of the great strengths of the United States is, although as I mentioned we have a very large Christian population, we do not consider ourselves a Christian nation or a Jewish nation or a Muslim nation; we consider ourselves a nation of citizens who are bound by ideals and a set of values."

There is no doubt that President Obama was declaring that America has fundamentally changed. And he applauded that change. But what is the change he is referring to? The essence of the change can be summed up with another quote from him. President Obama formally declared: "Now, therefore, I, Barack Obama, president of the United States of America, by virtue of the authority vested in me by the Constitution and the laws of the United States, do hereby proclaim June 2010 as Lesbian, Gay, Bisexual, and Transgender Pride Month. I call upon all Americans to observe this month by fighting prejudice and discrimination in their own lives and everywhere it exists."[93] And now the sin of pride is rampant! At a Human Rights Campaign dinner in 2009, the president stated: "My expectation is that when you look back on these years ... you will see a time in which we as a nation finally recognize relationships between two men and two women as just as real and

APOLOGETICS — SEPTEMBER 12

admirable as relationships between a man and a woman." In other words, we will look back and say, "We gave up Christian morality. Isn't that great?" The change from a worldview that viewed marriage as a special union between a man and a woman to one that redefines marriage as a relationship between any two individuals (man and man, or woman and woman) really sums up the change President Obama was referring to. It is really a change from building one's thinking on the Bible beginning in Genesis (where we learn about the origin of marriage when God made the first male and female) to a worldview in which mankind can redefine marriage. Increasingly, we see man redefining everything God defined.

What led to this change? In essence, this change reflects a shift between the world's two opposing religions. Ultimately, there are only two religions — one starts with God's Word, and the other starts with man's word. America — and the whole Western world — once built its worldview predominantly on the Bible. That doesn't mean they were Christian nations, but the dominant worldview was based on biblical morality. Now, a shift has occurred, as the West's worldview is being built on man's word. This change is reflected in a shift from Christianity's absolutes to the relative morality of human opinions — the secularization of the culture.

A secular humanist magazine once ran a cover story on "Fading Faith." The article stated: "A historic transition is occurring, barely noticed. Slowly, quietly, imperceptibly, religion is shriveling in America, as it already has in Europe, Canada, Australia, Japan — across the developed world. Increasingly, supernatural faith belongs to the third world. The first world is entering the long-predicted Secular Age, when science and knowledge dominate."

The president of the United States, the secular humanists, and Christians all recognized the change that was happening. However, is this change positive, as the secularists trumpet and as the U.S. president proclaimed? Sadly, this foundational change is affecting hearts and minds in regard to eternal matters. Fundamentally, the secularists have captured the hearts and minds of generations of kids. They have secularized their thinking by changing their starting point from God's Word to man's word — thus changing their worldview. After generations of such change, we now see the effect of the changing worldview of the Church and the whole culture. There's been a catastrophic generational loss from the Church that goes hand in hand with the secularization of the culture. The major way this change has occurred is through the education system and media, which teach that evolution over millions of years is a fact, causing many young people to doubt and ultimately disbelieve the Scriptures. Sadly, much of the Church and the majority of Christian academics aided this change by endorsing millions of years and evolutionary ideas while trying to instill a Christian worldview in other areas (such as Christian morality, marriage as one man and one woman, and abortion as murder).

"Whatever we once were we are no longer!" These words really mean that America as a nation no longer builds its thinking on God's Word, but man can determine truth for himself. America has changed religion — from Christianity to a man-centered religion, from worshipping God to worshipping man and the creation. This spiritual disaster is now reflected in this nation's economic and moral disaster. So, what is the solution? Whatever we once were we need to return to. But much more than that. The solution has always been God's Word and the gospel. As Psalm 11:3 states, *[I]f the foundations are destroyed, what can the righteous do?*

> The only solution for this nation (and every other nation) is to return to the authority of God's Word as the foundation for our individual and cultural worldviews.

SEPTEMBER 13
2 Corinthians 6:14-15

Church Compromise

One of the biggest challenges before us is not so much countering the teaching of evolution and millions of years in the secular culture — but dealing with this wrong teaching in the Church!

When I was speaking at an All-Asian Creation Conference in Malaysia one year, I wrote a blog entitled "Worldwide Epidemic Threatens Church." Here is basically what I said:

There were 20 countries represented at this conference, and I heard from people from nearly all of those nations pleading for a creation conference in their country. They all said to me something like, "Most of the pastors — Christian leaders — seminary professors — believe in evolution and millions of years."

Friends, disbelief in the Book of Genesis is a worldwide epidemic. Satan has used millions of years and evolution to permeate the Church around the world and undermine the authority of Scripture. It's what I call the Genesis 3 attack of our time that undermines the authority of the Word by attacking Genesis 1–11.

What a mission field we have to reach the "shepherds," the Christian teachers and leaders and pastors, around the world to call them out of compromise and back to the authority of the Word of God.

This one conference made me realize even more than ever how the pagan religion of millions of years and evolution has so permeated the Church around the world! What a mess! Sadly, countries like the USA and England have sent missionaries around the world teaching this damaging "compromise message" because they were trained in compromised colleges and seminaries. This makes me more burdened than ever to challenge church leaders who, whether wittingly or unwittingly, are allowing for or actively teaching compromise positions in regard to the Book of Genesis.

Just before I flew to Malaysia, a Christian academic from the United Kingdom had come to Malaysia to give presentations. But he was there to encourage the Church to believe in evolution and millions of years. This speaker was promoting the work of evolutionist Dr. Francis Collins, who founded the theologically liberal BioLogos Foundation.

Thankfully, biblical creation ministries have advanced around the world. Organizations like Answers in Genesis have been able to produce and distribute a plethora of resources (many are translated into other languages) to teach Christians how to defend the Christian faith beginning in Genesis.

At the same time, we have seen a corresponding increase in books and other resources by leaders in the Church who teach that evolution and millions of years are true and supposedly compatible with the Bible. And they are sending out their compromising "missionaries" around the world in an attempt to get the Church not to believe in a literal Genesis. As I have stated many times, such compromise undermines biblical authority, and it is a major reason there has been such a catastrophic collapse of the Christian worldview in our Western nations.

As part of our work to help stop this epidemic of compromise related to the inerrancy of Scripture, AiG staff also attend the Evangelical Theological Society (ETS) annual conference. This is a gathering of largely conservative evangelical scholars/Christian leaders who present and discuss papers on various topics.

CHURCH   SEPTEMBER 13

From our experience, though, probably the majority of Christians who attend the ETS meeting would either allow for or insist on believing in millions of years and in reinterpreting Genesis accordingly — not because the Bible teaches an old age, but because they have been indoctrinated by academics to accept millions of years (or they will be seen as "anti-scientific" or "anti-academic").

Yes, biblical compromise beginning in Genesis is an epidemic. It's now a global epidemic that is undermining biblical inerrancy and the authority of Scripture. I recognize that one of the biggest challenges before us is not so much countering the teaching of evolution and millions of years in the secular culture but dealing with this wrong teaching in the Church!

Christians need to realize that secular scientists reject God's Word. In fact, to compromise and make an idol out of millions of years/evolution — as secular scientists and many church academics have done — is no different than what the Israelites did when they compromised with the idol-worshipping Canaanite religion of their age. And the Church needs to understand that Genesis 1–11 is the foundation for everything!

My call to the Church is this: *Do not be unequally yoked with unbelievers. For what partnership has righteousness with lawlessness? Or what fellowship has light with darkness? What accord has Christ with Belial? Or what portion does a believer share with an unbeliever?* (2 Corinthians 6:14–15).

What agreement has the temple of God with idols? For we are the temple of the living God; as God said, "I will make my dwelling among them and walk among them, and I will be their God, and they shall be my people. Therefore go out from their midst, and be separate from them, says the Lord, and touch no unclean thing; then I will welcome you, and I will be a father to you, and you shall be sons and daughters to me, says the Lord Almighty" (2 Corinthians 6:16–18).

The Church needs to wake up to the fact that millions of years/evolution is really the pagan religion of this age.

SEPTEMBER 14
Nehemiah 2:19-20

Sanballats

Other than Genesis, one of my favorite books of the Bible is Nehemiah. There are so many lessons we can learn from the account of Nehemiah and the rebuilding of the wall in Jerusalem. I've often thought of Nehemiah as I've encountered various situations as we announced and moved ahead with the building of the Creation Museum and Ark Encounter. Over the years in the Answers in Genesis ministry, particularly during the time we were constructing the Creation Museum and full-sized Noah's Ark, we came across many "Sanballats."

Today, I can't help but think of how the analogy of Sanballat (a person from the Book of Nehemiah) relates more than ever to the people who oppose AiG's proclamation of the creation/gospel message. Let me explain. When Nehemiah announced he was going to rebuild the wall around Jerusalem, the Bible records the following: *But when Sanballat the Horonite and Tobiah the Ammonite servant and Geshem the Arab heard of it, they jeered at us and despised us and said, "What is this thing that you are doing? Are you rebelling against the king?" Then I replied to them, "The God of heaven will make us prosper, and we his servants will arise and build, but you have no portion or right or claim in Jerusalem"* (Nehemiah 2:19–20).

When AiG announced the building of the Creation Museum, secularists did not hide the fact that they despised us for attempting to build a Bible-upholding project. Even some people in the Church publicly spoke out against AiG. One of the most vocal museum opponents was a local pastor, who was quoted frequently in the press! Yes, we had our "Sanballats" when we built the Creation Museum.

Back then, a local atheist, speaking at a public meeting, declared that building our Creation Museum would be a violation of the so-called "separation of church and state" because it would not agree with evolution! And this was a project involving private funding on private land!

After some intense struggles with museum opponents (which made headline news throughout the region), we eventually purchased the land and obtained the necessary zoning. But a lawsuit was lodged against us, and we received additional intense opposition from atheists and others. It became a serious time of prayer for us.

Now, here is an example of when Nehemiah's Sanballat account comes in as it relates to the building of our Ark: *But when Sanballat and Tobiah and the Arabs and the Ammonites and the Ashdodites heard that the repairing of the walls of Jerusalem was going forward and that the breaches were beginning to be closed, they were very angry. And they all plotted together to come and fight against Jerusalem and to cause confusion in it. And we prayed to our God and set a guard as a protection against them day and night* (Nehemiah 4:7–9).

When we first announced the building of the Ark Encounter, and then when we actually started construction, AiG experienced the same sort of angry opposition as we did for the Creation Museum. In fact, the battles this time seemed to be at higher and more aggressive levels than with the museum construction. You see, the secularists realized that with the Ark Encounter, tens of millions of people would be presented with the truth of God's Word as they board the Ark and interact with its stunning exhibits.

As Nehemiah was rebuilding the wall, here is what happened: *Then Sanballat sent his servant to me as before, the fifth time, with an open letter in his hand. In it was written: It is reported among the nations, and Geshem*

RESOURCES

says, that you and the Jews plan to rebel; therefore, according to these rumors, you are rebuilding the wall, that you may be their king. And you have also appointed prophets to proclaim concerning you at Jerusalem, saying, "There is a king in Judah!" Now these matters will be reported to the king (Nehemiah 6:5–7; NKJV).

I was reminded of this passage when we learned that the anti-God group Americans United for Separation of Church and State had written to Kentucky politicians (including the governor) and also stirred up the media (such as the two left-leaning major newspapers in the state) to spread untruths and misinformation about the Ark project. Anti-Christian groups and the secular media launched a massive propaganda war (even continuing to this day) in their attempt to undermine the Ark Encounter. But I'm reminded of how Nehemiah responded:

Then I sent to him, saying, "No such things as you say have been done, for you are inventing them out of your own mind." For they all wanted to frighten us, thinking, "Their hands will drop from the work, and it will not be done." But now, O God, strengthen my hands (Nehemiah 6:8–9).

Now, we do answer the lying critics as we are able, and sometimes we just ignore them. But we didn't allow their opposition to be a distraction in building the life-sized, evangelistic Ark. We kept our focus on the fact that the Ark would be one of the greatest witnessing outreaches of our time! And it and the Creation Museum are.

Looking back on the opening of the Creation Museum in 2007 and the Ark in 2016, I am reminded of the passage from Nehemiah: *Now when the wall had been built …* (Nehemiah 7:1). Today, the Creation Museum and Ark Encounter continue to be blessed by God as they draw large crowds from whom we receive many life-changing testimonies.

The day the Creation Museum opened its doors, a few dozen atheists and other anti-Christians staged a protest at the front gate. To this day, many of the same vocal opponents are spreading falsehoods as a part of their attacks against the creation/gospel message. Atheists over the years have conducted a number of protest rallies outside the Ark Encounter. They sure are worried about these two God-honoring facilities.

Whenever I hear of such opposition, I am reminded of Nehemiah: *And when all our enemies heard of it, all the nations around us were afraid and fell greatly in their own esteem, for they perceived that this work had been accomplished with the help of our God* (Nehemiah 6:16).

There are many Sanballats active today, but we realize *there is nothing new under the sun* (Ecclesiastes 1:9). Yes, the opposition can be an annoyance. But with faith, knowing that God has opened the door, we declare that with the Creation Museum and the Ark Encounter, *this work had been accomplished with the help of our God* (Nehemiah 6:16).

Don't let the "Sanballats" distract you in your work for the Lord.

SEPTEMBER 15

1 Corinthians 15:3-4

Doors: Open and Shut

Over 6,000 years ago, a "door" was shut to a garden. Because Adam sinned, God sent Adam and Eve out of the Garden: *Then the LORD God said, "Behold, the man has become like one of us in knowing good and evil. Now, lest he reach out his hand and take also of the tree of life and eat, and live forever—" therefore the Lord God sent him out from the garden of Eden to work the ground from which he was taken. He drove out the man, and at the east of the garden of Eden he placed the cherubim and a flaming sword that turned every way to guard the way to the tree of life* (Genesis 3:22–24).

Because of Genesis 3:15, we understand that God told Adam and Eve that someone would come to open the "door," leading back to the tree of life: *"I will put enmity between you and the woman, and between your offspring and her offspring; he shall bruise your head, and you shall bruise his heel"* (Genesis 3:15). This is the first time the gospel is presented in God's Word.

In the Old Testament, prophets predicted that this someone would come: *For to us a child is born, to us a son is given; and the government shall be upon his shoulder, and his name shall be called Wonderful Counselor, Mighty God, Everlasting Father, Prince of Peace* (Isaiah 9:6).

We also understand that when God told Noah to place one door in the side of the Ark so that those who went through that one door would be saved from the judgment of the Flood, this door was a picture of the One (Jesus) who would come to open the "door," for He *set the door of the ark in its side* (Genesis 6:16).

Now, at Christmastime, we especially remember (as we should every day of the year) that this Someone has come and opened the door. God's Son stepped into history as the Babe in the manger so that as Jesus Christ, the God-man, He would suffer the penalty for our sin in Adam (i.e., death) by dying on the Cross. He then rose from the dead, conquering death, and now offers the free gift of salvation to those who receive it. The following verses about Christ come to mind:

"For unto you is born this day in the city of David a Savior, who is Christ the Lord. And this will be a sign for you: you will find a baby wrapped in swaddling cloths and lying in a manger" (Luke 2:11–12).

[T]hat Christ died for our sins in accordance with the Scriptures, that he was buried, that he was raised on the third day in accordance with the Scriptures (1 Corinthians 15:3–4).

[B]ecause, if you confess with your mouth that Jesus is Lord and believe in your heart that God raised him from the dead, you will be saved (Romans 10:9).

I am the door. If anyone enters by me, he will be saved and will go in and out and find pasture (John 10:9).

Yes, God's Son opened a "door" so that all who go through this door and receive the free gift of salvation shall be saved and will once again have access to the Tree of Life and live with our Creator and Savior forever:

"He who has an ear, let him hear what the Spirit says to the churches. To the one who conquers I will grant to eat of the tree of life, which is in the paradise of God" (Revelation 2:7).

Furthermore, *Blessed are those who wash their robes, so that they may have the right to the tree of life and that they may enter the city by the gates* (Revelation 22:14).

THEOLOGY — SEPTEMBER 15

There is only one way to heaven — only one door that people go through to be saved and have access to the Tree of Life: *"And there is salvation in no one else, for there is no other name under heaven given among men by which we must be saved"* (Acts 4:12).

The "door" is open for all who will receive the free gift of salvation. One day, however, that door will shut, just as God shut the door to the Ark. That will be when Jesus returns and then the final judgment.

It's interesting to note that there are a number of "doors" in Scripture to give us a picture/understanding of the gospel. There is the Ark Door, but then we learn of:

Doors	
The Passover Door in Exodus:	The blood shall be a sign for you, on the houses where you are. And when I see the blood, I will pass over you (Exodus 12:13). Jesus is our Passover, and His sacrificial death on the Cross takes away the sin of the world.
The Temple's Inner Doors:	For it is impossible for the blood of bulls and goats to take away sins (Hebrews 10:4). Though the blood of these animals could never fully take away man's sin, they pointed forward to the most important sacrifice of all. Jesus obtained eternal redemption for us through the sinless "once-for-all" offering of Himself to God as a sacrifice for sin.
The Sheep's Door:	I am the good shepherd. The good shepherd lays down his life for the sheep (John 10:11). As the good shepherd, Jesus said He would willingly die for the sheep, a reference to His sacrificial death on the Cross – the only means by which a person can be saved. He is able to save those who draw near to God through Him.
The Cross:	[B]ut God shows his love for us in that while we were still sinners, Christ died for us (Romans 5:8). But God so loved the world that He sent His Son to take our punishment by dying as our substitute on the Cross.
The Tomb's Door:	He is not here, for he has risen (Matthew 28:6). The Resurrection confirmed that Jesus Christ was exactly who He claimed to be – the Son of God. This spectacular miracle also demonstrated His power over sin and death, guaranteeing the hope of eternal life to all who repent of their sins and believe in Him.
The Narrow Door:	"Enter by the narrow gate. For the gate is wide and the way is easy that leads to destruction, and those who enter by it are many. For the gate is narrow and the way is hard that leads to life, and those who find it are few" (Matthew 7:13-14). Jesus Christ will return to this world in judgment, and most people are heading for that judgment on the wide road.

> The only way to be saved from the eternal consequences of your sin is to enter through the narrow gate, repenting (turning from your sin) and calling on the Son of God who gave His life for you.

SEPTEMBER 16

Matthew 7:24-27

Secularist Worldview

All of us have been impacted by the secular (anti-God) world. And all of us, to one degree or another, think at times in a secular way instead of with a biblical worldview based on the Bible. Most Christians have a predominantly secular worldview that they've tried to Christianize by adding God, the Bible, etc., into their thinking.

Over my many years of traveling and speaking, I've realized that even many Christians (mostly unwittingly) have adopted an evolutionary view of man's intelligence and achievements over the millennia. Consider this Scripture: *His brother's name was Jubal; he was the father of all those who play the lyre and pipe. Zillah also bore Tubal-cain; he was the forger of all instruments of bronze and iron. The sister of Tubal-cain was Naamah* (Genesis 4:21–22).

When we built the life-sized Noah's Ark for the Ark Encounter attraction, we received criticism from some Christians and non-Christians for using iron pegs, braces, etc. Now, the Ark is built as a true timber-frame structure and is the largest free-standing timber-frame structure in the world. Because of modern building codes, we had to use iron pegs, bolts, braces, etc. However, biblical history tells us that within seven generations of Adam, people used bronze and iron. So Noah could very well have used iron for various structural purposes on the Ark.

Because of the technologically advanced world we live in, with smart phones that connect to the world in astounding ways, jet planes, and spacecraft that land on Mars, we often think we are so much more intelligent today than our ancestors who lived hundreds or thousands of years ago. Most of us tend to think that people of past societies were somewhat "primitive."

We read that in the decades and centuries after the first two humans (Adam and Eve) were created by God, people invented and played musical instruments. And from the verse above, we know that there were talented people who worked with brass and iron prior to the Flood.

Now, Genesis 4 doesn't give us many details, but this section of the Bible tells us that these people had a high degree of sophistication in a certain technology. I know I don't have anywhere near that ability myself!

The fantastic technology we enjoy today is the result of an accumulation of knowledge gained over the past few hundred years. Think how far technology has advanced in a few hundred years! The beginnings of the technologies to build automobiles go back to the late 17th and early 18th centuries, and airplanes were invented just over 100 years ago.

I often try to imagine what many people must have invented by the time of Noah, about 4,400 years ago (about 1,600 years after Creation). Who knows what remarkable things were created by geniuses when Noah was building the great Ark? Those are questions we dealt with as we designed our Ark attraction.

After the global Flood, there would have been a catastrophic loss of technology. And we don't know what kinds of technological items, tools, and machines were brought on board the Ark by Noah. But after the Flood, and as people increased in numbers on the earth, no doubt technology once again exploded.

APOLOGETICS   SEPTEMBER 16

There is an exhibit on the third deck of the Ark at Ark Encounter that gives details of man's amazing achievements since the Flood. From an evolutionary perspective, most people today believe that ancient man originally communicated with grunts, eventually developed language, and then, over time, went from making "primitive" items (e.g., stone tools) to working with bronze and iron. However, the evidence collected from around the globe refutes this false, evolutionary view of human history. The evidence many have gathered over the years confirms what we would expect based upon reading God's Word about the world: humans have been highly intelligent from the beginning and could quickly gain knowledge to create sophisticated technology. The Bible, the true history of the universe, has revealed that truth to us in Genesis.

Certainly, there have been times when wars, catastrophes, or maybe even God's judgment on wicked rebellion have hindered knowledge and inventiveness. Some accumulated knowledge would have been lost. But afterward, humans would begin to accumulate information that allowed them to be inventive once again and develop new technologies.

Not only is it fascinating to learn of man's incredible achievements of the past (think of the remarkable Egyptian pyramids), but there is something more important to learn — the vital message concerning man's continual rebellion against his Creator. As we see nations remain on the path of wicked rebellion against the One who created all things and who owns us, we should be reminded that God has provided a way of salvation from our sin and rescued us from eternal separation from God.

Most people, even in our churches, have been indoctrinated in an evolutionary, secular worldview and don't even realize it. Statistics indicate that only 6% (I would say that the actual figure is much less) of Christian schools teach a biblical worldview. It's sad to see so many Christian schools using secular textbooks and trying to add some form of Christianity into them. It's either secular or Christian. The foundation is either man's word or God's Word. Make sure you're building your worldview on the rock of God's Word, not the sand of man's word.

"Everyone then who hears these words of mine and does them will be like a wise man who built his house on the rock. And the rain fell, and the floods came, and the winds blew and beat on that house, but it did not fall, because it had been founded on the rock. And everyone who hears these words of mine and does not do them will be like a foolish man who built his house on the sand. And the rain fell, and the floods came, and the winds blew and beat against that house, and it fell, and great was the fall of it" (Matthew 7:24–27).

> **We need to learn what it means to build our thinking on God's Word and develop a worldview that is truly Christian.**

SEPTEMBER 17

Isaiah 11:8

Suffering and Death

Over the years, I've had many people tell me that there had to be death and suffering before the Fall because creatures like snakes have venomous bites and many other creatures look like they are designed to kill in various ways. If God called His creation "very good," then why does it include dangerous venomous snakes today?

A major problem with people making such statements is that they are looking at today's world and using that to interpret the past. But if we take the history in Genesis, we know that the world today is not as God created it. The world we live in has gone through major events such as the Fall of man, the entrance of sin and death, the judgment of the curse, the Flood of Noah's day, and so on.

After Noah's Flood, God even changed the behavior of animals regarding their relationship with man: *The fear of you and the dread of you shall be upon every beast of the earth and upon every bird of the heavens, upon everything that creeps on the ground and all the fish of the sea. Into your hand they are delivered* (Genesis 9:2).

Animals were not part of the human diet originally, but God changed that after the Flood: *Every moving thing that lives shall be food for you. And as I gave you the green plants, I give you everything. But you shall not eat flesh with its life, that is, its blood* (Genesis 9:3–4).

The point is, we can't look at this world, which has had many changes since its creation, and use what we see today to then claim God created everything this way. Certainly, there's biological consistency in the sense that dogs reproduce dogs, etc., but much has changed since God called everything "very good." So, let's now get back to venomous snakes.

Are secular researchers on the right track as they examine the snake genome in order to find clues about gene evolution in humans? The answer is clear when you start with God's Word and remember that there are two kinds of science.

According to *Nature World News*, "A new study details the evolution of snakes and how they came to boast a venomous bite, challenging the conventional view of how the species got their toxic label."

Rather than just studying the genes related to venom production as previous studies have done, this study "used the genome to look at the rest of that picture" throughout the snake's whole body. Researchers are hoping that this new study will help "lead to improved anti-venom treatments as well as shed light on gene evolution in humans."

Now, improving anti-venom treatments because of a better understanding of snake genes is observational science because it's observable, testable, and repeatable. And it's great to do that in a fallen world to be of help to mankind. But examining these genes to try and understand how genes supposedly evolved in humans or how snakes supposedly evolved their venom is a different kind of science — historical science. This kind of science is not directly testable, observable, or repeatable. What you believe about the earth's history will largely determine how you interpret the evidence. In trying to make these evolutionary conclusions, the researchers have stepped outside the realm of observational science and are entering into the area of historical science.

APOLOGETICS

These researchers are also looking at snake venom from the wrong starting point! Contrary to the naturalistic ideas of many scientists, there never was "a core venom system [that] developed at one point in the evolution of snakes and lizards." There is no need to appeal to naturalistic processes to explain the complex structures and elements necessary for venom production and delivery. Venomous snakes show clear examples of having been designed. But how should we understand killer designs from a loving Creator?

Well, Scripture tells us that originally, all of creation — including snakes — was "very good" (Genesis 1:31). Genesis also says that the animals (and Adam and Eve) were originally vegetarians (Genesis 1:30). So, in a perfect world, there was no reason for snakes to kill or harm other creatures with venom. It wasn't until after Adam and Eve sinned and death and suffering came into the world that defense/attack structures, like venom, were necessary. These structures may have had a good purpose in the original creation and then were used for new purposes after the Fall, or they may have been expressed sometime after the Fall (mediated design) as snakes adapted to a fallen world.

Either way, deadly venom and the pain, suffering, and death caused by other attack structures are clearly consequences of the Fall and the curse — not an original part of a "very good" creation! Scripture talks about a coming time when we will no longer have to fear snakes' venom: *The nursing child shall play over the hole of the cobra, and the weaned child shall put his hand on the adder's den* (Isaiah 11:8).

If you start with man's word, then death and suffering have always been part of nature and always will be — they are the very things that are supposed to drive evolution. But if you start with God's Word, you get an entirely different picture. Death and suffering were not an original part of creation. They are the result of mankind's sin, and someday they will be removed from creation.

Then I saw a new heaven and a new earth, for the first heaven and the first earth had passed away, and the sea was no more. And I saw the holy city, new Jerusalem, coming down out of heaven from God, prepared as a bride adorned for her husband. And I heard a loud voice from the throne saying, "Behold, the dwelling place of God is with man. He will dwell with them, and they will be his people, and God himself will be with them as their God. He will wipe away every tear from their eyes, and death shall be no more, neither shall there be mourning, nor crying, nor pain anymore, for the former things have passed away" (Revelation 21:1–4).

Whether you start with man's word or God's Word makes a huge difference in how you interpret the world around you.

SEPTEMBER 18

Proverbs 13:24

Proper Child Rearing

Parents, if you desire to demonstrate biblical love to your children, then understand their sin nature and exercise biblical discipline. Our culture would greatly benefit from parents disciplining their children in God's way. Many Christians have known for a long time that discipline of children is a problem in our Western cultures. An article some years back from an Australian news source was titled, "Education experts claim discipline system in state schools is 'new-age and politically correct.'" In it, education experts argued that the disciplinary measures in Australian schools were not working.

Kevin Donnelly, director of the Education Standards Institute, not only identified a problem with the school system but also suggested that parents "needed to play a bigger role in teaching their children respect for authority." Surprisingly, he's right! Parents in American culture, like in Australia, do not discipline children God's way. They are not teaching their children respect for authority, and that has left us with many problems. Just as the culture has abandoned the foundation of God's Word for its worldview regarding such issues as marriage and the sanctity of life, so also it has abandoned the authority of Scripture in the discipline of children. Secular psychology rejects that children are sinners and instead teaches that children are basically "good." This is a false premise, and it will never lead to the exercise of biblical discipline of children. Children are no different than adults when it comes to sin, *for all have sinned and fall short of the glory of God* (Romans 3:23).

Many people, including some Christians, fail to realize that one God-given aspect of biblical discipline is corporal punishment — and God tells parents to use it in disciplining their children. Of course, there are some people who have abused children with force, and we at Answers in Genesis reject this misuse of corporal punishment. Physical punishment performed in a biblical manner is a socially unpopular component of biblical parenting, but there is more to parenting than just corporal punishment. Other aspects of biblical discipline include rewards and disincentives, "do's and don'ts," leadership by example (especially in faithfully following God's Word), and so on. Throughout the Book of Proverbs, biblical discipline is emphasized as the way to life and wisdom. Below are a variety of proverbs that speak to the issue of disciplining our children:

Whoever spares the rod hates his son, but he who loves him is diligent to discipline him (Proverbs 13:24).

Discipline your son, for there is hope; do not set your heart on putting him to death (Proverbs 19:18).

Train up a child in the way he should go; even when he is old he will not depart from it (Proverbs 22:6).

As part of the command to exercise biblical discipline, God also instructs parents not to "provoke" their children. In other words, discipline in all its aspects — positive and negative, physical and verbal — should be applied not abusively, but in a way that encourages the child to become the kind of person God intends (which incidentally is the sort of child both parents and teachers want to see):

Fathers, do not provoke your children to anger, but bring them up in the discipline and instruction of the Lord (Ephesians 6:4).

Any discipline, whether corporal or otherwise, must be motivated by love and concern for the best interests of the child. When we discipline our children, we are attempting to teach them wisdom and show them right from wrong. If we discipline biblically and in love, our children will grow to respect us as parents for it,

FAMILY SEPTEMBER 18

recognizing that we too are under God's authority. Furthermore, they will learn to respect those in authority outside of the home, whether teachers, government officials, or employers. The Bible commands us to discipline our children because it is a reflection of how God disciplines believers, who are His children:

And have you forgotten the exhortation that addresses you as sons? "My son, do not regard lightly the discipline of the Lord, nor be weary when reproved by him. For the Lord disciplines the one he loves, and chastises every son whom he receives." It is for discipline that you have to endure. God is treating you as sons. For what son is there whom his father does not discipline? If you are left without discipline, in which all have participated, then you are illegitimate children and not sons. Besides this, we have had earthly fathers who disciplined us and we respected them. Shall we not much more be subject to the Father of spirits and live? For they disciplined us for a short time as it seemed best to them, but he disciplines us for our good, that we may share his holiness. For the moment all discipline seems painful rather than pleasant, but later it yields the peaceful fruit of righteousness to those who have been trained by it (Hebrews 12:5–11).

Hebrews is clear: discipline from God our Father may be unpleasant, but the reward is the "fruit of righteousness." Likewise, when we practice biblical discipline with our children, we demonstrate that we love our children, and it teaches them wisdom and drives away foolishness. There are, however, many instances when God-honoring parents train their children in God's Word and discipline their children in a godly manner, only to have them rebel later in life. It can be deeply discouraging for parents to see their adult children walking away from the Lord. Parents often feel guilty because they believe such a rebellion was caused by something they failed to do during their children's younger years. However, when we look at Scripture, there are several instances of children rebelling against their parents. The following two accounts exemplify this.

The first account features Hophni and Phineas, the sons of Eli. Eli was a priest in Shiloh who was a personal caregiver to the child Samuel (1 Samuel 1:3). There is no doubt that Eli was a godly man who was seeking to please the Lord. However, his sons did not display the same godly character. Hophni and Phineas served as priests in Shiloh like their father, but they disregarded the duties of priesthood and engaged in illicit behavior (1 Samuel 2). God was not pleased with their actions, and they were eventually slain by the Philistines (1 Samuel 4:4).

The second account to consider is the parable of the prodigal son (Luke 15:11–31). While this may simply be a fictional narrative, Jesus used it to demonstrate God's love toward sinners. In this parable, the son requests and receives his inheritance from his father and wastes it in sinful living. The prodigal son realizes that the servants in his father's home are living in better conditions than he is. He comes home and is reconciled to his father.

Like these sons of old, our children might make decisions that contradict their godly upbringing. Ultimately, our children will have to make their own personal decisions to trust in Christ. Parents, if you desire to demonstrate biblical love to your children, then exercise biblical discipline. Our culture as a whole would benefit greatly from parents disciplining their children in God's way.

> **Our motivation for the discipline of our children is to show them their sinfulness and point them to Christ.**

SEPTEMBER 19
2 Chronicles 31:20-21

Lukewarm Churches: Part 1

So much of the Church today is lukewarm. Many churches in the West are more concerned about entertainment and music than the teaching of the Word! Associated with a lukewarm, compromising Church (so many church leaders compromise Genesis with evolution/millions of years) is a catastrophic generational loss from the Church. The next time you're tempted to despair at the hopelessness of our modern Church, consider Hezekiah. He faced similar challenges — and overcame them.

My mind constantly turns to the sad state of Christianity today and what Bible-believing Christians can do to turn things around. The task seems impossibly great, and the challenges overwhelming.

I was rereading our Answers in Genesis ministry's mission statement, and the Lord brought something to my mind that should encourage and warn every believer who is burdened to reach this world with the gospel. Our ministry's official goal is "to support the church in fulfilling its commission." To accomplish this goal, our vision statement says, "Answers in Genesis is a catalyst to bring reformation by reclaiming the foundations of our faith which are found in the Bible, from the very first verse." Note that our vision involves "bringing reformation."

When we think of the word "reformation," Christians usually think of the great reformer Martin Luther. However, there were reformers long before Martin Luther, from whom we can learn many lessons. One of the most valuable examples comes from the Bible itself, the reformer King Hezekiah. God ensured that details about Hezekiah's life and reforms would be written down in His holy Word so we could learn from what he did and be challenged in our own walk of faith.

God's Word says about the magnitude of Hezekiah's amazing reforms: *So there was great joy in Jerusalem, for since the time of Solomon the son of David king of Israel there had been nothing like this in Jerusalem* (2 Chronicles 30:26).

Hezekiah carried out reforms to destroy idol worship and restore temple worship. He reinstituted the Passover and did whatever he could and needed to do to get people back to obeying God's Word.

We certainly need that in our own culture. We need reformation in our churches because so many believers in this era have compromised God's Word, beginning in Genesis! We are also seeing the sad consequences (abortion on demand, gay "marriage," transgenderism, increasing violence, and so on) of a Western world that is becoming more anti-Christian and attempting to remove any vestiges of Christian influence and heritage.

So, what are the lessons we can learn from Hezekiah? What was different about Hezekiah compared to so many of the other kings of Israel and Judah who came before him? At the beginning of the 2 Chronicles account of Hezekiah, we read: *And he did what was right in the eyes of the Lord, according to all that David his father had done* (2 Chronicles 29:2).

And after Hezekiah instituted many of his reforms, we read more about his godly character: *Thus Hezekiah did throughout all Judah, and he did what was good and right and faithful before the Lord his God. And every*

CHURCH — SEPTEMBER 19

work that he undertook in the service of the house of God and in accordance with the law and the commandments, seeking his God, he did with all his heart, and prospered (2 Chronicles 31:20–21).

The lesson? If we want to impact the world around us, God's people first need to seek God and be obedient to His Word. Sadly, many Christians and Christian leaders today exalt man's word by taking man's religion of evolution and millions of years (an attempt to explain life without God) and adding it to God's infallible Word. This is, in reality, no different from the efforts by the people of Judah and Israel to adopt the pagan religion of their age and mix it with what God had instructed.

Yes, we first need to return to God's Word beginning in Genesis and give up the rampant compromise that has spread throughout the Church and Christian institutions. Reformation begins with a return to the authority of the Word of God and obeying God's revelation to man. But be warned, scoffers attack every good work. We read about some of Hezekiah's specific initiatives in 2 Chronicles 30:1 and 30:5:

Hezekiah sent to all Israel and Judah, and wrote letters also to Ephraim and Manasseh, that they should come to the house of the LORD at Jerusalem to keep the Passover to the LORD, the God of Israel.... So they decreed to make a proclamation throughout all Israel, from Beersheba to Dan, that the people should come and keep the Passover to the LORD, the God of Israel, at Jerusalem, for they had not kept it as often as prescribed.

Then, later, we find out about the negative response: *So the couriers went from city to city through the country of Ephraim and Manasseh, and as far as Zebulun, but they laughed them to scorn and mocked them* (2 Chronicles 30:10). As Hezekiah was calling on people to *return to the Lord* (2 Chronicles 30:9), many scoffed.

This is a reminder to anyone who shares the Word faithfully that there will be scoffers. In fact, we should expect scoffers. In 2 Peter 3, we are warned that the most basic teachings of God's Word — concerning creation, the Flood, and Christ's second coming and judgment by fire — will be scoffed at:

[K]nowing this first of all, that scoffers will come in the last days with scoffing, following their own sinful desires. They will say, "Where is the promise of his coming? For ever since the fathers fell asleep, all things are continuing as they were from the beginning of creation." For they deliberately overlook this fact, that the heavens existed long ago, and the earth was formed out of water and through water by the word of God, and that by means of these the world that then existed was deluged with water and perished (2 Peter 3:3–6).

So many in our world today scoff at those who stand on God's Word in Genesis and reject man's beliefs concerning the supposed big bang, billions of years, and evolution. At Answers in Genesis, we have experienced much scoffing too, and it has only increased with time.

Stay true to God's Word and contend for the faith (Jude 3), knowing we will have scoffers.

SEPTEMBER 20

2 Chronicles 29:34

Lukewarm Churches: Part 2

There is an interesting statement in 2 Chronicles 29:34 concerning the priests — that the common Levites were more diligent or conscientious than the priests, who were supposed to be the religious leaders:

But the priests were too few and could not flay all the burnt offerings, so until other priests had consecrated themselves, their brothers the Levites helped them, until the work was finished—for the Levites were more upright in heart than the priests in consecrating themselves.

All through the Old and New Testaments we are warned of shepherds (religious leaders) who lead the people astray. This is certainly not true of all leaders — but even in our world today, we find that the majority of church leaders compromise God's Word in Genesis or don't want to preach the hard things (like sin, repentance, and hell) for fear of upsetting people.

And then there's the problem of pride that threatens us all. Here is a very serious warning for all of us: the problem of pride. Even as great a man of God as Hezekiah was, his pride let him down. At first, he was humble, and God greatly blessed his faith. After the many reforms Hezekiah instituted, God allowed the king of Assyria to come against Judah, intent on war against Jerusalem. Hezekiah fortified the city, made weapons, and prepared for the battle. But most important, he encouraged the people to trust in God, who was on their side: *"Be strong and courageous. Do not be afraid or dismayed before the king of Assyria and all the horde that is with him, for there are more with us than with him. With him is an arm of flesh, but with us is the Lord our God, to help us and to fight our battles." And the people took confidence from the words of Hezekiah king of Judah* (2 Chronicles 32:7–8).

When the king of Assyria sent people to taunt the Jews and mock their God, Hezekiah did what we should all do for every challenge, every day: *Then Hezekiah the king and Isaiah the prophet, the son of Amoz, prayed because of this and cried to heaven* (2 Chronicles 32:20).

And because of this, God gave Hezekiah great victory, and I find it thrilling every time I read it: *And the Lord sent an angel, who cut off all the mighty warriors and commanders and officers in the camp of the king of Assyria. So he returned with shame of face to his own land. And when he came into the house of his god, some of his own sons struck him down there with the sword. So the Lord saved Hezekiah and the inhabitants of Jerusalem from the hand of Sennacherib king of Assyria and from the hand of all his enemies, and he provided for them on every side* (2 Chronicles 32:21–22).

But now comes the lesson every one of us must learn. The Scripture warns us about pride. Because of our sin nature, this is a problem we all have. After the great victory God gave Hezekiah, we read about this sad situation: *In those days Hezekiah became sick and was at the point of death, and he prayed to the Lord, and he answered him and gave him a sign. But Hezekiah did not make return according to the benefit done to him, for his heart was proud. Therefore wrath came upon him and Judah and Jerusalem* (2 Chronicles 32:24–25).

Because of the wonderful defeat of the Assyrian army, Hezekiah became proud! This should have been his downfall, but *Hezekiah humbled himself for the pride of his heart, both he and the inhabitants of Jerusalem, so that the wrath of the Lord did not come upon them in the days of Hezekiah* (2 Chronicles 32:26).

CHURCH

When we are involved in serving the Lord, no matter how great or small our role, we always need to remember to give God the glory and honor and to recognize it is easy for any of us to be lifted up in pride and set the wrong example for those looking at us. *One's pride will bring him low, but he who is lowly in spirit will obtain honor* (Proverbs 29:23).

There is one final lesson I want to bring to your attention. Hezekiah died, and we read that his son Manasseh became king in his place. But we are told: *And he did what was evil in the sight of the Lord, according to the abominations of the nations whom the Lord drove out before the people of Israel* (2 Chronicles 33:2).

It is hard to fathom how such a godly king as Hezekiah could end up with such an evil son as Manasseh to take his place. We don't know the circumstances or why Manasseh ended up the way he did. But what a warning to us that we must always be vigilant and do the very best we can to raise up offspring who will carry on the spiritual legacy to the next generation, and then the next, and so on. A lasting legacy requires vigilance. When we are involved in serving the Lord, we always need to remember to give God the glory and honor.

It's sad to observe the fact that most Christian institutions in our Western world have lost the biblical stand of their founders as compromise creeps in. Many such institutions have now become leaders in indoctrinating generations against the authority of the Word of God.

Yes, we need Hezekiah-type reformers today. But we need to understand the sober lessons from Hezekiah's life, which God put in His Word for our learning.

> Our focus needs to be on God's infallible Word, and we must always remember that hope for true reform rests in God alone.

SEPTEMBER 21

Genesis 2:24

The Bible Is Clear: Homosexuality Is Sinful

People can use the Bible to justify any position they want when they take words out of context or read into the text what is not there. On April 22, 2014, a new attack on the reliability and perspicuity of Scripture was released. *God and the Gay Christian* was a book that sought to teach readers that the Bible condones living a monogamous homosexual lifestyle. That attack continues today in the Church.

The author was Matthew Vines, an openly homosexual man and a professing Christian. Being an openly practicing homosexual and claiming to be a Christian often means the person has an agenda to attempt to make the words of Scripture fit with his worldview. This was certainly the case with Matthew Vines.

We carefully consider what God says in His Word and judge man's fallible ideas accordingly — which is what every church leader should be doing. If compromising church leaders were to judge Vines' words against Scripture, they would have to condemn his book for what it is — a work that misleads people to believe the author's homosexual lifestyle as a professing Christian is consistent with Scripture.

Vines offers many of the arguments typical of liberal-leaning Christians who wish to justify homosexual behavior, claiming ultimately that monogamous same-sex relationships were not what Scripture had in view in its condemnation of homosexual sin.

Dr. Mohler, president of Southern Baptist Theological Seminary, found Vines' book to be yet another confirmation that soon "there will be no place to hide, and there will be no way to remain silent" on the issue of homosexuality. He added that Vines simply divorces parts of Scripture from itself to make it mean whatever he wants it to: "The most radical proposal Vines actually makes is to sever each of these passages from the flow of the biblical narrative and the Bible's most fundamental revelation about what it means to be human, both male and female. He does not do this merely by omission, but by the explicit argument that the Church has misunderstood the doctrine of creation as much as the question of human sexuality. He specifically seeks to argue that the basic sexual complementarity of the human male and the female — each made in God's image — is neither essential to Genesis chapters 1 and 2 or to any biblical text that follows.

"In other words, he argues that same-sex sexuality can be part of the goodness of God's original creation, and that when God declared that it is not good for man to be alone, the answer to man's isolation could be a sexual relationship with someone of either sex. But that massive misrepresentation of Genesis 1 and 2 — a misinterpretation with virtually unlimited theological consequences — actually becomes Vines' way of relativizing the meaning of the six passages he primarily considers."[94] What Dr. Mohler claimed is no overstatement. In reading Vines' analysis of the creation account, it becomes evident that he has little regard for God's intention in making Adam and Eve male and female. Vines' agenda is clear: He must make room for same-sex relationships — from the very beginning of Scripture. He has to dismantle the Genesis account of creation.

Vines writes, "Let's start at the beginning." After offering a summary of the creation in Genesis 1, Vines goes on to say that "for everything God regarded as good about his creation, there was one thing he said was not good." It was not good for man to be alone. But Vines begins to twist Scripture here: "This story shows us what the world looked like before it became tainted by sin. Non-affirming Christians [i.e., those who believe

THEOLOGY

homosexual behavior is sinful] generally argue that the creation of Adam and Eve reveals the limits of God's blessing for sexual relationships: one man and one woman.... But the account of Eve's creation doesn't emphasize Adam's need to procreate. It emphasizes instead his need for a relationship."

It was not good for Adam to be alone, and Vines is correct in pointing out how Eve fulfilled the need for a relationship. However, one of the commands God gave when He created the first couple is to *be fruitful and multiply* (Genesis 1:28). This is a clear indication that humankind has a purpose: to fill the earth. Vines seems to be saying that God's command to be fruitful is secondary to finding a fulfilling relationship — the definition of which, according to Vines, is in the eye of the beholder. Even in Malachi 2:15, the prophet refers back to the "one flesh" of Genesis 2 when proclaiming one of the primary functions of marriage — to produce godly seed ("godly offspring"): *But did He not make them one, Having a remnant of the Spirit? And why one? He seeks godly offspring* (Malachi 2:15; NKJV).

And He answered and said to them, "Have you not read that He who made them at the beginning 'made them male and female,' and said, 'For this reason a man shall leave his father and mother and be joined to his wife, and the two shall become one flesh'? So then, they are no longer two but one flesh. Therefore what God has joined together, let not man separate" (Matthew 19:4–6; NKJV).

But Vines is not satisfied with just changing the definition of marriage in Scripture. Vines also reinterprets why Eve, in particular, was created for Adam, claiming that God's decision was based not on any sort of fixed definition of marriage but rather on "sameness."

How does Vines attempt to support his position? He uses God's process of bringing the animals to Adam to be named and Adam's failure to find a *helper comparable to him* among them (Genesis 2:20; NKJV) as evidence for his case that sameness — rather than marriage in God's design — is the focus. However, the vast majority of Christians would agree that the best kind of companionship for a human is with another human and that bestiality is sinful. God shows Adam through the naming process that there was no suitable helper for him among the animals. Of course, God could have stopped there in His provision of a companion for Adam, thus proving Vines' point that any human — male or female — will do. But He doesn't.

No, God gives Adam a human female companion — who also fits the exact definition of marriage God provides in Genesis 2:24. And when we consider this against the whole of Scripture (something Vines fails to do), God's provision of a woman as a suitable helper for the man Adam is consistent with Scripture's repeated warnings against same-sex and bestial relationships, and Christ's affirmation of marriage as it was described in Genesis 2. Scripture also refers back to Genesis (just like Jesus in Matthew 19), quoting the "one flesh" of Genesis 2 in Ephesians:

In the same way husbands should love their wives as their own bodies. He who loves his wife loves himself. For no one ever hated his own flesh, but nourishes and cherishes it, just as Christ does the church, because we are members of his body. "Therefore a man shall leave his father and mother and hold fast to his wife, and the two shall become one flesh" (Ephesians 5:28–31).

> **To emphasize another point, what Vines does in his attempts to justify gay "marriage" is no different than Christians who add millions of years and other evolutionary ideas to Scripture and reinterpret the words to fit their beliefs obtained from outside of Scripture.**

SEPTEMBER 22
1 Timothy 6:20

Creationists Can Be Scientists

I've often heard the claim from atheists that creationists can't be real scientists! What they really mean is if you are a scientist and a creationist, we (the atheists) will do all we can to discriminate against you and not allow you to be published because we are totally intolerant of Christianity. Answers in Genesis has a number of PhD scientists. One of them obtained his PhD from Harvard university. All of our PhD scientists actually obtained their qualifications from well-respected secular universities. Yes, they are real scientists and ardent (literal Genesis) creationists. I wanted to feature some of them for you and give you a summary of some of the research they are doing to show that observational science confirms the Bible's account of history.

To me, research can be both boring and exciting at the same time! Boring — because sometimes it seems to take millions of years for our researchers to meticulously carry out their investigations! Exciting — because after years of research, our speakers and writers (and others) can use the results to show people how observational science confirms the Bible's account in Genesis and devastates evolutionary ideas.

Take the research of Dr. Gabriela Haynes. She's a PhD paleontologist who came to work in AiG's research department from Brazil. Here, she explains some of her research: "Soft tissue in fossils was always something interesting for me as a paleontologist. Then, during my PhD research on Hymenoptera (wasps, ants, and bees) while I was looking for pollens, I found something that looked like blood cells in an insect fossil. As a creationist, that brought me a lot of excitement!

"At first my secular colleagues were excited to do some research, but then they concluded that those blood cells could not belong to the wasp since it is dated to supposedly 120 million years. They told me, 'It is contamination. Don't bother.' I just thought that their answer was not very scientific, and, as a creationist, I believed that there was a chance those blood cells were not the result of contamination. I tried to make them study the material, but it was in vain. They had already settled the case in their minds ... I did some research by myself, and all the results I had were pointing to soft tissue material and blood cells. Unfortunately, I didn't have the support from my secular colleagues to use the laboratory and run more tests." She is now continuing her research at Answers in Genesis and publishing papers in our technical publication, *Answers Research Journal*. In fact, there are now many examples of soft tissue found in fossils that are supposed to be millions of years old. Much more research needs to be done in this vital area, and our scientists will certainly be doing this.

Then there's our Harvard-trained PhD scientist, Dr. Nathaniel Jeanson. He published his monumental book *Replacing Darwin*. This ground-breaking book details his genetics research to clearly show that speciation, adaptation, and natural selection when properly understood, devastate Darwinian evolution.

Dr. Jeanson has also been conducting research into human genetics. He's looking into whether there's evidence from human populations to confirm the biblical account of history beginning about 6,000 years ago. Dr. Jeanson's research also has important things to say about the event of the Flood (i.e., all humans today are descendants of Noah's sons) and the account of the Tower of Babel. His research to date is blowing the evolutionary time scale out the window. Dr. Jeanson states: "In our culture, few things provoke more ridicule than the idea that the earth is just 6,000 years old. As a biologist, I've witnessed my anti-evolutionary colleagues critique evolution — and deftly avoid the contentious and embarrassing age question — for decades.

With the advent of modern genetics, this avoidance is no longer possible. For example, within each of our bodies, we have genetic 'clocks' that have marked the passage of time since the dawn of humanity. If anyone wants to explain the origin of mankind, they must deal with these genetic clocks. My published research has found evidence that these clocks have ticked for only 6,000 years. I'm now exploring an even more powerful implication of this finding: if the global genetic differences among humans reflect 6,000 years, then they should also bear the stamp of the known history of civilization. If evolution were true, this stamp would be very difficult to detect. Instead, my initial results are showing that 6,000 years are indeed the hero of the plot."

Now, evolutionists often use astronomy in an attempt to prove their billions of years/evolutionary history of the universe. There is so much more research needed in astronomy, and we praise the Lord that our PhD astronomer, Dr. Danny Faulkner, is involved in all sorts of such fascinating research. Dr. Faulkner states:"I have been working and publishing in the field of eclipsing binary stars for four decades. Two other creation astronomers who are close associates of mine also have studied eclipsing binary stars for years.

Then there's the ongoing research conducted by Dr. Andrew Snelling, who has been leading research on the massive folding of sedimentary strata in the Grand Canyon. This is the project that the Grand Canyon National Park and secular scientists tried to stop. It's that intolerance they have of anything Christian. A legal challenge was lodged on our behalf by the religious freedom group Alliance Defending Freedom. Because of clear and obvious violations of our First Amendment rights (discrimination because we were Christians) by the federal government, Grand Canyon officials were forced to settle, and all the necessary specimens were collected. Dr. Snelling's ongoing research at the Canyon is being published in a series of papers in our free *Answers Research Journal*. Dr. Snelling explains more about this research: "Evolutionary geologists claim the flat-lying sedimentary layers exposed like a stack of pancakes in the walls of the Grand Canyon were deposited grain by grain over 300 million years. Then some 150 million years later those layers were bent as the area was pushed up by earth movements to form a plateau. By that time, those layers were hard and brittle, so when they were bent, the rocks should have cracked and shattered. Or, because of the burial of these layers under a two-mile thickness of other layers above them, the pressure and heat may have made the rocks plastic enough to bend them smoothly as well. What we find is the layers are bent smoothly without any major cracking or shattering. So the layers had to have been bent while still soft. Thus, I have collected samples from these layers where they are bent and from well away from the bent layers for comparison. The laboratory and microscope examination results so far show no differences in either the minerals or the textures present in these sedimentary layers."

Now, it only took you a few minutes to read this article. But the research I've outlined for you can take many months — or even a few years — to complete. And yet, such research is vital for the Answers in Genesis apologetics ministry. I sometimes smile in my public talks as I share a particular piece of powerful evidence, but I take just a minute to do it! I know it may have taken two years of painfully meticulous work for a researcher to complete the work. Yes, I am passionate about our research team and their work. The ongoing research by our PhD scientists is so important in today's anti-Christian culture. *O Timothy, guard the deposit entrusted to you. Avoid the irreverent babble and contradictions of what is falsely called "knowledge"* (1 Timothy 6:20).

> It's crucial that Christians have the tools and the information they need to help refute the many attacks on the Bible.

SEPTEMBER 23
1 Peter 3:15

Rise of Scoffers

Ponder this verse: *A good name is better than precious ointment* (Ecclesiastes 7:1).

Over the many years of my personal, intimate experience in the biblical creation ministry (beginning in 1977), I have observed "evolving" (in the sense of "changing") tactics used by prominent secularists to respond to arguments from creationist scholars and researchers. Based on my experience, I would divide the interactions of biblical creationists and outspoken secularists into four basic eras:

The Debate Era of the 1970s: When I first became aware of the USA creation movement in the 1970s (while I was a teacher in Australia), I learned that the late Duane Gish (PhD in biochemistry from the University of California, Berkley) of the Institute for Creation Research was actively debating evolutionary scientists from various academic institutions.

At that time, creationist arguments against evolution largely consisted of arguments against so-called ape-men and arguments that the Cambrian Explosion and lack of transitional forms illustrated that Darwinian evolution did not happen. Evolutionists argued back with supposed counters to these arguments. For instance, they claimed that *Archaeopteryx* was a transitional form between reptiles and birds (since refuted), that the "mammal-like reptiles" (which are reptiles) were transitional forms, and so on. However, in the long run, such "evidence" was just interpreted differently by both sides according to their starting points — creation or evolution!

Nonetheless, the biblical creation movement began publishing more and more books, videos, and other materials; and the "creation versus evolution" issue rose to greater prominence in the culture and secular media. Secularist opposition to the creation movement intensified, with many articles in print. Although they included some ridicule, many articles tried to outline the supposed scientific reasons why creationists were wrong.

The Public School Controversies of the 1980s and Beyond: Frustrated with how evolutionary teaching had taken over much of the secular education system and seeing that creation (and critical thinking about origins) was outlawed from the classroom, many Christians tried (unsuccessfully) in the courts to force public (secular) school teachers to teach creation in their classes, or at least to allow critiques of evolution.

This era eventually sparked the rise of the non-Christian "Intelligent Design" movement — which many Christians thought might be the answer to the education problem but soon found it was not.

Secularists fought hard to falsely accuse creationists of being anti-science. They typically labeled belief in the Genesis account of history — or even the simple belief that God created — as just a "religious" view, while belief in Darwinian evolution was a supposed "scientific" view. But evolution is a religious view.

Some secularists have reverted to name-calling (intense ad hominem attacks) in a desperate attempt to discredit biblical creationists. No longer satisfied with arguing that creationists could not be real scientists and that belief in creation is anti-science, secularists began accusing creationists of being anti-technology. I began to see the (false) argument that people who believe in creation are inconsistent if they use modern technology, such as computers and airplanes, which are products of man's scientific ingenuity.

SCIENCE   SEPTEMBER 23

In an attempt to defame their integrity, increased name-calling against creationists began to appear, not just in newspaper articles but in various evolutionist books, blogs, and reputable science magazines. Biblical creationists were also often equated with terrorists, as secular writers used words like "fundamentalists" to describe both Christians and terrorists. All of this name-calling by unscrupulous secularists has been (and still is) part of a deliberate attempt to smear Christians and use fear tactics to brainwash people into a false understanding of what Christians/creationists believe.

This era also saw the rise of the "New Atheists," who began overtly attacking Christianity and preaching atheism around the world. This radical atheist movement was really spearheaded by Dr. Richard Dawkins of Oxford University, summed up in a quote from his best-selling book *The God Delusion*, in which he vehemently attacks the Christian God: "The God of the Old Testament is arguably the most unpleasant character in all fiction: jealous and proud of it; a petty, unjust, unforgiving control-freak; a vindictive, bloodthirsty ethnic cleanser; a misogynistic, homophobic, racist, infanticidal, genocidal, filicidal, pestilential, megalomaniacal, sadomasochistic, capriciously malevolent bully. Those of us schooled from infancy in his ways can become desensitized to their horror."[95]

Also troublesome were the accusations from different sources that creationists and Christians are "child abusers" (as I've mentioned at other times). Such an emotionally charged term was really meant to marginalize Christians in the culture. If the secular elite had total control of the culture, they could prosecute this in the courts. Richard Dawkins agrees that this term is appropriate for Christians who teach about the doctrine of hell, as he stated, "I am persuaded that the phrase 'child abuse' is no exaggeration when used to describe what teachers and priests are doing to children whom they encourage to believe in something like the punishment of unshriven mortal sins in an eternal hell."

When the Creation Museum opened near the Cincinnati International Airport on Memorial Day weekend 2007, secular scientists and an atheist group demonstrated outside the museum with signs simply mocking my name, such as "Behold, the curse of Ham," rather than using logical scientific arguments to argue their case. Resorting to such name-calling not only shows that this issue strikes deep spiritual problems but that those who can't prove their position by logic or science are driven by emotion. We can expect such name-calling in their attempts to marginalize Christians to increase as secularists become more frustrated in not being able to refute the powerful truth that the Creator is clearly seen and *In the beginning, God created the heavens and the earth* (Genesis 1:1).

A theme verse of my life and Answers in Genesis includes every Christian's duty to give answers "with gentleness":

[B]ut in your hearts honor Christ the Lord as holy, always being prepared to make a defense to anyone who asks you for a reason for the hope that is in you; yet do it with gentleness and respect (1 Peter 3:15).

We need to remember what God said in Proverbs 21:24: *"Scoffer" is the name of the arrogant, haughty man who acts with arrogant pride*. In contrast, God expects His people to take the higher ground and earn a reputation for kind and gentle words as we speak *the truth in love* (Ephesians 4:15).

    Ponder the verse again: "A good name is better than precious ointment" (Ecclesiastes 7:1).

SEPTEMBER 24
Ezekiel 3:17

AiG's Prophetic Message

What do I mean by saying that Answers in Genesis has been giving a "prophetic" message? When was the following written? The answer may surprise you: "Our declining society is an outward expression of an inward rejection of the Creator. And our freedoms are being eroded as Christianity is being slowly eliminated. Christians may wake up one day to find Christianity outlawed."

That certainly sounds like a description of America today, doesn't it? But it was published in 1988. The paragraph comes from page 97 of a book I co-authored as a companion to *The Genesis Solution*, a 16 mm film released in 1987 featuring a live presentation I gave that the Lord has used to build the Answers in Genesis ministry. We call it the "relevance of Genesis message."

Now back in the 1980s, I had been making the statement that "Christians may wake up one day to find Christianity outlawed." It was a major part of the talks I was giving in churches in both Australia and the USA. Frankly, many Christians laughed at me for even suggesting that such a change could happen. I remember some Americans back then saying something like, "No, not in America — it could never happen here!" At the time, I was also challenging the Church in the USA and Australia concerning what would happen if God's people continued to compromise Genesis with millions of years and evolutionary beliefs. For instance, I wrote this in *The Genesis Solution* book: "As 'the Genesis connection' is increasingly removed from modern society and replaced by belief in evolution and secular humanism, we can logically expect various tragic results:

- Decrease in marriage (fewer people will bother with it).
- Increase in suicides, 'mercy killings,' and euthanasia.
- Increase in promiscuity and pornography.
- Increase in public nudity. (The only moral basis for clothing and modesty is founded in Genesis.)
- Increase in homosexuality. (The only basis for forbidding it is in the Bible, in Genesis.)
- Decreasing respect for law.
- Increasing government control. Examples: Questioning parents' rights over their children; government legislation to 'protect' children from their parents … increasing government control over education; stifling of religious liberty."

Now, *The Genesis Solution* movie was shown in thousands of churches and other venues. Hundreds of thousands, if not millions, saw this film and heard the relevant message. There's no doubt the film had a dramatic impact on the Church, as it helped popularize the message that it was important that Christians stand on the literal truth of Genesis.

In some ways, the message I was giving in the 80s has been described as a "prophetic." Now, I am not suggesting that we should be compared to the real prophets of the Old Testament. I'm using a well-understood definition of the word "prophetic" as it is known today. The Merriam-Webster online Dictionary gives the following as one of the definitions of prophetic: "correctly stating what will happen in the future."[96] I believe the prophetic warning the ministry of AiG has been proclaiming for decades is being realized before our very eyes. For instance, here is a transcribed excerpt from the film *The Genesis Solution*, which was filmed in 1986 and released in 1987: "Let's sum all this up to see what we're saying. If you remove a basis of absolute authority from our culture, if you remove the creation basis, you would expect to see all the absolutes collapsing. And we do. We see the Christian ethic falling around us. Christians are saying the world is getting worse and worse. What's happening? Why is this so? Well, the more you remove the creation basis and the more you replace it with an evolutionary philosophy that says there is no God, the more you'll see the increase in all of these issues we have been talking about. People say to me: 'But are you therefore blaming evolution? Are you blaming evolution for what's happening in society?' The ultimate cause is a rejection of God as Creator. But let's be honest and let's face reality. What has become the scientific justification for rejecting God as Creator? Evolution."

I also stated in *The Genesis Solution*: "I would suggest to you that the more people will reject Christian ethics, the more we will see a rejection of marriage, and all the things that are associated with Christianity — the more you'll see an increase in abortion, homosexuality, pornography, lawlessness. Tell me, do you see those things? … The more people are taught they're just a product of random processes, and the more they're taught that they have animals in their ancestry, the more we would expect to see them acting like that. The more they are products of chance, then 'Why not do our own thing? Why not write our own rules? We can do whatever we want to do.' On the other hand, we understand that when it comes to these issues of homosexuality, drugs, abortion, infanticide, pornography, violence, divorce, promiscuity, and so on, they are not the results of animals in your ancestry. They are the results of sin. And as a result of sin, they should not be coddled and justified on the basis of evolution, but they should be condemned and judged, if not first repented and forgiven."

When I re-watched *The Genesis Solution* and re read the companion book, I realized that this "prophetic" message of the 1980s was being realized before our very eyes today! I actually first started preaching this message in the late '70s/early '80s in Australia. Because God's Word does not change, and the heart of man is sinful from conception, the message of *The Genesis Solution* is just as relevant — if not more so — in today's culture. In a sense, I believe God has raised up AiG to be one of those "watchmen," much like the one described in Ezekiel 3:17: *"Son of man, I have made you a watchman … give them warning from me."*

I believe God has called AiG to a special mission — not only to proclaim the gospel and stand unashamedly and uncompromisingly on God's Word beginning in Genesis but to warn the Church (as Ezekiel warned Israel) of the dire consequences of compromising God's Word. We must teach the current and coming generations to defend the Christian faith and build their worldview on the authority of the Word of God. AiG continues to stay true to its mission! If anything, I believe we have become stronger in our presentation of "the relevance of Genesis" and with our warning to the Church. I believe that's because we have become more intensely burdened than ever to do what we can (with the Lord's direction) to wake up Christians to what is going on in our anti-Christian world! And despite opposition from many compromising church leaders, we will continue to sound the warning bells in this increasingly secularized Church and culture. Secularists who oppose the Christian worldview are becoming increasingly intolerant of Christianity — in fact, trying to outlaw the Christian worldview in many places. They claim Christians are the intolerant ones, and yet many of these secularists are the most intolerant of all — particularly when it comes to Christianity.

That "prophetic" message of the 1980s is being realized before our eyes.

SEPTEMBER 25

Hebrews 11:35-38

Put Them in Fear

The topic of evolution has often been in the news over the years, especially regarding how politicians have responded when asked if they believe in evolution. The very liberal *Huffington Post* once published an article about the 2016 U.S. presidential election and stated: "The 2016 presidential campaign is already upon us and the debate is heating up over an unexpected issue — the theory of evolution. Of course, in an ideal world, evolution would never really become a campaign issue. But the anti-science wing of the Republican Party continues to voice skepticism. Apologists for this wing would dearly like to distract the media and the voting public from what is, frankly, a national if not a global embarrassment. In truth, the president of the United States needs to be scientifically literate."

The truth of the matter, however, is that such statements as those in this article and the questions about belief in evolution, when asked of politicians, actually portray their anti-God agenda. Just as the pro-evolution Bill Nye "the Science Guy" has done (and continues to do), the author of the *Huffington Post* article attempted to equate the rejection of evolution with the rejection of the whole of science, thus undermining studies in biology, genetics, diseases, and computing. Because of a commitment to the religion of naturalism (atheism), many evolutionists try to intimidate people through the use of terms like "anti-science" in their attempts to bully people into thinking that those who reject evolution are undermining technological advancement. I have observed that in most instances when the secular media write articles about Answers in Genesis, the authors will state we are against science and will use terms like "anti-intellectual," "anti-academic," and so on, and claim we are undermining the whole of what they call science. Then, when using the word "science," they will discuss technology and try to intimidate people into believing that organizations like Answers in Genesis will adversely affect America's technological achievements for the future. This has been the agenda of Bill Nye, as was seen in his debate with me in 2014 and as witnessed in his numerous interviews and lectures around the world.

That's why during my debate with Bill Nye, I concentrated on explaining that the word *science* means "knowledge." And then I explained the difference between historical science (beliefs about the past) and observational science (using our five senses, repeatable tests, and so on) that is used to build our technology. During the debate, I showed video clips of creation scientists who had developed some great technological achievements. I then asked Bill Nye a question (a question I have often asked publicly of all evolutionists — which secularists won't and cannot answer): Can you name one piece of technology that could only have been developed starting with a belief in molecules-to-man evolution? There is no such example! In fact, the real reason Bill Nye and reporters question politicians who are contemplating running for U.S. president, and bully and intimidate people about evolution is not because belief in molecules-to-man evolution is necessary for technological advancement. It's due more to the secular, humanistic, anti-God agenda they want to be implemented! If there is no God who created us — no God who is the absolute authority — then *Every way of a man is right in his own eyes* (Proverbs 21:2).

When the *Huffington Post* author stated, "In truth, the President of the United States needs to be scientifically literate," the author really is saying, "In truth, the President of the United States needs to be committed to the

APOLOGETICS

religion of naturalism and reject the absolute authority of the Word of God." Having abandoned the Bible as the authority, the president can then insist on supporting gay "marriage," abortion, and whatever else such a president deems is "right in his own eyes" (which is what we see happening).

That's why, at the Nye-Ham debate, I stated the following: "Public school textbooks are using the same word 'science' for observational and historical science. They arbitrarily define science as naturalism and outlaw the supernatural. They present molecules-to-man evolution as fact. They are imposing the religion of naturalism/atheism on generations of students." I also said at the Nye debate, "The creation/evolution debate is really a conflict between two philosophical worldviews based on two different accounts of origins or historical science beliefs." When politicians are asked about their beliefs concerning evolution, we are observing a conflict that has been building for many years. Think about it: the topic of evolution is often a major headline, usually just claiming evolution as fact. This is because the secularists can now assume that most people have been brainwashed concerning the word "science" and have accepted the contention that molecules-to-man evolution is a fact. Sadly, much of the Church has allowed this bullying to happen. In fact, by not teaching generations of kids how to defend the Christian faith, churches have contributed to the problem. Many of them have also told their young people that they could believe in evolution and/or millions of years.

Regardless of what the bullying secularists do, they can never thwart the outworking of history that God has ordained. But in all this, we as Christians must remain faithful and true to God's Word and never be like the Pharisees: *[F]or they loved the glory that comes from man more than the glory that comes from God* (John 12:43). And as Jesus stated to the Jews, *How can you believe, when you receive glory from one another and do not seek the glory that comes from the only God?* (John 5:44).

In Hebrews 11, we read of believers who were prepared to stand for God and His Word: *Women received back their dead by resurrection. Some were tortured, refusing to accept release, so that they might rise again to a better life. Others suffered mocking and flogging, and even chains and imprisonment. They were stoned, they were sawn in two, they were killed with the sword. They went about in skins of sheep and goats, destitute, afflicted, mistreated— of whom the world was not worthy—wandering about in deserts and mountains, and in dens and caves of the earth* (Hebrews 11:35–38).

Yes, we will be mocked, scoffed at, and called names like "science-deniers" and "anti-intellectual" because we stand publicly for the truth of God's Word in Genesis and reject the religion of evolution. We must honor the Word of God regardless! Are you prepared to stand and be counted? I will never forget my mother reminding me many times when I was a child that what's done for Jesus is what will last. I can still hear her reciting a line from the poem by a famous missionary, who was reported to have said, "If Jesus Christ be God and died for me, then no sacrifice can be too great for me to make for Him." He wrote a poem that included a line I remember my mother reciting to me: "Only one life, 'twill soon be past, Only what's done for Christ will last."

> **Secularists are not only aggressively imposing their religion of naturalism (atheism) on this current generation, but they are using intimidation techniques as a part of accomplishing their agenda, and so Christians need to stand up to the secularist agenda!**

SEPTEMBER 26

Revelation 21:8

Two Religions: Life and Death

What's happening in our culture is a war between the religion of life and the religion of death. We are seeing the results of the tree of death every day as a consequence of this sad war. This war started in a garden 6,000 years ago, and it's been raging ever since.

God made two trees in the Garden of Eden: *And the Lord God planted a garden in Eden, in the east, and there he put the man whom he had formed. And out of the ground the Lord God made to spring up every tree that is pleasant to the sight and good for food. The tree of life was in the midst of the garden, and the tree of the knowledge of good and evil* (Genesis 2:8–9).

Now, I call the tree of the knowledge of good and evil a tree of death. This is because God gave this instruction to Adam: *And the Lord God commanded the man, saying, "You may surely eat of every tree of the garden, but of the tree of the knowledge of good and evil you shall not eat, for in the day that you eat of it you shall surely die"* (Genesis 2:16–17).

Now, God's Word records that Adam (and thus all of us in Adam) disobeyed God, and this resulted in the judgment of death: *And to Adam he said, "Because you have listened to the voice of your wife and have eaten of the tree of which I commanded you, 'You shall not eat of it,' cursed is the ground because of you; in pain you shall eat of it all the days of your life; thorns and thistles it shall bring forth for you; and you shall eat the plants of the field. By the sweat of your face you shall eat bread, till you return to the ground, for out of it you were taken; for you are dust, and to dust you shall return"* (Genesis 3:17–19). Adam chose the tree of death instead of the tree of life. As a result, sin entered the world and the whole creation now groans (Romans 8:22), and death permeates the creation.

Now, in Genesis 3:15, God promised a Savior — one who would pay the penalty for our sins and the consequence of death. God's Son stepped into history to be our Savior and died on a Cross. Really, the Cross is a tree of life, as Jesus Christ conquered death so we can have eternal life with Him. All throughout the Bible, we see this contrast between life and death. It's portrayed in other ways as light and darkness, build your house on the rock or the sand, those who are for Christ and those who are against, and so on. Those who receive the free gift of salvation from this Savior will have eternal life with our Creator. Those who reject the free gift of salvation will suffer a "second death," eternal separation from God. *But as for the cowardly, the faithless, the detestable, as for murderers, the sexually immoral, sorcerers, idolaters, and all liars, their portion will be in the lake that burns with fire and sulfur, which is the second death* (Revelation 21:8).

Sadly, the majority of people have not received the free gift of salvation (there are more on the broad way than the narrow way), and as a result, we see the impact of the tree of death. For those who reject God as Creator and instead put their faith in naturalistic evolution, they believe death has always been a part of life. They believe death, bloodshed, disease, and suffering are a part of this supposed evolutionary process that they claim produces life. The evolutionary tree is a tree of death. And the consequence of those who reject the Creator and trust in the tree of death is death and more death. We live in a world where:

- Many people consider life ultimately meaningless, resulting in death through murder/violence, etc.

THEOLOGY

- Dictators like Hitler adopted evolutionary ideas, resulting in the deaths of millions.
- Many people kill millions of children in the womb — death.
- Margaret Sanger (founder of Planned Parenthood) promoted eugenics, resulting in the deaths of millions.
- Euthanasia results in death.
- People commit suicide — death.
- Many of those who adopt sinful lifestyles (homosexual behavior, adultery, fornication, etc.) can end up with diseases resulting in death.

Yes, we live in a world permeated by death. God's Word states: *"[B]ut he who fails to find me injures himself; all who hate me love death"* (Proverbs 8:36). However, what a difference for those who do find the Lord and trust in His Word and saving gospel: *For God so loved the world, that he gave his only Son, that whoever believes in him should not perish but have eternal life* (John 3:16).

Life! Yes, we need to be thinking about life in this world of death. And even though we live in a world permeated by death, God tells us that: *Then Death and Hades were thrown into the lake of fire. This is the second death, the lake of fire* (Revelation 20:14).

Death right now is an "enemy" (1 Corinthians 15:26). Sadly, many love this "enemy" instead of understanding it is a judgment because of our sin and should remind us of the need we all have to receive the free gift of salvation so we won't suffer the second death, eternal separation from God.

That's why I just can't understand Christians who compromise God's Word with millions of years and thus blame God for death. It's our sin that brought death. God, through death and Resurrection (the death of His Son on the Cross and His Resurrection), provides us with an offer of life to overcome the consequences of sin — death and eternal separation from God. Really, the Cross, even though it resulted in death, is a tree of life. Because of Christ's death and Resurrection (conquering death), God offers us the free gift of salvation. Christ conquered death!

[B]ecause, if you confess with your mouth that Jesus is Lord and believe in your heart that God raised him from the dead, you will be saved (Romans 10:9).

Because of our sin in Adam, God denied us access to the tree of life in the Garden of Eden. That's why the tree of death permeates our world. But one day in the future, for those who trust Christ, they will have access back to the tree of life:

Blessed are those who wash their robes, so that they may have the right to the tree of life and that they may enter the city by the gates. Outside are the dogs and sorcerers and the sexually immoral and murderers and idolaters, and everyone who loves and practices falsehood (Revelation 22:14–15).

"To the one who conquers I will grant to eat of the tree of life, which is in the paradise of God" (Revelation 2:7).

Where have you put your trust? In God's tree of life? Or in the tree of death?

For the wages of sin is death, but the free gift of God is eternal life in Christ Jesus our Lord (Romans 6:23).

Life and death are what this war raging about us is all about.

SEPTEMBER 27
Romans 3:4

Truth, Lies, and Science Educators

Secularists have attacked the ministry of Answers in Genesis, the Creation Museum, and the Ark Encounter over the years. But generally, I find the attacks are the same old tired accusations they continue to make, and we've answered in detail many times. For instance, back in 2012, the Creation Museum was attacked by a secularist who wrote an item in the renowned magazine *Scientific American*.

A guest columnist reported he visited the museum. Jacob Tanenbaum, who was a fourth- and fifth-grade science teacher, wrote the column titled, "A Science Teacher Draws the Line at Creation." The piece was originally published in the January 2013 print edition of *Scientific American* under the title "Creation, Evolution and Indisputable Facts." Unsurprisingly, Mr. Tanenbaum's "facts" about our exhibits weren't exactly accurate.

For instance, Tanenbaum claimed that when we teach about the global Flood, we teach that "Noah saved all animal species that we see today from the flood." This is a common equivocation that evolutionists make in regard to the animals on Noah's Ark. As we clearly teach in the Creation Museum, Noah didn't take representatives of every species of animal we see today — he took representatives of every "kind" (which is usually at the "family" level of classification) of land animal (not every type of animal). These animals would have had the genetic material within them to eventually produce the many species we see today.

Frankly, Tanenbaum's point in writing his column was not just to discuss the Creation Museum. Really, he wanted to show how inaccurate he believed biblical creation was. In doing so, Tanenbaum caricatured and misrepresented what biblical creationists, specifically those of us at Answers in Genesis, believe. Here is another example: "AiG's biblical literalists, on the other hand, hold that we are God's favorites. We live at the universe's center on a planet God made and maintains for us to use. Earth's resources are here for us to exploit. God protects us and promised he would not destroy Earth again until the end of days. In that scenario, we have little reason to safeguard our existence."

Many secularists claim that Christians don't bother to take care of the earth. However, in Genesis 1:26–28, the Bible makes clear (as we show in the museum) that man is to care for the earth when God told Adam and Eve to "have dominion" over it. The Bible talks about times and seasons for harvesting and planting (Ecclesiastes 3:2), implying that we must do so responsibly. We are even told in Proverbs 12:10 to treat animals well.

It is true that 2 Peter 3 is a prophecy of how God will destroy the heavens and the earth by fire one day. In the meantime, Answers in Genesis and the Creation Museum teach that man has a responsibility to care for and have dominion over the earth. We are to use it for man's good but God's glory.

There were other problems with Tanenbaum's column. He claimed, "Creationists begin with answers and work to prove that those answers are right.... Scientists who formed the idea of human evolution did not invent the idea and go looking for fossils."

What's interesting about this statement is that some form of the idea of evolution seems to have been around since at least the time of the ancient Greeks. Over 2,000 years ago, a group known as the Epicureans had a belief that there were no gods who intervened in the world. They also believed that over long ages, all life emerged from atom-like materials and that life gave rise to higher life, such as mankind. However, we do have an eyewitness account of the origin of the world — the Word of God Himself, the Creator and Sustainer of the universe. We don't have to rely on man's ideas (fallible speculations) of how the world may have come to be because the Bible tells us plainly how the universe and everything in it was created.

Creationists start with the answers in the Bible to enable them to have the correct basis to understand the world. For their part, atheists begin with the belief that there is no God and that the Bible has nothing to do with explaining reality. In other words, Christians and secularists all have their own starting point for their worldviews. They both start with beliefs. Creationists start with beliefs based on the Bible's historical account in Genesis, whereas atheists start with blind-faith beliefs based on the speculations of fallible man.

Tanenbaum also made the same mistake that TV host Bill Nye made in widely watched YouTube videos and on TV interviews: he confused historical science with observational science. He states:

"The danger is that 40 percent of the American electorate [referring to his earlier claim that 40 percent of U.S. adults believe that Genesis is literal] seems to have forgotten what science is. Considering that our nation put a man on the moon and invented the airplane and the Internet, this development is extraordinary."

The practice of historical science is very much dependent on a person's worldview. Men on the moon, airplanes, and the Internet all fall under the category of observational science. We often refer to this as "here and now" science because it is observed in the present and can be tested and repeated. Historical science, like studies in creation and evolution, involves past events that cannot be observed, tested, or repeated. The practice of historical science is very much dependent on a person's worldview. Do we start with man's ideas about the past when they were not there during the supposed billions of years of the earth's history? Or do we start with the eyewitness account of God, who inspired men to write the truth in His Word, the Bible?

Tanenbaum ended the article by stating that "if students do not understand how science works, we can destroy our country's future or even threaten our existence on this old Earth." Again, a student's beliefs about the past (historical science) generally have little bearing on the experiments they perform in the classroom (observational science). Imagine what would happen if students actually applied a belief that everything came about by random chance over eons of time to a chemistry experiment. They might just throw the chemicals together, leave the classroom, and not return!

The fact that the well-known *Scientific American* published this commentary was significant. To us, it meant the editors understood the importance of this battle over origins. In reality, it is a struggle over the question of authority. Who is the ultimate authority — man or God? Whatever authority you acknowledge will determine how you view moral issues such as gay "marriage" and abortion. If God is the authority (and He is), then marriage is one man and one woman, and abortion is a crime against God (it's murder). If man is the authority, then marriage can be whatever one wants to define it as — and abortion is just another way to kill an animal.

Let God be true though every one were a liar (Romans 3:4).

It does matter what you believe about where you came from and who your authority is.

SEPTEMBER 28

Genesis 1:1-2

Why Did (and Do) So Many in the Church Believe the Gap Theory?

The earth was without form and void, and darkness was over the face of the deep. And the Spirit of God was hovering over the face of the waters (Genesis 1:2). Grammatically, this verse is not a part of the sequence of the narrative in Genesis 1 but is really a commentary verse describing the earth in verse 1. There cannot be a gap of time (e.g., millions of years) between Genesis 1:1 and Genesis 1:2. When God created the earth, it was covered with water, so it didn't have the shape as it did when God formed the dry land on day two. Also, the earth was devoid of life until God created plants on day three. God created everything over a period of six days, so it all wasn't finished until the final events of the sixth day. But along the way, everything was "good," just not finished until it was then "very good." There cannot be a gap between the first verse and the second.

From what I've experienced, the most well-known position on Genesis within the Church to accommodate the supposed millions of years is what is called the gap theory. Now, there have been many different versions of the gap theory since the 1800s. The basic belief is there was an original creation that Lucifer ruled, but he rebelled. God judged the earth because of this rebellion and then recreated everything in six literal days. This proposed original earth and judgment is supposed to fit into millions of years between Genesis 1:1 and Genesis 1:2.

It is true that many great Bible teachers of the past held to the gap theory. To them, it was a way of fitting the millions of years idea into the Bible but still taking the stand that God created in six literal days as the Bible clearly teaches. And really, they had not studied all the issues involved concerning the supposed millions of years as we have had the opportunity to do in our day. Even the great expositional preacher of the twentieth century in England, Martyn Lloyd Jones, mentioned the gap theory. But from reading what he said about it, I believe he was not prepared to accept it because he had such a great emphasis on exegeting Scripture correctly. The details of the gap theory were popularized by Thomas Chalmers, the founder of the Free Church of Scotland in the 1800s. When you boil it all down, the gap theory really came about to try to explain the supposed millions of years. Thomas Chalmers placed those supposed millions of years into the Bible between the first two verses of Genesis 1.

So we need to understand that the motivation for the gap theory was to take a belief that actually came out of naturalism (atheism), attributing millions of years to the fossil record, and fit it into the Bible. Right there, this tells us the basic problem with the gap theory. It's called eisegesis, reading ideas into the Bible! That should make Christians immediately suspicious of this idea.

The gap theory was publicized in our modern times in the notes of the Scofield Reference Bible. But, as my father taught me, the notes in study Bibles are not inspired like the text, and the text of Scripture should always be used as the commentary on the notes! And look at this comment in the notes of the Scofield Bible: "Relegate fossils to the primitive creation, and no conflict of science with the Genesis cosmogony remains."

In other words, once you fit the millions of years into this proposed gap, then there's no conflict with what is referred to as "science." That's the issue — solving a conflict between the Bible's account of history and the historical science (beliefs) of the secular world. But this sadly fails, trying to "solve" this conflict by accepting man's beliefs and adding them into God's Word.

Now, I'm not going to go into a detailed refutation of the gap theory here, as we have an article dealing with that on the Answers in Genesis website. I just want to point out some of the basic problems, such as the one above concerning eisegesis.

Let me deal with two more major issues regarding the gap theory. Let's consider the topic of death and disease. The gap theory has millions of years of fossil layers with billions of dead things and bones with diseases like cancer before Adam and before Adam sinned. Thus, death and disease existed before sin! This is a major problem.

Another issue concerns a major inconsistency. The idea of millions of years came primarily out of atheism of the late 1700s–early 1800s. Atheists rejected the global Flood of Noah's day and claimed the fossil record was laid down slowly over millions of years. Now the classic gap theorists accepted the millions of years belief, put this in a supposed gap between Genesis 1:1 and 1:2, and then explained the fossil record with a flood called Lucifer's flood — a supposed judgment on the wicked world. So the gap theorist uses a global catastrophe to explain the fossil record, which then totally does away with the reason they wanted to gap in the first place — to explain the supposed millions of years based on the fossil record forming slowly over millions of years! And if they want to explain the fossil record with a flood, why not do it with a flood the Bible gives us an account of, Noah's Flood, instead of one it doesn't mention at all, the supposed Lucifer's flood?

What I've also seen generally historically, is that when one generation of Christians adhered to the gap theory, often the next generation would go further and become theistic evolutionists or accept some other compromise position that went much further than the gap theory. The point is, once one opens the door to adding ideas into Scripture, the next generation tends to open that door wider, and then wider, and then wider, until eventually they give up Genesis altogether. This also often puts them on a slippery slide of doubt and unbelief through the rest of Scripture.

The gap theory is actually an attack on the authority of Scripture beginning in Genesis. I'm not saying the many great Bible teachers who held to the gap theory were deliberately undermining Scripture, for they unwittingly were undermining the Word they were preaching authoritatively from. When I've had the opportunity to speak to such respected leaders about all we've now studied concerning the problems with the gap theory, I've usually found that those who don't want to ever compromise God's Word give up the gap theory quickly.

> **Christians need to look at whether they are taking ideas to Scripture or starting from Scripture to let God teach us what to believe.**

SEPTEMBER 29
Matthew 12:30

Naturalism Run Wild

Really, the current state religion in the USA (and really the entire Western world) of the public schools and government is that of atheistic naturalism. Almost all Americans have heard the phrase "separation of church and state." However, fewer realize the phrase is not in the Constitution. Yet, it has been used as something of a club to "beat down" and eliminate Christianity from public places, including symbols (like crosses), Bible reading and prayer in public schools, and the teaching of creation in science classes.

Now, where does the phrase "separation of church and state" come from? It is not a part of the original U.S. Constitution of 1787, as most people falsely believe, or in any of its amendments. In reality, the idea of a "wall of separation" between church and state came from a private letter from President Thomas Jefferson, and it has sadly been misused to slowly but surely eliminate Christianity from the public sector — and replace it with an anti-God religion.

Now, we need to understand something very important before we discuss this further. There is no neutral position. Through Scripture, we read that people are for or against Christ; they walk in light or darkness, they build their house on the rock or the sand, they gather or scatter, or they are on the broad way or the narrow way. There is no in-between. For instance:

Whoever is not with me is against me, and whoever does not gather with me scatters (Matthew 12:30).

"Everyone then who hears these words of mine and does them will be like a wise man who built his house on the rock. And the rain fell, and the floods came, and the winds blew and beat on that house, but it did not fall, because it had been founded on the rock. And everyone who hears these words of mine and does not do them will be like a foolish man who built his house on the sand" (Matthew 7:24–26).

[F]or at one time you were darkness, but now you are light in the Lord. Walk as children of light (for the fruit of light is found in all that is good and right and true) (Ephesians 5:8–9).

Secular does not mean neutral. Everyone has a worldview, a religion. Secular really means "anti-God." Think about that for those who send their children to the anti-God (secular) schools. That's how we need to say it to understand the religious indoctrination occurring in the government schools.

Now, the Establishment Clause in the First Amendment was intended to protect the Church from the (federal) government, not the government from the Church. Therefore, no "national" church or religion is allowed to be established by the federal government. I will highlight key words of the First Amendment: "Congress shall make no law respecting an establishment of religion, or prohibiting the free exercise thereof …"

You can see that the "separation of church and state" phrase is nowhere in the Amendment (or the rest of the Constitution). The 1802 letter from Jefferson was sent to the Danbury Baptist Association in Connecticut in response to the group's letter to him. Jefferson was trying to assure the Baptists that the federal government would never be permitted to interfere with the Church. In fact, in his letter, Jefferson states:

"Believing with you that religion is a matter which lies solely between man & his god, that he owes account to none other for his faith or his worship, that the legitimate powers of government reach actions only, and not opinions, I contemplate with sovereign reverence that act of the whole American people which declared that their legislature should make no law respecting an establishment of religion, or prohibiting the free exercise thereof, thus building a wall of separation between church and state."

Today, secular scholars have lifted the Danbury letter out of its entire historical context and have turned the so-called "wall" metaphor completely on its head. "Separation of church and state" is now used to protect the government from the influence of the Church — establishing a policy of freedom "from" religion, which, in reality, has become "separation of Christianity and state." This would have been an entirely foreign and unintended concept to the Founding Fathers.

Sadly, most Americans (Christians included) have also been duped into believing that the so-called "separation of church and state" requires eliminating the Christian God and creating a supposed neutral situation. But there is no such position as neutrality. Indeed, one is either for Christ or against Him (Matthew 12:30)!

The religion of naturalism (atheism) has been imposed on the public education system and on the culture as a whole. For instance, science textbooks in public schools now typically define science as naturalism (atheism), such as this example from a science textbook:

"Science requires repeatable observations and testable hypotheses. These standards restrict science to a search for natural causes for natural phenomena…. Supernatural explanations of natural events are simply outside the bounds of science."

In keeping with this pronouncement, these books teach molecules-to-man evolution based only on unproven natural processes as fact! In other words, they have eliminated the supernatural and replaced it with naturalism. In reality, they have eliminated the Christian worldview and replaced it with a secular, anti-God, atheistic one!

Thus, the secular (government) schools are indoctrinating students in a religion — the religion of naturalism. We live in a time where, when secularists use the term "religion," they usually mean Christianity. Thus, they claim they don't teach religion in secular schools, but secular (anti-God) schools are, in reality, churches of atheism, with many of the teachers being the priests of the secular religion.

When atheists have Nativity scenes, crosses, and other Christian symbols removed from public places, they claim they are removing religion from those places. But they didn't remove religion; they removed Christianity and replaced that with the religion of atheism! They are now imposing the atheist religion on people.

Sadly, because many Christians have falsely believed that there can be a neutral position and have also been duped regarding the so-called "separation of church and state," they are not prepared to boldly and unashamedly stand on the Word of God as they confront issues like abortion, gay "marriage," racism, etc. Now, we see the atheistic worldview (religion) dominating in the West.

> By shrinking back, believers have allowed the secularists to impose their anti-God atheistic religion on the public schools – and the culture as a whole.

SEPTEMBER 30
Psalm 14:1

Creation in Schools? Part 1

Public school teachers know that they can critically discuss different theories in regard to just about every issue — but not evolution. Even if a school board simply wants evolution to be critically analyzed (a good teaching technique, after all) without even mentioning creation or the Bible, the American Civil Liberties Union and other humanists are immediately up in arms. There are the usual accusations of trying to get "religion" into schools and that it's a front for what they label as "fundamentalist Christianity."

By the way, when the public school system threw out prayer, Bible readings, creation, and the Ten Commandments, they didn't throw out religion. They replaced the Christian worldview influence with an atheistic one. The public schools, by and large, now teach that everything a student learns about science, history, etc., has nothing to do with God but can all be explained without any supernatural reference. This is a religious view — an anti-Christian view with which students are being indoctrinated. Humanists know that naturalistic evolution is foundational to their religion — their worldview that everything can be explained without God. That is why they are so emotional when it comes to the topic of creation/evolution.

We are certainly encouraged at Answers in Genesis that there are moves in different places to stop the censorship of the anti-Christian propagandists in the public schools and allow students to, at the very minimum, question evolution. We are sure this is in part due to the influence of the creation ministry in society and the plethora of creationist and anti-evolutionist materials now available to parents and students. On the other hand, Christians have to understand that fighting the evolution issue in public schools is actually the same battle as fighting abortion, homosexual behavior, pornography, etc. In other words, just as these issues are symptoms of the foundational change in our culture (i.e., from believing that God's Word is the absolute authority to that of man's opinions being the authority), so the evolution issue is also a symptom of this same foundational change.

If you were to ask the average person if evolution is a religion, he would probably say no. However, evolution is actually one of the cornerstones of the religion of secular humanism. (Now keep in mind that evolutionists do use real observational science, such as natural selection, speciation, genetic studies, etc., as part of their overall argument. However, evolutionism in the sense of the belief aspects of evolution [life arising by natural processes, etc.] is a belief system — a religion.) Despite the vigorous objections of many humanists, humanism is a religion. Even a cursory reading of the "Humanist Manifesto I," penned in 1933, reveals that it is a religious document:

"FIRST: Religious humanists regard the universe as self-existing and not created.

"SECOND: Humanism believes that man is a part of nature and that he has emerged as a result of a continuous process.

"SEVENTH: Religion consists of those actions, purposes, and experiences which are humanly significant. Nothing human is alien to the religious. It includes labor, art, science, philosophy, love, friendship, recreation — all that is in its degree expressive of intelligently satisfying human living. The distinction between the sacred and the secular can no longer be maintained."

APOLOGETICS

Many other points in the document point to humanism as a religion that is to replace "the old attitudes" of traditional religions. John Dewey, considered the father of the modern American public school systems, was a signatory on the document. His application of his religious ideals to the education system cannot be denied. As a result, the public school system in America, and much of the world, is dominated by humanist philosophies. Later versions of the manifesto also include the idea that humans have evolved as part of nature with no supernatural intervention at all. Also presented are the beliefs that we can only know about the world around us by observation and experimentation — no biblical revelation is accepted — and that man is the measure of all things. All of these ideas are solidly anti-Christian in their sentiments.

Many humanists would call themselves secular humanists in order to avoid the connection to the word "religion." They have adopted a similar manifesto founded on the same basic principles but avoiding the religious phrasing.

"Separation of Church and State: Because of their commitment to freedom, secular humanists believe in the principle of the separation of church and state. The lessons of history are clear: wherever one religion or ideology is established and given a dominant position in the state, minority opinions are in jeopardy. A pluralistic, open democratic society allows all points of view to be heard. Any effort to impose an exclusive conception of Truth, Piety, Virtue, or Justice upon the whole of society is a violation of free inquiry."

Then, in the section on evolution, we read: "Today the theory of evolution is again under heavy attack by religious fundamentalists. Although the theory of evolution cannot be said to have reached its final formulation, or to be an infallible principle of science, it is nonetheless supported impressively by the findings of many sciences. There may be some significant differences among scientists concerning the mechanics of evolution; yet the evolution of the species is supported so strongly by the weight of evidence that it is difficult to reject it."

The secular humanists basically believe we should not "impose an exclusive conception of truth" unless it involves suppressing religious ideas (including creation) — it is mandatory that the "truth" of evolution can have exclusive reign in the science classrooms. What they fail to realize is that they are simply substituting one "article of religious faith" for another in an arbitrary way that fits their agenda; Christians could assert the opposite claim. If the documents from the humanists are not enough to be convincing about whether humanism (with the belief in naturalistic evolution as its foundation) is a religion that attempts to explain the meaning of life, the U.S. Supreme Court has also recognized humanism as a religion. In the 1961 case *Torcaso v. Watkins* regarding the legality of requiring a religious test for public office, the rationale for the finding includes the view that "religions in this country which do not teach what would generally be considered a belief in the existence of God, are Buddhism, Taoism, Ethical Culture, Secular Humanism, and others."

Humanism, whether secular or religious, is a religion, albeit a non-theistic one for most of its adherents. One of humanism's fundamental tenets — evolution by natural processes alone — is the sole view allowed to be taught in public school science classrooms. This demonstrates that the public school systems are indeed promoting one religious view over another in the science classrooms. Again, religion was not removed from schools; Christian views were simply replaced by secular humanistic views. There is indeed a state religion in the American and other government school systems — secular humanism!

Despite the assertion by humanists that evolution is an undeniable fact, is it really a scientific idea?

OCTOBER 1
Psalm 14:1

Creation in Schools? Part 2

The fool says in his heart, "There is no God" (Psalm 14:1).

Science is generally limited to those things that are observable, testable, and repeatable. Language in the humanist documents mentioned before would affirm this notion. When we are discussing operational science, conducting experiments, and building technology based on those principles, creationists and secularists have no disagreement. It is only when we look to explain the past that the disagreements occur. Everyone has the same evidence to examine, but we all look at the evidence in light of our pre-existing worldview. Evolutionists believe that life has evolved by natural processes, so they interpret the evidence in light of that belief. Creationists do the same but using God's Word, the Bible, as the standard. Since events of the past cannot be observed, tested, or repeated, we cannot ultimately call our understanding of those events scientific. Christians should trust what God has revealed in Scripture and build their thinking, in every area, on that foundation.

Some Christians who are teaching in the government schools sometimes find themselves in a situation where they can openly teach creation in the science classrooms. Teachers should understand what is allowed according to their state and local laws and statutes, and take advantage of those opportunities. However, there are often political implications to consider, and a teacher who even legally teaches biblical creation may face other repercussions. Also, many states have allowances for students to be released from school for special religious instruction. Consider supporting or starting a ministry that uses this time to teach students the true history of the earth from the Bible. Providing Christian students with this instruction will equip them to share this truth with teachers and other students. Additionally, these students should be equipped to share the gospel with their fellow students and teachers. Salvation is the ultimate goal for Christians in such a ministry, not just converting evolutionists into creationists.

We need bold Christians who will become active in their communities, school boards, and other organizations who will be prompting these changes from the bottom up. In these settings, Christians can start asking challenging questions about the exclusion of Christianity from schools, the acceptance of the religion of humanism, the absence of critical thinking when it comes to teaching evolution, etc. Based on the U.S. Constitution, no single religion should be endorsed in a government-run school, but everyone and every system has a religion! If no one stands up to challenge these ideas, the schools will continue to indoctrinate students with the religious beliefs of humanists.

Answers in Genesis is often misrepresented as trying to get creationist teaching into the public schools. AiG does not lobby any government agencies to include the teaching of biblical creation in the public schools. We do not believe that creation should be mandated in public school science classrooms. If teaching creation were mandated, it would likely be taught poorly (and possibly mockingly) by a teacher who does not understand what the Bible teaches and who believes in evolution. At the same time, it is not right that the tenets of secular humanism can be taught at the exclusion of Christian ideas. This type of exclusivity does not promote the critical thinking skills of students demanded by most science education standards. Teachers should be allowed the academic freedom to present various models of the history of life on Earth and teach the strengths

SCIENCE — OCTOBER 1

and weaknesses of those models. Recognizing that in the current political climate we can only expect to see evolution taught, it is only reasonable to include teaching the shortcomings of evolutionary ideas.

You are the salt of the earth (Matthew 5:13). If your state or country does not even permit the questioning of evolution or discussing creation, there are other options that will help keep a teacher from getting fired. There are many strategies that take the responsibility for any creation teaching away from the school and its administration:

- Offer an optional course after school that is free for students (perhaps once or twice a month) to refute some of the evolution and long-age teachings. You or someone you know who enjoys teaching creation can use many of the great biblically based, creationist resources. Show the students that they are not getting all of the information from their textbooks.
- Offer to be an adult sponsor for students who wish to start a Creation Club in the school. This student-led alternative can be very effective at getting outside speakers into the school to address the club and present information. Clubs can meet at lunch or after school, just like a Chess Club or any other.
- Have your local church youth group provide a short course to counter evolutionary claims. Students in the youth group can invite other students to attend and learn more about the issue. Use resources from Answers in Genesis to teach them.

As stated above, many U.S. states offer the option of "released time." Support or start a ministry in your community that would provide biblical instruction for public school students. Understand the limits a teacher has to discuss ideas with students outside of the classroom. The political climate in your district should be taken into consideration, as well as recognizing that you may face persecution. And consider how bold you are prepared to be. *Indeed, all who desire to live a godly life in Christ Jesus will be persecuted* (2 Timothy 3:12).

Have a local church or group of churches offer to bring students to the Creation Museum and Ark Encounter in the USA where they can be presented with biblical truths about God as the Creator. Students can help pass the word around at public schools. You can use the streaming platform Answers TV for a video tour.

As much as we want to see students know that true science confirms the creation account in Genesis and that molecules-to-man evolution is a blind-faith belief that flies in the face of much scientific evidence, in the long run the school battle will not be successful unless society as a whole (and the Church) returns to the Bible as the authority. That's why at AiG, we spend so much energy to equip the Church to restore biblical authority beginning with Genesis. Then, and only then, will the secular worldview of society be successfully challenged. More important, recognize that spreading the glorious gospel of Jesus Christ is the ultimate goal. If you are not directly involved in public schools in any way, pray for those who are and support Christian teachers and administrators who are trying to make a difference. Support and pray for families and students in the public schools. Volunteer to be a mentor or to assist in the public schools or teach a Sunday school class to help the students understand the origins issue.

> **Pray for Christian schools and homeschools that are being raised up to help parents disciple their children.**

OCTOBER 2

Mark 16:15

Christians and Elections

Should Christians be concerned about the outcome of elections? Elections have consequences. If the people in power reject God's Word, their anti-Christian agenda would certainly impact every area. But, regardless of who wins elections, some very important truths need to be understood as we build our thinking on God's Word. There are many areas of life where nothing should really change for us as Christians regardless of who wins elections. Let me explain why:

God is sovereign and in total control of everything. One of my friends often says to me, "God has yet to make His first mistake!" And of course, God never does.

Also, *who brings princes to nothing, and makes the rulers of the earth as emptiness* (Isaiah 40:23).

No matter how powerful a leader is, God can bring their plans to nothing! Human beings may think they're in charge, but remember what Jesus said to Pilate: *"You would have no authority over me at all unless it had been given you from above"* (John 19:11).

Even as we vote, we cannot divorce human responsibility from God's sovereignty—it is God (not the media and others) who ultimately controls who becomes the leader of a nation: *He changes times and seasons; he removes kings and sets up kings* (Daniel 2:21).

God even uses pagan rulers to accomplish His purposes. For instance, consider the Persian King Cyrus. God called him His "anointed": *Thus says the Lord to his anointed, to Cyrus, whose right hand I have grasped, to subdue nations before him and to loose the belts of kings, to open doors before him that gates may not be closed: "I will go before you and level the exalted places, I will break in pieces the doors of bronze and cut through the bars of iron"* (Isaiah 45:1–2).

The prophet Habakkuk was dismayed at pagan kings being used by God to judge his own people. *For the wicked surround the righteous; so justice goes forth perverted* (Habakkuk 1:4). And how did God answer the prophet? *Look among the nations, and see; wonder and be astounded. For I am doing a work in your days that you would not believe if told. For behold, I am raising up the Chaldeans, that bitter and hasty nation* (Habakkuk 1:5–6). So regardless of the outcome of the election, even if we are dismayed or discouraged like Habakkuk, we have to recognize that God is in control. But does that mean we should not be doing anything then? No. Responsibility and sovereignty go hand in hand, but only God can bring these together in ways we cannot understand.

As an example, I often use the parable of the Ten Minas. A nobleman (representing Jesus) left for another country to become king, and he entrusted resources to servants (representing followers of Jesus). They were told to "Engage in business until I come" (Luke 19:13). The lesson for us from this parable is that we must be faithful to serve our King Jesus until He returns. And how do we faithfully serve Him? Well, here are three of my favorite verses to remind me to be about the business of serving the King every day:

Preach the saving gospel: *And he said to them, "Go into all the world and proclaim the gospel to the whole creation"* (Mark 16:15).

THEOLOGY

Teach apologetics: *[B]ut in your hearts honor Christ the Lord as holy, always being prepared to make a defense to anyone who asks you for a reason for the hope that is in you; yet do it with gentleness and respect* (1 Peter 3:15).

Be actively involved in spiritual warfare: *Contend for the faith that was once for all delivered to the saints* (Jude 3).

We do our best to carry out these verses every day through the ministry of Answers in Genesis, the Creation Museum, and the Ark Encounter. And regardless of who is in power in government and the courts, while the Lord gives us open doors, we will do whatever we can to advance the business of the King—to stand uncompromisingly and unashamedly on the Word of God and proclaim the saving gospel!

Sadly, many of our church leaders have compromised God's Word, beginning in Genesis. This compromise is one of the major contributing reasons for why much of the Church is not impacting the culture as it should for the King.

Regardless of who is in power in our countries, we need to do all we can to equip and challenge people with the most vital message in the entire universe: the saving message of the gospel that is founded in Genesis and seen all the way through Scripture to the Book of Revelation.

Now, we'll probably have to deal with challenges and battles along the way. While the Israelites were given the Promised Land, they still faced battles at Jericho, Ai, and other places. Any Christian who is active in proclaiming God's Word and the gospel is involved in a war—a spiritual war.

We will have persecution—yes, we will have battles with enemies raised up against us. But while God gives us breath, let's work as hard as we can, with the resources the Lord has entrusted to us, to diligently do the work of the King.

Consider what we read in 1 Peter: *Beloved, do not be surprised at the fiery trial when it comes upon you to test you, as though something strange were happening to you. But rejoice insofar as you share Christ's sufferings, that you may also rejoice and be glad when his glory is revealed. If you are insulted for the name of Christ, you are blessed, because the Spirit of glory and of God rests upon you. But let none of you suffer as a murderer or a thief or an evildoer or as a meddler. Yet if anyone suffers as a Christian, let him not be ashamed, but let him glorify God in that name* (1 Peter 4:12–16).

And never forget: Whether it be the president of the United States, the head of the United Nations, a Supreme Court justice, a member of Congress, the Prime Minister of Australia or Canada, or any other person on Earth, we should be reminded of 1 Peter 4:5: *[B]ut they will give account to him who is ready to judge the living and the dead.*

And as I've quoted many times from God's Word: *It is a fearful thing to fall into the hands of the living God* (Hebrews 10:31).

God will have the final say.

OCTOBER 3
Romans 2:14–15

Atheists Hate God—and His People

At times I think I give many atheists much of their purpose and meaning in this life. Certain of them seem to follow every post, every blog, every article I write so they can attack me. They mock, they scoff, and sometimes get very emotional.

Why do atheists get so emotional and aggressive in opposing biblical Christianity? Why does it bother them? After all, when they die, from their perspective, they will not even know they ever existed. And most times they are forgotten as their name goes into oblivion. It's the rare exception someone is remembered in history, so why does it matter at all what Christians believe?

When Answers in Genesis announced plans to build the Creation Museum, a local atheist group began attacking the ministry and campaigning against the museum. When the museum was opened, the atheists gathered outside to protest the opening of this facility.

Atheists also aggressively opposed the building of a life-size Noah's ark, the Ark Encounter. But what is it to atheists if Christians build such a facility to proclaim the Christian message? After all, thousands of secular museums across the USA and other countries around the world are already proclaiming an atheistic, evolutionary message to the public. Government schools throughout the world indoctrinate hundreds of millions of the coming generations in naturalism—really atheism.

So why do atheists get so upset with a minority that stands for biblical Christianity?

During my debate with Bill Nye "the Science Guy" on February 4, 2014, Bill was asked where matter came from. He said it was a great mystery, but he loved the "joy of discovery" as he pursued such questions. In my responses to Bill's answers, I asked him why the joy of discovery mattered to him. I explained that from Bill's perspective, life is the result of natural processes and there is no biblical God, so when he dies, he won't know he ever existed or knew anything. Then, when others who knew him die, they won't know they ever knew him either. Eventually, from his perspective of naturalism, the whole universe will die and no one will ever know they ever existed. So what is the purpose of this "joy of discovery"? Really, the naturalistic view of life is ultimately purposeless and meaningless!

Think about the well-known atheist Richard Dawkins. Why does he spend so much time writing and speaking against Someone (God) he doesn't believe exists? Why is he so aggressive against biblical Christianity? In an ultimately purposeless and meaningless existence, why does it matter to him if people believe in the God of the Bible and the account of creation as outlined in Genesis? They claim that they care about people and argue that believing in creation is harmful to society. But something deeper is going on. They aren't fighting for the truth but suppressing it.

The fact that people like Bill Nye and Richard Dawkins and atheist groups in the USA like the ACLU, the Americans United for Separation of Church and State (AU), and the Freedom From Religion Foundation (FFRF) are so consumed with fighting against biblical Christianity, actually confirms the truth of God's Word.

APOLOGETICS   OCTOBER 3

In Romans 1 we read that God has given man the ability to know that He exists, so that if anyone rejects the God of the Bible, they are without excuse: *For what can be known about God is plain to them, because God has shown it to them. For his invisible attributes, namely, his eternal power and divine nature, have been clearly perceived, ever since the creation of the world, in the things that have been made. So they are without excuse* (Romans 1:19–20).

God's Word also makes it clear that the reason even atheists use words like right and wrong and good and bad is because God has given man a conscience—God's law written on our hearts: *For when Gentiles, who do not have the law, by nature do what the law requires, they are a law to themselves, even though they do not have the law. They show that the work of the law is written on their hearts, while their conscience also bears witness* (Romans 2:14–15).

In Genesis 3:5 we read that the temptation given to Adam and Eve was that they could "be like God." Because we succumbed to this temptation in Adam, we want to be our own god! Our fallen nature doesn't want to submit to the God who created us and owns us; we want to make our own rules! Romans 1 also explains that because of man's rebellious heart, fallen unregenerate man will *suppress the truth in unrighteousness* (Romans 1:18; NKJV).

Really then, when Bill Nye, Richard Dawkins, and others so aggressively oppose biblical Christianity, what they are doing is this: They are covering their ears and closing their eyes and saying, "I refuse to submit to the God who created me. I refuse to acknowledge that God is the Creator. I refuse to accept that I'm a sinner in need of salvation. I want to write my own rules! Therefore I must oppose anything that pricks my conscience and aggressively suppress the truth to justify my rebellion."

I was once speaking with an atheist when he said to me, "If there is a God, then why doesn't He come and show Himself to us?" I replied, "He did, and they nailed Him to a Cross." And, of course, I went on to talk about Jesus as the God-man, His death and Resurrection, and the gift of salvation that He offers.

In 2 Peter 3:5, we are told that those who scoff about God as Creator, the historical Flood, and coming judgment by fire are "willingly ignorant." Some translations say "deliberately reject." This means it is a deliberate action on their part not to believe, because they don't want to believe. They close their eyes and cover their ears, refusing to believe the truth and actively suppressing it.

So why do these who so aggressively oppose Christianity care? They care because they are desperately trying to justify their rebellion against the truth. They don't want to admit that they are sinners in need of salvation and thus need to submit to the God who created them and owns them.

> **These want to be their own god and reject the one true God who created them, owns them, and has a right to determine what is right and what is wrong, which is why they don't want God defining anything as they want to define everything themselves.**

OCTOBER 4

Deuteronomy 4:19

Star Dust Worship

In November 2023, Disney posted its first clip from the movie "I'm a Star." The words of this song are based on evolutionary naturalism (atheism) to teach kids (and everyone) that everything came from star dust! But this is nothing new.

We've heard so many times from secular groups like the Freedom from Religion Foundation (FFRF) or the Americans United for Separation of Church and State (AU) that students in science classrooms in public schools can't be taught about creation, as that would be teaching religion in government-funded schools. And yet, the government is allowing a religion to be imposed on public school students and using tax dollars to do it. Imagine if public school students in their science classes were encouraged to worship the sun. And yet this is happening! But how do they get away with it? Well, they just call worshipping the sun "science," and then claim they can teach this "science" in the public schools! Really the Disney song mentioned above is all about worshipping the sun and stars.

You see, the following statement is allowed to be made (and is being made in a number of instances) to public school science students: "Our ancestors worshipped the sun. They were far from foolish. It makes good sense to revere the sun and stars because we are their children. The silicon in the rocks, the oxygen in the air, the carbon in our DNA, the iron in our skyscrapers, the silver in our jewelry—were all made in stars, billions of years ago. Our planet, our society, and we ourselves are stardust."

That statement was made by Neil deGrasse Tyson in the *Cosmos* series he narrated. Evolutionists encouraged teachers to use this series in public school classrooms. Incidentally, Neil deGrasse Tyson is not the first disciple of naturalism to suggest a distinctly religious message in stardust. Tyson's statement echoes one that was made by a prominent atheist at the time who blasphemed the grace of Jesus Christ by casting stardust in the religious role of both "creator" and "savior." He said the following during a lecture: "You are all stardust. You couldn't be here if stars hadn't exploded, because the elements—the carbon, nitrogen, oxygen, iron, all the things that matter for evolution—weren't created at the beginning of time. They were created in the nuclear furnaces of stars, and the only way they could get into your body is if those stars were kind enough to explode. So, forget Jesus. The stars died so that you could be here today."

These atheists and the producers of this *Cosmos* series openly draw the battle lines between biblical Christianity and their own substitute religion of evolution. They not only wrongly claim that biblical Christianity is anti-science but also that evolutionary science satisfies a spiritual need. Tyson speaks in the series, not just about observational science overlaid heavily with his evolutionary claims but also extols the spiritual satisfaction he derives from his evolutionary beliefs. For instance, in this same episode ("Sisters of the Sun") Tyson says, "Accepting our kinship with all life on earth is not only solid science; it's, in my view, also a soaring spiritual experience."

Yet even before the series premiered, the producers made its religious position clear by defining scientific literacy as belief in evolution and blaming the exposure of students to creationism for rampant so-called "scientific illiteracy."[97]

APOLOGETICS — OCTOBER 4

I think it's about time Christians woke up and understood that even though there are Christian missionaries in the public (government) school system (and they need our prayers), by and large these schools are actually churches of atheism. Millions of students are being taught that all life and the universe arose by natural processes—by naturalism. But we need to call naturalism what it is: atheism. Regardless of where parents send their children to be educated, it does need to be understood that as these young people are sent to the public schools for around seven hours a day, they are largely being indoctrinated in an anti-God religion. If one is not for Christ, then one is against Christ—there is no neutral position. If the education system is not for Christ, it is against Christ. If the textbooks are not for Christ, they are against Christ! If the teachers aren't for Christ, they are against Christ!

Whoever is not with me is against me, and whoever does not gather with me scatters (Luke 11:23).

Around 85% of kids from Church homes attend public schools—and most are not surviving the system. Certainly, there are some Christian students (and they are the exception, not the rule) who can stand on God's Word, defend the faith and witness to the other students. But as I said, they are the exception! Most students from Church homes are adversely affected by the system.

God's Word certainly gives us the principles we need to understand so that we can teach and train our children. And how many parents are equipping their children with apologetics to defend the faith anyway? I think it would make a big difference in how parents view education and how they train their children if they started thinking this way: "Well, I'm sending my kids off to the church of atheism for seven hours today to be placed under the teaching of many who are priests of atheism for five days this week. I hope their one hour at church on the weekend enables them to survive."

Now there are parents who choose to homeschool or send their students to Christian school—and such decisions are between those parents and the Lord. But if parents truly understood what was going on, maybe so many students would not come through such a system and end up, in essence, worshipping the sun. What a reminder of the awesome responsibility parents have to do their best to teach their children to worship the Son—to put their faith and trust in the Lord Jesus Christ as their Creator Redeemer.

You shall love the Lord your God with all your heart and with all your soul and with all your might. And these words that I command you today shall be on your heart. You shall teach them diligently to your children, and shall talk of them when you sit in your house, and when you walk by the way, and when you lie down, and when you rise. You shall bind them as a sign on your hand, and they shall be as frontlets between your eyes. You shall write them on the doorposts of your house and on your gates (Deuteronomy 6:5–9).

And beware lest you raise your eyes to heaven, and when you see the sun and the moon and the stars, all the host of heaven, you be drawn away and bow down to them and serve them, things that the Lord your God has allotted to all the peoples under the whole heaven (Deuteronomy 4:19).

> **We need to be diligent and realize that every child conceived in a mother's womb is a being who will live forever in heaven or hell.**

OCTOBER 5

Romans 8:18

Suffering

There's been many books written about suffering and trying to explain how to understand death, suffering and disease, and a loving God. Atheists mock Christians who believe in a loving God by claiming such a God must be unjust and wouldn't allow children to suffer as we see in countries where there is starvation and horrible diseases. But these same atheists tell everyone to believe in evolution, yet this is the process they believe produced all this death, disease, and suffering! And how can an atheist, who has no absolute standard but their own subjective beliefs, accuse God (who they don't believe exists) to be unjust because of all the suffering we see and experience in this world?

These atheists don't accept this world of death and suffering we live in is a result of our sin! They don't want to acknowledge God created them and they (and all of us) are sinners because we, in Adam, rebelled against our Creator, our holy God. And we must suffer the consequences of our sin. A holy God must judge rebellion. And He did, but at the same time shows us His grace and mercy by providing a solution to our sin problem. Only God's Word can give us answers about suffering—and offer comfort.

It's heartbreaking to see children suffer, and our minds can wander to the inevitable question, "Why is someone so innocent suffering so badly?"

When we allow God's Word to inform our thoughts, however, we see a different picture. All children—in fact, all people—suffer to one degree or another while living on this earth because humanity is under the curse of sin (Romans 5:12).

God's Word emphasizes that all humans face the judgment of death. *And just as it is appointed for man to die once, and after that comes judgment* (Hebrews 9:27), it's also important to understand that the whole creation suffers because of our sin in Adam. *For we know that the whole creation has been groaning together in the pains of childbirth until now* (Romans 8:22). So it doesn't matter if we are a child or an adult, all are under the judgment of death, as all are sinners.

But it's also true that some people hurt more than others physically, mentally, emotionally, and spiritually. Does that necessarily mean their suffering is a direct result of a specific sin? Of course not! In Luke 13, Jesus spoke about 18 people who were killed when a tower fell on them.

Or those eighteen on whom the tower in Siloam fell and killed them: do you think that they were worse offenders than all the others who lived in Jerusalem? No, I tell you; but unless you repent, you will all likewise perish (Luke 13:4–5).

Those 18 weren't killed because they were worse sinners; it was their time to die. Jesus uses this to remind us that we are all under the judgment of death because of sin, and so all will face death. This is a stark reminder to make sure we have done what Jesus said: "Repent."

In other words, make sure you have received the free gift of salvation so you know with certainty that when you die, you will go to be present with the Lord for eternity. *[B]ut these are written so that you may believe that Jesus is the Christ, the Son of God, and that by believing you may have life in his name* (John 20:31).

APOLOGETICS   OCTOBER 5

Because we are responsible for the groaning creation (we all sinned in Adam), we have a responsibility to do whatever we can to help others who suffer.

For all have sinned and fall short of the glory of God (Romans 3:23).

Therefore, just as sin came into the world through one man, and death through sin, and so death spread to all men because all sinned (Romans 5:12).

Suffering is not God's fault; it's mankind's fault! It's a sad reminder of how bad sin is and what it's done to the world. And we can grieve as we see the results of our sin. We can also be reminded that because we are responsible for the groaning creation, we have a responsibility to do whatever we can to help others who suffer. We deserve nothing. We don't deserve to exist. But God loves us so much He provided a way (He paid the price Himself) for us to be reconciled to God. *For we know that the whole creation has been groaning together in the pains of childbirth until now* (Romans 8:22).

We can sometimes see specific ways God uses someone's suffering. How they cope with pain can be a witness to others who then listen to the gospel and receive the free gift of salvation. Think of people who have suffered, such as Joni Eareckson Tada. Yet even through her disability, Joni has had a spiritual impact on millions of people. Sometimes, God uses someone's suffering in their own life to bring them to Christ.

People sometimes look back over their lives and realize that, though they did not understand while they were suffering, they can now see the mighty hand of God working in marvelous ways through their suffering. Many times, we don't understand why someone suffers, but there's no doubt God has purposes which are beyond our understanding on this earth. Job learned this lesson when he stated:

I know that you can do all things, and that no purpose of yours can be thwarted. "Who is this that hides counsel without knowledge?" Therefore I have uttered what I did not understand, things too wonderful for me, which I did not know. "Hear, and I will speak; I will question you, and you make it known to me." I had heard of you by the hearing of the ear, but now my eye sees you; therefore I despise myself, and repent in dust and ashes (Job 42:2–6). Job learned he had to let God be God.

For my thoughts are not your thoughts, neither are your ways my ways, declares the Lord (Isaiah 55:8).

Living through horrendous suffering—or seeing loved ones hurting—can be very hard. But Paul offers some comfort through this: *For I consider that the sufferings of this present time are not worth comparing with the glory that is to be revealed to us* (Romans 8:18).

Our life on this earth is so short compared to eternity. Yet it's true that we struggle through this life, and our hearts go out to those who struggle more than others. We know that those who have trusted Christ have a beautiful future to look forward to when one day *[God] will wipe away every tear from their eyes, and death shall be no more, neither shall there be mourning, nor crying, nor pain anymore, for the former things have passed away* (Revelation 21:4).

But, *as it is written, "What no eye has seen, nor ear heard, nor the heart of man imagined, what God has prepared for those who love him"* (1 Corinthians 2:9).

What a day that will be!

OCTOBER 6
Revelation 3:15-16

Evolutionary Syncretism

When Christians compromise God's Word in Genesis with man's word concerning evolution/millions of years, they are actually mixing two religions! Such compromise contaminates the Word of God and undermines its authority. Ultimately, this exalts man, not God! Let me explain. The Bible makes it clear there are only two worldview positions a person can hold—we're either for Christ or against Him. *Whoever is not with me is against me, and whoever does not gather with me scatters* (Matthew 12:30).

Also, God's Word makes it clear there are only two ways to build a worldview—either on the rock or on the sand. *Everyone then who hears these words of mine and does them will be like a wise man who built his house on the rock.... And everyone who hears these words of mine and does not do them will be like a foolish man who built his house on the sand* (Matthew 7:24–26).

We're also told there are only two ways to walk in this world—in light or in darkness. *Jesus spoke to them, saying, "I am the light of the world. Whoever follows me will not walk in darkness, but will have the light of life"* (John 8:12). There are two roads: the broad way and the narrow way.

These teachings reflect the fact that, in an ultimate sense, there are only two religious views in the world—beliefs built on man's fallible word (darkness/sand) and the one that's built on the infallible Word of God beginning in Genesis (light/rock). These two views have been in conflict for about 6,000 years, and the battle that began in the Garden of Eden continues to rage before us today.

After God made Adam, He gave him an instruction to obey and then presented the consequences if he didn't. *The Lord God took the man and put him in the garden of Eden to work it and keep it. And the Lord God commanded the man, saying, "You may surely eat of every tree of the garden, but of the tree of the knowledge of good and evil you shall not eat, for in the day that you eat of it you shall surely die"* (Genesis 2:15–17).

In other words, Adam, who was to be the head of the entire human race (as from him all human beings would descend), was told to obey God's Word. It was a test of obedience.

The devil, however, came to Eve. Genesis 3 records: *Now the serpent was more crafty than any other beast of the field that the Lord God had made. He said to the woman, "Did God actually say, 'You shall not eat of any tree in the garden'?" And the woman said to the serpent, "We may eat of the fruit of the trees in the garden, but God said, 'You shall not eat of the fruit of the tree that is in the midst of the garden, neither shall you touch it, lest you die.'" But the serpent said to the woman, "You will not surely die"* (Genesis 3:1–4).

In other words, the devil claimed that you don't need to obey God's Word. You can be your own god and decide the truth for yourself.

Adam and Eve did just that, and they disobeyed God. *So when the woman saw that the tree was good for food, and that it was a delight to the eyes, and that the tree was to be desired to make one wise, she took of its fruit and ate, and she also gave some to her husband who was with her, and he ate* (Genesis 3:6).

And so began the battle of the only two religions. A battle between God's Word and fallible, sinful man's word—a religion of man being his own god and trusting his own word.

APOLOGETICS — OCTOBER 6

The same battle is raging today. Sadly, in our Western world, God's Word has been denigrated and has been thrown out of public schools. Now we have generations who largely believe they are their own god, and their worldview is predominantly one of moral relativism. Public schools have become, by and large, churches of atheism. Once you cease building your thinking on the absolute authority of God's Word, then ultimately anything goes, if you can get away with it.

Now, religions based on man's word take on many different forms: Hinduism, Buddhism, New Age, Baha'i faith, Zoroastrianism, Satanism, Jehovah's Witnesses, Deism, Taoism, Shinto, Unitarianism, Atheism, Agnosticism, Materialism, Christian syncretism with evolution, and other belief systems.

Now, when Christians take man's word concerning origins and reinterpret Genesis (e.g., add in millions of years and other evolutionary beliefs), they have added man's finite interpretations to the Word of the infinite God. Thus, they really have changed the starting point from God's Word to man's word. Once fallibility (man's fallible words) is added to God's infallible word, then such compromise means ultimately that the starting point is man's word.

You are the salt of the earth, but if salt has lost its taste, how shall its saltiness be restored? It is no longer good for anything except to be thrown out and trampled under people's feet (Matthew 5:13).

Salt loses its taste by becoming contaminated. Contamination destroys.

When Christians contaminate Genesis, they are undermining the authority of the Word and undermining the foundation of all doctrine, of the rest of the Bible, and of our biblical worldview.

I believe we can also apply what God's Word says about the Laodicean church:

I know your works: you are neither cold nor hot. Would that you were either cold or hot! So, because you are lukewarm, and neither hot nor cold, I will spit you out of my mouth (Revelation 3:15–16).

I apply this by saying that if one is "cold" (doesn't believe), then it is obvious, but if one is "lukewarm" then it's not so obvious and yet it's not "hot." Lukewarmness is a problem as contamination is a problem.

We need to be "hot"–believing God's Word in Genesis as written without compromise.

OCTOBER 7
1 Timothy 2:13-14
The Evolution of Adam Part 1

In 2012, Brazos Press released what I unhesitatingly call a heretical book, *The Evolution of Adam* by Dr. Peter Enns. I noted an irony as I read the book and then saw how the publisher describes its own mission.

"Brazos Press fosters the renewal of classical, orthodox Christianity by publishing thoughtful, theologically grounded books on subjects of importance to the church and the world. We serve authors and readers from all major streams of the historic Christian tradition, recognizing that the renewal of Christian orthodoxy transcends many traditional boundary lines and polarities ... publishing excellent and accessible works by leading thinkers on topics such as spirituality, the arts, the economy, popular culture, ethics, theology, biblical studies, and the social sciences. Our readers include clergy, educated laypersons, and students seeking clear, stimulating commentary on how the riches of the Christian tradition can be brought to bear on the struggles and hopes of the present day."

I especially took note of the publisher's claim that it seeks to uphold the "historic Christian tradition" as well as "Christian orthodoxy." I will put that claim to the test as I review this book. Before I summarize and give you my critique, some background is needed. Dr. Enns used to be a part of BioLogos, and they described him this way: "Pete Enns is the Abram S. Clemens Professor of Biblical Studies at Eastern University. He is a former Senior Fellow of Biblical Studies for BioLogos and author of many books and commentaries, including *Inspiration and Incarnation*, *The Evolution of Adam*, and *The Bible Tells Me So*. His most recent book is *The Sin of Certainty: Why God Desires Our Trust More Than Our 'Correct' Beliefs*." Here is a section extracted from one of my blogs posts, in which I quoted Dr. Enns (from what was on the BioLogos website).

[Enns:] "In my last post I suggested that the Adam story could be viewed symbolically as a story of Israel's beginnings, not as the story of humanity from ground zero.

"But some might ask, 'Why go through all this trouble? Why not just take it literally? The Bible says Adam was the first man. That's the end of it.'

"The biblical depiction of human origins, if taken literally, presents Adam as the very first human being ever created. He was not the product of an evolutionary process, but a special creation of God a few thousand years before Jesus—roughly speaking, about 6000 years ago. Every single human being that has ever lived can trace his/her genetic history to that one person.[98]

"This is a problem because it is at odds with everything else we know about the past from the natural sciences and cultural remains.[99]

[My comments:] "Enns accepts what the secular world teaches concerning evolution and millions of years, and it is so obvious this determines how he approaches the Bible. He does not have the same view of inspiration as I do. In fact, he doesn't have the biblical view of inspiration: *All Scripture is given by inspiration of God, and is profitable for doctrine, for reproof, for correction, for instruction in righteousness*" (2 Timothy 3:16; NKJV). The book is really divided into two sections. One section covers the Book of Genesis and one covers the topic of Paul and his statements about Adam in Romans and 1 Corinthians. On page xvi of his introduction, Dr. Enns stated, "After a virtual silence in the Old Testament, Adam makes a sudden and unprecedented

APOLOGETICS
OCTOBER 7

appearance in two of Paul's Letters (Rom. 5; 1 Cor. 15)." However, Peter Enns attempts to find alternate meanings for the word "Adam" whenever it appears in the Old Testament outside of Genesis 1–5. Although Enns acknowledges the mention of Adam in 1 Chronicles, he still does not believe Adam was a literal person. But, if Adam is not a literal person, then how can Adam appear in this genealogy? I assume Peter Enns would consider most of the others (including Abraham) in this list to be literal people. I have left out many names but included a number just to remind you of how detailed these lists of real people are.

Adam, Seth, Enosh, Cainan, Mahalalel, Jared, Enoch, Methuselah, Lamech, Noah, Shem, Ham, and Japheth. The sons of Japheth were Gomer, Magog, Madai, Javan, Tubal, Meshech, and Tiras. The sons of Gomer were Ashkenaz, Diphath, and Togarmah. The sons of Javan were Elishah, Tarshishah, Kittim, and Rodanim.

The sons of Ham were Cush, Mizraim, Put, and Canaan. ... The sons of Shem were Elam, Asshur, Arphaxad, Lud, Aram, Uz, Hul, Gether, and Meshech. Arphaxad begot Shelah, and Shelah begot Eber. To Eber were born two sons: the name of one was Peleg, for in his days the earth was divided; and his brother's name was Joktan. Joktan begot Almodad, Sheleph, Hazarmaveth, Jerah, Hadoram, Uzal, Diklah, Ebal, Abimael, Sheba, Ophir, Havilah, and Jobab. ... And Abraham begot Isaac. The sons of Isaac were Esau and Israel. The sons of Esau were Eliphaz, Reuel, Jeush, Jaalam, and Korah. And the sons of Eliphaz were Teman, Omar, Zephi, Gatam, and Kenaz; and by Timna, Amalek. The sons of Reuel were Nahath, Zerah, Shammah, and Mizzah (1 Chronicles 1:1–37; NKJV).

And then we see Adam showing up in this verse of Scripture: *But like Adam they transgressed the covenant; there they dealt faithlessly with me* (Hosea 6:7).

The above passage is obviously referencing the literal Fall (sin) of Adam in Genesis 3.1

Adam also appears in a detailed genealogy in the New Testament:

the son of Enos, the son of Seth, the son of Adam, the son of God (Luke 3:38).

Besides Romans 5 and 1 Corinthians 15 (cited by Peter Enns), Paul in 1 Timothy specifically referred to Adam being created first: *For Adam was formed first, then Eve; and Adam was not deceived, but the woman was deceived and became a transgressor* (1 Timothy 2:13–14).

Paul also referred to Adam in 1 Corinthians 11 when discussing the creation of Eve, relating men and women's roles to the historical creation account and how the woman was made from the man, just as Genesis 2 records (from his rib).

For man was not made from woman, but woman from man (1 Corinthians 11:8).

For as woman was made from man, so man is now born of woman (1 Corinthians 11:12).

Also, Jude references Adam and his specific place in the genealogy: *It was also about these that Enoch, the seventh from Adam* (Jude 1:14).

Peter Enns desperately tries to propose that Paul was not referencing a literal Adam as a real first man. He believes that "the Adam story in Genesis reflects its ancient Near Eastern setting and should be read that way" (p. 140). He insists this is really how Paul used Adam.

We need to take God at His Word and reject the fallible beliefs of fallible man.

OCTOBER 8
Proverbs 29:25

The Evolution of Adam Part 2

Continuing our discussion about *The Evolution of Adam*, a book written by Peter Enns to deny a literal Adam.

On page 95, Peter Enns wrote: "Paul engaged his Scripture against the backdrop of hermeneutical conventions of his day, not ours, and we must understand Paul in that context. In other words, in the same way that we must calibrate the genre of Genesis [my note: by rejecting it as literal history] by looking at the surrounding culture, we must also understand Paul's interpretation of the Old Testament within his ancient world."

On page 117, Enns concluded with the following: "When we keep in mind some of what we have seen thus far—the ambiguous nature of the Adam story in Genesis, Adam's functional absence in the Old Testament, the creative energy invested into the Adam story by other ancient interpreters, and Paul's creative use of the Old Testament in general—we will approach Paul's use of the Adam story with the expectation of finding there not a plain reading of Genesis but a transformation of Genesis. We will see that, whatever Paul says of Adam, that does not settle what Adam means in Genesis itself, and most certainly not the question of human origins as debated in the modern world. Paul was an ancient man with ancient thoughts, inspired though he was. Respecting the Bible as God's Word entails embracing the text in context."

It is obvious from how Peter Enns refers to Paul in a number of chapters in his book that he and conservative Evangelical scholars have totally different views of "inspiration." Enns obviously does not believe in the plenary inspiration (fully God-breathed) of the Scriptures as Paul makes clear in 2 Timothy 3:16: *All Scripture is breathed out by God and profitable for teaching, for reproof, for correction, and for training in righteousness.*

We must also point out that another New Testament person talked about Adam. Jesus Christ, Himself a descendant of Adam (Luke 3:23, 38), discussed the historicity of our first parents. Although He did not mention Adam by name, Jesus did refer to Adam and Eve when He discussed the subject of marriage and divorce with the Pharisees: *He answered, "Have you not read that he who created them from the beginning made them male and female, and said, 'Therefore a man shall leave his father and his mother and hold fast to his wife, and the two shall become one flesh'? So they are no longer two but one flesh. What therefore God has joined together, let not man separate"* (Matthew 19:4–6).

The Lord's statement that the two become one flesh in marriage would be baseless if there really wasn't a first man and woman in the early chapters of Genesis. If Enns is correct, then the biblical teaching on marriage (one man and one woman for life) has no basis in reality.

Also, Dr. Enns argues that "the presence of two different creation accounts is troublesome for readers who assume that Genesis 1 and 2 are historical in nature and that the Bible's first priority is to recount history accurately" (p. 52). This is a popular argument among those who seek to show that Genesis cannot be taken literally, and it's one that we have addressed many times. However, not only is it fairly easy to reconcile the apparent differences between Genesis 1 and 2, but also we need to realize that Jesus quoted from both chapters in His answer to the Pharisees and He wove the statements together seamlessly (Genesis 1:27 and 2:24). These chapters are complementary—Genesis 1 is an overview of creation chronologically (Days 1-7) whereas Genesis 2 is a more detailed account of the sixth day of creation. Since Jesus believed these chapters

APOLOGETICS — OCTOBER 8

to be historical, how can anyone who claims to believe in Christ reject His teaching by dismissing the historicity of Genesis 1 and 2?

Let me give two examples in which I actually agree with Enns (although it's very superficial once you get down into what he is saying):

First, Dr. Enns stated that he rejects the theistic evolution position (i.e., the view that God used evolution to create). He states it does not fit with Scripture. In fact, he says, "This hybrid view does not adhere to the Bible but rewrites it" (p. xv; introduction). I agree with that statement. Those Christians who compromise the Bible by adding evolution to it have to rewrite the words of the Bible. It's a point AiG has always made.

Second, Dr. Enns makes it clear that he believes the Bible does not teach that the earth is millions of years old. He states, "Since the eighteenth century, geology had made its presence known, showing by means of the fossil record that the earth is millions upon millions of years old—far older than most people had taken for granted, far older than a literal interpretation of the Bible allows" (p. 4). I certainly agree that taking Genesis literally does not allow for millions of years.

Dr. Enns, however, does believe that evolution is fact! And he accepts millions of years as fact! So, what is he really teaching about Genesis and God's Word? Here are just a few quotes from his book that sum up what he is trying to teach Christian leaders and laypeople in the Church. (By the way, the book's content fleshes out the points he gives in his talks, including a presentation he gave at Westmont College.)

"Evolution demands that the special creation of the first Adam as described in the Bible is not literally historical" (xvi; introduction).

"It is clear that, from a scientific point of view, the Bible does not always describe physical reality accurately" (xiv; introduction).

"If evolution is correct, one can no longer accept, in any true sense of the word 'historical,' the instantaneous and special creation of humanity described in Genesis specifically 1:26–31 and 2:7, 22" (xiv; introduction).

Frankly, I groaned many times when I read passages like these throughout the book. I groaned further when I thought how Dr. Enns is involved in producing a homeschool curriculum and how children will be affected by its biblical compromise. As I read the book, one thought came to my mind over and over: What about the perspicuity (i.e., the clarity) of Scripture? In his new book, Enns makes it clear that he accepts evolution as fact and that he also rejects a literal Adam and literal Fall—plus he rejects that the apostle Paul taught about a literal Adam in the Books of Romans and Corinthians. Enns states the following:

"A historical Adam has been the dominant Christian view for two thousand years. We must add, however, that the general consensus was formed before the advent of evolutionary theory. ... Evolution demands that the special creation of the first Adam as described in the Bible is not literally historical" (xvi; introduction).

Well, secular scientists today will argue that a man can't rise from the dead. Or that you can't have a virgin birth, or that a man can't walk on water. So shouldn't we (using the same approach as Dr. Enns) also give up the literal Resurrection and virgin birth of Christ?

> "The fear of man lays a snare, but whoever trusts in the Lord is safe" (Proverbs 29:25).

OCTOBER 9
1 Corinthians 15:22

The Evolution of Adam Part 3

Continuing our discussion on the book *The Evolution of Adam* by Peter Enns, what does Peter Enns believe about Genesis? He states: "The Genesis creation narrative we have in our Bibles today, although surely rooted in much older material, was shaped as a theological response to Israel's national crisis of exile. These stories were not written to speak of 'origins' as we might think of them today (in a natural-science sense). They were written to say something of God and Israel's place in the world as God's chosen people. …

"Placing Genesis in its ancient Near Eastern setting [among Israel's neighbors, such as the Canaanites and Babylonians] strongly suggests that it was written as a self-defining document, as a means of declaring the distinctiveness of Israel's own beliefs from those of the surrounding nations. In other words, Genesis is an argument, a polemic, declaring how Israel's God is different from all the other gods, and therefore how Israel is different from all the other nations" (pp. 5–6, bracketed content added).

Furthermore, Dr. Enns, at the end of the book, states the following: "One cannot read Genesis literally—meaning as a literally accurate description of physical, historical reality—in view of the state of scientific knowledge today and our knowledge of ancient Near Eastern stories of origins" (p. 137).

On page 12 we read the following as he discusses the historicity of Genesis: "Modern scholars have tended to focus on the historical questions raised by those ambiguities and inconsistencies; namely, how did such an ambiguous and inconsistent text come to exist in the first place."

What is he referring to? Enns lists a series of questions that, to him, mean Genesis can't be taken as literal history. You might be able to guess one or two. (Hint: they are the typical ones that atheists use today when they attempt to attack Genesis and all of God's Word, which we have answered many times). Here is Enns again: "If Adam and Eve are the first humans, and Cain their only surviving offspring, how can Cain be afraid of retaliation for murdering his brother (4:13–16)? Where did he get his wife (4:17)?" (p. 11).

He continues: "No doubt many reading this will recognize a good number of these questions, and one or two may even have been a source of embarrassment in teaching children's Sunday school. (What teacher has not been asked by a precocious eight-year-old where Cain found his wife?)" (p. 11). Notice that Enns does not mention that Genesis 5:4 provides the obvious answer: "And the days of Adam after he had begotten Seth were eight hundred years: and he begat sons and daughters."

Dr. Enns then lists more "tough" questions, and on page 13 he states the following: "These and other questions … led modern biblical scholars to question seriously—and eventually reject—the traditional view that Genesis and the Pentateuch were written in the second millennium BC by one man, Moses."

Sadly, Dr. Enns accepts some form of the Documentary Hypothesis (also known as the JEDP theory)—a thoroughly debunked idea put forth by anti-supernatural liberal critics that states the five books of Moses were written, or at least compiled, a thousand years after Moses died. In fact, Enns uses the liberal dating method for every book of the Old Testament and does not inform his readers that many scholars still hold to the traditional dates and have written extensively in support of those dates (pp. 30–32).

APOLOGETICS

Next, what does Dr. Enns say about the entrance of sin and death in the world? He struggles with this issue in chapter 7. Here we read the following excerpt: "By saying that Paul's Adam is not the historical first man, we are leaving behind Paul's understanding of the cause of the universal plight of sin and death. But this is the burden of anyone who wishes to bring evolution and Christianity together—the only question is how that will be done.

"Admitting the historical and scientific problems with Paul's Adam does not mean in the least that the gospel message is therefore undermined. A literal Adam may not be the first man and cause of sin and death, as Paul understood it, but what remains of Paul's theology are three core elements of the gospel: The universal and self-evident problem of death; The universal and self-evident problem of sin; and The historical event of the death and resurrection of Christ" (p. 123).

Basically, Dr. Enns is stating that you can't add evolution to the Bible and reinterpret the Bible. Yet he states evolution is fact. Therefore, the reader has to understand Genesis and what Paul wrote very differently. Enns gives no sense whatsoever that what Paul wrote in the New Testament is God's Word and God-breathed, but Enns makes it clear that he takes Paul's words as that of a fallible man writing his own thoughts. Furthermore, according to Enns, what Paul wrote needs to be understood in a totally different way. You see, Enns argues that the first Adam was not literal, yet what Paul wrote about Jesus and His Resurrection is literal.

It all raises the obvious question: How can Enns decide which parts of the Bible should be understood as literal history and which are not? His basic approach is that Bible readers can make the Bible say whatever they want it to (if scientists and critical scholars deem it necessary). Therefore, because it is Enns' opinion that Christians must believe in evolution and millions of years, they can fit those beliefs with the Bible—by changing their approach on how and why the Bible was written and how it is to be interpreted.

Nowhere in his book have I found Dr. Enns describe sin as rebellion against God—that all of us have rebelled (i.e., committed high treason against the God of creation). He seems to think of sin as just the bad or evil things that happen on Earth. (Of course, one could ask why something is considered "bad" or "evil" in the first place, but that's a discussion for another time.) He does not believe that because of a literal Fall of the literal Adam, all mankind inherits Adam's sinful nature, as Paul explained in Romans 5:12–21.

To summarize his book I would put it this way:

Evolution is a fact.

The Bible is written by humans and so it is really man's word (and contains some sort of spiritual message).

We must trust secular scientists' interpretation of the past.
The Bible is not God-breathed. Genesis is definitely not literal history.
There was no literal Adam, and there definitely was no literal Fall.
Paul's mention of Adam is not to be taken as if he believes Adam was a literal first man.

Dr. Enns obviously does not hold a high view of Scripture. Furthermore, near the end of his introduction he states, "It is always a difficult subject to suggest that something outside the Bible can significantly affect how the Bible is to be read" (pp. 19–20).

"For as in Adam all die, so also in Christ shall all be made alive" (1 Corinthians 15:22).

OCTOBER 10

Romans 1:16

The Evolution of Adam Part 4

Continuing our discussion of *The Evolution of Adam* book by Peter Enns, what does Peter Enns mean by stating, "It is always a difficult subject to suggest that something outside the Bible can significantly affect how the Bible is to be read."

Well, preceding this statement, we read his words, "At this moment in history, the state of scientific knowledge [Enns means evolution] is driving Christians to rethink some important issues. The challenge of evolution is here to stay, and its effect on how Christians read Genesis and Paul must be deliberately addressed."

Dr. Enns' thesis of his book can be summed up in his own words:

"Our thinking about Adam must change … I am not arguing in this book that Adam evolved. Rather, I am arguing that our understanding of Adam has evolved over the years and that it must now be adjusted in light of the preponderance of (1) scientific evidence supporting evolution and (2) literary evidence from the world of the Bible that helps clarify the kind of literature the Bible is" (p. xiii).

Then Dr. Enns makes a statement that just defies logic. "All of this can be done in a way that respects and honors the authority of the Bible" (p. xiii).

In the book's conclusion (p. 137), Dr. Enns declares, "Literalism is not an option … One cannot read Genesis literally—meaning as a literally accurate description of physical, historical reality—in view of the state of scientific knowledge today and our knowledge of ancient Near Eastern stories of origins."

Then on page 138, he states that for those of us who take Genesis literally: "Literalism is not just an outdated curiosity or an object of jesting. It can be dangerous. A responsible view of the biblical stories must account for the scientific and archaeological facts [i.e., evolution, millions of years, etc.], not dismiss them, ignore them, or—as in some cases—manipulate them."

Enns' approach to Scripture is captured in his own words on page 7: "Now the one-two-three-punch of biblical criticism, biblical archaeology, and science demanded a fresh synthesis of new and old." Note that all three of these areas come under the heading of "historical science"—that is, man's fallible attempts to interpret the past based on fallible assumptions.

So here is the book's bottom line: Dr. Peter Enns puts his trust in man's fallible ideas and then totally reinterprets the Word of God (and ultimately distorts it). He wants to adopt the philosophies of the world instead of bowing his knee to a holy, infinite, infallible God. Indeed, his is a low view of Scripture. And sadly, many church leaders are doing what Peter Enns does.

I will leave you with a challenge. There are Christian college and seminary professors who are enamored with academics like Dr. Enns, with their new ideas attempting to fit man's religion of evolution and millions of years into the Bible. In some respects, I think this view of scholarship is akin to gnosticism. Gnostics believe they possess some special knowledge to share with the world. And despite all the great men and women of God in the past who have treated Genesis as straightforward, literal history, it wasn't until this era that we now have new, special knowledge that will supposedly give us a correct understanding of the Word of God.

APOLOGETICS — OCTOBER 10

In essence, this academic is telling us that his approach is the new way to understand God's Word and what it means. Apart from using this novel approach to the Bible, argues Dr. Enns, you can't discern what the Scriptures teach.

It appears we have a dire situation in the Church today. There is a new "magisterium"—a group of theologians like Dr. Enns who want to tell us how and what to believe in regard to what God's Word states in Genesis (and now Romans too).

Frankly, I'm much more concerned about the disastrous influence of Bible scholars like Dr. Enns and his undermining of the Bible than I am by the outside attacks of atheists. Dr. Enns' attack on biblical authority should be a reminder to all Christians that they need to be equipped with answers. If more Christians properly armed themselves to combat compromise in the Church and were also more emboldened to share their faith with non-Christians, they could be a tremendous force in this world.

A book like Dr. Enns' should be a wake-up call to all Christians to courageously and boldly stand for the Christian faith in our culture—to be the salt and light we must be in our increasingly secularized world. As Paul wrote to Timothy, *Study to show thyself approved unto God, a workman that needeth not to be ashamed, rightly dividing the word of truth* (2 Timothy 2:15; KJV). Let's pray that all Bible-believing Christians will begin standing against those who compromise God's Word; let's make our voices heard in Christian colleges, seminaries, churches, and all of Christendom.

The following verses should be sober reminders for us all:

Beloved, although I was very eager to write to you about our common salvation, I found it necessary to write appealing to you to contend for the faith that was once for all delivered to the saints (Jude 1:3).

For I am not ashamed of the gospel, for it is the power of God for salvation to everyone who believes, to the Jew first and also to the Greek (Romans 1:16).

In my opinion, this author is (as Peter describes in 2 Peter 3) "willfully ignorant." He is deliberately rejecting the truth of God's plain teachings. Dr. Enns has accepted the views of fallible humans and sought the favor of academics. Perhaps he should consider the wisdom of Proverbs 29:25: *The fear of man lays a snare, but whoever trusts in the* LORD *is safe.*

So, after reading these quotes from Dr. Enns' book, would you call his beliefs "orthodox Christianity"? Do you agree that they are of the "historic Christian tradition"? No, this work of his is heretical.

In conclusion, I agree with Dr. Enns that a Christian shouldn't change God's Word to accommodate man's fallible ideas of evolution and millions of years. But I totally disagree with his idea that a Christian must come up with a different approach to understanding God's Word so that evolution and millions of years can be accepted. To do what Dr. Enns has done is really no different than those people who reinterpret the words of the Bible to fit in evolution. Dr. Enns is doing the same thing, just in a different way.

> **We need to take God at His Word and reject the fallible beliefs of fallible man, and we need to judge man's fallible ideas against the absolute authority of God's Word.**

OCTOBER 11

Genesis 3:1

Biblical Authority and Genesis Part 1

Now the serpent was more crafty than any other beast of the field that the LORD God had made. He said to the woman, "Did God actually say, 'You shall not eat of any tree in the garden'?" (Genesis 3:1).

The first attack was when the devil attacked the authority of God's Word in Genesis 3:1, and that attack has not stopped! Since the 1800s, that attack on the authority of God's Word has manifested as an attack on Genesis 1–11 in particular.

Let's look at biblical authority and Genesis.

If I have told you earthly things and you do not believe, how can you believe if I tell you heavenly things? (John 3:12).

Think about this verse very carefully as I apply it in a particular way. If you can't trust the Bible when it talks about geology, biology, and astronomy, then how can you trust the Bible when it talks about morality and salvation? The issues of morality and salvation are dependent upon the history in the Bible being true. God does not separate morality and salvation from geology, biology, and astronomy. However, it's popular today for liberal scholars to claim that the Bible doesn't speak about science.

Now, if we can't believe the Bible when it talks about earthly things—the rocks, the trees, and the animals and plants—then how can we believe the heavenly things (i.e., salvation) that are so important?

All of us, myself included, have been (to one degree or another during our lifetimes) what I call evolutionized. You might say you don't believe in evolution—bear with me.

When we hear the word evolution, it can mean many different things to many different people. We have to define what we mean by it. Evolution, in an ultimate sense, is more than a mechanism. It's a whole way of thinking—a philosophy of life that teaches that man, by himself and independent of God, determines truth. It's very important to understand that. Again, I believe we've all been evolutionized. Let me explain why.

We all go back to one man, Adam. We sin like Adam; Paul makes that very clear in Romans 5. As a result, all of us will have the same propensity that Adam had. We would rather listen to the words of fallible man than the Word of God. That's the bottom line. That was Adam's sin, wasn't it?

Now, we all have that nature. This leads us to be so easily influenced by the fallible words of sinful men who don't know everything and who weren't there instead of listening to the Word of the infallible God who knows everything and who's always been there.

Fallible men are trying to change the infallible Word of God. What I have come to recognize more and more is that if the Bible is a revelation from God to us, and if God has revealed the truth about the entire universe to enable us to understand who we are, what's happened, and why we're here, then everything that He has revealed in His Word has to be foundational to all our thinking in every area.

But, you see, we tend to take our ideas to the Bible. Our nature is such that we try to determine truth independently, by ourselves, and then add that to the Bible. But we need to understand that Christianity is founded in history. In fact, I call the Bible the history book of the universe. Christianity is not a pie-in-the-sky

APOLOGETICS

religion. Christianity is based in real history. Think about it: If the events of Jesus Christ's birth, death, and Resurrection didn't happen in history, how can we be saved? If we all don't go back to one man in history, a literal man in a literal garden, then who are we? Where did we come from?

As I travel around, sometimes I get so dejected when I talk to Christian leaders. A number of Christian leaders have told me, "Genesis is just a metaphor." I reply that if Genesis is a metaphor, then what about the account of Adam and Eve? Well, "It's a metaphor," they answer.

It's interesting to me that if we look up the genealogies in the Bible (e.g., Luke and Chronicles), something becomes quite clear: All the genealogies show that Jesus Christ was a descendant of Adam. So are we to believe that real people go back to real people... all the way back to a metaphor? In Jude 1:14, does Scripture say, "Enoch, the seventh from a metaphor"?

When I read my Bible, these real people trace back to a real person called Adam. Enoch was seventh from Adam. It's critical that we believe in the history of the Bible. If we don't believe it is real history, then who are we? Where did we come from? Why are we sinners? The history is foundational to understanding what Christianity is all about, and you see the importance of historical reality when you read through the Bible:

- A perfect creation is marred by sin, and death is a consequence.
- The catastrophe of Noah's Flood, with geological changes around the globe and biology onboard the ark.
- As a result of the confusion at the Tower of Babel, when God gave different languages, the population splits up into different people groups that move out over the earth. This division results in different characteristics of people groups, depending on what collections of genes they have.
- Jesus Christ becomes a man of flesh and blood; He dies on a Cross, and He is raised from the dead.
- One day, there's going to be a new heaven and a new earth.

The above lists what's happened in history, and we are now waiting for eternity. We have to understand that this biblical history should be like a pair of glasses. As I say to people, when we look at the universe, we should always have on our biblical glasses.

In a *Time* cover story once, astronomers speculated on how the universe will end. They began with evolutionary presuppositions, so the truth is that they really have no idea how the universe will end. Some say it will burn up; others claim it will freeze. Peter, the apostle, tells us through revelation that even the elements will burn up one day so that God can refashion the earth by purging it of its impurities. He will rid everything of the curse. *Time* magazine has it wrong.

I suggest that most people, even in our churches, have the wrong glasses on.

OCTOBER 12

Romans 10:17

Biblical Authority and Genesis Part 2

We're wearing evolutionized glasses, and we're trying to add God to our evolutionized understanding, and we wonder why we have all sorts of problems. Let me give a practical example. One of the questions I have been asked many times is this: "How do you fit dinosaurs with the Bible?" Are you ready for a shock? You don't fit dinosaurs with the Bible! Now, why did I say that?

Well, you don't take man's interpretation of the evidence and try to fit dinosaurs into the Bible. You use the Bible to explain dinosaurs. You use the Bible as history and put on your biblical glasses. Does the Bible tell us when God made land animals? Absolutely. Does He tell us what they ate before sin? Definitely! Does the Bible tell us anything about their history? Yes, they sailed on an ark. Where did they end up? In the Middle East. And then what? They came out of the ark. What happened to the dinosaurs that didn't get on the ark? They drowned. What would you expect to find? Dead ones. What do you find today in the fossil record? Dead ones.

The same approach works with the Grand Canyon. How do you fit the Grand Canyon into the Bible? You don't, but you use the Bible to explain the Grand Canyon. Do creationists and evolutionists, Christians and non-Christians, humanists and Christians all study the same world? Of course! Do we have the same animals? Do we have the same fossils? Do we have the same Grand Canyon? The same universe? Do we have the same facts? Yes! The facts are all the same. What is the difference?

The fight is not about facts—not about the evidence. The battle is about how you interpret evidence, which depends upon the history you believe to begin with. The real battle between Christianity and humanism, between creation and evolution, between Christian and non-Christian, is a battle between two different accounts of history—man's fallible view of history or God's infallible revelation of history. That's the real battle. We've got to recognize that the origins issue is one that concerns authority—God's Word versus man's word.

I was brought up in the secular education system, and it took me years to try to "de-evolutionize" myself. But all of us are evolutionized in some way. People come to me and say, "Look, I'm trying to witness to a non-Christian, and he says, 'Don't give me that Bible stuff; I don't believe the Bible. I want evidence; give me some evidence.'" When folks come to me with this dilemma, I say, "Don't let them set the terms of the debate." Again, the evidence is all the same. If you go out there and try to give them "evidence," what you're actually doing is giving them an interpretation of the evidence, and all they're going to do is reinterpret the facts. You need to set out to fit them with a new pair of glasses (biblical glasses) so that they will understand.

A girl came to me at a conference and said, "What you're saying makes sense. I go to Penn State University. We talk about ethics concerning using human embryos for research, and I have been telling my professors that it's wrong. However, I don't get anywhere with them." She paused, then continued, "I suddenly realized this morning that it's the glasses aspect I'm missing."

By and large, academics have a different foundation—a different set of glasses. We need to explain this to them by saying something like, "I can understand why you think the way you do. If you don't believe there's

APOLOGETICS

a God and you believe that we're a result of evolution, you're looking at the evidence and thinking, What's wrong with using human embryos? We're just animals anyway. But I want you to understand my position. I believe the Bible is the Word of God; you might not, but I do. And because of that, I have a particular way of thinking. That's why I interpret the evidence the way I do."

Thus, you simply explain where your thinking is coming from. Also, consider Romans 10:17: *So faith comes from hearing, and hearing through the word of Christ,* and thus: *How then will they call on him in whom they have not believed? And how are they to believe in him of whom they have never heard? And how are they to hear without someone preaching? And how are they to preach unless they are sent? As it is written, "How beautiful are the feet of those who preach the good news!"* (Romans 10:14–15).

It's the Word of God that convicts, that is sharper than a two-edged sword. I'm not going to divorce my presuppositions from the way I interpret the evidence. Thus, I can say, "You might not believe the Bible, but I do. And what I want to show you is that when I build my thinking on the Bible, I can make sense of the world. I can logically defend the Christian faith. I can show you that the statement, 'In the beginning, God created' (Genesis 1:1), is confirmed by science. I can show you that God created distinct kinds of animals and plants and that this is what we observe in the world. I can show you that a global Flood makes sense of a worldwide fossil record." I tell them that I can't prove this explanation to them because "without faith it is impossible" (Hebrews 11:6)—but the more I argue this way, the more I'm showing that the Bible is the best and correct explanation. I then go on to explain that they also need to listen to the rest of the Bible, including the gospel.

Sadly, most Christian adults and young people don't think like this. Let me give you a simple (but often overlooked) reason why so many believers fail to see the world through biblical glasses.

The Church has separated the Bible from the real world. They have been disconnected. As we'll see, the Church has accepted the world's teaching, and by doing so, it has undermined the authority of the Word.

Do churches really believe the Bible is the ultimate authority? The statement of faith at most churches reads something like this: The Bible is the ultimate authority in all matters of faith and practice. Is there anything wrong with that statement? No, not in itself; I agree with the statement. But there is a problem with it that we're not seeing. Let's look at it this way: Where the Bible touches on geology, can we trust it? What about biology, astronomy, and chemistry?

Of course, we can trust the Bible because it is the Word of God. But the Bible is not just the ultimate authority in all matters of faith and practice.

> The Bible is the ultimate authority in all matters of faith and practice and everything it touches upon.

OCTOBER 13

Genesis 1:29

Biblical Authority and Genesis Part 3

In the 18th and 19th centuries, the idea that the earth is millions of years old became very popular. The bulk of the Church basically said, "OK, we can believe what the world is teaching about geology, biology, and so on, as long as the Bible is recognized as a book that teaches about morality and salvation." All of a sudden, the Bible was disconnected from the real world. The next short step was that the Bible no longer connected to death and suffering, the Grand Canyon, dinosaurs, and so on. That is why Christians end up asking questions such as, "How do you fit dinosaurs into the Bible?" They no longer understand that the Bible connects to the real world. This thinking shows up in a big way in our Sunday school materials. In fact, I would say a lot of the Bible curricula that we use in the Church today totally miss the mark in many ways. Much of it is virtually worthless, because we have put the emphasis on cute animals and colorful packaging.

We teach Bible stories. Now, what's wrong with that? Isn't that what we're supposed to do? Shouldn't we teach the accounts of Jonah and the great fish, the feeding of the five thousand, Paul's missionary journeys, Noah and the ark, Adam and Eve? What's the problem with that?

Of course, I believe all those accounts. The problem, however, is that people grow up looking at the Bible as just a collection of stories. From there, it's a short leap to legend, myth, and fairy tales. Not surprisingly, many denominations today teach that the Old Testament, in particular, was spun from myths and campfire stories. This inevitably leads to a weakening of the faith and outright assaults on the inspiration of the Bible, as seen in the antics of the Jesus Seminar "scholars" who tell us, among other things, that only 18 percent of the words attributed to Jesus actually came from His mouth.

We criticize television networks for inaccurate depictions of Bible figures, but that's exactly what we do in Sunday school and in our Bible curriculum. We teach our children Bible stories. Now, here is what results from this shortsighted teaching method. These young people learn all these Bible stories, and then they go out into the big, "bad" world. Many end up in colleges and universities. They read magazines and books. But what they are taught in the world contradicts the Bible's history. Our young people are challenged by skeptics who ask questions that challenge the Bible's integrity. Questions such as:

- Where did Cain get his wife?
- Where did God come from?
- How did Noah get all the animals on the ark?
- Where did the races of people come from?
- What about the dinosaurs?
- How about carbon dating?
- How about continental drift?
- What about natural selection?

So it goes. Sadly, most churches are not teaching adults or students how to connect the Bible to the real world. By and large, they don't teach apologetics—how to defend the Christian faith and uphold the authority of the Word of God.

APOLOGETICS

Consider this: In Sunday school, do we usually teach children about geology, biology, and astronomy? No? Why not? Well, in Sunday school, we teach them about Jesus. If I can say this without being misunderstood, therein lies the major problem. The children end up thinking Sunday school and church is just about Jesus. Now, this is important, but it comes across in most instances as just a "story."

You see, the Bible teaches about geology. It states that there was a global Flood. The Bible also teaches about biology. God made distinct kinds of animals and plants. The Bible deals with astronomy. God made the sun, moon, and stars on day four for signs and for seasons. Now, the Bible doesn't deal with chemical equations or the laws of physics that helped put man on the moon, but the Bible does give the big picture in geology, biology, and other sciences to enable people to have the right way of thinking about the universe.

The Bible covers topics like the atmosphere and oceans. However, we usually teach the Bible as just a collection of stories. Thus, children grow up thinking the Bible is just a book about morality and salvation, but what they learn in the world about geology, biology, and astronomy—that's what they can trust concerning the history of the universe. Eventually, these students become consistent and say, "You know, if you can't trust the Bible's history, and you can't trust its geology, biology, and astronomy, why trust its morality and salvation?" And we lose these students to the world.

Increasingly, the world views Christians as fanatics fighting moral issues and trying to impose Christian morality on the culture. However, most Christians don't realize that the culture no longer has a foundation that takes the Bible seriously. The Church itself, when it compromises with billions of years of evolution, has effectively said, "Well, we don't really believe the Bible's history." Then we wonder why we've got problems.

At the Answers in Genesis headquarters in Kentucky, we have built the incredible Creation Museum. We had a four-year battle with the humanists over the right to use the property for a museum, but now visitors can walk in and learn how to put on biblical glasses. They tour exhibits that illustrate the whole history of the world through creation, corruption, the Flood, the Tower of Babel, Christ, the Cross, and consummation. They see how the Bible connects to the real world and learn answers to the questions of the age. We teach the doctrines that are built on the Bible's history, and we proclaim the gospel of Jesus Christ. With a 2,000-foot frontage on a major interstate, we are shouting to the world, "The Bible is true! We can logically defend the Christian faith. You're going to be challenged to believe its message." We do the same sort of thing at the Ark Encounter. If you take Genesis as history, at face value, and as written, Genesis 1:29 makes it very clear that God told Adam and Eve to eat fruit. *And God said, "Behold, I have given you every plant yielding seed that is on the face of all the earth, and every tree with seed in its fruit. You shall have them for food"* (Genesis 1:29). He told the animals to eat plants. He did not tell the animals to eat other animals. In fact, this is substantiated in Genesis 9:3; after the Flood, God told Noah he could now, for the first time, eat animals. That substantiates that Genesis 1:29 (and verse 30 as it's written in the same way as verse 29) teaches that man and animals were vegetarians originally. Why am I emphasizing this? At the end of the sixth day of creation, God said everything was "very good." Would the world at that time be full of cancer? Do you think God would look at such disease and say, "That's very good"?

> **If you take Genesis to Revelation consistently, I believe you can come to no other conclusion than that death, bloodshed, disease, and suffering of man and animals are a consequence of sin.**

OCTOBER 14

Matthew 19:4-5

Biblical Authority and Genesis Part 4

If you believe in millions of years before Adam, you have no option but to accept diseases like cancer, death, bloodshed, violence, thorns, suffering, and extinction as existing millions of years before man. There are some dinosaur bones in the fossil record (supposedly millions of years old) that show evidence of cancer. But the Bible's record makes it obvious such diseases are the result of Adam's sin. There are also thorns in the fossil record, supposedly hundreds of millions of years old, yet God specifically tells us that thorns are a result of the curse. The stomachs of some animals were fossilized with the remains of other animals that they had eaten. How could God describe all that as very good?

Let us consider the death issue in more detail by looking closely at the Book of Genesis. How did Jesus interpret Genesis? In Matthew 19, when asked about divorce and marriage, He referred to Genesis as history: *He answered, "Have you not read that he who created them from the beginning made them male and female, and said, 'Therefore a man shall leave his father and his mother and hold fast to his wife, and the two shall become one flesh'?"* (Matthew 19:4–5). What was Jesus teaching us? Do you want to understand the doctrine of marriage? The doctrine of marriage (and thus the meaning of marriage) is dependent upon its history being true. You become one. Why? It's based on the principle of "one flesh." Eve was taken out of Adam. If this event didn't happen in history, then how can you talk about oneness, as Jesus does in Matthew 19, and Paul in Ephesians 5? The woman couldn't have come from an ape-woman. To believe this is to destroy the whole basis of marriage. And we know it's to be a man and a woman and not a man and a man. Why? Because God made a man and a woman in history, not a man and a man. It grieves me, but it does not surprise me that the churches condoning homosexual behavior or ordaining homosexual pastors do not believe in a literal Genesis. If they did, they would realize that marriage could not be a man and a man, or a woman and a woman.

The history in Genesis 1–11 is foundational to the rest of the Bible. Incidentally, liberal teachers understand the best way to get rid of the Bible. First, get rid of the history (the geology and so on), because once the history's gone, it's then just some pie-in-the-sky religion, divorced from its foundation, and it will ultimately collapse. The Bible has been disconnected from the real world and relegated to just a collection of stories. No wonder people are leaving the Church. Since the 1960s, the United Methodist Church has lost millions of members and continues to decline. Today, there are more Muslims in America than Episcopalians. The cause of this shift is no mystery!

The Church has been destroying its own history by believing in millions of years, taking man's interpretation of the evidence, and adding it to the Bible. Discussions about Genesis and the whole issue of creation/evolution/millions of years is an issue of authority. Do we take God at His Word or not? Is the Bible the infallible Word of God? And what right do we have to tell God what we think He means instead of letting Him tell us what He said He did? That's the issue.

Another great controversy today concerning the history in Genesis is the length of the creation week. If you don't believe that God created in six days, as His Word clearly states, then why believe Jesus Christ rose from the dead? I'll tell you why I believe that Jesus Christ rose from the dead. Because the Bible clearly states that on the third day, He rose from the dead. Some people claim we know Jesus rose from the dead because of all the

APOLOGETICS

evidence. However, all evidence is circumstantial. It's all interpreted. Even though the evidence seems to overwhelmingly support the claim that Jesus rose from the dead, ultimately, it is not proof. The proof is what the Word of God states. You know why I believe that God created in six days? Because the Word of God clearly states this. You see, as soon as you question the six days of creation, you have lost the battle, and you may as well give up. Why? Let's consider the Scopes trial. Clarence Darrow persuaded William Jennings Bryan (a dear Christian gentleman) to get on the witness stand because he wanted to show the world (by using Bryan) that Christianity is a bankrupt religion. Darrow managed to get Bryan, representing Christianity, to be cross-examined concerning his faith, and it's interesting to read the transcript.

Darrow:	The morning and the evening were the first day," and "The morning and the evening were the second day," mean anything to you?
Bryan:	I do not think it necessarily means a 24-hour day.
Darrow:	You do not?
Bryan:	No.
Darrow:	Then when the Bible said, for instance, "And God called the firmament heaven. And the evening and morning were the second day," that does not necessarily mean twenty-four hours?
Bryan:	I do not think it necessarily does.
Darrow:	Do you think it does or does not?
Bryan:	I know a great many that think so.
Darrow:	What do you think?
Bryan:	I do not think it does.
Darrow:	You think those were not literal days?
Bryan:	I do not think they were 24-hour days.
Darrow:	Do you think those were literal days?
Bryan:	My impression is they were periods, but I would not attempt to argue against anybody who wanted to believe in literal days.
Darrow:	Have you any idea of the length of the periods?
Bryan:	No, I don't.
Darrow:	The creation might have been going on for a very long time.
Bryan:	It might have continued for millions of years.

Right then, the Christians lost the Scopes trial in the public mind. But didn't John Scopes get fined? Yes, even though it was overturned on a technicality. But I want you to think—that was 1925. Let's stand back and look at the big picture. Look at the culture. Is the culture today more pervaded by Christian influence or less than back in 1925? We would all agree it is much less Christian today. The Scopes trial was a turning point for Christendom in many ways. Christians lost the battle. Why? Because Clarence Darrow accomplished what he was seeking to do.

> Clarence wanted the world and the press to see that when it came down to the bottom line, Christians really didn't believe what the Bible clearly said.

OCTOBER 15
Romans 12:2

Biblical Authority and Genesis Part 5

Today, there is great debate about the Genesis account of early Earth history. Virtually any viewpoint is welcomed into the debating arena, except for the view that the Bible is plain in its language concerning the six literal days and, thus, a young earth. However, I also have to say that I dislike the term young-earth creationist. You see, when people use terms like young-earth creationist or old-earth creationist, they're setting up a straw man in a way. The priority is not whether you are a young-earth creationist. First and foremost, one needs to be a biblical creationist. For instance, the fact that I don't believe in billions of years is a consequence of biblical authority. It's not that I'm a young-earth creationist, and that's why I look at the Bible the way I do. It's because I look at the Bible the way I do that I cannot believe in billions of years, and, thus, I am a young-earth creationist.

Progressive creationist Hugh Ross, founder of Reasons to Believe, says that those he labels "young-earth creationists" are putting a stumbling block in people's way because they are telling people the world is not billions of years old when Ross says it is. Thus, Ross claims that if you let people believe in billions of years, it helps lead them to Christ because it helps them to accept the Bible. But the opposite is true. For instance, the late Dr. Carl Sagan said this: "If God is omnipotent or omniscient, why didn't he start the universe out in the first place so it would come out the way that he wants? Why is he constantly repairing and complaining? There is one thing the Bible makes clear, the biblical God is a sloppy manufacturer; he's not good at design, he's not good at execution, he'd be out of business if there was any competition."[100]

Notice what Sagan was saying: Look at this world out there, all the mistakes, all the mutations, and the death and suffering and disease. Where's a God of love? Where is your powerful God? I don't see a powerful God.

Now think about this question: Is this the world as God made it? No. There is some beautiful design in our present world, but that misses the point. Kids are given a false idea in our churches—ah, look at the beautiful world God made. Beautiful world God made? Go to Australia. It's a beautiful country with the world's most poisonous sea snake, most poisonous snake, most poisonous jellyfish, most poisonous octopus, most poisonous stonefish, and man-eating crocodiles.

Irven Devore from Harvard University said this: "I personally cannot discern a shred of evidence for a benign, cosmic presence. I look at evolution; I see indifference and capriciousness. What kind of God works with a 99.9 percent extinction rate?" Irven Devore is looking at a fallen world. We know it was once perfect, but that is true only if you believe the history in Genesis. The world now is a broken one. But when a person believes that the world is billions of years old and that the fossil record is millions of years old, then such a person is really saying that the death and disease in this present world have been here for millions of years. Thus, God is to blame for all the death and suffering and disease. But the Bible doesn't blame God. Sinful humans are to blame. Death and disease are the result of our sin. Now, think about this. Here is where the rubber meets the road. If Adam's in your history, then God made you, God owns you, and God sets the rules. But if that history can be reinterpreted on the basis of man's ideas, then man is the authority. Who then sets the rules? You do. Why not reinterpret the Bible's morality? Why not reinterpret the Bible's salvation? If the Bible's history is true, then the morality and salvation based on the Bible are true. However, if the geology, biology, and astronomy in the Bible can't be trusted, then why should one trust any of the Bible?

APOLOGETICS

The Christian who believes in millions of years reinterprets the geology in the Bible—then why shouldn't the rest of the Bible be reinterpreted on the basis of man's fallible ideas? Why not reinterpret marriage to allow for homosexual "marriage," for instance? However, when a Christian accepts that the Bible's history is true, then marriage is one man for one woman. One's worldview is built on the Bible because the Bible's history is true. And when Adam is in your history, salvation is found in the "last Adam." There is a spiritual battle in this world, and it's about time Christians are willing to stand up for what we believe, be bold, and deal with these issues. The biblical creation apologetics movement is part of a movement in which God has started to get people back to the foundation of His Word, beginning with Genesis.

In summary: The humanists are clever—how to try to get rid of Christianity? They know not to aim directly at the Resurrection or the virgin birth. They know to aim at the Bible's history of the world. Once the history's gone, the rest goes. And how have they done this? By convincing the Church to believe in millions of years and thus to reinterpret God's Word in Genesis. This unlocks the door to doubt in the authority of the Word, and this doubt spreads like cancer through the culture and through subsequent generations.

Harvard, Yale, Princeton—how many of them were once Christian? All of them. How many of them are Christian today? None of them. Why? When you look into their history, they started to reject the truth in Genesis. They unlocked the door to further doubt in the Word of God. Subsequent generations pushed that door of doubt open to lead to the unbelief that we see today.

I have a challenge for you and a plea to ensure that the Church stands on the Word of God from the very first verse. If we don't, the battle is lost. We might win little battles here and there, and we might see some successes with children. However, I wonder if, in 100 years, we would realize how even more devastating it had been for the Church to have allowed that door of compromise to stay open by accepting millions of years—just as we look back at the devastation wrought by the Scopes trial nearly 100 years ago. Would we realize that we had an opportunity to restore the foundations of biblical authority, but we lost it? While Christians take potshots at the "issues," the authority of Scripture is unraveling in people's minds. What do I mean?

We've spent millions of dollars fighting abortion. Guess what? It hasn't gone away. Why? Abortion is not so much the problem in itself; it's a horrific symptom of the problem. The real problem is the rejection of scriptural authority. This culture was once pervaded by a Christian influence, including prayer and Bible reading in the schools. But we have new generations coming through an education system devoid of the knowledge of God. The Bible's history is ridiculed. Increasingly, people don't understand the Christian message. Neither do they accept the morality of the Bible. They have been brainwashed to believe that the Bible's history is wrong—so its morality and salvation are suspect also.

The solution is we need to get out there and preach the authority of the Word of God without compromise. We need to show clearly that the Bible's history can be trusted. We need to give answers to the world's attacks on the Bible's history. The Church needs to tell the world that the millions-of-years belief is not true. The world needs to see Christians believing the Bible—not compromising with man's fallible words.

> "Do not be conformed to this world, but be transformed by the renewal of your mind, that by testing you may discern what is the will of God, what is good and acceptable and perfect" (Romans 12:2).

OCTOBER 16
Isaiah 55:9

The Foundations

A number of years ago, as a part of AiG's mission to reach churches around the world with the message of biblical authority, we stepped out in faith to equip Christian leaders and churches in Russian-speaking countries that desperately need apologetics training. We partnered with a missionary group, the Slavic Gospel Association (SGA), to translate and produce my Foundations DVD curriculum in Russian. We received some thrilling testimonies from Christian leaders who have been using these DVDs and the curriculum with great effectiveness. They came from Russia, Ukraine, Kazakhstan, and other countries of the former Soviet Union. I think this testimony from a Christian leader in Belarus really sums it all up and should challenge each of us:

"Ken Ham talks about problems in Western churches. And though he speaks about churches in the USA, his thoughts seem to me very urgent for our churches as well. Firstly, atheistic thinking spreads out all over the world very quickly. And nowadays, many of Europe's problems come to us, such as relativism, indifference to faith, biblical illiteracy, and the domination of evolution theory. Secondly, his lectures help me to understand what kind of problems are going to come to us in a few years—especially if we are talking about the neglect of biblical authority. Thirdly, thanks to his material, I see what I have to do in order to avoid threats. Ken shows where we are going, and what we can do to keep the church strong and faithful. We have to trust implicitly the Bible, to pay attention to his Word and the authority of the Bible. I thank you for the serious, qualitative, well-reasoned, steadfastness of faith of these Bible lectures."

After reading these comments, it really hit me. If the churches in these countries really become informed on the vital issue of biblical authority beginning with Genesis (so that they will have the right foundation for thinking), what a difference that could make for them. To understand this overseas situation further, I want you to read excerpts from a letter from the vice president of the SGA. I believe you will find this letter to provide some fascinating background, and it will remind you of how important the creation apologetics ministry is in helping the Church in Russia and other countries of the former Soviet Union.

Eric Mock, VP of SGA, wrote: "It is with great joy that I write to you regarding the Russian-language version of the Answers in Genesis Foundations DVD series.

"Russia and the countries of the former Soviet Union are in flux, and it is no different for their churches. Liberal Western thinking and similar European ideology have collided with generations of Christian believers who have stood for their faith for many years under the years of communism. During those years, our Lord, by his grace and will, protected the believers from much of the European liberal influence. They fought daily for each page of God's Word as if it was gold. They had no reason to believe that Genesis should be read in any fashion other than literally and they believed that God created the world in six literal days. At the same time, because evolution was taught in the schools, and they saw this teaching as false, they tended to push scientific practice away. Now, with the internet, smartphones, and the assault on the authority and sufficiency of God's Word, young Russian-speaking generations are growing up in a world where there is a need to equip them with the ability to view science and the world around them through a biblical lens. The Foundations DVD series provides the initial tools and has been graciously placed in their hands. By the way, the freedoms

APOLOGETICS

they have gained in the former Soviet Union are now the very freedoms we are on the verge of losing here in the West—and that's largely because of a massive attack on the authority of God's Word!"

Eric continued: "…SGA was able to translate, edit, layout, and produce 3,000 Russian-language copies of the Foundations DVD series. In addition, the leader's guide and student workbook were translated and posted on SGAMedia.org for electronic access. SGA works with indigenous Bible-teaching churches throughout the former Soviet Union, and seeks to equip these local churches as they reach their people with the life-saving gospel of Jesus Christ. An initial massive distribution occurred during several conferences, where pastors and leaders from Russia and nine additional countries were provided with DVDs to carry back to their countries for duplication and distribution. Plans have been made to copy and distribute around 1,000 copies to youth at a conference in the summer. Youth leaders in Russia are also making their own copies, and striving to put them in the hands of other youth leaders, who are ministering to more than 20,000 Russian-speaking youth. Distribution is ongoing as churches make more copies. In addition to distributions in Russia and Ukraine, we are very excited to tell you of the distribution of the Russian-language series within the limited and closed-access countries we serve. The Foundations DVD series has now made its way into the hands of believers in local churches in Belarus, Kazakhstan, Tajikistan, Turkmenistan, Uzbekistan, Kyrgyzstan, Azerbaijan, Armenia, Georgia, Albania, and now even in Israel. Believers in these countries are often stopped at the border if caught carrying Bibles, and they have limited resources. To now be encouraged and refreshed by the sound Bible teaching contained in the Foundations DVD series is a true blessing from God."

Who would have ever thought that God would use such a series in such a wonderful way? But we had no idea the Lord would take this video series and use it to impact churches in needy countries.

SGA also has been using this video series in Israel! Eric wrote: "Recently, SGA has begun serving the small and developing Russian-speaking churches in Israel. This is slow and difficult, but we are pleased to be serving them as they reach out to the Jewish community. With the fall of communism, a wave of Russian-speaking Jews returned to Israel, and among them, believers who began planting churches. Advancing the gospel in Israel is quite difficult. Upon receiving the Foundations DVD series, they were so excited that they requested us to provide them with a version in Hebrew as well! Imagine this: equipping Russian-speaking Jewish believers, who through various trials and tragic persecutions, have been placed in Israel for such a time as this to reach the nation. The potential impact of a Hebrew-language version of the Foundations DVDs for the sake of the gospel and for the Kingdom is great, and it is in our prayers. Additionally, it is our desire that this is only the beginning of providing Russian-language resources from Answers in Genesis to the Russian- and Hebrew-speaking peoples."

I'm reminded of a scripture (one I'm sure you are familiar with): *For as the heavens are higher than the earth, so are my ways higher than your ways and my thoughts than your thoughts* (Isaiah 55:9). There is no doubt: the Lord uses the biblical creation apologetics ministry in many ways to reach people, and it's not just in the West. The creation/gospel message is being heard in other parts of the world! It's a message for all people.

> **I trust this challenges you to ensure you are taking a bold stand on a literal Genesis and you are getting equipped to use creation apologetics teaching to impact the Church as well as the world.**

OCTOBER 17

1 Corinthians 14:8

Compromise Is Compromise

I find that many people in the Church reject the idea that man evolved from apelike creatures but don't necessarily reject the belief in millions of years. So many reject that the days of creation were six literal days; they claim they could represent millions of years or that we can't know what the days mean. But why do so many reject six literal days? The main reason is because they have been indoctrinated in the belief of millions of years and take this idea to Scripture to try to fit it in somewhere in the first chapter of Genesis. But this is a compromise. It compromises God's Word with man's fallible word (beliefs), thus undermining the authority of the Bible.

I'm sure that when many Christian leaders see the title of my book, *Six Days—The Age of the Earth and the Decline of the Church*, they shake their heads in disapproval. But I feel very strongly about the historicity of the teaching of God's Word on the six days of creation.

This book tackles a major problem that has plagued the Church from the 1800s to our modern era: compromise with the Book of Genesis and the six days of creation.

The Genesis compromise has been highly destructive to the Church regarding biblical authority. It has greatly contributed to the decline of the Church in America, including the exodus of so many young people from the Church.

I contend that many of our shepherds (our Christian leaders) have led their sheep (God's people) astray by allowing compromise with Genesis that undermines biblical authority. The compromise reveals that so many Christian scholars are exalting man's fallible word (e.g., secular "science"—historical science and beliefs, not observational science) above God's infallible Word.

Here is an excerpt from chapter two of my book *Six Days—The Age of the Earth and the Decline of the Church*:

And if the bugle gives an indistinct sound, who will get ready for battle? (1 Corinthians 14:8).

"Readers, many in the church are making an uncertain sound concerning Genesis 1–11, which could very well lead to an uncertain sound about Scripture as a whole. If believers are willing to deny God's clear Word in Genesis, why should they believe God's Word concerning the miracle of the Resurrection or the virgin birth?

"The mixture of millions of years and evolution with Scripture stems from secular ideas and philosophies. If we were to ask an evolutionist what he believes about the origin of the universe, he would likely tell us that there was a big bang 14 billion years ago, that 4.5 billion years ago, there was a hot molten blob that formed into the earth, and that the solar system then formed. He would tell you that billions of years ago, life formed in the oceans and then as life came out on land, one kind of animal changed into another, resulting in the many species we see today.

"He might even show you an evolutionary tree and tell you that ape-like creatures eventually became human, that writing was invented in the course of human evolution, and that man learned to grunt before he learned to speak.

"All of this is considered dogmatic, evolutionary fact—and that is how an evolutionist would treat it in his explanation. And think about it: the public school science texts and most of the teachers, the university textbooks and professors, many secular television programs, and evolutionary scientists all give the same basic message concerning origins. They are unified. They give their 'certain sound.'

"But if we were to ask the average Christian leader or pastor, or the average Christian academic or Christian college professor in America, or even just the average Christian what they believe when it comes to the origin of the universe, they are not unified—they do not give a 'certain sound.' Church leaders, church academics, and the average churchgoing person will give a variety of positions on Genesis—theistic evolution, progressive creation, gap theory, day-age theory, cosmic temple view, and many others.

"Some will say they do not believe in a literal Adam or Eve or a literal fall, or that Noah's flood was just local, and so on. Others will give all sorts of combinations of ideas. And the reason there are so many different views is because these people are trying to fit man's ideas about origins into the Bible. And every one of these compromise positions tries in some way to fit in the supposed millions of years.

"The reason there can be so many different views of Genesis to fit in the supposed millions of years is because none of them work! The only view that makes sense is what Genesis clearly states.

"There is an uncertain sound that permeates through much of the church. It is the secularists who are saying, 'We know what we believe.' The Christians are saying, 'Well, we don't know, but we'll accept what you believe and try to fit it in the Bible somehow.' That is what is happening, and we wonder why we have a problem.

"When you think about it, the secularists, by and large, are unified around man's beliefs about origins. The Christians want unity around man's beliefs, which is why they are not unified on what God's Word says. We need to be unified on God's Word and take it in its natural sense as it is meant to be taken, and then judge man's fallible ideas accordingly."

Ponder this verse: *And if the bugle gives an indistinct sound, who will get ready for battle?* (1 Corinthians 14:8).

> Does your church, with its leaders and curricula, give a certain or uncertain sound when it comes to God's Word in Genesis?

OCTOBER 18

Genesis 50:20

Taking Back Dinosaurs

When we first opened the Creation Museum, atheists expressed dismay that we had professional dinosaur models and authentic dinosaur fossil bones and were using them to teach adults and children the truth of God's Word in Genesis. One year, we had a special promotion using the phrase "Taking Back the Dinosaurs" as our theme. Some atheists seemed to go ballistic over this. It came across to me that, in a way, atheists considered dinosaurs their own. They almost saw them as some sacred item to be used in brainwashing people in the evolution religion.

So, at the time, I posted a blog item, "Do atheists own dinosaurs?" I commented on the widespread response to AiG's billboard campaign across America that promoted our Creation Museum.

I began my blog with, "It really has been amazing to see the atheists' blogs and Twitter posts going crazy about AiG's billboard campaign." Soon after, *the New York Times* covered our boards.

The secularists were really upset that the Creation Museum used dinosaurs to share our Christian faith. They acted as if creationists have no right to use dinosaurs—that these creatures only belong to the secularists. Why do these atheists get so upset and emotional?

Well, because they are aware that children love dinosaurs, and so atheists get incensed when we use dinosaurs to get young people to visit the Creation Museum and its several dinosaur exhibits. They can't stand that we deliberately use dinosaurs in our advertising!

For their part, atheists use dinosaurs to try to convince children there is no God—and that evolution and millions of years are fact. At the Creation Museum, we use dinosaurs in the opposite way: to tell adults and children the true history of the world from the Bible concerning the creation, the Fall, and the Flood, including the gospel message.

One reporter called and told me, "An educator I spoke to said you are intentionally using dinosaurs as bait to get kids to the museum. Do you admit it?"

My reply, though I did not care for the word "bait," was, "Of course we are! We're not just trying only to attract children, but dads and moms too. We wouldn't have gone to the effort of building a museum if we didn't want everyone to visit!"

The reporter then said, "Well, the educator I spoke to said what you are doing is false advertising. He says you use dinosaurs to get people in, and then you give them a religious message."

By the way, when secularists use the word "religious," they usually mean the Christian religion. What they won't recognize is that not believing in God is a religion itself—the religion of atheism. Secularists are very religious people. Evolution and millions of years are part of their religion—a religion based on naturalism. These atheists want to indoctrinate children in their religion of naturalism, which is why they so hate Christianity.

I responded to the reporter by observing that the word "creation" appears prominently on the billboards. It should give a very strong hint about the museum and its teachings, and that it is not pro-evolution.

Furthermore, the Creation Museum's website was prominently displayed on the billboards. We certainly don't hide who we are or what we believe. When people visit our site, the first paragraph makes it very clear that we present dinosaurs in a biblical context. We are very overt about what we believe and teach.

For years, evolutionists have been indoctrinating millions of young people and adults in evolution and against the Bible's account of creation. They don't care for it at all when we take what they consider are "their" dinosaurs to teach people the truth about them—from the Bible—and then share the gospel.

I had to smile when I read one atheist's comments about my blog, "Do atheists own dinosaurs?" This atheist wrote the following:

"Maybe the 'secularists' don't own the dinosaurs, but it was them [sic] who did all the discovery, data analysis, and interpretation that Ham is now parasitizing for his own gain." So, he really did think they owned them!

Are the billboards working? Here is an account that one of our staff members shared with me at the time:

"I talked to a couple from Texas in the museum. They had never heard of the Creation Museum until they happened to see a dinosaur billboard in Kingwood, Texas, in June."

The staff member continued.

"They were amused that the board said the Creation Museum was "only" 1,035 miles away! They already had plans for a trip to our region and decided to make a visit to the museum. Also, on the same day, a gentleman told me about seeing a billboard in Cleveland, about five hours away, and came here as a result."

Yes, that dinosaur billboard campaign certainly worked. Praise the Lord! Many more people now know about the Creation Museum. What's more, as the atheists became more vocal about these outstanding billboards, their public opposition helped fuel news reports across the nation, and more people began visiting the museum!

I've seen it over and over again with the atheist opposition to AiG and the highly evangelistic museum.

> "As for you, you meant evil against me, but God meant it for good, to bring it about that many people should be kept alive, as they are today" (Genesis 50:20).

OCTOBER 19
1 Samuel 16:7

Shades of Brown

Are there really "black" and "white" twins? Well, that's what people call them. Actually, they are very dark brown and light brown twins, as all humans have the same basic skin color—brown—but different shades. However, such twins are a vivid reminder that we are all members of one race.

The tragic legacy of Darwin's controversial speculations on evolution has led to terrible consequences taken to the deadliest extremes. The book I co-authored, *One Race One Blood*, reveals the origins of these horrors and the truth revealed in Scripture that God created only one race.

I was taking questions on a live Christian radio talk show and had just answered one about the origin of the supposed human races. I listened as the host patched in the next caller, who blurted out, "I'll believe we are all one race when you can show me two black people having a white baby and two white people having a black baby." I answered by first saying two poodles can't produce a wolf! I had to explain that poodles are called "pure-bred" dogs and don't have all the genetic diversity of dogs like wolves. I also said, "I can show you pictures of what are called 'black-and-white twins'—one twin is very dark and the other very light." (You can't show pictures on radio, unfortunately, so all I could do was to describe the picture to the caller.) "There is no way those two babies had the same father," the caller responded. "That is impossible. White people and black people do not belong to the same race."

Such prejudice, as betrayed by this caller, still exists in certain Christian circles in America and around the world, to my amazement (and disgust). But it is not just the Christian world where people find "black" and "white" twins incredible—it is also shocking to the secular world. They are surprised because they ignore the Bible's account that we all came from one race (begun by the first man and woman, Adam and Eve) and dispersed due to the Tower of Babel, which led to the formation of different people groups. They assume, instead, that human groups are deeply divided by significant variations over tens or hundreds of thousands of years and that different people groups originated from different "ancestral apes."

But are there really "black-and-white twins"? Over the last several decades, many examples of fraternal twins, where one is very dark (called "black") and one very light (called "white"), have been documented. Fraternal twins usually occur when two different eggs are fertilized by two different sperm cells and implanted in the mother's womb at the same time. Documented examples of fraternal twins being "black" and "white" include:

- The Hodgson-Horder twin girls (Born in April 2005 in England)
- The Biggs twin girls (Born in July 2006 in Australia)
- The Richardson twin boys (Born in July 2006 in England)
- The Grant twin girls (Born in 1983 in England)
- The Singerl twin girls (Born in May 2006 in Australia)

In reading over the various news reports on the above sets of twins, I noticed that one reporter called such occurrences "freak," and others quoted scientists saying that the chance of "black" and "white" twins was a million to one.

THEOLOGY

Some of the parents of these sets of twins have shared that people stopped and stared when they saw the "black" and "white" children. Some pointed, and others commented that they couldn't be from the same parents. Some even made racially prejudiced statements about one of the dark-skinned twins. Some believed the parents were lying about the twins having the same father.

But, in reality, such sets of twins are quite easy to explain and should not invoke such responses. So how can such "black" and "white" twins—though quite rare—be explained?

According to the Bible's history, all humans are descendants of Adam and Eve—thus, only one biological race exists. All humans in the world today are classified as Homo sapiens (same genus, species, and subspecies). When the Human Genome Project published a draft of its findings in 2000, *the New York Times* reported that "the researchers had unanimously declared there is only one race—the human race."

To form different people groups with distinguishing characteristics, the human population would need to be split up and isolated from each other. The Tower of Babel, as recorded in Genesis 11, provides the historical basis for the formation of such people groups. The human genome contains so much information that zillions of combinations are possible.

Yet all humans basically have the same skin color—a brown pigment called melanin. Although there are a couple of forms of melanin and other pigments and factors playing minor roles in skin color, every human basically has a brown color.

Lots of brown is called black, and a little brown color is called white. In actuality, no human really is "black," or "white." There are no different colors but different shades of one basic color: brown. While numerous genes and many factors are involved in determining skin color, and the steps are very technical, basic high school genetics can help us understand the most important principles.

Assume dominant genes result in lots of melanin and recessive genes result in little melanin. Adam and Eve were most likely a middle-brown color with both dominant and recessive genes for the pigment melanin in the skin. Children who received all the dominant genes would end up with a lot of color and be very dark. Children who received all the recessive genes would end up with only a little color and be very light. Children with a mixture of the genes would be middle brown.

Of course, many combinations are possible. But provided that the parents have mixtures of the dominant and recessive genes between them, children could exhibit a large range of skin shades. With fraternal twins, one twin could inherit genes for lots of melanin while the other could inherit genes for little melanin. So it's not just "black" and "white."

Bottom line: a person's skin shade (what is on the outside) should in no way invoke any sort of prejudiced or racist comments. What a difference we would see in our world if people reacted according to biblical principles, understanding that all humans are equal before God and all are sinners in need of salvation.

God reminded Samuel of this when he said, *For the Lord sees not as man sees: man looks on the outward appearance, but the Lord looks on the heart* (1 Samuel 16:7).

> **All of us need to build our thinking on the absolute authority of the Word of God, judging all beliefs and attitudes against the clear teaching of what our Creator God teaches us.**

OCTOBER 20

Proverbs 30:6

Men-Pleasing Shepherds

What is the motivation of theologians that compromise Genesis with the belief in millions of years? Sadly, my experience has shown that many theologically conservative theologians have adopted two different hermeneutical principles for interpreting Scripture. This inconsistency causes problems.

Now, I do have great respect for many such theologians. Take the late Dr. Norman Geisler. He was a prolific author who, for many years, contended for the faith and equipped Christians with some excellent apologetic arguments to defend the Christian faith against many secular attacks. At the same time, I assert that he and many others in Christian leadership (contrary to their sincerely good intentions) have unwittingly undermined the reliability and authority of the Scriptures they have loved and worked so hard to uphold.

Can such a serious allegation be substantiated? After my evolution/creation debate with Bill Nye "the Science Guy," on February 4, 2014, at the Creation Museum, there was a plethora of articles and blogs on the origins issue in secular and Christian media. On February 12, Dr. Geisler wrote an opinion piece for the online *Christian Post* titled, "Does Believing in Inerrancy Require One to Believe in Young Earth Creationism?"

In this commentary, Dr. Geisler attempted to use various arguments to discredit those who insist that God's Word clearly teaches a creation week of six, approximately 24-hour days (followed by a day of rest), and a relatively young age for the universe (approximately 6,000 years). Even though Dr. Geisler briefly discussed the meaning of the Hebrew word for day (yôm) and biblical genealogies (e.g., in Genesis 5), I suggest that his column article was really an attempt to justify a particular motivation he held as many other conservative theologians also hold.

For instance, Dr. Geisler in his *Systematic Theology* states:

"In addition to the biblical evidence for long periods of time, there are scientific arguments that the world has existed for billions of years. The age of the universe is based on

"(1) the speed of light and the distance of the stars;

"(2) the rate of expansion of the universe;

"(3) the fact that early rocks have been radioactively dated in terms of billions of years;

"(4) the rate that salt runs into the sea and the amount of salt there, which indicates multimillions of years.

"While all of these arguments have certain unprovable presuppositions, nonetheless, they may be true and, hence, point to a universe that is billions rather than thousands of years in age."[101]

In some of his other writings, Dr. Geisler made similar statements regarding a billions-of-years-old universe. Keep in mind that the belief in billions of years actually came out of naturalism, as fallible humans using autonomous human reasoning attempted to explain the origin of the earth and universe. When I study the writings of numerous contemporary Christian scholars, I find they propose a variety of ways to interpret Genesis. But they all have the same motivation. Somewhere in their writings, they admit to believing in or allowing for the supposed billions of years for the age of the universe.

APOLOGETICS

Now, when I read Dr. Geisler's writings where he dealt with the New Testament, I discovered that he never started with beliefs from secular scientists and took them to the Bible to interpret, say, the account of Jesus' Resurrection or virgin birth. He accepted those Scriptures as written. But when he looked at the account of origins in Genesis, Dr. Geisler did not take it as written but allowed ideas outside of God's Word to be reconciled to Scripture. As a consequence, he reinterpreted the plain meaning of God's written revelation.

I strongly and respectfully suggest that Dr. Geisler, along with many other Christian scholars, had one hermeneutical principle for Genesis chapters 1–11 (eisegesis) and a different one for the rest of Scripture (exegesis). Because of this approach, Dr. Geisler misrepresented biblical creationists who believe in a young earth/universe. For example, here is what he stated in his *Christian Post* commentary:

"For some, the belief in a young earth seems to be based on a kind of intuition or faith in what they believe an omnipotent God should do. It reasons that if God is all-powerful, then certainly he would not have taken millions of years to make the earth. However, by reduction ad absurdum, one could ask why God did not create it in six minutes or six seconds rather than six days? If he is all-powerful and can make something from nothing, then why did he not create the whole thing lock-stock-and-barrel instantaneously! Furthermore, it is not a question of what God could or should do; it is a question of what God actually did do. And it is presumptuous for a mortal to divine what God should have done."

At Answers in Genesis, we have always stated that it's a question of what God said He did! The priority is taking the Word of God naturally. There are many biblical and contextual reasons for concluding (as almost the whole Church did for 1,800 years) that Genesis 1–11 is straightforward literal history. Answers in Genesis has published numerous articles on the meaning of the Hebrew word for day in Genesis, the supposed gaps in the genealogies, and the problems with trying to determine the age of the earth using the various "scientific" methods. Perhaps one of the most thorough analyses we have of the Hebrew word for day comes from chapter 5 of my book *Six Days*.

It is true that many of the Church fathers and the early creeds did not deal with the age of the earth/universe. But that is because almost all of them were young-earth creationists, such as Augustine. He held to a global Flood, the great lifespans of the pre-Flood patriarchs, and that Adam lived less than 6,000 years before Augustine. He was only confused about the days in Genesis 1 (thinking creation was in an instant, not over millions of years) because of his faulty Latin Bible and his ignorance of Greek and Hebrew.

In addition, the famous reformer John Calvin believed that the world had not yet "completed its six thousandth year" (Calvin 2009, p. 90). Luther and Wesley also held to the young-earth view. In fact, this was the overwhelmingly dominant view in the Church till the early 1800s, when the idea of millions of years was developed in geology and so much of the Church accepted it. .

I assert that many great men of God in today's world are contributing to a generational loss of biblical authority because of their insistence on accommodating man's belief in billions of years with the infallible Word of God. Such a loss of biblical authority is contributing enormously to a massive exodus of young people from the Church and an increasing decline of Christian influence on the culture. Of course, for all Christians, compromising God's Word is a very serious matter.

"Do not add to his words" (Proverbs 30:6).

OCTOBER 21

Romans 8:22

Progressive Creation Compromise

There are many different, what I call "compromise positions" on Genesis, but they all have one thing in common: trying to fit the supposed millions/billions of years into Scripture. Let's look at one of these positions that has been fairly prevalent: progressive creation.

This position (popularized by Dr. Hugh Ross) allowed Christians to use the term "creationist" but still gave them supposed academic respectability in the eyes of the world by rejecting six literal days of creation and maintaining billions of years. In summary, progressive creation teaches:

- The big bang origin of the universe occurred about 13–15 billion years ago.
- The days of creation were overlapping periods of millions and billions of years.
- Over millions of years, God created new species as others kept going extinct.
- The record of nature (as interpreted by man) is just as reliable as the Word of God.
- Death, bloodshed, and disease existed before Adam and Eve.
- Man-like creatures that looked and behaved much like us existed before Adam and Eve but did not have a spirit that was made in the image of God, and thus had no hope of salvation.
- *The Genesis Flood* was a local event.
- The big bang origin of the universe.

Progressive creationists claim that the days of creation in Genesis 1 represent long periods of time and that day three of creation week lasted more than three billion years! This assertion is made in order to allow for the billions of years that evolutionists claim are represented in the rock layers of Earth. This position, however, has problems, both biblically and scientifically. The text of Genesis 1 clearly states that God supernaturally created all that is in six actual days. If we are prepared to let the words of the text speak to us in accordance with the context and their normal definitions without influence from outside ideas, then the word for "day" in Genesis 1 obviously means an ordinary day of about 24 hours. It is qualified by a number, the phrase "evening and morning," and for day one, the words "light and darkness."

As their name indicates, progressive creationists believe that God progressively created species on Earth over billions of years, with new species replacing extinct ones, starting with simple organisms and culminating in the creation of Adam and Eve. They accept the evolutionary order for the development of life on Earth, even though this contradicts the order given in the Genesis account of creation. Evolutionary belief holds that the first life forms were marine organisms, while the Bible says that God created land plants first. Reptiles are supposed to have predated birds, while Genesis says that birds came first. Evolutionists believe that land mammals came before whales, while the Bible teaches that God created whales first. Progressive creationists have stated that nature is "just as perfect" as the Bible and call nature the "sixty-seventh book" of the Bible.

Now, God tells us in Romans 8:22, *For we know that the whole creation has been groaning together in the pains of childbirth until now* because of sin. And not only was the universe cursed, but man himself has been affected by the Fall. So how can sinful, fallible human beings in a sin-cursed universe say that their interpretation of the evidence (nature) is as perfect as God's written revelation? Scientific assertions must use fallible

APOLOGETICS — OCTOBER 21

assumptions and fallen reasoning—how can this be the Word of God? It can't. Christians should build their thinking on the Bible, not on fallible interpretations of scientific observations about the past.

Progressive creationists believe the fossil record was formed from the millions of animals that lived and died before Adam and Eve were created. They accept the idea that there was death, bloodshed, and disease (including cancer) before sin, which goes directly against the teaching of the Bible and dishonors the character of God. But God created a perfect world at the beginning. When He was finished, God stated that His creation was "very good." The Bible makes it clear that man and all the animals were vegetarians before the Fall (Genesis 1:29–30). Plants were given to them for food (plants do not have a *nephesh* [life spirit] as man and animals do and thus eating them would not constitute "death" in the biblical sense). Concerning the entrance of sin into the world, progressive creationist Dr. Ross writes, "The groaning of creation in anticipation of release from sin has lasted fifteen billion years and affected a hundred billion trillion stars." However, the Bible teaches something quite different. In the context of human death, the Apostle Paul states, *[J]ust as sin came into the world through one man, and death through sin* (Romans 5:12). It is clear that there was no sin in the world before Adam sinned, and thus no death. Since evolutionary radiometric dating methods have dated certain humanlike fossils as older than Ross' date for modern humans (approx. 40,000 years), he and other progressive creationists insist that these are fossils of pre-Adamic creatures that had no spirit, and thus no salvation.

Progressive creationists accept and defend evolutionary dating methods, so they must redefine all evidence of humans (descendants of Noah) if they are given evolutionary dates of more than about 40,000 years (e.g., the Neanderthal cave sites) as related to spiritless "hominids," which the Bible does not mention. However, these same methods have been used to "date" the Australian Aborigines back at least 60,000 years (some have claimed much older) and fossils of "anatomically modern humans" to over 100,000 years. By Ross' reasoning, none of these (including the Australian Aborigines) could be descendants of Adam and Eve and so wouldn't have souls. However, Acts 17:26 says, *And he made from one man every nation of mankind to live on all the face of the earth, having determined allotted periods and the boundaries of their dwelling place.* All people who have lived on Earth are descendants of Adam. Progressive creationists will say they believe in a "universal" or "worldwide" Flood, but in reality, they do not believe that the Flood covered the whole earth. They believe in a local flood. They argue that the text of Genesis 7 doesn't really say that the Flood covered the whole earth. But read it for yourself and you will find the language overwhelmingly speaks of a Flood covering the entire earth and everything on it.

Now, it is true that whether one believes in six literal days does not ultimately affect one's salvation. However, we need to stand back and look at the "big picture." In many nations, the Word of God was once widely respected and taken seriously. But once the door of compromise is unlocked and Christian leaders concede that we shouldn't take the Bible as written in Genesis, why should the world take heed of it in any area? Because the Church has told the world that one can use man's interpretation of the world (such as billions of years) to reinterpret the Bible, it is seen as an outdated, scientifically incorrect "holy book," not intended to be taken seriously.

> **Beware of compromise positions that attempt to fit man's evolutionary/millions of years beliefs into the Bible.**

OCTOBER 22

Psalm 127:1

Boldly Proclaiming the Work of God's Hands

Over the years, God led me to other people committed to the search for biblically and scientifically sound answers to questions that most of the world believed could only be answered by evolution.

How can we see light from stars supposedly millions of light years away if the earth isn't millions of years old? Is everything we see in the night sky a result of a "big bang" that spread out all the matter in the universe? Is there life—even intelligent life—somewhere else in the universe?

The first time I encountered blatant evolutionary thinking about cosmology (how to understand astronomy and our universe), I didn't have any answers. I was 13, and the books, videos, radio programs, attractions, and websites we have today explaining cosmology from a biblical perspective just didn't exist.

When I began to explore the problem, a local clergyman even told me I could believe in evolution and just reinterpret the Bible! Maybe you've heard that too. But if we "reinterpret the Bible," change God's Word of creation, we compromise the foundation of the gospel.

I thank God for my Bible-believing father, who told me, "Son, just because we don't know the answers doesn't mean there aren't any. We just have to search for them and ask the Lord to reveal them to us." He explained how reinterpreting God's Word to try to fit man's beliefs undermined the authority of Scripture.

I began to search. In my final year at university, I found a couple of books that gave me a scientific background to help me defend the Christian faith against ideas about evolution and an old earth! When I showed the books to my father, he was just as excited as I was.

Over the years, God led me to other people committed to the search for biblically and scientifically sound answers to questions that most of the world believed could only be answered by evolution or an earth that was millions of years old. What has become known as Answers in Genesis was born, and God provided geologists, biologists, paleontologists, theologians, anthropologists, and others of deep faith who could help provide answers. I was able to use those answers in my talks and books so thousands (now millions) of people have answers to the skeptics of this age who reject God's Word.

It's important to understand that God provided the people. He brought them together. As we say, this ministry is a "God thing." He was building the ministry, calling various people to be involved.

Now I often had to say, "I don't know," to questions about astronomy and cosmology. I wanted to have better answers if possible. But I know as we are finite, there are things we will never be able to answer.

The Bible tells us that *the heavens declare the glory of God, and the sky above proclaims his handiwork* (Psalm 19:1). I wanted to hear their declaration loud and clear, and I wanted everyone else to hear it too!

I kept searching, and I kept speaking in churches and public forums and on the radio, battling the secular "explanations" that write God out of the history of the universe.

Later, I met an astrophysicist devoted to showing the world how the very skies declare God's work of creation. Praise God!

APOLOGETICS

He joined our AiG staff, wrote insightful, God-filled books, and provided guidance for our curricular materials. Many answers were provided for various questions. When it came time to build a planetarium at the Creation Museum, naturally, we turned to him.

Like everything else in the Creation Museum, the Stargazer's Planetarium is designed for excellence, with a state-of-the-art laser projection system and programs that unfold the wonder of God's heavenly creations. Hundreds of thousands—I'll even say millions—of people will get to sit in the planetarium and learn Bible-based answers in a field that so many have struggled with!

If only I'd had something like the Stargazer's Planetarium when I was a boy and first encountering the big bang belief and other ways secular scientists have described the heavens! When we first opened the planetarium, I sat there with the stars wheeling overhead, and a prayer of joyful praise rose in my heart:

- I praised the Lord for a father who taught me to search for answers.
- I praised the Lord for my heavenly Father who has allowed us to have answers.
- I praised the Lord for raising up creation scientists to research answers for us.
- I praised the Lord for modern technology that now allows us to disseminate these answers to multitudes of people of all ages.

Just think—if my father hadn't encouraged me to seek answers in line with the Bible, if I'd accepted that compromising clergyman's advice to just "reinterpret the Bible," Answers in Genesis (and the Creation Museum and Ark Encounter) might not exist today!

But God has brought hundreds of faithful Christians together to build a ministry that now impacts tens of millions each year with the gospel. But ultimately, it's God who built this ministry. It's God's ministry. We are just faithful stewards here to look after it.

"Unless the Lord builds the house, those who build it labor in vain" (Psalm 127:1).

OCTOBER 23
Matthew 5:14-16

Inadvertent Witnesses

You are the light of the world. A city set on a hill cannot be hidden. Nor do people light a lamp and put it under a basket, but on a stand, and it gives light to all in the house. In the same way, let your light shine before others, so that they may see your good works and give glory to your Father who is in heaven (Matthew 5:14–16).

This may surprise you, but really, in many ways, reporting by the secular and Christian media (from around the world) has certainly greatly contributed to seeing the gospel "preached in all the world."

As a testimony to all nations (Matthew 24:14).

The remarkable international media buzz surrounding the opening of the Creation Museum in 2007 and then the Ark Encounter in 2016 reminds me of the verse above from Matthew 24. The Creation Museum and Ark Encounter have certainly been something of a "testimony to all nations."

Secular newspaper, television, radio, and magazine reporters arrived here (and still do) from all over the globe to report on these two unique attractions. I'm particularly pleased to report that articles have appeared in the secular media across a very pagan Europe and even in Chinese media.

Two things really stand out to me about the secular media reporting:

Every reporter who comes to the Creation Museum and Ark Encounter hears the authority of God's Word upheld, Christianity defended, and the gospel proclaimed. Many of us, in representing AiG and the attractions to the press, answer their questions and often walk through the Ark and museum with them.

In fact, I found that some reporters become so involved in the experience, they even begin asking me questions that they personally wanted answered for themselves.

Second, as the Creation Museum's and Ark Encounter's continued success is reported around the world, many of the stories include details of what is taught at the attractions and what Answers in Genesis believes about the Bible.

These reports often include details about a perfect world marred by sin with death as a consequence (Genesis 3), the Flood of Noah's day, the dispersion at the Tower of Babel, and the message of Jesus' death and Resurrection!

Yes, the secular press has been teaching the Bible and the gospel message to millions around the world! Even when they have a very anti-Christian agenda, the media is still reporting on these two God-honoring facilities.

Whether it is the European press or the Australian or American media, reporters generally report on what is taught at the attractions even if they are mocking it.

Here are just two statements from the American media:

The Chronicle of Higher Education: "AiG's museum will proclaim the authority and accuracy of the Bible from Genesis to Revelation, and will show that there is a Creator, and that this Creator is Jesus Christ (Colossians 1:15–20), who is our Savior."

RESOURCES   OCTOBER 23

The New York Times: "The heart of the museum is a series of catastrophes. The main one is the fall, with Adam and Eve eating of the tree of knowledge; after that tableau the viewer descends from the brightness of Eden into genuinely creepy cement hallways of urban slums. Photographs show the pain of war, childbirth, death—the wages of primal sin…Then come the biblical accounts of the fallen world, leading up to Noah's ark and the flood, the source of all significant geological phenomena."

When the media have asked me to sum up what the ultimate aim of the Creation Museum is, I say something like: "To uphold the authority of God's Word beginning in Genesis, to show people clearly that the Bible's history is true, and thus its message of the gospel—based in that history—is true."

Indeed, at its very heart, the attractions are evangelistic centers. So please bring your unsaved family and friends to these exciting places. And when you see news articles, even if mocking, about the Ark or Creation Museum, praise the Lord that the message is getting out even through those who vehemently oppose it.

> **Remember:** "As for you, you meant evil against me, but God meant it for good" (Genesis 50:20).

OCTOBER 24
Psalm 119:160

The Power of a Photograph

When the Creation Museum first opened in 2007, almost every one of the scores of reporters from secular newspapers, magazines, and TV outlets who visited the museum photographed two children.

In the main hall of AiG's Creation Museum, visitors see two animatronic children next to a pond and a gorgeous nearby waterfall. Both children look real. In fact, the young girl is heard giggling as she feeds a squirrel, and the boy to her right is seen stirring a stick in the waterfall's pond.

These two children became famous around the world! How? Scores of reporters from secular newspapers, magazines, and TV outlets who visited the museum photographed these two children. Their photo has appeared in newspapers (even on the front page a number of times) and magazines around the world, plus on several websites and blogs. Video clips of the children have also been seen by untold millions via the major news networks worldwide.

But why did these two animatronic children capture the attention of the world's news media? It's because of what's beside them: two animatronic baby T. rex dinosaurs!

The two dinosaurs with the two children became one of the most photographed parts of the Creation Museum.

So why do dinosaurs and children together capture the attention of the secular world? It's not because they are really high-tech (although the animatronics are impressive). It's because these two children and two dinosaurs make one of the clearest visual statements possible against the earth being millions of years old and Darwinian evolution being possible.

One of the first things visitors to the Creation Museum near Cincinnati, Ohio, see as they enter the main lobby will be children playing alongside dinosaurs. You see, dinosaurs have become an icon for millions of years and molecules-to-man evolution. According to the evolution belief system, dinosaurs died out over 60 million years before humans evolved. Evolutionist museums and dinosaur books state this as fact. Most evolutionists are so dogmatic about this, that there is no possibility that dinosaurs and people could ever have lived at the same time. As soon as secular reporters walk into the main hall of the Creation Museum and see the young T. rex dinosaurs and children together, they recognize immediately that we're making very strong statements:

The supposed millions of years for the age of fossils (and the earth and universe) are simply not true. And molecules-to-man evolution is not true either.

All over the world, most children and adults have heard about dinosaurs. They automatically associate "millions of years" when they hear or see the word dinosaur—and they would also think that dinosaurs and humans didn't live at the same time.

Another statement that the animatronic dinosaurs and children convey here at the Creation Museum is that the Bible's history in Genesis is clear and true: God created the land animals (including what we today call dinosaurs) as well as the first two people (Adam and Eve) on the sixth day of creation.

SCIENCE OCTOBER 24

Evolutionary scientists must have millions of years in order to convince people that life has evolved. As people understand that the evolutionary idea of millions of years is not logical—from Scripture or from observable science—then they easily see that molecules-to-man evolution is impossible.

In the flood geology room of the Creation Museum, you will find a number of exhibits that tell visitors about the problems with the geologic dating methods and that there is actually overwhelming evidence that confirms a young age for the earth and fossils (of thousands of years). We also have such exhibits on the third deck of the Ark Encounter attraction that was opened in 2016.

In the flood geology room, guests receive a lot of scientific information that confirms what is seen in the main hall: that dinosaurs did not die out millions of years before people appeared. The teaching in these exhibits was researched by PhD scientists who are dedicated Christians who hold to a literal Genesis.

What a buzz one photograph of two dinosaurs and two children created! Truly, this photo is worth a thousand words and says it all: "The Bible is true!"

> "The sum of your word is truth, and every one of your righteous rules endures forever" (Psalm 119:160).

OCTOBER 25
John 6:11-14

One Body Together for the Gospel … Sort of Like the … Borg?

It's sad to see how millions, really billions, have been assimilated into an evil, anti-God collective. I believe I first heard the word collective while watching a Star Trek television program about something called the "Borg." Now, some of you may be thinking: "But many of Star Trek's programs are evolution-based." I know, but then … they are fiction after all, as is evolution!

The "Borg" are cyborgs who assimilate beings into their "collective" and take away their individuality—essentially brainwashing them. In a way, I believe what's happening in our culture is very much like the Borg collective! Those in power don't want people to think for themselves and want to impose upon them one way of thinking which is the religion of naturalism (atheism) and resulting moral relativism.

Now, that's totally different from our Creation Museum and Ark Encounter (and the entire creation ministry in general around the world), where we will challenge people to think critically (including those visitors who may have been indoctrinated and "assimilated" into the world's "collective" by the ideas of the secular world).

Answers in Genesis has been able to build family-friendly attractions with outstanding exhibits—"world-class" displays, as some visitors have described them—using cutting-edge technology. I want to tell you about a very special "collective" (very different from that referred to above) that God used to build the Creation Museum and Ark Encounter.

I have personally escorted dozens of professional people from the secular business world through our attractions. They often make statements like: "I can't believe you were able to build such world-class attractions that boldly present the Bible and the message of Christianity."

There's no doubt these attractions are impressive places. God brought tremendously talented people together as a "collective" to make it all happen. In fact, one of America's leading anti-creationists who once visited stated that the museum is "worrisome" because it is so first-class. You see, she was greatly concerned that children would be convinced by what's presented in the museum because it's so well-done!

I love endorsements like that! And actually, that's the standard all Christian facilities should show the world.

But how could places like this be built for such low costs (compared to what it would cost in the secular world) using only private donations (no government funding or for-profit investments)? After all, Disneyland or Universal Studios will spend well over $100 million just on one ride alone. Well, it's because of the "collective." Thousands of volunteers and supporters came together to provide the resources for this to happen. But it was not just volunteers and supporters! Groups of skilled sculptors, fabricators, painters, and graphic artists—in fact, every department of the AiG ministry has been involved in one way or another in the building of the Creation Museum and Ark Encounter. Reminds me of how God brought all sorts of people together to build the temple in Solomon's day.

Yes, what a "collective" the Lord has brought together in Northern Kentucky to fulfill a burden and vision that goes back many years! All I can do is praise Him for this miracle He has performed at the museum and the Ark. Like the boy with his meager lunch given to Jesus, our donations and abilities have been given to the

Lord, and He has multiplied them ... and now through His hand, He will "feed" multitudes—millions upon millions for years to come.

And that's my challenge to us. There's a massive remnant of sincere Bible-believing Christians in the West. There are many ways we can come together to be a "collective" to make a powerful impact on millions of people. We can all offer the Lord our loaves and fishes and ask Him to do great things to impact hearts and minds with God's Word and the saving gospel.

One of his disciples, Andrew, Simon Peter's brother, said to him, "There is a boy here who has five barley loaves and two fish, but what are they for so many?" Jesus said, "Have the people sit down." Now there was much grass in the place. So the men sat down, about five thousand in number. Jesus then took the loaves, and when he had given thanks, he distributed them to those who were seated. So also the fish, as much as they wanted. And when they had eaten their fill, he told his disciples, "Gather up the leftover fragments, that nothing may be lost." So they gathered them up and filled twelve baskets with fragments from the five barley loaves left by those who had eaten. When the people saw the sign that he had done, they said, "This is indeed the Prophet who is to come into the world!" (John 6:8–14).

> **God can multiply loaves and fishes, and God can multiply resources, talents, and gifts He's entrusted to us for His glory if we together do all we can to honor the Son and boldly preach God's Word and the gospel.**

OCTOBER 26
2 Peter 3:3-6

The Battle for Truth and Science

In a most nonacademic way, contrary to all one would expect from scientists dedicated to careful research, leading American atheist Dr. Eugenie Scott (who was at the time director of the National Center for Science Education, a somewhat misnamed organization because its primary mission is to oppose creationists) was convincing other scientists to sign petitions against the Creation Museum when its opening was announced in 2007, even though those scientists had not toured the museum. These people oppose Christianity, so it doesn't matter what biblical creationists say, to them it's wrong. And they don't need to listen to what is being said to "know" it's wrong!

In a letter about the museum sent to scientists in universities across the United States, Dr. John Pearse, then president of the Society for Integrative and Comparative Biology, stated: "Museum of make-believe facts being opened in the Cincinnati area. She [Eugenie Scott] is directing it mainly to our members in the Kentucky-Ohio-Indiana area, but the Core Officers and I think it should go out to all of you. The new museum could be a fun thing to go to if it was taken as a sort of Disneyland of anti-intellectualism. However, it is a serious frontal attack on evidence-based reasoning, and as such is a real threat to educating an informed, modern citizenry."

Pearse urged academics in Answers in Genesis' tristate area of Ohio, Indiana, and Kentucky to sign a petition that Scott said "will be made available to the press at the time of the opening." Part of the petition stated: "We, the undersigned scientists at universities and colleges in Kentucky, Ohio, and Indiana, are concerned about scientifically inaccurate material on display at the Answers in Genesis Museum."

I find it ironic that these academics, who are supposedly trained to check the evidence for themselves and not rely on secondhand sources, were worried about our alleged "attack" on "evidence" and yet they had not examined our museum at the time. And I doubt many (if any) of them have since. If a student of these professors even dared to conduct their research in this haphazard manner, they might fail them. But because we are Christians and believe God's account in Genesis, whatever we say is wrong to them, and they don't need to check it out. Again, it shows the spiritual nature of the battle. But it got even worse. Scott tried to scare parents and college-bound students when she also stated: "Students who accept such material as scientifically valid are unlikely to succeed in science courses at the college level. These students will need remedial instruction in the nature of science, as well as in the specific areas of science misrepresented by Answers in Genesis."

This seeming threat was not just directed against parents of students visiting the Creation Museum, but it was a way for her to intimidate parents of Christian school and homeschool students (or parents of public-school students who might take their children to the Creation Museum and now Ark Encounter) who take a stand on accepting the record of Genesis in the Bible. But what was Scott's real motive? Well, she was picked as the 1998 winner of the American Humanist Association's "Isaac Asimov Science Award" (she is an atheist). The organization she directed until 2014, the NCSE, is dedicated to propagating evolutionary beliefs and opposing creationists—she dogmatically equated "science" with "evolution." She had also been on the boards of a number of anti-God secular humanist organizations. In the letter she sent to Pearse, Scott stated: "This museum is viewed with dismay by teachers and scientists because it will present as scientifically valid religious views such as special creation, a 10,000 year old Earth, Noah's Flood, and the like." She was not just against the Creation Museum—she was against "special creation" and "Noah's Flood." Of course, this means that she must also be against the words of the Bible and Jesus Christ, for it was by Him that *all things were created* (Colossians 1). And Jesus Himself quoted from Genesis concerning the actual event of Noah's Flood.

There are thousands of secular evolutionist-based museums all across America and around the world. Almost all public (secular) schools teach naturalistic (atheistic) evolution as fact, evolutionary TV programs abound on various TV networks around the world, yet Scott and her colleagues were worried about one Creation Museum. Why were they so concerned? As Dr. Scott stated in her letter to Pearse: "The AIG museum is a multi-million dollar structure with first-rate exhibits, skillfully-crafted animatronic figures (of humans and dinosaurs coexisting), and a state-of-the-art planetarium. Students who are taken to this museum are very likely to consider it authoritative, to the detriment of science literacy."

Because, as the Lord has blessed, AiG and its supporters built a quality facility (and in 2016 opened another world-class facility, the Ark Encounter) that is first class in every way, Scott is greatly concerned that students will go through the museum and be convinced that the Bible is true! Secular humanists have had many victories in the West, and these museums must be seen by them as a setback. While creation, prayer, and the Bible have, by and large, been thrown out of public schools in the West, abortion has been legalized; gay "marriage" legalized; transgender openly promoted; and nativity scenes and the Ten Commandments have all but been thrown out of public places—all resulting in Christians being marginalized more and more. As God's Word states: *I have said these things to you, that in me you may have peace. In the world you will have tribulation. But take heart; I have overcome the world* (John 16:33).

The Creation Museum and Ark Encounter have become rallying places for Christians, taking on the atheistic evolutionary establishment and challenging both Church and culture to return to the authoritative Word of God. The uniqueness of these Christian facilities is that scientific research from biology, geology, astronomy, and anthropology is used to confirm the Bible's history in Genesis and demonstrate clearly the bankruptcy of evolutionary/millions-of-years ideas—and are made available to the public. At the same time, these attractions present the wonderful message of the gospel so that visitors will understand the true purpose and meaning of life. These anti-God evolutionists just don't want students and others to hear and see the information presented in the Creation Museum and Ark Encounter. If they did, then they would quickly recognize that the study of origins is very different from studying operational science that has built our modern-day technology. Actually, the students who are being taught evolution and millions of years as fact are the ones who need the "remedial instruction." They have been indoctrinated to a false understanding of what "science" is.

The Scriptures describe why Drs. Scott and Pearse and their colleagues believe as they do: *[S]coffers will come . . . following their own sinful desires. . . . For they deliberately overlook this fact, that the heavens existed long ago, and the earth was formed out of water and through water by the word of God, and that by means of these the world that then existed was deluged with water and perished* (2 Peter 3:3–6).

> It's about time Christians stand up to those who "suppress the truth" and are "willingly ignorant."

OCTOBER 27
Colossians 3:23

The Quality that the Queen of Sheba Saw

What does the Queen of Sheba have to do with the opening of the Creation Museum and Ark Encounter attractions?

I must admit I've been pleasantly surprised and amazed at the phenomenal interest that the secular media have expressed over the years about the opening of the Creation Museum and Ark Encounter Christian-themed attractions. I remember one particular Friday, we received 11 different calls or emails from media from Brazil, Switzerland, and, of course, the United States (including *The New York Times*).

The most unusual "press" interview I've had occurred with HBO comedian/commentator Bill Maher (formerly with the TV program *Politically Incorrect*). Maher actually broke our security protocols and "sneaked" into the AiG office to interview me. But that's another story about a secularist who used deceptive methods and lied to get the interview. With him, the end justified the means.

I recall when a BBC reporter came and soon after, a reporter for the Russian language version of *Newsweek* spent two hours with me in my office. And about the same time, a travel reporter with *The New York Times* interviewed me for an article on evolution exhibits in major museums around America (in New York City, Chicago, Boston, etc.) and how our Creation Museum compared to them.

The media list could go on and on—and media coverage continues as we often have requests from secular media to visit the attractions and conduct interviews.

But there's something I've heard over and over again from various members of the secular media that has been highly encouraging to me. It usually takes the form of a comment they almost always make: "We heard these were quality places, but we didn't realize they were so first class. Such quality. So professional." As one reporter said to me when I was touring him through the Ark, "You said this is the quality of Hollywood. No! This is way above Hollywood. For a start the wood is real."

The reporters often continue with words like: "I'd say the quality rivals anything you'd see at leading museums and even theme parks. Now, I don't necessarily agree with your message, but congratulations on how you've presented it."

As I think back on such comments, I am reminded of the account of the Queen of Sheba when she visited Solomon. Now, in no way are we comparing ourselves with the works accomplished by Solomon (e.g., the magnificent palace he built) or his great wisdom. But the Queen of Sheba, as recorded in 2 Chronicles 9:6, said: *And behold, half the greatness of your wisdom was not told me.*

To me, it's so exciting—so honoring to the God of Creation, to the Son—that the secular world is congratulating AiG and its talented museum staff on the professionalism of what has been accomplished with the two attractions. The quality helps people take our message more seriously that the Bible is true and that the gospel message of Jesus Christ is also true. And actually, I've experienced secular reports taking us more seriously as they see the quality of all that has been done. As a result, I've had many people over the years refer to the comment from the Queen of Sheba as they say, "Really, the half has not been told. These places are much more amazing than I thought they would be."

When you visit the two leading Christian-themed attractions in the world, I believe you too will make a comment similar to that of the Queen of Sheba's. I think it will surprise you what God has blessed us with at the Ark Encounter and Creation Museum.

People have often declared something like, "Wow—we didn't know it was like this!" Indeed, there is no way you can fully grasp what these places are like until you come to visit and like others exclaim, "the half . . . was not told me." You have to experience it.

I often think of my late father when I walk through the Creation Museum and Ark Encounter and consider the quality of what's been done by the late Patrick Marsh and his gifted design team that continues his legacy. My father, you see, always instilled in us as children that *whatever you do, work heartily, as for the Lord and not for men* (Colossians 3:23).

> So plan to visit the Creation Museum and Ark Encounter and get ready for your "Queen of Sheba" experience!

OCTOBER 28

Luke 13:4-5

The Consequences of Adam's Sin

How can we understand school violence? Over the years in America, there have been numerous instances of school shootings that have sent shock waves across the nation and around the world. For Christians, it is yet another sad reminder of the fact that we live in a fallen, cursed world. News reporters and others discuss such tragedies to try to understand why they happened.

When such terrible acts occur (and, sadly, random violence is occurring more frequently these days), they become the major topic of conversation on news and talk show programs. Quite often, church leaders are asked by reporters to give an explanation as to how someone can believe in a loving God when we see such tragedies happen.

When it comes to what people would call "natural evil" (e.g., earthquakes, tsunamis, hurricanes, etc.), I've heard many Christian leaders on television make statements such as: "We don't know why such things occur—we just have to have faith—and we just have to trust God." When it comes to "moral evil," such as a person shooting fellow human beings, some give the same answer that we don't really know and have to trust God, but some of these leaders would say that it was because of sin. However, if really pushed, many (just like the secular world) would not take all of Genesis 1–11 as literal history.

There's an inconsistency here in taking Genesis literally to accept sin to explain moral evil, such as the tragic school shootings, but not taking Genesis literally in their acceptance of millions of years of "natural evil" before man (e.g., death, violence, catastrophe, and extinction of animals). Now there's also a big problem with Christian leaders saying we don't know why these events occur. We do know. It's because of sin—our sin—and its resulting consequences on this earth.

At Answers in Genesis, we have written articles (and books) dealing with this often-asked question of how a good God can allow all this suffering and evil.

We explain that we now live in a fallen world where we have just a taste of what we really asked for in Adam, when the head of the human race disobeyed God's instruction. You see, when we accept Genesis as it was meant to be taken—as literal history—then we understand that death, disease, and violence are intrusions into this world and that they occurred after Adam was created. Paul tells us in Romans 8:19–23 that the whole of the creation is groaning because of sin.

So it's not God's fault that there is death and violence in the world—it's humanity's fault because we rebelled against our Creator. Certainly, the shooters committing these evil acts have to answer for their own sin. However, we still have to recognize that we now live in a fallen world where we have just a taste of what we really asked for in Adam, when the head of the human race disobeyed God's instruction not to eat the fruit of one particular tree. In a real sense, we are all responsible for the death and suffering we see around us.

It's also important to understand a concept that I present in my book *Divine Dilemma: Wrestling with the Question of a Loving God in a Fallen World*:

Only the person who believes in God has a basis to make moral judgments to determine what is "good" and what is "bad." Those who claim God does not exist have absolutely no authority upon which to call

APOLOGETICS — OCTOBER 28

something right or wrong. If God doesn't exist, who can objectively define what is good and what is bad? What basis could there be to make such judgments? The atheist has no basis upon which to call anything good or bad. They can talk about good and bad and right and wrong—but it's all relative, it's all arbitrary. What's "good" in one person's mind might be completely "bad" in another's.

Of course, from a biblical perspective, God must have morally good and just reasons as to why He allows bad things to happen. For instance, Christ's death on the Cross was an evil event, but God allowed this for a wonderful purpose: to redeem sinful human beings.

We live in an era when secular schools and colleges/universities have all but banned God from science classes. In these classrooms, students are taught that the whole universe, including plants and animals—and humans—arose by natural processes. Naturalism (in essence, atheism) has become the religion of the day and the foundation of the education system (and Western culture as a whole). The more such a philosophy permeates the culture, the more we would expect to see a sense of purposelessness and hopelessness that pervades people's thinking. In fact, the more a culture allows the killing of the unborn, the more we will see people treating life in general as "cheap."

I'm not at all saying that those who committed these murders were all driven by a belief in millions of years or evolution. Only God ultimately knows their heart and why they acted the way they did, except the obvious: that it was a result of sin. However, when we see such death and violence, it is a reminder to us that without God's Word (and the literal history in Genesis 1–11), people will not understand why such things happen.

There is another important lesson we need to be reminded of in the context of suffering and death in this world. In Luke 13:4–5, Jesus said: *Or those eighteen on whom the tower in Siloam fell and killed them, do you think that they were worse offenders than all the others who lived in Jerusalem? No, I tell you; but unless you repent, you will all likewise perish.*

Jesus was reminding people that every person will one day die and that they need to be ready! Those who were killed by this tower in Luke 13 didn't know that when they arose that morning, it would be their day to die. The Lord Jesus, in saying "unless you repent," was reminding everyone that they needed to be sure they were ready to face eternity.

This is the most important lesson for all of us to consider during this tragic time in American history and to be reminded of what the Apostle Paul wrote in Romans 10:9: *If you confess with your mouth that Jesus is Lord and believe in your heart that God raised him from the dead, you will be saved.*

Make sure you're ready if your time to die was today.

OCTOBER 29
Romans 8:22

Mutants Testify to the Truth

Despite what I say, please don't think I hate dogs like poodles or bichon frises, even though they are degenerate mutants.

We had a dog once, a bichon frise. My wife loved this little dog. She may have looked cute, but the science of genetics confirmed what I always said about her: "She's a degenerate mutant affected by sin and the curse." Of course, I was a bit worried I would personally have what we call in Australia "a dog's life" once my wife heard what I called her dog. But if I can use such little dogs to help people understand science and the Bible, then surely our dog could become a hero (actually, a heroine).

A report I read from the Associated Press stated:

"From the towering Great Dane to the feisty little Chihuahua, all dogs are brothers under the skin. Now, researchers have uncovered a reason why the animals wearing that skin vary so much in size. . . . Lark's Portuguese water dog, Georgie, had died and he was seeking a new one. Hearing he was a geneticist, the breeder urged him to work on dog genes. So he began the Georgie project, studying the genes of the Portuguese water dog, a breed that comes in a wide range of sizes from 25 pounds to 75 pounds."

The report continued:

"Ostrander and colleagues then extended that to a range of large and small breeds and the researchers located a section of DNA that varied between large and small breeds in most cases. Known as a regulatory sequence, the difference is on dog chromosome 15 next to a previously known gene named IGF1, for insulin-like growth factor 1. The hormone controlled by the IGF1 gene helps mammals—including people—grow from birth to adolescence. In small dog breeds a mutation in the sequence next to the gene kept them from growing larger, the researchers said."

This scientist discovered a mutation that caused certain dog breeds to remain small in size. So then my wife had no option but to admit that our dog was a mutant, for the scientist specifically mentioned this breed—the bichon frise:

"Overall, 21 researchers studied 3,241 dogs from 143 breeds, ranging from bichon frise, Chihuahua, Maltese, Pomeranian, toy poodle, pug and Pekingese to Saint Bernard, Newfoundland, mastiff, Great Dane, Irish wolfhound and standard poodle."

The article also stated (as many other secular articles have done) that "dogs are descended from wolves, having been domesticated 12,000 to 15,000 years ago." In other words, all dogs share the same gene pool.

So what is the point of all this? Well, as we've written many times before, all dogs are one "kind." Even though there is great variation within dogs, with many different species and varieties within certain species, all this variation only occurs within the dog kind. This has nothing to do with molecules-to-man evolution—on the contrary, the processes of natural selection and speciation result in a redistribution of genetic information or loss of genetic information (or mutations) that act on the information that is already there—as in the case of poodles or bichon frise—to corrupt information.

SCIENCE

There is no mechanism for brand-new information—which never previously existed—to be added into the gene pool for any kind. While we may see different characteristics (visible in the different species of dogs, like wolves, dingoes, coyotes, foxes, etc.), this is the result of new combinations of information from the original gene pool, not new information itself. And such species produced after the Flood were descendants of the two dogs that went on Noah's ark and carried an enormous amount of genetic diversity in their DNA.

Our domestic (many we call "purebred") dogs were produced by artificial selection—since humans do the selecting, rather than the environment or other factors. As is the case for most of our domestic dogs, we have selected for mutations (basically "mistakes") that we like but aren't necessarily good for the dog kind!

Also, this means that there were no degenerate mutants in the Garden of Eden! In fact, the correct definition of what we call our "pure" bred dogs (our domestic varieties like poodles, etc.) would go something like this:

"A poodle is a sin-cursed copy of the original once 'very good' dog that has suffered from the effects of sin and the curse to become the degenerate mutant that it is today living in a fallen world."

Another important point to make here is that most mutations (like this one concerning smallness in dogs) result from corruption of information. These are, by and large, detrimental—the opposite of what molecules-to-man evolution requires.

Even genetic studies in dogs confirm what we'd expect from the Bible concerning created kinds and the effects of sin and the curse! Perhaps the most important thing this "man's best friend" could ever do is tell us the truth concerning God's Word! Even dogs now "groan" because of the effects of sin:

> "For we know that the whole creation has been groaning together in the pains of childbirth until now" (Romans 8:22).

OCTOBER 30

Revelation 13:8

Slain from the Foundation of the World

Over the years, a number of reporters have asked me a question like the following: "What statement are you really making to the world through the Creation Museum and Ark Encounter?" My answer goes something like this: "Answers in Genesis wants the world to know that the Bible is not just a book of religion, or morality, or just a book of spiritual things—although it is all those things. We want people, including future museum visitors, to understand that the Bible is a book of history. And, because that history is true, the message of the gospel based in that history is true."

You see, the first book of the Bible relates to us the account of the biological, geological, astronomical, and anthropological history of the universe—and this history is confirmed by observational science in genetics, biology, geology, and astronomy. Because this history as revealed in the Bible is true, then the message of the Christian gospel (concerning salvation from our sin of rebellion in the first man Adam) is true—that the Son of God stepped into history to become one of us and to die (but as a sinless man) on a Cross (because death was the penalty for our sin), was raised from the dead (conquering death), and now offers a free gift of salvation (to live with God for eternity in a new heavens and earth—with no death) to those who will receive it. This is the statement of this Creation Museum.

I tell the reporters that the Creation Museum's centerpiece is a walk through the 7 C's of History: Creation, Corruption, Catastrophe, Confusion, Christ, Cross, Consummation. Visitors walk through the first four C's, where they not only experience the history of the world concerning creation, the Fall of man, the Flood of Noah's day, and the Tower of Babel (the giving of different languages that formed different people groups) but are also given numerous answers (using observational science) that confirm this history. Then there is a special exhibit giving the details of the last three C's, outlining who Jesus is and explaining the gospel.

I tell them that at the Ark Encounter, we also present the Bible's history but focusing on the Flood. The gospel is also presented clearly through exhibits and a movie on the third deck. We show a movie based on those last three C's at the Creation Museum at special times during the day. This high-quality dramatic presentation is a powerful visual presentation of the gospel. Various actors act out their parts so that everyone will clearly understand the gospel message based in true history.

At one stage, a woman acting the part of Mary talks about the Jewish sacrificial system. As you watch this presentation, you'll become so absorbed with it that it will be as if you're there. Mary says (in a passionate way): "Our sacrifice always had to be perfect—God required it. I have memories as a little girl, when my family would pick our best lamb from the flock. The priest took his knife and.... It always broke my heart, but my parents insisted that all of us were there. They wanted to make sure we each understood how terrible sin is, and just how much it costs to cover it." In the movie, you see Mary and her family watching this beautiful animal—and they see the priest's knife. The priest holds the lamb up above the altar, and you really sense what Mary and her family must have felt and experienced as the event broke their hearts.

Mary goes on: "One day, after I was engaged to Joseph, I was visited by an angel of God. He told me not to be afraid, and that I was to give birth to a child, and that I should call Him Jesus.

THEOLOGY
OCTOBER 30

"I asked how this could be, since I was still a virgin. The angel told me the power of the Most High would overshadow me, and my son would be called the Son of God. Of course, one day I learned that my son would be called something else as well—a lamb."

For me this brings to mind a number of things: The first time the gospel was preached was in Genesis 3:15. Right after Adam sinned, which separated himself and all his descendants from our Creator, God revealed He already had a plan to provide a way of salvation for sinners: *I will put enmity between you and the woman, and between your offspring and her offspring; he shall bruise your head, and you shall bruise his heel.*

God further illustrated His redemption plan when He made clothing for Adam and Eve from animal skins: *And the LORD God made for Adam and for his wife garments of skins and clothed them* (Genesis 3:21). This was the first blood sacrifice as a covering for their sin—a picture of what was to come in Jesus Christ, the Lamb of God, who would die and be raised from the dead to TAKE AWAY our sin.

Acts 2:23 states, *[T]his Jesus, delivered up according to the definite plan and foreknowledge of God, you crucified and killed by the hands of lawless men.*

Revelation 13:8 states, *[A]nd all who dwell on earth will worship it, everyone whose name has not been written before the foundation of the world in the book of life of the Lamb who was slain.*

Think about this: Before the universe was created, before time existed, before man was created, God knew that we (in Adam) would sin. He knew we would rebel against our Creator. And in the wisdom and love of God, He predetermined a plan so that we could receive a free gift of salvation. In eternity, God planned for the Son of God to step into history to provide the ultimate sacrifice—the sinless Son of God would suffer sin's penalty of death, be raised from the dead, thus providing a way of salvation. Hebrews 10:10 declares, *And by that will we have been sanctified through the offering of the body of Jesus Christ once for all.*

As you think about the fact that in eternity, God had predetermined that the Son of God would become a man to die for our sins, also contemplate these things:

- When God created the heavenly bodies on day four of creation *for signs and for seasons, and for days and years* (Genesis 1:14), He knew that one of the signs would be that the Son of God would become a man, born of a virgin in a town called Bethlehem.
- When God made the trees (and all plants) on the third day of creation (Genesis 1:11), He knew that a tree would one day be used for the most evil event of history: when evil men would crucify the Son of God. And yet, by God's foreknowledge and predetermined plan, this event would occur for the salvation of souls.
- When God made the land animals on day six (Genesis 1:24), He knew that soon He would sacrifice at least one of those animals because of our sin in Adam; He had predetermined that this would one day happen to the Son of God so we could receive the free gift of salvation.

> **Doesn't this make you want to fall on your knees and worship our Creator, praise Him, and continually thank Him for the Lamb slain from the foundation of the world?**

OCTOBER 31

2 Timothy 3:16-17

Who Begat Whom?

All Scripture is breathed out by God and profitable for teaching, for reproof, for correction, and for training in righteousness, that the man of God may be complete, equipped for every good work (2 Timothy 3:16–17).

Most of us love to read portions of Scripture that give accounts of victories, miracles, and such. What we enjoy far less are the Scriptures that outline where a certain person begat a son or daughter, who in turn begat a son, thus beginning a long list of begats. Most people feel the genealogies contain only dull details, but those of us who keep in mind that "every word is given by inspiration of God" see that even these so-called dull passages contain vital truth that can be trusted.

Genesis 5 and 11 contain two such genealogies, which some people think can be read to help them get to sleep. It may be hard to believe, but Genesis 5 and 11 are actually two of the more controversial chapters in the Bible, even in Christian circles.

Because so many Christians and Christian leaders have accepted the secular dates for the origin of man and the universe, they must work out ways that such dates can somehow be incorporated into the Bible's historical account. In other words, they must convince people that the Bible's genealogical records do not present an unbroken line of chronology. If such an unbroken line exists, then we should be able to calculate dates concerning the creation of man and the universe.

To fit the idea of billions of years into Scripture, many Christian leaders, since the early nineteenth century, have reinterpreted the days of creation to mean long ages. Biblical creationist literature has meticulously addressed this topic many times, showing clearly that the word *day*, as used in Genesis 1 (the context with a number, evening and morning connected to each day) for each of the six days of creation, means an ordinary, approximately 24-hour day.

Many Christian leaders also claim there are gaps in the Genesis genealogies. One of their arguments is that the word *begat*, as used in the timeline from the first man Adam to Abraham in Genesis 5 and 11, can skip generations. If this argument were true, the date for creation using the biblical timeline of history cannot be worked out.

In one debate, a well-known progressive creationist stated that he believed a person could date Adam back 100,000 years from the present. Since most modern scholars place the date of Abraham around 2000 B.C. (Ussher's date for Abraham's birth is 1996 B.C.), the remaining 96,000 years must fit into the Genesis 5 and 11 genealogies, between Adam and Abraham.

Now, if we estimate that 40 years equals one generation, which is fairly generous, this means that 2,500 generations are missing from these genealogies. But this makes the genealogies ridiculously meaningless.

Those who claim that there are gaps in these genealogies need to demonstrate this from the biblical text and not simply say that gaps exist. However, consider the following:

1. Although in the Hebrew way of thinking, the construction "X is the son of Y" does not always mean a literal father/son relationship, additional biographical information in Genesis 5 and 11 strongly supports

APOLOGETICS

the view that there are no gaps in these chapters. So we know for certain that the following are literal father/son relationships: Adam/Seth, Seth/Enosh, Lamech/Noah, Noah/Shem, Eber/Peleg, and Terah/Abram. Nothing in these chapters indicates that the "X begat Y" means something other than a literal father/son relationship.

2. Nowhere in the Old Testament is the Hebrew word for *begat* (*yalad*) used in any other way than to mean a single-generation (e.g., father/son or mother/daughter) relationship. The Hebrew word ben can mean son or grandson, but the word *yalad* never skips generations.

In the debate (mentioned previously), various biblical references were given as supposed proofs that the Hebrew word *yalad* does not always point to the very next generation. However, when analyzed carefully, these arguments actually confirm what we are asserting concerning the word *begat*, that it does not skip generations. A detailed article on the Answers in Genesis website attests to this fact.

The Scriptures themselves attest to the fact that the secular dates given for the age of the universe, man's existence on the earth, and so on, are not correct because they are based on the fallible assumptions of fallible humans. Nothing in observational science contradicts the timeline of history as recorded in the Bible. But there are two more reasons that these genealogies are vital. First, they are given in Scripture to show clearly that the Bible is real history and that we are all descendants of a real man, Adam; thus, all human beings are related.

Second, the Son of God stepped into this history to fulfill the promise of Genesis 3:15, the promise of a Savior. This Savior would die and rise again to provide a free gift of salvation to the descendants of Adam—all of whom are sinners and are separated from their Creator.

Without the genealogies, how can it be proven that Jesus is the One who would fulfill this promise? Indeed, perhaps the primary purpose of the genealogies is to show that Jesus fulfilled the promise of God the Father.

We can trust these genealogies because they are a part of the infallible, inerrant Word of God.

NOVEMBER 1

Jeremiah 10:2

Being Salt and Light, Not Desalted

Think about this: As society accepts evolutionary thinking and rejects the Bible's authority, the culture itself "evolves."

I have to admit (yes, somewhat sheepishly) that I'm a science fiction fan. I loved the original *Star Trek* TV series. Yes, I recognized the many evolutionary statements made by Captain Kirk (and others) as they traveled through the universe on the Enterprise.

With newer *Star Trek* programs, I became disillusioned. What I noticed was not just the typical evolutionary comments but also an agenda to promote things like gay "marriage," the homosexual lifestyle, abortion, etc.

Over the decades, the program has changed from mainly one of entertainment to one that often promotes anti-Christian lifestyles. This trend is also seen in many other television programs, like the popular program *CSI*. I prefer documentary detective shows (e.g., I occasionally watch *The Forensic Files*), where real-life detectives relate how they solved a particular crime. But these TV documentaries are very different from fictional forensic programs like *CSI* or *NCIS*.

While "vegetating" right after Christmas once, I happened to come across a *CSI* program—and quickly decided I wouldn't ever be watching this program again. *CSI*, a fictional program, has an emphasis on anti-Christian agendas (and they are overt about it). In the episode I watched, the issue came up of when life actually begins. A character (portrayed as a Christian) represented an organization that believed life began at fertilization. He was made to come across as ignorant and foolish.

A *CSI* detective rolled her eyes when she heard the Christian view and then made a big issue of the fact that life didn't begin until the baby moved in the womb. She then defended stem-cell research using cells from human embryos.

Later on, another *CSI* detective (named Grissom) quoted the Scripture verse about the life of the flesh being in the blood to argue that a life in the womb didn't begin until blood flowed through the baby. He then made the statement that "science" basically trumps theology anyway.

I point this out to remind all of us that we live in a world where even Christians can be susceptible to being influenced by the world. Many adults and children watch such programs and don't realize the effect these shows have on molding their worldview.

As such anti-Christian propaganda pervades television (and movies), the world is influencing the Church's coming generations … rather than those in the Church being the light of the world and influencing the culture. More and more children's programs (cartoons, etc.) are being permeated by the LGBTQ+ agenda.

Such programs as the one described above (and others, including *30 Rock, Studio 60, West Wing, Commander in Chief,* and even *The Simpsons*—and, of course, I could name many more) would not have been tolerated by the Christian community a few decades ago. But they are now the norm in many Christian homes—and the children in these homes are now accepting what appears to be the "norm" regarding social issues that are clearly unbiblical.

APOLOGETICS — NOVEMBER 1

In addition, as society accepts evolutionary thinking and rejects the Bible's authority, the culture itself "evolves." The secularists in Hollywood ensure that their evolving, anti-Christian agendas are being incorporated into the programs and films that reach millions (including churchgoers, teens, children, adults—everyone). This is another example of the secularization of the culture—and even the secularization of the Church.

Countering these things is one reason I believe the Lord has raised up Bible-upholding ministries like Answers in Genesis. We pray that through AiG, your family and mine can influence the Church and world for good and help stop (and even undo) the anti-God influence the world has had on the Church. Christians are often shocked when they read in the Bible of how the Israelites adopted pagan religions and worshipped idols. "How foolish could they be to do that?" they ask themselves.

And yet, so many of God's people today are no different in the way they have adopted pagan philosophies of the age (e.g., evolution, relative morality, etc.). They fail to see that they are no different than the Israelites.

As we read in Jeremiah 10:2: *Thus says the Lord: "Learn not the way of the nations."*

Please pray that God's people will be true salt and light in this increasingly secularized culture.

NOVEMBER 2
1 Peter 5:8-9

The War Between Christianity and Secular Humanism

We already know that the culture war is only heating up. And that it is really a war between two worldviews: Christianity versus secular humanism. At a foundational level, the debate is between these two factions: those who accept God as the Creator of life versus those who believe that natural processes are responsible for life. Either man is created in the image of God and accountable to his Creator, or man is an animal and answerable to no one but himself.

The influential British secular magazine *New Scientist* published an article that was a scathing attack on the homeschooling movement. The article stated: "These students are part of a large, well-organised movement that is empowering parents to teach their children creationist biology and other unorthodox versions of science at home, all centred on the idea that God created Earth in six days about 6000 years ago."

So the major argument presented against homeschooling in the United States and Britain is that most of the parents teach their children the biblical account of creation. The secularists recognize that if the account of creation in the Bible is true, then Christian doctrine and morality (marriage being one man and one woman, two genders only, abortion is murder, etc.) are also true—and that humans are accountable to their Creator God (who is the absolute authority in all things). Therefore, people who deny they are responsible to a Creator—and who demand that morality be relative to and lobby for the legalization of abortion, gay "marriage," etc.—are considered intolerant (and supposedly hateful) of those (i.e., biblical Christians) who oppose them.

As if this is a shocking state of affairs, the secular magazine continued: "For these parents, religious instruction and science are often intertwined. This bothers Brian Alters of McGill University in Montreal, Canada, who studies the changing face of science education in the US. He is appalled by some home-schooling textbooks, especially those on biology that claim they have scientific reasons for rejecting evolution. 'They have gross scientific inaccuracies in them,' he says. 'They would not be allowed in any public school in the US, and yet these are the books primarily featured in home-schooling bookstores.'"

The article continued: "One such textbook argues: 'Evolution is a concept that attempts to free man from God and his responsibility to his Creator.' Alters worries for the students who learn from such texts."

Yes, the secularists are worried. They are concerned because a minority of our young people—many of whom have shown they excel in their studies—are being taught that they are responsible to a Creator and that evolution (which is a religion based on naturalism) isn't true. As Dr. Alters stated in the quote above, public schools won't allow such material. In fact, I would say that public (secular) schools have, by and large, become churches of atheism. And as this *New Scientist* article made so clear, the creation/evolution debate is at the core of the battle between Christianity and secular humanism.

The article ominously hints at the need to give special tests to homeschool students (and notice the "hit" at Christian colleges as you read): "Until recently, most home-schoolers who were learning the evangelical version of science chose to go on to secular universities because such institutions tend to be more academically rigorous than Christian colleges. Many such universities today accept home-schooled students.

APOLOGETICS

"To judge home-school applicants, they rely mostly on standardised tests of factual knowledge. Such tests cannot, however, reveal whether or not a student understands scientific method [Note: By this, the magazine means believing in evolution, as it equates the scientific method with evolution], a compulsory subject in public schools but not for home-schoolers [Note: Homeschoolers do learn the scientific method; just check out their textbooks]." And what tests do secular universities need to be carried out according to him? Well, they are to determine if students believe in creation and have a Christian worldview! And if this is so, they would be denied access to secular universities.

Now, you might say that this is far-fetched. It wouldn't happen. Well, it has happened. For instance, some students from Christian schools were being denied entrance to state-run universities in California.

The Association of Christian Schools International (ACSI), in an issue of *Legal Legislative Update*, reported at the time that: "The University of California (UC) represents 10 university campuses such as UCLA, UC Berkeley, and UC San Diego. It has apparently decided that it will not accept new private-school course submissions for core curriculum subjects if they are based on the science textbooks." [Note: The texts were pictured in the ACSI update—some of the same kinds of Christian school textbooks that were referred to in the *New Scientist* article.]

The ACSI update continued: "For this reason, ACSI and the other plaintiffs have filed a court case against the University of California system. The goal of the case is to secure both religious and academic freedom in California by enjoining UC from engaging in viewpoint discrimination.

"UC did not have any objective evidence that students from religious schools are deficient in science when they arrive for their freshman year of college. The UC representatives indicated that there was no problem with the material facts in the [Christian] textbook—that if the Scripture verses that begin each chapter were removed the textbook would likely be approved for the science lab course requirement."

It became obvious to those representing Christian schools that the textbook decisions were highly subjective and appeared to be made because of discrimination against Christianity. Well, the Christian school and homeschool movements throughout the West continue to be embattled as the secular world comes against them. The secular humanists will not shy away from attacking Christian schools and homeschools over the creation/evolution issue. Their attacks will likely intensify. In Australia, there are moves in regard to anti-discrimination laws that could have a devastating effect on Christian schools. It's all part of the war against God in our culture. The Bible-upholding ministry of Answers in Genesis has been playing a major part in helping in all these battles—especially as we disseminate a tremendous number of resources to help Christians stand on the authority of God's Word.

Through our award-winning website, several publications, the Creation Museum and Ark Encounter attractions, curricula, radio programs, a video streaming service, a translations outreach, etc., Answers in Genesis is ministering at a core, foundational level in today's culture wars. And lives are being impacted. *Be sober-minded; be watchful. Your adversary the devil prowls around like a roaring lion, seeking someone to devour. Resist him, firm in your faith, knowing that the same kinds of suffering are being experienced by your brotherhood throughout the world* (1 Peter 5:8–9).

Rise up and make yourself ready for all the world is sending your way.

NOVEMBER 3

2 Corinthians 10:4-6

Battling Against Atheism on the Move

A number of years ago we started to hear the term "new atheists." We've warned you about them before on our website—but now, they're on a much more aggressive march all across America. No longer are they just staying in their classrooms or writing books and articles in the comfort of their offices. They are "the new atheists," and they are aggressively going after your children, your liberties, and your faith!

According to the print media and websites, the new atheists say that "evangelism is a moral imperative" to spread their "good news" in "persuading people of the virtues of atheism." They are "drawing on evolution" and are vocally "hostile to religions," especially "fundamentalist Christianity and Islam." They are "feeling a real need to convert people" and preaching an "un-gospel." In one media report, it was stated that "at some point there is going to be enough pressure that it is just going to be too embarrassing to believe in God."

One of the most outspoken of this new breed of atheists is the vehement anti-creationist Dr. Richard Dawkins of Oxford University in England; another is philosopher Sam Harris. *The Washington Post* wrote a major article about Harris and stated, "How exactly the faithful [Christians] will transition to a godless, Good Book-less cosmology is not exactly clear ... but he is heartened by countries such as Sweden, where he claims 80% of the populace do not believe in God."

These atheists are not just publicity seekers. They are very serious about their mission. For instance, Dawkins, from England, crusaded across America to proclaim his atheism to newspapers, websites, and at public meetings. Some people might say to me, "But there's no way Americans will go for atheism. Most people believe in God, even if they don't take the Bible seriously as AiG does." Think back to the 1950s. What if someone back then said to you, "Beware, the homosexual movement is on the march—if we don't do something, gay 'marriages' will be legalized across the country." Almost all of us at that time would have said that there's no way Americans would ever accept this. Most people believe that marriage is one man for one woman, so, no, this will never happen in America or most of the West. But as you know, it has happened and continues to happen throughout the West!

Interestingly, these new atheists likened their growing movement to that of the gay activists. One stated, "We're in the same position the gay movement was in a few decades ago. There was need for people to come out. The more people who came out, the more people had the courage to come out. That's the case with atheists. They are more numerous than anybody realizes." And in many ways, they have been successful. There's been a catastrophic generational loss from the Church. If you think this is all an exaggeration, just consider the popularity of two books associated with these new atheists: *The God Delusion* by Dawkins and *Letter to a Christian Nation* by Harris. Both books bitterly attack Christianity. Dawkins is more than just angry though. He has a purpose, says a reviewer: "The whole book is meant to change people's minds."

The God Delusion was #8 on *The New York Times* Best Sellers list, #10 on *Publishers Weekly*, and #2 on the Amazon bestseller rankings in November 2006. At the same time, *Letter* was #6 on *the Times* list and #8 in the Amazon rankings. An increasing number of atheists were attacking our Christian faith in several major newspapers and websites—with their evolutionary beliefs often presented.

It prompted me to ask: "Why are atheists now getting so much publicity and gaining ground? What's happened in the culture to allow this?" As we've been saying for years, there's been a change in this culture—at a foundation level. Generations have been indoctrinated by the secular education system and media to build their thinking on human reason, not the Word of God. And at the base of this is the creation/evolution issue. It's the spiritual war that's been raging for 6,000 years.

Naturalistic evolutionary indoctrination has produced generations (even in the Church) who doubt the Bible. Barna Research discovered that of teenagers today who call themselves born-again Christians, only a small percentage believe there is such a thing as absolute truth. These young people are ripe for "secular evangelists" like Dawkins and Harris.

Consider what else the media was saying about this "evangelistic" movement: "There is clearly an evolutionary explanation for the tools we have cognitively." "Dawkins is openly agreeing with the most stubborn fundamentalists that evolution must lead to atheism." Atheists "derive their own worldview from the theory of evolution."

Let me shock you further and illustrate how some of these God-haters think. Quoting Harris, a source reported: "If I could wave a magic wand and get rid of either rape or religion, I would not hesitate to get rid of religion."[102]

Dawkins insists that Christians have no right to indoctrinate their children in religious "nonsense." He continues, saying that children being brought up in Christian homes are being exposed to an "infection"—and Christianity is the most "dangerous thing in the world." One of Dawkins' "evangelistic" talks was actually given in a packed church (the First Parish in Cambridge, Massachusetts)! What times we live in! A news report stated: "At first his [Dawkins] words are greeted with laughter, and then with resounding applause." The words he preached were from his book: "The God of the Old Testament is arguably the most unpleasant character in all fiction: jealous and proud of it; a petty, unjust, unforgiving control-freak; a vindictive, bloodthirsty ethnic cleanser; a misogynistic, homophobic, racist, infanticidal, genocidal, filicidal, pestilential, megalomaniacal, sadomasochistic, capriciously malevolent bully."

All I can say is that I praise the Lord that He has raised up ministries like Answers in Genesis to engage the culture and the Church to return to the authority of God's Word. The militant atheists have been on the march. The creation/gospel message is vital today. God is using it at the front lines of the foundational battle in the lives of countless souls, like this one: "If it wasn't for your website, I don't know if I would be a Christian. I was really depressed last year because there were tons of questions I had about the world that no one could give me answers to. I started to think that if evolution was true as they taught me in school, why should I believe in God? You showed me that the Bible can be trusted"—C. T., Michigan.

For the weapons of our warfare are not of the flesh but have divine power to destroy strongholds. We destroy arguments and every lofty opinion raised against the knowledge of God, and take every thought captive to obey Christ, being ready to punish every disobedience, when your obedience is complete (2 Corinthians 10:4–6).

A reminder of how important it is to teach God's Word and equip people with answers to the attacks on His Word in our day.

NOVEMBER 4

Genesis 50:20

Battling the Brights

Did you know that in the late 1990s, a camp that was organized to train children in atheism/secular humanism started—not so coincidentally—in Kentucky, and in the same year, we had a highly publicized zoning battle over our Creation Museum a few miles away?

Now, who would have ever thought of Kentucky as a battleground between Christianity and humanism? We expect such battles in the liberal parts of the country—like the West and East Coasts—but not in relatively conservative, family-friendly states.

In the late '90s, we thought it would be easy to rezone a piece of property to build offices and a small (at the time) Creation Museum! But an atheistic organization called "Free Inquiry Group" (FIG), headed by an atheist attorney, the late Ed Kagin (who was at the time the director of American Atheists in Kentucky), led a charge in opposing the Creation Museum.

And what a battle it was! Answers in Genesis made front-page headlines on and off for months! On the evening news one night, a local Cincinnati TV station led off with a story about the opposition to the museum and then put President Clinton's renomination for president by the Democratic National Convention as the second story.

At first, it was so obvious that the opposition was because we were Christians. I remember being at a public zoning meeting where one person actually said that "the separation of church and state" forbade us from building a creation museum in Kentucky!

Think about it: a private museum—funded by private donations—shouldn't be built on privately owned land because of the (nonexistent) separation of church and state! Incredible!

At one of the zoning meetings, a lady stood up and pointed at me and vehemently said, "He's Jim Jones [the suicide cult leader], coming to get our kids!"

Actually, we were "AiG, coming to teach kids the truth concerning God's Word, praying that they would trust the Lord Jesus for salvation and thus live forever with the Lord in heaven!" The reality was that the atheistic/humanistic group that opposed us was out to get kids and train them in a philosophy of hopelessness and purposelessness that would keep them separated from God for eternity.

In the same year that the zoning battle began, so did this atheist group "Camp Quest" for children.

The late Mr. Kagin's website stated: "Camp Quest is the first residential summer camp in the history of the United States for the children of Atheists, Freethinkers, Secular Humanists, Humanists, Brights, or whatever other terms might be applied to those who hold to a naturalistic, not supernatural, world view."

On the same website, it was stated: "Camp Quest was conceived, and has been operated for the past ten years, as a summer camp for the children of the irreligious, for those who have accepted Atheism, or lack of a belief in a supernatural world, by whatever name such may be called, as a conclusion, not as a belief."

RESOURCES

Camp Quest then spread from Kentucky to Ohio, Minnesota, Michigan, Ontario (Canada), California, and Tennessee, and I'm sure many other places since then.

In 1997, when we were going to build the AiG offices and Creation Museum on the first property we were looking to buy, we had planned for a 30,000-sqare-foot building, and it was miles from the interstate.

Well, the Lord allowed the opposition (led by Mr. Kagin) and the subsequent loss of that first property to guide us to a new property beside I-275 instead. Because of the larger, much better located property, we decided to build a 95,000-square-foot building—over three times the size of the original plan! Over the years, I've often been reminded of this verse of Scripture: *As for you, you meant evil against me, but God meant it for good, to bring it about that many people should be kept alive, as they are today* (Genesis 50:20). And we have expanded the museum exhibits and grounds attractions over time.

In addition, the late Patrick Marsh, living in Japan at the time, contacted us to ask if he could be our exhibit designer. Patrick had worked with Universal Studios, the 1984 Olympic Games in LA, Asian theme parks, etc.

Patrick came on board, and during the delay in finding a suitable piece of land, we decided to take the Creation Museum to a whole new level of technology and exhibits—and thus a whole new level of excellence. As a result of Patrick's involvement, he set up a design studio that attracted very talented artists, sculptors, fabricators, etc., who wanted to use their talents for the Lord. This has been one of the great blessings to enable us to build world-class exhibits internally, saving multi-millions of dollars.

As a result of the opposition of the atheist group and others to the Creation Museum in 1996, the vision was greatly expanded so we could reach millions more with the truth of God's Word and the wonderful message of salvation! Yes, God had plans way beyond our expectations. And even though going through such battles is tough at the time, we can look back and see God's miraculous hand in all of it.

Truly, *[W]e know that for those who love God all things work together for good, for those who are called according to his purpose* (Romans 8:28). Note God doesn't say "all things will be good," but that "all things work together for good."

As the secular media and others visit, all are amazed at what has been accomplished. The quality—the professionalism—and the fact that the Creation Museum and later the Ark Encounter were built at a fraction of the cost of what it would take if we had to contract all the exhibits to outside firms.

Truly, what man means for evil God uses for good.

NOVEMBER 5

Genesis 1:20-21

Story Time: Once Upon a Time Dolphins Had Legs

It's amazing how people can be so easily brainwashed by embellished newspaper reports to believe in evolution! I remember when the following headline was featured Sunday morning (November 5, 2006) on the Fox News channel: "Japanese Researchers Find Dolphin with Remains of Legs." The reporters were surprised to find that this story was even more popular than Saddam Hussein's guilty verdict. One news reporter said, "I can't believe a story about a dolphin with legs beat out Saddam's verdict!" In a way, it is not surprising that a dolphin with supposed legs was the top story. The creation/evolution issue has been a hot one for years. Atheists like Richard Dawkins (probably the leading spokesperson for evolution today) with his book *The God Delusion* has certainly been on the march across the United States and the world.

Biblical creationists have been so successful in disseminating information that counteracts evolution/millions of years, that as soon as anything arises that remotely looks like it could in some way support evolutionists/millions of years, it almost immediately becomes headline news. It's almost as if people are desperate to accept anything that even hints at evolution supposedly being true. However, claims such as sea mammals with supposed legs have been made many times before (and will no doubt happen many times again). Answers in Genesis has written many articles about such supposed finds. Now, did that dolphin actually have legs? Well, what did researchers find? All we could go on at the time were the newspaper reports. That means one has to be very careful. Like many such news reports, one has to wait for a detailed paper/documentation before making definitive statements. And when one does, it so often turns out to be very different than what was hyped up in the media.

According to the Fox News report: "Japanese researchers said Sunday that a bottlenose dolphin captured last month has an extra set of fins that could be the remains of back legs, a discovery that may provide further evidence that ocean-dwelling mammals once lived on land."

So this dolphin had an extra set of fins (not legs). Still, they state it "could be the remains of back legs." Because of their obvious evolutionary bias, they had already jumped to a conclusion in interpreting those fins as back legs—before they had x-rayed the fins and carried out detailed research. (There was not even any mention of bones in these fins.) The article went on to quote one researcher as saying, "I believe the fins may be remains from the time dolphins' ancient ancestors lived on land ... this is an unprecedented discovery." So, without any detailed research and using phrases like "I believe" and "could be," this is already an "unprecedented discovery." But this is so typical of the media hype we experience on a daily basis.

The same news article stated categorically, "Fossil remains show dolphins and whales were four-footed land animals about 50 million years ago and share the same common ancestor as hippos and deer. Scientists believe they later transitioned to an aquatic lifestyle and their hind limbs disappeared." Now that's a fairy tale! The researcher was also reported as saying, "A freak mutation may have caused the ancient trait to reassert itself." It certainly seemed that this extra set of fins could have been a mutation—as the DNA of the dolphin already has the information for fins. A mutation could cause an extra set of fins to develop (e.g., researchers have seen mutations cause extra sets of wings in fruit flies, extra legs on a cow, etc.). However, to say that the mutation "caused the ancient trait to reassert itself" is an evolutionary interpretation of a phenomenon that is quite common—mutations resulting in an extra appendage based on the information already in the genes of the animal. And that's not evolution! The extra appendage is usually a big problem, not an evolutionary advancement.

It should be noted that the pectoral fins or flippers of the dolphin contain bones that are homologous (similar) to those of the human arm and hand (as well as the forelimbs of other mammals). The pectoral fin of the dolphin, for example, contains a short bone similar to the humerus (upper arm bone) of land-dwelling mammals which is attached by a ball socket-type joint to a scapula (shoulder blade). The humerus in turn articulates with a pair of side-by-side short bones similar to the radius and ulna (lower arm bones) of other mammals. Finally, the fin contains small bones roughly comparable to wrist bones and linear rows of bones that superficially resemble fingers. The homology argument does not support evolution but rather a common designer.

But there are significant differences in both structure and function between the fin bones of dolphins and the limb bones of terrestrial mammals. First, dolphins do not actually swim with their pectoral fins (this is largely a function of the tail flukes) but mostly use them to steer and to assist the flukes in stopping. Dolphins do not have a movable elbow joint and hold their pectoral fins rather rigidly out from the body. Their only mobile joint is at the shoulder. While this is an effective arrangement for simple steering and stopping, it is unsuitable for walking or grasping. The dolphin, like nearly all vertebrates, has five fingers or digits, but in the dolphin, there are many bones that make up the "fingers" (fin rays) rather than the typical sequence of three bones seen in the digits of humans and many other mammals. This serves to greatly lengthen the fin.

While cetaceans (dolphins, porpoises, and whales) lack hind limbs, they have pelvic bones that differ in males and females and appear to support the reproductive organs. Whether they also have rudimentary femurs and other leg bones is less certain. For evidence of whale "legs," many evolutionists cite a paper published by Struthers in 1881 which purports to describe a rudimentary "femur" in the adult Greenland right whale (*Balaena mysticetus*). Other more recent publications suggest embryonic stages in cetaceans that resemble limb bones.

Homologous structures are seen throughout the vertebrate phyla—but as creationists have pointed out so many times, the homology argument does not support evolution but rather a common designer. There are many problems with the homology argument. For example, the rudimentary male mammary gland and nipple are clearly homologous to those of the female, but they are not taken as evidence that males once nursed their young. Homology tells us something about embryology—not about evolution. It is unfortunate that reporters and others often jump to conclusions before real science can be done to provide proper conclusions. Evolutionists are constantly looking for transitional forms, grasping at straws—or even fins—for evidence that just isn't there.

And God said, "Let the waters swarm with swarms of living creatures, and let birds fly above the earth across the expanse of the heavens." So God created the great sea creatures and every living creature that moves, with which the waters swarm, according to their kinds (Genesis 1:20–21).

No evidence has ever contradicted that.

NOVEMBER 6

Job 42:2-4

Compromise Causes Unnecessary Confusion

One of the leading evolutionary spokespersons of our age has been Dr. Richard Dawkins of Oxford University in England.

In his book *The God Delusion*, Dawkins clenches both fists and attempts to "take on" the God of the universe! The publisher's blurb on the cover of the book states:

"Dawkins attacks God in all his forms, from the sex-obsessed, cruel tyrant of the Old Testament to the more benign, but still illogical, Celestial Watchmaker favoured by some Enlightenment thinkers. He eviscerates the major arguments for religion and demonstrates the ultimate improbability of a supreme being. He shows how religion fuels war, foments bigotry and abuses children."

I will bring just one of Dawkins' many points to your attention. Taken from chapter 7, the self-proclaimed atheist mocked the hypocrisy of compromising Christian theologians:

"The legend of the animals going into the ark two by two is charming, but the moral of the story of Noah is appalling. God took a dim view of humans, so he (with the exception of one family) drowned the lot of them including children and also, for good measure, the rest of the (presumably blameless) animals as well. Of course, irritated theologians will protest that we don't take the book of Genesis literally any more. But that is my whole point! We pick and choose which bits of scripture to believe, which bits to write off as symbols or allegories. Such picking and choosing is a matter of personal decision, just as much, or as little, as the atheist's decision to follow this moral precept or that was [also] a personal decision, without an absolute foundation. If one of these is 'morality flying by the seat of its pants,' so is the other."

At least Dawkins was being consistent. He recognized that his own "morality," based on his atheism, is relative! And he points out correctly: If theologians "pick and choose which bits of scripture to believe," then they too are actually saying that truth is relative—to be decided by humans!

For many years now, Answers in Genesis has been calling out to those Christian leaders who compromise the clear teaching of Genesis by accepting the secular idea of millions of years and evolution. Such compromise undermines people's acceptance of the authority of the Word of God. The very people these Christian leaders influence—both the "ordinary" church attenders and the leaders who teach and govern within the local body—soon join their pastors in believing that you can insert man's fallible ideas and reinterpret the clear meaning (the "hermeneutic") of Scripture. This has put many youths and adults on a slippery side—with tens of millions eventually rejecting the Bible as the Word of God. This is also connected to the catastrophic generational loss from the Church.

I think back to when I was given an initial overview of a major national poll for my book *Already Gone* published in 2009, that was commissioned by AiG (as a follow-up to the results of an alarming Barna Research poll of 2002 and a Southern Baptist poll around the same time). The AiG-commissioned poll clearly showed that a major reason many have left the Church is because they no longer believe the Bible is the absolute Word of God.

APOLOGETICS NOVEMBER 6

By the way, such compromise positions in the Church are seen by many as sheer hypocrisy—inside and outside the Church. They hear Christian leaders say that the Bible is infallible, but they watch as those same Christian leaders "pick and choose" which bits (particularly in Genesis) are to be accepted as written. Sadly, this compromise and hypocrisy is a pandemic through the Church and Christian institutions.

Many church leaders think that such compromise is necessary in order to appease the secular academics of the age. The reality, however, is that secular academics mock such compromise. Like Dawkins, they recognize that if you can't trust what the Bible clearly states in one area, you can't trust any of it! Seeing such compromise in the Church only fuels Dawkins' hatred of God and His Word. He is *not wishing that any should perish, but that all should reach repentance* (2 Peter 3:9).

Also, we need to pray for the many compromising church leaders—that they will accept and proclaim the authority of God's Word from the very first verse.

All Christians need to give up academic pride and intellectual peer pressure and get to the position Job arrived at when he recognized who God is and repented in dust and ashes: *I know that you can do all things, and that no purpose of yours can be thwarted. "Who is this that hides counsel without knowledge?" Therefore I have uttered what I did not understand, things too wonderful for me, which I did not know. "Hear, and I will speak; I will question you, and you make it known to me." I had heard of you by the hearing of the ear, but now my eye sees you; therefore I despise myself, and repent in dust and ashes* (Job 42:2–6).

We all need to be like Job and recognize compared to infinite Creator God we know just about nothing! We need to let God speak to us through His Word and not take our ideas to God's Word and reinterpret them to fit man's beliefs!

> We need to pray for atheists like Richard Dawkins. God is long-suffering–as He was in the days of Noah.

NOVEMBER 7

Daniel 3:13-18

Stand! Hold the Line!

Often, we will hear secularists accuse Christians of being intolerant. But who really are the intolerant ones? Let me give an example that happened to some staff of Answers in Genesis. It was a tense—and ironic—situation. One of our staff described the confrontation as "analogous to Rosa Parks being asked to go to the back of the bus."

AiG was actively witnessing and distributing thousands of materials at the annual National Education Association (NEA) teachers' convention in Florida. For many years, AiG, through a public school teacher, had manned the "Creation Science Educator's Caucus" booth at the world's largest gathering of educators. Through many generous AiG supporters, we saw thousands of dollars' worth of DVDs, books, and booklets get directly into the hands of thousands of teachers.

At the booth on this particular occasion, AiG boldly displayed three large banners. One of them stated: "Gay Marriage: Who Determines What Marriage Should Be?" At the bottom of the banner, it declared: "Genesis Is Literal History—God Created Them Male and Female." It was a clear message that the origin of marriage is in the Book of Genesis. In other words, we were displaying what the Bible clearly teaches.

But what caused the biggest stir—and what had NEA officials making unreasonable demands on us—was AiG's small gay "marriage" booklet. The NEA leadership demanded that the AiG booklet be moved to a back table. Apparently, some people were "offended by it." Here's how one of our staff—who led our effort—explained it to me:

"We received a press release from the American Family Association about a new NEA proposal that would 'promote homosexual marriage in public schools.'" Because of this new controversial proposal, AiG determined to actively engage in this battle.

"An official from the NEA leadership stopped by our booth. He requested/demanded that we move those gay marriage booklets to the back of our tables so they wouldn't be in plain view. If we didn't, he would take it to the next level—a not-so-veiled threat.

"If I was to acquiesce to the humanists' demands this time, what would be next? Surely sooner or later, someone would find our banners—or our creation message—to be offensive. If we backed down from preaching the whole counsel of God in this instance, it would not stop there. What we were doing did not go against the NEA by-laws (we checked). So we decided to 'obey God rather than men'" (Acts 5:29).

"An NEA official came by again. This man was noticeably nervous and repeated the request/demand that we move the gay marriage booklets to the back … or else face the consequences. With gentleness, I told him that we would not—and showed him the NEA by-laws.

"I mentioned to this gentleman that we felt like the late civil rights pioneer Rosa Parks being asked to move to the back of an Alabama bus. I told him, 'We will not go to the back of the bus. We will not move our booklets to the back.' And praise the Lord, we never heard back from them again. I'm so proud of our staff … they really do practice what we preach! What a challenge to all of us to stand on the Bible and not compromise."

APOLOGETICS

NOVEMBER 7

Once again at the NEA convention, several thousand Bible-proclaiming booklets and DVDs were distributed (free) to public school teachers and administrators (and they were also pointed to our website). Educators overall, we found, were very receptive!

What I notice in today's world is that many churches, church leaders, Christian institutions, and the leaders and board aren't standing up as they should on God's Word concerning LGBTQ+ issues, abortion, etc. Many soften their stand.

Oh, how we need more people like Daniel, Shadrach, Meshach, and Abednego who will stand their ground. And just because a Christian stands on God's Word concerning marriage and gender does not at all mean that's hate speech. In fact, if we as Christians truly love someone, we will point them to God's Word and the saving gospel. Yes, we must do this with gentleness and meekness but also being unashamed and with boldness.

Recall what happened with Shadrach, Meshach, and Abednego:

Then Nebuchadnezzar in furious rage commanded that Shadrach, Meshach, and Abednego be brought. So they brought these men before the king. Nebuchadnezzar answered and said to them, "Is it true, O Shadrach, Meshach, and Abednego, that you do not serve my gods or worship the golden image that I have set up? Now if you are ready when you hear the sound of the horn, pipe, lyre, trigon, harp, bagpipe, and every kind of music, to fall down and worship the image that I have made, well and good. But if you do not worship, you shall immediately be cast into a burning fiery furnace. And who is the god who will deliver you out of my hands?" Shadrach, Meshach, and Abednego answered and said to the king, "O Nebuchadnezzar, we have no need to answer you in this matter. If this be so, our God whom we serve is able to deliver us from the burning fiery furnace, and he will deliver us out of your hand, O king. But if not, be it known to you, O king, that we will not serve your gods or worship the golden image that you have set up" (Daniel 3:13–18).

I love these sentences they spoke which all Christians need to take note of:

"If this be so, our God whom we serve is able to deliver us from the burning fiery furnace, and he will deliver us out of your hand, O king. But if not, be it known to you, O king, that we will not serve your gods or worship the golden image that you have set up."

> **As Christians in this increasing secularized culture, we have to know where the line is (based on God's Word and a true Christian worldview) that we will not cross.**

NOVEMBER 8

Ephesians 6:12

God's Word vs. Man's Word

Are you aware that a well-known Oscar-nominated Hollywood actor once stated that Bibles should have a disclaimer pasted inside, warning that it's fiction? Could such stickers ever be placed inside Bibles? Actually, it wouldn't surprise me at all as those who are not for Christ are against Him!

Surely this wouldn't happen in America, the land of the free—the nation that was founded on the Bible. But then again, who would have thought 50 years ago that in once-Christianized countries:

- Abortion would be legalized, and gay "marriages" would be conducted?
- Prayer, Bible reading, and the teaching of creation would all but be banned from public (secular—anti-God) schools and other government-run places?
- The name of Christ would be increasingly taken out of Christmas?
- There would be threats to take the name of God out of the Pledge of Allegiance in America and that prayer would be banned at school graduations?
- The Ten Commandments and nativity scenes would be removed from public places?
- And the list goes on and on!

There's no doubt that Christians are becoming marginalized in America and the rest of the Western world.

Now someone actually did begin placing disclaimers in the front of Bibles in America! A Delta airlines pilot from Atlanta (and a friend of AiG) once found such a sticker in the front of a Gideon Bible placed in a drawer of his Salt Lake City hotel room. There's no telling how many of these stickers have been applied to other Bibles found in hotels (and other places).

This anti-Bible sticker was related to the creation/evolution (origins) issue. Now, where did this sticker's wording originate? It was applied to textbooks in Cobb County, Georgia, where the school board was concerned that science books were presenting evolution as fact to its students. The board had voted to place stickers in the front of some public-school biology textbooks to inform students that evolution should be studied critically.

As one compared the two stickers, it was easy to see that the sticker found in the hotel Bible was meant to mirror (mock) the textbook sticker. Such mockery just illustrated that the creation/evolution controversy is really a foundational issue in the battle between secular humanism and Christianity. It's the battle between God's Word and man's word.

At the rate we see the secularization of the West and the increasing anti-God sentiment, I must admit it wouldn't surprise me if some liberal judges would begin mandating that such stickers be placed in Bibles. In this vein, *The Da Vinci Code* movie was permeating the culture at the time of the sticker controversy with another blatant, anti-Christian propaganda message (though it's a work of fiction). One of its stars, Ian McKellen, a well-known gay activist/fundraiser (he also played Gandalf in the famous *Lord of the Rings* trilogy), answered a question about the movie on NBC-TV's *Today Show*. Here's the exchange:

APOLOGETICS

NBC reporter Matt Lauer: "How would you have all felt if there was a disclaimer at the beginning of the movie? Would it have been OK with you?"

McKellen: "Well I've often thought the Bible should have a disclaimer in the front saying this is fiction. I mean, walking on water? It takes an act of faith and I have faith in this movie—not that it's true—not that it's factual—but that it's a jolly good story."

Not long after this explosive interview, I read some Australian newspaper articles that reported on a number of hospitals that were banning Bibles from being placed in rooms. Australia's national newspaper, *The Australian* (akin to *USA Today*), reported:

"The banning of bibles in Queensland and Victorian hospitals was political correctness gone crazy, Health Minister Tony Abbott says."

In May 2006, Gideons International, which supplies Bibles to hospitals and hotels worldwide, said it had been banned from leaving Bibles at several Queensland hospitals to prevent giving offense to non-Christian patients. A Catholic news source in Australia reported:

"Almost all of Melbourne's main hospitals have withdrawn Bibles."

In Brisbane, the Royal Brisbane and Women's and Princess Alexandra hospitals were among the first to stop the Gideons' testaments from being left on patients' bedside tables. Staff said the Bibles were no longer in keeping with the "multicultural approach to chaplaincy."

Both news sources stated that the Bibles could be a source of infection! One said:

"It is also an infection-control measure… some claimed the Bibles were removed because they were a source of infection. Hospital spokeswoman Tanya Lobegeier said: 'If someone has a cold or anything and uses the Bible, their germs could be passed on to the next person who reads it.'"

You know, the Bible does talk about a kind of "infection"—one that we're all plagued with. It's called sin! And a resulting "infection" that arises from that sin is secular evolutionary humanism, which has spread through the education system and media. This infection (evolutionary humanism) is indoctrinating millions in our once-Christianized West to believe that Christianity is a problem—that it needs to be eliminated from the culture!

For our struggle is not against flesh and blood, but against the rulers, against the authorities, against the powers of this dark world and against the spiritual forces of evil in the heavenly realms (Ephesians 6:12; NIV).

A reminder–it's a spiritual battle.

NOVEMBER 9
Proverbs 13:22

What Legacy Are You Leaving Your Family?

When I think back on my Australian childhood (which seems like millions of years ago these days!), I fondly recall my mother's mother. We affectionately called her "Nana." In my mind's eye, I can still see Nana standing on the veranda of her and Grandfather's big farmhouse, waving her Bible at a couple of "fleeing" Jehovah's Witnesses who had dropped by to visit. They were virtually running away from her after she had passionately "preached" at them!

I can also recollect one particular scene of my other grandmother. It's of her sitting at my father's side, with all her grandchildren also beside her. (My grandfather on my father's side died when my father was a teenager, so I never knew him.) I recall sitting in church with my grandmother.

I also remember my mother and father teaching me the Word of God at home and ensuring we went to church each Sunday. My parents were active in the church, whether as Sunday school teachers or my father as an elder or deacon. I recall my parents starting Sunday schools, hosting missionaries, and organizing gospel outreach programs—it was at one such program where I dedicated my life to the Lord.

I praise the Lord that my siblings and I were taught to recognize our sinfulness and were given the opportunity to commit our lives to the Lord. (Our dear brother Robert is in heaven right now praising the Lord.) We, as imperfect as we are, did our best to train our children in the ways of the Lord, and we are so thankful to God that all of them are Christians and desire to serve the Lord in all they do.

The legacy my father left me—one that my wife and I have worked hard to pass on to our children—will be passed on to our grandchildren, great-grandchildren, and so on. What happens, though, when such a legacy (standing on the truth of God's Word) is not passed on to the next generation?

When the Australian Aboriginal people were discovered by Captain Cook in 1770 as he sailed up the eastern coast of Australia, they were an animist culture. They lived in fear of evil spirits and curses from witch doctors. They didn't know the God of the Bible. The Aborigines were considered "primitives." Sadly, some 100 years later, Darwinian evolution fueled such a view of these people. Of course, they were not "primitives" as some evolutionists claimed. In fact, they had lost something valuable that they once had.

On the basis of biblical history, the Aborigines had the same ancestor that we all have. Their great, great, great … grandfather, many generations ago, was ours: Noah. Noah, the great shipbuilder, worshipped and obeyed the true God. What happened, then, to the Australian Aborigines? Somewhere in their past, one of the generations lost the legacy of godly Noah. They failed to communicate it. And it only takes one generation to completely obliterate such a legacy.

In Judges 2:10–11, we read: *When all that generation had been gathered to their fathers, another generation arose after them who did not know the* Lord *nor the work which he had done for Israel. Then the children of Israel did evil in the sight of the* Lord, *and served the Baals [idols]* (NKJV). In just one generation, the legacy of the previous generation was lost!

FAMILY **NOVEMBER 9**

Dads and Moms, what legacy are you leaving your children? Are you doing what you should be to ensure that the next generation is not "primitive" spiritually? The best type of legacy any parent could leave their children is a love of the Lord and His Word.

The ministry of Answers in Genesis, the Creation Museum, and the Ark Encounter are all a legacy of my parents who taught us as a family to love God and His Word and trust in the Lord Jesus Christ for salvation. By example, they taught us to be unashamed and bold for the Christian faith. They also taught us to never knowingly compromise the Word of God.

"A good man leaves an inheritance [legacy] to his children's children" (Proverbs 13:22).

NOVEMBER 10
Matthew 6:19-21

A Life Well Lived

We all knew "the call" was coming and prepared ourselves as best we could. Dad had been sick off and on for some time, and this time we knew that he would not be getting better. I was in a hotel room in Indianapolis when the call came from my late brother Robert.

Dad and I had talked many times about what I should do if he were to die while I was conducting a seminar. Dad had told me, "Kenneth, if I die there's really no point in coming back, because I won't be here. It will be more important to preach God's Word so others can join me in heaven." So I decided to stay and speak—to honor what my father would want. By God's grace, I was able to complete the seminars over the next several days. Our family then flew to Australia.

During a special memorial service, my five siblings and I shared memories of Dad. We all used different words but conveyed the same basic theme: He always stood up for what he believed, he taught his children to love the Word of God, and he always insisted God's Word be authority over the fallible words of man. At the end of the service, a dear friend of the family came up and said, "After a service like that, I'm challenged to go home and ask my children what they're going to say about me when I'm dead!" His remark sparked a vision for a book to address the question that all parents should ask: What kind of legacy will you leave behind to future generations? The updated version of this book is called *Will They Stand: Parenting Kids to Face the Giants*.

My father's legacy began with his birth on October 22, 1928, on a little-known island near the northern tip of Australia (Thursday Island). When he was 16, his father died, so he turned to his heavenly Father for direction, stability, and leadership. In the words of the Bible, he found all he needed. He chose to become an educator, as his father had been, investing his career in the next generation as a teacher, administrator, and principal. With his new bride and his Bible, he set out to make an eternal difference. As his passion for truth and the lost grew, he became a powerful and articulate defender of his faith and the Word he so desperately loved.

Through his words and life, our father seized every day to influence his world for truth and to encourage his children to love God and His Word. He imparted lessons that will be forever etched in our hearts and minds. "Whatever you do, do it 100%." Dad never did anything half-heartedly. He had chosen to serve the world as an educator, but he approached the task with an intensity that reflected the truth in Colossians 3:23–24: *Whatever you do, work heartily, as for the Lord and not for men, knowing that from the Lord you will receive the inheritance as your reward. You are serving the Lord Christ.*

"What you do at the top filters down." Leaders have great responsibility because they influence their followers. In Luke 6:40, Jesus said, *A disciple is not above his teacher, but everyone when he is fully trained will be like his teacher.* By example, Dad illustrated this truth, both in school and at home. While other principals hit the pub after work and wondered why their teachers were sluggish in the morning, Dad upheld his moral integrity, and his faculty followed. His schools were simply the best in the territory.

"Invest where it counts." Our house was a well-known stopping point for missionaries. Generous with their meager finances, possessions, and time, our parents exhibited joy in helping others. They understood and practiced Matthew 6:19–21: *Do not lay up for yourselves treasures on earth, where moth and rust destroy and* where thieves break in and steal, but lay up for yourselves treasures in heaven, where neither moth nor rust destroys and where thieves do not break in and steal. For where your treasure is, there your heart will be also.

"Take action and take risks." If they were burdened that something should happen, they made it happen, and they rarely counted the costs. We saw, time and again, the provision of God. When I look at the history of Answers in Genesis, I am amazed. The people, the vision, the provision of God every step—it's miraculous. I doubt I would have ever learned to take risks (which are really just prayerful, thoughtful steps of faith) without my parents' model.

"Defend the faith wherever you are." Australia is about the same size as the continental United States; however, the population is less than a tenth of the United States. It is a land of rich natural resources; yet spiritually, it is a barren desert. The number of born-again Christians is probably only about 1–2%. Only a very small percentage attend church. In this land of great spiritual need, our parents instilled in us the conviction to be missionaries and defenders of the faith, no matter where we happen to be.

When I came home for my father's memorial service, it turned out that he had left one last earthly gift for me. In the months before Dad died, he constructed a model of Noah's ark. True to the dimensions in Scripture, he built the small craft to scale and weighted it properly so that it could withstand waves without turning over. My father wasn't a carpenter, but he put his heart and soul into making this model something special. When I arrived home, Dad's little ark was there, floating in the pool, flying miniature flags from both Australia and the United States. The ark my father built for me rests with pride in an exhibit with Dad's Bible in the lobby of Legacy Hall at the Creation Museum called, The Ham Family Legacy exhibit. Each time I look at it, I am reminded of the inheritance my parents gave me—an inheritance that is far more valuable than silver or gold. They left an everlasting spiritual inheritance—a love for the Creator and Savior and His infallible Word. The exhibit is there to challenge others as to what legacy they are leaving in their families.

Daily, Dad would study so he could defend the Christian faith. He was adamant that if you can't believe Genesis, then you can't trust the rest of the Bible. After all, every biblical doctrine is founded in the history of Genesis 1–11. My father understood that if Adam wasn't created from dust and didn't fall into sin, as Genesis states, then the gospel message of the New Testament couldn't be true. Dad started with the belief that God's Word is our sole authority in all matters of life and in every area it touches upon (geology, astronomy, anthropology, child raising, etc.). God used my father's biblical foundation like armor to deflect humanistic, evolutionary thinking. The Bible was the axiom of Dad's life, the central point of truth around which everything revolved.

You may need to sustain a godly heritage left by your ancestors, or you may need to recreate a legacy that has been lost. Either way, it is a great challenge—a vitally important one. The way we train our children will affect the way they train their children, generation after generation. From the genesis of his legacy on Thursday Island in 1928 to the revelation of his legacy at this memorial service in 1995, God used this simple and devoted man to reach his family and then the world for his Creator. May all praise go not to my father but to the Father he served—for that is the way both would want it.

What legacy are you leaving?

NOVEMBER 11
1 Timothy 6:20

Training Up Biblical Thinkers

In 2006, *The Times* and the U.K.'s *Guardian* newspapers featured lengthy stories about an increasing number of public school students who were challenging their instructors when evolution was being taught as fact.

Not surprisingly, many secular educators were up in arms about this! This is an example of how secularists only want their views to be taught to students. It's as if left-wing people want tolerance for their views only.

The Times reported: "Sometimes disruptive, but often sophisticated questioning of evolution by students has educators increasingly on the defensive."

The article wrote of a student who "considers it his Christian duty to expose his classmates to the truths he finds in the Bible, starting with the six days of creation."

The student, *The Times* said, "studies DVDs distributed by Answers in Genesis, a 'creation evangelism' ministry devoted to training children to question evolution."[103]

I've been involved in creation ministry since 1975. Ever since I left my teaching position (I taught science in public schools in Australia in the 1970s), the Lord burdened me—and the organizations I've been involved with—to disseminate books, videos, radio programs, web articles, etc. on biblical authority as widely as possible.

Our philosophy at AiG has always been that the more we make information available to the public, the more we'll see a grassroots change in the culture. That's true of the resources we produce and the exhibits at the Ark Encounter and Creation Museum attractions.

You see, trying to counter the teaching of molecules-to-man evolution as fact in public schools is, in reality, the same problem as trying to combat issues like abortion, gay "marriage," removing "Christ" from Christmas, and so on. The culture, including the West's secular education systems, have changed the foundation they were built upon (the Bible and resulting Judeo-Christian ethic) to a different foundation (that man determines truth).

Ultimately, the only way to effectively combat this phenomenon is for people to get back to the Bible's authority and then rebuild the culture/education system. So the solution has always been God's Word. Just another reminder, we are in a spiritual battle. Secularists will do all they can to stop people even questioning their false religion of evolution.

O Timothy, guard the deposit entrusted to you. Avoid the irreverent babble and contradictions of what is falsely called "knowledge" (1 Timothy 6:20).

God's Word and the saving gospel–that is the answer to all the issues in our cultures.

NOVEMBER 12
Proverbs 31:10-31

The Vital Importance of Godly Mothers

Just as God made the role of a diligent dad clear, He has also made His intentions known regarding the role of a godly mom. Like so many other essential doctrines, the role of the woman is first established in Genesis: *The LORD God took the man and put him into the garden of Eden to work it and keep it ... Then the LORD God said, "It is not good that the man should be alone; I will make him a helper fit for him" ... So the LORD God caused a deep sleep to fall upon the man, and while he slept took one of his ribs and closed up its place with flesh. And the rib that the LORD God had taken from the man he made into a woman and brought her to the man ... Therefore a man shall leave his father and his mother and hold fast to his wife, and they shall become one flesh* (Genesis 2:15–24).

In the midst of our fallen world, it is important to remember that this was God's good and original design. We would do well to reclaim as much of it in Christ as we can. God fashioned a woman to complete what was lacking in Adam, that she might become his helper, that the two of them would truly become one.

Many other passages from God's Word reveal the role that God has designed for wives and mothers. One of the more pointed and all-encompassing is found in Proverbs 31:10–31. (This was one of my father's favorite Scripture passages. I used to hear him quote it often in relation to his thankfulness for the gift of his wife, my mother.) The verses paint a beautiful picture of the woman God designed mothers to be. Here are some excerpts: *An excellent wife who can find? She is far more precious than jewels. The heart of her husband trusts in her ... She does him good, and not harm ... She rises while it is yet night and provides food for her household ... She considers a field and buys it; with the fruit of her hands she plants a vineyard ... She opens her hand to the poor ... Strength and dignity are her clothing ... She opens her mouth with wisdom.*

These passages reveal many virtues of a woman committed to building a godly legacy for her family. She is encouraged to be a woman of character, integrity, and action. The passages even endorse her role as a respected businesswoman in the marketplace. Certainly, mothers should also be involved in teaching their children spiritual truths. I praise the Lord for my godly mother who prayed with us when we were small and continued to pray daily for us until her time on Earth ended, standing as my father did on the authority of God's Word. There was no doubt that Dad was the spiritual head and that our mother supported him in this role one hundred percent. Whether it was cooking for visitors, supporting school functions, waiting up for Dad to return from school and church meetings—I never had any inkling that they didn't do everything together as one.

Mum also balanced out Dad in important ways. One of my brothers remembers it this way: "I can recall one fairly intimate chat that I had with Mum concerning our father's demeanor. She had told me of some of the many talks she had with him when he was in the process of defending God's Word. Often she would be behind the scenes reminding him to be gentle and gracious in his approach. The guiding persuasion of a godly wife was always in his ear, reminding him of his responsibility to use his words carefully and constructively."

I praise God that He has also given me a wife like this—a wife who loves me so much that she is willing to be honest enough to help me correct my faults in a way that will enhance and strengthen our partnership in ministry. Not only should husbands listen sincerely to their wives, but we should be seeking their input and hastening their comment. Apart from Christ, they know us better than anyone in this world!

FAMILY   NOVEMBER 12

Fathers are to be the overall spiritual head. Whenever and wherever possible, the father's leadership should be as obvious to the children as it is to the wife. But the task of raising godly children in an ungodly world takes teamwork. My wife, Mally, and I did this together when I was home, and she covered for me when I was on the road ministering. Overall, our children knew and observed that I took on the headship role and Mally took on the helpmate role. That is the way we were created to function, but in the modern world, we often see the opposite—where the mother is leading and the dad is following. This is even reinforced by most Christian children's books where mention of spiritual leadership is made. Many of these books will picture a mother with the Bible open, reading it to her children, or they will instruct the children to tell their mother something or ask for her advice. Look closely at the books you have for your children, and I am sure you will see that this is a characteristic of many children's materials available for the Christian market today. On top of this, more women are becoming increasingly domineering as they take over the position as head of the home. The more I travel and meet families around the world, the more obvious it appears to me that the feminist movement has affected many women in our churches—and this affects the whole family structure.

Over the years, I have observed a number of men in the Christian ministry who have had to give up the ministry or greatly limit what they set out to do because of an unsupportive spouse. I have also observed that some children of pastors and other full-time Christian workers rebel against Christianity. I know there are many reasons for such situations. However, from my own observations and experience in traveling around the world, I do believe a significant factor relates to the fact that their wives could not cope with the husband being away or spending so much time in the demands of Christian work. I've heard such wives question their husband's ministry in front of the children and others. The husband and wife were certainly not "one" in this regard. The wife's discontent was obvious to the children. Now it's also true that some men in Christian work have greatly neglected their wives and children, forsaking their priority to be diligent dads, and that is also a problem. Regardless, it's important for a mom to ask: "Am I fulfilling my role as a helpmate to my husband, or am I undermining his role as the spiritual head of our home?"

The old saying is true: "Behind every good man is a good woman." The Ham children were blessed in heritage to be able to say that of our mother. While so many women are burdened with a heart for the superficial and material things of life, God has given a much greater responsibility: that of supportive substance—the type of supportive substance that is also founded and grounded in His mighty Word and shines like a beacon as an example to wives everywhere. I can certainly say that God has provided not only a good wife and mother, but a good woman who is a mentor for women. Mally mentors our daughters and other women who seek her counsel. I'm truly blessed by the Lord every time I see committed, godly parents—those who are living according to the roles given to us in the Bible. Mally also rejoices when she sees parents who are totally committed to the truth of Scripture and display this to their children.

Mum's presence was a definitive factor in our father's legacy. My mother loved and supported him, and she endlessly cared for her children. After Dad's passing, she had had her share of health issues, and I witnessed my brothers and sisters rally to assist her—gratitude for the biblical heritage she also strove to supply. We see it as a true privilege and service not only to our mother but our sovereign Lord.

> **When parents choose to obey God and fulfill their God-given roles as described in Scripture, God's grace and blessings abound to all around and He is glorified.**

NOVEMBER 13
John 8:31-32

The Dire Consequences of Evolutionary Storytelling

In 2006, a permanent exhibit called "Evolving Planet" opened at the Chicago Field Museum. Now the unsuspecting public does not realize that there is "storytelling" going on in the guise of what is called "science."

In an interview with *Discover* magazine, John McCarter, who was at the time the highly vocal CEO and president of this world-famous Field Museum in Chicago, responded with the following when asked to comment on whether or not the purpose of science museums has been changing. In response to the statement that museums have switched from being repositories of artifacts and information and history to being advocates for a specific viewpoint, McCarter stated: "I don't think I'd call it advocacy. Again, I call it storytelling. For example, when we open our Pre-Columbian America exhibit in 2007, we will focus on a wonderful collection of artifacts ... what we are doing now is using the artifacts to tell a story."[104]

A major part of the interview with Mr. McCarter concentrated on the Field's new $17 million exhibit called Evolving Planet. In response to the question, "Why did the museum create this exhibit?" McCarter declared: "The fundamental goal is to improve scientific literacy."

However, the sad thing is that the way the exhibit portrays the issue of origins is promoting what I would call "scientific illiteracy"! Let me explain. When most people hear the word science, they think of computers, jet planes, modern medicine, cars, electricity, cell phones, and so on—our modern technology. The technology we are blessed to use today is a result of man gaining knowledge about the physical world (e.g., the properties of metals and how they can be used to develop machines, etc.). This is knowledge that is based on what we can observe and repeatedly test in the present—a process commonly referred to as "operational science" or "observational science."

Now, when it comes to the issue of origins (the topic of the Evolving Planet exhibit), this is very different from the observational science that has helped produce our technology. "Origins science" involves beliefs about the past that cannot directly be tested—beliefs about how the universe and life arose when there were no human witnesses.

Most visitors who go through evolutionary exhibits like Evolving Planet don't realize that they are being subject to "storytelling" about the past. It's a story (evolution) that is based on the belief that everything can be explained on the basis of natural processes. It's the religion of naturalism or atheism, even though a deity or "holy book" is not mentioned in this exhibit. A gullible public is being indoctrinated in an intense atheistic "storytelling" to lead them to think about life the way the scientists who constructed the exhibit want them to think.

Even if some of the scientists involved in the exhibit claim to believe in a god (or even the God of the Bible), the fact is that the exhibit portrays the origin of life as having occurred by natural processes—with no God involved at all. Thus the public is being indoctrinated in an anti-God religion and in the guise of what is called "science." But again, this is actually "origins science," which is totally different from "observational science."

The Answers in Genesis attractions—the Creation Museum and Ark Encounter—take the same facts (dinosaurs, other fossils, etc.) that the Field Museum uses but tell a different "story" (actually historical account) of

SCIENCE

NOVEMBER 13

origins—a true "story." It's from the Creator who was an eyewitness and had the true history of the universe written down for us in His Word, the Bible.

The Answers in Genesis attractions, though, do what the Field Museum doesn't: They teach the truth about the difference between "operational science" and "origins science." In that way, true scientific literacy will be greatly enhanced for the visitors who see the various exhibits.

At the same time, AiG clearly shows that observational science (the science of genetics, for example) overwhelmingly confirms the history (true "story") recorded in Genesis but does not confirm the evolutionary history (the false "storytelling") as promulgated by the Field Museum and other secular natural history museums. And museum directors be warned! The more you indoctrinate your visitors in the "story" that life and the universe evolved by natural processes, the more you are helping to mold the thinking of the coming generations concerning their morals. After all, if life is the result of natural processes, then who determines right or wrong? Why does anyone have a right to say what is good and what is bad?

As the Bible states concerning the Israelites: *In those days there was no king in Israel. Everyone did what was right in his own eyes* (Judges 17:6).

Evolutionary storytelling is teaching people there is no "king" over them—they "own" themselves and are not accountable to anyone. Thus, we can expect to see people becoming more and more consistent with their belief in naturalistic origins, and moral relativism will pervade the nations—and it is! Moral relativism now permeates the West.

What a refreshing change it is for people to be taught how to think correctly about science and origins at the Ark Encounter and Creation Museum. That's where people learn the truth.

> "If you abide in my word, you are truly my disciples, and you will know the truth, and the truth will set you free" (John 8:31–32).

NOVEMBER 14

Romans 1:22-23

The Hopelessness of Evolution

Is molecules-to-man evolution a proven fact?

In 2005, a cover story in the reputable journal *Science* proclaimed evolution as the "breakthrough of the year." Would you be thrilled to discover that scientists at a leading magazine proclaimed 2005 as the year of a phenomenal "breakthrough," one that will help people understand that:

- Everything is meaningless, "and you'd better live with it"?
- Parents want to adopt children because of "a kind of genetic mistake"?
- When you die, there is no afterlife, and "you're going to rot in the ground"?

How's that for a message of hope and meaningful existence? But that is the ultimate consequence of believing in atheistic evolution.

Aren't you now excited to help get schools to make sure they are teaching such a "breakthrough" to students? In reality, students already are being taught this truth-alternative (read "lie"), as you'll understand when you've finished this article.

Headlines appeared in many newspapers and at websites around the globe about a cover story in the reputable (albeit blatantly evolutionist) journal *Science,* where in its December 2005 issue, evolution was proclaimed the "breakthrough of the year."

After over a century of being presented as fact in science journals, secular schools, and mainstream media, evolution is now supposedly a breakthrough of some kind. For all these years, atheistic professors and scientists (the "high priests" of the evolution belief system) have been awaiting a breakthrough, while an unsuspecting public and generations of freshly minted teachers were confidently convinced by supposedly unbiased evolutionists that it had been proven.

Now, why was evolution called the "breakthrough of the year"? The magazine listed the supposed startling evidence for evolution—which is, in reality, much of the same old stuff we've been hearing for years (and we've been rebutting for years) and we're still hearing. Here it is:

- Animals produce different species (e.g., birds called European blackcaps produce different species, but we point out, they are still European blackcaps; AiG has written many articles over the years to refute such things).
- Chimps and humans are supposedly 96% similar (AiG also has a number of excellent articles about this on our website).
- Viruses mutate or "evolve" (for refutations, AiG has a number of web articles dealing with such topics).

None of these are "breakthroughs"—they are just the same old arguments used time and time again by evolutionists and refuted by AiG time and time again.

Be encouraged. Evolutionists are greatly concerned at the inroads the creation message is making in the culture. They are alarmed at the number of people who reject evolution as polls indicate. How could this be? I believe it's because of the impact of ministries like Answers in Genesis. You will continue to see (as is happening) a lot more of this sort of propaganda from the evolutionist community.

At the same time I read the *Science* article, I came across an interview conducted with atheist/evolutionist Dr. Richard Dawkins of Oxford University, probably the world's most famous believer in evolution today.

Dr. Dawkins was asked questions about his belief system, and some of his answers followed. What should be eye-opening for everyone who reads his responses are the real-life consequences that occur when people believe in molecules-to-man evolution. And these beliefs are being taught to tens of millions of young people in public schools virtually every day.

Q: "The idea of evolution and natural selection makes some people feel that everything is meaningless—people's individual lives and life in general."

A: (Dawkins): "If it's true that it causes people to feel despair, that's tough … If it's true, it's true, and you'd better live with it."

Q: "What do you see as the problem with a terminally ill cancer patient believing in an afterlife?"

A: "No problem at all. … If I could have a word with a would-be-suicide bomber who thinks he's going to paradise, … I would say, 'Don't imagine for one second you're going to paradise … You're going to rot in the ground.'"

Q: "Is atheism the logical extension of believing evolution?"

A: "My personal feeling is that understanding evolution led me to atheism."

Richard Dawkins even said that the reason parents want to adopt children could be understood in terms of a "genetic mistake": "You could think of it [i.e., accepting a child that is not biologically yours] as a kind of genetic mistake, in that human adults have strong parental instincts which make them long for a child. If they can't have a child of their own, they can then satisfy those parental instincts by adopting a child."

At least Dawkins is honest about his beliefs! He is being honest about the devastating consequences of rejecting God. So sad.

> "Claiming to be wise, they became fools, and exchanged the glory of the immortal God for images resembling mortal man and birds and animals and creeping things" (Romans 1:22–23).

NOVEMBER 15
Romans 10:14-15

Setting Prisoners Free from Their Chains

Did you know that creation apologetics teaching is supposedly a threat to prisoners. The truth is, rather than being "a threat to the safety" of prisoners, creation teaching (including through the web) is changing lives in prisons (and society). My heart breaks whenever I hear of people who are denied access to life-changing teaching resources about our sin nature, need of salvation, and the truths of Genesis. It's even more distressing when it's denied for use with prisoners by a Christian leader! In the words of one leader (a chaplain), the creation message is a "threat to the safety" of prisoners in jails. You see, he rejected a creation book an AiG supporter wanted to donate:

"I have reviewed your request ... I am approving the list, with the request that you drop from your syllabus *When Christians Roamed the Earth*. This book and most of the conversation regarding Creationism, Intelligent Design, Evolution, etc. causes unnecessary division within the church and has led to arguments on the yard in the past ... I do not believe that the average inmate with an educational level below the national average can properly process Christian apologetics and according to policy all programs must not be a 'threat to the safety of persons involved in such activity or that the activity itself disrupts order in the institution' ACA Standards 3.4459."

Many already know that we often say that some of the most ardent opposition to the creation message comes from Christian leaders. Be encouraged, however. Thankfully not all Christian leaders involved in prison ministry are like the one above. Read what another chaplain (at a different prison) said about AiG books that we donated to his prison ministry:

"I called on Monday requesting literature you suggested and it was at the jail on Friday. Wow, was I blessed. I [also] put the AiG DVDs on closed-circuit TV."

AiG has a prison outreach where we have donated thousands of resources to prison libraries (and sometimes directly to prisoners themselves).

So, rather than being "a threat to the safety" of prisoners, creation teaching (including through the web) is changing lives in prisons (and society). Consider these testimonies:

Lives saved—"I thank the Lord for your ministry ... God has used the truths of creation to significantly impact a number of lives in a ministry in our county jail."

"One man stated, 'I've gone to church all my life but I've been an atheist. Since coming to Bible study, I now believe in God.' In two weeks he placed his faith in Christ."

From a Bible study in a jail (California) we were sent this: "All of the Christian brothers meet on the yard every night that we are allowed to have 'night yard,' and I brought a Bible study on the AiG book *The Great Dinosaur Mystery Solved*. A very enlightening study. Some men just passing by were intrigued and stayed for the entire study. Praise God!!"

Booklets go like "hotcakes" (Florida)—"The booklets [witnessing booklets shipped by AiG] went like hotcakes. I think they stayed on the shelf only two days!"

RESOURCES

Well, it doesn't sound as if AiG materials are causing disruptive behavior or a safety threat! This is why we have donated thousands of dollars' worth of resources to jails each year. Sadly, many Christian leaders do not agree with Answers in Genesis in regard to our stand on a literal Genesis. And such leaders are leading many people astray and denying giving people the teaching they really need.

How then will they call on him in whom they have not believed? And how are they to believe in him of whom they have never heard? And how are they to hear without someone preaching? And how are they to preach unless they are sent? As it is written, "How beautiful are the feet of those who preach the good news!" (Romans 10:14–15).

> We all need to keep in prayer those who are incarcerated and see ways either personally or through the church or a specialized Christian jail ministry to do all we can to reach them with the truth of God's Word beginning in Genesis and the saving gospel.

NOVEMBER 16

Matthew 11:28-30

The Pilgrim Who Made Much Progress

Have you ever heard of the "pilgrim" who "preaches" from a grave? I'm sure you will recognize him. I want to bring to your attention the type of person everyone should look up to as one of the real heroes—a hero for the Christian faith: John Bunyan (who was saved from a rough background). He:

- Fixed pots and kettles for a living
- Voluntarily enlisted in the military
- Astonished people with his swearing
- Had over 60 published works
- Was indicted for preaching without a license
- Was known as a "non-conformist"
- Spent 12 years in jail
- Saw thousands flock to hear him preach
- Has a tomb that still "preaches" every day
- Is buried in a very famous graveyard in London
- Believed God created the universe in six literal days
- Had one of his books translated into over 2,000 languages
- Wrote the second best-selling book ever (second only to the Bible)

These are just some of the fascinating facts about one of the most famous preachers and writers in history. They describe the Englishman John Bunyan, author of what has been called the most successful allegory ever—*Pilgrim's Progress*.

In a day when so many people in the Church look to pagan movies, sports, music stars, and other non-Christian "media darlings" as heroes or heroines, I want to bring to your attention the type of person everyone should look up to as one of the real heroes—a hero for the Christian faith: John Bunyan.

John Bunyan was a non-compromiser. Back in 1656, he became one of the "non-conformists." After Cromwell's famous time of the "Protectorate" came to an end, the government in England tried to stop the growth of independent churches and forbade preaching by anyone other than those licensed to do so in the state church—the Church of England.

Bunyan refused to stop preaching the Word of God and was eventually imprisoned in 1660 in an attempt to get him to conform. But what men meant for evil, God meant for good. It was during one of his jail terms that he began writing the now-famous *Pilgrim's Progress* (the first edition being published in 1678).

Over 300 years later, *Pilgrim's Progress* is still a best seller, continuing to "preach" the gospel message to young and old alike. It came from the pen of a hero of the faith who stood on his convictions and would not compromise God's Word, which clearly tells us to preach the gospel to every human being.

THEOLOGY   NOVEMBER 16

The non-conformists at that time were not allowed to be buried in the normal church graveyards—they had to be buried in other locations. In London, one of the most famous non-conformist graveyards is called Bunhill Fields (opposite the chapel of John Wesley, the famed evangelist).

Bunyan's tomb stands in this graveyard right near a path that thousands walk on every day. I visited on one of my speaking tours to the United Kingdom and stood and watched all these people walking past his grave, most (if not all) oblivious to what they were passing. On each side of the tomb of this hero of the Christian faith are sculptures that sum up the message of *Pilgrim's Progress*. One sculpture shows the book's main character, Pilgrim, with the burden on his back, and one shows Pilgrim kneeling before the Cross with that burden falling off his back. What a summary of the gospel! And it's being "preached" from Bunyan's tomb every day.

Some great verses from Scripture that sum up part of the message of *Pilgrim's Progress* are these: *Come to me, all who labor and are heavy laden, and I will give you rest. Take my yoke upon you, and learn from me, for I am gentle and lowly in heart, and you will find rest for your souls. For my yoke is easy, and my burden is light* (Matthew 11:28–30).

> And, yes, as you would expect from such a non-compromiser, Bunyan believed in six literal days of creation, as he wrote in his exposition of the first 10 chapters of Genesis.

NOVEMBER 17

Ephesians 2:8

All Creation Groaning in Judgment

Understanding death, suffering, tragedy, and disease and how those mesh with the loving God of the Bible has been an ongoing struggle for people, whether Christian or not. After the 9/11 terrorist attacks on New York City and Washington, DC, after the massive tsunami in the Indian Ocean that killed thousands, and the deadly Hurricane Katrina disaster in 2005 on the Gulf Coast of America, people responded with the question: "Why does God allow this?"

Now in an article written by Nancy Gibbs for the online service of *Time* magazine (with references to the biblical account of Noah's Flood, God's rainbow promise, and Jesus' calming the wind and water), the writer searched for answers to the age-old question as to how to reconcile death and suffering with the loving God of the Bible. In reference to Noah's Flood, she stated: "The story holds the promise of the rainbow, but that does not ward off the painful search for meaning every time man's negotiations with the land and sea and air appear to have collapsed, as they have so often in the past year or so." She added that "the cataclysm of Katrina has been blamed on everything from SUV drivers to coastal developers to the Army Corps of Engineers." And, of course, we hear "climate change" blamed for everything from floods, to hurricanes, to even earthquakes!

Then this author moved on to quote "answers" from the religious community: "Then there is the response of those convinced they know God's Politics and are just as intent on seeing the guilt assigned. An ultraconservative Israeli rabbi declared that Katrina was retribution for U.S. support of the Israeli pullout from Gaza. Louis Farrakhan of the Nation of Islam called Katrina judgment for the Iraq war. The Christian Civic Group of Maine noted that the hurricane struck just as New Orleans was planning a huge gay-rights festival. A Kuwaiti official said, 'The Terrorist Katrina is One of the Soldiers of Allah.' There was, in other words, broad agreement in some far-reaching quarters that Katrina represented God's punishment, just no consensus on the sin." The author added that catastrophes like this result in "a revival of the familiar question, Why God Lets This Stuff Happen."

She continued: "The survivors often say God saved them—how many baby girls will be named Katrina?—but if he chose to save the living, did he choose to kill the lost? It is an occasion for atheists to remind believers of the flaws in the case for a benevolent God, and even the most mainstream pastors acknowledge that at times like this they are pressed for answers about how a loving God lets hateful things happen. 'Of course, this makes us doubt God's existence,' declared the Archbishop of Canterbury after the Asian tsunami, before calling his country to deeper prayer. The search for answers is part of the natural journey of faith; it is a mystery beyond our understanding, or a part of a larger plan, or the price we pay for free will, or God's tap on the shoulder, calling us to attention and mercy … [An evangelist] called Katrina 'perhaps the worst tragedy America has known since the Civil War.' But he added, 'It may be the greatest opportunity to demonstrate God's love in this generation.'"

I must admit that I often get frustrated at the Church when its leaders are not seen to be giving real answers. Nancy Gibbs noted that mainstream pastors acknowledge they are pressed for answers about this issue. And then there's the above quote from the Archbishop of Canterbury (considered the leader of the Church of England) admitting that such tragedies make us "doubt God's existence." Now, I believe the major reason

APOLOGETICS

most of the Church cannot (or does not) have logical answers to give the world is most have either given up or ignored the foundational importance of the history in Genesis 1–11. Because most Christian leaders have rejected the geology, biology, anthropology, and astronomy of Genesis 1–11, accepting instead the secular beliefs concerning the past (evolution and/or millions of years), they have disconnected the Bible's history from the real world. They just do not understand how the Fall affected everything, because the world of death they live in, to them, has gone on for millions of years. The Bible gives us an account of the major events of history concerning the past to enable us to understand the present.

- Why do we die? Because man rebelled against God (Genesis 3)—we are all sinners.
- Why are there fossil layers all over the earth? Because there was a global Flood—Noah's Flood.
- Why are there different languages and cultures?

The Bible gives us an account of the origin of sin and death and thus that we are living in a fallen world. This is not the world as God originally created it. Thus, the Bible's history connects to death, fossils, dirt, plants, animals—to everything. It is not just a book of moral and spiritual matters, but a book of history that connects to every aspect of reality and explains what we observe in this present world. As Christians, we should not be trying to fit death and suffering into the Bible but, using the history God has revealed to us, building the right way of thinking (worldview) to correctly understand the origin of death and suffering. Ultimately, because of man's sin, the whole creation is groaning in judgment (Romans 8:22) by this act of high treason committed against the God of creation. We human beings committed high treason (our sin) in Adam against the God of creation. We deserve nothing. We don't deserve to exist. Sin has consequences, and yet, we complain because we have to suffer those consequences. Yet, even with all that, God provided a way for us to come back to Him and have eternal life with our Creator. Christian leaders will not be able to even begin to give answers until they accept Genesis 1–11 as real history (and real science) and begin reconnecting it to the real world. Obviously, the author of this *Time* commentary was crying out for answers. But I really don't believe she would understand the real answer unless she changed her thinking about the Bible.

Non-Christians can't connect a loving God to tragedies because they have no understanding of Genesis 1–11 and how those chapters connect to reality. They have been so secularized in their thinking that they are looking at the issue from the wrong foundation. Most Christians can't connect a loving God to tragedies like Katrina because they either don't believe Genesis 1–11 is real history (and thus don't have a connection to the present to explain this present world) or they don't know how to connect Genesis 1–11 to the present even if they believe it because they have become so secularized in their thinking. In most instances, they can't even recognize this has happened. Until we are prepared to acknowledge we are all sinners (for we sinned in Adam) and not even deserving of the life we have, we will not understand tragedy issues. Until we are prepared to acknowledge that we (not God) are responsible for the mess of this world, we will not understand natural disasters. *For by grace you have been saved through faith. And this is not your own doing; it is the gift of God* (Ephesians 2:8).

> **Until we understand that our loving God stepped into history to save us from the mess we caused, we will not understand who He is and what He has done for us in providing a means of salvation so we can live forever with Him.**

NOVEMBER 18
Matthew 6:19-21

Real Tragedy: Lost Souls

My heart is saddened when I think of violent storms or tornadoes that take people's lives. Even while you read this, something catastrophic could be happening somewhere in the world that will result in people being killed. Bodies die and decay. And Paul in the New Testament describes our bodies as "tents" we live in (2 Corinthians 5:1). We will live forever either with God or separated from Him in hell—something we deserve because of our rebellion (sin).

I also realize that millions of dollars' worth of people's properties are often destroyed as a result of such catastrophic events. Beautiful old and new buildings alike can be destroyed.

In no way do I want to take away from people's grief at the loss of loved ones or of homes and businesses, but I want us to consider a perspective from the Bible. First, the Scripture tells us to "bear one another's burdens" (following Christ's example), and so we all need to help each other—and because we ALL sinned, and thus we are all (collectively) responsible for the mess this world is in, we all should help each other... particularly in a time of tragedy and disaster.

But the most important issue that we should all make our highest priority concerns the state of people's souls. After all, each soul will live forever in heaven or hell. Hebrews 9:27 says: *And just as it is appointed for man to die once, and after that comes judgment.*

When I was in Israel, my heart was greatly moved as I viewed the remains of various palaces built by Herod some 2,000 years ago. Herod wanted to be known as a great builder. He built a massive, luxurious palace at Caesarea Philippi, and he constructed three luxurious palaces on the top of the famous mountain known as Masada. Herod was not concerned about his soul—he was more concerned about the material things of this world (that don't last).

In Matthew 6:19–21, we read: *Do not lay up for yourselves treasures on earth, where moth and rust destroy and where thieves break in and steal, but lay up for yourselves treasures in heaven, where neither moth nor rust destroys and where thieves do not break in and steal. For where your treasure is, there your heart will be also.*

As far as we know from history, Herod's spiritual state was such that he died without receiving the Lord, and thus he faced eternal separation from God—suffering the "second death." His soul lives on forever, but the great buildings he had constructed as his memorial/legacy on Earth have all but crumbled into dust.

Yes, we grieve with our brothers and sisters when tragedy occurs. We should reach out to them if possible and help where we can as the Bible commands us. At the same time, we need to be ready to give answers about how Christians can reconcile a God of love with death, suffering and destruction. This, of course, enables one to explain how life came to be, what our problem is (sin), the resulting judgment of death, and what the solution is in Jesus.

In addition, be reminded that the most important thing in the whole universe is to be concerned for souls. People need to understand that the material things of this world will not last—but as real, living human beings, they will last forever.

APOLOGETICS *NOVEMBER 18*

There are many reminders in this fallen, groaning world that the things of this world are so fragile, so temporary. Let us pray that through the tragedies of destructive events, people will be convicted about the state of their souls, and many would turn to the God of creation and be saved:

[I]f you confess with your mouth that Jesus is Lord and believe in your heart that God raised him from the dead, you will be saved (Romans 10:9).

> Lives are often lost because of disastrous events, but if their souls are lost for eternity, that is the real disaster.

NOVEMBER 19

Genesis 9:13-16

Flood: Worldwide, Not Local—It Makes a Difference

I assert that those Christians who believe in evolution and/or millions of years destroy the fundamental nature of the Bible. Here is one major problem (there are many, but I want to focus on one): Those Christians who believe in evolution and/or millions of years just cannot allow "it." But what is the "it"?

To allow "it" would destroy the fundamental nature of what they believe.

To allow "it" would mean that their belief in the supposed millions of years in the fossil record never existed—this "it" would eliminate millions of years of supposed history.

The "it" would show that God does not break His promises. So to reject "it" would mean God breaks His promises!

So what is the "it"?

The "it" refers to the global Flood of Noah's day. Let me explain.

I find it fascinating that a compromiser like Dr. Hugh Ross from Reasons to Believe (a Christian organization that promotes the idea that God created over millions of years) recognizes that he can't believe in a global Flood and millions of years at the same time. He has accepted the millions-of-years time frame of the secular world. So he believes Noah's Flood was just a local event.

It is obvious that if there was a global Flood, this catastrophic event would have eroded billions of tons of sediments . . . and then would have deposited them all over the world. (As a comparison, just look at what happened with the small, local catastrophe of the 1980 eruption of Mount St. Helens and the almost immediate formation of massive sedimentary deposits.)

Think about it: If you accept a real global Flood, then you destroy (rightly) evolution's millions of years of history, as supposedly recorded in the fossils found in the layers of rock. You see, the eroding of these layers by the Flood—and then the "redepositing" of the sediments and the destroying of many of the fossils—would eliminate much of this "evidence" of these alleged millions of years. It's an important point.

In his book *The Genesis Question*, Ross states:

"Most skeptics (and even non-skeptics) assume that a Flood of such immense proportions would leave behind substantial evidence, a deposit that geologists should be able to find."[105] Ross doesn't believe such evidence exists.

Well, let me put it another way: if there really was a global Flood, you would expect to find billions of dead things buried in rock layers laid down by water all over the earth ... which is exactly what you do find! The evidence for a global Flood is "staring" at us from all over the world.

Now, recognizing there are massive sedimentary layers laid down by water all over the earth and full of dead things, Ross continues by stating:

APOLOGETICS — NOVEMBER 19

"The assumption that clear evidence 'should' remain must be challenged. The Flood, though massive, lasted but one year and ten days. A flood of such brief duration typically does not leave a deposit substantial enough to be positively identified thousands of years later."[106]

Of course, how could that be "typical" when he has never experienced such a flood of that duration? So what do you do when the evidence is obviously there? You just wave it away with a "magic wand" by saying there is no way an event we've never witnessed could do that (even though we've seen many local catastrophes cause massive erosion and enormous deposition of sediments)?

Consider this passage of Scripture:

I have set my bow in the cloud, and it shall be a sign of the covenant between me and the earth. When I bring clouds over the earth and the bow is seen in the clouds, I will remember my covenant that is between me and you and every living creature of all flesh. And the waters shall never again become a flood to destroy all flesh. When the bow is in the clouds, I will see it and remember the everlasting covenant between God and every living creature of all flesh that is on the earth (Genesis 9:13–16).

In Genesis 9, God promised that He would never again send a Flood to destroy all flesh and cover the earth—the rainbow being the sign of that promise. There have been lots of floods since Noah's day, but never a global one. To believe in a local flood, then, is to say that God broke His promise.

The Flood was a major event in Earth's history. Those who believe in millions of years ardently reject that this global event ever occurred. By doing so, they (whether Christian or non-Christian) are proclaiming that the words of Genesis 6–9 cannot be taken as written. If that's so, should anyone believe the rest of Genesis (or the rest of the Bible for that matter) as written?

Oh—and as I've detailed many times before in various articles, when a Christian believes in millions of years, then they have accepted that death and diseases like cancer have existed before man's sin. This blames God for death, disease, and suffering instead of our sin.

Now here is a lesson about the ark everyone needs to take seriously:

> Just as Noah and his family had to go through a doorway into the ark to be saved, so each of us needs to go through a doorway to be saved: Jesus Christ, the Son of God, is our ark of salvation.

NOVEMBER 20
2 Corinthians 10:4-6

Biblical Dinosaurs Make Secular Heads Spin!

Almost every time there's news in the secular press about Answers in Genesis, the reporter will mock the fact that we believe dinosaurs and humans have lived at the same time. They really cannot stand the fact that we reject the naturalistic evolutionary timeline of millions of years and accept God's Word in Genesis as literal history.

Indeed, evolutionists absolutely hate it when AiG uses dinosaurs to proclaim the falsity of the idea (religion) of evolution and the truth of the history in Genesis. Nearly every secular reporter who visits the AiG Creation Museum seems perplexed as to why we're including dinosaurs—and they often express amazement that we would even dare to do so.

Children and adults alike are fascinated by these creatures. Unfortunately, most people equate dinosaurs with millions of years and the evolutionary belief system. Dinosaurs have become almost icons for evolutionary teaching—they're treated as sacred "gods" that belong only to evolutionists for their purpose of indoctrinating generations (particularly children) in secular humanism.

Sadly, the Church, by and large, handed dinosaurs over to the "world" when so many Christian leaders abandoned the literal history so clearly communicated in Genesis and allowed belief in millions of years and evolutionary ideas (like the big bang) to be taught to generations. Well, over the years, we at Answers in Genesis have put the evolutionary secular humanists on notice when we stated: We're taking dinosaurs back!

For example, when you walk into the Creation Museum, you'll see animatronic dinosaurs and children together—you'll find a special dinosaur exhibit explaining them from a biblical worldview perspective—and you'll see them in books found in our museum gift store.

To the humanists, we are saying that we have invaded your evolutionary temples, and we have gone into your "holy of holies." We have captured the dinosaurs … and we're taking them back to give them their rightful place in history! They don't belong to you!

And, no, it's not ridiculous to believe dinosaurs and people lived at the same time (as the Bible makes very clear)—but it is ridiculous to believe life arose by itself from matter! It is ridiculous to believe dinosaurs grew feathers and changed into birds! It's ridiculous to believe humans are related to bananas as Bill Nye said to me—from an evolutionary perspective all life, animal and plant is related. Do you realize how absurd evolution really is? It's a religion—an anti-God religion where man worships the creature and not the Creator. It's Romans 1 happening before our eyes.

Now, think about it: According to evolutionary time, crocodiles have been around since the time of the dinosaurs—and yet, humans live with crocodiles today. So why is it ridiculous to think humans and dinosaurs lived at the same time?

But it's not just crocodiles—there are many other examples. On AiG's website, there's an article that quotes a leading evolutionist who said that finding what is called the Wollemi pine tree in Australia was like finding a "live dinosaur." This is because the tree, nicknamed the Wollemi pine, is known from fossils classed as so-called Jurassic age, supposedly around 150 million years ago, but not from fossils in rocks of later periods.

RESOURCES
NOVEMBER 20

Humans and the Wollemi pine tree live together today, and yet from an evolutionary perspective, the Wollemi pine dates back to the "time of the dinosaurs." That's why the evolutionists called it the "dinosaur tree."

While we don't find fossils of the Wollemi pine tree and humans together, we do know they live together—because both are alive today. So why then would it be so ridiculous to think that dinosaurs also lived beside humans but have died out in recent times? Even the news in March 2005 of soft tissue in dinosaur bones is consistent with this.

Of course, there's a lot of other interesting evidence, such as dragon legends, the description of Behemoth in Job 40, a number of petroglyphs that some believe look like dinosaurs, and so on.

Nothing in observational science contradicts the obvious conclusion based on the Bible's history:

- Dinosaurs (a word invented in 1841) were a subgroup of all land animals that were created alongside man around 6,000 years ago.
- Representative kinds of them were on Noah's ark.
- Most dinosaur fossils are from the Flood (about 4,500 years ago).
- Dinosaurs lived beside man after the Flood but, like lots of other animals and plants, have become extinct since that time.

No, as we proclaim in our Creation Museum, it's not ridiculous to believe dinosaurs and humans lived at the same time. In fact, it's the most logical belief based on the Scriptures and the fossils!

For the weapons of our warfare are not of the flesh but have divine power to destroy strongholds. We destroy arguments and every lofty opinion raised against the knowledge of God, and take every thought captive to obey Christ, being ready to punish every disobedience, when your obedience is complete (2 Corinthians 10:4–6).

More and more ground is being captured every day as we're reclaiming what rightfully belongs to the God of creation!

NOVEMBER 21
Genesis 26:18

Re-digging the Wells

This is a time when all Christians must "re-dig the wells." Let me explain.

One of my favorite preachers of all time (actually my favorite) is Martyn Lloyd Jones. I can't tell you how much I have benefited from his sermons. They are available on the Internet (and via an app) at MljTrust.org. David Martyn Lloyd Jones (December 20, 1899–March 1, 1981) was a Welsh Protestant minister, preacher, and medical doctor who was very influential in evangelical Christianity in the twentieth century. For almost 30 years, he was the minister of Westminster Chapel in London.

I was listening to a series he had on revival and loved his application on digging wells. After listening, I thought, "All of us need to be doing something that is so desperately needed for our nation's future—we need to be 're-digging the wells' that the Philistines had stopped up."

You see, in Genesis 26:18, we read: *Isaac dug again the wells of water which had been dug in the days of Abraham his father, which the Philistines had stopped after the death of Abraham.*

Isaac needed life-giving water to survive in the land. But the Philistines had stopped the flow of water from the wells by filling them in. To get to the vitally needed water supply, Isaac had to work hard to re-dig the wells and overcome what the Philistines had done.

Sadly, we're in the same situation today. Philistines (the secular humanists) have greatly affected the water supply (i.e., the life-giving water of God's Word) by filling in the wells (indoctrinating generations of students and their parents in evolutionary ideas and millions of years) and thus have adversely affected the flow of water. Most people today build their thinking on man's word instead of God's Word. Thus, moral relativism permeates the culture that was once very Christianized. For example, God's Word has been basically thrown out of public (secular, anti-God) schools, and the Christian worldview is being removed more and more from the culture.

Answers in Genesis is a ministry that we truly believe God has raised up to help God's people overcome the work of the Philistines through "re-digging wells." With this re-digging, the nation can again find what once flowed so freely through the culture—the "living water" of God's Word. We pour out this "living water" in many ways including through the two attractions, the Ark Encounter and Creation Museum.

The "Philistines," though, are great in number. And much more "digging" is still to be done. Indeed, the "water supply" has been greatly restricted in our Western nations.

Through all the various outreaches of AiG including our two attractions, we are working hard to "re-dig the wells" to see an abundant supply of God's "living water" that the culture so desperately needs. We all need to be re-digging wells.

The real difference between what AiG is doing in this day, compared to the great Christian leaders and outreaches of the past, is to promote an understanding of what the Philistines have done in our time to plug up the wells and stop people from knowing about the "living water" of His Word. We have an emphasis that

APOLOGETICS

is so needed on teaching people to think foundationally, to be equipped with apologetics, and to understand the saving gospel.

There's no doubt that the teaching of evolution and millions of years has been the key issue in our present era that has attacked and undermined the authority of the life-changing Word of God in the culture (and, sadly, also in much of the Church).

We understand the tools the enemy has used through the Internet, museums, social media, secular schools, etc. so we need to do our best to deal with this onslaught.

Make sure you are digging wells.

NOVEMBER 22

Romans 1:22

Newton, Pascal, Pasteur–Epitome of Stupidity?

Claiming to be wise, they became fools (Romans 1:22).

How would you like to fly in an airplane produced by chance random processes—no intelligence involved? Well, I challenged the terribly confused writer of the editorial entitled "They Have Designs on Darwin" from the *Philadelphia Daily News* back in 2005 to do just that! After all, if she really understood what she wrote in her editorial, that's a flight she might think twice about attempting!

For me, I want to ride in a plane that's been carefully designed and repeatedly tested by human intelligence—based in a real world with operating laws we can trust, not based on chance, random processes for construction. If any airplane manufacturer applied Darwinian evolutionary philosophy to its engineering, well, they would be out of business (actually, they wouldn't even get into business in the first place). Aerodynamics expert Professor Andy McIntosh of England has shown very clearly how flight requires precise design and that the design of birds is still giving us lessons today about flight.

In yet another slam against creationists (which seems to be the "in" thing for many secular journalists these days), the *Philadelphia Daily News* chief editorial writer, Carol Towarnicky, once wrote with the same gross misunderstanding of what the words *science* and *evolution* mean that continues plaguing the secular world—making what I could only say are quite silly statements about airplanes, medical technology, evolution, and so on. Quite often, if you don't have any substance to your arguments except generalizations (that are grossly inaccurate), you also resort to ad hominem arguments (i.e., "name calling"), stating things such as not believing in evolution but believing in creation is "stupidity." Fortunately for them, such journalists were not around in the days of such epitomes of so-called stupidity as Newton, Pascal, Maxwell, Pasteur, and the other creationist founders of modern science (many of whom were contemporaries of Darwin and rejected his views)!

Towarnicky stated, "Modern medicine is built on the truths of evolutionary biology." Of course, she hasn't the slightest qualifications in medicine. For further confirmation, I talked to the late Dr. David Menton, who was associate professor emeritus in anatomy at Washington University School of Medicine (one of the leading medical colleges in America) and someone who was once awarded the school's "Professor of the Year" award. I read the Philly editorial to him (by the way, he was an AiG speaker who accompanied me at many teaching conferences) and asked for his comments. He replied: "If evolution were thrown out of consideration, it would have no negative impact [in medicine]—it plays no necessary role in either the teaching or practice of medicine. This is not to imply it's not believed by most or that it doesn't come up. It does come up from time to time, but from the lectures I've attended, when it does come up, it's mentioned in passing as almost a confession of faith. It doesn't contribute materially to the topic. The professors can't spend too much time on evolution, as they have too much real medical knowledge to get across to the students. Spending a lot of time on evolutionary speculations just wastes time. If you remove evolution, there's nothing in the whole realm of empirical science that you can't pursue."

Dr. Menton added that he could give numerous specific examples where, in fact, evolutionary ideas have actually impaired our understanding of biology and medicine. For instance, Dr. Menton stated: "In the realm of medicine, many evolutionists say that the retina of the vertebrate eye in general is 'upside down,' which means the light-sensitive cells face away from the light rather than at the top facing the light. If there were a designer, you would expect it to be made 'properly,' with the cells facing forward. In evolution you expect things to be junk—to be poorly and inappropriately constructed. On the other hand, if there were a Creator you would expect the human body—including the retina—to be optimally constructed."

Dr. Menton more fully addresses the "proper" design of the eye in various articles and videos. I want to mention that evolutionists like Richard Dawkins (who has no qualifications in ophthalmology or optics) scoff at the idea that God created the eye. He states: "Any engineer would naturally assume that the photocells would point towards the light with their wires leading backwards towards the brain. He would laugh at any suggestion that the photocells might point away from the light" (*The Blind Watchmaker,* 93–94, 1986).

Dr. Menton said that on the basis of evolution, one would have no real reason to study why the retina is "upside down"—after all, that's what evolution did. However, he says: "Scientists who ignored the claims of evolutionists have looked to this nonintuitive arrangement of the retina and have found it to be optimally organized. When you do this, you find out all sorts of compelling reasons why this arrangement is optimum, which enables one to have a better understanding of the mechanisms involved." Thus, what you find is really what you would expect to find on the basis of an intelligent designer, not chance random processes. Dr. Menton continued, "The teaching of Haeckel's embryonic recapitulation, now known to be a fraud, actually put back embryology nearly 100 years. Haeckel's faked diagrams are still in many public school textbooks."

So we had a challenge for Carol Towarnicky: Please give one example where an engineer (of any sort—electrical, civil, etc.), a biochemist, or a medical technician would not have been able to develop technology or carry out their duties if they didn't base it on a naturalistic (i.e., evolutionist) belief concerning origins! And please don't give us again the example of "germ resistance" that you gave in your editorial for the medical technician's part—you need to first read articles on AiG's website to understand what is going on here. None of the mechanisms has anything remotely to do with "goo-to-you" evolution. Certainly, some of these mechanisms involve mutations and natural selection (note that the creationist Edward Blyth thought of natural selection 25 years before Darwin). However, properly understood, these actually illustrate that there is no mechanism to change one kind of creature into another. What is happening only involves either sorting already existing information or eliminating it and occurs within each kind of animal (and plant).

The trouble is that Towarnicky, like millions of others, had not been taught to understand "science" correctly. She couldn't distinguish between "operational science" (i.e., investigating cells, studying genetics, building airplanes, testing resistance in bacteria, and so on) and beliefs about the past. She's obviously been indoctrinated by an education system and media (like millions of others) to think that the belief aspect of Darwinian evolution is the same as operational science—and that's simply not true.

I do feel for these people and want so much to get the truth to them. In a way, they don't know what they're saying because they have been brought up in schools that have locked God out and won't even allow students to be taught correctly about how to think concerning science. Now they make foolish statements.

> **Next time you go to the doctor, take medicine, or fly in an airplane, be thankful that scientists using operational science (repeatable, testable science), without having any basis whatsoever in naturalistic evolution, produced the technology or product that is involved.**

NOVEMBER 23
Proverbs 1:7

Inherit the (Media) Windbags

It's not surprising, sadly, that such a prestigious newspaper as *The New York Times* would print such a disjointed, irrational, and absurd commentary as the one written by Maureen Dowd on February 3, 2005. She is still a columnist for *the New York Times* as I write this in 2024.

"It is a tale ... full of sound and fury; signifying nothing." This quote from Macbeth appropriately describes what was probably the most bizarre newspaper commentary dealing with the creation issue that I had ever seen. And that's saying something since I've seen "countless" such commentaries over the past 40+ years.

What an apt illustration of the verse of Scripture from Romans 1:22: *Claiming to be wise, they became fools.* The writer of this commentary was the winner of the 1999 Pulitzer Prize for distinguished commentary. But as a secular newspaper reporter said to me during an interview the day of the release of this bizarre commentary, "That's not the sort of article I would send to a prospective employer when applying for a journalism job!"

So what was I fussing about? Well, the commentary in question was titled "Inherit the Windbags." Apparently, this is taken from the anti-Christian and demonstrably deceitful Hollywood movie *Inherit the Wind*, supposedly based on the 1925 Scopes trial. Maureen Dowd, no doubt, thinks that the movie was a true account of the event, but it was a fictional version meant to denigrate Christians.

The commentary began by asking a question about male nipples and then informing people about the AiG Creation Museum near the Cincinnati airport. Interesting transition—male nipples to the Creation Museum and back to a creationist-mocking discussion about male nipples!

Dowd proceeded with more mocking commentary about creationists. Of course, as was usual, no real scientific issues were discussed—nothing of substance. And then, the clincher: She transitioned to Iraq and President Bush. Based on a statement Bush made in 2000, she mocks the president for apparently not believing evolution as fact. She mentions the warning stickers in textbooks in Cobb County, Georgia—then the tree of knowledge—then Dick Cheney and Newt Gingrich—Vietnam—"Happy Days"— *Roe v. Wade*—stem cells—and on to Bush's statements about social security!

Dowd obviously wanted to slam Bush for his views on social security. And how does one do that? Well, you start with male nipples and the AiG Creation Museum, of course!

So what was the connection? I'm not sure, but my (fallible) understanding of this article is that she seemed to be saying that belief in the Bible and creation are outdated, ridiculous ideas. She apparently sees creationists as dismantling the progress of modern thinking and returning to primitive ideas. She then connected Bush to the creation/evolution controversy and proceeded to blast him over his policies, claiming he was dismantling the advances of the whole twentieth century!

If columnists want to make such ridiculous statements about creationists, why not, instead of hiding behind their pen, agree to a real live debate! We publicly said at the time that "We're ready, Maureen Dowd—but a word of advice, don't debate like you wrote!"

SCIENCE
NOVEMBER 23

"The fear of the Lord is the beginning of knowledge; fools despise wisdom and instruction" (Proverbs 1:7).

NOVEMBER 24

2 Timothy 3:16-17

Standing on the Authority of the Word of God

One of my favorite phrases is, "Here I stand ... "

One of my favorite movies was *Luther*, a professionally dramatized account of the life of Martin Luther, the great reformer. Now, I know he, like each of us, was not perfect, and the movie didn't deal with many of his inconsistencies (which we all have), but despite whatever "warts" he had, he is one of my "heroes of the faith." God mightily used him. As I watched this gripping movie, I was moved time and again. At one point, as Luther stood in the bishop's palace and responded to the demand that he recant his writings about biblical authority, he purportedly said, "Here I stand. I can do no other. God help me." He was saying, "Here I stand on Scripture."

God used one man and his stand on God's Word to start a Reformation, which spread like wildfire around Europe. At that time, much of the Church had compromised on a major doctrine: justification by faith alone.

One of my favorite Bible teachers is Dr. Martyn Lloyd Jones. He is widely acclaimed as Britain's greatest preacher of the twentieth century. In one of his sermons on revival, he stated this, concerning the history of the Church:

"The concealing, and the neglect of certain truths, and certain aspects of Christian truth, has always been the chief characteristic of every period of declension [decline] in the long history of the Church."

He continued: "If you read the history of the Church, and look at these periods of declension, when the Church was moribund and did not seem to count at all, you will find that without a single exception the thing that has most characterized the life of the Church at such a time has been either a denial, or else a concealing, or else a neglect of certain vital truths which are essential to the whole Christian position."

Dr. Lloyd Jones exclaimed, "No revival has ever been known in the history of the churches which deny or ignore certain essential truths."

As we look at the West today, we see that the Church (or what is left of it from a local church perspective) is often emotionally excited (e.g., lots of praise teams and singing) but has not been experiencing true, life-changing revival. The Church is not reaching the culture as it once did. A Bible-based worldview does not pervade the thinking of the majority in churches as it used to.

- Christianity has all but been removed from public (secular) schools.
- Nativity scenes are thrown out of public places.
- The Ten Commandments are being removed.
- Gay "marriage" is rife across the West.
- Politicians are trying to normalize the LGBTQ worldview with transgender, etc.
- Abortions are prolific.
- The West is becoming less Christianized every day. Something is terribly wrong. Why does the Church seem so weak, especially in America when there is more Christian influence than any other nation on Earth?

APOLOGETICS

NOVEMBER 24

I suggest to you that Dr. Lloyd Jones was right. As has been the case all through Church history and as was the situation at the time of the Reformation, the reason the Church seems so weak and ineffective today is that there has been a "denial … a concealing … a neglect of certain vital truths which are essential to the whole Christian position."

And even though much of the Church today does not recognize a vital truth that has been compromised, I believe God has raised up ministries like Answers in Genesis to engage the Church and the culture (as Luther did), concerning a truth that has been denied and neglected.

The absolute authority and trustworthiness of God's written Word has been (and is increasingly being) denied, concealed, or neglected—and it starts with a gross neglect/compromise in a specific area.

So, what is the "truth" that has been compromised? It is the truth of the infallibility of God's Word—especially in the first book of the Bible, Genesis.

The absolute authority and trustworthiness of God's written Word has been (and is increasingly being) denied, concealed, neglected, and compromised in Genesis 1–11. Why? Because of the influence of fallible man's ideas concerning evolution and millions of years. The truth of Genesis 1–11 is "essential to the whole Christian position" because:

If the Church continues to reinterpret God's Word in Genesis based on man's fallible ideas, then the Church has opened the door to undermine the authority of all of God's Word. And Genesis 1–11 is the foundation for everything. Thus, rejecting the truth of Genesis 1–11, or neglecting it, is undermining the foundation for the rest of the Bible, for all doctrine, for the gospel, for a true Christian worldview, and, in fact, for everything.

By placing man's opinions in authority over the Bible, the authority of the Bible has been, by and large, lost from this culture. It is no longer a credible book (i.e., authoritative) in the eyes of the majority of people and particularly with Generation Z. There's been a catastrophic generational loss. Thus, the standard of morality based on the Bible (such as the immorality of gay "marriage," transgender, and abortion) is no longer accepted.

Every single doctrine of theology (e.g., marriage defined as one man for one woman, two genders—male and female, original sin, the gospel, etc.), whether directly or indirectly, is founded in the literal history of Genesis.

Many today are praying for revival. At the same time, I want to challenge the Church with the words of Dr. Lloyd Jones: "I am urging that there are certain truths which are always essential to revival. And while these truths are denied, or are neglected, or ignored, we have no right to expect the blessing of revival."

In many ways, I see the ministry of AiG as somewhat akin to that of Luther: to restore a truth that has been denied in the culture in this day (i.e., the truth of God's holy, inerrant Word, beginning in Genesis). Like Luther, we exclaim, "Here we stand [on Scripture]. We can do no other. God help us."

All Scripture is breathed out by God and profitable for teaching, for reproof, for correction, and for training in righteousness, that the man of God may be complete, equipped for every good work (2 Timothy 3:16–17).

> **We need to strive to help "rebuild the foundation" of God's Word beginning in Genesis in the Church and thus impact the culture.**

NOVEMBER 25
John 12:43

Unnecessary Compromise of Biblical Authority: Part 1

Why is it that so many Christian academics and leaders compromise God's Word in Genesis with evolution and millions of years? I want to explore this using the example of a well-known Christian scholar in the United Kingdom.

Dr. John Lennox, professor of mathematics at the University of Oxford (England), wrote a book titled *Seven Days That Divide the World* (Zondervan, 2011). Dr. Lennox is highly respected as an evangelical in the United Kingdom. There is no doubt he preaches the gospel and also is orthodox in his teaching of the Word of God (except when it comes to Genesis). Because he is obviously an active Christian with a very amenable disposition, he has a position of considerable influence on the conservative Church in the United Kingdom, in Eastern and Western Europe, and increasingly in the United States.

His book challenges biblical creation with a series of arguments that the staff members at Answers in Genesis have answered many times over. In fact, as I read Dr. Lennox's book, Ecclesiastes 1:9 came to mind, which states, *What has been is what will be, and what has been done is what will be done, and there is nothing new under the sun.*

Dr. Lennox is a much-admired Christian professor in the United Kingdom, but sadly, his book paints biblical creationists in a bad light. His arguments, which have all been used by others against biblical creation at one time or another, have been answered in various articles on the Answers in Genesis website.

I found it very interesting that Dr. Lennox referenced only one creationist article (from 1999) in his book, despite the breadth of current materials available. Answers in Genesis alone has published numerous books and articles written by experts in their fields. But Dr. Lennox instead chose to reference secularists and Christians who have compromised on Genesis. Not one of the well-known and respected biblical creationist researchers and writers (many with PhDs from respected secular universities) was referenced.

I watched a short video clip where Dr. Lennox was debating the famous atheist Dr. Richard Dawkins. On the surface, Dr. Lennox's response to Richard Dawkins made it seem as though Dr. Lennox is prepared to allow for God to use the evolutionary process in the creation of human beings. However, in his 2011 book *Seven Days That Divide the World*, he makes it clear that Adam was made from the dust of the ground and not from a preexisting creature (69–74). Regardless of which view of human origins that Dr. Lennox accepts, I suggest that Dr. Lennox has one hermeneutic (method of interpreting Scripture) for Genesis 1–11 but a different one for the rest of Scripture. There is no doubt that Dr. Lennox would not use his hermeneutical approach (taking ideas from outside the Bible to reinterpret the Genesis account of creation) when dealing with the virgin birth or the Resurrection.

In his book, one of Dr. Lennox's first attacks on biblical creation is to redefine what it means to read the Bible "literally." He writes, "When we are dealing with a text that was produced in a culture distant from our own both in time and in geography, what we think the natural reading is may not have been the natural meaning for those to whom the text was originally addressed" (22–23). Biblical creationists who believe the Genesis account of six literal days of creation are reading the Bible "literalistically," according to Lennox.

APOLOGETICS

At Answers in Genesis, we hold to a historical-grammatical hermeneutic.

Dr. Lennox tries to make his case that biblical creationists read the Bible "literalistically" by using as an example a line from Hannah's prayer in 1 Samuel. Hannah's prayer is not an account of cosmology, and Dr. Lennox should know better than to claim it as such. She was using figurative language—in this case, a metaphor, which is an implied comparison:

For the pillars of the earth are the Lord's, and on them he has set the world (1 Samuel 2:8).

Hannah is clearly referring to the might of God, who upholds the world by the word of His power. But Dr. Lennox sets up what is called a straw man argument (i.e., an argument by which a person misrepresents his opponent's position and proceeds to refute that misrepresentation rather than the actual claim). He implies that young-earth creationists cannot tell the difference between passages that are figurative and those that are not. But if one does a detailed comparison between poetic and narrative passages in the Old Testament, it is easy to show the vast differences between poetry and narrative.

As the book continues, readers find out that Dr. Lennox is very concerned about the reputation of Scripture.

"We don't wish to appear scientifically illiterate and bring the Christian message into disrepute.... Most of us would surely agree that it is important to distinguish between matters that belong to the core message of the Bible and issues that are less central" (32).

But my question for Dr. Lennox is, What about authority? If Scripture is inspired, then it contains no errors—and we can trust it as authoritative in all matters, including science. Scripture is not subject to the scientific opinions of the day. If the world reviles Scripture, let it be because the truth of Scripture is offensive, not because the world witnesses the blatant compromise going on within the Church.

I also suggest there is an issue here concerning how those Christians in academia are viewed by the academics of the world. One question we have been asked many times over the years, and even more so in recent times, is this: "Why is it that so many Christian academics and leaders compromise God's Word in Genesis with evolution and millions of years?"

Here is my hint for the answer:

> "[F]or they loved the glory that comes from man more than the glory that comes from God" (John 12:43)

NOVEMBER 26
John 12:43

Unnecessary Compromise of Biblical Authority: Part 2

Continuing to answer the question, "Why is it that so many Christian academics and leaders compromise God's Word in Genesis with evolution and millions of years, in reference to the writings of John Lennox from England?"

Having pondered this and carefully considered the reactions when we challenge such compromisers with what God clearly states in His Word, we believe it often comes down to the issue of academic/intellectual pride and academic peer pressure.

In an era when there has been so much emphasis on college education, there has been a great deal of peer pressure to fit in with the academia of our age. It seems to us that many Christian leaders and academics are prepared to be scoffed at for believing in the Resurrection or the virgin birth, but they do not want to be called "anti-intellectual," "anti-science," or "anti-academic" (even though such claims are false) for believing in six literal days, a young earth, a global Flood, and a literal Adam and Eve.

In that sense, perhaps the words of John are fitting here? *[F]or they loved the glory that comes from man more than the glory that comes from God* (John 12:43).

Because evolution and millions of years are really the anti-God religion of this age, the secular academics intimidate Christians into adopting their ideas (as many do, thereby compromising God's Word in Genesis) to avoid being deemed "anti-intellectual."

And it is true that it is almost impossible for a known six-literal-day, young-earth creationist to be published in the major journals of our day, whether the journals deal with science or theology.

On the issue of inspiration and authority, Dr. Lennox raises another common argument against a literal Genesis: "Genesis is, of course, a text that comes to us from a time and culture very different from our own. It is from the ancient Near East, so we cannot simply read it as if it were a contemporary Western document written to address contemporary Western concerns."[107]

Of course, when such an argument is used to deny the historicity of Genesis, it totally contradicts what Scripture says about its own perspicuity (i.e., clarity)! Paul said in 2 Timothy 3:16–17, *All Scripture is breathed out by God and profitable for teaching, for reproof, for correction, for training in righteousness, that the man of God may be complete, equipped for every good work.*

While Dr. Lennox is correct that it can be helpful to know the cultural context in which Genesis was written, many others who promote this argument wrongly believe that the Genesis account of creation originated in those pagan myths. This thinking about the ancient Near East falsely assumes that we cannot understand Genesis without first understanding the pagan myths from the time.

In regard to such arguments, most evolutionists do not believe the first humans could write. However, Genesis 5:1 states the following:

This is the book of the generations of Adam (Genesis 5:1).

APOLOGETICS

The Hebrew word translated book means "written account" and is translated as "book" or "scroll" elsewhere in the Old Testament. There is no reason not to believe that Adam could write and probably did write down the account of creation as revealed to him by God and also kept a written record of key historical events from the creation week until at least Genesis 5:5, which was passed down with the writings of the other patriarchs (Noah, Shem, Terah, Isaac, Jacob, etc.) eventually to Moses.

In more arguments that have been refuted multiple times, Dr. Lennox questions the meaning of the Hebrew word *yom*, translated day, and attempts to find ways to incorporate millions of years before and during creation week. He even offers detailed explanations of other "interpretations" of Genesis in the accompanying appendixes, including the idea that Genesis 1 and 2 allegedly contradict one another. AiG writers have refuted these "interpretations" many times before. Such articles are easily accessed on the Answers in Genesis website.

As the years go by, the arguments against a literal Genesis do not seem to change. And the arguments to counter them do not change either—because God's Word never changes. We have to be diligent in exposing the error that is prevalent even in the teachings of our churches and from fellow Christians such as Dr. Lennox. The above arguments are just some of the problems with Dr. Lennox's book. You can read a more technical review of *Seven Days That Divide the World* in the free online Answers Research Journal.

Dr. Lennox (quoted in part 1) preaches the gospel, and no doubt, people have been led to Christ through his teaching of God's Word. However, that does not discount the fact that his teaching on Genesis and his compromise with evolution and millions of years undermines the authority of the Word of God in spite of his sincere intentions to the contrary. Such collective compromise by numerous Christian leaders has been a major contributing factor to the demise of the Church in our Western world. In England, research indicates about two-thirds of young people do not believe in God, and church attendance plummeted from around 60% to about 5% of the population. Even though the gospel is preached in places, the big picture is one of a Church that has been devastated, leading to an almost spiritually dead culture in England.

This should be a warning to the West. Where England is today other countries including America will be tomorrow—for the same reasons. Increasing numbers of Christian academics take positions similar to that of Dr. Lennox.

> "[F]or they loved the glory that comes from man more than the glory that comes from God" (John 12:43).

NOVEMBER 27
2 Thessalonians 2:11

Yes, Evolution Is Still a Lie

In 1987, my first book was published. The title of that book, which is still in print, is *The Lie*. Where did the idea for that title come from? Well, consider this verse of Scripture:

Therefore God sends them a strong delusion, so that they may believe what is false (2 Thessalonians 2:11).

Yes, evolution is a lie. It is a false religion. The book, *The Lie: Evolution/Millions of Years,* became a bestseller. Even though I updated the book, it is still the main message of the Answers in Genesis ministry. We call that message "The Relevance of Genesis."

Many books simply go out of print after just a few years, but *The Lie* has remained quite popular, with new printings almost every year. I have received more testimonies of changed lives as a result of people reading *The Lie* than any other book I've authored or coauthored.

Back in 1999, I decided to celebrate the book's 25th anniversary by carefully reading through it and then updating and expanding it. As I read through *The Lie* 25 years after it was first published, I actually found the experience to be a heart-gripping and emotional one.

On a number of occasions, I stopped reading and said to myself, "Wow. I'm using the same arguments from the Bible today as I was back then to counter the arguments of people in the Church who compromise evolution/millions of years with the Bible."

I wondered why. But the answer quickly became clear. The Bible's teachings haven't changed. God's Word remains the same today as it was yesterday. Yes, if you stick with Scripture, the arguments against compromise don't change!

After I pondered the above observation, I also realized that the Answers in Genesis ministry has not wavered! We have stayed true to the proclamation of the creation/gospel message! Whereas so many leaders in the Church have been reinterpreting God's Word in Genesis to fit with man's fallible ideas of evolution/millions of years, the Lord has burdened us and enabled us to stand strong and maintain the purity of the message. I do not want to ever knowingly compromise God's Word. Yes, we continue to stand boldly without compromise on God's Word from the very first verse!

The title of *The Lie* is just as apt today as it was in 1987. You see, the book discusses the delusion that the Apostle Paul taught about in 2 Thessalonians 2:11. In fact, the delusion that began in Genesis 3 (*the lie* the devil used with Adam and Eve) continues today. That great lie is that God's Word cannot be trusted—and that man's word is more trustworthy than God's. Down through the ages, generations have been deluded by this lie.

In this era, the teaching of evolution and millions of years is a great delusion. It has led people, inside and outside the Church, to believe *the lie* that God's Word cannot be trusted for its history. Sadly, this mindset has led to a devastating loss of commitment to biblical authority, one that has greatly weakened the Church and nation spiritually. One consequence I believe is God's withdrawal of His blessing in the once-Christianized West.

APOLOGETICS — NOVEMBER 27

Over the years, many people have likened the reformation message of Answers in Genesis to that of a "prophetic"-type message. As I reread *The Lie*, I realized that the warnings the book presented for God's people in 1987 have actually come to pass before our very eyes: that is, we are experiencing the horrible consequences of the Church and culture not standing on God's Word beginning in Genesis.

The Lie is just as relevant, powerful, and eye-opening for the Church today as it was when first published. Its message is an essential one to help all of us to understand the great delusion that permeates our world! It is a vital message for our time. It's a message to help people understand that Genesis 1–11 is true—it's the true history God has revealed to us about the origin of life and the universe. And Genesis 1–11 is the foundation for all doctrine, for the gospel, for the rest of the Bible, and, in fact, for everything. We need to shout from the rooftops, "The history in the Bible beginning in Genesis is true, and that's why the gospel based in that history is true."

Sadly, *the lie* of evolution has led many people astray and caused them to reject the history in Genesis. Once they reject this history, they have rejected the foundational history for Christianity.

[I]f the foundations are destroyed, what can the righteous do? (Psalm 11:3).

Genesis 1–11 is like the foundation of a house. If the foundation is destroyed, then the structure collapses.

> So many Christians can't defend the Christian faith or explain what they believe and why because they don't believe and start with the foundational Book of Genesis.

NOVEMBER 28

Matthew 7:21

Don't Let the Door Shut on You!

We are seeing more and more "false prophets" arising in the Church today. These teachers ultimately deny the true, saving gospel that everyone needs to heed.

Let's consider this verse of Scripture: *[A]nd the door was shut* (Matthew 25:10).

In the Matthew 25 passage referred to above, we read the parable of the ten virgins. Five wisely kept their lamps lit as they awaited the return of the bridegroom, and five were foolish. From the context of this chapter and the preceding one, this passage helps expose the difference between nominal Christians (i.e., in name only) and true Christians.

John Gill, in his well-known Bible commentary, discusses the nominal and real Christians referred to in Matthew 25. He writes that there will be those who make "a profession of religion, and yet, at last, [will] be shut out of heaven."

The word *virgins* in the parable describes those who are betrothed to Christ. Five neglected their steadfast preparation and let their lamps go out and missed the joyful return of the bridegroom. They represent those who outwardly look like believers but inwardly are not true Christians.

I have sometimes wondered whether the "foolish virgins" could apply to many church leaders/academics today—those who say they are Christians but have rejected the authority of God's Word. They have relied instead on man's fallible ideas to determine truth. These leaders may have never truly been born again as the Bible teaches and, among other things, have put their trust in "the scholars" or other religious leaders rather than the Word, Jesus Christ. Now, don't misunderstand me, just because a church leader doesn't believe in six literal days of creation and a young earth does not mean they are not a Christian. But I do believe there are many church leaders who may not be truly saved.

In essence, such "Christians" have placed their faith in the writings of man over the clear teachings of the Word—and also over many biblical doctrines, including the Fall of Adam and Eve into sin (Genesis 3).

Sadly, we are seeing more and more "false prophets" arising in the Church today. These teachers deny the literal Fall and dismiss a sin nature inherited from a real Adam. Thus, they ultimately deny the true, saving gospel that everyone needs to heed.

These church leaders and academics outwardly profess to believe in Christ, but like the false prophets of Jeremiah's day (e.g., Jeremiah 23:9–40) and the Pharisees of Jesus' day (Matthew 23:11–36), they are leading God's people astray. One day, they will find that "the door is shut." It's all so very sad. We must "keep our lamps lit" (Matthew 25) and also continue our prayers for those who are not prepared for the return and judgment of Christ.

I pray that none of the readers of this article would be counted among the "foolish virgins" and that the door to heaven is not shut to them. Make sure your heart is truly right with God, that you are truly born again and believe God's Word.

THEOLOGY

NOVEMBER 28

In Genesis 7, we read the account of Noah and his family (eight people total) who went through the door of the ark to be saved from a watery judgment. These were the only people living in the pre-Flood world whose hearts were right with God and who believed God's promises.

Noah is also mentioned in the New Testament. In 2 Peter 2, the Apostle Peter warns us about false prophets in the Church—leaders who profess that their hearts are committed to the true God but are really false teachers. Outwardly, they were prophets/teachers, but inwardly, their hearts were not right.

In verse 5, Peter describes Noah as a "preacher of righteousness" and someone who was saved. But Peter points out that false teachers cannot expect to escape divine vengeance. Just as God shut the door when Noah and his family were on the ark and just as those whose hearts were not right with God suffered the judgment of the Flood, false teachers will not be on board today's ark of salvation, Jesus Christ, when He comes again (this time in judgment). The door will be shut to them.

At Answers in Genesis, we are burdened to proclaim the gospel of Christ and the fact that only those who go through the open door can be saved.

And the Lord shut him in (Genesis 7:16).

Jesus, the Son of God, said *I am the door. If anyone enters by me, he will be saved* (John 10:9).

I believe there is a great danger today in the Church—an increasing number of "Christian" academics and pastors who may intellectually believe in God, but inwardly (and only God knows), their hearts may not be right with God—like the "foolish virgins." And certainly, only Jesus, who is the Word, can ultimately judge their hearts (Hebrews 4:12).

Now I am not saying that if a person denies the creation account of origins and believes in evolution/millions of years, he or she can't be truly saved. After all, God's Word simply states that, *[I]f you confess with your mouth that Jesus is Lord and believe in your heart that God raised him from the dead, you will be saved* (Romans 10:9).

Please pray for these academics and pastors in Christendom who are leading so many people astray. Pray that the Lord will convict them to make their hearts right with God while the "door" (the Lord Jesus) is still open.

> **Remember, "Not everyone who says to me, 'Lord, Lord,' will enter the kingdom of heaven, but the one who does the will of my Father who is in heaven" (Matthew 7:21).**

NOVEMBER 29
Joshua 4:6–7

Show Them a Sign

After Joshua led the Israelites across the Jordan River in that miraculous event, he found 12 stones and built a memorial, so that *this may be a sign among you. When your children ask in time to come, "What do those stones mean to you?" then you shall tell them that the waters of the Jordan were cut off before the ark of the covenant of the LORD. When it passed over the Jordan, the waters of the Jordan were cut off. So these stones shall be to the people of Israel a memorial forever"* (Joshua 4:6–7).

Joshua's stones were to be a sign to remind future generations of what God had miraculously done for them so they would not forget.

In God's Word, we can read of a number of signs (or reminders) that help us never forget the truths of the Bible. For example, the rainbow of Genesis 9:13 was established as a sign that God would never again judge the world with a global Flood. Also, in 1 Corinthians 11, the cup and the bread were established as reminders to Christians not to forget what Christ has done for us in salvation.

When God told Noah to build the ark, it was meant to be a sign (or reminder) of three major things:

That God is Creator, and thus, we are accountable to Him. This is why He has a right to judge our sin with the penalty of death. He is a righteous, holy God and thus has to judge wickedness.

That God is a God of grace. Noah's ark was built as an ark of salvation. Those who went through the doorway were saved. In fact, even before man sinned (Genesis 3), God, from eternity, had established a way of salvation for man.

God keeps His Word. He established the rainbow as a covenant that He would never again judge the wickedness of man by a global Flood. However, God's Word makes it clear (2 Peter 3) that He will create a new heavens and a new earth after a final judgment (by fire).

In that passage from 2 Peter, we read that people are going to "willfully forget" (i.e., deliberately reject) that there was a creation and a global Flood and reject that God will keep His word concerning the coming judgment by fire:

For they deliberately overlook this fact, that the heavens existed long ago, and the earth was formed out of water and through water by the word of God, and that by means of these the world that then existed was deluged with water and perished. But by the same word the heavens and earth that now exist are stored up for fire, being kept until the day of judgment and destruction of the ungodly (2 Peter 3:5–7).

AiG stepped out in faith to build a life-size Noah's ark. It was built to be a sign—a reminder that:

God is Creator and thus we are accountable to Him. We are sinners under the judgment of death.

God is a God of grace. He has provided a way of salvation. Noah's ark is a "picture" of Jesus. As Noah and his family had to go through a door to be saved, so we need to enter through a door to be saved. Christ, in John 10:9, declared that: *I am the door. If anyone enters by me, he will be saved.*

APOLOGETICS

God keeps His Word. There will never be another global Flood, but there will be a final judgment—next time by fire. To be saved from the final judgment and its consequence of being eternally separated from God (because of our sin) in eternal fire (Matthew 25:41), we need to be in the ark of salvation: the Lord Jesus Christ.

In Noah's day, the majority of people did not believe God's warning about a coming Flood. The majority was wrong and was judged accordingly. Today, we live in an age when the majority of scientists mock the idea that there ever was a global Flood. Generations of young people are being indoctrinated to believe that the worldwide fossil graveyard is the record of millions of years of evolution. In reality, though, most of it is the graveyard of the Flood!

Our world needs a sign that shows millions of souls that God's Word is true and that He offers a free gift of salvation in Christ. Our sign is the building of the full-size Noah's Ark in Northern Kentucky. It serves to engage non-Christians with the truth of God's Word and affirm the faith of all who believe that the words of Jesus are true!

We have been in the last days since Jesus stepped into history to be the God-man. We pray that the life-size Ark will be a powerful sign to the world that God's Word is true, and people need to respond to the gospel message:

[K]nowing this first of all, that scoffers will come in the last days with scoffing, following their own sinful desires. They will say, "Where is the promise of his coming? For ever since the fathers fell asleep, all things are continuing as they were from the beginning of creation." For they deliberately overlook this fact, that the heavens existed long ago, and the earth was formed out of water and through water by the word of God, and that by means of these the world that then existed was deluged with water and perished. But by the same word the heavens and earth that now exist are stored up for fire, being kept until the day of judgment and destruction of the ungodly (2 Peter 3:3–7).

> **We live at a time when many reject that God created, that God sent a global Flood, and that Jesus will return and judge the earth with fire and make a new heaven and earth.**

NOVEMBER 30
Genesis 6:5–8

Fossils: Past Judgment, Future Judgment, and Salvation

The LORD saw that the wickedness of man was great in the earth, and that every intention of the thoughts of his heart was only evil continually. ... So the LORD said, "I will blot out man whom I have created from the face of the land, man and animals and creeping things and birds of the heavens, for I am sorry that I have made them." But Noah found favor in the eyes of the LORD (Genesis 6:5–8).

Where is the most horrific graveyard in the world?

It's a record of death, disease, and violence.

It's a record of billions of dead things buried in rock layers laid down by water all over the earth. We call it the fossil record.

But when did this graveyard of death occur—before Adam sinned?

Let us consider what the Bible teaches concerning life before Adam ate the forbidden fruit and sin entered the world, and compare it to the fossil record.

In Genesis 1:29–30, God instructed Adam and Eve to eat fruit and herbs, and He tells us that the animals ate plants. After the Flood, God told Noah he could now eat "everything," as he once ate plants (Genesis 9:3). In other words, Adam and Eve were originally vegetarian, but God changed the people's diet after the Flood.

Since God's instructions to animals were written in the same way as His instructions to Adam, it is obvious that the animals were originally vegetarian too. Look at these verses:

And God said, "Behold, I have given you every plant yielding seed that is on the face of all the earth, and every tree with seed in its fruit. You shall have them for food. And to every beast of the earth and to every bird of the heavens and to everything that creeps on the earth, everything that has the breath of life, I have given every green plant for food." And it was so (Genesis 1:29–30).

Every moving thing that lives shall be food for you. And as I gave you the green plants, I give you everything (Genesis 9:3).

The Bible makes no specific statement about when animals started eating each other. However, it had to be after sin—not before.

It is important to remember that the Bible is primarily a book about man and his relationship with God, not a book about animals. So we wouldn't expect to find detailed teaching concerning animals as we do man. Nevertheless, we can certainly apply what we do know from Scripture to an understanding of the animal kingdom.

At the end of creation week, when God had "finished" His work of creating, He described everything He had made, including all animals, plants, and Adam and Eve, as "very good" (Genesis 1:31).

When God uses the phrase "very good," what would that mean? Consider what happened when Jesus, the Creator, walked on the earth as the God-man. He had compassion on people who were sick, and He healed them. Would this same God call disease "very good"? In Luke 18:19, Jesus makes it clear there is only one who

APOLOGETICS — NOVEMBER 30

is "good," and that is God! When God described the creation as "very good," there would be no death, disease, suffering, or deterioration from old age. So, at the end of creation week, animals would not have been eating each other, they would not have suffered from any diseases, and they would not be dying from old age. It was a "very good," or perfect, creation.

Because of sin and as a part of the curse, God stated that "thorns and thistles it [the ground] shall bring forth for you" (Genesis 3:18). So there would have been no thorns in the creation before the curse.

What do we observe in the world today? We see animals eating each other, animals dying from diseases and old age, and thorns growing everywhere. Writing in the context of the effects of sin, the Apostle Paul says that the "whole creation has been groaning" (Romans 8:22).

Now, understanding all this, let us look at the most horrific graveyard in the world—the fossil record. Is it like the world today or the world before Adam sinned? We observe:

- Evidence of animals eating other animals
- Evidence of disease, such as cancer

Now secularists believe that most of the fossil record, which spreads over the majority of the earth's surface, was laid down over hundreds of millions of years—long before man appeared on the earth. (And, sadly, many Christians have adopted their ideas.)

I believe the Bible makes it quite clear that thorns, disease, and carnivory originated after Adam's sin. So the view that creatures lived and died millions of years before Adam's sin totally contradicts the Bible.

This horrific fossil graveyard had to be formed after Adam sinned—after the curse. So what formed the graveyard? The global Flood of Noah's day makes sense of the formation of such a fossil record.

The Garden of Eden could not have existed on top of this graveyard. Instead, most of this graveyard had to be formed by the burial of creatures during the Flood.

This horrific graveyard serves as a reminder that God's Word is true (He really did flood the whole earth, as recorded in Genesis 6–9). It is also a reminder that God will judge the world again, but next time by fire. This will be the final judgment.

Just as God provided an ark of salvation for Noah and his family (and anyone else, if they wanted to go through the door to be saved), so He has provided an ark of salvation for us—the Lord Jesus Christ.

Jesus said, *I am the door. If anyone enters by me, he will be saved* (John 10:9). My plea for you is that you would know for sure you are in the ark of salvation!

> **Let the horrific fossil graveyard always remind you of past judgment, future judgment, and the ark of salvation.**

DECEMBER 1
Hebrews 12:1-2

Should We Have Christian Heroes?

Some Christians call Hebrews 11 the "Believers' Hall of Fame." There, God recorded for us the names of some great (but not infallible, I might add) "heroes of the faith."

I have often thought about one of them, Noah (even more so with our huge Ark Encounter attraction). The only people to board the ark he built were his family and Noah himself. Now, have you ever thought about the fact that nowhere in Scripture does it indicate Noah knew how long he would stay on the ark? Noah had faith God would see him through.

I also think of other heroes of the faith like Martin Luther. In the sixteenth century, he was willing to stand on the authority of God's Word in spite of the powers that be—and regardless of the consequences. His actions helped launch something that we today know as the Reformation.

I definitely think of my parents as heroes. They trained me to stand uncompromisingly and boldly on the authority of God's Word. Also, I consider men like the late Drs. Henry Morris and John Whitcomb heroes of the faith; they started the modern creationist movement with the publishing of the book *The Genesis Flood* in 1961. In addition, I think of the late Dr. Duane Gish of ICR, who will always be known as the world's greatest creation/evolution debater.

Yet Another Hero

As a singer, dinosaur sculptor, author, teacher, and children's workshop leader, Buddy Davis became a "hero" for young and old at Answers in Genesis.

Over the years, parents have brought up their children to learn from various AiG speakers and writers. Many of them have said Buddy Davis (a talented musician and builder of many of the incredible dinosaurs in our Creation Museum who passed away in August of 2024) is their hero. Kids just love Buddy. I have seen many children run up to Buddy at seminars or at the museum to give him a hug or get his autograph.

Sometimes that "hero status" is given to other AiG speakers. Frankly, it was awkward to hear that at first. After all, we are just fallible humans. But then one mother told me: "I would rather my children look at AiG speakers as heroes than a pagan movie star, or some other famous non-Christian as their hero."

We soon realized a few things:

- It's good for children and teens (and adults) to have Christian heroes as models in their lives.
- At the same time, we know we have an incredible responsibility to ensure we don't let such praise "go to our heads"; we want to give the glory to the Lord Jesus in all we do.
- It's sobering too for AiG speakers and writers when they remember the verse: *Not many of you should become teachers, my brothers, for you know that we who teach will be judged with greater strictness* (James 3:1).

Buddy Davis, a hero to so many children, has many videos on our Answers TV streaming platform. Perhaps God will use it to make Buddy a Christian hero for many more kids!

THEOLOGY

DECEMBER 1

Young people need heroes like Buddy. Here's a man who stands on the Bible's authority, sings songs about God's Word, builds quality museum exhibits, and teaches the truth about God's Word beginning in Genesis.

I remember the first time I met Buddy. He and his wife Kay attended one of AiG's first conferences. There in Mt. Vernon, Ohio, in 1994, Buddy dropped off some of his dinosaur sculptures so they could be on display at our teaching conference.

After the conference, Buddy asked if I would go to his house nearby and see his other dinosaur models. When I saw them, I declared something like: "These dinosaurs will help give people a better understanding of what we want to put inside the future Creation Museum."

At that time, Buddy and his wife Kay shared with me that they too had a burden that their dinosaurs be used in a creation museum. That evening, I found out Buddy could also sing, and I asked him to perform a song. I was moved as he sang and decided right there that Buddy would perform that same song at the opening of the Creation Museum (which occurred 13 years later!). And he did just that.

Buddy Davis has become an "icon" of the AiG ministry and Creation Museum. And yes. I admit it! Buddy is one of my heroes too!

The Lord brought Buddy and Kay into our lives to be a key part in enabling the Creation Museum to become a reality and have used their talents in other ways to proclaim biblical truths. Praise God!

Buddy had some health issues that stopped him being active as he was, but his legacy lives on in the many videos and books he produced. He passed away in 2024.

After I read Hebrews 11, I love to read the next few verses in chapter 12:

Therefore, since we are surrounded by so great a cloud of witnesses, let us also lay aside every weight, and sin which clings so closely, and let us run with endurance the race that is set before us, looking to Jesus, the founder and perfecter of our faith, who for the joy that was set before him endured the cross, despising the shame, and is seated at the right hand of the throne of God (Hebrews 12:1–2).

> **Wouldn't you rather have your children look up to Christian heroes (like Buddy) than pagan movie, sports, and music stars?**

DECEMBER 2

Judges 21:25

Divine Judgment?

I've had people ask me in recent times, "Is the West under divine judgment?" Let me give you some insight in regard to America first. Is America under judgment? is a question I've been pondering, especially when we find examples like an evangelical pastor who was reported to have said the following according to a Christian news outlet:

"Materialism, drunkard pleasure seeking, arrogant conceit, defiant sinfulness, moral perversion, and corrupt leadership ... Do you not see [them] in America? ...

"[P]eople [ask] what is wrong with this country? They have rejected the Word, the law of the Lord, the Holy One Himself."

In explaining the use of his words *arrogant* and *conceit*, this pastor added that America was largely guilty of this sin because: "When a society does not want to hear from God but wants to be its own authority where every man does that which is right in his own eyes and feels that he is the ultimate authority, he is the ultimate source of truth."

Yes, I believe America is under divine judgment. To show you how, just consider some of the ways America has progressively been trying to remove God from this culture:

- In 1962, school prayer was ruled unconstitutional by the U.S. Supreme Court.
- In 1973, restrictions on abortion were lifted, and abortion clinics began to permeate the nation (through the infamous *Roe v. Wade* decision by the Supreme Court).
- In 1985, nativity scenes in public places were ruled to violate the so-called "separation of church and state."
- In 2003, laws against homosexual sodomy were ruled unconstitutional.
- In 2004, a federal court held it was unconstitutional for a school to teach intelligent design theory as an alternative to evolution.

The "blessings" and the "curses" seen in Deuteronomy 28 embody the principles of our Holy Creator and Judge. While they were meant for the covenant people of Israel, I can't help but see some similarities between what has happened in America to what we read in the Bible concerning Israel:

Blessings: *The Lord will cause your enemies who rise against you to be defeated before you. They shall come out against you one way and flee before you seven ways* (Deuteronomy 28:7).

Curses: *The Lord will cause you to be defeated before your enemies. You shall go out one way against them and flee seven ways before them. And you shall be a horror to all the kingdoms of the earth* (Deuteronomy 28:25).

I do believe America is under divine judgment. We could basically summarize today's culture with this one verse from the Book of Judges: *In those days there was no king in Israel. Everyone did what was right in his own eyes* (Judges 21:25). I was pondering all this while watching a TV news item about a high-profile case in which a mother was charged with murdering her daughter and was found not guilty by the jury. Millions of dollars were spent on this sad and tragic case about the death of a dear child. Now, in no way do I want to diminish the shocking nature of this tragedy. But I did not hear the secular media or the general public cry out that while the nation was focused on the death of one child, thousands of children a day were being murdered in the United States by their mothers in their wombs! Think of it another way: During the two months of this trial, about over 200,000 babies were "legally" murdered in America. How does God look at this? He cannot turn a blind eye. He is a Holy Judge.

Yes, over the decades, America has been singularly blessed as a nation. After all, it was originally built on principles based on the authority of the teachings of the Word of God. But I think of this verse: *Everyone to whom much was given, of him much will be required* (Luke 12:48). I do believe this nation today is under divine judgment. But I also believe the whole Western world is under divine judgment for the same basic reasons I've discussed above regarding America. But next, I must ask: Where is the Church during this time of immorality and rejection of the Bible? Well, that is another sad story. I've mentioned many times about two influential AiG books, *Already Gone* and *Already Compromised*. The first publication was based on research that explained why two-thirds of young people were leaving the Church. We discovered that one of the main reasons was "hypocrisy." Now, hypocrisy was defined as being told to believe the Bible by some Christian leaders who don't fully believe it.

The second book, *Already Compromised*, was based on research that was conducted into what Christian colleges were teaching about the authority of the Bible. This huge study found that compromise, particularly in Genesis regarding the acceptance of evolution/millions of years, was rife in Christian academia—even in many of our so-called "conservative" Christian colleges. How can we call society to repentance when much of the Church itself has compromised God's Word in Genesis and other parts of the Bible? Sadly, we see this low view of Scripture permeating much of Christendom in this nation.

I have heard many Christians declare: "We need to change this culture!" Actually, though, the Bible does not command us to go into all the world and change the culture but to go and preach the gospel and to make disciples. It is changing hearts and minds for Christ that influences and changes a culture. *For out of the abundance of the heart the mouth speaks* (Matthew 12:34). Unfortunately, much of the Church has allowed the secular world to capture the hearts and minds of so many of their children—and, thus, it has changed the culture for the worse.

At Answers in Genesis, our goal has always been to try to influence the hearts and minds of people first if we want to see society change. As God's Word instructs us: *For the weapons of our warfare are not of the flesh but have divine power to destroy strongholds. We destroy arguments and every lofty opinion raised against the knowledge of God, and take every thought captive to obey Christ* (2 Corinthians 10:4–5).

In fact, I believe both Church and culture are under divine judgment today. I believe we need a new reformation in both our churches and Christian colleges so that generations of young people will be raised to stand on the authority of the Word of God and thus help change this culture.

> "We destroy arguments and every lofty opinion raised against the knowledge of God, and take every thought captive to obey Christ" (2 Corinthians 10:5).

DECEMBER 3
Jude 3

The Culture War's Real Battle

The Creation Museum, a Christian-themed attraction in Northern Kentucky, is not just about the topic of origins. It is a center that walks people through the Bible, helping them to understand that the history in the Bible is true, and the gospel based in that history is true.

The Creation Museum has displays of world-class fossils and other magnificent exhibits, including the most powerful pro-life exhibit in the world. But it is so much more. Since the Creation Museum opened in 2007, I have met many museum visitors who have said something like this to me:

"I was expecting to come to a place that just had displays of fossils and other items, with signs explaining them from a creationist perspective. However, this place is not just about creation, evolution, and the age of the earth. It is a walk through the Bible."

The ministry that "powers" the Creation Museum is Answers in Genesis. When we followed the Lord's leading and began the ministry in 1994, we used a temporary name of Creation Science Ministries. At our first board meeting, the main agenda item was to decide what our main mission was to be and then choose a name consistent with that mission. It was really a historic moment for this ministry.

We determined that the issues of evolution and millions of years were a "Genesis 3 attack" on the culture and also on the Church (i.e., a questioning of the Bible's authority, represented in the Genesis 3 question: "Did God really say?"). Our ministry emphasis was to be one of standing upon the authority of the Word of God and proclaiming the gospel of Jesus Christ. That's why we are so passionate about calling out compromise on Genesis that undermines the authority of the Word of God.

Over the years, we have worked hard to position Answers in Genesis as a "biblical authority" ministry first and foremost. We share that the real battle in today's "culture war" is God's Word versus man's word. AiG recognizes that there is no point in converting people to be just creationists—creationists will end up in hell just like atheists if they don't trust in the Lord Jesus Christ for salvation.

And as "creation evangelists," we are engaged in the Great Commission to go into the world and preach the gospel. But in today's world, the teaching of evolution and millions of years has had a major detrimental effect on people believing that the Bible really can be trusted. Therefore, we do specialize in the teaching of—and providing resources for—creation apologetics.

We have also seen rampant compromise in the Church and Christian colleges/seminaries, particularly concerning Genesis 1–11. This has burdened us so much that we believe a large part of the mission the Lord has called us to is to help bring reformation to the Church—calling God's people back to the authority of the Word of God.

Years ago, we developed a mission statement that helps our staff and supporters understand that we are not just a creationist ministry. We are a Bible-affirming organization that has been raised up to defend the Christian faith, stand on the authority of the Word of God, and proclaim the gospel in today's secularized culture. We are, and always have been (and make no apologies for being), a biblical authority ministry.

RESOURCES — DECEMBER 3

The first few lines in our mission statement reveal this thrust:

"To support the church in fulfilling its commission, Answers in Genesis is a catalyst to bring reformation by reclaiming the foundations of our faith which are found in the Bible, from the very first verse. We proclaim the absolute truth and authority of the Bible with boldness."

Although the origins debate is still a hot one, the most strategic battle today in our culture is a spiritual one: a struggle over the authority of the Word of God.

At AiG, we stand boldly and uncompromisingly on God's Word—upholding the authority of the Word from the very first verse! It's what is proclaimed to our visitors at the Creation Museum and Ark Encounter attractions. It's all a part of contending for the faith, as the Book of Jude exhorts:

Beloved, although I was very eager to write to you about our common salvation, I found it necessary to write appealing to you to contend for the faith that was once for all delivered to the saints (Jude 3).

We all need to be contending for the faith as we proclaim the saving gospel message.

DECEMBER 4

Job 38:4

Were You There?

Over the years, atheists have mocked me for teaching children to ask the question "Were you there?" in regard to talking about origins, the age of the earth, and so on. In fact, atheists have gone ballistic over me teaching children this because I'm teaching them how to think correctly about origins. And atheists hate that. They don't want children to understand that evolution and millions of years are beliefs—all part of the religion of naturalism (atheism).

How can anyone know what happened in the beginning if none of us were there?

Now I've had atheists say to me, "Were you there?" in their efforts to mock me.

Well, the simple answer is "No, I was not there." And I have never claimed to have been there.

This question, "Were you there?" is based on one that God asked Job, *Where were you when I laid the foundation of the earth? Tell me, if you have understanding* (Job 38:4).

By asking a series of rhetorical questions, God demonstrated that Job's knowledge was finite. Compared to God, fallible humans know next to nothing!

Job responded correctly when he stated the following:

I know that you can do all things, and that no purpose of yours can be thwarted. "Who is this that hides counsel without knowledge?" Therefore I have uttered what I did not understand, things too wonderful for me, which I did not know. "Hear, and I will speak; I will question you, and you make it known to me." I had heard of you by the hearing of the ear, but now my eye sees you; therefore I despise myself, and repent in dust and ashes (Job 42:1–6).

When teaching children, we tell them they should politely ask the question, "Were you there?" when talking to someone who believes in millions of years and molecules-to-man evolution. If someone replies by asking the same question, as they have done, we say, "No, we weren't there, but we know someone who was there, someone who cannot lie, who knows everything and has always existed. And this One has revealed to us what happened in the past in his history book called the Bible. Are you interested in reading God's history book to find out what the Word of the One who was there tells us about the true history of the world?"

Really, the above simply illustrates the difference between historical and operational science. The word *science* primarily means "knowledge." Operational science (based on our five senses, repeatable, observable, etc.) has enabled man to build wonderful technology. Whether one is an evolutionist or creationist, Christian or atheist, we basically agree on operational science. The disagreement comes when considering historical science—knowledge concerning the past when we were not there.

There was once a high-profile murder trial in the USA. This trial highlighted the problem with historical science. The evidence presented by the prosecution was circumstantial evidence gathered in the present. Regardless of how much evidence they had, they could not absolutely prove (or prove beyond a reasonable doubt in the minds of the jurors) what happened in the past. In fact, there have been cases where people have been found guilty of a crime based on circumstantial evidence only to be found innocent later when more evidence (such as DNA) came to light. The only way we can know for sure how the universe and life were formed is if an infallible eyewitness revealed to us what happened.

The origins issue involves historical science. Certainly, operational science can be used in the investigation. For instance, scientists can observe bacteria becoming resistant to antibiotics, and even understand why this happens (in many instances, it is because of a loss of genetic information). Scientists can observe new species forming. However, such evidence in the present does not provide a mechanism for molecules-to-man evolution over millions of years where one kind of living creature turns into a totally different kind.

Evolutionists use such evidence from the present (such as speciation which is not evolution) and attempt to extrapolate back into history—claiming that the small changes they observe in the present ultimately lead to the big changes needed for molecules-to-man evolution. However, creationists claim that such changes do not provide the creation of brand-new genetic information, which is necessary for molecules-to-man evolution. The point is that the only way we can know for sure how the universe and life were formed is if an infallible eyewitness revealed to us what happened.

The Bible claims to be the Word of the One who was there, who is infinite in knowledge and wisdom, and who has revealed in His written Word an account of the history concerning our origins. So we can correctly understand the present since we have an inerrant record of the past.

No, we were not there, but God was there and has always existed. His record of history—concerning creation, the entrance of sin and death, the Flood of Noah's day, the Tower of Babel, and so on—correctly explains the present.

Who is this that darkens counsel by words without knowledge? Dress for action like a man; I will question you, and you make it known to me. "Where were you when I laid the foundation of the earth? Tell me, if you have understanding" (Job 38:2–4).

Evidence properly applied confirms the truth of this revelation.

DECEMBER 5
1 Corinthians 14:8

So Many Christian Colleges Are *Already Compromised*

I often use this verse when talking about compromise in the Church. An "uncertain sound" is being heard in many Christian institutions across the West. Oh, yes, professors and administrators will say their school is a "Christian college," but research detailed in the book titled *Already Compromised* (which I coauthored, and I discuss further on in this chapter) was both revealing and shocking. It was a wake-up call for parents and students to be much more vigilant and discerning when it comes to choosing among the schools that claim to be Christian colleges.

Over the years, I have met many people who have told me how their lives became shipwrecked because of professors who undermined biblical authority at what they thought was a solid Christian college. Praise the Lord for the testimonies of those whose confidence in God's Word was restored with the help of apologetics material from various organizations like Answers in Genesis—but not without suffering many negative consequences before their restoration. Now that they are parents, they have often told me they will be much more careful to whom they will entrust their children for higher education.

Sadly, many distressed parents have told me how their children's lives have already been shipwrecked. They found out too late that professors who taught at what they thought was a great Christian university were instilling doubts concerning God's Word. They can't believe they spent so much money and entrusted their children's hearts and minds to an institution, only to see their children walk away from the Christian faith.

From my experience of 30 years of itinerant ministry, I believe such instances have been repeated many times across the world. After working on the book *Already Gone*, which examined why two-thirds of young people leave the Church when they reach college age, I asked America's Research Group to do another study to determine what is really being taught at Christian colleges.

The results are detailed in the book *Already Compromised*. Researchers went directly to the presidents, vice presidents, academic deans, heads of the science departments, and heads of the theology/religion departments to find out what they believe and teach at each college.

On the one hand, we found nearly 100% agreement on New Testament issues such as belief in the virgin birth, Christ's substitutionary death on the Cross, a literal heaven and hell, and the bodily Resurrection of Christ. However, the minute we stepped into the Old Testament, and particularly the Book of Genesis, the more detailed our questions, the clearer it became that there were serious problems. But a disturbing pattern appeared: An "uncertain sound" is being given to students, which authors of the book dubbed a sort of "newspeak," to use George Orwell's word from *Nineteen Eighty-Four*. We could even call it a form of "Christian newspeak."

What we meant was that the words being used have one meaning to the hearers and another "new" meaning to the "speakers" (thus "newspeak"). In Orwell's novel, the bureaucrats of the all-powerful state manipulated words to hide the truth from the masses and to keep them under control.

APOLOGETICS

I believe we could say many Christian colleges are committing a form of newspeak. When they toss around words like infallibility, inspiration, inerrancy, literal, and as written, in many instances, the words do not convey the meaning that most parents and students think they convey.

For instance, many Christian professors say they believe in a worldwide Flood, but in reality, they believe in a local flood—to them "worldwide" means what they call "the known world," or some other limited area. They may say they take Genesis "literally," yet they believe the "days" of creation represent millions of years.

I have found over the years that some colleges don't really want parents to know what is being taught in their classes. So they tell parents comforting words like the ones listed above, knowing that the parents will automatically think the students are being taught the parents' biblical views—but that is not necessarily the case.

In the book *Already Compromised,* we detail that nearly half (49%) of the leaders at Christian colleges see themselves as "old-earth" Christians. Yet the majority of these same Christian leaders would say "yes" when asked whether they believe…

- "The Genesis account of creation as written."
  86% said "yes."
- "The Genesis 1–2 account of creation is literally true."
  78% said "yes."
- "God created the earth in six literal 24-hour days."
  52% said "yes."

And in a way, these educators' objective is "control," in the sense they want to put people at ease concerning what is being taught. But the research showed that Christians had ample reason to be uneasy about what was being taught. Based on this research, parents and students are advised to start asking professors and administrators very specific questions about what is being taught, to try to drill down to find what the words really mean.

It is vitally important that parents understand the gravity of this situation and spend much more time researching what is being taught at Christian colleges. Although in this sinful world there are no perfect colleges, nonetheless some (small minority) are doing their best to give a "certain sound" regarding the infallibility of God's Word.

And if the bugle gives an indistinct sound, who will get ready for battle? (1 Corinthians 14:8).

> If you have children who plan to choose a Christian college, please make sure you do your utmost to ensure they are fully prepared to make wise choices, despite the spiritual battle raging around us.

DECEMBER 6

Matthew 5:13

The Tsunami of Church Compromise

I remember waking up to the terrible news that a massive earthquake and tsunami had devastated Japan. I can still see images of the tsunami hitting the eastern coast of Japan in 2011. The mud, debris, and destruction were almost unbelievable. But there is a different kind of tsunami I want to write about. It's one that is also causing major destruction, and it's happening all around us. This tsunami is biblical compromise in the Church, and it's creating waves of spiritual destruction throughout the Christian world.

I have written a number of articles about Christian academics who are publishing books and articles—and giving talks—on topics relating to how they approach the Bible, and Genesis in particular. The blogs revealed that an increasing number of Christian academics teach ideas such as:

- Adam is just a metaphor for Israel and was not a real person.
- Genesis 1 is not a material account of origins but is supposedly about the creation of some "cosmic temple."
- God took two animals and gave them "animal amnesia" so they wouldn't remember all the death over the supposed millions of years that turned them into Adam and Eve.
- The image of God evolved in man over time.
- The Apostle Paul "would have flunked hermeneutics" (the practice of Bible interpretation).
- The "apostles were lousy at exegesis" (expositing the biblical text), etc.

And that's just some of the ideas that are permeating Christendom.

Over the past 150–200 years, church leaders have embraced all sorts of compromise positions about Genesis: theistic evolution, the gap theory, progressive creation, etc. These beliefs were attempts to add the secular ideas of evolution and/or long ages into the Bible. This wave of compromise is still hitting the Church and with even greater force today.

Over the years, biblical creation ministries like AiG have been successful in showing that a person cannot consistently add evolution/millions of years into the Bible and demonstrating that it is inconsistent for a Christian to believe that death, disease, animals eating each other, thorns (like those in the fossil record), etc. came before sin. This undermines the history in Genesis that is foundational to all Christian doctrine. The very Word of God is compromised.

Today, there is an increasing number of new organizations, books, articles, and conferences that are aggressively infiltrating institutions like Christian colleges and churches with teaching that undermines the authority of the Word of God in Genesis. One movement relegates the Bible to a fallible collection of works written in response to ancient Near Eastern writings. It also promotes evolution and millions of years.

An organization called the BioLogos Foundation (with funding from the Templeton Foundation) is headed by Christian academics who try to convince the Church to believe in evolution/millions of years and reject a literal Adam. The organization even produces a curriculum for homeschoolers to infiltrate the homeschool movement with its false teachings that compromise God's Word and thus undermine biblical authority.

CHURCH

We are now seeing an increasing number of conferences with Christian speakers who are promoting compromise positions in regard to Genesis (and the rest of Scripture). For example, one conference, called the Reading Genesis 1–2: An Evangelical Conversation, was held in Chattanooga. The conference was described as one where "current scholarly evangelical work on the Old Testament presents challenges to the traditional reading of Genesis 1–2."

Conference materials stated that: "Rather than assuming that Genesis presents a historical account of God creating man from the dust of the earth, that Adam was the common ancestor of all humans, and that human creation occurred in the relatively recent past, a newer consensual reading suggests acceptance of long ages of the earth and Darwinian evolution alongside a belief in the trustworthiness of Scripture."

Sadly, this growing wave of compromise has been washing over Christian colleges, seminaries, and churches for years. More than ever, Bible-believing Christians don't just have a spiritual battle with the secular world, but an enormous battle within the Church.

This is one of the reasons why we released the book *Already Compromised*—a sequel to our book on the youth exodus from our churches, *Already Gone*. This eye-opening book exposed what Christian colleges are really teaching their students. The results were shocking.

I think of the verse: *You are the salt of the earth, but if salt has lost its taste, how shall its saltiness be restored? It is no longer good for anything except to be thrown out and trampled under people's feet* (Matthew 5:13).

> **If we don't begin to turn back the tide of the tsunami of compromise, the Church in America will increasingly look like the declining Church (or what is left of it) in England and the rest of Europe.**

DECEMBER 7

2 Peter 3:3-7

The Bible Says ... It Was Not a Local Flood!

When we announced the construction of a full-size Noah's ark as a prominent part of the Ark Encounter attraction, we were drawing attention to that great yearlong Flood event described in Genesis 6–8.

Most of the evidence that secularists use for an old earth (i.e., the fossil record) is in reality evidence of the global Flood that occurred around 4,300 years ago. The Flood would have produced the kind of complex geological record of sedimentary rock layers and fossils that we see all over the earth. These fossil layers are not the evidence of millions of years. They are the graveyard of the Flood as a result of God's judgment.

In their attempt to compromise millions of years with the Bible, some church leaders claim that the Flood was just a local event and did not lay down most of the fossil record. However, that view will not stand up biblically. In the famous *The Genesis Flood* book (published in 1961), the authors (Whitcomb and Morris) dealt with this, giving many biblical reasons that Noah's Flood was a global event. For instance, consider the covenant of the rainbow. God told Noah that the rainbow was to be a sign there would never again be such a Flood. We've seen many local floods since, but never a global one!

We should also consider what the New Testament says about the Flood. Jesus and the New Testament writers provided abundant evidence that they took Genesis 1–11 (including the account of a global Flood) as literal history.

The New Testament also tells us something else that is important about the Flood: It is a forerunner of a coming judgment. 2 Peter 3:3-7 predicts that, just as there were scoffers during Noah's time, *scoffers will come in the last days with scoffing, following their own sinful desires. They will say, "Where is the promise of his coming?" ... For they deliberately overlook this fact ... that by means of these the world that then existed was deluged with water and perished. But by the same word the heavens and earth that now exist are stored up for fire, being kept until the day of judgment and destruction of the ungodly.*

As the Flood took people by surprise, so will Christ's future judgment. And just as no one outside the ark escaped that judgment, no one outside of Christ will escape the coming judgment. Only those who have repented of their sins and trusted in the sacrificial death and Resurrection of Jesus Christ will stand on judgment day and live with God forever in heaven.

This coming judgment is to be a global one—a judgment by fire. This will not be just a local event. Jesus also spoke of scoffers who reject Christ's second coming because they rejected ("deliberately overlook") God's original acts of creation (Genesis 1) and Noah's Flood. And they do this on the basis of assuming that "all things are continuing as they were from the beginning of creation."

Peter's statement almost 2,000 years ago accurately predicted the uniformitarian naturalistic worldview which now controls virtually all of modern science, which is why most scientists believe in evolution and millions of years. But one day, just as surely as God judged Noah's world with a Flood (and the evidence for that is all over the earth), all of humanity will face the Judge of all the earth at the final judgment.

APOLOGETICS

As the Apostle Paul said, *The times of ignorance God overlooked, but now he commands all people everywhere to repent, because he has fixed a day on which he will judge the world in righteousness by a man whom he has appointed; and of this he has given assurance to all by raising him from the dead* (Acts 17:30–31).

At the AiG website of AnswersInGenesis.org, the Creation Museum, and the Ark Encounter, you, your family, and friends can learn more about the truth concerning Noah's Flood and the reliability of the Word of God, which explains the gospel of Jesus Christ.

[K]nowing this first of all, that scoffers will come in the last days with scoffing, following their own sinful desires. They will say, "Where is the promise of his coming? For ever since the fathers fell asleep, all things are continuing as they were from the beginning of creation." For they deliberately overlook this fact, that the heavens existed long ago, and the earth was formed out of water and through water by the word of God, and that by means of these the world that then existed was deluged with water and perished. But by the same word the heavens and earth that now exist are stored up for fire, being kept until the day of judgment and destruction of the ungodly (2 Peter 3:3–7).

> **Understanding the biblical account of the Flood is crucial to our understanding of the age of the earth.**

DECEMBER 8

Proverbs 18:13

Jumping to Conclusions

Many Christians have been astounded at how the secular media and atheist bloggers responded so harshly when we announced Answers in Genesis was building a full-size Noah's ark in Northern Kentucky. But actually, we shouldn't be all that surprised. As Christians, we know that non-Christians "suppress the truth" and "hate knowledge," as the Scripture tells us. Secularists reacted the way we would expect based on what the Bible teaches us about the heart of man. We shouldn't be surprised at receiving opposition from the world, or how those who are lost behave.

As examples, let me share a few responses to a guest column written by three of AiG's PhD scientists that was published in a secular newspaper. Our article was intended to correct false information contained in an opinion piece that the paper had printed about the Ark and creation vs. evolution. Here's a sampling of comments to our rebuttal column:

"Why do you idiots make a living abusing innocent children? Are you too stupid to get a real job, or is being a dishonest [expletive deleted] more lucrative for you?"

"The problem is, Mr. Moron-For-Jeebus, your new facility is going to mentally abuse innocent children and it's going to make idiot America even more stupid."

"You three idiots should be put in prison for child abuse and excessive stupidity. You're a disgrace to your profession and a disgrace to the human race."

As nasty as these responses were, they were just the tip of the iceberg. So much more was written negatively about AiG and the Ark Encounter project. It should remind all of us of how anti-Christian the enemies of Christ are. Sadly, this anti-Christian sentiment is growing in our culture. However, what dismayed me the most about the attacks on the Ark was the response from Christians, for two (totally different) reasons:

First, there have been Christian leaders—even theologically conservative ones—who have written against the Ark Encounter (and also our first attraction, the Creation Museum). Some Christian leaders used the Ark project to voice their opposition to a literal interpretation of Genesis 1–11 and to speak out against Answers in Genesis and our attractions.

Second and most saddening, there have been Christians who contacted us to express opposition to the Ark Encounter because they actually believed some of the false information in a secular newspaper or websites. Because of these unfortunate responses, I thought I should use such opposition as a teaching point and to offer a reminder for all of us.

One of the most practical verses in the Bible is Proverbs 18:13: *If one gives an answer before he hears, it is his folly and shame.*

To paraphrase, it cautions believers not to hear just one side of a controversy and perhaps come to a (wrong) conclusion. Sometimes we can hear people give what sounds like a convincing case for their side of a controversy, but when we don't hear the other side, we don't really get the full story—and perhaps don't hear how unbiblical the "convincing" side might be.

RESOURCES

As you hear about new developments in the fight for biblical authority within the Church and in the secular world, you might hear something negative about a Christian organization like AiG—and perhaps even the Ark Encounter or Creation Museum. As I alluded to above, some Christians, reading articles in the secular press, have believed what they read and then wrote us to criticize the Ark project or how we supposedly conducted ourselves. But they didn't consider asking us first to see if the report was true. Frankly, these people violated Proverbs 18:13.

Sadly, jumping to conclusions occurs too often among Christians. You can probably recall a few disputes within your church—and between high-profile Christian leaders. As Christians, we need to follow Proverbs 18:13 (and other Scriptures) to make judgments about personal conduct, biblical soundness, etc. We really need to ensure we are like the Bereans of Acts 17 who searched the Scriptures to see if things were so.

> "Now these Jews were more noble than those in Thessalonica; they received the word with all eagerness, examining the Scriptures daily to see if these things were so" (Acts 17:11).

DECEMBER 9

Isaiah 55:11

Do All Creationists Go to Heaven?

Here is an interesting question for you. Do all creationists go to heaven?

The answer is no, not all creationists will go to heaven, but heaven awaits all creationists who place their trust in Jesus Christ, the Creator and Redeemer!

In Romans 1:20, Paul makes it clear that, from what we observe around us, a Creator obviously exists. If someone doesn't believe this, they are without excuse: *For his invisible attributes, namely, his eternal power and divine nature, have been clearly perceived, ever since the creation of the world, in the things that have been made. So they are without excuse.*

The Bible also plainly says in Romans 10:9 that we need to do more than recognize our Creator: *[I]f you confess with your mouth that Jesus is Lord and believe in your heart that God raised him from the dead, you will be saved.*

So even if a person believes in a Creator and is a creationist, he will be separated from God forever, just as an atheist will, unless he receives the free gift of salvation through Jesus Christ (see John 14:6). So, from a biblical perspective, it is not good enough for us just to see a person converted from evolutionism to creationism! God did not fill the universe with His glory just so we could be awed by it—He wanted us to turn to Him, to know Him, to submit our lives to Him, and to enjoy Him forever. From the perspective of understanding the ultimate meaning of life, merely seeing the wonders of creation and recognizing a Designer is a futile exercise unless a person comes to know the Creator/Redeemer, who is revealed in the written Word of God (the Bible).

After all, nature alone does not tell us what we need to know in order to be saved. Rather, we must turn to God's written revelation for the answers: *So faith comes from hearing, and hearing through the word of Christ* (Romans 10:17). Also, Isaiah 55:11 states, *[S]o shall my word be that goes out from my mouth; it shall not return to me empty, but it shall accomplish that which I purpose, and shall succeed in the thing for which I sent it.* The Word of God, not man's words, convicts people and brings them to faith in Christ.

This is why I have problems with what is called the "Intelligent Design" movement. I certainly understand this movement wants people to see that life could not have arisen by natural processes. But what's the point in trying to convert people to believe in an intelligent designer if we are not pointing them to the One who is that designer and helping them understand man's problem of sin and the solution our Creator has provided in Jesus Christ.

Certainly, in a world where evolutionary naturalism pervades the culture, we need to show people the evidence for the intelligent Creator. In the public schools, students are indoctrinated in the Darwinian view of the origin of life and man—they're taught that everything arose by natural processes with no supernatural activity involved. These people need to see how obvious it is that life could not have arisen through naturalism.

But it would be disastrous simply to show people the evidence for an intelligent Designer and not to pursue the topic any further. When we talk to people about an intelligent Designer, we must recognize the ultimate

THEOLOGY

need of each human. If we leave the Creator's identity a mystery, we invite people to consider all sorts of gods as this possible intelligence, instead of the one true Creator God.

Mankind's sinful heart is too corrupt to find God without the Scriptures. Jeremiah 17:9 states, *The heart is deceitful above all things, and desperately sick.*

Ephesians 2:1 explains that humans are "dead in trespasses and sins." Humans cannot raise themselves from the dead. Only the One who has ultimate power over death can do that—the infinite Creator God.

Romans 3:11 tells us that *"no one understands; no one seeks for God."*

If someone is convinced that some intelligence or creator must have designed the universe, their sinful heart will not want the true God. We are in rebellion against our Creator God. People are more likely to pursue a false god than the true One. The human heart does not want to submit to the Word of the One who created us. That is the very nature of our sin, inherited from Adam, after he rebelled against the words God clearly gave him in the Garden of Eden.

Christians use many powerful arguments to show people that they have no excuse for denying the Creator. Christians must also follow through, however, by sharing what the Bible reveals about the true God and His unique plan of salvation and restoration. Otherwise, their listeners might put their faith in good works and seek after a Hindu god, a New Age god, or the Muslim god.

As Paul teaches us in Romans 10:14–15, we must share the whole message of the Creator, including the sacrifice of His Son, Jesus Christ, to pay the penalty for our sins, which God planned before the beginning of time: *How then will they call on him in whom they have not believed? And how are they to believe in him of whom they have never heard? And how are they to hear without someone preaching? And how are they to preach unless they are sent? As it is written, "How beautiful are the feet of those who preach the good news!"*

It's not enough just to convert someone to be a creationist. As the Great Commission of Matthew 28 tells us, we need to preach the gospel—to see people saved and their hearts turned to their Creator! Where a person stands in relation to the Savior, the Lord Jesus Christ, is the most important thing in the entire universe.

Go into all the world and proclaim the gospel to the whole creation (Mark 16:15).

> **No, not all creationists will go to heaven, but heaven awaits all creationists who place their trust in Jesus Christ, the Creator and Redeemer!**

DECEMBER 10
Acts 17:18–34

The Cross–Stumbling Block or Foolishness?

A tremendous example of successful evangelism is Peter's sermon on the day of Pentecost in Acts 2. Peter boldly preached the message of the Cross and the Resurrection, and thousands were saved. The people who heard his message had an Old Testament background. They believed in the Creator God and understood sin and its penalty of death. When Peter was preaching to the Jews, it was like building a house, knowing that the foundation was already there. He could go straight to the structure to be built on the foundation.

In Acts 17:18–34, however, Paul preached to a totally different culture. Paul was speaking to the Greek philosophers. They had a different understanding compared to the Jews. Read through this passage and let me explain why this is so pertinent to us today:

Some of the Epicurean and Stoic philosophers also conversed with him. And some said, "What does this babbler wish to say?" Others said, "He seems to be a preacher of foreign divinities"—because he was preaching Jesus and the resurrection. And they took him and brought him to the Areopagus, saying, "May we know what this new teaching is that you are presenting? For you bring some strange things to our ears. We wish to know therefore what these things mean." Now all the Athenians and the foreigners who lived there would spend their time in nothing except telling or hearing something new. So Paul, standing in the midst of the Areopagus, said: "Men of Athens, I perceive that in every way you are very religious. For as I passed along and observed the objects of your worship, I found also an altar with this inscription: 'To the unknown god.' What therefore you worship as unknown, this I proclaim to you. The God who made the world and everything in it, being Lord of heaven and earth, does not live in temples made by man, nor is he served by human hands, as though he needed anything, since he himself gives to all mankind life and breath and everything. And he made from one man every nation of mankind to live on all the face of the earth, having determined allotted periods and the boundaries of their dwelling place, that they should seek God, and perhaps feel their way toward him and find him. Yet he is actually not far from each one of us, for 'In him we live and move and have our being'; as even some of your own poets have said, 'For we are indeed his offspring.' Being then God's offspring, we ought not to think that the divine being is like gold or silver or stone, an image formed by the art and imagination of man. The times of ignorance God overlooked, but now he commands all people everywhere to repent, because he has fixed a day on which he will judge the world in righteousness by a man whom he has appointed; and of this he has given assurance to all by raising him from the dead." Now when they heard of the resurrection of the dead, some mocked. But others said, "We will hear you again about this." So Paul went out from their midst. But some men joined him and believed, among whom also were Dionysius the Areopagite and a woman named Damaris and others with them (Acts 17:18–34).

The Greek culture had no concept of a personal, infinite God who was responsible for, transcendent to, and an upholder of His creation.

The Greeks did not have the Scriptures. While they saw "sin" and "evil" and recognized the importance of laws, they had no concept of an absolute authority, absolute truth, or the inherent sin nature of man.

APOLOGETICS

The Greeks had no understanding concerning their first ancestor, Adam, and original sin—nor had they received the Law of Moses. So these people could not understand or accept the absolute authority of the Creator God, the lawgiver.

How could Paul get them to understand?

Once they understood creation and our descent from the first man, Adam, Paul turned to the message of the Resurrection, the central part of the gospel. Paul knew that he could appeal to nature and their consciences to explain the concept of the true Creator God (Romans 1:20, 2:15).

For his invisible attributes, namely, his eternal power and divine nature, have been clearly perceived, ever since the creation of the world, in the things that have been made. So they are without excuse. For although they knew God, they did not honor him as God or give thanks to him, but they became futile in their thinking, and their foolish hearts were darkened. Claiming to be wise, they became fools, and exchanged the glory of the immortal God for images resembling mortal man and birds and animals and creeping things (Romans 1:20–23).

They show that the work of the law is written on their hearts, while their conscience also bears witness, and their conflicting thoughts accuse or even excuse them on that day when, according to my gospel, God judges the secrets of men by Christ Jesus (Romans 2:15–16).

So Paul explained the Christian message from the foundation upward. Paul pointed to one of their own altars that they had inscribed to the "unknown god." He explained this unknown god was, in reality, the true God. He urged them to repent from their erroneous ways and believe in the true God.

Finally, once they understood creation and our descent from the first man, Adam, Paul turned to the message of the Resurrection, the central part of the gospel.

Generations ago, in nations like America and England, evangelists could assume a foundation upon which the gospel could stand. However, there has been a major change—and the Church has sadly missed it.

Are our modern nations like the model in Acts 2—or like the very different situation in Acts 17? I suggest our Western nations were much like an Acts 2-type culture because of the significant Christian influence but have now become like the Greeks in Acts 17.

> **If God's people do not wake up to this change, they will increasingly be ineffective in reaching the coming generations with the truth of God's Word and the gospel.**

DECEMBER 11

1 Kings 19:18

A Generation Is Rising Up

A generation is rising up. Will you join them?

You probably recall the passage in 1 Kings 19:14 where Elijah was described as very discouraged. He was thinking that he was very alone in his stand for the Lord:

He said, "I have been very jealous for the Lord, the God of hosts. For the people of Israel have forsaken your covenant, thrown down your altars, and killed your prophets with the sword, and I, even I only, am left, and they seek my life, to take it away."

But then the Lord encouraged him in 1 Kings 19:18:

"Yet I will leave seven thousand in Israel, all the knees that have not bowed to Baal, and every mouth that has not kissed him."

I have quoted this passage a number of times over the years when I've been traveling and speaking in various cities. Why? You see, people have often come to me to say they feel so alone in their stand on the authority of God's Word beginning in Genesis as the culture around them becomes more secular and anti-Christian, and as more and more churches succumb to the woke agenda in various ways. They tell me that the leadership in their church won't support them, and others in their congregation just don't understand why AiG supporters are so strong about their biblical stand.

They often go on to tell me they feel so alone. These supporters then usually ask: "Do you think there are many people in the West anymore who believe as we do?" I get this when traveling in America, Canada, England, or Australia.

It's then that I remind them about Elijah, and that there are many more than 7,000 people in their nation who are prepared to stand uncompromisingly and unashamedly on God's Word—beginning with the very first book of the Bible. And it is so encouraging for them to be there at an AiG conference and realize there are many like-minded people in their area. For instance, when speaking at four conferences in Australia in 2024, it was amazing to see thousands of people pour into the auditoriums. This encouraged others that there is a large remnant (though a minority within the country) who do stand on the authority of the Word of God from Genesis.

I remember one day when there were thousands of visitors at the Creation Museum. I was greeting various guests on that day and sometimes apologizing for how crowded it was at the museum. However, the typical response I received (and I have heard this many times now from visitors at the Creation Museum and the Ark) went something like this:

"Oh, we don't mind at all—we're just so thrilled to know there are so many others who understand the importance of this ministry. It's so encouraging for us to see this many people visiting these God-honoring attractions." So I've come to realize that crowded days at the museum and Ark are really an encouragement to others—and to me as well!

CHURCH — DECEMBER 11

Be encouraged! There are thousands upon thousands of Christians in our Western nations who stand with Answers in Genesis on God's Word—and many thousands of people each week being influenced by AiG resources!

And there is something else I am finding—something that is ever so encouraging.

I've been active in the creation apologetics ministry now for over 30 years. I've heard so many testimonies from people who have been set "on fire for the Lord," or who have received the gift of salvation as a result of the Lord using Answers in Genesis in some way.

For instance, at one of our conferences, a 16-year-old girl told me she read our book *Already Gone* and realized she wasn't a Christian. So she asked her parents to pray with her, and she committed her life to the Lord. Also, a young man told me that he was heavily into pornography, but after watching AiG videos, he got back on track and became an on-fire Christian.

For many years now, I have been hearing one particular kind of testimony that really tugs at my heartstrings. In fact, I hear such testimonies many times during the year.

A young mom or dad will often come up and tell me that they had attended an AiG conference as a child—and/or that their parents purchased Answers in Genesis books for them as children. They grew up on AiG apologetics resources, and they meant so much to them and their stand on God's Word. They then introduce me to their children and tell me how they are now bringing their children up on AiG resources! That's the spiritual legacy being passed down from one generation to the next.

And what a thrill it is to speak to these children! I'm blown away by their enthusiasm for the Lord. Many of them tell me they want to be creation scientists, evangelists, and so on—they have such a love for God and His Word.

Yes, the effects of this ministry are spreading—not just across our Western nations and around the world, but even from generation to generation. I believe this next generation of "creationist kids" is going to be a formidable force in our culture—and who knows, maybe they will be the ones to launch a new Reformation, to bring the Church and culture back to the authority of God's Word.

I've often thought about how discouraging it must have been for Noah when he saw only eight people (his own family!) going on the Ark—he must have felt so alone. And how discouraged Abraham must have been when he found there were not even 10 righteous people in Sodom.

But, praise the Lord, we live in an era where thousands are standing up for biblical authority beginning in Genesis—and the "troops" are rallying!

A good man leaves an inheritance [legacy] to his children's children (Proverbs 13:22).

What legacy are you passing on to the next generation?

DECEMBER 12
Romans 1:18-20

Arguing Against Straw Men

For the wrath of God is revealed from heaven against all ungodliness and unrighteousness of men, who by their unrighteousness suppress the truth. For what can be known about God is plain to them, because God has shown it to them. For his invisible attributes, namely, his eternal power and divine nature, have been clearly perceived, ever since the creation of the world, in the things that have been made. So they are without excuse (Romans 1:18–20).

As I lined up with hundreds of others to get inside London's famed Natural History Museum to visit its new Darwin exhibition when England was celebrating Charles Darwin's 200th birthday in 2009, I couldn't help but wonder: Was this going to be some kind of attempt at mind control? After I went through the exhibition, there was no doubt!

The Darwin exhibit reminded me of one of those bizarre science fiction movies where people line up to be placed in a special machine and emerge like robots; these people now can't think for themselves, and they end up being like those people who brainwashed them.

In a related way, I found the Darwin exhibit to be a clever form of mind control, basically consisting of:

- Setting up straw-men arguments that totally misrepresent what Bible-believing Christians accept.
- Showing how wrong Christians are for believing the things they supposedly believe (which they don't believe in the first place!).
- Convincing visitors that Darwinian evolution is true, and that one is a fool to believe otherwise (and certainly foolish to believe the Bible).

Actually, this kind of mind control is already being used constantly on the West's children through the public education system, the secular media, and science museums (even in many Christian schools and colleges, sadly). Using London's Darwin exhibition, let's look at how they are using mind control to help us all to know what to look for at such places. Visitors read this display:

"Before Darwin was born most people in England accepted certain ideas about the natural world as given. Species were not linked in a single family tree. They were unconnected, unrelated and unchanged since the moment of their creation and earth itself was thought to be so young, perhaps only 6000 years old, that there would not have been time for species to change … Before Darwin, it was still possible to see the world as timeless, eternal and unchanging."

Wrong. That's a straw man. People who know and believe their Bible are aware that the earth has indeed changed because of what's recorded in Genesis (the entrance of sin, the event of Noah's Flood, and its account of the Tower of Babel). Those who believe God's Word know that two of every "kind" (seven of some) of land-dwelling animal were on Noah's ark. All the different species (there can be thousands of species within one kind) of land animals that are alive today descended from the "kinds" that got off the ark. Yes, animals have changed—and the earth has changed drastically since Adam sinned.

APOLOGETICS

In fact, before Darwin came along, people were breeding different sorts of dogs, cats, pigeons, and so on. Even in the Darwin exhibit, it is stated that "he [Darwin] was aware that people often bred animals with desirable traits and that over time such breeding exaggerated small differences. ... Dogs were dogs but a tiny lap dog and a large lean greyhound look nothing alike." I wonder how many visitors noticed this gross inconsistency as we read "dogs were dogs." Of course, everyone knows that animals change. The exhibition's straw-man argument—that Bible-believers think that animals within a species can't change—was set up so that the trustworthiness of the Bible can easily be knocked down. Now that the museum visitors were beginning to have their minds controlled to think that Bible-believers don't accept that things have changed, the exhibition's mind controllers state:

"Discoveries in geology had already challenged the idea that the world and all its species had been created at the same time a few thousand years ago. Fossils clearly show that in past ages the world had been inhabited by different species than those existing today..."

So Bible-believers supposedly don't believe animals change, but Darwin figured out that they do, proving the Bible wrong. These changes were his evidence of molecules-to-man evolution (e.g., apelike creatures turning to people).

This, too, is designed to make London's museum visitors think that they have to reject the Bible's account of origins and a young earth.

Now, here was the final step in indoctrinating visitors to disbelieve the Bible through mind control. They were indoctrinated to believe in an additional straw man: Creationists don't accept that new species can form. But we do. We have stated innumerable times that speciation occurs—and that natural selection happens (as we show at the Creation Museum and Ark Encounter). But we declare that speciation cannot result in Darwinian evolution— the idea that one totally different kind of creature (not species) changes into a totally different kind (e.g., the reptile kind becoming the bird kind). In other words, molecules-to-man evolution just does not happen. The London exhibit stated:

"Darwin's theory of evolution by natural selection is the only scientific explanation for the spectacular diversity of life on earth. It provides a powerful framework for understanding nature and is one of the essential theories of the very core of science. ... As Darwin himself anticipated some people have held to the conviction that species are the result of special creation through the action of a Creator. Some find incompatible with their religious beliefs the concept that humans share a common ancestry with earlier primates and that humans and other species evolved over immense spans of time. Creationism, including Intelligent Design, does not offer a scientific alternative to the theory of evolution by invoking the act of a Creator or an Intelligent Designer as the explanation for large diversity." Sad, isn't it?

The Bible warns us about such mind controllers at that Darwin exhibition and in secular museums and zoos and TV documentaries, etc.: It is *by their unrighteousness suppress the truth* (Romans 1:18).

Now I ask to what extent have the mind controllers of this age influenced you and your family, and not just with the creation/evolution question? Think about it.

Make sure you keep supplying yourself with answers to defend our Christian faith.

DECEMBER 13
Matthew 12:34-5

Teach People They Are Animals and They May Act Like It

Most people, when asked what they consider to be Charles Darwin's legacy, would quickly say "evolution." Indeed, evolution and Darwin are virtually synonymous, especially as evolutionists worldwide celebrated his 200th birthday in 2009. But what is not so commonly known is that there have been adverse parts of Darwin's legacy that many of his followers have either denied or kept from public knowledge.

Ideas, it is said, have consequences. What people believe about their origins and the purpose and meaning of life affects their entire worldview. It molds how they view themselves ... and others. Darwin's ideas concerning "molecules-to-man" evolution have left a significant negative legacy on society. For many secularists, his ideas were ammunition to eliminate any consideration of the supernatural. For example, in Darwin's house (now a museum) in England, there is an exhibit which comments on our Creator:

"[E]very living creature looked the way it did because God had designed it that way. Darwin's theory made nonsense of all of this."

The exhibit declares there is no God connected to why and how life exists. This idea dominates public (secular) school science classrooms. God has been outlawed there. Science is now defined as naturalism (really atheism)—it's the only explanation for the origin of life currently allowed. Any hint of the supernatural is not permitted.

The situation in public schools has only gotten worse in recent decades. Witness the Texas board of education ruling back in 2009 on the state's science curriculum, largely dictating that evolution cannot be questioned.

If we continue to have generations of students going through a public education system that teaches them that they are just animals and the result of natural processes (a *Scientific American* article stated, "We are all animals, descendants of a vast lineage of replicators sprung from primordial pond scum"), we will continue to see a growing moral collapse in society.

The horrible school shooting in Finland in 2007 was a prime example. The killer stated: "I am prepared to fight and die for my cause, ... I, as a natural selector, will eliminate all who I see unfit, disgraces of human race and failures of natural selection ... I am just an animal, a human, an individual, a dissident .... It's time to put NATURAL SELECTION & SURVIVAL OF THE FITTEST back on tracks!"

This student was only carrying out in practice what he had been taught concerning origins, as well as the lack of purpose and meaning he found in life. Herein lies Darwin's terrible legacy, which has affected all modern cultures.

Consider the continuing problem of racism. Darwin wrote that within humankind, some people groups were closer to their supposed apelike ancestors than others. No wonder the late evolutionist Stephen J. Gould stated: "Biological arguments for racism may have been common before 1859, but they increased by orders of magnitude following the acceptance of evolutionary theory."

An increase in abortion has gone hand in hand with the growing acceptance of evolution. Over the years, some women have told us that people at abortion clinics told them that when they get rid of their "unwanted"

APOLOGETICS   DECEMBER 13

baby, it's OK because it's just an animal. Some have been told that the baby as it develops in the womb retraces its evolutionary ancestry (e.g., saying that at a certain stage, they would just be getting rid of a "fetus" in its "reptile" stage).

Now don't get me wrong. Evolution is not the cause of violence, abortion, or murder, etc. Sin is the cause. But the more generations believe in naturalistic evolution, the more they will reject the moral absolutes based on God's Word, and the more they will decide "truth" for themselves. Their worldview then is subjective and their morality relative. What they believe about where they came from, who they are, and what life is all about determines what their worldview will be. Take note of what Jesus said when speaking to the religious leaders of their day: *You brood of vipers! How can you speak good, when you are evil? For out of the abundance of the heart the mouth speaks. The good person out of his good treasure brings forth good, and the evil person out of his evil treasure brings forth evil* (Matthew 12:34–35).

We should not be shocked when we see students only becoming more consistent in carrying out evolutionary beliefs. After all, they are acting out what they have been taught they are—animals.

> Such things in the culture remind me of Judges 17:6: "In those days there was no king in Israel. Everyone did what was right in his own eyes."

DECEMBER 14
Psalm 146:1-6

Christian Morality Is Based on Christianity

Atheists are very religious people. Everyone has a worldview, a way of thinking about life and the universe. Everyone has a religious belief.

I watched a TV news program where a representative of the group American Atheists was opposing the choice of Pastor Rick Warren by president-elect Barack Obama to give the inauguration prayer. It then hit me: Many people are oblivious to the fact that atheists—with a fervent belief there is no God—are aggressively trying to impose that belief on the culture.

We've already seen Nativity displays, Ten Commandments displays, crosses, and other important Christian symbols removed from public places in the West. And have you noticed that more and more people have been deleting the name "Christ" from Christmas, largely turning it into a secular/pagan "holiday"?

Sadly, millions of people have been brainwashed to believe that by deleting Christian symbols from society, the culture is becoming more "neutral." I would argue that there is no such thing as "neutrality." Matthew 12:30 clearly states: *Whoever is not with me is against me, and whoever does not gather with me scatters.* Everyone has a belief about life that determines how they view morality and therefore how they behave. Everyone has a religion.

Why did atheists protest against a Christian pastor offering the prayer at a presidential inauguration? Why did they not want the name of Jesus used in that prayer? Well, it's because the religion of the atheists is atheism. They want all references to the God of the Bible edited out of the culture, because they want their anti-God religion to be imposed instead. They are some of the most intolerant people around.

What would be the ultimate outcome if atheists were successful? Well, Friedrich Nietzsche, the famous atheistic German philosopher, is best remembered for his declaration: "God is dead." Now, just because he was an atheist and came to some wrong conclusions, that doesn't mean that everything he said was untrue. In fact, Nietzsche understood the moral issues of his day (the latter half of the 1800s) in a way that many in our society don't grasp today—but need to! I believe atheist Nietzsche was right when he wrote the following to a person more than a hundred years ago:

"When one gives up Christian belief one thereby deprives oneself of the right to Christian morality ... Christianity is a system, a consistently thought out and complete view of things. If one breaks out of it a fundamental idea, the belief in God, one thereby breaks the whole thing to pieces: one has nothing of any consequence left in one's hands. Christianity presupposes that man does not know, cannot know what is good for him and what (is) evil: he believes in God, who alone knows. Christian morality is a command: its origin is transcendent; it is beyond all criticism, all right to criticism; it has truth only if God is truth—it stands and falls with the belief in God."

Nietzsche was right! Indeed, the more this culture gets rid of the Christian God, the more we will see people depriving themselves "of the right to Christian morality." Charles Darwin's ideas are celebrated in this world by humanists as part of getting "rid of the Christian God" from the culture. What will be the ultimate end for

APOLOGETICS — DECEMBER 14

a culture that does this? Here's a warning from the Book of Judges: *In those days there was no king in Israel. Everyone did what was right in his own eyes* (Judges 21:25).

That is what is happening in the entire Western world right now. That is why a ministry like Answers in Genesis and its Ark and Creation Museum attractions are needed more urgently than ever—to call the Church and culture back to the authority of the Word of God, which is the foundation for Christian morality.

So many people still want to live by Christian morality, but they can't have Christian morality without Christianity. And they can't have Christianity without the Bible.

Praise the Lord! Praise the Lord, O my soul! I will praise the Lord as long as I live; I will sing praises to my God while I have my being. Put not your trust in princes, in a son of man, in whom there is no salvation. When his breath departs, he returns to the earth; on that very day his plans perish. Blessed is he whose help is the God of Jacob, whose hope is in the Lord his God, who made heaven and earth, the sea, and all that is in them, who keeps faith forever (Psalm 146:1–6).

> Finally, you can't have the Bible without the literal history of Genesis 1-11, which provides the foundation of all biblical doctrine–plus Christian morality.

DECEMBER 15
Romans 1:18-25

The Religion of Evolution

Two very famous people were born on the same date in the same year. Both men greatly impacted the world, but their legacies were quite different.

Abraham Lincoln and Charles Darwin were born on February 12, 1809. Among President Lincoln's famous achievements, of course, was the abolition of slavery in several states during the Civil War. At this same time, Darwin's famous book *On the Origin of Species* (published in 1859) was gaining popularity. But Darwin's view of dark-skinned people like the former slaves was different from that of Lincoln.

The subtitle of *On the Origin of Species* gives a hint to his racist beliefs: The Preservation of Favoured Races in the Struggle for Life. Now, Darwin is known to have used the word *races* to apply to animals, but his use of the term *races* as it also relates to people became clear a few years later (which he hinted at in the last section of the *Origin of Species* book) with his book *The Descent of Man*. In that book, Darwin called those with dark skin "degraded" and wrote that he would rather be descended from a monkey than such a "savage."

By the way, why haven't Darwin's books been banned from libraries and schools? I'll answer that later.

While most educated people in England during Darwin's time held similar views, Darwin's writings fueled racism. The late evolutionist Stephen J. Gould stated: "Biological arguments for racism may have been common before 1859, but they increased by orders of magnitude following the acceptance of evolutionary theory."

Sadly, evolutionist educators and scientists are celebrating a man with a terrible racist legacy. Interestingly, Darwin's defenders—in an attempt to revise history—in recent times have been stressing his humanitarian side to minimize his racist beliefs. The focus should really be on a man like Lincoln, who, while he may have said things that would be considered racist today, eventually wrote that all men are created equal and should be treated equally before the law and God. Despite his flaws, we should honor a man like Lincoln who saw all people as God's creation, not a man whose ideas spurred and justified the devaluing of human life.

Darwin also wrote in his book *The Descent of Man* that the Australian Aboriginal people were closer to the apes than those with light skin. In fact, the Aboriginal people were considered to be the supposed missing link in evolutionary history. Scientists sent people to Australia to kill the Aboriginal people and obtain their skins and skulls as specimens for museums—all in the name of evolution.

There's no doubt that Darwin's ideas fueled a particular type of racism. Of course, as I've said before, sin is the ultimate cause of racism. There is much documentation that Hitler used Darwin's ideas in justifying the killing of millions of people. Also, the founder of Planned Parenthood, Margaret Sanger, used Darwin's ideas to justify eugenics, resulting in the killing of tens of millions of children by abortion. Keep in mind that Planned Parenthood was founded by a woman who built her worldview on Darwin's beliefs about origins! The holocaust and tens of millions of children killed in abortion are both part of Darwin's legacy.

So why is Darwin protected from the cancel culture? Well, Darwin is, in reality, the high priest of the religion of naturalism. As you study Darwin's writings, you understand that Darwin's motivation was to come up with a way of explaining life by natural processes, which is atheism. Yes, atheism is a religion. It's a religion based

APOLOGETICS — DECEMBER 15

on the belief that all life came about through natural processes and no supernatural was involved. That's why Darwin is protected in libraries and the education institutions. The secularists have to protect the religion of atheism and its high priest Darwin at all costs. It doesn't matter how inconsistent or hypocritical they are, naturalism must be protected so generations of students and others can be indoctrinated in this religion.

Actually, the evolution religion is described in Romans 1:

For the wrath of God is revealed from heaven against all ungodliness and unrighteousness of men, who by their unrighteousness suppress the truth. For what can be known about God is plain to them, because God has shown it to them. For his invisible attributes, namely, his eternal power and divine nature, have been clearly perceived, ever since the creation of the world, in the things that have been made. So they are without excuse. For although they knew God, they did not honor him as God or give thanks to him, but they became futile in their thinking, and their foolish hearts were darkened. Claiming to be wise, they became fools, and exchanged the glory of the immortal God for images resembling mortal man and birds and animals and creeping things. Therefore God gave them up in the lusts of their hearts to impurity, to the dishonoring of their bodies among themselves, because they exchanged the truth about God for a lie and worshiped and served the creature rather than the Creator, who is blessed forever! Amen (Romans 1:18–25).

> **The more people are convinced that there's no God, the more they will abandon a worldview built on the Bible that saw all people being made in the image of God and equal in value before God.**

DECEMBER 16
Matthew 7:24-27

Building on the Right Foundation

I've visited England many times over the years. One year, I made a special effort to spend some time in the town of Shrewsbury.

On February 12, 1809, in the modest town of Shrewsbury, England, Susannah Darwin gave birth to her now-famous son Charles in their family home called The Mount. There are reminders of Darwin all over the town.

Darwin was born over 200 years ago, yet as you walk through the town of Shrewsbury, you sense Darwin's influence (his "ghost") all around. Darwin Street, Darwin Terrace, Darwin House, Darwin Gardens, and the Darwin Shopping Center are just a few of the landmarks that honor and immortalize this man.

Now, I don't believe in ghosts! But the ghost of Darwin is a very real phenomenon nonetheless. Before patrons enter the town library, they are greeted by a statue of an older Darwin and a plaque, which informs them that this is the very building where Darwin received his education. As area students enter their modern school, they see a prominent statue of a young Darwin, with sculptures of various animals he saw on the Galápagos Islands, which he used to support his idea of natural selection as part of the mechanism for molecules-to-man evolution.

Darwin's ghost also inhabits the classrooms of this school. There students are taught that Darwinian evolution is indisputable fact—the same "fact" that is taught in secular schools around the world.

Shrewsbury geared up for major celebrations in 2009, the 200th anniversary of Darwin's birth and the 150th anniversary of the publication of his famous work *On the Origin of Species by Means of Natural Selection, or the Preservation of Favoured Races in the Struggle for Life*. However, town officials did not just gear up for 2009. With the prospect of ongoing financial development through the promotion of Darwin's roots in Shrewsbury, they commissioned a 90-page, 30-year strategic plan centered on celebrating and commercializing Darwin. His ghost will become even better known and celebrated (not just in Shrewsbury, but around the world) and will be the focus for tourists visiting the area.

I saw another reminder of Darwin when I visited Westminster Abbey in London—Darwin's grave in the church. Isn't it ironic that Darwin—a man who popularized a philosophy destructive to the foundations of the Church—was honored by the Church of England by being buried in the foundations of the building. His grave is in the actual floor of Westminster Abbey.

The really sad aspect of all this is that Darwin's ghost has invaded the Church. Hundreds of thousands of churches around the world have adopted Darwinian evolution and reinterpreted the history in Genesis to fit with Darwin's anti-Christian beliefs. Theistic evolution (the belief that God used evolution) has become a dominant position in much of the Church in England and has spread from there around the world.

As a result of such compromise, which began in a big way in the Church of England during the nineteenth century, subsequent generations in the Church began rejecting more of the authority of Scripture. Observers note that whereas England's church attendance before World War II was 40–50 percent, by 2003, "Only 7.5 percent of the population went to church on Sundays and then down to 4 %." Where will it end?

CHURCH

The ghost of Darwin is also felt as one travels across England and sees church buildings that have been turned into shops, mosques, nightclubs, and worse. I saw a once-Protestant chapel that is now a Sikh temple, a religion formed in India nearly 500 years ago. Where the Bible was once proclaimed now sits a throne for the Guru Granth Sahib, their holy book.

England's education system and culture, as a whole, were once primarily built on the foundation of God's Word. The United States was also solidly founded on God's Word. However, Christians in England, America, and other Western nations have allowed that once-solid foundation to be replaced by the shaky foundation of man's word, particularly Darwin's evolutionary ideas and the belief in millions of years.

Darwinian thinking is seen in the pages of public (secular) school textbooks and in the humanistic mindset of the next generation. His ghost is present in empty church pews, in secular science, in revisionist history, in the hallowed halls of art museums, and in the signs, movies, and brochures at zoos and national parks worldwide. Christian morality has all but collapsed in Western society. The culture has been secularized, and young adults who were brought up in church, but with a naturalistic foundation, have been turning away from Christianity. These are a few results of evolutionary thinking and compromised doctrines that permeate even the Church today.

Christians should pray that the Lord rebuilds the foundations of His house that shifted from the firm ground of His Word (rock) and compromised because of the works of a man (foundation of sand). Such rebuilding must start with the literal history of Genesis 1–11—a return to the authority of the Bible. We need to build our thinking on the rock of God's Word and not compromise with the sinking sands of man's fallible words:

Everyone then who hears these words of mine and does them will be like a wise man who built his house on the rock. And the rain fell, and the floods came, and the winds blew and beat on that house, but it did not fall, because it had been founded on the rock. And everyone who hears these words of mine and does not do them will be like a foolish man who built his house on the sand. And the rain fell, and the floods came, and the winds blew and beat against that house, and it fell, and great was the fall of it (Matthew 7:24–27).

Christians must rally together to stop Darwin's ghost from destroying the culture.

DECEMBER 17
Psalm 11:3

When the Foundations Are Weak

During one of my speaking tours in England, I was able to visit Down House, the home of Charles Darwin.

In 1859, from his home near the small village of Downe in England, Charles Darwin wrote The *Origin of Species*. This book popularized the idea that life could be explained by natural processes, without God. A few years later Darwin published the book *The Descent of Man*, applying his evolutionary ideas to the origin of man and postulating that mankind evolved from apelike ancestors.

From this house spread a philosophy that attacked the authority of God's Word in Genesis—the foundational history for all Christian doctrine (including the gospel), and, in fact, for the entire Bible. This fact is clearly illustrated by a quote in the home's final exhibit, which is mounted on top of the silhouetted text of Genesis 1. It reads:

"Many Christians believed that the world and everything in it, including mankind, had been created by God in the beginning and had remained unaltered ever since. . . . Darwin's theory made nonsense of all of this. He said that the world was a constantly changing place and that all living creatures were changing too. Far from being created in God's own image, Darwin suggested that human life had probably started out as something far more primitive—the story of Adam and Eve was a myth."

The quote above sums up the legacy of Darwin. His ghost has spread around the world, and it is totally consistent with what Darwin himself wrote in his autobiography:

"I had gradually come, by this time, to see that the Old Testament from its manifestly false history of the world, with the Tower of Babel, the rainbow as a sign, etc., etc., from its attributing to God the feelings of a revengeful tyrant, was no more to be trusted than the sacred books of the Hindus, or the beliefs of any barbarian."

People need to understand that Darwin's motivation was to come up with a way of explaining life by natural processes—without God. In other words, a way of getting rid of God. Naturalistic evolution is a religion, a way of thinking that denies the supernatural and promotes materialism. Sadly, many church leaders over the years have accepted Darwin's ideas and compromised God's Word in Genesis.

Darwin was buried in Westminster Abbey. When I first saw his grave, I was surprised to see he was buried in the floor, the foundation of the church. I thought to myself, "Here's a man who popularized an idea that undermined the foundation of the Church, and he's buried in the foundation of the church. How symbolic is that!"

Sadly, Darwin's ideas have permeated the world including much of the Church and have done a lot of catastrophic damage as people have been led to believe the Bible is not true. Yes, evolution is certainly an attack on the foundation of the authority of the Word of God.

> "[I]f the foundations are destroyed, what can the righteous do?" (Psalm 11:3).

CHURCH

DECEMBER 17

DECEMBER 18
Romans 1:18-32

Life Doesn't Evolve, but It Does Revolve … Around Jesus Christ

As much as evolutionists wish otherwise, life doesn't evolve around Darwin—or at all.

Let me make a few observations about the culture in the West today. For instance, at Christmas, we don't sing carols such as the following, do we?

> Silent Night, Holy Night,
> All is calm, All is bright,
>
> For Charles Darwin we just want to say
>
> Thanks for showing us the evolutionary way
> We're glad we know we're an ape
> We're glad we know we're an ape

And we have never heard of anyone constructing a calendar like the following, have we?
B.C. (Before Charles) and A.D. (After Darwin)

If someone used this kind of calendar, we would, of course, be living in the year AD 200+. On this basis, Abraham lived around 3,800 BC.

The real "Silent Night" carol is about a special baby born in Bethlehem around 2,000 years ago, certainly not Charles Darwin. Jesus was the Son of God who became the "God-man" to be the Savior of the world. Here is another thing as it relates to the calendar. Our culture (as well as cultures around the world) base the workweek on a seven-day period, and it's not something that is just arbitrary. Ever wonder why? B.C. means "before Christ," and A.D. is Latin for "in the year of our Lord." Although some secularists have tried to change these designations, the event of Christ's birth had such an impact on the world that we still date our calendars from that miraculous event in Bethlehem.

Some people have unsuccessfully tried to change the seven-day week (basically, six days of work and one day of rest). Any other supposed "week" doesn't work. The seven-day week is not based on some arbitrary division of time, but on the Bible—specifically the fact that God created the universe and all life in six literal days and rested for one literal day. While the division of times we call day, month, and year come from astronomical observations, the seven-day week is based on the Bible—specifically, the fact that God created the universe and all life in six literal days and rested for one literal day. That is why God, through Moses, used the creation week in the fourth commandment (Exodus 20:11) as the foundation for our seven-day week today.

At the end of the year, I often think about how almost all Westerners once celebrated a special time of the year, Christmas, and its wonderful significance. Over the years, however, secularists have been increasingly successful in "gutting" the meaning of Christmas. They now refer to this time in December with the generic term "holidays." The media have followed suit, and today, the reason for Christmas—to celebrate Christ's birth—is ignored by a greater number of people. It has come to the point that I wouldn't be totally surprised if one day, secular Darwinists (who love to celebrate Darwin's birthday on February 12, 1809) come up with their own carols, with lyrics such as what I presented earlier tongue in cheek.

APOLOGETICS   DECEMBER 18

We live in a world in which evolutionists' ideas of Darwin permeate our education system, media, and culture as a whole. Darwin really is worshipped. Students are being taught as fact that man is just another animal that evolved from some apelike creature, that life is the result of natural processes, and that nothing supernatural was involved in the formation of the universe and the development of life.

The secular world (and sadly even a number of churches) now celebrates Darwin—almost in a sense of worshipping him as some kind of god. A number of years ago, nearly 60 members of Parliament in the United Kingdom signed an EDM (Early Day Motion, which was not necessarily expected to become a law but was intended to make a point) to suggest making February 12 an annual national public holiday: "Darwin Day." During Februrary 2009, the 200th birthday of Darwin, secular (and some church-based) educational institutions around the world spent millions of dollars to run special programs to promote Darwin and his evolutionary ideas. Many leading magazines gave Darwin their front cover promotion.

The truth is that life has not evolved, as Darwin believed. And the world does not evolve around Darwin. Not at all! But . . . The world actually revolves around our Creator and Savior, the Lord Jesus Christ. As I wrote before:

B.C. and A.D. attest to the birth of our Lord Jesus Christ as the "God-man" 2,000 years ago.

The seven-day week attests to the fact that God created the universe and life in six days and rested for one.

I point you to Romans 1:18–32:

For the wrath of God is revealed from heaven against all ungodliness and unrighteousness of men, who by their unrighteousness suppress the truth. For what can be known about God is plain to them, because God has shown it to them. For his invisible attributes, namely, his eternal power and divine nature, have been clearly perceived, ever since the creation of the world, in the things that have been made. So they are without excuse. For although they knew God, they did not honor him as God or give thanks to him, but they became futile in their thinking, and their foolish hearts were darkened. Claiming to be wise, they became fools, and exchanged the glory of the immortal God for images resembling mortal man and birds and animals and creeping things. Therefore God gave them up in the lusts of their hearts to impurity, to the dishonoring of their bodies among themselves, because they exchanged the truth about God for a lie and worshiped and served the creature rather than the Creator, who is blessed forever! Amen. For this reason God gave them up to dishonorable passions. For their women exchanged natural relations for those that are contrary to nature; and the men likewise gave up natural relations with women and were consumed with passion for one another, men committing shameless acts with men and receiving in themselves the due penalty for their error. And since they did not see fit to acknowledge God, God gave them up to a debased mind to do what ought not to be done. They were filled with all manner of unrighteousness, evil, covetousness, malice. They are full of envy, murder, strife, deceit, maliciousness. They are gossips, slanderers, haters of God, insolent, haughty, boastful, inventors of evil, disobedient to parents, foolish, faithless, heartless, ruthless. Though they know God's righteous decree that those who practice such things deserve to die, they not only do them but give approval to those who practice them.

> **Weep and pray—for this is our Western world today—and the adherence to Darwin's beliefs, and rampant compromise in the Church with Darwin's ideas, have greatly contributed to the demise of the West.**

DECEMBER 19

Psalm 118:8

There Is Only One Sure Foundation

In man we trust? Surely, that wouldn't happen in America. Right? Doesn't it say, "In God We Trust" on American currency?

Since 2000, Darwin's image has appeared on England's £10 pound note! Sadly, British society, including most of its churches, have enthusiastically embraced Darwin's ideas and in essence are therefore promoting trusting in man rather than God. The Judeo-Christian ethic once permeated the entire Western world. But things have greatly changed, and Darwin's ideas have greatly contributed to this change.

Now, in America, doesn't the Pledge of Allegiance say "one nation under God"? Yes, but does that statement still largely hold true for that country?

America was built on the foundation of God's Word—the Bible. Verses like Psalm 40:4 (*Blessed is the man who makes the LORD his trust*) and Psalm 56:11 (*[I]n God I trust*) led to the phrase "In God We Trust" being placed on U.S. currency.

I also discovered a couple of years ago (when standing in the U.S. Capitol's chamber of the House of Representatives) that a relief sculpture of Moses faces the Speaker of the House (and thus also faces the president when he gives his annual State of the Union address). So these people are faced by the lawgiver Moses as they stand in that place—a reminder that God is the absolute authority, and He determines what is right and wrong.

These are reminders of how important God's law was in determining the foundational principles for the United States. But America, like the rest of the West, has changed its foundation. What is happening in America is happening or has happened in the rest of the Western world.

Consider:

The public schools changed foundation.	They have now gone full circle and all but thrown out the God of the Bible, the Bible itself, prayer, and creation. The Bible and the Christian God are no longer part of the public education system; they have been replaced with the religion of naturalism (atheism). Students are now taught that all of reality (the universe, life, etc.) is explained by natural processes. So the foundation today? Man's opinions, not God's truth–not principles based on God's Word.
The court system changed foundation.	In many cases, the Ten Commandments have been banned from being displayed in courts and other public settings. Despite multiple depictions of the Ten Commandments in America's Supreme Court building, more and more judges are now deciding cases based on contemporary cultural values.

APOLOGETICS

The culture as a whole has changed foundation.	Nativity scenes, crosses, the Ten Commandments–anything that is connected to Christianity has, by and large, been eliminated from public places–whether by law or by pressure tactics like bullying from atheist groups. There is a continuing battle by some to remove "Christ" from Christmas in both public and private settings. Again, the culture as a whole has changed foundation from trusting in God to trusting in man.
Much of the Church has changed foundation.	Many church leaders (and so many of the people in the Church) have accepted the idea that the earth is millions of years old and the associated evolutionary ideas; they have reinterpreted God's Word in Genesis. These churchgoers have made man the authority instead of God. Generations of people in the Church have grown up believing they should trust man first. Also, about 85-90% of young people have attended public (secular) schools where they are taught to trust in man, not God.

No, America is no longer "one nation under God." It is now "one nation under man." This is now the situation in the entire once- very- Christianized West. This change is clearly illustrated in national elections, where it is obvious that most voters look to fallible, sinful man to solve their problems, instead of God and His Word. Oh, how we should be shouting from the rooftops to remind this nation that *the fear of man lays a snare, but whoever trusts in the Lord is safe* (Proverbs 29:25).

Many people celebrate this change from trusting God's Word to trusting man's word because it gives them supposed justification to do what they want to do with sex, etc. In other words, morality is relative, and everyone does what is right in his own eyes (Judges 21:25).

But God has a message for us:

It is better to take refuge in the LORD than to trust in man (Psalm 118:8).

Stop regarding man in whose nostrils is breath, for of what account is he? (Isaiah 2:22).

Now is the time to turn to God and to lead your loved ones to do the same.

DECEMBER 20

Proverbs 3:7

Seven Pounds Weighed and Found Wanting

The movie *Seven Pounds* tells the story of a man who decides that life is not worth living anymore. His deep emotional distress comes from both guilt and grief, and as he descends more and more into self-absorption, he kills himself to alleviate his suffering. At the film's beginning, you sympathize with this tormented soul and are moved by his altruistic acts toward many strangers. Even before he kills himself, Will Smith's character donates body parts so that others can live; his suicide provides additional body parts so that others (including one who turns out to be his love interest) can live.

Along with the themes of redemption and giving sacrificially to others, there are other spiritual allusions in the film (some of them from the Bible), but they ultimately do not sanitize what is, in reality, a dark movie about suicide. The film opened with Smith's character, Ben Thomas (we find out later that Smith's character is actually the brother of the real Ben Thomas), referencing the Bible with the comment, "In seven days, God created the world. In seven seconds, I shattered mine." He then calls a 911 operator about his intent to kill himself. The rest of the film is a flashback to what brought him to the 911 call.

Seven Pounds also had a few allusions to the number seven, the number of completion or perfection in the Bible. But not all the sevens in this film were positive ones. For example, while there are seven recipients of Thomas' generosity of seven body parts (apparently weighing a total of seven pounds, hence the movie's title), there were seven people, including his own fiancée, who died in a car accident that Thomas carelessly caused. But in his pursuit of redemption, Thomas' actions are far from perfect, with wrongdoings ranging from lying to impersonating a federal agent to the more profound: committing suicide. The movie has other spiritual allusions, such as scenes shot in a Catholic hospital. But this is not a film with a Christian message. Its redemption story is in the context of the secular sense of the word, for the movie's messages do not portray the biblical teachings of redemption and atonement. Now, in the Christian worldview, there are occasions when giving up one's life for others can be justified. Consider the nobility of a soldier who "takes a bullet" to save his comrades; but with this example, the soldier knew the risks of military service and the possibility of death in battle. More importantly, the soldier did not enlist with the intention of being killed. Also, think of the men who willingly gave up seats in the Titanic's lifeboats so that women and children could be saved. As with the first example, no forethought and planning were involved, and there was no selfish act on their part to end any personal suffering or assuage their guilt. The difference between these examples and the suicide in the movie has to do with the intent of the sacrifice.

The character's suicide, which ultimately helped others, might lead theatergoers to draw a parallel to Christ's willingness to sacrifice Himself on the Cross so that others might be saved. Indeed, Christ's death (and His ultimate victorious Resurrection) is the foremost example of laying down a life, but His death was not accomplished to relieve any personal suffering but rather to selflessly rescue people from their sins and give them spiritual life. The film's main character, on the other hand, is so racked with guilt over his mistakes that his suicide is more a selfish action on his part than it is a selfless act, even though it leads to his body being harvested for parts to help others. While some might argue that John 15:13 teaches that *Greater love has no*

APOLOGETICS

one than this, that someone lay down his life for his friends (and thus actions like Thomas' can be justified), it should be noted that Christ gave His life, not out of guilt and remorse but out of love (John 3:16).

Seven Pounds mirrors the secular mindset of our day: that people are accountable to nobody but themselves and that they own their bodies. Biblically, however, because we are created in God's image (Genesis 1:26), we are thus special to Him as His unique creation—He owns us. We have no right to take that which is rightly reserved for the Creator Himself. There are times when God delegates to humans the right to exercise judgment concerning life and death. For example, God permits the use of the death penalty against a person who takes the life of another, per Genesis 9:6. This demonstrates how God values human life and how serious a crime murder is. Thankfully, there can be forgiveness through Christ for any sinner, including those who unintentionally commit an act that leads to the deaths of others. Christ can save—and the Holy Spirit can indwell a person like the suicidal Ben Thomas and give him meaning and purpose in life. Just as Thomas asks a person in the film to promise to "live life abundantly," in reality, the abundant life—free of guilt—comes through Christ: *I am the door. If anyone enters by me, he will be saved and will go in and out and find pasture. . . . I came that they may have life and have it abundantly* (John 10:9–10). The remedy to hopelessness and guilt is not suicide but hope and faith in the giver of life: *Our soul waits for the Lord; he is our help and our shield. For our heart is glad in him, because we trust in his holy name. Let your steadfast love, O Lord, be upon us, even as we hope in you* (Psalm 33:20–22).

Admittedly, it's not illogical for the secular world, without a biblical foundation for thinking, to react as this critic did and consider suicide to be noble in the context the film depicts. Without the correct framework of thinking (i.e., God's Word), a nonbeliever can find it quite logical to view suicide as heroic if it alleviates guilt or depression. Of course, even the Christian who merely hears the Word but does not do what it says to do (James 1:22–24) is sinfully wasting what God owns too. Living apart from Christ, even for someone who does what the world deems "good," is inherently just as selfish as committing suicide. Furthermore, consider the connection between suicide and evolutionary thinking. For those who accept evolution as a foundation stone in their worldview—in which human life is just an accident in a purposeless universe—what meaning to life is there? Is it any wonder, then, that teen suicide is on the rise as public schools teach that there is no God and that life arose from chance processes?

There is a profound statement that occurs twice in the Book of Judges, (Judges 17:6, 21:25): *In those days there was no king in Israel. Everyone did what was right in his own eyes.* The more the Bible and its teachings are removed from the culture, and the more we see generations brought up in an education system that teaches young people that the whole of life is the result of natural process, the more we will see generations of people acting like the movie's Ben Thomas—doing what is "right" in their own eyes. The Bible warns us to *be not wise in your own eyes: fear the* Lord*, and turn away from evil* (Proverbs 3:7); furthermore, *The way of a fool is right in his own eyes, but a wise man listens to advice* (Proverbs 12:15). People must understand that there is a King to whom we are accountable, of whom the prophet said: *For you are our Father* (Isaiah 63:16). Our Father tells us that we are *the precious sons of Zion, worth their weight in fine gold* (Lamentations 4:2).

We are so valuable that He stepped into human history to give up His life on the Cross in the greatest selfless act that could ever occur so that we can be saved for eternity.

DECEMBER 21
1 John 5:20

We Can Know!

Several times over the years, I've encountered worshippers in what I would call the "Can't Know" religion. When I visited Shrewsbury, England, the birthplace of Charles Darwin, I walked past a Unitarian Church which had a plaque on the wall declaring that Darwin attended this church when he was a child. Right then, I groaned at the false teaching Charles Darwin would have received as a child.

Then on the door of the church, I read a sign: "No one has the only truth."

That's an interesting statement. I felt like going inside and asking if this was a "true" statement itself and see what kind of a reaction I would have received! This declaration is one that says that people can't know for sure if they have the truth—the "Can't Know" religion! Of course, if people claim they "can't know," then how can they be sure they do know they can't know?

Even when talking about "truth," people have to borrow from a biblical worldview to do so. Without an absolute authority, how can one determine ultimate "truth"? And as they talk about "truth," they are using the laws of logic, which only exist because God created them!

I once came across a devotee of the "Can't Know" religion while watching a film in a movie theater. Because of impending media interviews (the Creation Museum was featured in the film), I had to view what turned out to be a vulgar and blasphemous movie featuring the God-mocking comedian, Bill Maher: *Religulous*.

Even though Maher mocks Muslims and Jews in this movie, his venom was mainly directed against Christianity. His favorite phrase throughout the movie concerning the meaning of life—and also what happens after one dies—is that one simply "can't know."

Maher apparently doesn't realize that he is committing what's called a "logical fallacy." When he states that you "can't know," he is insisting that he himself knows that a person "can't know." I remember when Bill Maher interviewed me (that's another interesting story in how he deceived us to get this interview) that he got angry at me when I kept giving him answers to his questions. His producer even snapped at me saying something like, "Do you have answers for everything?" They didn't like a Christian defending the faith logically and giving answers to questions that attacked God's Word and the Christian faith. He was actually looking for a film clip for his movie to denigrate Christianity. Bill Maher kept saying to me that I can't say I know!

This is the same fallacy as this Unitarian church saying, "No one has the only truth." Or like the person who once told me that there are no absolutes—which, as I pointed out to him, was an absolute statement!

Now, Bill Maher thinks he is nonreligious—but he really has a religion: the "Can't Know" faith! That's his belief system. Maher thinks he can determine whatever truth he wants to believe. It is ultimately a trust he puts in man and his reasoning—instead of trusting in God. He thinks he can be his own god.

At Answers in Genesis, we proclaim a "Can Know" religion, Christianity!

As God's Word states in 1 John 5:13: *I write these things to you who believe in the name of the Son of God, that you may know that you have eternal life.*

THEOLOGY

And also in 1 John 5:20: *And we know that the Son of God has come and has given us understanding, so that we may know him who is true.*

The "Can't Know" religion destroys lives, leaving people with no purpose and meaning—and it ultimately separates them from their Creator forever. It is illogical and ignores the facts of both science and Scripture. It is a rebel's refuge most frequently disguised in intellectualism. It's a blind faith that lacks credulity.

Now remember, there's always a faith aspect as we are finite created human beings. But Christianity is not a blind faith. It's an objective faith—a faith, based in God's Word, that makes sense of all we observe and experience. It's the only true faith. And it's a faith that observational science confirms in many different ways over and over again.

And without faith it is impossible to please him, for whoever would draw near to God must believe that he exists and that he rewards those who seek him (Hebrews 11:6).

People can know Christ now and will spend eternity with their Creator forever. That's what Answers in Genesis is all about—changed lives for now and eternity. Wouldn't it be great to see a testimony from Bill Maher one day, showing that he's changed from the "Can't Know" religion to the "Can Know" one? Let's pray that Bill and atheists like him will come to know the Lord Jesus as their personal Savior.

The "Can Know" religion changes lives.

DECEMBER 22

Ephesians 6:12-13

Resorting to Fear Tactics

I have often found that since the evidence is not on their side, some skeptics resort to using fear tactics to attack Christianity. Yes, he actually said it: Creationism "may pose the greatest threat to the future of our children, your health, and the nation's economy."

This remarkable quote came from Arthur Caplan, who was chairman of the medical ethics department at the University of Pennsylvania and frequent TV commentator, when he wrote in a major newspaper, *The Philadelphia Inquirer*. What prompted this venomous attack? Vice-presidential candidate at the time, Sarah Palin, apparently believed in creation and was on record as saying that students should be allowed to "debate both sides" of the evolution question. She also added that creationism "doesn't have to be part of the curriculum." In Caplan's eyes, this simple desire to allow children to discuss both sides of the issue meant "a vote for Sarah Palin, or any creationist, is a vote for change, all right, a change back to the lifestyles of the 19th century." Attacks like these demonstrate better than anything I could ever say why the biblical apologetics ministry of Answers in Genesis is so crucial. We must be out on the front lines to combat the mixture of hysterics, misrepresentation, and scare tactics presented by secularists everywhere.

These secular "religious zealots" (of the religion of humanism) are out to eliminate Christianity from the culture—and they see the creation/evolution issue as foundational to that battle. At Answers in Genesis, we've been saying that for years. It may be the only thing on which we and the secularists agree. Actually, this battle has been going on since Genesis 3—the choice of believing in God's Word or man's word instead. If God is Creator and the Bible is true, then there is an absolute authority, and morality is not relative (as these secularists want it to be).

I just praise the Lord that for this time of history, He has raised up this apologetics ministry to stand on the authority of God's Word and uncompromisingly proclaim the truth of creation and the gospel of Jesus Christ. We want to do all we can to equip soldiers in this battle. It's a spiritual battle, but we all need to be equipped to know how to defend the Christian faith and proclaim the truth of God's Word and the gospel in an increasingly secularized culture.

Alarming Statistics: Now back in 2008, you would have thought that "creation" and the presidential election were synonymous. I had one of our researchers collect some statistics for me about Governor Palin and the creation/evolution issue at that time: Google News listed 2,000+ online stories mentioning Palin's purported creationist leanings.

PressDisplay, a digital newspaper service used by the AiG library (700 newspapers from 76 countries in 36 languages), reports over 170 articles mentioning Palin and creation. Besides the United States, newspapers from Australia, Canada, Mexico, United Kingdom, New Zealand, United Arab Emirates, China, South Africa, Belgium, Israel, Austria, Thailand, and others have run stories portraying Governor Palin as insisting that creation be taught in public schools. And well over 1,000 blog entries had discussed Palin and creationism.

Chris Matthews, host of *Hardball* on MSNBC, interviewed a guest from *The New Yorker* magazine who stated: "Now they're saying, OK, let's define her as a right-winger. You know, we'll talk about her views on creationism and some of these other extreme views." That elicited this from Matthews (who calls himself a Catholic Christian, by the way): "She's got a lot of strange views—they are pretty far over."

Hollywood celebrity Matt Damon was quoted in an Associated Press article headlined "Matt Damon Fears a Palin Administration." What's his biggest "fear" about Palin? Her belief about origins and the age of the earth. "I need to know if she really thinks that dinosaurs were really here 4,000 years ago. I want to know that. Because she's going to have the nuclear codes," says Damon.

Even the famous TV judge "Judge Judy" got into the discussion. On the program *The View*, host Barbara Walters and others discuss current events. *Newsbusters* reported (September 9, 2008) that the most famous judge in America, when prodded by Walters, expressed her discomfort with "the teaching of creationism in public schools." Well, as a judge, she has formed an opinion based on faulty information—Palin had not advocated the teaching of creation in public schools!

And then there was the attempt at a Muslim (and extremist) connection to biblical creationists like those at Answers in Genesis. On Salon.com (web traffic around 2.1 million visits a month at the time), it was stated (again totally misrepresenting what Palin has said): "Palin argued when running for governor that creationism should be taught in public schools, at taxpayers' expense, alongside real science. Antipathy to Darwin for providing an alternative to the creation stories of the Bible and the Quran has also become a feature of Muslim fundamentalism."

It's especially clear from these attacks that many evolutionists are not basing their arguments on scientific evidence. They know creationists have the answers readily available. So they resort to emotional arguments and scare tactics, just as the influential Dr. Caplan did in his article when he made these absurd statements: "But it will mean the United States can kiss goodbye any chance this nation has of using biomedical science to take on the rest of the world in biotechnology, alternative-energy technology, synthetic biology or genetics. And that means we can more or less kiss goodbye any chance we have of using our current prowess in biomedical science to drive our economy forward. . . . But what cannot be ignored is her view that a narrow religious account of how the world began and evolved belongs in the science classroom. If Palin's fundamentalist religious thinking are [sic] on display in the White House, then the odds are lower that America can tap biological science to work our way out of global warming, oil dependency, pollution, dying oceans, and finding new ways to grow healthy food."

Caplan's antagonism was even more concerning because he was prominent in his field. *Modern Health Care* magazine had voted him one of the 50 most influential people in American health care, so thousands of people would treat what he said as fact.

The sad thing is that this nonsense from Caplan above is what is being taught to most public (secular) school and college students. We need to get the truth out. We need to be equipped so we can be active in the battle: *For we do not wrestle against flesh and blood, but against the rulers, against the authorities, against the cosmic powers over this present darkness, against the spiritual forces of evil in the heavenly places. Therefore take up the whole armor of God, that you may be able to withstand in the evil day, and having done all, to stand firm* (Ephesians 6:12–13).

It's time to challenge Church and culture to get back to the authority of the Word of God.

DECEMBER 23

1 Samuel 16:7

Biblical Worldview in the Voting Booth

How should Christians approach elections? How should we pick among candidates? What is the "heart" of the issue? Would you vote for someone like Eliab if he were running for office? He was an impressive Old Testament character, a tall and handsome man! Surely, we should vote for such a person. After all, when comparing him to his little brother David (the future king of Israel), the prophet Samuel did!

The Lord said to Samuel, however: *Do not look on his appearance or on the height of his stature, because I have rejected him. For the LORD sees not as man sees: man looks on the outward appearance, but the LORD looks on the heart* (1 Samuel 16:7).

What should Christians do in voting for congressmen, senators, parliamentarians, prime ministers, premiers, and other offices? What about Christians in America who have opportunity to vote for the president of the most powerful nation on Earth (although things are changing in that regard).

Many years ago, my homeland of Australia passed legislation to allow its citizens to obtain citizenship in another country yet retain their Australian citizenship. My family and I (having lived in the United States for many years) immediately applied to become American citizens. Not long after, there was a presidential election. My wife and I had to decide whom we should we vote for, and I learned a lot in that process. Here's how we began to approach this issue.

First of all, as a Christian, I recognized that I needed to seek God's direction, just as the Apostle Peter and others did in Acts 1:24: *And they prayed and said, "You, Lord, who know the hearts of all, show which one of these two you have chosen."* So I now pray today: "Lord, please guide me as I take seriously this great responsibility to vote."

Second, we need to remember God's lesson to Samuel. It is not about how impressive a person is on the "outside"—it's what is on the "inside" that counts! I was also reminded of Matthew 12:34: *For out of the abundance of the heart the mouth speaks,* and how important it is that *I have stored up your word in my heart, that I might not sin against you* (Psalm 119:11).

Third, we need leaders who are wise and knowledgeable. How do we determine that? God's Word tells us that: *The fear of the LORD is the beginning of wisdom* (Psalm 111:10) and also: *The fear of the LORD is the beginning of knowledge* (Proverbs 1:7). Do they exhibit a reverence for the Lord and His Word?

Fourth, and probably the most applicable to each of us on a personal level, I should not consider someone's policies in light of what might benefit me materially. After all, the Scripture tells us: *Do not lay up for yourselves treasures on earth, where moth and rust destroy and where thieves break in and steal; but lay up for yourselves treasures in heaven, where neither moth nor rust destroys and where thieves do not break in and steal. For where your treasure is, there your heart will be also* (Matthew 6:19–21).

Now having said that, what if it's a choice between people you know all stand for policies totally against God's Word, some worse than others? Should we not vote at all? Would it depend on what party a candidate is with? Should Christians in Australia vote for the Liberal/National parties, Labor party, the Australian Greens, or some other party? What about American Christians? Should they vote Republican, Democrat, or

APOLOGETICS

Independent? What about Christians in the United Kingdom—which of the many parties should they vote for? It's vital for Christians to understand that the Bible (God's Word) is not just a guidebook to life. The Bible is a written revelation that is God-breathed (2 Timothy 3:16). As we're told in 1 Thessalonians 2:13, it is not just the word of men but, in truth, the Word of God: *And we also thank God constantly for this, that when you received the word of God, which you heard from us, you accepted it not as the word of men but as what it really is, the word of God, which is at work in you believers.*

Think about it. The Bible is the Word of One who is infinite in knowledge and wisdom and doesn't ever tell a lie. It's the Word of the One who is "the truth." Jesus said, *I am the way, and the truth, and the life. No one comes to the Father except through me* (John 14:6). The Bible describes Jesus as being the Word: *In the beginning was the Word, and the Word was with God, and the Word was God* (John 1:1).

When we start with God's Word, we learn that there is no such thing as a neutral position. The Bible tells us that we are either for or against Christ (Matthew 12:30), we walk in light or darkness (1 John 1:5–7), we build our "house" on the rock or the sand (Matthew 7:24–27), and we either gather or scatter (Luke 11:23). We are told that those who are not Christians are not neutral; they are, in fact, at enmity (at war) with God. *You adulterous people! Do you not know that friendship with the world is enmity with God? Therefore whoever wishes to be a friend of the world makes himself an enemy of God* (James 4:4). This principle enables us to understand that whenever we have opportunity to be of influence (to vote), and we choose to do nothing, we are not actually being neutral, but we are voting even in our silence.

Also, we are instructed in God's Word that we are to be "salt" and "light" in this world of darkness. *You are the salt of the earth, but if salt has lost its taste, how shall its saltiness be restored? It is no longer good for anything except to be thrown out and trampled under people's feet. You are the light of the world. A city set on a hill cannot be hidden. Nor do people light a lamp and put it under a basket, but on a stand, and it gives light to all in the house. In the same way, let your light shine before others, so that they may see your good works and give glory to your Father who is in heaven* (Matthew 5:13–16).

When we have the opportunity to "vote," we need to have a standard by which to judge the situation and vote accordingly. We do have a standard—an absolute standard—the absolute authority of the Word of God. And, yes, we have to judge—in fact, we do every day when we make decisions. But *Do not judge by appearances, but judge with right judgment* (John 7:24). So how do you vote?

As I ponder all these things, I also realize what King David said: *I know, my God, that you test the heart* (1 Chronicles 29:17). Only God can really know a person's heart. I can certainly judge a person's actions and words against Scripture as a test of the heart—but then I'm suddenly reminded: "But what about my own heart?" Oh, Lord, *Search me, O God, and know my heart! Try me and know my thoughts! And see if there be any grievous way in me, and lead me in the way everlasting* (Psalm 139:23–24). *Wretched man that I am! Who will deliver me from this body of death?* (Romans 7:24). But how I should fall on my face and thank God that He voted for me! You see, *God shows his love for us in that while we were still sinners, Christ died for us* (Romans 5:8). *Let us then with confidence draw near to the throne of grace, that we may receive mercy* (Hebrews 4:16).

We should ponder this: "Knowing my own heart, would I vote for me?"

DECEMBER 24
Romans 1:20

SETI? The Creator of the Universe Has Already Communicated

The Creator of the universe has already communicated with us, yet millions of dollars of taxpayer money have been used to try to communicate with supposed aliens and even to teach students how to communicate with the aliens!

Toward the end of the documentary *Expelled*, which was released in 2014, the famous atheist Dr. Richard Dawkins of Oxford University, in responding to a question from interviewer Ben Stein, stated that life could have been "seeded" on earth by aliens! What an astonishing admission! Dr. Dawkins didn't believe life was the result of any intelligence but instead had arisen out of chance processes—yet when pushed for an answer, he appealed to some sort of intelligence to explain life on Earth.

Such a comment is a testimony to the Scripture's truth concerning the sin nature of mankind. God's Word tells us that people (like Professor Dawkins) *by their unrighteousness suppress the truth* (Romans 1:18) and that *no one seeks for God* (Romans 3:11). Dr. Dawkins offered up some unknown alien intelligence to explain the purpose of life and all its complexity but totally dismisses the possibility of a God who made it all. He would rather believe in eternal alien existence than an eternal Creator God.

Unfortunately, Dr. Dawkins is not alone. The U.S. federal government, through groups like SETI (Search for Extraterrestrial Intelligence), has spent hundreds of millions of dollars searching for evidence of aliens so that scientists can contact and communicate with them.

Imagine the outcry in America, Australia, or the United Kingdom if it was discovered that tax dollars were being used by a government agency to teach people to communicate with God by prayer! So-called "civil liberties" groups in America like the ACLU would be up in arms, of course, and would threaten lawsuits. Activists who advocate a "separation of church and state" (nowhere in the U.S. Constitution, by the way) would be on CNN, CBS, and so on, demanding a stop to it.

Now the Creator of the universe has already communicated with us (through His Word), yet a U.S. agency used tax dollars to teach students how to communicate with aliens!

An article on the website of the University of Wyoming (a tax-supported school) stated: "English 4050/5560, otherwise known as 'Interstellar Message Composition,' is the first class to enlist creative writers in a potential cosmic conversation. Funded in part by the National Aeronautics and Space Administration's (NASA) Wyoming Space Grant Consortium, it's designed to fill a practical—if extremely theoretical—need."

The article continued: "'We've thought a lot about how we might communicate with other worlds, but we haven't thought much about what we'd actually say,' says Lockwood, a professor of natural science and humanities."

The piece went on to state: "During one of the semester's first classes, Lockwood asked the students to summarize the human condition in 250 words, then 50, then 10. . . . [S]ome students chose the poetics—'We are an adolescent species searching for our identity,' wrote English major Ann Stebner."[108]

THEOLOGY

People, of course, want to know who they are, where they came from, and what is the meaning/purpose of life. Some are now looking to aliens in hope of some answers! Sadly, such people refuse to even accept the possibility that the God of creation, as spoken of in the Holy Scriptures, is the intelligence for whom they are looking—the infinitely intelligent Creator. Why? It would mean that this Creator, the Lord Jesus Christ, is Lord over them and that they should kneel and worship Him and accept their sinfulness and the need for salvation.

If only they would realize that they don't have to waste other people's money trying to communicate with aliens. The infinite intelligence behind the universe has already communicated with us, and in different ways:

The heavens declare the glory of God, and the sky above proclaims his handiwork (Psalm 19:1).

For his invisible attributes, namely, his eternal power and divine nature, have been clearly perceived, ever since the creation of the world, in the things that have been made. So they are without excuse (Romans 1:20).

Long ago, at many times and in many ways, God spoke to our fathers by the prophets, but in these last days he has spoken to us by his Son, whom he appointed the heir of all things, through whom also he created the world (Hebrews 1:1–2).

The God of the universe has provided us with a written revelation, the Scriptures, and He came to Earth to be a man so He could pay the penalty for our sin to enable us to live for eternity with Him.

All Scripture is breathed out by God and profitable for teaching, for reproof, for correction, and for training in righteousness (2 Timothy 3:16).

> If only the students in that "Alien Communication 101" were taught about this kind of communication, and then were led to communicate with God in prayer, what a difference that would make for them.

DECEMBER 25
Genesis 3:15

Keep Christ in Christmas!

Christmas has been a time to celebrate the birth of a special baby, God's Son, who stepped into history to become the God-man. Even most secular stores in the West once played Christmas carols, and many even had nativity scenes on display. But things have greatly changed.

Why in the West has Christ, by and large, been taken out of Christmas as far as the culture is concerned? If you told the average person 50 years ago that "in the twenty-first century, countries in the West will take Christ out of Christmas and make it nothing but a pagan holiday," I'm sure most would have responded with something like, "No—that would never happen." But it has been happening.

At Christmastime, I think it's important to ponder where the West is as a culture and try to understand why this has been happening. Then Christians will be better equipped to impact the culture with the message of Christ. There are more Christian resources available today than at any time in its history—yet for all of that, the West is becoming less and less Christian every day from a worldview perspective. The battle over keeping Christ in Christmas is a sad example of this.

Abortion, gay "marriage," gender transition, Christian symbols ripped out of public places, and taking Christ out of Christmas—all of these issues are in reality symptoms of a much greater battle. Think about it. Who is Christ? He is our Creator (Colossians 1:16). He is our Redeemer (Galatians 3:13). He is the Word! *In the beginning was the Word, and the Word was with God, and the Word was God. He was in the beginning with God. All things were made through him, and without him was not any thing made that was made* (John 1:1–3).

The real reason many in today's culture don't want to keep Christ in Christmas is that they don't want to believe and obey the Word. This problem began in Genesis 3 when Adam and Eve rejected God's Word and wanted to decide truth for themselves. Ever since the Garden, this has been man's problem. Man wants to reject the Word and be his own god.

That is why Answers in Genesis must continue to stand up for the authority of God's Word in this era of history, called a "scientific age," where man has used supposed scientific evidence to discredit God's Word in people's eyes. As a result, generations have been led to believe that God's Word can't be trusted in Genesis. And subsequent generations have applied this more consistently and now believe God's Word cannot be trusted from Genesis to Revelation.

At Christmastime, as you ponder the reason for this battle about having Christ in Christmas, remember that the real battle is over the authority of the Word of God. That's why Answers in Genesis is all about upholding the authority of the Word beginning in Genesis—countering the false arguments of the age that attempt to discredit the Word—and proclaiming the gospel that Christ is the Word, He is the Creator, and He died and rose according to the Scriptures (1 Corinthians 15:3). That is why God offers us the free gift of salvation.

Answers in Genesis, the Creation Museum, and the Ark Encounter are on the cutting edge of this battle to proclaim Christ not just at Christmas, but all year long. This is because we're at the forefront of the battle in this age over the authority of the Word of God in the culture and in the Church. And a battle it is! It's one we can't fight alone, and I am challenging all Christians to be involved in this battle.

APOLOGETICS — DECEMBER 25

Remember, if the history in Genesis concerning our origins is not true, the significance of Christmas is removed. You see, if there never was a first Adam, there's no need for a last Adam! When the Christmas account is robbed of its context and historical foundation, it becomes meaningless and easily forgotten.

That's why the final stops on the Creation Museum tour are the powerful exhibits in the Christ, Cross, and Consummation section. When our museum guests reach this point, they have seen videos and exhibits bringing to life the miracle of Creation by God's own hand. They've seen the terrible consequences of the Corruption (entrance of sin), as the first Adam chose to disobey God.

Next, they witnessed the Catastrophe in a room dedicated to a cutaway biblical representation of Noah's ark and dioramas outlining the disaster that shaped the earth as we have it today. In the second-to-last exhibit of the museum, they've learned about the Confusion that God brought on by man's pride at the tower of Babel.

Then, when they understand the context of sin and devastation brought on our world by our own disobedience, they're ready at last to hear the message of the babe in the manger in a way many have never experienced before—full of meaning and hope for everyone.

We also show a gospel film called *The Last Adam*. It's a moving dramatization of Christ's life as seen through the eyes of the people He touched, from Mary His mother to the soldiers at the Cross. There's a moment I particularly enjoy when Mary places Christ's birth within the context of God's plan for all history:

"One day, after I was engaged to Joseph, I was visited by an angel of God. He told me not to be afraid and that I was to give birth to a son and that I should call him Jesus. I asked how this could be since I was still a virgin. The angel told me the power of the Most High would overshadow me and that my son would be called the Son of God. One day, I learned that my son would be called something else as well—a lamb."

All Seven C's work together until that blessed day when we reach the seventh, the Consummation, when God restores life to the perfection He originally designed, and those who are washed by Christ's blood can stand before Him forever.

It's no wonder most people think the Christmas account in the New Testament is no more than fiction, when the first four C's that give it meaning have been undermined and compromised by evolutionary and millions-of-years teaching! While the battle cries of God haters get louder and louder, while lawsuits over nativity scenes proliferate, while more and more of our society becomes entirely numb to the true meaning of Christ's birth... we must stand strong.

Oh, and how awe-inspiring it is to understand that the babe in a manger was promised right back at the beginning, in Genesis 3:15:

> "I will put enmity between you and the woman, and between your offspring and her offspring; he shall bruise your head, and you shall bruise his heel" (Genesis 3:15).

DECEMBER 26

Proverbs 13:22

A Good Well

The Answers in Genesis apologetics ministry provides resources through books, video streaming, radio programs, the Internet, and the Ark and Creation Museum attractions. In doing so, we are really digging new wells so the water of the Word will flow freely around the world. Let me explain.

On June 7, 2008, *The New York Times* published an editorial entitled, "The Cons of Creationism." The very first line was, "When it comes to science, creationists tend to struggle with reality." The editorial went on to describe belief in a Creator as "nonsense" and to claim that teaching about God belongs only in "church and social studies courses."

Remember back in Genesis 26:18, when Isaac re-dug Abraham's wells (the ones stopped up by the Philistines) and then went on to dig new wells? I couldn't help thinking of this passage as I read that *Times* editorial. You know how often Scripture uses water to symbolize the grace of the Spirit of God. The author of the editorial is clogging up the well of the Word of God, denying our children access to life-giving truth by banning the biblical God from the public school system where their thinking and worldview is formed.

It is important to understand that those who blast creation, as this *New York Times* editorial did, are not just against people believing in a literal Genesis account of origins. They are against the very first verse of the Bible. Now if that verse is not true, none of the Bible is true. If *in the beginning God created the heavens and the earth* (Genesis 1:1) is false—so is the Christian faith.

That's why we need to do all we can to clear the debris being thrown in our wells by modern-day Philistines and restore biblical authority to our schools, churches, and homes. Answers in Genesis is helping to do this through our two attractions and the resources we produce and disseminate. We trust by doing this we are also equipping others to help clear out these "wells" of water.

At Answers in Genesis, we challenge Christians concerning compromise and challenge churches to get back to the authority of God's Word—re-digging wells. As we provide resources through books, videos, radio programs, the internet, and the Creation Museum, we are also digging new wells so the water of the Word will flow freely through the nation and around the world. You're a vital part of that process every time you pray and give!

Now, I encourage you to re-dig wells and dig new ones of your own. We each need to work in our own homes and churches. If we're honest with ourselves, the "Philistines" have invaded here too. The wells have been stopped up. Many church leaders, Christian colleges, and seminary professors have compromised with evolution/the age of the earth, thus undermining the authority of the Word. Parents are neglecting the call to teach their children to stand on the authority of the Word and equip them to defend their faith in today's world. And, as you consider your family's education, think about how you can ensure they will experience that cleansing water of the Word and be equipped to stand firm in the spiritual battle for children and teens.

In a way, many church leaders have actually helped the modern-day Philistines to fill in the wells to stop the water of the Word flowing like it should.

APOLOGETICS   DECEMBER 26

My mother and father gave me the most tremendous possible gift—an abiding love for God and belief in the authority of His Word. This "well" that my parents dug and kept clean still flows freely today. Their legacy is seen in the impact of the truth of God's Word and the gospel on millions of people each year around the world. I pray that will be true of your family as well.

And Isaac dug again the wells of water that had been dug in the days of Abraham his father, which the Philistines had stopped after the death of Abraham. And he gave them the names that his father had given them. But when Isaac's servants dug in the valley and found there a well of spring water, the herdsmen of Gerar quarreled with Isaac's herdsmen, saying, "The water is ours." So he called the name of the well Esek, because they contended with him. Then they dug another well, and they quarreled over that also, so he called its name Sitnah. And he moved from there and dug another well, and they did not quarrel over it. So he called its name Rehoboth, saying, "For now the Lord has made room for us, and we shall be fruitful in the land" (Genesis 26:18–22).

"A good man leaves an inheritance [legacy] to his children's children" (Proverbs 13:22).

DECEMBER 27

Ephesians 6:13

It's a War for Hearts and Minds

A secular reporter once accused me of promoting violence. It was because he saw AiG's classic "castles illustration" we often use, which really sums up the spiritual battle AiG is fighting. Over the years, many people have told me those castle illustrations illustrate powerfully the spiritual battle over the Word of God.

The two castle illustrations are labeled "Problem" and "Solution." Our artist used cannons on the castles to symbolize the war between the secular and Christian worldviews. Now, I wonder what the same reporter might say if he saw some of the newer diagrams I use in my talks—today I'm using missiles instead of cannons. But it's all to symbolically represent the spiritual warfare that's raging around us.

What I'm doing with such illustrations is similar to what the apostle Paul did, as we read about in the Bible. He often used military language as he described the spiritual battle Christians are in. For instance, consider these passages from God's Word, penned by Paul:

- *Therefore take up the whole armor of God, that you may be able to withstand in the evil day, and having done all, to stand firm* (Ephesians 6:13).
- *The night is far gone; the day is at hand. So then let us cast off the works of darkness and put on the armor of light* (Romans 13:12).
- *[B]y truthful speech, and the power of God; with the weapons of righteousness for the right hand and for the left* (2 Corinthians 6:7).
- *For the weapons of our warfare are not of the flesh but have divine power to destroy strongholds* (2 Corinthians 10:4).
- *But since we belong to the day, let us be sober, having put on the breastplate of faith and love, and for a helmet the hope of salvation* (1 Thessalonians 5:8).

I liken the "missiles" fired by AiG to attacks on evolution's own "missiles," including its teaching of millions of years. I call ours "Christian Patriot Missiles." They are designed to counter the secular humanists' attacks on Christianity.

And what are Answers in Genesis' "missiles" of defense? They are our various Christianity-defending resources: the AiG website, our books, videos, curricula, CDs, *Answers* magazine, seminars, radio programs, Answers TV streaming platform, and all the teaching in the exhibits at the Ark and Creation Museum, etc.

Because Christians are engaged in a battle, they need a continual supply of "ammunition"—plus newer advanced "weapons" to counter the enemy's attacks and their ever-changing strategies against God's Word. To that end, AiG produces new "ammunition" each year in printed or digital form. We need to be reminded that as Christians, we're in a war. But as Paul states in Ephesians 6:12: *We do not wrestle against flesh and blood, but against the rulers, against the authorities, against the cosmic powers over this present darkness, against spiritual forces of evil in the heavenly places.*

APOLOGETICS

As we understand the cutting-edge spiritual battle raging today regarding the authority of Scripture, I trust you and your family will continue to obtain vital "ammunition" from AiG's powerful "arsenal." In this way, *By them you may wage the good warfare*—as was told by Paul to Timothy (1 Timothy 1:18).

Now did the secular reporter deliberately try to malign us by falsely accusing me of promoting violence or is it that he just has no clue as to what we are talking about regarding the spiritual battle? Well, it may be both, but I'm reminded of this passage of Scripture:

> "The natural person does not accept the things of the Spirit of God, for they are folly to him, and he is not able to understand them because they are spiritually discerned" (1 Corinthians 2:14).

DECEMBER 28

Romans 1:16

Faith Amidst Battles

The vision started in the late 1970s, when—as a public school science teacher in Australia—I took my students to a local natural history museum. Throughout, there were signs about millions of years and references to evolution—all presented as fact. As I watched my own students and hundreds of other young people there, I realized this same situation was playing out daily in cities around the world. That's where a "fire in my bones" started. I thought that a creation museum could reach generations of young people with the truth of God's infallible Word and refute evolutionary teaching.

Not long after, what was to become the leading creation apologetics ministry in Australia started in our home. One of the founding board members of the ministry and I talked about my burden to build a major creation-based museum. At one point, both of us stood on some land in Australia and prayed that the Lord would one day provide a place to build such a museum.

Despite our burden, nothing seemed to happen in answer to this prayer at first. However, the Australian ministry grew, and soon, I was invited to do speaking tours in America. In 1987, our family moved to the United States to become "missionaries to America" where I worked with the Institute for Creation Research (founded by Dr. Henry Morris). The goal was to help call the Church in the United States back to the authority of the Word of God, as so many had compromised God's Word in Genesis.

After seven amazing years at ICR, instead of returning to Australia, I saw the Lord opening the way for the Answers in Genesis ministry to be founded—and for the Creation Museum to be built in America. The Lord brought two very special men into my life while working with ICR. Mark Looy had worked in Christian radio in San Diego and had also helped ICR organize the major Back to Genesis conferences. Mike Zovath, who had just retired from the military, came to ICR to work with Mark as a seminar coordinator. In retirement, Mike wanted to do something significant for the Lord. Both of these men worked with me on speaking events.

Knowing my burden to build a major creation museum, Mark and Mike told me that they shared the same museum burden. The three of us, through a series of circumstances that could have only been orchestrated by the God of miracles, moved our families to Northern Kentucky (near Cincinnati, Ohio) to begin this new adventure in 1994.

We set up an office in a small strip mall in Florence, Kentucky (just south of Cincinnati), and started to tell people that the Lord had called us to start a biblical creation ministry and build a creation museum. When the secular press got wind of our vision, I remember one of them interviewing me and asking: "Where are you going to get the money for such a thing?" I answered, "We're Christians, and because we're sure the God of creation has called us to do this, He will provide the money through His people." I could see the reporter was not convinced. Her face suggested a scoffing attitude. But we stepped out in faith. With no money and no idea how it could happen, we moved ahead. AiG looked for land. We even signed a contract on a piece of property, only to lose it in a rezoning battle because the local secular humanist group stirred up intense opposition. The three of us couldn't believe how emotional a rezoning battle could become. Answers in Genesis was often front-page news for days on end as people lashed out at a ministry that wanted to build a creation museum! This was becoming a real spiritual struggle.

RESOURCES — DECEMBER 28

Yes, we were somewhat downcast at losing the rezoning battle, but God renewed our spirits, and we began looking for land again. Soon, the ministry found a beautiful piece of property a few miles west of the Cincinnati Airport—right at an exit and fronting Interstate 275. It was too good to be true. Yes, we had no money, but God had called us to do this. So, under the guidance of the godly AiG board, we approached the owners about buying the property interest-free over a few years, and they agreed! Only God could do this. We had more rezoning battles as the museum was opposed by the same secular humanists—there was even a court case—but the Lord had the right people in the right places at the right time, and this time the rezoning (after many stressful events) went through! AiG now had a superior property in a superior location, so the board decided to build a much bigger museum. The vision was growing. And truly, as AiG received opposition, we realized the promise of Genesis 50:20, *As for you, you meant evil against me, but God meant it for good.*

We hired a local architectural firm (who gave us a special discount), and soon, God's people were supporting this vision. Little by little the funds started to come in. Also, talented people who wanted to use their skills for the Lord began contacting us. Special mention should be made of Patrick Marsh, our museum's director of design. Patrick had worked for Universal Studios–Florida and was an exhibit designer for its King Kong and Jaws attractions; he had also designed theme parks in Japan and other Asian countries. He was a huge answer to our prayers.

When we opened the Creation Museum, a reporter asked me, "Where did you find such talent?" I replied, "It's the result of a miracle. Just as God brought the animals to Noah on the ark, so God brought these talented people to us!"

Yes, there were seemingly impossible difficulties to overcome. Donation issues were always keeping us on our toes (and more importantly, on our knees!). But just as God told the Israelites about conquering the promised land, we were reminded that *little by little I will drive them out from before you, until you have increased and possess the land* (Exodus 23:30).

On the museum's opening day, May 28, 2007, the same humanist group, who had opposed us on the first piece of property, helped organize a demonstration outside the museum property. A reporter asked me, "What do you think of the demonstrators at the gates?" I responded something like this, "Well, last time they opposed us, we ended up getting a far better piece of property and a far bigger vision to build a far bigger museum than we ever thought possible. I can't wait to see how the Lord uses their opposition this time!" Well, we received a lot of international press coverage that weekend, and, again, God used the "opposition" to help accomplish His plan! I am constantly reminded of the verse: *For I am not ashamed of the gospel, for it is the power of God for salvation to everyone who believes, to the Jew first and also to the Greek* (Romans 1:16).

As I look back and think about all the opposition AiG has faced, I can truly say that what was meant as evil, God meant for good, in order (as the rest of Genesis 50:20 says) *to bring it about that many people should be kept alive, as they are today.*

Yes, God uses the Creation Museum to save many people. It's the fulfillment of a vision that goes back many years to those high school teaching days. But with God's miraculous provision of several key people and tens of thousands of supporters, He has shown—again—that God's ways are higher than our ways.

All praise be to God.

DECEMBER 29

Proverbs 22:6

Never Too Young to Learn the Truth About Creation

Even with such intense atheistic indoctrination, secularists complain that creationists are increasingly successful in countering the evolution/long ages message.

I read an article once in which an evolutionist bemoaned the fact that biblical creationists are able to come across as very convincing to children. Now, I thought: If you go to one of those large secular bookstores, you can see a wide range of books on evolution/millions of years targeted at a young audience—designed to indoctrinate children in atheistic evolutionary ideas. Of course, public (secular) school science texts (and other resources in school libraries) also are geared to teach evolution/millions of years as fact, right from the youngest ages in the government-run education systems. And, sadly, there's an increasing number of books in secular stores, schools, and libraries pushing the LGBTQ worldview on children.

Even with such intense indoctrination, secularists complain that creationists are increasingly successful in countering atheism/evolution/long ages message. They say there's an urgent need for evolutionists to communicate their message more effectively to children.

Secular evolutionists/atheists know that if you can indoctrinate at a young age, it paves the way to brainwashing children with a naturalistic (atheistic) worldview. That's why the secularists are moving more and more to protect their ideology through legislation and litigation. They don't even want students to hear the difficulties with evolution or understand the observational evidence that contradicts it (evidence that actually confirms the Bible's account of creation).

Look at North Korea and how a dictator there takes children basically from when they are born and indoctrinates them in his own religious cult. Sadly, secularists have indoctrinated billions of children in anti-God ideas and are accelerating their efforts in order to gain an even stronger hold on the public education system. Such people are quick to accuse Christians (especially those believing in biblical creation) of indoctrinating children at a young age. Now the Bible instructs parents to:

Train up a child in the way he should go; even when he is old he will not depart from it (Proverbs 22:6).

Evolutionists and atheists thus work hard to kick Christianity out of the public school system (and other public places) and replace it with their own religion—the religion of naturalism (atheism). It's a worldview that teaches that the universe and all life have arisen by natural processes—and that man is just an animal who has no ultimate meaning and purpose. And the secularists have been very successful in accomplishing this. It's all part of the spiritual war that's been raging for 6,000 years.

Atheist Richard Dawkins actually stated that Christians who teach their children Christianity are committing "child abuse." Also, a person who used to be legal director for the group American Atheists (the same person who vehemently opposed the Creation Museum) was quoted as saying the following about creationism in general: "We might now be in the Dark Ages.... [There is a] need to oppose the terrorism of this ignorance, and the child abuse of teaching children that science is wrong and that faith and dogma trump truth."

APOLOGETICS — DECEMBER 29

Of course, Dawkins and this atheist should be labeled as "God haters," which is why they oppose creationists and want to impose their atheistic dogma on public school students (and society in general). In essence, they want schools to be churches of atheism with the teachers being the priests of that religion.

Such atheists often get livid when they see the effectiveness of the Creation Museum's and Ark Encounter's communication techniques, especially as they realize that such are reaching children with information they don't want them to know. God is doing a great work through the Ark and Creation Museum. We receive testimonies like this one that involved a very young museum booster:

"The Creation Museum is not lost on the really young. My 2-year-old son Elijah visited the museum (along with the rest of the family). Months later, he decided that he should pretend he is going to the Creation Museum. He lined up his [toy] dinosaurs, handed out tickets to us, and told us all the [dinosaur] names. . . . Our little boy (having not been to the Creation Museum in many months) described details of the museum—the brachiosaurus in the lobby that moves his head 'like this' (as our son demonstrated with his hand), and the planetarium where our 'seats went back to look at the stars on the ceiling.'

"He loves creation, and especially all the kinds of dinosaurs God made."

The more we train generations in the truth right from the earliest age (even at 2), the more they'll easily distinguish truth from error. Yes, the truth that God created as the Bible states is so obvious even a child gets it! We need such a generation of children to combat false teachings of "the children" of atheists.

[A]nd how from childhood you have been acquainted with the sacred writings, which are able to make you wise for salvation through faith in Christ Jesus (2 Timothy 3:15).

> Your children are never too young to learn the truth about creation, God's Word, and the saving gospel.

DECEMBER 30

2 Corinthians 4:4

A Frustrating Spiritual Blindness: Part 1

This article is based on how a secular reporter responded to my speaking tour in England back in 2008. But I have found that this is so typical of how most secular reporters respond to those like us at Answers in Genesis concerning our stand upon God's Word.

In their case the god of this world has blinded the minds of the unbelievers, to keep them from seeing the light of the gospel of the glory of Christ, who is the image of God (2 Corinthians 4:4).

The natural person does not accept the things of the Spirit of God, for they are folly to him, and he is not able to understand them because they are spiritually discerned (1 Corinthians 2:14).

Keep those verses in mind as you see how this reporter wrote about what he supposedly heard me say. Their unbelief also results in them deliberately wanting to malign Christians too. There's a spiritual blindness and a willingness (deliberate) to deceive people. A secular reporter from the United Kingdom's *Guardian* certainly let his spiritual state and resulting agenda shine through. *The Guardian* newspaper in Great Britain[109]—one of Britain's most influential papers and somewhat left-leaning—carried an article about my speaking tour in the land of Darwin. I was called "Richard Dawkins's [the atheist/evolutionist] worst nightmare" in the article. The reporter wrote: "Spending time with the creationist preacher Ken Ham is a profoundly disorientating experience. He inhabits a world that was created in six days, is around 6,000 years old and that started out with a pair of humans sharing a garden with every kind of animal on the planet—including fruit-eating dinosaurs and cuddly vegetarian tigers." Well, I never said tigers were in the Garden of Eden. We would say that the cat "kind" was represented. Tigers are a species that would have developed since the Flood.

He goes on: "Strangely, after two hours of his rapid-fire Australian drawl that world starts to seem vaguely plausible. Ham heads up the US-based organisation Answers in Genesis and, as the name suggests, he promotes a literal interpretation of the Bible. For him, there is no room for human interpretation or allegory." This is all somewhat misleading. I stated in my talk—and the reporter was in attendance—that I define literally as "naturally"—and that there is poetry in the Bible (e.g., Psalm) and that Jesus spoke in parables. I said that I take the Bible "naturally," according to the type of literature and language used. Where it is history, we should take it as history—as Genesis is written. Where it's poetry, like the Psalms, while it can teach great truths, we understand the poetic nature of the literature. The only reason that people make an allegory out of Genesis is to ignore the plain teaching and to read in their own ideas.

The reporter continued: "Ham, an Australian who has become very influential in his adopted country, has just come to the end of a two-week tour of the UK, bringing the literalist [Again, with the word literalist, he implies something different than what I clearly defined as reading the Scriptures "naturally"—as above] message to audiences from the Vale of Glamorgan to Bedford, Liverpool and London. He has been playing to significant, although not huge crowds—600 in Bedford, around 250 in Leicester, a similar number at a two-day conference in London. But in the US his organisation has had a much more dramatic effect. Its $27m (£13.5m) state-of-the-art 'creation museum' opened in Kentucky last May and clocked up 100,000 visitors in its first eight weeks. At Leicester's Parklands leisure centre last Thursday, Ham's pitch was that it is the atheists—and in particular "secular scientists"—who are the dogmatic ones sticking stubbornly to their bogus theories." Actually, I explained quite carefully that Christians and atheists both have starting points/ beliefs they are not willing to change. I did not say it was just the atheists who were dogmatic. My talk made it clear that both atheists and Christians insist upon their beliefs and are not willing to change their basic presuppositions.

The article continues: "In his first lecture, entitled Defending Creationism in an Evolutionary World, he claimed that by dismissing the idea that the Bible represents revealed truth, secularists are rigging the debate in their favour." Well, I did not use the word rigging. I said both groups—those who start with the Bible and those who start with atheistic beliefs—look at the same evidence and interpret it differently in regard to origins, because of the different starting points. However, it is true that a Christian giving up his starting points before a debate is foolish, as this article demonstrates.

The article continues: "'Bring [your children] up to understand that the Bible has to be the foundation for our thinking,' he told the faithful. 'We might not have the details.'" Actually, I said the Bible gives us many specific details concerning the history of the universe—and I went through these in considerable detail regarding Genesis 1–11, which give those specifics about the origin of all the basic entities of life and the universe. I spelled them out: origin of space, matter, time, earth, dry land, water, sea creatures, flying creatures, land creatures, man, woman, sin, death, clothing, language and languages, nations, cultures, seven-day week, etc.

Article continues: "But we have the big picture of history." I did explain that the Bible gives the big picture of history—but with many specific details that explain the present world. "I put it to him afterwards that radiometric dating methods applied to rocks from thousands of locations around the earth contradict the young earth idea. These methods rely on the rate at which certain radioactive forms of atoms decay, and point to a 4.5bn-year-old planet. His response is simple. This can't be correct because it would contradict the Bible." Here he is really twisting how I say that the Bible is our starting point in order to make out that we have blind faith in the Bible. Certainly, I said that the idea of an earth billions of years old contradicts the Bible, and I specifically spelled out problems regarding having death before sin.

He continues: "But it is the scientists who are blinded by dogma. 'If you are committed to the "millions of years" then you are going to cling to particular dating methods and particular results that you get,' said Ham. "Then comes an audacious falsehood. He states: 'Ninety per cent of those dating methods actually contradict the idea of millions of years and billions of years.'" No, not 90% of radiometric dating methods. I said that 90% of all dating methods—including those that are not radiometric—used to age-date the earth actually contradict the billions of years.

> It would take a great deal of space to list all of these, but a few examples are the magnetic field of the earth, Niagara Falls, helium, salt concentrations in the ocean, etc.

DECEMBER 31
1 Corinthians 2:14

A Frustrating Spiritual Blindness: Part 2

The natural person does not accept the things of the Spirit of God, for they are folly to him, and he is not able to understand them because they are spiritually discerned (1 Corinthians 2:14). Continuing to look at how a secular reporter is so blinded he misses the truth of what I as a biblical creationist taught, and misrepresents this in an article showing his agenda to undermine creationists.

The reporter continues in his article: "Sticking to the Biblical script involves some incredible mental gymnastics. Genesis says that eating flesh was not allowed in the Garden of Eden (before Eve messed things up)." Actually, it was Adam who "messed things up" for the human race, as Adam gets the blame for sin.

Article continues: "So all the animals happily got along by eating foliage and fruit—including the carnivores. If they were all herbivores originally, how can he say they were carnivores [that we see today] eating plants in the Garden? 'What do you think Adam was doing while T rex was considering lunch?' Ham asked his audience as part of a hypothetical dialogue to make his point."

Well, I would say I don't think Adam was worried at all. Not before the Fall anyway. Why the big teeth then? We've grown up in a fallen world and see sharp teeth on an animal like a lion or a tiger. So if we see another animal like that, we think they were always savage animals. In my presentation, I explained that just because an animal has sharp teeth doesn't mean it is a meat eater—it just means it has sharp teeth. I said that there are animals today that are carnivores, but before sin, they would have used their sharp teeth to eat plants.

The reporter stated: "According to Ham, all those adaptations for hunting and ripping flesh would have been put to different uses in Eden." That is not the way I would say such things. When I do talk about this, I generally say there were likely a lot of the features used for eating flesh today that would have had different uses before the Fall.

The reporter: "Afterwards I ask him about evolutionary biologist Richard Dawkins' assertion that labelling a child with a religion before they have had a chance to decide between different faiths or no faith at all amounts to child abuse. Answers in Genesis produces numerous books and DVDs for children." I may have become a little more forceful about this, as he was using the child abuse angle, saying AiG is producing all these books to influence and perhaps "infect" children. I wanted to emphasize that the world was indoctrinating children in a secular philosophy. Besides, God makes it clear we are to teach children: *Train up a child in the way he should go; even when he is old he will not depart from it* (Proverbs 22:6).

The reporter quoted me: "If you want to talk about child abuse I would say that Richard Dawkins is the one responsible for child abuse, because Richard Dawkins wants to train kids that there is no god, that there is no purpose and meaning in life." Yes, I said that. Take note that Dr. Dawkins is a signer of the Humanist Manifesto III, and is consistent with his professed religious views imposing them on students.

The reporter: "'Without this purpose, what's to stop them from killing their neighbour, having an abortion, becoming homosexual or taking drugs,' asks Ham." Well, that's his interpretation of what I said. In my talks, I explain that I can understand it if someone believes they are just an animal and thus sees nothing wrong with abortion. (It is not generally considered "wrong" to get rid of spare cats, so why not get rid of spare

APOLOGETICS   DECEMBER 31

humans—why should there be any difference?) I could see why such people would accept marriage to be whatever they want—two men together, two women, five men, etc.

The reporter: "And this is the nub of it. For Ham and his followers, if you start cherry-picking from the Bible (including dismissing Genesis as a metaphor) then you are on a slippery slope to moral ruin."

Well, I didn't say "slippery slope to moral ruin." But it would be a slippery slope to unbelief in the rest of Scripture—thus undermining biblical authority as a whole.

The reporter: "It's the familiar insulting and false idea that humanists and atheists are inherently amoral because we don't have a big God-shaped stick poised over our heads to beat us if we misbehave."[110]

I never said humanists and atheists were amoral. I said that they have no basis for absolutes—no ultimate basis for right and wrong. It is just subjective—just their opinion, and I even gave an example to explain this. It is interesting that Richard Dawkins makes it clear that from an evolutionary perspective, there is no right and wrong as he did in a debate with Jaron Lanier:

Jaron Lanier: "There's a large group of people who simply are uncomfortable with accepting evolution because it leads to what they perceive as a moral vacuum, in which their best impulses have no basis in nature."

Richard Dawkins: "All I can say is, That's just tough. We have to face up to the truth. Ken Ham's vision of a frugivorous T. rex sharing Eden with Adam and Eve requires some breathtaking intellectual dishonesty to sustain it. If this is the foundation for his moral edifice, I want no part of it."

The foundation of my moral edifice is not a "frugivorous T. rex sharing Eden with Adam and Eve" but building my thinking on the absolute authority of God's Word, which means, for example, that marriage is one man for one woman as taught in Genesis. Really, the point he misses is that, with a biblical worldview, morality is not the shifting, gray area that evolutionary thinking and moral relativism ultimately lead to. God's standard is the same no matter the location or the time period.

I have found that reporters who interview me about the creation/evolution issue and our stand on Scripture come in two basic types (with many variations of course). There are those who are just reporting—they want accurate quotes from me and then they will usually interview others who disagree with us and try to accurately quote them. Even though they don't always get it totally correct, they do try their best to report what we believe and what our opposition says about us. I am thankful for such reporters.

Then there are those (like this *Guardian* reporter) who have an agenda they want to publicly express. They are not concerned with trying to understand and/or present what we say and believe accurately. (It may be that they cannot [spiritual blindness] or don't want to understand, but, then again, why would it be important to report accurately if one doesn't believe in an absolute authority and has no basis for truth other than their own beliefs or agenda anyway?) They want to attack our position and put forward their own views. Thus they distort and misrepresent. One has to wonder: If evolution were true, then nothing matters when we die, so why are such reporters wasting their time attacking creation if it doesn't really matter?

> As the Scripture states in 2 Corinthians 4:4: "The god of this world has blinded the minds of the unbelievers, to keep them from seeing the light of the gospel of the glory of Christ, who is the image of God."

INDEX

A

abuse: 94, 255, 274, 277-278, 352, 355, 360, 362, 402, 452-453, 466, 474, 492, 537, 688, 730, 734

academic: 8, 33, 85, 95, 122, 213, 233-234, 266, 272-273, 337, 347, 349, 372-373, 414, 416, 516, 536, 552, 571, 585, 592, 617, 625, 664, 682

affirms: 274, 332

aliens: 11, 152-153, 206-207, 268-269, 720-721

Allies: 271, 456

anger: 31, 89, 114-115, 157, 194, 252, 333, 462-463, 526

anti-Christian: 5, 31, 36, 90, 226, 236, 251, 261, 266, 270, 278, 338, 356, 361-362, 370, 380, 385, 418, 424, 428-429, 437, 456, 486, 519, 528, 535, 539, 550-551, 554, 596, 614-615, 628, 658, 688, 694, 704

arguments: 17, 62-63, 92-93, 116, 138, 230, 237, 244, 248, 259-260, 271, 315, 340, 358, 382, 389, 402, 413, 446-447, 459, 510, 532, 536-537, 590, 612-613, 619, 624, 640, 642, 653, 656, 662, 664-666, 677, 691, 696, 698, 702, 717, 722

Arkophobia: 412-413

Arminian: 192

B

Babel: 9, 136, 147, 157, 191, 211, 217, 222, 236, 282-283, 320-321, 396, 458, 469, 511, 534, 573, 577, 588-589, 596, 610, 681, 696, 706, 723

banning: 408, 629, 724

begat: 19, 568, 612-613

Bereans: 95, 279, 287, 422, 441-442, 481, 496-497, 689

blindness: 732, 734-735

boldly: 13, 51, 54, 77, 96-97, 105, 114-115, 163, 196, 198-201, 208-209, 219, 226, 232-233, 240, 242, 255, 262, 266, 275, 277, 281, 315, 322, 328, 356-358, 361, 363, 370, 397-399, 409, 424, 434, 442, 484, 498-499, 549, 571, 594, 600-601, 626, 666, 674, 679, 692

Borg: 600

bread: 27, 42, 88, 159, 176, 480, 542, 670

burdened: 114, 201, 207, 214, 235, 238, 273, 280, 295, 323, 328, 332, 357-358, 436, 470-471, 478, 487, 516, 528, 539, 633-634, 637, 666, 669, 678

C

Cain: 68-69, 141, 148, 155, 160, 238, 300, 352, 404, 428-429, 450, 472, 568, 576

Calvinist: 192

cancer: 40-41, 83, 107, 123, 132, 139, 163, 168, 170, 226, 230, 258, 305, 335, 366-367, 415, 465, 482-483, 547, 577-578, 581, 593, 641, 651, 673

catastrophic: 25, 30, 36, 40-41, 79, 82-84, 126, 151, 162, 175-176, 187, 254-255, 287, 327, 348, 354, 420, 438-439, 441, 496-498, 504, 514-516, 522, 528, 618, 624, 648, 650, 661, 706

cavemen: 156, 164-165

chains: 98, 541, 642

Christmas: 318, 332, 340, 356, 384, 408, 432-433, 471, 614, 628, 634, 700, 708, 711, 722-723

climate: 13, 52, 60, 111, 174-175, 180-181, 254-255, 262-263, 326-327, 466-467, 553, 646

INDEX

college: 31, 33, 62, 82-84, 141, 146, 162, 168-169, 201, 223, 233, 239, 244, 259, 264, 292, 323-324, 328-329, 347, 349, 436, 443, 448, 470, 488, 491, 498, 567, 570, 585, 602, 617, 664, 682-683, 717

consequences: 13, 25, 31, 36, 77, 82, 87, 94, 111, 116, 125, 133, 148-149, 181, 202, 213, 218, 289, 334, 355, 369, 374, 380, 386, 389, 405, 420, 430, 482, 521, 525, 528, 532, 539, 543, 554, 560, 562, 588, 606, 626, 638, 641, 647, 667, 674, 682, 698, 723

Cross: 19, 58, 66, 70-71, 90, 102-103, 128, 132, 135, 228-229, 259, 268-269, 273, 281, 283, 287-289, 301, 313, 343, 374-375, 403, 433, 444, 453, 475, 484, 495, 501, 506, 513, 520-521, 542-543, 557, 573, 577, 607, 610, 627, 645, 675, 682, 692, 712-713, 723

CRT: 22-23

D

danger: 66, 235, 253, 446, 545, 669

Daniel: 8, 318, 360, 512, 554, 626-627

Desalted: 614

design: 62-63, 221, 224, 302-303, 305, 319, 329, 396, 462, 479, 501, 525, 533, 536, 580, 605, 621, 636, 642, 656-657, 676, 690, 697, 729

dinosaurs: 8, 34, 122, 141, 186, 214-215, 238, 240, 256-257, 277, 348, 397, 414, 436, 438, 468-469, 478, 480, 488, 574, 576, 586-587, 598-599, 603, 638, 652-653, 674-675, 717, 731-732

disease: 36-37, 39-41, 43, 62, 80-81, 83, 123, 127, 139, 168-170, 187, 191, 254, 258, 284, 334-335, 348-349, 360, 403, 444, 449, 465, 483, 489, 494, 542, 547, 560, 577, 580, 592-593, 606, 646, 651, 672-673, 684

divine: 28, 58, 62, 109, 173, 235, 351, 372, 463, 557, 591, 606, 619, 653, 669, 676-677, 690, 692-693, 696, 703, 709, 721, 726

DNA: 38, 56, 58, 60, 62, 86, 101, 116, 127, 136, 161, 211, 279, 303, 395, 415, 494, 558, 608-609, 622, 681

dolphins: 622-623

dominion: 13, 26, 46, 53, 73, 111, 124, 175, 255, 263, 303, 326-327, 356, 402-403, 461, 466, 544

doomed: 146-147, 202

dragon: 13, 468-469, 653

dust: 15, 20, 24, 35, 42, 44, 47, 70, 73, 85, 88, 96, 122, 124, 133, 184, 191-192, 194, 229, 285, 372, 396, 461, 488, 542, 558, 561, 625, 633, 648, 662, 680, 685

E

Easter: 70-71, 361, 471, 484

Eden: 42, 120, 205, 371-372, 400, 430, 496-497, 520, 542-543, 562, 597, 609, 636, 673, 691, 732, 734-735

evangelism: 60, 64-65, 224, 245, 248, 259, 343, 398, 401, 418, 490, 618, 634, 692

Exodus: 18-19, 73, 87, 109, 122-123, 130, 143, 158, 193, 208, 215, 227, 239, 247-248, 256, 281, 286, 293, 295, 301, 303, 322, 343, 390, 403, 436, 449, 494, 521, 584, 591, 685, 708, 729

F

facts: 17, 36, 72, 166-167, 256, 263, 267, 394, 422, 438, 441, 454, 458-459, 544, 570, 574, 602, 617, 638, 644, 715

Fallacies: 286, 288, 290

INDEX

father's: 13, 113, 115, 186, 194, 196, 198-199, 243, 290, 295, 301, 427, 477, 527, 630, 632-633, 636-637

fearfully: 86, 117, 302-303

fictional: 16-17, 206, 503, 527, 614, 658

fossils: 17, 30, 40, 83, 92, 101, 126-127, 151, 166-167, 186, 190-191, 246, 256-258, 264, 292, 423, 438, 440-441, 455, 464-465, 480, 482, 497, 534, 544, 546, 574, 593, 598-599, 638, 647, 650, 652-653, 672, 678, 686, 697

foundational: 38, 47, 72-73, 76-77, 93, 107, 123, 126-127, 146, 210-211, 218, 228-229, 236, 238, 247, 259, 281, 291, 297, 322, 325, 343, 349, 374-375, 406, 433, 454, 458, 484-485, 489, 510, 512, 514-515, 550, 572-573, 578, 616-617, 619, 628, 647, 667, 684, 706, 710, 716

future: 12, 19, 41-42, 82, 98, 117, 133, 146, 153, 169, 174-175, 239, 254-255, 275, 287, 323, 330, 335, 354-355, 367, 371, 376-377, 399, 401, 411, 423, 426, 435, 439, 448, 475, 483, 538, 540, 543, 545, 561, 610, 632, 654, 670, 672-673, 675, 686, 716, 718

G

gap theory: 24-25, 55, 73, 106, 122, 138, 186, 199, 347, 446, 488, 546-547, 585, 684

Garden: 7, 42, 64, 110, 120, 205, 258, 296-297, 337, 371-372, 400, 423, 430, 432, 496-497, 520, 542-543, 562, 572-573, 609, 636, 673, 691, 722, 732, 734

gender: 6-7, 13, 26, 48, 56, 66-67, 73, 76, 80, 90, 92, 96-97, 110, 146, 149, 154-155, 163, 179, 231, 236-238, 249, 336-338, 342, 356, 382, 390, 401, 404-405, 412, 450, 463, 490, 499, 504, 508, 627, 722

giant: 161, 215, 232, 267, 299

godly: 21, 27, 33, 54, 118, 124, 158-161, 177, 194-195, 197-198, 218-219, 227, 252-253, 257, 336-337, 339, 361, 380-381, 390-391, 397, 409, 437, 455, 471, 478, 503, 527-528, 531, 533, 553, 630, 633, 636-637, 729

groaning: 41, 43-44, 83, 132, 139, 153, 168-170, 175, 183, 254-255, 284, 332, 369, 464, 467, 483, 560-561, 592-593, 606, 609, 646-647, 649, 673

H

hands: 18, 21, 76, 87, 137, 150, 159, 184, 251, 260, 264, 287-288, 300, 302, 319, 333, 392, 422, 466, 475, 501, 512, 519, 555, 582-583, 594, 611, 626-627, 636, 692, 700

hate: 6-7, 42, 48, 88-89, 95, 125, 148, 172, 177, 185, 200-201, 237, 260, 262, 277-278, 298, 302, 310, 313, 328-329, 356-357, 379, 388, 404, 417, 543, 556, 586, 608, 627, 652, 680, 688

health: 20, 66, 76, 80-81, 87, 92, 116, 210, 250-251, 302, 337, 342, 360-361, 427, 629, 637, 675, 716-717

hell: 13, 31, 33, 147-148, 153, 188-189, 204, 207, 268-270, 281, 358, 362, 376, 401, 438, 452-453, 465, 499, 530, 537, 559, 648, 678, 682

Hezekiah: 380-381, 528-531

Hollywood's: 399, 502-503

homosexuality: 155, 184-185, 238, 362, 460, 512, 532, 538-539

hope: 5, 8, 31, 47, 61, 64, 109, 117, 146-147, 168, 189, 193, 195, 229, 244-245, 254, 264, 275, 277, 282, 293, 308, 314-315, 322-323, 330-331, 333, 350-351, 381, 407, 421, 428-429, 432, 436, 445-446, 451, 485-486, 495, 511, 514, 521, 526, 531, 537, 555, 559, 592, 640, 701, 713, 721, 723, 726

INDEX

hopelessness: 167, 330-331, 512, 528, 607, 620, 640, 713

humanism: 6, 48, 111, 116, 162, 253, 289, 312-314, 317, 355, 411, 462, 492, 494, 538, 550-552, 574, 616, 620, 628-629, 652, 716

I

inherit: 89, 155, 170, 184, 366, 482, 589, 658

Intelligent Design movement: 62

interpretation: 15, 17, 25, 36, 38, 109, 120-121, 138-139, 160, 166-167, 230-231, 237, 243, 267, 279, 324, 346, 395, 406, 416, 423, 440, 459-460, 476, 491, 566-567, 569, 574, 578, 587, 592-593, 622, 684, 688, 732, 734

interracial: 20-21

intolerance: 6, 48, 261, 297, 314-315, 342, 345, 356, 429, 462-463, 499, 535

intolerant: 6-7, 48, 90, 172-173, 181, 205, 299, 314-315, 343, 357, 362, 378, 382, 456, 462-463, 487, 534, 539, 616, 626, 700

J

Jeremiahs: 404

K

kinds: 79, 86, 88, 127, 142, 150, 183, 191, 225, 256-257, 360, 376, 402, 440-441, 468, 500, 503-504, 512, 522, 524, 575, 577, 609, 617, 623, 653, 696, 731

kings: 28, 118-119, 160, 208, 221, 318, 336, 377, 380, 424-425, 500, 528, 554, 694

knee: 275, 424-425, 570

L

language: 21, 38, 50-51, 56, 58, 60, 72-73, 99, 101, 130, 137, 139, 144, 147, 199, 211, 222-223, 246, 282, 292, 298, 342-343, 346, 371, 409, 413, 415, 422, 446, 506, 523, 552, 580, 593, 604, 663, 726, 732-733

leaven: 82-83, 480

legacy: 21, 31, 52-53, 157, 159, 161, 194-197, 232, 242-243, 252-253, 259, 294-295, 304, 324, 390-391, 426-427, 476-477, 531, 588, 605, 630-633, 636-637, 648, 675, 695, 698, 702, 706, 725

legends: 156-157, 216, 320, 446, 468-469, 502-503, 653

legs: 622-623

LGBTQ: 6-7, 13, 36, 47-48, 56, 73, 76, 97, 127, 148-149, 162, 172, 180-181, 226, 232, 236-238, 249, 251, 262-263, 279, 319, 356-357, 362, 380, 400, 404-405, 450, 454, 487, 490, 505, 514, 614, 627, 660, 730

lies: 13, 51, 97, 113, 119-120, 179, 186, 200, 205, 227, 259, 299, 308, 319, 328, 344, 347,

listen: 34, 52, 120-121, 131, 133, 141, 148, 159, 231, 272, 278, 282, 404, 427, 433, 435, 448, 459, 473, 561, 572, 575, 602, 636

local: 15, 40-41, 75, 85, 105, 114, 126, 142, 179, 190, 196, 218, 243, 246, 260-261, 266, 272, 330, 347, 414, 434, 477, 487, 497, 499, 518, 552-553, 556, 583, 585, 592-594, 620, 624, 650-651, 660, 683, 686, 728-729

lost: 31, 72, 92, 99, 105, 131, 137, 156-157, 161, 164-165, 187, 193, 195, 202, 259, 277, 316, 325, 331, 349, 378, 381, 387, 393, 419, 428, 442-443, 462, 490, 501-502, 523, 531, 563, 578-579, 581, 601, 630, 632-633, 646, 648-649, 661, 685, 688, 719, 731

loving: 27, 83, 89, 119, 121, 130, 148, 168-170, 225, 334-335, 445, 465, 525, 560, 606, 646-647

lukewarm: 7, 36-37, 49, 55, 72, 146, 162, 187, 190, 209, 230, 279, 325, 349, 400, 424, 490, 528, 530, 563

INDEX

M

marketing: 261, 276, 286-287, 479, 486-487, 507

Martians: 268

Men-Pleasing: 590

Menu: 42

minds: 15, 81, 97, 105, 113, 132, 213, 219, 227, 238, 269, 273, 277, 291, 308, 354-355, 360-361, 375, 378-379, 385, 388-389, 435-436, 448, 453, 456, 470, 493, 500, 508, 515, 534, 560, 581, 601, 618, 632, 677, 680, 682, 697, 726, 732, 735

mission: 64, 82, 203, 224, 294-295, 298, 304, 333, 375, 379, 399, 403, 417, 470, 491, 498, 516, 528, 539, 582, 602, 618, 678-679

missionaries: 196, 222-223, 253, 267, 292, 375, 435, 470, 478, 490-491, 516, 559, 630, 632-633, 728

mocked: 8, 34, 73, 85, 90, 215, 317, 319, 335, 370, 412, 414, 427, 452, 529, 541, 624, 680, 692

modern: 13, 16, 25, 30, 52, 68, 87, 111, 128, 141, 156, 180, 232, 268, 286, 288, 290, 302, 312, 368, 370, 389, 400, 406, 440, 447, 474, 478, 498, 522, 528, 535-536, 538, 546, 551, 566, 568, 584, 593, 595, 602, 612, 637-638, 656, 658, 674, 686, 693, 698, 704, 717

morality: 44, 68, 86, 92, 94, 135, 180-181, 268, 270, 333, 352-353, 361, 364, 370-371, 402-403, 411, 418, 492-495, 499, 513-515, 572, 576-577, 580-581, 610, 615-616, 624, 661, 699-701, 705, 711, 716, 735

mothers: 158-159, 302, 319, 332, 391, 402, 636, 677

movement: 48, 52, 62-63, 181, 212, 232-233, 240, 263, 302, 327, 356-357, 370, 388, 390, 400-401, 404, 406, 418, 420, 422, 450, 454, 460, 466-467, 478, 490, 498, 536-537, 581, 616, 618-619, 637, 674, 684, 690

Muslims: 188-189, 204, 359, 452, 578, 714

mutants: 608-609

N

Nehemiah: 114-115, 160, 478, 518-519

Nephilim: 160-161

neutral: 60, 94, 112-113, 232, 346, 362, 364, 386-387, 409-410, 412, 418, 430, 459, 480-481, 548-549, 559, 700, 719

Newton: 16, 305, 656

O

observational: 10-11, 16-17, 20, 56-57, 78-79, 93, 116, 126, 154, 166-167, 191, 215, 217, 269, 305, 308, 312-313, 315, 321, 396-397, 406, 438-441, 462-463, 474, 524, 534, 540-541, 545, 550, 558, 584, 610, 613, 638-639, 653, 715, 730

opposition: 177, 236, 260-261, 274-279, 298, 317, 344, 379, 398, 412-413, 429, 457, 474, 518-519, 536, 539, 587, 620-621, 642, 688, 728-729, 735

outer: 11, 152-153, 211, 268, 332

Overcoming: 260

P

pagan: 21, 28, 30, 41, 49, 87, 105, 123, 130-131, 160-161, 163, 170, 176, 180, 191, 195, 208, 213, 241, 250, 271, 273, 296, 374-375, 380, 390-391, 417, 490, 505, 509, 513, 516-517, 529, 554, 596, 615, 644, 664, 674-675, 700, 722

Paganization: 422

pandemic: 187, 270, 625

Pascal: 656

Pasteur: 656

INDEX

persecution: 48, 77, 209, 298, 339, 345, 360, 362-363, 384-385, 399, 553, 555

Pew Research: 31, 204, 473

Pilgrim: 644-645

planet: 11, 52, 60, 123, 146-147, 153, 180, 203, 207, 324, 326, 445, 466-469, 489, 544, 558, 638, 732-733

Pleases: 140

pride: 8-9, 37, 85, 88-89, 94-95, 122, 330, 347, 349, 377, 380-381, 414, 514, 530-531, 537, 625, 633, 664, 723

primitive: 156-157, 336, 522-523, 546, 631, 658, 706

prisoners: 642

progressive: 73, 122, 138, 347, 416, 446, 456, 488, 580, 585, 592-593, 612, 684

propaganda: 164, 253, 266-267, 274, 291, 312-315, 326, 345, 361, 394, 434, 519, 614, 628, 641

prophetic: 370, 404, 538-539, 667

Q

Queen: 28, 280, 440, 604-605

R

race: 11, 20-22, 42, 69, 102, 136-137, 146-147, 149, 153, 162, 164-165, 203, 206, 210-211, 216-217, 229, 243, 268-269, 278, 321-323, 342, 360, 373, 396, 404-405, 416, 430, 432-433, 444, 477, 562, 588-589, 606, 675, 688, 698, 734

rainbow: 12-13, 41, 156, 216, 320, 342, 356-357, 506, 646, 651, 670, 686, 706

raising: 33, 59, 65, 96-97, 108, 167, 194, 197, 245, 300, 361, 364, 391, 401, 449, 471, 501, 554, 595, 633, 637, 687, 692

ravenous: 36, 274-275, 317

Rearing: 526

redeeming: 104-105

re-digging: 176, 654, 724

reformation: 162-163, 208, 212-213, 227, 240-242, 380, 388-389, 400, 417, 422-423, 425, 439, 442-443, 476, 491, 498-499, 528-529, 660-661, 667, 674, 677-679, 695

relevance: 258, 322-323, 498, 538-539, 666

religions: 110, 180, 204-205, 225, 296, 313-314, 360, 371, 410-411, 417-418, 430-431, 474, 515, 542, 551, 562-563, 615, 618

religious: 28, 48, 59-60, 146, 188, 202-203, 224, 234, 253, 266, 271, 275, 314, 317, 345, 352, 360-361, 408-412, 418, 429-430, 439-440, 452, 456-457, 466-467, 492, 494, 502, 530, 535-536, 538, 548, 550-552, 558, 562, 586, 602, 616-617, 619, 646, 668, 692, 697, 699-700, 716-717, 730, 734

reparations: 23, 102-103

repentance: 89, 100, 144, 163, 245, 319, 331-332, 341, 385, 506, 530, 625, 677

rescue: 214-215, 238-239, 259, 277, 355, 363, 393, 465, 508, 712

responsible: 107, 132, 139, 294-295, 349, 465-467, 561, 570, 606, 616, 647-648, 692, 734

revival: 162-163, 213, 227, 389, 646, 654, 660-661

S

sacrifice: 71, 86-87, 90, 110, 117, 134-135, 141, 153, 181, 184, 206, 250, 286-291, 302, 310, 332, 336-337, 390, 465, 484, 511-513, 521, 541, 610-611, 691, 712

salt: 32, 75, 146, 187, 325, 349, 378-379, 387, 443, 490, 553, 563, 571, 590, 614-615, 628, 685, 719, 733

Sanballats: 518-519

INDEX

Savior: 14, 27-28, 46-47, 62-63, 70-71, 88, 93, 105, 129, 137, 153, 164, 191, 204, 206-207, 257, 287, 291, 301, 308, 315, 318, 343, 373-374, 398, 403, 419, 433, 465, 471, 484-485, 495, 501, 503, 507, 510, 512, 520, 542, 558, 596, 613, 633, 691, 708-709, 715

science, observational: 315

scoffers: 59, 100-101, 144, 275, 317, 384-385, 409, 505, 529, 536, 671, 686-687

Scopes: 428-429, 472, 579, 581, 658

secularist: 112, 213, 224, 232, 247, 261, 268, 312, 330, 348, 363, 382, 385, 388, 412-413, 418-419, 473, 522, 536, 541, 544, 604

shades: 21-22, 136-137, 147, 211, 217, 321, 588-589

Sheba: 28, 604-605

shepherds: 36, 214-215, 275, 283, 435, 516, 530, 584, 590

sinful: 8-9, 13, 25, 37, 80-81, 95, 102, 108, 110, 113-115, 135, 138, 144, 187, 205, 258, 273, 285, 317, 349, 365, 377, 384, 403, 431, 480-481, 486, 505-506, 513, 527, 529, 532-533, 539, 543, 562, 569, 572, 580, 592, 603, 607, 671, 683, 686-687, 691, 711

souls: 88, 193, 197, 227, 261, 331, 393, 408, 423, 432, 484, 487, 503, 593, 611, 619, 645, 648-649, 671

space: 10-11, 18-19, 46, 52, 57, 99, 152-153, 268-269, 374, 396, 440, 475, 503, 720, 733

star: 52, 362, 371, 474, 558, 600, 614, 674

stones: 30-31, 130, 157, 202, 252, 282, 295, 357, 670

suffering: 36-37, 39, 62, 73, 76, 83, 91, 107, 127, 132-133, 139, 168-170, 202, 233, 258, 284, 329, 335, 349, 360, 367, 403, 444-445, 465, 483-484, 494, 511, 524-525, 542, 560-561, 576-578, 580, 606-607, 617, 646-648, 651, 673, 682, 712

Sunday: 5, 104, 112, 114, 128, 158, 196, 226, 242, 245, 271, 280-281, 286-287, 289, 291-293, 295, 322-323, 343, 361, 371, 386, 434, 438-439, 443, 448-449, 471, 476, 508-509, 553, 568, 576-577, 622, 630

syncretism: 431, 491, 562-563

syndrome: 443, 448-449

T

tapestry: 478-479

technological: 78, 156, 164, 474-475, 522, 540

Testify: 269, 608

textbook: 78-79, 82-85, 168, 397, 419, 549, 616-617, 628

theologian: 8, 192, 420, 496

tolerance: 48, 343, 357, 462, 634

tragedy: 44, 284-285, 332, 368, 416, 646-648, 677

train: 31-32, 64, 66-67, 157, 195, 252, 354-355, 360-361, 375-376, 391, 419, 435-437, 448, 509, 526-527, 559, 620, 630, 633, 730-731, 734

training: 15, 31, 33, 50, 66, 72, 160, 227, 239, 249, 252, 322, 347, 361, 386, 391, 422-423, 437, 508-509, 566, 582, 612, 634, 661, 664, 721

transgender: 66, 80, 174, 336, 390, 450, 514, 603, 660-661

tsunami: 646, 684-685

INDEX

U

unashamedly: 105, 200, 208, 219, 225, 232, 242, 322, 328, 330, 357-358, 363, 378, 423-424, 427, 476, 486-487, 539, 549, 555, 694

unbelief: 9, 36, 50, 64, 82-83, 85, 106-107, 179, 186-187, 198, 201, 215, 218, 238, 240-241, 247-248, 270-271, 287, 293, 328, 366, 388, 465, 482, 490, 498, 547, 581, 732, 735

uncompromising: 130-131, 219, 227, 377, 498

unity: 54-55, 119, 191, 585

upholding: 74, 119, 679, 722

V

versus: 16-17, 92, 166, 230, 441, 536, 574, 616, 678

virus: 360, 438

vital: 14-15, 32, 46-47, 70, 72-73, 95, 141, 162, 189, 197-198, 203, 244, 264, 277, 292, 295, 301, 322-323, 342, 349, 375, 382, 386, 435, 464, 484, 507, 510, 512, 523, 534-535, 555, 582, 612-613, 619, 636, 660-661, 667, 719, 724, 727

voting: 386, 540, 718-719

W

wake: 187, 230, 232-233, 253, 399, 408, 517, 538-539, 693

wall: 209, 312, 345, 360, 398, 518-519, 548-549, 714

warfare: 392, 435, 555, 619, 653, 677, 726-727

watchmen: 398-399, 539

weather: 175, 344-345

wells: 176-177, 654-655, 724-725

Wild: 474, 548

Windbags: 658

witnesses: 5, 19, 563, 596, 630, 638, 663, 675

woke: 220, 236, 279, 490, 559, 694

wolves: 36, 274-275, 317, 588, 608-609

wonderfully: 86, 117, 302-303

worship: 13, 25, 34, 52, 60-61, 111, 130-131, 140-141, 149, 181, 238, 286-288, 290-291, 318, 380, 390, 403, 405, 413, 417, 428, 466-467, 475, 506, 528, 548, 558-559, 611, 627, 692, 721

Endnotes

1. Master Books, *Inside the Nye Ham Debate* (Green Forest, AR: Master Books, 2014).
2. Plass, Ewald, *What Martin Luther Says: A Practical In-home Anthology for the Active Christian* (St. Louis, MO: Concordia, 1959), 1523.
3. Natalie Angier, "Do Races Differ? Not Really, DNA Shows," *New York Times*, August 22, 2000, http://partners.nytimes.com/library/national/science/082200sci-genetics-race.html.
4. Pew Research Center, "Millennial Generation Less Religiously Active than Older Americans," Pew Research Center, February 17, 2010, https://www.pewresearch.org/religion/2010/02/17/religion-among-the-millennials/;
Pew Research Center, "Generation Z - Research and Data from Pew Research Center," Pew Research Center, May 26, 2021, https://www.pewresearch.org.
5. Lifesite News, "Michigan Lawmakers Set to Pass LGBT 'Civil Rights' Bill with No Religious Exceptions," Lifesite News, March 15, 2023, https://www.lifesitenews.com.
6. "Two Factors That Destroyed Christianity in Western Europe: Josef Ton's Testimony," New Life Christian Newspaper, January 23, 1982,
7. https://www.foxnews.com/entertainment/william-shatner-says-doesnt-have-long-live-reflecting-legacy.
8. Shatner, William, "People Ask About a Legacy," *The Guardian*, July 2, 2021, https://www.theguardian.com/culture/2021/jul/02/william-shatner.
9. Dawkins, Richard, "There Are Two Sexes, and That's All There Is to It," *Christian Post*, April 19, 2023.
10. Ibid.
11. Merriam-Webster Dictionary, s.v. "evangelism," accessed September 16, 2024, https://www.merriam-webster.com/dictionary/evangelism.
12. Merriam-Webster Dictionary, s.v. "religion," accessed September 16, 2024, https://www.merriam-webster.com/dictionary/religion.
13. Merriam-Webster Dictionary, s.v. "worldview," accessed September 16, 2024, https://www.merriam-webster.com/dictionary/worldview.
14. www.foxnews.com.
15. Ibid.
16. Ibid.
17. Merriam-Webster.com Dictionary, s.v. "science," accessed September 12, 2024, https://www.merriam-webster.com/dictionary/science.
18. WITF, "Dr. Rachel Levine is Named One of 12 'Women of the Year' by USA Today," WITF.org, March 16, 2022, https://www.witf.org.
19. Stump, J. B., and Chad V. Osborne, eds., *Understanding Scientific Theories of Origins: Cosmology, Geology, and Biology in Christian Perspective* (Downers Grove, IL: IVP Academic, 2021).
20. Bishop, Robert C., Larry L. Funck, Raymond J. Lewis, Stephen O. Moshier, and John H. Walton, *Understanding Scientific Theories of Origins: Cosmology, Geology, and Biology in Christian Perspective* (InterVarsity Press, 2018).
21. Stump and Osborne, eds., *Understanding Scientific Theories of Origins*.
22. Amnesty International, "My Body, My Rights," Amnesty.org, accessed October 2, 2024, https://www.amnesty.org/en/latest/campaigns/2014/02/my-body-my-rights/.
23. Wald, George, in *The New York Times*, April 27, 1958.
24. Lloyd Jones, Martyn, *The Revival of Religion in the Church*, (Edinburgh: Banner of Truth Trust, 2008).
25. biologos.org/.
26. Lloyd, Scott, and David K. C. T. L. Wong, eds., *Understanding Scientific Theories of Origins: Cosmology, Geology, and Biology in Christian Perspective* (Wheaton, IL: Crossway, 2021).
27. Merriam-Webster Dictionary, s.v. "religion."
28. Merriam-Webster Dictionary, s.v. "worldview."
29. Pew Forum on Religion & Public Life, "U.S. Religious Landscape Survey: Religious Beliefs and Practices," 2008, Washington, D.C.: Pew Research Center, https://www.pewforum.org/religious-landscape-study/.
30. Angier, "Do Races Differ?"
31. Collins, Francis S., and J. Craig Venter, "Mapping and Sequencing the Human Genome," *Science*, 2001, published by the National Institutes of Health, https://www.genome.gov.
32. Barna, George, "The State of the Church: 2016," Cultural Research Center at Arizona Christian University, 2016.
33. Barna, George, *America at the Crossroads:*

Explosive Trends Shaping America's Future and What You Can Do about It (Grand Rapids: Baker Books, 2016).

34 Gill, John, "A Commentary on the Gospel According to Matthew," Bible Study Tools, biblestudytools.com.

35 Plass, *What Luther Says.*

36 Emmert, Kevin P., "Should Pastors Stop Saying, 'The Bible Says'?" *Christianity Today*, accessed September 24, 2024, www.christianitytoday.com/2014/07/should-pastors-stop-saying-bible-says/.

37 https://obamawhitehouse.archives.gov/the-press-office/2013/04/26/remarks-president-planned-parenthood-conference.

38 Newton, Steven, "Creationism, Mr. Nye, and Dr. Pepper," Huffington Post Blog, http://www.huffingtonpost.com/steven-newton/creationism-mr-nye-and-dr-pepper_b_1934407.html.

39 www.huffpost.com/entry/neil-degrasse-tyson-ken-ham-aliens_n_5627239.

40 Sarah Gray on Salon, published on July 21, 2014.

41 Scott, Eugenie C., "The Teaching of Evolution in U.S. Schools: Where Politics, Religion, and Science Converge," American Association for the Advancement of Science Conference, September 2000.

42 *Los Angeles Times*, May 24, 2007.

43 *Vanity Fair*, February 2010.

44 *Architectural Record*, June 2008.

45 Beck, Glenn, and Daniel Lapin, "The Tower of Babel and Its Modern Symbolism," The Glenn Beck Program, Blaze Media, March 18, 2010, available at https://www.glennbeck.com.

46 "Religion Among the Millennials," Pew Forum, February 2010.

47 "Christianity in the United Kingdom," Faith Survey, August 13, 2018.

48 "Local Churches in Australia," NCLS, 2017; NCLS Church Life Pack Seminar Presentation, Sydney, 2016.

49 "Attitudes Towards Gay Rights," British Religion in Numbers, January 2017.

50 Kopplin, Zack, "Creationism is Not Science and Shouldn't Be in Public School Science Class—It's That Simple," *Science Progress*, Center for American Progress, February 16, 2013, https://www.scienceprogress.org.

51 Ibid.

52 Laats, Adam, "Creationism and Science Education: A Deeper Understanding," The American Conservative, January 22, 2015, https://www.theamericanconservative.com/articles/creationism-and-science-education-a-deeper-understanding/.

53 Merriam-Webster, s.v. "religion."

54 Merriam-Webster, s.v. "intolerance," accessed September 23, 2024, https://www.merriam-webster.com/dictionary/intolerance.

55 Merriam-Webster, s.v. "proselytize," accessed September 23, 2024, https://www.merriam-webster.com/dictionary/proselytize.

56 Sharp, Bill, "ACLU Stance on Tax Exemptions," *USA Today*, December 5, 2010.

57 Obama, Barack, "Oval Office Address on Terrorism," PBS NewsHour, December 6, 2015, https://www.pbs.org/newshour/show/full-speech-president-obama-says-freedom-is-more-powerful-than-fear.

58 Obama, Barack, "Statement by the President on the 37th Anniversary of *Roe v. Wade*," White House Office of the Press Secretary, January 22, 2010, https://obamawhitehouse.archives.gov/the-press-office/statement-president-37th-anniversary-roe-v-wade.

59 Merriam-Webster, s.v. "faith," accessed September 23, 2024, https://www.merriam-webster.com/dictionary/faith.

60 Dawkins, Richard, *The God Delusion* (Boston: Houghton Mifflin, 2006).

61 Becker, Jillian, "Religion is a Disease of the Human Mind," Ludwig von Mises Centre for Liberty, published July 20, 2012.

62 Ray, Darrel, *The God Virus: How Religion Infects Our Lives and Culture* (Bonner Springs: IPC Press, 2009).

63 "Can Your Child Be Too Religious?" *Time*, November 14, 2019.

64 Darwin, Charles, *The Descent of Man, and Selection in Relation to Sex* (London: John Murray, 1871).

65 Encyclopaedia Britannica, "Brave New World," Encyclopaedia Britannica, Inc., accessed October 7, 2024, https://www.britannica.com/topic/Brave-New-World-novel-by-Huxley.

66 Huxley, Aldous, *Ends and Means: An Inquiry into the Nature of Ideals and into the Methods Employed for their Realization* (London: Chatto & Windus, 1937).

67 Dembski, William, *End of Christianity* (Nashville: B&H Publishing, 2009), 155.

68 Bolt, Andrew, "Christians, Prepare for Persecution," *Herald Sun*, July 31, 2017, https://www.heraldsun.com.au/blogs/andrew-bolt/christians-prepare-for-persecution/news-story/fd5efd61324b0b31802b226427a48ca3.

69 BioLogos, "Ministry Description," ECFA, 2024, https://www.ecfa.org.

70 Dunphy, John J., "A Religion for a New Age," *The Humanist*, January-February 1983.

71 Merriam-Webster.com Dictionary, s.v. "phobia," accessed October 7, 2024, https://www.merriam-webster.com/dictionary/phobia.

72 https://ag.org/Beliefs/Position-Papers/The-Doctrine-of-Creation.

73 www.usatoday.com/story/opinion/2017/07/13/creationism-evolution-template-for-easing-divisions-tom-krattenmaker-column/467800001/.

74 The Victorian Society, "Redundant Churches: Who Cares?" *The Victorian*, November 2007.

75 Southern Poverty Law Center, "Finnish School Shooter Had Nazi Beliefs," March 1, 2008.

76 Horgan, John, "The New Social Darwinists," *Scientific American*, October 1995, 175–176.

77 Christian Post, July 27, 2019, www.christianpost.com.

78 Christian News, July 26, 2019, https://christiannews.net.

79 Christian Post, August 26, 2016, www.christianpost.com.

80 https://townhall.com/columnists/michaelbrown/2015/05/27/you-need-to-know-what-really-happened-in-ireland-n2004202.

81 Hare, Brian, and Vanessa Woods, "Being Gay Is Natural: Just Ask Bonobos," Live Science, March 28, 2014, https://www.livescience.com/44464-bonobo-homosexuality-natural.html.

82 Welsh, Jennifer, "Female Lemurs Benefit From Multiple Mates, Study Suggests," Live Science, October 4, 2011, https://www.livescience.com/16380-polyandrous-female-lemurs.html.

83 "The Origin of Humans Is Surprisingly Complicated," *Scientific American*, October 2016, https://www.scientificamerican.com/article/the-origin-of-humans-is-surprisingly-complicated1/.

84 "What Females Want | Real Swingers of the Animal Kingdom," PBS, March 12, 2010, https://www.pbs.org/wnet/nature/what-females-want-real-swingers-of-the-animal-kingdom/831/.

85 Liu, Ming-Jin, et al., "Biomechanical Characteristics of Hand Coordination in Grasping Activities of Daily Living," *PLOS ONE* 11, no. 1 (2016): e0146193, https://doi.org/10.1371/journal.pone.0146193.

86 Krauss, Lawrence M., *A Universe from Nothing: Why There Is Something Rather than Nothing* (New York: Simon & Schuster, 2012).

87 American Marketing Association, "Definition of Marketing," accessed September 24, 2024, https://www.ama.org/the-definition-of-marketing/.

88 LifeWay Research, "Pastors' Views on Creation and Evolution," December 2011, accessed September 24, 2024, https://research.lifeway.com/greatestneeds/.

89 Wald, George, "The Origin of Life," *Scientific American*, August 1954, p. 45.

90 Calvin, John, *Commentaries on the First Book of Moses Called Genesis*, trans. by William Pringle (Edinburgh: Calvin Translation Society, 1847).

91 http://hirr.hartsem.edu/.

92 CBS News, "Noah's Ark Continues to Capture the Imagination of the General Public," 2009, accessed October 7, 2024.

93 Obama, Barack, *The Audacity of Hope: Thoughts on Reclaiming the American Dream* (New York: Crown Publishers, 2006).

94 https://albertmohler.com/2014/04/22/god-the-gospel-and-the-gay-challenge-a-response-to-matthew-vines/.

95 Dawkins, Richard, *The God Delusion* (London, England: Black Swan, 2016), 31.

96 Merriam-Webster Dictionary, s.v. "prophetic." Merriam-Webster.com Dictionary. Accessed September 12, 2024. https://www.merriam-webster.com/dictionary/prophetic.

97 Neil deGrasse Tyson, *Cosmos: A Spacetime Odyssey* (Season 1, Episode 2, aired 2014).

98 Enns, Peter, "Paul's Adam, Part I," BioLogos, February 15, 2010, http://biologos.org/blog/pauls-adam-part-i/.

99 Ibid.

100 Sagan, Carl, *Contact* (New York, NY: Simon & Schuster, 1985), 285.

101 Geisler, Norman L., *Systematic Theology, Volume 1: Introduction, Bible* (Bloomington, MN: Bethany House, 2002).

102 Harris, Sam, *Letter to a Christian Nation* (New York: Alfred A. Knopf, 2006).

103 https://www.thetimes.co.uk.

104 www.discovermagazine.com.

105 Ross, Hugh, *The Genesis Question: Scientific Advances and the Accuracy of Genesis* (Colorado

Springs: NavPress, 2001).
106 Ibid.
107 Lennox, John C., *Seven Days That Divide the World: The Beginning According to Genesis and Science* (Grand Rapids, MI: Zondervan, 2011).
108 https://acalogcatalog.uwyo.edu/content.php?catoid=14&navoid=1193.
109 www.theguardian.com/uk.
110 Ibid.

THE LIE IS MORE THAN JUST A BOOK; IT IS A CALL TO ACTION.

Will you stand firm in your faith, reject the lie, and uphold the truth of God's Word from the very first verse?

Master Books®
A Division of New Leaf Publishing Group
www.masterbooks.com

ISBN-13: 978-1-68344-391-9

Our children are facing cultural "giants" that previous generations could never have imagined. Secularism, depravity, immorality, and apathy taunt Christians with a barrage of hate and intolerance. Will our children be equipped to stand strong against these giants or will they be overcome?

ISBN-13: 978-1-68344-256-1

Why is there so much suffering today, even for Christians?

In Divine Dilemma, Ken Ham confronts this topic head-on, using personal accounts of illness and loss from within his own family. You and your family will identify with these experiences in this powerful and practical book dealing with one of the most difficult questions we all must face. He understands that, as Christians, we do struggle and grieve in this world, and that is understandable. But, yes, there are answers from God's Word. And, no ... death is not the end. ISBN-13: 978-1-68344-355-1

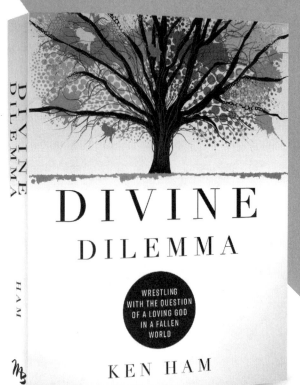

Master Books®
A Division of New Leaf Publishing Group
www.masterbooks.com